Sourcebook on Death and Dying

Reference Books Published by
Marquis Professional Publications

Sourcebook on Death and Dying

First Edition

Consulting Editor
James A. Fruehling, Ph.D.

Marquis Professional Publications
Marquis Who's Who, Inc.
200 East Ohio Street
Chicago, Illinois 60611

Library of Congress Card Number: 82-82013
International Standard Book Number: 0-8379-5801-6
Product Code Number: 031116

Manufactured in the United States of America
1 2 3 4 5 6 7 8 9 10

Preface

In recent years professionals and laymen alike have begun to explore and deal with a wide range of topics associated with death and dying. Death with dignity, the philosophy and psychology of grief, legal and medical definitions of death and their implications, alternatives to the "traditional" funeral, and the outlook for increasing the human life span are just a few issues of concern today. The realities of death and dying can no longer be ignored until the moment of death. Legal and financial complexities, for example, make it advisable to prepare in advance of death; ethical questions are raised by institutions involved in the care of terminal patients and their families; technologies for prolonging life present dilemmas in law, medicine, theology and philosophy.

This sourcebook is for professionals, scholars, and others interested in issues, facts, figures, and sources of additional information about death and dying. Part I, Current Issues, presents article reprints covering views of professionals in related fields. The section deals with aspects of the right-to-die movement, including euthanasia, patients' rights, and living wills (documents through which individuals assert their right to a "good death" or "death with dignity"). Another important issue is the question of when a human being is truly dead. Legal and medical forces are struggling to set a standard, and the articles included on this topic present the arguments among proponents of various points of view.

Also discussed here is the relatively new field of bereavement counseling, which is approached not so much from a clinical point of view as from a professional vantage point which examines the parts played by various professionals in assisting grieving persons.

This section also contains articles dealing with American funeral practices, hospice and terminal care, estate planning, and anatomical gifts.

Part II, Facts and Figures, supports Part I with U.S. and Canadian statistics and other background data on the same and additional subjects pertaining to death and dying.

Sources of Information and Assistance, Part III, includes comprehensive listings, with addresses and other information, for death-related associations and societies, support/self-help groups for the bereaved and terminally ill, and institutions that are or contain facilities for terminally-ill patients. Both the United States and Canada are covered. This section concludes with an extensive publications list which contains both a collection of periodicals that regularly address issues in this field and a bibliography of books and audiovisual materials.

To make this sourcebook especially useful—and easy to use—we have provided a glossary of terms used by professionals in the field of death and dying.

Marquis Professional Publications, a division of Marquis Who's Who, Inc., continually strives to provide the professional community with comprehensive, up-to-date information in the field of higher education. The staff of Marquis Professional Publications urges the users of this edition to inform us of corrections or additions to existing material and to suggest future improvements.

Contents

About the editor

James A. Fruehling, Ph.D. is Department Chairman, Department of Counselor Education, Northeastern Illinois University in Chicago. Dr. Fruehling is a registered psychologist and serves as a consultant for a number of organizations, including the National Selected Morticians.

Dr. Fruehling has written numerous articles on counseling, the role of the funeral director, and the professionalization of funeral service, and he regularly gives speeches and workshops on various aspects of death and dying.

PART 1

CURRENT ISSUES

In the Current Issues section of *Sourcebook on Death and Dying,* readers will find articles that present overviews on a number of special-interest topics. The editors chose these articles after reviewing various computer data bases representing journals (in law, psychology, sociology, medicine and finance), consumer-advocacy publications, and various professional newspapers. [*Note:* For most data bases, the articles chosen for review were published after 1976; for some, earlier articles were also examined.] From these bases, the editors evaluated approximately 1,500 English-language titles and abstracts representing both the United States and Canada.

The editors believe that their final selections will provide readers with a reasoned assessment of current issues—a solid base of up-to-date information on which to build.

THE RIGHT TO DIE— EUTHANASIA

Euthanasia: A Medical and Legal Overview

Howard N. Ward, M.D., J.D.

INTRODUCTION

The past decade has been a modern renaissance regarding the issues of death, dying, and euthanasia. Although many factors have no doubt contributed to this phenomenon, the following are deemed significant: 1) the flowering of modern scientific medicine with its technical ability to postpone the moment of death, 2) an alleged de-emphasis of compassion and a caring manner by physicians and nurses, and 3) the institutionalization of most dying patients in hospitals and nursing homes. In a primitive society, where medicine and science do not exist, man's natural right to die goes unchallenged. Hence, this rebirth of concern over a natural and inevitable process is both a reaction to medical progress as well as a recognition of the fact that until recently Americans have been using massive denial to avoid all contact with the realities of death and dying. Both the lay press and a variety of professional publications have been literally inundated with writings dedicated to the medical, legal, religious, social, ethical, emotional, and philosophical aspects of death, dying, and euthanasia. It will be the purpose of this paper to review these issues and where possible to offer suggestions that comport with modern man, his society and environment. Of course, it would be unmitigated arrogance to imply that one has the answers to such issues and no such intent is implied. But an opinion or suggestion based on experience and study is believed to be a meaningful place to start.

DEFINITION OF ISSUES AND PROBLEMS

In order to properly review euthanasia it is necessary to gain some understanding about death and dying in general. Firstly, death absent sudden causes such as trauma is a process and not an event. It is a natural and inevitable process. It is as natural as birth and indeed is the opposite end of the continuum. It is a biologically appropriate and necessary part of the regenerative cycle. If viewed in this context it is seen as no real threat but rather a normal part of the natural order of things within the framework of nature and God. Some have even given a euphemism to it by calling it the final stage of growth.[1] It can even be dealt with humorously, e.g., death is nature's way of telling you to slow down. Although physicians have been accused of depersonalizing the process, there are many institutions in society which more accurately deserve such criticism, with perhaps the military being the epitome in signifying a death of a human being as a mere KIA (killed in action). Actually, dying is so intensely and inherently a personal matter that its real significance can perhaps only be appreciated by those actually engaged in it. Overcoming the denial of death, so pervasive in American culture, has undoubtedly been a necessary step in getting people to be more congenial with their personal mortality.

When analyzed as a process rather than a momentary event, it becomes self-evident that life itself is a spectrum with varying degrees of energy, vitality, self-awareness, self-control, memory, a sense of futurity, of time, a capacity for interpersonal relationships, love, and a desire to live. Some have embodied these qualities into a concept of "personhood."[2/3] Thus, the degree of life possessed when the final moment approaches may be only a scintilla as compared to a healthy and vigorous person. A newborn does not have the qualities of personhood yet but may possess the potential absent severe congenital abnormalities. Although it is difficult to quantitate the qualities that make up personhood and hence it has been criticized by some, it is nonetheless a useful attempt to separate suffering and vegetative life from the reasonably pain-free, thinking and feeling form.[4] Thus, the degree of personhood that one possesses at any given moment will depend on a qualitative and quantitative assessment of that individual at that time. This is in no way intended to imply that the reverence and respect for life should vary with its stage or its degree of personhood. The privilege of life (or gift of it from a theological point of view) should be respected in all of its stages and in my view in all of its forms.

1. Kubler-Ross, E.: DEATH, The Final Stage of Growth. First Edition. Inglewood Cliffs, New Jersey, Prentice-Hall, Inc., 1975.

2. Engelhardt, H. T.: The Beginnings of Personhood: Philosophical Considerations. Perkins Journal 27:20-27, 1973.

3. Outler, A. C.: The Beginnings of Personhood: Theological Considerations. Perkins Journal 27:28-34, 1973.

4. Hudson, R. P.: Death, Dying and the Zealous Phase. Annals of Internal Medicine 88:696-702, 1978.

Reprinted courtesy of the Journal of the Kansas Bar Association, vol. 49, Winter, 1980.

Rather, it is an attempt to discriminate between meaningful and meaningless or hopeless existence. It is at this point that the subject of euthanasia becomes germane.

Euthanasia is derived from the Greek words eu, meaning normal, and thanatos, meaning death. Colloquially it has come to mean "mercy-killing." The definition in a medical dictionary is "an easy or painless death" or "mercy-killing." [5] A legal dictionary's definition is "the art or practice of painlessly putting to death persons suffering from incurable and distressing disease" or "an easy or agreeable death." [6] Thus, both professions' dictionaries recognize a non-criminal meaning of the word but in reverse order of preference.

Both legal and medical writers now recognize several types of euthanasia. Active or direct euthanasia is where an affirmative act directly results in death while passive euthanasia occurs when a person is allowed to die due to the natural consequences

---

Both legal and medical writers now recognize several types of euthanasia.

---

of their disorder due to an omission or non-act. Voluntary euthanasia involves the consent or personal wish of the patient (or another acting on his behalf) to bring about the act or non-act resulting in death while involuntary euthanasia occurs in the absence of the consent or wish of the patient or his representative. Thus, several combinations are possible. An example of voluntary-active (direct) would be intentionally giving someone, at their request, a fatal dosage of medication. Voluntary-passive (indirect) could occur by way of a living will, if respected by the physician, or by way of a natural death act where it has been enacted. Involuntary-active (direct) is obvious in that it involves deliberately performing an act resulting in death without the personal consent of the individual. Involuntary-passive (indirect) occurs when a non-act results in death without the consent of the person. Although subject to some dispute, the removal of life support apparatus

5. Dorland's Illustrated Medical Dictionary. Twenty-Fifth Edition. Philadelphia, W. B. Saunders Co. 1974, p. 553.

6. Black's Law Dictionary. Revised Fourth Edition. St. Paul, Minn., West Publishing Co. 1968, p. 654.

(e.g., mechanical respirator) has generally been interpreted as a passive or indirect procedure in spite of the fact that turning the switch to "off" or pulling the plug is an act. The reasoning behind this view is that the person dies from the natural consequences of the disease process rather than the act in this particular circumstance.

MEDICAL ISSUES

The physician and other health care providers by the nature of their work, play a major role in euthanasia decisions. Most physicians will acknowledge participating in voluntary-passive euthanasia where either the patient or someone acting on his behalf requests that further definitive treatment of the specific disorder not be continued and only comfort measures or symptomatic treatment be performed. Please note that the patient is not left devoid of all treatment as is sometimes implied. To the contrary, all measures which offer comfort, relief, and alleviation of pain and suffering are continued as aggressively as needed to maintain the patient, to the extent possible, in a state of comfort. This symptomatic therapy has been referred to in the legal literature as ordinary measures, whereas the omitted therapy has often been referred to as extraordinary or heroic measures. There is difficulty here in terminology for several reasons. Firstly, what was considered as extraordinary a few years ago may now be ordinary from the medical point of view. For example, antibiotics, intravenous fluids, transfusion of blood, and blood products, are now rather ordinary types of medical treatments and yet it is withholding such a therapeutic modality that may well permit or allow an elderly, vegetative patient to have his final wish. Pneumonia was once referred to as "an old man's best friend" and antibiotics can frustrate that person's very desire to allow God and nature to have their way. Secondly, the terms ordinary and extraordinary do not discriminate as precisely as definitive treatment (which may or may not include extraordinary measures) and symptomatic treatment in terms of what is actually done. To a physician, ordinary therapy is that therapy which is customary, common, and relatively safe. Extraordinary therapy would be those that are generally high risk or experimental, or very aggressive under the circumstances

(e.g., resuscitating a 90-year old person) or very expensive, or available on only a limited scale (e.g., small supply of a new drug). As can be seen, voluntary - passive euthanasia could involve the withholding of antibiotics in a variety of clinical settings. Most physicians would state that antibiotics represent ordinary thera-

---

The physician who accepts a patient has a duty, according to the law, to use ordinary means to preserve his patient's life but no corollary duty to employ extraordinary means.

---

py. The physician who accepts a patient has a duty, according to the law, to use ordinary means to preserve his patient's life but no corollary duty to employ extraordinary means. [7] Foreman defines ordinary treatment as all medicines, treatments, and operations which offer reasonable hope of benefit and which can be obtained and used without excessive pain or other inconvenience. Extraordinary treatment is those means which cannot be obtained and employed without considerable expense, pain, or other inconvenience and which provide no reasonable hope of lasting benefit. The central question is how reasonable hope and lasting benefit would be construed. If it is in a narrow sense, that is the patient's immediate illness, rather than a broad sense, that is the overall welfare of the patient, then the law would be very threatening to the physician and his ethical position of giving life to years rather than mere years to life. [8] Said in other words, it is not the mere number of days one lives but the quality of them that is most meaningful. The crucial judgment concerns benefit to the patient in its fullest sense. That infers that before a means is determined to be ordinary or extraordinary a judgment must be made regarding the patient's physical, mental, spiritual, psychological, and financial situation, and, most importantly, his personal wishes if known or ascertainable from another. [9]

7. Foreman, P.: The Physician's Criminal Liability for the Practice of Euthanasia. Baylor Law Review 27:54-61, 1975.

8. Barton, D. and Hollender, M. H.: Death Takes a Holiday—Reconsidered. The Pharos 36:20-22, 1973.

9. O'Rourke, K. D.: Active and Passive Euthanasia: The Ethical Distinctions. Hospital Progress 57 (11): 68-73, 1976.

Having suggested that definitive and symptomatic treatment is a more accurate classification than ordinary and extraordinary treatment, one must also point out that even the former terminology is not without some moral and clinical difficulties. This comes into focus if one notes that voluntary-passive euthanasia could involve withholding or withdrawing definitive therapy. That is, withdrawing definitive treatment measures could be morally different than merely not initiating it in the first place. To illustrate, definitive therapy (treatment aimed at controlling or correcting a specific disease state) could be directed at both the illness causing the terminal condition as well as other pre-existent disorders. An example could be an insulin requiring diabetic who acquires a malignancy and, when terminal, exercises his right of voluntary-passive euthanasia and requests only symptomatic care. There is no problem in discontinuing the chemotherapy aimed at his malignant disorder but what about withdrawing the insulin he has taken for many years? Clouser makes a persuasive argument that withholding therapy is morally different in kind than withdrawing therapy and furthermore withdrawing an aggressive or heroic measure (*e.g.*, mechanical respirator) is substantially different from withdrawing a routine, regularized, and expected item of care such as insulin for a diabetic or digitalis for a cardiac patient. This latter type of measure is expected and relied on by the patient and should be continued.[10] This reasoning could be used to help decide which definitive therapies should be continued when most are in fact being stopped in a given patient.

The role of the physician in involuntary-passive euthanasia would probably not be acknowledged so readily in view of the physician's sensitivity to legal liability. However, most physicians are faced at times with hopelessly ill patients who can no longer communicate their consent or personal wishes and for whom no relative or friend is available to act on his behalf. From a legal point of view such a situation would require appointing a guardian to exercise his or her "vote." This area will be discussed in more detail under the section on case law, infra, but in passing it should be mentioned that acting in a paternalistic fashion many patients have probably been treated as the physician thought best in his judgment at the time of the illness.

The role of the physician in active euthanasia (voluntary or involuntary) not only violates the law but is outside the scope and purpose of the medical profession and is unethical in my opinion. The legal aspects of deliberately terminating life as a direct result of an affirmative act will be dealt with later. The physician's role in society is to console, alleviate pain and suffering, and cure

---

To alleviate pain and suffering by not protracting the natural dying process is morally different than directly terminating life ...

---

when possible. To alleviate pain and suffering by not protracting the natural dying process is morally different than directly terminating life notwithstanding the views of others. Fletcher has stated that there is no moral difference between active and passive euthanasia. As a consequentialist, the result is the same whichever route is taken.[11] Even more iconoclastic is the view of Rachels which holds that active euthanasia is more humane than passive since the period of pain and suffering will actually be shortened.[12] These latter opinions fail to take into consideration the fact that the means to the end has a morality of its own and must be evaluated as to its nature and purpose.[9] Active euthanasia also presumes one has absolute dominion over his own life or that of another which is contrary to Judeo-Christian belief and the power of the State.

As mentioned previously, active euthanasia would seem to be outside of the scope and responsibility of the medical profession even if permitted by ethics, religion, and the law. The basic purpose of the physician is to preserve life. If he also served as the terminator of life, the trust a patient places in a physician could be seriously eroded. Once a patient (or the representative on his behalf) has elected to seek active euthanasia the physician is actually no longer needed except to certify that the medical condition is indeed hopeless. If ever permitted, this act could be performed by someone other than a physician for there is no technical difficulty in giving someone a lethal intravenous dose of a medicine. As Hudson points out, it is no trick to hit a vein with a dose of morphine as thousands of addicts prove daily.[4] By analogizing to the legal profession, the trier of fact whether it be judge or jury may yield a guilty verdict but neither is asked to execute or carry out the sentence.

In addition to the issues previously discussed, the physician-patient relationship can be complicated by factors perhaps not obvious to non-physicians. Firstly, a patient's apparent expression regarding his decisions concerning the dilemmas of dying may be spurious or inappropriate in some circumstances. Jackson and Younger have illustrated several clinical situations where the patient's "wish" may be distorted or erroneous due to depression, ambivalent feelings, an underlying unrecognized problem or an unjustified fear of treatment to mention only some. Such clinical situations could undercut what otherwise appears to be a sound decision on the part of the physician and patient and emphasizes the need for making euthanasia decisions only after the patient has been thoroughly and carefully evaluated.[13] Secondly, where the family is acting on behalf of an incompetent patient, the decision making process can be frustrated by the family being divided in its views, uncertain or lacking confidence in its position, or by abdicating this responsibility explicitly or implicitly. In such instances a physician may find himself "forced" into a paternalistic posture in the decision making process.[14]

Finally, how does one manage a subsequent illness or injury which is truly independent of an underlying terminal illness? An example could be a patient with advanced carcinomatosis who has an acute myocardial infarction. Logic and consistency would seem to dictate that since the illness responsible for the

10. Clouser, K. D.: *Allowing or Causing: Another Look.* Annals of Internal Medicine 87:622-624, 1977.

11. Fletcher, J.: *The "Right" to Live and the "Right" to Die.* The Humanist 34:12-15, 1974.
12. Rachels, J.: *Active and Passive Euthanasia.* New England Journal of Medicine 292:78-80, 1975.

13. Jackson, D. L. and Younger, S.: *Patient Autonomy and "Death With Dignity."* New England Journal of Medicine 301:404-408, 1979.
14. Relman, A. S.: *A Response to Allen Buchanan's Views of Decision Making for Terminally Ill Incompetents.* American Journal of Law & Medicine 5 (2):119-123, 1979.

underlying terminal state continues, then the approach to the new illness should be in concert philosophically with the treatment for the pre-existent illness. Hence, if only symptomatic measures are being rendered for the terminal disorder, then only symptomatic measures should be directed at the intervening disorder. Thus, in the example given above and if the patient had opted for voluntary-passive euthanasia, then only symptomatic treatment would be indicated for both the carcinomatosis and the acute myocardial infarction. Accordingly, such a patient should not be resuscitated for a cardiac arrhythmia or even admitted to any acute care unit since such treatment would be inconsistent and inappropriate for the patient's total condition.

To a certain extent, the ethical and legal dilemmas facing today's physician is a problem created by medical progress. The answers are not obvious but the questions must be examined critically with the hope of shedding wisdom and light where there is now confusion.

LEGAL ISSUES
A. Constitutional Law and Common Law

The United States Supreme Court has in recent years recognized a constitutional right of privacy as one of our fundamental rights. Within the protective ambit of this right comes such personal decisions as marriage, contraception, procreation, abortion, and the raising and educating of children.[15]/[16]/[17]/[18] Although the United States Constitution does not explicitly mention a right to privacy, it has been held to derive its roots from the First Amendment, Fourth Amendment, Fifth Amendment, Ninth Amendment, Fourteenth Amendment and the penumbras of the Bill of Rights.[17] The decisions assert that only those personal rights that can be deemed fundamental or implicit in the concept of ordered liberty are included in this guarantee of personal privacy. The Court in *Roe* based the right of privacy on the Fourteenth Amendment through its concept of personal liberty and restriction on state action. The Court also pointed out such rights are not absolute and must be balanced against the state's interests in safeguarding health, maintaining medical standards, and protecting life including that which is only potential. Today many commentators are asserting that the choice of death or the right to die also falls within this area of constitutional protection.[19]/[20] That is, the right of privacy includes the right to die since this too, is a fundamental decision affecting a person. State interests that could be asserted in balancing this qualified right include the following: 1) the duty to protect the lives of persons, 2) the maintenance of medical standards to prevent hasty or erroneous decisions, 3) the possibility that it is a violation of medical ethics, 4) the sanctity of life could be undermined, and that recognition of such a right could serve as an entering wedge for compulsory elimination of the aged, the unproductive, and the genetically defective, and 5) that society depends on the existence and productivity of its members and that death of some will leave dependents destitute and unable to care for themselves.[19] Those in favor of this right argue that the case for it is even stronger than abortion since no third being is involved. Furthermore, most of the state's interests diminish with time and are greatly attenuated in the cases of persons who are debilitated because of advanced age, whose medical condition is hopeless, and for whom continued medical treatment poses an unacceptable burden. Even prior to the United States Supreme Court decisions, Justice Cardozo, while a member of the New York Court of Appeals, stated that "every human being of adult years and sound mind has a right to determine what shall be done with his body," that is, a right of self-determination.[21] That would appear to include the right to be left alone mentioned in a United States Supreme Court case a decade ago.[22] Hence, it would appear that sound common law and constitutional arguments can be marshalled for asserting the choice of death as an aspect of the rights of self-determination and privacy respectively. Of course, one is not dealing with choice of death in

... it would appear that sound common law and constitutional arguments can be marshalled for asserting the choice of death as an aspect of the rights of self-determination and privacy respectively.

its inevitable sense but rather choice of the time and manner of death as a natural event without intervention by medical treatment.

B. The Physician's Criminal Liability

As pointed out by Foreman, whatever the definitional difficulties are regarding euthanasia (type, etc.) it is clear that *theoretically* the physician is criminally liable under almost any factual situation one can imagine. However, it is of interest that there have been few prosecutions and essentially no convictions in the history of American jurisprudence regarding this problem.[7] Involuntary-active euthanasia (*i.e.*, without consent by a positive act) is clearly murder, notwithstanding any kind or humane motive. This interpretation appears correct in terms of Kansas law where murder in the first degree is defined as "The killing of a human being committed maliciously,* willfully, deliberately, and with premeditation or committed in the perpetration or attempt to perpetrate any felony."[23]

Involuntary-passive euthanasia is perhaps less clear since the common law has imposed criminal liabilities for such deaths only where the person guilty of such an omission had a clear duty to act. This duty must be a legal one and not merely a moral one, and the omission of the duty must be the immediate and direct cause of death. A physician, once he or she accepts a patient, has a continuing obligation to use ordinary measures to preserve life, as a part of his contract with the patient. Hence, at least theoretically, if a physician voluntarily omits doing an act construed as ordinary treatment he could be criminally liable. As noted by Foreman, this liability appears to be only theoretical at present, since to his knowledge and that of several commentators there has never been a case dealing with this particular factual circumstance.

15. *Loving v. Virginia*, 388 U.S. 1, 87 S.Ct. 1817, 18 L. Ed. 2d 1010, 1967.
16. *Eisenstadt v. Baird*, 405 U.S. 438, 92 S.Ct. 1029, 31 L. Ed. 2d 349, 1972.
17. *Roe v. Wade*, 410 U.S. 113, 93 S.Ct. 705, 35 L. Ed. 2d 147, 1973.
18. *Wisconsin v. Yoder*, 406 U.S. 205, 92 S.Ct. 1526, 32 L. Ed. 2d 15, 1972.

19. Delgado, R.: *Euthanasia Reconsidered — The Choice of Death as an Aspect of the Right of Privacy.* Arizona Law Review 17:474-494, 1975.
20. Evans, F. J.: *The Right to Die—A Basic Constitutional Right.* The Journal of Legal Medicine 5 (8):17-20, 1977.
21. *Schloendorff v. Society of New York Hospitals*, 211 N.Y. 125, 105 N.E. 2d 92, 1914.
22. *Stanley v. Georgia*, 394 U.S. 557, 89 S.Ct. 1243, 22 L. Ed. 2d 542, 1969.

* Malice, legally, can mean a man-endangering state of mind and not necessarily an evil motive.
23. Kansas Statutes Annotated (K.S.A.) 21-3401.

Voluntary-active euthanasia would also appear to satisfy the criteria for murder since the common law has never recognized consent of the victim as a defense to criminal homicide. A lesser included crime under these circumstances would be that of assisted suicide. Here one merely aids or abets the suicide rather than deliberately taking the life, a subtle distinction (*e.g.*, preparing the poison as contrasted to giving it). Although suicide per se is no longer a crime in the majority of American jurisdictions, assisted suicide often is. In Kansas assisting suicide is "intentionally advising, encouraging, or assisting another in the taking of his own life." It is a Class E felony.[24]

Voluntary-passive euthanasia again raises the issue of whether or not the physician had a legal duty to act. If the patient disengaged or withdrew from treatment thereby cancelling the physician's legal duty to treat with ordinary measures, then no criminal liability would lie. Again, *theoretically*, if the physician-patient relationship still existed and the physician withheld ordinary measures then potential criminal liability could attach if the deliberate non-act or omission could be shown to be the direct and immediate cause of death (*e.g.*, withholding corticosteroids in a patient with adrenal insufficiency).

C. The Physician's Civil Liability

The common law did not provide a civil cause of action for death. In England one was created by statute under Lord Campbell's Act and in the United States American legislatures have followed this example by creating wrongful death statutes. Kansas has enacted such legislation in Kansas Statutes Annotated (K.S.A.) 60-1901 through 1905. The cause of action states as follows:

"if the death of a person is caused by the wrongful act or omission of another, an action may be maintained for damages resulting therefrom if the former might have maintained the action had he or she lived, in accordance with this article, against the wrongdoer, or his or her personal representative if he or she is deceased."

At present the aggregate sum of the damages other than for pecuniary loss cannot exceed $25,000.00.[25] The elements of damage which may be

recoverable include mental anguish, suffering or bereavement; loss of society, companionship, comfort or protection; loss of marital care, attention, advice, or counsel; loss of filial care or attention; loss of parental care, training, guidance or education, and the reasonable funeral expenses of the deceased. If no probate of administration for the estate of the deceased has been commenced, expenses for the care of the deceased which resulted from the wrongful act may also be recovered by any one of the heirs who paid or became liable for same. Neither the expenses for such care nor funeral expenses are included within the $25,000.00 limitation.[26] The action may be commenced by any one of the heirs at law of the deceased who sustained a loss by reason of the death.[27] Also to be considered would be the survival statutes which allow certain actions to survive notwithstanding the death of the person entitled to bring the action on the person liable for the same. It includes causes of action the deceased could have brought at common law for mesne profits, for injury to the person, or to the real or personal estate, or for any deceit or fraud, or for the death by wrongful act or omission.[28] Furthermore, no action pending shall abate by the death of either or both parties thereto, except an action for libel, slander, malicious prosecution, or for nuisance.[29]

At the outset it should be stated that there are no reported cases of civil liability for euthanasia.[30] Consequently, one can only discuss it from the point of view of theory, logic, and policy. Two doctrines, standard of care and informed consent, seem relevant to this area of liability. It is well established that a medical treatment or operation performed without consent, notwithstanding a good result, can be an intentional tort, i.e., a technical battery.[31/32] Thus, even if the physician does not deviate or depart from the standard of care, liability can attach for an intentional act absent consent. Conversely, in most situations, consent, absent deviation from the standard of care

will absolve the physician from civil liability. A situation that has been litigated several times involves the competent patient who refuses a lifesaving procedure, *e.g.*, refusal of blood transfusion with an underlying curable disorder. The courts are divided in compelling the treatment under such circumstances. On some occasions the presence of harm to others (*e.g.*, death of parent with young children) has been a factor in the outcome. Thus, it is a question of balancing the right of privacy previously discussed against the state interests involved. Assuming that a patient does have a right to choose his mode and manner of death and rejects life saving or prolonging treatment, does the physician have any civil liability? The answer appears uncertain at present but in legal theory the patient's right to refuse treatment coupled with the physician's duty to refrain from

> ... *if a competent terminal patient rejected life prolonging treatment, it would seem that the physician should not be liable.*

treatment absent consent would support a result of no liability for the physician. In reference to the previous statutory causes of action the underlying wrongful act must be of such a character that the patient would have been entitled to recover if alive. If the patient has the right to refuse treatment and the physician commits no wrongful act, then the statutory beneficiaries should not be able to recover since the patient himself could not. Thus, if a competent terminal patient rejected life prolonging treatment, it would seem that the physician should not be liable.

If a mentally competent patient requests or demands that a death inducing agent be given, a different situation arises since this is voluntary-active euthanasia. Traditionally, consent has vitiated the wrongfulness of an intentional tort. However, this factual situation is criminal and it is clear that one cannot consent to criminal conduct. Apparently jurisdictions vary on whether assent to a criminal act bars civil liability.[30] In Kansas this act would clearly violate the assisting suicide statute previously mentioned as well as possibly the murder statutes.

24. K.S.A. 21-3406.
25. K.S.A. 60-1903.
26. K.S.A. 60-1904.
27. K.S.A. 60-1902.
28. K.S.A. 60-1801.
29. K.S.A. 60-1802.
30. Sharp, Jr., T. H. and Crofts, Jr., T. H.: *Death With Dignity—The Physician's Civil Liability.* Baylor Law Review 27:86-108, 1975.
31. *Mohr v. Williams*, 95 Minn. 261, 104 N. W. 12, 1905.
32. Thurman, V.: *Euthanasia: The Physician's Liability.* The John Marshall Journal of Practice and Procedure 10:148-172, 1976.

If the patient is a minor, unable to express himself, or mentally incompetent, then any attempted consent would be ineffective and the physician's act or non-act at the instruction of this patient would be wrongful by law. This could technically, in the case of an act, be a battery and the statutory beneficiaries could pursue civil liability since the patient could have done so. When an incompetent or minor expresses himself or the patient is incapable of expressing himself, then the role of the family takes on great significance. If the responsible family members request an active or passive form of euthanasia, then there is a legal wrong to the patient (involuntary euthanasia), but since the family members participated in the wrong, they probably could not profit thereby by a subsequent cause of action. If some statutory beneficiary objected or did not participate in the decision, then that particular family member could probably bring a wrongful death action. Hence, if a physician committed an act or non-act at the request of all the statutory beneficiaries, he could be criminally liable but not civilly liable since the statutory beneficiaries should not recover for a wrong in which they participated.

The Kansas survival statute would appear to offer a potential recovery for wrongful death even if the responsible family members requested the act or non-act since the plaintiff would be the personal representative of the estate under that statute and this might not necessarily be one of the responsible family members.

In terms of standard of care, the usual guidepost is that skill, knowledge, and training possessed by an average member of the profession in the same or similar locality. However, technically speaking, active euthanasia is outside the scope of medical practice and the standard would not be relevant. If one assumes that this activity were part of medical practice, then the physician would be held to the same or similar locality standard for choosing the best means to achieve the desired result which in this case would be death.

All of the above discussion assumes that the physician was correct in diagnosing the patient's disorder and that death was inevitable. Otherwise, he would be potentially liable for medical malpractice within its orthodox meaning.

D. Definition of Death

A modern definition of death in the alternative (that is the traditional cardiorespiratory definition *or* in the alternative, brain death) is very helpful in all of these situations. It can often preclude criminal or civil liability since one cannot commit murder, assist suicide, or engage in wrongful death acts if the patient is already legally dead. K.S.A. 77-202 defines death as follows:

"A person will be considered medically and legally dead if, in the opinion of a physician, based on ordinary standards of medical practice, there is the absence of spontaneous respiratory and cardiac function and, because of the disease or condition which caused, directly or indirectly, these functions to cease, or because of the passage of time since these functions ceased, attempts at resuscitation are considered hopeless; and, in this event, death will have occurred at the time these functions ceased; *or*

A person will be considered medically and legally dead if, in the opinion of a physician, based on ordinary standards of medical practice, there is the absence of spontaneous brain function; and if based on ordinary standards of medical practice, during reasonable attempts to either maintain or restore spontaneous circulatory or respiratory function in the absence of aforesaid brain function, it appears that further attempts at resuscitation or supportive maintenance will not succeed, death will have occurred at the time when these conditions first coincide.

. . . this modern definition of death has relieved Kansas physicians of much anxiety and legal liability . . .

Death is to be pronounced before any vital organ is removed for purposes of transplantation.

The alternative definitions of death are to be utilized for all purposes in this state, including trials of civil and criminal cases, any laws to the contrary notwithstanding."

As one can see, this modern definition of death has relieved Kansas physicians of much anxiety and legal liability in any factual situation where there was either brain death or traditional death. Hence, disconnecting the respirator to permit the natural consequences of someone already "dead" under the statute would not be actionable. Our State was the first to enact a modern definition of death and is to be commended for its foresight. It is an outstanding example of the law keeping pace with advancements in society and science.

E. Natural Death Acts

Because of concern, perhaps inaccurate, by the public that many physicians and the law require a total commitment to preserving life at all costs some states have enacted natural death legislation. The first to be effective was in California as of January 1, 1977.[33] The acts recognize that a policy of all possible death prevention is not necessarily the wisest. The policy is that when the quality of life is no longer meaningful, that is the patient has a terminal condition, and the application of further life-sustaining procedures would only serve to postpone the final moment of death rather than prolong real life, then such procedures should be withheld or withdrawn so that the patient may die naturally. Such acts authorize a directive to physicians regarding the circumstances where the physician may withhold or withdraw treatment. In essence, the acts legally authorize voluntary-passive euthanasia when executed correctly. Presumably they do not affect the existing rights of physicians and families of terminally ill patients where the patient did not have the foresight to execute such a directive. Some commentators have doubted and others have championed the need for such legislation notwithstanding its limited application.[34/35] None of these acts authorize involuntary euthanasia or voluntary-active euthanasia (*i.e.*, Mercy Killing).

The 1979 Kansas Legislature passed a natural death act to take effect July 1, 1979.[36] The act authorizes a patient to make a written

33. California Health and Safety Code. Section 7185-7194, 1976.
34. Mills, D. H.: *California's Natural Death Act.* The Journal of Legal Medicine 5 (1):22-23, 1977.
35. Farabee, R.: *The Texas Natural Death Act.* Texas Medicine 73:91-95, 1977.
36. 1979 Session Laws of Kansas, Chapter 199, p. 970, K.S.A. 1979 Supp. 65-28101 *et. seq.*

declaration instructing a physician to withhold or withdraw life sustaining procedures in the event of a terminal condition. The written declaration must be witnessed by two or more persons at least 18 years of age and neither of whom signed the declaration for or at the direction of the declarant, is related to the declarant by blood or marriage, is entitled to any portion of the estate of the declarant by will, codocil, or the laws of intestacy, or is directly responsible financially for the declarant's medical care. Life sustaining procedures include any medical procedures or intervention which when applied to a qualified patient under the act would serve only to prolong the dying process and where in the judgment of the attending physician, death will occur whether or not such procedure or intervention is utilized.

A qualified patient is one who has executed a declaration in accordance with this act and who has been diagnosed and certified in writing to be afflicted with a terminal condition by two physicians who have personally examined the patient, one of whom shall be the patient's attending physician.

The declarant is responsible for notifying his or her attending physician of the existence of the declaration and the declaration or a copy thereof shall be made a part of the declarant's medical records.

The declaration is expressly inoperative during the course of an otherwise qualified patient's pregnancy. It may be revoked at any time by several methods including physical destruction if done in a manner indicating intent to cancel, written revocation if signed and dated by the declarant, and verbal revocation if performed in the presence of a witness at least 18 years of age who later signs and dates a writing confirming such intent. There shall be no criminal or civil liability for failure to act upon a revocation unless the person has actual knowledge of the revocation. Furthermore, the desires of a qualified patient shall at all times supercede the effect of the declaration.

The act requires the attending physician who is notified of the existence of a declaration and has diagnosed a terminal condition to take the necessary steps of confirming and certifying the terminal condition or if he refuses to do so then to effect a transfer of the qualified patient to

another physician. Failure of the physician to comply with either of the above procedures subjects him to discipline for unprofessional conduct under K.S.A. 65-2837(q).

It is a Class A misdemeanor to willfully conceal, cancel, deface, obliterate, or damage the declaration of another without consent or to falsify or forge a revocation. It is a Class E felony to falsify or forge a declaration of another or willfully conceal or withhold personal knowledge of the revocation of a declaration with the intent to cause a withholding or withdrawal of life sustaining procedures contrary to the wishes of the declarant and thereby directly causing life sustaining procedures to be withheld or withdrawn and death to be hastened.

Withholding or withdrawing life sustaining procedures in accordance with the act is expressly excluded as constituting the crime of assisted suicide. However, nothing in the act is to be construed to condone, authorize, or approve mercy killing or any affirmative or deliberate act or omission to end life other than to permit the natural process of dying as provided in the act.

Additionally, the act states that it does not in any way impair or supercede any legal right (*e.g.*, common law) or responsibility which any person may have to effect the withholding or withdrawal of life sustaining procedures in any lawful manner. The act also creates no presumption concerning the intention of an individual who has not executed a declaration to consent to the use or withholding of life sustaining procedures in the event of a terminal condition. Presumably this means that a patient who is competent, and has not executed a declaration, may still direct his own medical care and decisions.

A suggested declaration form is included within the statute and sub-

---

. . . Kansas now joins those states . . . which have created statutory natural death acts to authorize voluntary-passive euthanasia.

---

stantial compliance with the statutory form is required.

Hence, Kansas now joins those states (nine as of 1980) which have created statutory natural death acts to authorize voluntary-passive euthanasia. It will be interesting to see if the public and medical profession utilize this formal procedure in lieu of the traditional understanding between the physician and patient (or responsible family member). If the public perceives that their personal wishes and needs are not being met, then it should be used. In my own view, such a situation is not common and it is doubted that large numbers of people will flock to attorneys' offices to draw and execute their declaration.

F. Recent Case Law

Perhaps the two leading cases are those involving Karen Quinlan and Joseph Saikewicz.[37/38] The *Quinlan* case dealt with a twenty-two year old female who had sustained two respiratory arrests of several minutes duration (etiology unknown) prior to arrival at the hospital. She was treated aggressively including assisted mechanical ventilation, but in spite of therapy she failed to regain consciousness or a cognitive, sapient state. However, because of the fact that her electroencephalogram showed some activity, her cerebroarteriogram was normal, and certain clinical findings were present, she was not considered brain-dead as defined by the Ad Hoc Committee of Harvard Medical School.[39] Hence, her physician were unwilling to terminate her aggressive treatment program since the "Harvard Criteria" have often been acknowledged as the existing medical standard for brain death. However, it should be brought to the current reader's attention that many authorities now consider the "Harvard Criteria" to be too demanding and stringent.[40] Not withstanding the reluctance of the attending physicians to disconnect the mechanical respirator, they also admitted that she was in a persistent vegetative state and that there was no reasonable hope of her returning to a cognitive and sapient state. After Karen Quinlan

37. *In the Matter of Karen Quinlan*, 70 N.J. 10, 355 A.2d 647, 1976 Cert. Denied, *Garger v. New Jersey*, 429 U.S. 922, 97 S. Ct. 319, 50 L. Ed. 2d 289, 1976.

38. *Superintendent of Belchertown State School, et al. v. Joseph Saikewicz*, 1977 Mass. Adv. Sh. 2461, 370 N.E.2d 417, 1977.

39. Report of Ad Hoc Committee of the Harvard Medical School to Examine the Definition of Brain Death: *A Definition of Irreversible Coma.* Journal of the American Medical Association 205:337-344, 1968.

40. Black, P. McL.: *Brain Death.* The New England Journal of Medicine 299:338-344 and 299:393-401, 1978.

had been in this condition for a protracted period of time, her father sought to be appointed as guardian of her person and property and sought, by declaratory relief, the express power of authorizing on her behalf the discontinuance of all extraordinary procedures for sustaining his daughter's vital processes. The Superior Court, Chancery Division, denied authorization for termination of the life supporting apparatus, withheld letters of guardianship over the person of the incompetent (awarded to another individual) and the father appealed.[41] The Supreme Court of New Jersey held that a decision by the patient to terminate by natural forces a noncognitive vegetative existence was a valuable incident of her constitutional right of privacy and that this right, due to her incompetence, could be asserted by her guardian under the doctrine of substituted judgment. Furthermore, this relief could be granted in spite of the fact that the removal of the respirator would not conform to medical practice if the following criteria were met; upon the concurrence of guardian and family and should the attending physician conclude that there was no reasonable possibility of Karen ever emerging from her comatose condition to a cognitive, sapient state and that the life support apparatus now being administered should be discontinued, they shall consult the hospital "Ethics Committee" or like body and if that consultative body agrees with the attending physician's prognosis, then the life support system may be withdrawn and said action shall be without any civil or criminal liability therefor on the part of any participant whether guardian, physician, hospital or others. Furthermore, the Court expressly stated that they did not imply that a proceeding for judicial declaratory relief was required for the implementation of comparable decisions in the field of medical practice. To require application to a court for permission to withdraw life sustaining procedures would be generally inappropriate, not only as a gratuitous encroachment upon the medical profession's field of competence, but because it would be impossibly cumbersome. The Court also made clear that even though such removal could accelerate the moment of death, the ensuing death would not be homicide but rather expiration

41. In the Matter of Karen Quinlan, An Alleged Incompetent, 137 N. J. Super. 227, 348, A. 2d 801, 1975.

from natural causes. In addition, even if regarded as a form of homicide, it would not be unlawful since the termination of treatment pursuant to the right of privacy would be ipso facto lawful. Finally, this act of withdrawing treatment pursuant to the right of privacy would also negate an attempted prosecution for suicide or aiding suicide.

The Court recognized that the dilemma presented here was one constantly resolved in medical practice and acknowledged that the nature,

---

The Court recognized that the dilemma presented here was one constantly resolved in medical practice and acknowledged that the nature, extent, and duration of care is the responsibility of the physician.

---

extent, and duration of care is the responsibility of the physician. The morality and conscience of our society places this responsibility in the hands of the physician. However, if in deciding these matters, justiciable controversies arise between the parties to such a decision then an ultimate determination is a non-delegable judicial responsibility. In short, the physician, the patient (or his representative), family, and hospital ethics committee may resolve these decisions if *all* are in agreement. If not, then a declaratory judicial proceeding will be required in order to reach a lawful decision.

The *Saikewicz* case presented a factual situation where a markedly retarded person (I.Q. of 10 or about equal to age 2½ years), age 67, acquired acute myelomonocytic leukemia. The patient had spent most of his life institutionalized and could only communicate by grunts and physical gestures. On April 26, 1976, the superintendent of Belchertown State School filed a petition in the probate court for appointment of a guardian empowered to make decisions concerning Saikewicz's care and treatment. The guardian then rendered an opinion that treatment was not in the patient's best interests. A hearing on the guardian's report was held and after such the probate court agreed with the guardian. In so deciding the probate court weighed the following factors against treatment: 1) his age (older patients are less

responsive to currently available chemotherapeutic agents); 2) his ability to cooperate; 3) the predictable side effects; 4) small chance of remission; 5) the certainty that treatment would cause immediate suffering; and, 6) the quality of life possible after treatment. Factors favoring treatment were: 1) the chance that life might be lengthened; and 2) the fact that most people in this situation elect to undergo treatment. After entering the order agreeing with the guardian, the probate judge immediately reported the case to the Massachusetts Appeals Court. The Supreme Judicial Court of Massachusetts (hereinafter the Court) then allowed an application for direct appellate review. On July 9, 1976, the Court affirmed the action of the probate court and noted that a written opinion would follow. Saikewicz died on September 4, 1976, and on November 28, 1977, the Court handed down its decision. The decision deals with two distinct issues. The first involved the substantive rights of a competent or incompetent person to decline or refuse life-prolonging treatment. The second dealt with the procedures required to ensure the rights of an incompetent person.

With regard to refusing treatment the Court recognized, as in *Quinlan*, a constitutional right to privacy which in the instant case prohibits an unwarranted infringement of bodily integrity. This right must be weighed against the state's interests which were as follows: 1) the preservation of life; 2) the protection of interests of innocent third parties; 3) the prevention of suicide; and 4) maintaining the integrity of the medical profession. Thus, it is the suffering or "traumatic cost" of possible prolongation of life that must be balanced against the state interests, especially the preservation of life. The Court found that a right of privacy extends to both competent and incompetent persons since the value of human dignity extends to both. Thus, the substantive rights of a competent or incompetent person

---

. . . the substantive rights of a competent or incompetent person are the same in regard to the right to decline potentially life-prolonging treatment.

---

are the same in regard to the right to decline potentially life-prolonging treatment. The Court believed the right of privacy to be an expression of the sanctity of individual free choice and self-determination, as a fundamental constituent of life. No third parties' interests appeared to be involved here and, in fact, Saikewicz's family (two sisters) refused to participate in any aspect of the decision making process. The Court expressly made clear that permitting an incompetent to decline treatment was not to imply a denial of the state's power under the doctrine of *parens patriae*, to care for and protect the best interests of an incompetent person. The best interests of an incompetent person are not necessarily served by imposing treatment on an incompetent person not mandated as to competent persons similarly situated. Hence, it is a question of properly balancing applicable state and individual interests.

In allowing the guardian to decline treatment on behalf of Saikewicz, the Court adopted the principle of substituted judgment. The Court felt that in so doing, the principal test should not be what a majority of people do under such circumstances but rather, to ascertain as accurately as possible, the wants and needs of the individual involved. The decision should be that which would be made by the incompetent person, if the person were competent momentarily, but taking into consideration the present and future incompetency as one of the factors in the decision making process. Nevertheless, there is no way to ascertain what Saikewicz would want and it may be necessary in situations such as his to rely on objective criteria to a greater degree. The Court emphasized that in weighing one of the factors, namely the quality of life possible by him even if treatment brings about a remission, the guardian should not equate that with the value of life. The term quality of life would deal with the continuing pain and discomfort precipitated by the chemotherapy whereas the value of life would deal with social worth and its ramifications.

Finally the Court dealt with the procedure for handling these types of decisions with incompetent persons. After acknowledging that many health care institutions have developed medical ethics committees to deal with such issues, the Court went on to expressly reject the approach as adopted by the New Jersey Supreme Court in *Quinlan*. The Court did not believe this option should be transformed into a required procedure and, in fact, took a dim view of any attempt to shift the ultimate decision making responsibility away from the courts of proper jurisdiction and giving it to any committee, panel, group, ad hoc or permanent. Furthermore, the Court did not view judicial resolution of this most difficult and awesome question as constituting a gratuitous encroachment on the domain of medical expertise. Rather, such questions of life and death require the process of detached but passionate investigation and decision that forms the ideal on which the judicial branch of government was created. Achieving this ideal, is the responsibility of the judiciary and is not to be entrusted to any other group purporting to represent the morality and conscience of our society, no matter how highly motivated or impressively constituted.

The latter part of the opinion has been the subject of a raging controversy between the medical and legal professions. Distinguished physicians have accused the judges of ordaining themselves physicians and of casting a "no confidence vote" for medicine.[42] Some attorneys have suggested that the decision requires Massachusetts' physicians to go to court in every circumstance where it is believed that potentially life-prolonging treatment should be withheld from a person incapable of making his own decision.[43] The most enlightened, and hopefully correct, interpretation of the decision is that the power of granting civil and criminal immunity is to be retained by the courts. That is, one is not required or mandated to go to court for every non-treatment decision regarding an incompetent person but rather if the physician and other parties wish immunity it will only be granted by the judiciary and not delegated to private bodies such as ethics or prognosis committees. The Massachusetts procedure is a procedure whereby a physician, family, or hospital can ascertain their legal liability before the fact if they consider it either desirable or necessary.[44] In other words, a physician may continue to make such decisions in conjunction with other appropriate parties (*e.g.*, family, guardian), without going to court but he may later be held legally liable if the decision was substandard or unlawful. To preclude legal liability, civil or criminal, requires declaratory relief in a judicial proceeding.

Further evidence that this is the correct interpretation of *Saikewicz* is the fact that Justice Paul J. Liacos,

---

To preclude legal liability, civil or criminal, requires declaratory relief in a judicial proceeding.

---

the author of the decision, recently broke judicial tradition and shared his private views on the case.[45] Although his private opinion is not the law (the reported case is), this extra-judicial statement at least allows one to understand how the actual author of the opinion perceives it. Justice Liacos, in reference to the medical profession seeking civil and criminal immunity by a predetermination, stated, "*Saikewicz* permits that kind of procedure. Permits is not to say it requires it. On the other hand, a doctor can act and take the risks that traditionally doctors have always taken, and that is the risk of being judged by hindsight, and *Saikewicz* does not address that possibility."

Before this more limited view of *Saikewicz*, some commentators had accused the judiciary of legal imperialism since the decision could be interpreted to require a routine judicialization of all non-treatment decisions in incompetent patients. Secondly, the medical profession was alleged to oppose the *Saikewicz* decision and to assert that the physician should play the dominant role in these decisions under the doctrine of medical paternalism.[46] Actually, the polarization of absolute legal imperialism vis-a-vis absolute medical paternalism is more fictitious than real. The truth lies in between if one interprets *Saikewicz* as its own author does and defines the physician's role to include the family as

42. Relman, A. S.: *The Saikewicz Decision: Judges as Physicians.* The New England Journal of Medicine 298:508-509, 1978.

43. Vaccarino, J. M.: *If Your Patient is Hopelessly Ill Must You Go to Court.* Legal Aspects of Medical Practice 6 (7):50-51, 1978.

44. Glantz, L. H. and Swazey, J. P.: *Decisions Not to Treat: The Saikewicz Case and Its Aftermath.* Forum on Medicine 2:22-32, 1979.

45. Liacos, P. J.: *Dilemmas of Dying.* Medicolegal News 7 (3):4-7 and 29, 1979.

46. Buchanan, A.: *Medical Paternalism or Legal Imperialism: Not the Only Alternatives for Handling SAIKEWICZ-Type Cases.* American Journal of Law & Medicine 5 (2):97-117, 1979.

Relman does.[14] Relman believes that such non-treatment decisions for incompetent patients should be made by family members working together with the physicians and not by the physician alone unless the family is divided in views, abdicates responsibility, or defers to the physician. Where the family fails to carry its responsibility, Relman asserts the physician must take charge. In my view, it would seem, time permitting, that those circumstances Relman mentions are precisely the types of cases that might prompt a physician to implement the *Saikewicz* procedure so as to avoid legal liability. On the other hand, if the physician and family are in complete agreement, then one would take the traditional responsibility of being judged by hindsight.

Another option to this process is that of Buchanan who believes that the family of an incompetent should make such decisions after consultation with the physician. That is, the family plays the dominant role.[46] Actually, absent extenuating circumstances, such as the family forcing responsibility on the physician or advocating views clearly detrimental to the patient, this is probably a fair assessment of the current working relationship between physicians and families regarding incompetent patients. However, one must admit that families are greatly influenced by consultation with the physician. Thus, the dominant role of the family may be more apparent than real. Buchanan appears to have constructed a strawman (legal imperialism versus medical paternalism) and then delights in offering a family role that in my view is already acknowledged. He also asserts that such non-treatment decisions should be constantly reviewed in a retrospective fashion by an ethics committee which he defines as genuine only if it is composed of physicians, administrators, social workers, psychiatrists, psychologists, lawyers, and moral philosophers. Although this might be an admirable goal, this idea is as impractical as the routine judicialization some believed *Saikewicz* to require. As Relman points out, not only would this process be cumbersome and unattainable due to the large number of such decisions, but more importantly, unnecessary. The number of instances where the physician and family neglect the patient or worse yet, where the physician and family conspire

against the patient must be uncommon. In fact, the latter situation must be very rare.

Perhaps the most logical way to interpret the roles of the various figures in the treatment or non-treatment of incompetent patients where no prior expression of the patient is available is to view patient responsibility as a continuum. The principal attending physician has the immediate responsibility, and the judiciary has the ultimate responsibility. Other figures, such as consulting physicians, family, legal guardians, private groups (*e.g.*, ethics committees), and health care institutions lie between the principal attending physician and the judiciary. Among these other figures, the views of the family, after

---

Consultation with private groups or institutions should be elective and not mandatory and the views of such bodies should be advisory and not binding.

---

consultation with all physicians, should be held most controlling since the family is the entity most likely to know what the wishes of the patient would have been. If a legal guardian has been appointed, then the views of the guardian should become controlling notwithstanding the views of the family. Consultation with private groups or institutions should be elective and not mandatory and the views of such bodies should be advisory and not binding. Hopefully, the need to appeal to the ultimate authority, the judiciary, would arise infrequently. This would appear to be necessary only in a limited number of circumstances such as where there is disagreement between physician and family, a family refuses to accept its responsibility, there are conflicting family views, or no family member or legal guardian is available to act on behalf of the patient.

Fortunately, for Massachusetts' physicians, the full impact of *Saikewicz* has been modified by the Appeals Court of Massachusetts.[47] *In the Matter of Shirley Dinnerstein* involved a 67-year old woman with Alzheimer's disease who was de-

47. *In the Matter of Shirley Dinnerstein*, 1978 Mass. App. Adv. Sh. 736, 380 N. E. 2d 134, 1978.

mented and then sustained a cerebrovascular accident manifested by a left hemiparesis, inability to swallow without choking, and inability to communicate. The question presented was whether a physician attending a terminally ill patient may lawfully direct that resuscitative measures be withheld in the event of a cardiac or respiratory arrest. The Appeals Court distinguished *Saikewicz* by noting that case dealt with a non-treatment decision involving life prolonging therapy rather than a mere suspension of the dying process. Of interest is the fact that the Appeals Court in footnote 5 construed *Saikewicz* to not impair the traditional right of the family or guardian to consent to affirmative treatment decisions (as opposed to negative) on behalf of the patient without prior judicial approval. The Appeals Court held that where the patient is in essentially a vegetative state from an irreversible and terminal illness, then the law does not prohibit a course of medical treatment which excludes attempts at resuscitation in the event of a cardiac or respiratory arrest, and providing the physician and family are in agreement, the validity of the physician's order to that effect does not depend on prior judicial approval. However, the same question where the physician and family disagree was expressly reserved for a future concrete adversary proceeding. It is unfortunate that this case did not reach the Supreme Judicial Court of Massachusetts so that an answer more final in nature could have been achieved.

ADDENDUM

Since this paper was submitted for publication, there have been further developments in the case law dealing with the non-treatment (withdrawing or withholding) of incompetent patients. *In the Matter of Earle N. Spring*, again arising out of Massachusetts, The Supreme Judicial Court partially clarified *Saikewicz* by stating that neither *Spring* nor *Saikewicz* establish any requirement for prior judicial approval that would not otherwise exist.[48] However, such medical decisions, without judicial approval could theoretically lead to liability if the omission of the treatment was not made responsibly, in good faith and with due care. Such failure to treat, if erroneous, would be in the realm of civil negligence and not a battery and the negligence cannot be based solely on the failure to obtain prior judicial if the approval would have been given. With respect to criminal liability, the Court said little needs to be said since what precious little precedent there is suggests that the doctor will be protected if he acts in a good faith judgment that is not grieviously unreasonable by medical standards. The Court again stated its previous position that when a court is presented with the legal question of whether treatment may be withheld it must decide the question and not delegate it to some private person or group. The Court also approved of the result, but did not adopt the full opinion, in *Dinnerstein* which held that a prior judicial order is not necessary for a "no code" (do not resuscitate) order on the facts shown in that case.

At the same time, the Supreme Court, Appellate Division, Second Department, of New York faced this type of question for the first time and held that the hospital or physician *must* seek a court order before any life support system can be withdrawn from a terminally ill, incompetent patient.[49] This intermediate court then went on to establish an elaborate procedure whereby such decisions can be made under expedited conditions. Compliance with the procedure provides immunity from civil and criminal liability. The court beleived that the societal interests to be safeguarded are so great as to require judicial intervention on an individual, patient to patient, basis. In footnote 24, the court expressly excluded cases of brain death or any other medical situation in which "no code" orders would presently be written without judicial approval. This case is now under appeal to New York's highest court, the Court of Appeals, and hopefully the unreasonableness of the routine judicialization of one aspect of medical practice (*i.e.,* non-treatment decisions of incompetents) will be recognized and corrected. As argued by Paris, unanimity of family and physician opinion, when the physician's recommendation conforms to professional standards, has traditionally been, and ought to remain, the norm for a decision not to treat.[50] It should also be pointed

out that *Saikewicz, Spring,* and *Brother Fox* (the patient in the New York case) *all* died before their cases were fully adjudicated.

With respect to brain death, North Carolina has now provided statutorily that certain close relatives or the guardian may lawfully consent to terminating life support systems.[51] Furthermore, if none of the enumerated persons is available, then at the discretion of the attending physician the extraordinary means may be discontinued.

Finally, in December of 1980 in *Severns v. Wilmington Medical Center, Incorporated,* the Supreme Court of Delaware dealt with the issue of non-treatment of a terminally ill incompetent patient for the first time. The court held that the state's guardianship statute permitted the guardian (husband) of her person to assert any constitutional right she had including the right of privacy and the right to refuse medical treatment. However, the court required an evidentiary hearing to be held in such cases to determine what relief, if any, is appropriate under the circumstances. The court also earnestly invited the prompt attention of the legislature to these matters of transcendent importance.[52]

CONCLUSIONS

The subject of euthanasia and its various subtypes needs further clarification by appropriate legal institu-

---

The subject of euthanasia and its various subtypes needs further clarification by appropriate legal institutions.

---

tions. If decisions regarding death and dying indeed represent an aspect of the constitutional right of privacy then the United States Supreme Court should so state when an appropriate case arises. The wrongful death acts and criminal statutes of the several states should be construed so as to not make voluntary-passive euthanasia an unlawful activity. The setting of potential involuntary-passive euthanasia in an incompetent person is the place where, time permitting, a legal representative should be ap-

pointed to act on behalf of the patient under the doctrine of substituted judgment, hence transforming it into "voluntary-passive euthanasia." An alternative and better approach in most incompetent patients would be to permit the immediate family to lawfully act on behalf of the patient. This alternative approach needs to be recognized as a legal right since it is a method commonly used. Of course, the decisions of the physician and family made with this approach would be subject to judicial review if there is evidence of sub-standard or unlawful activity. If the physician or other parties desire absolute civil and criminal immunity, or a controversy arises among the various decision makers, then appropriate judicial declaratory relief should be sought. Hopefully the need for resorting to such proceedings will be infrequent. Involuntary - passive euthanasia in a competent person is unethical and should be subject to legal liability. Active euthanasia, if ever permitted by law, is in my opinion outside the scope of the healing professions. The physician's role in voluntary-active euthanasia would be to certify that the situation is indeed hopeless. At that point some type of judicial proceeding would seem to be imperative and if it concurred with the person's request, then the act of actually extinguishing the last remnant of life could be delegated to some highly supervised entity other than the medical profession. Obviously involuntary-active euthanasia should be legally reprehensible in both the criminal and civil sense. The role, if any, of private advisory groups (*e.g.,* ethics committees) is in my view one that should be an elective option available to the attending physician and family if desired. Its decisions should be clearly advisory and not binding on either the physician or the family. If one views patient responsibility as a continuum, the principal attending physician has the immediate responsibility and the judiciary has the ultimate responsibility with others such as consultants, family, private groups, and health care institutions lying between. Presumably, the need to exercise the court's ultimate authority would be infrequent since in most instances there will be among the responsible parties a concurrence of views and more importantly, no wrongdoing or unethical motives. Finally, the person's views and wishes

48. *In the Matter of Earle N. Spring,* 405 N.E. 2d 115, 1980.
49. *In the Matter of Eichner v. Dillon,* 426 N.Y.S. 2d 517, 1980.
50. Paris, John J.: *Court Intervention and the Diminution of Patients' Rights: The Case of Brother Joseph Fox,* New England Journal of Medicine 303:876-878, 1980.
51. General Statutes of North Carolina, Section 90-322(b).
52. *Severns v. Wilmington Medical Center, Inc.,* 421 A.2d 1334, 1980.

must be held paramount unless overturned by compelling state interests. In short, the physician and all others responsible for the person's care should respect his or her choice absent a lawful and compelling counter policy of such magnitude as to outweigh the right of privacy and its contained right of self-determination regarding one's physical self. To a substantial extent, within the framework of a free society, an individual has even the right to be wrong.

. . .To please no one will I prescribe a deadly drug, nor give advice which may cause death . . .
—Oath of Hippocrates.

Ten Laws and a Model Bill

Following is an analysis of the principal features of enacted legislation and a discussion of a Model Bill.

The YLS Model Bill was drafted in 1978 at the Yale School of Law in a Legislative Services Project sponsored by the Society for the Right to Die. Of the ten laws enacted to date, the Kansas statute (1979) most closely resembles the Model Bill.

It provides for an easily administered system of patient election secured by means of a document which can be executed *at any time*. A suggested form is included giving instructions to withhold or withdraw life-sustaining procedures in the event of a terminal condition as certified by two physicians. The bill makes clear that wishes expressed while the declarant is competent and never disavowed should remain valid in the event the declarant is no longer able to participate in medical treatment decisions. Provision is made for retraction by means of simple revocation procedures.

Although a declaration form is included in the bill, the document need only be followed "substantially," thereby permitting insertion of additional personalized directions or stipulations and allowing choices in areas where individuals may differ as to what they want or don't want at the end of their lives. The bill would also permit the declarant to designate a proxy. To protect the document's over-all validity such additions are severable.

The physician, while bound by standards of due care, is protected from civil and criminal liability for following a valid document. The obligations of the physician are clearly stated. It is his responsibility to follow the terms of the election in the same manner as an informed consent situation or to have the patient transferred to the care of another physician.

Although the bill does not contain a specific provision regarding withdrawal of treatment from minors, as does the New Mexico law, it does recognize the need for protection of the terminally ill minor. Thus, in the section which refers to competency the legislation states that "age of itself shall not be a bar to a determination of competency." A formal statement by a minor would serve as evidentiary evidence and would have advisory effect rather than directive effect.

Provisions are included to prevent abuse. For example, no one is required to sign a directive as a condition for receiving medical care; penalties are provided for forging a document or concealing knowledge of a revocation; witnesses to the document cannot stand to gain from the declarant's estate.

ARKANSAS

The Arkansas law (1977) omits many provisions usually contained in right-to-die legislation; on the other hand, its potential applicability is more comprehensive than any of the other statutes. It is one of two right-to-die laws which permits execution of a document on behalf of a terminally ill minor. (See New Mexico.) It also permits such action to be taken on behalf of an incompetent adult or someone otherwise unable to execute such a document on his or her own behalf.

Under Arkansas law, a person may state in writing an advance refusal of "artificial, extraordinary, extreme or radical medical or surgical means or procedures calculated to prolong his life. . ." Alternatively, he may request in writing that "extraordinary means" be used to "prolong life to the extent possible."

An individual indicates his or her choices as to treatment by means of a document which may be executed at any time. The document is drawn up with the same formalities as a will of property, requiring two witnesses and notarization.

The law contains no specific or suggested document form to be followed nor does it contain any provision for revocation of the document. Unlike other right-to-die laws, it contains no provision requiring physician certification of a terminal illness except when termination of treatment is requested on behalf of another.

Family members specified in the law or a legally appointed guardian can execute a document on behalf of a minor or an incompetent adult but only after written certification by two physicians that "extraordinary means would have to be utilized to prolong life."

CALIFORNIA

The California Natural Death Act (1976) is the nation's first right-to-die law. As such, it represented a constructive step toward establishing the right of the individual to determine the quality, time and dignity of his or her death. It is by no means a perfect piece of legislation. The history of its enactment is an example of legislative compromise and amendment and the law suffered from restrictions and limitations which were imposed.

A principal drawback of the California law is that the proscribed document is not legally binding unless it has been executed, or re-executed 14 days after the diagnosis of a terminal condition. If the directive is executed prior to this time it is left to the physician to decide "whether the totality of circumstances . . . justify effectuating the directive." It is also left to the physician to determine the validity of the patient's directive. The directive has a five-year expiration date. The need to continue to re-execute the document is an unreasonable requirement considering the ease with which the directive can be revoked under the law.

The simple and direct intent of the act can be understood by reading its preamble which sets forth the rationale of the law: the need to protect individual autonomy because of "considerable uncertainty . . . as to legality of terminating life-sustaining procedures when the patient has evidenced a desire that such procedures be withheld or withdrawn."

The individual's right is secured by means of a written directive, which must be in the form set out in the law. Guidelines are provided so that the physician, hospital, nurses and others involved in the patient's care can obey the directive without fear of liability.

Any California citizen over the age of 18 can execute the "Directive to Physicians" which instructs the attending physician to withdraw or withhold life-sustaining procedures in the event of a terminal condition and when death is "imminent," an unclear determinant which could be interpreted as hours, days, weeks or months.

Witnesses to the document cannot be family members, heirs or personnel connected with the attending physician or attached to the patient's health facility.

A physician's failure to comply with the directive of a "qualified" patient will be deemed unprofessional conduct unless he takes all steps necessary to transfer the patient to another physician who will effectuate the directive.

IDAHO

Idaho's Act Relating to the Right to Die (1977) is similar in many respects to the California Natural Death Act. It recognizes that an adult has the right to execute a written directive instructing his physician to withhold or withdraw life-sustaining procedures when such a person is in a terminal condition. The directive, which has a five-year expiration date, is legally binding only if executed after an individual has been diagnosed as having a terminal condition. Provisions regarding revocation procedures, immunity for health care personnel and insurance coverage are the same as California's law.

Idaho's law differs from the California Natural Death Act as follows:

• Its directive becomes operative only when a patient is comatose or otherwise unable to communicate with his physician.

• The directive requires notarization.

• Diagnosis of a terminal condition is by the attending physician only, with no second opinion required.

• There is no waiting period after the diagnosis of a terminal condition before a legally binding document can be executed.

• The physician is not required to determine the validity of the directive.

• The physician is not required to transfer a patient if he does not wish to comply with the patient's directive.

• The Idaho law contains no penalties for forgery or destruction of a declarant's document or for concealment of a revocation.

• The Idaho law does not contain California's exclusion of coverage of a dying woman, who is pregnant, nor does it contain special witnessing provisions for nursing home patients.

KANSAS

The Kansas law, enacted in 1979, represents the most effective legislation enacted to date, closely resembling the Model Bill.

Kansas is now one of four states which recognizes that a person in good health can execute, in advance, a legally binding directive to be honored when the declarant becomes terminally ill. The other states are Arkansas, New Mexico and Washington. This contrasts with California-style legislation (California, Idaho, Oregon and Texas) in which the directive is legally binding only if executed after the diagnosis of a terminal condition. It also contrasts with laws in Nevada and North Carolina where documents are advisory to the physician regardless of when they are executed.

Kansas law permits the same flexibility as does the Model Bill: it contains a document form but allowance is made for personalized instructions. The document must be dated, signed and witnessed. Excluded as witnesses are relatives, anyone who might benefit financially from the declarant's death and anyone financially responsible for the declarant's medical care. Should the declarant be incapable of signing a document, permission is granted to another person to sign the document in the declarant's presence and at the declarant's direction.

The patient is given the responsibility of notifying the physician of the existence of a legal document. The physician is then required to make it a part of the declarant's medical records. The physician is held legally responsible to act in accordance with the declaration or to arrange transfer of the patient to another physician. There is clear provision that no "presumption" can be inferred regarding the individual who has *not* executed a document, thereby protecting existing rights.

The Kansas law avoids most of the restrictive features of the California Natural Death Act. For example, as stated above, the declaration is legally binding whenever it is executed. There is no expiration date for the declaration so that it remains in effect unless revoked. The physician is not required to determine the validity of the declaration. It does not contain the determinant in the California Natural Death Act that medical procedures can be withdrawn only when "death is imminent."

NEVADA

Nevada's law (1977) sets forth a procedure whereby an adult executes a document requesting cessation of life-sustaining procedures when terminal, comatose or "otherwise incapable of communicating with his . . . physician."

The directive is never legally binding on the physician, who is required only to "give weight" to it but may also consider "other factors," which are unspecified.

The "Directive to Physicians" contained in the law states: "It is my intention that this directive be honored by my family and attending physician as the final expression of my legal right to refuse medical or surgical treatment and to accept the consequences of my refusal." Section 12 of the law states that if a terminal patient becomes comatose or incapable of communicating "the physician shall give weight to the declaration as evidence of the patient's directions . . . but may also consider other factors in determining whether the circumstances warrant following the directions."

The law contains a suggested document form. Immunity from criminal and civil liability is provided for the physician and other medical personnel who follow the written directions of the patient. The document must be witnessed, and Nevada law excludes the same categories of witnesses as does California. The law contains provision for revocation of the document as well as penalties for its falsification or forgery.

NEW MEXICO

The New Mexico "Right to Die Act" is a simple, well-drafted law. It is more comprehensive than most of the other statutes, however, in that it permits a document to be executed on behalf of a terminally ill minor by a family member under a careful system of safeguards, including provision for contrary indication by the minor and the need for court certification of the document.

It protects adults by providing that an individual of sound mind, having reached the age of majority, may execute a document directing that if he is ever certified by two physicians as suffering from a terminal illness then "maintenance medical treatment shall not be utilized for the prolongation of his life."

A physician who relies on the document and withholds treatment is "presumed to be acting in good faith" and is granted immunity for acting in accordance with the provisions of the law unless it is proved that he violated "reasonable professional care and judgment."

The law contains no document form. An individual can draw up his or her own statement, which must be witnessed and notarized. The document can be revoked by destruction or "contrary indication."

The section on terminally ill minors sets forth the following procedures: 1) certification of a minor's terminal condition by two physicians; 2) execution of a document on behalf of the minor by parent, guardian or adult spouse unless there is contrary indication by the minor or opposition by any of the above family members; 3) petition to the district court to certify the document. An evidentiary hearing may be held but is not required.

NORTH CAROLINA

The North Carolina statute, enacted in 1977 and amended in 1979, was proposed as the result of a two-year study by the General Statutes Commission. It is the only law which combines "natural death" and "brain death" in a single statute. It also establishes procedures to protect the irreversibly comatose patient who has not executed any prior declaration.

The North Carolina law contains a suggested declaration form which "authorizes" a physician to withhold or discontinue "extraordinary" means in the event of a terminal and incurable condition. The declaration must be signed, witnessed and certified by a notary public or clerk of the Superior Court.

North Carolina and Nevada are the only states where the physician is given discretion to interpret the patient's written dictates. The law states that the attending physician *may* rely upon an appropriate declaration to withhold or discontinue "extraordinary means" and is protected from criminal or civil liability for doing so. Confirmation of the declarant's condition by a second physician is required.

"Procedures for Natural Death in the Absence of a Declaration" permits family members to request cessation of extraordinary treatment of a patient who is comatose with no "reasonable possibility" of a return to a cognitive sapient state. The patient's condition must be "terminal," "incurable" and "irreversible" as confirmed by a majority of a committee of three physicians.

Those who can request the discontinuance of such measures are a spouse, a guardian or a majority of relatives of the first degree, in that order. If none of these are available it may be discontinued at the discretion of the attending physician.

Only North Carolina and Arkansas permit action to be taken by another on behalf of a incompetent adult patient. The North Carolina law, however, specifically addresses the problem of those patients, such as Karen Quinlan, who are in a persistent vegetative state, and the law only provides for the discontinuance of "extraordinary means." Presumably this would not include such maintenance measures as artificial feeding.

The North Carolina law contains a statutory definition of death which recognizes irreversible cessation of total brain function ("brain death") as a basis for such determination.

OREGON

Oregon's "Act Relating to the Right to Die" (1977) parallels the California Natural Death Act in most respects. The law contains a specific directive which must be used. An adult can execute the directive only on his own behalf. The directive is legally binding only when executed 14 days after the diagnosis of a terminal condition. The directive expires in five years.

The Oregon Law differs from California's as follows:
• It is not incumbent upon the physician to determine the validity of the directive. The directive is "valid on its face."
• There is no provision making the statute inapplicable to pregnant women.
• The Oregon law requires that the physician make a "reasonable effort" to transfer a qualified patient in the event that he feels unable to comply with the wishes set forth in a directive signed by the patient. There is no penalty for failure to do so.

TEXAS

The Texas "Natural Death Act" (1977) follows the California model. In 1979, the Texas legislature adopted two amendments proposed by Rep. Robert Bush: 1) to eliminate the five-year limitation on the effective duration of its "Directive to Physicians." 2) deletion of the 14-day waiting period after diagnosis of a terminal condition before a declarant could execute a binding directive.

Senator Ray Farabee, sponsor of the Texas Natural Death Act, and the Texas Medical Association have taken active measures to inform Texas residents of their rights under the law and to publicize and distribute its Directive to Physicians. It is Senator Farabee's opinion that the concepts embodied in the law have been broadly accepted but further improvements and simplifications could make it more effective.

WASHINGTON

The Washington Natural Death Act, sponsored by 20 state representatives and enacted in 1979, is a modification of the California Natural Death Act. It has effectively eliminated most of the unnecessary restrictions contained in the California statute.

Washington's "Directive to Physicians" is legally binding when-ever it is executed. A directive must follow "essentially" the form contained in the law but may also include other specific directions. Physicians and other health care professionals are protected from liability complying with the directive after confirmation of a terminal condition by two physicians. If a physician refuses to effectuate the directive, he must make a "good faith effort" to transfer the qualified patient to another physician but faces no penalty for failure to do so.

The Washington law retains an unfortunate requirement from its California model: medical procedures can be withheld or withdrawn only when "death is imminent." This is a vague time factor and subject to a wide latitude of interpretation. It leaves considerable discretion as to the appropriate time for stopping some or all life-prolonging treatment because it is left to the judgment of the attending physician to determine when death is "imminent."

Statutory Citations for Right-to-Die Laws

Arkansas Act 879
Ark. Stat. Ann. (1977 Supp.) Stat. 82-3801 *et seq.*

California Natural Death Act (A.B. 3060)
Cal. Stat. 1976, Chapt. 1439, Code §
Health and Safety, § 7185 *et seq.*

Idaho Natural Death Act (S.B. 1164)
Idaho Code 39-4501 *et seq.*

Kansas Senate Bill 99
K.S.A. 65-128, 101-109 (1979 Supp.)

Nevada Assembly Bill 8
Nev. Rev. Stat. § 449.540 *et seq.*

New Mexico Right to Die Act (S.B. 16)
N.M. Stat. Ann. (1977 Supp.) § 12-35-1 *et seq.*

North Carolina Right to Natural Death (S.B. 504)
N.C. Gen. Stat. 90-320 *et seq.*

Oregon Act "Rights with Respect to Terminal Illness" (S.B. 438)
Or. Rev. Stat. § 97.050 *et seq.*

Texas Natural Death Act (S.B. 148)
Vernon's Ann. Civ. St. Art. 4590h § 1 *et seq.*

Washington Natural Death Act (H.B. 264)
Rev. Code of Wash. 70.122.01 *et seq.* (1980 Supp.)

LANDMARKS OF THE RIGHT-TO-DIE MOVEMENT

1954 — Dr. Joseph Fletcher, theologian and biomedical ethicist, forced into the open a series of ethical issues surrounding medical care with his book *Morals and Medicine,* published in 1954. It dealt with the individual's freedom of action in a number of crucial decisions over life and death, among them human initiative in death and dying.

1957 — Address of Pope Pius XII distinguishing between "ordinary" and "extraordinary" means stating that it is unnecessary to use extraordinary means to prolong life when recovery is no longer possible.

1967 — Luis Kutner, a Chicago attorney, chairman of World Habeas Corpus, suggested a Living Will as a tangible way by which an individual could make his wishes known concerning his own dying.

1968 — Dr. Walter Sackett, a Florida legislator, introduced the first bill to make the Living Will a legally binding document.

1973 — Hearings on "Death with Dignity" before U.S. Senate Committee on Aging, chaired by Senator Frank Church.

1973 — American Hospital Association *Patients Bill of Rights* approved; included right of informed consent and right to refuse treatment.

1975 — Publication of first *Legislative Manual* by the Society for the Right to Die; published and analyzed ten "death with dignity" bills introduced in state legislatures up to that time.

1976 — New Jersey Supreme Court decision in *Quinlan* established that the privilege of choosing death, in certain circumstances, takes precedence over the duty of the state to preserve life.

1976 — California Natural Death Act signed into law.

1977 — Laws passed in Arkansas, Idaho, Nevada, New Mexico, North Carolina, Oregon, Texas. Right-to-die bills introduced in 42 states.

1978 — YLS Model Bill drafted by Yale law students as part of a Yale Legislative Services project, undertaken in conjunction with the Society for the Right to Die.

1979 — Washington enacts Natural Death Act (H.B. 264), sponsored by 20 legislators. Kansas enacts Senate Bill 99, which closely resembles the Model Bill.

1980 — World Federation of Right to Die Societies formed at Oxford, England. Sidney D. Rosoff, president of U.S. Society, elected president.

1980 — Vatican's "Declaration on Euthanasia" re-affirms that dying need not be prolonged by "burdensome" life-support systems.

1980 — Florida becomes 26th state to enact "brain death" legislation.

1980 — Opinions by state supreme courts in right-to-die cases increased to four as Florida and Delaware join New Jersey and Massachusetts.

MODEL BILL

Medical Treatment Decision Act

The following Model Bill was drafted at Yale Law School in a Legislative Services Project sponsored by the Society for the Right to Die. The use of * and ** is to indicate alternatives.

1. Purpose

The Legislature finds that adult persons have the fundamental right to control the decisions relating to the rendering of their own medical care, including the decision to have life-sustaining procedures withheld or withdrawn in instances of a terminal condition.

In order that the rights of patients may be respected even after they are no longer able to participate actively in decisions about themselves, the Legislature hereby declares that the laws of the State of .... shall recognize the right of an adult person to make a written declaration instructing his physician to withhold or withdraw life-sustaining procedures in the event of a terminal condition.

2. Definitions

The following definitions shall govern the construction of this act:

(a) "Attending physician" means the physician selected by, or assigned to, the patient who has primary responsibility for the treatment and care of the patient.

(b) "Declaration" means a witnessed document in writing, voluntarily executed by the declarant in accordance with the requirements of Section 3 of this act.

(c) "Life-sustaining procedure" means any medical procedure or intervention which, when applied to a qualified patient, would serve only to prolong the dying process and where, in the judgment of the attending physician, death will occur whether or not such procedures are utilized. "Life-sustaining procedure" shall not include the administration of medication or the performance of any medical procedure deemed necessary to provide comfort care.

(d) "Qualified patient" means a patient who has executed a declaration in accordance with this act and who has been diagnosed and certified in writing to be afflicted with a terminal condition by two physicians who have personally examined the patient, one of whom shall be the attending physician. (See Comment)

3. Execution of Declaration

Any adult person may execute a declaration directing the withholding or withdrawal of life-sustaining procedures in a terminal condition. The declaration shall be signed by the declarant in the presence of two subscribing witnesses *(who are not) **(no more than one of whom may be) (a) related to the declarant by blood or marriage, (b) entitled to any portion of the estate of the declarant under any will of declarant or codicile thereto then existing or, at the time of the declaration, by operation of law then existing, (c) a claimant against any portion of the estate of the declarant at the time of his decease at the time of the execution of the declaration, or (d) directly financially responsible for the declarant's medical care.

of the execution of the declaration, or (d) directly financially responsible for the declarant's medical care.

It shall be the responsibility of declarant to provide for notification to his attending physician of the existence of the declaration. An attending physician who is so notified shall make the declaration, or a copy of the declaration, a part of the declarant's medical records.

The declaration shall be substantially in the following form, but in addition may include other specific directions. Should any of the other specific directions be held to be invalid, such invalidity shall not affect other directions of the declaration which can be given effect without the invalid direction, and to this end the directions in the declaration are severable.

DECLARATION

Declaration made this _____ day of _____ (month, year).

I, _____, being of sound mind, willfully and voluntarily make known my desire that my dying shall not be artificially prolonged under the circumstances set forth below, do hereby declare:

If at any time I should have an incurable injury, disease, or illness certified to be a terminal condition by two physicians who have personally examined me, one of whom shall be my attending physician, and the physicians have determined that my death will occur whether or not life-sustaining procedures are utilized and where the application of life-sustaining procedures would serve only to artificially prolong the dying process, I direct that such procedures be withheld or withdrawn, and that I be permitted to die naturally with only the administration of medication or the performance of any medical procedure deemed necessary to provide me with comfort care.

In the absence of my ability to give directions regarding the use of such life-sustaining procedures, it is my intention that this declaration shall be honored by my family and physician(s) as the final expression of my legal right to refuse medical or surgical treatment and accept the consequences from such refusal.

I understand the full import of this declaration and I am emotionally and mentally competent to make this declaration.

Signed _____

City, County and State of Residence _____

The declarant has been personally known to me and I believe him or her to be of sound mind.

Witness _____

Witness _____

4. Revocation

A declaration may be revoked at any time by the declarant, without regard to his or her mental state or competency, by any of the following methods:

(a) By being canceled, defaced, obliterated, or burnt, torn, or otherwise destroyed by the declarant or by some person in his or her presence and by his or her direction.

(b) By a written revocation of the declarant expressing his or her intent to revoke, signed and dated by the declarant. The attending physician shall record in the patient's medical record the time and date when he or she received notification of the written revocation.

(c) By a verbal expression by the declarant of his or her intent to revoke the declaration. Such revocation shall become effective upon communication to the attending physician by the declarant or by a person who is reasonably believed to be acting on behalf of the declarant. The attending physician shall record in the patient's medical record the time, date and place of the revocation and the time, date and place, if different, of when he or she received notification of the revocation.

5. Physician's Responsibility: Written Certification

An attending physician who has been notified of the existence of a declaration executed under this act shall, without delay after the diagnosis of a terminal condition of the declarant, take the necessary steps to provide for written certification and confirmation of the declarant's terminal condition, so that declarant may be deemed to be a qualified patient, as defined in Section 1(d) of this act.

An attending physician who fails to comply with this section shall be deemed to have refused to comply with the declaration and shall be liable as specified in Section 7(a).

6. Physician's Responsibility and Immunities

The desires of a qualified patient who is competent shall at all times supercede the effect of the declaration.

If the qualified patient is incompetent at the time of the decision to withhold or withdraw life-sustaining procedures, a declaration executed in accordance with Section 3 of this act is presumed to be valid. For the purpose of this act, a physician or health care facility may presume in the absence of actual notice to the contrary that an individual who executed a declaration was of sound mind when it was executed. The fact of an individual's having executed a declaration shall not be considered as an indication of a declarant's mental incompetency. *(Age of itself shall not be a bar to a determination of competency.)

In the absence of actual notice of the revocation of the declaration, none of the following, when acting in accordance with the requirements of this act, shall be subject to civil liability therefrom, unless negligent, or shall be guilty of any criminal act or of unprofessional conduct:

(a) A physician or health facility which causes the withholding or withdrawal of life-sustaining procedures from a qualified patient.

(b) A licensed health professional, acting under the direction of a physician, who participates in the withholding or withdrawal of life-sustaining procedures.

7. Penalties

(a) An attending physician who refuses to comply with the declaration of a qualified patient pursuant to this act shall make the necessary arrangements to effect the transfer of the qualified patient to another physician who will effectuate the declaration of the qualified patient. An attending physician who fails to comply with the declaration of a qualified patient or to make the necessary arrangements to effect the transfer shall be civilly liable.

(b) Any person who willfully conceals, cancels, defaces, obliterates, or damages the declaration of another without such declarant's consent or who falsifies or forges a revocation of the declaration of another shall be civilly liable.

(c) Any person who falsifies or forges the declaration of another, or willfully conceals or withholds personal knowledge of a revocation as provided in Section 4, with the intent to cause a withhholding or withdrawal of life-sustaining procedures contrary to the wishes of the declarant, and thereby, because of such act, directly causes life-sustaining procedures to be withheld or withdrawn and death to thereby be hastened, shall be subject to prosecution for unlawful homicide.

8. General Provisions

(a) The withholding or withdrawal of life-sustaining procedures from a qualified patient in accordance with the provisions of this act shall not, for any purpose, constitute a suicide.

(b) The making of a declaration pursuant to Section 3 shall not affect in any manner the sale, procurement, or issuance of any policy of life insurance, nor shall it be deemed to modify the terms of an existing policy of life insurance. No policy of life insurance shall be legally impaired or invalidated in any manner by the withholding or withdrawal of life-sustaining procedures from an insured qualified patient, notwithstanding any term of the policy to the contrary.

(c) No physician, health facility, or other health provider, and no health care service plan, insurer issuing disability insurance, self-insured employee welfare benefit plan, or non-profit hospital plan, shall require any person to execute a declaration as a condition for being insured for, or receiving, health care services.

(d) Nothing in this act shall impair or supercede any legal right or legal responsibility which any person may have to effect the withholding or withdrawal of life-sustaining procedures in any lawful manner. In such respect the provisions of this act are cumulative.

(e) This act shall create no presumption concerning the intention of an individual who has not executed a declaration to consent to the use or withholding of life-sustaining procedures in the event of a terminal condition.

(f) If any provision of this act or the application thereof to any person or circumstances is held invalid, such invalidity shall not affect other provisions or applications of the act which can be given effect without the invalid provision or application, and to this end the provisions of this act are severable.

ARKANSAS
ACT 879 (H.B. 826)   ENACTED: March, 1977
Introduced by Representative Henry Wilkins III 2/24/77
Passed by House (52-3) 3/14/77
Passed by Senate (32-0) 3/17/77
Signed by Gov. David Pryor 3/30/77

BE IT ENACTED BY THE GENERAL ASSEMBLY OF THE STATE OF ARKANSAS:
SECTION 1.

Every person shall have the right to die with dignity and to refuse and deny the use or application by any person of artificial, extraordinary, extreme or radical medical or surgical means or procedures calculated to prolong his life. Alternatively, every person shall have the right to request that such extraordinary means be utilized to prolong life to the extent possible.

SECTION 2.

Any person, with the same formalities as are required by the laws of this State for the execution of a will, may execute a document exercising such right and refusing and denying the use or application by any person of artificial, extraordinary, extreme or radical medical or surgical means or procedures calculated to prolong his life. In the alternative, any person may request in writing that all means be utilized to prolong life.

SECTION 3.

If any person is a minor or an adult who is physically or mentally unable to execute or is otherwise incapacitated from executing either document, it may be executed in the same form on his behalf:

(a) By either parent of the minor;

(b) By his spouse;

(c) If his spouse is unwilling or unable to act, by his child aged eighteen or over;

(d) If he has more than one child aged eighteen or over, by a majority of such children;

(e) If he has no spouse or child aged eighteen or over, by either of his parents;

(f) If he has no parent living, by his nearest living relative; or

(g) If he is mentally incompetent, by his legally appointed guardian. Provided, that a form executed in compliance with this Section must contain a signed statement by two physicians that extraordinary means would have to be utilized to prolong life.

SECTION 4.

Any person, hospital or other medical institution which acts or refrains from acting in reliance on and in compliance with such document shall be immune from liability otherwise arising out of such failure to use or apply artificial, extraordinary, extreme or radical medical or surgical means or procedures calculated to prolong such person's life.

SECTION 5.

All laws and parts of laws in conflict with this Act are hereby repealed.

CALIFORNIA
A.B. 3060   ENACTED 1976
Introduced by Assemblyman Barry Keene, 2/13/76
Passed by Assembly (43-22), 6/17/76
Passed by Senate (22-14), 8/26/76
Signed by Gov. Edmund G. Brown, Jr., 9/30/76

THE PEOPLE OF THE STATE OF CALIFORNIA DO ENACT AS FOLLOWS:

NATURAL DEATH ACT

Sec. 7185.

This act shall be known and may be cited as the Natural Death Act.

Sec. 7186.

The Legislature finds that adult persons have the fundamental right to control the decisions relating to the rendering of their own medical care, including the decision to have life-sustaining procedures withheld or withdrawn in instances of a terminal condition.

The Legislature further finds that modern medical technology has made possible the artificial prolongation of human life beyond natural limits.

The Legislature further finds that, in the interest of protecting individual autonomy, such prolongation of life for persons with a terminal condition may cause loss of patient dignity, and unnecessary pain and suffering, while providing nothing medically necessary or beneficial to the patient.

The Legislature further finds that there exists considerable uncertainty in the medical and legal professions as to the legality of terminating the use of application of life-sustaining procedures where the patient has voluntarily and in sound mind evidenced a desire that such procedures be withheld or withdrawn.

In recognition of the dignity and privacy which patients have a right to expect, the Legislature hereby declares that the laws of the State of California shall recognize the right of an adult person to make a written directive instructing his physician to withhold or withdraw life-sustaining procedures in the event of a terminal condition.

Sec. 7187.

The following definitions shall govern the construction of this chapter:

(a) "Attending physician" means the physician selected by, or assigned to, the patient who has primary responsibility for the treatment and care of the patient.

(b) "Directive" means a written document voluntarily executed by the declarant in accordance with the requirements of Section 7188. The directive, or a copy of the directive, shall be made part of the patient's medical records.

(c) "Life-sustaining procedure" means any medical procedure or intervention which utilizes mechanical or other artificial means to sustain, restore, or supplant a vital function, which, when applied to a qualified patient, would serve only to artificially prolong the moment of death and where, in the judgment of the attending physician, death is imminent whether or not such procedures are utilized. "Life-sustaining procedure" shall not include the administration of medication or the performance of any medical procedure deemed necessary to alleviate pain.

(d) "Physician" means a physician and surgeon licensed by the Board of Medical Quality Assurance or the Board of Osteopathic Examiners.

(e) "Qualified patient" means a patient diagnosed and certified in writing to be afflicted with a terminal condition by two physicians, one of whom shall be the attending physician, who have personally examined the patient.

(f) "Terminal condition" means an incurable condition caused by injury, disease, or illness, which, regardless of the application of life-sustaining procedures, would, within reasonable medical judgment, produce death, and where the application of life-sustaining procedures, serve only to postpone the moment of death of the patient.

Sec. 7188.

Any adult person may execute a directive directing the withholding or withdrawal of life-sustaining procedures in a terminal condition. The directive shall be signed by the declarant in the presence of two witnesses not related to the declarant by blood or marriage and who would not be entitled to any portion of the estate of the declarant upon his decease under any will of the declarant or codicil thereto then existing or, at the time of the directive, by operation of law then existing. In addition, a witness to a directive shall not be the attending physician, an employee of the attending physician or a health facility in which the declarant is a patient, or any person who has a claim against any portion of the estate of the declarant upon his decease at the time of the execution of the directive. The directive shall be in the following form:

DIRECTIVE TO PHYSICIANS

Directive made this _____ day of _____ (month, year).

I _____, being of sound mind, willfully, and voluntarily make known my desire that my life shall not be artificially prolonged under the circumstances set forth below, do hereby declare:

1. If at any time I should have an incurable injury, disease, or illness certified to be a terminal condition by two physicians, and where the application of life-sustaining procedures would serve only to artificially prolong the moment of my death and where my physician determines that my death is imminent whether or not life-sustaining procedures are utilized, I direct that such procedures be withheld or withdrawn, and that I be permitted to die naturally.

2. In the absence of my ability to give directions regarding the use of such life-sustaining procedures, it is my intention that this directive shall be honored by my family and physician(s) as the final expression of my legal right to refuse medical or surgical treatment and accept the consequences from such refusal.

3. If I have been diagnosed as pregnant and that diagnosis is known to my physician, this directive shall have no force or effect during the course of my pregnancy.

4. I have been diagnosed at least 14 days ago as having a terminal condition by _____, M.D., whose address is _____, and whose telephone number is _____. I understand that if I have not filled in the physician's name and address, it shall be presumed that I did not have a terminal condition when I made out this directive.

5. This directive shall have no force or effect five years from the date filled in above.

6. I understand the full import of this directive and I am emotionally and mentally competent to make this directive.

Signed _____
City, County and State of Residence

The declarant has been personally known to me and I believe him or her to be of sound mind.

Witness_____   Witness_____

Sec. 7188.5

A directive shall have no force or effect if the declarant is a patient in a skilled nursing facility as defined in subdivision (c) of Section 1250 at the time the directive is executed unless one of the two witnesses to the directive is a patient advocate or ombudsman as may be designated by the State Department of Aging for this purpose pursuant to any other applicable provision of law. The patient advocate or ombudsman shall have the same qualifications as a witness under Section 7188.

The intent of this section is to recognize that some patients in skilled nursing facilities may be so insulated from a voluntary decision making role, by virtue of the custodial nature of their care, as to require special assurance that they are capable of willfully and voluntarily executing a directive.

Sec. 7189.

(a) A directive may be revoked at any time by the declarant, without regard to his mental state or competency, by any of the following methods:

1. By being canceled, defaced, obliterated, or burnt, torn, or otherwise destroyed by the declarant or by some person in his presence and by his direction.

2. By a written revocation of the declarant expressing his intent to revoke, signed and dated by the declarant. Such revocation shall become effective only upon communication to the attending physician by the declarant or by a person acting on behalf of the declarant. The attending physician shall record in the patient's medical record the time and date when he received notification of the written revocation.

3. By a verbal expression by the declarant of his intent to revoke the directive. Such revocation shall become effective only upon communication to the attending physician by the declarant or by a person acting on behalf of the declarant. The attending physician shall record in the patient's medical record the time, date, and place of the revocation and the time, date, and place, if different, of when he received notification of the revocation.

(b) There shall be no criminal or civil liability on the part of any person for failure to act upon a revocation made pursuant to this section unless that person has actual knowledge of the revocation.

Sec. 7189.5

A directive shall be effective for five years from the date of execution thereof unless sooner revoked in a manner prescribed in Sec. 7189. Nothing in this chapter shall be construed to prevent a declarant from reexecuting a directive at any time in accordance with the formalities of Sec. 7188, including reexecution subsequent to a diagnosis of a terminal condition. If the declarant has executed more than one directive, such time shall be determined from the date of execution of the last directive known to the attending physician. If the declarant becomes comatose or is rendered incapable of communicating with the attending physician, the directive shall remain in effect for the duration of the comatose condition or until such time as the declarant's condition renders him or her able to communicate with the attending physician.

Sec. 7190.

No physician or health facility which, acting in accordance with the requirements of this chapter, causes the withholding or withdrawal of life-sustaining procedures from a qualified patient, shall be subject to civil liability therefrom. No licensed health professional, acting under the direction of a physician, who participates in the withholding or withdrawal of life-sustaining procedures in accordance with the provisions of this chapter shall be subject to any civil liability. No physician, or licensed health professional acting under the direction of a physician, who participates in the withholding or withdrawal of life-sustaining procedures in accordance with the provisions of this chapter shall be guilty of any criminal act or of unprofessional conduct.

Sec. 7191.

(a) Prior to effecting a withholding or withdrawal of life-sustaining procedures from a qualified patient pursuant to the directive, the attending physician shall determine that the directive complies with Sec. 7188, and, if the patient is mentally competent, that the directive and all steps proposed by the attending physician to be undertaken are in accord with the desires of the qualified patient.

(b) If the declarant was a qualified patient at least 14 days prior to executing or reexecuting the directive, the directive shall be conclusively presumed, unless revoked, to be the directions of the patient regarding the withholding or withdrawal of life-sustaining procedures. No physician, shall be criminally or civilly liable for failing to effectuate the directive of the qualified patient pursuant to this subdivision. A failure by a physician to effectuate the directive of a qualified patient pursuant to this division shall constitute unprofessional conduct if the physician refuses to make the necessary arrangements, or fails to take the necessary steps, to effect the transfer of the qualified patient to another physician who will effectuate the directive of the qualified patient.

(c) If the declarant becomes a qualified patient subsequent to executing the directive, and has not subsequently reexecuted the directive, the attending physician may give weight to the directive as evidence of the patient's directions regarding the withholding or withdrawal of life-sustaining procedures and may consider other factors, such as information from the affected family or the nature of the patient's illness, injury, or disease, in determining whether the totality of circumstances known to the attending physician justify effectuating the directive. No physician, and no licensed health professional acting under the directive of a physician, shall be criminally or civilly liable for failing to effectuate the directive of the qualified patient pursuant to this subdivision.

Sec. 7192.

(a) The withholding or withdrawal of life-sustaining procedures from a qualified patient in accordance with the provisions of this chapter shall not, for any purpose, constitute a suicide.

(b) The making of a directive pursuant to Sec. 7188 shall not restrict, inhibit, or impair in any manner the sale, procurement, or issuance of any policy of life insurance, nor shall it be deemed to modify the terms of an existing policy of life insurance. No policy of life insurance shall be legally impaired or invalidated in any manner by the withholding or withdrawal of life-sustaining procedures from an insured qualified patient, notwithstanding any term of the policy to the contrary.

(c) No physician, health facility, or other health provider, and no health care service plan, insurer issuing disability insurance, self-insured employee welfare benefit plan, or nonprofit hospital service plan, shall require any person to execute a directive as a condition for being insured for, or receiving, health care services.

Sec. 7193.

Nothing in this chapter shall impair or supersede any legal right or legal responsibility which any person may have to effect the withholding or withdrawal of life-sustaining procedures in any lawful manner. In such respect the provisions of this chapter are cumulative.

Sec. 7194.

Any person who willfully conceals, cancels, defaces, obliterates, or damages the directive of another without such declarant's consent shall be guilty of a misdemeanor. Any person, who, except where justified or excused by law, falsifies or forges the directive of another, or willfully conceals or withholds personal knowledge of a revocation as provided in Section 7189, with the intent to cause a withholding or withdrawal of life-sustaining procedures contrary to the wishes of the declarant, and thereby, because of any such act, directly causes life-sustaining procedures to be withheld or withdrawn and death to thereby be hastened, shall be subject to prosecution for unlawful homicide as provided in Chapter 1 (commencing with Section 187) of Title 8 of Part 1 of the Penal Code.

Sec. 7195.

Nothing in this chapter shall be construed to condone, authorize, or approve mercy killing, or to permit any affirmative or deliberate act or omission to end life other than to permit the natural process of dying as provided in this chapter.

SECTION 2.

If any provision of this act or the application thereof to any person or circumstances is held invalid, such invalidity shall not affect other provisions or applications of the act which can be given effect without the invalid provision or application, and to this end the provisions of this act are severable.

SECTION 3.

Notwithstanding Section 2231 of the Revenue and Taxation Code, there shall be no reimbursement pursuant to this section nor shall there be any appropriation made by this act because the Legislature recognizes that during any legislative session a variety of changes to laws relating to crimes and infractions may cause both increased and decreased costs to local government entities and school districts which, in the aggregate, do not result in significant identifiable cost changes.

IDAHO

S.B. 1164   ENACTED: March, 1977

Introduced by Senator Arthur P. Murphy 2/15/77

Passed by Senate (27-6) 2/26/77

Passed by House (46-24) 3/10/77

Signed by Gov. John Evans 3/18/77

AN ACT

Relating to the right to die; adding a new Chapter 45, Title 39, Idaho Code; providing a short title; stating legislative findings and policy; defining terms; providing for a directive for withholding life-sustaining procedures in a terminal case; providing for revocation of the directive; providing for expiration of the directive; providing for immunity; making general provisions; and providing severability.

BE IT ENACTED BY THE LEGISLATURE OF THE STATE OF IDAHO

SECTION 1.

That Title 39, Idaho Code, be, and the same is hereby amended by the addition thereto of a NEW CHAPTER to be known and designated as Chapter 45, Title 39, Idaho Code, and to read as follows:

39-4501. Short Title

This act shall be known and may be cited as the "Natural Death Act."

39-4502. Statement of Policy

The legislature finds that adult persons have the fundamental right to control the decisions relating to the rendering of their medical care, including the decision to have life-sustaining procedures withheld or withdrawn in instances of a terminal condition.

The legislature further finds that modern medical technology has made possible the artificial prolongation of human life beyond natural limits.

The legislature further finds that patients suffering from terminal conditions are sometimes unable to express their desire to withhold or withdraw such artificial life prolongation procedures which provide nothing medically necessary or beneficial to the patient because of the progress of the disease process which renders the patient comatose or unable to communicate with the physician.

In recognition of the dignity and privacy which patients have a right to expect, the legislature hereby declares that the laws of this state shall recognize the right of an adult person to make a written directive instructing his physician to withhold or withdraw life-sustaining procedures when such person is suffering from a terminal condition and unable to instruct his physician regarding such procedures because of the terminal condition.

39-4503. Definitions

The following definitions shall govern the construction of this chapter:

1. "Attending Physician" means the physician licensed by the state board of medicine, selected by, or assigned to, the patient who has primary responsibility for the treatment and care of the patient.

2. "Terminal condition" means an incurable physical condition caused by disease or illness which reasonable medical judgment determines shortens the lifespan of the patient.

3. "Qualified patient" means a person of sound mind at least eighteen (18) years of age diagnosed by the attending physician to be afflicted with a terminal condition.

4. "Artificial life-sustaining procedure" means any medical procedure or intervention which utilizes mechanical means to sustain or supplant a vital function which when applied to a qualified patient, would serve only to artificially prolong the moment of death and where, in the judgment of the attending physician, death is imminent whether or not such procedures are utilized. Artificial life-sustaining procedures shall not include the administration of medication or the performance of any medical procedure deemed necessary to alleviate pain.

39-4504. Directive For Withholding Procedures

Any qualified patient may execute a directive directing the withholding or withdrawal of artificial life-sustaining procedures when such patient becomes unconscious or unable to communicate with his attending physician because of the progress of the terminal condition resulting in his inability to voluntarily determine whether such procedures should be utilized, and if such procedures would serve only to prolong the moment of his death and where his attending physician determines that his death is imminent whether or not such procedures are utilized. The directive shall be signed by the qualified patient in the presence of two (2) witnesses who shall verify in such directive that they are not related to the qualified patient by blood or marriage, that they would not be entitled to any portion of the estate of the qualified patient or codicil thereto then existing, at the time of the directive, or by operation of law then existing. In addition, the witnesses shall verify that they are not the attending physician, an employee of the attending physician or a health facility in which the qualified patient is a patient or any person who has a claim against any portion of the estate of the qualified patient upon his demise at the time of the execution of the directive. The directive shall be in the following form:

DIRECTIVE TO PHYSICIAN

Directive made this _____ day of _____.

I, _____, being of sound mind, willfully and voluntarily make known my desire that my life shall not be artificially prolonged under the circumstances below:

1. In the absence of my ability to give directions regarding the use of artificial life-sustaining procedures as a result of the disease process of my terminal condition, it is my intention that such artificial life-sustaining procedures should not be used when they would serve only to artificially prolong the moment of my death and where my attending physician determines that my death is imminent whether or not the artificial life-sustaining procedures are utilized.

2. I have been diagnosed and notified that I have a terminal condition known as _____ by _____, M.D., whose

address is _____ and whose telephone number is _____
_____.

3. This directive shall have no force or effect after five years from the date filled in above.

4. I understand the full impact of this directive and I am emotionally and mentally competent to make this directive.

_____
(Name)
(City, County and State)

_____   _____
Witness   Witness

STATE OF IDAHO
County of Ada

We, _____, _____, and _____
_____, the Qualified Patient and the witnesses respectively, whose names are signed to the attached and foregoing instrument, being first duly sworn, do hereby declare to the undersigned authority that the Qualified Patient signed and executed the Directive and that he signed willingly and he executed it as his free and voluntary act for the purposes therein expressed; and that each of the witnesses, in the presence and hearing of the Qualified Patient signed the Directive as witness and that to the best of his knowledge the Qualified Patient was at the time 18 or more years of age, of sound mind and under no constraint or undue influence. We the undersigned witnesses further declare that we are not related to the Qualified Patient by blood or marriage; that we are not entitled to any portion of the estate of the Qualified Patient upon his decease under any will or codicil thereto presently existing or by operation of law then existing; that we are not the attending physician, an employee of the attending physician or a health facility in which the Qualified Patient is a patient, and that we are not a person who has a claim against any portion of the estate of the Qualified Patient upon his decease at the present time.

_____
Qualified Patient

_____   _____
Witness   Witness

SUBSCRIBED, sworn to and acknowledged before me by _____
_____, the Qualified Patient, and subscribed and sworn to before me by _____ and _____, witnesses, this _____ day of _____, 19___.

_____
Notary Public for the State of Idaho
Residing at Boise, Idaho

39-4505. Revocation

1. A directive may be revoked at any time by the qualified patient, without regard to his mental state or competence, by any of the following methods:

(a) By being cancelled, defaced, obliterated or burned, torn or otherwise destroyed by the qualified patient or by some person in his presence and by his direction.

(b) By a written revocation of the qualified patient expressing his intent to revoke, signed by the qualified patient.

(c) By a verbal expression by the qualified patient of his intent to revoke the directive.

2. There shall be no criminal or civil liability on the part of any person for failure to act upon a revocation of a directive made pursuant to this section unless that person has actual knowledge of the revocation.

39-4506. Expiration Of Directive

A directive shall be effective for five (5) years from the date of execution unless sooner revoked in a manner described in section 39-4505, Idaho Code. Nothing in this chapter shall be construed to prevent a qualified patient from re-executing a directive at any time. If the qualified patient becomes comatose or is rendered incapable of communicating with the attending physician, the directive shall remain in effect for the duration of the comatose condition or until such time as the qualified patient's condition renders him able to communicate with the attending physician.

39-4507. Immunity

No physician or health facility, which, acting in accordance with a directive meeting the requirements of this chapter, causes the withholding or withdrawal of artificial life-sustaining procedures from a qualified patient, shall be subject to civil liability or criminal liability therefrom.

39-4508. General Provisions

1. This chapter shall have no effect or be in any manner construed to apply to persons not executing a directive pursuant to this chapter nor shall it in any manner affect the rights of any such persons or of others acting for or on behalf of such persons to give or refuse to give consent or withhold consent for any medical care, neither shall this chapter be construed to affect Chaper 43, Title 39, Idaho Code, in any manner.

2. The making of a directive pursuant to this chapter shall not restrict, inhibit or impair in any manner the sale, procurement, or issuance of any policy of life insurance, nor shall it be deemed to modify the terms of existing policy of life insurance. No policy of life insurance shall be legally impaired or invalidated in any manner by the withholding or withdrawal of artificial life-sustaining procedures from an insured qualified patient, notwithstanding any term of the policy to the contrary.

3. No physician, health facility or other health provider and no health care service plan, insurer issuing disability insurance, self-insured employee, welfare benefit plan, or nonprofit hospital service plan, shall require any person to execute a directive as a condition for being insured for, or receiving, health care services.

SECTION 2.

The provisions of this act are hereby declared to be severable and if any provision of this act or the application of such provision to any person or circumstance is declared invalid for any reason, such declaration shall not affect the validity of remaining portions of this act.

KANSAS

Senate Bill 99   **ENACTED: April, 1979**

Introduced by Senator Wint Winter

Be it enacted by the Legislature of the State of Kansas:

Section 1. The legislature finds that adult persons have the fundamental right to control the decisions relating to the rendering of their own medical care, including the decision to have life-sustaining procedures withheld or withdrawn in instances of a terminal condition.

In order that the rights of patients may be respected even after they are no longer able to participate actively in decisions about themselves, the legislature hereby declares that the laws of this state shall recognize the right of an adult person to make a written declaration instructing his or her physician to withhold or withdraw life-sustaining procedures in the event of a terminal condition.

Section 2. As used in this act:

(a) "Attending physician" means the physician selected by, or assigned to, the patient who has primary responsibility for the treatment and care of the patient.

(b) "Declaration" means a witnessed document in writing, voluntarily executed by the declarant in accordance with the requirements of Section 3.

(c) "Life-sustaining procedure" means any medical procedure or intervention which, when applied to a qualified patient, would serve only to prolong the dying process and where, in the judgment of the attending physician, death will occur whether or not such procedure or intervention is utilized. "Life-sustaining procedure" shall not include the administration of medication or the performance of any medical procedure deemed necessary to provide comfort care or to alleviate pain.

(d) "Physician" means a person licensed to practice medicine and surgery by the state board of healing arts.

(e) "Qualified patient" means a patient who has executed a declaration in accordance with this act and who has been diagnosed and certified in writing to be afflicted with a terminal condition by two physicians who have personally examined the patient, one of whom shall be the attending physician.

Section 3. (a) Any adult person may execute a declaration directing the withholding or withdrawal of life-sustaining procedures in a terminal condition. The declaration made pursuant to this act shall be: (1) In writing; (2) signed by the person making the declaration, or by another person in the declarant's presence and by the declarant's expressed direction; (3) dated; and (4) signed in the presence of two or more witnesses at least eighteen (18) years of age neither of whom shall be the person who signed the declaration on behalf of and at the direction of the person making the declaration, related to the declarant by blood or marriage, entitled to any portion of the estate of the declarant according to the laws of intestate succession of this state or under any will of the declarant or codicil thereto, or directly financially responsible for declarant's medical care. The declaration of a qualified patient diagnosed as pregnant by the attending physician shall have no effect during the course of the qualified patient's pregnancy.

(b) It shall be the responsibility of declarant to provide for notification to his or her attending physician of the existence of the declaration. An attending physician who is so notified shall make the declaration, or a copy of the declaration, a part of the declarant's medical records.

(c) The declaration shall be substantially in the following form, but in addition may include other specific directions. Should any of the other specific directions be held to be invalid, such invalidity shall not affect other directions of the declaration which can be given effect without the invalid direction, and to this end the directions in the declaration are severable.

DECLARATION

Declaration made this _____ day of _____ (month, year). I, _____, being of sound mind, willfully and voluntarily make known my desires that my dying shall not be artificially prolonged under the circumstances set forth below, do hereby declare:

If at any time I should have an incurable injury, disease, or illness certified to be a terminal condition by two physicians who have personally examined me, one of whom shall be my attending physician, and the physicians have determined that my death will occur whether or not life-sustaining procedures are utilized and where the application of life-sustaining procedures would serve only to artificially prolong the dying process, I direct that such procedures be withheld or withdrawn, and that I be permitted to die naturally with only the administration of medication or the performance of any medical procedure deemed necessary to provide me with comfort care.

In the absence of my ability to give directions regarding the use of such life-sustaining procedures, it is my intention that this declaration shall be honored by my family and physician(s) as the final expression of my legal right to refuse medical or surgical treatment and accept the consequences from such refusal.

I understand the full import of this declaration and I am emotionally and mentally competent to make this declaration.

Signed _____

City, County and State of Residence _____

_____

The declarant has been personally known to me and I believe him or her to be of sound mind. I did not sign the declarant's signature above for or at the direction of the declarant. I am not related to the declarant by blood or marriage, entitled to any portion of the estate of the declarant according to the laws of intestate succession or under any will of declarant or codicil thereto, or directly financially responsible for declarant's medical care.

Witness _____

Witness _____

Section 4. (a) A declaration may be revoked at any time by the declarant by any of the following methods:

(1) By being obliterated, burnt, torn, or otherwise destroyed or defaced in a manner indicating intention to cancel;

(2) By a written revocation of the declaration signed and dated by the declarant or person acting at the direction of the declarant; or

(3) By a verbal expression of the intent to revoke the declaration, in the presence of a witness eighteen (18) years of age or older who signs and dates a writing confirming that such expression of intent was made. Any verbal revocation shall become effective upon receipt by the attending physician of the above mentioned writing. The attending physician shall record in the patient's medical record the time, date and place of when he or she received notification of the revocation.

(b) There shall be no criminal or civil liability on the part of any person for failure to act upon a revocation made pursuant to this section unless that person has actual knowledge of the revocation.

Section 5. An attending physician who has been notified of the existence of a declaration executed under this act, without delay after the diagnosis of a terminal condition of the declarant, shall take the necessary steps to provide for written certification and confirmation of the declarant's terminal condition, so that declarant may be deemed to be a qualified patient under this act.

An attending physician who fails to comply with this section shall be deemed to have refused to comply with the declaration and shall be subject to subsection (a) of Section 7.

Section 6. The desires of a qualified patient shall at all times supersede the effect of the declaration.

If the qualified patient is incompetent at the time of the decision to withhold or withdraw life-sustaining procedures, a declaration executed in accordance with Section 3 of this act is presumed to be valid. For the purpose of this act, a physician or medical care facility may presume in the absence of actual notice to the contrary that an individual who executed a declaration was of sound mind when it was executed. The fact of an individual's having executed a declaration shall not be considered as an indication of a declarant's mental incompetency. Age of itself shall not be a bar to a determination of competency.

No physician, licensed health care professional, medical care facility or employee thereof who in good faith and pursuant to reasonable medical standards causes or participates in the withholding or withdrawing of life-sustaining procedures from a qualified patient pursuant to a declaration made in accor-

dance with this act shall, as a result thereof, be subject to criminal or civil liability, or be found to have committed an act of unprofessional conduct.

Section 7. (a) An attending physician who refuses to comply with the declaration of a qualified patient pursuant to this act shall effect the transfer of the qualified patient to another physician. Failure of an attending physician to comply with the declaration of a qualified patient and to effect the transfer of the qualified patient shall constitute unprofessional conduct as defined in K.S.A. 1978 Supp. 65-2837, as amended.

(b) Any person who willfully conceals, cancels, defaces, obliterates or damages the declaration of another without such declarant's consent or who falsifies or forges a revocation of the declaration of another shall be guilty of a class A misdemeanor.

(c) Any person who falsifies or forges the declaration of another, or willfully conceals or withholds personal knowledge of the revocation of a declaration, with the intent to cause a withholding or withdrawal of life-sustaining procedures contrary to the wishes of the declarant, and thereby, because of such act, directly causes life-sustaining procedures to be withheld or withdrawn and death to be hastened, shall be guilty of a class E felony.

Section 8. (a) The withholding or withdrawal of life-sustaining procedures from a qualified patient in accordance with the provisions of this act shall not, for any purpose, constitute a suicide and shall not constitute the crime of assisting suicide as defined by K.S.A. 21-3406.

(b) The making of a declaration pursuant to Section 3 shall not affect in any manner the sale, procurement, or issuance of any policy of life insurance, nor shall it be deemed to modify the terms of an existing policy of life insurance. No policy of life insurance shall be legally impaired or invalidated in any manner by the withholding or withdrawal of life-sustaining procedures from an insured qualified patient, notwithstanding any term of the policy to the contrary.

(c) No physician, medical care facility, or other health care provider, and no health care service plan, health maintenance organization, insurer issuing disability insurance, self-insured employee welfare benefit plan, nonprofit medical service corporation or mutual nonprofit hospital service corporation shall require any person to execute a declaration as a condition for being insured for, or receiving, health care services.

(d) Nothing in this act shall impair or supersede any legal right or legal responsibility which any person may have to effect the withholding or withdrawal of life-sustaining procedures in any lawful manner. In such respect the provisions of this act are cumulative.

(e) This act shall create no presumption concerning the intention of an individual who has not executed a declaration to consent to the use or withholding of life-sustaining procedures in the event of a terminal condition.

Section 9. Nothing in this act shall be construed to condone, authorize or approve mercy killing or to permit any affirmative or deliberate act or omission to end life other than to permit the natural process of dying as provided in this act.

Section 10 amends K.S.A. 1978 Supp. 65-2837 which lists acts of "unprofessional conduct." It adds the following: "(q) Failure to effectuate the declaration of a qualified patient as provided in subsection (a) of Section 7."

Section 11 amends K.S.A. 77-202 on "definition of death."

Section 12. K.S.A. 77-202 and K.S.A. 1978 Supp. 65-2837 are hereby repealed.

Section 13. This act shall take effect and be in force from and after its publication in the statute book.

NEVADA

A.B. 8   ENACTED: May, 1977

Introduced by Assemblyman Steven A. Coulter, et al 1/17/77

Passed by House (28-11) 3/21/77

Passed by Senate (14-6) 4/21/77

Signed by Gov. Mike O'Callaghan 5/6/77

AN ACT relating to life-sustaining procedures; permitting any adult person to direct cessation of such procedures for himself if he is in a terminal condition and becomes comatose or otherwise incapable of communicating with his attending physician; and providing other matters properly relating thereto.

THE PEOPLE OF THE STATE OF NEVADA, REPRESENTED IN SENATE AND ASSEMBLY, DO ENACT AS FOLLOWS:

SECTION 1.

Chapter 449 of NRS is hereby amended by adding thereto the provisions set forth as sections 2 to 16, inclusive, of this act.

SECTION 2.

As used in sections 2 to 16, inclusive, of this act, unless the context otherwise requires, the words and terms defined in sections 3 to 7, inclusive, have the meanings ascribed to them in those sections.

SECTION 3.
"Attending physician" means the physician, selected by or assigned to a patient, who has primary responsibility for the treatment and care of the patient.

SECTION 4.
"Declaration" means a written document executed by an adult person directing that when he is in a terminal condition and becomes comatose or is otherwise rendered incapable of communicating with his attending physician, life-sustaining procedures shall not be applied.

SECTION 5.
"Life-sustaining procedure" means a medical procedure which utilizes mechanical or other artifical methods to sustain, restore or supplant a vital function. The term does not include medication or procedures necessary to alleviate pain.

SECTION 6.
"Physician" means any person licensed to practice medicine or osteopathy.

SECTION 7.
"Terminal condition" means an incurable condition which is such that the application of life-sustaining procedures serves only to postpone the moment of death.

SECTION 8.
Any adult person may execute a declaration directing that when he is in a terminal condition and becomes comatose or is otherwise rendered incapable of communicating with his attending physician, life-sustaining procedures be withheld or withdrawn from him. The person shall execute the declaration in the same manner in which a will is executed, except that a witness may not be:

1. Related to the declarant by blood or marriage.
2. The attending physician.
3. An employee of the attending physician or of the hospital or other health care facility in which the declarant is a patient.
4. A person who has a claim against any portion of the estate of the declarant.

SECTION 9.
The declaration shall be in substantially the following form:

DIRECTIVE TO PHYSICIANS

I, _____, being of sound mind, intentionally and voluntarily declare:

1. If at any time I am in a terminal condition and become comatose or am otherwise rendered incapable of communicating with my attending physician, and my death is imminent because of an incurable disease, illness or injury, I direct that life-sustaining procedures be withheld or withdrawn, and that I be permitted to die naturally.

2. It is my intention that this directive be honored by my family and attending physician as the final expression of my legal right to refuse medical or surgical treatment and to accept the consequences of my refusal.

3. If I have been found to be pregnant, and that fact is known to my physician, this directive is void during the course of my pregnancy.

I understand the full import of this directive, and I am emotionally and mentally competent to execute it.

Signed _____

City, County and State of Residence _____

The declarant has been personally known to me and I believe _____ _____ to be of sound mind.

Witness _____
Witness _____

Section 3 of the declaration form should be omitted for male declarants.

The executed declaration, or a copy thereof signed by the declarant and the witnesses, shall be placed in the medical record of the declarant and a notation made of its presence and the date of its execution. A notation of the circumstances and date of removal of a declaration shall be entered in the medical record if the declaration is removed for any reason.

SECTION 10.
1. A declaration may be revoked at any time by the declarant in the same way in which a will may be revoked, or by a verbal expression of intent to revoke. A verbal revocation is effective upon communication to the attending physician by the declarant or another person communicating it on behalf of the declarant. The attending physician shall record the verbal revocation and the date on which he received it in the medical record of the declarant.

2. No person is liable in a civil or criminal action for failure to act upon a revocation of a declaration unless the person had actual knowledge of the revocation.

SECTION 11.
No hospital or other health and care facility, physician or person working under the direction of a physician who causes the withholding or withdrawal of life-sustaining procedures from a patient in a terminal condition who has a declaration in effect and has become comatose or has otherwise been rendered incapable of communicating with his attending physician is subject to criminal or civil liability or to a charge of unprofessional conduct or malpractice as a result of an action taken in accordance with sections 8 to 14, inclusive, of this act.

SECTION 12.
1. If a patient in a terminal condition has a declaration in effect and becomes comatose or is otherwise rendered incapable of communicating with his attending physician, the physician shall give weight to the declaration as evidence of the patient's directions regarding the application of life-sustaining procedures, but the attending physician may also consider other factors in determining whether the circumstances warrant following the directions.

2. No hospital or other health care facility, physician or person working under the direction of a physician is subject to criminal or civil liability for failure to follow the directions of the patient to withhold or withdraw life-sustaining procedures.

SECTION 13.
1. A person does not commit suicide by executing a declaration.

2. The executive of a declaration does not restrict, inhibit or impair the sale, procurement or issuance of any policy of insurance, nor shall it be deemed to modify any term of an existing policy of insurance. No policy of life insurance is impaired or invalidated in whole or in part by the withholding or withdrawal of life-sustaining procedures from an insured person, regardless of any term of the policy.

3. No person may require another to execute a declaration as a condition for being insured for or receiving health care services.

SECTION 14.
1. Any person who willfully conceals, cancels, defaces, obliterates or damages the declaration of another without the consent of the declarant is guilty of a misdemeanor.

2. Any person who falsifies or forges a document purporting to be the declaration of another, or who willfully conceals or withholds personal knowledge of a revocation, with the intent to cause a withholding or withdrawal of life-sustaining procedures contrary to the wishes of the declarant and thereby directly causes life-sustaining procedures to be withheld or withdrawn and death to be hastened is guilty of murder.

SECTION 15.
Nothing in sections 8 to 10, inclusive, of this act permits any affirmative or deliberate act or omission which ends life other than to permit the natural process of dying.

SECTION 16.
Nothing in sections 9 to 14, inclusive, of this act limits the right or responsibility which a person may otherwise have to withhold or withdraw life-sustaining procedures.

SECTION 17.
An instrument executed before July 1, 1977, which clearly expresses the intent of the declarant to direct the withholding or withdrawal of life-sustaining procedures from him when he is in a terminal condition and becomes comatose or is otherwise rendered incapable of communicating with his attending physician shall, if executed in a manner which attests voluntary execution and not subsequently revoked, be given the same effect as a declaration prepared and executed in accordance with sections 2 to 16, inclusive, of this act.

NEW MEXICO

S.B. 16   ENACTED: April, 1977

*Introduced by Senators John E. Conway
and William K. Valentine 1/18/77*

Passed by Senate (36-3) 2/15/77

Passed by House (35-33) 3/17/77

Signed by Gov. Jerry Apodaca 4/7/77

AN ACT Relating to medical treatment of terminally ill patients.

**BE IT ENACTED BY THE LEGISLATURE OF THE
STATE OF NEW MEXICO**

SECTION 1. Short Title

This act may be cited as the "Right to Die Act".

SECTION 2. Definitions

As used in the Right to Die Act:

A. "maintenance medical treatment" means medical treatment designed solely to sustain the life processes;

B. "minor" means a person who has not reached the age of majority;

C. "physician" means an individual licensed to practice medicine in New Mexico; and

D. "terminal illness" means an illness that will result in death as defined in Section 1-2-2.2 NMSA 1953, regardless of the use or discontinuance of maintenance medical treatment.

SECTION 3. Execution of a Document

A. An individual of sound mind and having reached the age of majority may execute a document directing that if he is ever certified under the Right to Die Act as suffering from a terminal illness then maintenance medical treatment shall not be utilized for the prolongation of his life.

B. A document described in Subsection A of this section is not valid unless it has been executed with the same formalities as required of a valid will pursuant to the provision of the Probate Code.

SECTION 4. Execution of a Document for the Benefit of a Terminally Ill Minor

A. If a minor has been certified under the Right to Die Act as suffering a terminal illness, the following individual may execute the document on his behalf:

(1) the spouse, if he has reached the age of majority; or

(2) if there is no spouse, or if the spouse is not available at the time of the certification or is otherwise unable to act, then either the parent or guardian of the minor.

B. An individual named in Subsection A of this section may not execute a document:

(1) if he has actual notice of contrary indications by the minor who is terminally ill; or

(2) when executing as a parent or guardian, if he has actual notice of opposition by either another parent or guardian or a spouse who has attained the age of majority.

C. A document described in Subsection A of this section is not valid unless it has been executed with the same formalities as required of a valid will under the Probate Code, and has been certified upon its face by a district court judge pursuant to Subsection D of this section.

D. Any person executing a document pursuant to the provisions of this section shall petition the district court for the county in which the minor is domiciled, or the county in which the minor is being maintained, for certification upon the face of the document. The court shall appoint a guardian ad litem to represent the minor and may hold an evidentiary hearing before certification. All costs shall be charged to the petitioner. If the district court judge is satisfied that all requirements of the Right to Die Act have been satisfied, that the document was executed in good faith and that the certification of the terminal illness was in good faith, then he shall certify the document.

SECTION 5. Certification of a Terminal Illness

A. For purposes of the Right to Die Act, certification of a terminal illness may be rendered only in writing by two physicians, one of whom is the physician in charge of the individual who is terminally ill. A copy of any such certification shall be kept in the records of the medical facility where the patient is being maintained. If the patient is not being maintained in a medical facility, a copy shall be retained by the physician in charge in his own case records.

B. A physician who certifies a terminal illness under this section is presumed to be acting in good faith. Unless it is alleged and proved that his action violated the standard of reasonable professional care and judgment under the circumstances, he is immune from civil or criminal liability that otherwise might be incurred.

SECTION 6. Revocation of a Document

A. An individual who has executed a document under the Right to Die Act may, at any time thereafter, revoke the document. Revocation may be accomplished by destroying the document, or by contrary indication expressed in the presence of one witness who has reached the age of majority.

B. A minor may revoke the document in the manner provided under Subsection A of this section. During the remainder of his terminal illness, any such revocation may constitute actual notice of his contrary indication.

SECTION 7. Physician's Immunity From Liability

A. After certification of a terminal illness under the Right to Die Act, a physician who relies on a document executed under that act, of which he has no actual notice of revocation or contrary indication, and who withholds maintenance medical treatment from the terminally ill individual who executed the document, is presumed to be acting in good faith. Unless it is alleged and proved that the physician's actions violated the standard of reasonable professional care

and judgment under the circumstances, he is immune from civil or criminal liability that otherwise might be incurred.

B. A physician who relies on a document executed on behalf of a terminally ill minor under the Right to Die Act and certified on its face by a district court judge pursuant to Section 4 of that act, and who withholds maintenance medical treatment from the terminally ill minor on whose behalf the document was executed, is presumed to be acting in good faith, if he has no actual notice of revocation or contrary indication. Unless it is alleged and proved that the physician's actions violated the standard of reasonable professional care and judgment under the circumstances, he is immune from civil or criminal liability that otherwise might be incurred.

C. In the absence of actual notice to the contrary, a physician may presume that an individual who executed a document under the Right to Die Act was of sound mind when the document was executed.

D. Any hospital or medical institution or its employees which act or refrain from acting in reasonable reliance on and in compliance with a document executed under the Right to Die Act shall be immune from civil or criminal liability that otherwise might be incurred.

SECTION 8. Insurance

A. The withholding of maintenance medical treatment from any individual pursuant to the provisions of the Right to Die Act shall not, for any purpose, constitute a suicide.

B. The execution of a document pursuant to the Right to Die Act shall not restrict, inhibit or impair in any manner the sale, procurement or issuance of any policy of life insurance, nor shall it be deemed to modify the terms of an existing policy of life insurance. No policy of life insurance shall be legally impaired or invalidated in any manner by the withholding of maintenance medical treatment under the Right to Die Act from an insured individual, notwithstanding any term of the policy to the contrary.

C. No physician, health facility or other health care provider, and no health care service plan, insurer issuing disability insurance, self-insured employee welfare benefit plan or nonprofit hospital service plan shall require any person to execute a document pursuant to the Right to Die Act as a condition for being insured for, or receiving, health care service.

SECTION 9. Cumulative Provisions

Nothing in the Right to Die Act shall impair or supersede any existing legal right or legal responsibility which any person may have to effect the withholding or nonutilization of any maintenance medical treatment in any lawful manner. In such respect the provisions of the Right to Die Act are cumulative.

SECTION 10. Penalties

A. Whoever knowingly and willfully conceals, destroys, falsifies or forges a document with intent to create the false impression that another person has directed that no maintenance medical treatment be utilized for the prolongation of his life or the life of a minor, or whoever knowingly and willfully conceals evidence of revocation of a document executed pursuant to the Right to Die Act, is guilty of a second degree felony, punishable by imprisonment in the penitentiary for a period of not less than ten years nor more than fifty years or a fine of not more than ten thousand dollars ($10,000) or both.

B. Whoever knowingly and willfully conceals, destroys, falsifies or forges a document with intent to create the false impression that another person has not directed that maintenance medical treatment not be utilized for the prolongation of his life is guilty of a third degree felony, punishable by imprisonment in the penitentiary for a term of not less than two years nor more than ten years or a fine of not more than five thousand dollars ($5,000) or both.

C. Whoever executes a document under the Right to Die Act for the benefit of a terminally ill minor and who either has actual notice of contrary indications by the minor who is terminally ill, or, when executing as a parent or guardian, has actual notice of opposition by either another parent or guardian or a spouse, is guilty of a second degree felony, punishable by imprisonment in the penitentiary for a period of not less than ten years nor more than fifty years, or by a fine of not more than ten thousand dollars ($10,000) or both.

SECTION 11. Application

The Right to Die Act applies to all persons executing documents in conformity with that act on or after the effective date of the Right to Die Act.

NORTH CAROLINA

S.B. 504   ENACTED: June, 1977

Introduced by Senator William G. Smith et al 4/13/77

Passed by Senate (44-3) 4/28/77

Passed by House (80-23) 6/27/77

Ratified 6/29/77 by: The Hon. James C. Green, President of the Senate

The Hon. Carl J. Stewart, Jr., Speaker of the House

AN ACT to provide a procedure for the exercise of a person's right to a natural death; and to add expressly the criterion of irreversible cessation of brain function to the other criteria for establishing a person's death.

THE GENERAL ASSEMBLY OF NORTH CAROLINA ENACTS:

Section 1.

Chapter 90 of the General Statutes is hereby amended by adding a new Article thereto to read as follows:

ARTICLE 23.
RIGHT TO NATURAL DEATH; BRAIN DEATH

Sec. 90-320. General purpose of Article.

(a) The General Assembly hereby recognizes that an individual's rights as a citizen of this State include the right to a peaceful and natural death. This Article is to establish a procedure for the exercise of that right and to state expressly the extent of a physician's obligation to preserve the life of his patient in situations where artificial means may be used to sustain the circulatory and respiratory functions for an indefinite period.

(b) Nothing in this Article shall be construed to authorize any affirmative or deliberate act or omission to end life other than to permit the natural process of dying.

Sec. 90-321. Right to a natural death.

(a) As used in this Article the term:
1. "Declarant" means a person who has signed a declaration in accordance with subsection (c);
2. "Extraordinary means" is defined as any medical procedure or intervention which in the judgment of the attending physician would serve only to postpone artificially the moment of death by sustaining, restoring, or supplanting a vital function;
3. "Physician" means any person licensed to practice medicine under Article I of Chapter 90 of the laws of the State of North Carolina.

(b) If a person has declared, in accordance with subsection (c) below, a desire that his life not be prolonged by extraordinary means; and the declaration has not been revoked in accordance with subsection (e); and
1. It is determined by the attending physician that the declarant's present condition is
    a. terminal; and
    b. incurable; and
2. There is confirmation of the declarant's present condition as set out above in subdivision (b) (I) by a physician other than the attending physician;

then extraordinary means may be withheld or discontinued upon the direction and under the supervision of the attending physician.

(c) The attending physician may rely upon a signed, witnessed, dated and proved declaration:
1. which expresses a desire of the declarant that no extraordinary means be used to prolong his life if his condition is determined to be terminal and incurable; and
2. which states that the declarant is aware that the declaration authorizes a physician to withhold or discontinue the extraordinary means; and
3. which has been signed by the declarant in the presence of two witnesses who state that they (i) are not related within the third degree to the declarant or to the declarant's spouse and (ii) would not be entitled to any portion of the estate of the declarant upon his death under any will of the declarant or codicil thereto then existing or under the Intestate Succession Act as it then provided, and (iii) are not the attending physician, an employee of the attending physician or of a health facility in which the declarant is a patient, or of a nursing home or any group care home in which the declarant resides and (iv) is not a person who has a claim against any portion of the estate of the declarant at the time of the declaration; and
4. which has been proved before a clerk or assistant clerk of superior court who certifies substantially as set out in subsection (d) below.

(d) The following form is specifically determined to meet the requirements above:

DECLARATION OF A DESIRE FOR A NATURAL DEATH

I _____, being of sound mind, desire that my life not be prolonged by extraordinary means if my condition is determined to be terminal and incurable. I am aware and understand that this writing authorizes a physician to withhold or discontinue extraordinary means.

This the _____ day of _____, _____.

Signature _____

I hereby state that the declarant, _____, signed the above declaration in my presence and that I am not related to the declarant by blood or marriage and I would not be entitled to any portion of the estate of the declarant under any existing will or codicil of the declarant, or as an heir under the Intestate Succession Act if the declarant died on this date without a will. I also state that I am not the declarant's attending physician or an employee of the declarant's attending physician, or an employee of a health facility in which the declarant is a patient or an employee of a nursing home or any group care home where the declarant resides. I further state that I do not now have any claim against the declarant.

Witness _____
Witness _____

The clerk or the assistant clerk may, upon proper proof, certify the declaration as follows:

CERTIFICATE

I, _____, Clerk (Assistant Clerk) of Superior Court for _____ County hereby certify that _____ and _____, witnesses, appeared before me and swore that they witnessed _____, declarant, sign the attached declaration; and also swore that at the time they witnessed the declaration (i) they were not related within the third degree to the declarant or to the declarant's spouse, and (ii) they would not be entitled to any portion of the estate of the declarant upon the declarant's death under any will or the declarant or codicil thereto then existing or under the Intestate Succession Act as it provided at that time, and (iii) they were not a physician attending the declarant or an employee of an attending physician or of a health facility in which the declarant was a patient or of a nursing home or any group care home in which the declarant resided, and (iv) they did not have a claim against the declarant. I further certify that I am satisfied as to the genuineness and due execution of the declaration.

This the _____ of _____, _____.

_____
Clerk (Assistant Clerk) of Superior
Court for the County of _____.

The above declaration may be proved by the clerk or the assistant clerk in the following manner:
1. upon the testimony of the two witnesses; or
2. if the testimony of only one witness is available, then
    a. upon the testimony of such witness, and
    b. upon proof of the handwriting of the witness who is dead or whose testimony is otherwise unavailable, and
    c. upon proof of the handwriting of the declarant, unless he signed by his mark; or upon proof of such other circumstances as will satisfy the clerk or assistant clerk of the superior court as to the genuineness and due execution of the declaration.
3. If the testimony of none of the witnesses is available, such declaration may be proved by the clerk or assistant clerk
    a. upon proof of the handwriting of the two witnesses whose testimony is unavailable, and
    b. upon compliance with paragraph c. of subdivision (2) above.

Due execution may be established, where the evidence required above is unavoidably lacking or inadequate, by testimony of other competent witnesses as to the requisite facts.

The testimony of a witness is unavailable within the meaning of this subsection when the witness is dead, out of the State, not to be found within the State, insane or otherwise incompetent, physically unable to testify or refuses to testify.

If the testimony of one or both of the witnesses is not available the clerk or the assistant clerk of superior court may, upon proper proof, certify the declaration as follows:

CERTIFICATE

I _____, Clerk (Assistant Clerk) of the Court for the Superior Court of _____ County hereby certify that based upon the evidence before me I am satisfied as to the genuineness and due execution of the attached declaration by _____, declarant, and that the declarant's signature was witnessed by _____, and _____, who at the time of the declaration met the qualifications of G.S. 90-321 (c) (3).

This the _____ day of _____, _____.

_____
Clerk (Assistant Clerk) of Superior
Court for _____ County.

(e) The above declaration may be revoked by the declarant, in any manner by which he is able to communicate his intent to revoke, without regard to his mental or physical condition. Such revocation shall become effective only upon communication to the attending physician by the declarant or by an individual acting on behalf of the declarant.

(f) The execution and consummation of declarations made in accordance with subsection (c) shall not constitute suicide for any purpose.

(g) No person shall be required to sign a declaration in accordance with subsection (c) as a condition for becoming insured under any insurance contract or for receiving any medical treatment.

(h) The withholding or discontinuance of extraordinary means in accordance with this section shall not be considered the cause of death for any civil or criminal purposes nor shall it be considered unprofessional conduct. Any person, institution or facility against whom criminal or civil liability is asserted because of conduct in compliance with this section may interpose this section as a defense.

Amendments to

1977 NORTH CAROLINA RIGHT TO A NATURAL DEATH; BRAIN DEATH

Senate Bill 771, Ratified in 1979 Session

(New language is in italics. Section 90-322 was entitled "Brain Death" in 1977 law.)

Section 90-332. *Procedures for natural death in the absence of a declaration.*

(a) If a person is comatose and there is no reasonable possibility that he will return to a cognitive sapient state, and:

    1. It is determined by the attending physician that the person's present condition is:
        a. terminal; and
        b. incurable; and
        c. irreversible; and
    2. There is a confirmation of the person's present condition as set out above by this subsection, by a majority of a committee of three physicians other than the attending physician; and
    3. A vital function of the person is being sustained by extraordinary means;

then, *extraordinary means may be discontinued in accordance with subsection* (b).

(b) If *a person's condition has been determined to meet the conditions set forth in subsection (a) and no instrument has been executed as provided in G.S. 90-321* the extraordinary means to prolong life may be discontinued upon the direction and under the supervision of the attending physician at the request (i) of the person's spouse, or (ii) of a guardian of the person, or (iii) of a majority of relatives of the first degree, in that order. If none of the above are available then at the discretion of the attending physician the extraordinary means may be discontinued under the direction and under the supervision of the attending physician.

(c) The discontinuance of such extraordinary means shall not be considered the cause of death for any civil or criminal purpose nor shall it be considered unprofessional conduct. Any person, institution or facility against whom criminal or civil liability is asserted because of conduct in compliance with this section may interpose this section as a defense.

Section 90-323. Death; determination by physician. The determination that a person is dead shall be made by a physician licensed to practice medicine applying ordinary and accepted standards of medical practice. Brain death, defined as irreversible cessation of total brain function, may be used as a sole basis for the determination that a person has died, particularly when brain death occurs in the presence of artificially maintained respiratory and circulatory functions. This specific recognition of brain death as a criterion of death of the person shall not preclude the use of other medically recognized criteria for determining whether and when a person had died.

OREGON

S.B. 438   ENACTED: June, 1977

Introduced by Senator Ted Hallock, et al 2/4/77
Passed by Senate (17-12) 3/30/77
Passed by House (33-23) 5/18/77
Signed by Gov. Robert W. Straub 6/9/77

AN ACT Relating to the right to die.

BE IT ENACTED BY THE PEOPLE OF THE STATE OF OREGON:

SECTION 1. As used in this Act:

(1) "Attending physician" means the physician with primary responsibility for the care and treatment of a patient.

(2) "Directive" means a written document voluntarily executed by a declarant in accordance with the requirements set forth in section 2 of this Act.

(3) "Life-sustaining procedure" means any medical procedure or intervention that utilizes mechanical or other artificial means to sustain, restore or supplant a vital function of a qualified patient that is used to maintain the life of a person suffering from a terminal condition and serves only to artificially prolong the moment of death and when death is imminent whether or not such procedures are used. "Life-sustaining procedure" does not include the administration of medication or the performance of any medical procedure deemed necessary to alleviate pain.

(4) "Physician" means an individual licensed to practice medicine by the Board of Medical Examiners for the State of Oregon.

(5) "Qualified patient" means an individual, 18 years of age or older, whom the attending physician and one other physician, upon diagnostic examination of the patient, certify to be suffering from a terminal condition.

(6) "Terminal condition" means an incurable condition caused by injury, disease or illness which, regardless of the application of life-sustaining procedures would within reasonable medical judgment produce death, and where the application of life-sustaining procedures serves only to postpone the moment of death of the patient.

SECTION 2.

(1) An individual of sound mind and 18 years of age or older may at any time execute or reexecute a directive directing the withholding or withdrawal of life-sustaining procedures should the declarant become a qualified patient. The directive shall be in the following form:

DIRECTIVE TO PHYSICIANS

Directive made this _____ day of _____ (month, year). I _____ _____, being of sound mind, wilfully and voluntarily make known my desire that my life shall not be artificially prolonged under the circumstances set forth below and do hereby declare:

1. If at any time I should have an incurable injury, disease or illness certified to be a terminal condition by two physicians, one of whom is the attending physician, and where the application of life-sustaining procedures would serve only to artificially prolong the moment of my death and where my physician determines that my death is imminent whether or not life-sustaining procedures are utilized, I direct that such procedures be withheld or withdrawn, and that I be permitted to die naturally.

2. In the absence of my ability to give directions regarding the use of such life-sustaining procedures, it is my intention that this directive shall be honored by my family and physician(s) as the final expression of my legal right to refuse medical or surgical treatment and accept the consequences from such refusal.

3. I have been diagnosed and notified at least 14 days ago as having a terminal condition by _____, M.D., whose address is _____ _____, and whose telephone number is _____. I understand that if I have not filled in the physician's name and address, it shall be presumed that I did not have a terminal condition when I made out this directive.

4. This directive shall have no force or effect five years from the date filled in above.

5. I understand the full import of this directive and I am emotionally and mentally competent to make this directive.

Signed _____
City, County and State of Residence _____

I hereby witness this directive and attest that:

(1) I personally know the Declarant and believe the Declarant to be of sound mind.

(2) To the best of my knowledge, at the time of the execution of this directive, I:

    (a) Am not related to the Declarant by blood or marriage,
    (b) Do not have any claim on the estate of the Declarant,
    (c) Am not entitled to any portion of the Declarant's estate by any will or by operation of law, and
    (d) Am not a physician attending the Declarant or a person employed by a physician attending the Declarant.

(3) I understand that if I have not witnessed this directive in good faith I may be responsible for any damages that arise out of giving this directive its intended effect.

Witness _____   Witness _____

(2) A directive made pursuant to subsection (1) of this section is only valid if signed by the declarant in the presence of two attesting witnesses who, at the

time the directive is executed, are not:

    (a) Related to the declarant by blood or marriage; or

    (b) Entitled to any portion of the estate of the declarant upon his decease under any will or codicil of the declarant or by operation of law at the time of the execution of the directive; or

    (c) The attending physician or an employee of the attending physician or of a health facility in which the declarant is a patient; or

    (d) Persons who at the time of the execution of the directive have a claim against any portion of the estate of the declarant upon the declarant's decease.

(3) One of the witnesses, if the declarant is a patient in a house for the aged licensed under ORS Chapter 442 at the time the directive is executed, shall be an individual designated by the Department of Human Resources for the purpose of determining that the declarant is not so insulated from the voluntary decision-making role that the declarant is not capable of wilfully and voluntarily executing a directive.

(4) A witness who does not attest a directive in good faith shall be liable for any damages that arise from giving effect to an invalid directive.

(5) A directive made pursuant to this Act may be revoked at any time by the declarant without regard to his mental state or competency by any of the following methods:

    (a) By being burned, torn, canceled, obliterated or otherwise destroyed by the declarant or by some person in his presence and by his direction.

    (b) By a written revocation of the declarant expressing his intent to revoke, signed and dated by the declarant.

    (c) By a verbal expression by the declarant of his intent to revoke the directive.

(6) Unless revoked, a directive shall be effective for five years from the date of execution. If the declarant has executed more than one directive, such time shall be determined from the date of execution of the last directive known to the attending physician. If the declarant becomes comatose or is rendered incapable of communicating with the attending physician, the directive shall remain in effect for the duration of the comatose condition or until such time as the declarant's condition renders him able to communicate with the attending physician.

SECTION 3.

A directive that is valid on its face is valid as to any physician for the purposes of this Act unless the physician has actual knowledge of facts that render the directive invalid or is under the direction of a court not to give effect to the directive.

SECTION 4.

(1) It shall be lawful for an attending physician or a licensed health professional under the direction of an attending physician, acting in good faith and in accordance with the requirements of this Act, to withhold or withdraw life-sustaining procedures from a qualified patient who has properly executed a directive in accordance with the requirements of this Act.

(2) A physician or licensed health professional or health facility under the direction of a physician who, acting in good faith and in accordance with the requirements of this Act, causes the withholding or withdrawal of life-sustaining procedures shall not be guilty of any criminal offense, shall not be subject to civil liability and shall not be in violation of any professional oath, affirmation or standard of care.

(3) A physician or licensed health professional or health facility shall not be guilty of any criminal offense, shall not be subject to civil liability and shall not be in violation of any professional oath, affirmation or standard of care for failing to assume the duties created by or for failing to give effect to any directive or revocation made pursuant to this Act unless that physician has actual knowledge of the directive or revocation.

SECTION 5.

(1) Except as provided in this section, no physician, licensed health professional or medical facility shall be under any duty, whether by contract, by statute or by any other legal requirement to participate in the withdrawal or withholding of life-sustaining procedures.

(2) (a) An attending physician shall make a directive or a copy of a directive made pursuant to this Act part of the patient's medical record.

    (b) An attending physician shall record in the patient's medical record the time, date, place and manner of a revocation and the time, date, place and manner, if different, of when he received notification of the revocation. If the revocation is written, the attending physician shall make the revocation or a copy of the revocation a part of the patient's medical record.

(3) A physician or medical facility electing for any reason not to participate in the withholding or withdrawal of life-sustaining procedures in accord with a directive made pursuant to this Act shall:

    (a) Make a reasonable effort to locate a physician or medical facility that will give effect to a qualified patient's directive and shall have a duty to transfer the qualified patient to that physician or facility; or

    (b) At the request of a patient or of the patient's family, a physician or medical facility shall transfer the patient to another physician or medical facility that will reconsider circumstances which might make this Act applicable to the patient.

SECTION 6.

(1) Before withdrawing or withholding life-sustaining procedures from a qualified patient who is mentally competent in the opinion of the attending physician, the attending physician shall determine that the directive is valid under the requirements of this Act and shall determine that all steps proposed to be taken are in accord with the desires of the qualified patient.

(2) Before withdrawing or withholding life-sustaining procedures from a qualified patient who is not mentally competent in the opinion of the attending physician, the attending physician shall determine that the directive is valid under the requirements of this Act and shall weigh the directive with other surrounding circumstances such as information from the affected family or the nature of the patient's illness, injury or disease to determine if the steps proposed to be taken are, in the opinion of the attending physician, in accord with the known desires of the qualified patient. If the declarant was a qualified patient at least 14 days before executing or reexecuting the directive, the directive shall be conclusively presumed, unless revoked, to be in accord with the desires of the qualified patient for the purposes of this subsection.

SECTION 7.

(1) Except as provided in subsection (2) of this section, the making of a directive pursuant to this Act shall not restrict, inhibit or impair in any manner the sale, procurement or issuance of any policy of insurance, nor shall it be deemed to modify the terms of an existing policy of insurance.

(2) No physician, health facility, health care service plan, insurer issuing disability insurance, self-insured employee welfare benefit plan, nonprofit hospital service plan or other direct or indirect health service provider shall require any person to execute a directive as a condition for being insured for, or receiving, health care services.

(3) No policy of insurance shall be legally impaired or invalidated in any manner by the withholding or withdrawal of life-sustaining procedures from an insured qualified patient.

SECTION 8.

Nothing in this Act shall be construed to condone, authorize or approve mercy killing, or to permit any affirmative or deliberate act or omission to end life other than to permit the natural process of dying as provided in this Act.

SECTION 9.

Nothing in this Act shall impair or supersede any legal right or legal responsibility which any person may have to effect the withholding or withdrawal of life-sustaining procedures in any lawful manner. In such respect the provisions of this Act are cumulative.

SECTION 10.

The withholding or withdrawal of life-sustaining procedures from a qualified patient in accordance with the provisions of this Act shall not, for any purpose, constitute a suicide.

SECTION 11.

(1) No person shall by wilfully concealing or destroying a revocation or by wilfully falsifying or forging a directive cause the withdrawal or withholding of life-sustaining procedures.

(2) No person shall by wilfully concealing or destroying a directive or by wilfully falsifying or forging a revocation cause an individual's intent with respect to the withholding or withdrawal of life-sustaining procedures not to be given effect.

SECTION 12.

(1) Violation of subsection (1) of section 11 of this Act is a Class A felony.

(2) Violation of subsection (2) of section 11 of this Act is a Class A misdemeanor.

(3) Failure to perform the duties prescribed in sections 5 and 6 of this Act shall constitute unprofessional conduct for purposes of ORS 677.190.

TEXAS

S.B. 148   ENACTED: June, 1977

Introduced by Senator Ray Farabee 1/17/77

Passed by Senate (18-13) 3/23/77
Passed by House (74-56) 5/26/77
Signed by Gov. Dolph Briscoe 6/15/77
Amended in 1979 by H.B. 571

BE IT ENACTED BY THE LEGISLATURE OF THE STATE OF TEXAS:

SECTION 1.

This Act shall be known and may be cited as the Natural Death Act.

SECTION 2.

In this Act:

(1) "Attending physician" means the physician selected by, or assigned by the physician selected by, the patient who has primary responsibility for the treatment and care of the patient.

(2) "Directive means a written document voluntarily executed by the declarant in accordance with the requirements of Section 3 of this Act. The directive, or a copy of the directive, shall be made part of the patient's medical records.

(3) "Life-sustaining procedure" means a medical procedure or intervention which utilizes mechanical or other artificial means to sustain, restore, or supplant a vital function, which, when applied to a qualified patient, would serve only to artificially prolong the moment of death and where, in the judgment of the attending physician, noted in the qualified patient's medical records, death is imminent whether or not such procedures are utilized. "Life-sustaining procedure" shall not include the administration of medication or the performance of any medical procedure deemed necessary to alleviate pain.

(4) "Physician" means a physician and surgeon licensed by the Texas State Board of Medical Examiners.

(5) "Qualified patient" means a patient diagnosed and certified in writing to be afflicted with a terminal condition by two physicians, one of whom shall be the attending physician, and the other shall be chosen by the patient or the attending physician, who have each personally examined the patient.

(6) "Terminal condition" means an incurable condition caused by injury, disease, or illness, which, regardless of the application of life-sustaining procedures, would, within reasonable medical judgment, produce death, and where the application of life-sustaining procedures serves only to postpone the moment of death of the patient.

SECTION 3.

Any adult person may execute a directive for the withholding or withdrawal of life-sustaining procedures in the event of a terminal condition. The directive shall be signed by the declarant in the presence of two witnesses not related to the declarant by blood or marriage and who would not be entitled to any portion of the estate of the declarant on his decease under any will of the declarant or codicil thereto or by operation of law. In addition, a witness to a directive shall not be the attending physician, an employee of the attending physician or a health facility in which the declarant is a patient, a patient in a health care facility in which the declarant is a patient, or any person who has a claim against any portion of the estate of the declarant upon his decease at the time of the execution of the directive. The signature of the declarant shall be acknowledged, and the witnesses shall subscribe and swear to the directive before a notary public. The directive shall be in the following form:

DIRECTIVE TO PHYSICIANS

Directive made this _____ day of _____ (month, year).

I _____, being of sound mind, willfully and voluntarily make known my desire that my life shall not be artificially prolonged under the circumstances set forth below, and do hereby declare:

1. If at any time I should have an incurable condition caused by injury, disease, or illness certified to be a terminal condition by two physicians, and where the application of life-sustaining procedures would serve only to artificially prolong the moment of my death and where my attending physician determines that my death is imminent whether or not life-sustaining procedures are utilized, I direct that such procedures be withheld or withdrawn, and that I be permitted to die naturally.

2. In the absence of my ability to give directions regarding the use of such life-sustaining procedures, it is my intention that this directive shall be honored by my family and physicians as the final expression of my legal right to refuse medical or surgical treatment and accept the consequences from such refusal.

3. If I have been diagnosed as pregnant and that diagnosis is known to my physician, this directive shall have no force or effect during the course of my pregnancy.

4. I have been diagnosed and notified as having a terminal condition by _____, M.D., whose address is _____, and whose telephone number is _____. I understand that if I have not filled in the physician's name and address, it shall be presumed that I did not have a terminal condition when I made out this directive.

5. This directive shall be in effect until it is revoked.

6. I understand the full import of this directive and I am emotionally and mentally competent to make this directive.

7. I understand that I may revoke this directive at any time.

Signed _____

City, County, and State of Residence _____

The declarant has been personally known to me and I believe him or her to be of sound mind. I am not related to the declarant by blood or marriage, nor would I be entitled to any portion of the declarant's estate on his decease, nor am I the attending physician of declarant or an employee of the attending physician or a health facility in which declarant is a patient, or a patient in the health care facility in which the declarant is a patient, or any person who has a claim against any portion of the estate of the declarant upon his decease.

Witness _____

Witness _____

STATE OF TEXAS
COUNTY OF _____

Before me, the undersigned authority, on this day personally appeared _____, _____, and _____, _____, known to me to be the declarant and witnesses whose names are subscribed to the foregoing instrument in their respective capacities, and, all of said persons being by me duly sworn, the declarant, _____, declared to me and to the said witnesses in my presence that said instrument is his Directive to Physicians, and that he had willingly and voluntarily made and executed it as his free act and deed for the purposes therein expressed.

Declarant _____

Witness _____

Witness _____

Subscribed and acknowledged before me by the said Declarant, _____ _____, and by the said witnesses, _____ and _____, on this _____ day of _____, 19 _____.

_____
Notary Public in and for
_____ County, Texas

SECTION 4.

(a) A directive may be revoked at any time by the declarant, without regard to his mental state or competency, by any of the following methods:

(1) by being canceled, defaced, obliterated, or burnt, torn, or otherwise destroyed by the declarant or by some person in his presence and by his direction;

(2) by a written revocation of the declarant expressing his intent to revoke, signed and dated by the declarant. Such revocation shall become effective only on communication to an attending physician by the declarant or by a person acting on behalf of the declarant or by mailing said revocation to an attending physician. An attending physician or his designee shall record in the patient's medical record the time and date when he received notification of the written revocation and shall enter the word "VOID" on each page of the copy of the directive in the patient's medical records; or

(3) by a verbal expression by the declarant of his intent to revoke the directive. Such revocation shall become effective only on communication to an attending physician by the declarant or by a person acting on behalf of the declarant. An attending physician or his designee shall record in the patient's medical record the time, date, and place of the revocation and the time, date, and place, if different, of when he received notification of the revocation and shall enter the word "VOID" on each page of the copy of the directive in the patient's medical records.

(b) Except as otherwise provided in this Act, there shall be no criminal or civil liability on the part of any person for failure to act on a revocation made pursuant to this section unless that person has actual knowledge of the revocation.

SECTION 5.

A directive shall be effective until it is revoked in a manner prescribed in Section 4 of this Act. Nothing in this Act shall be construed to prevent a declarant from reexecuting a directive at any time in accordance with the formalities of Section 3 of this Act, including reexecution subsequent to a diagnosis of a terminal condition. If the declarant has executed more than one directive, such time shall be determined from the date of execution of the last directive known to the attending physician. If the declarant becomes comatose or is rendered incapable of communicating with the attending physician, the directive shall remain in effect for the duration of the comatose condition or until such time as the declarant's condition renders him or her able to communicate with the attending physician.

SECTION 6.

No physician or health facility which, acting, in accordance with the requirements of this Act, causes the withholding or withdrawal of life-sustaining procedures from a qualified patient, shall be subject to civil liability therefrom unless negligent. No health professional, acting under the direction of a physician, who participates in the withholding or withdrawal of life-sustaining procedures in accordance with the provisions of this Act shall be subject to any civil liability unless negligent. No physician, or health professional acting under the direction of a physician, who participates in the withholding or withdrawal of life-sustaining procedures in accordance with the provisions of this Act shall be guilty of any criminal act or of unprofessional conduct unless negligent. No physician, health care facility, or health care professional shall be liable either civilly or criminally for failure to act pursuant to the declarant's directive where such physician, health care facility, or health care professional had no knowledge of such directive.

SECTION 7.

(a) Prior to effecting a withholding or withdrawal of life-sustaining procedures from a qualified patient pursuant to the directive, the attending physician shall determine that the directive complies with the form of the directive set out in Section 3 of this Act, and, if the patient is mentally competent, that the directive and all steps proposed by the attending physician to be undertaken are in accord with the existing desires of the qualified patient and are communicated to the patient.

(b) If the declarant was a qualified patient prior to executing or reexecuting the directive, the directive shall be conclusively presumed, unless revoked, to be the directions of the patient regarding the withholding or withdrawal of life-sustaining procedures. No physician, and no health professional acting under the direction of a physician, shall be criminally or civilly liable for failing to effectuate the directive of the qualified patient pursuant to this subsection. A failure by a physician to effectuate the directive of a qualified patient pursuant to this subsection may constitute unprofessional conduct if the physician refuses to make the necessary arrangements or fails to take the necessary steps to effect the transfer of the qualified patient to another physician who will effectuate the directive of the qualified patient.

(c) If the declarant becomes a qualified patient subsequent to executing the directive, and has not subsequently reexecuted the directive, the attending physician may give weight to the directive as evidence of the patient's directions regarding the withholding or withdrawal of life-sustaining procedures and may consider other factors, such as information from the affected family or the nature of the patient's illness, injury, or disease, in determining whether the totality of circumstances known to the attending physician justifies effectuating the directive. No physician, and no health professional acting under the direction of a physician, shall be criminally or civilly liable for failing to effectuate the directive of the qualified patient pursuant to this subsection.

SECTION 8.

(a) The withholding or withdrawal of life-sustaining procedures from a qualified patient in accordance with the provisions of this Act shall not, for any purpose, constitute an offense under Section 22.08, Penal Code.

(b) The making of a directive pursuant to Section 3 of this Act shall not restrict, inhibit, or impair in any manner the sale, procurement, or issuance of any policy of life insurance, nor shall it be deemed to modify the terms of an existing policy of life insurance. No policy of life insurance shall be legally impaired or invalidated in any manner by the withholding or withdrawal of life-sustaining procedures from an insured qualified patient, notwithstanding any term of the policy to the contrary.

(c) No physician, health facility, or other health provider, and no health care service plan, or insurer issuing insurance, may require any person to execute a directive as a condition for being insured for, or receiving, health care services nor may the execution or failure to execute a directive be considered in any way in establishing the premiums for insurance.

SECTION 9.

A person who willfully conceals, cancels, defaces, obliterates, or damages the directive of another without such declarant's consent shall be guilty of a Class A misdemeanor. A person who falsifies or forges the directive of another, or willfully conceals or withholds personal knowledge of a revocation as provided in Section 4 of this Act, with the intent to cause a withholding or withdrawal of life-sustaining procedures contrary to the wishes of the declarant, and thereby, because of any such act, directly causes life-sustaining procedures to be withheld or withdrawn and death to thereby be hastened, shall be subject to prosecution for criminal homicide under the provisions of the Penal Code.

SECTION 10.

Nothing in this Act shall be construed to condone, authorize, or approve mercy killing, or to permit any affirmative or deliberate act or omission to end life other than to permit the natural process of dying as provided in this Act.

SECTION 11.

Nothing in this Act shall impair or supersede any legal right or legal responsibility which any person may have to effect the withholding or withdrawal of life-sustaining procedures in any lawful manner. In such respect the provisions of this Act are cumulative.

SECTION 12.

The importance of this legislation and the crowded condition of the calendars in both houses create an emergency and an imperative public necessity that the constitutional rule requiring bills to be read on three several days in each house be suspended, and this rule is hereby suspended, and that this Act take effect and be in force from and after its passage, and it is so enacted.

WASHINGTON

H.B. 264   ENACTED: March, 1979

BE IT ENACTED BY THE LEGISLATURE OF THE STATE OF WASHINGTON:

Section 1. This act shall be known and may be cited as the "Natural Death Act".

Section 2. The legislature finds that adult persons have the fundamental right to control the decisions relating to the rendering of their own medical care, including the decision to have life-sustaining procedures withheld or withdrawn in instances of a terminal condition.

The legislature further finds that modern medical technology has made possible the artificial prolongation of human life beyond natural limits.

The legislature further finds that, in the interest of protecting individual autonomy, such prolongation of life for persons with a terminal condition may cause loss of patient dignity, and unnecessary pain and suffering, while providing nothing medically necessary or beneficial to the patient.

The legislature further finds that there exists considerable uncertainty in the medical and legal professions as to the legality of terminating the use or application of life-sustaining procedures where the patient has voluntarily and in sound mind evidenced a desire that such procedures be withheld or withdrawn.

In recognition of the dignity and privacy which patients have a right to expect, the legislature hereby declares that the laws of the state of Washington shall recognize the right of an adult person to make a written directive instructing such person's physician to withhold or withdraw life-sustaining procedures in the event of a terminal condition.

Section 3. Unless the context clearly requires otherwise, the definitions contained in this section shall apply throughout this chapter.

(1) "Attending physician" means the physician selected by, or assigned to, the patient who has primary responsibility for the treatment and care of the patient.

(2) "Directive" means a written document voluntarily executed by the declarer in accordance with the requirements of Section 4 of this act.

(3) "Health facility" means a hospital as defined in RCW 70.38.020(7) or a nursing home as defined in RCW 70.38.020(8).

(4) "Life-sustaining procedure" means any medical or surgical procedure or intervention which utilizes mechanical or other artificial means to sustain, restore, or supplant a vital function, which, when applied to a qualified patient, would serve only to artificially prolong the moment of death and where, in the judgment of the attending physician, death is imminent whether or not such procedures are utilized. "Life-sustaining procedure" shall not include the administration of medication or the performance of any medical procedure deemed necessary to alleviate pain.

(5) "Physician" means a person licensed under chapters 18.71 or 18.57 RCW.

(6) "Qualified patient" means a patient diagnosed and certified in writing to be afflicted with a terminal condition by two physicians one of whom shall be the attending physician, who have personally examined the patient.

(7) "Terminal condition" means an incurable condition caused by injury, disease, or illness, which, regardless of the application of life-sustaining procedures, would, within reasonable medical judgment, produce death, and where the application of life-sustaining procedures serve only to postpone the moment of death of the patient.

(8) "Adult person" means a person attaining the age of majority as defined in RCW 26.28.010 and 26.28.015.

Section 4. (1) Any adult person may execute a directive directing the withholding or withdrawal of life-sustaining procedures in a terminal condition. The directive shall be signed by the declarer in the presence of two witnesses not related to the declarer by blood or marriage and who would not be entitled to any portion of the estate of the declarer upon declarer's decease under any will of the declarer or codicil thereto then existing or, at the time of the directive, by operation of law then existing. In addition, a witness to a directive shall not be the attending physician, an employee of the attending physician or a health facility in which the declarer is a patient, or any person who has a claim against any portion of the estate of the declarer upon declarer's decease at the time of the execution of the directive. The directive, or a copy thereof, shall be made part of the patient's medical records retained by the attending physician, a copy of which shall be forwarded to the health facility upon the withdrawal of life-sustaining procedures. The directive shall be essentially in the following form, but in addition may include other specific directions:

DIRECTIVE TO PHYSICIANS

Directive made this _____ day of _____ (month, year).

I _____, being of sound mind, wilfully, and voluntarily make known my desire that my life shall not be artificially prolonged under the circumstances set forth below, and do hereby declare that:

(a) If at any time I should have an incurable injury, disease, or illness certified to be a terminal condition by two physicians, and where the application of life-sustaining procedures would serve only to artificially prolong the moment of my death and where my physician determines that my death is imminent whether or not life-sustaining procedures are utilized, I direct that such procedures be withheld or withdrawn, and that I be permitted to die naturally.

(b) In the absence of my ability to give directions regarding the use of such life-sustaining procedures, it is my intention that this directive shall be honored by my family and physician(s) as the final expression of my legal right to refuse medical or surgical treatment and I accept the consequences from such refusal.

(c) If I have been diagnosed as pregnant and that diagnosis is known to my physician, this directive shall have no force or effect during the course of my pregnancy.

(d) I understand the full import of this directive and I am emotionally and mentally competent to make this directive.

Signed _____

City, County, and State of Residence _____

The declarer has been personally known to me and I believe him or her to be of sound mind.

Witness _____ Witness _____

(2) Prior to effectuating a directive the diagnosis of a terminal condition by two physicians shall be verified in writing, attached to the directive, and made a permanent part of the patient's medical records.

Section 5. (1) A directive may be revoked at any time by the declarer, without regard to declarer's mental state or competency, by any of the following methods:

(a) By being canceled, defaced, obliterated, burned, torn, or otherwise destroyed by the declarer or by some person in declarer's presence and by declarer's direction.

(b) By a written revocation of the declarer expressing declarer's intent to revoke, signed, and dated by the declarer. Such revocation shall become effective only upon communication to the attending physician by the declarer or by a person acting on behalf of the declarer. The attending physician shall record in the patient's medical record the time and date when said physician received notification of the written revocation.

(c) By a verbal expression by the declarer of declarer's intent to revoke the directive. Such revocation shall become effective only upon communication to the attending physician by the declarer or by a person acting on behalf of the declarer. The attending physician shall record in the patient's medical record the time, date, and place of the revocation and the time, date, and place, if different, of when said physician received notification of the revocation.

(2) There shall be no criminal or civil liability on the part of any person for failure to act upon a revocation made pursuant to this section unless that person has actual or constructive knowledge of the revocation.

(3) If the declarer becomes comatose or is rendered incapable of communicating with the attending physician, the directive shall remain in effect for the duration of the comatose condition or until such time as the declarer's condition renders declarer able to communicate with the attending physician.

Section 6. No physician or health facility which, acting in good faith in accordance with the requirements of this chapter, causes the withholding or withdrawal of life-sustaining procedures from a qualified patient, shall be subject to civil liability therefrom. No licensed health personnel, acting under the direction of a physician, who participates in good faith in the withholding or withdrawal of life-sustaining procedures in accordance with the provisions of this chapter shall be subject to any civil liability. No physician, or licensed health personnel acting under the direction of a physician, who participates in good faith in the withholding or withdrawal of life-sustaining procedures in accordance with the provisions of this chapter shall be guilty of any criminal act or of unprofessional conduct.

Section 7. (1) Prior to effectuating a withholding or withdrawal of life-sustaining procedures from a qualified patient pursuant to the directive, the attending physician shall make a reasonable effort to determine that the directive complies with Section 4 of this act and, if the patient is mentally competent, that the directive and all steps proposed by the attending physician to be undertaken are currently in accord with the desires of the qualified patient.

(2) The directive shall be conclusively presumed, unless revoked, to be the directions of the patient regarding the withholding or withdrawal of life-sustaining procedures. No physician, and no licensed health personnel acting in good faith under the direction of a physician, shall be criminally or civilly liable for failing to effectuate the directive of the qualified patient pursuant to this subsection. If the physician refuses to effectuate the directive, such physician shall make a good faith effort to transfer the qualified patient to another physician who will effectuate the directive of the qualified patient.

Section 8. (1) The withholding or withdrawal of life-sustaining procedures from a qualified patient pursuant to the patient's directive in accordance with the provisions of this chapter shall not, for any purpose, constitute a suicide.

(2) The making of a directive pursuant to Section 4 of this act shall not restrict, inhibit, or impair in any manner the sale, procurement, or issuance of any policy of life insurance, nor shall it be deemed to modify the terms of an existing policy of life insurance. No policy of life insurance shall be legally impaired or invalidated in any manner by the withholding or withdrawal of life-sustaining procedures from an insured qualified patient, notwithstanding any term of the policy to the contrary.

(3) No physician, health facility, or other health provider, and no health care service plan, insurer issuing disability insurance, self-insured employee welfare benefit plan, or nonprofit hospital service plan, shall require any person to execute a directive as a condition for being insured for, or receiving, health care services.

Section 9. Any person who wilfully conceals, cancels, defaces, obliterates, or damages the directive of another without such declarer's consent shall be guilty of a gross misdemeanor. Any person who falsifies or forges the directive of another, or wilfully conceals or withholds personal knowledge of a revocation as provided in Section 5 of this act with the intent to cause a withholding or withdrawal of life-sustaining procedures contrary to the wishes of the declarer, and thereby, because of any such act, directly causes life-sustaining procedures to be withheld or withdrawn and death to thereby be hastened, shall be subject to prosecution for murder in the first degree as defined in RCW 9A.32.030.

Section 10. The act of withholding or withdrawing life-sustaining procedures when done pursuant to a directive described in Section 4 of this act and which causes the death of the declarer, shall not be construed to be an intervening force or to affect the chain of proximate cause between the conduct of any person that placed the declarer in a terminal condition and the death of the declarer.

Section 11. Nothing in this chapter shall be construed to condone, authorize, or approve mercy killing, or to permit any affirmative or deliberate act or omission to end life other than to permit the natural process of dying.

Section 12. Sections 1 through 11 of this act shall constitute a new chapter in Title 70 RCW.

Section 13. If any provision of this act or the application thereof to any person or circumstances is held invalid, such invalidity shall not affect other provisions or applications of the act which can be given effect without the invalid provisions or application, and to this end the provisions of this act are severable.

SOCIETY FOR THE RIGHT TO DIE

PURPOSE

To work for the recognition of the individual's right to die with dignity; to accomplish this purpose by:

- An educational program directed to the general public, health related professionals, clergy, and those concerned with the judicial and legislative processes.
- Support of judicial and legislative action.
- Publication and distribution of literature.

THE SOCIETY . . .

- Believes that the basic rights of self-determination and of privacy include the right to control decisions relating to one's own medical care.
- Works to advance legislation enabling individuals, by means of a legally binding document, to limit the futile prolongation of dying.
- Opposes the use of medical procedures which serve to prolong the dying process needlessly, thereby causing unnecessary pain and suffering and loss of dignity. At the same time we **support** the use of medications and medical procedures which will provide comfort care to the dying.
- Recognizes that a terminally ill patient may become unable to take part in medical care decisions and that a patient's previously expressed wishes may not be observed by physician and/or hospital.
- Seeks to: 1) protect the rights of a dying patient, and 2) protect physicians, hospitals and health care providers from the threat of liability for complying with the mandated desires of those who wish to die with medical intervention limited to the provision of comfort care.

Physicians' Opinions Toward Legislation Defining Death and Withholding Life Support

Harold J. Wershow, DSW, Ferris J. Ritchey, PhD, and Thomas H. Alphin, MD†
Birmingham, Alabama

ABSTRACT: We explored attitudes and practices of Alabama physicians regarding two bills considered in the 1978 State Legislature. One bill defined death to permit the withdrawal of life supports; the other permitted the cessation of active treatment when demanded by terminal patients. Members of the Medical Association of the State of Alabama (MASA) in practices permitting independent action in such cases composed the sample. Twenty percent of 1,300 questionnaires were returned. Most participants idealistically resented legislative interference but realistically were resigned to or welcomed legal clarification of physicians' rights and responsibilities. Respondents encountering demands for life-support withdrawal generally acceded, usually after consultation with family and/or colleagues. Most used analgesics to control pain, if necessary, even to a point compromising respiration. Most considered withdrawal of life support, and most approved of "living wills." Alabama physicians are in the mainstream of American medicine in this area of bioethical concern.

This study reports data from two opinion polls of members of the Medical Association of the State of Alabama (MASA). The polls were designed to determine the range of opinion within the medical community on two legislative bills introduced in the 1978 session of the Alabama Legislature. One poll centered on a bill to permit the withholding of "extraordinary" life-preserving measures (LPM) from moribund patients, a practice often referred to as *passive euthanasia.* The second centered on a bill which outlines circumstances and procedures under which a moribund patient may be defined as *dead.* The polls were conducted by mail in May 1978. Although the bills died in committee, they have been reintroduced in the 1979 session, where they have received more vigorous support.

This paper is designed to report the opinions of the medical community to its members and the legislature. In addition, the survey provides estimates of how frequently and under what circumstances physicians actually withhold LPM and/or take actions which may hasten the death of moribund patients. Such death-hastening measures (DHM) are often spoken of as *active euthanasia.* Before reporting our findings, a brief review of the research literature concerning LPM and DHM is warranted.

Current State of Knowledge

A search of the literature has disclosed four papers with a sound data base dealing with actual practices of physicians regarding LPM and DHM. Brown et al[1] conducted a study of 418 physicians in Seattle, Washington, and found "a generally favorable response to the omission of LPM but opposition to DHM." Travis et al[2] found that nearly half of all responding physicians in Iowa "frequently" (a term left undefined) omitted LPM. Crane,[3] in a book widely touted as "dealing with the actual behavior of physicians" regarding LPM, really only described what physicians *say they would do* in certain specified hypothetic situations. One small section revealed that, in routine practice with "service" patients in one university hospital, many fewer patients are actually resuscitated than physicians claimed for hypothetic situations. Duff and Campbell[4] discussed physicians' actual practices relating to issues of LPM. Their study considered only a limited range of possible cases in a neonatal intensive care unit in a New England university hospital. They found that LPM were withheld from 14% of the babies in this unit, largely from those with multiple severe anomalies, anencephaly, spinal cord anomalies, and others whose chance of survival and meaningful life were poor to nonexistent.

Additional papers report specifically on physicians' attitudes and opinions concerning LPM and DHM.[5-7] For example, Carey and Posavac,[5] in a survey of Chicago area physicians who dealt with terminally ill people, found that 90% of physicians approved of passive and 17%, active euthanasia. These figures appear to be representative of the mainstream of medical opinion, that passive euthanasia is practical and ethical, while active euthanasia is somewhat

†From the Department of Sociology and the Office of Health Affairs Administration (Dr. Alphin), University of Alabama in Birmingham.

Reprint requests to Room 237, Ullman Bldg, University Station, Birmingham, Ala 35294 (Dr. Wershow).

Supported by funds from the UAB University Research Council.

Reprinted by permission from the *Southern Medical Journal,* vol. 74(2), pp. 215–220, February, 1981.

controversial and less practiced. It should be noted, though, that their definition of active euthanasia was very strict, and its practice may be underestimated.

The passing of legislation pertinent to LPM, DHM, and defining death may have both direct and indirect effects on medical practice in this area. Towers,[6] in a discussion of the effects of the Natural Death Act in California, agreed that the Act (similar to the one presented to the Alabama Legislature) was useful as a positive force "in encouraging patients and their families to discuss the (previously taboo) subject of terminal illness. . . . The primary significance of the Act may lie in its symbolic value, in that it makes clear the right of a patient [under certain unduly restricting provisions which, incidentally, are absent in the Alabama Act] to keep his or her autonomy and control over what may and may not be done to him or her, right up to the last."

Alabama physicians, we will show, are similar to others in this country in their attitudes and practices in these areas of ethical controversy.

METHODS

Sample Procedure. The population of physicians from which the two samples were drawn are actively practicing physicians in MASA who have a direct interest in death-related legislation. Names for mailed questionnaires were selected from the then current MASA *Membership Directory* of members living and practicing in the state. The two samples came from the population of physicians who generally met the following criteria: (1) those in types of practices that might provide patients in life-threatening situations, and

TABLE 1. Attitudes Toward Legislation Allowing Patients to Direct Physicians to Withhold Life Support

Response	No.	%
(1) Strongly approve of it.	11	9.6
(2) Approve of it.	49	42.6
(3) Undecided.	11	9.6
(4) Disapprove of it.	18	15.7
(5) Strongly disapprove of it.	13	11.3
(6) No response.	13	11.3
Total	115	100.1*

*Percentages do not add up to 100 because of rounding.

(2) those in a position to make independent judgments about withholding life support. On the basis of the first criterion the population of interest is limited to general and family practice, neurology and neurosurgery, internal medicine and its subspecialties, obstetrics and gynecology, and pediatrics. Dermatologists and psychiatrists, among others, were disregarded. On the basis of the second criterion, physicians were disregarded who were retired or engaged in the full-time practice of a profession or business other than medicine or who were working in areas not providing direct patient care. Interns, residents, and fellows in teaching hospitals or on active duty in the Armed Forces were also excluded from the sample population. After these were eliminated from consideration, around 1,300 names remained, which were systematically divided into two groups of roughly 650 names each. One group was mailed a questionnaire dealing with legislation on life support, and the

TABLE 2. Circumstances Under Which a Physician Would Inform Patients of Their Option to Withhold Life Support if Pertinent Legislation Were Passed

Response	No.	%
(1) Would make the choice widely known through the dispersion of literature in waiting rooms.	15	13.0
(2) Would inform those with terminal illnesses or their families or trusted advisors (eg, lawyers, minister).	38	33.0
(3) Would be highly selective in choice of patients given this information.	16	13.9
(4) Would not make the information known, but would generally support the decision of a patient asking about such documents.	20	17.4
(5) Would urge all patients who request an opinion not to execute such a document.	2	1.7
(6) Would not care to serve patients who have executed such a document and would urge them to choose another doctor.	10	8.7
(7) No response.	14	13.2
Total	115	100.9*

*Percentages do not add up to 100 because of rounding.

other group received a questionnaire on legislation that defines the point at which a moribund patient may be pronounced dead. From the part of the study dealing with the bill to permit withholding of life support, 115 questionnaires were returned, for a response rate of 17.7%. This sample is called sample 1. From the part of the study dealing with the bill to define death (sample 2), 142 questionnaires were returned, for a response rate of 21.8%.

TABLE 3. The Practice of and Disposition of Respondents Toward Withholding Life Support (Sample 1)

Response	No.	%
(1) Have withheld life support on at least one occasion.	37	32.2
(2) Have not withheld life support but would if legal right to do so were clear.	15	13.0
(3) Generally disapprove of withholding life support but would do so if patient desired it and legal right to do so were clear.	22	19.1
(4) Would never consider withholding life support as a professional option.	3	2.6
(5) No response.	38	33.1
Total	115	100.0

An examination of the demographic features of the two samples revealed that both indeed came from the same population of physicians. In the returned questionnaires there was no statistically significant difference between samples 1 and 2 with respect to the age of the respondents, their religious affiliation, and their political orientation (conservatism or liberalism). Roughly 80% of the respondents in both samples practiced in hospitals with 101 or more beds. There were no significant differences in the proportions of the samples in given medical specialties: taking the samples together, 33.1% of the respondents were general or family practitioners, 25.2% were surgeons, 22.8% specialized in internal medicine, 10.6% in obstetrics and/or gynecology, and 8.3% in pediatrics. Since the two samples appeared to come from the same population, they were combined where appropriate.

To maximize response rates, a support letter from Dr. Leon C. Hamrick, then President of MASA, was solicited and graciously granted. Only one wave of questionnaires was mailed. There were no recalls because the principal investigator left the country temporarily in June 1978. Further, methodologic problems were encountered in the computer coding and statistical analysis which make it more cost-efficient to revise the questionnaire and draw new samples rather than make recalls. With these limitations in mind, the reader should view this report as a first approximation. It is hoped that this study may be redesigned to account for response contingencies not initially recognized.

FINDINGS

In both questionnaires, the respondents were given the following statement and asked whether they agreed with it:

Physicians have inescapable responsibilities for life and death decisions, which they can and must carry out. Therefore under these circumstances, laws are neither necessary nor advisable when they restrict, govern or limit the individual physician's responsibility and judgment, aided by whatever advice or consultation that physicians may deem advisable.

TABLE 4. Disposition of Sample 2 Respondents Toward a Legislative Bill to Define Death

Response	No.	%
(1) Approve the proposed legislation.	56	39.4
(2) Approve the legislation if additional safeguards are proposed.	8	5.6
(3) Think a determination of death is best left loosely defined, to be made by physicians (with whatever consultation each physician may choose to employ in specific cases). Believe the present legal status is, therefore, satisfactory.	53	37.3
(4) Do not believe in shutting off life-sustaining apparatus under any circumstances. Believe it should be forbidden.	1	0.7
(5) Other.	16	11.3
(6) Did not respond.	8	5.6
Total	142	99.9*

*Percentages do not add up to 100 because of rounding.

TABLE 5. Physicians' Opinions Regarding the Acceleration of Death via Positive Acts

Response	No.	%
(1) Believe there may be circumstances and physicians should have that responsibility, with adequate safeguards and legal protection.	51	35.9
(2) Believe that under no circumstances should such a responsibility be given to physicians or anyone else.	59	41.5
(3) Other.	13	9.2
(4) No response.	19	13.4
Total	142	100.0

Out of the combined samples, 257 respondents, 172 or 66.9% agreed that the physician has ultimate and sole responsibility for life and death decisions; 18.3% disagreed, and the remaining 14.8% did not respond. Also, 41% of the 257 indicated agreement that "clarification of physicians' responsibilities and authority is vitally necessary and some legislation (not necessarily that proposed) *is needed*," while 39.3% disagreed. Finally, of the 257, 43.8% indicated that, while legislation is not necessary, clarification of the physicians' responsibilities and authority is desirable in any legislation that may be passed. Taken together, these three categories of responses suggest that the majority of physicians believes the physician has ultimate responsibility for life and death decisions, without legislation; but that if relevant legislation is indeed passed, it should not impose limits on the individual physician's judgments and responsibilities. While this general question suggests that the majority is *not* in favor of legislation, questions about specific legislative bills reveal that the majority supports certain ones. Attention is now turned to specific bills.

Findings From Sample 1: Attitudes Toward Legislation to Permit Withholding Life Supports

The respondents in sample 1 were given a summary of a bill recently introduced in the Alabama Legislature which

"allows a terminally ill patient to direct his physician to withhold or withdraw life-sustaining medical procedures" because "adult persons have the fundamental right to control the decisions relating to rendering their own medical care."

Specific situations where this right is accorded the patient and qualifications safeguarding the physician from liability were detailed. The respondents were then asked: "In general, how do you feel about such legislation?" The results are shown in Table 1. Of the 115, 60 (52.2%) approved or strongly approved of this legislation, 27.0% disapproved or strongly disapproved of it, with 9.6% undecided and 11.3% not responding. In sum, over half of the respondents favored such legislation.

The respondents were then asked: "If such a bill is enacted, would you inform patients of this option?" The responses to this question are presented in Table 2. Nearly half (46.0%) of the physicians said they would take positive steps to inform patients of their option to withhold life support, and an additional third (31.3%) would inform some patients. Only 10.4% would avoid involvement with legal documents relating to life support.

How Common is the Practice of Withholding Life Supports? Of the 115 respondents in sample 1, 43 (37.4%) indicated that they had in the past two years encountered a situation in which a patient had requested withdrawing or withholding life support. Of these 43, 37 withdrew life support on at least one occasion. These actions were taken after consultation with a responsible family member(s). The majority of those withholding life support also consulted with a colleague(s) (29 of the 37).

Of the 62 who had never encountered a situation where a patient has requested the withholding of life support, 15 indicated that they "would consider doing so, if the legal right to do so were clear." Another 22 indicated that they generally disapprove of withholding life support but would consider doing so if they believed the patient clearly desired it and the legal right to do so were clear. Only three indicated that they would never consider such actions as a professional option, while 38 reserved comment. In sum, around one third of the respondents in sample 1 have withheld life support, and another one third would do so under certain circumstances. Less than 3% chose to express the opinion that they would never consider doing so.

Legislation Concerning the Hastening of Death. The respondents in sample 1 were also asked the following:

Would you approve of such a bill being extended to permit "the administration of any medical procedures deemed necessary to alleviate pain," even if these procedures might hasten death (the intent of the bill in this regard is unclear)?

Nearly half (48.7%) of the 115 respondents indicated they would approve of such legislation. About one fifth (20.9%) indicated disapproval, with 20.9% undecided and 9.6% not responding.

A specific instance of these types of death-hastening procedures is the use of drugs. Thus, the following question was included:

Would you approve of extending this legislation to permit prescribing large doses of narcotics to alleviate pain, even if it may be necessary to administer sufficient amounts to eventually compromise respiration?

Of the 115 respondents, 46 (40.0%) said "yes" and 23.5% said "no," with 25.2% undecided and 11.3% not responding. From the information available to us it is not clear whether those who disapprove of this do so because of the nature of the procedure itself or because such legislation is so specific as to infringe upon the practitioner's right to consider treatment options. Follow-up studies will attempt to clarify this.

The respondents were then asked if they had in the past two years encountered such a situation. Of the 33 (28.7%) who indicated they had, 24 administered the drug. One may thus speculate that around 70% of physicians who encounter this situation take measures to alleviate pain for terminally ill patients, even at the risk of hastening death.

While the questionnaire mailed to sample 1 respondents did not center on the question of when a patient on life support may be declared legally dead, the respondents were asked whether they approve of legislation that

clarifies the definition of death in cases where artificial means are employed to maintain cardiac and/or respiratory function, permitting a physician to determine that death has occurred based on "usual and customary standards. . . ." [D]eath may be pronounced before artificial means of maintaining vital functions are terminated. . . .

Eighty-seven (75.7%) of the respondents approved of legislation clarifying the procedures for declaring a patient dead. Nine (7.8%) disapproved, 7.8% were undecided, and 8.7% failed to respond. In sum, roughly three fourths of the respondents approved of legislation defining *death*. Data from sample 2, the findings of which are reported next, are intended to expound on this issue.

Findings From Sample 2: Opinions on Legislation "Defining" Death

The 142 respondents in sample 2 were familiarized with proposed "death defining" legislation by the following:

A bill has been introduced into the Alabama Legislature which in effect, permits physicians to turn off life-sustaining cardiac and respiratory supports when *"there is no spontaneous respiratory or cardiac function,* and there is no expectation of recovery." The major criterion is "usual and customary standards of medical practice in his (the physician's) general neighborhood." A subsidiary clause provides for a determination of death if "there is total and irreversible *cessation of brain function.* Death may be pronounced in this circumstance before artificial means of maintaining respiratory and cardiac function are terminated . . . with independent confirmation of the death by another medical doctor." Nothing in this Act shall prohibit a physician from using other procedures based on "usual and customary standards of medical practice . . . as exclusive basis for pronouncing a person dead."

Additional safeguards are proposed in the bill for use when "a part of the donor is proposed to be used for transplantation," which does not concern the vast majority of practicing physicians, and is not part of this inquiry.

The Act exempts from criminal prosecution or civil action a physician "acting in good faith in terms of this Act."

They were then asked with which of several results they were in accord. The results are reported in Table 4. More than one third (37.3%) of the respondents believed the status quo was adequate, that no legislation was needed. Forty-five percent of the respondents approved of the legislation in one form or another. It was of particular interest that only one of the 142 respondents was unalterably opposed to the cessation of life-sustaining measures and believed that shutting them off should be forbidden.

Positive Euthanasia. While shutting off life-sustaining apparatus is an intentional act on a practitioner's part, the subsequent death of a moribund patient is only a passive result. This act may be distinguished from those intended to hasten or accelerate death, acts that may be called types of positive euthanasia. Without being given an explicit definition of what is meant by *positive euthanasia,* the respondents were asked:

Do you believe that circumstances may arise (beyond the intent of the bill) when physicians should allow the process of death to accelerate by positive acts?

The response categories and frequencies are presented in Table 5. The respondents seemed to be close to evenly divided on this question, with slightly more against the idea of taking "positive acts" to hasten death. In sample 1 (already reported) only 23.5% expressly opposed legislation that approves hastening death through administering heavy doses of narcotics to relieve pain. When the situation is described in less precise terms, using the words "positive acts," the opposition rises to 41.5%.

Opinions Regarding Living Wills. Other legislation has been proposed concerning patients' rights to request the withholding of life-sustaining procedures through the legal document summarily called a "living will." The respondents of sample 2 were asked about this generally as follows:

Would you in general approve of permitting people to write a "living will" making known to one's family, physician and others, one's desire not to have life sustaining procedures used on oneself, and holding those who obey the provisions of such a will free of blame for criminal prosecution, civil action and/or charges of professional misconduct?

Nearly three fourths of the respondents, 106 of them (74.6%), said "yes." Another 15 (10.6%) were undecided, with 17 (12.0%) saying "no" and four (2.8%) not responding. It may be concluded that substantial opposition to living wills does not exist at this time.

CONCLUSIONS FROM FINDINGS

The reader should keep in mind that the population of Alabama physicians studied here included only those physicians directly concerned with "death" legislation. Thus, the findings may not be generalized to the medical profession as a whole. Further, the findings in this study are tentative and additional investigation is warranted. Notwithstanding this, the following findings are worthy of note.

(1) Two out of three respondents believe that the physician has ultimate and sole responsibility for life and death decisions.

(2) About two fifths of the respondents are of the opinion that legislation is needed to clarify the physician's responsibility and authority regarding life-and-death situations, while a like proportion disagrees. Slightly more respondents (43.8%) are of the opinion that such legislation is desirable but not necessary.

(3) About half of the respondents approve of legislation giving terminally ill patients the right to direct a physician to withhold life support, while about one fourth disapprove of such legislation.

(4) The physicians were asked, if such legislation were passed, if they would inform patients of the opposition to withhold life support. Nearly half would take positive steps to inform patients and an additional third would inform some patients under some circumstances. About one tenth would avoid involvement with legal documents pertaining to the patient's request.

(5) More than one third of sampled physicians had in the past two years encountered a situation in which a patient had requested withdrawal or withholding of life support.

(6) Most of the respondents who had been requested to withhold or withdraw life support consented to do so on at least one occasion. These actions were taken after consultation with responsible family member(s) and/or physician colleague(s).

(7) Of those physicians who had *not* encountered a request for the withholding of life support, about one half indicated they would withhold support under certain circumstances. The remainder were undecided or failed to answer, save roughly 3% who said they would never consider doing so.

(8) Nearly half of those asked indicated that they would approve of legislation permitting the administration of analgesics to alleviate pain, though the amount may be such that death may be hastened. About one fifth expressed disapproval. The proportion of respondents approving of death-hastening legislation diminishes by one fifth to 40% when asked about extending the legislation to include the *specific* procedure of giving "large doses of narcotics" known to compromise breathing.

(9) In the previous two years about three of ten physicians responding had encountered a situation in which death-hastening measures using drugs might be appropriate. About 70% of those who encountered that situation administered drugs for pain relief even at the risk of compromising respiration.

(10) Respondent physicians in one sample were asked straightforwardly if they approved of legislation clarifying the legal procedures for declaring a moribund patient dead. Three fourths approved of such legislation. Respondents in the second sample were asked about legislation clarifying the legal definition of death and were given the option of indicating that the present legal status is adequate. Thirty-seven percent chose that response category, while another 45% approved of such legislation in one form or another.

(11) About one of three physicians asked believes there may be circumstances under which it is appropriate to accelerate the death of a moribund patient via "positive acts." A slightly greater proportion (41.5%) believe that under no circumstances should such a responsibility be given to physicians or anyone else.

(12) Three fourths of physicians indicated approval of permitting people to write "living wills." About 12% disapprove of living wills.

(13) In any question where respondents were given the option of indicating that they would never consider the withholding of life supports as a professional option, less than 3% chose that response.

(14) Taking together those questions asking respondents to approve or disapprove of legislation, the average percentage approving was 53.9, while the average percentage disapproving was 24.1.

(15) A comparison of these findings to those of similar studies shows that the opinions and practices of Alabama physicians are in harmony with those of physicians elsewhere in the United States.

Acknowledgments. We thank Dr. Jennie Kronenfeld, formerly with the Department of Public Health and Epidemiology, University of Alabama in Birmingham (UAB), who collaborated in designing the study; Dr. John Packard, Director of Medical Education, Birmingham Baptist Hospitals, who helped in questionnaire design; and Dr. Leon C. Hamrick, Past-President of the Medical Association of the State of Alabama, for his aid in gaining acceptance of the medical community for this study.

References

1. Brown NK, Bulger RJ, Laws EH et al: The preservation of life. *JAMA* 211:76-81, 1970
2. Travis TA, Noyes R Jr, Brightwell DR: The attitudes of physicians toward prolonging life. *Int J Psychiatry Med* 5:17-26, 1974
3. Crane D: *The Sanctity of Social Life.* New York, Russell Sage Foundation, 1975
4. Duff RS, Campbell AGM: Moral and ethical dilemmas in the special care nursery. *N Engl J Med* 289:890-894, 1973
5. Carey RG, Posavac EJ: Attitudes of physicians on disclosing information to and maintaining life for terminal patients. *Omega* 9:67-76, 1978
6. Towers B: Report from America: the impact of the California Natural Death Act. *J Med Ethics* 4:96-98, 1978
7. Fox RC, Swazey JP: *The Courage to Fail.* Chicago, University of Chicago Press, 1974

Is It Right?

. . . TO TURN OFF LIFE SUPPORT?
. . . TO KEEP A BODY ALIVE FOR ITS ORGANS?
. . . TO GIVE ILLEGAL NARCOTICS TO THE DYING?

'Plug-pulling' is a major national controversy—among laymen. But for nurses, with their intimate knowledge of the new life-sustaining technology and its often pathetic results, there's little debate. The question, they say, is not *whether* the plug should be pulled on an artificially sustained patient, but, rather, *who* should make the terminal decision.

The 12,500 nurses who answered *RN*'s "ethics" questionnaire earlier this year were, in fact, virtually unanimous on the basic issue: Only 1% said they would *never* advocate an end to heroic measures. Beyond that, however, all consensus ends. Four out of ten nurses said they'd accept the patient's request as sufficient reason to terminate artificial life-support (See "Who should decide?", page 39). "Too often medical personnel forget that a patient's body is not *their* possession," said one. "As nurses we offer services; the patient has a right to refuse at *any* time."

But almost half the nurses responding said it isn't that simple. They feel the decision to withdraw life support must also include the family and/or clinical personnel. Here's one nurse's description of the complications that can arise:

"Sometimes a patient says 'I want to die' when he is in pain or depressed. If he can be made well or comfortable the call for death fades away. Sometimes families let their emotions rule and order futile life-sustaining measures. I think patients' and family members' wishes should be heard, and they should have every move explained to them, but they cannot have a final say-so in many cases."

Another nurse paints a somewhat different scenario:

"I think a living will is a great idea and I guess it protects me. But what if I have a patient who's signed a living will and is too sick to reconsider, the family is in a hurry for him to die (yes, I've had that kind!), and the doctor and I are convinced the patient can recover?"

Interestingly, the need for input from clinical personnel drew less support among younger nurses and students than from more experienced nurses (see "With experience comes faith in clinical judgment," page 39). This may be because emphasis on patient and family rights has been taught vigorously to recent nursing school graduates. Or it could be that younger nurses simply have not yet come across some of the complications that can arise.

Making decisions about the death of an individual is delicate and difficult, and we heard many tales of abuse. Nurses who found the space on our survey form inadequate wrote letters telling of 90-year-old terminal cancer patients undergoing repeated defibrillations; of terminal children suf-

---

Reprinted with permission from *RN*, vol. 43(12), December, 1980.

LIFE-SUPPORT: WHO SHOULD DECIDE?

Asked when life-sustaining measures should be stopped,
respondents chose to place their confidence in the patient's wishes or a mutual consensus.

Cease measures when:

Patient requests it	40%*	Medical panel recommends it	11%
Family requests it	29%	Joint decision of some or all of above	46%
All clinical personnel agree there's no hope of survival	25%	Other	6%
*Multiple responses		Never	1%

WITH EXPERIENCE COMES FAITH IN CLINICAL JUDGMENT

Younger nurses and students are less willing to leave the decision
to clinical personnel or medical panels.

Age	Stop life support when clinical personnel agree there's no hope	Stop life support when a medical panel recommends it
Under 25 years	19%	7%
45 and older	27%	14%
Position		
Student	18%	9%
Staff nurse	25%	10%
Supervisor	28%	12%

fering prolonged, paintul deaths; of patients on ventilators with flat EEGs, sustained by IVs, tube feedings, and antibiotics while their families paid enormous hospital bills.

But despite abuses and the difficulty of making joint patient-family-clinical personnel decisions, the vast majority of RNs do *not* want such decisions taken out of the hands of those directly involved in each case. Only one out of ten nurses favors calling in a medical panel to decide when to withdraw life supports. Supervisors and nurses over 45 tend to support this idea slightly more than younger nurses and students. But even here, support is minimal. This seems to reflect a basic faith that most of the time—despite fears of legal suits—the family and clinical personnel (and the patient, if conscious) do have the courage to make the correct decision.

Nurses are, in fact, noticeably more liberal on this issue than they are on the even hotter question of abortion. Only 5% of those nurses who oppose abortion under any circumstances were willing to reject plug-pulling totally (see "On life-support, everyone's a liberal," page 40). It seems that, at least in this instance, omission (of artificial life-support) is easier to accept than commission (deliberate abortion).

So someone else may live

Ethical decisions are always easiest to make when there is only one potential good at stake. Where a peaceful, timely death is possible, almost all nurses are willing to go along with termination of life support. But what if a possible good can come from keeping a patient alive on a respirator, such as a chance to harvest his kidneys, heart, or corneas for transplant use? Should heroic measures be used in these cases?

"Yes," said more than six out of ten RNs. *If* the patient has previously arranged to donate. *If* the family agrees. *If* a transplant recipient is readily available. And only within limits: "I would not object to something like the continued use of a respirator for a few hours to preserve kidneys, for example, until a recipient could be found. But measures to prolong the dying process for days or weeks could not be justified." Other typical comments were that the body is a natural incubator or storage unit for organs; that there is no reason to "waste" organs if they can save another life; and that harvesting organs may help the family accept the patient's sudden death.

But almost four out of ten nurses do ethically object to keeping a patient alive so that organs can be transplanted. Typical comments: "We should never prolong suffering for any reason"; "This puts the family through too much"; "It's not necessary; organs can be obtained without heroic measures." One nurse told of this anguish: "We maintained a boy on a respirator. It took a few hours to 'harvest' his kidneys. Knowing he was declared dead but having to act as if he weren't made those the most difficult hours I have ever worked."

The older nurses surveyed were less comfortable about using heroic mea-

ON LIFE-SUPPORT, EVERYONE'S A 'LIBERAL'

Even if they firmly oppose abortion, most nurses will accept a deliberate decision
to cease prolonging a terminal patient's life.

Cease measures when:	Plug-pulling sentiment among nurses who oppose abortion*	Plug-pulling sentiment among nurses who favor abortion**
Patient requests it	32%	47%
Family requests it	22%	34%
All clinical personnel agree there's no hope of survival	21%	29%
Medical panel recommends it	8%	14%
Joint decision of some or all of the above	47%	42%
Other	6%	6%
Never	5%	‡

*Those who do not approve of abortion under any circumstances

**Those who approve of abortions for any unwanted pregnancy

‡Less than 1%

LAYMEN AND 'THE RIGHT TO DIE': A VERY DIFFERENT VIEW

Almost all nurses favor moderation in the use of artificial life-support;
but not so among laymen, as the answers to these two Harris Survey questions show.

"Do you think that a patient with a terminal disease ought to be able to tell his doctor to let him die, or do you think this is wrong?"

Ought to be allowed	78%
It is wrong	19%
Not sure	3%

"Do you think that a patient who is terminally ill ought to have the right to tell his doctor to put him out of his misery, or do you think this is wrong?"

Ought to be allowed	56%
Is wrong	41%
Not sure	3%

Harris Survey. 1981 study of cross-section of 1,513 households
Copyright © 1981 by the *Chicago Tribune*

sures to permit organ transplants than younger nurses. Perhaps the younger ones take it for granted. But the six-to-four split in opinion among all nurses shows this *is* a controversial question. The underlying fear may be what one nurse expressed: "Once those sup-port systems are implemented it be-comes very difficult to remove them."

The basis of this difficulty is that as a society we no longer agree about how to define death. When *RN* asked nurses for their personal definitions of clinical death, many mentioned "brain death" or the "Harvard criteria" (24 hours' unresponsiveness to pain; a flat EEG; no reflexes; no spontaneous res-pirations) or another brain-death crite-rion (three flat EEG lines, 72 hours apart). But some stuck to an older defi-nition, which establishes death as "no heartbeat, no respirations."

Currently 25 states have laws that define death as the irreversible cessation of brain function. Three more have ruled that this criterion may be applied in some cases. But the remaining states equate only heart and respiratory failure to death. And when the President's Commission for the Study of Ethical Problems in Medicine tried to reach a definition of death, it too wound up hopelessly divided.* All the physicians who testified before the commission urged that the brain-death definition be adopted. But the theologians disagreed, not only with the physicians, but even with their own co-religionists. Thus two Rabbis presented opposing views, as did two Catholic theologians.

The public, too, has trouble with life-and-death decisions. Harris Survey results show that six out of ten people believe terminal patients have the right to tell their doctors to allow them to die (see "Laymen and 'the right to die,'" page 40). But only four out of ten feel a doctor should actively speed the death of a terminal patient—even if the patient requests it. Again, the distinction seems to lie between passive acceptance of death and efforts to actually bring it about. One nurse crystallized it this way:

"If I make a decision not to resuscitate a badly deformed baby who has not breathed at birth, I don't want to be sued and I accept the emotional trauma my decision costs me. Yet if the baby does breathe and is put in an isolette, no medical committee could make me go in and turn off the heat and oxygen."

The distinction between a "no code" order and active euthanasia is certainly germane when a terminal patient is receiving pain meds. In some cases, doses and drug types sufficient to give good pain control may also shorten the patient's life. Yet administration of such

*Panel asks "When is a person dead?" *Science* 209:669, 1980.

drugs doesn't seem to bother most nurses. When asked what *they* would do if the wife of a terminal hospital patient were slipping him extra morphine, the majority opted for little, if any, interference. Few would, for instance, order the morphine confiscated (they went so far as to cross that off the list of options). One out of four would do nothing at all. And many others would do no more than inform the patient's physician.

"Tell physician and request med increase or change" was one common recommendation. "I don't know of many doctors," added one nurse, "who would not increase the medication to make the patient comfortable. Only if this failed would I turn my back and do nothing."

'Snowing' the patient

A few nurses mentioned they would warn the wife that the morphine might be enough to kill the patient, and a few others said they'd encourage the wife to give the medicine. "Keep the patient comfortable by whatever means," was their refrain. One nurse came right out and said: "I believe in 'snowing' patients."

The number of nurses who said they would, in fact, do nothing seems to indicate that many feel pain medication prescriptions are often inadequate. So it's interesting that only one out of four said "Yes" to the question: "Should currently illegal narcotics be given for intractable pain?" Three-fourths evidently feel there are enough legal, tested drugs on the market to control pain. The problem would therefore appear to lie in the amount of analgesic prescribed. And, in fact, many nurses noted that they thought MDs tended to underprescribe.

Brompton's elixir—a mixture of medications, including heroin, used in England to control cancer pain—was mentioned by several nurses as a pos-

sibly beneficial use of currently illegal drugs. But one experienced nurse had this to say:

"I worked in a hospice in Sheffield, England for two weeks. The heroin they use has less effect on the respiratory system, but it did not do that much better in controlling symptoms than the mix of morphine, methadone, and compazine we use here. The problem we have is not in the drugs we use but in our reluctance to give them regularly, so patients wouldn't have to wait until the pain is upon them."

Concern with contributing to the crime problem was another objection to using illegal pain meds: "Illegal is illegal. Maybe we need to change the laws, though, to allow certain medical uses for heroin and marijuana." Several nurses criticized the tendency to rely on drugs rather than a total pain evaluation, which might reveal the need for psychological or surgical pain-relief measures.

The one-out-of-four nurses who *do* favor the use of currently illegal drugs focused on the need to relieve terminal pain by whatever method. "Ad lib, prn," scribbled one nurse. "Use them when other pain meds no longer work and there's no chance of long-term addiction," wrote another. "They can prevent the patient from reaching his pain threshold and keep him lucid." And a motif that ran through all the survey answers: "We must allow the patient to die as *he* wishes."

Whether or not they agree on the specifics of how to help a patient exercise his rights, there's clearly a strong consensus among nurses on what those rights should be. Among the amendments they'd add to the usual "patient's bill of rights" are the patient's right to:
- die free of pain,
- donate his organs if he wishes, *and*
- die in peace, undisturbed by medical procedures that offer little hope for recovery.

The Polls:
Changing Attitudes
Toward Euthanasia

John M. Ostheimer

Euthanasia, long a dilemma of medical ethics, has quietly been taking on new significance over the past decade. Developments in medical technology have contributed to a growing number of situations that suggest the euthanasia alternative: individuals who a few years ago would have died can now be sustained beyond the point which even they themselves would desire.

The "politics" of euthanasia has been developing apace. The Euthanasia Society, recently renamed Concern for Dying, grew rapidly during the 1970s. Although it has no membership as such, its growth can perhaps be measured by its mailing list, which expanded from 10,000 in 1967 to 160,000 by August 1979.[1] The second major national organization, the Euthanasia Educational Council, grew from 600 members to 30,000 from 1969 to 1974, according to the New York Times (July 21, 1974).

Congressional hearings on "death with dignity" have been published.[2] Most significant, some relevant laws have been enacted.[3] Although these actions have occurred only at the state level, it is worth remembering that abortion liberalization also began that way. The development of a "politics of euthanasia" probably stands about where abortion did in the early 1960s, the plights of Karen Ann Quinlan and others serving as issue stimulants just as the thalidomide and rubella tragedies did during the years that led up to abortion liberalization.

Poll questions on euthanisia have varied between "passive" and "active" situations. These terms distinguish between merely allowing a person to die a more natural death by not using "heroic" measures of life support or resuscitation (passive), and actually taking some step such as injecting air or administering some chemical to a terminal patient in order to hasten death (active). Comparison of the two Harris questions suggests that passive euthanasia, the first alternative offered respondents, is more acceptable to the public.

[1] Personal communication with Concern for Dying.
[2] U.S. Senate, Special Committee on Aging, "Death with Dignity," 1972.
[3] See Robert M. Veatch, Death, Dying and the Biological Revolution (New Haven: Yale University Press, 1976).

John M. Ostheimer is Associate Professor of Political Science, Northern Arizona University.

Reprinted by permission of the publisher from "The Polls: Changing Attitudes Toward Euthanasia," by John M. Ostheimer, Public Opinion Quarterly, vol. 44(1), Spring, 1980, pp. 123–128. Copyright 1980 by The Trustees of Columbia University.

The present state of euthanasia polls suggests several methodological problems. First, questions asked on polls are not appropriate for the types of controversial situations that have so far dominated the issue. Except for the Texas poll, the available data deal only with situations in which the dying person's wishes have been clearly stated, whereas most publicized cases have involved incompetent patients such as accident, stroke, or overdose victims, deformed infants, or unconscious terminal illness sufferers. We do not know very much about the public's views in such situations.

The wording of available poll questions also leaves much to be desired. The base question of the Gallup-NORC poll is ambiguous. What does it mean to "end the patient's life by some painless means"? Our understanding of public attitudes is weakened by the imprecision inherent in the question, and attention should be given to clarifying the hypothetical situations posited. Questions should be worded so as not to precondition a negative response. For example, the low support for the Harris 2 question may derive partly from its wording: to be "put out of one's misery" is somewhat reminiscent of shooting one's trusty horse.

The "base question" for euthanasia attitudes, Gallup-NORC, now covers a 30-year period. Its results indicate a growing acceptance of the idea of euthanasia over that time. Acceptance has grown among all major population subgroups, but change has been greatest among Catholics and the younger age groups.

The data show a general absence of significant sex differences, although, on a related issue, a 1975 Institute of Life Insurance poll showed that women think about death more than men do.[4] The Texas poll shows some tendency for men to be slightly more tolerant of passive euthanasia.

Hostility to the idea of euthanasia is obviously greater among older respondents. However, in the California 1 poll a large number of "qualified" or "don't know" answers among the oldest group may indicate that although the elderly are comparatively hostile to euthanasia, the contemporary debate, particularly intense in California, where one of the first Right to Die laws was enacted, may be causing reconsideration.

Socioeconomic variables show largely predictable subgroup differences. Those with more education tend to have more "liberal" attitudes on euthanasia. Although other demographic variables, such as income, occupation, and region also show correlations with euthanasia attitudes, the nature of the issue leads to the hypothesis that age, religion, and educational differences are responsible for these other relationships.

Finally, the NORC and Ohio results show race to be important. Racial differences on most political issues are usually dismissed as merely a function of the fact that nonwhites are less educated and more fundamentalist. A 1975 Gallup poll on suicide by those with terminal medical conditions also showed strong racial differences, but the 1973 Gallup euthanasia poll did not.

The polls mentioned are reported here with the permission of the following research organizations:

California	Field Research Corp., and *Current Opinion*
Gallup: 1930s	*G.H. Gallup, The Gallup Poll: Public Opinion 1935–1971*
Gallup	*Gallup Poll, Princeton, N.J.,* and *Gallup Opinion Index*
Harris	The Harris Poll, and *Current Opinion*
IOLI	Institute of Life Insurance, & *Current Opinion*
NORC	National Opinion Research Center
Ohio	The Ohio Poll, and *Current Opinion*
Texas	The Texas Poll, and *Current Opinion*

HARRIS

1. All doctors take an oath saying they will maintain, restore, and prolong human life in their treatment of patients. It is now argued by some people that in many cases people with terminal diseases (those which can only end in death) have their lives prolonged unnecessarily, making them endure much pain and suffering for no real reason. Do you think a patient with a terminal disease ought to be able to tell his doctor to let him die rather than to extend his life when no cure is in sight, or do you think this is wrong? . . . .

	Ought to Be Allowed	It Is Wrong	Not Sure
1973 National total	62	28	10

[4] See *Current Opinion* IV, 5 (May 1976): 47.

2. Do you think the patient who is terminally ill, with no cure in sight, ought to have the right to tell his doctor to put him out of his misery, or do you think this is wrong?

1973 National total	Ought to Be Allowed	It Is Wrong	Not Sure
	37	53	10

GALLUP
Do you favor mercy deaths under government supervision for hopeless invalids?

	Yes	No
Nov. 1936: National total	46	54
Sex		
Males*		
Females	48	52
Age		
21–24	54	46
Region		
New England	43	57
Middle Atlantic	54	46
East Central	40	60
West Central	32	68
South	38	62
Mountain	63	37
Pacific	64	36
Jan. 1939: National total	46	54
Sex		
Males	49	51
Females	42	58
Age		
21–29	52	48
30–49	44	56
50+	41	59

GALLUP-NORC BASE QUESTION
When a person has a disease that cannot be cured, do you think doctors should be allowed to end the patient's life by some painless means if the patient and his family request it? (Percentage in agreement)

	GALLUP 1947	GALLUP 1950	GALLUP 1973	IOLI 1975	NORC 1977
National total	36	36	53	52	62
Sex					
Males		38			67
Females		34			58
Age					
18–49	(18–49) 39	(21–29) 39	(18–24) 68	(18–34) 60	(18–24) 68
		(30–49) 37	(25–29) 65		(25–29) 65
			(30–49) 51		(30–49) 51
				(35–54) 45	
50+	(50+) 31	(50+) 30	(50+) 44	(55+) 49	(50+) 44
Religion					
Protestant	36		53		60
Catholic	28		48		63
Jewish	54		60		76
					(no religion) 82

*No figures given in original document.

CALIFORNIA

1. Should an incurably ill patient have the right to ask for and get medication that would pain-lessly end his or her life?

	Should	Should Not	Qualified Don't Know
1975 statewide total	63	29	8
Sex			
Men	67	29	4
Women	60	30	10
Age			
18–24	70	25	5
25–34	76	19	5
35–49	62	36	2
50–69	57	31	12
70+	41	36	23
Religion			
Catholics	49	43	8
Non-Catholics	67	25	8

2. Should an incurably ill patient have the right to refuse medication that would painlessly end his or her life?

	Should	Should Not	Qualified Don't Know
1975 statewide total	87	10	3
Sex			
Men	84	12	4
Women	89	9	2
Age			
18–24	91	6	3
25–34	94	4	2
35–49	83	13	4
50–69	84	12	4
70+	82	16	2
Religion			
Catholics	77	15	8
Non-Catholics	90	8	2

OHIO

Do you favor or oppose authorizing a doctor, by law, to painlessly end the life of a patient who is terminally ill, if the patient and his family request it?

	Favor	Oppose	Don't Know
1974 statewide total	44	41	15
Male	44	40	16
Female	44	42	14
Age groups			
18–30	52	39	9
31–45	48	38	14
46–64	43	43	14
65+	41	39	20
Religion			
Protestant	48	37	15
Catholic	34	50	16
Jewish	76	16	8
Race			
white	45	40	15
black	37	48	15
Income			
under $15,000	42	44	14
over $15,000	54	35	11

TEXAS

Some persons who are gravely ill, with no chance of recovery, are kept alive by life support machines. Do you think the immediate relatives of these persons should or should not have the right to decide if these machines should be turned off? (Percentage in favor of giving relatives the right)

1976 statewide total	63
Sex	
Male	67
Female	59
Age	
18-24	69
25-34	64
35-49	62
50-64	60
65+	62
Religion	
Protestant	64
Catholic	61
Other	61

GALLUP, NORC BASE QUESTION: FURTHER BREAKDOWN

When a person has a disease that cannot be cured, do you think doctors should be allowed to end the patient's life by some painless means if the patient and his family request it? (Percentage in agreement)

	Gallup 1973	NORC 1977	NORC 1978
National total	53	62	60
Race			
White	54	65	62
Nonwhite	53	(Blacks) 39	45
Education			
Some college	61	70	69
High school	54	64	62
Grade school	39	57	41
Occupation			
Professional and business	58		
White collar	63		
Farmers	42		
Manual workers	52		
Religion			
Catholic	48	63	59
Atheist/Agnostic		82	81
Jewish	60	76	75
Protestant	53	60	58
Baptist		55	54
Methodist		67	63
Lutheran		63	71
Presbyterian		71	67
Episcopalian		68	73
Politics			
Republican	50		59
Democrat	49		60
Independent	49		63
Ideology			
Liberal		70	66
Slightly liberal		62	67
Moderate		66	60
Slightly conservative		61	61
Conservative		56	51
Region			
East	51		
Midwest	51		
South	48		
West	64		

Income			
$15,000 and over	60	67	64
$10,000–14,999	54	64	62
$7,000–9,999	48	60	62
$5,000–6,999	55	63	55
$3,000–4,999	46	51	51
Under $3,000	45	58	61
Community size			
1 million people plus	52	68	
50,000–999,999	55	62	
2,500–49,999	53	63	
Under 2,500	48	58	

Mercy Killing and the Law—A Psychoanalytically Oriented Analysis

C. G. Schoenfeld, Esq.

Traditional arguments for and against mercy killing are first discussed, and it is concluded that this is a subject upon which moral and intelligent men may disagree. Then, the disparity between the law's condemnation of mercy killing and society's usual failure to punish it is stressed, as are the ways in which modern medical technology has intensified the plight of the hopelessly ill and their families. Much of this is then detailed in an analysis of the celebrated Quinlan *case. Problems faced by physicians in dealing with the hopelessly ill are considered, as is the view—found wanting—that these physicians should have the right to decide whether terminally ill patients should live or die. Finally, a psychoanalytic explanation of the disparity between the law in words and the law in action is offered.*

The past few years have witnessed a re-awakening of the public's interest in mercy killing. This revived concern with mercy killing, and particularly with ending the torment of the hopelessly ill (and their families), is in large measure a result of the much-debated *Quinlan* case.[1] In this case, the possibility of a 21-year-old girl living on indefinitely in a vegetative state—one of a host of problems that modern medical technology has spawned—was vividly dramatized. Written in response to the renewed public interest in mercy killing, this paper will seek—with the aid of psychoanalytic tools and insights—to help its readers to decide whether current laws regarding mercy killing (laws that, in general, equate mercy killing with murder) ought to be changed.

Mercy killing is a subject upon which moral and intelligent men may disagree. Almost two thousand years ago, Seneca urged that "If one death is accompanied by torture and the other is simple and easy, why not snatch the latter? . . . Just as a long-drawn-out life does not necessarily mean a better one, so a long-drawn-out death necessarily means a worse one."[2] As Yale Kamisar pointed out in a celebrated essay on euthanasia in 1958, however,

the consequences of mistake, of course, are always fatal . . . [and] the incidence of mistake of one kind or another is likely to be quite appreciable . . . [Further, there is] the danger that legal machinery initially designed to kill those who are a nuisance to themselves may some day engulf those who are a nuisance to others.[3]

The main contention of many of those who oppose mercy killing is grounded in the belief that life is sacred—indeed, sacrosanct—and that the only proper attitude towards it is one of awe, reverence, and respect. To tamper with life, to experiment with it—and certainly to end it by mercy killing—is a profanation of the sacred. Related is the view of the Roman Catholic Church that life belongs not to man but to God; and that consequently, only God has the right to decide when life (which men are deemed to hold in trust) may be ended.[4]

It is no gentle irony, however, that many of those who speak of the sacredness of life in the context of mercy killing seem quite willing to justify its loss in such other contexts as punishment and war.

[T]he objection is often heard that to take steps to end life is playing God, for it is God's prerogative to determine the end of life. . . . Interrogation, however, usually reveals that the objector does not object to killing in war. There, apparently, we have a permit from God to go at it. . . .[5]

Such observations aside, those who dispute the view that life is so sacred that it must be preserved at all costs, point out that this view is based upon the highly questionable assumption that every life, no matter what its quality or circumstance, is worth living and must be lived. Rather, they insist that the value of life lies in its quality, not its span—that "being human is more important than being alive."[6] Indeed, some of them contend that wars are often fought because of the conviction that "a change in the quality of life is more important than submissive behavior that would probably let more people live but in conditions that are intolerable."[7]

The one reason most usually stressed for the quality of life being so poor as to make mercy killing acceptable is the presence of pain—intolerable and unending pain, particularly when there is no hope of recovery. It is frequently contended, for example, that when a patient is dying and in excruciating pain, the first duty of a doctor is to relieve suffering, rather than prolong life.[8] For those persons who reason from the premise that pain is an absolute evil, mercy killing in such a situation may be "not only morally permissible but mandatory."[9]

But is pain an absolute evil? Surely not always, since pain often serves as a much-needed signal that a part of the body is malfunctioning and requires attention. Also, many deeply religious persons believe that pain provides an opportunity for spiritual growth and for making amends

Reprinted from *The Journal of Psychiatry and Law*, vol. 6(2), Summer, 1978, © Federal Legal Publications, Inc., 157 Chambers Street, New York, New York 10007, pp. 215-244.

for sin. In fact, it has been contended that the pain of approaching death is "part of the sacrifice that God demands for the sins and faults of life."[10]

Whether or not these contentions are valid, there can be little doubt that intense pain may render men incapable of making rational decisions, particularly when they have been heavily drugged. If so, should such persons be permitted to make life or death decisions concerning themselves? Are they not likely to make serious—indeed, fatal—mistakes? Surely the rapid strides made by medical science since World War II suggest that cures may be found in the near future for many presently painful and incurable ills (though, admittedly, there is a difference between a vague hope for a medical miracle and a realistic expectation of a cure being discovered). Such are the questions and observations of those who dispute the view that pain or any other quality of life criterion ought to be used in making decisions concerning mercy killing. They contend that to employ such criteria as a basis for mercy killing is to abandon the firm ground of morality for the shifting sands of tastes and preferences.[11]

Metaphysical arguments concerning the value of life aside, however, what possible social interest is served by preserving the lives of men so painfully and hopelessly ill that they are a burden both to themselves and to others? How are these men, and the community to which they belong, aided by a prolongation of their suffering? Wouldn't both these men and society benefit if such suffering were brought to a merciful end? These and similar questions are asked by persons who believe that "in place of the right to live, a criterion of the value of an individual life to the community . . . [should be] substituted."[12] It can also be argued that, because society's resources are necessarily limited, to expend these resources on the hopelessly ill—and thereby inevitably reduce the availability of society's resources to others who are more likely to contribute to the lives of their fellowmen—is immoral.

The most usual objection, perhaps, to using a man's presumed value to the community as the reason for helping him to survive—or, conversely, for accelerating his death—is that doing so is likely to lead to horrendous abuses. Still within memory are the abominations of the Nazi euthanasia program under which more than 275,000 so-called "useless eaters" (the aged, the incurable, the insane, and so on) were put to death on the grounds that they were unable to contribute anything of value to the community.[13]

But are not abuses likely to occur regardless of whether the criterion for euthanasia is uselessness to the community, pain and certain death, or whatever? Such is the view of many opponents of mercy killing who, believing that its legalization must inevitably undermine the inviolability of life and upset the delicate balance of forces that restrain killing, contend that if mercy killing is legalized in but one circumstance (no matter how carefully circumscribed), it will eventually be legalized in others—in fact, in an ever-widening variety of circumstances.

Once the respect for human life is so low that an innocent person may be killed directly at his own request, compulsory euthanasia will necessarily be very near. This could lead easily to killing all incurable charity patients, the aged who are a public care, wounded soldiers, captured enemy soldiers, all deformed children, the mentally afflicted, and so on. Before long the danger would be at the door of every citizen.[14]

This is the celebrated "wedge" argument. It is the contention that to permit mercy killing in a single instance is to allow the entry of "a most dangerous wedge,"[15] one that will eventually cause "a complete breakdown of accepted standards"[16] and ultimately result in "mass euthanasia and genocide."[17] If mercy killing is permitted in one instance, according to Joseph V. Sullivan, "there is no way of stopping the advancement of that wedge."[18]

The obvious difficulty with this argument is that it is contradicted by experience. Mercy killings have been sanctioned in a number of ancient and modern societies, without any noticeable breakdown in accepted standards or genocidal results, at least in most of these societies.[19] Further, as will be pointed out later, mercy killing (particularly by physicians) has existed on a *de facto* basis in the United States for many years, and one would be hard put to document either a resultant moral collapse or genocidal consequences. Indeed, as many law reformers have observed, the wedge argument is employed almost reflexively whenever changes are proposed in the law; and, as experience has shown, the dramatic consequences to which it points rarely if ever occur.[20] Clearly, just because something *can* be abused does not mean that it *will* be abused.

To list other arguments and counterarguments concerning mercy killing requires little perspicacity. For example, it has been contended that a physician who participates in mercy killing violates his commitment to heal and undermines "the confidence of all patients in their physicians."[21] But, surely, attempting to counter this argument—or detailing additional arguments—is unnecessary to reveal that, as was observed at the beginning of this discussion, mercy killing is a subject upon which moral and intelligent men may disagree.

Because a gap between the law in words and the law in action is not at all unusual when the public is of two or more minds about a matter,[22] it is tempting to speculate that the disagreements about mercy killing detailed above have found expression in extraordinary contrast between the letter of the law concerning mercy killing and the way this law is carried out. In any event, there can be no doubt that the letter of Anglo-American law has traditionally condemned mercy killing. Now, as in the past, mercy killing is typically labeled murder (or some form of felonious homicide); and if the victim cooperated or consented, he is deemed to be guilty of the felony of suicide (though, in an increasing number of states, suicide is no longer a crime[23]). As Glanville Williams has put it:

If the doctor gives the patient a fatal injection with the intention of killing him, and the patient dies in consequence, the doctor is a common murderer because it is his hand that has caused the death. Neither the consent of the patient, nor the extremity of his suffering, nor the imminence of death by natural cause, nor all of these factors taken together is a defence.[24]

Despite the severe sound of all of this, the law regarding mercy killing has rarely proven to be harsh in practice. Even though mercy killings are probably more common than is usually supposed (surveys among physicians reveal a considerable incidence of mercy killing, particularly when pain-ridden and terminally ill cancer patients are involved[25]), prosecutions are comparatively rare. "[P]rosecutors and grand juries tend not to indict those who kill . . . to relieve suffering or to prevent a prolonged unconscious existence when there is no hope of recovery."[26] Moreover, even when indictments are handed down, juries usually vote for acquittal. "[J]uries are prone to acquit on [the] grounds of temporary insanity or [because of a] lack of a showing of causation."[27] Further, the punishments ordinarily imposed for mercy killing tend to be mild—and then, are frequently alleviated by pardons. Thus, as pointed out above, a considerable gap exists between the letter of the law regarding mercy killing and the way this law is carried out.

This lack of congruence between the law of mercy killing in words and in action has sometimes been defended on the ground that it permits mercy killing where needed, and yet avoids the unsettling effect upon the populace—"the 'unwanted repercussion on the delicate forces which restrain killing'"[28]—that official approval of mercy killing might well entail. But, surely, for the law to denounce certain conduct and then to allow it in practice constitutes an open invitation to lawlessness—one that is certain to evoke the epithet "hypocritical" and bring the law into serious disrepute. Further, the contrast between the legal condemnation of mercy killing and the all too frequent failure to prosecute and convict those who engage in it offers cold comfort to physicians and others faced with the life or death decision implicit in mercy killing. The possibility always exists—especially when a conscientious prosecutor is involved—that an offender will be indicted, convicted and punished. Indeed, the inequities in the treatment of offenders (coupled with abuses of official discretion) that are likely to result from gross divergences between the letter of the law and its enforcement, has caused a number of authorities on the law—most notably the legal philosopher Lon Fuller—to condemn such divergences as clear violations of "the internal morality of the law."[29]

But if it is unwise to permit a wide gap to exist between law in words concerning mercy killing and law in action, what ought to be done? Should the gap be narrowed by strict and vigorous enforcement of the law? Or should the law be changed? If so, how? To do nothing at all and hope that, somehow, the quandary will disappear, seems unrealistic—especially since modern medical technology has spawned a host of insistent problems that have exacerbated the situation.

Largely because of what can only be described as incredible advances in medical knowledge and skill (and comparable advances in related scientific disciplines), life expectancy in the United States has risen since 1900 from 47 to 70 years. In fact, "it has been estimated that one-quarter of all human beings who have ever reached the age of 65 are alive today."[30] Unfortunately, however, this presumably welcome increase in man's life expectancy seems to have brought with it some highly unwelcome consequences. For example, an ever-increasing number of the aged now live in, and spend much of their time shuttling back and forth between, nursing homes and hospitals. In an earlier era, these aged persons would probably have been taken care of in their own homes, or in the homes of members of their family. But now, in part because of the inability of physicians to offer privately the highly sophisticated medical care available in hospitals (and, of course, partly because of changes in family life), an increasing number of the aged spend their final years, apart from family and friends, in nursing homes and hospitals.

At the turn of the century, most Americans died in their familiar lodgings. In 1958, 60.9 percent of all deaths in America occurred in hospitals or other institutions such as nursing homes . . . and estimates now range near 80 percent.[31]

The physicians who minister to the needs of patients in nursing homes and hospitals (and who, particularly in large modern hospitals, have access to the most advanced resuscitative and other equipment) tend to regard keeping their patients alive as their prime responsibility. For this reason, perhaps, many persons who would probably have died at home in the past (possibly mercifully so), are now kept alive in nursing homes and hospitals, often by means of respirators, dialysis machines, and other advanced medical techniques. Have such efforts to keep the aged and the infirm alive been *too* successful, however? The use of resuscitative and other modern medical equipment frequently results in patients being isolated from their fellows; and what is worse, many of these patients ultimately end up existing—often for a very long time—on what can only be described as a vegetative level. In the words of Joseph Fletcher: "Whereas the so-called human vegetable . . . was once an infrequent problem in terminal wards of hospitals, it is now a common daily problem because of medical success."[32] Indeed, one of the basic reasons for the increasingly worrisome debate over how to define "death"—whether, for example, to equate it with the cessation of cerebral activity, or only with pulmonary and cardiovascular failure—is that sophisticated medical techniques are now being employed to keep people "alive" who, by any test other than pulmonary and cardiovascular activity, are "dead."

The possibility of a patient existing indefinitely in a vegetative state was, of course, vividly illustrated in the *Quinlan* case. The case began when Joseph Quinlan, the father of Karen Quinlan, petitioned a court to be appointed her guardian and to be given the right to authorize the discontinuance of all so-called "extraordinary" medical procedures that were sustaining her vital processes. Karen's brain had been profoundly, and apparently irreparably, damaged; and she was being kept alive in the intensive care unit of a hospital by means of a variety of advanced medical techniques and equipment, including a nasal-gastro feeder, a catheter to remove wastes, and (most importantly, perhaps) an MA-l respirator: "a sophisticated machine which delivers a given volume of air at a certain rate and periodically provides a 'sigh' volume, a relatively large measured volume of air designed to purge the lungs of excretions."[33] Despite all this, and despite the ministrations of a team of doctors and nurses on a 24-hour-a-day basis, Karen remained in "a chronic and persistent vegetative state"[34]—a state that appeared to be irreversible.

All of the parties to the suit appeared to agree with the court that "no form of treatment which can cure or improve that condition is known or available. As nearly as may be determined...she can *never* be restored to cognitive or sapient life."[35] In addition, by the time that the case had reached the highest court of New Jersey, Karen had lost 40 pounds and was "undergoing a continuing deteriorative process."[36] In the words of the court: "[Karen's] posture is . . . fetal-like and grotesque; there is extreme flexion-rigidity of the arms, legs and related muscles and her joints are severely rigid and deformed."[37]

The court granted Joseph Quinlan's request to be Karen's guardian and authorized the discontinuance of the "life support apparatus" under certain specified conditions. In so doing, the court discussed several distinctions sometimes made in regard to the termination of life, such as the distinction between acts of *commission*—for instance, the deliberate infliction of deadly harm—and acts of *omission*—the failure to employ "artificial life support or radical surgery," for example.[38] In addition, the court cited the distinction taken by the Catholic Church between "ordinary" and "extraordinary" methods of preserving life, noting that under Catholic doctrine a physician was bound to use only ordinary medical procedures, and indicating that the medical procedures to be discontinued regarding Karen were clearly "extraordinary."[39] Further, the court held that although the State of New Jersey had a legitimate interest in protecting Karen's life, this interest was superseded by Karen's "right of privacy," under which her father (and guardian) could order the discontinuance of her life support apparatus. In the court's words: "We do not question the State's undoubted power to punish the taking of human life, but that power does not encompass individuals terminating treatment pursuant to their right of privacy."[40]

The court's reliance upon Karen's right of privacy to authorize the discontinuance of her life support apparatus may seem to many persons to be contrived. The "right to privacy" was originally the brainchild of Samuel D. Warren and Louis D. Brandeis, who, in a celebrated law review article in 1890, suggested that its existence be inferred so as to provide a basis in law for prohibiting newspapers from exposing men's private lives to public view.[41] It is certainly arguable that to use a person's right to privacy as the legal basis for authorizing his guardian to discontinue medical procedures that are keeping him alive, is to strain this concept beyond recognition. It should also be noted that the court's labeling the medical techniques used to keep Karen alive "extraordinary" rather than "ordinary"—and authorizing the discontinuance of these "extraordinary" techniques—can have little or no precedential value. As many writers on euthanasia have pointed out, "the same procedure may be ordinary for one patient but extraordinary for another, depending on the extent of the problems the patient has."[42] The court itself seemed to recognize this, for it declared that "the use of the same respirator . . . could be considered 'ordinary' in the context of the possibly curable patient but 'extraordinary' in the context of the forced sustaining by cardio-respiratory processes of an irreversibly doomed patient."[43]

To turn now to the distinction mentioned by the court between acts of commission and acts of omission in regard to the termination of life, there can be no doubt that the line of demarcation between them—between pulling out the plug of an oxygen machine that is keeping a dying patient alive, and simply not replacing the tank of oxygen when it runs out—is hard to maintain. One cannot help wondering what the moral difference really is between deliberately killing a person, or letting him die by omitting a needed and available medical remedy, so long as the death is intended. Little wonder, perhaps, that many people regard the difference, if there is one, between mercy killing and letting a patient die by omitting a life-sustaining treatment as "a moral quibble."[44]

If all this is so, did the court in the *Quinlan* case actually begin to legalize mercy killing in New Jersey—albeit in carefully circumscribed circumstances—and thereby begin to narrow the gap between the letter of the law regarding mercy killing and the way this law is usually enforced? One might think so, particularly since the court admits that the termination of Karen's treatments "would accelerate Karen's death."[45] Yet on the other hand, the court fails to mention, or even to allude to, mercy killing by name. Similarly, in a statute enacted in California in 1976—the country's first "Death with Dignity" act—the California Legislature provides that "any adult person may execute a directive . . . [authorizing] the withholding or withdrawal of life-sustaining procedures [by his physicians] in a terminal condition";[46] but in a later section of the law, the legislature specifically declares that "nothing in this . . . [statute] shall be construed to condone, authorize, or approve mercy killing. . . ."[47] One is left confused.

It is also noteworthy that the *Quinlan* court was very much concerned not simply with Karen's fate, but also with the terribly difficult problems faced by physicians who attempt to minister to the hopelessly ill. "There must be a way," in the words of the court, "to free physicians . . . from possible contamination by self-interest or self-protection concerns [fear of malpractice suits, for example, or of prosecution] which would inhibit their independent medical judgments for the well-being of their dying patients."[48] To this end, the court considered at length the views of Dr. Karen Teel, an advocate of shared medical judgments and diffusion of medical responsibility. And, when rendering its final judgment, the court held that

upon the concurrence of the guardian and family of Karen, should the responsible attending physicians conclude that there is no reasonable possibility of Karen's ever emerging from her present comatose condition to a cognitive, sapient state and that the life-support apparatus now being administered to Karen should be discontinued, they shall consult with the hospital 'Ethics Committee' or like body of the institution in which Karen is then hospitalized. If that consultive body agrees that there is no reasonable possibility of Karen's ever emerging from her present comatose condition to a cognitive, sapient state, the present life-support system may be withdrawn and said action shall be without any civil or criminal liability therefor, on the part of any participant, whether guardian, physician, hospital or others.[49]

The *Quinlan* court's ruling that the discontinuance of Karen's life-support apparatus required the cooperation of the hospital ethics committee and the agreement of her physicians seems consistent with the view expressed with increasing frequency today that once a hopelessly ill patient (or his guardian) requests that his death be accelerated, that the decision ultimately be made by the physicians involved. A well-known exposition of this view is to be found in *The Sanctity of Life and the Criminal Law*, in which the author urges that we trust the "good sense" of physicians regarding mercy killing and that we grant them "a wide discretion" concerning it.[50] In fact, Professor Williams goes on to propose a law under which a physician who deliberately accelerates the death of a seriously ill patient is to be held legally blameless, unless it is proven "that the act was not done in good faith with the consent of the patient and for the purpose of saving him from severe pain in an illness believed to be of an incurable and fatal character."[51]

There are many reasons why such a law may prove of value. For one thing, it might help to free doctors from the fear of malpractice suits, prosecution, and the like, and thereby enable them to concentrate completely upon relieving the suffering of their patients. As was noted earlier in this paper, mercy killing—particularly by physicians—has existed on a *de facto* basis in the United States for many years. In an editorial in 1970 in the *Journal of the American Medical Association*, for example, the senior editor Dr. Alister Brass declared that euthanasia was practiced by physicians to a "wide extent"[52]—an observation that has gained considerable support since then from the responses given by physicians (especially those physicians who deal with terminal cancer patients) to questionnaires submitted to them.[53] Indeed, the *Quinlan* court itself observed that "humane decisions against resuscitative or maintenance therapy are frequently a recognized *de facto* response in the medical world to the irreversible, terminal, pain-ridden patient. . . ."[54]

Paradoxically, perhaps, authorizing physicians to accelerate the death of hopelessly ill patients might help to prevent mistakes by these doctors. If mercy killing were legalized, there would then seem to be no good reason why doctors would fail to consult with their colleagues concerning it. Under the law proposed above, a doctor could "confer with a colleague in the usual way and so obtain help and advice in his onerous duty."[55] But what about the possibility of mistakes being made by physicians concerning the wishes of their patients regarding mercy killing? How can physicians be certain that when they accelerate a patient's death (either by failing to employ a needed treatment, or otherwise), that they are really acting in accordance with the patient's wishes?

Use of a so-called "living will" is the solution to this problem that advocates of euthanasia frequently suggest.[56] In essence, a "living will" is a formal legal document, signed and witnessed in much the same manner as an ordinary will, in which a man declares that if certain extreme circumstances arise (if he becomes painfully and hopelessly ill, for instance), that he wants his death accelerated—or, at least, not prolonged by Herculean measures. Under the California "Death with Dignity" act, for example, physicians are absolved of civil and criminal liability if they act in accordance with and under the authority of a formal legal document (signed by a patient in the presence of two disinterested witnesses) which provides that if a patient's physicians determine that his/her death is imminent "whether or not life-sustaining procedures are utilized," that these procedures be withheld or withdrawn and that the patient be permitted to "die naturally."[57] Though it is possible to debate the merits of this law—and the "living will" for which it provides—endlessly, there can be no doubt that it serves the useful psychological function of helping to assuage the almost inevitable guilt of doctors who engage in mercy killing.[58]

Convincing though the foregoing arguments in favor of doctors making the ultimate decisions regarding mercy killing may appear to be, they lose their persuasiveness when weighed in the balance against other considerations. To begin with, doctors may not want to make the ultimate, or any, decisions concerning mercy killing. As Kamisar has pointed out, the possibility that doctors will simply refuse to accept responsibility for mercy killing is "a problem of major proportions."[59] Also, is it really advisable to continue to expand the power of physicians over their patients, especially when these powers may already be (in the words of Jerry B. Wilson) "unbearably great"?[60]

Alerted by such writers as Thomas Szasz and Nicholas Kittrie to what has increasingly come to be known as the "tyranny of experts," the courts have already begun to circumscribe the powers of doctors.[61] Further, if physicians were given the responsibility for determining whether the death of their terminally ill patients ought to be accelerated, a conflict might well arise between the interests of these patients and the bias of many physicians in favor of investigatory medicine.[62] In addition, permitting doctors to make life or death decisions regarding their patients might well "weaken medical research by taking away the incentives to find cures for painful diseases."[63]

As psychoanalysts, especially, are aware, patients tend to regard their physicians as parent substitutes. "[T]he patient . . . will do his best to push . . . [his doctor] into the place of parental authority, and will make use of . . . [his doctor] as parental authority to the utmost."[64] Again, a doctor represents for most people "some combination of man-of-science, father-confessor, advisor, and even a bit of magician. Just as a sick child looks to his parents, so a sick adult looks to his doctor to make him 'all better.'"[65] If so, then it is little wonder that patients tend to exaggerate greatly the ability of their physicians and to endow them with far more knowledge and wisdom than they actually have—including the knowledge and wisdom needed to determine if and when life ought to be terminated.

Unfortunately, however, medical schools usually avoid formal consideration of mercy killing; and perhaps as a result, there is precious little serious discussion of it during a physician's years in training. Also, studies reveal that the judgment of doctors in regard to mercy killing is often based not upon their medical training or expertise, but rather upon their "philosophical and religious upbringing."[66] As Reiser has noted, there is little or no evidence that physicians have acquired, along with "substantial technical ability to prolong lives," a knowledge of moral principles that would enable them to know "when to apply or withhold...[life-saving] remedies."[67] In short, there seems to be no basis in fact for believing that the education or medical expertise of physicians enables them to determine when a patient's death ought to be accelerated.

Another major objection to authorizing doctors to engage in mercy killing is the likelihood that doing so will tend to undermine the confidence of patients in their physicians. If doctors were authorized to accelerate the death of patients, then patients might begin to regard them not only as healers with whom openness and frankness is desirable, but rather as possible destroyers to whom symptoms are to be disclosed only with the greatest of caution. It has been argued that "if the public once came to think that their doctors might exchange the role of preserver for that of destroyer, their suffering in anxiety would far outweigh that now attributable to the unnecessary prolonging of life."[68]

In addition, to ask doctors to engage in mercy killing is to ask them to violate the Hippocratic Oath. This oath contains the pledge that: "I will use treatment to help the sick according to my ability and judgment, but never with a view to injury and wrongdoing. Neither will I administer a poison to anybody when asked to do so, nor will I suggest such a course." Mercy killing and the Hippocratic Oath are irreconcilable.[69]

Another frequently mentioned objection to giving doctors the right to make life or death decisions concerning their patients has to do with the delicate subject of medical incompetence. Even though such a law as the California "Death with Dignity" act may protect doctors who fail to employ Herculean life-sustaining procedures,[70] it is diffi-cult to understand how the state can—or would want to—shield these doctors from suits charging, for example, that they made egregious mistakes of fact concerning such matters as the condition of their patients, the desire of these patients that their death be accelerated, or the nature of the medical procedures withheld. Also, a doctor who engages in mercy killing runs the very great risk of having his professional reputation besmirched by "accusations of neglect and foul play by those who feel guilty over their relationships with the deceased."[71]

It is a commonplace that close relatives of a deceased often feel extremely guilty about his death; and to help assuage this guilt, accuse the physicians who took care of him of neglect or worse. The process of "projection"—an unconscious mental mechanism whereby a person attributes to others his own guilty thoughts and feelings—may well be responsible for a considerable percentage of the suits for malpractice and the like brought against doctors by the relatives of a deceased.[72]

A final reason why authorizing doctors to make the ultimate decisions regarding mercy killing is likely to prove unsuccessful has to do with the psychology of doctors themselves. Surprisingly, perhaps, many physicians experience a great deal of difficulty in facing up to death. They seem to have what has been described as "a marked aversion to the fact of death";[73] and as a result, are often unable to help their patients, and the families of these patients, come to grips with it.[74] One well-known sign of the difficulty experienced by doctors in dealing with death is their almost routine failure to let dying patients know that they are dying.

Surveys show consistently that more than 80 percent of physicians routinely do not tell terminally ill patients that they are terminally ill. Of course it goes without saying that they do not, therefore, discuss with them their illness, different alternatives regarding treatment, and certainly not the problem of dying and how that might affect them.[75]

Another sign of the reluctance (or inability) of many doctors to face up to death is their tendency to avoid—and even to abandon—dying patients. Studies have shown that a physician is likely to use a variety of techniques to avoid dying patients, including "prescrib[ing] life-sustaining techniques he knows will not provide a cure."[76] Indeed, when a physician seeks to avoid or abandon dying patients by having them spend their final days, isolated and alone, on respirators, dialysis machines, and the like, he may be venting his aggression and sadism upon them. As psychoanalytic investigations have revealed, the helpless and the dying frequently arouse in others not so much sympathy and compassion, as aggression and sadism.[77]

One reason why a doctor is likely to find it extremely difficult to deal with patients who are terminally ill is that (in the words of August M. Kasper) "they simply will not feed the doctor's narcissism by responding and getting well. Their care is demanding, frustrating, and far from helpful to the medical magician's self-esteem."[78] Dying patients, in short, pose a threat to a doctor's narcissism and self-esteem. Further, doctors often become seriously depressed when terminal patients whom they have taken care of finally die. In fact, it has been contended that the depression that physicians experience as a result of the trauma "of 'saying goodbye' . . . is enormous . . . [and] second only to the depression that exists in intensive care unit nursing staffs and coronary care unit nursing staffs."[79] Whether or not this is so, there can be no doubt that because of the difficulties experienced by many doctors in facing up to death, they hardly seem to be the appropriate parties to engage in, or to make the ultimate decision regarding, mercy killing.

If, as has been seen, there are many persuasive reasons why doctors should not be called upon to make life or death decisions concerning their patients, there would seem to be no point in trying to impose this responsibility upon them. Moreover, assigning to judges or to some other authoritative figures the task of making the ultimate decisions in regard to mercy killing would also seem to be pointless, since there is no firm societal consensus concerning mercy killing that could help to guide them.

As was noted earlier in this paper, evidence of this lack of a societal consensus regarding mercy killing may well be seen in the striking contrast between the law's vigorous condemnation of mercy killing and society's usual failure to convict or punish those who engage in it. Indeed, because this gap between the law in words and the law in action concerning mercy killing is probably the central legal problem of mercy killing today, the balance of this paper will be devoted to trying to determine—with the aid of psychoanalytic tools and insights—why this gap exists and what can be done about it.

As has been suggested, the disparity between the law's vigorous condemnation of mercy killing and society's usual failure to punish or convict those who engage in it may well be related to the fundamental societal disagreements concerning it detailed at the beginning of this paper. There is reason to believe, however, that the disparity between the letter of the law regarding mercy killing and the way this law is usually carried out may also reflect a conflict between the use of the criminal law to denounce mercy killing on the one hand and the realities or practicalities of life on the other.

One of the basic purposes of the criminal law—a purpose emphasized in the works of the great Victorian judge and historian of the criminal law, James Fitzjames Stephen—is to denounce behavior that society regards as morally approbrious: "to express in emphatic form moral condemnation of the offender and...[thus] 'ratify' the morality which he has violated."[80] In more modern psychoanalytically oriented terminology, one of the basic functions served by the criminal law is to help to express the strictures of man's moral faculty—of his superego. Thus, when the law condemns mercy killing, labeling it at the very least "felonious homicide," the law is probably helping to

satisfy the demands of man's superego that mercy killing be denounced as an immoral—indeed, as an outrageously immoral—act.

Even though mercy killing may offend man's moral faculty or superego, the fact is that it is rarely punished. This suggests that either the punishment of mercy killing is impracticable—or, what is more likely, that to punish it violates man's understanding of the necessities or realities of life. To employ psychoanalytic terminology once again, society's usual failure to punish mercy killing may well reflect the influence or activity of that agency of the mind responsible for reality testing—of the ego.[81]

To suggest that the disparity between the letter of the law concerning mercy killing and the lack of vigor with which this law is usually enforced reflects a possible conflict between two agencies of the mind, is to suggest nothing that is unique to the law dealing with mercy killing. The contrast between the law in words and the law in action in regard to so-called "victimless" crimes—gambling, homosexuality, drinking, prostitution, and so on—is equally striking.[82] Just as society's failure to punish gambling, homosexuality, drinking, and prostitution with severity—or indeed at all—probably reflects the operation of man's reality oriented ego, so the law's vigorous condemnation of these "victimless" offenses undoubtedly reflects in part the moral demands of man's superego. In fact, the insistence of so many people that the criminal law continue to denounce gambling, homosexuality, drinking, prostitution, and the like—offenses which, as psychoanalysts have learned, are more like illnesses than anything else[83]—may well serve (as has been suggested elsewhere) to reinforce "their moral faculty or superego in its attempts to curb the temptation within themselves to engage in these very acts."[84]

Finding reasons why man's moral faculty or superego is likely to oppose mercy killing is not at all difficult. In fact, a number of these reasons were detailed in the first section of this paper. Considerable attention was devoted, for example, to the so-called "wedge" argument—to the contention that to allow mercy killing in a single instance would be to permit the entry of a wedge that would eventually cause a complete breakdown of accepted standards and result in mass euthanasia and genocide. When viewed in the light of reality, however, this argument is obviously fallacious, since mercy killing has existed on a *de facto* basis in the United States for many years, without any resultant moral collapse or genocidal consequences. On the other hand, the wedge argument does make *emotional* sense. It reflects the fear that any relaxation in the present strong prohibitions against killing would inevitably result in "abuses and errors."[85] Or, as Freud's disciple A.A. Brill expressed it more than 40 years ago:

the lust for killing can only be held in leash with the greatest effort, and like the proverbial sleeping dog it is best not to disturb it. . . . [M]ercy killing by physicians, no matter how humanely applied, would be bound to demoralize society. . . . It would revive . . . [man's] dormant and repressed sadism and destroy the sacredness of human life.[86]

The fear that the legalization of mercy killing (or any other relaxation in the ban on killing) might "destroy the 'Thou shalt not kill' upon which the whole fabric of orderly society [rests]"[87] is based in part upon the realization that man is, innately, an incredibly aggressive creature.[88] In the words of Anthony Storr:

The sombre fact is that we are the cruellest and most ruthless species that has ever walked the earth; and that, although we may recoil in horror when we read in newspaper or history book of the atrocities committed by man upon man, we know in our hearts that each one of us harbours within himself those same savage impulses which lead to murder, to torture, and to war[89]

One of the superego's original and prime functions is to oppose and attempt to mute this aggressiveness—and, particularly, to try to prevent homicide.[90] To succeed in doing so, however, it needs all the help that it can get from religion, custom, morality, and the law. Fortunately, the law is often able to offer this needed help: indeed, it has been contended that *the prime operative duty of law is the control of human aggressiveness.*"[91]

Whether or not this is so, there can be no doubt that when the law denounces mercy killing, declaring that it is a form of murder, the law is thereby lending support to the superego in the task of opposing and attempting to mute man's furiously aggressive—and often frankly homicidal— urges. In so doing, the law is helping (in the phraseology of West) "to remedy our inability to control our own aggressive selves."[92]

There may be other reasons why the law's condemnation of mercy killing may offer the superego much-needed support. For example, to the extent that the elderly or others may consciously or unconsciously identify themselves with the terminally ill, the law's opposition to mercy killing (particularly when coupled with religious doctrine[93]) may help the superego to prevent suicides.[94] In any event, the possible conflict suggested above between the morally oriented superego and the reality oriented ego concerning mercy killing confronts the would-be law reformer with a serious dilemma. If, as was pointed out earlier in this paper, the conflict between the law in words and in action regarding mercy killing cannot be permitted to continue indefinitely, what is the law reformer to do? Should he/she act in accordance with the presumed demands of the superego and insist that the law continue to oppose mercy killing? Or should he/she conform his/her behavior to the presumed wishes of the ego and urge that, at least under some circumstances, mercy killing be legalized?

Clearly, these questions admit of no easy answers. Man certainly cannot ignore the wishes of the superego—particularly if, as Edmund Bergler has insisted, the superego's use of guilt to enforce its demands makes it the "real master of the personality."[95] Indeed, Bergler has contended

that at least "fifty percent of man's psychic energy is . . . expended in his attempts to ward off the constant avalanche of . . . [guilt] flowing from the superego."[96]

On the other hand, the practice of psychoanalysis teaches that it is not only desirable—but also quite possible—to extend the hegemony of the ego. It is the rare psychoanalysis in which id and superego have not been replaced to some extent by the ego—and in a successful psychoanalysis, to a significant extent. Freud always insisted that man's "best hope for the future" lay in the ego's ability to "establish a dictatorship over the human mind."[97]

By no means is this to say that no compromise concerning mercy killing is possible between the ego and the superego. One of the ego's prime functions other than reality testing is to try to find ways of reconciling the conflicting demands of the id, the superego, and the outside world.[98] Indeed, compromises regarding mercy killing between the ego and the superego may well be found in the law of other countries. In West Germany, for instance, mercy killings are placed in a special category—"homicides upon request"—and are usually punished with comparatively light sentences; in Switzerland, judges are empowered to mitigate the punishments imposed by the law when mercy killing is involved; and in Uruguay, mercy killings have been legalized by statute—provided that they are "motivated by compassion" and performed at "the victim's own request."[99]

It should also be noted that mercy killing may be in accordance with, rather than contrary to, the demands of the moral faculty of many people. One can hardly doubt that moral fervor moved Lord Moynihan when he urged in an historic debate over mercy killing before the British Parliament in 1936, "that in cases of advanced and inevitably fatal disease, attended by agony which reaches, or oversteps, the boundaries of human endurance, the sufferer, after legal inquiry and due observance of all safeguards, shall have the right to demand and be entitled to release."[100]

In short, there would seem to be a number of alternatives to the present system in the United States of declaring mercy killing to be murder and then failing to convict or punish most of those who engage in it. If and when a new consensus is achieved in the United States regarding mercy killing—a consensus that, as the *Quinlan* case seems to indicate, may well be formed as a result of the problems spawned by modern medical technology—there should be no hesitation in changing the law, both in words and in action, to conform to this consensus.

Notes

1. *In re* Karen Quinlan, An Alleged Incompetent, 70 N.J. 10 (1976).

2. Norman St. John-Stevas, *Life, Death and the Law* (Bloomington, Ind.: Indiana University Press, 1961), p. 264.

3. Yale Kamisar, "Euthanasia Legislation: Some Non-Religious Objections," in Samuel Gorovitz et al., *Moral Problems in Medicine* (Englewood Cliffs, N.J.: Prentice-Hall, 1976), pp. 402, 403.

4. See Glanville Williams, *The Sanctity of Life and the Criminal Law* (New York: Knopf, 1957), p. 314.

5. Daniel C. Maguire, *Death By Choice* (Garden City, N.Y.: Doubleday, 1974), p. 141.

6. Joseph Fletcher, "The 'Right' to Live and the 'Right' to Die," in Marvin Kohl, *Beneficent Euthanasia* (Buffalo, N.Y.: Prometheus Books, 1975), pp. 44, 48.

7. Maguire, *supra* note 5, at 154.

8. See Jerry B. Wilson, *Death by Decision: The Medical, Moral, and Legal Dilemmas of Euthanasia* (Philadelphia, Pa.: Westminster Press, 1975), p. 54.

9. Stevas, *supra* note 2, at 268.

10. Williams, *supra* note 4, at 314-315.

11. See, *e.g.*, Susan Sherwin, "Moral Problems Concerning Life and Death: Introduction," in Gorovitz et al., *supra* note 3, at 242, 243.

12. Stevas, *supra* note 2, at 269.

13. See Koessler, "Euthanasia in the Hadamar Sanatorium and International Law," 43 *J. Crim L.C. & P.S.* 735-755 (1953).

14. Joseph V. Sullivan, "The Immorality of Euthanasia," in Kohl, *supra* note 6, at 19, 24.

15. *Id.*

16. Williams, *supra* note 4, at 333.

17. Maguire, *supra* note 5, at 131.

18. Sullivan, *supra* note 14, at 24.

19. See, *e.g.*, Maguire, *supra* note 5, at 41-43.

20. See Williams, *supra* note 4, at 334-335.

21. John E. Schowalter, Julian B. Ferholt, and Nancy M. Mann, "The Adolescent Patient's Decision to Die," in Gorovitz et al., *supra* note 3, at 414, 420.

22. Of particular relevance here is the extended discussion of "victimless" crime (in the chapter titled "The Overreach of the Criminal Law") in Norval Morris and Gordon Hawkins, *The Honest Politician's Guide to Crime Control* (Chicago: University of Chicago Press, 1970).

23. See Sissela Bok, "Euthanasia and the Care of the Dying," in John A. Behnke and Sissela Bok, *The Dilemmas of Euthanasia* (New York: Doubleday, 1975), pp. 1, 19.

24. Williams, *supra* note 4, at 319.

25. See, *e.g.*, Diana Crane, "Physician's Attitudes Towards the Treatment of Critically Ill Patients," in Behnke and Bok, *supra* note 23, at 107, 111; Maguire, *supra* note 5, at 43; Wilson, *supra* note 8, at 43.

26. Wilson, *supra* note 8, at 149.

27. Norman L. Cantor, "Law and the Termination of an Incompetent Patient's Life Preserving Care," in Behnke & Bok, *supra* note 23, at 69, 74.

28. Wilson, *supra* note 8, at 156.

29. Lon Fuller, *The Morality of Law* (New Haven, Conn.: Yale University Press, 1964), p. 81; see also Lon Fuller, *Anatomy of the Law* (New York: New American Library; Mentor Books, ed., 1969), p. 19.

30. Maguire, *supra* note 5, at 4.

31. Bok, *supra* note 23, at 11.

32. Fletcher, *supra* note 6, at 47.

33. *In re* Quinlan, *supra* note 1, at 25.

34. *Id.* at 26.

35. *Id.*

36. *Id.*

37. *Id.*

38. *Id.* at 43.

39. See *id.*, at 48.

40. *Id.* at 52.

41. See S.B. Warren and L.D. Brandeis, "The Right to Privacy," 4 *Harv. L. Rev.* 193 (1890).

42. Schowalter et al., *supra* note 21, at 420.

43. *In re* Quinlan, *supra* note 1, at 48.

44. Wilson, *supra* note 8, at 118.

45. *In re* Quinlan, *supra* note 1, at 51.

46. Cal., A. 3060 § 7188 (1976).

47. *Id.* at § 7195.

48. *In re* Quinlan, *supra* note 1, at 49.

49. *Id.* at 55.

50. Williams, *supra* note 4, at 339.

51. *Id.* at 340.

52. Wilson, *supra* note 8, at 43.

53. See Crane, *supra* note 25, at 111.

54. *In re* Quinlan, *supra* note 1, at 47.

55. Williams, *supra* note 4, at 342.

56. See, *e.g.*, *Death With Dignity: Legislative Manual* (New York: Society for the Right to Die, 1976).

57. Cal., A. 3060 § 7188 (1976).

58. See Bok, *supra* note 23, at 19.

59. Kamisar, *supra* note 3, at 406.

60. Wilson, *supra* note 8, at 58.

61. See, *e.g.*, such leading cases concerning the rights of the mentally ill as O'Connor v. Donaldson, 422 U.S. 563 (1975) and Lessard v. Schmidt, 349 F. Supp. 1078. (E.D. Wis. 1972).

62. See Maguire, *supra* note 5, at 181.

63. Wilson, *supra* note 8, at 58.

64. Anna Freud, "The Doctor-Patient Relationship," in Gorovitz et al., *supra* note 3, at 200, 203.

65. Bernard V. Strauss, "The Role of the Physician's Personality in Medical Practice (Psychotherapeutic Medicine)," 51 *New York State Journal of Medicine*, (1951), reprinted in *Elmcrest Classic of the Month* (Portland, Conn.: Elmcrest Psychiatric Institute, June 1977), Vol. 2, No. 6, p. 2.

66. Maguire, *supra* note 5, at 181.

67. Stanley Joel Reiser, "The Dilemma of Euthanasia in Modern Medical History: The English and American Experiences," in Behnke & Bok, *supra* note 23, at 27, 29.

68. Wilson, *supra* note 8, at 58.

69. See, *e.g.*, the discussion of the Pythagorian views upon which the Hippocratic Oath is based in Wilson, *id.* at 21.

70. See Cal., A. 3060 § 7190 (1976).

71. Wilson, *supra* note 8, at 111.

72. For a discussion of the relationship between projection and the law, see C.G. Schoenfeld, *Psychoanalysis and the Law* (Springfield, Ill.: Charles C. Thomas, 1973).

73. Maguire, *supra* note 5, at 182.

74. See Wilson, *supra* note 8, at 111.

75. Article by George J. Annas, in *Changing Attitudes Toward Euthanasia: Excerpts from Papers Presented at the Eighth Annual Euthanasia Conference, New York, N.Y., December 6, 1975* (New York: The Euthanasia Educational Council), pp. 9, 10.

76. Bok, *supra* note 23, at 11.

77. See, *e.g.*, Erich Fromm, *The Anatomy of Human Destructiveness* (New York: Holt, Rinehart & Winston, 1973), p. 291.

78. August M. Kasper, "The Doctor and Death," in Gorovitz et al., *supra* note 3, at 69, 70.

79. Article by Samuel C. Klagsbrun in *Changing Attitudes Toward Euthanasia*, *supra* note 75, at 4, 5.

80. H.L.A. Hart, *Law, Liberty and Morality* (Stanford, Calif.: Stanford University Press, 1963), p. 63.

81. For a short but authoritative discussion of the activities of the ego—and particularly reality testing—see Charles Brenner, *An Elementary Textbook of Psychoanalysis* (Garden City, N.Y.: Doubleday; Doubleday Anchor Books ed., 1957), pp. 62 *et seq.*

82. See note 22 *supra*.

83. See, *e.g.*, Edmund Bergler, *The Psychology of Gambling* (New York: Hill and Wang, 1957).

84. C.G. Schoenfeld, "Psychoanalysis, Criminal Justice Planning and Reform, and the Law," 7 *Criminal Law Bulletin* 313, 317 (1971) (emphasis deleted).

85. Bok, *supra* note 23, at 8.

86. A.A. Brill, "Reflections on Euthanasia," 84 *Journal of Nervous and Mental Diseases* 1, 10 (1936).

87. *Id.* at 12.

88. For what is, perhaps, the classic psychoanalytic statement concerning man's aggressiveness, see Sigmund Freud, *Civilization and Its Discontents* (London: Hogarth Press, 1955), p. 85.

89. Anthony Storr, *Human Aggression* (New York: Atheneum, 1968), Introduction.

90. See Freud, *supra* note 88, at 105.

91. Ranyard West, *Conscience and Society* (New York: Emerson Books, 1945), p. 165 (emphasis in the original).

92. *Id.* at 166.

93. See, *e.g.*, Sidney Hook, "The Ethics of Suicide," in Kohl *supra* note 6, at 57, 58.

94. This is not to deny, however, that the pressure exerted by the superego on the ego may be a prime *cause* of suicides. See, *e.g.*, Jacob A. Arlow and Charles Brenner, *Psychoanalytic Concepts and the Structural Theory* (New York: International Universities Press, 1964), p. 92.

95. Edmund Bergler, *The Superego* (New York: Grune & Stratton, 1952), p. *vii* (emphasis deleted).

96. *Id.* at x.

97. Sigmund Freud, *New Introductory Lectures on Psychoanalysis* (New York: Norton, 1933), p. 234.

98. *Id.* at 108.

99. Maguire, *supra* note 5, at 41-42.

100. Bok, *supra* note 23 at 2.

Euthanasia

A Paper for Discussion by Psychiatrists*

R. C. A. Hunter, M.D.[1]

Background

As part of an ongoing and lengthy review of Canadian Law, the Law Reform Commission of Canada (LRCC) has released a number of study or working papers in what is called the "Protection of Life Series" (7). These documents are the following:

1) Criteria for the Determination of Death†
2) Sterilization†
3) Sanctity of Life or Quality of Life†
4) Cessation of Treatment‡
5) Informed Consent§
6) Treatment in Criminal Law§
7) Human Experimentation‡
8) Behaviour Modification — Control‡
9) The Meaning of Person in Law‡

The issue of the "Right to Life" is a continuing theme in all this. Euthanasia, one aspect of which is the "right to die" is another.

"Cessation of Treatment" is scheduled for publication in the spring of 1981 and the LRCC hope that it will be given wide circulation and will lead to discussion and feedback. Following this the LRCC will generate final views which will be advanced in the Commission's Report to the Minister of Justice and Parliament whence any or all recommendations may or may not find their way into Canadian Legislation.

As medical doctors and psychiatrists we are inescapably involved in decisions regarding treatment and the cessation of treatment. It is logical, therefore, for us to advance such views as we possess in an attempt to influence the LRCC's final recommendations in the direction we deem proper.

Definition of Euthanasia

The Concise Oxford Dictionary and Funk and Wagnall's provide the following definitions: "Gentle and easy death: bringing about of this in cases of incurable and painful disease. Mercy killing".

The word is derived from the Greek "Eu" — meaning "well" and "Thanatos" meaning "death".

In the context of present day discussions it is customary to distinguish between active and passive euthanasia.

Active euthanasia means intentionally doing something that will induce death. This is indistinguishable from killing (the prefix "mercy" notwithstanding), regardless of the motivation that leads to the act. An example is ordering or giving a lethal dose of morphine.

Passive euthanasia means the intentional avoidance or discontinuation of steps to prolong life, for example, the intentional discontinuation of life support measures such as machines.

As the term "mercy killing" suggests, it is not always possible to distinguish between active and passive euthanasia, since discontinuation of some vital treatment modality can be construed as a positive and intentional act and thus is not passive but active in interpretation. Nevertheless, as psychiatrists we cannot avoid being aware of the differences in the physician's motivation and emotional reaction

*Manuscript received March 1980.
[1]Professor of Psychiatry, University of Toronto; Senior Consultant in Psychiatry, Sunnybrook Medical Centre, 2075 Bayview Avenue, Toronto, Ontario M4N 3M5 (reprint address)
†Published in 1979
‡Not yet published
§Published in 1980

between intentionally administering a lethal dose of some drug or discontinuing or not embarking upon heroic measures for the maintenance of life. There does appear to be a difference in the physician's emotional context between active and passive euthanasia even if they are not readily distinguishable operationally and legally.

Some Important Clarifications

At this point a number of clarifications seems in order to further our discussion:

1. It is now medically possible to maintain the circulation of the blood and the function of respiration indefinitely by means of machines which are, generally, external to the patient. Such measures can be continued long after there is any realistic medical expectation that the patient can recover spontaneous and/or independent cardiac and respiratory functions.

2. This situation has led to the need to define death in ways that are not dependent on cardiac and respiratory function and ways that will allow the physician to make accurate judgements concerning the probability of the recovery of function. The principal definition at the moment is that death is that state in which there is cessation of brain function, judged by clinical, and where possible, electroencephalographic means. Whereas this seems fairly cut-and-dried, it should be recognized that the definition is primarily useful as a description of an end-state. It is not reliable as a predictor of whether brain function may not return if resuscitation measures are employed or continued. For instance, children's brains can withstand longer periods of anoxia than can the brains of adults. Pathological conditions which lead to hypoxia are more damaging than brief total anoxia. Body temperature is a crucial variable in judging ultimate viability. Thus, the common medical rule-of-thumb that four minutes of continuous anoxia is incompatible with recovery of brain function is unreliable. To illustrate this the Intensive Care Unit physicians at a major teaching hospital in Toronto do not discontinue life maintenance systems until after 48 hours of absent brain waves and the appropriate clinical signs (for example, fixed pupils).

3. In the event that respiratory and cardiac functions fail, but brain function has not irrevocably ceased, life-sustaining machines may be used to tide over clinical situations which would previously have caused death, until such time as cardiac and respiratory function can be regained by the individual. For instance, in some forms of cardiac surgery the maintenance of the patient's blood flow is relegated to a machine which is later to be discontinued when the patient's heart can once more resume its task. In some situations therefore, the physician must make a judgement about the likelihood of independent functioning when life support measures are discontinued.

4. There are pharmacological means for controlling intractable even severe pain for relatively long periods, without major risk to the development of tolerance and addiction or severe side effects. An example of such a preparation is the so-called "Brompton Cocktail" (morphine, cocaine, ethyl-alcohol, and flavouring). Thus the physician has the capability for a substantial degree of analgesia at very reduced risks to the patient for protracted periods of weeks or even months.

The upshot is that medicine now possesses a considerable capacity for prolonging life of a sort. But of what sort? It is here that the notion of "the quality of life" enters in and this is discussed briefly in 1(c) below.

The Problem of Euthanasia for Medicine, The Law and Religion

1. *Practical Medical Problems*

From what has gone before the practical medical problems appear to be as follows:

(a) Difficulties in establishing the fact that death has occurred (in acute situations).

(b) Difficulties in prognosticating accurately about ultimate recovery (in acute, sub-acute and chronic situations).

(c) In the terminal, pain-ridden, or hopelessly ill patient, how does medicine make the judgement to cease supporting life?

This question brings into focus discussions concerning "the quality of life." Continued existence may be of such painful, uncomfortable, handicapped or otherwise poor quality that insisting that the patient continue to live may not seem humane. The sources of information on which judgements concerning this general issue can be based are as follows: The patient's wishes and preferences, assuming that the patient is able and competent to express them; the wishes and preferences of the patient's relatives; society's wishes as codified in religion, moral philosophy, the law, the medical profession, and the personal conscience of the medical attendant.

2. Problems with the law appear to be disarmingly simple. As the Criminal Code stands now, there is no provision for mercy killing, either actively or passively. Any action or avoidance of action which is done on an intentional basis by the medical profession and which results in the death of a patient is illegal and open to prosecution.

3. In addition to a plethora of views advanced by columnists and editorial writers in the media there is a wide range of opinion to be found in the religious and codified moral attitudes on the issue of euthanasia. These opinions vary between denominations and within denominations. One polar view is that expressed by the Anglican Church of Canada (9) which proposes that it might be morally right: (a) to actively end the lives of newborn infants with severe CNS damage; (b) to approve of passive euthanasia in the case of terminally ill adults; (c) to recognize that there may be cases amongst adults when active euthanasia may be both moral and compassionate.

    The other polar extreme is the religious contention that God gives life and only God should be able to take it away. That is to say that life does not belong to any person or individual but only to God.

4. Those responsible for funding in health care systems have concerns that the uncontrolled proliferation of life-maintenance systems, which are mostly in hospitals, would increase costs tremendously in the years ahead. The topic of euthanasia, however, is so emotionally loaded that there is much reticence in publicly stating this concern, and so it is seldom discussed.

Psychiatric Variables

Physicians qua Physicians

The majority of physicians are men and women of sensibility, humaneness and good judgement, but as psychiatric clinicians we are aware that some physicians harbour omniscient and omnipotent fantasies which they may find either reassuring or tormenting. We are also aware that such fantasies can have an effect on professional judgement and this intrusion may in fact impair the objectivity and quality of professional judgement in the area of euthanasia. There comes to mind a patient whom I once treated. This man was an anaesthetist who experienced anxiety and guilt because of conscious omnipotent fantasies that in his daily work he put patients to death and then resurrected them.

Some physicians suffering from a rather obsessional personality organization have grave difficulties in making judgements as profound as those which we are discussing. I once knew a physician who became so preoccupied with what the law would permit him to do that in fact he became ineffectual and was unable to act with good medical judgement for fear of breaking the law and exposing himself to litigation or legal punishment. Some physicians with obsessional personalities have reduced ability to tolerate uncertainty or the patient's suffering. Variants of this include identification with the victim and of course with the Saviour, as well as considerable components of reaction formation. I knew a surgeon once, much involved in heroic and dramatic surgery, who wept when his car squashed a squirrel.

Unfortunately not all our colleagues have their sadistic impulses under sufficient control and on several occasions I have witnessed the effects of the intrusion of sadistic impulses into clinical situations. One can only assume that some of the physicians who collaborated in Hitler's Germany with barbaric human experimentation would belong in this group. In addition, a narcissistic ambitious involvement in clinical experimentation may on occasion eventuate in behaviour towards patients which is not humanitarian.

I have not listed frank psychiatric disturbances such as severe depression, schizophrenia or paranoid states which in themselves, necessitate psychiatric consultation with the physician who suffers from them and which may preclude the freedom to practice. The same can be said for states of addiction.

Patient Variables

The literature on what is now called thanatology is sometimes trite or pretentious: that which is not is complex and difficult to generalize and apply. This is not surprising in view of the methodological difficulties that surround research in this area. Both the human subjects that have been studied and the techniques that have been used to study them vary widely. The kinds of patients that have been studied include those who are chronically or terminally ill, oftentimes in considerable pain. Such for instance were the populations studied by John Hinton and Elizabeth Kubler-Ross (3,6). Information has also been gathered on people involved in trauma or sudden threats to life, for example, Otto Pfister, Kalich, Hunter (5,4). Weisman and Hackett studied patients facing major surgery and spoke of those with a "predilection to death" (10). Philosophers from Socrates to Sartre have offered their views on death and its meaning.

Some of the investigative methods that have been used include retrospective accounts, the so-called psychological autopsy, interviews, psychological testing, questionnaires and philosophical discourse.

This literature by now is vast and is rapidly growing. Hardly a quarter-year goes by without the appearance of some book on death or dying. It is beyond the scope of this essay to attempt to summarize this work, but it is necessary for purposes of orientation, to indicate broadly some of its findings.

In people who find themselves faced with a potentially lethal chronic illness, it is not unusual for a period of disbelief, protest or denial to give way to a sapping of energies and resistance and thence to a loss of hope, resignation or acceptance. Sometimes there may be altruistic elements as when chronically ill patients wish to die to relieve their beloved ones of the burden of their continued existence. I have firsthand knowledge of patients in the United States in whom a fiscal motive (the high cost of dying) played a major role in their requesting active euthanasia. Healthy people who are unexpectedly faced with death can often become panicky and show acute fear reactions. When the threat to life has been removed some of these may follow a discernible pattern as Caplan and others have shown (1).

The actual process of dying itself (sometimes paradoxically called "the act of dying") can be free of distressing affect and may even be pleasant. Opinions have been advanced that this is a more likely outcome if the patient has been suitably prepared for death by spiritual or psychological counselling and has made satisfactory practical plans for his dependents. There is also some belief that such substances as cannabis may smooth out this process.

Thus, it would seem prudent that in considering any particular patient, care should be given to assessing the patient's individual reactions to both the thought and fantasy of dying—the idiosyncratic meaning of death—and the fact of death itself. To risk a generalization it seems to me that one of the most significant factors about death is the finality of the separation it entails. To quote from Iris Murdoch "Death . . . separates one more than anything else" (8).

Noteworthy also is the fact that some potential killer-diseases in themselves affect the patient's mood and therefore outlook. These include patients who suffer from such diseases as carcinoma of the pancreas, cancer of the stomach, liver disease, lupus erythematosis, patients who are in great pain or who hold themselves responsible for their illnesses and therefore are guilt-ridden, and patients who are depressed for whatever reasons; these and others may be only too willing to request the termination of their lives. In addition I have witnessed aged people (and I think of one physician's mother in her 80's) who wanted to die in order to bring an end to their suffering and in an altruistic way to free their family from the burden of themselves and their illnesses. In one patient there was also a wish to come face-to-face with her God, an event which she joyfully anticipated, having been a religious woman all her life.

Organized Medicine and Euthanasia

The views of the Ontario Medical Association, the College of Physicians and Surgeons of Ontario and the Royal College of Physicians and Surgeons of Canada lean heavily on the Canadian Medical Association's code of ethics. On this subject the Code can be summarized as follows:

1) "An ethical physician will allow death to occur with dignity and comfort when death of the body appears inevitable. He will support the body when clinical death of the mind has occurred, but need not prolong life by unusual or heroic means." This statement with very minor variations in wording occurs in both the CMA Code of

Ethics and the Transactions of General Council, 1969. It also appears to have achieved fairly wide acceptance by the Provincial organs of organized medicine. 2) There is awareness that such action as is set out in the Code of Ethics, may contravene the provisions of the Criminal Code of Canada and it is understood that "A physician acting on the policy of the CMA could find himself in contravention of one or more parts of the Criminal Code." 3) The legal implications of the written order "no resuscitation" in the order book has prompted the recommendation that such an order should not be written under any circumstances. The College of Physicians and Surgeons of Ontario has taken the position that, "Where there are considerations of impending and inevitable death, the judgement of the physician possessing knowledge of the facts will decide at the time whether or not to resuscitate. There should be no need to chart an order of 'no resuscitation' in advance of the situation."

Jacques Genest, in his presentation to the Royal College of Physicians and Surgeons (2), has provided clear and crisp views concerning the field of bioethics before conception, in situations connected with pregnancy, and after birth. Because of his obvious orientation, his section on active euthanasia is worth quoting *in extenso:*

"Active euthanasia has been discussed extensively in Great Britain, probably more than in any other country. It can be said from a review of British literature that any serious regulation of active euthanasia of terminally pain-stricken incurable cancer patients, as well as of patients with senile dementia, or severely defective children, is caught between over-elaborate legal safeguards on the one hand or grossly inadequate protection for the patient and his family on the other. It is not sufficient to rely on the good sense of the medical practitioner because in some cases, he may be minimally competent or even part of a scheme set up by heirs anxious to obtain their inheritance. Again, as for abortion, the case for active euthanasia is too often built around carefully constructed abstract and hypothetical presentations. It does not take into account the experience of expert clinicians who know that severely ill patients often show distorted judgement and decreased capacity for rational thinking, and the decisions by such patients can vary a great deal whether they are in a state of severe depression and suffering or during a period of remission and greater mental clarity. It also fails to take into account the wishes of the family who may find euthanasia repulsive because the care of the patient may be for family members, the last and greatest proof of their love and devotion.

"The argument used by some that the quality of life is a major reason for euthanasia has already been used by the Hitler regime. It is unfortunately based only on the material and physical aspects of life and neglects the importance of exemplary courage, fortitude and self-control shown by many suffering or terminal patients which so often have a lasting influence on all those who come in contact with such patients.

"If the law will not allow active euthanasia by a minimally competent practitioner because of possibility of diagnostic error, should we resort to so-called 'euthanasiasts' selected and nominated by the State for the job? Who amongst us after giving the Hippocratic Oath of protecting life at all costs would take on and enjoy such a position? It is certainly of interest to note that active euthanasia was not considered for a moment by society for the Thalidomide babies who were so severely deformed and destined for such a severely handicapped life."

Conclusions

There seems little doubt that the problems of the quality of life, the right to live and the right to die will increase in number and complexity for members of the medical profession. In attempting this survey of the field I have tried to indicate the issues as dispassionately and simply as I could.

I will offer my own views in summary fashion. They may act as a catalyst for discussion by members of our specialty.

Personally I am very uncomfortable with the idea of active euthanasia. Whatever the qualities may be which would make a physician able to cope with active euthanasia (compassion? megalomania? courage? sadism?) they are not represented strongly enough in my temperament to facilitate my comfortable use of this device. Nor can I think of any clinical experience which I have had in which passive euthanasia could not have achieved the desired end, although admittedly I have had no experience with stigmatized neonates or severe birth defects. Nevertheless, I believe that active euthanasia places too heavy a burden on the conscience of the physician. I also have the conviction that inflexible postures for or against passive euthanasia are undesirable. Clearly, medical and humanitarian concerns indicate that opening the door too widely to passive euthanasia is to expose the profession, the patient and the public to considerable risk. Similarly, an absolute prohibition of euthanasia will expose some patients and their families to long drawn out suffering and a life whose quality is perforce reduced to levels which may be intolerable to the patient and to those who love him.

In my opinion, therefore, we should strive towards the judicious (conservative) use of passive euthanasia. For this to be permissible there would need to be a system of controls, or checks and balances, which would get as near as possible to the professional ideal of preserving life and reducing pain and suffering.

The only valid justification for the use of passive euthanasia should be the suffering of the patient. Justification on pragmatic grounds, which only too often boil down to the patient being unwanted, imperfect, or socially or aesthetically embarrassing, should be avoided.

The achievement of this goal would involve a high degree of cooperation between medicine, the law, the religions, and the public. Whether such a system could be established remains to be seen. I do not think that doctors have any advantage over other people in terms of morality, scruples and so on, but they are in the firing line. Medical people, therefore, are best qualified to contribute primarily in the area of medical expertise. The doctor, however, would be the person who would have to carry out the euthanasia, and in any or all cases this may impose an unfair burden on any of us. At any particular time or in any particular case, if the decision to carry out passive euthanasia were reached, arrangements should exist which will permit the transfer of responsibility from any physician who requests that this be done, to one who is willing to accept it.

Acknowledgements

In preparing this document, the view of the Ontario Medical Association, the College of Physicians and Surgeons of Ontario and the Royal College of Physicians and Surgeons of Canada were canvassed. All these organizations were generous and cooperative and in the face of a subject of this delicacy, I am more than indebted to them.

Summary

There are two factors that are focusing attention, both public and professional, on euthanasia. These are: (i) the increasing ability of medicine to maintain life; (ii) the activity of the Law Reform Commission of Canada which might result in new legislation. Euthanasia raises problems medically, legally, morally and ethically. These difficulties are placed in context and discussed. The author offers a personal opinion on euthanasia in an attempt to mobilize Canadian psychiatric opinion.

References

1. Caplan, G.: *Support Systems and Community Mental Health.* New York: Behavioral Publications, 1974.
2. Genest, J.: Bioethics and the leadership of the medical profession. *Ann Roy Coll Phys Surg (C),* 10: 129-38, 1977.
3. Hinton, J.: Physical and mental distress of dying. *Q J Med,* 32: 1-21, 1963.
4. Hunter, R.C.A.: On the experience of nearly dying. *Am J Psychiatry,* 124: 122-26, 1967.
5. Kalish, R.A.: "Experience of persons reprieved from death" in Kutscher, A.H. (ed) *Death and Bereavement.* Springfield, Ill.: Charles C. Thomas, 1969, pp. 84-98.
6. Kubler-Ross, E.: *On Death and Dying.* New York: MacMillan, 1969.
7. Law Reform Commission of Canada, Ottawa.
8. Murdoch, I.: *Henry and Cato.* St. Albans, Herts: Triad-Panther Books, 1977, p. 337.
9. Task Force Report on Human Life: Dying, Considerations Concerning the Passage From Life to Death. Toronto: Anglican Church of Canada, 1979.
10. Weisman, A.D., Hackett, T.P.: Predilection to death: Death and dying as a psychiatric problem. *Psychosom Med,* 23: 232-56, 1961.

THE RIGHT TO DIE— LIVING WILLS AND PATIENT RIGHTS

Euthanasia: Due Process for Death with Dignity; The Living Will

Luis Kutner

Euthanasia, or mercy killing, has become a subject of increasing interest of late—and while no longer of mere theoretical concern, it is no less a controversial topic.[1] Indeed, the word "euthanasia" has such an emotional impact itself that a new word, "benemortasia," has been coined for use in its stead.[2] Perhaps an even better term here is "death with dignity," which means ceasing to use extraordinary or heroic means to prolong the life of a dying person.[3]

"Euthanasia" is derived from two Greek words which essentially translate into "easy death."[4] *Eu*, the first component part, means easy or painless, while the other word, *thanatos*, means death.[5] There are two broad types of euthanasia: active euthanasia is the actual rendering of a life-shortening agent;[6] passive euthanasia is when certain measures that might postpone death are not taken, though neither is anything done to hasten death. In the latter case, as Dr. D. B. Hiscoe of Michigan State University sees it, "[W]e are not really deciding who will die—everyone dies. We are really deciding who will be made to live."[7]

The act of euthanasia involves either a person taking his own life in order to relieve his suffering or an outside person who takes the life of another for the same reason.[8] Thus, euthanasia is usually considered in connection with a patient who is irrevocably unconscious or a terminal patient who himself might request some sort of action to shorten his life.[9] Resolving the life-death decision in favor of death can be made by the individual himself[10] or by another individual who, in the context of this paper observes a person suffering in pain from an incurable disease or, perhaps, a genetic deformity, and is hence motivated—not by malice or

---

[1] Whittingham, *Debating Death with Dignity*, Chicago Tribune, September 27, 1974, at 10, col. 6 [hereinafter cited as Whittingham].

[2] Note, *Informed Consent and the Dying Patient*, 83 YALE L.J. 1632, 1632 (1974) [hereinafter cited as *Informed Consent*].

[3] Whittingham, *supra* note 1.

[4] *Id.*

[5] Kutner, *Due Process of Euthanasia: The Living Will, A Proposal*, 44 IND. L. J. 539, 540 n.3 (1969) [hereinafter cited as Kutner].

[6] *Informed Consent, supra* note 2, at 1632 n.5.

[7] Snider, *Why Patient's Death Wish Isn't Heeded*, Chicago Daily News, Sept. 23, 1973.

[8] Whittingham, *supra* note 1.

[9] *Informed Consent*, at 1632.

[10] Marcus, *The Forum of Conscience: Applying Standards Under Free Exercise Clause*, 1973 DUKE L.J. 1217, 1254 [hereinafter cited as Marcus].

Reprinted with permission from the *Indiana Law Journal*, 54(2), 1979, and Fred B. Rothman & Co., Littleton, Colorado 80127.

personal profit, but out of a very human desire of compassion–to end that suffering.[11] Beside the pain and suffering of a terminally-ill patient, among other considerations here may be the possible exhaustion of his family's financial resources in providing health care that would merely delay death through the use of expensive mechanical devices, contrary to the will of both patient and family.[12] (In speaking of a terminally-ill patient, reference is made to a person facing imminent death; beyond such a general definition medical science itself has been unable to go, given the problem of lucid intervals and remissions which the patient might go through in turn.[13])

Euthanasia raises a myriad of philosophical, medical, legal and theological questions,[14] although this debate has gone on for centuries without any resolution.[15] The wish of a terminally-ill patient to forego further medical treatment in order to prolong his life may conflict with the interest and committment of those who provide health care, as well as with existing state laws against suicide and homicide.[16] But can this be called murder? It is one question that invariably arises in connection with euthanasia.[17] Another is: "Why make an exception permitting death?" Instead, perhaps a better question to ask is "What exceptions should be made?"[18]

Such questions suggest problems which could be created if euthanasia were sanctioned. For example, since insurance companies do not pay life insurance in the case of a suicide, would not euthanasia then become a "luxury" for the wealthy? And what of a dying assault victim: if he were put to death, would his attacker then be charged merely with assault or with murder?[19] Evidently, voluntary euthanasia seems too direct for most of society, which, according to Ely, would prefer an "indirect" taking of life as opposed to the shattering illusion of a direct one—with as much adverse psychological impact on people here as the refusal of treatment itself.[20] Some see proposals for voluntary euthanasia as opening the door for mass genocide because they think it incapable of providing the necessary safeguards.[21]

So euthanasia remains a moral-legal tangle in need of unravelling.[22] This paper shall endeavor to do that.

Some Case Studies

That a person can lose his will to live is illustrated by the true story of a marine who had been in a Viet Cong prison camp for two years. Major F. Harold Kushner, a physician who himself spent five-and-a-half years as a prisoner of war, related how this marine had, at first, maintained his physical and mental health on assurances from the Viet Cong that he would be released in time. But, when he finally learned he was not to be released afterall, he soon grew depressed, refused to eat, and just lay on

---

[11]Kutner; *supra* note 5, at 539-40.
[12]*Informed Consent*, at 1632.
[13]*Id.*
[14]Kutner, *supra* note 5, at 540.
[15]Marcus, *supra* note 10, at 1254.
[16]*Informed Consent, supra* note 2, at 1632, 1635.
[17]Kutner, *supra* note 5, at 539.
[18]*Informed Consent, supra* note 2, at 1648.
[19]Whittingham, *supra* note 1.
[20]*Informed Consent, supra* note 2, at 1647, 1669.
[21]Kutner, *supra* note 5, at 549.
[22]Whittingham, *supra* note 1.

his bed in a stupor. His fellow POWs were unable to bring him around and, shortly thereafter, he died. This is but one case of a person who had simply given up all hope that had previously sustained him.[23]

More appropos to the subject matter of this paper is the case of columnist Bob Considine's younger brother who was suffering from the effects of inoperable cancer of the pancreas. Out of brotherly devotion, Considine took him to New York and registered him in Memorial Hospital, where he was given pills, drugs, radiation treatment and placed in an oxygen tent. Finally, Considine's brother said, "I know I'm dying. Tell...those doctors to stop doing all these painful things to me. Tell...them to let me die in peace."[24]

The late Stewart Alsop, himself suffering from leukemia, wrote of his hospital room-mate, another terminal cancer patient, who would pitifully cry out in pain all through the night. Alsop allowed that if the fellow were a dog he would be chloroformed. "No human being with a spark of pity could let a living thing suffer so, to no good end," concluded Alsop.

> [A] human being's life is his own, to keep or to leave.... [A] man of sound mind has every right to decide that the time has come for his life to end....I am...suggest[ing] that a terminal patient in full command of his faculties should be permitted to ask a committee of experienced doctors about his future, and if he is told that it holds nothing but suffering, and death at the end, he should have the right to demand, and to receive, a pill or some other painless means of ending his life. But the right to end his own life should be his, not a doctor.[25]

Take, further, the example of an elderly woman, hellishly lingering in her terminal illness for days or even weeks in a hospital room where she is surrounded by tubes, bottles and other assorted apparatus meant to treat her—but which has weakened her as much as the disease from which she suffers; the combined torture of pain and drugs has so confused her mind that she cannot recognize her own family; if she can think at all, perhaps her thoughts are simply of being relieved from her suffering.[26] Or, what of the Jehovah's Witness who voluntarily enters a hospital for treatment? When advised that unless she is given a blood transfusion she will die, the Witness tells her doctor she cannot consent to that because of her deeply-held religious beliefs.[27]

There is also the case of Robert Waskin, a young college student, who, on the pleading of his cancer-stricken mother, shot her three times as she lay in her hospital room. Previously, he had tried to administer sleeping pills to her. The Grand Jury of Cook County, Illinois, returned an indictment of murder in the first degree against him, but after a trial of one week, Waskin was freed by a jury, having deliberated only forty minutes, on the determination that he was temporarily insane when he committed the act. "He knew he shot his mother. That was not disputed," said the jury foreman, "but prosecution failed to show he was of sound mind when he did it." But Waskin himself had a very different response to the verdict. "The moral issue of euthanasia...was not taken up...," he said after the trial. "[I]t should have been faced squarely. Some day it will have to be."[28] That is the primary purpose of this paper.

---

[23]*Submissive Death: Giving up on Life*, PSYCHOLOGY TODAY, May 1974, at 80.
[24]Consodine, *The Right to Die With Dignity*, IRISH ECHO, Aug. 3, 1974, at 13.
[25]*See*, Alsop, *The Right to Die With Dignity*, GOOD HOUSEKEEPING, Aug. 1974.
[26]Whittingham, *supra* note 1.
[27]Marcus, *supra* n. 10, at 1251.
[28]Kutner, *supra* note 5, at 539.

LEGAL PROBLEMS

Suicide & Homicide Laws

Related to euthanasia is the law on suicide, which under early common law, was regarded as a criminal offense. Suicide was a felony, to be punished by driving a stake through the body of the one who had committed suicide and then burying the corpse under a public highway; in addition, all lands, goods and chattel of the suicide victim were forfeited to the king. This rule in England was tempered in 1824 to allow such bodies to be buried in a churchyard—yet only between the hours of 9 o'clock p.m. and midnight, and *without* religious ceremonies. Gradually, sanctions against both body and property were removed as legal attitudes toward suicide began to mellow, though an attempt by a person to end his life is still considered an attempt to commit a felony in England, albeit not an attempt to commit murder within the offenses against the Person Act of 1861. Further, while suicide is no longer a crime under English law, the aiding and abetting of suicide is.[29]

English common law on suicide was never fully accepted in the United States, and while once a crime, suicide is no longer such in some jurisdictions, such as California. In Michigan, suicide is neither a statutory nor common law crime. New York state has declared that suicide is not a crime, but it nonetheless censured by statute as a great "public wrong" and promoting the attempt is a felony under penal law: the distinction between accessory and principal have been abolished, and those so involved are treated as principals in a homicide.[30]

So, assistance in euthanasia could amount to the crime of aiding and abetting suicide.[31] While some jurisdictions appear to distinguish situations where one has instigated or suggested to another that he commit suicide from those situations where the idea came originally, the law, as a rule, does not permit one to assist another in committing suicide regardless of motive or if done at the request of the suicide victim. Any immunity from suicide today actually means immunity of attempted suicide, with the law varying in different jurisdictions as to aiders and abettors. Where punishment of accessories is predicated on the criminal character of the act of the principal, the aider or abettor enjoys immunity—the act of the principal not being a crime, as prevailing in Germany and France. Other statutes specifically define aiding and abetting as an independant crime.[32]

Texas was possibly the only state that viewed aiding suicide as noncriminal, absent statute. Prior to 1974, anyone who aided or abetted suicide was innocent of any violation of law inasmuch as suicide was not a crime under state law. However, now aiding or attempting to aid a suicide has become a statutory crime in Texas. Still, other states, absent statute, are not precluded from adopting the old Texas common law view on aiding and abetting suicide; and in Switzerland, a doctor is permitted to put poison in a patient's hand but not to actually administer said poison himself, thus the final act is performed solely by the patient and the involvement of the third party is minimized—somewhat similar to the Texas view before 1974.[33]

---

[29]*Id.* at 543; *Informed Consent, supra* note 2, at 1659-60, 1662.

[30]Kutner, *supra* note 5, at 543; *Informed Consent, supra* note 2, at 1660.

[31]*Informed Consent, supra* note 2, at 1660.

[32]Kutner, *supra* note 5, at 543-44.

[33]*Informed Consent, supra* note 2, at 1661.

Suicide itself remains a crime in yet a few jurisdictions, as in North Carolina, where it is regarded as a misdemeanor; or, in South Carolina, where suicide retains its common law character as a felony. The argument advanced for such prohibitions against suicide are usually that every life has a value to society—and if a life is taken the cost would be too great in terms of psychological damage to that society, not to mention the loss of productive potential; moreover, it is argued that one cannot take his life without self-destruction. These decisions on self-destruction may not be firmly held and may merely be pleas for help. That is certainly the case of certain classes of people—though many take their own lives out of a strong determination to do so, for reasons of physical or social calamity, or the loss of a loved one. A study of suicides among the elderly found just that, and they were neither insane nor mentally abnormal.[34]

Generally, the law does not appear to condone suicide, but the law has proven to be adaptive to some situations where assistance to commit suicide is given to one who freely requests it.[35] It would seem that sanctions against suicide would be less defensible when particularly applied to a dying patient seeking some form of euthanasia.[36] Nevertheless, the law treats mercy killing no different from other cases involving the taking of human life, at least conceptually. Common law does not recognize motive as an element of homicide. If the proven facts establish that a defendant did, in fact, kill wilfully (that is, had the intent to kill, as a result of premeditation and deliberation), then there is murder in the first degree regardless of motive; relevant evidence is needed only to establish the degree of murder or homicide (premeditated).[37] If another assists a person to end his life, he is liable by this assistance to prosecution for murder even though the victim requested it, since consent is not defense to homicide—except in some sports contests.[38] Even so, prosecutors, judges, and juries have approached mercy killing cases differently, thus making an exception to the rule of law existing as far as practice is concerned. This has also served to create a gap within the legal system with regard to euthanasia, and this absence of any governing standards in this area certainly leaves much to be desired. The state of law on euthanasia, such as it is, really lacks any definitiveness or objective criteria.[39]

Tracing Case Law

Sans symmetry of case law on euthanasia, it is perhaps best to review chronologically how the courts have handled individual cases which have had a legal bearing on this subject.

One of the earliest cases[40] held that if elements of wilful premeditation exist, the perpetrator of the act stands equally condemned regardless of the fact that he might have acted from an impulse of mercy. It is a precept that had been reaffirmed since the time of this early nineteenth century case in the United States, as well as in England.[41]

---

[34]*Id.* at 1660-2.
[35]Kutner, *supra* note 5, at 544.
[36]*Informed Consent, supra* note 2, at 1662.
[37]Kutner, *supra* note 5, at 542, 540.
[38]*Informed Consent, supra* note 2, at 1650.
[39]Kutner, *supra* note 5, at 542-43.
[40]People v. Kirby, 2 Park Crim. Rep. (N.Y.) 28 (1823).
[41]State v. Ehlers, 98 N.J.L. 326, 119 A. 15 (1922); Rex v. Simpson, 84 L.J.R. (n.s.) 1893 (K.B. 1915).

An important doctrine emerged out of medical malpractice suits and the courts began to deal with the rendering of some treatment to which a patient had not consented.[42] From such cases came the doctrine of informed consent, and the landmark case in the area was *Schloendorff v. Society of New York Hospital.*[43] It was in that case that Judge Cardozo opined that the principle of informed consent was meant to protect the self-determination of individuals of sound mind,[44] the basic premise being that every adult of sound mind had the right to determine what should be done with his own body. Hence, it followed that if a competent patient retains control over any decision about treatment, this right to consent presupposes the right to refuse as well; for a patient's right to informed consent would make no sense unless there was a right to an informed refusal. Every man has the right, then, to forego treatment or even a cure if it involves what, to *him,* seem intolerable consequences or risks, no matter how distorted such values may be viewed by the medical profession, just as long as the law itself does not regard them as incompetent. The implication is that there exist categories of decisions that an individual must be permitted to make, even if the individual decides irrationally or incorrectly. Basically, it is thus for the competent patient, who has the right to define what his *best* interests are under the self-determination principle of informed consent, to be able to withdraw his consent at any time and discontinue treatment.[45]

The underpinnings of the informed consent axiom of self-determination over one's body, according to *Schloendorff,* might be further explained in terms more commonly applied in the law of torts from the standpoint that tort law seeks to achieve an efficient allocation of resources. While it also seeks other goals, general tort doctrine is concerned with placing the responsibility for a particular decision on those individuals who can best avoid whatever costs arise from such decision-making. The cost of avoidance here includes those attempts to reduce the number and severity of incorrect decisions, as well as the costs of gathering and considering information that go into making the decisions. It is in terms of cost avoidance that decision-making for purposes of informed consent might be evaluated, to wit: medically, a doctor, who is considered to be an expert in diagnosis and treatment, can better determine than can a patient—and at less expense—the desirability of a particular treatment; yet, the doctor is *not* equipped to evaluate treatment in terms of a patient's non-medical needs—psychological, social, and business—and, moreover, the cost to the physician in discovering all these obligations would be far too great. So, only the patient can sufficiently know his own value preference, his own capacity for pain and suffering, his religious beliefs and his uncompleted business and social plans for the future in order to evaluate the desirability and maximum satisfaction of deciding on a particular treatment. And, by alone knowing what is best for him as an individual, he becomes the optimal cost avoider.[46]

Still, this issue of informed consent (which involves the right to a natural death) has remained unsettled—although it has always received considerable attention from the courts and commentators, many of the latter viewing the doctrine as not really central to euthanasia. Courts have applied the doctrine regularly in non-terminal cases and even in

---

[42]Pratt v. Davies, 118 Ill. App. 161, 166, *aff'd* 224 Ill. 300, 79 N.E. 562 (1906).

[43]Schloendorff v. Society of New York Hospital, 211 N.Y. 125, 105 N.E. 92 (1914).

[44]*Id.* at 129, 105 N.E. at 93.

[45]*Informed Consent, supra* note 2, at 1634, 1643, 1648-49, 1664.

[46]*Id.* at 1643, 1645-6, 1648.

some cases of terminal illness. The concern has been with voluntary euthanasia, rather than with the involuntary euthanasia in a case of brain death—although even that has been accepted by some courts.[47]

In the meantime, however, the decision in the *People v. Roberts*[48] case rendered at the beginning of the decade of the 1920s was of special import to the matter of mercy killing. The defendant in this case was a husband who had prepared poison and made it available to his wife, upon her request, by placing it within her reach. The dying wife, confined in bed with arteriosclerosis, drank the poison. The husband was found guilty of murder in the first degree by the judge because he had assisted his wife, who wished to die, by providing a means for her to commit suicide. Such assistance was held to be murder and the man was sentenced to life imprisonment.

This particular case is noted because it was one of few where a mercy killer has been convicted for murder. Perhaps this was due to the fact that the case was *not* a jury trial, for juries have often disregarded the dictates of the law and superimposed their own beliefs in mercy killing cases, as evidenced by the case of Robert Waskin, previously mentioned here. Thus, what takes place at the trial level on mercy killing cases indicates that the law in theory is actually quite malliable in practice. In the judicial process dealing with mercy killings, the decision is often based on what "is" rather than what "ought" to be, as there is a high incidence of failure to indict, suspended sentences, acquittals (such as finding a defendant innocent because of insanity), or a finding of guilt for a lesser offense than murder when a killer has had mercy as a motive. It would seem that, while there is opposition to mercy killing, there is, nonetheless, sympathy for the killer, that is, the defendant. Since there is usually a human interest aspect to mercy killing cases, they receive wide press coverage and public attention. Unlike other acts of murder, the public does not have the same revulsion toward mercy killings. The tendency is to side with the defendant and not to favor the same type of punishment society inflicts on other murders. During the Waskin trial, for example, the judge, the defendant's father and lawyer all received letters urging mercy be shown. And over forty years after *Roberts*, the case of Suzanne van de Put, a Belgian woman who had killed her eight-day-old, thalidomide-deformed daughter, gained international attention. Mrs. van de Put went on trial in Liege for murder, along with her husband, mother, sister and family doctor who were arraigned as abettors. The defendants claimed to have acted from what they felt were unselfish motives and popular sympathy was with them. The trial lasted only six days, with the jury finally acquitting all five defendants—a verdict that was met with general exultation.[49]

Throughout the 1930s and 1940s, U.S. courts considered a number of relevant cases involving suicide;[50] but also during the latter decade there was decided a case in the area of competency to consent, whereby it was held that, while informed consent need not be obtained from an incompetent patient, it must be obtained from said patient's guardian.[51] Later, in

---

[47]*Id.* at 1645, 1634.

[48]People v. Roberts, 211 Mich. 187, 178 N.W. 690 (1920).

[49]Kutner *supra* note 5, at 540-42.

[50]*See,* Stiles v. Clifton Springs Sanitarium Co., 74 F. Supp. 907, 909 (W.D.N.Y. 1947); State v. Campbell, 217 Iowa 848, 850, 251 N.W. 717, 718 (1933); Huntert v. Commercial Travelers' Mut. Accident Ass'n. of America, 244 App. Div. 459, 460, 279 N.Y.S. 555, 556 (1935).

[51]Bonner v. Moran, 75 U.S. App. D.C. 156, 157-8, 126 F.2d 121, 122-3 (1941).

the *In re Serferth* case,[52] decided in the following decade, there was no guardian, however.

The year 1958 brought several important decisions from various jurisdictions. One case[53] illustrates how one trial court approached mercy killing. The sixty-nine year-old defendant had suffocated his wife, a hopeless cripple bedridden by arthritis. In arraignment proceedings, the state waived the murder charge and permitted the defendant to enter a guilty plea to the charge of manslaughter. The court then found the defendant guilty of this charge on his stipulated admission of killing. After hearing testimony of the defendant's children and pastor concerning his unfailing care for and devotion to his wife's two-year illness, and reading a letter from the deceased's doctor attesting to her excruciating pain and mental despair, the court allowed the defendant to withdraw his plea and entertained a plea of "not guilty," then so found him not guilty because under the circumstances the jury "would not be inclined to convict." Because there was no reason to be concerned about recidivism, the court withheld the "stigma" of a finding and judgement of guilty by allowing the defendant "to go home...and live out the rest of [his] life in as much as [he] can find it in [his] heart to have." In following such a procedure in this case, the court was acting out of a sense of justice; the decision was based on the motives of the defendant—although this was unauthorized by statute. While the court had discretion to permit a defendant to withdraw a guilty plea, that discretion was limited to those particular instances where it would appear that there is doubt as to a defendant's guilt, or that he has any defense at all worthy of consideration by a jury, or, further, that the ends of justice will be served by submitting the case to a jury. However, these criteria were absent in this particular case.[54]

The number of cases dramatically increased in the 1960s and early 1970s, especially insofar as informed consent was concerned. As the decade of the 1960s began, the *Schloendorff* axiom on an individual's self-determination was restated by a Kansas court in the noted case of *Natanson v. Kline*.[55] The court, basing its opinion on the premise of thoroughgoing self-determination under Anglo-American law, held that each man must then be considered to be the master of his own body, and so may expressly prohibit the performance of surgery to save his life or any other medical treatment—provided he was of sound mind. While a doctor might feel an operation or some form of treatment was desirable or necessary, the court stated that the law would not permit him to substitute his own judgement for that of the patient by any form of artifice or deception.

Following *Natanson* during the 1960s, however, some courts refused to recognize the doctrine of informed consent[56] and enforced the overruling by doctors of patients' refusal of treatment. Such a case was that decided in 1964 (among others) where the Appellate Court of the District of Columbia "determined to act on the side of life" overruled the refusal of a blood transfusion by a Jehovah's Witness.[57] The court maintained that the woman needed the transfusion to save her life and she was not in a mental condition to make such a lifesaving decision. The decision sug-

---

[52]In re Serferth, 309 N.Y. 80, 127 N.E.2d 280 (1955).

[53]People v. Werner, Crm. No. 58-3636 (Cook Co. Ct., Ill. 1958).

[54]Kutner, *supra* note 5, at 541.

[55]186 Kan. 393, 350 P.2d 1093, *rehearing denied*, 187 Kan. 186, 354 P.2d 670 (1960).

[56]*Informed Consent, supra* note 2, at 1633.

[57]Application of Pres. and Directors of Georgetown College, Inc., 331 F.2d 1000 (D.C. Cir. 1964).

gested that there was authority to apply anti-suicide sanctions to individuals seeking euthanasia for religious purposes, the court having noted that when death results "from failure to extend proper medical care, where there is a duty of care" it is manslaughter in the District of Columbia.[58]

Future Supreme Court Chief Justice Warren Burger, then a circuit judge, dissented because he felt a hospital's effort to compel a person to accept a blood transfusion against her will was not justifiable. "Some matters of essentially private concern and others of enormous public concern," he wrote, "are beyond the reach of private concern and others of enormous public concern are *beyond the reach of judges*." [Emphasis added]. Discussing the allocation of decision-making powers, Burger quoted Mr. Justice Brandeis on "the right to be let alone" and averred that such privacy includes refusal of medical treatment even at great risk, no matter how foolish, unreasonable or absurd that notion may seem.[59] Of course, implicit in the weighing of interests competing in decision-making is resolution by free choice.[60] Yet, one need only look at motorcycle crash helmet cases, for example, to see the difficulty in the allocation of decision-making power for choices that apparently affect only a given individual: in the same year one court found the helmet requirement invalid, since an individual was not held accountable to society, in the eyes of that court, for any actions that concern no one but himself;[61] but another court held the requirement valid.[62]

Some courts accepted the Burger pronouncement that resolving the issue of avoiding treatment is "beyond the reach of judges." In such life-and-death decisions, the "free exercise" clause of the First Amendment of our Constitution, which occupies a "preferred position" with other constitutionally protected rights, began to take on a wider scope and application in the courts—whereas before its newfound judicial flexibility, individuals asserting the clause had not been very successful in state or federal courts. Still other courts agreed with the majority opinion in the D.C. case and saw the state as having the power to protect its citizens against themselves even in the face of the "free exercise" clause.[63] In the same year as the above D.C. case was decided, another court held that a woman may be compelled to accept a blood transfer for her unborn child since the unborn child is entitled to the law's protection.[64] Also in the following year, a court again took the position of protecting a citizen's life even though this protection was against the individual's wishes.[65]

Nevertheless, no proper legal outcome to the question was settled upon during that decade—and especially in one jurisdiction, New York, the lower courts were most inconsistent. After *Natanson* but before the D.C. case previously cited, a New York court followed the patient's wishes in the interest of self-determination, ruling that a terminal patient, just as one who is non-terminal, is entitled to refuse treatment.[66] It extended the right to refuse to the dying patient, giving him a choice on proffered

[58]*Id.* at 89 n.18.

[59]*Id.* at 98.

[60]*Informed Consent, supra* note 2, at 1643.

[61]American Motorcycle Association v. State Police, 11 Mich. App. 351, 158 N.W.2d 72, 73-4 (1968).

[62]State ex. rel. Colvin v. Lombardi, 104 R.I. 28, 241 A.2d 625 (1968), *aff'd.* State v. Lombardi, 110 R.I. 776, 298 A.2d 141 (1972).

[63]Marcus, *supra* note 10, at 1218, 1220, 1254, 1271.

[64]Raleigh Fitkin - Paul Morgan Mem. Hosp. v. Anderson, 42 N.J. 421, 423, 201 A.2d 537, 538, *cert. denied* 377 U.S. 985 (1964).

[65]United States v. George, 239 F. Supp. 752 (D. Conn. 1965).

[66]Erickson v. Dilgard, 94 Misc.2d 27, 252 N.Y.S.2d 705 (S. Ct. 1962).

treatment like in any other medical situation. An Illinois case adopted a similar approach three years later: the State Supreme Court upheld the refusal of a blood transfusion by a Jehovah's Witness, a competent adult who had steadfastly asserted her religious belief against such a transfusion—despite the fact she was *in extremis*. The court noted that there were no minors involved and no clear and present danger to society.[67] However, in New York the same year as the D.C. case (1964 was evidently a banner year for cases of this sort), a court compelled treatment.[68] Two years thereafter, though, a New York judge refused to intervene in the dispute or treatment of an eighty year-old person suffering from gangrene; thus, the patient's apparent refusal of an operation prevailed.[69]

Those courts that purported to apply the *Schloendorff* principle (as restated in 1960 by *Natanson*) actually developed a wide variety of formulations that served to inhibit realization of ultimate patient control. Courts overlooked the patient's self-determination by either focusing on the therapeutic privilege to withhold information or by basing its determination of the physician's liability on the disclosure standards of the local medical community.[70] Such judicial deviations appeared in a mix of cases throughout the 1960s. Early in the decade one jurisdiction held that the duty of disclosure was based on community standards requiring only the disclosure of risks consistent with the practice of the local medical community.[71] That ruling was in common with most other jurisdictions in the United States.[72] But within a year one court had abolished medical community standards and adopted in their place new disclosure standards, while utilizing the reasonable man standard to retain some limits on physicians liability.[73] Also that year, another court found liability for psychic injury—but only if disclosure was grossly negligent, capricious, not well-founded and inducing harmful therapy.[74] Further, in connection with *Natanson*, "any conflict between [the doctor's primary duty to do what is best for the patient] and that of frightening disclosure," opined a court four years after, "ordinarily should be resolved in favor of the primary duty."[75] And, as some courts began adopting a negligence theory for informed consent in the mid-1960s, it too differed greatly from jurisdiction to jurisdiction as to what constituted risk.[76]

Through-out the decade of the 1960s a few cases stand-out because of their relation to the subject of euthanasia, running from a case in which assistance in a suicide was found to be manslaughter[77] to a later case in which the court said that "protection of the safety of all...against consequences of their own actions" was a legitimate use of a state's police powers.[78] Also worthy of note here is the dictum in the *People v. Conley* case, where the strong indication was given that complicity in active euthanasia even by a well-intentioned physician would constitute suffi-

---

[67]In re Brooks' Estate, 32 Ill.2d 361, 205 N.E.2d 435 (1965).

[68]Collins v. Davis, 44 Misc.2d 622, 2524 N.Y.S.2d 624 (S. Ct. 1966).

[69]Petition of Nemser, 51 Misc.2d 616, 273 N.Y.S.2d 624 (S. Ct. 1966).

[70]*Informed Consent, supra* note 2, at 1633.

[71]DiFilippo v. Preston, 53 Del. 539, 550, 173 A.2d 333, 339 (1961).

[72]*Informed Consent, supra* note 2, at 1637.

[73]Woods v. Brumlop, 71 N.M. 221, 377 P.2d 520 (1962).

[74]Draus v. Speilberg, 37 Misc.2d 519, 236 N.Y.S.2d 143 (S. Ct. 1962).

[75]Watson v. Clutts, 262 N.C. 153, 159, 136 S.E.2d 617, 621 (1964).

[76]*Informed Consent, supra* note 2, at 1633.

[77]Persampieri v. Commonwealth, 343 Mass. 19, 175 N.E.2d 387 (1961).

[78]Bisonius v. Karns, 42 Wis.2d 42, 52, 165 N.W.2d 377, 382, *appeal dismissed* 395 U.S. 709 (1969).

cient malice for a murder prosecution. "[O]ne who commits euthanasia bears no ill will toward his victims and believes his act is morally justified," said the court, "but he nonetheless acts with malice if he is able to comprehend that society prohibits his act regardless of his personal belief."[79]

Although the present decade has not yet ended, the volume of cases already decided in this area is quite large, indeed.

A number of cases decided during 1971 took in the wider issue of constitutional rights along with that of informed consent. This was initiated by the *John F. Kennedy Memorial Hospital v. Heston,*[80] where the court ordered a blood transfusion in the interest of protecting a citizen's life, thereby compelling a twenty-two year-old Jehovah's Witness to receive the life-sustaining transfusion over her objections. The patient was paid to have submitted to the doctor's "professional standard" by requesting treatment and the doctor was to treat accordingly, not to terminate such treatment before death.[81] But in another 1971 case, involving a Christian Scientist, the court reversed the prior holding of a lower New York state court, which in league with a health care provider, had forced a patient, involuntarily committed to a hospital for treatment of an alleged mental illness, to take tranquilizers over her religious objections. In its reversal, the court found there was a cause of action under the 100 year-old Civil Rights Act of 1871.[82] Thus, the court drew a connection between the constitutional doctrine of freedom of religion and the doctrine of informed consent, with the former seeming to be a foundation for the latter. The majority of the court had also based its decision on the distinction between instances of harm to others and to self, which was "rarely if ever...relevant in actuality because others are affected by virtually any action...an individual takes or fails to take," according to the dissent of one judge.[83]

Further, in 1972, it was held in *In re Osborne,* again involving a Jehovah's Witness, that a competent and informed adult patient was entitled to refuse treatment on religious grounds over and against state intervention—even if that treatment were to save the patient's life. The court distinguished earlier cases involving compulsory rendition of medical care to which patients objected on religious grounds, noting that some cases involved comatose patients or other incompetents while, in other cases, lives of unborn or the welfare of survivors were at stake.[84] It particularly distinguished *Heston* as protecting the lives of unborn children.[85] (That distinction may have later been weakened by *Roe v. Wade,*[86] which legalized certain abortions as within the zone of constitutionally protected privileges. But even before *Roe,* in the same year as *Osborne,* a court had suggested in a New Jersey case striking down a state abortion statute as unconstitutional that there was no authority for a state to infringe on constitutional rights for the purposes of general welfare.[87] Still, it should be noted that the Supreme Court in *Roe* did not say that there was any right to do with one's body as one pleased.[88]

---

[79]People v. Conley, 64 Cal.2d 310, 322, 411 P.2d 911, 918, 49 Cal. Rptr. 815, 822 (1966).
[80]John F. Kennedy Memorial Hosp. v. Heston, 58 N.J. 576, 279 A.2d 670 (1971).
[81]*Id.* at 583, 279 A.2d at 673.
[82]Winters v. Miller, 496 F.2d 65 (2d Cir.), *cert. denied* 404 U.S. 985 (1971).
[83]*Id.*
[84]In re Osborne, 294 A.2d 372, 374-75 (D.C. App. 1972).
[85]*Id.* at 374.
[86]401 U.S. 113 (1973).
[87]Y.W.C.A. v. Kugler, 342 F. Supp. 1048, 1073 (D.N.J. 1972).
[88]Roe v. Wade, 410 U.S. 113 (1973).

Osborne stressed that whether the patient's "current choice is competently maintained" is to be the important thing.[89]

In a final 1972 case, *In re Green*, involving a family of Jehovah's Witnesses, the state of Pennsylvania brought an action to have a guardian appointed for a 14-year-old patient whose parents would not allow him to have a blood transfusion for a spinal fusion operation. The court failed to find any showing that the child's life was in imminent danger and upheld the free exercise interest of the patient (which interest had been expanded in the Supreme Court culminating in a case decided during this same year).[91] However, the court in *Green* remanded the case to determine if the child agreed with his parent's decision concerning the blood transfusion.[92] Courts have appointed requested guardians if the patient was a minor or mentally incompetent, but there is also conflict whenever an individual is capable of making rational choices.[93]

As commentators Harper and James have declared, "Individual freedom... is guaranteed only if people are given the right to make choices which would generally be regarded as foolish ones. Thus, the Jehovah's Witness should have the legal right to refuse—on religious grounds which seem mistaken to most of us—the blood transfusion which is needed to save his life...."[94]

A trial of cases from 1972—*Cobbs*,[95] *Wilkinson*,[96] and *Canterbury*[97] abolished medical community standards on disclosure and formed new tests for disclosure by each taking different approaches toward that issue.

In *Cobbs* the court opted for a standard more protective of the patient's rights, requiring disclosure of known risks of death or serious bodily harm. The court was viewing insufficient disclosure of risks and alternatives as a failure to exercise due care, the failure of obtaining informed consent being a tort of negligence.

In speaking of the patient's need for information, the court says the test for adequate disclosure encompasses "whatever is material to the decision."[98] But that standard is left undefined and no clear test is arrived at as to whether the court is talking about an objective test (based on the so-called "reasonable man") or subjective test (based on the individual patient).

Moreover, *Cobbs* allowed a waiver of the right to disclosure by a competent patient; and if he expresses that wish the doctor is then advised to exercise therapeutic privilege in withholding information from him.[99]

The Rhode Island Supreme Court in *Wilkinson* decided that a patient must be given all necessary material information, the charter of which could not be determined by "a local medical group" having no knowledge of the individual or unique situations involved. It was further noted that informed consent is based on the right of the patient "to be the final judge to do with his body as he wills"—a right that "should not be delegated to a local medical group." *Wilkinson* employed a reasonable

---

[89]In re Osborne, 294 A.2d at 375.
[90]In re Greene, 448 Pa. 338, 292 A.2d (1972).
[91]Wisconsin v.Yoder, 406 U.S. 205 (1974).
[92]In re Greene, *supra* note 90.
[93]Marcus, *supra* note 10, at 1252.
[94]Quoted in *Informed Consent, supra* note 2, at 1748.
[95]Cobbs v. Grant, 8 Cal. 3d 229, 502 P.2d 1, 104 Cal. Rptr. 505 (1972).
[96]Wilkinson v. Vesey, 110 R.I. 606, 295 A.2d 676 (1972).
[97]Canterbury v. Spence, 464 F.2d 722(D.C. Cir.), *cert. denied,* 409 U.S. 1064 (1972).
[98]Cobbs. v. Grant, 8 Cal.3d 229, 245, 502 P.2d 1, 11 (1972).
[99]*Id.*

man test—the objective standard—with regard to the withholding of information.[100] The test was "isolated" and "concentrated" to apply only to determining the required scope of disclosure.[101] The doctor was held responsible only for disclosing all facts and risks a reasonable man would deem material.

The court in *Wilkinson* recognized that a physician might feel a patient would be "upset" by information and so withhold relevant facts on the familiar grounds of therapeutic privilege. From that, it concluded that no disclosure was necessary if "it would unduly agitate or undermine an unstable patient."[102]

The situation in the *Canterbury* case is similar to that of *Wilkinson* in that the treatment performed was not consented to. The court in *Canterbury* said that informed consent requires a competent, non-terminal patient in a non-emergency situation to be given a chance to consent or refuse. The court stressed the competency of the patient out of recognition of the importance of comprehending the information conveyed. Because the patient lacks the expertise of a doctor, he must rely heavily on the doctor for information about the nature and quality of the treatment.[103]

On a patient's refusal, the court in *Canterbury* noted that an ideal rule governing disclosure should require that all risks which the patient would feel material be revealed; yet, the court was aware that such a subjective rule would place an "undue demand" on a doctor to "second-guess" the patient. So the court applied *both* the reasonable man test and an objective causation test. Under this combined test, the more severe or likely the risk, the more probable the facts are material.[104] The focus here is on the magnitude of risks and the liklihood of their occurance as perceived by the reasonable man. In so doing, the test would seem to clearly put a doctor on notice as to the necessity of disclosure.[105]

The *Canterbury* opinion also moved in the direction of viewing the invocation of therapeutic privilege as the equivalent of asserting a patient incompetent. The court rejected likening the claim of therapeutic privilege to conceal information to that of asserting the community standard against disclosure. Instead, it cut back on therapeutic privilege. The "privilege to withhold information for therapeutic reasons must be carefully circumscribed," decided the court so that it would not "devour the disclosure rule itself." While placing only an outer limit on the privilege, the court still suggested that if the privilege were exercised there should be disclosure to the closest relative.[106]

Another 1973 case, similar to a 1966 case from the same jurisdiction, as previously cited, resulted very differently result when a judge appointed a guardian to consent to an operation on an 84-year-old suffering from gangrene despite a dispute as to what his wishes were.[107] But when a sixty year-old woman suffering from cancer refused life-saving surgery, giving as a reason that she had fears over such an operation—fears other witnesses suggested were based on the belief that the surgery would prevent a movie career, a lower court in Pennsylvania held that this chronic

---

[100]Wilkinson v. Versey, 110 R.I. 606, 626, 295 A.2d 676, 689 (1972).
[101]*Informed Consent, supra* note 2, at 1642.
[102]Wilkinson v. Vesey, 110 R.I. at 628, 295 A.2d at 689.
[103]Canterbury v. Spence, 464 F.2d at 780-83, 790-91.
[104]Canterbury v. Spence, 464 F.2d at 780-83, 790-91.
[105]*Informed Consent, supra* note 2, at 1690.
[106]Canterbury v. Spence, 464 F.2d at 789.
[107]Center v. Levitt, 73 Misc.2d 395, 342 N.Y.S.2d 356 (S. Ct. 1973). *See* note 74,*supra.*

undifferentiated schizophrenic was nevertheless sufficiently competent to refuse, although some might consider her reasons irrational. But the court allowed her to make this decision, using as its test that of the patient's capacity to comprehend the situation's risks and alternatives, *sans* any examination of whether the patient's choice is rationally or dispassionately conceived. So, in the eyes of the court, a terminal patient who had decided to die for reasons irrational to others should have that decision honored, since informed consent protects all the decisions of a competent patient.[108]

In upholding this schizophrenic's right to refuse, the court in *Yetter,* above, recognized a connection between that right and the right of privacy, referring to *Roe v. Wade,* where the U.S. Supreme Court based its decision on the 14th Amendment right to privacy *vis-a-vis* the interests of the state.[109] Of course, the constitutional right to privacy had already been recognized by the Supreme Court in *Griswold v. Connecticut.*[110] The Court in *Roe* claimed that the committment to self-determination and privacy presupposes a disposition to permit activities whose adverse impact on others would be only psychological.[111] Said the lower court in *Yetter*:

> In our opinion the constitutional right of privacy includes the right of a mature competent adult to refuse to accept medical recommendations that may prolong one's life and which, to a third person at least, appear to be in his best interests, in short, that the right of privacy includes a right to die with which the state should not interfere where there are no minor or unborn children [actually departing from the sum and substance of the *Roe* ruling here] and no clear and present danger to public health, welfare or morals. If the person was competent while being presented with the decision and in making the decision which she did, the court should not interfere even though her decision might be considered unwise, foolish or ridiculous.[112]

It now appeared that informed consent was being viewed as a manifestation of constitutionally protected rights.[113] Another case from 1973 seems to have borne this out when it was further decided that the denial of retirement benefits to an employee whose religion prohibited life-saving surgery, thus rendering her disabled, was an unconstitutional infringement on her free exercise of religion.[114]

Two of the most recent decisions rendered have further contributed to case law here. They are important, each in their own way: In *Lacy,* the court overtly ignored the individual values of the patient. The facts of the case were that a blood transfusion was recommended for an infant in Florida, but the child's parents were Jehovah's Witness and flew the boy to a Texas hospital which treated such patients without transfusions. It was alleged that the doctor in Florida notified the hospital and welfare unit in Texas that the infant was in immediate danger of death. The welfare unit then obtained a court order—*sans* notice— making the child a ward of the state. The sheriff next transferred the infant to a general

---

[108]In re Yetter, Civil No. 1973-533, at 2-3, 5 (Pa. C.P. N'ampton Co., June 6, 1973).
[109]410 U.S. 113 (1973).
[110]381 U.S. 476 (1965).
[111]Roe v. Wade, 410 U.S. 113,152-56 (1973).
[112]In re Yetter, *supra* note 108 at 4.
[113]*Informed Consent, supra* note 2, at 1644.
[114]Montgomery v. Board of Retirement, 33 Cal. App.3d 447, 109 Cal. Rptr. 181 (1973).

hospital where the boy received a blood transfusion over the complaints of the plaintiffs.[115] Some feared this action might lead others in similar circumstances to avoid or delay consulting a physician because their values might be disregarded, and, by neglecting to seek medical advice, risk the deterioration of health standards at the cost of society.[116]

In the second current case, it was held that the Department of Health, Education, and Welfare regulations were arbitrary and unreasonable since they did not sufficiently protect welfare clients against coercion.[117] In the regulations in question, HUD had defined the doctrine of informed consent as "the knowing consent of an individual or his legally authorized representative, so situated as to be able to exercise free power or choice without undue inducement or any element of force, fraud, deceit, duress and other forms of constraint or coercion...."[118] Coerced consent could take the form of subtle pressure from others, unconscious motivation, or simply a failure to comprehend information in the form conveyed. Particularly vulnerable to the influence of family members, drugs, pain, and financial problems is the terminal patient. That poses a special problem, increasing the number and frequency of incorrect and irreversible decisions on the part of the patient. There is a greater cost to society here imposed than if the responsibility were placed on the state, for example. But, indeed, the thrust of the above decision implies that the state should do more to protect an individual from such coercion. In formulating a suitable test in order to handle the problem of coercion, it has been suggested that the state can structure its approach along those lines whereby the relatively uncoerced patient can alone make the ultimate decision as to treatment, with the state itself striving to assure that he makes it with true understanding. It may be asserted, on the other hand, that the state, if it has an interest here, should then override the expressed will of the patient.[119] Yet, as can be seen through-out this chronological review of case law, it has been questioned from time to time as to whether the mere fact an individual wishes to resolve the decision of life or death in favor of the latter should automatically give rise to any strong state interest whatever.[120]

In case law effecting euthanasia, the judicial process has treated mercy killing differently than murder with malice.[121] However, few cases on the issue of liability for euthanasia ever reach the courts, due, in part, to prosecutorial discretion, or, for the larger part, difficulty of proof, or, more simply, failure of authorities to discover the act (morphine, for example, is an easily disguised death-inducing agent). Moreover, criminality of inaction by physicians has not been generally decided by the courts, especially in America.[122] As a matter of fact only two prosecutions of doctors for murdering dying patients have been recorded in American and British law. Yet, those courts that have upheld the doctrine of informed consent in the numerous cases cited above, have, in fact, recognized the right of a competent patient to forego treatment.[123]

Although some courts, questioning the validity of the *Schloendorf* axiom, have stressed concerns countervailing that principle, most recent

---

[115]Lacy v. Harris Co. Welfare Unit, Civil No. 74-H-129 (S.D. Tex., filed Jan. 22, 1974).
[116]*Informed Consent, supra* note 2, at 1646.
[117]Relf v. Weinberger, 392 F. Supp. 1196 (D.D.C. 1974).
[118]Quoted in *Informed Consent, supra* note 2, at 1633.
[119]*Id.* at 1656-57.
[120]Marcus, *supra* note 10, at 1254.
[121]Kutner, *supra* note 5, at 549.
[122]*Id.* at 548.
[123]*Informed Consent, supra* note 2, at 1662, 1664.

cases abolishing the medical community standard rule on disclosure have returned to a position of greater consistency with *Schloendorf*.[124] So case law has evidently come full-circle. Concerns over the psychological impact on society of refusing treatment has not been strong enough to overcome the law's committment to an individual's decision-making with regard to his or her own medical treatment.[125] Such decisions must rest with the patient, and the law will recognize the right to consent to or refuse treatment—even when a patient is *in extremis*—whether it be an infection or an operation to extend life, *providing* the patient is capable of giving consent and that that consent is both voluntary and informed. This right has been further buttressed by the constitutionally recognized right to privacy. If a patient is incapable of giving his consent (he may be unconscious), constructive consent to life-saving treatment may be presumed, but how far such constructive consent should be extended is to be answered on the basis of the best available evidence according to the rule of law that merciful termination of life shall be decreed.[126]

The courts must take care so there will be no accretions of the doctrine of informed consent that will diminish the patient's entitlement to receive information on risks involved and to consent before treatment. These two elements—information and consent—are, of course, essential to the doctrine, but they are not as settled in the courts as is a third element: the concept that a patient must comprehend the information conveyed, which the courts have more fully developed since the notion of informed consent itself came into being. Some courts have joined the concept of determining competency with the use of therapeutic privilege (which a doctor could abuse as a loophole through which to avoid providing information for informed consent). These courts expand therapeutic privilege into the presumption of incompetency, resulting in a possible denial of a patient's right to make his own decision on euthanasia. To safeguard patients' interests, adequate legal tests on competency should be carefully formulated by the courts instead, in order that patients will not be so manipulated. Unfortunately, courts have been lax in considering such tests. In addition to the judicial permissiveness of therapeutic privilege, courts trending in the direction of holding a doctor liable for even honest, though frightening, disclosures should re-examine such an approach, for it may impede the flow of material information to the patient. In its place, the law should concentrate on developing the duty to inform the patient fully, yet tactfully, of material information, however distressing, so that, in the interest of informed consent, he can make an informed decision.[127]

Another area that has not received extensive attention (at least not on the appellate level) is the measure of damages to be recovered in an informed consent tort action, as the cases above demonstrate. For there to be cause for tort liability, it would have to be proven that damages resulted from concealment; though any requirement that the patient show he would have been better off had he undergone alternative treatment would lead to the introduction of highly speculative considerations in many cases as to proofs for damage. It is for the courts, however, to develop a tort doctrine on informed consent—and only they can achieve it.[128]

---

[124]*Id.*, at 1631.
[125]*Id.*, at 1664.
[126]Kutner, *supra* note 5, at 547, 549-50.
[127]*Informed Consent, supra* note 2, at 1631, 1636-7, 1651-2, 1659.
[128]*Id.*, at 1641, 1644.

Legislative Responses

Euthanasia has also been a subject of legislative, as well as judicial, consideration.[129] Given the uncertainties of suicide and homicide laws, legislation authorizing some sort of euthanasia seems to be desirable.[130] But, for others, legislative ends are to preserve human life, and, to date, all proposals to legalize voluntary euthanasia have been rejected.[131]

Noted legal scholar Glanville Williams long urged enactment of a statute to permit voluntary mercy killing, which was backed by proponents of euthanasia in both the United States and England. It was originally designed to establish a means of immunizing relatives or physicians in administering means of ending life upon the request of a patient who was suffering great pain from an incurable, fatal disease.[132] The Williams proposal would recognize the *de facto* power of the health care provider by leaving the rendition of euthanasia to the discretion of the doctor and, thus, minimizing the risk of litigation. However, by legally utilizing the doctor's discretion over the decision of euthanasia, rather than having it made by the patient himself, Williams disregarded informed consent.[133]

The House of Lords in England defeated a bill to allow voluntary euthanasia for Britain in 1969. The opponents charged that it would allow "suicide by proxy." This is one of many arguments raised against voluntary euthanasia proposals. It is further asserted that such laws would prove too cumbersome if applied and could not provide the necessary safeguards.[134] To be sure, in order to provide the latter, the sick room would have to become overly "bureaucratized," and the period between the request for euthanasia and its actual rendition could be quite long.[135] But the greatest objection to such proposals seems to be the fear that they could open the door to possible mass euthanasia and genocide to eliminate the aged or the congenitally defective. This "entering wedge" theory finds support in the Nazi experience in Germany: euthanasia was expanded from the "voluntary" stage to the elimination of the mentally ill and defective, and finally as a rationale for genocide. Thought was even given to eliminating all cardiac patients, as well. (Today, under the German legal system, though, the approach toward mercy killing is that there should neither be exculpation nor reduction of sentence where death is administered for the benefit of persons other than a suffering patient. The failure of a doctor to artificially prolong a painful life is not regarded as a homicide as long as the victim is incurably ill. Otherwise, there is a duty to act and intent to cause death is punishable as homicide.)[136] That legalized voluntary euthanasia might soon lead to involuntary euthanasia ignores the main difference between the two: informed consent—a greater difference than exists between active or passive euthanasia (act *vis-a-vis* omission). So, the legal definition of euthanasia could be limited to include only those terminal patients who gave their informed consent, thus preventing mercy killing of any non-consenting terminal patients.[137]

---

[129]Marcus, *supra* note 10, at 1253.

[130]*Informed Consent, supra* note 2, at 1659.

[131]Kutner, *supra* note 5, at 545, 549.

[132]*Id.,* at 544-45.

[133]*Informed Consent, supra* note 2, at 1650-51, 1659.

[134]Kutner, *supra* note 5, at 547, 549.

[135]*Informed Consent, supra* note 2, at 1663.

[136]Kutner, *supra* note 5, at 545-6, 548.

[137]*Informed Consent, supra* note 2, at 1663.

Euthanasia legislation has fared little better in America than in England. Despite bills in many state legislatures relative to absolving physicians of any liability, none has yet been passed.[138] The American Euthanasia Society supported one proposal that was unsuccessfully introduced in bill form in both the Nebraska and New York legislatures. Under the proposal, an eligible patient would have petitioned for euthanasia in the presence of two witnesses. The petition would then be filed, along with a certificate from an attending physician in a court of appropriate jurisdiction. This court would next appoint a committee of three, at least two of whom would be physicians. The committee would forthwith examine the patient and other such persons as they deemed advisable or the court might direct. Within five days the committee was to report back to the court on whether or not the petition should be granted.[139]

Other legislative attempts at legalizing passive euthanasia were made in Florida and Oregon. Opponents of the bill in the Florida legislature were successful in memorializing Congress to pass a constitutional amendment to prohibit both active and passive euthanasia before the passive euthanasia bill could again be re-introduced. The Oregon bill died in committee, though the state medical society was behind it; the general public, however, was not. This brought the sponsor of the bill to the realization that such a bill was not politically feasible but a "political liability" instead. Therefore, he "reluctantly" concluded not to re-introduce the bill and to "depend on social education" to change public opinion before going the legislative route again. And although a Patient's Bill of Rights was enacted in Minnesota, it did not include the right to refuse treatment.[140]

Still, lawmakers need to generate adequate legal measures that will permit death with dignity, and, to that end, legislation should dispel any fear of possible criminal liability in cases of voluntary euthanasia. Legislation reducing fear of liability for complicity in certain forms of voluntary euthanasia would allow the patient's wishes to be honored, for, with liability removed, more deference to the patient's wishes would surely be expected.[141] Criminal codes can be adapted to meet the situation. One suggestion is to return to motive (rather than intent) in criminal law here as other legal systems have done. For example, under modern European codes motive is considered relevant in classifying offenses. There could then be a milder punishment than in other homicides for an accused who had killed at the request of the victim suffering in great pain from an incurable disease. So, if the renderer of euthanasia has good motive he will be punished—if punished at all—for a lesser offense than murder.[142] Further, the prohibition of suicide could be limited to non-terminal cases by changing the definition of suicide to clearly exclude voluntary passive euthanasia.[143]

ETHICS & EUTHANASIA

Medical & Theological Ethics

Doctors feel they have a duty to act in the best interest of their

---

[138]Reinhold, *Facing the Last Taboo: Death*, Chicago Tribune, July 28, 1974, Sec. 2, at 1 [hereinafter cited as Rheingold].
[139]Kutner, *supra* note 5, at 544-45.
[140]*Informed Consent, supra* note 2, at 1634.
[141]*Id.* at 1659, 1663-64.
[142]*Id.* at 1651; Kutner, *supra* note 5, at 546, 549.
[143]*Informed Consent, supra* note 2, at 1662.

patients, as they perceive that duty, according to professional standards based on the theory of medicine under which they are trained.[144] Medicine is seen as the implacable foe of death,[145] and, given the advancements in medical technology,[146] it is possible today for medical science to prolong life artifically through mechanical methods to keep such vital functions as circulation and respiration going;[147] moreover, operations to transplant human organs, like a heart or kidney, have now become routine due to these advances: they give patients a second chance at life.[148] But in other cases, it is not human life that is prolonged but merely vegetation.[149] Still, as one doctor admits about many of his colleagues, they "have a dread of death so great they can scarcely function in its presence."[150] Thus, doctors usually follow the route of doing everything within their power to prolong life.[151] That is how they are psychologically oriented: to "win."[152]

Yet what of the best interest of the patients as the patient himself views it? That should be the primary duty of the physician when he acts. Indeed, there is evidence to show that a majority of the American public want to be able to tell their doctors to let them die if they are suffering from an incurable disease. Of those sampled in a 1973 Harris Poll, 62% favored this approach, while 28% felt it was wrong and 10% were undecided.[153] And in a Gallup Poll, 52% said they would support a law to end a patient's life by some painless means, at his request or that of his family, if he had an incurable disease.[154] The result of that poll certainly represented a change of attitude, for in 1950 only 36% thought a doctor should be allowed to induce painless death for an incurable patient if that patient or his family so requested.[155]

There is also evidence, however, that doctors themselves may be changing their own attitudes toward euthanasia. Surprisingly, in a survey reported in mid-1974, 79% of physicians responding expressed some belief in the right of the patient to have a say about his death.[156] The subject of death has also become an important part of medical school curriculum, whereas in the past there was a tendency to neglect it in other than a strictly clinical sense.[157] Moreover, at its annual conference, the austere American Medical Association formally adopted the following policy statement: "The cessation of the employment of extraordinary means to prolong the life of the body where there is irrefutable evidence that biological death is imminent is the decision of the patient and-or his immediate family...." This provided doctors with a sanction for what many had actually been doing for some time, since the practice of turning off machines, for example, to allow death to come to a patient whom only the machine is keeping alive is a fairly common practice for hospitals.[158]

---

[144]*Id.* at 1649.
[145]Rice, *Euthanasia: A Time to Live and A Time to Die--How Physicians Feel,* PSYCHOLOGY TODAY, Sept. 1974 at 29 [hereinafter cited as Rice].
[146]Reinhold, *supra* note 138.
[147]Whittingham, *supra* note 1.
[148]Dempsey, *Who Shall Live...and Who Shall Die?,* Chicago Daily News, Oct. 19, 1974, at 19.
[149]Whittingham, *supra* note 1.
[150]*Informed Consent, supra* note 2, at 1658.
[151]Snider, *supra* note 7.
[152]*Informed Consent, supra* note 2, at 1648.
[153]*Id.* at 1649, 1658; Whittingham, *supra* note 1.
[154]*Informed Consent, supra* note 2, at 1658.
[155]Reinhold, *supra* note 138.
[156]Rice, *supra* note 145, at 29.
[157]Reinhold, *supra* note 138, at 1.
[158]Whittingham, *supra* note 1.

As a matter of fact, doctors at the Yale University School of Medicine willingly acknowledged that they had quietly allowed 43 severely deformed infants to die by withholding treatment after the parents agreed there was little chance for "meaningful life." The doctors disclosed this in hopes of breaking down "a major social taboo."[159]

Returning to the physician's poll mentioned above, what objections there were to euthanasia seemed to be based on religious grounds rather than on the major specialties or age groups of the responding doctors. Of the 933 doctors who answered the questionaire, those with no religious affiliation were most likely to be found among the 20% who totally agree that patients should "have a right to choose how they die by making their wishes known to their physicians before serious illness strikes." (Overall, 38% in the random sample agreed with that in most cases, and another 21% agreed in some cases.) However, Catholics were the least likely to accept the idea that a patient had a right to influence his own death. Likewise, when asked what they would do "if ... a member of your family were suffering from terminal illness, which you as a physician knew carried little or no hope for survival"—a question to which nearly two-thirds reacted by saying that would "take no heroic measures" to keep the patient alive, most Catholic doctors opted for keeping the patient alive; among those 11% who would resort to the positive action of ending the suffering (euthanasia, of course), two-thirds were either Jewish or without religion.[160]

The position of Catholic theologians has been that a doctor is obliged to take all ordinary means, including those medicines and treatments which can be used without causing unnecessary pain or expense (as may be coincident with the legal obligation to exercise due care), in order to preserve a patient's life; but this excludes any extraordinary means.[161] The Vatican has now issued an authorative statement on the ethics of mercy killing and the parameters within which it shall be acceptable. A majority of other churches in the United States have also subscribed to similar points of view.[162] Furthermore, last year a Jesuit priest, Father Richard G. McCormick of the Kennedy Center for Bioethics at Georgetown University, proposed that grossly deformed infants should be allowed to die if their "potential for human relationship...is simply non-existent or would be utterly submerged and undeveloped in the mere struggle to survive." Father McCormick noted that though modern medicine has increased the power to preserve life, with that has come the added responsibility to make judgements about the quality of life to be saved. To that end, he has proposed the following guidelines "that may help in the decision about sustaining...lives": the individual decision to end life of such infants must be borne by the parents in consultation with their doctor, and the decision should only be made in terms of what is good for the child. He also offered some caveats, allowing that mistakes will be made because human decisions are involved and cautioning that the death of these infants does not imply that some lives are more valuable than others or that there is such a thing as a life not worth living. Still, Father McCormick concludes, "It is neither inhuman nor un-Christian to say that there comes a point where an individual's condition itself represents the negation of any truly human potential."[163]

---

[159]Reinhold, *supra* note 138, at 1.
[160]Rice, *supra* note 145, at 29-30.
[161]Kutner, *supra* note 5, at 548.
[162]Whittingham, *supra* note 1.
[163]Hausner, *Jesuit Backs Mercy Death for Grossly Deformed Babies*, Chicago Daily News, July 8, 1974, at 38.

It has been asserted that the Judeo-Christian ethic forbids taking a life—even if that life will irreversibly end in painful death.[164] But some theologians claim that forms of religion stressing the promise of life after death merely use religion for selfish purposes. "This enormous emphasis on immortality," announced Krister Stendahl, Dean of Divinity at Harvard University, "was not in Judaism or early Christianity...." Perhaps, now there will be a return to a purer form of religion based simply on faith in God. At any rate, theologians are giving new attention to what human mortality means and they are raising those long neglected questions over the real purpose of human existence.[165]

New Standards of Ethics--A Right to Die

Out of society's concern for preserving human life, the state may feel justified in forbidding voluntary euthanasia. After all, the underlying values of our society and Constitution uphold the right to life—and its protection is basic to any legal system. That is the prime justification, in fact, for the state's existence, according to Hobbes. However, it may well be argued that to forbid voluntary euthanasia is an infringment of the constitutionally recognized right of privacy, as derived from the 4th or 9th Amendments or the due process clause of the 5th Amendment.[166] In the interest of privacy, society ought to opt for an approach that will encourage self-determination, for voluntary euthanasia is not espoused merely as a relief for pain; rather, it is to preserve for the terminal patient his last meaningful freedom: control over the time of his death. Certainly, in such a case, there is the same right of self-determination for death as there is for life.[167]

Strangely enough, though, given our advocacy of man's free will and the constitutional rights of the individual, he cannot relieve his suffering when all hope for recovery is lost.[168] Glanville Williams, the strong proponent of voluntary euthanasia, held there was a human freedom to end one's life. He contended that the law could not forbid conduct that, albeit undesirable, did not adversely affect the social order.[169] This view was similar to that advanced by John Stuart Mill, who based his concept of freedom of choice on instances which had a direct adverse effect on no one but the decision-maker himself.[170] "Each is a proper guardian of his own health, whether bodily or mental or spiritual," wrote Mill. "Mankind are great gainers by suffering each other to live as seems good to themselves, than by compelling each to live as seems good to the rest." And for Mill, "the sole end for which mankind are warranted...in interfering with liberty of action..., is self-protection."[171] But Mill did make an exception to his doctrine of an individual's sovereignty over his own mind and body by applying it to the mature only, since he did not feel a child or young person not yet of age legally should be asked to make such life and death decisions; the minor was to be under the protection of the state.[172]

In the conflict that arises between the right of the competent terminal patient to time his own death and the right of society to prolong death in

---

[164]Whittingham, *supra* note 1.
[165]Reinhold, *supra* note 138, at 1.
[166]Kutner, *supra* note 5, at 539, 545.
[167]*Informed Consent, supra* note 2, at 1657-58.
[168]Whittingham, *supra* note 1.
[169]Kutner, *supra* note 5, at 545.
[170]*Informed Consent, supra* note 2, at 1643-44.
[171]J. S. MILL. ON LIBERTY 6, 8 (People's ed. 1873).
[172]Marcus, *supra* note 10, at 1252.

the interest of preserving life, there is, of course, disagreement over whether society owes any reimbursement to the terminal patient and his family for the full costs of being deprived his right to timing his own death. But, granting the competent terminal patient the choice of when he shall die need not conflict with society's concern to preserve life. Such a patient who prefers a more rapid end should not have a continuation of life forced upon him. The sanctity of life is not an absolute concept which implies that society should deny the decision of a terminal patient who elects euthanasia. That decision should really include both alternatives of euthanasia—passive, for a prolonged death, or active, for a quicker death—in order to allow the maximum choice of timing death so that the patient will maintain what he regards as his dignity.[173]

THE LIVING WILL

When an individual patient has no desire to be kept in a state of complete and indefinite vegetated animation with no possibility of recovering his mental and physical faculties, that individual, while still in control of all his faculties and his ability to express himself, could still retain the right of privacy over his body in determining whether he should be permitted to die by way of a document known as a "living will,"[174] providing least two witnesses who would affirm that the declarant was of sound mind and acted of his own free will.

Each individual case would be referred to a hospital committee, board, or a committee of physicians which would consider circumstances under which the document was made to determine the patient's intent and whether or not his condition had reached the point where he would no longer want treatment. If physicians found some doubts existed as to the

---

[173]*Informed Consent, supra* note 2, at 1658, 1650.
[174]A typical living will may read as follows:

I,_____, of the City of _____, State of _____, U.S.A., Declarant, being of sound mind and disposing memory, herewith make this, my LIVING WILL, to be effective upon the following conditions:

That when an event occurs wherein it appears that I am physically or physiologically irreversibly ill, maimed or disabled, I request that a NON-JUDICIAL BOARD be convened comprised of three duly accredited Doctors of Medicine, a member of the Clergy of my faith (_____), and two lay persons;

That after total evidence has been presented to my irreversible conditions, and under my constitutional rights and my right to determine the integrity of my person, I then direct and request that I be given any appropriate method of EUTHANASIA. In so doing, I hold harmless and exonerate the members of my EUTHANASIA BOARD, individually and collectively;

That in the event legislation is in force authorizing the existence and functioning of a EUTHANASIA BOARD, as suggested in substance above, I agree to be bound by the legislative parameters.

I herewith subscribe to my LIVING WILL, this _____day of _____, in the presence of my two witnesses who shall Attest to my sound mind and disposing memory and shall so Attest in my presence and the presence of each other.

LIVING WILL DECLARANT

Address   City

ATTESTED:

Name   Address   City

Name   Address   City

patient's intent, they could give treatment pending a resolution of the matter—but a patient should not be compelled to undergo treatment, such as taking certain drugs, receiving innoculations or therapy, or undergoing surgery, expressly contrary to his will. In instances where a hospital board might decline to assume responsibility, a patient's living will could be adjudicated by courts and supported by medical and lay testimony and evidence to create affirmative inactive termination of a patient's life.

These living wills by which persons of sound mind can specifically request no extraordinary life-preserving means be taken for their incurable illnesses are not as yet legally binding,[175] but thousands of Americans have already signed them to express in advance their wishes to be allowed to die when there is not reasonable expectation of recovery from a disability.[176]

The individual could carry this document on his person at all times, while his wife, physician, lawyer, or confidant would have the original copy. Personal possession of the document would create a strong presumption that one regards it as binding. The document carried on the patient's person could indicate what people should be contacted if the patient reaches a comatose state.

At any time before reaching the comatose state, an individual could revoke the document; and, because statements or actions subsequent to the written document might indicate contrary consent, if the maker of the will is subsequently adjudged incompetent, the will would also be revoked (though the revocation would not apply where incompetency resulted from a medical condition contemplated in making the decision). The approach of the living will here is analogous to the concept of a revocable or conditional trust, with the patient's body as the *res,* the patient himself as the beneficiary and grantor, and the doctor and hospital as trustees. The doctor is given authority to act as trustee of the patient's body by virtue of the patient's consent to treatment. But the patient, as grantor, is free at any time to revoke that trust relationship created between him and the doctor. In creating the document, it is the intent of the patient to cover contingencies wherein he would be able to grant or withhold consent to treatment. That would include incompetency due to mental illness. Mental illness might present a problem to the concept of the living will, but the mentally ill patient has the same rights as any other patient. So, *via* the will, an individual may anticipate mental illness and limit his consent to treatment accordingly. If, in the course of that illness, the patient enters an incurable comatose state, treatment may cease. The problem might arise in that a court may find the patient, upon becoming mentally ill, to be incompetent and appoint a guardian for him. Still, the will would remain in effect; the guardian could not nullify it. Sometimes mentally ill patients have moments when their minds are lucid. During such instances, he might indicate to his guardian or physician if he wishes the will revoked and the guardian could then act accordingly to revoke the will.

To those who feel that living wills are too vague to offer any confidence in the adequacy of their safeguards, it might be pointed out that these documents could be individually tailored to mitigate some of the uncertainties as to the actual intent under particular circumstances.[177] A

[175]Whittingham, *supra* note 1.
[176]Reinhold, *supra* note 138, at 1.
[177]*Informed Consent, supra* note 2, at 1664.

Jehovah's Witness, opposed to blood transfusions on religious principles, could so provide in such a document. A Christian Scientist could indicate he does not wish any medical treatment through such a document.

Further, living wills can only be made by adults capable of giving their consent—patients who have a right to decide whether they will receive treatment. That does not apply to minors, those institutionalized or adjudged incompetent. Nor could a parent acting on behalf of his child make such a declaration, so that while an adult patient may himself refuse to undergo an operation or receive a blood transfusion to save his life, a parent could not deprive a child of such treatment.

As long as public policy does not condone euthanasia, the living will may still be used as a means to direct a doctor to act passively through inaction (thereby permitting the patient to die) in much the same way a patient may refuse to sign the legal statement required to indicate his consent to undergo surgery or other treatment.

The Living Will:
The Final Expression

Cynthia H. Baker

Death is the most certain event in life. We do not know when it will come, or how it will come, but sooner or later it does come to us all. Some of us may deny it, while some of us will accept it, and attempt to meet it on our own terms. The Living Will is such an attempt to specify those terms—to control one's destiny as much as possible.

The Living Will presents two challenges to the legal and medical world: 1) does a patient, by refusing life-prolonging treatment, have the right to die? and 2) should a physician implementing the request, by omitting or withdrawing treatment, be held civilly or criminally liable for his actions?

THE RIGHT TO A NATURAL DEATH

If adult persons have the right to make decisions concerning their medical care, should it follow that it includes the right to decide to have life-sustaining procedures withheld or withdrawn upon a terminal condition?

It is an accepted fact that modern medical technology can artificially prolong human life well beyond natural limits. But, what if a patient is in such a terminal condition, *eg* comatose, and cannot express his wish not to prolong or sustain the artificial life? Who should have the burden of that decision? The physician and/or the patient's family? Realistically, some person (or persons) is already making that decision. Should he be subject to legal repercussions?

An American writer, Richard Oulahan Jr,[1] reported that at a mid-west meeting of physicians, when asked to raise their hands if they had *never* practised euthanasia, not a hand was raised. There was no distinction made between "passive" and "active" euthanasia. Assuming that euthanasia is now being practised, charges of liability seldom reach the courts. This may be due, perhaps, to prosecutorial dis-

cretion, difficulty of proof or simply failure of authorities to uncover the situation. And practically speaking, one cannot bring the dead person back to life.

Undoubtedly, the same circumstances exist in Canada. Every day in some hospital, passive euthanasia is probably being practised; either on the decision of the doctor alone, by the doctor respecting the verbal wishes of his patient or the wishes of the patient's family. This situation places an enormous burden of responsibility upon the physician. It seems logical that legal recognition of a Living Will would clarify the cloudy conspiracy.

Suppose the family and doctor cannot agree? Dr Yutaka Kato[2] believed in his right to exercise medical judgment. He believed treatment should continue for a partially brain damaged female patient. The husband wished a sustaining respirator turned off and went to court for an opinion. Chancellor Herschel Franks ruled that if, in Dr Kato's judgment, there was no reasonable possibility that treatment would cure the patient or that she would recover from her coma, Dr Kato could not continue treatment without patient consent. Dr Kato appealed, saying no physician can guarantee treatment and the court should not make his decision. The case was moot, however, since the patient died. This case does point out the conflict when a family disagrees with the doctor. Usually a family will get another physician when they disagree, but the family in this case desired to have Dr Kato remain on the case.

An American legal opinion[3] states that under present law, "disconnecting a life support mechanism falls within the definition of homicide", and if a patient consents or demands removal of life-sustaining procedures, he may be guilty of committing suicide (if successful). It is also a crime for a physician to aid or abet suicide.

In Canada, the Criminal Code[4] sets out the duty of persons undertaking acts dangerous to life.

s198 Every person who undertakes to administer surgical or medical treatment to another person or to do any other lawful

Cynthia H Baker BA LLB (Alberta).

Reprinted with permission from *Legal Medical Quarterly*, vol. 4, Spring, 1980.

acts that may endanger the life of another person is, except in cases of necessity under a legal duty to have and to use reasonable knowledge, skill and care in so doing.

s199 Everyone who undertakes to do an act is under a legal duty to do it if an *omission* to do the act is or may be dangerous to life. (Emphasis added)

Section 205 (1) states:

A person commits homicide when, directly or *indirectly,* by any means, he causes the death of a human being . . . (5) A person commits culpable homicide when he causes the death of a human being, (a) by an unlawful act . . . (Emphasis added)

Finally section 212 (a) says:

Culpable homicide is murder where the person who causes the death of a human being (1) means to cause his death, or (2) means to cause him bodily harm that he knows is likely to cause his death, and is reckless whether death ensues or not . . . .

Thus, we see that a physician, undertaking the care of another, has a legal duty of reasonable care, and the legal duty includes not to omit an act if it is or may be dangerous to life. Section 205(1) says the doctor may be charged with homicide if he directly, or indirectly, by any means, causes the death of a human being. This logically would cover the situation where he withdraws the life-prolonging or sustaining technology from a dying patient (*ie* he "pulls the plug").

It is a rare occurrence for any doctor in Canada to be charged under these sections. Either the law is being ignored or else passive (and perhaps "active") euthanasia are considered exceptions to the legislation in this area.

Very few reported cases in the United States have specifically dealt with the right of the individual to refuse life-sustaining medical care. The courts, generally, have permitted competent, adult patients without dependents, to knowingly refuse consent to treatment, even though life could be sustained or prolonged. The cases reported involved collateral issues such as constitutionality, or a religious conviction opposed to proposed treatment,[5] or advanced age combined with radical surgery which only offered limited quality of life.[6]

Meyers[7] feels that the personal and individualized relationship between patient and doctor is best left to common law informed consent and individual freedom of choice and good, ethical medical practice. He suggests the public wish for certainty regarding their care and treatment as they approach death should involve more candid discussion rather than legislation. At the same time the Natural Death Act of California has pointed out the recognition of the need for proper medical limits for care of the dying.

EUTHANASIA

Euthanasia is sub-divided into two categories: passive or active. Passive euthanasia is non-intentional or "benemortasia"—*ie* permitting natural death, to stop the use of extraordinary means. Active euthanasia is a positive, intentional act, which causes death. One gets into a cloudy area where an act or omission cannot be sharply differentiated as either active or passive euthanasia.

For example, suppose a patient is being kept alive by some mechanical device. The doctors agree there is no possibility of recovery, and without the machine, life would soon cease. Maintaining the patient on the machine is an "active" care, but if the physician unplugs the machine, it could be classified as an "omission to take care" or an act of active euthanasia. The latter definition would suggest that presently, physicians, even though they have the consent of patient or family, are practising *active* euthanasia which is punishable under the Criminal Code.

Fletcher[8] has argued that turning off the respirator is an omission rather than a positive act. The omission is defined as a failure to continue treatment, thus "permitting" the patient to die.[9] The argument goes that the omission would not cause criminal liability, because liability only attaches to a commission which *causes* a result and not to an omission which *permits* a result to occur. It all must turn upon the duty the doctor has to his patient; and how far that duty goes.

However, Kennedy[10] feels this is "logic chopping" and semantical. Instead he proposes that "the crucial medico-legal decision is not switching off a respirator but rather *switching it on,* either initially or after having once turned it off."[11] Kennedy bases his argument upon the definition of death as being "brain-death", in which state a person will not breathe nor will his heart beat if the brain stem does not function. Thus he posits, in order to ascertain if brain death has occurred, the respirator must be turned off. If there is no heart beat or respiration the patient is legally dead; and the machine need not be switched on again. All the arguments put forth illustrate the difficulty of assessing when recovery is irreversible or the condition is terminal.

Kennedy agrees that a doctor, who acts in good faith and takes all due care, by turning off a respirator does nothing to warrant criminal sanction. He also feels that requests to be taken off machines, such as respirators and kidney dialysis machines, are so rare that the criminal law should make them justifiable exceptions. Kennedy reaches this point by proposing that a lucid patient has the right to withdraw consent to further treatment.

Criminal law establishes that any affirmative act of euthanasia is homicide. A person cannot legally consent to another inflicting death upon himself.[12] The courts have shown sympathy to persons accused of euthanasia. On the other hand, the legal status of the physician who withholds treatment at the request of the patient is in dispute. The legality of this omission is uncertain. Glanville Williams[13] feels the doctor's inaction at the patient's request is probably lawful. No physician has ever been convicted of such a crime.

Withholding treatment is a murky area, and administration of pain-relieving medication, even though it may shorten life, is apparently not regarded as illegal. The point is often ultimately reached when medical treatment does not preserve life, but *prolongs dying.* At this point, "extraordinary" techniques are not needed to maintain life.

The physician-patient relationship has been analyzed in a contractual concept.[14] The patient-offeror communicates his offer to the physician by seeking his services. The physician may accept or refuse. If he accepts, a contract is formed and the usual elements of a valid contract must exist. Both physician and patient retain the right to revoke the contract at will, with reasonable notice. This patient-physician contract has been described as a "mutual participation" comprised of continuing offers by the patient that ripen into contracts as the physician provides his services.

Once the physician accepts the patient's offer, verbally or by his conduct, the law imposes a duty to continue treatment as long as it is required. If the physician does not perform in accordance with the agreement, and the patient is injured he could recover for breach of contract.

Following this contractual analysis, if the patient wishes to end treatment, he can terminate the contract, discharging the physician from further duty. In effect, this is what the Living Will purports to do: discharge the physician from contractual duty and legal liability.

Refusal of medical treatment is a patient's right, and the doctor must respect the patient's decision even though it may result in further deterioration and eventual death.[14.1] Exercise of the right may place the physician's ethical and legal duties in conflict, since preservation of life and health is his professional commitment. However, the patient is not legally required to preserve his own health or life. Therefore, if the doctor proceeded with forbidden treatment, thus following his professional ethical standards, he invites potential liability. Employing this reasoning, a court could find a doctor liable for "wrongfully saving life", but damages would probably be nominal.[14.2]

Every physician-patient relationship proceeds upon the doctrine of informed consent. The physician cannot give appropriate medical treatment unless the patient has voluntarily consented. A consent is only considered valid if the patient has capacity and competence. It must meet the criteria of being voluntary, with no feeling of constraint or duress; it must be an informed consent, and any deviation from the procedure consented to will be actionable.[15]

Failure to obtain consent can be an assault for a mere touching, or for battery, now often called surgical battery. Most malpractice suits are based on negligence of the medical or hospital staff. In emergency situations, where it is impossible to obtain the necessary consent, it is assumed the patient would have given consent, and persons rendering emergency treatment are protected from liability.[16]

Consent to treatment has different orientations for the health care world and the legal world. The latter focuses on the *rights* of individuals; the former aims to concentrate on the *needs* of the individuals as determined by the standards of hospital and medical practice. The rights and needs of the patient are not always the same, and the consent to treatment is the link between the two.[17]

WITHDRAWAL OF CONSENT

If a patient withdraws consent and he refuses to be touched by a doctor, any further touching will be unlawful and may give rise to criminal and civil liability. "A patient has the right to decline operative investigation or treatment however unreasonable or foolish this may appear in the eyes of the medical advisors."[18]

Professor Glanville Williams writes: "Some doctors seem to fail to realize that if an adult patient has positively forbidden particular treatment, they act illegally if they administer it, and could be . . . prosecuted for assault."[19] He also refers to a patient's right to self-determination to be an "upstart notion."[20]

Cardozo J held in the landmark case of *Schloendorff* v *Society of New York Hospital*[21] that "every human being of adult years and sound mind has a right to determine what shall be done with his own body."

In Canada, the case of *Mulloy* v *Hop Sang,*[22] doctors were held liable when Hop Sang's hand was amputated contrary to his expressed wish. In *Beausoleil* v *Soeurs de la Charitee*[23] a patient expressly forbad the use of a spinal anaesthetic, but was later persuaded to consent while under sedation. The operation resulted in permanent paralysis from the waist down. It was held that a doctor "may not overrule his patient and submit him to risks that he is un-

willing and in fact has refused to accept. And if he does so and damages result he will be responsible without proof of negligence or want of skill."[24] The key in these two cases appears to be the right to self-determination.

Kennedy[25] premises that the right to self-determination is undermined by paternalism of the medical profession. Decisions regarding a particular person's fate are made *for* him rather than *by* him. In many instances the patient is willing to have such decisions made on his behalf. But when he expressly, either orally or by writing, refuses a certain course of treatment, then those wishes, if made with full capacity and competence, should be respected. Kennedy asserts that present formal legal rules are adequate in most circumstances: what needs to change are administrative and procedural practice.[26] The Living Will would probably be an exception to the usual practice of dealing with the dying, and such a document should be validly recognized, and provision made for it by changes in administration and procedure.

As early as 1929[27] Canadian courts held that a patient had the right to refuse treatment, and tried to balance this right with the goals of the health care profession. In *Masny,* the patient had refused consent to a necessary operation, which resulted in a painful wait for death. Mr Justice Knowles of the Saskatchewan Court of King's Bench said:

> Three months ago the medical men knew this would all happen, but according to our present legislation, they were helpless. The poor immigrant, through ignorance or foolhardiness, or both, forbade them putting forth the hand which would have saved his life. Should not society protect such a man from his own foolishness?[28]

If courts will accept an oral refusal to treatment, should they not also accept a written refusal such as the Living Will?

If consent is required prior to treatment, the logical extension is that the consent can also be withdrawn, or revoked. Consequently, it is argued, a patient should have the right to refuse treatment offered, even if his refusal will shorten his life. Generally, in the United States, when persons have refused life-saving treatment, the medical profession has resorted to the courts for a mandatory order to treat the patient. The American courts have considered various states' interests involving children being left orphaned, doctor's conscience and professional oaths, conservation of life, and protection of a viable fetus within a patient.

There have been a few cases where the patient's right to refuse life-saving blood transfusions was upheld. One case was based upon 1) the patient being fully informed as to consequences of refusal; 2) no minor children involved; 3) execution of documents releasing doctor and hospital from civil liability; and 4) there appeared otherwise no clear and present danger to society.[29]

These cases were, however, non-terminal cases, and the Living Will is meant to deal with instances where there is no reasonable hope of recovery. If the doctrine of informed consent can be applied to non-terminal cases, it seems more logical that it should be extended to terminal cases.

The patient's right to an informed consent makes no sense if the right does not extend to include an informed refusal. This right should be open to the dying patient, for his decision on proffered treatment is no different than another patient's. Only that particular individual best knows his own values, capacity for pain and suffering, and his unfinished business and family obligations. He knows what he can afford in all these areas.[30] In all the articles reviewed the economic costs of maintaining terminal patients on machines is passed over. Perhaps it is considered vulgar to speak of money in connection with dying. Nevertheless, as the ratio of older and consequently dying patients increases, the economic burden will escalate and have to be faced. Will values change when costs are greater to maintain the traditional values?

No matter how one analyzes the present situation, as contractual or an act or omission accompanied by a duty, we are either consciously or unconsciously ignoring what is going on. Legislation, giving the patient the right to withdraw his consent to further treatment, would clarify and recognize this reality.

CONCEPT OF THE LIVING WILL

The Living Will has been defined as a document in which a competent adult expresses his desire that if ever the time comes when there is no reasonable expectation of his recovery from physical or mental disability, that he be allowed to die rather than be kept alive by artificial means or heroic measures. In effect it sanctions passive euthanasia.

A Living Will, distributed by the Euthanasia Council, *(infra)* in 1974 had been signed by perhaps 750,000 Americans who hoped to have a death with dignity.[31]

Euthanasia, literally meaning "good death" has, as we have noted, both passive and active definitions. The latter involves the commission of an act which hastens death; the former, the omission of an act. "Mercy killing" is synonymous for active euthanasia. The discussion will deal almost exclusively with passive euthanasia, or antidysthanasia, defined as "the failure to take positive action to prolong life."

The Living Will directs one's physician to cease affirmative treatment under certain specified circumstances. It applies to the situation where a person is in a terminal condition and lapses into the final stage of illness, as well as the situation where an individual injured in an accident deteriorates into a vegetative condition.

The Living Will resembles a testamentary document. It is notarized and at least two witnesses attest to the competence and voluntariness of the maker. This procedure safeguards the patient against the influence of pain or future family financial ruin at the time he executes the document.

As an advance declaration, it signifies the competence of the declarant; whereas a patient in a critical medical condition could well be influenced by the emotional stress of his illness, his doctor's attitude, his desire to satisfy his relatives' wishes, and concern over finances. Psychological studies have also shown there is a suppressed longing for death in all persons—a "release." Another factor is the lack of knowledge of the patient's true condition. These considerations all point to the wisdom of an advance directive, as against a bed-side decision of life and immediate death.

As well, many debilitating illnesses incapacitate a person, such as strokes or sudden accidents, and he would be unable to make a competent choice at that precise time. Then the customary consent to treatment would be given by others for the patient. The Living Will foresees such possibilities and endeavors to prepare for such occurrences.

The Living Will allows the individual, while considering his religious convictions, personal desires, and financial circumstances, to control his own medical destiny. It is worthwhile noting that a prolonged illness in the US could ruin a family financially. At the present time, under provincial and federal health care schemes in Canada, almost unlimited care is available. It is totally unrealistic to assume that any scheme could stand the financial strain of unlimited prolongation of life for unlimited numbers of the population.

While testamentary documents are authorized by statute, generally Living Wills are not. The Living Will is really a moral request to one's physician. In Canada and most of the US they have no legal force, which the document itself recognizes with its statement that "this document is not legally binding." Although, as will be seen, several American states, including California, have enacted legislation giving a form of Living Will legal recognition.

The advance declaration releasing the hospital and physician from liability has been criticized as contrary to public policy. While the advance statement may be unenforceable as a waiver, it could be evidence of lack of consent to proposed treatment. Alternatively, it may be considered as a contract not to sue in consideration for not administering treatment.

The Living Will requests "not to be kept alive by artificial means or heroic measures", *ie* a refusal to extraordinary means of treatment. This clause has been criticized on the basis that what is considered "extraordinary" at the present time, in the near future may be considered "ordinary." One only has to think of antibiotics as a simple example. However, this problem could be overcome by a classification by a physician's committee, or the declarant himself could specify what means he did not wish.

Another critical problem with the Living Will is the interpretation of "reasonable expectation of recovery." It presumes that a physician can accurately determine the hopelessness of each particular case. Even in terminal cases there is always a slight percentage of cases where recovery occurs. Hospital committees are suggested to verify a physician's prognosis of "hopelessness," if he wishes confirmation. It is not known what procedure is followed at the present time.

The physician and hospital are dedicated to providing quality medical care, and as technology can prolong life the situation becomes muddled. How far does the medical duty extend to become the legal duty? The Living Will affords one alternative to the present system. Until the Living Will is legitimized it cannot afford effective protection for the medical profession. Legitimization, such as Natural Death Acts, passed by California and other American states, is a possible solution.

The Living Will document should be readily accessible. A physician or hospital should not have to chase around to find if one exists, when time for treatment may be crucial. The onus should be on the patient to indicate he has executed a Living Will. He should carry a copy of the document with his necessary identification and give another copy to his family doctor. Future miniaturization on a plasticized card is a suggestion.

REVOCATION

A person may change his mind regarding the disposition of his property, and similarly the maker of a Living Will may change his mind respecting treatment of his person. In the model Living Will, there is no provision for revocation; although it has been suggested it should be updated regularly.

Commentators describe the dilemma of the physician who is confronted with a patient in an emergency situation who says he has changed his mind. Immediately the question of competency arises. If the physician proceeds to treat the patient following Living Will instructions, he could be liable for a wrongful death action, but if he honors the revocation, he could be faced with a charge for assault and battery.

Proper standards for an effective revocation could be set out, without undermining the value of the document.[32]

ADMINISTRATION OF PAIN-RELIEVING DRUGS

The model Living Will instructs for pain-relieving drugs:

> I ask also that drugs be mercifully administered to me for terminal suffering even if in relieving pain they may hasten the moment of death. . . .

If this clause authorizes affirmative action intending death, it is an illegal act. If the clause is ineffective, it could mean an extremely painful death which some would consider a death without dignity.

It is often necessary to continually increase the dosage of drugs which eventually results in the patient's death. There is American authority indicating that the administration of pain-relieving drugs is considered illegal if they hasten death, although they may have been given with the intention to alleviate pain. It is argued that although the Living Will points out the difficulty in this area, it already exists even without the presence of the Living Will. The Roman Catholic Church, although opposed to euthanasia, approves the use of such drugs to reduce pain, but not to cause death.[33]

Generally, there seems to be agreement that as long as the purpose of administration of drugs is to relieve pain, the action is morally correct, and legally sanctioned. Lord Justice Coleridge said: "It is not correct to say that every obligation is a legal duty, but every legal duty is founded upon a moral duty."[34]

CURRENT LIVING WILL LEGISLATION

American Legislation

Several American states have enacted "Natural Death Acts" to clarify the terminally ill patient's right to refuse treatment.

California was the first to enact legislation, The Natural Death Act, under the California Health and Safety Code. An overview of the Act reveals that basically the signor legally directs that in the event of becoming terminally ill, and life-sustaining procedures will clearly only postpone the moment of death, such procedures be withdrawn or withheld. Briefly, the California legislation specifies that 1) only adults of sound mind may execute a directive, and 2) if an individual is diagnosed as terminally ill by his attending physician (and confirmed by a second physician), he then becomes a "qualified patient" and the directive is legally enforceable, and 3) if the signor is not a "qualified" patient at time of execution, the directive is not legally binding but only *advisory* to the physician. The doctor is to give weight to the directive as evidence of the patient's directions, but *may* consider other factors such as information from the affected family or the nature of the patient's illness, injury or disease in determining whether all the circumstances justify implementing the directive. 4) If a person executes a directive and subsequently is diagnosed as terminally ill, he must re-execute a directive to make it legally binding. The order remains in force for five years unless revoked by the patient,

and may not be enforced until at least 14 days after execution. 5) Witnesses are required, but individuals with specified conflicts of interest such as being related by blood or marriage, being entitled to any portion of the estate, and attending physician and employees of that physician or health facility where the declarant is a patient, are not eligible as witnesses. 6) Revocation is simple—it can be verbal, written or by destroying the directive. 7) Any licensed health professional who complies with the directive is granted immunity by law from criminal or civil liability. Compliance with the directive does not constitute suicide under the law, and, importantly, cannot affect the signor's life insurance in any manner. 8) It is deemed unprofessional conduct for the physician if he fails to comply with a valid directive, has not made arrangements to implement instructions, or fails to transfer the patient. Concealment of, or damage to, a directive is considered a misdemeanor. Any act "contrary to the wishes" of the declarant, which has been achieved by falsification or forgery of a directive which quickens death constitutes unlawful homicide. 9) In no instance does this law approve mercy killing. Deliberate and affirmative actions to end life are expressly forbidden. The purpose of the law is only to allow natural death to occur as the qualified patient has directed. 10) Amendments to the Act include 1) a directive by a qualified patient is not enforceable if she is pregnant; and 2) recognizing the often coercive setting of a nursing home, therefore one witness for a nursing home patient must be a State Department of Aging designated ombudsman or patient advocate.

Seven other states (including Idaho, Arkansas, New Mexico, Oregon, North Carolina) have enacted Natural Death Acts based on the California model with some modifications. Idaho does not prohibit pregnant women from issuing a directive; nor does it make special provision for nursing home residents, and does not require a waiting period for the directive to become effective. Arkansas goes even further, and does not require a specific form for the directive. New Mexico follows Arkansas, and merely requires formalities similar to a valid will.

California and Oregon place the burden on the physician of determining that a directive has been lawfully executed before he carries out the directive. New Mexico eliminates the burden on the doctor and presumes he will act in good faith, and also has the presumption that the individual was competent upon execution of the directive. Arkansas and New Mexico permit the execution of a legally enforceable directive at any time. Thus terminal illness is not required at the time of execution.

Relman,[34.1] commented on more recent legislation[34.2] in Michigan which introduces the concept of a proxy designated by the patient who makes a decision for the patient when he has become incapable of doing so. The physician still has a major role in defining medical options and explaining their implications to the patient's surrogate, but the doctor and surrogate work closely together.

Relman has recognized the basic purpose of a "living will" as ensuring the patient's right of self-determination. However, he feels that the abstract and general terms of "living will" cannot adequately cover very unique clinical situations. As well, "living will" legislation tends to put pressure on physicians to allow apparently incurable patients to die, since they would be legally liable if they did not comply with the patient's declaration.

The proposed proxy concept, in the case of the incompetent patient, is seen by Dr Relman as an effective method of overcoming some of the deficiencies of the "living will."

Several bills have tried to incorporate a definition of brain death in their Natural Death Act. Since brain death is determined by various changing clinical practices and determination of moment of death, it is usually considered apart from a Natural Death Act. Fundamentally, Natural Death legislation is the affirmation of the continuing right of the patient to refuse treatment.

CRITICISM OF NATURAL DEATH ACTS

A brief summary indicates the various criticism of Natural Death legislation.[35]

1 Generally one would expect objections on moral grounds, but few have been presented by the major religious groups. Most of the clergy define artificial or extraordinary life supports as intervening with the natural process of death. In 1957, Pope Pius XII spoke out against prolonging the dying process by means of extraordinary medical intervention. He urged consideration of the needs of the patient, and the economic and emotional stress of prolonged dying upon the family and medical staff.[36]

2 Some physicians argue that the clinical setting is sufficiently adequate for discussion of appropriate care between patient, family, and attending physician, and, therefore, no legislation is needed. This ignores the fact that some patients do not have a personal family physician, nor a family. As well, why should others make the decision for an individual who has taken the time and reflection to decide how he wishes to have his own body treated?

3 The medical profession objects that the legislature should not interfere in the clinical setting. Since courts have already defined "informed consent," natural death legislation would simply affirm the right of a class of patients, ie the terminally ill, who experience special problems concerning that right to give or withhold consent to treatment.

4 A further objection is the small number of people who fill out directives, and such legislation is therefore not required. One could point out the increasing numbers of individuals who do fill out living wills, thus attempting to express their desires. As well, somewhere along the line decisions are made by someone to prolong life or permit a natural death. Should not the wishes of the patient concerned have paramount importance? Or has the terminally ill patient truly become a "thing," a "non-being" or a "statistic" to be handled according to someone else's values and standards?

5 If natural death is permitted, will that mean society will soon permit and accept mercy killings? The hypothetical of allowing mercy killing of retarded people is always cited. However, all the Acts prohibit mercy killing or affirmative acts which hasten death.

6 Is a five-year renewal clause necessary? This may place an undue hardship on patients suffering from degenerative diseases, or the elderly, who due to senility may not be able to express themselves clearly five years hence. In contrast, it is pointed out that there is no such requirement concerning a will disposing of one's personal estate.

7 The "cooling-off" period of 14 days has been criticized as being severe in some cases. Perhaps a provision for bed-side directives could be made in exceptional circumstances eg a burn patient. Again, properly executed bed-side wills are legally enforceable, therefore, logically, bed-side "living wills" should be accepted if there is mental competence.

8 Differentiation between a directive signed by a diagnosed terminally ill patient which is legally enforceable, and a healthy individual's directive which is merely advisory, seems incomprehensible. Should not such a directive have more weight in a situation where the individual is not under emotional and physical stress? As well, a testamentary disposition is considered valid if properly executed by a terminally ill person or a healthy person. Is this distinction really necessary in the case of Living Wills?

9 An accurate comprehensive list of what is considered "extraordinary measures" should be drawn up for the guidance of attending medical staff. Annual review could be made to keep abreast with new medical technological achievements.

10 A statutory definition of death, eg "absence of brain activity," would also clarify possible conflicting situations.[37] The definition of death is particularly important when organ donations are anticipated.

11 Two physicians must concur when a patient is in a terminal condition, but only one physician is needed to determine the imminency of death. "Imminent" has not been defined in the Act, and, therefore, inconsistency could result. Steinberg[38] has argued that these requirements should be included in the directive for the declarant's information. Although "imminent" was not defined, it could be interpreted differently by various physicians, thereby giving flexibility. The sponsor of the California legislation, Assemblyman Barry Keene, suggested that about two weeks would seem reasonable.[39]

Meyers[40] points out that to be a "qualified patient" one must be in "imminent danger" for 14 days, but if the directive is issued prior to the terminal stage, then the directive is merely advisory, even though executed by a healthy, fully competent individual. On the other hand, if the patient must be in a critical condition for 14 days, would he be sufficiently mentally alert to execute the directive and make it binding? This apparent ambiguity seems to defeat the purpose of the legislation by taking away the force of the directive issued prior to becoming terminal.

12 The Act provides that the physician will not be criminally or civilly responsible if he has no actual knowledge of revocation of a Living Will. While the California legislation protects the doctor from liability, and removes the onerous burden of ascertaining whether there has been a revocation, at the same time it relegates the interest of preserving human life and protecting human autonomy to a second rate position.[41] What may occur is an expedited death for an individual who does not desire it.

13 Steinberg[42] points out that physician autonomy has been paramount in the California Act, rather than patient autonomy. The physician has a great discretion concerning the competency of the patient, thus overriding the patient's directive. The physician has been granted sole power to decide whether or not a directive should be fulfilled, and when an individual becomes a qualified patient after making his directive. The doctor has also been provided with a discretion to consult the family which would appear to destroy the whole reason for the Living Will. All the provisions seem to reinforce the time-honored authority and autonomy of the physician over the patient.

As well the doctor is subject to a misdemeanor penalty at law, for example if he loses a directive; but, if he does not follow the patient's instructions on the directive, he is only subject to professional discipline for this deliberate misconduct. It was felt these changes were made to get support of the California Medical Association. Are physicians above the law, when control is exercised by their own medical profession? Steinberg[43] reiterates that criminal sanctions are justified when physicians do not adhere to a patient's human right, (eg to be transferred to another doctor who will follow his instructions) and California society's fundamental interest in seeking legal redress was violated by the legislation.

BRITISH LEGISLATION

Voluntary euthanasia bills were introduced in the British House of Lords in 1936, and again in 1969. Basically, the provisions of the 1969 version were similar to the 1977 California legislation, but it had many ambiguities.

Weaknesses pointed out in the legislation included: the extreme difficulty in ensuring true consent at all necessary stages; the impossibility of a doctor being certain that there was presence or absence of a consent in a patient unable to communicate for any reason; the realization that unintentional subtle pressures could influence a patient's decision to request euthanasia; the possibility of defects in the Euthanasia Act going beyond the voluntary principle. The conclusion was that safeguards which would adequately avoid these pitfalls would be so complex they would be unworkable.

There was much objection to clause 8 of the proposed bill which declared that all terminal patients could receive whatever quantity of drugs required to keep them entirely free from pain, and could be made and kept entirely unconscious. The section applied whether the patient was a declarant or not. In essence, many felt that opening the door to voluntary euthanasia could easily proceed to involuntary euthanasia.

In Britain, as in the US, there were semantical, as well as philosophical distinctions. Mr Justice Devlin (now Lord Devlin) said in R v Adams[44]:

If the first purpose of medicine—the restoration of health—can no longer be achieved, there is still much for the doctor to do and he is entitled to do all that is proper and necessary to relieve pain and suffering even if the measures he takes may incidentally shorten life . . . But it remains the law that no doctor has the right to cut off life deliberately.

Hence the test is not the outcome of what the doctor directs, but his intent with which he gives the direction. Essentially this is the Reasonable Man test, whereby he intends the consequences of his act(s), and, therefore, is more onerous. Gould and Craigmyle[45] contend that "the law is clear, and consistent with medical practice."

Parliamentary debates included the British Medical Association's condemnation of euthanasia and opposition to the bill. On the other hand, information was offered that antibiotics are often withdrawn to help their patients "over the edge." A national opinion poll showed that approximately 76 percent of doctors agreed that some of them help their patients "over the last hurdle"; as well, 36.6 percent of doctors would be willing to administer euthanasia.[46] It was argued by Lord Raglan, who introduced the Bill, that a declaration would give the doctor ethical guidance as to the patient's desires.

After both well-reasoned and emotional debate, evidence of conflicting attitudes, morals and experiences, the bill was defeated 61/40.

CANADA AND THE LIVING WILL

Thus far the medical situations in Canada and the United States appear to be analogous. In the United States the right to die proposal has been supported by five amendments to the federal constitution. They include the right to privacy, the free exercise clause (under freedom of religion) and the Fourth Amendment which provides the right to be let alone.

The Canadian Criminal Code, without other legislation, would appear to hold a physician criminally responsible if he accedes to the request to die in a Living Will.[47]

The Canadian Bill of Rights also, provides in Part I:

s1 It is hereby recognized and declared that in Canada there have existed and shall continue to exist . . . the following human rights . . . (a) the right of the individual to life, liberty, security of the person . . . and the right not to be deprived thereof except by due process of law.

Ontario introduced a private members bill, which failed to pass when the 1977 provincial election intervened.[48] It was similar to the California legislation.

The distribution of legislative powers is different in Canada than in the United States. In Canada, the criminal powers and residual constitutional powers are federal, whereas the reverse is true in the United States. As well, criminal powers reside with the various state legislatures.

The Canadian Criminal Code[49] sets out statutory prohibitions concerning the taking of someone's life. These were detailed earlier.[50] Also everyone who counsels, procures or aids a person to commit suicide, whether suicide follows or not, is guilty of an indictable offence. It would appear, therefore, that the proposed legislation in Ontario[51] (in addition to that proposed in Alberta) goes against the Canadian Criminal Code.

The doctor in Canada can be charged in a civil action with assault or negligence if he does not meet the appropriate standard of care. The purpose of the civil action is to compensate the aggrieved patient. Duties are also imposed by law upon the doctor, and are set out in sections 197 and 198 of the Criminal Code. If he fails to live up to the imposed duty, he could be guilty of criminal negligence which has a higher standard than for civil negligence. In R v Bateman[52] it was said that to establish criminal liability one must show that "the negligence or incompetence of the accused went beyond a mere matter of compensation and showed such disregard for the life and safety of others as to amount to a crime against the State and conduct deserving punishment." Thus, a doctor found liable for death by criminal negligence would be charged under s203 and would be subject to a maximum penalty of life imprisonment; if found liable for bodily harm, the charge would be under s204, carrying a maximum penalty of 10 years imprisonment.

Doctors are rarely charged with criminal negligence in the Canadian courts; and when they are, it would appear that most end in an acquittal. However, as people become more aware that they have rights concerning the care and the withdrawal of such care, doctors should be aware of their potential liability. At present it appears, in many cases, they have assumed the sole responsibility for deciding how long a patient should have extraordinary care.

A private members bill[53] was also introduced into the Alberta legislature in 1977. The purpose of the bill was "to provide a means whereby an individual may limit the effect of a general or implied consent to medical treatment to prevent the use of life-sustaining procedures while in a terminal condition."[54] However, it never progressed beyond first reading.

CONCLUSION

Formerly when death occurred "naturally" from most causes, it was easy to avoid discussion of an unenjoyable fact and leave those matters to the doctor. Now that science has made available mechanical, chemical and other artificial means which can prolong the semblance of life—or prolong dying as some prefer to call it—it does not seem fair to leave the whole responsibility of decision-making to the physician. Society and the individual should share the burden by becoming fully informed about the limits of medical science, the economic costs, and should delineate appropriate limits for the prolongation of life. Gallup (1974) and Harris (1973) polls in the United States indicate the majority of Americans think a doctor should allow his patient to die if he requests it.[55]

Recognition of a Living Will would respect the individual's integrity and freedom of choice. He would retain his right to refuse further medical treatment. On the other hand, if a person has not issued a directive, he would be deemed to have left the matter to whomever is giving consent for him, or to the discretion of the doctor.

The doctor who "pulls a plug" upon the legally sanctioned instructions of his patient would not incur liability for an omission covered under the "extraordinary measures" provision which formerly would be classified as an omission or failure of care on his part.

The Living Will expresses the intent and goal of securing autonomy and death with dignity for the individual. Legislation setting forth standards and procedures has been recommended to recognize this reality so that what is lawful is clearly stipulated. It would also recognize the reality of the situation as it presently exists (who is really making the decision?), and clarify the right of the individual.

REFERENCES

1. Richard Oulahan Jr *Euthanasia, Should One Kill A Child?* Life August 1962.
2. Jane A Raible *The Right To Refuse Treatment And Natural Death Legislation* (fall 1977) 5 Medicolegal News No 4 at 10.
3. *Id.*
4. Criminal Code RSC 1970 c C-34, as am ss 198, 199, 205(1) and 212(a).
5. In Re Brooks' Estate (1965) 32 Ill 2d 361, 205 NE2d 435.
6. In Re Raasch (1972) 455-996 (at 331) Probate Division, Milwaukee County Court—a 77 yr old woman refused leg amputation.
7. Meyers *The California Natural Death Act: A Critical Appraisal* 1977, July/August CalifStBJ 383.
8. Fletcher *Prolonging Life* (1966-67) 42 UWashLRev 999.
9. *Id* at 1007.
10. Kennedy *Switching Off Life Support Machine: The Legal Implications* (1977) CrimLRev 443.
11. *Id* at 445.
12. Cantor *A Patient's Decision To Decline Life-Saving Medical Treatment: Bodily Integrity versus The Preservation Of Life* (1973) 26 RutLRev 228.
13. Glanville Williams The Sanctity of Life And The Criminal Law 326 (1956 Knopf New York).
14. Strand *The Living Will: The Right To Die With Dignity* (1976) 26 CaseWResLRev 485, 491.
14.1. Marshall v Curry [1933] 3 DLR 260, 274 (NSSC).
14.2. *See* Lepp v Hopp (1977) 2 CCLT 183, 195 (AltaSC) and Ellen Picard, Legal Liability Of Doctors And Hospitals In Canada 70 (1978 Carswell Toronto).
15. Mulloy v Hop Sang [1935] 1 WWR 714 (AltaCA).
16. Emergency Medical Aid Act RSA 1970 c122 s3 (am 1975(2) c26 s82 (21)).
17. Rozovsky *Consent To Treatment* (1973) 11 Osgoode Hall LJ 1, 103.
18. Smith v Auckland Hospital Board [1965] NZLR 191, 219 per TA Grasson J.
19. Glanville Williams *Euthanasia* 41 MedLJ 14, 24.
20. *Id* at 17.
21. Schloendorff v Society of New York Hospital 211 NY 125 (1914).
22. [1935] 1 WWR 714 (AltaCA).
23. (1966) 53 DLR (2d) 65.
24. *Id* at 68 per Casey J.
25. Kennedy *Legal Effect Of Request By Terminally Ill And Aged Not To Receive Further Treatment From Doctors* (1976) CrimLRev 217.
26. *Id* at 220.
27. Masny v Carter-Halls-Aldinger Co Ltd [1929] 3 WWR 741.
28. *Id* at 745.
29. In re Estate of Bernice Brooks, alleged incompetent, 32 Ill2d 361, 205 NE2d 435 (1965).
30. Montagne *Informed Consent And The Dying Patient* (1974) 83 Yale LJ 1632.
31. Vaughan *The Right To Die* (1974) 10 CalifLRev 613, 625.
32. The Natural Death legislation has dealt with this area.
33. Address of Pope Pius XII February 24 1957, 49 AAS at 146 quoted in *The Living Will supra* note 14 at 520.
34. R v Instan (1893) 17 CoxCrCases 602, 603, (QB).
34.1. Relman *Michigan's Sensible "Living Will"* May 1979 NewEng JMed 300.
34.2. Michigan House Bill 4058.
35. *See* especially Raible *supra* note 2.
36. The Pope Speaks 3-4 (1956-58): 393-98.
37. See *Sanctity Of Life* Protection of Life Series Study Paper, Law Reform Commission of Canada at 49.
38. Steinberg *The California Natural Death Act—Failure To Provide For Adequate Patient Safeguards And Individual Autonomy* (1977) 9 ConnLRev 203.
39. Meyers *supra* note 7 at 328.
40. *Id* at 327.
41. Steinberg *supra* note 38 at 214.
42. *Id* at 215.
43. *Id* at 216.
44. R v Adams unreported [1957] CrimLRev 365, 773.

45. Craigmyle Baron and Gould Your Death Warrant? 70 (1971) Arlington House New Rochelle NY.
46. *Id* at 51.
47. *See* discussion herein from note 2 to 5.
48. Stephens *The Right To Die* (1977) 1 LMedQ 111.
49. Criminal Code RSC 1970 c C-34.
50. *See* note 47.

51. Stephens *supra* note 48 at 113. Note that 20 members heard 40 minutes of debate on the Private Members bill. The vote following second reading was 51–40 in favor of the bill. The June 1977 election intervened before final reading.
52. R v Bateman (1925) 41 TLR 557, 559 (CCA).
53. Bill 242. Dr. Walter Buck, Private Members Bill.
54. Alta Hansard 3rd session 18th legislature at 1337.
55. Montagne *supra* note 30 at 1658.

THE LIVING WILL

TO MY FAMILY, MY PHYSICIAN, MY CLERGYMAN, MY LAWYER: If the time comes when I can no longer actively take part in decisions for my own future, I wish this statement to stand as the testament of my wishes.

If there is no reasonable expectation of my recovery from physical or mental and spiritual disability, I, _____ , request that I be allowed to die and not to be kept alive by artificial means or heroic measures. I ask also that drugs be mercifully administered to me for terminal suffering even if in relieving pain they may hasten the moment of death. I value life and the dignity of life, so that I am not asking that my life be directly taken, but that my dying not be unreasonably prolonged nor the dignity of life be destroyed.

This request is made, after careful reflection, while I am in good health and spirits. Although this document is not legally binding, you who care for me will, I hope, feel morally bound to take it into account. I recognize that it places a heavy burden of responsibility upon you, and it is with the intention of sharing this responsibility that this statement is made.

_____

_____
Witness

_____
Witness

Place, and date

A Living Will

To make best use of your LIVING WILL

1. Sign and date before two witnesses. (This is to insure that you signed of your own free will and not under any pressure.)

2. If you have a doctor, give him a copy for your medical file and discuss it with him to make sure he is in agreement.

   Give copies to those most likely to be concerned "if the time comes when you can no longer take part in decisions for your own future". Enter their names on bottom line of the Living Will. Keep the original nearby, easily and readily available.

3. Above all discuss your intentions with those closest to you, NOW.

4. It is a good idea to look over your Living Will once a year and redate it and initial the new date to make it clear that your wishes are unchanged.

IMPORTANT

Declarants may wish to add specific statements to the Living Will to be inserted in the space provided for that purpose above the signature.

Possible additional provisions are suggested below:

1. a) I appoint _____
      to make binding decisions concerning my medical treatment.
                          OR
   b) I have discussed my views as to life sustaining measures with the following who understand my wishes

      _____,
      _____,
      _____.

2. Measures of artificial life support in the face of impending death that are especially abhorrent to me are:
   a) Electrical or mechanical resuscitation of my heart when it has stopped beating.
   b) Nasogastric tube feedings when I am paralyzed and no longer able to swallow.
   c) Mechanical respiration by machine when my brain can no longer sustain my own breathing.
   d) _____

3. If it does not jeopardize the chance of my recovery to a meaningful and sentient life or impose an undue burden on my family, I would like to live out my last days at home rather than in a hospital.

4. If any of my tissues are sound and would be of value as transplants to help other people, I freely give my permission for such donation.

Reprinted with permission from Concern for Dying, 250 W. 57th Street, New York, New York 10107.

To My Family, My Physician, My Lawyer and All Others Whom It May Concern

Death is as much a reality as birth, growth, maturity and old age—it is the one certainty of life. If the time comes when I can no longer take part in decisions for my own future, let this statement stand as an expression of my wishes and directions, while I am still of sound mind.

If at such a time the situation should arise in which there is no reasonable expectation of my recovery from extreme physical or mental disability, I direct that I be allowed to die and not be kept alive by medications, artificial means or "heroic measures". I do, however, ask that medication be mercifully administered to me to alleviate suffering even though this may shorten my remaining life.

This statement is made after careful consideration and is in accordance with my strong convictions and beliefs. I want the wishes and directions here expressed carried out to the extent permitted by law. Insofar as they are not legally enforceable, I hope that those to whom this Will is addressed will regard themselves as morally bound by these provisions.

Signed_____

Date _____

Witness_____

Witness_____

Copies of this request have been given to _____

_____

_____

_____

Living Will Declaration

Declaration made this _____ day of _____ (month, year).

I, _____, being of sound mind, willfully and voluntarily make known my desire that my dying shall not be artificially prolonged under the circumstances set forth below, do hereby declare:

If at any time I should have an incurable injury, disease, or illness regarded as a terminal condition by my physician and if my physician has determined that the application of life-sustaining procedures would serve only to artificially prolong the dying process and that my death will occur whether or not life-sustaining procedures are utilized, I direct that such procedures be withheld or withdrawn and that I be permitted to die with only the administration of medication or the performance of any medical procedure deemed necessary to provide me with comfort care.

In the absence of my ability to give directions regarding the use of such life-sustaining procedures, it is my intention that this declaration shall be honored by my family and physician as the final expression of my legal right to refuse medical or surgical treatment and accept the consequences from such refusal.

I understand the full import of this declaration and I am emotionally and mentally competent to make this declaration.

Signed _____

City, County and State of Residence _____

The declarant has been personally known to me and I believe him or her to be of sound mind.

Witness _____

Witness _____

Patient's Bill of Rights

The American Hospital Association presents a Patient's Bill of Rights with the expectation that observance of these rights will contribute to more effective patient care and greater satisfaction for the patient, his physician, and the hospital organization. Further, the Association presents these rights in the expectation that they will be supported by the hospital on behalf of its patients, as an integral part of the healing process. It is recognized that a personal relationship between the physician and the patient is essential for the provision of proper medical care. The traditional physician-patient relationship takes on a new dimension when care is rendered within an organizational structure. Legal precedent has established that the institution itself also has a responsibility to the patient. It is in recognition of these factors that these rights are affirmed.

1. The patient has the right to considerate and respectful care.

2. The patient has the right to obtain from his physician complete current information concerning his diagnosis, treatment, and prognosis in terms the patient can be reasonably expected to understand. When it is not medically advisable to give such information to the patient, the information should be made available to an appropriate person in his behalf. He has the right to know by name, the physician responsible for coordinating his care.

*3. The patient has the right to receive from his physician information necessary to give informed consent prior to the start of any procedure and/or treatment. Except in emergencies, such information for informed consent, should include but not necessarily be limited to the specific procedure and/or treatment, the medically significant risks involved, and the probable duration of incapacitation. Where medically significant alternatives for care or treatment exist, or when the patient requests information concerning medical alternatives, the patient has the right to such information. The patient also has the right to know the name of the person responsible for the procedures and/or treatment.

*4. The patient has the right to refuse treatment to the extent permitted by law, and to be informed of the medical consequences of his action.

5. The patient has the right to every consideration of his privacy concerning his own medical care program. Case discussion, consultation, examination, and treatment are confidential and should be conducted discreetly. Those not directly involved in his care must have the permission of the patient to be present.

6. The patient has the right to expect that all communications and records pertaining to his care should be treated as confidential.

7. The patient has the right to expect that within its capacity a hospital must make reasonable response to the request of a patient for services. The hospital must provide evaluation, service, and/or referral as indicated by the urgency of the case. When medically permissible a patient may be transferred to another facility only after he has received complete information and explanation concerning the needs for and alternatives to such a transfer. The institution to which the patient is to be transferred must first have accepted the patient for transfer.

8. The patient has the right to obtain information as to any relationship of his hospital to other health care and educational institutions insofar as his care is concerned. The patient has the right to obtain information as to the existence of any professional relationships among individuals by name, who are treating him.

*Reprinted by Concern for Dying, 250 West 57th Street, New York, N.Y. 10107.

*9. The patient has the right to be advised if the hospital proposes to engage in or perform human experimentation affecting his care or treatment. The patient has the right to refuse to participate in such research projects.

10. The patient has the right to expect reasonable continuity of care. He has the right to know in advance what appointment times and physicians are available and where. The patient has the right to expect that the hospital will provide a mechanism whereby he is informed by his physician or a delegate of the physician of the patient's continuing health care requirements following discharge.

11. The patient has the right to examine and receive an explanation of his bill regardless of source of payment.

12. The patient has the right to know what hospital rules and regulations apply to his conduct as a patient.

No catalogue of rights can guarantee for the patient the kind of treatment he has a right to expect. A hospital has many functions to perform, including the prevention and treatment of disease, the education of both health professionals and patients, and the conduct of clinical research. All these activities must be conducted with an overriding concern for the patient, and, above all, the recognition of his dignity as a human being. Success in achieving this recognition assures success in the defense of the rights of the patient.

DEFINING DEATH

On the Definition and Criterion of Death

James L. Bernat, M.D.; Charles M. Culver, M.D., Ph.D.; and Bernard Gert, Ph.D.

The permanent cessation of functioning of the organism as a whole is the definition underlying the traditional understanding of death. We suggest the total and irreversible loss of functioning of the whole brain as the sole criterion of death; this has always been an implicit criterion of death. If artificial ventilation is present, only completely validated brain dysfunction tests should be used to show that this criterion of death is satisfied. In most cases without artificial ventilation, permanent loss of cardiopulmonary function is sufficient. We propose a statutory definition of death based on the criterion of total and irreversible cessation of whole brain functions but allowing physicians to declare death according to their customary practices in most cases.

Much of the confusion arising from the current brain death controversy is due to the lack of rigorous separation and ordered formulation of three distinct elements: the definition of death, the medical criterion for determining that death has occurred, and the tests to prove that the criterion has been satisfied. This confusion can be reduced by the formulation of a definition of death that makes its ordinary meaning explicit, the choice of a criterion of death that shows that the definition has been fulfilled, and the selection of tests that indicate with perfect validity that the criterion is satisfied.

Another source of confusion has been introduced by the definitions of death that appear in legal dictionaries and the new statutory definitions of death. These do not account for what the layman actually means by death, but merely state the criteria by which physicians legally determine when death has occurred. "Death," however,

is not a technical term, but a common term in everyday use. We believe that a proper understanding of the ordinary meaning of the word or concept of death must be developed before a medical criterion of death is chosen. We must decide what is commonly meant by death before physicians can decide how to measure it.

Agreement on the correct definition and criterion of death is literally a life and death matter. Whether a spontaneously breathing patient in a chronic vegetative state is classified as dead or alive depends on our understanding of the definition of death. Even given the correct definition, the status of a patient with a totally and permanently dysfunctional brain who is being maintained on a ventilator depends on the criterion of death employed. Providing the definition is primarily a philosophical task; the choice of the criterion is primarily medical; and the selection of the tests to prove that the criterion is satisfied is solely a medical matter.

The Definition of Death

DEATH AS A PROCESS OR AN EVENT

Death has often been described as a process rather than an event (1). Evidence for this claim is found in the fact that a series of degenerative and destructive changes occurs in the tissues of an organism, usually following but sometimes prior to the irreversible cessation of spontaneous ventilation and circulation. These changes include: necrosis of brain cells, necrosis of other vital organ cells, cooling, rigor mortis, dependent lividity, and putrefaction. This process actually persists for years, even centuries, until the skeletal remains have disintegrated. Further, this process could be viewed as beginning with the failure of certain organ systems during life. Because these

▶ From the Division of Neurology, Department of Medicine and the Departments of Psychiatry and Philosophy; Dartmouth Medical School and Dartmouth College, Hanover, New Hampshire; and the Department of Medicine, Veterans Administration Hospital, White River Junction, Vermont.

changes occur in a fairly regular and ineluctable fashion, stipulation of any particular point in this process as the moment of death seems arbitrary.

We believe that a definition of death stipulating that it occurs at a more or less definite time is preferable to a definition that makes death a process. If we regard death as a process, then either the process starts when the person is still living, which confuses the "process of death" with the process of dying, for we all regard someone who is dying as not yet dead, or the "process of death" starts when the person is no longer alive, which confuses death with the process of disintegration. Death should be viewed not as a process but as the event that separates the process of dying from the process of disintegration.

Although the definition of death as a process has value as a description of biological events and allows the avoidance of choosing between the various definitions of death discussed below, this view makes it impossible to precisely declare the time of death. This is not a trivial issue. There are pressing medical, legal, social, and religious reasons to declare the time of death with precision, including the interpretation of wills, burial times and procedures, mourning times, and decisions regarding the aggressiveness of medical support. There are no compensatory reasons to regard death as a process and not an event in the formulation of a definition of death. We shall say that the event of death occurs at some definite if not precisely determinable time.

CHOICES FOR A DEFINITION OF DEATH

The definition of death must encompass the common usage of the term, for "death" is a word used by everyone, and not primarily in the fields of medicine or law. Because certain facts are assumed in its common usage, we shall assume them as well and not attempt to answer the speculations of science fiction, such as if the brain continues to function independently of the rest of the organism (2, 3). Thus, we assume that all and only living organisms can die, that the living can be distinguished from the dead with fairly good reliability, and that the moment when an organism leaves the former state and enters the latter can be determined. We know that literally death is permanent. Although there are religious theories about death involving the soul leaving the body, when a person dies, religious persons and secularists do not disagree in their ordinary use of the term "dead." We acknowledge that the body can remain physically intact for some time after death and some isolated parts of the organism may continue to function (for example, it is commonly believed that hair and nails continue to grow after death).

We define death as the permanent cessation of functioning of the organism as a whole. We do not mean the whole organism, for example, the sum of its tissue and organ parts, but rather the highly complex interaction of its organ subsystems. Also, the organism need not be whole or complete, it may have lost a limb or an organ (such as the spleen), but it still remains an organism. The spontaneous and innate interrelationship of all or most of the remaining subsystems and the interaction of the per-

haps impaired organism with its environment is to be regarded as the functioning of the organism as a whole.

After the organism as a whole has permanently ceased to function, individual subsystems may function for a time. While this is not true for spontaneous ventilation, which ceases either immediately after or just before the permanent cessation of functioning of the organism as a whole, it is true for spontaneous circulation, which with artificial ventilation may persist for up to 2 weeks after the organism as a whole has ceased to function.

The functioning of the organism as a whole means the spontaneous and innate activities carried out by the integration of all or most subsystems (for example, neuroendocrine control), and at least limited response to the environment (for example, temperature change and responses to light and sound). However, the integration of all of the subsystems is not necessary. Individual subsystems may be replaced (such as, by pacemakers, ventilators, pressors) without changing the status of the organism as a whole.

Temperature regulation is one example of an activity of the organism as a whole. The control of this complex process is located in the hypothalamus and is important for normal maintenance of all cellular processes. It is lost when the organism as a whole has ceased to function. Although consciousness and cognition are sufficient evidence for the functioning of the organism as a whole in higher animals, even for them these functions are not necessary. Lower organisms never have consciousness and when a higher organism is comatose, proof of the functioning of the organism as a whole may still be evident, such as temperature regulation.

We believe that this definition encompasses the traditional meaning of death. Death is considered a biological occurrence not unique to humans, and other higher animals would be considered dead according to the same definition. As a biological phenomenon, death should apply equally to related species. When we talk of the death of a man we mean the same thing as we do when we talk of the death of a dog or a cat. This is supported by our ordinary use of the term death, by law, and by tradition. It is also in accord with social and religious practices and is not likely to be affected by future changes in technology. In their recent monograph, Grisez and Boyle (4) reach similar conclusions.

The definition of death as the irreversible loss of that which is essentially significant to the nature of man (5) seems initially very attractive but we disagree with it on several grounds. First, it does not contain what is commonly meant by the term. According to common usage, stating that a person has lost that which is essentially significant to the nature of man, but is still alive is not self-contradictory. For example, we acknowledge that permanently comatose patients in chronic vegetative states are sufficiently brain-damaged that they have irreversibly lost all that is essentially significant to the nature of man but we still consider them to be living (for example, Karen Ann Quinlan [6]).

The patients described by Brierley and associates (7) are also in this category. These patients had complete neocortical destruction with preservation of brainstem and diencephalic structures. They had isoelectric EEGs and were permanently comatose, although they had normal spontaneous breathing and brainstem reflexes; they were essentially in a permanent, severe, and chronic vegetative state (8). They retained many of the vital functions of the organism as a whole, including neuroendocrine control and the control of circulation and breathing.

This proposed definition actually states what it is for an organism to cease to be a person rather than stating what it is for that organism which is a person to die. The concept "person" is not biological but rather a concept defined in terms of certain kinds of abilities and qualities of awareness. It is inherently vague. Death is a biological concept. Thus in a literal sense, death can be applied directly only to biological organisms and not to persons. We do not object to the phrase "death of a person" but the phrase in common usage actually means the death of the organism which was the person. For example, one might overhear in the hospital wards, "The person in room 612 died last night." Obviously, in this common usage one is referring to the death of the organism that was a person. By our analysis, Veatch (5) and others have used the phrase "death of a person" metaphorically, applying it to an organism that has ceased to be a person but has not died.

Without question, consciousness and cognition are essential human attributes. If they are lost, life has lost its meaning. A patient in a chronic vegetative state is usually regarded as living only in the most basic, biological sense. But this basic biological sense is essential to our definition of death. We must not confuse the death of an organism which was a person, with an organism's ceasing to be a person. Immediately aware of the loss of personhood in these patients, we are repulsed by the idea of continuing to treat them as if they were persons. But considering these chronic vegetative patients as actually dead leads to some serious problems. First, a slippery slope condition would be introduced wherein the question could be asked: how much neocortical damage is necessary before we declare a patient dead? Surely patients in chronic vegetative states, although usually not totally satisfying the tests for neocortical destruction, have permanently lost their consciousness and cognition. Then what about the somewhat less severely brain damaged patient?

By considering permanent loss of consciousness and cognition as a criterion for ceasing to be a person and not for death of the organism as a whole, the slippery slope phenomenon is put where it belongs: not in the definition of death, but in the determination of possible grounds for non-voluntary euthanasia. The justification of non-voluntary euthanasia must be kept strictly separate from the definition of death. Most of us would like our organism to die when we cease to be persons, but this should not be accomplished by blurring the distinctions between biological death and the loss of personhood.

A practical problem also arises in considering chronically vegetative patients with spontaneous ventilation to be dead. To bury such patients while they breathe and have a heartbeat, most would view as at least esthetically unacceptable. Then how will these vital signs be stopped and by whom? Disconnecting a ventilator from a recently declared dead patient fulfilling tests of permanent loss of whole brain functioning is one thing; suffocating a spontaneously breathing patient is another.

The Criterion of Death

Having argued that the correct definition of death is permanent cessation of functioning of the organism as a whole, we will proceed to inspect the two competing criteria of death: the permanent loss of cardiopulmonary functioning and the total and irreversible loss of functioning of the whole brain.

CHARACTERISTICS OF OPTIMUM CRITERIA AND TESTS

Given that death is the permanent cessation of functioning of the organism as a whole, a criterion or set of tests will yield a false positive if it incorrectly denies the possibility for that organism to function as a whole. By far the most important requirement for a criterion of death and for a test is to yield no false positives.

Of secondary importance, the criterion and tests should produce few and relatively brief false negatives, such as the prediction that the organism as a whole may again function when it will not. Current tests may produce many false negatives during the 30-minute to 24-hour interval between the successive neurologic examinations required for the determination of irreversible whole brain dysfunction. Certain sets of tests, particularly those requiring electrocerebral silence by EEG, may produce false negative determinations if EEG artifact is present and cannot confidently be distinguished from brain wave activity. Generally, a few brief false negatives are tolerable, and even inevitable since tests must be delineated conservatively in order to eliminate any possibility of false positives.

Further, as has been noted (9), every physician should be able to use the tests easily to determine that the criterion is satisfied. Also, although the tests are established, validated, applied, and interpreted by medical professionals, they must originate in a criterion with significance understandable to a layman.

PERMANENT LOSS OF CARDIOPULMONARY FUNCTIONING

The permanent termination of heart and lung function has been a criterion of death throughout history. The ancients observed that all other bodily functions ceased shortly after cessation of these vital functions, and the irreversible process of bodily disintegration inevitably followed. Thus, loss of spontaneous cardiopulmonary function was found to predict permanent nonfunctioning of the organism as a whole, therefore serving adequately as a criterion of death.

Because of current ventilation/perfusion technology, the loss of spontaneous cardiopulmonary functioning is no longer necessarily a prediction of permanent nonfunctioning of the organism as a whole. To consider a conscious, talking patient with apnea from bulbar poliomyelitis requiring an iron lung and who has developed asystole requiring a permanent pacemaker as dead is absurd.

Also, now that ventilation and perfusion can be mechanically maintained, an organism with permanent loss of whole brain functioning can have permanently ceased to function as a whole days to weeks before the heart and lungs cease to function with artificial support. In this light, the heart and lungs seem to have no special relationship to the functioning of the organism as a whole. Continued artificially supported cardiopulmonary function is no longer perfectly correlated with life and the loss of spontaneous cardiopulmonary functioning is no longer perfectly correlated with death.

TOTAL AND IRREVERSIBLE LOSS OF WHOLE BRAIN FUNCTIONING

The criterion for cessation of functioning of the organism as a whole is permanent loss of functioning of the entire brain. This criterion is perfectly correlated with the permanent cessation of functioning of the organism as a whole because the brain is necessary for the functioning of the organism as a whole. It integrates, generates, interrelates, and controls complex bodily activities. A patient on a ventilator with a totally destroyed brain is merely a group of artificially maintained subsystems since the organism as a whole has ceased to function. Korein (10) has made a further defense of the brain as the critical system controlling the organism as a whole, using thermodynamics and information theory.

The brain generates the signal for breathing through brainstem ventilatory centers, and aids in the control of circulation through medullary blood pressure control centers. Destruction of the brain produces apnea and generalized vasodilatation; in all cases, despite the most aggressive support, the adult heart stops within 1 week, and that of the child within 2 weeks (11). Thus, when the organism as a whole has ceased to function, the artificially supported "vital" subsystems quickly fail. Many other functions of the organism as a whole including neuroendocrine control, temperature control, food searching behaviors, and sexual activity, reside in the more primitive regions (hypothalamus, brainstem) of the brain. Thus total and irreversible loss of functioning of the whole brain and not merely the neocortex is required as the criterion for the permanent loss of the functioning of the organism as a whole.

Using permanent loss of functioning of the whole brain as the criterion for death of the organism as a whole is also consistent with tradition. Throughout history, whenever a physician was called to ascertain the occurrence of death, his examination importantly included the following signs indicative of permanent loss of functioning of the whole brain: unresponsivity, lack of spontaneous movements including breathing, and absence of pupillary light response. Only one important sign, lack of heartbeat, was not directly indicative of whole brain destruction. Yet the heartbeat stops within several minutes of apnea and permanent absence of the "vital signs" is an important sign of permanent loss of whole brain functioning. Thus, permanent loss of whole brain functioning has in an important sense always been the underlying criterion of death.

The Tests of Death

Given the definition of death as the permanent cessation of functioning of the organism as a whole, and the criterion of death as the total and irreversible cessation of functioning of the whole brain, the next step is examination of the available tests of death.

CESSATION OF HEARTBEAT AND VENTILATION

The physical findings of permanent absence of heartbeat and respiration are the traditional tests of death. In the vast majority of deaths not complicated by artificial ventilation, these classic tests are still applicable. They show that the criterion of death has been satisfied since they always quickly produce permanent loss of functioning of the whole brain. However, when mechanical ventilation is being used, these tests lose most of their utility due to the production of numerous false negatives for as long a time as days to weeks, for example, death of the organism as a whole with still intact circulatory-ventilatory subsystems. Thus determination of the circulation-ventilation tests will suffice in most instances of death, and only in the case of artificial maintenance of circulation or ventilation will the special brain dysfunction tests be needed.

IRREVERSIBLE CESSATION OF WHOLE BRAIN FUNCTIONING

Numerous formalized sets of tests have been established to determine that the criterion of permanent loss of whole brain functioning has been met. These include, among others, the publications of the Harvard Medical School Ad Hoc Committee (12) and the National Institutes of Health Collaborative Study of Cerebral Survival (13). They all have been recently reviewed (14, 15). What we call tests have sometimes themselves been called "criteria," but it is important to distinguish these second-level criteria from the first-level criteria. While the first-level criteria determining the death of an organism must be understood by the layman, the second-level criteria or tests determining permanent loss of functioning of the whole brain need not be understood by anyone except qualified clinicians. To avoid confusion, we prefer to use the designation tests for the second-level criteria.

All the proposed tests require total and permanent absence of all functioning of the brainstem and both hemispheres. They vary slightly from one set to another, but all require unresponsivity (deep coma), absent pupillary light reflexes, apnea, and absent cephalic reflexes including corneals, gag, oculovestibulars, and oculocephalics. They also require the absence of drug intoxication, and the newer sets require the demonstration of a structural brain lesion. Isoelectric EEGs are generally required, and tests disclosing absence of cerebral blood flow are of confirmatory value (13). All tests require the given dysfunction to be present for a particular time interval, which in the case of absence of cerebral blood flow may be as short as 30 minutes.

There are ample studies (reviewed by Veith and associates [16]) which show perfect correlation between the brain dysfunction tests of the Ad Hoc Committee of the

Harvard Medical School and total brain necrosis at post-mortem examination. Veith and associates (16) conclude that "the validity of the criteria must be considered to be established with as much certainty as is possible in biology or medicine." Thus, when a physician ascertains that a patient fulfills the validated brain dysfunction tests, he can be confident that the loss of whole brain functioning is permanent. Physicians should only apply tests which have been completed validated.

The Determination of Death

The consideration of several examples of death to illustrate the applications of our analysis is helpful. We will review deaths by primary respiratory arrest, primary cardiac arrest, and primary brain destruction. In each case the process of dying, the event of death, and the process of disintegration will be identified.

Death by Hanging: In a properly executed hanging, a displaced fracture of the odontoid process ("hangman's fracture") occurs which acutely compresses the cervical spinal cord and produces instantaneous apnea. Some degree of airway compromise and carotid artery compression undoubtedly also occurs, but we will restrict our attention to the principal fatal effect, that of primary respiratory arrest.

As apnea persists, progressive hypoxemia and acidosis produce cardiac arrest within several minutes. Throughout this time, the brain is becoming progressively ischemic and finally, within a short period after cardiac arrest, suffers total infarction. Cooling, lividity, rigor mortis inevitably follow.

While stating that death occurs at the moment of the neck fracture may sound plausible, clearly this is not the case. The neck fracture and subsequent respiratory and cardiac arrests are part of the process of dying. Only once the whole brain has become irreversibly dysfunctional by the cardiopulmonary arrest has the event of death occurred. This event is then followed by the process of disintegration. If the victim had been placed on a ventilator immediately after the neck fracture, permanent loss of whole brain functioning would have been prevented. Thus the process of dying would have been reversed and death prevented. A similar, and even more dramatic example, is death by decapitation, though at present there may be no way to reverse this process.

Death by Chronic Disease: Many patients dying of chronic diseases suffer spontaneous ventricular fibrillation. As cardiac output ceases, so does cerebral blood flow so that the brain becomes progressively ischemic. When medullary ischemia occurs, apnea is produced which accelerates the loss of brain and other organ functioning. Finally the brain becomes totally infarcted, and events of disintegration proceed.

While ventricular fibrillation may be said to be the proximal cause of death, clearly the patient is not dead at the moment the heart stops or even at the time the respirations cease. At these times he is dying. Death occurs when the brain has become totally and irreversibly dysfunctional by ischemic infarction. A timely resuscitation prior to total loss of brain functioning would reverse the process of dying. Death, of course, is irreversible by definition.

Death by Massive Head Injury: These injuries are often complicated by immediate and severe cerebral edema. When the resulting increased intracranial pressure exceeds that of systolic blood pressure, cerebral blood flow ceases and whole brain infarction occurs. At the time of head injury or minutes later when whole brain infarction is proceeding, medullary failure produces apnea. Progressive hypoxemia and acidosis then produce ventricular fibrillation or asystole. Untreated, the organism undergoes the process of cooling, dependent lividity, and rigor mortis.

However, if the patient were placed on a ventilator immediately after irreversible whole brain dysfunction but prior to cardiac arrest, the circulatory functioning could probably be maintained for a few days. If bedside testing confirmed fulfillment of validated brain dysfunction tests, the difficult situation of preserved circulatory-ventilatory subsystems despite the cessation of functioning of the organism as a whole would be present. Death would have occurred at the time the brain had totally and permanently lost all functioning. In this case, mechanical ventilation and other aggressive therapeutics would have delayed the process of disintegration, although the event of death has already occurred.

The Statute of Death

Veith and colleagues (17) have recently emphasized the need for recognizing the role of the brain in determining death in statutory definitions of death. The model statute of Capron and Kass (18), the best-known and adopted by five states reads:

> A person will be considered dead if in the announced opinion of a physician, based on ordinary standards of medical practice, he has experienced an irreversible cessation of spontaneous respiratory and circulatory functions. In the event that artificial means of support preclude a determination that these functions have ceased, a person will be considered dead if in the announced opinion of a physician, based on ordinary standards of medical practice, he has experienced an irreversible cessation of spontaneous brain functions. Death will have occurred at the time when the relevant functions ceased.

The Capron-Kass statute, like the Kansas statute (19) that it criticizes, has two distinct criteria: first, irreversible cessation of spontaneous respiratory and circulatory functions; and second, when this cannot be determined, irreversible cessation of spontaneous brain functions. No explanation is given for the reason irreversible cessation of spontaneous brain functions should be used only when one cannot determine that the other criterion is satisfied. And indeed, there is no reason for limiting its use in that way. If someone has his head cut off or completely crushed, there is no need to determine that he has also suffered an irreversible cessation of spontaneous respiratory and circulatory functions.

Recognizing that the Capron-Kass statute had two distinct criteria, in 1975 the American Bar Association (A.B.A.) published their model statute of death (20). It states: "For all legal purposes, a human body with irreversible cessation of total brain function, according to usual and customary standards of medical practice, shall be considered dead."

Because this statute has a single criterion of death, the irreversible cessation of whole brain functioning, it is an improvement over that of Capron-Kass. However, it has a shortcoming which Capron and Kass have avoided. It does not state that physicians can declare death in their customary fashion, using the circulation-ventilation tests in the overwhelming majority of deaths not complicated by artificial ventilation.

We propose a statute with a single criterion that does not require any change in current medical practice. It states:

> A person will be considered dead if in the announced opinion of a physician, based on ordinary standards of medical practice, he has experienced an irreversible cessation of all brain functions. Irreversible cessation of spontaneous respiratory and circulatory functions shall be considered sufficient proof for the irreversible cessation of brain functions in the absence of any medical evidence to the contrary. Death will have occurred at the time when the brain functions have irreversibly ceased.

This statute has several advantages over the Capron-Kass proposal. First, it meets all of the standards that they proposed for an acceptable statute. It does not result in Brierley's (7) patients being declared dead. Indeed, all and only those patients determined to be dead by the Capron-Kass statute meet the criterion of this statute. Thus it allows for the change in the declaration of death they desire, without going too far. It is incremental, but unlike their statutory definition, it proposes a single criterion. Irreversible cessation of whole brain functioning is the criterion of death. Additionally, this statute allows physicians to make their determinations of death in exactly the way they do now, which is an improvement over the A.B.A. statute.

By using the irreversible cessation of spontaneous circulatory and respiratory functions as a test for irreversible loss of whole brain function, our proposed statute allows us to answer the question raised by Jonas (21): "Why are they alive if the heart, etc., works naturally but not alive when it works artificially?" Spontaneous circulation and ventilation proves that at least part of the brain continues to function whereas artificial support does not show this. Thus in the latter case one needs to discover directly if the whole brain has permanently ceased to function.

Finally, our statute explicitly states the fact that it is the brain, not the heart and lungs, which is important in the functioning of the organism as a whole. Thus it allows for new technological advances such as a totally implantable artificial heart which may continue to function after the brain has ceased to function.

In conclusion, we include only what we really believe to be the criterion for death in our statutory definition: the irreversible cessation of total brain functions. We use irreversible cessation of spontaneous ventilation and circulation as the usual method for determining death, as the Capron and Kass statute prescribes, but unlike them, we do not elevate this method into a criterion of death. Rather, it is considered as presently used, the most common test for determining that the criterion of death—irreversible total cessation of whole brain functioning—has been satisfied.

ACKNOWLEDGMENTS: Grant support: Dr. Gert is a recipient of a Sustained Development Award, OSS-8018088, National Science Foundation.

▶ Requests for reprints should be addressed to James L. Bernat, M.D.; Division of Neurology, Department of Medicine; Dartmouth Medical School; Hanover, NH 03755.

References

1. MORISON RS. Death: process or event? *Science.* 1971;**173**:694-8.
2. GERT B. Can the brain have a pain? *Philosophy and Phenomenological Research.* 1967;**27**:432-6.
3. GERT B. Personal identity and the body. *Dialogue.* 1971;**10**:458-78.
4. GRISEZ G, BOYLE JM JR. *Life and Death with Liberty and Justice. A Contribution to the Euthanasia Debate.* Notre Dame, Indiana: University of Notre Dame Press; 1979.
5. VEATCH RM. *Death, Dying and the Biological Revolution: Our Last Quest for Responsibility.* New Haven: Yale University Press; 1976.
6. BERESFORD HR. The Quinlan decision: problems and legislative alternatives. *Ann Neurol.* 1977;**2**:74-81.
7. BRIERLEY JB, ADAMS JH, GRAHAM DI, SIMPSOM JA. Neocortical death after cardiac arrest. *Lancet.* 1971;**2**:560-5.
8. JENNETT B, PLUM F. Persistent vegetative state after brain damage: a syndrome in search of a name. *Lancet.* 1972;**1**:734-7.
9. TASK FORCE ON DEATH AND DYING OF THE INSTITUTE OF SOCIETY, ETHICS, AND THE LIFE SCIENCES. Refinements in criteria for the determination of death: an appraisal. *JAMA.* 1972;**221**:48-53.
10. KOREIN J. The problem of brain death: development and history. *Ann NY Acad Sci.* 1978;**315**:19-38.
11. INGVAR DH, BRUN A, JOHANSSON L, SAMMUELSSON SM. Survival after severe cerebral anoxia with destruction of the cerebral cortex: the apallic syndrome. *Ann NY Acad Sci.* 1978;**315**:184-214.
12. BEECHER HK. A definition of irreversible coma: report of the Ad Hoc Committee of the Harvard Medical School to examine the definition of brain death. *JAMA.* 1968;**205**:337-40.
13. A COLLABORATIVE STUDY. An appraisal of the criteria of cerebral death: a summary statement. *JAMA.* 1977;**237**:982-6.
14. BLACK PM. Brain death. *N Engl J Med.* 1978;**299**:338-44, 393-401.
15. MOLINARI GF. Review of clinical criteria of brain death. *Ann NY Acad Sci.* 1978;**315**:62-9.
16. VEITH FJ, FEIN JM, TENDLER MD, VEATCH RM, KLEIMAN MA, KALKINES G. Brain death: I. A status report of medical and ethical considerations. *JAMA.* 1977;**238**:1651-5.
17. VEITH FJ, FEIN JM, TENDLER MD, VEATCH RM, KLEIMAN MA, KALKINES G. Brain death: II. A status report of legal considerations. *JAMA.* 1977;**238**:1744-8.
18. CAPRON AM, KASS LR. A statutory definition of the standards for determining human death: an appraisal and a proposal. *Univ Penn Law Rev.* 1972;**121**:87-118.
19. KENNEDY IM. The Kansas statute on death—an appraisal. *N Engl J Med.* 1971;**285**:946-50.
20. House of Delegates redefines death, urges redefinition of rape, and undoes the Houston amendments. *Am Bar Assoc J.* 1975;**61**:463-4.
21. JONAS H. *Philosophical Essays: From Ancient Creed to Technological Man.* Englewood Cliffs, New Jersey: Prentice-Hall; 1974:134-40.

Definition of Death: An Emerging Consensus

Dennis J. Horan

In the past 10 years 26 state legislatures have passed statutes "defining death,"[1] and three state supreme courts and several trial courts have adopted "brain death" definitions.[2] This flurry of legal activity has been precipitated by much scholarly legal, medical, and ethical writing addressing this topic, loosely described as definition of death legislation.[3] That description is imprecise since what really is at issue is not a definition of death but a decision as to whether an additional criterion for determining death may be made legal.

The phrase "brain death" is inartful and somewhat confusing. Death is diagnosed when a person is dead. "Brain death" is merely a descriptive, shorthand way of referring to the debate on whether this additional method of diagnosing death may be used by physicians when circumstances so warrant.

Obviously the issue is not an additional definition of death since what has been true remains true: you are dead when you are dead. One does not suddenly redefine the fact that you are dead unless someone intends to define that as dead which is not dead. Such intended definitions have been part of the problem surrounding this issue as shall be discussed later.

Death is a diagnosis. Physicians have diagnosed death without the aid of statutes for ages. Why then in the last 10 years has it become necessary for state legislatures and courts to embark on a sea of legislative controversy to do for the medical profession what it heretofore has been capable of doing for itself? Why, indeed, did the medical profession itself see a necessity for promoting legislative determination of brain death?

Part of the answer lies in the problems created by technology. As resuscitative technology became more and more sophisticated its use became more and more common. That use created a problem. People were maintained on machinery after a resuscitative crisis, but they never regained consciousness. Physicians soon realized that that state of unconsciousness had become irreversible, and that the brain was no longer functioning. The machinery was maintaining heart and pulse rate, but was it maintaining the life of a person? A conceptual problem became obvious at this point.

In the past the diagnosis of death had always been based on the customary standards of medicine for making such a diagnosis: absence of circulatory and respiratory functions. Even the law accepted this standard, although its inquiry into the problem had been practically non-existent.[4] In the current problem, however, circulatory and respiratory functions were present because a machine was causing them to be present. On what basis, then, could a person whose circulatory and respiratory functions were being maintained by machinery be declared dead?

A little common sense reflection at this point would have solved the problem and headed off much of the unnecessary great debate which followed: circulatory and respiratory functions ceased when the brain ceased functioning and thereby caused the circulatory and respiratory systems to stop. In short, death occurred when the brain died.[5]

Instead, several movements began at this time among certain circles which caused even greater confusion. The brain is composed of several parts which include the medulla, cerebellum, midbrain, and cerebrum. Cognitive function is thought to be a product of the cerebrum. One group of commentators proposed to society that once the cognitive function was lost then that person should no longer be considered a person and should be defined as dead. Cognition, they said, makes you human. Your thoughts are your humanum, and when the power to think is gone the humanum is gone. Death of the cerebrum alone, they argued, was the equivalent of death of the person.[6] In the brain death debate this position presents the greatest danger to a value system which rejects euthanasia.

Two more groups of physicians added to the confusion. Fear of litigation made one group hesitant to arrive at the very common-sense notion that a brain is dead. Since circulation and respiration were being maintained, albeit artificially, they wondered if declaring such a person dead might lead to malpractice suits or criminal prosecution. This fear rendered them unable to act.[7]

Another group of physicians was interested in developing the medical art of transplanting organs from one

Reprinted with permission from *TRIAL* Magazine, The Association of Trial Lawyers of America, December, 1980.

person to another. In recent years organ transplantation had become possible, and advances in technology were speeding its use. Organ transplantation, however, had to take place as soon as possible after the donor's death in order that the donor organs would be optimally viable in order to facilitate successful transplants. Delays in diagnosing death, it was said, make organ transplantation difficult if not impossible. This group of physicians saw brain death as a possible acceptable social means for curing what they had considered an important problem stalling medical progress.[8]

A movement began to resolve the impasse. The medical profession was split on the issue, but enough physicians feared the growing momentum of litigation to feel it necessary to seek legislative help in an area that should have been solved by the common-sense use of customary medical practice.

The impasse was broken by the passage of the first brain death statute in Kansas in 1970. Since that time 25 other states have passed similar statutes.[9] These statutes attempt to retain the traditional standards of absence of respiration and circulation for diagnosing death while adding the standard of brain death.

The statutes generally follow one of four different types.[10]

The first is modeled after the Kansas law, which provides for alternative definitions of death—one based on brain death, the other based on absence of spontaneous respiratory and cardiac functions. The "brain death" section is as follows:

"A person will be considered medically and legally dead if, in the opinion of a physician, based on ordinary standards of medical practice, there is the absence of spontaneous brain function; and if based on ordinary standards of medical practice, during reasonable attempts to either maintain or restore spontaneous circulatory or respiratory function in the absence of aforesaid brain function, it appears that further attempts at resuscitation or supportive maintenance will not succeed, death will have occurred at the time when these conditions first coincide. Death is to be pronounced before artificial means of supporting respiratory and

circulatory function are terminated and before any vital organ is removed for purposes of transplantation."

Maryland, New Mexico, and Virginia have enacted statutes substantially similar except that the Virginia statute requires the additional opinion of a consulting physician who is "a specialist in the field of neurology, neurosurgery, or electroencephalography." Commentators have criticized this alternative definition approach on the basis that in reality there are not two different ways of dying as the statute seems to imply.[11]

A second type of statute provides a determination of death based on absence of brain function, to be used only when the heart and lungs are maintained artificially. This approach is illustrated by the Michigan provision:

"A person will be considered dead if in the announced opinion of a physician, based on ordinary standards of medical practice in the community, there is the irreversible cessation of spontaneous respiratory and circulatory function. If artificial means of support preclude a determination that these functions have ceased, a person will be considered dead if in the announced opinion of a physician, based on ordinary standards of medical practice in the community, there is the irreversible cessation of spontaneous brain function. Death will have occurred at the time when the relevant functions ceased."

Statutes in Alaska, Hawaii, Iowa, Louisiana, and West Virginia are substantially similar except that the Iowa and Hawaii statutes require the opinion of a consulting physician as well as the attending physician.

The Tennessee statute is an example of a third type of statute which follows the American Bar Association (ABA) model and which reads: "For all legal purposes, a human body, with irreversible cessation of total brain function, according to usual and customary standards of medical practice, shall be considered dead."

This type differs in that there is no explicit provision made for determination of death based on respiratory and cardiac cessation, the traditional means used to diagnose death, although such is implied since brain death is a clinical diagnosis, and it

was not intended by the ABA that traditional means of determining death were to be superseded by the statute. This approach is also followed in California, Idaho, Illinois, Montana, and Oklahoma. California and Idaho require independent confirmation of death by a second physician.

A fourth type of statute provides that a person *may be* pronounced dead if he or she has suffered irreversible cessation of spontaneous brain function. This type of statute permits, but does not require, a physician to pronounce a person dead if brain function cessation has occurred. The Georgia statute is of this type, stating: "A person may be pronounced dead if it is determined that the person has suffered an irreversible cessation of brain function. There shall be independent confirmation of the death by another physician." Oregon is similar.

Several states make provisions within their statutes for organ donation. The California, Hawaii, and Louisiana statutes provide that a physician who makes a determination of brain death may not participate in the removal or transplantation of any organs of the deceased. Most ethical commentators see such a provision as necessary in order to remove potential conflicts of interest for the physician making the determination of brain death.[12]

The Courts' Responses

Several courts have had the opportunity to deal with the brain death problem. Their basic approach has been to accept the testimony of the neurological experts on this issue. That testimony generally is provided so that instructions can be drafted which will indicate to the court and jury an intelligible meaning and definition of brain death. In *Tucker v. Lower,* for example, which was one of the earliest cases to present the question of definition of death in the context of organ transplantation, the court instructed the jury that death occurs at a precise time, and that it is defined as the cessation of life, the ceasing to exist, a total stoppage of the circulation of the blood and a cessation of the animal and vital functions consequent thereto such as respiration and pulsation. This court initially refused to employ a medical concept of neurological or brain death in establishing a rule of law. In its charge to the jurors, however, the court did allow all possible causes of death to be considered by them, including brain death. Unfortunately, the case was never appealed, and there is no reported precedent. In addition, the instructions are somewhat confusing.[13]

The Massachusetts supreme court accepted the concept of brain death in the case of *Commonwealth v. Golston*.[14] The court instructed the jury that brain death occurs "when in the opinion of a licensed physician based on ordinary and accepted standards of medical practice, there has been a total and irreversible cessation of spontaneous brain functions and further attempts at resuscitation or continuous support of maintenance would not be successful in restoring such functions." In *New York City Health and Hospitals Corporation v. Sulsona*,[15] a New York trial court in a declaratory judgment suit construed the definition of death in the context of the anatomical gift statute. The court held that the word "death" implies a definition consistent with generally accepted medical practice. Doctors are qualified to testify as to what the general standards are, and a general standard of death based upon the diagnosis of brain death was found acceptable by the court.

Recently the supreme courts of Arizona and Colorado have accepted brain death.[16] The Colorado opinion is illustrative. A seventeen-month-old child was discovered to have breathing difficulty and was unresponsive. He was taken to a hospital where it was determined that he had been grossly abused and was not breathing. He was placed on a respirator. Subsequently the mother was arrested for child abuse, and custody of the child was taken from her and placed with the Department of Social Services. The child's attending physician and consulting neurologist as well as the court-appointed neurologist testified that the child had suffered total brain death caused by extensive brain damage resulting from head trauma. The child had sustained multiple bruises, was completely comatose, was not breathing spontaneously, and his respiration

was maintained entirely by artificial means. He had no spontaneous muscular movements, no reflexes, including stretch or tendon reflexes, and no response to even the most intense pain or other stimuli. Corneal reflexes were absent, his pupils were dilated and fixed, electroencephalograms were flat. The unanimous opinion of the physicians was that the respirator and any other artificial mechanisms supporting the vital functions of the child's body should be discontinued since the child had suffered brain death.

The court viewed the case as one involving the definition of death in Colorado. Conceivably it said the common law might be interpreted broadly enough to include permanent cessation of brain functions as one of the definitions of death since one of the common law definitions of death was "cessation of life." The court rejected this definition as applicable to the circumstances here where respiration and circulation were being maintained artificially.

The court then proceeded to discuss modern scientific views, judicial decisions, and comparatively recent legislation in other states as well as model legislation offered by the American Bar Association, the American Medical Association (AMA), and the National Conference of Commissioners on Uniform State Laws. As the rule of this case the court adopted the provisions of the Uniform Brain Death Act which was created by the National Conference of Commissioners on Uniform State Laws.

The Colorado and Arizona cases illustrate the courts' willingness to act in instances where legislative activities have not provided a solution. Of significance is the Colorado supreme court's view that: "Under the circumstances of this case we are not only entitled to resolve the question, but have a duty to do so. To act otherwise, would be to close our eyes to the scientific and medical advances made worldwide in the past two or three decades."[17]

In *State v. Fierro*[18] the Arizona supreme court was faced with the issue of brain death when the defendant argued that the victim's death was not caused by the bullets he fired but rather by the physicians who, after declaring the victim brain-dead,

removed his life support systems. The court reflected this view, stating that when supported by expert testimony, either the Harvard criteria or the standard created by the National Commissioners is appropriate.

The ABA, the AMA, and the National Commissioners have each adopted a recommended brain death statute. In each case the wording varies slightly, but the substance is the same. Each requires irreversible cessation of all brain function which can be determined in accordance with reasonable medical standards. The AMA version adds legal immunity for the physician.

The version adopted by the National Commissioners reads: "For legal and medical purposes, an individual with irreversible cessation of all functioning of the brain, including the brain stem, is dead. Determination of death under this act shall be made in accordance with reasonable medical standards."[19]

This definition is very similar to the definition adopted by the ABA in 1975 which states as follows: "For all legal purposes, a human body with irreversible cessation of total brain function, according to the usual and customary standards of medical practice, shall be considered dead."

The determination of death provision in the AMA model bill states as follows: "A physician, in the exercise of his professional judgment, may declare an individual dead in accordance with accepted medical standards. Such declaration may be based solely on an irreversible cessation of brain function."

Fortunately, it was early recognized that the use of cerebral or cortical death alone as an equivalent for brain death was unacceptable to medicine and society and constituted the introduction of euthanasia into our society.[20] Consequently, all of the brain death statutes require total brain death or its equivalent as an acceptable standard. That standard is usually expressed as irreversible cessation of total brain function or equivalent language.

Model Statute

Recently a full day meeting was held in Chicago which was attended by the chairman of the Medicine and Law Committee of the ABA, two attorneys from the AMA, the executive director of the National Commissioners, and three of its board members, as well as the executive director of the President's Commission for the Study of Ethical Problems in Medicine and Biomedical and Behavioral Research. As a result of that meeting, an agreement was reached by the participants on language for a model statute concerning death:

"Uniform Determination of Death Act. An individual who has sustained either (1) irreversible cessation of circulatory and respiratory functions, or (2) irreversible cessation of all functions of the entire brain, including the brain stem, is dead. A determination of death must be made in accordance with accepted medical standards."

Each participant agreed to return to the respective associations and begin the process whereby the associations would determine whether or not to adopt the proposed definition. Adoption by each association is highly likely.

The brain death statutes constitute a legislative determination which is really no different than the commonsense insight that should have been made by the physicians 10 to 15 years ago. When the brain has irreversibly ceased to function, then the person is dead in spite of the fact that respiration and circulation are maintained artificially.

This is not to say that determining when the brain has irreversibly ceased to function is an easy diagnosis to make or that it is made easier by the existence of legislation supporting it.[21] What these statutes and cases are simply saying is that when the brain has irreversibly ceased all of its functions the person is dead. We should not confuse that acceptable medical fact with the also-acceptable medical fact that in any given case it may be difficult to prove that the brain has irreversibly ceased all of its functions.

Irreversibility, of course, is the key. The diagnosis of brain death as irreversible is made with caution in the cases of children or drug-induced coma states. Experience has shown the difficulty of making the diagnosis in these instances.[22] That difficulty, however, is no greater than the difficulty medical practitioners experience in making many diagnoses and should not deter entry into the area of diagnosing brain death. The customary concern and caution of physicians, including even transplant physicians, will deter hasty diagnoses and will protect patients. The history of the slow development of brain death and its cautious use by the medical profession is proof of the profession's concern for the well-being of patients, even dying patients.

Another key is the universally accepted criterion that brain death must be total. All brain centers must be dead. Death of the cortex alone has been correctly rejected by state legislatures and ethical commentators as the introduction of euthanasia which is contrary to our law. Karen Quinlan is in deep coma; she is not dead, nor is she brain dead.

Some have argued that brain death is an acceptable criterion for death only if the words "brain death" were merely other words for saying the complete destruction of the entire brain.[23] If by "destruction" what is meant is the irreversible cessation of all neuronal activity, then understanding the issue in that fashion presents no insurmountable problems.[24] However, it seems that some understand that word "destruction" in its anatomical sense, thus arguing that brain death is only acceptable when it involves the anatomical destruction of brain tissue. We do not ordinarily wait for anatomical destruction of tissue before determining that death has occurred, having almost universally accepted permanent and irreversible loss of function as the standard.[25]

A more significant problem in my judgment is what direction the law would take in the absence of the currently existing statutes.

All of the currently existing statutes require total brain death, obviating the fear of introduction of euthanasia through brain death.[26] Without such legislation the avenue is left open for courts through judicial pronouncement to accept other but lesser standards of brain death if supported by competent neurological testimony. If that testimony supports only cerebral brain death as death, only a judge very sophisticated in these medicolegal problems would understand and be able to overcome the trust of such ideologically oriented expert testimony.

The important problem is that without brain death legislation requiring total brain death, courts may unwittingly accept a much lesser standard and create even greater problems for society. Thus, legislation limiting the concept of brain death to the irreversible cessation of total function of the brain, including the brain stem, is beneficial and does not undermine any of the values we seek to support. Indeed, total brain death legislation enhances those values by prohibiting euthanasia and allowing only those to be declared dead who are really dead. The definition also serves a teaching function by clearly delineating the distinction between the living, the dead, and the "virtually" dead, a problem which has confused and plagued the definition-of-death issue for many years.[27] Medical treatment is terminated for the dead because one does not treat a dead patient. Medical treatment may be terminated for the virtually dead, but not because they are dead. Rather, it is terminated in those cases because it has become useless, offering no hope of benefit for the patient and only serving to prolong unduly the dying state. The distinction, however, is vital and, if not understood, causes great confusion.

In addition, it is interesting to note that the acceptance of brain death as an additional diagnosis for the determination of death may represent one **of the first broad consensuses on bioethical issues in our country.**

REFERENCES

Ala. Act. 165, 1979; Alaska Stat. §09.65.120; Ark. Stat. Ann. §82–537; Cal. Health & Safety Code §1780; Conn. Public Act 79–556; Ga. Code §88–1715.1; Haw. Rev. Stat. §327 C-1; Idaho Code §54–1819; Ill. Rev. Stat. Ch. 110 1/2, §302; Iowa Code §702.8; Kan. Stat. §77–202; La. Civ. Code Ann. Art. 9–111; Md. Ann. Code Art. 43, §54F; Mich. Comp. Laws §14.228(2); Mont. Rev. Codes Ann. §50–22–101; Nev. Stats. Ch. 451 (S.B. No. 5, Ch. 162, Sixtieth Sess., 1979); N.M. Stat. Ann. §1–2–2.2; N.C. Gen. Stat. §90–322; Okla. Stat. Tit. 63 §1–301; Or. Rev. Stat. §146.087; Tenn. Code Ann. 53–459; 1979 Tex. Sess. Law Serv., p. 368; Va. Code §54–325.7; W. Va. Code §16–19–1; Wyo. Stat. §35–19–101; and Fla.: 5B 293.

² *Lovato, et al. v. District Court, et al.* (S.Ct. Col.), No. 79 SA 407 Dec. 10-15-79; *Commonwealth v. Golston,* ___Mass.___, 366 N.E.2d 744 (1977), cert. den. 434 U.S. 1039, 98 S. Ct. 777, 54 L.Ed.2d 788 (1978) (court adopts brain death as alternative definition of death); *Arizona v. Fierro* (Ariz. Sup.Ct.), 124 Ariz. 182, 603 P.2d 74. *See also: State v. Shaffer,* 223 Kan. 244, 574 P.2d 205 (1977) (upholding constitutionality of Kansas brain death statute); *Cranmore v. State,* 85 Wis.2d 722, 271 N.W.2d 402 (1978) (error not to instruct jury on what constitutes death); *State v. Brown,* 8 Oreg.App. 72 (1971) (gunshot wound rather than termination of life supports was cause of death); *Tucker v. Lower,* No. 2381 Richmond, Va., L & Eq. Ct., May 23, 1972 (jury instructed that it can consider brain death as an alternative definition of death); *People v. Lyons,* 15 Criminal Law Reporter 2240, Cal. Sup.Ct. (1974) (court instructed jury that victim legally dead from gunshot wound because of brain death before respirator turned off); *New York City Health and Hospitals Corp. v. Sulsona,* 367 N.Y.S.2d 686 (1975) (court declares brain death as an alternative definition of death).

³ *See,* e.g.: "Euthanasia and Brain Death: Ethical and Legal Considerations;" Horan, D.J. *Annals of the New York Academy of Sciences,* Vol. 315, pp. 363–375, Nov. 17, 1978 (this entire volume is devoted to the issue of brain death); Conway, "Medical and Legal Views of Death: Confrontation and Reconciliation," 189 *St. Louis U.L.J.* 1972 (1974); Arent, "The Criteria for Determining Death in Vital Organ Transplants— A Medical-Legal Dilemma, 38 *Mo. L. Rev.* 220 (1973); Biorck, "When is Death?," 1968 *Wis. L. Rev.* 484; Black, "Brain Death, Part I," 299 *N. Eng. J. Med.* 338 (1978); Black, "Brain Death, Part II," 299 *N. Eng. J. Med.* 393 (1978); Cantor, "Quinlan, Privacy, and the Handling of Incompetent Dying Patients," 30 *Rutgers L. Rev.* 243 (1977); Collestar, Jr., "Death, Dying and the Law: A Prosecutorial View of the Quinlan case," 30 *Rutgers L. Rev.* 304 (1977); Frederick II, "Medical Jurisprudence—Determining the Time of Death of the Heart Transplant Donor," 51 *N.C.L. Rev.* 1972; Friloux, Jr., "Death, When Does it Occur?," 27 *Baylor L. Rev.* 10 (1975); Hirsh, "Brain Death," 1975 *Med. Trial Tech. Q.* 377; Hoffman and Van Cura, "Death—The Five Brain Criteria," 1978 *Med. Trial Tech. Q.* 377; note, "The Tragic Choice: Termination of Care for Patients in a Permanent State," 51 *N.Y.U.L. Rev.* 285 (1976). Wasmuth, Jr., "The Concept of Death," 30 *Ohio St. L. Rev.* 32 (1969). "Refinements in Criteria for the Determination of Death: An Appraisal." 221 *J.A.M.A.* 48 (1972). "An Appraisal of the Criteria of Cerebral Death, A Summary Statement," 237 *J.A.M.A.* 982 (1977). Capron and Kass, "A Statutory Definition of the Standards for Determining Human Death: An Appraisal and a Proposal. 121 *U. Penn. L. Rev.* 87 (1972).

For an excellent review of this subject *see,* Van Till, A., "Diagnosis of Death in Comatose Patients Under Resuscitation Treatment: A Critical Review of the Harvard Report," *American Journal of Law and Medicine,* Vol. 2, No. 1, 1976, pp. 1–40; *See also,* Veith, F., *et al.,* "Brain Death," *J.A.M.A.,* Vol. 238, No. 15, pp. 1651–1655, Oct. 10, 1977; and *J.A.M.A.,* Vol. 238, No. 16, pp. 1744–1748, Oct. 17, 1977; Byrne, *et al.,* "Brain Death—An Opposing Viewpoint," *J.A.M.A.,* Vol. 242, No. 13, pp. 1985–1990, Nov. 2, 1979; Editorial, *J.A.M.A.,* Vol. 242, No. 18, pp. 2001, 2002, Nov. 2, 1979; Horan and Mall, *Death, Dying and Euthanasia,* University Publication of America, Inc., Washington, D.C., 1977.

⁴ Under the common law a person was considered dead when there was, "total stoppage of the circulation of the blood, and a cessation of the animal and vital functions consequent thereon, such as respiration pulsation, etc." *Black's Law Dictionary* (4th Ed. 1951), p. 488.

⁵ The common law can be interpreted broadly enough to include permanent cessation of brain functions as one of the definitions of death. One of the common law definitions of death was "cessation of life." *Bouvier's Law Dictionary* (Rawle's Ed.) p. 775 (1914); *Cyclopedic Law Dictionary,* p. 285 (1922).

⁶ Olinger, S.D., "Medical Death," *Baylor L. Rev.* Vol. 1, 1975, pp. 22–26 (1975) (the entire issue of the law review is devoted to euthanasia).

⁷ *See,* e.g., Editorial, *J.A.M.A.,* Nov. 2, 1979,Vol. 242, No. 18, pp. 2001, 2002 where Robert M. Veatch, Ph.D., says: "But the historical evolution has slowed. While approximately 20 states have adopted legal changes in the years after the Harvard report, the rate of change has recently decreased. Physicians are, or should be, bound by law. Where the definition of death has not been changed, newer criteria for death pronouncement based on brain function should not be used."

⁸ *See* the discussion in: Paul Ramsey, *The Patient as a Person,* Yale University Press, New Haven & London, 1979.

⁹ Note 1, *supra.*

¹⁰ For these classifications I am thankful to the legislative department of the Public Affairs Division of the American Medical Association, January 1979 memo.

¹¹ Capron and Kass, *Op. Cit,* note 3, at pp. 108–111.

¹² Note 8, *supra,* at p. 101.

¹³ Note 2, *supra.*

¹⁴ 366 N.E.2d 744 (Sup.Ct. Mass., 1977).

¹⁵ 376 N.Y.S.2d 686 (1975).

¹⁶ *Lovato,* note 2, *supra,* slip opinion.

¹⁷ Ibid., p. 20.

¹⁸ *Arizona v. Fierro,* note 2, *supra.*

¹⁹ Uniform Brain Death Act drafted by the National Conference of Commissioners on Uniform State Laws, approved at its annual conference July 28–August 4, 1978.

²⁰ Horan, D.J., "Euthanasia and Brain Death: Ethical and Legal Considerations, *Annals of the New York Academy of Sciences,* Vol. 315, pp. 363–375, Nov. 17, 1978.

²¹ That the diagnosis may be medically difficult to make is made clear by Vol. 315 of the *Annals of the New York Academy of Sciences,* the entire volume of which is devoted to the subject of brain death on a medical, scientific, legal, and moral basis.

²² "An Appraisal of the Criteria of Cerebral Death," *J.A.M.A.* Vol 237, No. 10, pp. 982–986, Mar. 7, 1977.

²³ Byrne, *et al.,* "Brain Death—An Opposing Viewpoint, *J.A.M.A.,* Vol. 242, No. 18, pp. 1985–1990, Nov. 2, 1979.

²⁴ *See,* Van Till, *Op. Cit.,* note 3, at pp. 8–12. In his rebuttal editorial to the Byrne article, Veith praises the Byrne article as a challenge to be more precise in specifying what it is whose irreversible loss signals death of the person.

[25] Robert M. Veach, *J.A.M.A.,* Nov. 2, 1979, Vol. 242, No. 18, pp. 2001, 2002.

[26] Note 19, *supra.*

[27] Paul Ramsey, *Statement on Matters Related to the Definition of Death,* Testimony submitted to the President's Commission for the Study of Ethical Problems in Medicine and Biomedical and Behavioral Research, July 11, 1980.

A New "Definition" of Death?

Dorothy Rasinski Gregory, M.D., J.D., F.C.L.M.

The problems of deciding when death occurs and of establishing guidelines for the determination of death are ones that have plagued American medicine recently, with the advent of respirators, ventilators, pacemakers, and similar wonders of modern technology. We physicians have recently had to ask ourselves, when an individual's brain has ceased to function but life-support mechanisms, capable of stimulating or supporting respiration and heartbeat (the traditional vital signs relied upon by the law to determine when death has occurred) exist and are available, can or should that person be considered dead? The problems generated by the gap between our medical capabilities and the rules of law have been matters of concern not only to the patient, whose life or death may be at issue, but also to the treating physician and to surviving family members. Legal standards established by our society in this context will also affect decisions on inheritance, insurance payments, criminal liability, distribution of scarce medical resources, and medical costs to be borne by the family, the community, and insurance or Federal reimbursement funds. Unfortunately, not all jurisdictions within the United States have maintained the same pace regarding this very troublesome question. Some states still follow the old "common law" definition, holding that death occurs only when there is a total cessation of circulatory and respiratory functions. In other jurisdictions, the concept of "brain death" has been adopted, as amplified by the "Harvard criteria," and other parameters are employed in determining when an individual should be considered dead.

The President's Commission for the Study of Ethical Problems in Medicine and Biomedical and Behavioral Research, established by Congress in 1978, has studied this topic extensively to determine whether our modern society needs a nationwide uniform definition of death, or whether the multiple definitions legislated by the several states (the current situation) are adequate. In addition, it has asked whether it is appropriate to wait for judges to rule on these matters in some states on a case-by-case basis. In deciding that a uniform approach is appropriate, the Commissioners observed that an individual who might be regarded as dead in one state might well be alive according to the laws of a neighboring state. They consider this a solvable dilemma.

The Commission recently announced its proposed "Uniform Determination of Death Act," with the recommendation that it be adopted in all jurisdictions within the United States. The language is that of the model statute proposed by the American Medical Association, the American Bar Association, and the National Conference of Commissioners on Uniform State Laws. It is as follows:

An individual who has sustained either (1) irreversible cessation of circulatory and respiratory functions, or (2) irreversible cessation of all functions of the entire brain, including the brain stem, is dead. A determination of death must be made in accordance with accepted medical standards.

Reprinted from *Legal Aspects of Medical Practice*, vol. 9, no. 8, August, 1981. Reprinted with permission.

This language has also been endorsed by the American Academy of Neurology and the American Encephalographic Society.

Included in the Commission's report is a set of guidelines to assist in the clinical determination of death. These guidelines represent the consensus of some 50 neurologists, neurosurgeons, cardiologists, and other medical experts and consultants who advised the Commission in this very complex and troublesome area. Their recommendations have not been the subject of Commission deliberation or action.

The model statute presupposes that the medical community at large acknowledges the existence of "accepted medical standards" to be applied in determining whether a patient has died. In the majority of cases, the traditional criteria will continue to be applied—i.e., total irreversible cessation of cardiac and respiratory functions. In those clinical situations where the use of artificial life-support systems preclude reliance on the traditional tests, the use of accepted medical standards to measure human death by other than traditional means will be permitted. These standards have changed dramatically since the concept of brain death was first proposed and the Harvard criteria were enunciated. The sophisticated technology by which brain function, or the absence thereof, is tested will permit even more exquisite and precise determinations. The guidelines, as published, are but one statement of such standards to aid in the implementation of the model statute. In all cases, the use of sound, prudent medical judgment by a careful, competent, and judicious physician who is experienced in the clinical examination of these patients and in the relevant procedures is critical.

The Commission's conclusions are essentially as follows:

1. Recent developments in medical treatment necessitate a restatement of the standards traditionally recognized for determining that death has occurred.

2. Such a restatement preferably should be a matter of statutory law.

3. Such a statute should remain a matter for state law, with federal action at this time being limited to areas under current federal jurisdiction.

4. The statutory law should be uniform among the several states.

5. The "definition" contained in the statute should address general physiological standards rather than medical criteria and tests, which will change with advances in biomedical knowledge and refinements in technique.

6. Death is a unitary phenomenon which can be accurately demonstrated either on the traditional grounds of irreversible cessation of heart and lung functions or on the basis of irreversible loss of all functions of the entire brain.

7. Any statutory "definition" should be kept separate and distinct both from provisions governing the donation of cadaver organs and from any legal rules on decisions to terminate life-sustaining treatment.

The full guidelines, as prepared by the Commission's Medical Consultants on the Diagnosis of Death, follow:

GUIDELINES
Introduction

The criteria that physicians use in determining that death has occurred should:
(1) eliminate errors in classifying a living individual as dead,
(2) allow as few errors as possible in classifying a dead body as alive,
(3) allow a determination to be made without unreasonable delay,
(4) be adaptable to a variety of clinical situations, and
(5) be explicit and accessible to verification.

Because it would be undesirable for any guidelines to be mandated by legislation or regulation or to be inflexibly established in case law, the proposed Uniform Determination of Death Act appropriately specifies only "accepted medical standards." Local, state, and national institutions and professional organizations are encouraged to examine and publish their practices.

The following guidelines represent a distillation of current practice in regard to the determination of death. Only the most commonly available and verified tests have been included. The time of death recorded on a death certificate is at present a matter of local practice and is not covered in this document.

These guidelines are advisory. Their successful use requires a competent and judicious physician experienced in clinical examination and the relevant procedures. All periods of observation listed in these guidelines require the patient to be under the care of a physician. Considering the responsibility entailed in the determination of death, consultation is recommended when appropriate.

The outline of the criteria is set forth below in capital letters. The text that follows each outline heading explains its meaning. In addition, the two sets of criteria (cardiopulmonary and neurologic) are followed by a presentation of the major complicating conditions: drug and metabolic intoxication, hypothermia, young age, and shock. It is of paramount importance that anyone referring to these guidelines be thoroughly familiar with the entire document, including explanatory notes and complicating conditions.

The Criteria for Determination of Death

An individual presenting the findings in either section A (cardiopulmonary) or Section B (neurologic) is dead. In either section, a diagnosis of death requires that both *cessation of functions,* as set forth in subsection 1, and *irreversibility,* as set forth in subsection 2, be demonstrated.

A. AN INDIVIDUAL WITH IRREVERSIBLE CESSATION OF CIRCULATORY AND RESPIRATORY FUNCTIONS IS DEAD.

1. *CESSATION* IS RECOGNIZED BY AN APPROPRIATE CLINICAL EXAMINATION.

Clinical examination will disclose at least the absence of responsiveness, heart beat, and respiratory effort. Medical circumstances may require the use of confirmatory tests such as an EKG.

2. *IRREVERSIBILITY* IS RECOGNIZED BY PERSISTENT CESSATION OF FUNCTIONS DURING AN APPROPRIATE PERIOD OF OBSERVATION AND/OR TRAIL OF THERAPY.

In clinical situations where death is expected, where the course has been gradual, and where irregular agonal respiration or heart beat finally ceases, the period of observation following the cessation may be only the few minutes required to complete the examination. Similarly, if resuscitation is not undertaken and a monitored patient develops ventricular fibrillation and standstill, the required period of observation thereafter may be as short as a few minutes. When a possible death is unobserved, unexpected, or sudden, the examination may need to be more detailed and repeated over a longer period of time, while appropriate resuscitative effort is maintained as a test of cardiovascular responsiveness. Diagnosis in individuals who are first observed with rigor mortis or putrefaction may require only the observation period necessary to establish that fact.

B. AN INDIVIDUAL WITH IRREVERSIBLE CESSATION OF ALL FUNCTIONS OF THE ENTIRE BRAIN, INCLUDING THE BRAINSTEM, IS DEAD.

The "functions of the entire brain" that are relevant to the diagnosis are those which are clinically ascertainable, subject to confirmation (where indicated) by laboratory tests as described below. Consultation with a physician experienced in this diagnosis is advisable.

1. *CESSATION* IS RECOGNIZED WHEN EVALUATION DISCLOSES FINDINGS OF **a** *AND* **b**:

a. CEREBRAL FUNCTIONS ARE ABSENT, AND

There must be deep coma, that is, cerebral unreceptivity and unresponsivity. Medical circumstances may require the use of confirmatory studies such as an EEG or blood flow study.

b. BRAINSTEM FUNCTIONS ARE ABSENT.

Reliable testing of brainstem reflexes requires a perceptive and experienced physician using adequate stimuli. Pupillary light, corneal, oculocephalic, oculovestibular, oropharyngeal, and respiratory (apnea) reflexes should be tested. When these reflexes cannot be adequately assessed, confirmatory tests are recommended.

Adequate testing for apnea is very important. An accepted method is ventilation with pure oxygen or an oxygen and carbon dioxide mixture for ten minutes before withdrawal of the ventilator, followed by passive flow of oxygen. (This procedure allows $PaCO_2$ to rise without hazardous hypoxia). Hypercarbia adequately stimulates respiratory effort within theirty seconds when $PaCO_2$ is greater than 60 mm Hg. A ten-minute period of apnea is usually sufficient to attain this level of hypercarbia. Testing of arterial blood gases can be used to confirm this level. Spontaneous breathing efforts indicate that part of the brainstem is functioning.

Peripheral nervous system activity and spinal cord reflexes may persist after death. True decerebrate or decorticate posturing or seizures are inconsistent with the diagnosis of death.

2. *IRREVERSIBILITY* IS RECOGNIZED WHEN EVALUATION DISCLOSES FINDINGS OF **a** *AND* **b** *AND* **c**:

a. THE CAUSE OF COMA IS ESTABLISHED AND IS SUFFICIENT TO ACCOUNT FOR THE LOSS OF BRAIN FUNCTIONS, AND

Most difficulties with the determination of death on the basis of neurologic criteria have resulted from inadequate attention to this basic diagnostic prerequisite. In addition to a careful clinical examination and investigation of history, relevant knowledge of causation may be acquired by CT scan, measurement of core temperature, drug screening, EEG, angiography, or other procedures.

b. THE POSSIBILITY OF RECOVERY OF ANY BRAIN FUNCTIONS IS EXCLUDED, AND

The most important reversible conditions are sedation, hypothermia, neuromuscular blockage, and shock. In the unusual circumstance where a sufficient cause cannot be established, irreversibility can be reliably inferred only after extensive evaluation for drug intoxication, extended observation, and other testing. A determination that blood flow to the brain is absent can be used to demonstrate a sufficient and irreversible condition.

c. THE CESSATION OF ALL BRAIN FUNCTIONS PERSISTS FOR AN APPROPRIATE PERIOD OF OBSERVATION AND/OR TRAIL OF THERAPY.

Even when coma is known to have started at an earlier time, the absence of all brain functions must be established by an experienced physician at the initiation of the observation period. The duration of observation periods is a matter of clinical judgment, and some physicians recommend shorter or longer periods than those given here.

Except for patients with drug intoxication, hypothermia, young age, or shock, medical centers with substantial experience in diagnosing death neurologically report no cases of brain functions returning following a six-hour cessation, documented by clinical examination and confirmatory EEG. In the absence of confirmatory tests, a period of observation of at least twelve hours is recommended when an irreversible condition is well established. For anoxic brain damage where the extent of damage is more difficult to ascertain, observation for twenty-four hours is generally desirable. In anoxic injury, the observation period may be reduced if a test shows cessation of cerebral blood flow or if an EEG shows electrocerebral silence in an adult patient without drug intoxication, hypothermia, or shock.

Confirmation of clinical findings by EEG is desirable when objective documentation is needed to substantiate the clinical findings. Electrocerebral silence verifies irreversible loss of cortical functions, except in patients with drug intoxication or hypothermia. (Important technical details are provided in: American Electroencephalographic Society, *Guidelines in EEG 1980,* Section 4: "Minimum Technical Standards for EEG Recording in Suspected Cerebral Death," pp. 19–24, Atlanta, 1980.) When joined with the clinical findings of absent brainstem functions, electrocerebral silence confirms the diagnosis.

Complete cessation of circulation to the normothermic adult brain for more than ten minutes is incompatible with survival of brain tissue. Documentation of this circulatory failure is therefore evidence of death of the entire brain. Four-vessel intracranial angiography is definitive for diagnosing cessation of circulation to the entire brain (both cerebrum and posterior fossa) but entails substantial practical difficulties and risks. Tests are available that assess circulation only in the cerebral hemispheres, namely radioisotope bolus cerebral angiography and gamma camera imaging with radioisotope cerebral angiography. Without complicating conditions, absent cerebral blood flow as measured by these tests, in conjunction with the clinical determination of cessation of all brain functions for at least six hours, is diagnostic of death.

Complicating Conditions

DRUG AND METABOLIC INTOXICATION

Drug intoxication is the most serious problem in the determination of death, especially when multiple drugs are used. Cessation of brain functions caused by the sedative and anesthetic drugs, such as barbiturates, benzodiazepines, meprobamate, methaqualone, and trichloroethylene, may be completely reversible even though they produce clinical cessation of brain functions and electrocerebral silence. In cases where there is any likelihood of sedative presence, toxicology screening for all likely drugs is required. If exogenous intoxication is found, death may not be declared until the intoxicant is metabolized or intracranial circulation is tested and found to have ceased.

Total paralysis may cause unresponsiveness, areflexia, and apnea that closely simulates death. Exposure to drugs such as neuromuscular blocking agents or aminoglycoside antibiotics and diseases like myasthenia gravis are usually apparent by careful review of the history. Prolonged paralysis after use of succinylcholine and related drugs requires evaluation for pseudo-cholinesterase deficiency. If there is any question, low-dose atropine stimulation, electromyogram, peripheral nerve stimulation, EEG, tests of intracranial circulation, or extended observation, as indicated, will make the diagnosis clear.

In drug-induced coma EEG activity may return or persist while the patient remains unresponsive, and therefore the EEG may be an important evaluation along with extended observation. If the EEG shows electrocerebral silence, short-latency auditory or somatosensory-evoked potentials may be used to test brainstem functions, since these potentials are unlikely to be affected by drugs.

Some severe illnesses (e.g., hepatic encephalopathy, hyperosmolar coma, and preterminal uremia) can cause deep coma. Before irreversible cessation of brain functions can be determined, metabolic abnormalities should be considered and, if possible, corrected. Confirmatory tests of circulation or EEG may be necessary.

HYPOTHERMIA

Criteria for reliable recognition of death are not available in the presence of hypothermia (below 32.2°C core temperature). The variables of cerebral circulation in hypothermic patients are not sufficiently well studied to know whether tests of absent or diminished circulation are confirmatory. Hypothermia can mimic brain death by ordinary clinical criteria and can protect against neurologic damage due to hypoxia. Further complications arise since hypothermia also usually precedes and follows death. If these complicating factors make it unclear whether an individual is alive, the only available measure to resolve the issue is to restore normothermia. Hypothermia is not a common cause of difficulty in the determination of death.

CHILDREN

The brains of infants and young children have increased resistance to damage and may recover substantial functions even after exhibiting unresponsiveness on neurological examination for longer periods than do adults. Physicians should be particularly cautious in applying neurologic criteria to determine death in children less than five years old.

SHOCK

Physicians should also be particularly cautious in applying neurologic criteria to determine death in patients in shock, because the reduction in cerebral circulation can render clinical examination and laboratory tests unreliable.

How Does Your State Define Death?

William H. L. Dornette M.D., J.D., F.C.L.M.

THE NEED for a new definition of death began to germinate in the middle of this century. In the 1950s, scientists and engineers responded to the needs of anesthesiologists, internists, pneumotologists, other clinicians, and respiratory therapists by developing the intermittent positive pressure breathing device.

The manufacture of such equipment and its application in intensive care medicine—a new field—for the first time in medical history allowed physicians to prolong the lives of those who because of injury, disease, poisoning, or other reasons, had lost the ability to breathe spontaneously.

Where the absence of spontaneous respiration was only transient, use of one of these devices literally became life-saving. Unfortunately, however, not all such respiratory impairment was transient. In a significant number of instances, respiratory and intensive care did not save a life but only postponed inevitable death. The attempts to salvage the so-called neurologic vegetable taxed the resources of families, health care providers, and third-party payers, to say nothing of the anguish created among next of kin. With time, the number of such instances increased. In some cases, litigation arose between family members who recognized the inevitable and

This article is based on a presentation by the author at the symposium, "Geriatrics: The V.A. Challenge of the Eighties." at Alexandria, Va., September 12, 1979.

Address reprint requests to William H.L. Dornette, M.D., J.D., F.C.L.M., 22650 Shaker Blvd., Shaker Heights, Ohio 44122

health care providers who felt bound by medical ethics and legal precedent to maintain a semblance of "life" at all costs.

Another factor creating a need for a modern definition of death was the perfection of techniques for organ transplantation. This development of the 1950s and early '60s occurred principally in this country, and to a lesser extent abroad. Increasing activity in transplant surgery and tissue-typing immunology in turn created a widespread need for viable organs—a need that realistically could only be met from cadaveric sources.

It is, of course, well recognized that if a cadaveric organ is to be viable, it must be removed within minutes of the moment effective circulation of the "donor" ceases—and preferably before. To await the cessation of all signs of life through natural death precludes the availability of many potentially useful organs for transplantation.

Unless brain death is recognized, that is just what can happen. A victim of an assault or automobile accident suffers "brain death" by modern standards. Were a transplant surgeon to remove the needed organ before the heart had stopped beating spontaneously, however, he might be held liable for interfering with justice. The lawyer for the criminal who assaulted the victim could allege that it was the surgeon's knife rather than his client's blows that terminated the victim's life. A modern definition of death would cure such problems.

Modern medical science responded to the intensified need for a better definition. In 1968, a committee of the Harvard Medical School faculty, chaired by Dr. Henry Beecher, Dorr professor of research in anesthesia, published a set of criteria that would constitute "irreversible coma" if present in an unconscious patient. These criteria are:

1. Unreceptivity and unresponsivity;
2. Absence of movements and spontaneous respiration;
3. Absence of reflexes;
4. Similar findings 24 hours later;
5. Absence of any factors (*e.g.*, pharmacologic, hypothermia) that would or might depress central nervous system activity.[1]

The committee also noted that the electroencephalogram could be used to confirm these clinical findings.

These criteria soon became widely recognized and accepted. Their acceptance was a major step in helping place a modern definition of death before the public. But publication of these criteria did little to change the common law definition of death then prevailing in all U.S. jurisdictions. To change the legally recognized definition in any state would require either legislation or litigation. The courts could change the common law definition judicially if a new determination were upheld on appeal.

In the same year the Harvard criteria were published, two other events gave great impetus to the development and ultimate adoption of a definition of brain death. The first of these sprang from the activities of the Conference of Commissioners on Uniform State Laws, a group made up of representatives from each U.S. jurisdiction. It was established to draft model acts that could be adopted by each state legislature, thus promoting uniformity of laws across the nation. In 1968, the commission adopted the Uniform Anatomical Gifts Act. This act, ultimately passed by the legislatures of all U.S. jurisdictions, helped assure the availability of cadaveric sources of organs. But without the concomitant statutory definition of brain death, viability of the organs that did become available was not necessarily assured. Enactment of the Uniform Anatomical Gifts Act spurred the need for recognition of brain death.

Kansas became the first state to enact a statutory definition of brain death. The same year the Harvard study was published and the Uniform Anatomical Gifts Act adopted, a group at the University of Kansas College of Medicine sought a medical-legal opinion on how best to have brain death legally recognized in the state. Don Harper Mills, a physician-lawyer, was consulted. Recognizing the uncertainties of litigating the issue, he recommended approaching the legislature.

His three-page opinion letter in essence became the text of the Kansas statute, enacted in 1970. This statute provides:

A person will be considered medically and legally dead if, in the opinion of a physician, based on ordinary standards of medical practice, there is the absence of spontaneous respiratory and cardiac function and, because of the disease or condition which caused, directly or indirectly, these functions to cease, or because of the passage of time since these functions ceased, attempts at resuscitation are considered hopeless; and, in this event, death will have occurred at the time when these functions ceased; or

A person will be considered medically and legally dead if, in the opinion of a physician, based on ordinary standards of medical practice, there is the absence of spontaneous brain function; and if, based on ordinary standards of medical practice, during reasonable attempts to either maintain or restore spontaneous circulatory or respiratory function in the absence of aforesaid brain function, it appears that further attempts at resuscitation or supportive maintenance will not succeed, death will have occurred at the time these conditions first coincide. Death is to be pronounced before artificial means of supporting respiratory and circulatory function are terminated and before any vital organ is removed for purposes of transplantation.

These alternative definitions of death are to be utilized for all purposes in this state, including the trials of civil and criminal cases, any laws to the contrary notwithstanding.[2]

Four other states—Maryland, New Mexico, Oregon, and Virginia—now have similar statutes.

The Mills report to the University of Kansas faculty—and the subsequent statute—in essence contained the old common law definition as well as a modern one. Does the presence in the statute of these dual (or alternative) definitions impair the application of the statute? Two faculty members at the University of Pennsylvania thought so. In 1972, A.M. Capron and L.R. Kass published a law review article[3] criticizing the Kansas statute. They proposed a definition of their own, which they call the "Capron-Kass model." Their definition provides that:

. . . death is to be pronounced when a person has experienced irreversible cessation of spon-

taneous respiratory and circulatory functions, and that in the event that artificial means of support precluded determination that these functions had ceased, a person will be considered dead if in the announced opinion of his or her physician (basing judgment on ordinary standards of medical practice) he or she has experienced irreversible cessation of brain functioning.

Seven states—Alaska, Hawaii, Iowa, Louisiana, Michigan, Texas, and West Virginia—have adopted legislation incorporating versions of the Capron-Kass definition.

In 1974, a standing committee of the American Bar Association, the Committee on Law and Medicine, chaired by McCarthy DeMere, M.D., LL.B., developed a definition of death. This definition was adopted by the ABA House of Delegates the following year. The shortest of all the models proposed to date, it reads:

For all legal purposes, a human body with irreversible cessation of brain function, according to usual and customary standards of medical practice, shall be considered dead.

Illinois, Montana, and Tennessee have adopted this definition.

For a number of years, a committee of the Conference of Commissioners on Uniform State Laws had been working to draw up a model act defining death. Many of the model definitions were returned to committee by the commissioners. Finally, on August 3, 1978, the commission adopted the following definition, which is embodied in the Uniform Brain Death Act:

For all legal and medical purposes, an individual who has sustained irreversible cessation of all functions of the brain, including the brain stem, is dead. Determination of death under this section must be made in accordance with reasonable medical standards.

Nevada adopted the uniform act.

The Wyoming legislature incorporated portions of the ABA definition into the uniform act. The Wyoming definition reads:

For all legal purposes, a human body with irreversible cessation of total brain function, including the brain stem, according to usual and customary standards of medical practice, is dead. Total brain function shall mean purposeful activity of the brain as distinguished from random activity.[4]

This statute was signed into law February 22, 1979, making Wyoming the 23rd U.S. jurisdiction to enact legislation on this subject.

The legislatures of seven other states—Arkansas, California, Connecticut, Georgia, Idaho, North Carolina, and Oklahoma—have adopted statutes defining death in ways different from the four statutory types just cited. The one adopted by the California legislature, for example, has a second "catchall" paragraph that allows the physician to use traditional signs for determining death (*i.e.*, those based in the common law). The statutory language is:

A person shall be pronounced dead if it is determined by a physician that the person has suffered a total and irreversible cessation of brain function. There shall be independent confirmation of the death by another physician.

Nothing in this chapter shall prohibit a physician from using other usual and customary procedures for determining death as the exclusive basis for pronouncing a person dead.[5]

The statutes refer to neurologic activity in a variety of ways, including "all functions of the brain," "brain function," "total brain function," and "total brain function including brain stem." Whatever the nomenclature used, all focus on loss of function of the entire brain. The majority of neurologists, neurosurgeons, and other clinicians who urge adoption of the concept of brain death—and the legislators these physicians advise—advocate loss of essentially all intracranial function before the diagnosis of brain death is made. Some clinicians, however, feel strongly that the destruction of the neocortex kills the "person" as he or she was known.

For those concerned that all states have not adopted the same definition of death, it would be well to point out the number of definitions of neurologic death in the medical literature. Consider the following:

Apallic Syndrome—destruction of neocortical structures within the cerebrum; synonymous with neocortical death.

Brain Death—destruction of all neuronal structures within the cranial vault; flat EEG; apnea.

Brain Stem Death—destruction of brain stem; apnea with some EEG activity.

Cerebral Death—destruction of both cerebral hemispheres, neocortex as well as deeper structures; brain stem intact; flat

EEG; some respiratory activity.

Neocortical Death—bilateral destruction of cortical neurons; thalamus, basal ganglia, cerebellum, and brain stem intact; some EEG and respiratory activity.[6]

Less than half of the U.S. jurisdictions have adopted statutory definitions of death. In the others, the common law definition presumably still prevails.

Why have not all the states adopted the Uniform Brain Death Act (as they did the Uniform Anatomical Gifts Act)? The Uniform Brain Death Act was not finalized until 1978—after most of the states took legislative action in this area. I believe the lack of uniformity of definition poses no problem in patient care. Therapy (or its termination) can be governed only by the laws of the jurisdiction in which the health care facility is located.

Each state legislature is a separate entity, responding only to the needs of the citizens of that jurisdiction (the people who elect the lawmakers). In many ways, legislators are similar to appellate jurists. Any issue that is not brought before them is not considered. I suspect most state legislators find themselves so busy during the lawmaking session that they are reticent to introduce legislation not germane to immediate problems. As the medical and societal needs in the states without a modern definition of death continue to grow, however, their legislators, too, will respond with meaningful statutes.

For health care providers in those 27 states without a statutory definition, a few thoughts on the legislative process may be in order. Statutes are drafted in a process that is sometimes protracted while many individuals—some with expertise, some with political clout, some with both, and some with neither—attempt to mold or amend the proposed bill in their own best interests (or kill it altogether). In the absence of a well drafted model statute to be used as a pattern, a bill may become so watered down that its main thrust is lost.

Which statutory definition is the best model? In reviewing the definitions discussed in this article, I find them all acceptable. In my opinion, the application of any one of them in the appropriate case should help promote justice, humanity, and sound medical practice—as well as good common sense.

State Statutes Defining Death

Alaska Statutes §09.65.120

1977 Arkansas Acts 879

California Health & Safety Code §7180

Georgia Code §88-1715.1

Revised Hawaii Statutes §327C-1

1977 Idaho Session Laws, ch. 130, §1

Illinois Statutes, ch. 3, 522(b)

Iowa Code, ch. 1, §208

Kansas Statutes §77-202

Louisiana Revised Statutes §9:111

Code of Maryland, art. 43, §54F

Michigan Compiled Laws §326.8b

Revised Code of Montana §69-7201

Nevada Revised Statutes, ch. 393

1977 New Mexico Laws, ch. 287

1977 North Carolina Adv. Legislative Service, ch. 815, §90-320

Oklahoma Statutes, ch. 63 §1-301(g)

1977 Oregon Laws, §438

Tennessee Code §53-459

Texas Codes, art. 45.90h

Code of Virginia, ch. 19.2 §32-3643:1

West Virginia Code §16-19-1(c)

Wyoming Statutes §35-20-101

REFERENCES

1. A definition or irreversible coma: report of the Ad Hoc Committee of the Harvard Medical School to examine the definition of brain death, *JAMA* 205:337-340 (1968).
2. KAN. STAT. §77-202 (1970).
3. CAPRON AM, KASS LR: A statutory definition of the standards for determining human death; an appraisal and a proposal, *U Pa L. Rev.* 121:87-118 (1972).
4. WYO. STAT. §35-20-101 (1979).
5. CAL. HEALTH & SAFETY CODE §7180 (1976).
6. Adapted from KOREIN J: Terminology, definitions and usage, *Ann NY Sci* 180:6-9 (1978).

What is Death?

Thomas E. Kelly

WEBSTER'S Third New International Dictionary defines death as "the ending of all vital functions without the possibility of recovery."

This definition, of course, does not discuss the precise *time* of "the ending of all vital functions." Nor does it discuss how one can be sure that there really is "no possibility of recovery."

In recent years these have become key points.

The great fear in the past was that a live person could be considered dead, leading, perhaps, to premature burial. Some people today also believe this danger exists, and accordingly, that a corpse be treated as if it were still alive.

As the situation now stands, a person may be considered alive in one hospital and considered dead according to another definition employed in a hospital across town.

This quandary stems from two major problems in defining the biological event of death. First, death has no positive characteristics that can be recognized and written down to pinpoint the moment of death. As Richard G. Benton points out in his excellent book, *Death and Dying,* death is always recorded as the *absence* of some function. The patient no longer breathes, the heart no longer beats, the electoencephalograph no longer registers any electrical activity in the brain.

Second, the whole body does not die at once. Individual cells die at a slower rate than the systems that make up a human being's vital functions: heartbeat and breath. Those vital functions may cease to operate but the individual cells can live on.

The whole process of organ transplants rests on that biological fact.

A person may be pronounced dead, but his heart may still be alive and able to function in a living person. The practice of organ transplanting also makes establishment of the precise moment of death more important, as the viability of the organ is limited once the vital functions have ceased.

Back in the year 1836 a British physician named M. Ryan observed, "Individuals who are apparently destroyed in a sudden manner, by certain wounds, diseases, or even decapitation, are not really dead, but are only in conditions incompatible with the persistence of life."

This observation, still completely valid, recognizes the distinction between what scientists call somatic death, the extinction of personality, and molecular death, the actual death of the cells which make up the body.

Somatic death. Molecular death. We shall discover that there are, according to the scientists, several additional kinds of death.

Somatic death is the cessation of all vital functions such as the heartbeat and respiration. Molecular or cellular death follows.

But how soon?

Many cells in the body respond, for instance, to electrical stimulation up to two hours, a fact documented as long ago as 1811. In that year a French physician used the electrical current test to diagnose death. When muscles failed to contract when the current was applied, the patient was dead.

Checking for reflexes long has been a common — if not always accurate — way to determine whether death has taken place. The earliest tests were simple, visual observation of vital signs. Hold a feather to the lips, a mirror to the nostrils. Shakespeare had his characters use both (the feather in *Henry IV, Part Two;* the mirror in *King Lear*), and the feather test proved false. In *Romeo and Juliet* "no pulse . . . no warmth, no breath, shall testify thou livest." But she did. Shakespeare, who died in 1616, was well aware of the fallibility of the life tests of his time, and so were his contemporary physicians.

The fear of premature burial drove people to demand more precise medical definitions and prompted some bizarre requests, such as decapitation and surgical incisions. The traditional signs that are still useful in diagnosing death include absence of heartbeat, which is indicated by absence of pulse; absence of breathing, which is indicated by blueing of the extremities, mouth and lips; and lack of reflexes in the pupil of the eye.

In addition, as the whole body dies the skeletal muscles of the head, neck and lower extremities stiffen in *rigor mortis.* The body temperature falls to that of the environment (*algor mortis*), and a purple-red discoloration of body parts results from the settling of the blood (*livor mortis*). As *rigor mortis, algor mortis* and *livor mortis* appear at generally predictable intervals after death, they are useful in identifying the moment of death. *Algor mortis* is especially useful. Since bodily tem-

Reprinted with permission from *American Cemetery*, June, 1981.

perature decreases at a rate depending on the temperature of the external environment, the time elapsing between death and the discovery of the body can be calculated if the external temperature is known and has been consistent.

The traditional signs of death are not mere excerpts from ancient history. They appear in medico-legal books today. But these traditional signs are only part of the definitions of death that now appear in these standard reference works. An additional part of the definition indicates an entirely new era in medicine. The addition has to do with the cessation of activity in the brain — brain death.

In lay terms, the brain functions to integrate the activities of the central nervous system. When blood ceases to flow to the brain's cells, supplying them with oxygen, these cells die in a relatively short time. Obviously, the flow of vital fluids, breath and blood — represents a crucial factor in the life of the brain. In the ordinary sequence of events, the heart and lungs cease functioning, and then the brain cells die. As one observer put it, "Under normal circumstances a person is as dead today as he was a thousand years ago if his heart does not beat for five minutes."

New machines include the artificial respirator, cardiac resuscitation units, heart and lung machines, and machines for cleansing the blood. Cardiac shock and electric massage can start a heart beating again — and can do this even after the five minutes it takes for a brain to be irreversibly damaged.

The ordinary sequence of events no longer is the necessary sequence of events. The vital flow of fluids can be maintained mechanically after the brain has ceased to function.

The brain is divided into three parts: the cerebrum, or cerebral hemisphere; the cerebellum, and the brain stem. In addition to its role as "message conveyor," the brain stem also controls breathing. Since the heart's controlling center lies mostly within itself, it is possible for someone to sustain an injury that destroys the cerebrum and still continue to have breath and heartbeat without the aid of machinery.

The term "brain death" thus refers usually to the absence of activity in all three parts of the brain, not just in one part. Some physicians and thanatologists think that the "whole-brain" definition of brain death is too conservative and results in ministering to dead bodies as though they were alive.

The machine most often mentioned in accounts of brain death is the electroencephalograph (EEG), an apparatus with amplifiers and a write-out system for recording the electric activity generated by the brain and obtained from leads placed on the scalp.

Normally, people generate four different kinds of brain waves, depending on their emotional states, what activities they are engaged in, and whether or not they are asleep. These four kinds of impulses register on the EEG write-out system as various kinds of wavy lines. A flat (isoelectric) line indicates no brain activity.

Once the brain registers a straight EEG line, there are only two circumstances in which recovery is believed possible. One is in the case of a drug overdose; the other occurs when the body temperature has been lowered to the point where the body is effectively in hibernation.

(Chilling the body to induce a flat EEG reading is a procedure used in modern heart surgery. When the patient is warmed up after the operation, the vital functions spontaneously begin pulsating the vital fluids again and the patient is restored, even though the brain registered a "brain death" and the heart registered a "heart death.")

The EEG machine is not infallible. But supporting its use as an indicator of death is a study of 2,642 comatose patients whose brains were dead — all registered flat EEGs. Of the 2,642, only three recovered, and all three had taken drugs. They therefore could be excluded from consideration with the overwhelming empirical data that a brain-dead person does not return to the world of consciousness.

There are two main controversies centering on the identification of the whole brain with the death of an individual. The primary controversy focuses on the statement that the death of the brain is the same as the death of the individual. The second, and equally important, controversy turns on the question whether the whole brain should be considered the location where death takes place, or whether we are interested in man's consciousness; in his ability to think, reason, feel, experience, and interact with others.

Human consciousness does not take form in the brain stem, but in the cerebrum. Therefore, this reasoning goes, it is only necessary for the cerebrum to die; then death has occurred. This is the theory's conclusion, although it is possible for the cerebrum to be destroyed and the heart and lungs still to function.

Identifying the brain as the essence of the individual, so that when the brain dies it can be said that the person dies, represents another highly controversial judgment. An important difference exists between the statement that the brain no longer functions and the pronouncement that a person has died. The first statement is based on observations such as the EEG. But the second statement is not an empirical criterion of death; it is a judgment about what is vital to the nature of a human being — a value judgment on what constitutes the essence of human existence.

The belief that brain death means final, absolute death attributes the essence of human life to the brain. This might be very convenient to people who work in hospitals. The physician must know whether he is dealing with a human being or a "vegetable." The family and friends must know, for reasons having to do with their psychological situations. They all must know for reasons having to do with the estate of the deceased. Also, there is the very real (and often pressing) question of what is to be done with the corporeal remains of the deceased.

And what if one disagrees with the contention that brain death does not mean final, absolute death? There seems to be plenty of evidence for this lack of belief.

At least one student of this very real problem, Robert M. Veatch of the Hastings Institute of Society, Ethics, and the Life Sciences, Hastings-on-Hudson, N.Y., said, "Terms such as brain death or heart death should be avoided because they tend to obscure the fact that we are searching for the meaning of the death of the person as a whole."

Philosophers and others have been searching for such meaning certainly since the origin of writing, and almost certainly since before that. Their apparent failure (as most would say) does not mean that people in 1981 and the years to come should quit the quest. The new names for various conditions — all of them carrying the word "death" — appear not really to have added any light to what Dr. Veatch calls "the meaning of the death of the person as a whole."

"Life must be sustained under any circumstances," runs one argument (highly questionable in itself, many would say). Some extremely sincere people (ignoring this idea's basic premise) reply, "Where nothing more than the artificial appearance of life is maintained, any hope must be equally artificial."

But suppose someone important to you has retained the lower brain functions after the higher brain functions have ceased, and is able to breathe in what apparently is a normal manner, even though you have been assured, and know quite well, that all the higher brain functions have ceased?

The controversy over which parts of the brain are to be considered important in brain death is the second key point in the brain-death thesis. The rather rare but definitely possible situation of a breathing but otherwise vegetating person has led some to reject the "whole-brain" definition of brain death. They want to refine the concept of whole-brain death, not because there might occur a few cases of breathing people who were declared dead, but because those persons might *not* be declared dead.

The whole-brain death concept has been rejected on the basis of two interlocking points. First, those who wish to redefine the brain-death concept assumes that the presence of some of the reflex action controlled by the lower brain stem does not necessarily indicate an additional functioning in the cerebrum. Says Dr. Veatch, "If we can make this assumption, it seems very doubtful that the ability to contract and dilate the pupils and to execute any other reflex arc which happens to pass through the brain stem is in any way a significant sign of human living."

Secondly, the redefiners hold that a person's inability to interact socially is as important, if not more important, as the ability to integrate bodily functions. Says Dr. Veatch, "The ability to maintain nerve circuitry to carry out reflexes does not really add significantly to man's integrating capacity. Certainly it does not directly measure capacity to experience or interact socially."

One school of thought, therefore, distinguishes between brain death and cerebral death, holding that heart and lung machines should be shut off when the patient is cerebrally dead. Therefore, once a flat line appeared on the EEG machine, and if drugs or lowered body temperature could be ruled out, then the patient could be ruled dead.

The question now to be raised is: What kind of brain activities are crucial to man as a social animal? Obviously the emotional and rational activities of human beings are the ones that are part of daily life. The very ability to live together, to communicate, to participate in some way in general human society all represent important humanness.

Aristotle made a similar observation when he defined man as a social animal. But Aristotle was not establishing a medical definition that was intended to be functional in medical practice.

What is Death?
Part Two

Thomas E. Kelly

ARGUMENTS, dilemmas, and legal, moral and philosophical problems abound concerning the various definitions of death.

Consider: Consciousness and the capacity for any sort of social action can be absent, but some physical reactions may still persist in a patient. If death is defined as "the irreversible loss of consciousness or the capacity for social intercourse," and if that situation can be established by giving the electroencephalograph (EEG) test, then physicians may use this test as the major criterion in determining death.

Yet some vital functions may be spontaneously present. This leads to the question, "Would you bury a breathing body?"

There is something utterly repugnant about the thought of behaving toward a breathing body as though it were dead. It may be far better to err by treating a dead person as if alive, rather than mistake a living person for a dead one.

The purpose of settling on a medical definition of death once was primarily the prevention of burial of someone who was still alive. Fear of pronouncing dead someone who is still alive remains the primary restraint on those who must decide whether to pronounce a person dead. The advent of organ transplants has increased the need for publicly-stated medical definitions of death. Or at least it has caused several major medical organizations to try to come to terms with the definition of death and offer terms for medical guidance.

The World Health Organization defined death as the permanent disappearance of life, with no possibility of resuscitation. The United Nations Vital Statistics Office has defined death as the permanent disappearance of every sign of life. Some physicians would like to change that to read, "Death has occurred when every spontaneous vital function has ceased permanently."

But even that refinement has critics. What happens, some ask, if we apply that definition to someone who has met a violent death — someone beheaded or hanged. Spontaneous vital functions may still be present.

The general medical definitions are unsatisfactory because it has become necessary to know when, exactly, death occurred, especially if organ transplanting is involved.

There was the case of Bruce Tucker, a 56-year-old laborer who fell and sustained massive brain injury on May 24, 1968. The next day he was taken to the Medical College of Virginia where he was operated on in an attempt to relieve the pressure on his brain. After the operation, he was fed intravenously, given medication, and kept breathing with a respirator. The treating physician soon noted, "prognosis for recovery is nil and death imminent." A neurologist tested for brain waves and found virtually nothing but flat lines.

The respirator was turned off in the afternoon. Five minutes later Mr. Tucker was pronounced dead and the respirator was turned on again to preserve his organs.

Not quite an hour later his heart was removed and implanted in the chest of a heart-transplant patient.

The incision to remove the defective heart of the transplant recipient had been made two minutes *before* Mr. Tucker was pronounced dead. (The recipient died about one week later.)

Mr. Tucker's brother, William, sued for $100,000 damages, charging that the transplant team was engaged in a "systematic and nefarious scheme to use Bruce Tucker's heart and hastened his death by shutting off the mechanical means of support."

In 1972 a jury in Richmond decided in favor of the physicians. The head of the transplant team said the decision "brings the law up to date with what medicine has known all along — that the only death is brain death."

The Tucker case brought to light several problems. The doctors had to make a moral decision with standards quite apart from any medical criteria that ever will be available. They decided that the essential thing to Bruce Tucker was his brain, or the functions which his brain performed. They disregarded the fact that his heart still was beating. They also took all the responsibility for that decision upon themselves. No attempt was made to contact the brother, even though William Tucker's address was in Bruce Tucker's pocket. The brother obviously disagreed about the patient's status.

Then there is the case of Brother Joseph Charles Fox, an 83-year-old

Reprinted with permission from *American Cemetery*, July, 1981.

member of the Marianist order, who lapsed into a coma on Oct. 2, 1979, after a hernia operation. He breathed with the help of a respirator, but showed no other signs of life. He was fed, washed and cared for by attendants. He was conscious of nothing, not even his own existence. Doctors agreed that he was in an "irreversible vegetative state."

The Rev. Philip K. Eichner, a priest representing the Marianist order, after some months asked that all life-support equipment be turned off. Justice Robert C. Meade ruled at Mineola, N.Y., that the respirator could be turned off but that intravenous feeding had to continue. He also stipulated that a prior condition be the certainty of physicians that no reasonable expectation exist that the patient would ever again be able to function as a conscious human being.

The Nassau County district attorney appealed the decision on the grounds that two neurologists had concluded that Brother Joseph was not brain dead and improvement therefore was theoretically possible. The case became moot when Brother Joseph's lungs stopped breathing and his heart stopped beating.

The Brother Joseph case, like the Karen Ann Quinlan case, is an example of the enormous complexity of the questions being raised.

Some thanatologists have advocated establishment of new guidelines on death so that what formerly would have been considered unethical might be considered ethical in the future. Robert M. Veatch of the Hastings Institute of Society, Ethics and the Life Sciences, Hastings, N.Y., says, "While the potential for use of human organs for therapeutic transplantation should never justify the adoption of a new understanding of what is essentially significant to human life and death, it may require a philosophically responsible clarification of imprecise use of these terms adequate only in a time when little morally critical was at stake."

In plain English, what that amounts to is calling a patient dead who would have been considered alive according to older standards. Thus one neatly avoids such issues as mercy killing, and the problem of preferential treatment of a patient in need of an organ of a dying patient.

In his excellent, book, *Death and Dying,* Richard G. Benton quotes a Princeton theologian as qualifying the physician's duties this way:

"Never abandon care of the dying except when they are irretrievably inaccessible to human care. Never hasten the dying process except when it is entirely indifferent to the patient whether his dying is accomplished by an intravenous bubble of air or by the withdrawal of useless ordinary natural remedies such as nourishment."

Dr. Benton comments, "Such 'guidelines' inevitably raise questions. How is the physician to know when the patient is 'indifferent' to being alive or dead?"

Dr. Benton suggests that one way may be to establish brain death. Most of the medical definitions that came out of the 1960s and the laws that some states established in the 1970s are concerned primarily with criteria for brain death.

The French Academy of Medicine in 1968 accepted the death of the brain as an indication of the "irrevocable loss of function of an indispensable organ." That same year the 22nd World Medical Assembly published detailed guidelines for physicians seeking to diagnose death.

They included, total lack of response to external stimuli; no reflexes, flat EEG, and no muscular movements, especially breathing. If the patient is on a mechanical respirator, it may be turned off for three minutes to establish whether he is capable of breathing without it.

The most often cited criteria for defining death also were published in 1968 by the *Ad Hoc* Committee of the Harvard Medical School to Examine the Definition of Brain Death. They covered essentially the same points as the World Medical Assembly: unreceptivity and unresponsivity, no movements or breathing, no reflexes, and a flat EEG.

Noting that the EEG is "of great confirmatory value," the Harvard committee also recommended that the EEG test be repeated at least 24 hours later because EEG data can be invalid in cases of lowered body temperature and drug poisoning.

The Harvard committee's criteria actually are used to identify irreversible coma. The committee hedged on the issue of identifying irreversible coma with death, or death with irreversible coma. This may have been wise; suggesting guidelines for physicians falls in a different category than establishing either legal definitions or ethical recommendations.

Many believe that, in cases where respirators or similar machines have been employed, the physician should not be the person to rule on death or non-death. Margaret Mead, the noted anthropologist, is among these, saying, "The real issue that we are talking about is the issue of whether the physician should ever be asked to perform, on a patient who has any life left in him at all, an operation (transplant) which means certain death."

D. C. Maguire, in his book, *Death by Choice,* speaks of a growing tendency to see the patient, "as datum among data." This tendency, he believes, has been generated by the trend toward experimentation which can create a conflict between what is good for the patient and what is good for the experiment.

Mr. Maguire also says, "In consigning the decision over death to a physician, you are actually adopting his particular religion or philosophical bias as determinative of wisdom and morality." He also stresses that doctors have no special training in moral decisions and that some are not even competent as physicians.

Different levels of responsibility are involved in any definition of death. The *material* responsibility could be defined as the various tests to determine brain death, or to check heartbeat or lung function. The *efficient* responsibility would be what are called "operational criteria" — the traditional criteria of the flow of vital fluids, and the more recently suggested criteria of irreversible cessation of spontaneous brain functions.

The *formal* responsibility could be assigned as the definition of the area of the body whose functioning is critical. The *final* responsibility consists of the philosophical concept of death itself.

Obviously, the physicians are in charge of the material responsibility, for the physicians administer the tests. And just as obviously, the physicians must bear the efficient responsibility of deciding which tests best determine the material criteria.

The formal responsibility is by no means a matter for the physicians alone as it involves choosing which part of the human being is the most important in determining vitality. Is it the brain alone, or is it the heart and lungs, the cardiopulmonary system? Legal authority may have its place at this level.

The final responsibility belongs neither to individual physicians nor to the organized medical profession. The basic concept of death is essentially a philosophical matter.

Examples of possible definitions of death include "permanent cessation of the integrated functioning of the organism as a whole," "departure of the animating or vital principle," or "irreversible loss of personhood."

The choice of basic concept will determine to a great extent the for- mal general standards, the general standards will limit the efficient operational criteria, and the operational criteria will determine the material tests. All the levels of the definition of death are governed by the final responsibility for the definition.

Responsibility for the final defini- tion of death traditionally has been borne by society itself, along with religious leaders. In more recent times changes in medical science, social consensus, and religious tradi- tion also contributed to the formal definition of death.

Because it is fundamental to American democracy to preserve the rights of an individual, it seems that some flexibility must be allowed in both the final and formal definitions of death. That means that medical practice on the efficient and formal levels of criteria would not every- where and always be consistent. But individuals — the family as well as the patient — have the right to their beliefs and the right to expect hospital treatment that is consistent with those beliefs. Affirmation of that right may require legislation.

A county probate judge, Michael T. Sullivan, writing in the *New England Law Review,* thinks that the individual alone "should decide whether he will employ the Harvard criteria or some other definition for his death." Judge Sullivan con- tinues, "The polestar of any legisla- tion must be the dying person's right to make decisions concerning all his interrelationships. This is because death decisions as well as life deci- sions belong to him."

What is Death? Part Three

Thomas E. Kelly

FROM A legal point of view, it is not entirely satisfactory to allow each individual to formulate his own definition of death. A need exists for some kind of rules or guidelines that might guard the individual's rights and control medical practice without forcing a doctor to risk a lawsuit every time he makes a decision.

The law traditionally has had much to say about the circumstances of death, but until recently the major legal distinctions were concerned with the causes of death: accidental death, suicide, homicide, natural causes. There also are laws concerning the presumption of death.

The first U.S. legislative action establishing a definition of death other than the traditional cessation of all vital functions came in 1968 in Kansas. The statute was prepared specifically to permit organs to be procured for transplantation.

Conveniently, the law seems to provide two definitions of death, suitable for varying situations. It reads:

"A person will be considered medically and legally dead if, in the opinion of a physician, based on ordinary standards of medical practice, there is the absence of spontaneous respiratory and cardiac function and, because of the disease or condition which caused, directly or indirectly, these functions to cease, or because of the passage of time since these functions ceased, attempts at resuscitation are considered hopeless; and, in this event, death will have occurred at the time these functions ceased; or

"A person will be considered legally and medically dead if, in the opinion of a physician, based on ordinary standards of medical practice, there is the absence of spontaneous brain function; and if, based on ordinary standards of medical practice, during reasonable attempts to either maintain or restore spontaneous circulatory or respiratory function in the absence of aforesaid brain function, it appears that further attempts at resuscitation or supportive maintenance will not succeed, death will have occurred at the time when these conditions coincide. Death is to be pronounced before artificial means of supporting respiratory and circulatory function are terminated and before any vital organ is removed for transplantation."

The most obvious criticisms of this statute concern the law's purpose — facilitating transplants — and on the alternate definitions. J.M. Kennedy, writing in the *New England Journal of Medicine,* observed mildly, "To draft a statute on death inspired apparently by the desire to facilitate what must still be considered experimental surgical procedures must serve to disturb the man on the street."

Although the Kansas statute has alternative definitions, the law does not allow the patient to choose. The alternative definitions in the statute may lead to some difficult situations. A patient, under the Kansas law, might be considered dead if a doctor wanted to transplant organs, but alive if no organs were needed.

This situation reduces the individual to the status of an object to be used as the circumstances require.

At press time, 19 states had statutory definitions of death: Alaska, California, Georgia, Hawaii, Idaho, Illinois, Iowa, Kansas, Louisiana, Maryland, Michigan, Montana, New Mexico, North Carolina, Oklahoma, Tennessee, Virginia, and West Virginia.

Maryland was the second state to adopt such a law, and it was virtually identical to the Kansas Statute. So is the New Mexico law. The Virginia statute is quite similar, but requires the opinion of a consulting physician who is "a specialist in the field of neurology, neurosurgery, or electroencephalography" in addition to the opinion of the attending physician that there is an absence of spontaneous brain function.

The law adopted in Michigan reads: "A person will be considered dead if in the announced opinion of a physician, based on ordinary standards of medical practice, there is the irreversible cessation of spontaneous respiratory and circulatory functions. If artificial means of support preclude a determination that these functions have ceased, a person will be considered dead if in the announced opinion of a physician, based on ordinary standards of medical practice in the community, there is the irreversible cessation of spontaneous brain functions. Death will have occurred at the time when the relevant functions ceased."

In this type of legislation the determination of death based on the

Reprinted with permission from *American Cemetery,* September, 1981.

absence of brain function may be used only when the heart and lungs are artificially maintained. Much the same approach is taken by the statutes in Alaska, Hawaii, Iowa and Louisiana. Hawaii and Iowa require a second opinion.

The law in Tennessee reads: "For all legal purposes, a human body, with irreversible cessation of total brain function, according to the usual and customary standards of medical practice, shall be considered dead."

This type of statute does not provide for determination of death based on respiratory and cardiac cessation. Similar laws are in effect in California, Idaho, Illinois, Montana and Oklahoma. California and Idaho require a second opinion; the other states do not.

The law in Georgia reads: "A person may be pronounced dead if it is determined that the person has suffered an irreversible cessation of brain function. There shall be independent confirmation of the death by another physician."

This type of statute permits a physician to pronounce a person dead if the brain has stopped functioning, but does not require him to do so.

The American Medical Association, an extremely influential body, has prepared "model" legislation which seems more concerned with the welfare of the physician than of the patient. It reads in part:

"Section 1. A physician, in the exercise of his professional judgment, may declare an individual dead in accordance with accepted medical standards. Such declaration may be based solely on an irreversible cessation of brain function.

"Section 2. A physician who determines death in accordance with Section 1 is not liable for damages in any civil action or subject to prosecution in any criminal proceeding for his acts or the acts of others based on that determination.

"Section 3. Any person who acts in good faith in reliance on a determination of death by a physician is not liable for damages in any civil action or subject to prosecution in any criminal proceeding for his act.

"Section 4. If any provision of this Act is held by a court to be invalid, such invalidity shall not affect the remaining provisions of the Act, and to this end the provisions of this Act are hereby declared to be severable."

The National Conference of Commissioners on Uniform State Laws recently adopted a "model" Uniform Brain Death Act which reads:

"For legal and medical purposes, an individual with irreversible cessation of all functioning of the brain, including the brain stem, is dead. Determination of death under this act shall be made in accordance with reasonable medical standards."

This definition is very similar to the definition adopted by the American Bar Association in 1975:

"For all legal purposes, a human body with irreversible cessation of total brain functions, according to the usual and customary standards of medical practice, shall be considered dead."

Note that these last two definitions specify "total" brain death, in one instance specifically including the brain stem, while the AMA definition could be interpreted to mean only cerebral death. Similarly, the Tennessee version of the state laws already enacted specifies "total" brain death; the others do not. And none of these laws, "model" or enacted, lists specific criteria.

Attorney Walter C. Ward, writing in the *University of Florida Law Review* in 1970, said, "There is no need for a specific legislative definition of death. Such an effort would be futile in that the use of a flexible definition is required for differing circumstances."

The AMA, in 1979, said, "Physicians have always based their determination of death upon medical criteria accepted at that particular time."

Judicial decisions have been important in this field. In Commonwealth vs. Golston, a 1977 Massachusetts case, the judge instructed the jury that brain death occurs "when, in the opinion of a licensed physician, based on ordinary and accepted standards of medical practice, there has been a total and irreversible cessation of spontaneous brain functions and further attempts at resuscitation or continued supportive maintenance would not be successful in restoring such functions." On appeal, the judge's interpretation was upheld.

In a 1975 case, New York City Health and Hospitals Corp. vs Sulsona, the court accepted a definition of death which would make the Anatomical Gift Law a practical reality in New York State. It accepted the idea of a diagnosis of death before the body was so long dead that any use of organs for transplant became impossible. The court also asked the State Legislature to pass a law on the problem. (At this writing, the State of New York has no statutory definition of death.)

A.M. Capron and L.R. Kass, writing in the November, 1972, edition of the *University of Pennsylvania Law Review,* suggested five principles to govern the formulation of a statute on death:

The statute should concern the death of the human being, they wrote, not the death of his cells, tissues, or organs, and not the death or cessation of his role as a fully functioning member of his family or community. This first principle leaves the *final* responsibility for defining death to the individual.

A statute should preserve continuity with tradition. That is, a state should supplement the standards now in practice.

The statute should express a change in method, not a new meaning for life and death.

The standards of determining death should apply uniformly to all people, without regard to an individual's possible status as a donor.

The statute should leave room for medical advances.

To those principles Robert M. Veach of the Hasting Institute of Society, Ethics and the Life Sciences, Hastings, N.Y., would add that "the physicians pronouncing death should be free of significant conflict of interest — whether the interest focuses on a respiring patient, research, continued treatment fees, or transplantation."

Virtually all the legislation, "model" or enacted, and almost all the court decisions, have had to do with physicians and the medical profession. There are those who think that the patient, and his family, ought to have some say in the matter.

Judge Michael T. Sullivan, writing in the August, 1973, edition of the *New England Law Review,* proposed a "statutory" declaration that "the constitutional right securative of life encompasses the individual's right within lawful means to choose his path of death."

Judge Sullivan also proposes that it be further specified that people have the right to prescribe their death style, and that there be "particularly statutory creation of a proctorship to ensure enforcement" of relationship with physicians, clergy, hospitals, nurses, paraprofessionals, and family; death definition and organ donations; and funeral directions.

Dr. Veach, somewhat along the same lines, has suggested that the authority to make death decisions be transferred to the next of kin or a legal guardian. He words his proposal for a "freedom of choice statute:

"It is provided . . . that no person shall be considered dead even with the announced opinion of a physician solely on the basis of an irreversible cessation of spontaneous cerebral functions if he, while competent to make such a decision, has explicitly rejected the use of this standard, or, if he has not expressed himself on the matter while competent, his legal guardian or next of kin explicitly expresses such rejection.

"It is further provided that no physician shall pronounce the death of any individual in any case where there is significant conflict of interest with his obligation to serve the patient (including commitment to any other patients, research, or teaching programs which might directly benefit from pronouncing the patient dead)."

A law such as this would require an individual to object specifically to organ removal. It also would appear to be too aggressively in favor of the brain death criteria.

To be more in keeping with current trends in American ethics, it might be appropriate to propose a statute which specifies that no organ "harvesting" may be made unless the patient has consented, or the next of kin or legal guardian permits it.

Such permission places the authority for the definition of death in the hands of the individual. It also assures that any medical procedures performed on the patient would be consistent with that patient's definition of death.

It well may be that in its eagerness to push ahead in the organ transplant program, the medical profession has given the public the erroneous impression that the harvesting of human organs is more important than the absolute assurance that the donor of an organ is dead.

Any new definition of death must take this into consideration.

FUNERAL PRACTICES—
ISSUES AND ALTERNATIVES

Coping with the Present and the Future

Gordon W. Rose, Ph.D.,
and Leandro Rendon, M.S.

The voluntary adoption and profession-wide implementation of professional performance standards in embalming is a necessary first step to assure improved and standardized services to the public. This is especially important in light of recent developments, e.g., the review of licensing board functions in several states, which suggest strongly the need for precise definitions of the values of embalming.

Many questions are being raised about the need for embalming. When the true functions of embalming are questioned, we must be able to offer answers that are based on experimental data and confirmatory evaluations. As knowledgeable licensees know, it is easier to provide meaningful responses if they can refer to standards of performance that have reproducibly resulted in a high quality of professional service. Without such adopted standards, how does one predict acceptable results that should be based on a program of quality assurance?

The goal, therefore, should be to make certain that when embalming is performed, a measure of uniformity of minimum professional skills are employed by all licensees. To achieve such a goal or set of goals, it is necessary to delineate those techniques and procedures that have been confirmed to be most effective. Such procedures should be adopted as "the minimal standards of professional practice" when embalming is to be performed.

From the available experimental evidence, it is obvious that embalming is effective and useful as it relates to the primary purposes, namely, disinfection and preservation. This is consistently true when the embalming chemicals are used in **proper concentrations adequate total volumes,** and are administered **under conditions of proper techniques.** This was first emphasized by Dr. Edward

Reprinted with permission from *NRIC's National Reporter,* National Research & Information Center, vol. 2(9), September, 1979.

Francis, United States Public Health Service, in 1915!
[1] More recent investigations [2, 3] have confirmed
and updated the data originally reported by Dr. Francis.

A review of such available data, emphasizing those
techniques and procedures which must be considered
when establishing a set or profile of minimum standards
for the practice of embalming, is especially important at
this time. Our procedural recommendations which follow are based on practical experience and laboratory
evaluations, are realistic, defensible, and enforceable:

1. The use of techniques that insure the widest
   possible distribution of the disinfectant/pre-
   servative solution. According to Dr. Francis
   and many of today's practitioners, multiple
   point (more than one) injection-drainage
   methods assure the most effective contacts
   with all receptive tissue sites, both deep and
   superficial. Such methods are more effective
   than single point injection-drainage and in
   practice, require little additional time and effort to employ. Unless maximal contact of
   receptive tissues is effected, the long-term
   effectiveness of embalming may be greatly
   reduced.

2. Moderate rate of flow (12-15 minutes to inject
   each gallon) and use of sufficient pressure to
   maintain that rate of flow, usually two to ten
   pounds. [2] Time is required for the injected
   disinfectant/preservative chemical to exert its
   influence on tissue. Mere circulation of the injected solution through the circulatory system
   does not guarantee adequacy of embalming. It
   is necessary to accomplish diffusion into, and
   saturation of, all soft tissue areas to achieve
   desirable levels of disinfection and preservation
   of those areas.

3. Use of the intermittent or restricted type of
   drainage procedure after surface discolorations
   have cleared (usually after the first gallon or so
   injected). [2] This is one of the most effective
   methods of insuring good distribution of the
   solution being injected. It has the effect of
   causing solution pressure to build up in the circulatory system and force a "flooding" of soft
   tissue areas instead of possibly by-passing them
   through continuous drainage. If proper drainage has been established, this technique will
   not impede drainage. Solutions under pressure
   tend to follow routes of least resistance, and
   through continuous drainage may cause loss of
   the injected solution before it has had an opportunity to disinfect and preserve body

tissue. This technique actually should result
in maximum usage of the injected solution.

4. Use of at least three, and preferably four, gallons of total solution. [2, 3] Many years ago,
   studies indicated that use of modifying and surface active agents (surfactants such as "penetrating," "wetting," "emulsifying," "tension
   breakers," etc.) in embalming formulations
   made it possible for about 50 percent or more
   of the injected solutions to be drained from the
   body. This is predicated on technique that
   insures adequate distribution, diffusion and saturation into soft tissue areas. During the embalming technique, some one (1) to one and
   a half (1½) gallons of blood and body liquids
   are removed. To restore a natural appearance
   to the remains and prevent over-dehydration
   effects, it is necessary to replace the volume
   removed. Since about 50 percent of the injected solution will leave the body through
   drainage (especially continuous drainage) it is
   necessary to inject a total solution volume of
   some three (3) to four (4) gallons.

5. Research data from recent studies [2, 3] as
   well as the special studies by Dr. Edward
   Francis of the United States Public Health Service have established rather conclusively that
   embalming solutions, to be effective in achieving sanitation and preservation of tissue, must
   be used in stronger concentrations than at
   present. The data from Burke and Sheffner of
   the Snell Laboratories [3] show that formaldehyde solutions must be used in concentrations
   ranging from 2.3 percent to 3.0 percent to reduce bacterial populations in excess of 95
   percent. It is reasoned that a 2 percent alde-
   hyde concentration will produce reductions in
   microbial densities in excess of 70 percent
   which is considered a significant reduction.
   There is documentation for this type of usefulness for embalming.

Separate and independent work at Wayne
State University [Hockett, et al, 2], shows
that use of aldehydes in combination of 2
percent concentrations is effective in killing
significant numbers of bacteria — in excess of
95 percent! This research data has also been reported in a technical journal and been presented before the annual meeting of the American
Public Health Association.

It is important to also acknowledge that a 1
per cent formaldehyde solution may produce

fixation and firmness of tissue. However it takes more formaldehyde to kill significant numbers of bacteria. According to E.H. Spaulding [4], formaldehyde is a "high level" germicide if used in concentrations of 3 to 8 percent.

6. No less than one bottle of "cavity" chemical should be used in the treatment of each major or primary cavity. [3] The techniques employed in the treatment of such anatomic sites should effect maximal contact with all tissues organs, and viscera, assuring thorough perfusion and perforation. Again, such techniques and procedures have been confirmed to be effective through scientific evaluations.

7. Naturally, minimum standards should also list those procedures that are important in safeguarding the hygienic well-being of all concerned. These should include procedures in **concurrent** disinfection (pertaining to the remains, the embalmer and the immediate environment) as well as **terminal** disinfection in the same general areas. General information on public health guidelines already has been made available to funeral licensees. [5]

Other factors and considerations could well be discussed as they relate to standardization of practices and quality assurance of services performed. In all cases, however, they should be based on reliable and reproducible experience and evaluation data. In other words, when requirements are set forth in a profile of performance standards, the needs for such standards should be substantiated.

What can one say, then, about the usefulness and purpose of embalming? Perhaps, the most concise and accurate statement that can be made, based on available documentation, is that EMBALMING IS PERFORMED FOR REASONS OF SANITATION AND THE PRESENTABILITY OF REMAINS. The art and science of embalming can achieve such expectations within the professional framework of practical and defensible MINIMUM STANDARDS FOR THE PRACTICE OF EMBALMING.

BIBLIOGRAPHY

[1]. Francis, Edward, **Embalming: A Satisfactory Method of Performing**, U.S. Public Health Service Reports, Vol. 30, No. 31, July 30, 1915.

[2]. Hockett, Robert N., Leandro Rendon, and Gordon W. Rose, **In-Use Evaluation of Glutaraldehyde As A Preservative-Disinfectant In Embalming**, Abstracts of Annual Meeting of the American Public Health Association, Session 449, Contributed Papers: Microbiology-Immunology, November, 1973.

[3]. Burke, Peter A., and A.L. Sheffner, **The Anti-Microbial Activity of Embalming Chemicals and Topical Disinfectants On the Microbial Flora of Human Remains**, HEALTH LABORATORY SCIENCE, Vol. 13, No. 2, October, 1976.

[4]. Spaulding, E.H., **Role of Chemical Disinfection in the Prevention of Nosocomial Infections**, Proceedings of the International Conference on Nosocomial Infections, Center for Disease Control, August, 1970.

[5]. **Expanding Encyclopedia of Mortuary Practice**, Issue No. 465, March, 1976, The Champion Co., Springfield, OH 45501.

Funeral Industry Practices

A Proposed Trade Rule

Sec.

Section 453.1 Definitions

(a)   Accounting year. "Accounting year" refers to the particular calendar year or other one year period used by a funeral provider in keeping financial records for tax or accounting purposes.

(b)   Alternative container. An "alternative container" is a non-metal receptacle or enclosure, without ornamentation or a fixed interior lining, which is designed for the encasement of human remains and which is made of cardboard, pressed-wood, composition materials (with or without an outside covering) or pouches of canvas or other materials.

(c)   Cash advance item. A "cash advance item" is any item of service or merchandise described to a purchaser as a "cash advance," "accommodation," "cash disbursement," or similar term. A cash advance item is also any item obtained from a third party and paid for by the funeral provider on the purchaser's behalf. Cash advance items may include, but are not limited to, the following items: cemetery or crematory services; pallbearers; public transportation; clergy honoraria; flowers; musicians or singers; nurses; obituary notices; gratuities and death certificates.

(d)   Casket. A "casket" is a rigid container which is designed for the encasement of human remains and which is usually constructed of wood, metal, or like material, and ornamented and lined with fabric.

(e)   Commission. "Commission" refers to the Federal Trade Commission.

(f)   Cremation. "Cremation" is a heating process which incinerates human remains.

(g)   Crematory. A "crematory" is any person, partnership or corporation that performs cremation and sells funeral goods.

(h)   Direct cremation. A "direct cremation" is a disposition of human remains by cremation, without formal viewing, visitation, or ceremony with the body present.

(i)   Funeral goods. "Funeral goods" are the goods which are sold or offered for sale directly to the public for use in connection with funeral services.

(j)   Funeral provider. A "funeral provider" is any person, partnership or corporation that sells or offers to sell funeral goods and funeral services to the public.

(k)   Funeral services. "Funeral services" are any services which may be used to care for and prepare deceased human bodies for burial, cremation or other final disposition; and arrange, supervise or conduct the funeral ceremony or the final disposition of deceased human bodies.

(l)   Immediate burial. An "immediate burial" is a disposition of human remains by burial, without formal viewing, visitation, or ceremony with the body present, except for a graveside service.

(m)   Outer burial container. An "outer burial container" is any container which is designed for placement in the grave around the casket including, but not limited to, containers commonly known as burial vaults, grave boxes, and grave liners.

(n)   Person. A "person" is any individual, partnership, corporation, association, government or governmental subdivision or agency, or other entity.

Language approved by Commission for transmittal to the Office of Management and Budget, September 1981.

Federal Trade Commission, Bureau of Consumer Protection, Washington, D.C., 1981.

(o)   Services of funeral director and staff. The "services of funeral director and staff" are the services, not included in prices of other categories in Section 453.2(b) (4) which may be furnished by a funeral provider in arranging and supervising a funeral, such as conducting the arrangements conference, planning the funeral, obtaining necessary permits and placing obituary notices.

(p)   Unfinished wood box. An "unfinished wood box" is an unornamented casket made of wood which does not have a fixed interior lining.

Section 453.2 Price disclosures

(a)   Unfair or Deceptive Acts or Practices

In selling or offering to sell funeral goods or funeral services to the public, it is an unfair or deceptive act or practice for a funeral provider to fail to furnish price information disclosing the cost to the purchaser for each of the specific funeral goods and funeral services used in connection with the disposition of deceased human bodies, including at least the price of embalming, transportation of remains, use of facilities, caskets, outer burial containers, immediate burials, or direct cremations, to persons inquiring about the purchase of funerals. Any funeral provider who complies with the preventive requirements in Section 453.2(b) is not engaged in the unfair or deceptive acts or practices defined here.

(b)   Preventive Requirements

To prevent these unfair or deceptive acts or practices, as well as the unfair or deceptive acts or practices defined in Section 453.4(b) (1), funeral providers must:

(1)   Telephone Price Disclosures

(i) Tell persons who call the funeral provider's place of business and ask about the terms, conditions, or prices at which funeral goods are offered, that price information is available over the telephone.

(ii) Tell persons who ask by telephone about the funeral provider's offerings or prices any accurate information from the price lists in Sections 453.2(b) (2) through (4) which reasonably answers the question and any other information which reasonably answers the question and which is readily available.

(2)   Casket Price List

(i) Give a printed or typewritten price list to people who inquire in person about the offerings or prices of caskets or alternative containers. The funeral provider must offer the list upon beginning discussion of, but in any event before showing caskets. The list must contain at least the retail prices of all caskets and alternative containers offered which do not require special ordering, enough information to identify each, and the effective date for the price list. In lieu of a written list, other formats, such as notebooks, brochures, or charts may be used if they contain the same information as would the printed or typewritten list, and display it in a clear and conspicuous manner. *Provided however,* that funeral providers do not have to make a casket price list available if the funeral providers place on the general price list, specified in Section 453.2(b) (4), the information which is required by this Section 453.2(b) (2) (i).

(ii) Place on the list, whether a printed or typewritten list or other format is used, the name of the funeral provider's place of business and a caption describing the list as a "casket price list."

(3)   Outer Burial Container Price List

(i) Give a printed or typewritten price list to persons who inquire in person about outer burial container offerings or prices. The funeral provider must offer the list upon beginning discussion of, but in any event before showing the containers. The list must contain at least the retail prices of all outer burial containers offered which do not require special ordering, enough information to identify each container, and the effective date for the prices listed. In lieu of a written list, the funeral provider may use other formats, such as notebooks, brochures, or charts, if they contain the same information as the printed or typewritten list, and display it in a clear and conspicuous manner. *Provided however,* that funeral providers do not have to make an outer burial container price list available if the funeral providers place on the general price list, specified in Section 453.2(b) (4), the information which is required by this Section 453.2(b) (3) (i).

(ii) Place on the list, whether a printed or typewritten list or other format is used, the name of the funeral provider's place of business and a caption describing the list as an "outer burial container price list."

(4)   General Price List

(i) Give a printed or typewritten price list for retention to persons who inquire in person about funeral arrangements or the prices of funeral goods or funeral services. When people inquire in person about funeral arrangements or the prices of funeral goods or funeral services, the funeral provider must offer them the list upon beginning discussion either of funeral arrangements or of the selection of any funeral goods or funeral services. This list must contain at least the following information:

(A)   The name, address, and telephone number of the funeral provider's place of business;
(B)   A caption describing the list as a "general price list";
(C)   The effective date for the price list; and
(D)   In immediate conjunction with the price disclosures required by §453.2(b) (4) (ii), the statement: "This list does not include prices for certain items that you may ask us to buy for you, such as cemetery or crematory services, flowers, and newspaper notices. The prices for those items will be shown on your bill or the statement describing the funeral goods and services you selected."

(ii) Include on the price list, in any order, the retail prices (expressed either as the flat fee, or as the price per hour, mile or other unit of computation) and the other information specified below for at least each of the following items, if offered for sale:

(A)   Forwarding of remains to another funeral home, together with a list of the services provided for any quoted price;
(B)   Receiving remains from another funeral home, together with a list of the services provided for any quoted price;
(C)   The price range for the direct cremations offered by the funeral provider, together with: (1) a separate price for a direct cremation where the purchaser provides the container; (2) separate prices for each direct cremation offered including an unfinished wood box or alternative container; and (3) a description of the services and container (where applicable), included in each price;
(D)   The price range for the immediate burials offered by the funeral provider, together with: (1) a separate price for an immediate burial where the purchaser provides the casket; (2) separate prices for each immediate burial offered including a casket or alternative container; and (3) a description of the services and container (where applicable) included in that price;
(E)   Transfer of remains to funeral home;
(F)   Embalming;
(G)   Other preparation of the body;

(H) Use of facilities for viewing;

(I) Use of facilities for funeral ceremony;

(J) Other use of facilities, together with a list of facilities provided for any quoted price;

(K) Hearse;

(L) Limousine;

(M) Other automotive equipment, together with a description of the automotive equipment provided for any quoted price; and

(N) Acknowledgment cards.

(iii) Include on the price list, in any order, the following information:

(A) Either of the following:

(aa) The price range for the caskets offered by the funeral provider, together with the statement: "A complete price list will be provided at the funeral home."; or

(bb) The prices of individual caskets, disclosed in the manner specified by Section 453.2(b) (2) (i); and

(B) Either of the following:

(aa) The price range for the outer burial containers offered by the funeral provider, together with the statement: "A complete price list will be provided at the funeral home."; or

(bb) The prices of individual outer burial containers, disclosed in the manner specified by Section 453.2(b) (3) (i); and

(C) Either of the following:

(aa) The price for the services of funeral director and staff, together with a list of the principal services provided for any quoted price and, if the charge cannot be declined by the purchaser, the statement: "This fee for our services will be added to the total cost of the funeral arrangements you select. (This fee is already included in our charges for direct cremations, immediate burials, and forwarding or receiving remains.)"; or

(bb) The following statement: Please note that a fee for the use of our services is included in the price of our caskets. Our services include [specify]." The statement must be placed on the general price list together with the casket price range, required by Section 453.2(b) (4) (iii) (A) (aa), or together with the prices of individual caskets, required by Section 453.2(b) (4) (iii) (A) (bb).

(5) Statement of Funeral Goods and Services Selected

(i) Give an itemized written statement for retention to each person who arranges a funeral or other disposition of human remains, at the conclusion of the discussion of arrangements. The statement must list at least the following information:

(A) The funeral goods and funeral services selected by that person and the prices to be paid for each of them;

(B) Specifically itemized cash advance items. (These prices must be given to the extent then known or reasonably ascertainable. If the prices are not known or reasonably ascertainable, a good faith estimate shall be given and a written statement of the actual charges shall be provided before the final bill is paid.); and

(C) The total cost of the goods and services selected.

(ii) The information required by this Section 453.2(b) (5) may be included on any contract, statement, or other document which the funeral provider would otherwise provide at the conclusion of discussion of arrangements.

(6) Other Pricing Methods

Funeral providers may give persons any other price information, in any other format, in addition to that required by Section 453.2(b) (2), (3), and (4) so long as the statement required by Section 453.2(b) (5) is given when required by the rule.

Section 453.3 Misrepresentations

(a) Embalming Provisions

(1) Deceptive Acts or Practices

In selling or offering to sell funeral goods or funeral services to the public, it is a deceptive act or practice for a funeral provider to:

(i) Represent that state or local law requires that a deceased person be embalmed when such is not the case;

(ii) Fail to disclose that embalming is not required by law except in certain special cases.

(2) Preventive Requirements

To prevent these deceptive acts or practices, as well as the unfair or deceptive acts or practices defined in Sections 453.4(b) (1) and 453.5(2), funeral providers must:

(i) Not represent that a deceased person is required to be embalmed for direct cremation, immediate burial, a funeral using a sealed casket, or if refrigeration is available and the funeral is without viewing or visitation and with a closed casket when state or local law does not require embalming; and

(ii) Place the following disclosure on the general price list, required by Section 453.2(b) (4), in immediate conjunction with the price shown for embalming: "Except in certain special cases, embalming is not required by law. Embalming may be necessary, however, if you select certain funeral arrangements, such as a funeral with viewing. If you do not want embalming, you usually have the right to choose an arrangement which does not require you to pay for it, such as direct cremation or immediate burial."

(b) Casket for Cremation Provisions

(1) Deceptive Acts or Practices

In selling or offering to sell funeral goods or funeral services to the public, it is a deceptive act or practice for a funeral provider to:

(i) Represent that state or local law requires a casket for direct cremations;

(ii) Represent that a casket (other than an unfinished wood box) is required for direct cremations.

(2) Preventive Requirements

To prevent these deceptive acts or practices, as well as the unfair or deceptive acts or practices defined in Section 453.4(a) (1), funeral providers must place the following disclosure in immediate conjunction with the price range shown for direct cremations: "If you want to arrange a direct cremation, you can use an unfinished wood box or an alternative container. Alternative containers can be made of materials like heavy cardboard or composition materials (with or without an outside covering), or pouches of canvas." This disclosure only has to be placed on the general price list if the funeral provider arranges direct cremations.

(c)　Outer Burial Container Provisions

(1) Deceptive Acts or Practices

In selling or offering to sell funeral goods and funeral services to the public, it is a deceptive act or practice for a funeral provider to:

(i) Represent that state or local laws or regulations, or particular cemeteries, require outer burial containers when such is not the case;

(ii) Fail to disclose to persons arranging funerals that state law does not require the purchase of an outer burial container.

(2) Preventive Requirements

To prevent these deceptive acts or practices, funeral providers must place the following disclosure on the outer burial container price list, required by Section 453.2(b) (3) (ii), or, if the prices of outer burial containers are listed on the general price list, required by Section 453.2(b) (4), in immediate conjunction with those prices: "In most areas of the country, no state or local law makes you buy a container to surround the casket in the grave. However, many cemeteries ask that you have such a container so that the grave will not sink in. Either a burial vault or a grave liner will satisfy these requirements."

(d)　General Provisions on Legal and Cemetery Requirements

(1) Deceptive Acts or Practices

In selling or offering to sell funeral goods or funeral services to the public, it is a deceptive act or practice for funeral providers to represent that federal, state, or local laws, or particular cemeteries or crematories, require the purchase of any funeral goods or funeral services when such is not the case.

(2) Preventive Requirements

To prevent these deceptive acts or practices, as well as the deceptive acts or practices identified in Section 453.3(a) (1), Section 453.3(b) (1), and Section 453.3(c) (1), funeral providers must identify and briefly describe in writing on the statement of funeral goods and services selected (required by Section 453.2(b) (5) any legal, cemetery, or crematory requirement which the funeral provider represents to persons as compelling the purchase of funeral goods or funeral services for the funeral which that person is arranging.

(e)　Provisions on Preservative and Protective Value Claims

In selling or offering to sell funeral goods or funeral services to the public, it is a deceptive act or practice for a funeral provider to:

(1) Represent that funeral goods or funeral services will delay the natural decomposition of human remains for a long-term or indefinite time;

(2) Represent that funeral goods have protective features or will protect the body from gravesite substances when such is not the case.

(f)　Cash Advance Provisions

(1) Deceptive Acts or Practices

In selling or offering to sell funeral goods or funeral services to the public, it is a deceptive act or practice for a funeral provider to:

(i) Represent that the price charged for a cash advance item is the same as the cost to the funeral provider for the item when such is not the case;

(ii) Fail to disclose to persons arranging funerals that the price being charged for a cash advance item is not the same as the cost to the funeral provider for the item when such is the case.

(2) Preventive Requirements

To prevent these deceptive acts or practices, funeral providers must place the following sentence in the general price list, at the end of the cash advances disclosure, required by Section 453.2(b) (4) (ii) (C): "We charge you for our services in buying these items," if the funeral provider makes a charge upon, or receives and retains a rebate, commission or trade or volume discount upon a cash advance item.

Section 453.4 Required purchase of funeral goods or funeral services

(a)　Casket for Cremation Provisions

(1) Unfair or Deceptive Acts or Practices

In selling or offering to sell funeral goods or funeral services to the public, it is an unfair or deceptive act or practice for a funeral provider, or a crematory, to require that a casket other than an unfinished wood box be purchased for direct cremation.

(2) Preventive Requirements

To prevent this unfair or deceptive act or practice, funeral providers must make an unfinished wood box or alternative container available for direct cremations, if they arrange direct cremations.

(b)　Other Required Purchases of Funeral Goods or Funeral Services

(1) Unfair or Deceptive Acts or Practices

In selling or offering to sell funeral goods or funeral services, it is an unfair or deceptive act or practice for a funeral provider to condition the furnishing of any funeral good or funeral service to a person arranging a funeral upon the purchase of any other funeral good or funeral service, except as required by law or as otherwise permitted by this part.

(2) Preventive Requirements

To prevent this unfair or deceptive act or practice, funeral providers must:

(i) Place the following disclosure in the general price list, immediately above the prices required by Sections 453.2(b) (4) (ii) and (iii):

"The goods and services shown below are those we can provide to our customers. You may choose only the items you desire. If legal or other requirements mean you must buy any items you did not specifically ask for, we will explain the reason in writing on the statement we provide describing the funeral goods and services you selected."

Provided, however, that if the charge for "services of funeral director and staff" cannot be declined by the purchaser, the statement shall include the sentence: "However, any funeral arrangements you select will include a charge for our services" between the second and third sentences of the statement specified above herein; and

(ii) Place the following disclosure on the statement of funeral goods and services selected, required by Section 453.2(b) (5) (ii): "Charges are only for those items that are used. If we are required by law to use any items, we will explain the reasons in writing below."

Section 453.5 Services provided without prior approval

(a) Unfair or Deceptive Acts or Practices

In selling or offering to sell funeral goods or funeral services to the public, it is an unfair or deceptive act or practice for any provider to embalm a deceased human body for a fee unless:

(1) State or local law or regulation requires embalming in the particular circumstances regardless of any funeral choice which the family might make; or

(2) Prior approval for embalming (expressly so described) has been obtained from a family member or other authorized person; or

(3) The funeral provider is unable to contact a family member or other authorized person after exercising due diligence, has no reason to believe the family does not want embalming performed, and obtains subsequent approval for embalming already performed (expressly so described). In seeking approval, the funeral provider must disclose that a fee will be charged if the family selects a funeral which requires embalming, such as a funeral with viewing, and that no fee will be charged if the family selects a service which does not require embalming, such as direct cremation or immediate burial.

(b) Preventive Requirements

To prevent these unfair or deceptive acts or practices, funeral providers must include on the contract, final bill, or other written evidence of the agreement or obligation given to the customer, the statement: "If you selected a funeral which requires embalming, such as a funeral with viewing, you may have to pay for embalming. You do not have to pay for embalming you did not approve if you selected arrangements such as a direct cremation or immediate burial. If we charged for embalming, we will explain why below."

Section 453.6 Retention of documents

To prevent the unfair or deceptive acts or practices specified in Section 453.2 and Section 453.3 of this rule, funeral providers must retain and make available for inspection by Commission officials true and accurate copies of the price lists specified in Section 453.2(b) (2) through (4), as applicable, for at least one year after the date of their last distribution to customers, and a copy of each statement of funeral goods and services selected, as required by Subsection 453.2(b) (5) for at least one year from the date on which the statement was signed.

Section 453.7 Comprehension of disclosures

To prevent the unfair or deceptive acts or practices specified in Section 453.2 through Section 453.5, funeral providers must make all disclosures required by those sections in a clear and conspicuous manner.

Section 453.8 Declaration of intent

(a) Except as otherwise provided in Section 453.2(a), it is a violation of this rule to engage in any unfair or deceptive acts or practices specified in this rule, or to fail to comply with any of the preventive requirements specified in this rule;

(b) The provisions of this rule are separate and severable from one another. If any provision is determined to be invalid, it is the Commission's intention that the remaining provisions shall continue in effect.

(c) This rule shall not apply to the business of insurance or to acts in the conduct thereof.

Section 453.9 State exemptions

If, upon application to the Commission by an appropriate state agency, the Commission determines that:

(a) There is a state requirement in effect which applies to any transaction to which this rule applies; and

(b) That state requirement affords an overall level of protection to consumers which is as great as, or greater than, the protection afforded by this rule;

then the Commission's rule will not be in effect in that state to the extent specified by the Commission in its determination, for as long as the state administers and enforces effectively the state requirement.

ANY NAME FUNERAL HOME

100 Main Street
Hometown, Iowa
(123) 456–7891

GENERAL PRICE LIST

(These Prices are Effective as of July 1, 1981)

The goods and services shown below are those we can provide to our customers. <u>You may choose only those items you desire</u>; however, any funeral arrangements you select will include a charge for our services. If legal or other requirements mean you must buy any items you did not specifically ask for, we will explain the reason in writing on the statement we provide describing the funeral goods and services you selected.

This list does not include prices for certain items that you may ask us to buy for you, such as cemetery or crematory services, flowers, and newspaper notices. The prices for those items will be shown on your bill or the statement describing the funeral goods and services you selected.

DIRECT CREMATIONS: $400.00 to $700.00

Our charge for a direct cremation (without ceremony) includes:

* removal of remains and transportation to crematory
* cremation
* necessary services of staff and authorizations

If you want to arrange a direct cremation, you can use an unfinished wood box or an alternative container. Alternative containers can be made of materials like heavy cardboard or composition materials (with or without outside covering), or pouches of canvas.

1. Direct cremation with container provided by purchaser $400.00
2. Direct cremation with cardboard box $500.00
3. Direct cremation with unfinished pine box $700.00

IMMEDIATE BURIALS: $600.00 to $800.00

Our charge for an immediate burial (without ceremony) includes:

* removal of body
* local transportation to cemetery
* necessary services of staff and authorizations

1. Immediate burial with container provided by purchaser $600.00
2. Immediate burial with unfinished pine box $700.00
3. Immediate burial with beige cloth covered soft-wood casket with beige interior $800.00

FUNERAL ARRANGEMENTS:

<u>Transfer of Remains to Funeral Home</u> (within 50 mile radius) $25.00

<u>Services of Funeral Director and Staff</u> $335.00

Our charge includes arrangement of funeral and consultation with the family and clergy, direction of the visitation and funeral, preparation and filing of necessary notices, and authorizations and consents.

This fee for our services will be added to the total cost of the funeral arrangements you select. (Such a fee is already included in our charges for direct cremations, immediate burials, and forwarding or receiving remains.)

<u>Embalming</u> $75.00

Except in certain special cases, embalming is not required by law. Embalming may be necessary, however, if you select certain funeral arrangements, such as a funeral with viewing. If you do not want embalming, you usually have the right to choose an arrangement which does not require you to pay for it, such as a direct cremation or immediate burial.

<u>Other Preparation of the Body</u> (if no embalming is performed) $20.00

<u>Use of Facilities for Viewing</u>

Main stateroom (per day) $75.00
Smaller stateroom (per day) $50.00

<u>Use of Facilities for Funeral Ceremony</u>

Chapel $75.00
Smaller stateroom $35.00

<u>Other Use of Facilities</u>

Tent and chairs for graveside service $100.00

<u>Hearse</u> $45.00

<u>Limousine</u> $35.00

<u>Other Automotive Equipment</u>

Flower car $25.00
Family car $35.00

Acknowledgment Cards $5.00

Caskets . . . .$175.00 to $2,500.00

    (A complete price list will be provided at the funeral home.)

Outer Burial Containers . . . .$200.00 to $3,100.00

    (A complete price list will be provided at the funeral home.)

Other:

    Pallbearers (6) $120.00
    Burial clothing. . . . .$50.00 to $250.00

Forwarding of Remains to Another Funeral Home $200.00

    This charge includes removal of remains, services of staff, necessary authorizations, embalming, and local transportation (but not shipping charges).

Receiving of Remains from Another Funeral Home $100.00

    This charge includes services of staff, care of remains, and transportation of remains to cemetery or crematory.

Alternative 2

ANY NAME FUNERAL HOME

100 Main Street
Hometown, Iowa
(123) 456-7891

GENERAL PRICE LIST

(These Prices are Effective as of July 1, 1981)

The goods and services shown below are those we can provide to out customers. <u>You may choose only those items you desire;</u> however, any funeral arrangements you select will include a charge for our services. If legal or other requirements mean you must buy any items you did not specifically ask for, we will explain the reason in writing on the statement we provide describing the funeral goods and services you selected.

This list does not include prices for certain items that you may ask us to buy for you, such as cemetery or crematory services, flowers, and newspaper notices. The prices for those items will be shown on your bill or the statement describing the funeral goods and services you selected.

___

DIRECT CREMATIONS: $400.00 to $700.00

Our charge for a direct cremation (without ceremony) includes:

    * removal of remains and transportation to crematory
    * cremation
    * necessary services of staff and authorizations

If you want to arrange a direct cremation, you can use an unfinished wood box or an alternative container. Alternative containers can be made of materials like heavy cardboard or composition materials (with or without outside covering), or pouches of canvas.

1. Direct cremation with container provided by purchaser $400.00
2. Direct cremation with cardboard box $500.00
3. Direct cremation with unfinished pine box $700.00

IMMEDIATE BURIALS: $600.00 to $800.00

Our charge for an immediate burial (without ceremony) includes:

    * removal of body
    * local transportation to cemetery
    * necessary services of staff and authorizations

1. Immediate burial with container provided by purchaser $600.00
2. Immediate burial with unfinished pine box $700.00
3. Immediate burial with beige cloth-covered soft-wood casket with beige interior $800.00

FUNERAL ARRANGEMENTS:

Transfer of Remains to Funeral Home (within 50 mile radius) $25.00

Embalming. $75.00

Except in certain special cases, embalming is not required by law. Embalming may be necessary, however, if you select certain funeral arrangements, such as a funeral with viewing. If you do not want embalming, you usually have the right to choose an arrangement which does not require you to pay for it, such as a direct cremation or immediate burial.

Other Preparation of the Body (if no embalming is performed) $20.00

Use of Facilities for Viewing

Main stateroom (per day) $75.00
Smaller stateroom (per day) $50.00

Use of Facilities for Funeral Ceremony

Chapel $75.00
Smaller stateroom. $35.00

Other Use of Facilities

Tent and chairs for graveside service $100.00

Hearse $45.00

Limousine $35.00

Other Automotive Equipment

Flower car $25.00
Family car $35.00

Acknowledgement Cards. $5.00

Forwarding of Remains to Another Funeral Home $200.00

This charge includes removal of remains, services of staff, necessary authorizations, embalming, and local transportation (but not shipping charges).

Receiving of Remains from Another Funeral Home $200.00

This charge includes services of staff, care of remains, and transportation of remains to cemetery or crematory.

Caskets

Please note that a fee for the use of our services is included in the price of our caskets. Our services include arrangement of funeral and consultation with the family and clergy, direction of the visitation and funeral, preparation and filing of necessary notices, and authorizations and consents.

1. Beige cloth-covered soft-wood with beige interior $510.00
2. Taupe embossed cloth-covered soft-wood with pleated beige crepe interior $531.00
3. 22 gauge bronze colored metal with white interior $545.00
4. 22 gauge silver toned metal with blue crepe interior $582.00
5. 20 gauge copper toned metal with mauve interior $627.00
6. 20 gauge rose colored metal with beige pleated interior $716.00
7. Oak stained soft-wood with pleated blue crepe interior $794.00
8. Mahogany finished soft-wood with maroon crepe interior $828.00
9. Solid white pine with beige crepe interior $835.00
10. 20 gauge lead coated steel with silver tone finish and white crepe interior $957.00
11. 20 gauge lead coated steel with bronze tone finish and tan crepe interior $974.00
12. 18 gauge steel with pale blue finish and off-white interior $1106.00
13. 18 gauge steel with bronze highlights and tan crepe interior $1253.00
14. Solid mahogany with tufted beige velvet interior $1641.00
15. Hand-finished solid cherry with pale blue velvet interior $1904.00
16. 16 gauge bronze finished with maroon velvet interior $2505.00

Outer Burial Containers

In most areas of the country, no state or local law makes you buy a container to surround the casket in the grave. However, many cemeteries ask that you have such a container so that the grave will not sink in. Either a burial vault or a grave liner will satisfy these requirements.

1. Concrete grave liner. $150.00
2. Standard concrete vault $200.00
3. Deluxe asphalt steel-lined vault $539.00
4. Solid copper vault. $3100.00

Other

Pallbearers (6) $120.00
Burial clothing. . . . .$50.00 to $250.00

Pre-need— Prearranging and Pre-financing Funerals

Facts: There are persons who will record essential personal data to indicate what they want in the way of a funeral or alternative often mentioning how much money they wish to have spent. Persons also "prearrange" a funeral or alternative by making specific arrangements with a particular funeral home/mortuary and sometimes "pre-finance" the "prearrangements" that have been made. Historically perhaps the first pre-financing of a funeral was with the birth of life insurance when a group of clergypersons bonded together over a century ago to set up an organization to provide for death insurance. However, before and since then, there have been groups or societies which have pooled funds in a mutual interest to have some monies to pay for the post-death expenses of their members.

The "modern" history of making arrangements for immediate post-death activities dates back to the depression of the 1930s when burial insurance came on the scene in the South.

There are many people within and outside of funeral service who feel that burial insurance and funeral insurance are synonymous. They are not! The generally accepted view is in the following explanatory definitions:

Funeral insurance is payable in cash to any designated beneficiary to use in any manner they choose, but intended to be applied toward funeral expenses. Most such insurance is provided by carriers other than a funeral home/firm owned company although in some areas funeral homes/firms endorse a carrier/plan.

Burial insurance is payable in merchandise and service or as a credit toward merchandise and service, with a lesser benefit often payable in cash when the person dies and final disposition occurs outside the service area of the funeral establishment that services that burial association.

Many burial associations had their origins during the Great Depression as a means of avoiding community assistance in providing funds for funerals of persons whose families were unable to provide such funds themselves. Most of these specified the services and merchandise to be received, and also placed a value on those benefits. The values were sometimes as low as $50.00 and seldom over $150.00.

As the country grew out of the depression and more people became able to provide funeral services beyond these basic minimum services, the benefit of belonging to a burial association decreased. To adjust for this, many asso-

ciations increased the value of their benefits by increasing their membership fees. It was also during this post-depression era that most burial association benefits simply became a credit toward merchandise and service that could be purchased from the funeral establishment which sponsored the association. However a recent court decision which could be a precedent holds that benefits be paid in cash if the named funeral home or association sponsored by the funeral home is not used

Pre-financed funerals are those where an individual(s) pays a lump sum or in installments for a prearranged funeral, including services, facilities and merchandise. Or a person places a sum of money in trust leaving the final decision as to merchandise and services to their survivors. This is especially applicable in states that allow a stipulated sum not counted as an asset in determining eligibility for a welfare benefit. In neither instance are these to be confused with the pre-need purchase of a particular piece of funeral or burial merchandise which most times is bought from some vendor other than a funeral firm separate and distinct from a funeral.

The purpose of this statement is not to probe into all facets of burial or funeral insurance or the multiplicity of funeral plans arranged in advance of need. NFDA has had two special study committees presently reviewing these matters. However, action taken by the House of Delegates in New Orleans precludes going beyond what follows.

Changes Occurring/Issues

The position NFDA took for years relative to burial insurance and funeral insurance as well as prearranged and pre-financed funerals was deemed in the public interest. Various units of government, courts of law, and organizations including many in funeral service felt and still feel that specific arrangements paid in advance were "fraught with the danger of fraud" unless "properly regulated." Proper regulation as to pre-financed funerals was to deposit "every penny" in a trust account with earnings accruing to the account and the person doing the pre-financing having the right to withdraw the corpus and interest at any time without penalty. The resolution encompassing these principles passed at the 1952 NFDA Convention became known as the basis for the 100% trust law concept.

Reprinted from "Tradition in Transition," The Report of the 21st Century Committee of the National Funeral Directors Association, October 26, 1981.

Today, while some still strongly support these former NFDA policies, the situation is changing.

• The average age at the time of death grows each year with an increasing number of persons dying without funds for the kind of post-death activities they would like. The purchasing power of the dollar goes down as prices go up.

• As previously stated, by 1982, the federal government will make about $225,000,000 less available in SSA lump sum payments and VA allowances. The elderly will suffer the most. These cutbacks are also bound to affect state welfare programs.

• Soliciting funerals in advance of need used to be looked upon as only a quasi-legitimate if not an illegitimate type of operation. Now it has gained legitimacy in most areas by upgrading of procedures and the climate of the day.

• There is an increase in the number of pre-need plans available. The very nature of most funeral directors mitigates against their soliciting—especially the doorbell-pushing variety of solicitation.

• In some states funeral directors are bound by a more stringent law than other sellers of pre-financed funerals—laws which allow up front money to other than funeral directors. Even where there is a 100% law, some competitors of funeral directors have other sources of funds paid to them by the consumer they can use to finance pre-need plans without waiting for the time of payment when the pre-need contract requirements are filled.

• A growing number of people feel that a most important factor in arranging a funeral/alternative is the wishes of the deceased.

The issue is the extent to which NFDA in response to requests of its affiliated states gets into proposing laws to control and regulate the prearranging and pre-financing of funerals, suggests plans for them and how to market such plans. The following questions are most pertinent.

1. What state agency controls, regulates, or has the responsibility for overseeing pre-need trust agreements?
2. What funeral merchandise, facilities and service are covered by such agreement?
3. Is a permit required for the firm making the pre-financing agreement, and does the funeral home hold such a permit?
4. How much of the total amount paid must be placed in the trust account?
5. How much, if any, of the income derived from the funds is to remain as part of the trust?
6. How much, if any, of the trust can be withdrawn on demand?
7. Is the price in the pre-financing agreement firm/guaranteed?
8. To what extent, if at all, is the agreement/contract portable?
9. Should a firm charge for the "service" of prearranging a funeral even though it will benefit by the prearrangement because it will provide the services, merchandise and facilities when death occurs?

Impact/Projections

The impact of the need often preceded by a demand for the pre-financing of funerals or alternatives in many areas of the country warrants increased attention and programming. However, because (1) the existence or exposure to pre-need, pre-financed plans in some states is not as great as in others or may be minimal, (2) there is a variance of state laws where they exist with some states having no pre-need law, and (3) where plans are in operation the intensity of competition varies, this report will give scenarios of what can be done regarding pre-financing a funeral and/or pre-arranging and pre-financing.

• Funerals can be pre-financed by the sale of burial or funeral insurance or by old line life insurance not designated as funeral insurance although there could be a stipulation that $X be used for a funeral. The plus here is that some, if not sufficient, funds will be available for the funeral and final disposition. The minus is the dollar and other limitations on burial insurance and their lack of portability. Also some funeral insurance plans do not involve specific prearrangements with a funeral director or facets of the plan are not legal in some states. The equalizer is that laws are being changed and state associations can adapt to funeral insurance plans as some have without the funeral director being the seller/solicitor of the insurance.

• Prearranged and pre-financed funerals can be sold where permitted by law, by a third party for funeral homes. The plus is the expertise of those who sell these plans and the fact that they solicit sales—not the funeral director. The minus is the cost involved (a percentage of the price of the service prearranged) and the third party representations which are sometimes less than dignified. The questions spelled out previously affect these plans.

• Funerals can be prearranged and pre-financed by individual funeral firms in accordance with state law. The questions referred to are pertinent. The plus is the direct association between the person making the prearrangement and the funeral director while meeting needs of a clientele and securing a future for the firm. The minus could be what is allowed by law versus what is essential for a successful operation vis a vis the entrusting funds range from 70% to 100%; trusts can be revocable or irrevocable and the contract can be open ended or fixed.

Our projection is there will be more prearranging and pre-financing of funerals in the future. We also project:

• A diminution of burial insurance with existing firms owned or associated with funeral homes going to a life/funeral insurance program.

• More state associations will have funeral insurance programs with the size of the policies offered increasing in dollar amounts.

• Competition and the climate of the day will result in some states lowering the percentage of funds to be trusted below 100%, allowing funeral directors and other providers of prearranged plans to get "up front" monies and not have to wait for the death of the person for whom the service has been prearranged for some income.

• There will be a move toward programs with irrevocable contracts to permit eligibility for SSI and other welfare programs.

• A key to most plans will be a provision to guarantee that the funeral selected or something similar will be provided when death occurs. Having to deposit less than 100% and/or retaining some or all of the earnings on the trust will provide funds to permit this guarantee.

• There will be an increasing number of states or areas within a state which will establish a trust into which pre-need funds can be placed to benefit by the money market through a central office management rather than that of individual funeral homes.

Planning a Funeral at a Fair Price

FEW FUNERAL HOMES advertise prices. Some won't quote prices over the telephone. When the time comes to do business with one of them, it's all too easy to overspend.

Being a wise shopper isn't the first thing on your mind at such a moment. As the funeral director runs down his list of wares and services, you're expected to make instant decisions on each item. And you do, although you hardly have any idea which choices are best, or even necessary, much less what it all may cost.

Some funeral directors make a genuine, conscientious effort to provide suitable service without pushing expenses you can do without. Others are not above taking advantage of your grief—and your feelings of guilt at being cost conscious—to steer you into overspending.

The average cost of a funeral in the U.S. is about $1,400, according to one member of a House of Representatives subcommittee that looked into proposed funeral regulations. But with all of the various charges added up, a funeral, including casket, funeral home services and burial, can cost as much as $8,000 or more.

Some funeral homes quote totals rather than item-by-item prices for their funerals. In either case, it's important to know in advance the principal items and typical charges you'll be dealing with. Here, while you can consider them calmly, are the items and charges that will probably confront you.

Embalming. Funeral directors sometimes assume, without permission, that they should embalm the body. At a relatively low priced mortuary, the charge for this may be about $175. Elsewhere it may be $225 to $250. The price includes cosmetic treatment for a lifelike appearance. Charges for burial clothes, if they are needed, are often $45 to $65 in a low-priced funeral home, $85 to $125 for those that charge average prices.

Embalming is generally necessary if the body is to be displayed for any length of time. If burial is within two to three days, embalming may not be necessary.

State laws on embalming vary. Some don't require it at all. In many others the time a body can be held for burial or cremation without embalming ranges from 24 to 72 hours. Some states don't require embalming if the body is held under refrigeration, but few funeral homes are equipped to do this. Embalming is usually required if the person died of a communicable disease or if the body is to be shipped across state lines. It is sometimes required if the body is to be shipped within a state.

Ask what your state laws demand, and bear in mind that routine embalming is mainly for esthetic purposes rather than for preservation.

Caskets. The least expensive casket generally is the pine box, covered inside and out with doeskin fabric, which sells for about $200. The top-of-the-line items—at $3,000 or more—are of copper or bronze with innerspring mattresses and elaborate satin or velvet linings.

The funeral director will often attempt to steer you to the most expensive casket he thinks you will buy. A casket is a high-profit item, frequently retailing for three, four or five times its wholesale price. This markup prevails even when the funeral home doesn't stock the caskets but takes you to a wholesale dealer to make your selection.

The pressure can be great to select a high-priced model, perhaps one designed to preserve the body for a long time, although the casket is but one of the factors affecting a body's resistance to decomposition. Many people end up choosing something in the middle price range. Most of these caskets are made of steel or of expensive hardwoods, such as walnut or mahogany, crafted like expensive furniture. Prices run from $1,000 to $1,500 or more.

Extras. These can add up fast. Use of the funeral home for visiting hours, with the casket on display, is often a minimum of $150 for the first day and an additional $25 to $50 for each extra day. More frequently the charge is $350 to $450 for one afternoon and evening of viewing.

Charges are also made if the funeral service is to be held in the funeral home. You can, of course, arrange to have the service in a church or synagogue, which makes no charge. You are expected to give an honorarium to the officiating clergyman, anywhere from $25 to $75, depending on local practices. Some funeral homes charge for making the arrangements for a service elsewhere.

Transportation can also be expensive. Picking up the body at the hospital and taking it to the funeral home can cost $75 to $85. Additional charges are made for taking the body from the funeral home to the church and to the cemetery. Charges for a flower car, if you want one, and for each limousine are somewhat less. Nevertheless, the total transportation cost can be several hundred dollars.

If pallbearers are needed, the charge is about $12 to $15 each, so for six, the usual number, that charge comes to $72 to $90. If arranged by the funeral director, live music may cost $35 to $60.

Some funeral directors price death certificates at cost —$1 or $2 each—and do the same for newspaper death notices, which can be $18 to $20 a day in a big-city paper. Others add a service charge, bringing the cost of the newspaper notice to $30 or $40.

Funeral directors will also help you file for government death benefits—$255 in almost all cases where the deceased is insured by social security, $300 for veterans with an honorable discharge and another $150 if the veteran requires a plot outside a national cemetery.

Graves and mausoleums. Prices for these have been rising rapidly. Although it is possible to buy a grave plot in many places for $150 or so, charges of $575 to $600 are fairly common. This is for an average plot. One next to an oak tree or beside the chapel may cost from $1,200 to $1,500.

Mausoleum crypts are generally more expensive than grave plots. They can cost from $700 to $3,000.

There are other charges as well. In some places it costs $300 or more to open and close the grave. Some cemeteries charge extra for burial on weekends or holidays. In many cemeteries you must buy some sort of grave liner, a simple concrete box, designed not to protect the casket but to keep the ground above the grave from sinking, which makes mowing difficult. These can cost $90 to $190. The more elaborate concrete or metal vaults that funeral directors often try to sell, some guaranteed waterproof for a period of years, start at $275 to $400 and rise to $700 to $1,500. Simple monuments or markers cost $125 to $200; engraving is extra.

Cremation and medical donation. Cremation has been gaining wider acceptance. Most Protestant denominations allow it. Roman Catholics may request permission from the chancery in their diocese. Greek and Jewish Orthodox faiths oppose cremation, as do some Lutheran and fundamentalist Protestant groups.

A low-cost funeral home might charge under $400—about $250 if it owns the crematory—to go to the hospital, pick up the body, obtain the necessary certificates and permits, take the body to the crematory, pick up the ashes and deliver them to the relatives. An ornate urn for the ashes may be as low as $75 to $125 but can go to several hundred dollars. There may be an extra charge if you want the bone fragments pulverized so that you can scatter the ashes. Some states and local jurisdictions restrict scattering ashes, so check before making plans to do so.

Though crematories can be much less expensive than traditional burial, the funeral home may try to sell an expensive casket. Some crematories require that the body be in a casket, but it need be only hardboard or cardboard, which costs as little as $25 or $30. Embalming the body is generally unnecessary, but an effort may be made to sell you on that, too. Some states, however, require that bodies to be cremated be held for 48 hours and that bodies held longer than 24 hours be embalmed or refrigerated, so you have to pay for one or the other.

If the deceased had made arrangements to donate organs or his entire body to medical science and the hospital or medical school accepts the gift, it may also arrange for transportation.

Prearrangement and prefinancing. Some people make all the arrangements beforehand, picking out the items and services they want and discussing them with their families and a funeral director. Most funeral homes will record your choices and keep them on file.

You can also work out some sort of prepayment arrangement. Most states require that some or all of the money paid in advance to a funeral home be deposited in a trust fund or savings account.

Obviously, before entering into one of these arrangements, you have to consider whether the firm will still be in business when the need arises, whether you'll still be living in the same area, whether and how the contract can be canceled and whether you can get a refund. Further, you should know whether the total price will remain fixed or whether the survivors will have to pay an additional amount. You might want to get legal advice.

Organizations that help plan

Funeral and memorial societies are nonprofit organizations aimed at helping people arrange in advance for simple, dignified services at low cost. They're an alternative to the unplanned, "at time of need" arrangements.

They do this by working directly with funeral directors who are willing to provide at greatly reduced prices the kinds of merchandise and services members want.

There are about 170 such groups throughout the country, with a total membership of nearly 1,000,000. One-time membership fees generally are $10 to $20, although some charge as little as $5.

The societies can arrange for traditional funerals with casket, funeral home services and burial, or for cremation. They can also advise you on donating your body to science.

You can get information about societies in your area by writing to the Continental Association of Funeral and Memorial Societies, Suite 1100, 1828 L St., N.W., Washington, D.C. 20036.

Funerals
The Memorial-Society Alternative

The average American funeral and burial costs about $2000 these days. A purchase that large usually deserves careful shopping, but the key decisions about funerals and burial must typically be made within a matter of hours, often by people too burdened by grief to think clearly. As a result, consumers are particularly vulnerable to deception and exploitation by undertakers.

To remedy that situation, the Federal Trade Commission has spent several years developing a set of regulations that could help consumers resist the tactics some undertakers use to sell high-priced funerals. Earlier this year, however, the FTC softened and weakened several portions of its proposed rule. The report beginning on page 492 explains what happened and why.[1]

One provision that did survive the FTC's last-minute changes was a ban on anticompetitive practices. That should make it easier for consumers to obtain information on cremation, memorial societies, and other alternatives to the traditional funeral. In general, those alternatives can save hundreds of dollars in funeral and burial expenses and spare survivors painful and difficult decisions when a death occurs. The report that follows* describes the workings of memorial societies, so you can decide if that is an option you wish to explore.

In 1939, a group of parishioners of a Seattle church formed the nation's first memorial society. Angered by the high cost of extravagant funerals, the founders of the People's Memorial Association set out to find an alternative to the elaborate and costly services pushed by many undertakers. Members wanted a simple, dignified funeral at a cost their families could afford.

A committee of volunteers from the People's Memorial Association eventually found the key to the plan's effectiveness—a Seattle mortician who was willing to cooperate with the membership. An agreement negotiated with the mortician provided, among other things, that members would be charged special low rates for direct cremation or direct burial—undertaker services that do not include embalming, viewing of the body, and other often costly features of a conventional funeral.

That same firm of Seattle morticians, Bleitz Funeral Home, is still affiliated with the People's Memorial Associa-tion and still provides services for members at special low rates. For many years, there wasn't much profit for the Bleitz Funeral Home in its work for the organization. Membership grew slowly. By 1952, there were only about 650 in the association. But by mid-1979, there was an adult enroll-ment of 57,000 with some 300 adults, on average, joining the memorial society each month.

According to Friend Deahl, an accountant and early member of the People's Memorial Association, the member-ship has saved a sizable sum on funerals. Between 1965 and 1974, for example (the decade for which Deahl has compiled data), 6956 services for members cost a total of $1.67-mil-lion, or an average of about $240 per service. If conven-tional funerals had been arranged in regular mortuaries at the prevailing average costs, Deahl told CU, they would have cost upward of $1400 each, on average, for a total of some $10-million.

The nation's second memorial society was organized in New York City just a few months after the Seattle associa-tion was formed. But the memorial-society idea was slow to catch on. By 1950, only seven societies had been estab-lished in the United States.

During the 1950's, however, the movement began to spread more quickly. New societies were formed in many states, particularly among Protestant religious groups, pro-fessional people, the highly educated, and the affluent. Most of these groups patterned themselves after the People's Memorial Association. There are now some 160 memorial societies in the United States, with nearly a million mem-bers in all.

How They Work

Memorial societies are by no means alike. They vary in size, in their operation, and in their arrangements with a mortu-ary. They do share certain characteristic features, however. All are non-profit, democratic, and cooperative. Nearly all memorial societies are members of the Continental Associa-tion of Funeral and Memorial Societies or its Canadian counterpart, the Memorial Society Association of Canada. (Occasionally, illegitimate "memorial societies" are set up as fronts for undertakers; these groups ask a much larger fee than usual and sometimes try to sell "members" a funeral or a cemetery lot well in advance of need.)

---

*Adapted from a chapter on memorial societies in "Funerals: Consumers' Last Rights," pub-lished by Consumer Reports Books.

[1] Report does not appear in this volume.

Memorial societies—consumer movements organized in reaction to high funeral and burial costs—are the watchdogs of the funeral industry at the local, state, and Federal level. They keep an eye on current funeral policies and practices. They are quick to bring to public attention the more noisome practices of undertakers, funeral establishments, and related businesses. Most societies are affiliated with churches, ministerial associations, cooperatives, labor unions, or civic organizations and are staffed almost entirely by volunteers.

All memorial societies stress simplicity, dignity, economy, and the right of individuals to arrange the disposition of their own body. All provide literature about low-cost funerals, cremation, donor programs (bequeathal of the body or body organs to medical science), and other pertinent information relating to death arrangements.

All memorial societies see their prime mission as educational: to encourage open discussion of funeral arrangements in advance of need. The societies urge people to discuss their wishes about such arrangements with family members. This, they say, helps people face the reality and inevitability of death.

Anyone may join a memorial society; there are no restrictions. Those who become members pay a onetime fee that rarely exceeds $25 for a family membership. Lists of legitimate memorial societies are available from: Continental Association of Funeral and Memorial Societies, 1828 L Street N.W., Washington, D.C. 20036; Memorial Society Association of Canada, Box 96, Weston, Ontario M9N 3M6.

The Three Types

A memorial society may be one of three types: a contract society, a cooperating society, or an advisory society.

Contract societies have formal agreements with local undertakers to provide society members with prearranged services at moderate costs. Because of the likelihood that the membership will turn to them in time of need, contract undertakers are, in effect, guaranteed sufficient volume to set lower prices for society members. However, the undertakers continue, in most cases, to conduct their regular funeral business for others at their normal prices.

In contract societies, the new member is given a set of forms and literature that describes the types and prices of services available, gives names of cooperating undertakers, and provides information about donor programs. After going over the material provided by the memorial society, the new member selects a specific plan and fills out the necessary forms. With a family membership, each adult fills out a separate form. Minor dependent children are also usually covered by the family membership.

Normally, three or four copies of each form are required, one for the member's records, one for the memorial society's files, one to be sent to the undertaker, and one for the clergy, if desired.

Many memorial societies include space on the membership form for biographical data that can be used for an obituary. This ensures that the information given to newspapers is accurate and spares survivors additional stress and inconvenience at a difficult time.

Contract undertakers usually keep a separate file for the forms of memorial-society members and know exactly what is to be provided when notified that a member has died. Memorial societies generally believe that survivors can expect fair treatment from a contract undertaker. If disputes arise, societies try to mediate.

Memorial-society contracts with undertakers usually offer at least two basic plans—one for direct cremation and another for direct burial. (Such kinds of disposition are often followed by a memorial service held a few days or weeks later.) Total costs for either of the two basic plans are usually less than $500, and many societies have been able to obtain much lower prices. (Rates for members of the People's Memorial Association include $230 for direct cremation and $304 for direct burial. Direct burial with a memorial service is also available, for $440.)

Groups frequently offer a number of other plans at set prices or arrange with undertakers for extra items at special prices. Additions to the basic plan could include such things as: higher-priced caskets, embalming, dressing of body, cosmetology, viewing, and use of the funeral home's chapel. Members of a contract memorial society, according to estimates made by the Continental Association, can typically save 50 percent in funeral costs, no matter what type of arrangements they make.

Cooperating society. A memorial society without a formal contract with a mortician may still be able to assist members with funeral arrangements. The society may have an understanding or verbal agreement with a local funeral home. In that way, it might save members the task of searching for low-cost facilities.

For example, the Greater Kansas City Memorial Society (about 500 members) has had a long-standing relationship with a cooperating mortician who offers direct cremation (for $325 to society members) and direct burial (for $425, exclusive of cemetery costs), as well as conventional funerals at reduced rates.

On the other hand, the Blackhawk Memorial Society in Davenport, Iowa, reports that its special relationship with a local mortician has deteriorated to the point that it no longer refers members to his funeral home. The reluctance of that cooperating undertaker to continue his arrangement with the society appears to have been caused by pressure from other morticians, the former president of the society told CU. Blackhawk, thus far, has been unable to work out a new relationship with any undertaker in the area.

Advisory society. Some societies serve only in an advisory capacity, usually because they can't find an undertaker willing to agree in advance to low-cost arrangements—or an undertaker willing to cooperate in any way with a memorial society. (On occasion, morticians who do agree to cooperate are subjected not only to pressure and ostracism from other moriticians but also even to disciplinary measures from the state board of funeral directors. In some cases, state boards have prevented a special relationship between a memorial society and an undertaker.) Even so, an advisory society seeks to offer members useful assistance in planning for death or in dealing with arrangements when a death occurs.

Some Common Themes

No matter the type of memorial society, when a member dies it is never the society that carries out the funeral arrangements; that is up to survivors. Nor does a society ever prescribe or recommend a specific plan. It provides information to members about options available—funerals, burial, cremation. A society will also know which medical schools in the area may need bodies to assist with instruction of students and what organ-donor programs exist in community medical centers.

Other aspects common to memorial societies include the following:

Memorial services. Memorial societies strongly encourage survivors to include some kind of memorial service as part of the funeral arrangements. A talk or series of short talks, a prayer, or music can all be part of a memorial gathering.

Low budgets. Most memorial societies are supported by the one-time membership fee; there are no annual dues. It is largely the unpaid work of members and volunteers, who answer mail and phones and maintain records, that makes it possible for the societies to function. Only a few of the larger societies have part- or full-time paid office workers.

Reciprocity. If a member dies while on a visit to another community, and survivors wish disposition to be arranged there, they can get in touch with the nearest memorial society in the area. If a member moves permanently to another community with a functioning memorial society, membership can be transferred at little or no cost.

Even if there were no nearby memorial society to consult, the home society of a traveling member would assist the member or survivors with information about possible arrangements in the new locality or with advice about transportation home and similar matters.

Participating in a Society

Many memorial societies are offsprings of larger organizations—often a church, consumer cooperative, or senior citizens group. In some cases, however, concerned friends and neighbors—sometimes as few as three people—have come together to organize a group. The Continental Association publishes a handbook for memorial societies, which gives detailed instructions on organizing and operating a memorial society. (The book costs $3.50.) On request, the Association will send "How to Organize a Memorial-Funeral Society," a free summary of its handbook.

Prospective members of a memorial society need not adopt any particular philosophy or point of view. The great majority of memorial-society members choose cremation or the donation of their body to medical science and stress memorial meetings rather than funeral services. However, other members, because of personal preference or for religious reasons, choose conventional funerals.

Participation in society activities is encouraged but not mandatory. People are free to join for whatever reason is most important to them. Memorial societies are pragmatic, realistic, consumer-oriented organizations that usually help their members to save money. They also seek to lower funeral costs for everyone in the community and to heighten consumer awareness of shoddy practices. For many members, memorial societies also help foster a healthy awareness and acceptance of the inevitability of death.

About Funeral and Memorial Societies

There are now Memorial Societies in 193 cities in Canada and the U.S., representing nearly a million members. Most Canadian societies are united in the Memorial Society Association of Canada, Box 96, Station A, Weston, Ontario M9N 3M6. Most U.S. societies belong to the Continental Association of Funeral & Memorial Societies, Suite 1100, 1828 L St., N.W., Washington, D.C. 20036. The two groups work closely and membership is reciprocal between them.

How Funeral and Memorial Societies Work

Q. What is a memorial society?

A. *A memorial society is a voluntary group of people who have joined together to obtain dignity, simplicity and economy in funeral arrangements through advance planning.*

Q. Is it run by funeral directors?

A. *No. It is an organization of consumers that helps its members to make dignified funeral arrangements at reasonable cost.*

Q. How is it controlled?

A. *It is a democratic organization managed by an unpaid board of directors elected from its membership.*

Q. Who organizes memorial societies?

A. *Usually they have been started by a church or ministerial association; occasionally by labor, civic or educational groups; sometimes by a few concerned individuals.*

Q. Is membership limited?

A. *No. Membership is open to all regardless of creed, color, occupation or nationality, even though a society may be organized by a church or other group.*

Q. How are memorial societies supported?

A. *Most have a single modest membership fee for individual or family memberships. A few have annual dues. Some receive gifts or bequests. Some make a small charge which is remitted to them by the funeral director at time of death.*

Q. Who does the work?

A. *The members. Most societies are run by unpaid officers and committees, some by church staffs. A few larger ones have part or full time paid secretaries.*

From *A Manual of Death Education and Simple Burial* by Ernest Morgan. Reprinted with the permission of Celo Press. If you wish to have a copy of the Manual, it can be obtained for $3.50 (ppd.) from Celo Press, Route 5, Burnsville, NC 28714.

Q. What happens when you join?

A. *The society lets you know what kinds of funeral services are available and at what cost. You talk it over in your family and decide on your preference, then fill out forms provided by the society.*

Q. Can these plans be cancelled or changed?

A. *Certainly. Any time.*

Q. How does preplanning help at time of death?

A. *In several ways:*

1. *You know what you want, how to get it and what it will cost. You don't have to choose a casket or negotiate for a funeral.*
2. *Your family understands what is being done. Simplicity will reflect dignity rather than lack of respect.*
3. *By accepting in advance the reality of death, and by discussing it frankly, you and your family are better able to meet it when it comes.*

Q. Does planning really save money?

A. *The amounts vary greatly, but memorial society members usually save several hundred dollars on a funeral. One large society estimates that its members save upwards of a million dollars a year by belonging to the organization.*

Q. What is the basis of these savings?

A. *Simplicity. A dignified and satisfying funeral need not be costly if you are not trying to demonstrate social status or compete with the neighbors. There is also the element of collective bargaining in your favor and the advantage of knowing where to go to get the desired services at moderate cost.*

Q. Can these savings be made without a memorial society?

A. *Theoretically, yes. But it rarely happens. One has to search carefully and inquire widely to discover all the possibilities, something few families are prepared to do, especially at a time of death.*

Q. How do I join a memorial society?

A. *Phone or write the nearest society and ask for their literature. They will send you information about the help they can give you and membership fee.*

Q. What if there is no society nearby?

A. *Write the Continental Association or the Canadian Association to find out if there is a society that serves your area or if one is being formed. If you are interested in helping start a society, the Association will supply information and frequently local contacts as well.*

Q. What if I move to another place?

A. *There are memorial societies in 193 cities in the U.S. and Canada, affiliated with the Continental or Canadian Association. They accept transfers of membership with little or no charge.*

Q. Are all societies alike?

A. *Memorial societies vary in their arrangements and mode of operation. Their common characteristic is that they are democratic and non-profit. Occasionally pseudo memorial societies have been set up as "fronts" for funeral directors.*

Q. How can I tell the real thing from the imitation?

A. *In two ways:*

1. *Virtually all genuine memorial societies are members of one of the two Associations. The Associations screen their members with care.*
2. *A bona fide society has no commercial interests. Membership rarely costs over $20. If an organization calling itself a memorial society tries*

to sell you a cemetery lot, or if it asks a large membership fee, you had better investigate it carefully.

Q. What does a memorial society have to do with funeral directors?

A. *Some societies serve only in an advisory capacity, informing their members where specific services may be had at specific costs. Most societies, however, have contracts or agreements on behalf of their members with one or more funeral directors.*

Q. Does the society handle the business details of a funeral?

A. *Not ordinarily. The society commonly brings the family and the funeral director together on a pre-arranged understanding of services and terms. The family itself deals directly with the funeral director.*

Q. Are funerals necessary?

A. *Survivors have important social and emotional needs which should not be ignored. A funeral is one way of meeting some of these needs.*

Q. Are there other ways?

A. *Yes. Disposition of the body can be made immediately after death and a memorial service held later.*

Q. What is the difference?

A. *In a funeral the focus of attention tends to be the dead body; the emphasis is on death. In a memorial service the center of concern is the personality of the individual who has died, and the emphasis is on life. In addition a memorial service generally involves less expense and can be held in a greater variety of locations.*

Q. What are memorial services like?

A. *They vary, taking into account the religious customs of the family and the personal relationships of the one who has died. The distinctive thing is that they stress the ongoing qualities of the person's life rather than his death. Each service can be worked out to meet the needs and circumstances of the particular family.*

Q. Is there any essential difference between funeral societies and memorial societies?

A. *No. Both types of service are arranged by most societies. In every case, however, the family is encouraged to make the type of arrangements most congenial to its background and religious beliefs.*

Q. Is embalming mandatory?

A. *If the body is to be kept several days for a funeral service or, in some cases when it is to be transported by common carrier, yes. Otherwise embalming serves no useful purpose and except in one or two states is not legally required.*

Q. Why then is embalming usually practiced in this country?

A. *Funeral directors assume that unless otherwise advised, there will be viewing of the body, and a service in its presence, and that embalming and ''restoration'' are desired. If this is not the case, the funeral director can be instructed to omit embalming.*

Q. What appropriate disposition can be made of a body?

A. *There are three alternatives:*

   1. *Earth burial was once the simplest and most economical arrangement. With increasing population, rising land values, cost of caskets, vaults and other items usually required, it is becoming more and more costly.*
   2. *Cremation, a clean orderly method of returning the body to the elements, is economical and is rapidly increasing in use.*

3. *Bequeathal to a medical school (as is done by many public spirited people) performs a valuable service and eleminates funeral expense. In many areas there is great need.*   *Back-up arrangements should be made through a memorial society in case the body cannot be accepted. Bear in mind also, a body from which any organs other than eyes have been removed cannot be accepted by a medical school.*

> I bequeath myself to the dirt to grow from
>   the grass I love,
> If you want me again look for me under
>   your boot-soles.
>
> You will hardly know who I am or what I mean,
> But I shall be good health to you nevertheless,
> And filter and fibre your blood.
>
> Failing to find me at first keep encouraged,
> Missing me one place search another,
> I stop somewhere waiting for you.

from Walt Whitman's *Song of Myself*

The Memorial Society Association of Canada and the Continental Association of Funeral & Memorial Societies

History

Starting in 1939, the first societies were successful but attracted little attention and had little contact. By 1960, however, they had become a continental movement and in 1963, on the initiative of the Co-op League they formed the Continental Association with its own office and executive. In 1971 a separate Canadian Association was formed, in close cooperation with Continental, which gave great impetus to the movement in Canada.

Purposes

1. To stimulate and assist in the formation of new societies wherever they are needed.
2. To provide by careful screening of each society applying for membership, a basic credential whereby the public may know it is dealing with a democratic, non-profit service organization and not with a private promoter.
3. To foster, through its leadership and services, the improvement of member societies.
4. To provide for universal reciprocity of membership and service among member societies.
5. To provide information to persons making inquiries and, where possible, to forward inquiries to local societies for follow-up.
6. To provide a central voice for the memorial society movement.
7. To join with other consumer groups to protect basic consumer interests, especially in the area of funeral practices.

Services Provided by the Canadian Association

1. Vigorous organizational help is given to Canadian societies in process of formation.

2. Well-qualified speakers are available to assist with organizing and to speak at annual meetings and on TV programs, etc.
3. A bulletin is issued, carrying news of special interest to Canadian societies.
4. Dominion-wide meetings are held at suitable intervals.
5. An excellent teaching unit on Death and Dying is provided (Available to U.S. societies as well.)

Services Provided by the Continental Association

1. Continental has published the *Handbook for Memorial Societies,* to give detailed instructions on organizing and operating a memorial society. Supplementing the *Manual,* it contains instructions on negotiations with funeral directors, bylaws, financial arrangements, tax regulations, publicity, annual meetings, forms and literature, etc. Especially important, it sets forth organizational guidelines for use by new societies in writing their constitutions and bylaws. Most of these guidelines are merely suggested but a few basic ones are mandatory to membership in the Association. The *Handbook* is provided for $3.50 to member societies and groups in the process of organizing. The Association also:
2. Sends a quarterly *Bulletin* to trustees and directors of member societies reporting news of the movement, new organizations, changes of address, announcements of books and pamphlets, discussion of memorial society operations, legal and legislative developments, etc.
3. Handles—at the national level—legislative problems, contacts with other organizations, and public relations. It responds to thousands of inquiries each year, then channels them to the appropriate societies.
4. Holds Biennial Meetings to formulate Association policy and exchange ideas; encourages regional workshops in alternate years.
5. Provides free, to each member society (courtesy of Celo Press) a copy of each new edition of *A Manual of Death Education and Simple Burial*, now in its ninth edition, to be kept as an office copy and up-dated with revisions as they appear in the *Bulletin*. Most societies keep *Manuals* for sale; many supply a copy to each new member. It sells for $2.50. Quantity discounts are shown on the inside back cover.
6. Makes available a set of forms, *Putting My House In Order*, which is two sheets printed on both sides. This provides for a comprehensive and concise record of financial and property matters and preferences for funeral and other arrangements at time of death. This can be a great relief to survivors, who in addition to their shock and grief, often find the financial records of the deceased in disarray. Many memorial societies give a set to each member family. The forms may be ordered from Continental.
7. Supplies *Uniform Donor Cards* to member societies who wish them.
8. Prepares directories, brochures and other printed material for responding to inquiries and for use by memorial societies. (Samples and prices of this material may be ordered from Celo Press.)
9. Published in 1973, jointly with the Canadian Association, *Proposals for Legislative Reforms Aiding the Consumer of Funeral Industry*, still a valuable sourcebook. (149 pp. Paperback. $5 postpaid.) Also an annotated Bibliography on Funeral Costs, edited by Ruth Harmer. ($1 postpaid.)

Routines of Reciprocity of Membership and Service

When a member moves to an area served by another society, he sends his old membership card (with any transfer or equalizer fee which may be charged) to the new society and fills out such forms as are required for membership in that society. The new society should send a postcard to the former society informing them of the transfer. (People who regularly spend substantial time in two areas of the country should join *both* societies.)

In case of death away from home the family should contact directly the society closest to the place of death who will assist in making arrangements. A directory of memorial societies is in this *Manual* and is also published as a separate folder. If necessary, the decedent's society can also make the contact with the society closest to the place of death.

Cremation in advance of a ceremony or shipment of the body home can usually be arranged in this way. If bequeathal is wanted, the society has a record of medical schools that desire bequeathals and, if one is near, can help with the necessary arrangements.   Bequeathal of eyes or other organs must take place more rapidly, based on instructions on the wallet card.

In every case, of course, appropriate authorizations must be signed, and any financial responsibilities involved must be assumed by the next of kin.

Societies should keep an up-to-date file of addresses and telephone numbers of reciprocating societies to facilitate prompt contact. Each society is also responsible for clearing the reciprocal arrangement with its cooperating funeral directors.

To Organize a Memorial Society

Groups wishing to organize a memorial society should order a copy of the *Handbook of Memorial Societies* ($3.50) from the Continental Association and should ask for any available names and addresses of interested persons located in the area. Canadian groups should, in addition, get in touch with the Canadian Association.

Nearly All Societies are Members

As we go to press only two of the 193 bona fide memorial societies in Canada and the U.S. are not in one or the other association. They are the Memorial Society of British Columbia, 207 W. Hastings, Vancouver, BC V6B 1J3; and Tri-County Memorial-Funeral Society, Box 114, Midway City, CA 92655.

For Consumer Advocate Information

The Continental Association of Funeral and Memorial Societies, 1828 L St. NW, Washington DC 20036.

The Memorial Society Association of Canada, Box 96, Weston, Ontario M9N 3M6

St. Francis Burial Society, 3421 Center St., Washington DC 20010

Books & Bibliographies

A Consumer Bibliography on Funerals, Edited by Ruth Harmer. $1. Available from the Continental Association, listed above.

Funerals: Consumers Last Rights, Consumers Union

The American Way of Death, by Jessica Mitford.

Report of the Federal Trade Commission

Checklist of Things to Be Done

Assuming that the family belongs to a memorial society and that the matters above have been taken care of, there still remain numerous details, many of which can be taken care of by friends though others require the attention of the family. Scratch off the items in the following checklist which do not apply; check the others as they are taken care of:

☐ Decide on time and place of funeral or memorial service(s).

☐ Make list of immediate family, close friends and employer or business colleagues. Notify each by phone.

☐ If flowers are to be omitted, decide on appropriate memorial to which gifts may be made. (As a church, library, school or some charity.)

☐ Write obituary. Include age, place of birth, cause of death, occupation, college degrees, memberships held, military service, outstanding work, list of survivors in immediate family. Give time and place of services. Deliver in person, or phone, to newspapers.

☐ Notify insurance companies, including automobile insurance, for immediate cancellation and available refund.

☐ Arrange for members of family or close friends to take turns answering door or phone, keeping careful record of calls.

☐ Arrange hospitality for visiting relatives and friends.

☐ Arrange appropriate child care.

☐ Coordinate the supplying of food for the next days.

☐ Consider special needs of the household, as for cleaning, etc., which might be done by friends.

☐ Select pall bearers and notify. (Avoid men with heart or back difficulties, or make them honorary pall bearers.)

☐ Notify lawyer and executor. Get several copies of death certificate.

☐ Plan for disposition of flowers after funeral (hospital or rest home?).

☐ Prepare list of distant persons to be notified by letter and/or printed notice, and decide which to send each.

☐ Prepare copy for printed notice if one is wanted.

☐ Prepare list of persons to receive acknowledgments of flowers, calls, etc. Send appropriate acknowledgments. (Can be written notes, printed acknowledgments, or some of each.)

☐ Check carefully all life and casualty insurance and death benefits, including Social Security, credit union, trade union, fraternal, military, etc. Check also on income for survivors from these sources.

☐ Check promptly on all debts and installment payments. Some may carry insurance clauses that will cancel them. If there is to be a delay in meeting payments, consult with creditors and ask for more time before the payments are due.

☐ If deceased was living alone, notify utilities and landlord and tell post office where to send mail. Take precaution against thieves.

Suggestions to Those Who Plan My Funeral

National Selected Morticians

Use this form wisely. Consider well your entries. Be moderate. Be clear. Remember that you can neither explain nor change your comments after you are gone.

Do not feel compelled to complete this form in full. Keep in mind that you may harm your family by trying to give too much guidance. Help those you love to help themselves.

About My Family and Friends:

These persons should be notified of my death as soon as possible:

Name	Relationship	Address	Telephone Number

The following persons because of age, infirmity, or other reasons should be notified personally by their clergyman, a friend, or an associate:

My clergyman is_____

My physician is_____

My lawyer is_____

My funeral director is_____

About Personal Data:

The following information will be needed for official certification. Accuracy is very important. Claims, benefits, and legal procedures may be involved. This will become a permanent record and could be important to your family many generations hence.

Full Name:_____

        First   Middle   Last

Also any other name, if commonly used

Usual residence:_____

    Street number or location if rural

City:_____ County: _____ State:_____ Length of Residence:_____

Birthdate: _____ Birthplace: _____

Usual occupation: _____ Kind of business or industry: _____

Employer: _____ Retired?_____

Spouse: _____ Birthplace: _____

    Full maiden name

Father: _____ Birthplace: _____

    Full name

Mother: _____ Birthplace: _____

    Full maiden name

Social Security Number: _____

If ever employed by a railroad, list company and dates:

If ever in Armed Services, Service Serial Number:_____

Dates of Service:_____

If in Service under any other name:_____

Attach a listing of biographical information, family relationships, church, fraternal, vocational, professional, club, or union affiliation, etc. Although not necessarily required, this might be useful.

About My Estate:

I have ☐   I have not ☐   executed a will.

If "yes" it is dated:_____ and will be found:_____

My executor is:_____

My bank is:_____

I have Safety Deposit Box No._____ in _____

                Bank

It is held jointly with_____

Valuable papers not in this box will probably be found: _____

_____

(or attach separate notations, if advisable.)

_____

About The Ceremonies:

This form is intended to convey suggestions only. Except as hereinafter provided, your comments will be treated as suggestions only, not binding instructions. Unless otherwise indicated, your family will assume that this is only for their information, that you have not dictated firm decisions, and that they are free either to confirm, or not confirm, your suggestions. It will be ONLY in connection with items that you ENCIRCLE AND INITIAL that it will be considered that your instructions shall prevail insofar as may be possible under the applicable laws.

Unless in conflict with the legal rights of others, I desire that the preferences of _____
                                                                                                              name
my_____ shall be given special consideration in connection with
                    relationship
the ceremonial arrangements. If not possible, I designate _____
                                                                                                        name
_____ under the same conditions.
                    relationship
My preferred clergyman:_____

   Alternate, if necessary:_____

My preferred funeral director:_____

   Alternate, if necessary:_____

I prefer to have the ceremony held at_____

_____
                          (church, funeral home, residence or other location)

I desire that final disposition shall be:

   ☐ Burial in_____
                                                      Cemetery

Where I do ☐   Do not ☐   Have space.

If you do, describe:_____

Where is the cemetery lot certificate?_____

   ☐ Entombment_____ Where?_____

   ☐ Cremation   Disposition of cremated remains:_____

_____

I do ☐   do not ☐ desire to comment on the costs or qualities of caskets, vaults, funeral services, et cetera.

If you do, make appropriate notations:_____

_____

_____

_____

Outline as much detail of the funeral service as you feel necessary. Avoid such terms as "usual" or "customary." Such terms can be meaningless. You might want to suggest such things as scripture, music, or other ceremonial details. If lodge, or other semi-secular services are to be considered, make a notation — but DO NOT specify such preferences UNLESS FULLY DISCUSSED with your family and your clergyman.

_____

_____

_____

_____

You might note here the "little" things which could make a big difference: (Clothing, hairdresser, glasses, bearers, flowers, or anything else)

_____

_____

_____

If you are considering donating tissue or organs from your body for medical research, you should first discuss this thoroughly with your family, your doctor and your funeral director. Ordinarily, such wishes cannot be fulfilled unless preparations are made IN ADVANCE. In any event, your comments on the funeral are still appropriate. Donation does not usually interfere with the body being present for services.

I have_____or have not_____made payment of any costs. If yes, attach copy of receipt or a notation as to where it will be found.

In subscribing to all the foregoing, I state that I have set forth these suggestions only in a spirit of helpfulness. I recognize that it is impossible for me to anticipate accurately all the circumstances that might affect my funeral. Therefore, *excepting only such things as I may have encircled and initialed*, the effect of which has already been noted in this folder, I specifically direct that the preferences of my family shall prevail.

Date:_____   _____
                                                                  Signature

Copies of this form should be given to persons who will be available and able to act at any time. An extra copy is attached for this purpose. Relatives, close friends, or your clergyman might be considered. If your selection of funeral director is definite, he should have a copy since he or an associate must be constantly available. DO NOT put it in your safety deposit box.

Clergy Views of Funeral Practices: Part One

Frank Minton, Ph.D.

THE SURVEY

Since funeral directors must interact regularly with clergy of numerous religious affiliations, it is important for them to become aware of the relationship between the belief systems and practices of major religious groups. Also, the funeral director will be better equipped both to serve the public and to have a good professional relationship with clergy if he knows their preferences. This study has attempted to address these areas based on a national survey of clergy from thirty-two Jewish and Christian groups. [1]

This is the first survey ever attempted of this scope and with these objectives. The most similar was the excellent 1959 study by Robert Fulton entitled "Attitudes of Clergymen Toward Funerals and Funeral Directors in the United States." That study, however, focused primarily on what religious leaders thought about funeral practices and funeral directors and did not inquire about clergy preferences regarding the religious content of the funeral, nor make any attempt to correlate theology and practice. Various other studies, such as the one sponsored by the Casket Manufacturers Association in 1974 entitled "American Attitudes Toward Death and Funerals," have been based on surveys of the general public rather than clergy. These have tended to emphasize the grieving process and attitudes towards the industry, especially with reference to pricing.

> . . . the sample is comprehensive in the sense that the thirty-two bodies selected do represent 85% of all persons in this country who are affiliated with a religious organization. Furthermore, the sample reflects much of the diversity within Protestantism, for the list includes denominations identified as liturgical and free, conservative and liberal, evangelical and confessional.

The thirty-two institutions selected for the present survey include most religious groups in the United States which have 500,000 or more members. Also included in the sample are certain smaller Protestant denominations having historical or cultural importance. The sample is confined to groups within the Judeo-Christian tradition although, because of the great multiplicity of sects in the United States, many of these could not be surveyed. Most of those omitted are relatively small and highly localized. Only a few of the major groups had to be omitted. One was the Church of Jesus Christ of Latter Day Saints, which has no professional clergy; another was the National Baptist Convention U.S.A., which has a policy not to release clergy lists. Nevertheless, the sample is comprehensive in the sense that the thirty-two bodies selected do represent 85% of all persons in this country who are affiliated with a religious organization. Furthermore, the sample reflects much of the diversity within Protestantism, for the list includes denominations identified as liturgical and free, conservative and liberal, evangelical and confessional. Three of the major black churches are included, as well as churches representing various socio-economic strata.

In addition to religious affiliation, the survey questionnaire was designed to measure the responses according to three other variables concerning the respondent: his geographical region, his age, and the size of his community. The number of questionnaires sent to the clergy of each religious group was proportional to the total membership of that group and, likewise, the number sent to each of the nine geographical regions was proportional to membership distribution. For example, since 16% of Roman Catholics reside in the West North Central Region, 16% of the total questionnaires allocated to Roman Catholic clergy were sent to priests within that region. In every instance the actual selection of names was made purely at random.

A total of 2,037 questionnaires were mailed and 1,105 completed questionnaires were received making a return rate of 54.2%. These were sufficiently distributed so that every variable could be adequately tested. This excellent response demonstrates that there is an intense interest in the subject by clergy, a conclusion further confirmed by the fact that several hundred of the respondents requested the results of the survey.

Different versions of the questionnaire were sent to Jewish and Christian clergy, but both were designed to elicit three basic categories of information from the respondents: the elements they include in funeral services, their present views of funerary practices, and their theology of death. Using this data it was possible to draw conclusions regarding their beliefs concerning the function of the funeral ritual, their perceptions of the funeral industry, the practices they find to be of value and those they would like changed, and the relationship of their theology to their funeral preferences.

Part One of this report focuses on those conclusions which relate to practices in which the funeral director plays a major role. Part Two will concentrate to a greater extent on the liturgical preferences and theological assumptions of clergy.

TYPE OF SERVICE

Questions regarding the funeral service would never arise if we could follow one minister's advice and "abolish death," but as long as death is with us most clergy agree that it should be acknowledged through an appropriate rite of passage. Furthermore, the overwhelming majority agree that this should be a public rite. To merely dispose of the body is unacceptable to them because it diminishes the dignity of human life, and to have a strictly private service deprives the family of the support of the community in dealing with their grief.

In religious practice two basic services have emerged. One is the traditional public service followed by interment. Normally in this type, there are stated times during which friends may call at the funeral parlor to view the remains and express condolences to the family. At the service, which may be either in the church or in the funeral chapel, the casket will be present. Afterwards, if there is to be a ground interment, guests will process behind the family to the cemetery for a brief committal service. If there is to be a cremation, the service normally concludes at the place of worship with a committal and benediction.

In the other type of service the body is not present at all. There is either a private ground interment, cremation, or donation of the body followed by a public memorial service held at some later time. This may be scheduled within a few days after death, or it may be postponed a week

Reprinted with permission from NRIC's *National Reporter,* the National Research and Information Center, Evanston, Illinois, April, 1981.

or more until distant relatives and friends can arrive. It is most likely to be held at the place where the person worshipped, but may also be held at a convocation hall if the deceased was well-known.

Actually, the second type of service is found primarily among Protestants since Roman Catholic, Orthodox, and Jewish clergy overwhelmingly prefer a public service with the body present, followed by interment. Generally speaking, clergy from the more liberal Protestant denominations tend to favor the memorial service, while those from the more conservative denominations tend to favor the traditional service.

TYPE OF SERVICE PREFERRED

Clergy Group	Traditional	Memorial	Other*
Jewish	100.0%	0.0%	0.0%
Orthodox (Christian)	100.0	0.0	0.0
Roman Catholic	94.3	1.2	4.5
Protestant	73.1	21.5	5.4
African Methodist Episcopal Church	100.0	0.0	0.0
African Methodist Episcopal Zion Church	90.9	9.1	0.0
American Baptist Churches	52.2	39.1	8.7
American Lutheran Church	76.6	17.0	6.4
Assemblies of God	73.7	0.0	26.3
Christian Church — Disciples of Christ	53.3	43.3	3.4
Christian Churches & Churches of Christ	70.0	15.0	15.0
Church of the Brethren	30.0	70.0	0.0
Church of God	61.5	30.8	7.7
Church of the Nazarene	100.0	0.0	0.0
Churches of Christ	86.8	10.5	2.7
Episcopal Church	90.2	7.3	2.5
Friends United Meeting	0.0	100.0	0.0
Lutheran Church in America	66.7	17.8	15.5
Lutheran Church — Missouri Synod	75.0	22.7	2.3
Mennonite Church	33.3	55.6	11.1
National Baptist Convention of America	100.0	0.0	0.0
Presbyterian Church in the United States	50.0	33.3	16.7
Reformed Church in America	60.0	36.0	4.0
Salvation Army	91.7	4.2	4.1
Seventh-Day Adventists	90.9	9.1	0.0
Southern Baptist Convention	86.6	9.0	4.4
Unitarian-Universalist Association	21.4	78.6	0.0
United Church of Christ	57.8	31.1	11.1
United Methodist Church	75.5	20.0	4.5
United Presbyterian Church	37.5	50.0	12.5

*"Other" includes (1) private service and interment with only the family present, (2) simple disposal and elimination of the funeral service entirely, and (3) various combinations of the options.

The memorial service is more popular among Protestant and Roman Catholic clergy who reside in the Pacific region. According to a survey of funeral directors from all nine geographical regions a higher proportion of funerals in the Pacific region do, in fact, involve immediate disposition with a memorial service held at a later time. [2]

The memorial service is more popular among Protestant and Roman Catholic clergy who reside in the Pacific region.

TYPE OF SERVICE PREFERRED
COMPARISON OF PACIFIC REGION AND TOTAL UNITED STATES

All Christian Clergy	Traditional	Memorial	Other
Pacific Region	66.7%	23.1%	10.2%
United States	84.2	10.9	4.9
Protestant Clergy Only	Traditional	Memorial	Other
Pacific Region	56.7%	30.0%	13.3%
United States	73.1	21.5	5.4

There are probably several reasons why the traditional service remains very popular. One is simply that it is traditional. At a time of loss the family may derive comfort from following a familiar pattern, one which may have been sustaining in the past — for instance, at the death of a parent or grandparent. Or a family may be reluctant to deviate from tradition for fear of criticism from friends and relatives.

There are probably several reasons why the traditional service remains very popular. One is simply that it is traditional. At a time of loss the family may derive comfort from following a familiar pattern, one which may have been sustaining in the past — for instance, at the death of a parent or grandparent. Or a family may be reluctant to deviate from tradition for fear of criticism from friends and relatives. Equally important are the powerful psychological reasons for following this familiar ritual. Having the body present may help the mourners confront the reality of death and work through their grief. Also, the presence of the body can serve as a focus for the memorial to the deeds of the deceased. Finally, remaining with the body until it is interred can be a comforting expression of devotion to the loved one.

Those who favor the memorial service point out that it has the practical advantage of allowing flexibility in scheduling, but they also feel it has a strong appeal both psychologically and symbolically. For one thing, it relieves the family of the emotional strain of repeatedly confronting their loss through the visible casket and allows them instead to focus on the beauty of relationships they share with the deceased.

Those who favor the memorial service point out that it has the practical advantage of allowing flexibility in scheduling, but they also feel that it has a strong appeal both psychologically and symbolically. For one thing, it relieves the family of the emotional strain of repeatedly confronting their loss through the visible casket and allows them instead to focus on the beauty of relationships they share with the deceased. One minister put it this way, "Reminiscence of the past life is more uplifting than dwelling upon the throes of death." Other ministers who choose the memorial service observe that celebrating a life without the body present is the most positive affirmation that hope is not bound to the flesh. The fact that the deceased has been buried and that mourners have resumed life's routine by the time the memorial service takes place conveys the thought that people are able to recall and retain relationships in a way that is not life-defeating, but life-generating.

LOCATION AND TIME OF THE SERVICE

The questionnaire which was sent to Christian clergy asked for their

By an overwhelming majority they want the service for church members to be held in the church. This is true for Roman Catholics, Orthodox, and Protestants of every denomination included in the survey.

preferences regarding the location of the funeral service. By an overwhelming majority they want the services for church members to be held in the church. This is true for Roman Catholics, Orthodox, and Protestants of every denomination included in the survey. Most consider it more appropriate for non-member services to be held in the funeral chapel, though a significant minority would also hold these in the church. It is possible that some Roman Catholic and Orthodox respondents interpreted "non-member" to mean a person who is not a member of that particular parish rather than a person who is not Roman Catholic or Orthodox, for the customary practice of these two churches is to bury from the church only those persons who were of their religious persuasion. Many Protestant denominations, on the other hand, do allow non-member services within the church. This practice is most common for "friends" of the church — persons who regularly attend and participate in the life of the church but do not actually belong, or for spouses, parents, and children of members. The more liturgical Protestant churches are the most insistent that member services be held in the church and more inclined to conduct non-member services in the funeral home.

LOCATION PREFERENCES OF
MEMBER AND NON-MEMBER SERVICES

Location of Member Services

Clergy Group	Funeral Home	Church	No Preference
Protestant	6.8%	76.6%	16.6%
Roman Catholic	1.2	96.4	2.4
Orthodox	0.0	97.9	2.1

Location of Non-Member Services

Clergy Group	Funeral Home	Church	No Preference
Protestant	54.2%	22.2%	23.6%
Roman Catholic	60.5	24.7	14.8
Orthodox	60.5	37.2	2.3

No question about the location of the service was included on the questionnaire sent to Jewish clergy, for the Christian practice of bringing the casket into the church and conducting the funeral in the house of worship is foreign to Judaism. Jewish funerals, traditionally held in the home, are now usually held in Jewish mortuaries where the directors are familiar with Jewish ritual. Thus, the location of the service is simply not an issue.

This is very much an issue for Christian clergy, for they would like to reverse the trend that has developed in recent years to conduct the funeral service in the mortuary rather than in the church. Rightly or wrongly they perceive funeral directors as encouraging the use of their facilities in order to avoid the inconvenience of transporting the casket and equipment to the church. They want member services moved back to the church to make possible a service of worship with congregational participation. The mortuary chapel may be well equipped with stained glass windows, lectern, chancel, and organ, but it usually contains few specific symbols because it must be acceptable to all faiths. In the church, on the other hand, there is an opportunity to have hymn singing, readings and responses, and music by those familiar with the liturgy of the church. Moreover, as many clergy point out, it is most fitting that the transition which culminates life should be celebrated in the place where the stages along life's way — baptism, confirmation, and marriage — have also been marked.

Although the questionnaire contained no question about time of the

service, a surprisingly large number of clergy suggested that the service be held in the evening so that a greater number of friends and relatives could participate. This recommendation came as much from those who prefer the traditional service with the body present as from those who opt for the memorial service and seems to reflect a perceived need to adapt to sociological change. In an earlier time, when society was more agrarian, the whole community could pause from the daily round and rally to the support of the family at the funeral. In this urban age, however, when families live anonymously and work miles from their bedroom communities and when approximately sixty percent of the women are in the work force, it is increasingly difficult for people to attend daytime funerals unless the deceased is a close relative. The policy of many companies is to give released time to employees only for the funeral of an immediate family member. Consequently, the tendency is for acquaintances to call at the parlor during evening visitation hours and for only the closest friends and relatives to attend the funeral itself. Many clergy feel this deprives the family of a powerful support system and renders impossible a corporate celebration of the life of the deceased.

. . . a surprisingly large number of clergy suggested that the service be held in the evening so that a greater number of friends and relatives could participate.

The model which an increasing number of ministers are proposing has the evening service as the focal point. Some suggest one evening of visitation, a public service the following evening, and private interment or cremation the next day with only family and intimates present. Others would compress the visitation and public service into a single evening. Still others would have the public memorial service the evening immediately following the private burial. Common to all of these recommendations are the public celebration in the evening and the private leave-taking during the day. This would put increased demands on the funeral staff and facilities during the evening hours, but the demand on facilities would be reduced if the other recommendation to locate more services in the church were implemented.

VIEWING AND VISITATION

Whether viewing the body helps the bereaved accept the reality of death is a point on which Christian and Jewish clergy are sharply divided. By a margin of 80.3% to 19.7% Christian clergy say that it does help, but 93% of Jewish rabbis do not find viewing the body to be of value. In sharpest contrast to Jewish clergy are Roman Catholic and Orthodox priests, of whom 84.2% and 98.8% respectively find viewing the body to be helpful. Although the majority of Protestant ministers of nearly every denomination take the same position, a somewhat larger minority, 24.3%, find no correlation between viewing the body and a healthy acceptance of death.

Whether viewing the body helps the bereaved accept the reality of death is a point on which Christian and Jewish clergy are sharply divided. By a margin of 80.3% to 19.7% Christian clergy say that it does help, but 93% of Jewish rabbis do not find viewing the body to be of value. In sharpest contrast to Jewish clergy are Roman Catholic and Orthodox priests of whom 84.2% and 98.8% respectively find viewing the body to be helpful.

Some rabbis say that when there is viewing, it should be restricted to the immediate family. They say that modesty and dignity should prevail, and they oppose any display of the corpse in a lavish casket that would obscure the equality of all persons before the Lord. Few Christian clergy would confine viewing to the family, but their comments reveal that they would definitely like to limit the time for viewing. Almost unanimously, they strongly object to re-opening the casket following the funeral service. The consensus is that the casket should be permanently closed prior to the beginning of the service. A Lutheran minister expresses the sentiments of

. . . the "body should be viewed beforehand — so the family is aware of the reality of death and so that they can 'say goodbye emotionally'," and . . . "opening the casket after the service has an adverse psychological effect on the family and takes away from the message of hope in the service."

many clergy from other Christian churches as well when he grants that the "body should be viewed beforehand — so the family is aware of the reality of death and so that they can say 'goodbye emotionally', " and also when he observes that "opening the casket after the service has an adverse psychological effect on the family and takes away from the message of hope in the service."

A visitation period when friends may call on the bereaved family is endorsed by all groups, Jewish and Christian. It should be noted, however, that visitation is not necessarily equated with viewing. Rabbis, the majority of whom oppose viewing except possibly for the immediate family, do favor a visitation period. In fact, 73.2% say that such a period is "very helpful," 11.3% say that it is "somewhat helpful," and only 15.2% say that it is "not helpful at all." They would seem to have reference to the mourning period during which the bereaved have an opportunity to work through their grief, and especially to the first two stages of the mourning period: (1) the time between death and the funeral when friends may come and bring comfort to the family, and (2) to the Shiva period, the seven days of mourning beginning with the day of the funeral. Some rabbis, while acknowledging the emotional support friends may offer during the mourning period, nevertheless oppose formal visitation hours. One rabbi observes that these tend to take on a "party atmosphere." Another rabbi commented that he would like to see Jewish funerary customs "move away from our 'Western' influence of prior visitation, open casket, expensive caskets, and the centrality of the funeral home."

A visitation period when friends may call on the bereaved family, is endorsed by all groups, Jewish and Christian. It should be noted, however, that visitation is not necessarily equated with viewing.

In a Christian context, visitation normally means gathering at the funeral home both to view the remains and to express condolences to the family. Depending on local custom and the prominence of the deceased, the visitation may extend through either one or two evenings. Christian clergy generally find value in scheduled visitation hours as indicated in the following table:

VALUE OF A SCHEDULED VISITATION PERIOD

Clergy Group	Very Helpful	Somewhat Helpful	Not Helpful At All
Protestant	49.6%	45.4%	5.0%
Roman Catholic	71.2	25.8	3.1
Orthodox	69.6	28.3	2.2

A number of Christian clergy, although on record as favoring visitation hours, suggest that they be shortened. They would limit the visiting hours to a single evening and avoid having it prolonged to the extent that it would be taxing to the family. Nearly all believe that the family derives great comfort from a community of friends who demonstrate by their presence respect for the deceased and compassion for the survivors. However, they are concerned that what should be a source of comfort may become an ordeal if the family must be in a receiving line or have their grief either repressed or put on display for an inordinate period of time. Some would move the visitation to a church setting, and some would have a closed casket and simply a picture of the deceased. Yet these latter issues do not appear to be as significant to most clergy as the duration of the visitation period.

CREMATION

Cremation appears to be gaining acceptance, at least by most religious groups. Only Orthodox clergy have not altered their historical opposition to it. The majority of Protestants and Roman Catholics have come to the conclusion that the Christian faith is neutral as to the practice. This is a moderation of their historical position, which held cremation to be a pagan practice without biblical warrant, advanced in an effort to deny the Christian doctrine of the resurrection. Jewish clergy, by contrast, are overwhelmingly in opposition to cremation, though it does not appear that the actual practice of Jewish families necessarily parallels this opposition. Note the following table for a comparison of these respective groups:

ATTITUDES TOWARD CREMATION

Clergy Group	Favor	Oppose	Neutral
Protestant	24.6%	14.1%	61.3%
Roman Catholic	16.1	13.7	70.2
Orthodox (Christian)	2.1	89.6	8.3
Jewish	1.5	78.5	20.0

As might be expected, the number of clergy favoring cremation is greater in the densely populated New England and Middle Atlantic States and in the Pacific region.

As might be expected, the number of clergy favoring cremation is greater in the densely populated New England and Middle Atlantic states and in the Pacific region. This probably reflects the fact that the practice of cremation is more prevalent in those areas and that persons from urban areas are more directly aware of the need to conserve space. This study disclosed that the percentage of clergy from major metro areas who favor cremation is double that of clergy from rural areas. Geographical region and community size are not, however, the only pertinent factors. The relative dispersal of religious denominations and the spread of theological convictions partially determine the practice of a given region. For example, Southern Baptists are heavily concentrated in the South Atlantic and East South Central Regions, while the Episcopal Church and the United Church of Christ are well represented in the New England and the Middle Atlantic states. Observe the correlations:

ATTITUDES TOWARD CREMATION

	Favor	Oppose	Neutral
New England	39.2%	17.6%	43.1%
Middle Atlantic	33.6	14.0	52.4
Episcopal	48.8	2.4	48.8
United Church of Christ	61.7	2.1	36.2
South Atlantic	18.9	16.2	64.9
East South Central	15.1	23.7	61.3
Southern Baptist	6.0	40.3	53.7

It might be predicted that those who are opposed to cremation on theological grounds would also be opposed to organ transplants and the willing of the body to medical science. Yet, there is scarcely any opposition to this practice by Christian clergy — only 1.9%; and more than two-thirds (67.6%) are on record as favoring it. The only exceptions are Orthodox and Conservative rabbis, of whom 81% and 35%, respectively, oppose the practice, no doubt largely due to ritualistic prohibitions about treatment of the dead. Only a very small minority of Reform rabbis (9%) express any opposition. One wonders why most of those who have reservations about cremation do not have a problem with transplants and dissection. Perhaps burning implies a finality and cessation of being which cutting the body does not. And perhaps some realize that, at some point, a transplant could lengthen their own lives.

Clergy Views of Funeral Practices: Part One Continued

Frank Minton, Ph.D.

USE OF RENTAL CASKETS

Apparently the idea of rental caskets has not yet penetrated the country, for, when asked their opinion of them, many penciled in incredulous comments. There is a general receptivity to this idea by Protestants (44.2% in favor, 17.2% opposed, and 40.6% neutral) and by Roman Catholics (41.2% in favor, 21.8% opposed, and 37% neutral), though the reaction varies widely among Protestant denominations. Both Orthodox Christian clergy and Jewish rabbis are opposed to the idea. It is difficult to find a pattern among the Protestant responses. Some of the more liberal groups such as the United Methodist and United Presbyterian are strongly in favor, but so are some of the more conservative and evangelical bodies such as the Assemblies of God and the Salvation Army. More black clergy oppose the idea than favor it and, in the huge Southern Baptist Convention, those opposed outnumber those in favor by 31.8% to 25.8%.

Apparently the idea of rental caskets has not yet penetrated the country, for, when asked their opinion of them, many respondents penciled in incredulous comments. There is general receptivity to this idea by Protestants (42.2% in favor, 17.2% opposed, and 40.6% neutral) and by Roman Catholics (41.2% in favor, 21.8% opposed, and 37% neutral) though the reaction varies widely among Protestant denominations. Both Orthodox Christian clergy and Jewish rabbis are opposed to the idea.

A sharp difference is found between age groups on this particular question. Christian clergy thirty years of age and younger definitely endorse the rental casket (51.9% in favor, 5.4% opposed, and 42.7% neutral), while those sixty and over are decidedly against the idea (23 9% in favor, 40.5% opposed, and 35.6% neutral).

It would seem plausible to find a correlation between attitudes toward cremation and preferences regarding the rental casket. That is, one should expect those who favor cremation to be more inclined toward the rental casket and vice versa. Indeed, as the following table displays, this hypothesis is confirmed:

PREFERENCES REGARDING RENTAL CASKETS

	Favor	Oppose	Neutral
Those favoring cremation	65.8%	9.6%	24.6%
Those opposing cremation	22.6	42.6	34.8
Those neutral about cremation	38.5	16.6	44.9

Thus, one may suppose that as the practice of cremation continues to increase, the marketability of rental caskets will correspondingly increase.

OPEN/CLOSED CASKET

Protestant, Catholic, and Jewish clergy unanimously prefer a closed casket during the religious service. They are divided, however, on the question of whether it should remain closed throughout the entire proceedings or be opened prior to the service and then closed.Most Protestants favor a viewing period before the service, though there is considerable variation among the individual denominations on this point. In eight of the twenty-six Protestant denominations sampled, a majority of the clergy prefer not to open the casket at all. Roman Catholics, by more than a two-to-one margin, want the casket to remain closed both before and during the mass. Virtually all Jewish clergy insist that the casket not be opened. Only Orthodox Christian clergy request that the casket be open for viewing throughout the religious services.

Although some regional differences are to be found, which no doubt reflects local customs, in none of the nine geographical regions do more than a small minority of clergy, other than those from the two Orthodox bodies, want the casket to remain open for viewing. Yet, they are even

Protestant, Catholic, and Jewish clergy unanimously prefer a closed casket during the religious service. They are divided, however, on the question of whether it should remain closed throughout the entire service or be opened prior to the service and then closed.

more insistent that the casket should be present at the traditional funeral. They find it appropriate to have the bodily remains present when the person's life is being celebrated. But they want the mourners to shift their attention from the physical form and focus on the enduring spiritual qualities.

PREFERENCE REGARDING THE CASKET

Clergy Group	Remain Open	Remain Closed	Open Then Closed	Not Present
Protestant	8.0%	38.8%	49.6%	4.6%
Roman Catholic	10.1	64.6	25.3	0.0
Orthodox (Christian)	87.5	6.3	6.3	0.0
Jewish	0.0	95.8	2.8	1.4

QUALITY OF PROFESSIONAL SERVICES

Clergy are generally satisfied with the quality of the services offered by funeral directors. Of Christian clergy, 49.2% rate these services as "excellent," while 46% rate them as "good." Only 4% consider them to be "fair," and a mere 0.8% find them to be "poor." The evaluations of Jewish clergy are very similar: 54.9% "excellent," 36.7% "good," 4.2% "fair," and 4.2% "poor."

Reprinted with permission from NRIC's *National Reporter,* the National Research and Information Center, Evanston, Illinois, May, 1981.

Clergy are generally satisfied with the quality of the services offered by funeral directors. Of Christian clergy, 49.2% rate these services as "excellent," while 46% rate them as "good." Only 4% consider them to be "fair," and a mere 0.8% find them to be "poor." The evaluations of Jewish clergy are very similar: 54.9% "excellent," 36.7% "good," 4.2% "fair," and 4.2% "poor."

However, many respondents — even among those who give funeral directors high marks for their professionalism — advocate simpler, less costly funerals. While finding little fault with the quality of services performed, they frequently criticize the funeral industry for conveying the impression that dignity and respect for the deceased requires an elaborate burial. A rabbi expresses the criticism of many Jewish clergy in his charge that Jewish morticians "seem intent on a lavish 'production' and are the biggest stumbling blocks to rabbinic desire to preserve traditional simplicity." Typical of Christian clergy is the priest who recommends "more reverent simplicity, less ostentation and superfluity of massive floral and such other displays, less expensive accomodations (caskets, funeral home, cemetery, and other 'consumer' services)." The conclusion reached from the numerous comments volunteered on this subject is that clergy experience most funeral directors as honest, compassionate individuals with a high level of competence but they believe that funeral directors, as businessmen, have a vested interest in selling expensive packages.

The familiar charge, popularized by certain exposes, that funeral directors cynically exploit emotional vulnerability to sell these "expensive packages" occurs infrequently in the clergy comments. Even the clergy who are the most discontent with present practices do not criticize funeral directors as much for a lack of professional integrity as for a lack of flexibility. They contend that the funeral industry has tied the profitability of the business to a certain norm for the funeral and consequently, that the industry resists certain changes that may be in the public interest. Prominently displaying less expensive caskets, encouraging memorial gifts to charity instead of lavish floral displays, de-emphasizing elaborate cosmetology, and possibly substituting a simple shroud for the dress suit are examples

The familiar charge, popularized by certain exposes, that funeral directors cynically exploit emotional vulnerability to sell these "expensive packages" occurs infrequently in the clergy comments. Even the clergy who are the most discontent with present practices do not criticize funeral directors as much for a lack of professional integrity as for a lack of flexibility.

of changes which many clergy recommend but feel are resisted by the industry.

Relatively few clergy raised the issue of embalming. Possibly, the lack of comments on this subject was due to the fact that it was not raised on the questionnaire. However, the absence of any direct question on funeral costs did not deter numerous clergy from commenting on that subject. Thus, it may be that most clergy, except for those who believe religious law prohibits embalming, are not dissatisfied with this practice.

Thus, it may be that most clergy, except for those who believe religious law prohibits embalming, are not dissatisfied with this practice.

The clergy with the most positive image of the funeral director are found in small towns and rural communities. Ratings by urban clergy, though still quite favorable, are noticeably lower. Restricting the sample to clergy from rural areas and villages under 5,000 population, the quality of services are judged 55.5% "excellent," 40.6% "good," and 3.6% "fair." The sample from cities over 100,000 population rate the services as 39.3% "excellent," 52.2% "good," and 7.7% "fair." One reason may be the natural tendency of clergy to respond more warmly to the funeral director who is regularly encountered as a small town acquaintance than to the more anonymous big city professional.

ROLE OF THE FUNERAL DIRECTOR

Judging by the comments on the questionnaire, the clergy's most serious criticism is not directed at funeral costs, although these are definitely a matter of concern, but is rather directed at the enlarged role of the funeral director. They believe that many prerogatives, which properly belong to them, have been assumed by the funeral director. They resent the fact that they are often not called until all arrangements have been made and that they must then adapt to customs and rituals which they believe are neither helpful to the mourners nor compatible with their faith. Comments such as the following appear frequently on the questionnaires: "Encourage funeral directors to work WITH ministers and families in arranging services. Too often the service is completely set up without any input from the clergyman."

Judging by the comments on the questionnaire, the clergy's most serious criticism is not directed at funeral costs, although these are definitely a matter of concern, but is rather directed at the enlarged role of the funeral director.

If clergy were called before the service was planned, they say that they would have an opportunity to discuss with the family such matters as holding the service in the church, scheduling it during evening hours, requesting memorial gifts instead of flowers, opening the casket, and seating of the family. Particularly objectionable to many clergy is the use of a special "family room" which prevents eye contact by the speaker and eliminates the symbolic support of being surrounded by a community of friends. From the clergy's standpoint, the funeral director has an important role to play but is not the master of ceremonies. In short, clergy resist being relegated to a twenty minute slot after all arrangements have been made. They see the entire ritual, beginning at the point of death and extending through the visitation and final rites, as an opportunity to minister to the mourners and to celebrate their faith. There appears to be a conflict in the perception of roles with ministers struggling to regain a greater degree of control.

Control is particularly important to the minority who consider present practices regarding disposal of the dead to be inconsistent with the Christian faith. Greatest dissatisfaction was evidenced by Orthodox priests, 23.8% of whom checked "inconsistent." Least critical are Catholic priests, only 7.8% of whom say that present funeral practices are inconsistent with the Christian faith. Protestants fall in between with 15.8% marking "inconsistent." However, there is wide variation between the individual Protestant bodies. Generally, those bodies traditionally identified as "liberal" or "mainline Protestant" tend to be most dissatisfied with present practices while the more "evangelical" groups tend to be less critical. For example, 36.8% of Episcopalian clergy say "inconsistent" while the figure for Southern Baptists is only 7.6%.

No comparable question was included on the questionnaire sent to Jewish rabbis, but their comments indicated that they experience similar role conflicts. For Jews, as for Christian, many of the rites once performed by religious institutions have been assumed by the professional funeral director. Some rabbis advocate a return to the tradition of having the volunteer burial society (Chevra Kadisha) take responsibility for all arrangements. Others, who recognize the practicality of having the funeral director handle the physical and mechanical aspects of the funeral, at least want greater control by boards of rabbis over Jewish mortuaries.

CLERGY HONORARIUM

Clergy were asked whether in those situations in which they do accept an honorarium, they prefer to be paid by the funeral director or by the family. A number point out that they do not accept an honorarium for conducting the funeral of a church member. When payment is appropriate, however, the majority prefer to receive it from the funeral director. On this point there is surprisingly little variation among the three major Christian groups; for 63.5% of Protestants, 63.9% of Roman Catholics, and 68.2% of Orthodox clergy express a preference for payment by the director. Jewish rabbis are more evenly divided on this issue as 53.4% prefer payment through the funeral establishment and 46.6% want to be paid by the family.

Many clergy observe that the size of the payment has not kept pace with inflation and that it is not adequate compensation for the time invested. One Protestant minister complained, "People think nothing of paying a surgeon $1,000 and a funeral director $3,000, then pay the preacher $25.00." Another notes that he receives the same amount for non-member services today as he did fifteen years ago. Some clergy apparently depend on honoraria to supplement marginal salaries. Others regard member funerals as one of their pastoral or rabbinical functions for which they are paid by their church or synagogue, but see non-member funerals as an individual service carried out largely on their own time for which a truly professional fee is warranted.

NOTES

[1] The thirty-two groups included in the survey consisted of the following. PROTESTANT: African Methodist Episcopal Church, African Methodist Episcopal Zion Church, American Baptist Churches, American Lutheran Church, Assemblies of God, Christian Church—Disciples of Christ, Church of the Brethren, Church of God, Church of the Nazarene, Churches of Christ, Episcopal Church, Friends United Meeting, Lutheran Church in America, Lutheran Church—Missouri Synod, Mennonite Church, National Baptist Convention of America, Presbyterian Church in the United States, Reformed Church in America, Salvation Army, Seventh-Day Adventists, Southern Baptist Convention, Unitarian-Universalist Association, United Church of Christ, United Methodist Church, United Presbyterian Church; JEWISH: Conservative, Orthodox, Reform; ORTHODOX (CHRISTIAN): Greek Orthodox, Orthodox Church of America; ROMAN CATHOLIC.

[2] According to research conducted by Vanderlyn R. Pine and reported in his book CARETAKER OF THE DEAD (NY: John Wiley & Sons, 1975), of funeral directors operating in the Pacific region, 60% report that "almost none," 29% that a "few," and 11% that "some or most," of their funerals involve immediate disposition with a memorial service. The figures for the United States as a whole are 89%, 9%, and 2% respectively.

Clergy Views of Funeral Practices: Part two

Frank Minton, Ph.D.

Most clergy conduct under twenty-five funerals per year, and the majority of Protestant and Orthodox clergy report that they officiate at ten or less. The number for Roman Catholic and Jewish clergy is higher because the average size of their congregations is larger.

NUMBER OF FUNERAL SERVICES CONDUCTED EACH YEAR

Clergy Group	10 or less	11-25	26-50	Over 50
Protestant	59.4%	32.6%	6.8%	1.2%
Roman Catholic	21.3	41.4	24.9	12.4
Orthodox (Christian)	55.3	29.8	14.9	0.0
Jewish	35.2	45.1	11.3	8.4

Nearly all believe that the funeral has both psychological and religious value, and only a negligible number from the more than 1,100 responses suggest abolishing the service or surrendering their prerogative to the funeral director. However, they are far from being of one mind about the religious content of the service. This article will first examine their preferences on the liturgy, the sermon, and the form of member and non-member services. Then it will explore some of the theological presuppositions of those preferences.

Nearly all believe that the funeral has both psychological and religious value, and only a negligible number from the more than 1,100 responses suggest abolishing the service or surrendering their prerogative to the funeral director.

THE LITURGY OF THE FUNERAL SERVICE

The word "liturgy" is used here in the broadest sense to refer to all elements of the religious service other than the sermon. The very word would be objectionable in some Protestant circles because of its connotation of formality. With the qualification that it does not necessarily refer to an elaborate or prescribed order of worship, it can be a convenient term for discussing the music, prayers, readings, and, indeed, the whole tone of the service. None of the questions dealt explicitly with these elements, so a statistical analysis is not possible. However, many clergy volunteered opinions and recommendations from which the following four impressions have been gathered.

Some single out such hymns as "In the Garden," Beyond the Sunset," and "I Believe" as prime examples of "tear-drawing" music which counteracts the message of joy and hope the minister is trying to convey through the spoken word.

The first is that there is a general dissatisfaction with music played in the funeral chapel. Clergy find much of it to be excessively sentimental and pseudo-religious. Some single out such hymns as "In the Garden," "Beyond the Sunset," and "I Believe" as prime examples of "tear-drawing" music which counteracts the message of joy and hope the minister is trying

to convey through the spoken word. One minister even goes so far as to say he would "ban 90% of present vocal music now being used at funerals." Though their particular choice of hymns varies, the genre preferred by most is the hymn of hope and victory. Generally, they want more substantial hymns of worship, joyous songs, music of praise and faith.

. . . clergy would like to see the funeral service become a time for celebration and affirmation rather than a time for wallowing in grief.

A second impression, closely related to the first, is that clergy would like to see the funeral service become a time for celebration and affirmation rather than a time for wallowing in grief. A Roman Catholic priest charges that "the general atmosphere of funeral directors and their establishments is one of grief — controlled and repressed, but grief none the less." Many clergy, however, fault themselves and their congregations for having perpetuated the somber mood. As one minister explains, services don't have to "act" sad in order to convey sensitivity toward sadness and grief. "They should take sadness and grief seriously" but come across as "triumphant and courageous." Another minister recalls a note he received following a service: "I came to the funeral wishing the ordeal was over but left feeling so uplifted." A great many clergy want to make the funeral less of an ordeal and more of a celebration of the person's life by the community of faith.

One way to accomplish an attitudinal change, in the opinion of these clergy, is to introduce more congregational participation into the service. Comments to this effect were received from Roman Catholic, Protestant, and Jewish respondents. Basically they feel the funeral service should be an experience of worship which contains congregational singing, Scripture readings and responses, and prayers spoken by all. Several proposed that members of the family and close friends might share memories about the deceased. The officiating clergyman can speak of the religious faith of the community but the eulogizing and personalizing can better be done by those who were close to the person. One Christian clergyman summarized the views of many of his colleagues when he said, "A funeral should never be something done by a professional for others, but a corporate act of Christian worship." The desire to make it an act of the entire religious community is, of course, the primary reason why most Christian clergy would like to hold member services in the church.

Basically they feel the funeral service should be an experience of worship which contains congregational singing, Scripture readings and responses, and prayers spoken by all.

The third impression, that clergy advocate wider participation in the funeral service, is substantiated statistically, at least with reference to Christian clergy; for 65.9% of them indicated on the questionnaire that they prefer a funeral in which the congregation and family members participate. Fully 82% of Roman Catholic priests recommend a change in this direction, a position in accord with the trend of Roman Catholic worship since Vatican II. The majority of the Orthodox Christian (75%) and Jewish (70.4%) groups would continue to have the funeral conducted entirely by officiating clergy. Certain Protestant denominations, especially

Reprinted with permission from NRIC's *National Reporter,* the National Research and Information Center, Evanston, Illinois, June, 1981.

the more evangelical groups, are in agreement. The more liberal and liturgical groups, on the other hand, overwhelmingly endorse greater participation by the family and congregation. Whatever the degree of congregational participation in the chapel service, the committal service at the cemetery is usually conducted solely by the clergyman.

The responses on the questionnaires reveal no consensus about this service, but they do indicate that many clergy are troubled by it. Some believe that the procession to the cemetery destroys the hopeful mood which has been established through corporate worship. Others observe that the committal service is redundant and that the cemetery is certainly not a favorable setting for repeating the affirmations which were spoken earlier in the chapel. Those who favor the memorial service would, of course, solve the problem by having a private interment precede the public service of celebration operating within the context of the traditional service, some clergy would have only the funeral director, or the funeral director and the minister accompany the body to the grave, while others would include the family, but delay the committal until the day after the funeral service. A few clergy suggest that confrontation of the reality of death and leave-taking would be more complete if the casket were visibly lowered into the grave during the committal service. In summary, this fourth impression about the funeral liturgy is that clergy are groping for new ways to handle the committal. It is definitely a topic which clergy and funeral directors should candidly discuss.

In summary, this fourth impression about the funeral liturgy is that clergy are groping for new ways to handle the committal. It is definitely a topic which clergy and funeral directors should candidly discuss.

THE FUNERAL SERMON

As the following table demonstrates, a sermon or meditation is an integral part of the funeral service conducted by most Christian and Jewish clergy.

INCLUSION OF A SERMON IN THE FUNERAL SERVICE

Clergy Group	Always	Often	Seldom	Never
Protestant	81.0%	12.6%	4.6%	1.8%
Roman Catholic	93.5	4.7	1.8	0.0
Orthodox (Christian)	87.5	12.5	0.0	0 0
Jewish	86.1	13.9	0.0	0.0

Reform Jewish clergy are more likely to delete the sermon than either Orthodox or Conservative rabbis, for 32% of them marked "often" in contrast to only 6% of the other two groups. Among Protestants, clergy of the Episcopal church and the Presbyterian Church in the United States are the least likely to include a sermon. Nearly half the respondents from both groups marked either "seldom" or "never." Some ministers, especially from the more liturgical churches, consider the liturgy itself sufficient to carry the message without the necessity of a sermon.

The majority preach sermons of ten minutes or less, and the most popular length is six to ten minutes. Protestant ministers of the more evangelical churches preach longer than the average; and, based on the responses, the sermons are longest in the black churches. The list of churches with clergy who state that the average length of their funeral sermon is more than ten minutes includes: African Methodist Episcopal Church, African Methodist Episcopal Zion Church, Assemblies of God, Christian Churches and Churches of Christ, Church of the Nazarene, Churches of Christ, National Baptist Convention of America, Seventh-Day Adventists, and Southern Baptist Convention. Whatever their religious affiliation, clergy seem to become more long-winded with advancing age. Of those thirty-five and younger, 22.5% say they preach sermons in excess of ten minutes but for the fifty-one and older group the percentage preaching over ten minute sermons increases to 35.2%.

More important than the length of the sermon are the themes within the sermon, for these determine the impact on the mourners. The one theme common to the preaching of all clergy is assurance to the bereaved that they will find the strength to sustain the loss and re-construct their lives. There is a consensus that the speaker has a primary responsibility to speak a word of comfort, and nearly all clergy do emphasize the love of God and the caring community. Beyond this one central theme, there are apparently widely differing opinions regarding what a funeral sermon should accomplish. Some are inclined to make the meditation primarily a memorial to the deceased. In those cases, they comment extensively on the life of the person and try to portray the unique qualities of that life. This is particularly the emphasis of rabbis, 88.7% of whom always personalize their message and 97.2% of whom always or often stress the uniqueness of the life of the deceased. Not surprisingly, those Christian clergy most attracted to the memorial service rather than the traditional funeral are the ones most inclined to fashion the sermon into a personal tribute to the deceased. Hope for life after death is another prevalent theme in the sermons of Christian clergy, but less so in the meditations of Jewish clergy except for Orthodox rabbis. For Christian clergy, the degree of explicitness about life after death seems related to two factors. To the extent that the minister is agnostic about life after death and interprets heaven and hell in symbolic terms, he or she will stress the life of the deceased rather than eternal destiny. For example, 71.4% of Unitarian-Universalist ministers either disbelieve in or doubt life after death, and correspondingly 66.7% seldom or never express hope for life after death. At the opposite end of the theological spectrum, ministers who are absolutely convinced that the individual lives after death in either heaven or hell will conscientiously avoid offering assurance if there is any doubt about the person's being one of the "saved." This accounts for why the majority of a clergy group such as the Salvation Army, though very firm in belief, stated that they "often" rather than "always" offer assurance of life after death for the deceased.

More important than the length of the sermon are the themes within the sermon, for these determine the impact on the mourners. The one theme common to the preaching of all clergy is assurance to the bereaved that they will find the strength to sustain the loss and re-construct their lives.

In the case of Jewish clergy there is a very definite correlation between theological belief about human destiny and the presence or absence of the theme of life after death in their funeral meditations.

RELATIONSHIP BETWEEN PERSONAL BELIEF IN LIFE AFTER DEATH AND EXPRESSION OF HOPE IN SERMON (JEWISH CLERGY)

Believe in Life after Death	Express Hope for Life after Death in Sermon

ORTHODOX CLERGY

92% — Definitely	48.5% — Always
8% — Probably	33.3% — Often
0% — Probably Not	16.7% — Seldom
0% — Definitely Not	4.2% — Never

CONSERVATIVE CLERGY

32% — Definitely	8.7% — Always
41% — Probably	21.7% — Often
18% — Probably Not	34.8% — Seldom
9% — Definitely Not	34.8% — Never

REFORM CLERGY

9% — Definitely	0% — Always
24% — Probably	9% — Often
29% — Probably Not	14% — Seldom
38% — Definitely Not	77% — Never

SERVICES FOR MEMBERS AND NON-MEMBERS

The majority of Christian clergy (80.3%) make a distinction between the services of church members and non-members. Most Jewish rabbis make no such distinction, but the situations are different. A "non-member" from the standpoint of a rabbi would normally be a Jewish person who does not belong to his synagogue, but who would still be accorded a funeral in the Jewish tradition, whereas a "non-member" from the standpoint of a Christian clergyman often means a person with no church affiliation and possibly not even a professing Christian.

Christian services from more liturgical churches use different forms for the two services. Roman Catholics and Orthodox, for instance, reserve the requiem mass for members and have a special liturgy of prayers and scripture for non-members. Similarly, in the Episcopalian church the norm for a church member is a requiem Eucharist at the church, while that for the non-member is the burial office in a funeral home. Most Lutherans also employ different liturgies, and some are hesitant to officiate at all unless the deceased can be assumed to be a Christian. Non-liturgical churches are more apt to use similar forms but vary the content, particularly of the sermon.

Some variation is necessitated because non-members are usually less well-known to the clergy than their own parishioners are. The funeral service for a relative stranger will necessarily contain more generalized expressions of hope and comfort, or what one minister describes as a "stock funeral home service." Part of the difference in content, however, arises from the fact that many clergy perceive different destinies for the "churched" and "unchurched" or "saved" and "unsaved." When conducting a non-member funeral these clergy are more apt to emphasize the comfort of God's love to the living rather than a sense of joy for the deceased. Some will even construe that the primary need of the bereaved is to pay attention to their own salvation and thus make the non-member service evangelistic in tone. In the words of one minister with this point of view, "there should be a clear statement at funerals of the salvation that is open to all (yes, all attending the funeral) if they will turn to Christ." Other ministers strongly criticize "combining a funeral with a revival" as an insensitive exploitation of vulnerable emotions.

To test the hypothesis that clergy are more likely to differentiate between the services of members and non-members if they have definite beliefs about eternal rewards and punishments, the responses of three control groups were compared. Group 1 consists of those who regard heaven and hell as places of reward or punishment; Group 2 consists of those who interpret heaven and hell as states of being where the individual experiences fulfillment or alienation; and Group 3 consists of those who interpret heaven and hell as symbols for a full or meaningless life here and now. If the hypothesis is correct one should expect a higher percentage of Group 1 clergy to have different services for members and non-members, and a progressively diminishing percentage for Groups 2 and 3.

RELATIONSHIP OF THEOLOGICAL BELIEFS TO DIFFERENCES BETWEEN MEMBER AND NON-MEMBER SERVICES

	Services Differ	Services Do Not Differ
Group 1	76.0%	24.0%
Group 2	67.5	32.5
Group 3	53.5	46.5

The conclusion is that clergy who believe in some ultimate judgment will tend to categorize their funerals, while those who do not presume to probe the future are more apt to dwell on the grace of God and the life of the deceased — themes that lead to less differentiation

HOW THEOLOGY INFLUENCES TYPE OF SERVICE PREFERENCE

Either the traditional funeral service with the body present or the memorial service without the body could be compatible with either belief

In fact, however, Christian clergy who are agnostic about life after death are more inclined to the memorial service than those who are definite about life after death.

or disbelief in personal survival of death. In fact, however, Christian clergy who are agnostic about life after death are more inclined to the memorial service than those who are definite about life after death. Rabbis present a special case because traditional Jewish rites can accomodate differing personal theologies. Orthodox, Conservative, and Reform rabbis have sharply contrasting beliefs about human destiny, but they do not display comparable differences on the type of service preferred. For Christian clergy — particularly for Protestants and to some degree Roman Catholics — practice is a function of theology, as the following graphs make clear.

RELATIONSHIP OF PERSONAL BELIEF ABOUT LIFE AFTER DEATH TO SERVICE PREFERENCE

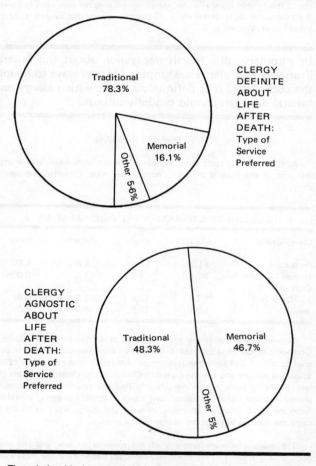

CLERGY DEFINITE ABOUT LIFE AFTER DEATH: Type of Service Preferred

Traditional 78.3%
Memorial 16.1%
Other 5.6%

CLERGY AGNOSTIC ABOUT LIFE AFTER DEATH: Type of Service Preferred

Traditional 48.3%
Memorial 46.7%
Other 5%

The relationship between belief and practice is further borne out by correlating type of service preferences with concepts of heaven and hell. Those who interpret heaven and hell as places are most in favor of the traditional service, those who interpret them as states of being are somewhat less so, and those who interpret them symbolically are least of all. This information is summarized in the table on the following page.

It is clear that theology is a significant determinant of service preference, but it is not the only factor. There are conservative clergy who prefer the memorial service because it is more adaptable to an experience of worship, and there are liberal clergy who prefer the traditional service because they feel it better helps the mourners confront the reality of death

RELATIONSHIP OF CONCEPTS OF
HEAVEN AND HELL TO SERVICE PREFERENCE

Clergy Group	Traditional Service	Memorial Service	Other
Interpret heaven and hell as places of reward and punishment	85.3%	9.7%	5.0%
Interpret heaven and hell as states of fulfillment and alienation	71.2%	24.2	4.6
Interpret heaven and hell as symbols of fullness and meaningfulness here & now	45.2	52.4	2.4

and work through their grief. Nor do liberal and conservative clergy necessarily draw the same conclusions. A person who believes in the resurrection of the dead may find the memorial service to be the best setting to make the point that resurrection is not a resuscitation of the corpse, lying there in state, but a new creation, a "spiritual body." On the other hand, a person who believes survival is through the memory of the mourners may wish the body present as a focus for the memory. Still, the prevailing opinion is that the memorial service is the more natural setting in which to shift the emphasis from possible survival of death to the enduring contributions of life, whereas the presence of the body calls attention to the deceased's present status and raises the question of existence in another realm.

SUMMARY

A single clergy view of funeral practices has not emerged from this study. Indeed, clergy views vary widely, and these variations are largely the result of differing theological presuppositions. Nevertheless, certain generalizations are possible, both about problem areas that concern all clergy and about preferences of the different groups.

PROBLEM AREAS

— Most clergy conceive of themselves as the "director" of the funeral service, and they believe that the funeral director's role has been enlarged at the expense of their own.

— While most clergy are satisfied with the quality of professional services performed, they believe that the funeral has become unnecessarily elaborate and costly.

— All Christian clergy groups want services for church members to be held in the church, and they resist the trend to shift them to the mortuary.

— Clergy, except for Orthodox Christian, do not want the casket open during the funeral service, and in communities where this custom prevails they would like it discontinued.

— Although most consider viewing helpful in confronting the reality of death, they want viewing restricted to a single evening out of consideration for the family.

— The present committal service is troubling to many clergy, and they are groping for alternatives.

PREFERENCES

— The traditional service continues to be the accepted norm except among the more liberal Protestant clergy, a significant number of whom prefer the memorial service.

— An increasing number of clergy — those who prefer the traditional service as well as those who prefer the memorial service — wish to schedule the funeral service during evening hours.

— Most Protestant and Roman Catholic clergy are not opposed to cremation, but Orthodox Christian and Jewish clergy reject the practice.

— Likewise, most Protestant and Roman Catholic clergy approve the idea of a rental casket, while it is opposed by the other groups.

— When an honorarium is appropriate, the majority of clergy prefer to be paid by the funeral director.

— Nearly all clergy include a sermon in the funeral service, and the themes reflect their views of life after death.

— A number of clergy would like more family and congregational participation in the service, a change they believe can more easily be accomplished when the service is held in the church.

The preferences that characterize the different religious groups need to be understood in light of their theology. Therefore, it is suggested that colleges of mortuary science and funeral directors' associations make a greater effort to educate their constituencies regarding the basic beliefs of religious organizations in the United States. With this background, funeral directors would be better equipped to adapt their services to the particular needs of people from diverse religious groups.

BEREAVEMENT COUNSELING

The Many Faces of Counseling

James A. Fruehling, Ph.D.

Counseling is a multi-faceted concept. And that is both a good and bad thing. It is good in that counseling embodies many of the qualities that are characteristic of all good human relations. Glimpses of those qualities can be seen every day during "special" moments between parent and child; husband and wife; teacher and student; lover and lover; friend and friend. One person caring for the person of another. Counseling's focus then, is on the deeper qualities of human relating; the feelings shared, the actions taken, and the meanings created. These qualities are, however, by and large intangible constructs and it is this apparent intangibility that is a bad thing. There is a very fine, almost imperceptible line between authoritarian and appropriate discipline, between love and exploitation, between counseling and advice giving. Today we are deluged with counselors of various sorts. The Easy Money Lending Company offers financial counseling, Wanda's Wiggery offers beauty counseling and the Body Beautiful Health Club offers figure counseling. You can even receive counseling regarding any pest control problems you might have. When counseling turns to advice-giving; when advice-giving leads to the sale of goods and services provided by the advice giver, there is a disturbing question as to whether it is the "deeper qualities of human relating" that is the primary focus.

The funeral director has for some time now been encouraged to explore his role as a counselor as it pertains to the psychological well being of his bereaved clients. He has been exhorted to become an expert in grief, a crisis interventionist, a thanatologist, a preventive psychiatrist, and a death educator. No small task; even for Horatio Alger. I am afraid, however, that the exhorters have not been terribly helpful to the funeral directors in helping them to understand what counseling is, where it can be found in their professional role, and how they can do it. I am further certain that those who have helped funeral directors append these awkward titles to their professional identity have failed to help many funeral directors fully grasp this single simple truth: that it is the person of the funeral director (who he is, how he thinks, how he feels, and how he behaves) that is the single most important factor in understanding the implications of counseling for his

or her professional role. It is the object of this article to examine four of the many faces of counseling as they apply to contemporary funeral service. The four faces to be presented include: THE FACES OF OPPORTUNITY, THE FACES OF RELUCTANCE, THE INTERFACE BETWEEN COUNSELING AND BUSINESS, AND THE FACE OF THE FUNERAL DIRECTOR.

PROBLEMS IN PROFESSIONAL HELPING

Before presenting a definition of counseling, it might be instructive to consider some existing parallels between funeral directors and psychologists. Both groups ostensibly deal with persons experiencing emotional pain. Both groups offer services to respond to the needs of their respective clients. Both groups charge a fee for their professional service. In fact, funeral directors are far from alone in facing accusations that they overcharge for their services and that they profit from pain. Psychiatrists and psychologists face the same criticism. That criticism is, perhaps most eloquently stated in this little story paraphrased from the popular Ziggy cartoon strip.

Ziggy goes to see his psychiatrist feeling very alone and very depressed.

"Doc, I just can't stand it any more. I don't have one real friend in the whole world."

"I see," replied the hundred dollar per hour analyst.

"No matter what I do, I still can't seem to find a friend. I never miss a birthday, always pick up the check at the restaurant and still find myself irrevocably alone."

"Ziggy my boy, how many times have I told you that you can't purchase friendship?"

"I know Doc, (sobbing) but I'm desperate. I'd give anything just to have one friend."

"But Ziggy, I'm your friend."

"I know Doc, but you're a little more than I wanted to spend."

As you can see, that imperceptible line between caring and exploitation is equally thin for psychologists and psychiatrists. In fact, there has been a fair amount of

Reprinted with permission from *National Selected Morticians*, Spring, 1977.

academic research that suggests that the primary outcome of professional counseling has been the client's adoption of the counselor's values and a recognition on the part of the client of the necessity of the counselor's services.

TOWARD A DEFINITION OF COUNSELING

One of the reasons for confusion surrounding counseling and its implications for funeral directors is that it is in fact an ambiguous concept. There are more than a hundred different definitions for counseling in professional texts and journals. It may be accurate to say that the definition of counseling is totally dependent on who is doing the defining. There are some common characteristics, however, and these have been identified by one impertinent member of the field. He defines counseling as follows:

> Counseling is an ambiguous process of uncertain outcome which is both difficult to describe and impossible to evaluate. For this, many years of advanced academic training are required.

Funny or not, the foregoing definition does make a serious point. Satire, after all, is only humorous when it captures a small kernel of truth. If a concept like counseling is so ambiguous, is it really anything at all? Or is it an entitlement bestowed randomly on a group of graduate students who have endured the necessary academic demands to achieve credentials that will allow them to act out a role? Put more succinctly, does counseling achieve identifiable, concrete, positive outcomes for the individuals it is supposed to help or is it simply a means of enhancing the self-image of another group of "experts." There is one school of thought that suggests that there may be a direct relationship between the emphasis an individual places on his credentials and expertise and his unexpressed belief that he really has very little to offer in the way of tangible assistance.

This phenomenon may account for what some have identified as the over-expertizing of our society. Experts are available regarding every facet of life. From cradle to grave there are individuals who possess specialized knowledge regarding circumscribed events in life. One of the consequences of this over emphasis on expertise is that people have begun to not trust their own thoughts and feelings. The answers to their human concerns no longer reside within themselves; they need to be purchased from outside sources. Dr. Benjamin Spock, author of perhaps the best selling self-help book of all time, noted that one of the negative side effects of his publication was that the locus of responsibility gradually shifted from the individual to the expert. Responsible individuals can make appropriate use of experts. Experts, however, cannot replace the individual or assume a responsibility that perforce must remain the individual's.

The purpose of this preamble is simply this: counseling as a concept either has a real meaning and application to funeral service or it does not. Those funeral directors who would assume the trappings of counselors without the concommitant knowledge and skills are destined for personal and professional disaster. Those funeral directors who appropriately refuse to present themselves as something they are not will retain their integrity. They may, however, run the risk of becoming anachronistic in a future that will increasingly emphasize the personal meaningfulness of a funeral experience. Those funeral directors who do come to understand and accept the implications of counseling may find their practice more responsive to the ebb and flow of change, more sensitive to individual differences in clients; and more personally and professionally rewarding.

DEFINITION OF COUNSELING

> COUNSELING IS A HELPING RELATIONSHIP IN WHICH ONE PARTY SEEKS TO FACILITATE THE DEVELOPMENT OF INFORMED CHOICES AND MEANINGFUL ACTIONS AT A CRITICAL TIME WITHIN THE CONTEXT OF ANOTHER'S LIFE.

Four points must be emphasized regarding this definition. Counseling is a *helping* relationship. It needs to be distinguished from other care-giving relationships. Counseling is not simply extending the feelings of sympathy for the circumstances of another individual. Counseling is not nursing in the "take-care-of" sense. It is something more than pouring care into an individual on the assumption that that caring will make him or her better. The counselor does not tell the client what to take or what to do in order to get better. *Both* the client and the counselor have responsibilities for engaging in a relationship that will produce new understandings, choices, and actions. A helping relationship implies action; not passivity. It does not, however, imply abdication of responsibility or active participation on the part of the client. It is a mutual process in which the ultimate decision making responsibility rests with the client. It is the client who must make the "informed choices" and take the "meaningful actions."

Second, most counseling takes place at *critical points within individuals' lives*. That is the central concept of crisis intervention. Crises force change on individuals. The quality of their response to forced change can either be creative and growth oriented or it can be maladaptive. Maladaptive responses to forced change situations can produce life-long problems. Many of the numerous pseudo-counselors simply do not deal with people at truly critical times in life. It isn't truly critical whether you should be counseled to select Acapulco or the Riviera for your next vacation or whether you should select the Farrah Fawcett Blonde Wig or the Little Orphan Annie curls for your next social affair. How one responds to the myriad of changes brought on by a death, however, may well be *the* critical moment in life.

Third, and perhaps most important, all of this helping, choosing, and acting must take place *within the context of the client's life*. It is within his or her frame of reference that decisions and actions will take on meaning. Different people experience similar situations in widely different ways. Unless you are ready to assert that you have somehow cornered the market on life's truths, then you can only attempt to enter the client's world and see and feel things as the client sees and feels them. One of the primary stumbling blocks in most human relations is the apparently universal tendency for human beings to try to impose beliefs, attitudes, and decisions on others. Generally, this practice results in resistance and hostility initially or bitter disappointment later when the client's experience turns out to be substantially at odds with the "truth" he adopted.

Finally, counseling implies *a professional relationship* between the helper and the person being helped. The counselor is, in effect, an advocate for the client. He stands in the stead of his client. The implicit assumption is that the individual being helped will emerge from the counseling relationship in a better condition than if he had not sought assistance. A counseling point of view offers a clarity of values in complex human situations. The client's betterment reigns supreme. The sole reason for being in a helping relation is the facilitation of growth and understanding on the part of the client. All progress must be measured by this standard. Did it help the client in some tangible way? This thought is not at odds with a simple, naive understanding of good business relations. This client-centeredness is captured in those old-fashioned slogans:

Your satisfaction guaranteed.
The customer is always right.

A counseling point of view measures the effectiveness of a service on the benefits that accrue to the client. And, incidentally, concrete, meaningful service has always been worth its cost.

Perhaps, Alfred Benjamin in his book, *The Helping Interview,* provides the best perspective regarding a counseling point of view in everyday human encounters. His basic premise is that thousands of individuals engage in potential helping communications everyday. At home, at school, at the office, individuals must communicate with each other. They must get and give information in order to problem solve; in order to choose and act. These interchanges can either be productive or they can become disasters. By the way, isn't it true that despite the economy, the recession, and the energy shortage, that the most persistent problem faced by business is "people problems?" These problems could be rectified, according to Benjamin, if individuals understood and practiced helping interview techniques.

Helping is an enabling act so that those who are helped recognize, feel, know, decide, and choose how to change. In providing a helping relationship, interviewers give their time, their capacity to listen, and their ability to understand. In short, they call upon their fullest resources to enable others to live more insightfully and meaningfully.

(Benjamin p. IX)

HOW DOES ONE *DO* COUNSELING?

It really does not profit anyone a great deal to simply define and talk in general terms about counseling.

The important point is the translation of those concepts and values into specific action on the part of the funeral director. It would be foolish to attempt to present elaborate skills and techniques in an article of this nature. There are no short-cuts to the acquisition of knowledge or to the polishing of specific helping skills. One cannot, for example, simply append the title "Par Golfer" to his or her name and legitimately expect to shoot a round in the low seventies. Such skill development requires instruction, study, and continual practice. The same is true of counseling. One life is not long enough to read all of the books that provide foundation knowledge and the subsequent subtlety and nuance necessary for increased understanding of human behavior. Numerous formal training programs and informal workshops exist to help the sincere student of counseling grow and develop. Also, there is a lifetime in which to practice and hone the interpersonal skills that will increasingly be necessary to serve a dynamic and constantly changing clientele. If one is going to claim the role of a professional, one must be willing to pay the price necessary to acquire the knowledge and skills of that profession.

One of the beauties of counseling is that many of the most important basic skills do not require highly specialized, advance training. A proper understanding of the counseling role provides a broad foundation for behaviors that are easily within the domain of funeral directors right now. If it can be agreed that the person being served is at the center of our attention, there are four specific behaviors that funeral directors can perform that reflect a counseling point of view.

1. *TAKE TIME.* Simply taking the time to be with another human being at a critical point in that individual's life is a prerequisite for any counseling relationship. Good human relations take time. There are no shortcuts. Perhaps a good example of taking time can be found in the case of a sick child. You probably have all had the experience of attending a child who has been leveled by a fever or some other minor ailment. Your presence, your simple presence, is a major curative agent. You don't even need to say anything. Your willingness to be present at a trying moment is reassuring. Generally, you can't *do* anything to immediately stop the illness. Your presence, however, assures the young child that the illness will not be faced alone. Funeral directors need to offer clients their time. No one can say for certain how that offering of time will be used or that it will be used at all. The extension of time, however, creates an opportunity for the client to express thoughts, feelings or desires that will be meaningful within his frame of reference. More than one funeral has been spoiled by an overly efficient funeral director who was more concerned with time than he was with people. By taking sufficient time to be with the client, the counseling funeral director will discover numerous opportunities to create a more personalized and meaningful funeral.

2. *LISTEN.* The second skill is to become a good listener. Good listeners are at a premium in our

society. Generally, we are so anxious to respond with our own thoughts and feelings that we fail to accurately hear what is being said. We live in a competitive society and one unfortunate side effect is that our conversations frequently turn in to wars of words. True communication, however, begins in silence. Recall, if you will, one moment in your life when you had an enormously important thought or feeling that you simply had to share with someone. If you found a good, understanding listener, you may remember that sharing as one of your life's most intimate moments. If, on the other hand, you encountered a deaf ear or a stinging response, you may still recall that moment with bitterness. Good listeners help people feel more comfortable with themselves. Good listeners allow individuals to explore their feelings. Good listeners provide the kind of quiet, supportive, attentive environment that encourages individuals to think through rather be frightened by their own feelings. Good listeners do not pre-judge or impose their values on the communications of others. Funeral directors who will take the time to listen sensitively will tap a veritable ocean of material that can be used to effectively place the bereaved at the heart of the funeral.

3. *CLARIFY AND REFLECT*. Good listening is an active, not a passive process. Good listening cannot be done by a mechanical manikin. It requires intense concentration on the part of the listener. It is hard work. The object is to capture the emotional essence and meaning of the client's statements. This is accomplished in two ways. First, some statements need to be clarified. In order to verify that the listener has accurately understood the client, his understanding must be checked. "If I understand what you are saying . . ." might be an example of a clarifying statement. How often have you had the experience of telling somebody something in perfectly clear English only to discover (generally after the fact) that he didn't really understand at all? Perhaps he even got the exact opposite meaning of your original intent. Our society has almost institutionalized this breach of communication with the cliche, "If you want something done right, you had better do it yourself." A better thought might be, "If you want to say something to someone, you had better make sure (clarify) that he understands." Funeral directors have a special need to clarify client's thoughts and feelings. *After* the funeral, there is no opportunity to repair misunderstandings.

Reflection is another component of active listening. By reflecting back to the client his thoughts and feelings, the listener provides the feedback link that is necessary for the client to know that he is being understood. Reflection lets the client know that you are with him. If a listener is able to reflect accurately he has the potentiality to go anywhere with his client. He no longer needs to "know" what to say. That develops naturally. Effective reflections permit an almost harmonious movement through an apparent quagmire of conflicting feelings and thoughts. This paraphrasing also allows the client to re-experience his feelings with, perhaps, new understanding. The client is permitted to re-focus his experiencing. It also encourages the client to continue his exploring until he is comfortable with his thoughts. It is through reflection and clarification that good listeners help clients develop a personalized framework for meaning for their experience. The death of someone close is certain to spawn innumerable thoughts and feelings that need to be experienced and integrated. It is the counseling funeral director that has the opportunity to provide those conditions that will legitimize and facilitate this exploration. This simple act may be one of the critical determinants of effective grieving. It is only after the client has had this opportunity to be heard in depth that he is genuinely ready to participate meaningfully in a funeral. It is only after the bereaved individual has experienced what is in himself that he can make knowledgeable choices regarding a funeral service.

4. *SUPPLY RELEVANT INFORMATION*. Funeral directors are veritable encyclopedias of information regarding the events surrounding death. Funeral directors deal daily with events that are unknown to many and frightening to most. Funeral directors virtually become guides for the bereaved in a strange and unknown land. The information they possess is invaluable for the ritual that marks that a life has been lived. It is also maximally useful in the reorganization of the lives of the individuals who continue. Rules, regulations, traditions, and benefits are only some of the areas of specialized knowledge that funeral directors possess that their clients need. Good decisions are based on good information. Funeral directors need to share as much information with the public as possible in order for the funeral to be of maximum benefit to survivors. Ignorance breeds fear; and people will seek to avoid those things they fear. Knowledge, however, leads to understanding and the opportunity for a comprehensible participation in the funeral process. It is a mistake for funeral directors to equate counseling with information giving. Remember, the same information leads to different conclusions among different clients. A commitment on the part of the counseling funeral director to full disclosure of any and all useful information is the same as a commitment to the client being served.

THE FACES OF OPPORTUNITY

Where does the funeral have the opportunity to do these things? It would be easy to simply state that the opportunity to engage in a helping relationship presents itself every time a funeral director is in contact with someone seeking his professional assistance. There are, however, a number of reasonably clearly marked opportunities during post-death events that appear particularly apt for the funeral director's counseling skills.

A. *PRE-NEED ARRANGEMENTS*. One of the

prime opportunities for effective funeral director counseling may actually occur prior to a death. There is no better time for individuals to contemplate their own death than before they are directly confronted with it. People who will take the time to become informed prior to their need have the time necessary to encounter their feelings and share them with those they love. The counseling funeral director may find this a unique opportunity to see the direct benefits of the time he has extended and the listening he has done. He might also see how his clarifications and reflections have enabled a family to put to use in an integrated fashion the specialized information he has communicated.

B. *THE ARRANGEMENT CONFERENCE.* This is traditionally the most common opportunity for the funeral director to employ his counseling skills. Information needs to be given and received. The client-centered funeral director will provide ample time for the bereaved family. He will provide an environment that gives permission for the bereaved to experience and express their feelings. He will listen carefully and help clarify the bereaved's desires. His accurate reflection of the client's feelings will permit the creation of a funeral that will accurately capture the essence of the life that has been lived from the point of view of the survivors. Most importantly, the counseling funeral director will convey through his behavior that the bereaved will have every opportunity to design and actively participate in the funeral that is being arranged.

C. *FINANCIAL ADVISING.* Financial concerns are a part of the funeral process. Dollars are important to people. Colleges have even created positions for financial advisors to help parents and students handle the costs of a college education in workable ways. The same concerns are true regarding funeral service. Counseling funeral directors serve as advocates for their clients. It is the responsibility of every client-centered funeral director to do everything within his power to assure that bereaved individuals can be served within their means. It would be a cruel misuse of counseling skills for the funeral director to inadvertently allow a client to create a funeral that might result in a financially crippling condition. Financial decisions are, however, reached in the same fashion as all other decisions. It is the funeral director that will take ample time to communicate accurate information and to clarify preferences within the life context of the client that will assure appropriate financial decisions. Remember, it is the whole life of the client being served, not simply the isolated instance of the funeral. Carelessly made financial decisions may eradicate the meaning inherent in any funeral and add a more specific economic grief to the original loss. A funeral that adds grief to grief is not a funeral; it is a bad purchase.

D. *POST FUNERAL SERVICES.* A reasonably new opportunity for counseling can be found in the services of the funeral director to the bereaved following death. These services may be as specific and limited as helping individuals apply for certain benefits. They may elaborate to the point of contacting the bereaved a month following the funeral simply to see how things are going. Client-centered funeral directors may become active to the point of making referrals to widow-to-widow programs. Funeral directors may even help initiate such programs in their communities. If the primary purpose of the funeral director is to facilitate the grieving process, it is short-sighted to think that the funeral director's helping role ends with the funeral. The usefulness of any funeral cannot be evaluated until a client has successfully grieved. Many individuals experience heightened grief around anniversaries of the death. Counseling funeral directors may soon recognize a need for an additional memorial service one year following the death either to mark the end of grieving or to facilitate further grief work.

Other opportunities for counseling exist. Funeral directors may find unique counseling opportunities during the first call, during family visitations, or even during the ride to the cemetery. In fact, it may be said that funeral directors have a limitless horizon of opportunities to behave in a counseling capacity. The question is not whether or not funeral directors have opportunities to counsel. The question is whether they will recognize and effectively make use of the many opportunities they have. The funeral director's professional role places him by definition in a helping capacity at a critical time. Those funeral directors who succeed in employing their counseling skills will also succeed in achieving the betterment of the clients they serve.

THE FACES OF RELUCTANCE

Many funeral directors are reluctant to incorporate counseling concepts into their professional role. These hesitancies can be articulated through statements that typically account for funeral director reluctance. Three such statements are offered below.

1. I DO NOT HAVE THE TIME TO ENGAGE IN COUNSELING. I AM A BUSINESS MAN AND TO A BUSINESS MAN TIME IS MONEY.

This statement of reluctance implies that a business man is something different than a person. It at least implies that a business man does not have time to be responsive to the customers he serves. It also implies a product orientation rather than a person orientation. This statement of reluctance also represents a shortsighted business philosophy. Behind every goods or service is a human need or desire. *People* purchase the goods and services of the funeral director; and it is people who must be touched in meaningful ways as a result of the funeral director's service. When people are no longer touched by the goods and services of the funeral director, they will seek other alternatives. When people no longer find meaning in the goods and services that comprise the funeral, they will look upon expenditures for such things as wasteful. This source of reluctance may, in truth, simply bare witness to the fact that many funeral directors lack a structure for being duly compensated for their professional time. The counseling funeral director, however, places his client at the center of the funeral. By helping the bereaved to create a personally expressive funeral, the counseling funeral director assures his viability as a helper to those in need. People do not seek alternatives to things that are personally meaningful. People do not complain about services they helped to create. It is incumbent on every funeral director to create a structure that allows him maximal flexibility in meeting the needs of the clients he serves.

2. I LACK THE TRAINING. THAT IS NOT MY JOB. I LEAVE PSYCHIATRY TO THE PSYCHIATRISTS. I AM NOT ABOUT TO OPEN A PANDORA'S BOX OF EMOTIONS THAT I AM NOT QUALIFIED TO DEAL WITH. MY FAMILY BUILT THIS BUSINESS ON INTEGRITY AND WE ARE NOT ABOUT TO DESTROY THAT DIGNITY IN THE PUBLIC EYE BY GETTING INTO AREAS WE HAVE NO BUSINESS GETTING INTO.

This source of reluctance may have some partial validity. The curriculum of the typical college of mortuary science has up until recently provided very little in the way of training and background in the behavorial sciences. Recent curricular revisions have sought to make changes in that deficit. It remains, however, an uncontested fact that there is a great deal of learning to be accomplished in the areas of science, business administration, psychology, and embalming, and a very limited amount of time in which to accomplish it. It is necessary to point out, however, that *listening* and *responding sensitively* is not the isolated domain of the psychiatrist, psychologist, or social worker. In fact, the vast majority of all counseling or "helping" is done informally by mothers, fathers, husbands, wives, and friends. Just plain ordinary persons; like you and me.

There is a reasonable body of research that indicates that college students would most likely seek the counsel of a friend before they would seek professional assistance with a pressing problem. People are simply too important a source of assistance not to include them in any discussion of helping. Everyone has the capacity to serve as a helper to one degree or another. In fact, there is an earnest movement afoot to take the basic psychological skills out of the exclusive domain of a professional elite and put them in the hands of the population at large. Paraprofessionals, indigenous workers and lay personnel have received training in basic skills and have demonstrated that they can be effective. As a sidelight, it may be worth mentioning that at times, formal academic training actually mitigates against the development of effective helping skills. To the extent that professional counselors hide behind their professional role, formal training serves as a barrier. Given the proper motivation, most people can master the basic helping skills. Funeral directors are no exception.

3. I LACK THE PERSONALITY FOR COUNSELING. I'M JUST NOT THE TYPE. ALL THAT TALKING MAKES ME NERVOUS.

Counseling is founded on a set of specific skills. It is not simply an expression of personality. Counselors are made; not born. Some just have to work harder than others. Stop and think for a moment. Have you ever heard anyone say, "I don't have the personality to be a father." Personality is not a fixed thing. It changes and is subject to directed change. People can change in ways that will improve the quality of their inter-

personal skills. Perhaps some individuals feel that counseling connotes something less than a masculine image. To three generations of men raised on the tall-in-the-saddle-John Wayne-man-of-action stereotype, counseling may threaten their masculinity. The truth, however, is that counseling as defined is much more than sympathetic listening. It is effective communication that leads toward action-oriented decision-making in life's critical areas. In counseling, there is no truth except in action. The decisions that clients reach they will enact. Both men and women funeral directors are needed to facilitate that kind of growth in clients. Funeral directors by virtue of their calling have already placed themselves "Where the action is."

There has been considerable research regarding the personality of an effective helper. Dugald Arbuckle places the person of the helper at the center of the counseling universe.

The evidence would at least seem to imply that it is the humanness, the very person of the counselor that is *the* critical factor in a successful counseling process. It is generally accepted that a successful counseling process is precluded without the establishment of a close relationship between the two parties.
(Arbuckle: p. 85)

Research into counselor effectiveness begins to paint a picture of those qualities that characterize the effective counselors. In summary, effective counselors are:

A. Warm and sensitive to others.

B. Open to their own experience as well as to the experience of others.

C. Able to listen with understanding.

D. Positive in their outlook on life.

E. Able to communicate a sense of commitment to others.

F. Able to respond flexibly.

Perhaps the single most important counselor trait is the ability to be empathic. Empathy is the ability to enter another person's world and see it as if it were your own without losing the *as if* quality. Empathy is a necessary quality because people do see different things in different ways. This understanding was brought home most forcefully to the author in a college biology class. The biology professor was completing a discussion regarding the perception of color. He asked each member of the class to view various multi-colored plates and to record any numbers found there. This writer discovered a series of numbers readily. They were, however, the wrong numbers. Every member of the class viewed the same templates and every member of the class saw a series of numbers that were different than those seen by this writer. It is a thought provoking experience to discover that after twenty plus years one is color-blind. For twenty years, I had been looking at the same things other friends and relatives had seen; yet unknowingly I had been seeing them differently. One has to wonder in how many more subtle areas of life one has been looking at something and erroneously assumed that others were seeing the same things. Since different people see and experience different things in different ways, it is imperative that funeral directors develop sufficient empathic abilities to enter the world of their clients; to see as they see. It is only when the funeral director achieves this ability that he will be able to construct funerals from the inside out; starting from the inside of his client and building out to the funeral.

In summary, the effective helper is the individual who has the courage to fully be who he or she is and has the even greater courage not only to permit, but to actually *help* another person become the individual he or she would be.

THE INTERFACE BETWEEN COUNSELING AND BUSINESS

The primary purpose of this section is to assure funeral directors that one of the implications of counseling is not that concern for economics must be abandoned. Counseling and good business practices are not antithetical. In fact, it could be said that counseling is excellent business. Not excellent business in the sense that the Federal Trade Commission has implied. No, counseling is not good business because it creates a professional image that lulls the consumer into a false sense of security. No, it is not good business in the sense that in the name of human concern that the funeral director may enhance his ability to market a more profitable funeral. Counseling does, however, provide a clarity of value to the economic aspect of the funeral. With the client at the center of the funeral experience, it is client benefit that represents the primary concern. Individuals who are tangibly benefited are happy customers.

One of the oldest business maxims is "Give the customer what he wants." In order to accomplish this task, however, it is necessary for the funeral director to be in intimate contact with his client. This requires the use of the counseling skills identified earlier in this article. The counseling funeral director must provide his clients with accurate information and ample time to clarify their own thoughts and feelings. Many purchasers of funeral services genuinely do not know what they want when a death occurs. It is during this period following a death that the funeral director's counseling skills can help insure that the decisions reached by his clients have been informed decisions. This can only be achieved if the counselor has succeeded in communicating to his client that the fullest possible range of options is open to him and that the counselor is committed to enacting the client's informed choices. UNDER NO CIRCUMSTANCES CAN THIS BE INTERPRETED AS AN OPPORTUNITY TO SELL THE CLIENT MORE EXPENSIVE MERCHANDISE. Since different clients will have different needs, it is absolutely essential that the funeral director use his counseling skills to insure that the choices accurately reflect those needs. The funeral director who fails to clarify and verify the informed choices of his client runs the risk of creating a funeral that does not add meaning to the life of the bereaved. Funerals that are devoid of meaning are comparable to faulty products. Funerals that do not tangibly help the bereaved are the equivalent of advertisements against funerals. Funerals that do not successfully place the bereaved at the center of the funeral experience in meaningful ways debase the dignity of Man.

In order to provide individuals with the widest array of choices, funeral directors must develop a model that will enable them to give the customer what he *genuinely* wants at a price that provides sufficient incentive to the funeral director to keep his service in operation. All service costs; and good service has always been a bargain. The funeral director of the future will have to become more flexible to provide the options that a wide distribution of customers will require. Funeral directors will also have to develop pricing systems that will allow them to be compensated for everything that they do in order to enact their client's informed choices. The funeral director's counseling skills are a prerequisite to the design and implementation of the particular types of funeral service their clients will choose.

THE FACE OF THE FUNERAL DIRECTOR

This section is devoted entirely to the person of the funeral director. The funeral director is one member of the helping professions that is present at life's critical moments. By choosing to work at the raw edges of life, funeral directors expose themselves to the wide expression of life's full power. Psychiatrists, doctors, and psychologists also choose to venture out of life's more comfortable illusions to encounter the emotions of life and death squarely. This can be tremendously rewarding. It is also personally expensive. Being that kind of a professional extracts very real, personal costs. Members of the helping professions, people who should know better, have nonetheless been negligent regarding their personal costs. Every businessman knows that you can't spend more than you take in for very long and still remain in business. Unfortunately, many helping professionals disregard that simple truth with disturbingly dire consequences. Psychiatrists, for example, have an unusually high rate of suicide. Doctors have an unusually high rate of drug abuse. Psychologists have an unusually high rate of divorce. Funeral directors, for their part, are frequently cited as high users of alcohol. There is an irony that borders on tragedy when a significant fraction of a helping profession turns in on itself in self-destructive ways.

Funeral directors need to treat themselves with the same respect and caring that they treat their clients. Funeral directors' role demands are considerable. If funeral directors fail to take in a sustaining amount of input, there will eventually be no output. If funeral directors take in an inferior quality of life-supporting energies, there will be diminishing reserves to give out. To paraphrase a common computor saying, "Garbage in—garbage out." The final premise of this article is that those funeral directors who burn out the quickest are those funeral directors who are the most out of touch with the counseling nature of their vocation. By simply performing a role, the funeral director robs himself of the enriching human exchanges that are part and parcel of every funeral transaction. By placing the client at the center of the funeral of each funeral experience, the counseling funeral director will be open to the personal gains both he and his client can achieve. At that point, the intangibles of counseling become good points. The intangibles of client growth, shared feelings, and mutual meanings can be professionally and personally sustaining.

Are you a counselor? Ask yourself these questions put to all helpers by Carl Rogers, one of the country's leading humanistic psychologists.

Can I *be* in some way which will be perceived by the other person as trustworthy, as dependable or consistent in some deep sense?

Can I be expressive enough as a person that what I am will be communicated unambiguously?

Can I let myself experience positive attitudes toward this other person—attitudes of warmth, caring, liking, interest, respect?

Can I be strong enough as a person to be separate from the other?

Am I secure enough within myself to permit him his separateness?

Can I let myself enter fully into the world of his feelings and personal meanings and see those as he does?

Can I receive him as he is? Can I communicate this attitude?

Can I act with sufficient sensitivity in the relationship that my behavior will not be perceived as a threat?

Can I free him from the threat of external evaluation?

Can I meet this other individual as a person who is in the process of becoming, or will I be bound by his past and by my past?

(Shertzer and Stone: p. 8)

Hopefully, this article has introduced you to some of the many faces of counseling. There are, however, as many faces of counseling as there are facets to your existence. There are as many faces of counseling as there are faces that will turn to funeral directors for assistance at the time of death. There are as many faces of counseling as there are emotions associated with grief. The question is not whether funeral directors should be counselors. To one degree or another, they already are. The only question that remains is how well they are going to do their job. For as Robert Carkhuff has observed in his book, *Helping and Human Relations*, there is nothing part way regarding human relations. You are either part of the solution or you are part of the problem.

REFERENCES

1. Arbuckle, D. S., *Counseling Philosophy, Theory, and Practice*. Boston: Allyn and Bacon, Inc., 1966.

2. Benjamin, A., *The Helping Interview*. Boston: Houghton Mifflin Company, 1969.

3. Carkhuff, R. R., *Helping and Human Relations*. New York: Holt Rinehart and Winston, Inc. 1969.

4. Patterson, C. H., *Theories of Counseling and Psychotherapy*. New York: Harper and Row, 1973.

5. Shertzer, B., and Stone, S. C., *Fundamentals of Counseling*. Boston: Houghton Mifflin Company, 1974.

Should the Funeral Director Be Considered a Counselor?

Frank W. Miller, NSM Executive Secretary – **Pro**

Counseling has been defined as "a face-to-face situation in which by reason of training, skill, or confidence vested in him by the other, one person helps the second person to face, perceive, clarify, solve and resolve adjustment problems." (1) While this definition is, I believe, an accurate one it does not entirely remove the confusion that exists between the terms *counselor* and *advisor.* A counselor listens, asks, reassures and attempts to understand the client so that he (the counselor) can serve the client most effectively and help him resolve his problem. An advisor, on the other hand, explains, instructs, directs, and informs . . . and plays the dominant role in the interview.

Some confusion also exists over the terms *counseling* and *psychotherapy.* A counselor deals primarily with normal individuals who are under moderate stress. The psychotherapist deals with neurotics and other individuals who are exhibiting abnormal behavior. However, uncertainty over the role of the funeral director in counseling is due to a number of factors other than confusion over the terms advising, counseling, and psychotherapy. Some funeral directors are more interested in business activity than in people. Some feel that they lack the proper personal characteristics: others feel that they lack the necessary training and experience. Some are playing an active role as counselors without realizing it and some are forced to accept responsibilities beyond their training and experience simply because no other qualified person appears to be available.

There are two important reasons why the funeral director must be considered a counselor. First, counseling automatically implies concern for the client *as a person,* in terms of his physical, emotional, and financial welfare. Therefore, funeral directors who are counseling-oriented will work out funeral arrangements with the bereaved that are consistent with the latter's emotional and financial resources. Secondly, funeral directors have a certain advantage over specialists in serving as counselors in that they have already established a "helping" relationship with their client; this relationship offers a more natural counseling opportunity than does a scheduled interview with a psychologist, psychiatrist or clergyman in a relatively strange office.

In most cases funeral directors lack the training to deal with mentally disturbed clients or those with deep-seated problems. This causes them to ask "Should the funeral director ever counsel?" The answer is that there are different levels of counseling. There will be times when counsel-

ing the bereaved will be well within the scope of the funeral director's professional competence. Stress and emotional discomfort that is not too deep-seated may be alleviated through a type of "surface" counseling involving sympathetic attention, reassurance, and suggestions of a positive nature. By just being a good listener, the funeral director may help to release tensions that are interfering with recovery of emotional balance. Thus, while it may not be accurate to state that every funeral director is a counselor, every funeral director will profit by the use of certain counseling techniques.

Funeral directors have another counseling responsibility. A bereaved person, under extreme stress, sometimes needs prompt referral to a psychologist, psychiatrist, clergyman or other specialists. Funeral directors must be able to recognize the symptoms of extreme stress and must know the proper person or agency to whom referral should be made.

Although the funeral director is an important member of the counseling team, there is some debate over whether *all* funeral directors can perform the aforementioned functions. There are obvious limitations to the counseling role of *any* funeral director, yet some funeral directors have found it difficult to recognize and accept counseling responsibilities that are being fulfilled adequately by their colleagues. In an attempt to distinguish between the *rationalizations* of a few funeral directors who wish to avoid counseling responsibilities and the practical *limitations* on all funeral directors as counselors, let us analyze three statements often heard in this connection.

1. *Funeral directors lack the time for counseling.* Unfortunately, there is some truth to this statement. It is sometimes difficult for the funeral director to arrange his schedule so that he can be an unhurried listener or a relaxed conversationalist. However, I believe funeral directors are misleading themselves if they believe that their counseling responsibilities require extra time. Counseling is as much an *attitude* as it is an act. Where the responsibility is more of an attitude than an act, the question of time loses its importance.
2. *Funeral directors lack the training and experience for counseling.* There is an element of truth in this statement also. It is unfair to expect funeral directors to perform specialized counseling functions if they have not had special training. However, the counseling functions previously discussed involve the same type

Reprinted with permission from *National Selected Morticians,* September, 1975.

and degree of training and experience that is necessary for establishing *any* effective personal relationship. The skills necessary for the successful performance of these functions should have been obtained as part of the funeral director's pre-service education. Until all funeral directors receive this type of pre-service education, an in-service training program should be established to serve as a temporary substitute.

3. *Funeral directors lack the personality for counseling.* This statement is misleading. The implication seems to be that the personality necessary for counseling is different from the personality necessary to develop a close and warm, working relationship with individuals who are temporarily under stress. Some funeral directors *may* lack the personal characteristics necessary for effective counseling, but one questions whether they have desirable personal traits for effective funeral directing. Are they not, instead, "getting by" with certain personal traits in a complex and ever-changing group situation that become a more obvious liability in a one-to-one relationship.

SUMMARY

All of us have problems and it has been estimated that 90% of these problems are treated by laymen (husbands, wives, friends, next-door neighbors) in informal settings. The funeral director's role as a counselor is extremely important. He has certain advantages over specialists in performing some counseling functions; he is at a disadvantage in attempting to perform others. It is necessary that we distinguish between the rationalizations of a few funeral directors who wish to avoid counseling responsibilities and the limitations on all funeral directors in the performance of *certain* counseling functions. The development of counseling skills should receive more adequate attention in the pre-service training programs for funeral directors. As a temporary measure these skills can be built in funeral directors through seminars, workshops, and other types of in-service education programs.

(1) Williamson, E. G. and J. D. Foley, *Counseling and Discipline.* New York: McGraw-Hill Book Company, Inc. 1949, p. 192.

Brannon B. Lesesne — Con

This is a very interesting question and one which seems to be commanding much attention amongst a certain part of our industry.

Let's try to interpret what we mean by "counselor." My dictionary, among other interpretations which are not relevant, says that counseling is (and I quote) "the use of psychological methods in testing the interest of and giving professional guidance to individuals." To me, this signifies a person especially trained in the use of psychology, such as a psychiatrist, a psychologist, a minister or priest. I cannot picture a funeral director as having this type of ability, and I think there would be danger in so assuming.

Rather, I think a funeral director, because of his training and long experience, is capable of guiding a family— advising and assisting—in the many details of funeral service. I feel he may offer advice as to the service itself, advice as to certain legal matters—helping with claims to governmental divisions, to insurance companies, to unions. He may also advise as to cemetery memorialization, filing wills, acknowledging flowers and other kindnesses, and be of similar assistance. But after the service is over, claims have been made, and the funeral bill settled, I feel

it would be an intrusion for the funeral director (except in his own family or that of a very close friend) to continue to contact that family, offering further advice and service. The family of a deceased person is faced with a terrible problem of readjustment. They must reorient their lives, face the future without their deceased member, seek guidance and advice from their minister, their attorney, their banker, and in some cases, their psychiatrist. The funeral director, in my opinion, would only serve as a reminder of the trauma through which the family has gone. He should be available for advice if called on, but, in my mind, he should not impose himself on a family after he has completed the work he is employed to perform.

It would be well for him to know who is available for counseling if he is asked, but when he has completed that which he is asked to do, he must remain in the background and permit this family to re-organize and re-align themselves for the future.

Advise and assist—yes. But to attempt counseling beyond the scope of his knowledge and experience would be an exercise in foolishness and must be avoided.

Bereavement: The Role of the Family Physician

Marian G. Secundy, MSW

Much has been written regarding attitudes of patients, families, and physicians in managing death and subsequent grief reactions. Here at Howard University College of Medicine, we are constantly aware of our educational responsibility to insure that our students and residents achieve certain levels of awareness, acquire certain basic and specific information, and be afforded an opportunity to ventilate and discuss issues of death, dying, and bereavement as they relate to their current or future encounters with patients and their families. We are specifically interested in the roles and responsibilities of the family physician.

Certain observations must be made about social processes in today's world which make it more difficult than it used to be for people to grieve. Certain coping mechanisms used historically no longer appear to be operative or seem to serve us now. Lazare at Massachusetts General Hospital has spoken of an absence of a proper social matrix.[1] Mobility prevents the establishment of stable relationships and close ties, often making it necessary for people to try to grieve alone and forcing an internalization of the process which can be quite detrimental. The hospital, often viewed as a place to hide those who enter its doors, is characterized by massive depersonalization. The actual organization of the hospital disrupts the natural processes of grief more often than not. Restricted visiting hours for family members, no visiting hours for children, and large sterile impersonal machinery all contribute to the sense of isolation of those in the throes of suffering losses. Our modern bureaucracies are indifferent to grief. One or two days are allowed to attend funerals of *immediate* family only. One is expected to return to work promptly and efficiently as opposed to days gone by when one's employer allowed "as much time as you need." Further, perhaps with the devaluing of life in our society over this past generation, there have been major movements away from the healing effects of faith, belief, and the comforts of the ritualized service. We no longer have readily available in our dogmas consistent interpretations of life and death. What can one really feel about death when one has been anesthetized by daily television depictions of Vietnam dead, thousands of dead on regular TV programming, and our indifference to and resistance to asking or answering questions about abortion, where termination of life is alright and socially negated as loss of life.

In light of these observations then, what types of grief reactions ought family physicians anticipate?

Adult Grief

Elizabeth Kubler-Ross and others observe that family members confronted with death of loved ones may go through the five stages of denial, hostility, bargaining, depression, and acceptance which terminally ill adults experience.[2] Burstein notes that the "initial phase of denial probably constitutes an emergency shutdown of psychological process in the face of overwhelming stress," and that anger is an "expression of reaction to injustice."[3] There are several possible dimensions to normal grief. Grieving persons describe a range of feelings, experiences, and reactions. Among them are a sense of loss, pining, yearning, preoccupation of thoughts, visual imageries, motor coordination difficulties, loss of appetite, inability to sleep, inability to remember or concentrate, feelings of anger, guilt, restlessness, bewilderment, numbness, disbelief, frustration, despair, disorganization, helplessness, bitterness, and irritability. They may experience excessive anxiety (free floating, sexual, or financial); a desire to withdraw; physical symptoms; and actual illness. Many believe they are actually going mad. Hinton has reported that one third to one half of the immediate relatives of deceased persons come to doctors within a few months to obtain help with their problems connected with loss.[4] Further, Parkes reported in his

Reprinted with permission from the *Journal of the National Medical Association,* vol. 69(9), September, 1977.

study of bereavement that widows needed to consult physicians much more than usual during the first six months of widowhood.[5]

The family physician must be able to assess and learn about the bereaved persons' prior experiences with health care and death in the context of previous physician, health professional, and institutional responses. Knowledge of ways in which people coped with other kinds of losses is often helpful as a clue to their capacity and methods for coping with the death of a loved one, eg, such losses as those experienced through separation, divorce, drafting of a son, marriage of a child, etc. Cultural background, social class, religious beliefs, and individual capacity to cope with stress are also relevant. The reactions to the death of a family member may be determined by the importance which the person played in the family and individual member's life, the feeling the individual family member possessed for the deceased, the place the deceased held in the family group, ie, his/her roles and functions, and the implications of the death for the future status and financial well-being of the family. For example, the more the mourner's sense of identity, meaning, and purpose of life and responsibility has been involved in the interaction with the lost partner, the more demanding may be the task of readaptation after death.[6] Some women report a sense of emptiness and permanent incompleteness. The mourner whose interaction with the deceased has been frustrating, humiliating, frightening, or otherwise unpleasant is left with a set of conflicts to solve and adjustments to make in the course of mourning that differ from those of a mourner who has been engaged in satisfying interaction.[7]

Circumstances of death and age of the deceased are also factors which may affect adaptations. Reaction to the death of a child may vary considerably from reactions to the death of an elderly parent. Some authoritative observers have noted that the loss of a child for most people is the most difficult for which to compensate. Stronger emotions are often displayed overtly for a longer period of time. Overt psychiatric problems may result more frequently. Consider the impact of the

loss of the breadwinner. What changes will have to be made in the standard of living? What new roles must be assumed? Consider the adjustments necessary in the loss of a young mother. Who will replace her nurturing and caring functions?

Whether or not a family has had time to prepare for death may be crucial in latter adaptations. This is a critical point to be considered by family physicians. There appears to be some observable difference in reactions of family members when there has been time for anticipating grief shared with the dying member as opposed to situations of sudden death. Generally, where an opportunity has existed for anticipating grief, adjustments appear to take place more "comfortably." This is so despite the vicissitudes of emotion which have been experienced during prolonged illness. More problems seem to exist where family members have anticipated death but have operated in a system of "closed awareness," ie, a conspiracy of silence in relation to the patient prior to his death. Secretiveness and evasiveness often take severe toll. Family members begin final grief work with varying degrees of guilt, a sense of not having finished the important business of saying goodbye in their own ways, and without having benefitted from the deceased's response to their feelings and needs. In situations of sudden, unexpected death there is a certain lack of reality and a degree of shock and numbness which must be overcome before grief work can begin at all.

The psychological aspects of grief are invariably translated into physiological reactions, some of which contribute, if not lead directly, to the death of the bereaved. There appears to be a true change in the functioning of the total body organism. Research is being done currently relative to the relationship of bereavement to immunity mechanisms. Statistically there appears to be a correlation between the onset of myocardial infarctions and cardiac diseases with loss. Rheumatoid arthritis, bronchial asthma, and ulcerative colitis also all appear to be positively correlated with loss. Many persons in grief states put themselves at great risk by virtue of their often

impulsive activities after the death of a loved one. Families who have recently experienced sudden or unexpected death show an increased risk of higher morbidity and mortality rates occurring within the first year after bereavement.[8] Physiologically the bereaved person is in a precarious health state. Losses in middle and later years tend to arouse in the mourner intense preoccupation with his own future terminal illness, dying and being dead, and fears of being physically or emotionally alone when having to face death.[6]

Anger is often associated with feelings of guilt. If the anger is tolerated by the family physician, for example, he/she may be able to help family members take great steps towards acceptance without guilt. Relatives are often guilt ridden for very valid reasons. To urge them not to feel guilty may not deal effectively with the reality of their situations at all.

Hostility may be directly related to actual negative experience with physicians or other health professionals during the deceased's illness. Often these must be talked out in order for individuals to obtain significant relief. If left to simmer unchecked, such hostility may surface in future physician encounters or may haunt the bereaved indefinitely.

It is well understood that many pathological depressions are the result of grief work which has not been completed. There is not universal agreement as to what constitutes a period of "normal" grief in our society. Lindemann, in 1944, described a period of six months of active grief as within normal limits. After six months he suggested that pathological elements might be present.[9] Experts have suggested the possibility that *pain* of loss never ends, although it does abate.[9] Bereavement for some may continue for years — even indefinitely — and be reactivated by anniversaries, holidays, and other personal reminders of the deceased.

Children and Grief

The family physician should be aware that a child's ability to understand death is directly related to the developmental process. Briefly, in children under three, the concept of death as irreversible is not generally understood. In children aged four or five, one may see some delineation of awareness of death as a sleep state. The child may express distinctive fears of separation but death is not viewed as permanent. Dead things and people are thought to be living elsewhere. In the child between ages five and nine, death begins to be accepted with the idea of finality but the acceptance is not universal. It excludes the child and all loved ones. Death is personified. In the child older than age nine there are the beginnings and refinements of adult formulation.[10] Yudkin[11] has pointed to several critical areas relative to childhood grief. Children may experience guilt feelings, blaming themselves for the death of a family member due to "bad thoughts" they have had about the other person. If not managed properly the guilt can manifest itself in extreme ways, ie, superego accusations, depressive withdrawal, accident prone behavior, punishment-seeking provocative actions, and exhibitive use of guilt and grief. Children may develop distorted concepts of illness and death or disturbed attitudes toward doctors, hospitals, or God. Death phobias may become manifest.

Discussion

Grief work is to be encouraged and is essential for the achievement of physical and emotional well-being. The family physician is in a unique position to provide the necessary support to individuals and families. It is incumbent upon him/her to develop the necessary skills, openness and acceptance of attitudes which are most helpful to his/her patients. He/she knows the family best, its needs, weaknesses, and strengths. Specifically, the family physician can provide reassurances for families even when or if the deceased

patient was in the care of a consultant or other specialist. He/she can function as liaison to the family. His/her continual presence as a caring human being is critical. The family physician can function as a listener, encourage expression of feelings, attempt to answer questions which the family may still have, and refer to others who have more time and additional therapeutic skills as necessary. He/she can help family members to understand the grief state and the processes of grief which in themselves, without comprehension, can be terrifying.

Lynn Caine in her book *Widow* says,

I am convinced that if I had known the facts of grief before I had to experience them, it would not have made my grief less intense, not have lessened my misery, minimized my loss or quietened my anger. No, none of these things. But it would have allowed me hope. It would have given me courage.[12]

She further describes going over and over the circumstances leading to her husband's death. Once able to talk, she admits to the alleviation of some of the fears.[12]

The family physician can help patients provide appropriate truthful reassurances to children, and help parents to avoid contributing unwittingly to the child's guilt through neglectful behavior, deception, total exclusion from this critical family experience, or refusal to allow the child to grieve if he/she feels the need to do so. The family physician should be well versed in child development theory and psychology in order to clarify for parents or parent normal vs abnormal responses of their children.

Further, the family physician can perform a meaningful job of health education if he/she does not oversedate the bereaved, thereby preventing the necessary grief work, or if he/she does not treat the grieving

person's functional complaints as if they were organic. Roy and Jane Nichols,[13] in a recent anthology on death, suggest that, "In death and grief we do not need as much protection from painful experiences as we need the boldness to face them. We do not need as much tranquilization from pain as we need the strength to conquer it. Mourning is a healing process — a very necessary, very helpful way of diminishing . . . . grief." Finally, the Nichols further suggest that "there is a real value to ourselves and to others to pausing from our well-meant efficiency as professionals to care, to gentle, to share, to listen, to feel, to respond to each other and to ourselves . . . ."[13] So the challenge for appropriate responses is placed before the family physician.

Literature Cited

1. Lazare A: Commentary on Death and Dying. Address made at the first Annual Conference on Death and Dying, Harvard University, November 1975
2. Kubler-Ross E: On Death and Dying. New York, MacMillan Co, 1969, pp 4-10
3. Burstein A: The fearful, depressed patient. In Bowden and Burstein A: Psychological Basis of Medical Practice. Baltimore, 1974, Williams and Wilkins, pp 64-65
4. Hinton J: Dying. Baltimore, Penguin Books, 1967, p 196
5. Parkes CM: Effects of bereavement on physical and mental health — a study of medical records of widows. Br Med J 1:274-279, 1964
6. Gut E: Some aspects of adult mourning. Omega 5:327-335, 1974
7. Cassem NH: Commentary. Address made at the first Annual Conference on Death and Dying, Harvard University, November 1975
8. Rees WD, Lutkins SG: The mortality of bereavement. Br Med J 4:13-16, 1967
9. Lindemann E: Symptomatology and management of acute grief. Am J Psychiatry 101:141-148, 1944
10. Kubler-Ross E: Coping With Death. Audiotape Lectures, The Dying Patient, tape #4, Children and Death, 1969
11. Yudkin S: Children and death. Lancet 1:37-41, 1967
12. Caine L: Widow. New York, Bantam, 1974, pp 69 and 110
13. Nichols R, Nichols J: Funerals: A time for grief and growth. In Kubler-Ross E: Death: The Final Stage. Englewood Cliffs, NJ, Prentice-Hall, 1975, p 96

Object Loss and Counseling the Bereaved

Dr. Ronald R. Lee

Persons interested in the subject of death, dying and grieving need a better understanding of object relations. Object relations theory (Fairbairn, 1963), with its interest in the way people become attached to or detached from other persons, places, things or even ideas, is useful in helping persons with the fears and sorrows of bereavement. More importantly, the theory is basic knowledge for ministers and funeral directors, the professional helpers of the bereaved. Ministers need to understand object relations theory not only because of their role with the bereaved but because they encounter a whole range of people, from those who cannot invest emotions in anything to those who become so heavily invested that the loss of the object of investment leaves them emotionally crippled. Funeral directors need to understand object relations theory to better help persons during acute grieving. This paper will mainly focus on one aspect of object relations, the problems of detachment associated with object loss.

The theory of object relations could be considered as having two major components: object attachment and object detachment.

Object attachment means the investment of feelings—feelings which are no longer involved when object detachment takes place. The process of object detachment where there is no investment of feelings is a contradiction in terms. Degrees of investment mean degrees of attachment. Such an attachment can be simply diagrammed as a person A (circle) being attached to a person B (square).

Diagram I: OBJECT ATTACHMENT

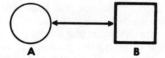

Yet it is more than this. Person A really contains the image of B inside him/herself (Klein, 1940)

Diagram II: OBJECT ATTACHMENT, REVISED

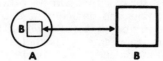

Thus the death of B always poses a problem for A if a deep emotional investment exists and hence B is already an image in the mind of A. The death of B means that A has to work at retaining the image or let it fade. The latter choice involves the process called grieving or mourning (Freud, 1917), and a lot of unpleasant or painful feelings of sadness, yearning, and even anger.

Object loss is a more general term than death, because death is usually restricted to the loss of persons or animals, while object loss includes severing a relationship with things, places or ideas, necessitating the same grief process as with death itself. Hence, in this article, death is seen as a special form of object loss.

Object loss is an internal state. If persons die or things are taken away but little or no emotional attachment has occurred, the sense of loss will not be great. No serious dilemma will then exist. If the loss is real because an attachment or emotional investment existed, the person has the choice of retaining or resolving the internal image of the lost object. There is often a third choice involved, that of displacing the lost object with some substitute.

Diagrammatically, object retention, displacement, and resolution will look something like the following:

Diagram III: OBJECT RETENTION

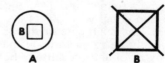

Diagram IV: OBJECT DISPLACEMENT

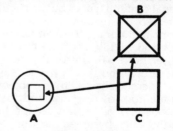

Diagram V: OBJECT RESOLUTION

Reprinted with permission from NRIC's *National Reporter,* the National Research and Information Center, Evanston, Illinois, March, 1979.

In object retention the external object is lost but the internal object is retained by whatever method it takes. With object displacement the internal object is retained as long as the new external object (C) is able to play a function similar to that played by the lost object. Under object resolution neither the external nor internal attachments exist. Some memories remain, but these do not have the emotional investment they formerly did.

A. Object Retention.

Edgar Jackson (1947) describes a case of object retention where two elderly unmarried sisters, who had lived together all their lives, were separated because the dominant one died suddenly of a heart attack. The survivor did not mourn and explained this by saying, "I know my sister is not really dead. She is here with me now just as she always was. She couldn't die, not my sister."

After the funeral the pattern became clearer. The surviving sister worked hard at retaining the illusion of her sister's presence. Two places were always set at the table, though she served no food for the dead sister, explaining, "In the spirit body we don't need food. We just don't want to be ignored." She kept flowers in her sister's bedroom and left her clothes hanging in the closet untouched except for an occasional cleaning. As much as possible, the presence of her sister as a spiritual being was accepted. When guests came, she would say, "I know that my sister would want me to thank you for coming." Christmas cards were always signed by both sisters.

It needs to be understood that object retention may not always lead to some kind of pathological results. An assumption often made is that all persons who suffer bereavement need to go through grieving, that is, object resolution. This is not necessarily so. One reason could be the absence of a strong attachment. If a strong attachment is lacking, how could grieving, which is the process of detachment, possibly take place? Another reason relates to this point about object retention. There seems to be a tremendous difference in the way a 70 year old person copes with object loss as compared to a 35 year old. The main goal of the 35 year old person would probably be to go through the grieving process which leads to object resolution. For the 70 year old there may be little or no grieving because the major goal is object retention. What is being stated is that the needs accompanying object loss will vary not only because of personal circumstances but particularly because of age. All research in the grieving process needs to take age into account and concentrate on samples of persons of young adult and middle age where object resolution is a much clearer need. All persons suffering object loss have needs, of course, but these needs may have to focus more on memorializing than object resolution. Honoring the memory of a spouse and fostering object retention can possibly add years to the lifespan of an otherwise healthy aging bereaved person.

B. Object Displacement.

Object displacement is where some object is used as an identical replacement for the one which has been lost. It is really a special case of object retention. In the author's first parish, the people were strongly attached to their church building even though the old Tasmanian mining town had declined from a population of 10,000 to 300, and the old Methodist church, built to hold 400 worshippers, had a total membership of 10. The building was old and dangerous, especially when the winds blew, because the high pitched roof acted like a sail and made the old timber structure, exposed by the absence of surrounding buildings, sway and creak so that the sanctuary lights could sometimes move in a two-foot arc.

Despite the persistent efforts of several ministers to have the building demolished, the faithful remnant clung tenaciously to their church, gaining the sympathy and support of the whole town. Eventually the church people were persuaded to build a small chapel on empty land opposite the old building and use pieces of the old furnishings to help in the transition. Once the new building was a fact, there was no resistance when the old church was demolished and the sales of the old lumber were used to clear the new church of debt. The same fierce loyalty and attachment was then focused on caring for the new building.

Object displacement, like object retention, can be a constructive or maladaptive way of coping with object loss. For example, object displacement is generally not a satisfactory way of adapting to a marital breakup because of death, divorce or separation. If a person rushes into a new marriage within weeks or months after the death or divorce of a spouse, he/she is risking a great deal of trouble in the future relationship. Object displacement saves the person the pain of grieving, but it also imposes an impossible burden on the new partner. He/she must now live up to the behavior of the "ghost" of the old spouse which remains internalized, unresolved, in the person. In such cases, object resolution is recommended before any new attachments are made.

C. Object Resolution.

Object resolution is what many people mean by grieving or mourning. In the grieving process there is a gradual diminishing of the attachment to the internal image of the lost object (Freud, 1917). The object is still remembered, but no longer has the same claim on the attention or energy of the person. Emotional investment in the object is weakened sufficiently so that new investments can occur without these investments being a form of object displacement. In object resolution the task of the griever is to accept the finality of the loss with mind, feelings and behavior. In complete grieving, we believe the loss, we feel its pain, and we adjust to the consequences in our lives.

Sometimes grieving is presented as if there are clear, distinct stages to the process. Kubler-Ross (1969) defines five stages: denial, anger, bargaining, depression, and acceptance, but her scheme, evolved from the self-grieving of dying persons, needs modification if applied to grievers. Bargaining generally does not apply to the grieving process, for example. On the other hand, terms like protest, despair and detachment also occur in the literature to describe stages (Bowlby, 1969, 1973). Whatever theoretical frame is selected, its value would seem to be mainly didactic. Any theory is open to misuse if taken too literally and applied too rigidly. These stages, meant as guides to help in a confusing array of behaviors, can never represent reality itself. Misapplied, they can result in increased guilt and hence retardation of object resolution (Klein, 1940).

The four "stages" used in this paper are:
1. shock (special stage);
2. cognitive (intellectual) resolution;
3. affective (feeling) resolution;
4. conative (behavior) resolution.

Evidence for this theoretical framework comes from the following areas:

i. grief studies, such as those by Colin Parkes (1972);

ii. infant studies, such as those by John Bowlby (1969, 1973);

iii. animal studies, such as those conducted by Konrad Lorenz (1963);

iv. natural disasters, such as those studied by James Taylor (1970) or R. J. Lifton (1967);

v. the author's clinical experience with grievers.

1. Shock (special stage)

Shock as a stage of object resolution is most evident in cases of sudden object loss, and even with such cases, is limited to a small percentage of persons who suffer bereavement. As one widow said, "I felt numb for a week. It's a blessing. Everything goes hard inside you like a weight" (Parkes, 1972).

The physical signs of shock, well known to physicians, can also be present. These are queasiness, sore pains in the stomach, throbbing head, cottony mouth, and heart palpitations. Stated physiologically, in the shock stage the body functions under the control of the sympathetic part of the autonomic nervous system which in turn mobilizes the muscular system for emergency performance.

In natural disasters, shock is always the initial reaction. The tornado that hit Topeka, Kansas in 1966 struck a 200-yard swathe diagonally across town for about four or five miles. As persons emerged form their cellars they beheld trees and electricity wires down, houses flattened and everything in chaos. The city's services were temporarily immobilized. Many persons were found walking around stunned (Taylor, 1970). In another situation, Robert J Lifton (1967) tells how the survivors of Hiroshima reacted to the atomic bomb explosion with shock and disbelief. The devastating impact of the bomb damage was underscored by the fact that the city had been untouched by conventional bombing.

2. Cognitive (intellectual) Resolution

One of the most important studies done in the area of object detachment took place in the Tavistock Child Center in London with children who were separated from their parents for a week or two (Bowlby, 1969) These children reacted initially to the withdrawing of their parents by indicating protest behavior. They kicked, screamed, cried, and tried to follow the parents unless restrained. In this way they expressed their hope that the separation was not really taking place.

Resistance to accepting object loss intellectually manifests itself in many more ways than protest. Parkes indicates that a lot of pining and searching behavior is displayed in adults in the early stages of loss and reaches a peak of intensity somewhere between the first and second weeks. This pining, traditionally known as the "pangs of grief," is also described in animal studies. Konrad Lorenz (1963) explains the effects of separating a greylag goose from its mate. "The first response to the disappearance of a partner consists of an anxious attempt to find him again. The goose moves about restlessly by day and night, flying great distances and visiting places where the partner might be found, uttering all the time the penetrating tri-syllable long-distance call for which this bird is known. The searcher s expeditions are extended further and further, and quite often the searcher itself gets lost or succumbs to an accident. All the objective observable characteristics of a goose's behavior on losing its mate are roughly identical with human grief. Studies of other animals such as domestic dogs, orangutans, chimpanzees and jackdaws indicate the same restless behavior in bereavement." Such behavior reveals that in the deeper recesses of the mind the object loss has not been fully believed.

3. Affective (feeling) Resolution

The cognitive stage of object resolution closely resembles an attempt at object resolution, but on a temporary basis. When the person is forced to face reality, the hope disappears and a firm belief in the loss is experienced. The resulting despair may be expressed as open hostility, as depression, or as displaced anger that gets acted out on the mortician, minister or physician associated with the loss. People can become irritable, bitter or just apathetic. Milder forms of despair may be identified as an overwhelming sense of sadness.

In the Tavistock Child Center, once it became evident to the infants that their parents would not return immediately, despair set in and much anger was directed at the members of the staff. The infants refused to be dressed or undressed, to eat, to potty, to pick up, etc. Some children displaced their hostility, directing it by hitting and kicking other children. Others had periods of withdrawal and depression. Behind such despair was the realization that the parent was indeed "lost." Soon, however, adjustment or reorganization took place. The children gradually began to cooperate with the nurses at the center. By the time the mothers returned, the children refused recognition of them, even retreating when the mothers entered the room. It is important for us to recognize that these expressions of feelings enabled the children to start emotionally detaching themselves from their parents.

Those who serve people in grief must be prepared to support them through despair and be ready to accept feelings in a variety of forms, even anger, without retaliating, yet keeping these feelings from becoming too destructive. Ministers particularly, if they have not accepted their own internal anger, are generally unable to facilitate this process, which is so necessary for people if they are to resolve their attachment to the old object.

4. Conative (behavioral) Resolution

This final stage of object resolution is sometimes referred to as the reorganization stage. This can mean:

a. clearing out drawers and closets in the loved one's room;

b. giving away the clothes, tools and books

of the deceased;

c. getting a job or driving license;

d. finding new interests;

e. going to more social functions and
returning to or joining a church.

Such reorganizing behavior manifests itself three or four months after the bereavement, according to two-thirds of those who were involved in the London Study (Parkes, 1972), but it is generally more evident after six months.

If the first stage of shock is seen as a special stage in a minority of persons, there are essentially three main stages of grieving. Another way to state this is that for grieving to take place resulting in a detachment from the internal image of the lost object and a reinvestment of energy in new interests and attachments, a person has to accept the loss cognitively, affectively and conatively. This acceptance is demonstrated by the way the person is able to acknowledge the reality of the loss and plan for the future without the active presence of the deceased person. While normally intellectual acceptance precedes the other two, and affective acceptance precedes behavioral reorganization, the important point is that eventually the death or loss is fully accepted in these three ways, no matter what the order of acceptance, given object resolution as the goal.

The unfolding of behavior which indicates that a person is going through the three main stages of grieving is more likely to appear when the object loss is sudden and extremely unexpected. Where the object loss is expected, some preparatory grief can take place, leading to changes in the grieving process after death. For example, it is possible that a grieving person has so prepared for the loss that after some feelings of sadness for a brief period of time, the person is able to move into reorganization behavior very soon after the death. Watching a loved one slowly die of cancer can mean that much of the grief work of the first two main stages of grieving has taken place by the time of actual death. Death can be experienced by both the dying person and the bereaved as a release. This enables reorganization to take place soon after the death without feelings of inappropriateness or guilt.

Of course, with so little real knowledge about the grieving process, much of the theorizing of the last decade of renewed interest in the subject has been crude guessing at best. It may be comforting to believe there are definite stages for the course of each person s grieving, but this process may be more affected by factors such as a person's character structure or by social pressure than by some innate process. We really don't know. Thus, an action-oriented person may be able to express the growing acceptance of the loss of a spouse through reorganization behavior more than through crying or through other expressions of feelings. Does it matter which comes first as long as full acceptance of the loss eventually takes place?

In addition to a theoretical understanding of object relations, the person trying to help those who have experienced object loss needs to have some rudimentary knowledge of psychopathology. Unfortunately, ministers and funeral directors, the two main professional groups who work with the bereaved receive little, if any, training in this area. Yet persistently the questions raised by both these groups in continuing education seminars center around cases where there is a pathological reaction to object loss. Acting out (the funeral director is physically assaulted), suicidal or hallucinatory behavior will occur in situations involving object loss. Psychotic depression, frantic spending of large sums of money, alcoholic or drug binges are also indicators of extensive psychopathology. Such reactions, needing, as they do, psychiatric referral, are frequent enough to justify larger funeral homes being required to have psychiatric or psychological consultants. Preferably, one of the staff members of a funeral home needs to have training not only in grief counseling but in psychopathological assessment and in ways of making effective referral (Lee, 1976). Ministers in local parishes need to have a consulting relationship with pastoral counseling specialists or with secular therapeutic professionals.

Percentages of pathological reactions to object loss can only be guessed. In studies of the bereaved it would seem that about two out of three go through a relatively normal grieving process where the symptoms of grieving, if present, are not extreme or are only on a temporary basis. Even for the one-third of reactions to object loss which could be considered pathological, there will be a range in the seriousness of the pathology, with not all of the cases being as severe as have been mentioned in the preceding paragraph. However, more moderate reactions of a neurotic nature such as sexual frigidity or impotence need just as much professional attention as the more extreme forms. And like psychological casualties of war, the sooner the pathological reactions are treated, the better the prognosis (Menninger, 1948). This is all the more reason for an early referral by ministers and funeral directors, who are the professional gatekeepers for the bereaved.

Pathological reactions to object loss do not necessarily occur when a person has a history of psychopathology. For all persons who suffer object loss, with or without a prior mental illness, rites of passage (Van Gennep, 1960) and rituals associated with cultic or religious traditions can be of inestimable benefit. The sacraments, prayer, scripture reading, hymn singing, eulogizing, viewing the body, the gathering of family and friends are all acts which can facilitate adaptation to object loss, especially object resolution, even among those with severe psychopathology.

One illustration of this fact occurred when a 38 year old charge nurse of a mental hospital ward suddenly died, and the entire ward decided to attend the funeral (Schmiedeck, 1972). In the church there was a highly emotional scene. Hymns were sung, people punctuated the service with "Amen's," and the relatives cried and called on the deceased by name. Then as the ward doctor described it, "As the chanting and crying grew louder and the rhythm intensified, we could feel the pressure increase and I began to be concerned that the patients might not be able to tolerate it and might lose psychic control. **However, the opposite happened** (author's emphasis). As more and more people joined in the singing and crying, the patients joined in too. Suddenly we were all singing, weeping and trembling. Nobody remained untouched." Most significantly, the doctor said that after the patients returned to their hospital ward they did not have setbacks which would normally be anticipated with the loss of such an important ward mother figure.

Those who are intrinsically religious will turn naturally to the resources of their faith at a time of object loss. Those extrinsically oriented to their faith need to know that the utilization of religious resources can be very helpful and that these religious resources can help avoid major psychotherapeutic bills later in life. Those who are not prepared to utilize religious resources for intrinsic or extrinsic reasons need to perform some of the rituals of termination associated with their own social customs because these too can help even though the rites may be severed from their religious origins. Rites of termination, for example, the closing of the casket, the lowering of the casket into the grave, the filling in of the grave, and so forth, signify the reality of the death.

While it could be demonstrated that religious and termination rituals are of great adaptive value to the bereaved, these rites sometimes need to be supplemented with counseling on an individual, family or group basis. Such counseling occurs in the pre- or post-burial period. The pre-burial counseling generally evolves out of a need to make decisions about the disposal of the body and funeral arrangements. In the context of such decision-making all kinds of feelings may erupt and miscommunications arise. Helping persons who are seen as skillful generally have capacities essential to all who counsel in a multitude of situations: to listen, to evaluate, to educate, to assure, to facilitate, and to refer.

To listen seems simple enough, but it is difficult for some persons to do for personality or other reasons. To listen means that the listener must be prepared to make the agenda of the client primary and the listener's own need secondary. To listen means that the counselor does not have all the answers and needs the communication of the client to know how to respond in the most appropriate and useful way. Those ministers who have an agenda of indoctrination or those funeral directors who are seeking to oversell something are generally poor listeners.

To evaluate means that the counselor has to be alert to signs of pathological reaction to object loss and to the possiblities of a psychiatric or psychological consultation or referral. To evaluate means some theoretical understanding of the options open to a person who has experienced object loss, and particularly an ability to understand behavior associated with the grieving process.

To educate is an important part of counseling the bereaved. Unfortunately, many persons avoid understanding the processes associated with death until they actually face a bereavement. Sometimes persons are too upset to be able to understand or remember anything. However, many persons have just the reverse reaction after a loss, especially when they think the counselor cares and has some knowledge to share. A brief indication of the "stages" of grieving can be very useful to the bereaved. It is important for the persons to know they are not becoming mentally ill as they experience irrational feelings associated with an important loss.

To assure follows naturally from educating. It is assuring to know that what the person is going through is normal and necessary as a part of grieving. To be openly assured so, repeatedly, may be necessary through the early stages of the grief process if a person is obsessionally angry or internally feels out of control. It is assuring to have someone like a minister or funeral director as a guarantor to the fact that one day the grieving person can be free from the burden of the bereavement and live again. It is assuring to other family members to know that a grieving parent or loved one is going

through a basically healthy process and has every good chance of enjoying life again.

To facilitate, provided this comes after listening, evaluating, educating and assuring, can be a beneficial part of a counselor's skills. This may involve suggesting alternatives to the bereaved or the family members, sharing expertise about many of the technicalities associated with death, and assisting the person to fill in forms. Aiding in the decision making, all the time being careful to play the secondary role, and helping make arrangements, always consulting with the bereaved, can relieve the grieving person of a great deal of the confusion associated with the loss of a loved object.

To refer is a necessary skill, which when taken seriously is a more difficult process than many first assume (Lee, 1976). Anyone can suggest a referral, although not enough do, but for the referral to actually take place demands counseling skills in discussing the surface and deeper reasons for the resistance to referral which normally will appear. The appearance of resistance and the skillful handling of this is often the acid test of whether a counselor is really an effective professional or not.

The most neglected area of counseling the bereaved is during the first six months after the funeral. Years ago, when home visitation was a regular part of the clergy's work, a lot of post-burial contacts were made with the bereaved. Unfortunately, pastoral visitation is slipping as a clergy practice even though some individual pastors are as faithful in their performance of this duty as ever. Funeral directors generally have felt this post-burial period was beyond their area of responsibility, so have been slow to "take up the slack." Hence, monitoring the grief needs of the bereaved from the critical period approximately one month post-burial to the fifth or sixth month becomes the most urgent need for those going through the process of bereavement.

Ministers and funeral directors are recommended to set up grief groups in churches and funeral homes (Clinebell, 1966). These groups should be educational and sharing in nature, should be for those in the early phases of grieving only, and should be "open." By open it is meant that persons join and keep dropping out all the time in a flow-through approach to group membership. Length of time in a bereavement group needs to be **strictly** limited to three months. Where possible there should be co-leaders, who preferably ought to be qualified ministers or funeral directors and not professional people normally associated with mental illness. Groups set up like this for normal grievers are designed to be as clearly distinguishable from group therapy as possible. They are also designed to minimize the distortions (transferences) which can evolve in closed groups. Persons who need more than three months of education and sharing of a bereavement group and are resistant to leaving it need to be referred to other groups in churches or in the community. If necessary, they can be referred to a therapy group if long-term needs emerge during the bereavement group sessions.

One view of counseling the bereaved is that it is a necessary but unpleasant task as a byproduct of living. Another is that bereavement and the task of adapting to object loss is central to what life is all about. Along with the many reasons for the recent revival of interest in the subject, at a deep level there seems to be an awakening to the reality that life from when we are born until when we die is nothing but a series of object losses.

From when we lose our omnipotent innocence as an infant to when we face our own demise as a physical, earthly being, we undergo nothing but hurt. These hurts may be seen as mini-deaths. How we handle such losses determines who we are and what we are able to contribute as useful and meaningful members of society. Point out a wise or contented person and you will find he or she has learned to accept object loss as a reality, adapt to these losses, and make the most of the opportunities which come along. Understanding object loss in the form of bereavement, and the question of how it may be adaptively coped with is a paradigm for the struggle of persons in modern society. To the extent that we learn to cope with object loss, there is always a future.

REFERENCES

1. Bowlby, John. ATTACHMENT AND LOSS, 2 vols. N.Y.: Basic Books, 1969 & 1973.
2. Clinebell, H. BASIC TYPES OF PASTORAL COUNSELING. N.Y.: Abingdon, 1966.
3. Fairbairn, W. R. D. "Synopsis of an object-relations theory of the personality," INT. JOURNAL OF PSYCHOANALYSIS, 44 (1963).
4. Freud, S. "Mourning and Melancholia," in STANDARD EDITION OF COMPLETE WORKS OF S. FREUD, 14 (1917) 243-258.
5. Jackson, Edgar N. UNDERSTANDING GRIEF, N.Y.: Abingdon, 1947.
6. Klein, M. "Mourning and its relation to manic-depressive states," in LOVE, GUILT AND REPARATION AND OTHER WORKS, N.Y.: Delacorte Press, 1975.
7. Kubler-Ross, E. ON DEATH AND DYING. N.Y.:Macmillan, 1969.
8. Lee, R. R. "Referral as an act of pastoral care," JOURNAL OF PASTORAL CARE, 30 (1976), 3, 186-197.
9. Lifton, Robert J. DEATH IN LIFE. N.Y.: Random House, 1967.
10. Lorenz, K. ON AGGRESSION. London: Metheun, 1963.
11. Menninger, W. PSYCHIATRY IN A TROUBLED WORLD. N.Y.: Macmillan, 1948.
12. Parkes, Colin. M. BEREAVEMENT. N.Y.: International Universities Press, 1972.
13. Schmiedeck, R. A. "The funeral of a psychiatric aide," BULL. MEN. CLIN., 36 (1972), 6, 641-645.
14. Taylor, James, Louis A. Zurcher and William H. Key. TORNADO. Seattle, Wash.: University of Washington Press, 1970.
15. Van Gennep, A. THE RITES OF PASSAGE. Chicago: University of Chicago Press, 1960.

Surviving the Loss Of a Loved One: An Inside Look at Grief Counseling

Marv Miller, Ph.D.

The telephone rings at an inopportune moment.

"Dr. Miller?"

"Yes?"

"This is Mrs. Baker."

"Yes, Mrs. Baker."

"Doctor, my husband . . . my husband is . . . (crying may be heard for the next 30 seconds). I'm sorry, doctor, I really must stop crying so much."

"Don't be sorry for expressing what you actually feel, Mrs. Baker. You may have a very understandable reason for crying so much. Now what was it you were starting to tell me?"

"My husband died recently and my life has been an absolute mess ever since. A friend of mine saw you on television and told me about your work. Doctor, I must see you soon."

"I will see you soon, but first I'd like to mail you some information about grief counseling so you'll know just what to expect when we get together."

"The mail will take forever. I can't wait that long. I feel like I'm losing my mind. I need to see you today . . . right now. Please, can I come over right now?"

"Mrs. Baker, I'm expecting someone in ten or fifteen minutes. Suppose I see you in two hours. It will probably take you that long to get dressed and drive here anyway. How does that sound?"

"You're right, it would take me that long. Okay, I'll see you at eleven o'clock."

That's how grief counseling typically begins and there is usually a typical ending, but what happens in between may be as trying, frustrating, and emotionally painful as any experience a person ever encounters.

Every day in the United States, more than 5,200 people die; that's more than two million deaths each year. The overwhelming majority of those deaths are among the elderly and often mark the involuntary end of a marriage. Survivors then face what many psychologists feel is the greatest single adjustment that life calls on us to make—adjusting to the loss of a loved one.

As long as mourners have solicited answers and consolation from those around them, there has been, in a very informal sense, a type of grief counseling. Recently, however, a new professional has evolved who specializes exclusively in the resolution of grief reactions. Most grief counselors entered their profession through the back door. That is, they had been involved in related work or had experienced a personal calamity, and were thrust into the realization that the need for such counselors was acute and steadily increasing. Few, if any of them, had realized when they were

young that they would be doing this type of work.

In my own case, I had been teaching courses on old age, suicide, and dying on several campuses. I began to notice that each semester my courses would attract some students (of all ages) who had never fully come to terms with their unresolved grief. A few had even quietly crossed that hypothetical line which separates mourning from pathological grief by grieving too much or too little.

Invariably these students would identify themselves by continually seeking my time, attention, and succor outside of the classroom. They were in touch with their feelings enough to realize that they needed assistance in dissipating their grief, but they did not know specifically where they could turn for help. Most felt that they did not need the services of a psychiatrist because they were not suffering from a mental or emotional illness. From their family doctors, who were usually overworked, they were given prescriptions for anti-depressants and/or sleep-inducing drugs, but little else. In addition, many had not been consoled by their clergyman's cliches concerning the deceased loved ones in heaven.

Years later I also heard similar tales of frustraton from a large group of widows I had interviewed while conducting research. What all of those

Editor's Note: Marv Miller, Ph.D., is Founder and Director of The Center for Information on Suicide, and is presently a Consultant in Suicidology. Miller has authored several articles relating to grief, thanatology, and suicide. He has taught at several universities and is currently a lecturer at the University of California/Irvine, and San Diego State University/San Diego.

Reprinted with permission from the Michigan Funeral Directors Association "Journal," February, 1980.

bereaved people felt they needed was not more platitudes, but a "nuts and bolts" type of guidance in relation to successful coping patterns. In short, they needed advice on how to survive emotionally. It was through my interactions with such students and the widows who had described their plight to me, that I finally decided to become a grief counselor in private practice.

Unlike therapy, in which patients may be seen for years in an attempt to resolve many complex and stubborn problems, grief counseling focuses on only one major issue: "How can the survivor most effectively deal with his/her grief in an optimal amount of time?" Therefore, grief counseling tends to work or not work very quickly. By that I mean that if positive results are to be obtained, they will almost invariably become conspicuous by the fifth session. If no salubrious change is apparent by the fifth session, then it's a fairly safe assumption that significant change will not be forthcoming from the association of that client with that particular counselor.

What about the cases in which no improvement is seen after several sessions with the counselor? Bear in mind that many people in emotional pain do not truly want their problems to abate. Therefore, they are unwilling to bring about change in their lives even when their happiness is contingent upon such change. These people often enter grief counseling under duress. They have been pressured into coming by their friends or relatives, and their prime motivation is merely to decrease the familial or peer pressure.

Such people are, of course, poor candidates for grief counseling and the chances of their successfully resolving their difficulties is severely diminished as a result. However, there is a rule of thumb to help identify these people in advance. They don't call to make an appointment; for any number of reasons they are unable or unwilling to do so. It is often the Good Samaritan who calls in their behalf—either a child, a sibling, or a friend. Usually it is the caller who is pressuring the grieving person into entering a therapeutic relationship.

Another observation, which shouldn't surprise anyone in the helping professions, is that women are much more likely to seek grief counseling than are men. My supposition is that the "big-boys-don't-cry ethic," which is such a powerful influence in our culture, precludes the majority of men from reaching out for the help which they may desperately need. Perhaps this is at least a partial explanation for the plurality of male suicides in our country.

Dynamics of Grief Counseling

My experience has indicated that the crucial factor which determines the success of grief counseling is the attitude of the client. If the client, who is usually a widow, believes that the counselor can wave a magic wand and breathe life back into her deceased husband, then our efforts are only perpetuating a fantasy. Therefore, I attempt to explain to each prospective client that there is nothing magical about grief counseling. However, if the client begins with the desire to work with the counselor in a partnership, then we are certainly starting off on the right foot. By working together, we are able to regenerate the client's life by refocusing her attention and energy.

The initial telephone conversation with the counselor may reveal that the client has several questions for which there are no answers. An example would be: "How many sessions with you will it take until I'm better?" Naturally, at that point, such a question makes as little sense as asking a medical doctor for a prognosis before he's had a chance to examine the patient. The motivations behind those questions are easier to understand if you consider that recently bereaved people tend to be much more emotional than logical. A question similar to the one quoted above is merely a reflection of the mourner's desire to work through his or her grief as quickly as possible, which is not an unreasonable ambition.

One of the primary purposes of grief counseling is to give the client permission to grieve. As strange as it may sound, many families cannot tolerate open expressions of grief. They will chastise and criticize the mourner for doing something as natural as crying. These relatives will often advise: "For your own good, don't cry so much!" Actually, they are sending a coded message which translates into: "When you cry, you upset *me* and I can't tolerate your grief. On the contrary, the counselor will not only encourage the mourner to cry, but will purposely say things calculated to induce tears. By giving the grief-stricken survivor permission to cry openly and to discuss any aspect of the deceased's life, a special service in itself is rendered.

An example that readily comes to mind was the widow whose sister would not "allow" her to cry. Whenever she cried in her sister's presence, the sister told her in no uncertain terms that she was crazy and needed to see a psychiatrist. Although her sister may have been acting in what she perceived as good faith, she was depriving my client of the requisite permission to grieve. When I handed the widow a handkerchief and told her my office had been especially designed for people to cry in, I was serving notice that tears were a plus not a minus. I continued to reward her for crying by speaking of her obvious ability to show that she was human and had suffered a profound loss. I not only convinced her that she was sane, as her sister had questioned, but also that she was probably a lot healthier mentally than those who don't cry or don't let others around them cry.

The resulting change in this woman's demeanor was so drastic that even her co-workers and supervisor noticed it the morning after our first session. Yet, all that I had done was give her "permission" to be exactly what she already was: human, deeply in need of support, racked with grief, and filled with tears.

The Stages of Grief

As documented by John Bowlby, a British researcher who has written extensively on the subject of grief, bereaved people typically experience three stages in the resolution of their grief. The first has been termed the "impact stage" because it is characterized by a numbness (which may be physical and/or emotional) and stoicism. The stoic behavior is indicative of the shock that survivors feel. In fact, they may be feeling very little else because they have been so traumatized. In other words, in a very realistic sense, it is still much too soon for them to truly recognize the depth of their loss.

After the ephemeral impact period, mourners move into the deeply disturbing "recoil stage." It is during this second phase that the reality of the loss begins to "sink in." An empty bed and a pervasive feeling of loneliness force the mourner into a rude awakening. The reality of the depth of the loss can no longer be denied. Widows will later recall: "That was the time that I really began to believe that my husband was never coming home again; prior to that point, I tended to think of him as being away on a long vacation. Whenever the phone or doorbell rang, I used to believe it was my husband, but I can no longer sustain myself on fantasies."

The recoil stage is characterized by depression and anger. It is during this stage that the risk of suicide among widows and widowers is at its peak. During the first year after bereavement, the risk of suicide is two and a half times as high as it is among married people in the same age group. Several studies have indicated that the mortality rate in general is much higher during the first year after bereavement than it is for married people of similar age. Mourners are also much more susceptible to disease than are their counterparts with intact marriages.

The survivor's anger sometimes has an irrational edge to it which may be directed at the nearest object, whether appropriate or not. Such objects often include the physician ("If he hadn't been playing golf while my husband was having his heart attack, my husband would be alive today!"), the funeral director ("That man manipulated me into ordering a very expensive funeral!"), or the clergyman ("Where was God when we needed Him the most?"). It is also not uncommon for the mourner's hostility to be directed at fate ("Why now, just when he was gaining a foothold on his career?"), or even at the deceased himself ("We had three young children to

raise and he just died. How could he do that to me?").

A big part of my job as a grief counselor is to help my clients to acknowledge their feelings of guilt, ambivalence, and anger. Naturally we can more adequately deal with the effects of such feelings once the mourner has admitted their presence. Ventilation of the grief-stricken person's anger has a salubrious, cathartic effect in itself, and is therefore an integral part of the healing process. Unfortunately some mourners never move beyond the recoil stage. That may be because they simply do not wish to heal. When I once observed that a middle-aged widow was still wearing her wedding band almost four years after the death of her husband, she remarked: "My husband is dead, but we're still married." Her comment could be construed as a poignant, romantic reaction. However, consider how such an attitude might seriously detract from her chances of ever again regenerating happiness and love in her life. Another way of interpreting her remark might be: "I died when my husband died."

Fortunately, the overwhelming majority of mourners are able to transcend their grief during the third and final stage, known simply as the "recovery (or adjustment) phase." While in the recovery stage, the bereaved sever their strong emotional ties with the past and reorient themselves toward the present and future. Renewed optimism about the future is one of the earmarks of the recovered mourner. Other signs that I look for would include: removal of the wedding rings, giving away the decedent's clothing and/or personal effects, redecorating the home, changing the listing in the telephone directory, removing the deceased's name from the mailbox, etc. Depending on the survivor's age, I might also look for a desire to begin dating or at least sharing companionship with those of the opposite sex.

Sudden Death vs. Chronic Illness

When a person is declared to be "terminally ill," his/her family has time in which to prepare for the inevitable loss it is about to bear.

However, regardless of how much "preparatory grief" is experienced prior to the loved one's death, there is almost invariably a resurgence of grief when death finally occurs. This tendency may be observed no matter how far in advance the family becomes aware of the impending death.

When a sudden death occurs, such as in an accident or a fatal first heart attack, there is no time to prepare psychologically for the shock of the event. As a result, he or she is much more likely to remain in the impact stage for an inordinately long time. Also, the anger of survivors of sudden death victims is likely to be specifically directed—for example, at a drunken driver ("He murdered my daughter the same as if he had used a gun."). Feelings of guilt may also be more common among such survivors ("If only I had urged her to have that annual physical exam . . ." or "If only I hadn't been out shopping, I could have called an ambulance or done something.").

Surviving a Suicide

When a loved one dies by suicide, a vastly complex set of mixed emotions is usually the legacy. Guilt is often the salient feeling of the survivors. Adding insult to injury, the community is likely to stigmatize and/or ostracize the surviving relative of a suicide victim. It is as though the society were pointing its collective finger and hypothetically asking: "Why weren't you more supportive of the deceased?" or "What in the world did you do to drive the deceased to suicide?"

In addition, while survivors of a death brought about by natural causes, an accident, or a homicide, will usually experience having their friends and relatives rallying around them, survivors of suicides will often find that they are denied similar support. In fact, people surviving those who commit suicide may even be treated as though suicide were transmitted by a virus. Unfortunately, such stigmatization serves to reinforce the mourner's own already overdeveloped sense of guilt.

Because people who experience a suicide in their immediate families have a greatly enhanced risk of becoming a suicide in the future, grief counseling can accomplish some of its most important goals in these situations. As indicated, those surviving suicides are often devastated by guilt. However, their guilt may be quickly ameliorated once they become convinced that the origins of suicide are often traceable to the deceased's childhood. It also helps survivors to know that suicide is typically the result of a long-term, progressive inability to adapt. As such, it is rarely a spontaneous act. Therefore, in most cases, one person's suicide cannot be said to actually have been "caused" by another person's specific act. As survivors are shown through counseling that they need not accept nor carry the emotional scars of a suicide for the remainder of their lives, their own mental health can be vastly improved. It is in this manner that bereavement counseling could become a major suicide prevention technique. Unfortunately, at present, very few families that experience a suicide are ever exposed to the prophylactic and healing effects of such counseling.

Creative Grieving

In terms of self-image, there is a vast difference between a woman thinking of herself as "Mrs. Bob" and "Mary." Very often, the manner in which she perceives herself will determine what image she projects to the outside world, and conversely, how that world reacts to her. The "Mrs. Bob's" tend to have severe reactions to the death of their spouses since such women have not really existed as individuals—usually they were extensions of their mates and lived in the shadows of their husbands.

By moving directly from their parents' homes into marriages, many "Mrs. Bob's" may have denied themselves the important opportunity to spread their wings and find out how far and in which direction they could have flown. Instead, as a result of having lived in their husbands' "protective custody," these women may have never written a check, pumped gasoline into an automobile, replaced a fuse, or changed a light bulb. However, as constricting as the "Mrs. Bob" situations tend to be for the wife as long as the husband is alive, they do present unusual opportunities for personal growth after the onset of widowhood. Perhaps for the first time in many years, or in her entire life, the recently bereaved widow is involuntarily presented with a distinct period which is uniquely conductive to discovering or reaffirming her individual identity.

By helping the widow to focus on certain crucial questions (viz., who she really is, what she is, what she wants to do with the remainder of her life, with whom she wants to do it, where she wants to do it, etc.) during this unusual period in her life, the grief counselor is in an ideal position to promote the personal and emotional growth of his/her clients. In fact, mourners may emerge from their grief with a commitment to further their formal educations, to change careers, or to begin a career.

It is not unusual to see clients become aware of sources of strength and ambitions that they hadn't previously realized were lying dormant within their own personalities. For example, one young widow had thought seriously of becoming a nun prior to her marriage. Through counseling she was able to see how she had substituted her husband and marriage for religion. She had worshiped her husband's multiple abilities and was in awe of his education and profession. While in bereavement counseling she began to discover her own inner strengths and become convinced that she could control her own life. She does now and is preparing for graduate education and a professional career. Her grieving was indeed creative, and through it she realized that the "Mary" who had been residing all of those years inside of her "Mrs. Bob" was a worthwhile person in her own right.

Hospice Programs

AMA Council on Medical Service

Over the past few years, both the scientific and popular literature has reflected growing awareness of the value of the hospice approach to care of the terminally ill. In 1978, this House of Delegates approved "the physician directed hospice concept to enable the terminally ill to die in surroundings more home-like and congenial than the usual hospital environment," reflecting increased professional recognition of the need for and use of this approach.

The purpose of the present report is to briefly summarize for the House of Delegates the origin, development, and present status of hospice programs, to identify issues regarding further study in this area, and to respond to Resolution 40 (A-80) which was referred to the Council for study.

Definition

A hospice is not necessarily a specific facility or institution, but rather a program and concept of care. The National Hospice Organization (NHO) organized in 1978, has proposed the following preliminary definition of a hospice program:

Hospice is a medically directed, nurse coordinated program providing a continuum of home and inpatient care of the terminally ill patient and family. It employs an interdisciplinary team acting under the direction of an autonomous hospice administration. The program provides palliative and supportive care to meet the special needs arising out of the physical, emotional, spiritual, social and economic stresses which are experienced during the final states of illness and during dying and bereavement. This care is available 24 hours a day, seven days a week and is provided on the basis of need regardless of (ability) to pay. Such care of necessity requires careful record keeping for coordination of patient care as well as for use in education and research.

Thus, hospice care may be provided in a specially built free standing facility, in a specific section of a

EDITOR'S NOTE: This is a report of the AMA Council on Medical Services to the House of Delegates at its Interim Meeting in December, 1980.

hospital or nursing home, in the patients' homes (often as part of a coordinated home care program)—or in all these settings in a given program. The prime purpose of such care is to improve the quality of life of the patient and his family by alleviating pain, whether that pain be physical, emotional, social or spiritual. The program provides an environment for the family to be involved in the care of the patient, and to be involved in the patient's dying in such a way as to enable the patient and the family to accept the death process as much a part of life as the birth process. Following the death of the patient, the hospice may provide bereavement counseling for the family, as a preventive health care measure.

The type of atmosphere sought in such programs is described by Leonard M. Leigner, M.D., in the December 8, 1975, issue of JAMA, reporting on his visit to St. Christopher's Hospice in London, England:

"Although I arrived with an initial resistance to continual contact with the dying patient, the actual experience was quite different from what I had expected. Instead of a terminal care or "death house" environment with cachectic, narcotized, bedridden, depressed patients, I found an active community of patients, staff, families, and children of staff and families.

"Each bed has a colorful curtain around it... Personal touches... give a feeling of warmth... there are family rooms for visits and a large room for group activities... There is close face-to-face and bodily contact between the staff member and the arriving patient... Visiting hours are liberal with as many visitors as desired allowed (8 a.m. to 8 p.m. daily except Monday)."

Origins and Current Status

St. Christopher's Hospice in London, founded in 1967, is generally recognized as the program upon which the modern hospice concept as implemented in the United States and elsewhere is patterned. The St. Christopher's Hospice is a free-standing facility with inpatient beds, and is not affiliated with any hospital. It also provides hospice care in the patients' homes when

Reprinted with permission from *Connecticut Medicine*, 45(6), June, 1981; and from the American Medical Association.

their condition has stabilized sufficiently to permit discharge to that setting. Reportedly, all of Great Britain's other hospices—about 31 in number—are patterned after the St. Christopher's model.

The hospice movement in the United States is relatively new, with the first U.S. hospice opening its doors in 1974; growth since that time, however, has been vigorous. By September 1978, according to a 1979 U.S. General Accounting Office report, there were 59 operating hospices and 73 additional in developmental stages in the U.S. Figures supplied by the National Hospice Organization would seem to indicate that vigorous growth is continuing. As of September 1980, the NHO claimed 118 provider members and 87 cooperating members. (Provider members are operating hospices, while "cooperating" members are those in the development phases).

Of the 59 operating hospice programs identified in the GAO report, 24 were operated by and part of a hospital, five were free-standing inpatient facilities, two were operated by HMOs and one by a skilled nursing facility. The remaining 27 operated as home care programs, with no inpatient facility. Professional administrators supervised about half the hospice programs. Others had registered nurses, social workers, physicians, clergy, or psychologists directing the program.

Hospice Services and Staffing

According to the 1979 GAO report, most of the 59 operating hospices provided home health, nursing and aide services, bereavement followup counseling and referral to other agencies for services, as well as various other medical and supportive services.

Only about half of the hospices provided 24-hour-a-day, 7-day-a-week home nursing care, which many individuals consider an essential element of hospice care. However, five additional hospices said they planned to expand their home care nursing programs to provide 24-hour-a-day, 7-day-a-week services.

According to the GAO report, hospices that provide psychiatric consultation indicated that this service is primarily provided to the hospice staff rather than the patient and family. The psychiatrist gives the staff emotional support and helps the team determine how best to serve the patient and his/her family. A few hospices, however, indicated that the psychiatrist or a psychiatric nurse may have individual sessions with either the patient or family member.

A significant feature of hospice operation is the extensive reliance on volunteer staff in many of the programs. According to the GAO report, paid staff totaled about 340 full-time equivalents for the 39 hospices reporting paid staff, and volunteer staff totaled 2,251 persons for the 53 hospices that reported such data. Paid staff ranged from a low of 0.1 full-time equivalents to a high of 51.5 (in a free standing facility

hospice), while active volunteer staff ranged from 1 to 160 persons. The ratio of paid to volunteer staff ranged from 1 full-time equivalent to 0.2 volunteers to 1 full-time equivalent to 134 volunteers.

Most paid staff were medical personnel (mainly nurses, with some physicians, therapists, and technicians); the rest were administrative and clerical staff. In contrast, most volunteers were persons trained by the hospices to provide personal care services and give emotional support to the patient and family.

Hospice Regulation and Accreditation

Only Connecticut and Florida license hospices as such. In other states, hospice programs are operated by licensed hospitals, skilled nursing facilities, home health agencies, and/or psychiatric hospitals. Some states do not license home health agencies but permit their operation; or permit hospice operation where the services it provides itself do not require licensure. The latter is the case, for example, where nursing services are the only service subject to licensure and these are provided for the hospice under contract by the Visiting Nurses Association. The licenses held by the 59 operating hospices in the GAO study were as follows:

License Held	Number of Hospices/a
Hospital	24
Psychiatric Hospital	2
Skilled Nursing Facility	5
Home Health Agency	19
No license held/b	28

a - Does not total 59 because some hospices hold multiple licenses.

b - Hospices providing no medical services requiring licensure.

There is currently no national program in operation to evaluate the quality of care provided in hospice programs. The National Hospice Organization has developed and approved standards which identify essential principles and characteristics of hospice care, as a potential base for development of a national accreditation program for hospices, and has discussed the feasibility and source of such a program with other groups including the Joint Commission on Accreditation of Hospitals. In August 1980, the JCAH received a grant from the Kellogg Foundation to study and make recommendations to the JCAH Board of Commissioners as to the needs for quality assurance in the field of hospice care, and the role of the JCAH in meeting such needs. Results of this feasibility study are expected in early 1981.

Costs and Financing of Hospice Care

Hospices in the GAO study were not able to provide sufficiently detailed data to enable valid comparisons of the cost of caring for patients in a hospice program vs. care in the traditional health delivery system.

Some estimates of cost savings achieved by specific hospice programs are available. An article in the May

1979 issue of the Joint Commission on Accreditation of Hospitals *Quality Review Bulletin* noted claimed savings by Hospice, Inc., of Connecticut of $1,800 per patient served, on the basis that care provided under the program avoided the need for an average of two weeks of hospital care. In that same article, Royal Victoria Hospital in Montreal, Canada, is reported to have admitted 522 patients to its palliative care unit during a 26-month survey period, for an average stay of 24 days. During the same period, it treated 351 patients on its home care program an average of 59 days. The hospital projected that without this program, the same patients would have spent 50.5 percent of these days in the hospital, and estimated that its home care program saved the hospital $1.5 million during its 26-month experience. However, information to date is too limited to permit generalization to all hospices—and in fact seems inconsistent from one program to the next. For example, the average per patient cost in a British hospice has been found to be approximately 80 percent of the cost of care in a British hospital.

Not surprisingly, the GAO study found that the requirements for initial hospice funding as well as the amount of operating costs depended in great measure on the hospice's staffing pattern and the number and mix of services performed. Data on 6-month operating costs obtained from 19 hospices showed that hospices having inpatient facilities had relatively high costs compared to those offering only homecare services. One of the free-standing hospices which had an inpatient facility and provided most of the medical/supportive services commonly performed had operating expenses of $668,560 for a year's period. This program served 182 patients and had 29.8 paid staff in full-time equivalents. In comparison, one nonfacility-based program which provided relatively few medical and supportive services had operating expenses for one year of only $17,202. This program served 171 patients with 30 volunteers and 3 part-time paid staff (2 nurses and 1 secretary) and placed a value of $190,000 on the professional services donated without charge.

Forty-two hospices provided data on the sources and amount of funds needed to begin providing services. They indicated that initial funding, ranging from $100 to $3 million, came from five major sources—private donations; membership fees; hospital revenues that exceeded expenses; federal, state, and local grants and contracts; and private grants. Private organizations providing grants to hospices included the American Cancer Society, the Kaiser Foundation and churches. A few hospices said they received some federal funds from the National Cancer Institute and the Comprehensive Employment and Training Act program.

Nineteen hospices—ranging from free standing facility-based programs to purely home care programs—provided the GAO with relatively detailed data on the sources and amounts of operating funds. Revenue in these programs ranged from $1,125 to $302,610 from six major sources during varying periods of time between January 1977 and July 1978. The following table illustrates by major source, the amount of revenue these hospices received and the number receiving operating funds from each source.

SOURCES AND AMOUNTS OF OPERATING FUNDS FOR 19 HOSPICES FROM JANUARY 1977 - JULY 1978/a

Source of operating funds	Amount of funds received	Number of Hospices
Medicare	$160,685	2
Medicaid	2,650	1
Commercial insurance and self-paying patients	110,526	3
Contributions	95,075	16
Endowments, trusts, and memorials	10,452	4
Grants and contracts/b	157,800	12
Other	101,180	5
Total	$638,368	

a - The hospices had been operating for various periods. (1 month, 6 months, 12 months, etc.) and their financial reporting periods varied. The data in this table are provided on a total of 155 months of operation between January 1977 and July 1978.

b - This category includes federal grants under the Comprehensive Employment and Training Act and Older Americans Act, federal contracts with NCI, revenue sharing funds, state grants, and private grants.

It is noteworthy that only two facility-based hospices reported receiving any Medicare reimbursement, and only three any reimbursement from commercial insurance and self-paying patients. Of the funds paid in these two categories, one free standing facility-based hospice received 84 percent.

Private and public third party payment for hospice care has up to the present been primarily for specific inpatient or home care services covered under existing contracts or regulations, rather than for any benefit package identified as "hospice care" per se. Existing provisions for covering the services of physicians and other health professionals at home and for inpatient care in hospitals or skilled nursing facilities may well apply at different times during a patient's receipt of "hospice care." However, other services provided under a hospice program—particularly those of a supportive rather than medical nature—may not be covered, or be covered only in part.

More recently, both private and public payors are experimenting with broader coverage for hospice care, in pilot studies to determine the cost, utilization and quality of such services when provided through an integrated program. According to representatives of the Blue Cross or Blue Shield Associations who discussed this subject with the Council, a number of local Blue Cross/Blue Shield plans have extended coverage on a pilot basis to hospice care provided in a number of settings including the home, the skilled nursing facility, the chronic hospital and the acute hospital-based unit. Among the coverage issues under study are terms and methods of payment for services, identifying proper financial requirements, keeping adequate records, and establishing incentives for sound financial management and appropriate utilization. To assist local plans in implementing and evaluating such studies, the National Association adopted in 1978 an "Initial Statement on Hospice Care and Hospice Services," which suggests three criteria as the basis for local plan support of hospice programs:

1. There must be demonstrated community needs for hospice services or programs.

2. There must be assurances that the care provided meets medically acceptable standards of quality and sound principles of health care administration.

3. There must be assurances that the delivery of hospice care is performed in an efficient and economical manner and physical setting that make effective use of existing community resources.

The statement also makes more detailed recommendations concerning the operation of and payment for hospice programs. These recommendations call for hospice care to be a coordinated program of home health and inpatient services, which is made available only on the basis of written, well-defined criteria addressing patient condition and prognosis and home and family conditions. There should be suitable linkages with existing providers to assure that all necessary levels of care can be made available. The care given should be subject to utilization review and quality assurance, and there should be compliance with state and local health planning requirements and with eventual accreditation standards.

The recommendations further call for initial payment arrangements on a pilot demonstration basis only, followed by thorough evaluation. As far as possible, use should be made of existing benefit provisions, with necessary benefit modifications also being tested on a limited basis. Reimbursement should be made only for patients and services meeting specific benefit and other relevant criteria. Plan and subscriber liability must have limits related to medical necessity and appropriateness of care. Finally, care should be delivered both effectively and economically, without exceeding costs of more traditional services.

The Health Insurance Association of America has issued a special advisory on hospice care to member plans, summarizing current information on such programs and identifying a number of issues requiring consideration in any expansion of coverage to hospice services.

HCFA "Waiver" Project: In September 1980, the Health Care Financing Administration initiated a study of the impact on the Medicare and Medicaid programs of paying for hospice services not presently covered under these programs. In 26 hospice programs selected from a number of applicants, Medicare restrictions or exclusions on payment for such services as custodial care, bereavement counseling and provision of pain killing drugs and biologicals which can be self-administered at home will be waived for the two-year duration of the study.

The specific statutory and regulatory requirements or exclusions of coverage that will be waived in the study are as follows:

1) *For in-home hospice services*

   a. Waiver of the "home bound" requirement for home health services.

   b. Waiver of the exclusion of drugs and biologicals provided in the home. Palliative drugs medically recognized and accepted will be reimbursed by the Medicare program. HCFA will determine on an individual hospice basis whether coverage and reimbursement will extend to prescription drugs such as antiemetics, antidepressants, and steroids.

   c. Waiver of the "skilled nursing requirement" so that payment will be made for services which are considered a custodial level of care.

   d. Waiver of the requirement for a new plan of treatment upon a patient's discharge following reinstitutionalization. Because some hospice patients will be institutionalized to stablize their conditions, the current Medicare requirement that a new plan of treatment be established at each discharge may be waived.

   e. Waiver of the current limits of 100 home health visits allowed under Part A of Medicare. Coverage of in-home hospice services may be expanded under Part A of the Medicare home health benefit with no numerical limits.

   f. Waivers of the Medicare provisions relating to a 3-day prior hospital stay, establishment of a plan of treatment by a physician within 14 days of discharge from a hospital or SNF and treatment for a condition treated in the hospital or SNF.

   g. Waiver of exclusion of reimbursement for bereavement counselling to the family by a nurse or other qualified professional after the death of a hospice patient.

   h. Waiver of restrictions on reimbursement for visits by psychologists, psychiatrists, and other qualified professionals made to the hospice patient and family.

   i. Waiver of restrictions on reimbursement for visits made by the hospice team to hospice patients who have been reinstitutionalized.

   j. Waiver of applicable coinsurance and deductible for hospice services which are approved during the demonstration.

   k. Waiver of the current Medicare cost reimbursement principles for hospice services if respondent proposes and HCFA accepts an alternative reimbursement system (e.g., capitation, prospective rates, etc.)

l. Waiver of the requirement that a patient must be in need of skilled nursing care, physical therapy, or speech therapy in order to utilize home health benefits.

2) *For inpatient hospice services*

a. Waiver of current Medicare cost reimbursement principles for service provided by hospitals and skilled nursing facilities (SNF's) if a respondent proposes and HCFA accepts an alternative reimbursement system.

b. Waiver of the level of care reimbursements which must be satisfied before a patient can receive covered hospital or SNF services.

c. Waivers of the Medicare requirements for a 3-day prior hospital stay, transfer within 14 days of discharge from a hospital, and treatment for a condition treated in the hospital.

d. Waiver of the current limits on hospital and SNF days, scope and duration of benefits such that limits on the stay in a hospital-hospice and SNF-hospice will not be applied.

e. Waiver of deductible and coinsurance for a patient admitted to an institutional hospice.

f. Waiver of the limitations of the "benefit period" for admission to and coverage of services provided by institutional hospices.

For the above waivers to apply, four other conditions must be met:

a. Beneficiaries must have a life expectancy of less than 6 months as certified by a physician who has treated the patient or can be shown to have complete knowledge of the patient's medical status.

b. The hospice home care program must assure that a primary care person is available on an "around the clock" basis. (This can be a family member, friend, or hired help.)

c. Plans of treatment must be established within 3 days of admission to the home care hospice and within 2 days of admission to the inpatient hospice.

d. Beneficiaries must give informed consent, in writing, to the hospice plan of treatment.

At the 1980 Annual Meeting, the House of Delegates referred Resolution 40, "Reimbursement for Charges in Voluntary Home Treatment of Terminally Ill," to the Board of Trustees for study. The resolution would have the AMA urge "the government and private health insurance programs to designate as reimbursable all medical charges and costs incurred by individuals electing to remain at home for the period of medical treatment required in the case of a terminal illness, thereby encouraging alternative, less costly treatment settings."

The Council on Medical Service has had the benefit of further comment on this resolution from representatives of its sponsor, the Colorado Medical Society, and has discussed the subject with government officials and representatives of the health insurance industry. The Council believes that the HCFA Waiver project described above, as well as the comparable studies underway in the private health insurance industry, will provide much needed additional information on the actual cost of providing coverage for hospice services, on appropriate criteria for quality and utilization of such services, on the feasibility of providing benefits for such services as bereavement counseling, which are extended to the family rather than the named insured, and on methods for coordinating the multiple levels of care which a given patient in a hospice program may require. Such information is an important prerequisite, in the Council's opinion, to consideration of any broad scale expansion of third-party coverage—particularly to services less directly related to medical care.

The results of these studies should provide a body of actuarial experience on which to develop reasonable payment mechanisms and coverage plans which can best meet the needs of patients who can benefit from hospice care. Pending their completion, the Council believes that a policy advocating blanket extension of third party coverage to *all* medical expenses involved in hospice care at home would be premature.

The Council on Medical Service believes that the concept of hospice care is a complex one, involving as it does multiple levels of medical and supportive care for both the patient and patient's family, but that the potential of such programs for alleviating human suffering and reducing the isolation of the dying patient is immense. The Council intends to monitor development in this area carefully, with particular reference to issues concerning third party coverage, accreditation, quality assessment and coordination of services, the need for closer physician direction and supervision, sources for program administration, and admission and utilization criteria, and will submit further reports to this House of Delegates as appropriate.

The Council recommends that:

1. The following statement be adopted in lieu of Resolution 40 (A-80):

The American Medical Association strongly supports continuation of studies by private and public third parties in paying for hospice care with the goal of designing coverage for medical charges and costs incurred by individuals electing to remain at home for the period of treatment required in the case of terminal illness, thereby encouraging alternative, less costly treatment settings.

2. The remainder of this report be filed.

Hospice: Comprehensive Terminal Care

Robert F. Rizzo, Ph.D.

Within the last two decades, we have heard a great deal of talk about death and dying. One may wonder how national and international events of the 1960s may have compelled us to look at reality more closely, and in looking we have taken more conscious note of death, the inescapable reality of our existence. Whatever may have been the overall impact of the movements and events of the 1960s and early 1970s, there are those pioneers, individual men and women, whose influence is unmistakable in helping us to become more aware of the dying person and his or her needs and in working toward answering these needs. Herman Feifel, who was chief clinical psychologist at the Veterans Administration Mental Hygiene Clinic in Los Angeles, was one of the pioneers in the late 1950s and early 1960s. In 1959, *The Meanings of Death,* which he edited, appeared on the scene to give us insights into the various attitudes toward death. In this work, Feifel[1] underscored society's difficulty in dealing with the subject. He saw that until it was removed from the status of taboo to that of a relevant topic, there could be no significant psychology of death. His own endeavors met with resistance, an experience shared by others like him. This resistance from health care professionals as well as from laymen is an attitude which has become widely researched.[2] Another outstanding leader is Elizabeth Kubler-Ross, M.D., a Swiss psychiatrist, who practices in Chicago. Her book, *On Death and Dying,*[3] has made us aware of the various "stages" of the dying process and has helped us relate practically to the dying patient as well as aiding the patient to relate to himself. Another physician in the vanguard of terminal care is Cecily Saunders, a clinical pharmacologist and medical director of St. Christopher's Hospice near London, a 44-bed inpatient facility with a home care program. It serves terminal patients with neurologic and malignant diseases. Before founding St. Christopher's in 1967, Saunders[4] worked six years at St. Joseph's Hospice, Hackney, a 150-bed facility established by the Irish Sisters of Charity in 1905 for the care of the dying and long-term sick. It is the hospice program which is the focus of this article.

Significance of the hospice program

There are several reasons why the hospice program is being considered. First, it is significant because in reality, as Saunders[4] points out, "the basic principles or components" of hospice care and terminal care are one and the same. These principles can be realized in different contexts, examples of which will be given shortly. The principles of hospice are neither esoteric nor provincial. They have universal meaning and application whatever the context. The second significance is that these principles have been applied in what might be called a special hospital, an inpatient facility designed specifically to meet the special needs of the terminal patient and staff. Such facilities as St. Christopher's, St. Joseph's, and St. Luke's, all in England, have become models for others built in England and the United States, and, as in the case of St. Christopher's, this kind of care facility with well-trained staff and proper procedures and environment can become a teaching center of terminal care in different contexts. A third reason for examining hospice is the movement in the United States for the establishment of the hospice program on both an inpatient and home care basis. There is already the National Hospice Organization with representatives from a number of states. At a recent meeting, a definition of hospice and hospice care was formulated. It is worth citing it as a basis of further analysis:

Reprinted by permission from the NEW YORK STATE JOURNAL OF MEDICINE, copyright by the Medical Society of the State of New York, vol. 78(12), October, 1978.

Hospice is a medically directed multidisciplinary program providing skilled care of an appropriate nature for terminally ill patients and their families. Hospice care helps patients and families to live as fully as possible until the time of death—helps relieve symptoms and provide support during the distress (physical, psychological, spiritual, social, economic) that may occur during the course of disease, dying, and bereavement.

Since the early 1970s, such care has developed in various parts of the United States, and the National Cancer Institute is committed to further the development by offering six grants for a three-year period. Guidelines for support are a home care program of 65 to 125 patients and an inpatient facility not exceeding 24. Emphasis is placed on volunteer participation, with a staff-volunteer ratio of 1 to 12. Patients must be terminal with a life expectancy of only a short time. This is to remove any notion of the hospice as an extended-care facility.[5]

The following are three examples of how the principles of hospice care can be realized in somewhat different contexts. The Vince Lombardi Cancer Center at Georgetown University, which already has much experience in home care, is applying for NCI (National Cancer Institute) funds to establish inpatient service for 25 terminal patients in a remodeled floor of the Washington Home for Incurables.[5] Hospice of New Haven has also had a strong home care program since 1974. With funds from the NCI and other sources, the New Haven program is nearing completion of a 44-bed inpatient facility, modeled after St. Christopher's. The design of the building lends support to staff as well as to patients and families.[6] There are spaces on either side of the chapel where people can be alone to rest or to talk with others. Since children are a welcomed part of the community, a day care center is provided for the workers. Essential services are provided by "a pharmacy with a full-time pharmacist; diagnostic radiation; oxygen and suction systems at every bed; and a small laboratory for frequently administered tests."[6] Next to the patient wings is the Home Care Service. At the center of the building is the chapel for spiritual renewal and ecumenical services. The rooms are spacious enough to accommodate four beds with comfortable space for visitors. Terraces, living rooms, and dining rooms are all designed for comfort and companionship. According to the objectives of hospice, the new inpatient service will strengthen the home care program with its present staff of physicians, registered and licensed practical nurses, social worker, director of volunteers, trained volunteers, and consultant clinical pharmacist. The expanded staff will continue to work toward the ideal of home care with inpatient service as a backup. Another

This article focuses on the hospice as a program of inpatient and home care of the terminally ill. It examines its methods and guiding principles and the issues raised by their application. It poses questions concerning the integration of the hospice into our health care system. The article is timely in view of the hospice movement in the United States and the programs already providing home care and inpatient/home care, some of which are being supported by the National Cancer Institute. Its relevance is highlighted by the recent introduction of bills in the California and New York legislatures to promote pilot programs.

variety of hospice is Hospice at St. Luke's Hospital Center in New York City. It began in 1975 with St. Christopher's as its model. The hospice team is made up of clinical nursing specialists with one as program coordinator, psychiatrists, a cancer specialist, a social worker, a chaplain, and several highly trained volunteers. Financial reasons limit participation to a part-time basis for all except the coordinator. In the words of the hospice's brochure, "the Hospice team functions as consultants and catalysts, establishing and maintaining channels of communication with other health professionals at St. Luke's who care for terminal cancer patients." The aforementioned are three ways in which the principles of hospice care can be realized.

On June 23, 1978, a bill introduced by Sen. Hugh T. Farley to establish a "hospice demonstration program" was passed by an unanimous vote of the New York State Senate. The bill now awaits a vote in the Assembly where it was introduced by Assemblyman Alan Hevesi. This bill and a similar one in California will be examined later. However, before doing so, it would be well to look at the various features and issues of the hospice program.

Control of pain

Management of pain is a primary concern of the hospice program. Saunders'[7] interest in hospice grew out of her care for cancer patients with severe intractable pain and with only a few months to live. She found that "for 70 percent the main problem is pain although this is rarely the only symptom." The chronic or constant pain associated with certain degenerative diseases is "a very complicated condition different from acute pain."[8] Acute pain can be protective as in the case of the stinging sensation at the touch of a hot object or the stabbing sensation of a sideache warning us to find the cause. It can be the postoperative pain whose cause the patient may understand and tolerate because there is the expectation of its short duration. Unlike acute pain, chronic pain has the qualities of seeming "timeless and endless as well as meaningless."[8] Moreover, Saunders[7] found that anticipation can make the pain much more intense and that "pain itself is the strongest antagonist to successful analgesics and if it is ever allowed to become severe the patient will then increase it with his own tension and fear."

From clinical experience, pain is understood as a complex phenomenon with psychologic as well as physiologic components. John Bonica, M.D., who has made a long study of pain, points out the complexity of both types. His observations parallel those of Saunders in regard to the differences between chronic and acute pain. According to Bonica,[9] there is a greater recognition today that the total pain experience embraces and is affected by a number of different but interrelated factors, namely, physiologic, motivational, affective, cognitive, personality, perceptual, ethnic, cultural, learning, and environmental, and in particular that anxiety, depression, and attention have a significant impact on reducing pain tolerance or increasing pain behavior. The factors influencing chronic pain are similar, but the effects of chronic pain, because of its duration, are more complex, making its relief much more difficult as "one of the major national and world health problems."[9] It would be well worth citing in full some of the differences Bonica[9] sees between acute and chronic pain.

Chronic pain is characterized by physiologic, affective, and behavioral responses which are quite different from those of acute pain. When pain due to disease or injury persists, the immediate automatic reflex responses become progressively less and, within a short period of time, disappear, probably because they are no longer useful. Many patients undergo a progressive physical deterioration caused by disturbance in sleep and appetite and often by excessive medication, all of which contribute to general fatigue and debility. Sleep disturbances are likely to occur with concern about the meaning and prognosis of the pain.

Many patients with chronic pain undergo serious emotional, affective, and behavioral changes. The anxiety of acute pain is replaced by reactive depression and hypochondriasis—two important characteristics of chronic pain, whether due to somatic or psychologic factors. Some patients with pain due to known but unremovable pathology (e.g., arthritis, cancer) cannot give meaning or purpose to the pain and become depressed and develop feelings of hopelessness, helplessness, and despair. These, like the sleeplessness, spiral to greater proportion as the patient goes from one doctor to another and one clinic to another. Each time he or she experiences hopefulness and the disappointment and, gradually, increasing bitterness and resentment toward the doctors.

This analysis gives us insight into the complexity of chronic pain, whose "mechanisms . . . probably involve prolonged dysfunctions of the neurologic and psychologic substrates of pain."

Hospice care is designed to meet the problem of the total pain experience presented by chronic pain in the terminally ill. Such care requires an interdisciplinary medical approach.[4] This is demanded by the very nature of chronic pain which, as noted, involves many interrelated dimensions. Although it is the major function of the physician to assess the patient's overall condition and prescribe symptomatic care and medication, he or she must work closely with other staff members because of concern for the whole person whose needs range beyond the physiologic and biologic. In addition to the pharmacist who has an important part in the assessment of the patient's need for analgesics and medication in general, there are the nurses, the social workers, the counselors, the chaplains, the volunteers, the cooks, and the aides, who must collaborate in attending to the stresses and needs which have a cumulative impact on the total pain experience. Saunders[4] recommends consultation beyond the confines of the hospice to gain the respect and cooperation from the physicians of the patients admitted and to foster a mutually informative exchange.

Saunders[7] outlines the major features of treatment of intractable pain to give us a good picture of comprehensive terminal care. The staff first makes an evaluation of the troublesome symptoms. These symptoms, which often accompany chronic illness, cannot only be a major source of physical pain but also of mental distress. They can be a source of embarrassment and repugnance to the patient, provoking shame, anxiety, depression, and bitterness. The staff can help immeasurably by being attentive to such symptoms as nausea, vomiting, dyspnea, sore mouth, diarrhea, and constipation. Shortness of breath, for instance, is a very frightening experience, which can only aggravate the patient's physical and mental distress. Saunders[7] feels that, if careful attention to symptoms and complaints can eliminate or reduce them, "a great deal of pain can be relieved without the use of analgesics at all, or the need can be greatly reduced."

Constant pain requires constant attention and treatment. Saunders[7] has discovered from experience that analgesics should be given routinely so that the patient does not have to ask for them out of pain. Although she remarks that this may not seem novel since they are often prescribed on four-hourly schedule, she notes:

All too often, however, the letters "p.r.n." are added in practice. At this stage, the patient should not have to ask for relief of his pain, nor should analgesics be withheld until it becomes severe.

At most, the patient should just begin to become dimly aware of pain when another dose is routinely given. The ideal is that the patient never know pain. The schedule of pain relief is not rigid because of inevitable fluctuations in condition and sleep patterns. The goal is to avoid severe pain which leads to a vicious cycle of tension, fear, and increased pain. Saunders[7] concludes that the balanced routine eliminates the need to raise the dosage frequently. The kinds and amount of drugs are tailored to the patient's needs. This takes trial and error. In England, the key component of pain relief is the "Brompton mixture," which contains diacetylmorphine or heroin, cocaine, alcohol, that is, gin, and sometimes the syrup of one of the phenothiazine group. Although synthetic analgesics prove effective for some patients, the hospices in England rely mainly on the opiates. Diacetylmorphine is the chief one, since in most cases it seems to provide the greatest relief without creating severe drowsiness and confusion. Tranquilizers and sedatives are also introduced to avoid a too-great and rapid increase in diacetylmorphine. Small doses of steroids are used in combination with the other drugs to reduce the need for opiates as well as to improve the symptom control and sense of well-being. Saunders[7,8] sees the problem as one of balancing clarity and reduction of pain. This demands careful assessment of the patient's needs and then the prescription of the proper combination of analgesics, tranquilizers, and sedatives. It also requires clinical evaluation of the drugs, particularly diacetylmorphine, in controlled studies.[10] For those concerned about the use of heroin, it should be mentioned that substitutes are being tried in combination with other drugs. The Vince Lombardi Cancer Center uses morphine sulfate in its "Brompton mixture."[5]

The question of addiction obviously arises at this point. From a clinical viewpoint, Saunders[7] does not find this a grave problem. With proper management of drugs and attention to symptomatic care and mental stress, the factors that build up chronic pain are held in check. Tension and fear, two important factors which increase the pain experience, are minimized. There may be a physical dependence on the drugs, but addiction, that state of mind characterized by "an emotional and demanding dependence," can be avoided by a well-balanced program. Saunders does not downplay the problem of addiction as a serious concern for all involved. When it does occur in a newly admitted patient or begins to occur in a patient under care, it can be alleviated by the addition of steroids and tranquilizers. The multidisciplinary approach can best respond to the needs of the patient. This is made eminently clear when we see pain in its total dimension and not narrowly defined in terms of its physical aspects.

The patient in chronic pain is prone to a weariness more difficult to endure than pain. There are the feelings of depression and guilt, isolation, and hopelessness. It is not unusual that patients feel that they are failing others as well as that their bodies are failing them. This is bound to generate self-hostility, guilt, and depression. These emotions may in turn be projected outward, becoming hostility and resentment toward those who care. There is that hopelessness that comes from an inability to find meaning in all the suffering.[7,11] At times like these, a caring person willing to reach out and to listen is the greatest asset in terminal care. Here all members of the hospice staff can help to assuage the feelings of hopelessness that "can be the hardest pain to bear."[8,12,13] It is here that the large number of volunteers organized and trained in the hospice program can be of great assistance. The time spent with patients and family can be invaluable in working through these feelings. Recruitment and training of volunteers is an important feature of the hospice program.[14]

Family

Immediate attention is given to the family, and this concern continues throughout inpatient and home care and into bereavement. There are a number of ways that the family can be helped and in turn become a part of the caring team. They can be given the opportunity to voice their feelings, especially those of weariness and impatience, over which they are likely to feel guilty. They should be given information in regard to what symptoms to expect and be assured that pain and distress can be adequately managed. Death, the unknown and feared, can be discussed with them in terms of the signs of death and attitudes of the patient.[3,11] Finally, home care will require strong support from the staff. Here the caseworker will be a valuable liaison between the hospice and home. In bereavement, the family may also need support. The program is designed to identify and aid those in special need.[14]

Question of euthanasia

The hospice movement and the movement for the legalization of euthanasia have different perspectives on terminal care and the values embodied in that care, and hence they differ in their moral evaluation of euthanasia. By euthanasia is meant the termination of the patient's life by direct intervention, for example, by a narcotic overdose. Simply it means the direct killing of the patient. It can be either voluntary, that is, at the request of the patient, or involuntary, at the request of another party because of the patient's incompetence to make the decision. Some like to term direct killing active or direct euthanasia, while they call omission of artificial life supports passive or indirect euthanasia. For supporters of active euthanasia, passive is a logical and humane first step, which could be followed by active in the proper circumstances; they are now focusing on the legalization of voluntary euthanasia.[15,16]

These views are not shared by those prominent in hospice care for several good reasons. They do not support active euthanasia in any form. They see a moral distinction between omission of artificial life supports in the proper circumstances and active euthanasia. The latter is killing, a negative and defeatist approach; the former is an exercise of humane judgment as to what will benefit or aggravate the patient's condition in concrete circumstances. This distinction is supported by religious and legal traditions deeply rooted in our culture. Moreover, to discuss terminal care bleakly in terms of active and passive euthanasia is to narrow our perception. Terminal care is much more comprehensive in its objectives, methods, and content. It does not reduce itself simply to omission of artificial life supports. In hospice care, when certain supports or therapies are omitted, other kinds of supports take their place. The patient still receives care, but the kind of care changes to suit his or her needs and condition. This is a somewhat broader and richer perspective than that presented by supporters of euthanasia.

The hospice approach is backed by religious, moral traditions. Within the Catholic tradition, there has developed the principle that the patient does not have the absolute moral obligation to use morally extraordinary means of preserving life and therefore has the right to refuse or accept them. By morally extraordinary is meant "all medicines, treatments, and operations, which cannot be obtained or used without excessive expense, pain, or other inconvenience, or which, if used, would not offer a reasonable hope of benefit."[17] Briefly stated, a practical decision of what means are morally extraordinary can be made only after an appraisal of each patient's condition, which takes into account age, type of illness, medical history of the disease and treatment, diagnosis of present condition, and prognosis. The rights of the patient in regard to morally extraordinary means is a moral principle which does not set to rest all problems. However, it is a principle which has a twofold function. It expresses a value to be upheld, a goal to be achieved, that is, the personal integrity and freedom of the patient. In so doing, it establishes a perspective from which the implications of the physical-patient relationship can be better perceived in concrete cases. It also indicates a norm

of conduct, of which physician and patient should be aware for the benefit of both. However, like all principles, it needs to be properly interpreted.

There is a strong convergence between the Catholic and Jewish traditional teachings. While both are opposed to active euthanasia, they accept the moral validity of omission of morally extraordinary means in the proper circumstances. Sherwin,[18] a professor of Jewish thought, notes a consensus among Orthodox, Conservative, and Reform rabbinic authorities. He writes:

> The obvious reason for this rare phenomenon of consensus is the *apparently* clear and unequivocal position taken by the classical sources on the subject . . . . Though active euthanasia is forbidden, passive euthanasia, in certain circumstances, is permitted by Jewish law. One is permitted, but not obliged, to remove any artificial means keeping a terminal patient alive because such activity is not considered a positive action.

There are also supporters of this moral position in Protestantism.[19] It is based on the premise that in certain grave circumstances the moral obligation to preserve life by every possible means is not absolute. It depends on the reasonableness of using specific means in these circumstances. It is based on a commonsense appraisal of the usefulness and reasonableness of these means, which weighs the cost benefit of their use under specific conditions. This analysis takes into account the spiritual, social, psychologic, as well as the physical and economic values, weighing the values to be achieved against those to be sacrificed in the employment of specific measures. Such an evaluation of means and values is out of concern for what constitutes the most humane and reasonable care in view of the patient's condition.[20]

There is a sound legal difference between euthanasia and omission of morally extraordinary means. As Robitscher,[21] psychiatrist and lawyer, notes, the Anglo-Saxon legal system, while protecting life against aggressive acts, recognizes the patient's right to refuse treatment. Court rulings have offered some insight into the legal interpretation of the right without, however, removing all uncertainty and ambiguity. After a thorough examination of court rulings, Veatch[22] reaches the broad conclusion that "competent individuals may refuse any medical treatment they desire for whatever reason they desire (unless they are prisoners) if treatment is offered for their own good." In regard to the mentally incompetent, the courts have not clearly resolved the issue "whether a death-prolonging or truly lifesaving treatment may be refused on the grounds that it is unreasonable—because of its uselessness or the burden it generates."[22] The ruling of the Supreme

Court of New Jersey in the Karen Quinlan case, although not setting to rest all the issues, concurs with the direction of a developing moral consensus that treatment which serves no purpose other than to prolong the dying process or which causes the patient more burden and suffering than can be justified by its benefits can be rightly refused by the guardians.[23] As for the practical application of these moral and legal principles, a more personalized relationship between physician, patient, and family, reinforced by frank and sensitive communication, would lessen in practice a number of difficulties foreseen arising out of a crisis situation.

The hospice approach is a practical application of sound moral principles rooted in tradition and common sense. Saunders[4] expresses it in this fashion:

> There are, as it were, two complementary systems of treatment—one concerned with the drive to eliminate a controllable disease and the other with the drive to relieve the symptoms of the relentless progress of an incurable disease. There should be openness and interchange between the two systems so that each is available at the time a patient needs it . . . . A patient should no more undergo aggressive treatment, which not only offers no hope of being effective but which may cause him further distress and thus isolate him from all true contact with those around him, than he should merely receive control of symptoms when the underlying cause is still treatable or has once again become so.

This presents the soundness of the hospice approach as it addresses the realities of terminal care and expresses the need for flexibility. Hospice does not embrace active euthanasia because, as Saunders[8] states, it "is an admission of defeat, and a totally negative approach."

Separate facility

There is some concern that hospices designed and run as separate facilities will be an unnecessary addition to an already overgrown health care system with plenty of unused acute care beds and duplicating programs. Those who raise such objections are not necessarily against the hospice principles. They would prefer to see them incorporated into already existing systems. Mel Krant, M.D., Director of Cancer Programs at the new University of Massachusetts School of Medicine, poses several objections. Although he admires the English hospice, he feels that imported into the American scene it will add another specialty, care of the dying, to a field already full of specialties. Instead of fostering integration, it will contribute to the existing fragmentation. Second, he fears that the necessary elements that

make hospice a success in England may not be found in America. The spirit of voluntary service and community cooperation, together with devoted leadership, as given by Saunders, are essential if the hospices are not to turn into ordinary nursing homes. Krant feels that terminal care is a responsibility of the hospital and that in the long run, integration of such care into the hospital is better than the creation of an independent facility, which "would help relieve hospitals and physicians of their true responsibilities, which should include more community involvement . . . ."[5] These comments, as reported, pose serious objections to the hospice as a separate facility. They come from a physician who recognizes that at present the general hospital has difficulty in caring for the dying patient because it is geared for cure and rehabilitation and not palliative care.[24]

Saunders and other promoters of the hospice program are not at odds with the contention that hospitals can serve the terminal patient. If we understand their point of view which expresses concern for the essential principles of terminal care first and foremost, it should become clear that these objections, although well taken, may paradoxically point up the need for hospices as separate facilities in various locations. Saunders[4] sums up well her view in this way:

> The basic principles or components of hospice or terminal care are set out below. They may be interpreted in a variety of ways and need not be limited to care in a geographically separate unit. At present, for example, they are being developed by a symptom control team operating throughout a general hospital, in special wards attached to hospitals and in some oncology units. Most new ventures offer a consulting service and are developing Home Care programmes and family follow-up care. Wherever they may be, hospice care staff have a special obligation to develop liaison with the doctors previously treating their patients, to continue to involve them and to encourage interest and skills in the investigation and control of distress of all kinds.

There is, therefore, no opposition to incorporation of the basic principles into hospitals, whether general or specialized. However, given the present problems confronting hospitals in general and given the need for special training and environment for terminal care, it could be asked whether some geographically separate units are not just what is needed at this time. The hospice would become a model and training center for personnel serving in palliative care units of hospitals. Staff from nursing homes would also benefit from such training.

A number of studies have examined "two fundamental issues" and their impact on terminal care:

"the range of skills, attitudes, and behaviors of the health professions" and "the organization of a complex social system . . . created to organize these skills and to make available the technological resources of the therapeutic and diagnostic arts."[25-29] The conclusion has been that the organizational structure of hospitals in general and the priorities, objectives, and training of their staffs are more attuned to cure and rehabilitation than to care of the dying patient. Strauss and Glaser,[30] sociologists who have done extensive research, recommend:

> Training for giving terminal care should be amplified and deepened in schools of medicine and nursing. The changes need to be fairly extensive. Experimentation will be necessary before faculties can be satisfied that they have provided adequate training in the aspects of terminal care—psychological, social, and organizational—now relatively neglected. How and when to teach these matters—these are questions.

This is not an indictment of anyone. Those who work in a hospital realize that the staff has limited physical and emotional resources which need replenishment. The turnover of staff in intensive care units indicates this. Moreover, not everyone is suited for the care of the terminal patient. A frank admission of limitations and an open recognition of the special physical, social, emotional, and spiritual needs of the dying person and family make all the more obvious that the answer to Glaser's and Strauss's questions as to how and when are centers specifically designed, equipped, and staffed for terminal care. Not only can the needs of the patient and family be better met, but much could be experientially learned by physicians and nurses who would staff the palliative care units of hospitals. The hospice as a separate facility can be a vital teaching center like St. Christopher's in London and also a place for research into the various aspects of terminal care.

The fear that the hospice as a separate facility will add to the fragmentation, overspecialization, and discontinuity in American medicine seems based on a misconception. At this time, the experience emanating from the hospice movement does not raise the specter of detracting from the hospital services and responsibilities. First of all, home care should be the primary goal of palliative care units in hospitals, as it is in the hospice program. Hospice inpatient service can do much to train palliative care staff in fostering a smooth transition from inpatient care to home care. Second, in view of the organizational structure, staffing, mentality, training, and environment of hospitals, it hardly seems realistic to expect a quick shift to comprehensive terminal care within the hospital system. Third, as already mentioned, an inpatient hospice facility can be a learning, teaching, and research center, which in turn can spur the development of palliative care units in hospitals, thus promoting improvement of hospital care. This is important in view of the fact that many dying patients will still find their way into hospitals. The trend toward institutional deaths, which began in the 1940s, seems to be holding steady.[31,32] There are already good examples of palliative care in hospitals, such as Mount Calvary Hospital in New York, Hospice at St. Luke's, and the Palliative Care Unit at the Royal Victoria Hospital in Montreal. But studies have shown that much more needs to be done if comprehensive terminal care is to find a place in the hospital setting. An inpatient hospice facility can be a vital bridge to such care.

Cost

With emphasis on home care, the hospice program can help significantly to reduce the medical costs which mount because of long stays in the hospital during terminal stages. Just a few days away from institutional care can result in sizable savings, particularly if the institution is a hospital.[31] If home care is combined with hospice inpatient care, the savings would be substantial. For example, the projected cost of a hospice room is $105 as compared with the estimated $190 per day in a general hospital in the same area.[31]

A cost-benefit analysis must focus on the serious question of whether the expense of an inpatient facility for a limited number of patients is warranted by the service. The New Haven annual report for 1975 gives $1,325,000 as the projected cost for the planning and building of a 44-bed facility.[31] This figure is somewhat lower than the $2.7 million cited as the target for a fund-raising campaign in its newsletter of December, 1974. Will this end in being a large expense for special care of a minority, while the majority continue to receive present institutional care? Balfour Mount, M.D., is reported as raising this point "in reference to St. Christopher's, which serves 54 patients within a 6-mile radius."[31] The figure of 54 can be misleading. The number is much larger because the hospice provides short-term inpatient care rather than long-term chronic care. With its emphasis on home care, the total program allows for a great patient turnover. For example, in reference to St. Christopher's, Saunders states that "during the first full year (1968) we admitted 380, and during 1971 we admitted 489; during 1972, 519; and during 1973, 579."[33] Inpatient care is not inexpensive, bed cost being about 70 percent of a teaching hospital and 80 percent of a general hospital bed. But its costs per week are higher than most other hospices because it is a teaching center.[4] As a teaching center, its range of service and influence extends beyond its geographic boundaries. Benefits accruing from the immediate expenses cannot be readily estimated because they derive from the long-term home care fostered and provided by the trainees of the hospice.

Another factor to be considered is the fact that 85 percent of expense goes to staff salaries.[5] The significance of this can best be understood by looking at the apportioning of hospital expenditures. About 60 percent goes toward labor costs, the remainder to drugs, medical hardware, and overhead in general.[34] It has been the contention of the hospital industry that the astronomic rise in costs has been due to salary raises. However, evidence points to nonlabor costs as a more decisive factor, as, for example, the cost of medical technology.[35,36] In *Technology as a Shaping Force*, Bennett[35] makes a distinction between "definitive technology" and "half-way technologies—measures which merely palliate the manifestation of major diseases whose underlying mechanisms are not yet understood and for which no definitive prevention, control or cure has yet been devised." It is the use of this latter kind of technology which is behind the rapid rise in medical cost, a view shared by Thomas.[37] He cites the savings accruing from the technologic advances that have effected cures, prevention, and greater skill and efficiency. But he underscores the great extent to which the half-way technologies prevail along with overuse of diagnostic technology to increase cost. Unlike hospitals, hospice costs are unlikely to rise so rapidly because of a lack of investment in and use of such technology.

If we take an overall picture of the hospice program, considering the hidden factors as well as the obvious ones, the benefits both in terms of human welfare and financial savings can be substantial, even if expenditures are made for a new facility built along the lines of New Haven Hospice. Moreover, it may be possible that some existing facilities, such as nursing homes, could be remodeled to meet the standards of hospice care. The home care program should be underlined as a service whose potential for human welfare and economic savings cannot be overestimated, particularly in view of the increasing number of people dying from degenerative diseases.

Health care category

An important question is under what category would hospice come if incorporated into our health care system. This is relevant to reimbursement for the levels of care provided by hospice. For example, under Medicare, there exists a problem for anyone moving from a long stay at home to a nursing home. The requirement for reimbursement is a three-day stay in a hospital. This kind of shuttle can result in unnecessary stays in the hospital and increased costs.[31] There is concern whether this might not happen in regard to the hospice and whether the rates of reimbursement will be high enough to cover inpatient care. Section 414.1 of the New York State Hospital Code stipulates that for an institution with beds for inpatient care by or under the supervision of a physician to be designated hospital it must meet specific requirements. The first one makes it impossible to categorize the hospice as a hospital. It reads: "(1) provides diagnostic and therapeutic services for medical diagnosis, treatment and care of injured and sick persons and has, as a minimum, laboratory and radiology services and organized departments of medicine and surgery . . . ." The specific requirement of an organized department of surgery in itself eliminates hospice from this category. Obviously hospice does not require such a department to meet the needs of the patient. Moreover, whenever palliative care warrants, recourse will be made to some of the services provided by nearby hospitals, for example, palliative x-ray. However, by virtue of the nature and scope of terminal care, hospice does not fit into the category of nursing home; there are a number of differences. The patients in a nursing home are not all terminal. There is a much greater range of conditions, while in the hospice all are terminal, requiring specialized palliative care. This care demands personalized attention with a nurse-patient ratio of 1:1.25.[33] Hospice is also a short-term care facility; nursing homes tend to be long-term. In addition, the hospice has a more complex facility with a built-in diagnostic laboratory and radiology departments along with a first-rate pharmacy, all under the direction of a physician. Another significant difference is in regard to the family, which in the hospice program is a unit of care, receiving attention during the illness and bereavement. Moreover, the family is brought into the caring team as much as possible so that ultimately home care can be possible under the direction of staff. This concern for the family and home care places special demands on the staff's skills and energies. Nursing homes do not aim at developing a strong home care program. These differences make it imperative that hospice be given a special designation and place in our health care system.

Legislation

The legislatures in California and New York would establish pilot projects or demonstration programs under the supervision of their respective health agencies. A major objective is to test whether and where the hospice program can be integrated in the system and codes. An allied objective is to work out ways for adequate reimbursement. The quality and cost effectiveness of the program in both its inpatient and home care with its large staff of trained lay volunteers must also be examined in comparison with traditional care systems. A further issue is the extent of present and future demand for such care and the need to construct new facilities or use existing ones. These are the issues the Hart bill in California singles out for evaluation.[38] They are implied in Sen. Hugh T. Farley's bill when it authorizes "the public health council . . . to establish a hospice demonstration program to evaluate the use of hospices within the health care system of the state and to aid in the establishment of regulations governing subsequent certification and operation of hospices including a reimbursement methodology showing cost benefit."[39]

The Farley bill clearly defines the features of hospice care.

"Hospice" means a coordinated program of home and in-patient care which treats the terminally ill patient and family as a unit, employing an interdisciplinary team acting under the direction of an autonomous hospice administration. The program provides palliative and supportive care to meet the special needs arising out of physical, psychological, spiritual, social, and economic stresses which are experienced during the final stages of illness, and during dying and bereavement.[38]

The bill goes on to emphasize the pivotal importance of home care by stating that "the hospice demonstration program shall consist of three hospice models, one each to evaluate the hospice program of homecare with back-up in-patient beds provided: (a) in a special, autonomous unit of a general hospital or of a nursing home; (b) in a free-standing hospice facility; and (c) in whatever unit of a general hospital to which the patient may be admitted."[39] The importance of this emphasis on home care and of the inclusion of the concept of autonomy in such legislation is readily seen from the analysis of the special nature and scope of the hospice program.

Conclusion

Hospice is a comprehensive interdisciplinary approach to terminal care which embraces patient and family. Its principles can be applied in different settings. As a separate facility of short-term care, hospice can serve many patients and at the same time be a great community resource as a learning, teaching, and research center. Advances in these areas would benefit hospitals in their palliative care units and nursing homes. The hospice program can give impetus to home care, for which there is a growing need. It should not be viewed as competing with other established institutions and methods of care. Rather, it should be seen as complementing them. It is certainly not designed to remove the patient's physician from the scene. One of its principles is to involve in the program those who have cared for the patient. In the development of comprehensive terminal care, the direction and services of the physician are essential to the caring team.

Addendum

Senator Farley's hospice bill, which passed the New York State Senate on June 23, passed the Assembly on July 18 and was signed into law by Governor Carey on August 7, 1978.

346 N. Elliott Street
Williamsville, New York 14221

References

1. Schneidman, E. S., Ed.: Death: Current Perspectives, Palo Alto, California, Mayfield Publishing Company, 1976, p. 423.
2. Kastenbaum, R., and Aisenberg, R.: The Psychology of Death, New York, Springer Publishing Company, 1972, p. 237.
3. Kubler-Ross, E.: On Death and Dying, New York, Macmillan, 1969.
4. Saunders, C.: Hospice Care and Cancer, unpublished paper, London, St. Christopher's Hospice, October, 1976.
5. Holden, C.: Hospices: for the dying, relief from pain and fear, Science 193: 389 (July 30) 1976.
6. Hospice . . . A Vision, Newsletter, New Haven, Hospice, Inc., December, 1974, p. 1.
7. Saunders, C.: Management of intractable pain, Proc. Roy. Soc. Med. 56: 195 (1963).
8. Idem: The moment of truth: care of the dying person, in Scott, F. G., and Brewer, R. M., Eds.: Confrontations of Death, Corvallis, Oregon, A Continuing Education Book, 1971, p. 116.
9. Bonica, J. J.: Pain mechanisms, presented at the Lakes Area Medical Education Program, Buffalo, New York, January 20, 1975, pp. 3, 21, 22.
10. Horwitz, H.: London hospice eases plight of the dying, Hospital Tribune, February 11, 1974, p. 10.
11. Saunders, C.: Terminal illness, excerpted from proceedings, Health Congress of the Royal Society of Health at Blackpool, April 24–28, 1961, p. 113.
12. Feifel, H.: Attitudes toward death: a psychological perspective, in Schneidman, E. S., Ed.: Death: Current Perspectives, Palo Alto, California, Mayfield Publishing Company, 1976, p. 423.
13. Feder, S. L.: Attitudes of patients with advanced malignancy, in ibid., p. 430.
14. Dobihal, E. F., Jr.: Talk or terminal care?, Connecticut Med. J. 38: 364 (1974).
15. Downing, A. B., Ed.: Euthanasia and the Right to Death, London, Peter Owen, Ltd., 1969, p. 19.
16. A plea for beneficent euthanasia, The Humanist 34: 5 (1974).
17. Kelly, G.: The duty to preserve life, Theological Stud. 22: 228 (1961).
18. Sherwin, B. L.: Jewish views on euthanasia, The Humanist 34: 19 (1974).
19. Ramsey, P.: The Patient as Person, New Haven and London, Yale University Press, 1970, p. 113.
20. McCormick, R. A.: The quality of life, the sanctity of life, Hastings Center Rep. 8: 30 (Feb.) 1978.
21. Robitscher, J. B.: The right to die, ibid. 2: 11 (1972).
22. Veatch, R. M.: Death, Dying and the Biological Revolu-

tion, New Haven and London, Yale University Press, 1976, p. 162.

23. In the Matter of Karen Quinlan, An Alleged Incompetent, N.J. 355 A. 2d 645 at 633 (1976).

24. Hendin, D.: Death as a Fact of Life, New York, W. W. Norton & Co., 1975, P. 112.

25. Mauksch, H. O.: The organizational context of dying, in Kubler-Ross, E., Ed.: Death: The Final State of Growth, Englewood Cliffs, New Jersey, Prentice-Hall, Inc., 1975, p. 22.

26. Glaser, B. G., and Strauss, A.: Time for Dying, Chicago, Aldine, 1968.

27. Sudnow, D.: Passing On, New York, Prentice-Hall, Inc., 1967.

28. Verwoerdt, A.: Communication with the Fatally Ill, Springfield, Illinois, Charles C Thomas, 1966.

29. Cartwright, A., et al.: Life Before Death, London, Routledge & Kegan Paul, 1973.

30. Strauss, A., and Glaser, B.: Patterns of dying, in Brim, O. G., Jr., et al., Eds.: The Dying Patient, New York, Russell Sage Foundation, 1970, p. 153.

31. Ryder, C. F., and Ross, D. M.: Terminal care—issues and alternatives, Pub. Health Rep. 92: 20 (Jan.–Feb.) 1977.

32. Lerner, M.: When, why and where people die, in Brim, O. G., et al., Eds.: The Dying Patient, New York, Russell Sage Foundation, 1970, p. 20.

33. Saunders, C.: St. Christopher's hospice, in Schneidman, E. S., Ed.: Death: Current Perspectives, Palo Alto, California, Mayfield Publishing Co., 1976, p. 518.

34. Ginzberg, E.: Power centers and decision-making mechanisms, in Knowles, J. H., Ed.: Doing Better and Feeling Worse, New York, W. W. Norton & Co., Inc., 1977, p. 209.

35. Bennett, I. L., Jr.: Technology as a shaping force, in ibid., p. 129.

36. Law, S. A.: Blue Cross, What Went Wrong, New Haven and London, Yale University Press, 1974, p. 91.

37. Thomas, L.: On the science and technology of medicine, in Knowles, J. H., Ed.: Doing Better and Feeling Worse, New York, W. W. Norton & Co., 1977, p. 37.

38. Assembly Bill 1586, introduced by Assemblyman Hart, California, April 12, 1977, amended in Assembly August 12, 1977, section 2.

39. Senate Bill 9725-B, New York State, introduced by Sen. Hugh T. Farley, April 26, 1978; passed by Senate, June 23, 1978, as amended by Committee on Health, sections 2 and 3.

Note: The English are now using a simpler mixture [than the Brompton mixture] administered orally. Called the "Hospice Mix," it includes morphine (instead of heroin) in a sweet (cherry) syrup with phenothiazine. The other ingredients of the "Brompton mixture" are left out. I just heard about this recently and as yet, have no literature on the controlled studies that led to the change.

Hospice Care Update: Many Questions Still to Be Answered

M. Caroline Martin

Hospice care is emerging in this country as a workable alternative to traditional hospital care, but the successful integration of this concept of care requires that hard work be done. In November 1980, Parks identified research possibilities in the area of hospice. She said, "It is time to study hospice care through controlled scientific means to prove that hospice care is an effectual, replicable and cost-effective form of care for dying patients and their families."[1]

This article will look at those areas that need to be worked on and will seek to determine how much progress is being made.

Hackley listed a series of steps that have been necessary for granting third-party coverage for most modalities of health care.[2] These steps are:

- Professional acceptance of a new modality of care.
- Development of a universally accepted definition of the service and development of criteria and standards of performance, quality, and eligibility.
- Programs of licensure, certification, and accreditation.
- Significant public demand for the service.
- Government agencies' extension of partial or full coverage of the service (Medicare or Medicaid).
- Almost universal coverage of the service.
- Proliferation of the service until it is considered generally available.

Although it would be nice if reimbursement implementation progressed along such a neat series of steps, reality is frequently more sporadic, out of step, and oftentimes includes gaps or a combination of steps. The growth of hospice is no exception.

Acceptance

From the beginning of 1979 until December of the same year, the number of states having laws relating to hospice increased from 1 to 11. The United States General Accounting Office noted in a 1979 publication that there were approximately 59 hospice organizations in operation; the current number would certainly be greater. The National Hospice Organization (NHO) counts hundreds of programs among its membership, and there are many others that operate without NHO affiliation.[3]

Acceptance of hospice as an appropriate way to answer "the health care vacuum" that has existed for the dying patient can be seen by the number of new programs evolving, the media coverage, and the private and public financial support that is given to hospice programs at all levels. Nevertheless, there still are many unresolved problems and unanswered questions.

In fact, acceptance is a factor in the dilemma facing hospice today. Anthony J. Amado, chairman of the NHO Committee on Reimbursement and Licensure, observed, "This accelerated program development is considerably ahead of any significant advancements in the preparedness of health insurers and rulemakers to reimburse or license what is distinctly hospice care."[3]

Universal Definition

NHO defines hospice as a coordinated program of home and inpatient care, employing an interdisciplinary team that treats the terminally ill patient and his family as a single unit. The program provides palliative and supportive care to meet the special needs arising out of physical, psychological, spiritual, social, and economic stresses that are experienced during the final stages of illness and during bereavement.

In reviewing the licensure language of the 11 states that address hospice care, most contain similar definitions of "hospices." Nearly all of the states emphasize services to the terminally ill and their families to meet their physical, psychological, social, and spiritual needs. Most state definitions also specify the use of an interdisciplinary team, inpatient and home care, and follow-up care through the bereavement period.

Licensure

On the national level, the Joint Commission on Accreditation of Hospitals (JCAH) currently is involved in a pilot project concerning the development of a standards and accreditation program in the field of hospice care.

The JCAH study will look at trend indicators to measure the growth and size of hospice programs. It also will analyze "impact indicators" in an attempt to measure the effect of hospice programs on other health systems.

Reprinted, with permission, from *Hospitals,* published by the American Hospital Publishing, Inc., copyright May 16, 1981, Vol. 55, No. 11.

To determine what is the appropriate role, if any, for JCAH to play in the field of hospice care, the Commission proposes to examine hospice care through analysis of the literature and to use ongoing observations of hospice programs as a way to develop draft standards and survey procedures. JCAH will use this information to conduct field test surveys using formally trained surveyors, to revise the standards and survey procedures as necessary, and to develop an educational program in the field.

As standards are developed, the special interests of regulators and providers must be merged. In an unpublished study of the development of standards and criteria, Sister Catherine Sanders found that "regulators were stronger in their responses to the standards that deal with cost, excess number of acute care beds, and health planning standards." Providers were more egalitarian and sought a high utilization rate in order to make the program financially feasible.[4]

Licensure will legitimize hospice and ensure that the care provided is consistent with accepted hospice practice. In addition, licensure will place hospice in a better position to approach third-party payers for funding.[3]

The Oregon Legislative Task Force on Hospice addressed the issue of licensure and stated, "There is a public need to regulate hospice programs in order to ensure consumer protection, preserve the unique aspects of the hospice philosophy, facilitate incorporation of the hospice philosophy into the existing health care delivery system, and encourage the development of a stable financial base for hospice services."[5]

NHO's Committee on Reimbursement has developed three "models" that could be used by hospice organizations when working with state regulators and lawmakers. The material includes a regulatory document for use by state departments of health, a model bill for use by state legislators, and a prototypical health insurance contract that describes eligibility requirements and covered benefits. The documents are being forwarded to the National Governor's Conference, the National Conference of State Legislators, the Council of State Governments, the Health Insurance Association of America, and the national Blue Cross and Blue Shield Associations. Without data to demonstrate the cost-effectiveness and high quality of service provided by hospice care, third-party payers will continue to be reluctant to reimburse for hospice care services.

Health care planners, as well as providers and consumers, are understandably interested in research studies that focus on the cost-effectiveness of hospice care. Hospice advocates contend that hospice care costs no more than traditional care of terminally ill patients, and may even cost less because of its emphasis on home health care.[5] Skeptics fear that hospice care may turn out to be an additional layer of services imposed on the existing health care delivery system that will increase total costs for health care delivery by adding new service expectations and costs or by causing underutilization of existing resources.

It is obvious that the cost-effectiveness of hospice care cannot be determined until sufficient data has been gathered, and this data will need to be uniform with regard to definitions, standards, and procedures for service delivery. Studies by both private and public sectors are helping to gather this needed data. For example, a cooperative effort between the nation's Blue Cross Plans, NHO, and the AHA resulted in a 1979 study to determine how many Blue Cross Plans provided reimbursement for hospice care and to what extent. Thirty-six responding plans indicated that they were considering hospice service coverage.

In Virginia, the state legislature launched a hospice study that is being conducted by the Department of Health through a hospice advisory committee. The lawmakers have requested recommendations relating to standards for quality of care, as well as criteria for licensure and reimbursement of both home care and inpatient services. Unpublished studies also yield a wealth of information on the difficult unresolved issues. *A Development of Criteria and Standards for Hospice Care Programs* by Sister Catherine Sanders is a prime example. The thoroughness of this piece of work could serve as a base or framework to begin the responsibility of health planning and development.[4]

A study by Gravely uses three parameters to ensure that the hospice component of total hospital operations continues to be cost-effective. The parameters are: cost of acute hospice care related to cost of acute nonhospice care; patient capacity within the present program; and operational indexes.[6]

Another study identifying unresolved issues relating to the future of hospice is *Hospice: A Massachusetts Perspective.*[7] Furthermore, the federal government's interest in hospice, most notable through HCFA demonstration projects, is evidence at the national level of commitment and research.

Coverage

Today, more than 95 percent of the population is covered by some form of public or private health insurance, making third-party reimbursement crucial to hospice development. Medicare, Medicaid, and many third-party payers now reimburse for many elements of hospice care, that is, hospitalization and services provided by hospitals, nurses, and various therapists who visit the home, in addition to medical equipment needed at home. Still, there are hospice care elements such as bereavement and religious counseling, homemaker services, respite caregivers, shopping, transportation aides, and so forth, that are not reimbursable by the usual sources. Members of the Reimbursement and Licensure Committee of NHO feel that "the third-party payers will base their decision to recognize and reimburse for hospice services based on the following considerations: popular and business demand for hospice reimbursement; the results of HCFA's three-year hospice demonstration that permits reimbursement for hospice care that is provided to Medicare and Medicaid beneficiaries; organization of hospice services as part of the health service system; and licensure requirements governing delivery of hospice services."[3]

Currently, third-party payers are reluctant to develop subscriber benefit packages because of a lack of uniform regulations and utilization review criteria.

General Availability

One of the principal obstacles that needs to be overcome before a sufficient number of providers will be willing to develop a program of hospice care is reimbursement. The Committee on Reimbursement and Licensure of NHO plans to collect financial data concerning the operation of various hospices and to survey state and federal action concerning legislation and regulations that will have an impact on hospice care programs. The most important aspect of this process, however, will be communicating these findings to local and federal lawmakers and to third-party payer decision makers. The same holds true for the JCAH and others who are studying hospice care.

Other issues raised in making hospice care available to the general population are concerns about licensing and quality of care in hospice programs, governmental assistance to start new programs, and total increases or decreases in health care costs resulting from a changed demand for services. Hospitals interested in the development of hospice programs have voiced concern over the certification-of-need issue. Generally speaking, the newness of the hospice program means that there are almost no criteria on which to base a certification-of-need decision.[8]

Conclusion

The conversion of a philosophy into practice is never accomplished without growing pains. Daniel Hadlock, M.D., NHO president, said, "The challenge now is to convert the concept or philosophy of hospice into practical terms that relate to the realities of quality control and reimbursement without losing the uniqueness which evolved out of the response to the needs of the terminally ill that are not being met by standard health care programs."[9]

Hospice care providers are reminded that continued hard work is needed to meet the challenge of establishing hospice care as a credible and competent health care service.— M. CAROLINE MARTIN, *senior vice-president, Riverside Hospital, Newport News, VA.*

References

1. Parks, P. Evaluation of hospice care still needed. *Hospitals.* 54:56, Nov. 16, 1980.
2. Hackley, J. A. Financing and accrediting hospices. *Hosp. Prog.* 60:51, Mar. 1979.
3. *Annual Report to the Membership of the National Hospice Organization.* McClean, VA: National Hospice Organization, 1980, p. 24.
4. Sanders, Sister C. Development of criteria and standards for hospice care programs. Unpublished study, Medical College of Virginia/Virginia Commonwealth University, Richmond, VA, Nov. 1979.
5. *Legislative Task Force on Hospice: Report and Recommendations.* Salem, OR: Aug. 1980, p. 10.
6. Gravely, G. E. Financial and statistical evaluation of the hospice program at Church Hospital Corporation. Unpublished study, Medical College of Virginia/Virginia Commonwealth University, Richmond, VA, Feb. 1980.
7. *Hospice: A Massachusetts Perspective.* Boston, MA: Regional Cancer Control Committee, 1980.
8. *Hospice.* Washington, DC: Intergovernment Health Policy Project, 1980.
9. Hadlock, D. President's message. *NHO Membership Newsletter,* Nov./Dec. 1980.

The Hospice Concept Integrated with Existing Community Health Care

Katherine A. Meyer, R.N. M.S.

Interest in establishing hospice programs as supplementary hospital functions has been growing in this country. Rising health care costs are a major issue in the health system today and should be considered in the planning of any new hospice program. The needs of terminal cancer patients and their families can be met by using existing inservice and community resources with a minimal capital cost to the health care system.[1]

Historically, the hospice concept has been considered appropriate for terminal cancer patients when curative therapies have failed.[2] Its focus includes patients and their families. Psychological and social support is provided to the family and every effort is made to alleviate pain and symptoms for the sick member. Hospice is a philosophy of care and is therefore not dependent on the availability of a particular kind of facility for implementation. A variety of hospice models have been established; a hospice program that combines the resources of an existing hospital and an existing home health agency may be the model best able to use available resources and therefore more cost efficient because of the low capital expenditure.

Hospitals and long-term care facilities are currently showing the most interest in the hospice movement. The advantages they have are availabilities of an existing structure, supportive services (laundry, laboratory, kitchen facilities, administrative structure) and multidisciplinary personnel and the ability to bill third party payment sources for services provided. The disadvantages of an autonomous hospital hospice program are the organizational tendency to assign currently employed hospital personnel to the new hospice positions and the need to create a new department for home care.

Pitfalls in Implementation

The disadvantages can unknowingly become pitfalls for the success of a program. When trying to use available personnel for the home care portion of the program, hospital administrators err in assuming that hospital personnel can automatically deliver care in the home. This is a fallacy. Hospital-based and home-based nurses, social workers and health aides learn to emphasize separate skills that are inherent to their work setting.

Attitudes and values also differ. Hospital personnel are more action and result oriented, whereas skilled home nurses learn to deliver services with patients maintaining control in patients' home territory. Hospital personnel are less skilled in working with families because they have limited and controlling exposure to family members in an environment that places the family in a vulnerable position. Hospitals should turn to their local home health agencies where these agencies already exist. The local home health agency will have the structure in place for delivering home care, in addition to the professional staff skilled in delivering care in the home and in working with families of sick and dying people.

Joint Team Effort

The presence of two existing organizations that can each contribute a portion of their operation to a new concept allows the administration to focus on the modifications needed to adapt their structures to enhance their appropriateness for the new function and its process. Administrators of each organization will meet jointly to set goals and formulate the appropriate plans.

Reprinted from *Nursing Administration Quarterly,* Spring, 1980, "The Hospice Concept Integrated with Existing Community Health Care" by Katherine A. Meyer, by permission of Aspen Systems Corporation, ©1980.

Figure 1. Team and Family Relationships

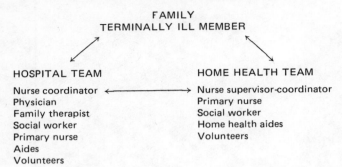

FAMILY
TERMINALLY ILL MEMBER

HOSPITAL TEAM   HOME HEALTH TEAM

Nurse coordinator ⟷ Nurse supervisor-coordinator
Physician   Primary nurse
Family therapist   Social worker
Social worker   Home health aides
Primary nurse   Volunteers
Aides
Volunteers

Each organization will be responsible for providing a team of professionals and nonprofessionals with expertise in oncology care and dealing with death and dying in addition to the skills inherent for each work setting. Figure 1 illustrates the relationships of the teams and the family.

Each team will be autonomous and responsible to its own administration; however, their major goals are to create a climate of coordination to provide the best possible care for terminally ill individuals and their families.

Hospice Program Requirements

If the process is to produce the expected outcomes successfully, administrations of both facilities need to recognize the importance of providing highly skilled personnel in the professional positions. Their functions will include assessment, supervision, teaching, coordination and support to the family, sick member and other team members.

Team Support

Members of each team require support from within their system. It is important that teams not subdivide tasks in a vertical manner but that all members bring their professional skills and strengths to the group and assist one another in caring for the dying person. Nonprofessional personnel of

---

A reciprocal and complementary relationship between teams and team members will improve the overall skill level of the teams and enhance the quality of care given to patients.

---

course are accountable to the professionals, but much of their support comes from sharing their insights and experiences and establishing their credibility with other team members. A reciprocal and complementary relationship between teams and team members in the long run will improve the overall skill level of the teams and enhance the quality of care given to the patients.

Home Health Aides

An advantage of the hospice program in the home is the assistance of family in the care of the patient. However, few of these programs can be successful without the availability of home health aides. One of the most frequent reasons for rehospitalization is inadequate staffing and inability of family to cope for such an extensive period of time without this type of intensive help.

Communication

The key to coordination and cooperation between teams is communication.[3] This is perhaps the most costly part of the program because it will directly affect productivity of the staff. Much time will necessarily be spent in team conferences (within the team and between teams) to share information and knowledge and to arrive at plans and goals with which both teams can agree. There will be occasions when it is appropriate to include the family in these conferences. The outcomes of the conferences should be a harmonious consensus of the group; otherwise the client and family will find themselves in the middle of a very difficult situation.

Coordination

Coordinating with the other team could become problematic as the patient is transferred from institution (hospital) to home or vice versa. A key person on each team can be assigned this responsibility, as demonstrated in Figure 2.

Figure 2. Coordinating Patient Care

HOSPITAL TEAM   HOME CARE TEAM

Nursing coordinator ⟷ Nursing supervisor
    ↓ ↑   ↑ ↓
Physician   Staff nurse

The home coordinator of the hospital team is responsible for discharge planning with the family and home care team so that appropriate services are in place when the patient is discharged. This person keeps the home care team up to date on the status of the patient and informs the home care supervisors of family and team conferences, which will be held in hospital during the hospitalization. Selected and vital members of the home care team have a responsibility to attend to aid in continuity of care and agreement of goals.

The home care nursing supervisor assumes the role of coordinator when the patient returns home. The supervisor has responsibility for keeping the hospital nursing coordinator informed of the patient's status (while in the home) and communicating medical management problems to the hospital team. It is not unusual for the hospital physician and the nursing coordinator to make home visits and sometimes team and family conferences are held in the home.

Maintaining Patients at Home

It is extremely important that a hospice program emphasize services and patient management to facilitate patients' abilities to stay in their own homes. Efforts to maintain patients in their own homes as long as possible are rewarded by appreciation on the part of the patient and family and a feeling of having done a good job as all members of the team sense the family's comfort and satisfaction. This allows dying persons to be persons—not patients—in their own environments, where they are able to maintain certain controls. The relaxation that occurs as a result of not being in a depersonalized and technological environment in turn generally allows patients to maintain comfort with a lesser amount of pain medication.[4] They are therefore more alert and able to function at a more optimal level.

Skills Required

Maintaining the patient at home requires many skills on the part of the home care team. Professional members, with psychosocial assessment skills, can better assess the potential of families to maintain a patient in the home. Families are a key to the success of the community hospice program, and the program may not be appropriate for all families. Professional nurses and social workers are able to assess those family qualities that can contribute to or negate such an experience.

Cultural Values

Cultural values are a major factor in a family's decision of how to care for a dying member. Not all of the cultures in society will condone support of a dying person in the home; in fact, such an act might be considered neglectful by some people. Because the families will have to live with their feelings and environment after the death occurs, their present and future well-being is an important consideration and needs to be a part of the assessment and decision.

Family Acceptance

What is the patient's and family's understanding of the diagnosis and prognosis? Do they perceive what is happening to them and are they able to refocus to function in this framework? A family that is not ready to accept this will often continue to search for the "something else," and the patient will be rehospitalized for every minor complaint. When families do not initially accept the prognosis, the hospice program can be effective and helpful to the families if the cultural values are consistent with the program and the family strengths are strong.

It is not realistic to expect that the team can maintain a dying individual in the home if there are no bonds that are strong enough to tolerate the emotional and role stresses that will occur. In the early stages there is a discrepancy between a client's and family's cognitive and affective acceptance of death. One of the goals of the program should be to increase the congruency for the family by the time the sick person dies. This in turn usually diminishes the severity of the postdeath bereavement.

Family members need to be encouraged to carry on with their individual responsibilities to the extent they feel is appropriate. Encouragement on the part of the professional staff to realign family roles assists the family to accept that the family member will soon be departing and reduces their fears of how they will manage or adapt without this member. They are then better able to function following the death.

As families assist in the care of their loved one, they see and perceive the gradual failure of the sick person. As acceptance of this increases, professional staff can encourage the family to begin the funeral arrangements. Contact and agreement with a funeral director prior to the death will make for a smoother transfer of the body following death. This in turn enhances the comfort of the family by making them feel that they did everything they could to maintain their loved one's integrity and comfort.

Families are usually grateful for their participation regardless of whether the death occurred in hospital or home. The multidisciplinary professional respect and development that occur are strong side benefits. This approach should be examined wherever a home health agency exists because the approach is easily implemented; it is cost efficient and satisfying to the participants.

References

1. Osterweis, M. and Champagne, D. S. "The U.S. Hospice Movement: Issues in Development." *American Journal of Public Health* 69:5 (May 1979) p. 492-496.
2. The American Cancer Society. "Hospice: Family Centered Care for the Dying." *Cancer News* 32:3 (Fall 1978) p. 10-13.
3. Ward, B. "Hospice Home Care Program." *Nursing Outlook* (October 1978) p. 646-649.
4. Parks, P. "Hospice Care: Implications for Hospitals." *Hospitals, JAHA* 53:6 (March 16, 1979) p. 58-59.

Hospice Care: The Challenge of Change

Greg Owen and Robert Fulton
98th NFDA Convention, October, 1979
St. Louis, Missouri

Mr. President, distinguished guests, ladies and gentlemen, I am pleased to have the opportunity to address you today and to share with you some research notes from our investigation of hospice care in the United States. In our research, we have been able to accumulate a wide variety of information about hospice care for dying persons and the ways in which this form of care has involved funeral directors since its introduction into the United States just a few years ago. In my discussion, I would like to raise four questions concerning the role of funeral directors in hospice care and offer some recommendations about how funeral directors might extend the potential for human service in conjunction with this new form of care. While we can offer no definitive answers at this time, the nature of the evidence to date suggests that funeral directors have a very significant role to play in hospice care and that this role will be shaped by the kind of service and cooperation that you demonstrate in these early formative years of hospice in America.

Before providing you with a brief description of the origins and growth of hospice care, let me introduce the questions that served to guide our investigation:

First, does hospice care change the involvement of the funeral director at the time of death?

Second, what expectations do hospice caregivers have of funeral directors?

Third, does hospice care change the attitudes of families toward funeral pre-planning, and if so, in what way?

Fourth, and finally, what are the implications of hospice caregiver involvement in funeral pre-planning?

It has been our desire since the beginning of the study to examine hospice programs throughout the country. Unfortunately, the hospices that we have contacted outside of the metropolitan Minneapolis and St. Paul area have been less than enthusiastic about participating in this research. This is not surprising given the following facts.

First, every program director is hesitant to provide information that they feel could be used for purposes of evaluation. At a time when the National Hospice Organization is preparing materials for standards and accreditation, it is understandable that hospice caregivers are reluctant to provide specific details concerning their programs, especially if they fall short of NHO provisional standards. Moreover, most programs are now in the developmental or pilot stage and most directors are choosing not to share information until care plans are more formalized.

Second, hospice programs are being saturated with questionnaires and requests for data. One hospice director I spoke with said that she had received nearly two dozen questionnaires in a two-month period. It is not surprising, therefore, that many requests go unanswered.

Third, the nature of terminal illness and its often debilitating effects upon the family make the hospice caregivers understandably protective of their charges. Of the nearly fifty questionnaires which we distributed to various hospices to be completed by patients and family members. Only three were returned. This means that they are either not distributing any questionnaires or else they are not providing much encouragement for patients and families to complete them. This is unfortunate, but again, not altogether surprising given the sensitivity and intimacy of the various question areas as a result of these difficulties, we have made the decision to localize our investigation, develop and nurture personal contacts within the Minneapolis and St. Paul community, and implement a research design that explicitly compares hospice care and its effects upon caregivers, patients and families with non-hospice methods of terminal care. In addition to funds provided by the National Funeral Directors Association, a grant from the Northwest Area Foundation in St. Paul to the Amherst H. Wilder Foundation, also of St. Paul, has greatly facilitated this work. The Wilder

Reprinted with permission from the Michigan Funeral Directors Association "Journal," January, 1980.

Foundation has retained me to direct an investigation of hospice in this community and at the same time has provided me with a full time research staff to assist in the project. This generous support has allowed me to expand the scope of the original study.

As it turns out, Minneapolis-St. Paul is an excellent community in which to initiate a comparative study because of the diversity and scope of hospice activity here. There are three inpatient hospices, eight hospices with home care programs and bereavement followup, and at least as many programs in various stages of development. Additionally, there is a wide range of alternative services for terminally ill persons, including a cancer home operated by Catholic sisters, several home nursing associations, 37 acute care hospitals and 174 long-term care facilities. Every one of these facilities provides care to terminally ill persons. Let me describe how we have proceeded to date.

Beginning earlier this year, we initiated contacts with local hospice directors and described the nature of the study we had planned. By securing the cooperation of several key persons in the community, including two hospice directors on the board of the NHO, several physicians, including the President of the local medical society, and two widely respected oncologists, as well as many caregivers who have at one time or another, participated in death and dying classes with Professor Fulton or me, we have been able to gain momentum within the community and support for the project.

Additionally, and through the cooperation of the Minnesota Registrar of Vital Statistics, we have selected a random sample of death certificates for the Ramsey County area. Copies of the certificates are being sent to the physicians who have signed them, along with a letter from the President of the Ramsey County Medical Society encouraging their cooperation. We are asking each physician to notify us of the cases that were preceded by a period of terminal illness so that we might go out and interview bereaved family members to learn about the nature of terminal care, the problems that were experienced during the period of illness, the method by which funeral arrangements were made and the nature of these arrangements. This sample will allow us to speak with much more accuracy and validity regarding comparisons of terminal care programs and their relative impact on funeralization.

We are also securing interviews at various facilities in which care is provided so that we may contrast treatment programs, care philosophies and caregiver responses and at the same time gain access to patients and families in the process of making decisions about the future.

What I am discussing is based on a thorough review of available literature, ten in-depth interviews with hospice directors, and the experience of rallying community support for research in a sensitive but vital area of concern.

I hope that the preliminary observations we offer can provide you with a compass by which you can chart your future efforts in the care and service of bereaved families.

First, let me offer a thumbnail sketch of the hospice movement and the place that it has established for itself in America.

It is proper to begin this scenario in Great Britain where the modern methods of care for the dying were pioneered both at St. Joseph's Hospice in Hackney and St. Christopher's Hospice in Sydenham. But to begin there would be to neglect the historical roots and benevolent missions of so many religious persons throughout history. For example, we can look back to the religious work of Ste. Bridget in Ireland during the Fifth Century, A.D., at a time when there was widespread pagan worship, brutal atrocities and savage warfare shaking the land. As the daughter of a slave, Ste. Bridget became the predominant power in the Church of Ireland following the death of St. Patrick. Her heroism, courage and mercy to the sick were well known as she cared for the leperous and dying and attempted to bring persons under her charge back to the bosom of their own families. This is not so different from what hospice attempts to do today, albeit under far less difficult conditions.

We might also mention the missions of the Hospitaler Knights of St. John in Jerusalem during the Eleventh and Twelfth Centuries, A.D. Under the direction of Brother Gerard and his poor brethren, a way station was built for the sick and weary pilgrims where they were cared for and comforted. But soon, the group moved to the Island of Malta and in 1306 established a hospital. Here, for the first time, a place was created where patients with incurable diseases were separated from all others and cared for. This special care for incurable patients was not unlike that offered by Brother Vincent De Paul and his Sisters of Charity who ministered to the sick and dying of Paris in the early part of the 17th Century. Nor was it unlike the care offered by Rev. Fleidner of Kaiserworth in Prussia, the first Protestant hospital in history to have an order of nursing sisters dedicated to the care of the ill and dying.

We may speak of the Catholic priests, like Father Damien, who cared for lepers on the Island of Molowkai, or Quakers like Elizabeth Fry who dedicated herself to hospital reform in 19th Century England. Wherever we may look, under whatever spiritual mandate we might examine, the impulse to provide care, comfort and relief to persons confronted by the visage of death is an ancient as it is inspiring. The modern professional caregiver has no corner on the palliative care market in today's world. We are latecomers who must look to the dedication and devotion of those who have preceded us in the service of God and their fellow human beings.

When we turn to the more immediate origins of the modern hospice movement as it has taken form in the United States in the last few years, we can ask - Where has it come from? Where is it going? How does it change the nature of, and the response to, death?

The story is now told in several places of how a contemporary of Florence Nightingale, Sister Mary Aikenhead, founded the Irish Sisters of Charity in Dublin in 1815, the year of the Battle of Waterloo. Mother Mary, as she was known, who was herself crippled and in constant pain, directed the work of the sisters from her bed, and they, through her leadership, established hospitals for the sick and refuges for the poor and homeless. Dublin at this time was plaqued with epidemics of cholera and typhus and the Irish sisters were able to bring relief to the needy in the tenements and streets where they could be found. News of this charitable work soon spread overseas and in 1900 the sisters were invited to London by Cardinal Vaughan.

St. Joseph's, the first British hospice, was established in 1905. The first patient was a hackney tram driver dying of consumption. He was carried in by his friends on Jan. 14, of that year. From this small beginning at the threshold of the 20th Century, we can now count over 30 hospices in Great Britain and more than 200 operating hospice programs in the United States.

Although cancer has quickly replaced cholera, typhus and consumption as the modern scourge, the kind of comfort and affection which was provided to patients nearly 80 years ago in England and elsewhere is still the kind of care that human beings so desperately need during the last months and weeks of life. This is not to say, however, that modern hospice care has not advanced in its methods. In fact, it was the perfection of pharmacological agents for the relief of pain of cancer patients whose felt needs went unmet in acute care hospitals that combined to bring English hospice care to the forefront in the late 1960s.

The founder of the American hospice movement is Cicely Saunders, a woman who has been described as a modern saint by TIME Magazine. The influence of her work in the United States and her repeated visits here in the 60's and 70's were major catalysts for the first hospice program in New Haven, Connecticut. It is clear, however, that the responsiveness of American audiences to this form of care was conditioned in an important way by Elisabeth Kubler-Ross's book, ON DEATH AND DYING. Kubler-Ross exposed a very sensitive nerve in the health care delivery system of the United States. In her widely read book, she gave a vivid account of the deplorable conditions under which dying persons were cared for in this country. She described the loneliness, isolation, lack of family involvement, and physical pain that came to be synonomous with conditions of care for dying persons in acute care hospitals. It is easy to see how such a message could stir the American people, given the fact that out of all of the deaths that occur in any given year one out of every five would be the result of cancer.

It's important to note, too, that at the time Cicely Saunders first came to the United States, there was an alternative proposal being vigorously proposed in the form of the enthanasia movement. Persons in this movement advocated the right to die either by assisting the patient to end his or her life, or allowing the patient to discontinue treatment. In 1977, Robert Veatch of the Hastings Center reported that 40 pieces of legislation were introduced into state legislatures in an attempt to legalize one or another aspect of enthanasia. The effect of the hospice movement on this range of activity is not to be underestimated. Hospice proponents emphasized the quality of remaining life and the ability of those attending to provide comfort and care rather than the extreme solution of enthanasia for patient distress. The hospice philosophy, in confronting the enthanasia philosophy head on, has not only illuminated the problems of dying as never before, but has also provided a more humane and acceptable manner of dealing with these problems. The success and acceptance of the hospice movement by profes-sional, as well as lay persons, can be measured by the fact that the enthanasia organization has recently seen fit to change its name to "concern for dying" as an expression of their support and belief in the principles of the hospice movement.

Thus, we are confronted with a serious problem and a seemingly perfect solution at the same instant. Is it any wonder, then, that in the past five years we have seen the number of hospice programs in the United States rise from 2 to over 200 with virtually every small and large city now involved in some kind of hospice planning? This is no accident; it is no fad; and it is not likely to be a temporary enthusiasm. Major insurance companies, including Blue Cross and Blue Shield and American Family, are now providing some kind of hospice benefits and are exploring ways to expand their coverage. Major newspaper columnists, like Sylvia Porter, are addressing the issue in a week long series of articles. All of the major news magazines are covering the very rapid developments in hospice care. In fact, the 1979 Nobel Peace Prize Laureate is a Catholic nun, Mother Teresa, who has devoted herself to the care of the dying in Calcutta. In a world in which technology threatens to undermine our sense of humanity and meaning, hospice has appeared with the promise of restoring the familial and religious ideals that have allowed us to progress as we have as a nation.

Let us turn now to what we believe are four major issues that must be addressed in order to understand the challenge which the hospice movement poses to funeral service in the decade ahead. There can be no doubt that the 1980's will be the decade of hospice in the United States. Hospice, home and humanitarian care will be the watchwords for many.

The first question is, does hospice care change the involvement of the funeral director at the time of death? The answer to that question, we believe, is yes. From the interviews we have conducted to date, we have seen with increasing frequency that funeral directors come into contact with family members and caregivers in the hospital ward, rather than with the morgue attendant. In some cases, this has required that the funeral directors be in attendance with the family prior to the removal of the body for up to two or three hours. This leads to the possibility that the funeral director in the future will meet with the family not only at an earlier point in time following the death, but also in a different setting with different participants being present. Moreover, whether the death occurs at home or in the hospital, those various participants and professional caregivers, by virtue of their involvement, become important in the decision making process. In fact, in some cases, families will turn to the caregivers for answers to questions which were formerly dealt with by immediate survivors. For example, the strong religious and spiritual commitment that is intrinsic to the hospice movement may mean that in the future there will be a higher frequency of funerals being conducted within the church.

The second question, what expectations do hospice caregivers have of funeral directors can be best answered by simply stating that caregivers at this point in time have no specific expectations of what the funeral director can or should do. In the interviews we have conducted, caregivers are stating that they really do not understand or have much knowledge of the role of the funeral director. This is primarily the result of two facts: First, many of the caregivers have not had any personal involvement with loss themselves, and second, they have never been this intimately involved with the death of a virtual stranger. This means that there is a tremendous opportunity for funeral service to articulate the role they believe they can play in this particular setting. At the same time it points to the need for educational and informational efforts directed toward the caring group.

The third and fourth points we want to address involve funeral pre-planning. Does hospice care effect

the attitudes of families in this area and do caregivers become involved in this decision process? First, it needs to be strongly emphasized that the funeral director should not feel that the caregiver is intruding in an area that is not of his or her concern. From Colonial days and the sharing of that first Thanksgiving to the barnraising and quilting bees of the best century to modern day organ donations, America's strength and character has been built on the voluntary efforts of friends and stranger alike. Dying is a public event, as well as a private concern and now, more than ever, the family has others who are by their side responding to this momentous event. We know that during this time, human lives can be quickly and profoundly welded together in a context of care and concern. The work of Mary Vachon and her colleagues at the Clarke Institute, University of Toronto, has demonstrated that the stress of caregivers is as high, if not higher, than the stress of family members at the death of a family member. The funeral director, therefore, cannot neglect or fail to respect this new role of the caregiver in response to those in need. Rather, it is for the funeral director to realize the new opportunities for service, as well as the new responsibility for dealing sensitively for those who also care. For the funeral director to expand his or her own role, enlarge upon his or her philosophy of service, and realize the challenge that is there is not only to live up to the highest standards that funeral service providers have set for themselves, but it is also to meet the needs of **all** those who mourn.

With respect to pre-planning, per se, the more firmly established hospices have taken a role in suggesting to the family that some kind of plans should be made. To the degree to which caregivers enjoy the trust of families they serve, it would behoove the funeral director to afford them the same respect they have always accorded surviving family members. It is too early at this time to speculate as to the direction that funeral pre-planning may

go as a result of caregiver involvement. However, we should keep in mind two things with regard to the issues of viewing, public services and disposition of the body. One is highly religious and traditional character of the volunteer caregivers in this setting and two, the centrifugal force of hospice care in potentially restoringthe family and community, as well as the caregivers themselves to a vital social group.

It would be our prediction that this rejuvenation of the family and its spiritual values that hospice so often provides should not only preserve the funeral as a significant and meaningful ceremony, but indeed we may well see in the next decade its refinement and enhancement as a rite for the dead and a cherished right of the living. However, this may take somewhat different forms from what we have known previously, as well as what we have come to expect.

With regard to the traditional practice of viewing, for example, several observations need to be made, especially with regard to the cancer victim and the physical effects often seen from that disease. Since hospice care at this point in time is primarily cancer care, there may be an appreciable change observed with regard to the survivor's desire for review. This is related to the fact that the surviving group has suffered with the patient over a considerable length of time and has lived day after day with the spectre of death. The need to confirm the reality of death for those who have been in constant attendance would appear not to be as great as those who die away from home in a hospital or nursing home. Care and tact must be observed, therefore, in reminding the intimate survivors and caregivers that others less involved with a particular dying experience may need or desire the confirmation of the death. For the immediate survivors who have suffered through the pain and agony of the last days, such confrontation may appear unnecessary, if not an affront. It is to be remembered, too, that the contemporary hospice program is a middle class movement and that the ravages of cancer, to say nothing of death itself, constitute an embarrassment to many. This is particularly so among middle aged men and women whose elderly parents have died of cancer. Again, middle class attitudes and tastes do not reinforce the display of an aging parent's body that has suffered significant alteration of features as a result of disease. Body image is an important factor in all of human life and not the least at the time of death. While it is paradoxical, we do not find it contradictory to suggest to you that, while family members and survivors might involve themselves more actively in funeral rites, they at the same time may not wish or feel the need for reviewal. In the case of a child's death, however, where denial may be a more prominent feature of the parent's reaction, the advice of the funeral director to confront the death openly can seldom be amiss.

Finally, let us look at hospice in the broader perspective. As I have already suggested, hospice is more than a place or a particular program of care. It is a philosophy; a philosophy that has the potential to change our view of what good health care is and to reorient our values such that the patient and his or her family, rather than a specific disease entity, become the focal point of the caregiver's attention. This idea is well expressed in the remark of one non-terminal patient upon hearing about the hospice method of care. "Do you have to die to get that kind of care," he asked. The question is well put and serves to frame the perspective of most any person who must confront our health care delivery system and its massive and sometimes overwhelming technology. Humane and dignified care would seem to be a worthy goal, regardless of whether the patient is expected to recover. If, as one hospice director has suggested, "hospice has the potential to change our system of health care from the inside out," it behooves us, not only as professionals, but as individuals, also, with families and loved ones of our own, to promote the hospice concept of care wherever we may find it.

Hospice is not a new and unique institution. It is an institution that has been with us for hundreds of years. It is families giving care to their own family members. It is ministers, priests and rabbis comforting the dying and the bereaved. And it is nurses and physicians recognizing the individuality of the patient and attending to the patient's mental, as well as physical distress. Hospice is a reenactment of traditional values; the values that have produced and sustained the American ways of caring for and honoring the living - as well as the dead.

It is clear that funeral directors who are able to gain the trust of hospice caregivers early in this movement and who demonstrate their own call to service on behalf of the families they serve will reap the fruits of that service in the years ahead. The decision is yours to decide what part you will play and how responsibe you will be to those who must confront death: the universal human crisis.

ESTATE PLANNING

Planning Your Estate
Death and Taxes

George J. Laikin

The principal objectives of estate planning are the preservation of an estate for the maintenance and welfare of family and dependents and for appropriate ultimate distribution in accordance with the estate owner's desires. To attain these objectives, there must first be ascertained the factors which cause an estate to shrink in value at death. Then, plans to minimize such shrinkage, including ways and means to reduce the burden of taxes and other estate expenses and losses, must be formulated, as well as plans to provide sufficient funds with which to pay such death costs and taxes as will inevitably remain to be paid. Finally, plans for distribution in accordance with estate owner's desires must be formulated and implemented.

In the formulation and implementation of such plans, many legal instrumentalities and procedures are used. Principal among them are the will, trust, life insurance, gift, business protection and buy-out agreement; also, the partnership, corporation, joint venture, pension plan, profit sharing plan, deferred compensation agreement, and a great spectrum of other tools available in our legal and economic systems. However, since this discussion will emphasize personal planning and tax considerations, rather than business planning, only those procedures most commonly used in personal planning will be discussed.

Recent Tax Law Changes

Tax law changes in recent years which make necessary a review of existing programs include the following: (1) unification of estate and gift tax exemptions and transfer taxes; (2) unlimited expanded marital deduction; (3) availability of the marital deduction for "qualified terminal interest property" or trust—the QTIP; (4) increase in the "exemption equivalent" for federal estate and gift tax purposes; (5) increase in annual federal gift tax exclusion; (6) the generation-skipping trust and resultant tax effect; (7) elimination of rule requiring inclusion in an estate of gifts made within three years of death; (8) new rules for taxing joint tenancy property; (9) special methods of valuing farm lands and valuing real estate of closely held businesses; (10) new rules relating to extension of time for payment of death taxes in certain cases; (11) new rules with respect to pension plans; (12) income tax law changes relating to capital gains

taxes and holding period; and (13) additional restrictions on tax sheltered investments and similar concepts.

UNIFIED TRANSFER TAX CREDITS
Exemption Equivalents

Year of Death	Unified Credit	Exemption Equivalents
1981	$ 47,000	$175,625
1982	62,800	225,000
1983	79,300	275,000
1984	96,300	325,000
1985	121,800	400,000
1986	155,800	500,000
1987	192,800	600,000
Thereafter	192,800	600,000

Factors Causing Estate Losses

The basic factors which bring about estate shrinkage and losses at death are: (1) the various costs and expenses relating to the probate of an estate, which range from four to five percent for most estates; (2) the decedent's normal debts, which range from four to six percent for most estates; and (3) federal estate taxes which may range from virtually nothing, where the entire estate is left to a surviving spouse, to from 30% to 50% (and more) on large estates, where the surviving spouse receives less than the entire estate, or where there is no surviving spouse. State inheritance taxes are in addition to the federal estate taxes and vary from state to state. They can range from 0% to 15% depending on the state and on the relationship of the heirs and beneficiaries to the decedent. Additional losses, which cannot readily be calculated in advance, result from the forced sale of assets or business interests in order to raise cash with which to pay these costs. While significant relief is available to

George J. Laikin is a member of the Bars of Wisconsin, California, New York, Illinois, and the District of Columbia. He is a partner in Laikin & Laikin, s.c., Milwaukee. He was formerly Special Assistant to the Attorney General of the United States, Tax Division. He is counsel for the Wisconsin and Milwaukee Associations of Life Underwriters. Mr. Laikin is also certified as a Specialist in Taxation Law by the California Board of Legal Specialization.

Mr. Laikin has lectured at the New York University Institute on Federal Taxation and numerous other tax institutes. He is co-author of *Estate Planning Techniques* and *Basic Estate Planning* and a frequent contributor to numerous legal and tax periodicals, including *Trusts & Estates, Taxes,* and the *CLU Journal.*

This article was originally published in *Trusts & Estates* in 1980 and revised to date.

married individuals who leave substantial portions of their estates to spouses, each individual must also plan for the possibility that he or she will die unmarried, in which case the burden can be very great.

The following table shows the average amount of shrinkage brought about by federal death taxes for estates of various sizes.

ESTATE SHRINKAGE
Examples of Estate Tax Burdens*

Taxable Estate*	1982	1984	1986	1987
$ 500,000	$ 93,000	$ 59,899	$ 0	$ 0
1,000,000	283,000	249,500	190,000	153,000
2,000,000	718,000	684,500	625,000	588,000
3,000,000	1,228,000	1,194,500	1,120,000	1,083,000

Note: To the above must be added state inheritance taxes, where applicable, plus the cost of probating an estate and debts, in order to obtain a better picture of shrinkage at death.

*For an unmarried person. For a married person the estate tax could range from virtually none upward, depending upon how much of the unlimited marital deduction was utilized.

Some of the factors causing shrinkage may be controlled through appropriate planning and the use of permissive tax-reducing concepts, such as the marital deduction, the unified transfer tax credit, the gift and the trust, as well as the considered use of wills, life insurance and business protection and buy-out agreements.

Marital Deduction

A transfer made by a husband to his wife, or by a wife to her husband, either at death, or as a gift during lifetime, may qualify for the marital deduction if the transfer is "outright," that is, if the spouse becomes the absolute owner of the property transferred. If the transfer is made through the use of a trust, the marital deduction will apply if all of the income from the property so transferred is payable at least annually, and she (if the wife is the donee of the gift) is given the right to dispose of the trust property, either during her lifetime, or by her will, or both, including to herself or her estate.

The marital deduction will also apply to "Qualified Terminal Interest Property" or a "Qualified Terminal Interest Trust" ("QTIP" or "QTIT"), if a wife receives all of the income from the property or trust during her lifetime, and no one else may receive such income or property during her lifetime, and if the executors (or the donor, if a gift was involved) elect to have such property or trust qualify for the marital deduction.

Viewed simply, the marital deduction provides a married individual with an exemption for estate and gift tax purposes which applies ahead of the unified transfer tax credit (discussed later) and which may cover all, or almost all, of the amount transferred.

For gift tax purposes, the marital deduction applies to the full amount transferred to a wife. Therefore, as to transfers to a wife after January 1, 1982, either during her lifetime, via gift, or death, through inheritance, the annual exclusions and exemption equivalents are irrelevant—because all transfers between husbands and wives are tax free under the marital deduction. Moreover, such transfers can be made either outright, or through a trust with a power of appointment (discussed later) or with a "QTIP" trust, without a power of appointment.

Example: A husband has an estate after debts and administration expenses of $700,000. In 1982, he makes a gift to his wife of $100,000. This gift is free of federal gift taxes, being a transfer from one spouse to another. He dies in 1983 and leaves the balance of his estate—$600,000—to his wife. This, too, is free of federal estate taxes (but may be subject to state inheritance taxes). It would be estate tax free whether the amount were left outright, to the surviving spouse, or through the conventional marital deduction trust with

a general power of appointment, or with a QTIP trust, whereunder the surviving spouse receives all income, is the sole beneficiary of principal distributions during lifetime, and the executor elected to qualify such trust for the marital deduction. A combination of the foregoing methods could be used.

However, it should be noted that the amount inherited tax free by the wife will be taxed at her death to the extent she still owns the inherited assets.

Now, if at the husband's death in 1983 he was still worth $600,000, the exemption equivalent of $275,000 were placed in a "by-pass trust" which did not qualify for the marital deduction, $275,000 would pass tax free at the husband's death, and would not be taxed at the wife's death. The remainder of the estate, $425,000, would pass tax free to the wife because of the marital deduction. Then, assuming the wife died in 1984, when the exemption equivalent will be $325,000, only $100,000 would be subject to the estate tax. If she died in 1987, when the exemption equivalent reached $600,000, there would be no tax. Thus, it is important to plan for realization of the tax benefits which the exemption equivalent provides for both estates, particularly where a surviving spouse is the beneficiary of the entire estate. If children or others are beneficiaries of part of the estate, the amount allocated to them might absorb all or part of the exemption equivalent. The point is, consideration should be given to the full use of the exemption equivalent before taking advantage of the marital deduction.

Prior to January 1, 1982, the marital deduction was limited to one-half of the adjusted gross estate—roughly one-half of the estate calculated for federal tax purposes after reduction for debts, claims and expenses, but before federal estate taxes. Now, the marital deduction can cover virtually the entire estate. Prior to January 1, 1982, the gift tax marital deduction covered one-half of the amount given to a wife. Now, all gifts between husband and wife are exempt under the new unlimited marital deduction concept. The QTIP trust can also be used for this purpose. So, it behooves all married people to review their programs to determine whether all or less than all of the full marital deduction should be utilized.

In this regard, it should be noted that the marital deduction formula clauses used prior to the 1981 tax laws are still usable and viable where the estate owner wants less than all of the estate to pass under the unlimited marital deduction; for example, where part of the estate is to pass to children or others.

The marital deduction is a tax concept; it does not affect property rights or create new ones. It does not automatically give a wife ownership of one-half of her husband's property or his income, or vice versa. It is not to be confused with a true community property system. It merely provides a method for determining the amount of tax to be paid so that the tax burden on residents of common law states is, theoretically at least, equalized with that of residents of community property states, who prior to the development of the marital deduction concept enjoyed lower federal estate tax costs.

How the Gift Tax Works

One of the basic procedures involved in estate planning relates to the use of lifetime gifts for the purpose of dividing a large estate into smaller units. Both estate and income taxes can frequently be reduced through such divisions. Since rates are higher in the upper brackets, lower overall taxes will result by increasing the number of taxpayers with respect to a given situation, thus lowering the applicable brackets.

The taxpayer can benefit from four important aspects of the gift tax laws: the annual exclusion, gift splitting, the marital deduction, and the exemption equivalent. Each year, the first $10,000 of a gift which a donor gives to a donee is excluded from taxable gifts. Also, a gift made by a husband to a third party may be considered as a gift made one-half by his wife, if she consents. Gift splitting between husband and wife will result in use of lower tax brackets, permits the use of two $10,000 exclusions per donee, and permits the use of the exemption equivalent of both husband and wife, thereby adding substantially to the amount of gifts that may be made tax free.

These gift tax principles may be illustrated as follows: Black is a widower. He this year makes gifts of $10,000 to each of his three sons. None of the gifts is subject to tax. If Black makes gifts of $25,000 to each of them, he still will not be required to pay a gift tax because the first $10,000 of each gift will be covered by the annual exclusion of $10,000, and the remaining $15,000 of each gift, or a total of $45,000, will be applied against his exemption equivalent.

If in future years gifts of $25,000 are again made to each son, $10,000 of each gift will again be tax free because of the exclusion, and the remainder of the gifts will be applied against the transfer tax equivalent until it is exhausted.

Suppose White, who also has three sons and is married, wishes to make gifts to them. He elects, with the consent of his wife, to "split" the gifts with her, i.e., to use her exemptions even though White is making the gifts. He and his wife will each be entitled to the annual gift tax exclusion of $10,000, or a total of $20,000, for each son. Thus, White can, with exemption equivalents available in 1982 ($225,000 for White and for his wife), make gifts of $170,000 in 1982 to each of his sons without paying a tax thereon, because the first $20,000 of each gift would be subject to the annual exclusions and the remaining $150,000 of each gift, or a total of $450,000, would be covered by the exemption equivalent of $225,000 available to each White and Mrs. White.

Gift splitting is not utilized for gifts to a spouse. Each has the benefit of the marital deduction and the entire gift to a spouse is tax free. Even the annual exclusion is no longer relevant for such gifts. But, it should be expressly noted that to the extent the exemption equivalent is used for gift tax purposes, it will not be available for estate tax purposes later. This becomes important (1) where less than the whole estate is left to a spouse; and (2) at the death of the spouse, when the marital deduction is not available.

Unified Credit

Estate and gift transfers are taxed under a unified system so that transfers, whether made during lifetime or at death, are taxed cumulatively and at the same but at progressive rates. Against this tax there is allowed a new series of tax credits which are being phased in over a five-year period starting in 1982 with a $62,800 credit and increasing each year to $192,800 in 1987 and thereafter. This credit has the equivalent effect of reducing a taxable estate so that an otherwise taxable estate or gift of $225,000 in 1982 will incur no federal transfer tax, and in 1987 one $600,000 will incur no federal transfer tax.

It should be noted that the credit is computed after the estate or gift is reduced by any applicable marital deduction. Thus, if the entire estate passes to a spouse under the now available unlimited marital deduction, the credits become irrelevant—but, as pointed out elsewhere, it should not be wasted (depending on the size of the estate). However, if less than the whole estate passes under the marital deduction, the unified credit becomes very relevant because it offsets taxes payable on the portion of the estate on which a tax is payable.

An example of the gift tax and the correlation of the gift tax with the estate tax is presented in the cases of Jones and Brown. Both have equal estates of $1,009,840—an arbitrary figure to make the examples clearer. Jones made no taxable gift before 1981, but then he made a gift of $200,000. Brown had made a gift of $100,000 in 1971, and in 1981 he also made a gift of $200,000. Brown paid a gift tax of $15,525 in 1971 on the $100,000 gift. In 1981, they each had estates of $1,009,840. In 1981, the unified transfer tax credit is $62,800 and the exemption equivalent is $225,000.

JONES' AND BROWN'S ESTATES
(Gift and Estate Tax—Integration)

Assume that, in 1981, Jones and Brown had equal estates of $1,009,840 and that each then made a $200,000 gift. Jones has never made a taxable gift before; Brown made a taxable gift of $200,000 in 1971 and, at that time, paid a gift tax of $15,525.

Their respective gift taxes in 1981 were computed as follows:

	Jones	Brown
1. 1981 Gift	$ 200,000	$ 200,000
2. Less Annual Exclusion*	3,000	3,000
3. 1981 Taxable Gift	197,000	197,000
4. Add Previous Taxable Gifts	-0-	100,000
5. Total Taxable Gifts Through 1981	197,000	297,000
6. Tentative Tax	53,840	86,780
7. Less Tentative Tax on Previous Taxable Gifts	-0-	23,800-computed on 1981 gift tax rates
8. Transfer Tax Total Gifts	53,840	62,980
9. Less Unified Credit–1981	47,000	47,000
10. Gift Tax Paid in 1981	6,840	15,980

Assume Jones and Brown both die in 1985. Their respective estate taxes would be computed as follows:

11. Original Estate Values in 1981	$1,009,840	$1,009,840
12. Less Gifts in 1981	200,000	200,000
13. Less Gift Tax Paid in 1981	6,840	15,980
14. Taxable Estate in 1985	803,000	793,860
15. Add Adjusted Taxable Gifts	197,000	197,000
16. Taxable Amount	1,000,000	990,860
17. Tentative Estate Tax	345,800	342,235
18. Less Transfer Tax on 1981 Gift	6,840	15,980
19. Adjusted Tentative Estate Tax	338,960	326,255
20. Less Unified Credit–1985	121,800	121,800
21. Estate Transfer Tax Due in 1985	217,160	204,455
Total Tax on Post-'76 Transfers:		
Gift Tax	$ 6,840	$ 15,980
Estate Tax	217,160	204,455
	$ 224,000	$ 220,435

*$10,000 in 1982 and thereafter

An examination of the respective columns will show how the gift tax for 1981 is computed. Jones' situation is rather clear cut. The $200,000 is reduced by the $3,000 annual exclusion $10,000 in 1982 and thereafter, leaving $197,000 taxable and having no previous gifts results in a transfer tax before credit of $53,840. Taking off the unified credit (line 9) of $47,000 results in a gift tax in 1981 of $6,840.

With Brown, starting with the same $200,000, taking off $3,000 for the annual exclusion leaving $197,000; the original 1971 taxable gift of $100,000 is added back so that the total of all taxable gifts made through 1981 is $297,000. The tentative gift tax before credit is $86,780. From this is subtracted the tax on the $100,000—not the $15,525 actually paid in 1971 but $23,800—computed on the basis of the current 1981 transfer tax rates, leaving a tax before the unified credit of $62,980. From this the unified transfer tax credit of $47,000 is taken off, with the resulting tax of $15,980. You will note that Brown received a credit for his 1971 gift of $23,800, although he only paid $15,525. So, in effect, it cost Jones $6,840 to give away $200,000 and it cost Brown $15,980 to give away $300,000. Cost was proportionately more because he gave away $100,000 in 1971, $100,000 more than Jones had given.

Assume both Jones and Brown died in 1985. The estate tax would be computed as follows: Jones' original estate was $1,009,840. Take off the $200,000 gift he made and take off the gift tax of $6,840. This leaves an estate of $803,000. Then add back the taxable gift made after 1976 of $197,000 so that the total amount is $1,000,000. The tentative estate tax on this is $345,000. He is entitled to a credit for the $6,840 in gift taxes he paid in 1981 so the amount is reduced to $338,960. Applied against this amount is the unified credit of $121,800, leaving an estate tax of $217,800. Note that the credit has increased so that in 1985, it is $121,800.

In Brown's case the starting point is also an estate of $1,009,840. From this is subtracted the $200,000 gift and the $15,980 in paid gift taxes, leaving an estate of $783,860. Added back are taxable gifts made after 1976, or $197,000, to reach the amount of $990,860. The tentative estate tax is $326,255. Taking a credit for his 1981 gift tax of $15,980 reduces this to $326,255, against which is applied the unified credit of $121,800, leaving an estate tax due of $204,455.

Of course Brown actually gave away an additional $100,000 in 1971 and paid an additional gift tax of $15,525 at that time. His estate was larger to begin with. But the cases show the interrelationship between the two taxes and the unified transfer tax credit.

While not applicable to the foregoing calculations, because of the size of the estate, it should be noted that there is a gradual reduction in the federal estate tax rates so that by 1985, the maximum rate will be 50% on an estate of $2,500,000 or more. The tax table shows how this maximum reduction takes place.

MAXIMUM TRANSFER TAX RATES
Estate and Gift Taxes

Year	Rate	Taxable Amounts Over
1981	70%	$5,000,000
1982	65%	4,000,000
1983	60%	3,500,000
1984	55%	3,000,000
1985	50%	2,500,000
Thereafter	50%	2,500,000

Reducing Estate Taxes by Gifts

The taxable gifts made after 1976 are added back into the donor's estate when computing his estate tax (with a credit, however, for gift taxes paid). A lifetime gift is therefore taxed like a transfer at death. It does, though, allow the donor to take advantage of the annual exclusion and the marital deduction and serves two other significant purposes. First, a gift can keep future appreciation of the gift asset out of the donor's estate. For example: if a donor makes a gift of an asset with a taxable value of $50,000 at the time of the gift, only that $50,000 is calculated as if it were part of the donor's estate at death even though the asset might then be worth $150,000. Second, the amount of the gift taxes paid will be excluded from such calculation. Thus, if a donor makes a taxable gift to a child of $100,000, with respect to which $20,000 is paid in taxes, only the $100,000 will be included in his estate for tax computation purposes. If he had not made the gift, but would have made a bequest of the same amount to a child, his estate would be taxed on the full $120,000.

The foregoing illustrations do not take into consideration the decrease in probate expense as a result of the reduction in the size of the estate passing through probate. On the other hand, residents of Wisconsin, which imposes state gift taxes, must take them into consideration in order to properly calculate the anticipated savings.

Property transferred as gifts carries the donor's basis into the donee's hands. But, appreciated property receives an increase in basis for that part of the gift tax paid which bears the same ratio as the net appreciation in value of the gift bears to the amount of the gift. To illustrate: a gift of securities with a fair market value of $30,000, having a basis of $20,000 on which donor paid a $6,000 gift tax, would have a new basis of $22,000 ($20,000 + $2,000 of the $6,000 gift tax payable).

Prior to 1982, a gift made within three years of death was included in the donor's estate and any gift tax paid with respect thereto was also added back to the estate. (This did not apply to gifts of $3,000 or less per year.) Thus, deathbed gifts for the purpose of taking the gift tax out of the estate were not possible. Moreover, for estate tax purposes, the value of gifts made within three years of death in excess of $3,000 was the value on the date of the decedent's death. If the gift was of life insurance, the full value of the policy at the time of death was includable in the donor's estate.

Commencing with 1982, gifts within three years of death are no longer includable in the estate, except gifts in the form of life insurance premiums; nor is the gift tax paid with respect to such gifts includable in the estate.

Joint Tenancy

The creation of a joint tenancy, in which one joint tenant pays for the asset, may constitute a gift to the other joint tenant and be subject to the gift tax. However, the gift tax marital deduction, which applies to gifts between spouses, is also applicable to a gift to a spouse which results from the creation of a joint tenancy. Such a gift would be tax free. If the gift were to a child, the annual exclusion and the exemption equivalent would be applicable. With respect to a gift between husband and wife creating a joint tenancy, the tax problem relates to the basis of the gift property in the hands of the surviving spouse (only one-half of the property will receive a stepped-up basis at the death of a joint tenant) and the qualification for special use valuation, estate tax payment deferral, or qualified redemption of stock.

It should be expressly noted that joint tenancy precludes the use of some flexibility in planning. Joint tenancy precludes the ability to direct who will inherit the property after the death of the second joint tenant. It may, for example, be desirable for the surviving spouse's protection to leave the deceased spouse's entire estate in trust. Or, the property may be needed by the decedent to fund a bypass trust. If the property is jointly held, it will pass outright to the surviving spouse automatically for ultimate disposition as the surviving spouse wishes. Nevertheless, joint tenancy is much less troublesome now from a tax viewpoint than it was previously.

Where property is jointly owned by husband and wife, the estate of the first to die will include one-half of the value regardless of who furnished the consideration for the property. This rule applies to estates developing in 1982 and thereafter.

Gifts of Life Insurance

Life insurance makes an excellent gift. It is popular as a gift to a child. Not only are taxes saved for the donor, but the future security of the child is enhanced. Premiums may qualify not only for the exemption equivalent but also for the annual $10,000 exclusion.

An individual may pay premiums with respect to insurance on his own life and avoid subjecting the proceeds to the estate tax at his death so long as he retains none of the incidents of ownership in the policy. Thus a policy on the life of the insured may be owned by his child or wife and he may pay the premiums thereon without the proceeds being taxed in his estate. The law enhances the significance of life insurance as a medium for gifts and encourages the use of a properly conceived life insurance trust.

If the insurance made subject of a gift is to be on the life of the child who is the donee, the donor should not retain any incidents of ownership in the policy. It should become the absolute property of the donee without any restrictions. To be safe, only the donee and his estate should be named beneficiary; a contingent beneficiary should not be designated by the donor, but only by the donee.

Trusts

A gift may be made in trust for an individual as well as directly to him. The trust, an old and important legal instrumentality, is used extensively in estate planning. It may be either a "living trust," which is established during lifetime, or a "testamentary trust," which comes into existence at death, pursuant to a will.

The living trust may be further classified as "revocable" or "irrevocable." If the creator of the trust may terminate it and retake the assets, it is revocable. If not, it is irrevocable. This difference is basic and affects the tax results. Property transferred to a revocable trust is not, for tax purposes, given away, since it may be retaken. Hence, if estate taxes are to be reduced, the trust must be irrevocable.

If property is given to a trust for the benefit of a wife, and it is also intended that the marital deduction be utilized, the provisions relating to the marital deduction or the QTIP must be scrupulously followed. As already noted, if the conventional marital trust is used the trust must provide that the wife shall receive all of the income therefrom at least annually during her lifetime, and that she have the right to dispose of the principal of the trust either during her lifetime or at her death through a general power of appointment. If the QTIP trust is used, it must provide for all income to the wife, no one but her may receive any principal during her lifetime, and she may not have a general power of appointment.

Short Term Trusts

The short term trust has been used extensively for the purpose of minimizing the family income tax. Such a trust must exist for a period of not less than ten years. It may provide either for the accumulation of income or for the current distribution thereof to the beneficiary. At termination, the principal must be returned to the individual who established the trust.

The short term trust is a means for reducing the income tax rather than the estate tax. The value of the principal to be returned to the creator of the trust will be included in his estate in the event of his death. While gift taxes may be payable upon the transfer of assets to such trust, the tax is not on the entire value of the property transferred but only on the value of the right to the income therefrom for the number of years the trust will remain in force. This is because such a trust provides for the transfer of income for a period of years but requires the return of the principal at the end of the period.

Trusts for Minors

Normally, where a gift is made in trust for a person under 21 and such trust is to continue after he becomes 21, the $10,000 annual exclusion is not available. However, if the trust fund is payable to the minor when he attains age 21—or to his estate, or as he directs, if he should die before 21—the $10,000 annual exclusion will be available.

Before such a trust is used, it is necessary to weigh the advantage of obtaining the $10,000 gift tax exclusion against the disadvantage of distributing a trust at the early age of 21.

Reducing Income Taxes

The division of an estate by gift can also result in the reduction of income taxes. A gift of income-producing assets will divide between two or more individuals the income that would ordinarily be received by the estate owner alone and been taxed in a higher bracket. Such savings are also possible through gifts in trust, depending on the kind and purpose of the trust.

While the use of a joint income tax return permits the "splitting" of income between husband and wife, the possibility of dividing income with children and other dependents should not be ignored.

Moreover, an unmarried, divorced, or widowed individual may have a great need to reduce taxes because the right to file a joint return does not apply.

Reducing Second Tax

Thus far the discussion has related largely to one basic procedure in estate planning; namely, the division of large estates into smaller units through the medium of gifts. A second basic procedure involves the use of trusts to eliminate the second, and possibly the third, set of death charges and taxes with respect to all or part of an estate. Even though the marital deduction is used to the fullest extent, the importance of the problem at the death of the second spouse cannot be overemphasized.

It is true that the burden of double or triple federal estate taxes is somewhat ameliorated by the law which provides for a decreasing credit with respect to taxes paid on inherited property, depending upon the number of years between the first death and the second. The credit ranges from 100%, if the second death occurs within two years, to 20% if the second in the ninth or tenth year. No credit is given if death occurs after the tenth year. But, the basic problem of double or triple taxation remains because the interval between deaths obviously cannot be predicted.

The problem may be illustrated as follows: Assume an estate of $875,000, that no taxable gifts had been made, and that death takes place in 1983 when the exemption equivalent is $275,000. Assume the entire estate was left to the spouse so that it passed virtually estate tax free by reason of the marital deduction. The exemption equivalent is wasted in that when the survivor dies in 1987, when the exemption equivalent is $600,000, the amount over $275,000— $225,000—will be subject to a tax of $54,800. This tax of $54,800 could have been saved. Had the husband's will first used up the 1983 exemption equivalent of $275,000 and passed the balance of $600,000 via the marital deduction, and had a trust in the will been used for the $275,000 so that there would have been no tax on the death of the wife when it passed to the children, her estate would have been entitled to an exemption equivalent of $600,000, which would have covered the $600,000 she received via the marital deduction from her husband. Thus consideration should be given to placing first emphasis on using up the exemption equivalent rather than on the marital deduction.

In any event, the trust can be used to eliminate successive sets of death charges and taxes. Thus, a married man might provide in his will that one-half of his estate pass to his wife in such a way as to be tax free via the marital deduction, and the other half be kept in trust so as to provide income to her for life, then to his son, and finally to be distributed to his grandson at the death of his son. Under such an arrangement, death charges and taxes need not again be paid at the death of the wife or son upon the half with respect to which taxes were paid (after the exemption equivalent applied). Even if only one set of death charges and taxes is eliminated, substantial savings might result. But, it should be remembered that the portion kept in trust for the wife will be subject to the estate tax to the extent that the amount involved exceeds the exemption equivalent.

Generation Skipping Trusts

The generation-skipping trust, to which reference has just been made, has long been a valuable tool in estate planning. It has—and does now to a more limited extent in larger estates—permit an individual to transfer assets into a trust for the benefit of his children, his grandchildren and even for his great grandchildren with reduced tax costs.

Some examples will illustrate the law and problems. A father creates a trust (either testamentary or living) and provides that income may be distributed to his son, in the discretion of the trustee. Upon the son's death, any undistributed income and the remaining trust principal are to be distributed to the son's children, the grandchildren. Because the son has a right to income (albeit in the discretion of the trustee), the value of the trust—to the extent it exceeds $250,000—will upon his (the son's) death be taxed as if it were part of his estate when the assets pass to his children.

If a father has two sons and two daughters and created trusts for them (either testamentary or living), giving them rights to principal and income, each of those children would be entitled to have $250,000 excluded from their portions of the trust upon their respective deaths and the transfer over to the next generation. So, for this father's estate there would be total exclusions of $1,000,000 before the generation-skipping tax would be imposed. The values that would make up the $250,000 for each child would be determined at the time of the child's death. The amount in excess of $250,000 would be included in the child's estate for tax computation purposes. The taxes due would be paid by the trust, not by the child's estate. Any unused unified transfer tax credit of the child could be applied against the amount thus taxable to his estate. The marital deduction for the child's estate would be increased because his taxable estate would be increased.

The so-called generation-skipping tax does not apply to any trust which was created and which was irrevocable on June 11, 1976, except to the extent that additions are made after that date. Nor does it apply to trusts created by will, or by a revocable trust, which was in existence on June 11, 1976, and was not amended prior to death, and death occurs before January 1, 1983. This suggests that wills executed prior to June 11, 1976 for estates where the generation-skipping tax would be a significant problem should not be revised (if revision can be avoided) until after January 1, 1983.

Planning for the generation-skipping tax might involve, in proper situations, a trust for a child and a separate trust for grandchildren. In this way the passing from one younger generation to another younger generation would be eliminated to an extent, and the problem of generation-skipping tax minimized. Actually this is not a new concept because trusts have always been used in proper cases for the various generations if the estates were large enough to so permit. It has not been unusual to have a will with a marital portion for a wife, trusts for children and separate trusts for grandchildren.

The generation-skipping tax has created many problems both in planning and in the administration of the tax. As of this writing, there is a movement towards eliminating the tax, but nothing definite by way of change has as yet occurred.

Trusts and Marital Deduction

In planning for the use of trusts, it should be recognized that a married estate owner is not compelled to use the marital deduction. He has the choice of so arranging his estate program that a tax upon his entire estate will be paid at his death and eliminating entirely the tax on his wife's death; or of arranging the marital deduction so that a tax will be paid upon only a part, or none, of his estate, recognizing that the portion passing tax free to his wife will be taxed at her death, to the extent that she is then still possessed of such portion.

In making the choice, the estate owner will want to compare the total death charges and taxes payable after the death of both himself and his wife, under plans calling for all or part of the marital deduction, with those under plans where the marital deduction is not used; the availability of liquid assets in his estate and in his wife's estate wherewith to pay death charges and taxes; the advantages of the immediate tax savings; the possibilities of changes in the law and economic conditions; whether family circumstances preclude granting the wife or husband the type of control required for the power of appointment marital deduction; the size of the wife's own estate; and the possibility of integrating both the husband's and the wife's estate programs to take fullest advantage of the tax savings permitted by the law. In most instances, the use of the marital deduction will be warranted for at least part of the estate.

Since the advantages of the marital deduction will be denied to an estate owner if his wife predeceases him, basic planning—the division of a large estate into smaller units through the medium of gifts, the wise use of trusts, and so on—should still take place. Then, if the marital deduction becomes available, because the wife survived, additional economies will be affected.

Gifts to Charity

It should be remembered that charitable gifts and bequests can be made free of the gift tax and the estate tax, and can have substantial income tax advantages.

Stepped-up Basis

Property sold after death has as its basis the value determined for federal estate tax purposes—"stepped-up basis." However, it should be remembered that property made subject of a gift has a basis in the hands of the donee, for the purpose of computing again, equal to the donor's basis plus a portion of the gift tax paid. For computing loss, the basis is the higher of the market value as of the date of the gift for the donor's basis, plus a portion of the gift tax paid. In view of the present integrated transfer tax, which covers both the estate tax and the gift tax, an estate owner is confronted with the problem of whether an asset should be given away during lifetime or held until death. A "stepped-up basis" will not occur unless the asset is transferred at death. Against this must be weighed the advantage to the donee of receiving the income now, and not waiting till death. Also to be considered is whether the asset is apt to appreciate after the transfer. There are economic considerations which need to be considered as well as the tax consideration.

Disclaimers

A beneficiary or heir named in a will or trust may disclaim the assets or interests designated for him, thus, in effect, changing the instrument which designated him and the amount he was to receive so as to eliminate him as such heir or beneficiary and have the assets devolve to others instead. The disclaimer permits "second guessing" of the decedent's or donor's plans. It is therefore a very useful "after-the-fact" planning tool. It will be valid for federal estate and gift tax purposes if it's timely made and the disclaiming persons accepts no personal benefits from such disclaimer. The disclaimer must be made within nine months after the date on which the disclaiming individual's interests come into being.

Planning for Liquidity

Another basic procedure in estate planning is arranging for sufficient liquid assets to meet those death charges and taxes which cannot be further reduced as well as the debts and liabilities. This is particularly true for an unmarried estate owner for whom the marital deduction is not available.

One thing the estate owner can do during his lifetime is to convert valuable but difficult-to-sell assets—like a closely held business, unproductive real estate, or even objects of art—into liquid assets, thus avoiding a forced sale at death.

Or, the estate owner might try to accumulate liquid assets over a period of time by regularly setting aside a specified sum. One defect in this method is that the estate owner may not live long enough to complete the accumulation. Another serious weakness is that it is expensive: The amount accumulated must first be earned, then it is subject to income tax, and ultimately it increases the size of the estate and is itself again subject to tax at death.

In planning for the future one must keep in mind the potential increase in the dollar value of an estate by reason of growth and inflation and the potential tax burden notwithstanding the increase in exemption equivalents. Assuming an average rate of growth and inflation of 10 percent, the following table illustrates the possibility of increasing estate tax burdens:

INCREASING ESTATE TAX BURDENS
Ten Percent Growth Rate

Year	Taxable Estate*	Exemption Equivalent	Subject to Tax
1981	$ 500,000	$175,625	$ 324,375
1983	605,000	275,000	330,000

1985	732,000	400,000	332,000
1987	885,780	600,000	285,780
1991	1,296,871	600,000	696,871
2001	3,363,749	600,000	2,763,749

*After expenses and debts but prior to exemption equivalents and taxes.

Liquidating Business Interest

Practical estate planning requires considering the effect of death upon a business, whether it is a partnership, a corporation, or a sole proprietorship. It is not always possible for a wife or other members of a family to continue the business. They may be prevented from doing so because of age, inexperience or inability to get along with surviving associates. Moreover, it may not be prudent to have the future welfare and support of a wife and children dependent upon the uncertainties of business.

This suggests that arrangements for the sale of a business interest at death should be explored. Such arrangements are generally accomplished with buy and sell agreements, implemented by life insurance for the purpose of providing the necessary cash. The purchase price—or a formula for determining it—should be included in the agreement, thus minimizing friction at a critical time. If the agreement is properly conceived, the price determined in accordance with its provisions will also fix the value for estate tax purposes.

In partnership or corporation situations, such an agreement may take the form of a buy-out by the surviving partners or stockholders, or a buy-out by the partnership or corporation itself. If a corporate stock redemption is contemplated, consideration must be given to the attribution rules in Section 318 of the Internal Revenue Code, which may make such redemptions vulnerable under the income tax laws where members of the same family are stockholders or have certain other defined relationships with each other.

The law does provide, however, some relief for estates which contain a private business interest. If certain requirements are met, the estate tax attributable to such business interest—but not the entire estate tax—may be paid in installments over a period of 15 years with interest only payable during the first five years, and a low interest of 4% on the first $1,000,000 attributable to the value of the closely held business. To qualify the business interest must be at least 35% of the estate reduced by estate expenses, losses and indebtedness. The decedent must also have owned 20% of the value of the particular business, and the business must have 15 or fewer shareholders or partners.

Another type of relief is provided by Section 303 of the Internal Revenue Code. It permits a corporation to redeem its shares held by an estate for the purpose of providing the estate with liquid funds wherewith to pay death taxes and administrative costs—provided the value of the shares held by the estate is less estate expenses, losses and debts.

A redemption under Section 303 will normally result in little tax so long as the stepped-up basis is available. However, any gain to the estate would be taxed as capital gains rather than ordinary income, which may offer substantial tax savings.

Life Insurance

Providing funds for such a redemption can best be accomplished through the medium of life insurance. In fact, insurance upon the life of the estate owner is generally the best solution to the problem of estate liquidity. Life insurance can provide the necessary funds when needed, thus permitting the estate to be transferred to beneficiaries with a minimum of shrinkage. New forms of policies and methods of financing and paying premiums are constantly being devised to facilitate the acquisition and maintenance of adequate coverage.

If life insurance is used to provide cash and to offset shrinkage, it should, whenever possible, be so arranged that the proceeds will not be subject to estate and inheritance taxes in the insured's estate. This can be accomplished if someone other than the insured is the owner. The insured must not have any rights in the policies. The proceeds should not be payable to his estate. But he may pay the premiums.

Thus, Mrs. Jones might apply for insurance on the life of Jones, pay the premiums out of her own funds and name herself as beneficiary. Upon Jones' death she will receive the proceeds. They will not be taxes as part of Jones' estate. With the insurance proceeds, Mrs. Jones might purchase assets from her husband's estate. The executor will then receive cash with which to pay the death costs and she will receive assets which might otherwise be sacrificed in order to obtain cash.

Life Insurance Trust

The same procedure may be followed with a life insurance trust. This may be the only solution where the wife herself possesses a substantial estate. She could, for example, create such a trust for her children, pay for insurance on her husband and cause the proceeds to be payable to the trust. Upon the husband's death, the trustee could transfer cash to his estate by purchasing assets from it.

If properly programmed, the proceeds of such insurance would not be taxed in the estate of the husband nor increase the estate of the wife. The premiums would be considered as gifts from the wife to the beneficiaries of the trust. If an insurance trust is not used, insurance purchased by the wife on her husband would increase her own estate.

Insurance for Wife

While it has always been good practice to plan the estates of husband and wife simultaneously, it is doubly important to do so if the marital deduction is to be used. If all or a substantial portion transferred to a wife, provision must be made for liquid assets to meet the charges and taxes imposed at her death. Again, life insurance is the most economical and efficient way of providing such liquidity for her estate.

Life insurance for the wife may accomplish other purposes as well. Thus, a husband planning for the use of the marital deduction may be deprived of its benefits if his wife should predecease him. Insurance on his wife will reimburse him for the extra tax he must pay under such circumstances. And, if she does not survive him, the insurance will provide liquidity for her estate.

Life insurance should be programmed and correlated with the rest of the estate. Effective use of the settlement options is important. Because insurance may receive the benefits of the marital deduction, it must be arranged with due regard for technicalities relating thereto, essentially similar to the requirements for a trust. For example, insurance arrangements pursuant to which installment payments are made to a wife during her lifetime must give her the right to dispose of any balance at her death. Insurance may also be used with a QTIP trust.

In programming life insurance, it should also be remembered that if the proceeds are payable under an installment option, $1,000 of the interest forming part of each year's installment payments is free of income taxes if, but only if, the wife is the beneficiary.

Employee Benefit Plans

A substantial portion of the estate owner's assets may consist of an interest in an employee retirement or other similar plan—pension, profit sharing, stock bonus, employee stock ownership plan, an individual retirement account (IRA)—which is qualified under the tax laws for special treatment both during his lifetime and at his death.

When the employee dies before that interest is distributed to him, the manner in which the pay-out is made to his estate or beneficiaries may significantly affect the taxes paid on the distribution. Depending on the terms of the plan, the employee (or, possibly, his beneficiaries) may choose one of two basic methods of pay-out: (1) a lump sum pay-out in which all plan benefits are distributed within one year, or (2) a payment schedule spread over a period of time.

If the distribution is made over a period of time, it will not be included in the employee's estate for estate tax purposes. It will, however, be subject to income taxes, but is eligible for special treatment, including partial capital gains and a 10-year forward averaging.

The correct choice depends on a number of factors including the amount of the employee benefit plan distribution, the size of the estate and the income tax brackets of the estate and its beneficiaries. Because of the important tax consequences, however, the choice must be considered by both the estate owner and the distribution beneficiaries.

Estate plans must be reviewed frequently because of ever changing family circumstances, economic conditions and tax laws. Moreover, a flexible rather than a rigid program is to be preferred.

The estate planning process, at its most effective level, requires the cooperation of those trained in the law, accounting, life insurance, and trusts. The wise estate owner will seek their advice.

The Push to Prune Social Security Benefits

ONLY three and a half years ago Congress strengthened the social security system by increasing taxes on wages and changing the formula for computing benefits. Those amendments were supposed to maintain the system in sound financial shape through the rest of the century.

Now we are told social security faces a new crisis that requires immediate action if the system is to stay alive. And again, people are plagued by the fear that this pillar of their economic well-being may be collapsing. In a public survey taken by the American Council of Life Insurance, 55% said they believed the statement that social security will be unable to meet its commitments within ten years unless something is done.

Is the social security system really in trouble? Yes. The old age and survivors insurance (OASI) part of the program is running short of money and might not be able to meet all its obligations by middle to late 1982 unless it receives additional funds. The other parts of social security—disability insurance (DI) and the hospital insurance (HI) plan that covers Part A of medicare—are not involved in the current financial problems.

Is the system in danger of collapse? No. There's no reason for such a catastrophe because the financial imbalance of the social security system can be quickly corrected.

Will it be necessary to reduce benefits severely to make up the shortfall in funds? Not necessarily. The short-term strain can be relieved by a combination of measures that won't materially alter the system. An easing in inflation and unemployment pressures, which are at the bottom of the difficulties, would help turn the situation around. The long-range problems foreseen by experts in and out of the government might ultimately dictate fundamental changes in benefits. However, Congress and the President have a number of solutions available, and many don't entail any cataclysmic cutbacks.

The more you look into the financial affairs of social security, the more you may be inclined to agree with Robert J. Myers, one of the most knowledgeable people in the field, that the system is viable and not in mortal danger. Myers headed the actuarial department of the Social Security Administration (SSA) for 23 years. He was a member of the social security task force set up by President Reagan before he took office.

How the system works

To see why there are grounds for optimism, start with a few basic facts.

Social security depends on monthly payroll taxes to meet its current bills. It is unlike private pension programs in that it does not accumulate special funds to pay retirees and survivors of workers covered by the law. In fact, any effort to accumulate such immense sums could conceivably upset the economy. But the pay-as-you-go arrangement makes the system very sensitive to adverse economic developments.

Out of the 6.65% of workers' incomes to be paid this year by both employees and employers, 4.7% will go into old age and survivors insurance, 0.65% into disability insurance, and 1.3% into hospital insurance. The three funds are separate: Money allocated to one program cannot be used to pay benefits provided by another. Thus, one part of the system may be incurring deficits while another enjoys a surplus.

Although benefits are not funded in advance, each program in the system does maintain safety reserves, called trust funds. They are designed to bridge temporary fluctuations in income and outlays, absorb transient deficits and give time for action if deficits persist.

Preliminary estimates indicate that the government will distribute 173.2 billion dollars in benefits this year and take in 173.6 billion dollars in taxes. To keep this vast financial machine running properly, the Social Security Administration and its official advisory organizations must plot future income and outgo for short- and long-term periods, taking into account such factors as trends in wage levels, prices and unemployment, and the rates at which people are likely to marry, bear children, divorce, retire, and become disabled.

The SSA develops three sets of forecasts that are based on "optimistic," "pessimistic" and "intermediate" assumptions about the course of those economic and demographic factors. Actuaries then extract from the computations estimates of future surpluses and deficits for each part of the system.

Keep in mind that all social security projections are no more than estimates built on varied assumptions, usually the intermediate set. In a world in which you can't be sure how much a loaf of bread will cost next week, it's hardly surprising that the forecasters sometimes miss the mark by a substantial margin—or, looked at from the other side, that real events deviate widely from the predictions.

Even seemingly small assumption errors can throw the final figures off by millions of dollars. And the estimates become less reliable the further ahead the forecasters push the numbers.

What went wrong

The current social security crisis is rooted in the general economic deterioration that began in the latter part of the 70s. A report prepared by the Congressional Research Service of the Library of Congress points out that overly favorable assumptions were factored into the social security forecasts made in 1972 and 1977, when Congress last enacted major changes in benefit and tax provisions. For example, it was assumed that real wages—earnings covered by social security adjusted for cost-of-living increases—would continue to rise during the 1970s as they did in the previous two decades. In actuality, only twice between 1972 and 1980 did the gain in real wages come up to or exceed the forecast rate. Moreover, real wages fell in four of those years as the cost of living rose faster than paychecks.

Real wages strongly influence social security's financial condition. Revenues depend in part on how much each person covered by social security earns during the year, but most of the benefits increase automatically with the cost of living. Therefore, when real wages decline, expenditures tend to mount faster than revenues.

Unemployment, another crucial factor, turned out to be higher than expected. The fewer people working, the fewer pay social security taxes. For every 1,000,000 people laid off for just one month last year, social security lost an estimated $100,000,000 in tax income. High unemployment also encourages early retirements, thereby adding to benefit costs.

Lawrence H. Thompson, an SSA policy planning official, observes that the government's 1977 assumptions

How bad is the problem?

The seemingly precise figures on social security deficits and surpluses actually fluctuate a great deal depending on the assumed rate of future changes in prices, wages and other factors. The table shows the deficits and surpluses of the three social security programs and the combined account as forecast on three occasions. The left-hand bars for each program represent the estimates from social security's early 1980 reports, the middle bars reflect revised assumptions made in midyear, and the right-hand bars are based on the previous administration's budget for fiscal year 1982.

billions of dollars

old-age and survivors insurance	disability insurance	hospital insurance	combined programs
1981 +4.1 / −10.4 −7.4 −5.8	−1.2 −0.9	+6.6 +6.4 +7.0	+0.3 / −2.2 +0.4
1982 +5.7 +3.9 +4.0 / −12.4 −13.6 −15.5		+7.5 +6.7 +7.5	+0.9 / −3.1 −4.0
1983 +7.8 +5.6 +5.8 / −14.2 −18.3 −23.1		+7.7 +6.4 +8.6	+1.2 / −6.2 −8.7
1984 +10.0 +7.4 +7.6 / −16.2 −20.9 −28.9		+7.1 +6.0 +9.3	+0.9 / −7.4 −11.9

(+) = surplus
(−) = deficit

were no more wrong than the predictions of many private economists. It was the unforeseen setback in the economy that undermined the 1977 amendments and turned the anticipated surpluses into deficits.

Finding solutions

There's no scarcity in the number of proposals to remedy all the ills that afflict social security. The difficulty is in trying to put together an economically effective program that is also politically acceptable. That may prove even more difficult this year, given the new party divisions in Congress.

Among the measures seen most likely to be seriously considered during 1981 are the following.

Make funding more flexible. One way to offset the deficits in the OASI program to some extent would be to tap the disability and health insurance trust funds. Congress moved a step in that direction last year when it reallocated some of the disability insurance tax revenues to OASI for two years, 1980 and 1981. Congress could extend this and perhaps supplement it by giving the SSA authority to borrow from one fund to help another.

Early last year it was thought that such reallocation and interfund borrowing would be enough to balance the system's accounts for a few years. However, more recent estimates indicate that accounting changes alone might not be enough to forestall new deficits that would further reduce the already meager trust funds. But reallocation and interfund borrowing are widely recommended as essential reforms. And since they don't involve any real structural change in the system, they are less subject to partisan controversy.

Borrow from the Treasury. The SSA could be authorized to borrow from the Treasury to handle financial emergencies, as some other government agencies are permitted to do.

Change the index for benefit adjustments. Inflation by itself doesn't necessarily harm social security, provided wages rise faster than the cost-of-living index, by which benefits are adjusted each year. It's the decline in real wages that upsets the system. One proposal would limit automatic increases in benefits to the gain in the average wage when the cost-of-living index rises more than the average. This plan is backed by the National Commission on Social Security, which was set up during the Carter administration but made its final report after President Reagan took office. Another proposal would change the index used for automatic adjustments to one that more accurately measures the living costs of retirees.

Increase social security taxes. The tax rates and the amount of earnings subject to taxes were raised this year, and further tax rate increases are already scheduled for 1982, 1985, 1986 and 1990. The amount of earnings subject to tax may also go up again because that is tied to a wage index.

Raising taxes or imposing the planned increases sooner might be less objectionable to the public than is often assumed. A survey of randomly selected adults taken for the National Commission on Social Security showed that 63% would favor raising the payroll tax to prevent a reduction in retirement benefits. A smaller majority, 51%, would prefer higher taxes to an increase in the retirement age to 68. And 49% would rather pay higher payroll taxes than higher income taxes to support social security.

Use general revenues. Whether some of social security's costs should be financed out of general tax funds (individual and corporate income taxes) has long been a highly controversial issue. Support has come largely from liberals, but use of general revenues has been advanced as a possibility by Sen. Robert Dole, the Kansas Republican who heads the Senate Finance Committee, which deals with social security matters.

One roundabout way of tapping general revenues, suggested by the National Commission on Social Security, would be to have the government pay part of the costs of hospital insurance and make it up by imposing a surcharge on income taxes.

Eliminate less important benefits. What's unimportant to one person may be highly important to another, so reducing any benefit is bound to trigger opposition. Here are two of the candidates for elimination now being discussed.

▶ *The minimum benefit.* Everyone eligible for social security who retires at 65 or becomes disabled is entitled to a minimum $122 monthly payment. The minimum protects the needy who have earned very little over a lifetime. However, it also produces a windfall for, say, a government employee who retires on a government pension but has worked just long enough in outside jobs to qualify for social security.

President Reagan has proposed eliminating the minimum benefit of $122 a month, which would affect nearly 3,000,000 retirees. Income lost by the truly needy would be made up by aid under the Supplemental Security Income program for those who are at least 65, blind or disabled. Doing away with the minimum would save one billion dollars in fiscal year 1982.

▶ *Student benefits.* Eligible children get benefits up to age 18 and from 18 through 21 if they are full-time students. President Reagan has recommended eliminating benefits for youngsters who become eligible for those payments in the future. Benefits for students currently receiving money would be reduced 25% a year. Those changes would save an estimated $700,000,000 in fiscal year 1982.

Reduce disability outlays. Although the disability program is in better shape than the retirement plan, the Reagan administration has indicated it would like to scale down disability insurance expenditures for budgetary reasons. This could be done by imposing tougher eligibility rules, cutting payments to take into account benefits the disabled person may be receiving from workers' compensation and other government programs, and weeding out people incorrectly classified as disabled.

The long-range problems

Those are only some of the ideas likely to be offered this year to take care of the short-term financial difficulties of social security. But you can also expect appeals to be made for fundamental revisions aimed at solving such long-term problems as the rising proportion of older people in the population.

One proposal calls for an increase from 65 to 68 in the age at which you would be able to draw full pensions. Another would extend social security to government workers and employees of nonprofit organizations.

Bringing in those groups would raise social security outlays as well as revenues, but the program would gain on balance because it would reduce benefits paid to government employees who held part-time private jobs.

Such large-scale changes could not be instituted quickly, even if adopted this year. The age increase provided for in most of the proposals would be phased in very gradually, starting around the year 2000. Similarly, coverage of government workers would be extended in stages, first to people on the payroll who are not in a retirement program and later to new workers who would have been eligible to join present government pension programs. The President's Commission on Pension Policy recommended last year that social security be made universal, covering virtually all employees in government and private business, but that too would be done by extending the system to new workers, leaving others with their present retirement plans.

The Future of Social Security

Richard S. Schweiker

We are facing the most serious crisis in the 46-year history of the Social Security system—a crisis both in financing, and in public confidence in the system. No one questions that the Social Security system faces a major financial crisis—the facts and figures show that the OASI system will not have enough on hand to pay benefits at some time after mid–1982. The question is how to meet this crisis.

The American public has been told over and over again in the last several years that the system will not go bankrupt. Yet, in the same period, the actuarial reports have shown the prospects of deficits in the near future and the threat of bankruptcy. It has become clear that stop-gap and Band-Aid approaches will not work . . .

None of the solutions to these problems will be easy, popular, or painless. There are really only three kinds of choices available to us: restrain the growth of benefits, increase payroll taxes, or turn to some other revenue source.

We are prepared to work with all interested parties to develop a reasonable set of proposals to deal with the fundamental problems. As the President has [previously] indicated . . . our sole commitment is to three basic principles: first, the integrity of the Social Security trust fund and the basic Social Security benefit structure that protects older Americans; second, holding down the tax burden on current workers supporting the Social Security system; and third, the elimination of the abuses in the current system that rob the elderly of their rightful legacy . . .

Whatever changes are made will be difficult and may even be unpopular. But as things now stand, without changes, the cumulative Social Security trust fund deficit of income needed to adequately meet benefit outgo would, under pessimistic economic assumptions, be as high as $111 billion during the next 5 years. Over the long term—75 years—under the 1980 Board of Trustees intermediate assumptions, there is an average deficit of 1.52 percent of taxable payroll, and the projections based on pessimistic assumptions are much worse—a deficiency of 6.17 percent of taxable payroll.

Raising the Social Security tax rates to cover whatever the current program requires would be both unfair to current taxpayers who have to bear the tax burden and a serious drag on the economy. The apparent alternative of turning to general revenues for additional financing, whether these general revenues come from current taxes or some type of new tax, would still mean that additional taxes would be paid by—and be a burden on—the same people who now pay Social Security taxes. The congressional budget process we are all going through now makes it clear to all of us that there really are not any excess general revenues to turn to for Social Security—there is a deficit to reduce and you don't balance the budget by adding the Social Security deficit to the existing general revenue deficit. . . .

Over the past few months since the initial budget proposals, the Administration has conducted an intensive review and analysis of the entire Social Security program in order to develop a set of proposals to address the Social Security crisis facing us. We developed proposals aimed at restoring Social Security to programmatic and financial soundness by:

- Reducing the social-adequacy or welfare-oriented elements which duplicate other programs and which have been over emphasized in recent years in the Social Security program;
- Relating disability benefits more closely to a worker's work history and medical condition;

This article is adapted from testimony given before the House Ways and Means Subcommittee on Social Security.

• Reducing the opportunity for "windfall" benefits—that is, relatively high monthly benefits for persons who spend most of their working lifetime in non-covered employment and only a short time in covered work, especially as compared with low-wage earners who have spent a lifetime contributing to the system;

• Encouraging workers to stay on the job—at least until the traditional Social Security retirement age of 65;

• Lowering future *replacement rates* (that is, the initial benefit as compared with recent preretirement earnings) by moderating, for 6 years, the indexing of the initial benefit formula computation. This would be done in order to adjust for benefit over-liberalizations in the early 1970's which substantially exceeded increases needed to keep pace with changes in the economy.

I would like to emphasize that these reforms would have virtually no impact on the 36 million beneficiaries now on the rolls or on the several million persons now aged 62 or over and eligible to be on the rolls. For example, the proposal for reducing the amount payable at age 62 affects no one who will be 62 or over before next January.

The Administration's package of proposals would not only put Social Security back on sound financial ground, but also lessen, in the future, the taxes required to support the system.

Even under relatively "worst case" economic assumptions, we would be able to reduce the increase in the Social Security tax rate now scheduled for 1985, and to decrease Social Security tax rates for 1990.

This means that the young person with average earnings who enters the labor force next year would pay $33,600 less in Social Security taxes over his/her lifetime, a reduction of slightly more than 10 percent.

Employment

Computation Period:

The first proposal would change the benefit computation point from age 62 to 65. Under the present law, the period used to calculate the number of years on which average earnings for computing Social Security benefits are based ends when the worker reaches age 62. Under the proposal, the averaging period would be extended to the year in which the worker reaches age 65. There would be no change in the number of years of low earnings that can be disregarded under present law in calculating the average earnings.

The computation closing point was first lowered to age 62 for women in 1956 when reduced benefits were made available to women workers at age 62. When reduced benefits were made available to men in 1961, this change was not made. The 1972 amendments inappropriately provided the age-62 computation point for men, instead of conforming the computation closing age for

Comparison of Social Security Employee Taxes and Federal Income Taxes for Workers at Various Earning Levels in 1980.

Earning Level	Wages	Social Security Tax	Federal Income Tax*	
			Single	Married**
Low	6228	382	463	116†
Average	12455	764	1717	1148
Maximum	25700	1588	5061	4316

*Assumes no income other than wages, standard deductions, and one exemption for single case, two for married.
**Assumes spouse has no income and joint return is filed.
†Social Security tax equals Federal Income Tax.
SOURCE: U.S. Department of Health and Human Services

women to that for men. Restoring the basic period used in figuring a worker's earnings to age 65, rather than age 62, reinforces age 65 as the "normal" retirement age. To underscore the value of working at least to age 65, our proposal would include these three additional years in figuring the average earnings on which a worker's initial benefits are based.

Early Retirement:

The second proposal would increase the permanent reduction made in benefits for retirement at ages 62 through 64. Persons retiring at age 62 would get 55 percent of what they would get at age 65, rather than 80 percent as they now do. This is a reduction of 1¼ percent per month, as opposed to 5/9ths of 1 percent per month under present law. The same reduction that applies to the worker's benefit (1¼ percent per month) would also apply to the spouse's benefit; no change would be made in the reduction provision affecting widow's or widower's benefits.

Although this proposal has been criticized for the increase in the reduction for early retirement, it should be looked at in terms of the incentive for deferred retirement that it offers. For each additional year of continued work at ages 62-64, an additional 15 percent of the basic benefit will be payable. Indeed a worker retiring at age 63 and 8 months would receive 80% of what he would get at age 65. Also, of course, additional earnings during this period may increase the average earnings on which the worker's benefits are based.

Benefits for Children of Early Retirees:

Benefits would not be paid for the children of workers getting retirement benefits before age 65. However, children's benefits would remain payable as under current law when the worker reaches age 65.

Currently, children under 18, or under 22 if in school, and disabled adult children, can receive benefits if a parent is getting a retired worker's benefit. Elimination of benefits for the children of retired workers under age

65 would remove another incentive for people to retire and claim Social Security benefits before age 65.

Thus, under these proposals, early retirement under Social Security will be a less attractive option than it is today and there will be greater positive incentives for people to remain in the labor force until, at least, age 65.

The Earnings Test:

Another change—the phase-out of the earnings test for people aged 65 and older—would remove a disincentive for people to continue working beyond age 65. Under current law, if the earnings of a beneficiary aged 65 to 72 (age 70 in 1982) exceed an annual exempt amount ($5,500 in 1981 and $6,000 in 1982), Social Security benefits are reduced $1 for each $2 earnings above that amount. Under the proposal, the exempt amount for this group would be raised to $10,000 in 1983, $15,000 in 1984, and $20,000 in 1985. In 1986, the earnings test would be eliminated entirely for those aged 65 and over. There would be no change in the earnings test for those under age 65; as under present law the exempt amount for this group, now $4,080, would increase in the future as average wages increase.

The Administration's proposal to phase out the earnings test over a 3-year period for those aged 65 and over will remove a strong disincentive for this group to continue working. In effect, the present test operates as a 50-percent tax on earnings above the exempt amount, and such earnings are further reduced by Federal, State, and local income taxes, as well as the expenses connected with working . . .

Our senior citizens should not be penalized because they choose to remain in or reenter the work force, thereby continuing to contribute their valuable skills to our Nation's productive effort, while supplementing their Social Security benefits.

The proposal would increase Social Security costs by approximately $6.5 billion in the 1982 through 1986 period. However, there would be some increase in Social Security tax revenues as a result of additional people deciding to continue working after age 65. Moreover, there would also be an increase in Federal income tax revenue as a result of people continuing to work.

Elimination of windfall benefits

We would also eliminate "windfall" benefits for persons who have been in noncovered employment for most of their working lifetimes, but who acquire sufficient covered employment to qualify for Social Security benefits. Currently, it is possible for a person, such as a retired Federal employee who works in Social Security covered employment for only a few years, to receive dispropor-

tionately high Social Security benefits. Our proposal would use a different formula to compute benefits for persons with pensions from noncovered employment—so as to eliminate the heavy weighting in the current benefit formula, which is intended for long-term, low-wage workers. This would have the effect of removing the unintended advantage that Social Security now provides for persons who have substantial pensions from noncovered employment.

Disability insurance reforms

The Administration is proposing four changes in the disability-benefits area which are designed to restore the Social Security disability program to its original intent and scope by relating benefits more directly to work history and to medical condition.

• The first change relates to the Social Security definition of disability. Under current law, a worker may qualify for Social Security disability benefits based either on medical factors alone or on a combination of medical and nonmedical, vocational factors, such as age, education, and work experience. The great majority of people (about 75 percent) who are awarded Social Security disability benefits qualify based on medical factors alone. If both awards and denials are considered, the present procedures require an evaluation of vocational and other nonmedical factors in 50 percent of the cases; this type of determination is very subjective and makes it very difficult to reach consistent decisions in all cases.

The present use of vocational factors in making the determinations of disability goes far beyond the original intent of the Congress and introduces a degree of subjectivity that is undesirable in a national disability benefits system. We believe that the definition of disability should be returned to the original intent. The revised definition of disability would apply only to people becoming entitled to disability benefits after 1981.

• The next change relates to the disability-prognosis requirement. Again, under the original disability provisions, "permanent" disability was clearly intended by the phrase "of long continued or indefinite duration." The provision for a prognosis requirement of only 12 months was added in 1965. To return to the original intent and assure that disability benefits will not be awarded to individuals with temporary disabilities, we propose that a person's disability must have lasted, or be expected to last, 24 full months. This would restore the disability program to its original purpose. Temporary disability protection should, as was initially intended, be provided by other means such as sick-leave plans, private insurance, and State programs. This change would apply only to people becoming entitled to disability benefits after 1981.

• Under the third disability benefit proposal, the waiting period would be restored to the 6 months which it was when the program began. Presently, there is a 5-month waiting period after a person becomes disabled before he or she begins receiving Social Security disability benefits.

• The fourth change in the disability program involves the insured status requirements. Under current law, generally a worker may qualify for Social Security disability benefits if he or she has 20 quarters of coverage (about 5 years of work covered under Social Security) in the 40-quarter period (10 years) preceding disability. We are proposing that this requirement be changed so that a person need 30 quarters of coverage (about 7½ years of covered work) in the 40-quarter period in order to qualify. This proposal would be in addition to the budget proposal which would require that the worker have 6 quarters of coverage during the 13-quarter period preceding disability.

We are concerned that people are qualifying for disability benefits even though they have not demonstrated that they have a substantial recent attachment to the covered work force. Increasing the amount of work necessary to qualify for disability benefits is in line with the basic purpose of the program—to provide benefits only to people who have a strong and recent attachment to the workforce and who have suffered a loss of their livelihood because they have become disabled and unable to work.

Welfare reduction

Benefits for Children of Early Retirees:

I described earlier one proposal that is designed both to reduce excessive benefits and to help encourage people to remain in the labor force until at least age 65. This is the proposal not to pay benefits for the children of workers getting old age benefits until the worker has reached age 65.

Disability Family Maximum on Benefits to Retirement and Survivor cases:

The disability maximum family benefit would be extended to retirement and survivor cases. The 1980 disability amendments changed the maximum family benefit, so that Social Security benefits for the disabled worker's family would not exceed the lesser of 85 percent of the worker's average indexed earnings or 150 percent of the worker's benefit amount (but not less than 100 percent of the worker's benefit). This limitation is intended to assure that family benefits based on the worker's earnings will not exceed the worker's previous net take-home pay. Extending this maximum on family benefits to old-age and survivor cases would assure that

benefits for these cases would be more closely related to the worker's previous take-home pay and not excessive.

One additional proposal would have substantial long-range impact on the scope and cost of the Social Security program. This proposal woud phase in gradually over the next six years and would correct past over-expansions of general benefit levels by ultimately reducing replacement rates—the ratio of the initial benefit to the earnings immediately before retirement—for future beneficiaries by an average of about 10 percent. Thus for an average worker, his replacement rate would be reduced from 42 percent to 38 percent. Under present law, the 3-step benefit formula is adjusted for people newly eligible for benefits each year by increasing the bend points—the dollar amounts that determine the levels of average earnings to which the three benefit percentage factors apply—by 100 percent of the annual increase in average wages. Under the proposal, for each of the adjustments for new eligibles in the six years, 1982-1987, the annual adjustments would be based on 50 percent of the annual wage increase. By the end of this period, replacement rates for new cohorts of beneficiaries will be restored to the levels generally intended by the Congress through the 1950s and 1960s.

Fiscal-Year Benefit Increases:

We are proposing to shift the effective date for paying the automatic cost-of-living increases from July to October—the beginning of the fiscal years. The full amount of the 1982 increase would be paid, but there would be a 3-month deferral. Therefore, increases would occur each October. This change is the only one that will have some impact on current beneficiaries.

Coverage of Sick Pay:

We propose taxing and crediting under Social Security all sick pay made by an employer for the first 6 months of illness. Under present law, sick pay within this 6-month period is taxed and credited only if it is not made under a plan or system established by an employer. Some employers have complained about the difficulty and expense of keeping records of sick pay for as little as one hour at a time, so that the sick payments can be excluded from Social Security wage reports. Also, some employers do not understand current law and incorrectly report sick pay as wages—or, conversely, fail to report sick pay that is not paid under a plan or system. Sick pay made more than 6 months after the employee last worked for the employer would continue to be exempt from Social Security taxes.

Conclusion

Assuming the enactment of these reform proposals, and those included in the Administration's budget, we will have a Social Security system that is actuarially sound both in the short-range and over the long-range future. And we can say this without qualifiers concerning the state of the economy. This statement is true on the basis of "worst case" economic assumptions. The system is shown to be in even more favorable financial condition under the more realistic economic assumptions based on the Administration's Program for Economic Recovery.

Under these proposals, and assuming interfund borrowing authority, the combined Social Security trust funds will not fall below 17 percent of expenditures under the worst-case economic assumptions. The low point is 22 percent next year under the Administration's expected economic conditions. It will be possible to have a smaller Social Security tax increase in 1985 than that now scheduled and, in 1990, to actually decrease Social Security taxes below the current level, even under the worst-case economic assumptions.

The present tax rate for employers and employees of 6.65 percent each is scheduled to go to 7.05 percent in 1985 and 7.65 percent in 1990. If these proposals are enacted, the 1985 tax rate could be 6.95 percent and the 1990 tax rate could be 6.45 percent, even under worst-case assumptions. If the economy improves at a more rapid rate, as we anticipate it will under the President's Program for Economic Recovery, the tax rates could be further reduced.

The Administration's proposals deserve to be given serious and objective consideration. They are reasonable and practical solutions for an extremely difficult problem. They would not be the first proposals adopted by Congress which reduced the Social Security program. In 1977, and again in 1980, the Congress made changes in the Social Security program to reduce and control the

level of Social Security benefits—in 1977 by stabilizing the overall replacement rates at a lower level than currently payable, and in 1980 by putting a ceiling on the amount of benefits payable to the family of a worker drawing disability benefits. But these changes, difficult as they were, did not solve the problem. Nor did the large increase in taxes enacted in 1977 solve the problem.

If strong actions are not taken, the system faces financial insolvency, and the economic security of the 36 million people who receive Social Security benefits will be threatened. Continuation of the status quo cannot guarantee the future economic-security protection of those who now pay Social Security taxes, and are counting on receiving benefits in the future. Under the Administration's proposals, financial security will be assured, and future benefits will be paid, even under the worst-case economic assumptions.

We recognize that there are other possible ways to deal with the financial problems in the Social Security system and we are willing to work with the Congress to try to develop mutually agreeable solutions to the Social Security financing crisis.

The Administration's proposals avoid the need to increase taxes or to resort to general revenues; in fact we propose tax reductions. Our proposals eliminate work disincentive of the earnings test, encourage longer work lives, reduce the over emphasis on the social adequacy or welfare aspect of Social Security, restore the integrity of the disability program, and strengthen the basic social insurance character of the program. We believe that these are reasonable objectives and criteria for any set of proposals and offer them as a starting point for the bipartisan effort to restore the confidence of the people in their Social Security system.

Pending Proposals for Social Security Reform

Virtually everyone involved in the Social Security debate agrees that something must be done to keep the system solvent. The disagreement arises as to what that something is.

The Reagan administration has proposed a package of major reforms in Social Security legislation. But the 97th Congress has other options: Rep. J. J. Pickle (D.-Tex.), Chairman of the Ways and Means Subcommittee on Social Security, and Sen. Lawton Chiles (D.-Fla.) have both introduced their own proposals.

None of the three recommends raising the payroll taxes that now go into the three trust funds—Old Age and Survivors (OASI), Disability (DI), and Medicare Hospital (HI). In fact, both the administration and Chiles proposals would reduce payroll taxes.

To balance the books, the three plans include a variety of cost-saving benefit reductions and eligibility changes, and provisions for general revenue infusions to substitute for higher payroll taxes. Their similarities and differences are outlined below.

A major feature of the administration's package is a proposal to reduce benefit levels to early retirement.

Under current law, those who elect to retire at 62 receive 80 per cent of the benefits to which they would be entitled at 65. The administration proposed to reduce these early retirement benefits to 55 per cent at age 62.

The Pickle bill contains a similar provision, proposing to reduce benefits at age 62 to 64 per cent.

The intended effect of reducing early retirement benefits is to keep potential retirees in the labor force—and off Social Security rolls—longer, so they cost less and pay more in payroll taxes.

But retirement could also be delayed by raising the retirement age from 65 to 68. Pickle and Chiles favor this; the administration opposes it.

Under both the Pickle and Chiles bills, the retirement age would be raised gradually. Pickle would phase this provision in from 1990 to 1999; Chiles from 2000 to 2012.

The administration "will stand by the traditional retirement age of 65; we will not raise it."

Still other measures have been proposed to create greater work incentives for older workers. Under current law, a Social Security beneficiary loses 50 cents in benefits for each dollar of earnings—a marginal "tax" rate of 50 per cent—above $5,500.

The administration plan would phase out this "earnings test" by raising the amount successively starting in 1983, and eliminating it entirely in 1986.

The Chiles bill includes a similar provision, eliminating the earnings test for those over 65 starting in 1986, with the age rising gradually to 68 by 2012. Chiles also proposes eliminating payroll taxes on workers over 65, raising the tax exemption in step with the retirement age. Chiles also wants to eliminate mandatory retirement at age 70.

The administration is also proposing to "reduce the welfare-oriented elements which duplicate other programs and which have been introduced over the years into the social security system," and "restrain the growth of non-retirement portions of the program which are out of control."

These changes would eliminate "windfall" benefits for workers who enter Social Security covered employment late in their work histories, then retire collecting a pension from non-covered employment (for example, Civil Service) plus, Social Security.

The eligibility requirements for disability benefits would be tightened under the administration proposal, requiring a longer (2 year) prognosis of disability, and defining disability in purely medical terms, rather than considering age, education and work experience as determinants. The administration also proposes requiring a longer period of "recent work" before granting disability retirement.

Current law provides that children of retirees can receive benefits if they are under 18, or under 22 if in school. The administration proposes eliminating these benefits in early retirement cases. Chiles would like to do away with them completely over a four year period, and Pickle over a six year period.

Both the Chiles bill and the administration proposal would eliminate the "minimum benefit" for retirees, which was originally conceived as a form of income support for the elderly poor. The current minimum is $122 at age 65; $97.50 at 62.

The administration also wants to pare down the benefit formula itself, which determines retirement benefits on the basis of earnings histories. According to the Congressional Research Service, "the age-65 retiree with average steady earnings over his career could expect to receive equal to 38 per cent of his earnings in his final year of work, rather than 42 per cent," if this proposal is adopted.

The Pickle and Chiles bills seek to ease Social Security's financial problem through general revenue financing.

The Pickle bill proposes permanently allocating half of the payroll tax revenues that currently finance Medicare Hospital Insurance to OASDI, with an equivalent reimbursement to the HI fund from general revenues.

The Chiles bill would phase in general revenues for HI—50 per cent now, 70 per cent in 1983 and thereafter—and use the revenue surplus to provide a 13 per cent reduction in payroll taxes over the next 10 years.

Both bills would allow the nearly bankrupt OASI fund to borrow from the more solvent HI and DI funds. With general revenue infusions to the HI fund, the interfund borrowing provisions of both the Pickle and Chiles bills could act as a pipeline for general revenues to flow into the retirement fund.

The administration opposes general revenue financing, which it characterized as "not a valid, or even honest, solution."

How to Save Social Security

A. F. Ehrbar

Last spring, when Washington was carrying on its brief flirtation with a balanced budget, some people in the Carter Administration and on Capitol Hill actually were talking out loud about cutting Social Security benefits. Specifically, they proposed holding the automatic cost-of-living raise that beneficiaries got on July 3 to something less than the 14.3% increase in the consumer price index. Would-be cost cutters in the Office of Management and Budget and the Congressional Budget Office figured it would be fair to trim $4.7 billion from the scheduled $16.8-billion increase because the C.P.I. has been overstating inflation recently.

Hardly anyone took the proposal seriously, of course. The survival instinct still stops politicians from reducing transfer payments to 31 million voters in an election year. Yet the fact that responsible officials mentioned the proposal at all suggests that an across-the-board cut in Social Security benefits may no longer be politically unthinkable. Even many liberals agree that benefits must be trimmed—especially those promised to workers now in their 30s or younger.

The cost of carrying the aged and disabled in the style we have become accustomed to promising them may ultimately be more than workers are willing to pay. If no changes are made in the Social Security system, the tax rate needed to finance benefits 50 years from now will be double or possibly even triple the current rate, which will raise $150 billion or so this year. Happily, though, a couple of comparatively modest changes—raising the retirement age in the next century and revising the benefit formula—could avert such horrific costs, provided the changes are made soon.

Next year alone, the Social Security tax rate jumps from 6.13% to 6.65%—for a combined employer-employee rate of 13.3%—and the taxable wage base scoots up from $25,900 to $29,700. The new rate and wage base work out to a maximum tax per employee of $1,975, nearly $400 more than this year's maximum. Adding in the employer-paid portion, which most economists agree is passed back to employees as lower wages, high-income workers will pay $3,950 in Social Security taxes next year.

A congressional flip-flop

Onerous as the 1981 tax hike may be, it is only the fourth of eight increases mandated by Congress in 1977. By 1990 the combined employer-employee tax rate will climb another two percentage points to 15.3%, and after next year the wage base will rise at the same pace as average wages. If wages increase at a real rate of 1.5% through the Eighties, high-income workers in 1990 will pay Social Security taxes of $5,300—in 1981 dollars.

Congress began scrounging around for ways to roll back those increases just a month after it voted for them. Chairman Al Ullman of the House Ways and Means Committee, for instance, has been touting a value-added tax as a replacement for part of the payroll levy, and Senator William Roth Jr., cosponsor of the Kemp-Roth tax-cut bill, suggested using some of the tax on "windfall" oil profits to eliminate the 1981 increase. Congress may still substitute a less visible tax for part of the Social Security increases, but it's unlikely to reduce total tax collections.

In fact, Congress may well raise taxes even higher. The package of tax increases legislated in 1977 was supposed to put Social Security on a solid footing, but it hasn't kept the system out of the red. Rapid inflation has ballooned benefits while high unemployment and meager real wage gains have depressed revenues. As a result, the Social Security Administration has been depleting the trust funds that are its working capital.

The Old Age and Survivors Insurance trust fund will be exhausted by late next year or early 1982. The administrators can continue paying benefits after that if Congress allows them to borrow excess reserves from the disability- and hospital-insurance trust funds. But there is a good chance that the combined funds won't be adequate to finance benefits by early 1984.

Every year, Social Security actuaries make three projections of future costs and revenues—optimistic, intermediate, and pessimistic. In this year's intermediate projection, which assumes the current recession will be mild and short, the combined trust funds squeak through 1984 with a small

---

Research Associate: Matthew Nemerson

---

safety margin and then rebuild to a comfortable level. But many, including some liberal congressional aides who ordinarily play down Social Security problems, say the intermediate projection is too optimistic. In the pessimistic projection the system goes broke in January 1984, and stays broke.

When baby-boomers retire

The immediate financial crunch is a mere inconvenience compared to the one that's coming when the baby-boom generation starts retiring 30 years from now. As the multitudes born in the philoprogenitive years following World War II leave the labor force after 2010, the retired population will mushroom. Meanwhile, the population of revenue-producing workers will stagnate because the baby boom was followed by the comparatively barren Sixties and Seventies. By 2030, when the last of the boomers will be over 65, the combined payroll tax rate needed to finance benefits probably will be at least 25% of taxable payroll, and could be as high as 36%.

Those estimates are derived from the Social Security Administration's intermediate and pessimistic projections (few rational adults heed the optimistic one). Most of the striking difference between the two estimates reflects different assumptions about future fertility and mortality rates. In the pessimistic estimate, the fertility rate continues to fall, as it has in all industrialized countries for the last 150 years, and life expectancy improves at a rapid pace. Those factors combine to lift the number of beneficiaries per 100 workers from 31 today to 68 in 2030 and 84 in 2050 (the number of persons aged 20 to 64 actually declines after 2010). The intermediate estimate assumes a slower gain in life expectancy and an increase in the fertility rate; the number of beneficiaries per 100 workers reaches 52 in 2030 and remains fairly constant after that.

As with the shorter forecasts, many pension experts believe the intermediate projections are too optimistic. One is Thomas Woodruff, executive director of the President's Commission on Pension Policy, a group studying the effects that the baby boom will have on all retirement systems. Woodruff believes the pessimistic projection is more realistic, though the President's Commission is using the intermediate one so its forecasts will be comparable to those of other researchers.

The problem of paying for the retirement of the baby-boom generation is more urgent than it might appear. The only way to avoid sky-high payroll tax rates is to reduce promised benefits, and that should be done soon if it is to be done at all. Cutting benefits may be politically impossible if we wait until the Nineties, when the oldest of the postwar generation will be only ten or 15 years away from collecting them. Moreover, it's questionable whether society should alter long-standing commitments so soon before they come due. Says William Agee, chairman of Bendix Corp. and one of the few businessmen who has made a close study of Social Security: "Procrastinating until the burden forces the breaching of promises will only make the problem worse. Young and old will be pitted against one

another in a fearful battle over the remains of a shrinking economy."

Two simple changes would eliminate the need for any payroll tax increases beyond the level now set for 1990. One is to raise the retirement age, starting in the year 2000, from 65 to 68. A new study by four economists at the National Bureau of Economic Research shows that such a change would eliminate the long-term deficit in the Old Age and Survivors portion of Social Security. Using the Social Security Administration's intermediate projection, the economists calculated that the present value of the old-age deficit is about $885 billion. That is, the old-age benefits that will be paid over the next 75 years—discounted to the present at a 3% real interest rate—are $885 billion more than the old-age portion of the payroll taxes that will be collected.

The total deficit, including the hospital portion of Medicare and disability benefits, is much larger. Stanford economist Michael J. Boskin, who headed the National Bureau study team, figures that the hospital and disability deficits come to 50% to 70% of the old-age deficit. That puts the present value of the total Social Security deficit at $1.3 trillion to $1.5 trillion—more than double the national debt.

When Boskin's team calculated the effect of raising the retirement age to 68, they came up with a $200-billion surplus in the old-age portion of the system. Says Boskin, a 34-year-old baby-boomer who advocates later retirement: "Altering the length of retirement by a single year, by changing either the retirement age or life expectancy, raises or lowers the Social Security deficit by about $350 billion."

A case for later retirement

While raising the retirement age obviously amounts to a benefit cut, it wouldn't mean a large reduction in the length of retirement. Robert Myers, a former chief actuary of Social Security and another proponent of later retirement, estimates that a man 68.9 years old in the year 2000 will have the same life expectancy a 65-year-old had when the Social Security Act was passed in 1935; for women, life expectancy at 72.5 will be the same as it was at age 65 in 1935.

Boskin and Myers have a lot of support in their call for a later retirement age. The National Commission on Social Security, set up by Congress to evaluate possible changes in the system, has tentatively endorsed a plan to raise the eligibility age to 68 over a 12-year period starting in 2000. The President's Commission has recommended that Congress consider raising the age, and the last two Social Security Advisory Councils have supported the idea. The councils are groups that assess the state of the system every four years.

Most of the opposition to later retirement comes from Social Security expansionists like former Commissioner Robert Ball, old-age lobbyists like the American Association of Retired Persons, and Congressmen. In 1977, Barber Conable, the ranking Republican on the Ways and Means Committee, proposed a plan similar to the one endorsed by the National Commission. Conable couldn't even muster the support of the Republicans on the committee, but he did draw 3,000 letters from enraged Gray Panthers.

Price indexing vs. wage indexing

The other change that would bring large savings is an adjustment in the benefit formula that Congress adopted in 1977. That formula ties initial benefit levels to average wages. That is, future retirees will be entitled to benefits that rise by the same amount as average wages until a person is 60; after that, an individual's benefits are tied to the C.P.I. Since wages rise faster than prices over the long run, benefits paid to future retirees will be higher than the present ones, even in constant dollars. The idea behind the formula, called "wage indexing," is to assure that pensions replace a constant percentage of pre-retirement income.

An alternative is to index initial benefits to prices instead of wages. Under that formula Social Security would gradually replace a smaller percentage of pre-retirement income, but it would provide future retirees with at least as much purchasing power as persons retiring this year. In fact, the formula for determining initial benefits would cause them to continue to rise in real terms, though at a slower rate. In 1977, a congressional consulting panel headed by Harvard economist William C. Hsaio estimated that a worker with average earnings who retires in 2050 would get a pension with a real value of triple the current benefit under wage indexing and double the present benefit under price indexing. Hsaio, who favors price indexing, figures it would save roughly the same amount as raising the retirement age.

In addition to reducing costs, price indexing would boost private savings and economic growth. Social Security cuts into savings by diminishing the need to provide for retirement—though the magnitude of the effect is a matter of hot dispute. Studies by Martin Feldstein, president of the National Bureau of Economic Research and another price-indexing proponent, indicate that Social Security may reduce private savings by as much as 38%.

If we changed the benefit formula and raised the retirement age, the combined cost savings would wipe out the entire long-term Social Security deficit and leave room for a payroll tax cut sometime after the year 2000. The lower costs would also give Congress the flexibility it will need to correct some of the system's deficiencies, such as the inequitable treatment of working wives.

Billion-dollar nibbles

Under current law a couple gets 150% of the husband's basic pension while both are alive, and the survivor gets 100% after one of the two dies. That benefit usually is greater than what working wives can collect on their own earnings (they can't take both), so most of them get nothing in return for the payroll taxes they pay. Since Congress isn't likely to repeal the 50% bonus for housewives, correcting the mistreatment of working wives will be expensive. And with a majority of wives now in the labor force, voters are bound to demand some such change.

Unfortunately, Congress has no similarly simple options for dealing with Social Security's short-term financial troubles. Slashing benefits to current retirees still is politically unthinkable; it also would be morally indefensible to cut payments to persons who depend on Social Security just to get by. However, a handful of unnecessary benefits could be eliminated without harming the truly needy. The cuts would be puny relative to total costs, but just nibbling at Social Security can save several billion dollars a year.

One potential cut is the payment to survivors between 18 and 21 years old who are full-time students. The benefit was added in 1965, before Congress created the panoply of college-assistance programs available now. Another benefit that could go is the payment to surviving spouses with 16- and 17-year-old children. The reasoning behind the benefit is that single parents aren't able to work, but that obviously isn't the case when children reach 16. A third prospective cut is the $255 lump-sum death benefit, originally meant to cover burial costs.

The benefit most deserving of elimination is the so-called minimum payment, intended to help persons whose covered earnings were too low to qualify for even a subsistence-level pension. The prime beneficiaries now are federal employees. Though exempt from Social Security taxes, many moonlight in order to qualify for the minimum pension. The Congressional Budget Office estimates that those four cuts, all of which were proposed by President Carter last year, would save $3.2 billion a year by fiscal 1985.

Penalizing the industrious

Two other desirable reforms would actually entail higher costs, but would make the system fairer. One is to get rid of the earnings test for retirees between 65 and 72. They now lose 50 cents in benefits for every dollar they earn over $5,000. The provision, which exacts a large penalty from poor retirees who want to supplement their benefits, doesn't affect those with substantial capital income or private pensions. In effect, the system applies a means test to beneficiaries who work but not to those who are idle.

Eliminating the earnings test for people 65 and over would be surprisingly cheap. Last year the Social Security Administration saved only $2.1 billion by reducing the benefits of workers who earned too much. The full cost wouldn't even be that high because many retirees would work more—and so pay more Social Security and income taxes—if they didn't have to sacrifice benefits.

The second reform, and the most controversial of all possible changes, is to reverse the income-tax treatment of Social Security—tax the benefits and exempt the payroll taxes. The common view, of course, is that benefits should be tax-exempt because retirees paid for them with after-tax dollars. In fact, Social Security is a welfare system that dispenses benefits on the basis of past earnings instead of need, with proportionately larger payments going to low earners. The Internal Revenue Service (not Congress) originally exempted the benefits from income taxes in 1940 precisely because they were welfare payments. Moreover, the taxes a worker pays have no direct relation to the benefits he receives; taxes are determined by the cost of paying benefits to others during the years he works.

The case for taxing Social Security benefits rests on the enormous wealth transfers the system effects—not just from high earners to low earners, but also from one age group to another. One estimate of the intergenerational transfers was calculated by Boskin and his associates. They defined a transfer as the difference between the pension benefits a person will receive and what he could have earned by investing the old-age portion of his taxes (including the part paid by the employer) in an annuity with a 3% real return. They found that persons born before 1913 who survived to collect benefits will, on average, receive net transfers of nearly $60,000 in 1980 dollars. In other words, persons born before 1913 "paid for" only 14% of the benefits they will collect. The other 86% is a windfall. In contrast, persons born between 1943 and 1952 will pay $374 more in taxes than they'll collect in retirement benefits, and persons born after 1952 will suffer successively larger losses.

A subsidy for high earners

Some wealth transfer from the richer working-age generation to the poorer retired generation is justifiable. But Social Security makes glaringly inequitable transfers from poor young workers to rich retirees. As Boskin says, "It makes little sense for current unskilled workers to surrender income to subsidize retired doctors and lawyers beyond fair returns on the taxes they paid."

Reversing the tax treatment would help redress that imbalance. Exempting young workers from income taxes on their "contributions" would reduce their total Social Security losses somewhat because the value of the tax savings would be greater than the taxes they would eventually pay on benefits. The deduction would be worth more to high-income individuals in higher tax brackets, but they ultimately would pay higher taxes on benefits; on balance, over their lifetimes, the change probably wouldn't have much effect on the wealth transfers among workers the same age.

The change would be fair to retirees as long as they were taxed only on benefits over and above the payroll taxes they paid into the system—a tax treatment identical with that now given to employee thrift plans, where workers invest after-tax dollars and pay taxes only on the earnings. Including benefits in taxable income wouldn't penalize the elderly poor; some 60% of Social Security recipients would pay no taxes at all.

A case can be made that an elderly couple with $15,000 of income from Social Security and a private pension deserves preferential tax treatment. But a stronger case can be made for a worker with a wife and two or three children and the same income. His Social Security payroll deduction this year will be $919.50, on which he'll pay another $130 or more of income taxes.

In 1978, the change would have cost $5.4 billion in lost income-tax revenues. Mickey D. Levy of the American Enterprise Institute made a study of the effects of various tax treatments of Social Security and found that exempting payroll taxes would have reduced income-tax revenues by $9.4 billion in 1978. Including benefits (in excess of payroll taxes paid) in the recipients' taxable income would have increased revenues by $4 billion, and taxing all benefits would have boosted revenues $6.9 billion.

A passion for camouflaging costs

The political history of Social Security gives little reason for optimism about any of these reforms, with the possible exception of eliminating the earnings test. Congress has frequently boosted benefits over the years, comfortable in the knowledge that the full bill for its vote-getting largess would come due only in the distant future. In the process, Social Security has evolved from a reasonably modest program to keep the elderly out of extreme poverty into a full-blown federal pension system.

Congressmen frequently talk of reforming the system, especially now that some of the formerly distant costs are driving up the tax rate. But the talk focuses more on camouflaging costs than on reducing them. Says Jake Pickle, chairman of the Ways and Means subcommittee on Social Security: "We've had 120 bills to freeze the taxes, but nobody's talking about cutting those benefits. If somebody does say he's going to cut benefits, we may want to freeze him."

The forces working against change are formidable. Cutting current benefits would anger the elderly, more of whom vote than any other age group, yet it wouldn't save enough to permit a sizable tax cut. Cutting future benefits is politically expensive because the elderly, ever watchful, see any reduction as a precedent that threatens their own benefits.

"This craven collective"

Barber Conable, weary and bent from previous battles, is despondent about the prospects for heading off the long-term crisis. "We should be able to design a system based on the facts of the baby boom," he says. "But it's going to take a Congress that is politically accountable, and this Congress is not. This craven collective will break and run as soon as they get 300 letters on a subject."

Still, under pressure from a public indignant over big increases in an extremely visible tax, Congress and the White House may be starting to move away from the traditional politics of Social Security. President Carter's proposal to cut certain benefits last year was a remarkable event. Though Congress rejected the cuts out of hand, a few Democrats on Ways and Means are starting to talk as though some reductions might really be possible at last. Pickle, for one, has been saying that a later retirement age might be possible. And Jim Jones of Oklahoma, an influential young member of the committee hopes to engineer a major overhaul of the system next year.

Jones believes that public outrage over next January's payroll tax increase, combined with the looming 1984 deficiency in the trust funds and the bad news about the long-term deficit that will be coming out in the final reports of the National Commission and the President's Commission, will force Congress to act. "The average Congressman has put Social Security out of his mind," Jones says. "But the events of history are converging, and the public will demand that we do something." Jones's assessment that the nation at last has an opportunity to get control of the largest "uncontrollable" in the budget seems correct, but the opportunity is sure to dwindle if Congress delays for long.

A Nightmarish Tax Burden

The Social Security tax increases that have had Americans screaming lately are nothing compared with what's coming when the baby boom starts retiring around 2010. This year the combined Social Security tax rate—including both the employer's and employee's "contributions"—is 12.26% of taxable payroll. Under present law, the levy will rise to 15.3% in 1990. The rates for 2010, 2030, and 2050 were derived from Social Security Administration estimates of the cost of benefits stated as a percentage of the taxable payroll under three sets of assumptions —optimistic, intermediate, and pessimistic. The "intermediate" tax rates in the projections are 16.6% in 2010, 25.4% in 2030, and 25.0% in 2050. According to the "pessimistic" projection, the combined Social Security tax will come to an incredible 21.4%, 36.3%, and 45.3% in those three years. Most pension experts think the intermediate tax rates are about the lowest Americans can reasonably hope for unless benefits are reduced.

Where the Windfalls Fall

Year of Birth	Net Transfer Received
Before 1913	$59,445
1913–22	$41,126
1923–32	$31,894
1933–42	$18,242
1943–1952	($375)
After 1952	"Large, negative"

The pay-as-you-go method of financing Social Security has produced handsome windfalls for people collecting benefits now, but it will make net losers of the baby-boom generation. The table shows the average per-family windfall, or net transfer, for various age groups. Economist Michael Boskin and associates, who developed these numbers, define a transfer as the difference between the benefits a person will collect, provided he lives past 65, and what he could have received by investing in an annuity with a 3% real rate of return. The figures are in 1980 dollars, with future amounts discounted to the present at the 3% real rate.

An Idea Whose Time Has Passed

During the next year or two in Washington, a lot of sound and fury is likely to burst forth over proposals to change the way Social Security benefits are kept even with inflation. At present, benefits are indexed to the consumer price index, which critics at the Office of Management and Budget and the Congressional Budget Office charge has overstated inflation. A better index, some say, is the personal consumption expenditures component of the G.N.P. deflator—or P.C.E. If benefits had been tied to that index for the last five years, Social Security would cost $11 billion less in fiscal 1981.

The problem with the C.P.I. is that it counts higher mortgage interest rates as higher living costs. But mortgage rates merely reflect anticipated inflation, which lifts house values by more than enough to offset the higher interest costs. In addition, the C.P.I. includes house prices, even though an increase in the price of houses constitutes a higher cost only for those who don't already own one. The P.C.E. avoids those pitfalls by treating home ownership as an investment; it defines the cost as the rental income owners forgo by living in a house themselves.

Even so, people who advocate switching indexes now are beating the wrong end of a dead horse. Most of the recent difference between the two indexes was caused by rising mortgage rates. Now that mortgage rates are falling, the C.P.I. will understate inflation. By switching to the P.C.E. at this point, the nation would lock in benefits at an artificially high level and miss out on the coming correction.

Organ Donor Recruitment

Need for Organ Donors

The quality of life of patients with end-stage renal disease on a hemodialysis regimen has improved steadily in recent years, and the incidence of renal transplantation procedures has been constant. The latter has been both because the quality of life after transplantation remains imperfect and donor organs are in short supply. Nevertheless, renal transplantation frees the patient from his dialysis apparatus and is less costly than long-term hemodialysis: the extra cost of surgery is offset by dialysis savings within 18 months after transplantation. It is likely that new improvements in the control of the rejection phenomenon during the next few years will further enhance the desirability of this option for at least half of those approximately 50,000 Americans now undergoing long-term hemodialysis.

The imminent acceptance of cardiac transplantation as a reimbursable procedure will further increase the demand for brain-death donors. The major limiting factor in the number of renal transplants now done (about 3,000 in 1979) and the principal deterrent to more widespread progress in cardiac transplantation has been the shortage of organs. Each transplant program in the country

From the Council on Scientific Affairs, American Medical Association, Chicago.

Reprint requests to Council on Scientific Affairs, American Medical Association, 535 N Dearborn St, Chicago, IL 60610 (Richard J. Jones, MD).

has a long list of end-stage renal disease patients awaiting a suitable kidney. To address these problems until truly acceptable artificial organs can be manufactured, it becomes imperative to make available from acceptable donors a larger supply of organs.

Organs removed from a cadaver after breathing and heart action have ceased have sustained serious ischemic injury and, except for cornea, bone, and skin, are rarely suitable for transplantation. Death from brain injury, tumor, or infarction may permit hours or days of normal circulation, especially if controlled mechanical ventilation is maintained, which will allow preservation of heart and kidney until they can be removed, cooled, and properly preserved for transplantation. There are more than enough such deaths in the United States (estimate, 20,000) to provide a surfeit of organs, if there were a satisfactory method of bringing all such cadavers into the pool of donors. Now that there is a cadaver graft survival of transplanted hearts or kidneys of 50% to 70% and kidney host survival of up to 90% for two years, it has become important that our society find ways to improve donor recruitment.

Donor Recruitment

The Uniform Anatomical Gift Act has been adopted by all 50 states and allows the donor's wishes to be binding after his death. The legal instrument is the wallet-sized donor card,

which has been made available through many organizations, including the American Medical Association, and which has been placed on the back of vehicle driver's licenses in 17 states. In 1968, a Gallup poll indicated that 70% of Americans were willing to donate organs for transplantation at the time of their death. A subsequent poll of physicians in 1969 suggested that more than 70% supported the concept of routine organ salvage from cadavers. In contrast to these poll findings, a recent survey in the state of Maryland, where the donor card is on the driver's license, found that only 1.5% elected to sign the donor contract.

Unless there has been a signed donor card of which the family is actively aware, obtaining family consent may be difficult—even in an altruistic society. The physician's failure to save the patient, his fancied exposure to legal liability, the family's grief, the often acute nature of brain injury, and any complexity in obtaining the cooperation of a transplant team all militate against considering the brain-death patient as a potential donor. This may be true even if the individual was generous and thoughtful enough to sign the consent form on his vehicle driver's license. It is a rare physician who will overcome these considerations and initiate a discussion with the family to request its consent in the absence of a donor card. It is reasonable to hope that this will change, as the population with successfully transplanted organs increases and contributes to a promotion of the concept. However, something more needs to be done if a meaningful increase in donors is to be seen in the near future.

Presumed Consent

It has been suggested that donor recruitment might be enhanced by providing for routine salvage of cadaver organs except when there has been prior objection by the decedent or current objection by the nearest of kin. There was an earlier suggestion that a carefully drawn statute could be made acceptable to a majority of people in the United States and could refer to the experience in other countries.[1] However, the experience needs to be carefully assessed.

A questionnaire mailed to renal transplant programs in 40 countries brought responses fom 28. Thirteen countries used presumed consent as a basis for removing organs for transplantation, although seven employed donor cards along with presumed consent. Thirteen other countries required a donor card or family consent, but permitted a hospital official or coroner to give consent in the absence of a donor card when the nearest of kin could not be found. The European Committee on Legal Cooperation of the Council of Europe has favored presumed consent and European countries are expected to move further in this direction. However, it is by no means certain that national acceptance of this presumption would correct the organ shortage.

Even though nations with presumed consent statutes have not dramatically reduced their need for organs, all still have continuing waiting lists for renal transplantation. It may be relevant to note that most English-speaking countries do not have such statutes. Even when consent may be presumed, or at least freely given, several hurdles to efficient donor recruitment remain.

One additional program that might encourage more people, if not the full 70% who agree to the idea in the abstract, to sign an organ donor card would be a requirement that every adult younger than 65 years respond to the donor card provision on his vehicle license by either accepting or rejecting that responsibility.

While presumed consent laws might promote public awareness and enhance the likelihood of organ salvage after a prospective donor has been identified, they do nothing to aid physicians and nurses in that identification. Currently, most organ retrieval is limited to those hospitals with active transplant programs where there exists a high level of awareness to the need and ready access to an organ recovery team. The recruitment of donors in hospitals remote from such centers has been difficult whether consent is direct or presumed.

Hospital Surveillance System

A group of physicians at the Centers for Disease Control, Atlanta, that has studied cadaver donor problems has concentrated on one method for encouraging greater recruitment of brain-death patients for cadaver donors.[2] They organized a recruitment network that related the transplant team to certain hospital areas, such as the intensive care unit and the emergency room, through a transplant nurse-coordinator who served as an intermediary between the attending staff of the hospital and the organ recovery team. This individual alerted the attending physician to the possibility and, only after he had declared the patient dead and given his permission, discussed the prospect of organ donation with the family. In the event that consent was given, the transplant team was contacted and arrangements for organ salvage made by the coordinator.

Beginning in 1976, thirty-four Georgia hospitals instituted such active donor-surveillance procedures for a total of 900 hospital-months of effort, in collaboration with the two transplant programs in the state. Criteria for donor selection were established at each hospital. These included the donor's age, the circumstances of death, the absence of infection, the absence of malignancy, the general health prior to admission, and the renal status. Each hospital was studied to determine which service units were likely to yield the most potential donors. Specific sys-

tem programs were established in each hospital for professional education, active surveillance by a transplant coordinator, continuous medical record surveillance, and evaluation of the organ retrieval process efficiency. It was estimated that one nurse or physician's assistant could serve as transplant coordinator for five to eight hospitals, or 3,000 to 5,000 deaths in a year.

In a preparative phase of chart review for the 37 hospitals of Georgia, it was found that 229 potential donors could be identified out of 12,531 deaths or 1.8% of in-hospital deaths. A potential donor was generally a white male, between 5 and 55 years of age, who died of CNS trauma, hemorrhage, or tumor in a critical care unit within three days of admission to an acute-care hospital that had more than 350 deaths per year. Only ten kidneys were retrieved in this year.

During the 2½-year study period, 555 potential donors were identified among 23,846 deaths. Of these 82, or 15%, became actual donors. During each of the last two years of the prospective effort, 88 and 90 kidneys, respectively, were obtained. Thus, through this mechanism the yield of actual donors was enhanced about ninefold. Perhaps more important is the fact that an ongoing analysis of factors involved in organ donation at 34 hospitals in Georgia is continuing and may hope to provide further increments in success at retrieving acceptable organs.

The Georgia effort suggests that this plan, which can be used by any group of motivated physicians, is capable of substantially increasing the recruitment of organ donors. It has worked in other locations where active transplant teams have attempted similar organization of the effort. However, the Georgia program has documented dramatically how much more success can be achieved.

Conclusion

It is apparent that the number of donors contributing to transplant surgery, especially in the areas of cardiac and renal transplantation, needs to be greatly increased if transplant surgery is to realize its full potential. This issue will become even more critical when cardiac transplantation becomes more generally reimbursable and greater control is gained over the rejection phenomenon (events that are both likely to occur in the near future). Continued efforts to inform the medical community and the general public about transplantation and the need for identification of potential donors must be pursued. In addition, society at large must recognize the importance of extending the voluntary gift act through a greater willingness to consider one's own death and the potential gift he may, thereby, make to the life of another. Social and ethical discussions to bring

a greater awareness of this possibility should be pursued at all levels of society.

Until the possibility of organ donation becomes a routine consideration at every hospital death, the Council recommends that the AMA take the following steps: (1) continue to urge the signing of donor cards by the enlightened citizens of the land; (2) continue to teach physicians through continuing medical education courses and the lay public through health education programs about transplantation issues in general and the importance of organ donation in particular; (3) encourage state govern-

ments to attempt pilot studies on promotional efforts that stimulate each adult to respond "yes" or "no" to the option of signing a donor card; and (4) encourage and lend moral support to the development of an active surveillance system based on an organ donor coordinator as employed in the Georgia program.

References

1. Stuart FP, Veith FJ, Crawford RE: Brain death laws and patterns of consent to remove organs for transplantation from cadavers in the United States and 28 other countries. *Transplantation* 1981;31:238-244.

2. Bart KJ, Macon EJ, Humphries AL, et al: Increasing the supply of cadaveric kidneys for transplantation. *N Engl J Med*, to be published.

Anatomical Gifts

Facts: There always have been some bodies available for medical science purposes. Previously most of them were made available through public channels—bodies unclaimed for funeralization/disposition. Public welfare funds and other allowances (Social Security and Veterans allowances) reduced the supply as survivors claimed the body for a then termed "Christian funeral and burial." The balance of the bodies available were donated with the next of kin having the right to negate the gift under some circumstances and medical institutions not accepting a body where there was a likelihood of objection by a next of kin.

In 1968 a Uniform Anatomical Gift Act was recommended by the National Conference of Commissioners on Uniform State Laws. Within a couple of years every state had enacted this law in one form or another. Section 7 of the Uniform Act "Rights and Duties at Death," applicable in most states says:

"(a) The donee may accept or reject the gift. If the donee accepts a gift of the entire body, he may, subject to the terms of the gift, authorize embalming and the use of the body in funeral services. If the gift is of a part of the body, the donee, upon the death of the donor and prior to embalming, shall cause the part to be removed without unnecessary mutilation. After removal of the part, custody of the remainder of the body vests in the surviving spouse, next of kin or other persons under obligation to dispose of the body."

Changes Occurring/Issues

While states were passing the Uniform Anatomical Gift Act or something similar to it, there was a concern about organ and tissue transplantation, as well as donations of the entire body. Most of the concerns related to problems families and funeral directors might have as to bodies from which an organ was transplanted. The fears were never realized. Post-death activities were not interfered with or changed beyond special procedures that had to be followed, sometimes in the preparation of a body for viewing and funeralization. Therefore, a decade later, there is no concern which relates to the gift of a part of the body and funeralization and memorialization following the transplant.

However, there are well-founded fears about body donations insofar as most institutions do not assure the acceptance of every gift. Some reasons for rejection are:

- An oversupply of bodies
- Body has been autopsied
- Body is mutilated
- A limb is missing
- There has been a transplant of a major organ
- The body is too tall or too short or too obese or too emaciated

Impact/Projections

In 1980, one hundred fifty-four (154) of the institutions which accept bodies for medical science were surveyed. One hundred twenty (120) of those which responded reported receiving over 10,000 bodies in 1979. This is more than the total number needed by these institutions for anatomical study even though there is continued publicity claiming a shortage of bodies. Most schools allow a funeral with the body present prior to delivery of a body to the medical institution if this is requested by the donor or family. Also, most of these institutions allow for some sort of memorialization when there is the disposition of the residue of the body following its use. However, some do not. Others discourage it. And there are some schools which accept bodies for medical science study even though they do not use them because they are not needed or acceptable.

There have been occasional requests for bodies claiming a donated body helps medical science and avoids funeral disposition costs. One anatomist stated he felt it is the obligation of his state through the medical school with which he was associated to accept all bodies for use *and* disposition regardless of whether or not they were used for study purposes.

Most medical schools will continue to get enough bodies for study. They will become more selective and expand their "needs" by requiring more bodies for the same number of students.

Medical schools' sensitivity to a next of kin of the donor will continue. However, as "needs" remain constant or increase there could be a surge of donations with public institutions having difficulty refusing the gifts. They could accept and dispose of the bodies. If this became a reality, it would be a form of direct disposition, most times without the survivors aware that the donation was not one to aid medical science.

Reprinted from "Tradition in Transition," The Report of the 21st Century Committee of the National Funeral Directors Association, October 26, 1981.

How the Dead Can Help the Living

There are many ways in which people can arrange while they are living to serve the needs of their fellow men after they have died. Many lives can be saved, and health and sight can be restored to thousands through the intelligent ''salvaging'' of organs and tissues. (Except for corneas and ear bones, the donor should be under 60.) Medical and dental training requires thousands of bodies each year, for anatomical study. (All ages are acceptable.) Medical research, too, needs cooperation, in the form of permission for autopsies (not permissible if the body is left to a medical school) and the bequeathal of special parts, such as the ear bones of people with hearing difficulties.

If we truly accept our own mortality and genuinely identify ourselves with humanity, we will gladly help in every way we can. These ways are steadily increasing. This section of the *Manual* deals with some of them.

1. Permission for Autopsy

Such permission should routinely be granted *except* when the body is destined for a medical school. Autopsy is often very helpful in improving the knowledge and experience of doctors and in some cases is more valuable than bequeathal. Sometimes it directly benefits the family.

2. Bequeathal to a Medical School

3. Bequeathal of Eyes to an Eye Bank

4. Bequeathal of Ear Bones to a Temporal Bone Bank

More than 18 million people in the U.S. alone—three million of them children—suffer partial or total deafness. Since 1960, thanks to the John A. Hartford Foundation and other financial donors, research into the causes and cure of deafness has been greatly accelerated.

Persons with hearing problems or other ear disorders are urged to bequeath their inner ear structures for research. A medical history is obtained from the donor's doctor. The removal of the ear structures is a specialized task and arrangements are made by the National Temporal Bone Banks Center of the Deafness Research Foundation at the time of death. For more information and necessary forms write: The Deafness Research Foundation, 342 Madison Ave., New York, N.Y. 10002.

5. Bequeathal of Kidneys

Thousands of kidney transplants have been made but thousands of Americans are still living on kidney machines (expensive and awkward!). More kidneys are urgently needed. A kidney transplanted from a brother or sister has a survival

From *A Manual of Death Education and Simple Burial* by Ernest Morgan. Reprinted with the permission of Celo Press. If you wish to have a copy of the Manual, it can be obtained for $3.50 (ppd.) from Celo Press, Route 5, Burnsville, NC 28714.

rate of about 90%; from an unrelated donor the rate is 50 to 60% and rising. Transplants are coordinated by the National Kidney Foundation, 116 E. 27th St., New York, N.Y. 10016.

6. Regional Tissue Banks

This is a recent development, typified by the Northern California Transplant Bank, 751 South Bascom Ave., San Jose, Calif. 95128. (408-998-4550; after hours, 408-289-8200). It is a unified regional approach to the problems of procurement, processing, storage and distribution of tissues for transplant. Included in the organization are transplant units concerned with bone, ear, eye, heart, heart valve & artery cartilage renewal and skin. A donor to such an institution can be assured of maximum "recycling." We will appreciate learning of similar institutions.

7. Pituitary Glands

An estimated 10,000 children in the U.S. are suffering from serious pituitary deficiency. Each of these children needs the hormone extracted from about 200 pituitary glands to maintain normal growth for one year. Only 1,400 to 1,500 children are getting it. An estimated additional 50,000 children have a partial deficiency and could be helped by growth hormone. Pituitary glands should be collected whenever possible. They can be kept frozen, or in acetone and sent periodically to the National Pituitary Agency, Suite 503-7, 210 W. Fayette St., Baltimore, Md. 21201.

8. Donor Clearing Houses

The Living Bank, P.O. Box 6725, Houston Texas 77005 (713-528-2971) is a non-profit registry which coordinates the disposition of anatomical gifts. It supplies donor cards and records donor data for instant retrieval.

9. Recording of Medical Data

Medic Alert, Turlock, Calif. 95380 (209-632-2371) provides emergency identification of hidden medical problems and anatomical gift instructions through the use of a bracelet or necklace on which the information is engraved, plus a wallet card. Emergency personnel can phone collect to the number engraved on the emblem and receive full medical data in a matter of seconds.

Medical Data Bank, Inc., 7920 Ward Parkway, Kansas City, Mo. 64114 (816-333-2080) provides microfilm chips containing a person's complete medical history and anatomical gift instructions.

10. The Naval Medical Research Center

The Tissue Bank, Naval Medical Research Institute, NNMC, Bethesda, Md. 20014 (202-295-1121) is reported to be doing an outstanding job and accepts donations of anatomic material, particularly from persons under 35 who die within the National Medical Center or at San Diego Naval Hospital. The bodies must be cremated or buried at the family's expense.

11. Skin for Dressing and Grafting

For persons suffering from serious burns, skin taken from a person who has just died can be extremely valuable. Such skin commonly constitutes the most desirable kind of dressing, and in some cases can be successfully grafted.

12. Artificial Implants

Persons having artificial implants, either internal or external, can perform an important service by making the appropriate portions of their bodies available for study after their death. Such study is vital in improving the quality and workability of the growing variety of valuable artificial implants.

13. The American Association of Tissue Banks

This new, non-government-sponsored group includes physicians, nurses, lawyers, technicians and the general public. Long range goals include setting up standards for tissue banking and establishing regional tissue banks. The address: 12111 Parkinson Drive, Rockville, Md. 20852

14. Recycling of Non-Organic Materials

Glasses left by the dead can be sent to: New Eyes for the Needy, Inc., Short Hills, N.J. 07078. Over a million persons have benefitted.

Pills from a patient's last illness can be salvaged. Their use in Canada and the U.S. is illegal, but missionary doctors abroad are commonly desperate for medicines. They must be clean and in their original containers. Likewise tooth fillings of gold can be recycled by dental schools serving needy patients. These materials (and eye-glasses as well) may be sent to: Inland Empire Human Resources Center, c/o Congregational Church, 2 W. Olive Avenue, Redlands, Calif. 92373.

UNIFORM DONOR CARD

OF_____
Print or type name of donor

In the hope that I may help others, I hereby make this anatomical gift, if medically acceptable, to take effect upon my death. The words and marks below indicate my desires.

I give: (a) _____ any needed organs or parts
(b) _____ only the following organs or parts

_____
Specify the organ(s) or part(s)

for the purposes of transplantation, therapy, medical research or education;
(c) _____ my body for anatomical study if needed.

Limitations or special wishes, if any:_____

Signed by the donor and the following two witnesses in the presence of each other:

_____   _____
Signature of Donor   Date of Birth of Donor

_____   _____
Date Signed   City & State

_____   _____
Witness   Witness

This is a legal document under the Uniform Anatomical Gift Act or similar laws.

The Uniform Donor Card, designed for the donor's wallet, is a legal document in most states and provinces.

Copies of the Uniform Donor Card may be obtained without charge from:
Eye Bank Association of America, 3195 Maplewood Ave., Winston-Salem NC 27103
Living Bank, Hermann Professional Building, P.O. Box 6725, Houston TX 77005
Medic Alert, Turlock CA 95380
National Pituitary Agency, Suite 501-9, 210 W. Fayette St., Baltimore MD 21201
National Society for Medical Research, 1000 Vermont Ave., Washington DC 20005

Most states now have donor forms on the back of drivers licenses. These should be used in addition to wallet cards. Be sure to fill yours in.

15. Cadaver Blood

This is a controversial subject. In 1980 approximately 11.5 million units (pints) of blood will be transfused in America—up from 6.5 million in 1970. A large percentage of this will be "commercial" blood for which the "donor" was paid. This commercial blood will account for nearly all of the thousands of cases of post-transfusion hepatitis which will occur.

To minimize the use of commercial blood the New York Blood Center alone is importing some 200,000 units per year, mainly from Europe. Clearly, increased supplies of non-commercial blood are needed.

Dr. J. Garrott Allen, of Stanford University Medical Center, writes, "The use of cadaver blood has not increased in recent years though there is no reason why its use should not be pressed, provided precautions are taken to minimize the possibility that the cadaver was from the high risk group. With improvement of legislation to enable the obtaining of blood under proper circumstances, this source could become an important and integral part of our national blood program."

The Red Cross has pointed out that cadaver blood, as obtained by Russian Blood banks, is very expensive. In reply it is argued that with equipment of appropriate design, this cost might be reduced below that of commercial blood.

Cadaver blood for transfusion has three important advantages: a. it is less prone to coagulate; b. there is sufficient blood from a single "donor" to make careful testing economical; and c. a recipient is better off to have several units from one donor than one unit each from several donors.

With the rising need for blood in this country, a vigorous effort should be made to develop this valuable source.

Then too, better procedures are needed for collecting and allocating blood, to avoid the substantial waste which frequently takes place.

THE "UNIVERSAL DONOR" PRINCIPLE

A promising breakthrough in the transplanting of tissues and organs appears to be on the way. By injecting the recipient with antigens from the donor, the patient is apparently enabled to accept transplants which otherwise would be rejected.* This offers hope for thousands and will, if it materializes, enormously increase the need for tissues and organs for transplant and therapy.

Alas, the work of collecting anatomical materials is seriously fragmented. One organization collects kidneys, another eyes, a third pituitary glands, and so on. They do their best but the supply is pitifully short. 20,000 people are being kept alive on kidney machines; 30,000 blind people could have their sight restored if corneas were available.** Ten times as many pituitary glands are needed as can presently be obtained.

The answer to this problem is two-fold. First is Uniform Legislation authorizing the salvaging of needed material from anyone who dies anywhere in the country—except persons carrying some indication to the contrary or whose families object. (Nothing compulsory about it!) It would not apply to persons leaving their bodies to a medical school.

The other part of the answer is in regional tissue banks to coordinate procurement, processing, storage and distribution of tissues for transplant and therapy.*** Ideally such banks will, in the future, accept the entire body and dispose

---

*From papers presented in 1979 at the British Association for the Advancement of Science, as quoted in "The Economist."
**Summer, 1978, Newsletter, Inland Empire Human Resource Center.
***The American Association of Tissue Banks, 12111 Parklawn Drive, Rockville MD 20852 is the U.S. clearing house for tissue bank information and technology. Human Parts Banks of Canada, 5326 Ada Blvd., Edmonton, Alberta T5W 4N7 is the Canadian clearing house.

of the remains without cost to the family. The removal of a needed organ or tissue is a routine matter, in no way interfering with funeral display if that is wanted. It is unthinkable to burn or bury precious human tissues which might be providing "The Gift of Life."

Consider what this can mean. *You* are in the emergency room suffering from severe burns. You need skin at once. Down the hall a patient has just died from an auto accident. Skin is available without delay.

You are blind and need a corneal transplant to restore your sight. The necessary corneas are available immediately.

Your child is stunted and needs growth hormones. He gets all he needs.

You need an organ transplant to save your life. You get it right away.

Shortages of tissues and organs are ended once and for all. This gives a new and creative dimension to death.

ABOUT EYE BANKS

One important service we can render at death is to leave behind our eyes to relieve the blindness of others. In America alone there are about 30,000 blind people whose sight could be restored if enough corneas were available.

Eye donations are increasing, but the demand is increasing even more, as new techniques are perfected and new uses are found for the donor-eye. Today the corneal transplant operation is effective in restoring sight in 90% of the most common corneal diseases. All vision defects cannot be cured by transplants. It is not possible to transfer the entire eye. To pledge your eyes call or write the nearest Eye Bank. Carry a Uniform Donor Card and check the Eye Bank square. Let your physician know (in writing) and be sure to clear your plans with your family. No matter if you wear glasses, or what your age, race or blood type may be.

Eyes must be removed within 2 to 4 hours of death. This can be done in the hospital or at home, assuming Eye Bank personnel are available. An increasing number of funeral directors are being trained to do this. Eyes may not be bequeathed to specific individuals. They will be used on a first-come first-served basis, regardless of ability to pay. Airlines fly them to their destinations without charge.

CANADIAN EYE BANKS

BRITISH COLUMBIA-YUKON: 350 E. 36th Ave., Vancouver, B.C. V5W 1C6
ALBERTA DIVISION: 12010 Jasper Ave., Edmonton, Alta. T5J 2L4
SASKATCHEWAN DIVISION: 2550 Broad St., Regina, Sask. S4P 3E1
MANITOBA DIVISION: 1031 Portage Ave., Winnipeg Man. R3G 0R9
ONTARIO DIVISION: 1929 Bayview Ave., Toronto M4G 3E8
QUEBEC DIVISION: 1181 Guy St., Montreal, P.Q. H3H 2K6
MARITIME DIVISION: 6136 Almon St., Halifax, N.S. B3J 2Z1
NEWFOUNDLAND & LABRADOR DIVISION: 70 Boulevarde, St. John's, Nfld. A1A 1K2

U.S. EYE BANKS

ALABAMA: BIRMINGHAM: Alabama Lions Eye Bank, 708 18th St. 35233   205-933-8251
TUSKEGEE: Eye Bank of Central Alabama, 620 N. Water St. 36083   205-727-6553

ARIZONA: PHOENIX: Arizona Lions Eye Bank, PO Box 13609 85002   602-258-7373, Ext 568
ARKANSAS: LITTLE ROCK: Arkansas Eye & Kidney Bank, 4301 W. Markham 72205   501-664-4990
CALIFORNIA: SAN DIEGO: Eye Bank of San Diego, 4077 5th Ave. 92103 714-294-8267
TORRANCE: Southern California Eye Bank & Research Foundation, 4201 Torrance Blvd., Suite 380 90503   213-540-5832
COLORADO: DENVER: Colorado Eye Bank, Univ. of Colorado Health Sciences Center, 4200 9th Ave. 80262 303-377-1087
CONNECTICUT: NEW BRITAIN: Connecticut Eye Bank, New Britain Gen. Hosp. 06052   203-224-5550
D.C.: WASHINGTON: Lions Eye Bank & Research Foundation, 919 18th St. NW Suite 121 20006 202-393-2265
FLORIDA: GAINESVILLE: North Florida Lions Eye Bank, Box J-382 32610 904-392-3135
TAMPA: Central Florida Lions Eye Bank, Box 21, N. 30th St. 33612   813-977-1300 or 971-4500
GEORGIA: ATLANTA: Georgia Lions Eye Bank, Inc., 1365 Clifton Rd. NE 30322   404-321-9300
AUGUSTA: Georgia Lions Lighthouse Foundation, Inc. 30912 404-724-1388
ILLINOIS: CHICAGO: Illinois Eye Bank, 53 W. Jackson Blvd.,

Room 1435   60604   312-922-8710
CHICAGO: Illinois Eye Bank Lab. and Eye & Ear Infirmary, 1855 West Taylor St.   60612   312-996-6507
BLOOMINGTON: Watson Gailey Eye Foundation Eye Bank, 807 N. Main St.   61701   309-828-5241
INDIANA: INDIANAPOLIS: Indiana Lions Eye Bank, Inc., 1100 W. Michigan St.   46223   317-264-8527 or 635-8431
IOWA: IOWA CITY: Iowa Lions Eye Bank, University Hospitals   52242   319-356-2215 or 356-1616
KANSAS: TOPEKA: Kansas Odd Fellows Eye Bank, P.O. Box 1851   66601   913-233-4652
KENTUCKY: LOUISVILLE: Kentucky Lions Eye Foundation, 301 E. Walnut St.   40202   502-584-9934
LOUISIANA: NEW ORLEANS: Southern Eye Bank, 145 Elk Place   70112   504-523-6343
MAINE: See New England Eye Bank, Boston MA
MARYLAND: BALTIMORE: The Medical Eye Bank of Maryland, 505 Park Ave.   21201   301-986-1830
BETHESDA: International Eye Bank, 7801 Norfolk Ave. 20014   301-986-1830
MASSACHUSETTS: BOSTON: New England Eye Bank, 243 Charles St.   02114   617-523-7900
MICHIGAN: ANN ARBOR: Michigan Eye Bank, 1000 Wall St., Parkview Medical 48109 313-764-3262 or 764-4244
DETROIT: Michigan Eye Bank, 540 E. Canfield Ave. 48201   313-577-1329
MARQUETTE: Upper Michigan Lions Eye Bank, 420 W. Magnetic St. 49855   906-228-9440, Ext. 438 or 800-562-9781
MINNESOTA: MINNEAPOLIS: Minnesota Lions Eye Bank, Box 493, Mayo Hosp. 55455   612-373-8425 or 373-8484
MISSISSIPPI: JACKSON: Mississippi Lions Eye Bank, Inc. 2500 N. State St.   39216   601-987-3500 or 987-5899
MISSOURI: COLUMBIA: Lions Eye Tissue Bank, 404 Portland 65201   314-443-1471 or 443-1479
KANSAS CITY: Eye Bank of Kansas City, 3036 Gillham Rd. 64108   816-531-1066
ST. LOUIS: Lions Eye Bank in St. Louis, 1325 S. Grand 63104 314-771-7600
St. Louis Eye Bank, 660 S. Euclid 63104 314-454-2150 or 454-2666
NEBRASKA: OMAHA: Nebraska Lions Eye Bank, 42nd & Dewey Streets 68105   402-541-4039
NEW HAMPSHIRE: see New England Eye Bank, Boston MA
NEW JERSEY: NEWARK: New Jersey Eye Bank, Eye Institute of New Jersey, 15 S. 9th St. 07107   201-456-4626
NEW MEXICO: ALBUQUERQUE: New Mexico Lions Eye Bank, 201 Cedar S.E., Suite 501 87106   505-843-9211
NEW YORK: ALBANY: Sight Conservation Society of N.E. N.Y., 628 Madison Ave. 12208 518-445-5199 or 377-5761
BUFFALO: Buffalo Eye Bank & Research Society, Inc., 2550 Main St. 14214   716-832-5448 or 835-8725
NEW YORK CITY: Eye Bank for Site Restoration, 210 E. 64th Street 10021   212-838-9155 or 838-9211
ROCHESTER: Rochester Eye & Human Parts Bank, 220 Alexander St.   14607   716-546-5250
SYRACUSE: Central N.Y. Eye Bank & Research Corporation, P.O. Box 21   13201   315-471-6060
NORTH CAROLINA: WINSTON-SALEM: N.C. Eye & Human Tissue Bank, 3195 Maplewood Ave. 27103   919-765-0932
NORTH DAKOTA: WILLISTON: Williston Lions Eye Bank, Box 1627   58801   701-572-7661
OHIO: CINCINNATI: Cincinnati Eye Bank, 231 Bethesda Ave.

Room 6004   45267   513-861-3716
CLEVELAND: Cleveland Eye Bank, 1909 E. 101st St. 44106 216-791-9700
COLUMBUS: Central Ohio Lions Eye Bank, Inc., 456 Clinic Dr. UHC 43210   614-422-1111
YOUNGSTOWN: Melvin E. Jones Eye Bank, 2246 Glenwood Ave. 44511   216-788-2411
OKLAHOMA: OKLAHOMA CITY: Oklahoma Lions Eye Bank 608 Stanton L. Young Dr. 73104   405-271-5691
OREGON: PORTLAND: Oregon Lions Sight & Hearing Foundation, Inc., 1200 NW 23rd St.   97210   503-229-7523
PENNSYLVANIA: BETHLEHEM: N.E. Pennsylvania Lions Eye Bank, 1916 Rockingham Dr.   18018   215-867-9696
PHILADELPHIA: Eye Foundation of Delaware Valley, 1601 Spring Garden St. 19130   215-569-3937
PITTSBURGH: Medical Eye Bank of Western Pennsylvania, 3515 5th Ave.   15213   412-687-8828
PUERTO RICO: SAN JUAN: Lions Eye Bank of Puerto Rico, G.P.O. Box 5067   00936   809-763-8050
RHODE ISLAND: see New England Eye Bank, Boston MA
SOUTH CAROLINA: COLUMBIA: South Carolina Eye Bank, 110 Lexington Medical Mall   29169   803-796-1304
TENNESSEE: KNOXVILLE: East Tennessee Eye Bank, 509 Cedar Bluff Rd. 37921   615-693-4991
MEMPHIS: Mid-South Eye Bank, 188 S. Bellevue, #215 38104 901-726-8264
NASHVILLE: Lions Eye Bank, Research & Service Center, Suite 634 Medical Arts Bldg.   37212   615-322-2662
TEXAS: AMARILLO: Lions Hi-Plains Eye Bank, PO Box 1717 79105   806-359-5101
DALLAS: Lions Sight & Tissue Foundation, Room G7-250, 5323 Harry Hines 75235   214-688-3908
EL PASO: West Texas Lions Eye Bank, 2901 McRae 79925 915-598-6306 or 598-5948
FT. WORTH: Lions Organ & Eye Bank of District 2-E2, c/o Carter Blood Center, 1263 W Rosedale 76104 817-335-4935
HOUSTON: Lions Eyes of Texas Eye Bank, 6501 Fannin, Suite C-307   77030   713-797-9270
LACKLAND: Central USAF Eye Bank WHMC/SGHSE, Lackland AFB   78236   512-670-7841
LUBBOCK: District 2-T2 Lions Eye Bank, Box 5901   79417 806-762-2242
MIDLAND: District 2-A1 Lions Eye Bank, P.O. Box 4283 79701 915-682-7381
SAN ANTONIO: Eye Bank at Baptist Memorial Hosp., 111 Dallas   78286   512-222-8431, Ext. 2338
TYLER: East Texas Regional Eye Bank, P.O. Drawer 6400 75711   214-597-0351
UTAH: SALT LAKE CITY: Lions Eye Bank of Univ. of Utah, 50 N. Medical Dr. 84132   801-581-6384
VERMONT: see New England Eye Bank, Boston MA
VIRGINIA: RICHMOND: Old Dominion Eye Bank, 408 N. 12th Street 23219   804-648-0890
ROANOKE: Eye Bank of Virginia, P.O. Box 1772 24008 703-345-8823
WASHINGTON: SEATTLE: Lions Eye Bank of Wash. & N. Idaho, Dept. of Opthalmology—RJ10, Univ. of Wash. 98195 206-543-5394 or 223-3010
WISCONSIN: MADISON: Wisconsin Eye Bank, 600 Highland Ave. 53792   608-263-6223
MILWAUKEE: Wisconsin Lions Eye Bank, 8700 Wisconsin Ave. 53226   414-257-5543

THE BEQUEATHALS OF BODIES TO SCHOOLS OF MEDICINE AND DENTISTRY

If you wish to perform an important service at time of death, you may leave your body for education or science where it is urgently needed.

Bodies may only be given. They may not be sold.

Our 1979 survey showed a surplus of bodies in a few areas and shortages in others. 36 schools reported "urgent" need, the same number as in 1976, against 34 in 1974 and 30 in 1972. Bequeathals are increasing, but not fast enough. Also, greater sharing is needed between areas of surplus and shortage.

Why They are Needed

Thousands of bodies are needed each year for the training of future doctors and dentists. New medical schools are opening, and the supply of unclaimed bodies is steadily diminishing. Only the rapid increase in the practice of bequeathing bodies has averted a nationwide crisis.

Procedure at Time of Death

If there is to be no service in the presence of the body, as when a memorial service is held instead of a funeral service, then the body may be removed immediately to the medical school. In this case the directory of medical schools in the *Manual* should be consulted and a phone call made to the Anatomy Department of the nearest school listed as accepting bequeathals. Transportation details can be worked out on the phone. A funeral director usually takes the body to the school though an ambulance service is sometimes used or the school may have its own conveyance. If no funeral director is used, someone else must handle the legal papers.

A Deeply Meaningful Experience

The papers are simple. The attending physician makes out a death certificate. This is taken to the county Board of Health where a transportation permit is issued. The body is then transported to the medical school where it is signed for. The family may prefer to take the body themselves, using a station wagon. The legal papers remain the same. The body may be placed in a box or on a stretcher or a plain canvas cot, or simply wrapped in a blanket. People are repelled by death and often shrink from handling a dead body. In practice, however, the privilege of helping to care for the body of a friend is a deeply meaningful experience. Too often in modern life we withdraw from reality or call in a professional to do things we should do for ourselves.

If a service is to be held in the presence of the body, embalming or refrigeration is needed and a funeral director is necessary. The funeral director should phone the medical school to find out what embalming is acceptable.

How to Transport the Remains

Some medical schools pay no transportation expense. Most pay the expense within the state or within a certain radius (see the directory). Expenses beyond that distance are paid by the family. Incidentally, Amtrac offers fast, cheap service to some 300 points. In warm weather the body should be gotten to the medical school in 24 hours, unless dry ice is used. The school will dispose of the remains or, if desired, will return the ashes to the family.

If a common carrier is used, such as an airline or Amtrac, the body must be packed in a certain way, requiring the services of a funeral director. If the body is to be held for a funeral service or sent by common carrier, the funeral director should ask the medical school what kind of embalming is acceptable to the school. If the body is delivered promptly, in a private vehicle, no embalming is necessary.

It is wise to have alternate plans, preferably through a memorial society, since death may occur in an area where there is no need for bodies, or the body may not be acceptable. Some medical schools assume responsibility for the final disposal of a body which has been rejected. Others don't. A body which has been mutilated or autopsied, or from which organs other than eyes have been removed, is not acceptable.

PART 2

FACTS
AND FIGURES

Life-Spans

Frederick G. Vogel

SOMEWHERE between the longest life-span possible to imagine — that of the universe, which is already some 20 billion years old and still going strong — and the shortest — a group of subatomic particles known as the unstable hadrons, which last only one one-hundred-sextillionth of a second — lies mankind.

With a life-span of 70-plus years, human beings are relatively long-lived members of the animal kingdom. (The black Seychelles tortoise lives for 170-plus years.) Through the 250 millennia or more of man's life on earth, the "expectable" span of his lifetime has risen gradually over most of history, sharply over the past 100 years. What we cannot yet do is explain death itself or, ultimately, the aging process that makes death inevitable. And both death and the process of aging are as much a part of a life-span as life itself.

These are only several of the fascinating observations contained in a new book by Frank Kendig and Richard Hutton entitled *Life-Spans, Or How Long Things Last* (Holt, Rinehart & Winston, 383 Madison Ave., New York, N.Y. 10017; 265 pp; $5.95).

For those interested in how to tell a fish's age by examining its scales; how long those mythical gnomes live; what occupations are regarded as the most hazardous to health; and how best to store an egg or a jar of caviar, this is the book. What it is is a brightly written treasure trove of scientific data, with just a little of the fanciful (albeit factual) thrown in.

But the most interesting parts of the book concern the human life-span, especially the aging process already referred to. The authors write:

"Probably the most misunderstood aspect of aging and death is old age — what it is and what it does. Simply speaking, old age is the latter stages of a constant, continuing, and inexorable decline in the ability of the body to carry out its own functional requirements and to resist and bounce back from disease and trauma. Even if we somehow escape the ravages of war, accidents, and deadly diseases, this decline proceeds at a steady pace, so that, for most of us, there is a good chance that we will succumb to physical ailments between the ages of 65 and 80. What this means is that there really is no such thing as death *by* old age. What the elderly are actually dying from is a combination of disease or disorder and the inability of their bodies to respond to the challenge any longer.

By 1974, the average life-span of Americans was almost double that of Copper Age Man — 71.9 years *vs.* 36 years.

As Alex Comfort noted in his book, *Aging: The Biology of Senescence,* if we kept throughout life the same resistance to stress, injury, and disease that we had at the age of 2, about half of us here today might expect to survive another 700 years."

The medical profession has done much to combat the external causes of death that we face daily, they continue. It has learned to patch and sew up many traumatic injuries, fight dangerous germs with friendlier varieties, and even replace some of our bodily parts as they become defective. But it has barely begun to deal with the most fundamental causes of death — the general disintegration and ultimate breakdown of our bodies.

Many scientists believe that our genes carry some form of self-destruct mechanism that ends our lives at predetermined times. Dr. Leonard Hayflick is one scientist who subscribes to this *death clock* theory. Working first at Philadel-

Human Life-Spans	
	Life-span (years)
Neanderthal man	29
Cro-Magnon man	32
Man in the Copper Age	36
Man in the Bronze Age	38
Greek and Roman man	36
Fifth-century man (England)	30
Fourteenth-century man (England)	38
Seventeenth-century man (Europe)	51
Eighteenth-century man (Europe)	45*

* Epidemics in urban areas were the cause of this drop in life-span.

Reprinted with permission from *American Cemetery*, May, 1981.

phia's Wistar Institute and then at Stanford University, Dr. Hayflick has found that animal cells, cultured or grown in the laboratory, are able to divide only a limited number of times before they stop.

All animals, including man, contain cells that continue to divide throughout their lives. But while cells taken from young animals and grown in the laboratory divide many times before their cultures die out, those from senile animals divide only once or twice. In man, cells can reproduce through about 50 cellular generations; then the line dies out. Can it be that we die because our cells can no longer reproduce? Dr. Hayflick is certain of it.

Other researchers reject both the notion of an internal clock that eventually shuts off the body's cells and the theory that chemical alterations in our tissues cannot be prevented. Instead, they believe that senescence is the result of random forces, that we age because some accidental, repetitive injury eventually destroys our vitality. Typical of these theories, and one of the most highly regarded, is the *error catastrophe hypothesis* proposed by

Dr. Leslie Orgel of the Salk Institute in La Jolla, California. Dr. Orgel believes that in building its component proteins, the body occasionally makes a mistake and creates a defective protein.

Whatever function that protein was to perform then goes unfulfilled. For example, an enzyme required for energy transport within the cell might be unable to do its job. This would cripple the cell and slightly impair the function of the organ containing it. Because some proteins aid in the reproduction of DNA — the genetic material that controls all life processes — defects in the protein would return as errors in the DNA. When too much damage accumulates, the system breaks down and the organism dies.

Other researchers have suggested that other highly reactive chemicals called *free radicals* promote crosslinking and are possibly the cause of aging. They have found that drugs that destroy free radicals also extend the life-spans of test animals. Between them, these experiments provide strong proof that crosslinking is at least a contributor to

the aging process.

According to the authors, a baby born in the United States today has an expected life-span of 71.3 years. But there are babies and there are babies. According to a 1974 study by the National Center for Health, a white baby born in the United States has an expected life-span of 72.7 years; a nonwhite baby, only 67 years. And, as is the case in virtually all species, females can expect to outlive males: a female white baby born in 1975 has a projected life-span of 77.2 years, whereas a male white baby can expect to live only 69.4 years. In some countries the difference is astounding: a woman's life expectancy in Gabon, Africa, for example, is 45 years; that of her spouse is only 25.

"No matter what your category," Kendig and Hutton say, "your projected life-span increases as you get older. Statistically, you become a survivor. A woman who reaches 70, for example, has a projected lifespan of 83.6 years. By the time she reaches 85, her projected life-span is up to 90.8 years. Curiously, the situation with respect to race and color seems to reverse with increasing age. Whereas a white female child can expect to outlive her nonwhite counterpart, a nonwhite woman over 70 can expect to outlive a white woman of the same age."

Most scientists feel that a human body's potential life-span has always been the same — about 100 years. There are, of course, reports of human beings living well over 100 years, and even some suggestion that humans have approached 200 years, but such claims have not held up to investigation. According to the *Guinness Book of World Records*, the longest authenticated life-span of a human being is 113 years, 214 days.

The great decline in infant mortality in Western society did not begin until the first few decades of the twentieth century, with improvements in the sterilization of food, the pasteurization of milk, the development of disinfectants, and modern medical advances. By 1915 neonatal deaths had declined to 4 percent in the United States, with only 9 percent of American infants failing to survive the the first year. Succeeding decades brought even more spectacular gains in the industrialized countries of the world — and infant mortality rates con-

Life Expectancy (Years) at Birth in the United States, by Race and Sex: 1900-1974

Year	Total Both sexes	Male	Female	White Both sexes	Male	Female	Black and other races Both sexes	Male	Female
1900	47.3	46.3	48.3	47.6	46.6	48.7	33.0	32.5	33.5
1905	48.7	47.3	50.2	49.1	47.6	50.6	31.3	29.6	33.1
1910	50.0	48.4	51.8	50.3	48.6	52.0	35.6	33.8	37.5
1915	54.7	52.5	56.8	55.1	53.1	57.5	38.9	37.5	40.5
1920	54.1	53.6	54.6	54.9	54.4	55.6	45.3	45.5	45.2
1925	59.0	57.6	60.6	60.7	59.3	62.4	45.7	44.9	46.7
1930	59.7	58.1	61.6	61.4	59.7	63.5	48.1	47.3	49.2
1935	61.7	59.9	63.9	62.9	61.0	65.0	53.1	51.3	55.2
1940	62.9	60.8	65.2	64.2	62.1	66.6	53.1	51.5	54.9
1945	65.9	63.6	67.9	66.8	64.4	69.5	57.7	56.1	59.6
1950	68.2	65.6	71.1	69.1	66.5	72.2	60.8	59.1	62.9
1955	69.6	66.7	72.8	70.5	67.4	73.7	63.7	61.4	66.1
1960	69.7	66.6	73.1	70.6	67.4	74.1	63.6	61.1	66.3
1965	70.2	66.8	73.7	71.0	67.6	74.7	64.1	61.1	67.4
1970	70.9	67.1	74.8	71.7	68.0	75.6	65.3	61.3	69.4
1974	71.9	68.2	75.9	72.7	68.9	76.6	67.0	62.9	71.2

Source: U.S. Department of Health, Education, and Welfare, Public Health Service, National Center for Health Statistics, *Vital Statistics of the United States, 1973*, vol. 2; *Monthly Vital Statistics Report*, vol. 24, no. 11, supp. 1. Reprinted in U.S. Department of Commerce, *Social Indicators 1976* (Washington, D.C.; U.S. Government Printing Office, 1977), p. 190.

This table, in *Life-Spans, Or How Long Things Last*, indicates how long each of us may expect to live according to race and sex.

tinue to decline.

The authors continue:

"In the health-conscious 1970s changing habits are significantly affecting our projected longevity. According to Dr. Norman M. Kaplan of the University of Texas, reduced smoking and the growing tendency to avoid animal fats in our diets along with better care and treatment of high blood pressure, have already added a couple of years to our lifespans."

How does life expectancy in other parts of the globe compare with our own? It may come as a surprise that the United States does not even rank among the top 10 nations. Ahead of us are Sweden, the Netherlands, Iceland, Norway, Denmark, The Ryukyu Islands, Canada, France, Japan, and the United Kingdom.

"There are astounding variations in life-spans around the world. A Swede, for example, can expect to live twice as long as a Nigerian and nearly three times as long as a male from Guinea, whose average life expectancy is only 26 years.

"These variations are attributable to many factors. The standard of living (itself determined by such crucial factors as the quality of medical care and nutrition), climate, cultural and social traditions (particularly the kinds of stresses found in each society) are only a few."

It goes without saying that anyone concerned about wealth and happiness should choose his occupation carefully. But the job you take also influences your life-span. Professionals — doctors and lawyers — have the longest lifespans. Administrators, managers, and technicians follow; then farmers and agriculture workers; small businessmen, salesmen, and skilled workers; semiskilled workers; and finally unskilled laborers. Insurance companies and others who develop such statistics break down the categories even further. The lifespan of a miner, for example, actually depends on the material he mines. Miners of metals and stone outlive petroleum workers, who, in turn, outlive coal miners.

For high-risk occupations, actuaries estimate the number of additional deaths per thousand that are likely per year: For astronauts, it is 30 extra deaths; race-car drivers, 25; aerial performers and professional prizefighters, 8. But for steeplejacks, it is only 3. So if you

John Adams and Herbert Hoover were the longest-lived U.S. Presidents; four others lived at least to age 80.

Presidential Life-Spans		
U.S. President	Term of service	Age at death
John Adams	1797-1801	90
Thomas Jefferson	1801-1809	83
James Madison	1809-1817	85
James Monroe	1817-1825	73
John Quincy Adams	1825-1829	80
Andrew Jackson	1829-1837	78
Martin Van Buren	1837-1841	79
John Tyler	1841-1845	71
Millard Fillmore	1850-1853	74
James Buchanan	1857-1861	77
Rutherford B. Hayes	1877-1881	70
Grover Cleveland	1885-1889	71
	1893-1897	
William Howard Taft	1909-1913	72
Herbert Hoover	1929-1933	90
Harry Truman	1945-1953	88
Dwight D. Eisenhower	1953-1961	78

like speed, heights, or violence, be prepared for an early demise.

Strange as it seems, according to the authors, there is growing medical evidence that still other aspects of our lives influence our life-spans precisely because they have so much to do with whether we are happy or discontented. Emotional and physical well-being are more closely linked than many realize.

"The connection is easiest to see in our relationships with other people. Loneliness and feelings of isolation are among the most potent forces that destroy our health and shorten our lives, a fact convincingly borne out by mortality figures in the United States. People who are single, widowed, or divorced are far more likely to die of a wide variety of illnesses than those who are married. Divorced women, for example, die of cervical cancer almost twice as often as married women. In many potentially fatal diseases, the strain of being divorced or widowed is one of the strongest predictors of death. Even being single is comparatively unhealthy. The death rate from heart disease is markedly higher for singles than for those who are married. From suicide and stroke, it is nearly twice as high; from cirrhosis of the liver, nearly three times.

"In short, the old macho idea that people who need people are weaklings has nothing going for it. Medically speaking, everybody needs somebody just to survive."

Although claims of reaching extremely advanced age have been exposed as false, it is nevertheless true that in certain remote mountain regions of the world unusual numbers of people — though plagued with minor health problems, such as rotten teeth — live to ripe and active old age. For example, according to the 1970 Soviet census, there were 2,500 centenarians residing in the Soviet republic of Azerbaidzhan, a figure representing 20 times the percentage of the population over 100 in the United States.

The life histories of such people underscore the importance environment plays in the aging process. Dr. David Davies, a British gerontologist, spent several years in Ecuador among the "centenarians of the Andes" and isolated the following environmental factors he believes contribute to their longevity. They inhabit high-altitude regions near the equator, geographic areas having a dry climate and even temperature; they subsist on an austere, relatively unvaried diet low in calories, sugar, and animal fats, but with plenty of fruits and vegetables; they make elaborate use of medicinal herbs; they lead physically vigorous but unharried lives and are not subjected to the kinds of tensions and stresses experienced by individuals living in urban industrialized societies; there is little air pollution; the aged are not segregated and continue to fulfill important social functions.

Furthermore, the aging process itself seems different. The elderly remain physically more youthful — and sexually active; but eventually they go into a swift decline as death approaches. A good deal more research needs to be done before any solid conclusions can be drawn.

For those still searching for the Fountain of Youth, but unwilling to move to Vilcabamba, the states with the greatest percentage of population over 65 are Kansas, Texas, Missouri, parts of Arizona and Oklahoma, and, of course, Florida; however, Mrs. Delina Filkins, the person with the world's longest authenticated life-span — 113 years, 214 days — lived in New York.

Only seers and tea-leaf readers claim to know for sure how long each of us will live, but we can make a reasonable stab at establishing our own life-span with the following enlightened exercise in addition, which the Messrs. Kendig and Hutton append to the opening section. First, however, look up your statistical life-span on the age/sex/race table. Taking that number, apply the following factors:

HEREDITY

1. If two of your grandparents lived past 80, add 2 years to your life expectancy. If all four made it to 80 or beyond, add 5.

2. If anyone in your immediate family died of heart attack or stroke before age 50, subtract 4.

3. For a parent, brother, or sister who has cancer, a heart condition, or diabetes, subtract 3.

LIFE-STYLE

1. If you live in a large (2 million plus) city, subtract 1; if you live in a small (10,000 or under) town, add 1.

2. If your work keeps you sitting behind a desk, subtract 2; if it involves physical activity, add 2.

3. If you are living with someone, add 4; if not, subtract 1 for each decade along since 25.

4. If you use seat belts and stay within speed limits when driving, add one; if you got a speeding ticket this year, subtract one. (Auto accidents are among the top five killers.)

5. If you make over $50,000, subtract 2. (High-income jobs yield short life expectancy.)

6. If you are a college graduate, add 1; if you received any postgraduate degree, add 2.

7. If you're 60 or older and still working, add 3.

HEALTH HABITS

1. For smokers: If you consume two packs a day, subtract 8; one to two packs, subtract 6; one pack or less, subtract 3.

2. For every ten pounds you are overweight, subtract 1.

3. For exercising three times weekly or more, add 3.

4. Checkups: for men over 40, add 2 if you have annual checkups; for all women who have at least one checkup annually, add 2.

5. If you sleep 9 hours or more, subtract 4.

ATTITUDES

1. For the intense, aggressive, easily angered person, subtract 3; for the easygoing, passive person, add 3.

2. For those unhappy with life, subtract 2; for those who are happy, add 2.

The number you get gives a reasonable estimate of your life expectancy based on what is known about various factors and how they work for or against us in everyday life.

Mr. Kendig is a former executive editor of *Omni,* the new science and science fiction magazine; Mr. Hutton, a freelance writer, has collaborated on several books on medical science and nutrition, including *The Food Connection.*

Life Tables

Abridged Life Tables by Color and Sex: United States, 1978

AGE INTERVAL	PROPORTION DYING	OF 100,000 BORN ALIVE		STATIONARY POPULATION		AVERAGE REMAINING LIFETIME
PERIOD OF LIFE BETWEEN TWO EXACT AGES STATED IN YEARS	PROPORTION OF PERSONS ALIVE AT BEGINNING OF AGE INTERVAL DYING DURING INTERVAL	NUMBER LIVING AT BEGINNING OF AGE INTERVAL	NUMBER DYING DURING AGE INTERVAL	IN THE AGE INTERVAL	IN THIS AND ALL SUBSEQUENT AGE INTERVALS	AVERAGE NUMBER OF YEARS OF LIFE REMAINING AT BEGINNING OF AGE INTERVAL
(1)	(2)	(3)	(4)	(5)	(6)	(7)
x to $x+n$	$_nq_x$	l_x	$_nd_x$	$_nL_x$	T_x	$\overset{\circ}{e}_x$
TOTAL						
0-1	0.0138	100,000	1,379	98,796	7,330,600	73.3
1-5	.0027	98,621	270	393,856	7,231,804	73.3
5-10	.0017	98,351	165	491,312	6,837,948	69.5
10-15	.0017	98,186	169	490,573	6,346,636	64.6
15-20	.0051	98,017	496	488,960	5,856,063	59.7
20-25	.0067	97,521	656	485,986	5,367,103	55.0
25-30	.0066	96,865	636	482,735	4,881,117	50.4
30-35	.0070	96,229	672	479,538	4,398,382	45.7
35-40	.0094	95,557	900	475,679	3,918,844	41.0
40-45	.0147	94,657	1,389	470,041	3,443,165	36.4
45-50	.0233	93,268	2,177	461,238	2,973,124	31.9
50-55	.0366	91,091	3,330	447,647	2,511,886	27.6
55-60	.0545	87,761	4,780	427,499	2,064,239	23.5
60-65	.0853	82,981	7,079	398,024	1,636,740	19.7
65-70	.1165	75,902	8,846	358,257	1,238,716	16.3
70-75	.1739	67,056	11,659	307,056	880,459	13.1
75-80	.2629	55,397	14,565	241,082	573,403	10.4
80-85	.3659	40,832	14,941	166,202	332,321	8.1
85 AND OVER	1.0000	25,891	25,891	166,119	166,119	6.4
MALE						
0-1	0.0153	100,000	1,527	98,665	6,949,897	69.5
1-5	.0031	98,473	304	393,193	6,851,232	69.6
5-10	.0019	98,169	191	490,336	6,458,039	65.8
10-15	.0022	97,978	214	489,458	5,967,703	60.9
15-20	.0073	97,764	713	487,224	5,478,245	56.0
20-25	.0101	97,051	982	482,830	4,991,021	51.4
25-30	.0096	96,069	919	478,010	4,508,191	46.9
30-35	.0096	95,150	916	473,539	4,030,181	42.4
35-40	.0126	94,234	1,189	468,380	3,556,642	37.7
40-45	.0189	93,045	1,762	461,112	3,088,262	33.2
45-50	.0300	91,283	2,740	450,008	2,627,150	28.8
50-55	.0480	88,543	4,254	432,769	2,177,142	24.6
55-60	.0721	84,289	6,076	407,074	1,744,373	20.7
60-65	.1143	78,213	8,936	369,643	1,337,299	17.1
65-70	.1590	69,277	11,018	319,603	967,656	14.0
70-75	.2324	58,259	13,539	257,893	648,053	11.1
75-80	.3354	44,720	14,999	185,712	390,160	8.7
80-85	.4461	29,721	13,259	114,046	204,448	6.9
85 AND OVER	1.0000	16,462	16,462	90,402	90,402	5.5
FEMALE						
0-1	0.0122	100,000	1,224	98,934	7,718,382	77.2
1-5	.0024	98,776	234	394,554	7,619,448	77.1
5-10	.0014	98,542	137	492,339	7,224,894	73.3
10-15	.0012	98,405	121	491,753	6,732,555	68.4
15-20	.0028	98,284	272	490,787	6,240,802	63.5
20-25	.0033	98,012	328	489,254	5,750,015	58.7
25-30	.0036	97,684	355	487,562	5,260,761	53.9
30-35	.0044	97,329	428	485,642	4,773,199	49.0
35-40	.0064	96,901	617	483,068	4,287,557	44.2
40-45	.0106	96,284	1,022	479,030	3,804,489	39.5
45-50	.0169	95,262	1,615	472,510	3,325,459	34.9
50-55	.0258	93,647	2,413	462,545	2,852,949	30.5
55-60	.0381	91,234	3,475	447,939	2,390,404	26.2
60-65	.0591	87,759	5,187	426,535	1,942,465	22.1
65-70	.0813	82,572	6,710	397,033	1,515,930	18.4
70-75	.1284	75,862	9,741	356,263	1,118,897	14.7
75-80	.2125	66,121	14,051	296,800	762,634	11.5
80-85	.3178	52,070	16,546	219,198	465,834	8.9
85 AND OVER	1.0000	35,524	35,524	246,636	246,636	6.9

From *Vital Statistics of the United States 1978,* vol. II–Section 5, "Life Tables," U.S. Department of Health and Human Services, Public Health Service, National Center for Health Statistics, 1980.

Abridged Life Tables by Color and Sex: United States, 1978—Con.

AGE INTERVAL	PROPORTION DYING	OF 100,000 BORN ALIVE		STATIONARY POPULATION		AVERAGE REMAINING LIFETIME
PERIOD OF LIFE BETWEEN TWO EXACT AGES STATED IN YEARS	PROPORTION OF PERSONS ALIVE AT BEGINNING OF AGE INTERVAL DYING DURING INTERVAL	NUMBER LIVING AT BEGINNING OF AGE INTERVAL	NUMBER DYING DURING AGE INTERVAL	IN THE AGE INTERVAL	IN THIS AND ALL SUBSEQUENT AGE INTERVALS	AVERAGE NUMBER OF YEARS OF LIFE REMAINING AT BEGINNING OF AGE INTERVAL
(1)	(2)	(3)	(4)	(5)	(6)	(7)
x to $x+n$	$_nq_x$	l_x	$_nd_x$	$_nL_x$	T_x	$\overset{\circ}{e}_x$
WHITE						
0-1	0.0120	100,000	1,201	98,946	7,395,375	74.0
1-5	.0025	98,799	245	394,633	7,296,429	73.9
5-10	.0016	98,554	156	492,353	6,901,796	70.0
10-15	.0016	98,398	162	491,648	6,409,443	65.1
15-20	.0051	98,236	502	490,032	5,917,795	60.2
20-25	.0063	97,734	616	487,135	5,427,763	55.5
25-30	.0058	97,118	561	484,178	4,940,628	50.9
30-35	.0060	96,557	582	481,392	4,456,450	46.2
35-40	.0080	95,975	772	478,082	3,975,058	41.4
40-45	.0128	95,203	1,214	473,204	3,496,976	36.7
45-50	.0212	93,989	1,995	465,297	3,023,772	32.2
50-55	.0337	91,994	3,102	452,735	2,558,475	27.8
55-60	.0511	88,892	4,545	433,750	2,105,740	23.7
60-65	.0817	84,347	6,890	405,342	1,671,990	19.8
65-70	.1143	77,457	8,856	366,074	1,266,648	16.4
70-75	.1695	68,601	11,630	314,950	900,574	13.1
75-80	.2580	56,971	14,699	248,730	585,624	10.3
80-85	.3702	42,272	15,648	171,651	336,894	8.0
85 AND OVER	1.0000	26,624	26,624	165,243	165,243	6.2
WHITE, MALE						
0-1	0.0134	100,000	1,337	98,825	7,019,639	70.2
1-5	.0028	98,663	280	394,014	6,920,814	70.1
5-10	.0018	98,383	179	491,440	6,526,800	66.3
10-15	.0021	98,204	206	490,604	6,035,360	61.5
15-20	.0074	97,998	723	488,360	5,544,756	56.6
20-25	.0095	97,275	925	484,072	5,056,396	52.0
25-30	.0084	96,350	806	479,688	4,572,324	47.5
30-35	.0082	95,544	787	475,820	4,092,636	42.8
35-40	.0107	94,757	1,014	471,426	3,616,816	38.2
40-45	.0163	93,743	1,527	465,182	3,145,390	33.6
45-50	.0274	92,216	2,523	455,217	2,680,208	29.1
50-55	.0445	89,693	3,990	439,187	2,224,991	24.8
55-60	.0681	85,703	5,837	414,767	1,785,804	20.8
60-65	.1101	79,866	8,793	378,308	1,371,037	17.2
65-70	.1572	71,073	11,171	328,269	992,729	14.0
70-75	.2294	59,902	13,744	265,672	664,460	11.1
75-80	.3330	46,158	15,372	192,039	398,788	8.6
80-85	.4528	30,786	13,939	117,620	206,749	6.7
85 AND OVER	1.0000	16,847	16,847	89,129	89,129	5.3
WHITE, FEMALE						
0-1	0.0106	100,000	1,058	99,072	7,779,221	77.8
1-5	.0021	98,942	209	395,283	7,680,149	77.6
5-10	.0013	98,733	130	493,314	7,284,866	73.8
10-15	.0012	98,603	117	492,749	6,791,552	68.9
15-20	.0028	98,486	272	491,793	6,298,803	64.0
20-25	.0031	98,214	301	490,325	5,807,010	59.1
25-30	.0031	97,913	308	488,818	5,316,685	54.3
30-35	.0038	97,605	372	487,151	4,827,867	49.5
35-40	.0055	97,233	530	484,938	4,340,716	44.6
40-45	.0093	96,703	899	481,430	3,855,778	39.9
45-50	.0153	95,804	1,462	475,598	3,374,348	35.2
50-55	.0235	94,342	2,214	466,511	2,898,750	30.7
55-60	.0352	92,128	3,246	452,973	2,432,239	26.4
60-65	.0557	88,882	4,953	432,730	1,979,266	22.3
65-70	.0785	83,929	6,589	404,187	1,546,536	18.4
70-75	.1232	77,340	9,530	364,287	1,142,349	14.8
75-80	.2062	67,810	13,980	305,546	778,062	11.5
80-85	.3208	53,830	17,269	226,259	472,516	8.8
85 AND OVER	1.0000	36,561	36,561	246,257	246,257	6.7

Abridged Life Tables by Color and Sex: United States, 1978—Con.

AGE INTERVAL	PROPORTION DYING	OF 100,000 BORN ALIVE		STATIONARY POPULATION		AVERAGE REMAINING LIFETIME
PERIOD OF LIFE BETWEEN TWO EXACT AGES STATED IN YEARS	PROPORTION OF PERSONS ALIVE AT BEGINNING OF AGE INTERVAL DYING DURING INTERVAL	NUMBER LIVING AT BEGINNING OF AGE INTERVAL	NUMBER DYING DURING AGE INTERVAL	IN THE AGE INTERVAL	IN THIS AND ALL SUBSEQUENT AGE INTERVALS	AVERAGE NUMBER OF YEARS OF LIFE REMAINING AT BEGINNING OF AGE INTERVAL
(1)	(2)	(3)	(4)	(5)	(6)	(7)
x to $x+n$	$_n q_x$	l_x	$_n d_x$	$_n L_x$	T_x	$\overset{\circ}{e}_x$
ALL OTHER						
0-1	0.0212	100,000	2,115	98,178	6,923,402	69.2
1-5	.0038	97,885	377	390,638	6,825,224	69.7
5-10	.0022	97,508	210	486,963	6,434,586	66.0
10-15	.0021	97,298	200	486,067	5,947,623	61.1
15-20	.0048	97,098	469	484,461	5,461,556	56.2
20-25	.0092	96,629	890	481,028	4,977,095	51.5
25-30	.0116	95,739	1,115	475,964	4,496,067	47.0
30-35	.0135	94,624	1,274	470,076	4,020,103	42.5
35-40	.0189	93,350	1,767	462,557	3,550,027	38.0
40-45	.0278	91,583	2,544	451,853	3,087,470	33.7
45-50	.0383	89,039	3,414	437,034	2,635,617	29.6
50-55	.0592	85,625	5,073	415,948	2,198,583	25.7
55-60	.0834	80,552	6,716	386,533	1,782,635	22.1
60-65	.1196	73,836	8,834	347,716	1,396,102	18.9
65-70	.1347	65,002	8,754	303,538	1,048,386	16.1
70-75	.2186	56,248	12,298	250,712	744,848	13.2
75-80	.3175	43,950	13,953	184,120	494,136	11.2
80-85	.3175	29,997	9,523	125,313	310,016	10.3
85 AND OVER	1.0000	20,474	20,474	184,703	184,703	9.0
ALL OTHER, MALE						
0-1	0.0233	100,000	2,325	97,990	6,498,841	65.0
1-5	.0042	97,675	410	389,731	6,400,851	65.5
5-10	.0026	97,265	251	485,643	6,011,120	61.8
10-15	.0027	97,014	259	484,544	5,525,477	57.0
15-20	.0069	96,755	664	482,342	5,040,933	52.1
20-25	.0139	96,091	1,337	477,287	4,558,591	47.4
25-30	.0177	94,754	1,678	469,603	4,081,304	43.1
30-35	.0200	93,076	1,858	460,889	3,611,701	38.8
35-40	.0271	91,218	2,473	450,181	3,150,812	34.5
40-45	.0385	88,745	3,418	435,533	2,700,631	30.4
45-50	.0499	85,327	4,259	416,409	2,265,098	26.5
50-55	.0777	81,068	6,295	390,181	1,848,689	22.8
55-60	.1075	74,773	8,041	354,310	1,458,508	19.5
60-65	.1545	66,732	10,308	308,386	1,104,198	16.5
65-70	.1746	56,424	9,850	257,749	795,812	14.1
70-75	.2612	46,574	12,166	202,363	538,063	11.6
75-80	.3567	34,408	12,272	140,249	335,700	9.8
80-85	.3781	22,136	8,370	88,614	195,451	8.8
85 AND OVER	1.0000	13,766	13,766	106,837	106,837	7.8
ALL OTHER, FEMALE						
0-1	0.0190	100,000	1,899	98,372	7,356,333	73.6
1-5	.0035	98,101	342	391,574	7,257,961	74.0
5-10	.0017	97,759	169	488,325	6,866,387	70.2
10-15	.0014	97,590	140	487,638	6,378,062	65.4
15-20	.0028	97,450	274	486,635	5,890,424	60.4
20-25	.0049	97,176	474	484,756	5,403,789	55.6
25-30	.0064	96,702	622	482,031	4,919,033	50.9
30-35	.0080	96,080	766	478,609	4,437,002	46.2
35-40	.0122	95,314	1,161	473,844	3,958,393	41.5
40-45	.0189	94,153	1,779	466,549	3,484,549	37.0
45-50	.0282	92,374	2,604	455,668	3,018,000	32.7
50-55	.0431	89,770	3,866	439,592	2,562,332	28.5
55-60	.0618	85,904	5,312	416,770	2,122,740	24.7
60-65	.0895	80,592	7,211	385,637	1,705,970	21.2
65-70	.1024	73,381	7,514	348,644	1,320,333	18.0
70-75	.1823	65,867	12,009	299,802	971,689	14.8
75-80	.2850	53,858	15,351	230,635	671,887	12.5
80-85	.2751	38,507	10,594	165,528	441,252	11.5
85 AND OVER	1.0000	27,913	27,913	275,724	275,724	9.9

Number of Survivors at Single Years of Age, Out of 100,000 Born Alive, by Color and Sex: United States, 1978

AGE	TOTAL			WHITE			ALL OTHER		
	BOTH SEXES	MALE	FEMALE	BOTH SEXES	MALE	FEMALE	BOTH SEXES	MALE	FEMALE
0	100,000	100,000	100,000	100,000	100,000	100,000	97,885	97,675	98,101
1	98,621	98,473	98,776	98,799	98,663	98,942	97,762	97,543	97,987
2	98,528	98,367	98,698	98,714	98,563	98,872	97,660	97,433	97,894
3	98,456	98,286	98,635	98,649	98,489	98,816	97,577	97,342	97,819
4	98,399	98,222	98,584	98,597	98,431	98,771	97,508	97,265	97,759
5	98,351	98,169	98,542	98,554	98,383	98,733	97,452	97,200	97,711
6	98,310	98,123	98,507	98,516	98,340	98,701	97,405	97,145	97,672
7	98,273	98,081	98,477	98,482	98,301	98,672	97,365	97,097	97,641
8	98,240	98,042	98,450	98,450	98,265	98,646	97,330	97,054	97,614
9	98,211	98,008	98,426	98,422	98,232	98,623			
10	98,186	97,978	98,405	98,398	98,204	98,603	97,298	97,014	97,590
11	98,163	97,952	98,386	98,377	98,180	98,585	97,267	96,975	97,566
12	98,140	97,925	98,367	98,356	98,156	98,567	97,234	96,934	97,542
13	98,112	97,891	98,345	98,330	98,124	98,546	97,197	96,886	97,515
14	98,072	97,839	98,318	98,291	98,074	98,520	97,152	96,828	97,485
15	98,017	97,764	98,284	98,236	97,998	98,486	97,098	96,755	97,450
16	97,944	97,662	98,242	98,162	97,894	98,443	97,033	96,666	97,409
17	97,855	97,536	98,191	98,071	97,764	98,392	96,956	96,560	97,362
18	97,752	97,389	98,134	97,966	97,613	98,334	96,864	96,432	97,308
19	97,640	97,226	98,074	97,852	97,448	98,274	96,756	96,277	97,246
20	97,521	97,051	98,012	97,734	97,275	98,214	96,629	96,091	97,176
21	97,396	96,866	97,949	97,613	97,095	98,154	96,482	95,873	97,097
22	97,266	96,670	97,884	97,489	96,908	98,094	96,316	95,625	97,009
23	97,132	96,469	97,818	97,363	96,718	98,034	96,134	95,351	96,913
24	96,998	96,267	97,751	97,239	96,531	97,974	95,941	95,059	96,810
25	96,865	96,069	97,684	97,118	96,350	97,913	95,739	94,754	96,702
26	96,735	95,877	97,615	97,001	96,177	97,853	95,529	94,437	96,588
27	96,607	95,690	97,546	96,887	96,012	97,792	95,311	94,107	96,468
28	96,481	95,508	97,475	96,776	95,853	97,731	95,086	93,768	96,342
29	96,355	95,328	97,403	96,667	95,698	97,669	94,857	93,424	96,213
30	96,229	95,150	97,329	96,557	95,544	97,605	94,624	93,076	96,080
31	96,102	94,973	97,252	96,446	95,391	97,538	94,388	92,726	95,943
32	95,973	94,796	97,172	96,334	95,238	97,468	94,147	92,371	95,801
33	95,840	94,616	97,087	96,219	95,083	97,394	93,897	92,006	95,651
34	95,702	94,430	96,997	96,100	94,924	97,316	93,633	91,624	95,490
35	95,557	94,234	96,901	95,975	94,757	97,233	93,350	91,218	95,314
36	95,403	94,027	96,799	95,843	94,580	97,145	93,046	90,785	95,121
37	95,238	93,807	96,688	95,701	94,392	97,050	92,720	90,326	94,910
38	95,060	93,571	96,567	95,549	94,191	96,947	92,370	89,836	94,680
39	94,867	93,318	96,433	95,384	93,975	96,832	91,992	89,310	94,428
40	94,657	93,045	96,284	95,203	93,743	96,703	91,583	88,745	94,153
41	94,427	92,750	96,118	95,005	93,492	96,559	91,140	88,135	93,853
42	94,176	92,429	95,934	94,788	93,218	96,399	90,661	87,480	93,526
43	93,900	92,080	95,731	94,548	92,917	96,221	90,148	86,787	93,171
44	93,598	91,699	95,507	94,283	92,585	96,023	89,607	86,067	92,787
45	93,268	91,283	95,262	93,989	92,216	95,804	89,039	85,327	92,374
46	92,907	90,829	94,993	93,663	91,806	95,562	88,445	84,569	91,931
47	92,512	90,334	94,698	93,303	91,353	95,296	87,820	83,786	91,455
48	92,080	89,792	94,376	92,906	90,853	95,005	87,151	82,958	90,940
49	91,608	89,197	94,026	92,471	90,301	94,687	86,423	82,058	90,380
50	91,091	88,543	93,647	91,994	89,693	94,342	85,625	81,068	89,770
51	90,526	87,824	93,235	91,471	89,024	93,966	84,751	79,978	89,106
52	89,910	87,037	92,788	90,900	88,289	93,557	83,801	78,792	88,387
53	89,243	86,184	92,306	90,279	87,490	93,115	82,780	77,519	87,613
54	88,527	85,268	91,788	89,610	86,628	92,639	81,695	76,176	86,785
55	87,761	84,289	91,234	88,892	85,703	92,128	80,552	74,773	85,904
56	86,945	83,249	90,643	88,124	84,715	91,580	79,357	73,321	84,974
57	86,075	82,141	90,010	87,301	83,657	90,992	78,106	71,813	83,992
58	85,135	80,947	89,326	86,408	82,510	90,354	76,782	70,229	82,945
59	84,108	79,643	88,579	85,428	81,252	89,654	75,363	68,541	81,815
60	82,981	78,213	87,759	84,347	79,866	88,882	73,836	66,732	80,592
61	81,744	76,648	86,858	83,156	78,343	88,031	72,184	64,788	79,259
62	80,401	74,953	85,876	81,858	76,688	87,100	70,420	62,725	77,824
63	78,966	73,144	84,824	80,465	74,912	86,098	68,593	60,598	76,330
64	77,462	71,246	83,720	78,994	73,036	85,039	66,772	58,481	74,836
65	75,902	69,277	82,572	77,457	71,073	83,929	65,002	56,424	73,381
66	74,292	67,244	81,381	75,856	69,029	82,767	63,308	54,455	71,983
67	72,621	65,141	80,134	74,184	66,900	81,542	61,662	52,552	70,614
68	70,873	62,954	78,814	72,428	64,677	80,240	59,997	50,657	69,200
69	69,024	60,664	77,396	70,571	62,347	78,845	58,215	48,684	67,642
70	67,056	58,259	75,862	68,601	59,902	77,340	56,248	46,574	65,867
71	64,971	55,742	74,208	66,519	57,348	75,722	54,087	44,319	63,869
72	62,772	53,126	72,431	64,327	54,694	73,986	51,760	41,946	61,672
73	60,449	50,413	70,507	62,013	51,943	72,106	49,279	39,479	59,269
74	57,992	47,608	68,410	59,563	49,095	70,054	46,666	36,955	56,660
75	55,397	44,720	66,121	56,971	46,158	67,810	43,950	34,408	53,858
76	52,671	41,764	63,638	54,241	43,145	65,367	41,160	31,865	50,894
77	49,828	38,760	60,971	51,385	40,076	62,731	38,328	29,345	47,813
78	46,890	35,733	58,138	48,423	36,974	59,918	35,492	26,867	44,673
79	43,882	32,710	55,163	45,377	33,868	56,945	32,697	24,454	41,545
80	40,832	29,721	52,070	42,272	30,786	53,830	29,997	22,136	38,507
81	37,766	26,797	48,881	39,130	27,760	50,588	27,454	19,953	35,645
82	34,712	23,973	45,615	35,973	24,820	47,232	25,142	17,957	33,051
83	31,696	21,284	42,291	32,823	21,999	43,772	23,144	16,210	30,825
84	28,747	18,767	38,923	29,700	19,330	40,214	21,554	14,785	29,074
85	25,891	16,462	35,524	26,624	16,847	36,561	20,474	13,766	27,913

Expectation of Life at Single Years of Age, by Color and Sex: United States, 1978

AGE	TOTAL			WHITE			ALL OTHER		
	BOTH SEXES	MALE	FEMALE	BOTH SEXES	MALE	FEMALE	BOTH SEXES	MALE	FEMALE
0	73.3	69.5	77.2	74.0	70.2	77.8	69.2	65.0	73.6
1	73.3	69.6	77.1	73.9	70.1	77.6	69.7	65.5	74.0
2	72.4	68.6	76.2	72.9	69.2	76.7	68.8	64.6	73.1
3	71.5	67.7	75.2	72.0	68.3	75.7	67.9	63.7	72.1
4	70.5	66.7	74.3	71.0	67.3	74.8	66.9	62.8	71.2
5	69.5	65.8	73.3	70.0	66.3	73.8	66.0	61.8	70.2
6	68.6	64.8	72.3	69.1	65.4	72.8	65.0	60.8	69.3
7	67.6	63.8	71.4	68.1	64.4	71.8	64.1	59.9	68.3
8	66.6	62.9	70.4	67.1	63.4	70.8	63.1	58.9	67.3
9	65.6	61.9	69.4	66.1	62.4	69.9	62.1	57.9	66.3
10	64.6	60.9	68.4	65.1	61.5	68.9	61.1	57.0	65.4
11	63.7	59.9	67.4	64.2	60.5	67.9	60.1	56.0	64.4
12	62.7	58.9	66.4	63.2	59.5	66.9	59.2	55.0	63.4
13	61.7	58.0	65.5	62.2	58.5	65.9	58.2	54.0	62.4
14	60.7	57.0	64.5	61.2	57.5	64.9	57.2	53.1	61.4
15	59.7	56.0	63.5	60.2	56.6	64.0	56.2	52.1	60.4
16	58.8	55.1	62.5	59.3	55.6	63.0	55.3	51.1	59.5
17	57.8	54.2	61.6	58.3	54.7	62.0	54.3	50.2	58.5
18	56.9	53.2	60.6	57.4	53.8	61.1	53.4	49.3	57.5
19	56.0	52.3	59.6	56.5	52.9	60.1	52.4	48.3	56.6
20	55.0	51.4	58.7	55.5	52.0	59.1	51.5	47.4	55.6
21	54.1	50.5	57.7	54.6	51.1	58.2	50.6	46.5	54.7
22	53.2	49.6	56.7	53.7	50.2	57.2	49.7	45.7	53.7
23	52.2	48.7	55.8	52.7	49.3	56.2	48.8	44.8	52.8
24	51.3	47.8	54.8	51.8	48.4	55.3	47.9	43.9	51.8
25	50.4	46.9	53.9	50.9	47.5	54.3	47.0	43.1	50.9
26	49.5	46.0	52.9	49.9	46.5	53.3	46.1	42.2	49.9
27	48.5	45.1	51.9	49.0	45.6	52.4	45.2	41.4	49.0
28	47.6	44.2	51.0	48.0	44.7	51.4	44.3	40.5	48.1
29	46.6	43.3	50.0	47.1	43.8	50.4	43.4	39.7	47.1
30	45.7	42.4	49.0	46.2	42.8	49.5	42.5	38.8	46.2
31	44.8	41.4	48.1	45.2	41.9	48.5	41.6	37.9	45.2
32	43.8	40.5	47.1	44.3	41.0	47.5	40.7	37.1	44.3
33	42.9	39.6	46.2	43.3	40.0	46.6	39.8	36.2	43.4
34	41.9	38.7	45.2	42.4	39.1	45.6	38.9	35.4	42.5
35	41.0	37.7	44.2	41.4	38.2	44.6	38.0	34.5	41.5
36	40.1	36.8	43.3	40.5	37.2	43.7	37.2	33.7	40.6
37	39.1	35.9	42.3	39.5	36.3	42.7	36.3	32.9	39.7
38	38.2	35.0	41.4	38.6	35.4	41.8	35.4	32.0	38.8
39	37.3	34.1	40.5	37.7	34.5	40.8	34.6	31.2	37.9
40	36.4	33.2	39.5	36.7	33.6	39.9	33.7	30.4	37.0
41	35.5	32.3	38.6	35.8	32.6	38.9	32.9	29.6	36.1
42	34.6	31.4	37.7	34.9	31.7	38.0	32.0	28.9	35.3
43	33.7	30.5	36.7	34.0	30.8	37.1	31.2	28.1	34.4
44	32.8	29.6	35.8	33.1	29.9	36.1	30.4	27.3	33.5
45	31.9	28.8	34.9	32.2	29.1	35.2	29.6	26.5	32.7
46	31.0	27.9	34.0	31.3	28.2	34.3	28.8	25.8	31.8
47	30.1	27.1	33.1	30.4	27.3	33.4	28.0	25.0	31.0
48	29.3	26.2	32.2	29.5	26.5	32.5	27.2	24.3	30.2
49	28.4	25.4	31.3	28.7	25.6	31.6	26.4	23.5	29.3
50	27.6	24.6	30.5	27.8	24.8	30.7	25.7	22.8	28.5
51	26.7	23.8	29.6	27.0	24.0	29.8	24.9	22.1	27.8
52	25.9	23.0	28.7	26.1	23.2	29.0	24.2	21.4	27.0
53	25.1	22.2	27.9	25.3	22.4	28.1	23.5	20.8	26.2
54	24.3	21.5	27.0	24.5	21.6	27.3	22.8	20.1	25.5
55	23.5	20.7	26.2	23.7	20.8	26.4	22.1	19.5	24.7
56	22.7	19.9	25.4	22.9	20.1	25.6	21.5	18.9	24.0
57	22.0	19.2	24.5	22.1	19.3	24.7	20.8	18.3	23.3
58	21.2	18.5	23.7	21.3	18.6	23.9	20.1	17.7	22.5
59	20.5	17.8	22.9	20.6	17.9	23.1	19.5	17.1	21.8
60	19.7	17.1	22.1	19.8	17.2	22.3	18.9	16.5	21.2
61	19.0	16.4	21.4	19.1	16.5	21.5	18.3	16.0	20.5
62	18.3	15.8	20.6	18.4	15.8	20.7	17.8	15.5	19.9
63	17.6	15.2	19.8	17.7	15.2	19.9	17.2	15.1	19.3
64	17.0	14.6	19.1	17.0	14.6	19.2	16.7	14.6	18.6
65	16.3	14.0	18.4	16.4	14.0	18.4	16.1	14.1	18.0
66	15.7	13.4	17.6	15.7	13.4	17.7	15.5	13.6	17.3
67	15.0	12.8	16.9	15.0	12.8	16.9	15.0	13.1	16.7
68	14.4	12.2	16.2	14.4	12.2	16.2	14.4	12.5	16.0
69	13.7	11.7	15.4	13.7	11.6	15.5	13.8	12.0	15.4
70	13.1	11.1	14.7	13.1	11.1	14.8	13.2	11.6	14.8
71	12.5	10.6	14.1	12.5	10.6	14.1	12.8	11.1	14.2
72	12.0	10.1	13.4	11.9	10.1	13.4	12.3	10.7	13.7
73	11.4	9.6	12.8	11.4	9.6	12.7	11.9	10.4	13.2
74	10.9	9.2	12.1	10.8	9.1	12.1	11.6	10.0	12.8
75	10.4	8.7	11.5	10.3	8.6	11.5	11.2	9.8	12.5
76	9.9	8.3	11.0	9.8	8.2	10.9	11.0	9.5	12.2
77	9.4	7.9	10.4	9.3	7.8	10.3	10.8	9.3	11.9
78	9.0	7.5	9.9	8.8	7.4	9.8	10.6	9.1	11.7
79	8.5	7.2	9.4	8.4	7.1	9.3	10.4	8.9	11.6
80	8.1	6.9	8.9	8.0	6.7	8.8	10.3	8.8	11.5
81	7.8	6.6	8.5	7.6	6.4	8.3	10.2	8.7	11.3
82	7.4	6.3	8.1	7.2	6.1	7.9	10.1	8.6	11.1
83	7.1	6.0	7.7	6.8	5.8	7.5	9.9	8.5	10.9
84	6.7	5.8	7.3	6.5	5.5	7.1	9.6	8.2	10.5
85	6.4	5.5	6.9	6.2	5.3	6.7	9.0	7.8	9.9

Life Table Values by Color and Sex: Death-Registration States, 1900-1902 to 1919-21, and United States, 1929-31 to 1978

[Alaska and Hawaii included beginning in 1959. For decennial periods prior to 1929-31, data are for groups of registration States as follows: 1900-1902 and 1909-11, 10 States and the District of Columbia; 1919-21, 34 States and the District of Columbia. For 1900-1902 to 1929-31, figures for "All other, male" and "All other, female" include only the black population. However, in no case did the black population comprise less than 95 percent of the corresponding "All other" population]

| AGE, COLOR, AND SEX | NUMBER OF SURVIVORS OUT OF 100,000 BORN ALIVE (l_x) | | | | | | | | |
	1978[1]	1969-71[1]	1959-61	1949-51	1939-41	1929-31	1919-21	1909-11	1900-1902
WHITE, MALE									
0	100,000	100,000	100,000	100,000	100,000	100,000	100,000	100,000	100,000
1	98,663	97,994	97,408	96,931	95,188	93,768	91,975	87,674	86,655
5	98,383	97,671	97,015	96,403	94,150	91,738	88,842	82,972	80,864
10	98,204	97,441	96,758	96,069	93,601	90,810	87,530	81,519	79,109
15	97,998	97,208	96,503	95,728	93,089	90,074	86,546	80,549	78,037
20	97,275	96,480	95,908	95,104	92,293	88,904	84,997	79,116	76,376
25	96,350	95,524	95,106	94,294	91,241	87,371	83,061	77,047	73,907
30	95,544	94,716	94,401	93,489	90,092	85,707	80,888	74,810	71,219
35	94,757	93,843	93,589	92,543	88,713	83,812	78,441	72,108	68,245
40	93,743	92,631	92,427	91,173	86,880	81,457	75,733	68,848	64,954
45	92,216	90,725	90,533	89,002	84,285	78,345	72,696	65,115	61,369
50	89,693	87,690	87,424	85,601	80,521	74,288	69,107	60,741	57,274
55	85,703	83,001	82,463	80,496	75,156	68,981	64,574	55,622	52,491
60	79,866	75,969	75,485	73,172	67,787	61,933	58,498	48,987	46,452
65	71,073	66,343	65,834	63,541	58,305	52,964	50,663	40,862	39,245
70	59,902	54,138	53,825	51,735	46,739	41,880	40,873	31,527	30,640
75	46,158	40,324	40,207	38,104	33,404	29,471	29,205	21,585	21,387
80	30,786	25,885	25,993	24,005	19,860	17,221	17,655	12,160	12,266
85	16,847	13,527	13,065	12,015	9,013	7,572	8,154	5,145	5,252
ALL OTHER, MALE									
0	100,000	100,000	100,000	100,000	100,000	100,000	100,000	100,000	100,000
1	97,675	96,592	95,301	94,911	91,696	91,268	89,499	78,065	74,674
5	97,265	96,038	94,570	93,921	89,920	88,412	85,195	68,589	64,385
10	97,014	95,716	94,234	93,453	89,211	87,311	83,768	66,377	61,730
15	96,755	95,385	93,874	92,965	88,417	86,152	82,332	64,478	59,667
20	96,091	94,293	93,108	91,941	86,770	83,621	79,057	61,426	56,733
25	94,754	92,267	91,825	90,285	84,055	79,516	74,540	57,736	53,285
30	93,076	90,106	90,270	88,327	80,865	75,083	70,344	54,073	49,867
35	91,218	87,597	88,331	85,940	77,185	70,049	65,873	49,865	46,541
40	88,745	84,378	85,744	82,832	72,830	64,710	61,353	45,414	42,989
45	85,327	80,163	82,075	78,686	67,514	58,432	56,589	40,563	39,230
50	81,068	74,748	77,239	72,891	60,766	51,748	51,880	35,427	34,766
55	74,773	67,808	70,351	65,122	52,867	44,436	46,581	29,754	29,987
60	66,732	59,396	61,669	55,535	44,370	36,790	40,506	23,750	24,194
65	56,424	49,607	51,392	45,198	35,912	29,314	34,042	17,836	19,015
70	46,574	39,025	39,914	35,018	27,688	21,741	26,923	12,295	13,829
75	34,408	27,789	29,064	25,472	19,765	14,419	18,854	7,494	8,892
80	22,136	17,999	19,994	16,904	12,352	8,239	11,615	3,894	4,831
85	13,766	10,811	11,620	9,898	6,492	3,660	5,605	1,747	2,030
WHITE, FEMALE									
0	100,000	100,000	100,000	100,000	100,000	100,000	100,000	100,000	100,000
1	98,942	98,468	98,036	97,645	96,211	95,037	93,608	89,774	88,939
5	98,733	98,203	97,709	97,199	95,309	93,216	90,721	85,349	83,426
10	98,603	98,042	97,525	96,960	94,890	92,466	89,564	83,979	81,723
15	98,486	97,902	97,375	96,756	94,534	91,894	88,712	83,093	80,680
20	98,214	97,618	97,135	96,454	93,984	90,939	87,281	81,750	78,978
25	97,913	97,299	96,844	96,072	93,228	89,524	85,163	79,865	76,588
30	97,605	96,945	96,499	95,605	92,320	87,972	82,740	77,676	73,887
35	97,233	96,474	96,026	94,977	91,211	86,248	80,206	75,200	70,971
40	96,793	95,762	95,326	94,080	89,805	84,256	77,624	72,425	67,935
45	95,804	94,649	94,228	92,725	87,920	81,780	74,871	69,341	64,677
50	94,342	92,924	92,522	90,685	85,267	78,572	71,547	65,629	61,005
55	92,128	90,383	89,967	87,699	81,520	74,321	67,323	61,053	56,509
60	88,882	86,726	86,339	83,279	76,200	68,462	61,704	54,900	50,752
65	83,929	81,579	80,739	76,773	68,701	60,499	54,299	47,086	43,806
70	77,340	74,101	72,507	67,545	58,363	49,932	44,638	37,482	35,206
75	67,810	63,290	60,461	54,397	44,685	37,024	32,777	26,569	25,362
80	53,830	48,182	44,676	38,026	28,882	23,053	20,492	15,929	15,349
85	36,561	30,490	26,046	21,348	14,487	10,937	9,909	7,152	7,149
ALL OTHER, FEMALE									
0	100,000	100,000	100,000	100,000	100,000	100,000	100,000	100,000	100,000
1	98,191	97,235	96,172	95,913	93,318	92,796	91,251	81,493	78,525
5	97,759	96,772	95,543	95,055	91,710	90,185	87,149	72,768	68,056
10	97,590	96,546	95,265	94,679	91,092	89,201	85,607	70,508	65,111
15	97,450	96,353	95,057	94,343	90,363	88,088	83,954	68,218	62,384
20	97,176	95,917	94,660	93,544	88,505	85,078	80,154	64,764	59,053
25	96,702	95,247	94,005	92,336	85,961	81,067	75,359	61,430	55,795
30	96,080	94,370	93,070	90,799	83,147	76,816	70,643	58,281	52,773
35	95,314	93,123	91,670	88,805	79,879	72,192	65,857	54,595	49,567
40	94,153	91,247	89,676	86,052	75,908	67,271	61,130	50,568	46,146
45	92,374	88,608	86,793	82,257	71,061	61,365	56,234	45,947	42,279
50	89,770	84,964	82,979	77,007	64,886	54,920	50,780	40,886	37,681
55	85,904	80,162	77,362	70,196	57,419	47,074	44,742	35,415	33,124
60	80,592	73,984	69,941	61,758	49,102	38,761	37,954	28,908	27,524
65	73,381	66,064	60,825	52,358	40,718	30,852	31,044	22,302	21,995
70	65,867	56,375	51,274	42,612	32,579	23,341	24,107	15,871	16,140
75	53,858	44,841	40,540	32,981	24,668	16,576	17,216	10,657	11,066
80	38,507	33,373	30,315	23,712	17,157	10,822	11,151	6,324	6,708
85	27,913	22,763	19,744	15,550	10,658	6,033	5,972	3,029	3,567

[1]Deaths of nonresidents of the United States were excluded beginning in 1970.

Life Table Values by Color and Sex: Death-Registration States, 1900-1902 to 1919-21, and United States, 1929-31 to 1978—Con.

[See headnote at beginning of table]

AGE, COLOR, AND SEX	AVERAGE NUMBER OF YEARS OF LIFE REMAINING $(\mathring{e}_x)$								
	1978[1]	1969-71[1]	1959-61	1949-51	1939-41	1929-31	1919-21	1909-11	1900-1902
WHITE, MALE									
0	70.2	67.94	67.55	66.31	62.81	59.12	56.34	50.23	48.23
1	70.1	68.33	68.34	67.41	64.98	62.04	60.24	56.26	54.61
5	66.3	64.55	64.61	63.77	61.68	59.38	58.31	55.37	54.43
10	61.5	59.69	59.78	58.98	57.03	54.96	54.15	51.32	50.59
15	56.6	54.83	54.93	54.18	52.33	50.39	49.74	46.91	46.25
20	52.0	50.22	50.25	49.52	47.76	46.02	45.60	42.71	42.19
25	47.5	45.70	45.65	44.93	43.28	41.78	41.60	38.79	38.52
30	42.8	41.07	40.97	40.29	38.80	37.54	37.65	34.87	34.88
35	38.2	36.43	36.31	35.68	34.36	33.33	33.74	31.08	31.29
40	33.6	31.87	31.73	31.17	30.03	29.22	29.86	27.43	27.74
45	29.1	27.48	27.34	26.87	25.87	25.28	26.00	23.86	24.21
50	24.8	23.34	23.22	22.83	21.96	21.51	22.22	20.39	20.76
55	20.8	19.51	19.45	19.11	18.34	17.97	18.59	17.03	17.42
60	17.2	16.07	16.01	15.76	15.05	14.72	15.25	13.98	14.35
65	14.0	13.02	12.97	12.75	12.07	11.77	12.21	11.25	11.51
70	11.1	10.38	10.29	10.07	9.42	9.20	9.51	8.83	9.03
75	8.6	8.06	7.92	7.77	7.17	7.02	7.30	6.75	6.84
80	6.7	6.18	5.89	5.88	5.38	5.26	5.47	5.09	5.10
85	5.3	4.63	4.34	4.35	4.02	3.99	4.06	3.88	3.81
ALL OTHER, MALE									
0	65.0	60.98	61.48	58.91	52.33	47.55	47.14	34.05	32.54
1	65.5	62.13	63.50	61.06	56.05	51.08	51.63	42.53	42.46
5	61.8	58.48	59.98	57.69	53.13	48.69	50.18	44.25	45.06
10	57.0	53.67	55.19	52.96	48.54	44.27	45.99	40.65	41.90
15	52.1	48.84	50.39	48.23	43.95	39.83	41.75	36.77	38.26
20	47.4	44.37	45.78	43.73	39.74	35.95	38.36	33.46	35.11
25	43.1	40.29	41.38	39.49	35.94	32.67	35.54	30.44	32.21
30	38.8	36.20	37.05	35.31	32.25	29.45	32.51	27.33	29.25
35	34.5	32.16	32.81	31.21	28.67	26.39	29.54	24.42	26.16
40	30.4	28.29	28.72	27.29	25.23	23.36	26.53	21.57	23.12
45	26.5	24.64	24.89	23.59	22.02	20.59	23.55	18.85	20.09
50	22.8	21.24	21.28	20.25	19.18	17.92	20.47	16.21	17.34
55	19.5	18.14	18.11	17.36	16.67	15.46	17.50	13.82	14.69
60	16.5	15.35	15.29	14.91	14.38	13.15	14.74	11.67	12.62
65	14.1	12.87	12.84	12.75	12.18	10.87	12.07	9.74	10.38
70	11.6	10.68	10.81	10.74	10.06	8.78	9.58	8.00	8.33
75	9.8	8.99	8.93	8.83	8.09	6.99	7.61	6.58	6.60
80	8.8	7.57	6.87	7.07	6.46	5.42	5.83	5.53	5.12
85	7.8	6.04	5.08	5.38	5.08	4.30	4.53	4.48	4.04
WHITE, FEMALE									
0	77.8	75.49	74.19	72.03	67.29	62.67	58.53	53.62	51.08
1	77.6	75.66	74.68	72.77	68.93	64.93	61.51	58.69	56.39
5	73.8	71.86	70.92	69.09	65.57	62.17	59.43	57.67	56.03
10	68.9	66.97	66.05	64.26	60.85	57.65	55.17	53.57	52.15
15	64.0	62.07	61.15	59.39	56.07	53.00	50.67	49.12	47.79
20	59.1	57.24	56.29	54.56	51.38	48.52	46.46	44.88	43.77
25	54.3	52.42	51.45	49.77	46.78	44.25	42.55	40.88	40.05
30	49.5	47.60	46.63	45.00	42.21	39.99	38.72	36.96	36.42
35	44.6	42.82	41.84	40.28	37.70	35.73	34.86	33.09	32.82
40	39.9	38.12	37.13	35.64	33.25	31.52	30.94	29.26	29.17
45	35.2	33.54	32.53	31.12	28.90	27.39	26.98	25.45	25.51
50	30.7	29.11	28.08	26.76	24.72	23.41	23.12	21.74	21.89
55	26.4	24.85	23.81	22.58	20.73	19.60	19.40	18.18	18.43
60	22.3	20.79	19.69	18.64	17.00	16.05	15.93	14.92	15.23
65	18.4	16.93	15.88	15.00	13.56	12.81	12.75	11.97	12.23
70	14.8	13.37	12.38	11.68	10.50	9.98	9.94	9.38	9.59
75	11.5	10.21	9.28	8.87	7.92	7.56	7.62	7.20	7.33
80	8.8	7.59	6.67	6.59	5.88	5.63	5.70	5.35	5.50
85	6.7	5.54	4.66	4.83	4.34	4.24	4.24	4.06	4.10
ALL OTHER, FEMALE									
0	73.6	69.05	66.47	62.70	55.51	49.51	46.92	37.67	35.04
1	74.0	70.01	68.10	64.37	58.47	52.33	50.39	45.15	43.54
5	70.2	66.34	64.54	60.93	55.47	49.81	48.70	46.42	46.04
10	65.4	61.49	59.72	56.17	50.83	45.33	44.54	42.84	43.02
15	60.4	56.60	54.85	51.36	46.22	40.87	40.36	39.18	39.79
20	55.6	51.85	50.07	46.77	42.14	37.22	37.15	36.14	36.89
25	50.9	47.19	45.40	42.35	38.31	33.93	34.35	32.97	33.90
30	46.2	42.61	40.83	38.02	34.52	30.67	31.48	29.61	30.70
35	41.5	38.14	36.41	33.82	30.83	27.47	28.58	26.44	27.52
40	37.0	33.87	32.16	29.82	27.31	24.30	25.60	23.34	24.37
45	32.7	29.80	28.14	26.07	24.00	21.39	22.61	20.43	21.36
50	28.5	25.97	24.31	22.67	21.04	18.60	19.76	17.65	18.67
55	24.7	22.37	20.89	19.62	18.44	16.27	17.09	14.98	15.88
60	21.2	19.02	17.83	16.95	16.14	14.22	14.69	12.78	13.60
65	18.0	15.99	15.12	14.54	13.95	12.24	12.41	10.82	11.38
70	14.8	13.30	12.46	12.29	11.81	10.38	10.25	9.22	9.62
75	12.5	11.06	10.10	10.15	9.80	8.62	8.37	7.55	7.90
80	11.5	9.01	7.66	8.15	8.00	6.90	6.58	6.05	6.48
85	9.9	7.07	5.44	6.15	6.38	5.48	5.22	5.09	5.10

[1]Deaths of nonresidents of the United States were excluded beginning in 1970.

Estimated Average Length of Life in Years, by Color and Sex: Death-Registration States, 1900-1928, and United States, 1929-78

For selected years, life table values shown are estimates

AREA AND YEAR	TOTAL			WHITE			ALL OTHER		
	BOTH SEXES	MALE	FEMALE	BOTH SEXES	MALE	FEMALE	BOTH SEXES	MALE	FEMALE
UNITED STATES									
1978[1]	73.3	69.5	77.2	74.0	70.2	77.8	69.2	65.0	73.6
1977[1]	73.2	69.3	77.1	73.8	70.0	77.7	68.8	64.6	73.1
1976[1]	72.8	69.0	76.7	73.5	69.7	77.3	68.4	64.2	72.7
1975[1]	72.5	68.7	76.5	73.2	69.4	77.2	67.9	63.6	72.3
1974[1]	71.9	68.1	75.8	72.7	68.9	76.6	67.0	62.9	71.3
1973[1,2]	71.3	67.5	75.2	72.1	68.4	76.1	65.9	61.8	70.1
1972[1,2,3]	71.1	67.4	75.0	72.0	68.2	75.9	65.6	61.4	69.9
1971[1,2]	71.1	67.4	75.0	71.9	68.2	75.8	65.6	61.6	69.7
1970[1,2]	70.8	67.1	74.7	71.7	68.0	75.6	65.3	61.3	69.4
1969[2]	70.5	66.8	74.4	71.4	67.7	75.3	64.5	60.6	68.6
1968[2]	70.2	66.6	74.1	71.1	67.5	75.0	64.1	60.4	67.9
1967[2]	70.5	67.0	74.3	71.4	67.8	75.2	64.9	61.4	68.5
1966[2]	70.2	66.7	73.9	71.1	67.5	74.8	64.2	60.9	67.6
1965[2]	70.2	66.8	73.8	71.1	67.6	74.8	64.3	61.2	67.6
1964[2]	70.2	66.8	73.7	71.0	67.7	74.7	64.2	61.3	67.3
1963[2,4]	69.9	66.6	73.4	70.8	67.4	74.4	63.7	61.0	66.6
1962[2,4]	70.1	66.9	73.5	70.9	67.7	74.5	64.2	61.6	66.9
1961[2]	70.2	67.1	73.6	71.0	67.8	74.6	64.5	62.0	67.1
1960	69.7	66.6	73.1	70.6	67.4	74.1	63.6	61.1	66.3
1959	69.9	66.8	73.2	70.7	67.5	74.2	63.9	61.3	66.5
1958	69.6	66.6	72.9	70.5	67.4	73.9	63.4	61.0	65.8
1957	69.5	66.4	72.7	70.3	67.2	73.7	63.0	60.7	65.5
1956	69.7	66.7	72.9	70.5	67.5	73.9	63.6	61.3	66.1
1955	69.6	66.7	72.8	70.5	67.4	73.7	63.7	61.4	66.1
1954	69.6	66.7	72.8	70.5	67.5	73.7	63.4	61.1	65.9
1953	68.8	66.0	72.0	69.7	66.8	73.0	62.0	59.7	64.5
1952	68.6	65.8	71.6	69.5	66.6	72.6	61.4	59.1	63.8
1951	68.4	65.6	71.4	69.3	66.5	72.4	61.2	59.2	63.4
1950	68.2	65.6	71.1	69.1	66.5	72.2	60.8	59.1	62.9
1949	68.0	65.2	70.7	68.8	66.2	71.9	60.6	58.9	62.7
1948	67.2	64.6	69.9	68.0	65.5	71.0	60.0	58.1	62.5
1947	66.8	64.4	69.7	67.6	65.2	70.5	59.7.	57.9	61.9
1946	66.7	64.4	69.4	67.5	65.1	70.3	59.1	57.5	61.0
1945	65.9	63.6	67.9	66.8	64.4	69.5	57.7	56.1	59.6
1944	65.2	63.6	66.8	66.2	64.5	68.4	56.6	55.8	57.7
1943	63.3	62.4	64.4	64.2	63.2	65.7	55.6	55.4	56.1
1942	66.2	64.7	67.9	67.3	65.9	69.4	56.6	55.4	58.2
1941	64.8	63.1	66.8	66.2	64.4	68.5	53.8	52.5	55.3
1940	62.9	60.8	65.2	64.2	62.1	66.6	53.1	51.5	54.9
1939	63.7	62.1	65.4	64.9	63.3	66.6	54.5	53.2	56.0
1938	63.5	61.9	65.3	65.0	63.2	66.8	52.9	51.7	54.3
1937	60.0	58.0	62.4	61.4	59.3	63.8	50.3	48.3	52.5
1936	58.5	56.6	60.6	59.8	58.0	61.9	49.0	47.0	51.4
1935	61.7	59.9	63.9	62.9	61.0	65.0	53.1	51.3	55.2
1934	61.1	59.3	63.3	62.4	60.5	64.6	51.8	50.2	53.7
1933	63.3	61.7	65.1	64.3	62.7	66.3	54.7	53.5.	56.0
1932	62.1	61.0	63.5	63.2	62.0	64.5	53.7	52.8	54.6
1931	61.1	59.4	63.1	62.6	60.8	64.7	50.4	49.5	51.5
1930	59.7	58.1	61.6	61.4	59.7	63.5	48.1	47.3	49.2
1929	57.1	55.8	58.7	58.6	57.2	60.3	46.7	45.7	47.8
DEATH REGISTRATION STATES									
1928	56.8	55.6	58.3	58.4	57.0	60.0	46.3	45.6	47.0
1927	60.4	59.0	62.1	62.0	60.5	63.9	48.2	47.6	48.9
1926	56.7	55.5	58.0	58.2	57.0	59.6	44.6	43.7	45.6
1925	59.0	57.6	60.6	60.7	59.3	62.4	45.7	44.9	46.7
1924	59.7	58.1	61.5	61.4	59.8	63.4	46.6	45.5	47.8
1923	57.2	56.1	58.5	58.3	57.1	59.6	48.3	47.7	48.9
1922	59.6	58.4	61.0	60.4	59.1	61.9	52.4	51.8	53.0
1921	60.8	60.0	61.8	61.8	60.8	62.9	51.5	51.6	51.3
1920	54.1	53.6	54.6	54.9	54.4	55.6	45.3	45.5	45.2
1919	54.7	53.5	56.0	55.8	54.5	57.4	44.5	44.5	44.4
1918	39.1	36.6	42.2	39.8	37.1	43.2	31.1	29.9	32.5
1917	50.9	48.4	54.0	52.0	49.3	55.3	38.8	37.0	40.8
1916	51.7	49.6	54.3	52.5	50.2	55.2	41.3	39.6	43.1
1915	54.5	52.5	56.8	55.1	53.1	57.5	38.9	37.5	40.5
1914	54.2	52.0	56.8	54.9	52.7	57.5	38.9	37.1	40.8
1913	52.5	50.3	55.0	53.0	50.8	55.7	38.4	36.7	40.3
1912	53.5	51.5	55.9	53.9	51.9	56.2	37.9	35.9	40.0
1911	52.6	50.9	54.4	53.0	51.3	54.9	36.4	34.6	38.2
1910	50.0	48.4	51.8	50.3	48.6	52.0	35.6	33.8	37.5
1909	52.1	50.5	53.8	52.5	50.9	54.2	35.7	34.2	37.3
1908	51.1	49.5	52.8	51.5	49.9	53.3	34.9	33.8	36.0
1907	47.6	45.6	49.9	48.1	46.0	50.4	32.5	31.1	34.0
1906	48.7	46.9	50.8	49.3	47.3	51.4	32.9	31.8	33.9
1905	48.7	47.3	50.2	49.1	47.6	50.6	31.3	29.6	33.1
1904	47.6	46.2	49.1	48.0	46.6	49.5	30.8	29.1	32.7
1903	50.5	49.1	52.0	50.9	49.5	52.5	33.1	31.7	34.6
1902	51.5	49.8	53.4	51.9	50.2	53.8	34.6	32.9	36.4
1901	49.1	47.6	50.6	49.4	48.0	51.0	33.7	32.2	35.3
1900	47.3	46.3	48.3	47.6	46.6	48.7	33.0	32.5	33.5

[1]Excludes deaths of nonresidents of the United States.
[2]Figures are revised, and therefore, may differ from those published in volumes of <u>Vital Statistics of the United States</u>, Vol. II, Mortality, Part A, for 1976 and earlier years; see Technical Appendix.
[3]Deaths based on a 50-percent sample.
[4]Figures by color exclude data for residents of New Jersey; see Technical Appendix.

Annual Summary of Births, Deaths, Marriages, and Divorces: United States, 1980

A summary of monthly provisional reports shows that there were more births, marriages, divorces, and deaths in the United States in 1980 than in 1979. The rates per 1,000 population for births, marriages, and deaths were also higher in 1980 than in 1979. The divorce rate, however, remained at the same level as the previous year. Although the number of infant deaths was the same in both years, the infant mortality rate per 1,000 live births was lower in 1980 than in 1979. The population bases used to compute rates for 1979 and 1980 were the same as those used for the monthly series published in Vol. 29, nos. 1-12 and, therefore, are not consistent with estimates based on the 1980 census enumeration (see Technical notes).

Natural increase

As a result of natural increase, the excess of births over deaths, 1,612,000 persons were added to the population during 1980. The rate of natural increase was 7.3 persons per 1,000 population compared with 7.1 for 1979. This increase was due to the increase in the birth rate.

Table B. Seasonally adjusted birth and fertility rates, by month: United States, 1979 and 1980

[Rates on an annual basis. Birth rates per 1,000 population and fertility rates per 1,000 women aged 15-44 years]

Month	Birth rate		Fertility rate	
	1980	1979	1980	1979
January	15.3	15.5	65.8	67.0
February	15.8	15.2	67.6	65.9
March	16.3	15.3	70.0	66.3
April	16.3	15.7	69.9	68.0
May	16.3	15.9	69.8	68.4
June	16.2	15.6	69.4	67.5
July	16.1	15.9	68.7	68.5
August	16.5	16.5	70.6	71.1
September	15.9	15.5	67.9	66.5
October	17.0	15.7	72.7	67.6
November	15.8	16.8	67.4	72.3
December	16.6	15.8	70.9	67.7

Deaths

During 1980 an estimated 1,986,000 deaths occurred in the United States. The crude death rate for 1980 (892.6 deaths per 100,000 population) was 3 percent higher than the provisional rate for 1979

Vital Statistics of the United States

Item	Rate per 1,000 population								
	1980[1]	1979[1]	1978	1977	1976	1975	1974	1973	1972
Births	16.2	15.8	15.3	15.4	14.8	14.8	14.9	14.9	15.6
Deaths	8.9	8.7	8.8	8.8	8.9	8.9	9.2	9.4	9.4
Natural increase	7.3	7.1	6.5	6.6	5.9	5.9	5.7	5.5	6.2
Marriages	10.9	10.7	[2]10.5	10.1	10.0	10.1	10.5	10.9	11.0
Divorces (est.)	5.3	5.3	5.2	5.0	5.0	4.9	4.6	4.4	4.1

[1]Provisional.
[2]Beginning with 1978, data include nonlicensed marriages registered in California; see Technical notes.

From *Monthly Vital Statistics Report,* vol. 29, no. 13, U.S. Department of Health and Human Services, Public Health Service, National Center for Health Statistics, September 17, 1981.

Table C. Deaths and death rates, by month: United States, 1979 and 1980

[Rates on an annual basis per 1,000 population]

Month	Number		Rate	
	1980	1979	1980	1979
Total	1,986,000	1,906,000	8.9	8.7
January	173,000	169,000	9.2	9.1
February	177,000	160,000	10.1	9.5
March	181,000	164,000	9.6	8.8
April	165,000	160,000	9.1	8.9
May	161,000	157,000	8.6	8.4
June	153,000	152,000	8.4	8.4
July	163,000	158,000	8.6	8.5
August	160,000	154,000	8.5	8.3
September	150,000	147,000	8.2	8.1
October	163,000	160,000	8.6	8.5
November	160,000	160,000	8.7	8.8
December	179,000	165,000	9.5	8.8

(866.2 per 100,000).

Except for November, monthly death rates in 1980 were the same or higher than the corresponding rates for 1979. Rates for February, March, and December were substantially higher in 1980 than in 1979 (table C). This is attributable to the outbreak of influenza during the early and late parts of 1980 in contrast to the absence of an influenza outbreak for the corresponding periods in 1979.[1,2,3]

The age-adjusted death rate increased by 1 percent between 1979 and 1980. The provisional rate for 1980 was 594.1 deaths per 100,000 population compared with a provisional rate of 587.4 for 1979. Age-adjusted rates control for changes and variations in the age compositions of the population. Therefore, they are usually better indicators than crude death rates in showing changes in the mortality risk over time, between race-sex groups within the population, and among causes of death.

Expectation of life

The estimated expectation of life at birth in 1980 was 73.6 years for the total population compared with 73.8 years in 1979. The decrease of 0.2 years between 1979 and 1980 was the first decrease in annual life expectancy in the United States since the decrease of 0.3 years between 1967 and 1968. Both declines reflect higher death rates associated with the influenza epidemics in 1968 and 1980. For the race-sex groups, estimated life expectancies at birth in 1980 were as follows: white females, 78.1 years; all other females, 74.0 years; white males, 70.5 years; and all other males 65.3 years. The expectation of life at birth represents the average number of years that a group of infants would be expected to live if throughout life they were to experience the age-specific death rates prevailing during the year of their birth.

Based on the respective annual age-specific death rates, the expectation of life at birth for the total population for 1967-80 was as follows:

1980 (est.)	73.6	1973	71.3
1979 (est.)	73.8	1972	71.1
1978	73.3	1971	71.1
1977	73.2	1970	70.8
1976	72.8	1969	70.5
1975	72.5	1968	70.2
1974	71.9	1967	70.5

Death rates by age, race, and sex

Age differentials.—Between 1979 and 1980, provisional death rates increased for every age group except under 1 year, 5-14 years, and 35-44 years. The largest increase, about 5 percent, was for the age groups 1-4 years and 85 years and over. The largest decrease, 9 percent, was for the age group 5-14 years (table D).

Race differentials.—The age-adjusted death rate for the population of all other races increased in 1980 more than the rate for the white population, a little over 2 percent compared with a little less than 1 percent. The rate for the population of all other races (790.5 per 100,000 population) was nearly 40 percent higher than the rate for the white population (567.9). Death rates for each 10-year age group under 85 years were higher for the population of all other races than those for the white population.

Sex differentials.—Between 1979 and 1980, the age-adjusted death rate for females increased more than the rate for males, nearly 2 percent compared with almost 1 percent. The rate for 1980 for the male population (787.6 per 100,000) was 80 percent higher than the rate for the female population (437.5). For 1980, death rates were higher for males than for females in each age group.

Table D. Death rates by age: United States, 1979 and 1980

[Based on a 10-percent sample of deaths. Rates per 100,000 population in specified group]

Age	1980 (est.)	1979 (est.)	Percent difference
All ages[1]	892.6	866.2	3.0
Under 1 year	1,310.7	1,372.5	−4.5
1-4 years	65.7	62.7	4.8
5-14 years	31.5	34.8	−9.5
15-24 years	118.8	118.2	0.5
25-34 years	140.7	139.1	1.2
35-44 years	225.9	227.9	−0.9
45-54 years	590.7	588.5	0.4
55-64 years	1,381.1	1,371.1	0.7
65-74 years	2,968.5	2,921.9	1.6
75-84 years	7,178.4	7,014.0	2.3
85 years and over	14,489.6	13,831.0	4.8

[1] Figures for age not stated included in "All ages" but not distributed among age groups.

Major causes of death

Deaths assigned to the 15 leading causes in 1980 accounted for nearly 90 percent of the total number of estimated deaths (table E). The list of the leading causes for 1980 remained unchanged from the list based on data for 1979. Age-adjusted death rates are shown for 13 of the 15 leading causes. Since deaths from the other two causes (Congenital anomalies and Certain conditions originating in the perinatal period) occur almost entirely at ages under 1 year, age-adjusted rates for these causes are not shown.

The age-adjusted rates were higher for 11 of the 13 leading causes for 1980 than they were for 1979 (table F). These causes were Diseases of heart; Malignant neoplasms including neoplasms of lymphatic and hematopoietic tissues; Chronic obstructive pulmonary diseases and allied conditions; Pneumonia and influenza; Diabetes mellitus; Chronic liver disease and cirrhosis; Atherosclerosis; Suicide; Homicide and legal intervention; Nephritis, nephrotic syndrome, and nephrosis; and Septicemia. The age-adjusted rates were lower in 1980 than they were in 1979 for Cerebrovascular diseases and for Accidents and adverse effects.

Diseases of heart.—An estimated 763,060 deaths from Diseases of heart (the leading cause of death in the United States) occurred in 1980, accounting for

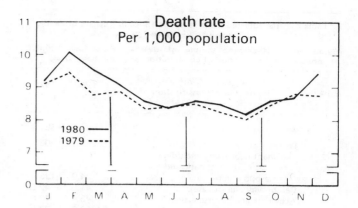

38 percent of all deaths. The age-adjusted death rate for 1980 (205.3 deaths per 100,000 population) was 1 percent higher than the rate for 1979 (203.0). For Diseases of heart, death rates for all age groups 65 years and over increased between 1979 and 1980, while death rates for the age groups 35-64 years decreased.

Malignant neoplasms, including neoplasms of lymphatic and hematopoietic tissues.—In 1980 there were an estimated 414,320 deaths (21 percent of all deaths) from Malignant neoplasms, including neoplasms of lymphatic and hematopoietic tissues, the second leading cause of death. The age-adjusted rate (134.2 deaths per 100,000 population) was slightly higher than the rate for 1979 (133.4). Death rates for Malignant neoplasms increased between 1979 and 1980 for the age groups 55-84 years and decreased for the age groups 25-54 years and 85 years and over.

Cerebrovascular diseases.—An estimated 170,420 persons died from Cerebrovascular diseases in 1980. This third leading cause of death accounted for about 9 percent of all deaths. The age-adjusted death rate decreased 2 percent between 1979 and 1980, from 42.5 per 100,000 to 41.5, the lowest rate ever recorded for this cause in the United States. A decrease occurred in all age groups 35 years and over.

Accidents and adverse effects.—An estimated 106,550 deaths were attributed to Accidents and adverse effects in 1980, including 54,200 deaths from Motor vehicle accidents and 52,350 from All other accidents and adverse effects. The age-adjusted rate for Accidents and adverse effects and for its two component causes—Motor vehicle accidents and All other accidents and adverse effects—each decreased less than 1 percent between 1979 and 1980.

Chronic obstructive pulmonary diseases and allied conditions.—In 1980 there were an estimated 55,810 deaths from Chronic obstructive pulmonary diseases and allied conditions. The age-adjusted death rate for this cause increased 9 percent between 1979 and 1980, from 14.8 to 16.2 deaths per 100,000 population. Death rates for the age groups 45 years and over increased for this cause.

Table E. Death rates for 15 leading causes of death: United States, 1980

[Based on a 10-percent sample of deaths. Rates per 100,000 population. See table 8 for category numbers of causes of death]

Rank	Cause of death (Ninth Revision International Classification of Diseases, 1975)	Death rate	Percent of total deaths
...	All causes	892.6	100.0
1	Diseases of heart	343.0	38.4
2	Malignant neoplasms, including neoplasms of lymphatic and hematopoietic tissues	186.3	20.9
3	Cerebrovascular diseases	76.6	8.6
4	Accidents and adverse effects	47.9	5.4
...	Motor vehicle accidents	24.4	2.7
...	All other accidents and adverse effects	23.5	2.6
5	Chronic obstructive pulmonary diseases and allied conditions	25.1	2.8
6	Pneumonia and influenza	23.7	2.7
7	Diabetes mellitus	15.4	1.7
8	Chronic liver disease and cirrhosis	14.1	1.6
9	Atherosclerosis	13.4	1.5
10	Suicide	12.7	1.4
11	Homicide and legal intervention	11.3	1.3
12	Certain conditions originating in the perinatal period	10.1	1.1
13	Nephritis, nephrotic syndrome, and nephrosis	7.8	0.9
14	Congenital anomalies	6.2	0.7
15	Septicemia	4.1	0.5
...	All other causes	94.9	10.6

Table F. Age-adjusted death rates for 15 leading causes of death, 1979 and 1980: United States

[Based on a 10-percent sample of deaths. Rates per 100,000 population. For method of computation, see Technical notes]

Rank[1]	Cause of death (Ninth Revision International Classification of Diseases, 1975)	1980 (est.)	1979 (est.)
...	All causes	594.1	587.4
1	Diseases of heart	205.3	203.0
2	Malignant neoplasms, including neoplasms of lymphatic and hematopoietic tissues	134.2	133.4
3	Cerebrovascular diseases	41.5	42.5
4	Accidents and adverse effects	43.4	43.6
...	Motor vehicle accidents	23.7	23.9
...	All other accidents and adverse effects	19.6	19.7
5	Chronic obstructive pulmonary diseases and allied conditions	16.2	14.8
6	Pneumonia and influenza	12.6	11.1
7	Diabetes mellitus	10.1	9.9
8	Chronic liver disease and cirrhosis	12.6	12.3
9	Atherosclerosis	5.8	5.6
10	Suicide	12.2	12.0
11	Homicide and legal intervention	11.4	10.6
12	Certain conditions originating in the perinatal period	(2)	(2)
13	Nephritis, nephrotic syndrome, and nephrosis	4.7	4.5
14	Congenital anomalies	(2)	(2)
15	Septicemia	2.6	2.5

[1] Based on numbers of deaths for 1980; see Technical notes.
[2] Since deaths from these causes occur primarily among infants, rates adjusted to the total population of the United States in 1940 are not shown. See table H.

Pneumonia and influenza.—An estimated 52,720 deaths in 1980 were attributed to Pneumonia and influenza. The age-adjusted death rate for this cause increased about 14 percent, from 11.1 per 100,000 population in 1979 to 12.6 in 1980, reflecting the presence of influenza epidemics in 1980 and the absence of one in the previous year. For Pneumonia and influenza, death rates increased for the age groups 35 years and over.

Diabetes mellitus.—In 1980 an estimated 34,230 persons died from Diabetes mellitus. The age-adjusted death rate increased 2 percent between 1979 and 1980, from 9.9 to 10.1 deaths per 100,000 population.

Chronic liver disease and cirrhosis.—Chronic liver disease and cirrhosis accounted for 31,330 deaths in 1980. The age-adjusted rate for this cause increased 2 percent, from 12.3 deaths per 100,000 population in 1979 to 12.6 in 1980.

Atherosclerosis.—An estimated 29,830 persons died from Atherosclerosis in 1980. The age-adjusted death rate (5.8 deaths per 100,000 population) was close to 4 percent higher than the rate for 1979 (5.6).

Suicide.—An estimated 28,290 persons in the United States committed suicide in 1980. The age-adjusted death rate was nearly 2 percent higher for

1980 (12.2 deaths per 100,000 population) than for 1979 (12.0).

Homicide and legal intervention.—There were an estimated 25,090 deaths from Homicide and legal intervention in 1980. The age-adjusted death rate of 11.4 deaths per 100,000 population for 1980 was the highest ever recorded in the United States and 8 percent higher than the rate of 10.6 for 1979. Death rates for Homicide and legal intervention increased for most age groups between 1979 and 1980, with the age groups under 1 year and 45-54 years showing the largest increases.

Certain conditions originating in the perinatal period.—An estimated 22,570 deaths were attributed to Certain conditions originating in the perinatal period. Since nearly all of the deaths from this cause occurred among infants under 1 year of age, mortality change for this cause was measured by the infant mortality rate per 100,000 live births. On this basis, the rate for 1980 (623.4 infant deaths per 100,000 live births) was close to 5 percent below the rate for 1979 (653.6).

Nephritis, nephrotic syndrome, and nephrosis.—In 1980 there were an estimated 17,390 deaths from Nephritis, nephrotic syndrome, and nephrosis. The age-adjusted death rate of 4.7 deaths per 100,000 population for 1980 was about 4 percent higher than the provisional rate of 4.5 for 1979. Between 1979 and 1980, death rates for this cause increased for the age groups 35 years and over.

Congenital anomalies.—In 1980 an estimated 13,730 deaths were assigned to Congenital anomalies. Since two-thirds of these deaths (9,150) were to infants under 1 year of age, the number of infant deaths per 100,000 live births was used to measure the change in the risk of dying from this cause. This

Table G. Infant mortality rates by age: United States, 1950, 1960, 1965, and 1970-80

[For 1979 and 1980, based on a 10-percent sample of deaths; for all other years, based on final data. Rates per 1,000 live births]

Year	Under 1 year	Under 28 days	28 days to 11 months
1980 (est.)	12.5	8.4	4.1
1979 (est.)	13.0	8.7	4.2
1978	13.8	9.5	4.3
1977	14.1	9.9	4.2
1976	15.2	10.9	4.3
1975	16.1	11.6	4.5
1974	16.7	12.3	4.4
1973	17.7	13.0	4.8
1972[1]	18.5	13.6	4.8
1971	19.1	14.2	4.9
1970	20.0	15.1	4.9
1965	24.7	17.7	7.0
1960	26.0	18.7	7.3
1950	29.2	20.5	8.7

[1] Based on a 50-percent sample of deaths.

Table H. Infant mortality rates for 10 selected causes of death, 1970 and 1976-80; and comparability ratios, 1976: United States

[For 1979 and 1980, based on a 10-percent sample of deaths; for all other years, based on final data. Rates per 100,000 live births]

Cause of death (Ninth Revision International Classification of Diseases, 1975)	Year						Compara-bility ratio
	1980 (est.)	1979 (est.)	1978	1977	1976	1970	
All causes	1,251.4	1,296.7	1,378.4	1,412.1	1,523.6	2,001.1	1.0000
Certain gastrointestinal diseases 008-009,535,555-558	8.1	10.7	23.0	20.8	24.2	24.1	0.4678
Pneumonia and influenza 480-487	28.1	33.1	46.0	50.6	61.9	168.9	0.7471
Congenital anomalies 740-759	254.3	257.7	252.1	253.1	263.4	301.7	1.0071
Disorders relating to short gestation and unspecified low birthweight 765	107.8	100.5	110.3	111.6	125.5	234.6	0.9630
Birth trauma 767	25.3	31.7	57.4	53.9	57.2	64.2	0.7154
Intrauterine hypoxia and birth asphyxia 768	42.2	48.4	88.7	98.3	113.6	252.9	0.3270
Respiratory distress syndrome 769	139.8	155.8	99.7	107.8	119.7	119.5	(1)
Other conditions originating in the perinatal period 760-764,766,770-779	308.2	317.3	[2]403.3	[2]438.3	[2]485.4	[2]605.5	0.8492
Sudden infant death syndrome 798.0	146.8	142.8	148.9	142.8	137.5	---	(1)
All other causes .... Residual	190.4	199.0	[3]397.6	[3]385.5	[3]392.2	[3]349.1	0.5455

[1]Comparability ratio has not been computed for this cause; see Technical notes.
[2]Includes deaths from Respiratory distress syndrome; see Technical notes.
[3]Includes deaths from Sudden infant death syndrome; see Technical notes.

infant mortality rate for Congenital anomalies decreased from 257.7 infant deaths per 100,000 live births in 1979 to 254.3 in 1980, a reduction of 1 percent.

Septicemia. –There were an estimated 9,230 deaths from Septicemia in 1980. The age-adjusted death rate for 1980 (2.6 deaths per 100,000 population) was 4 percent higher than the rate for 1979 (2.5). Between 1979 and 1980, death rates for this cause increased for most age groups.

Maternal and infant mortality

In 1980 the deaths of an estimated 250 women were assigned to Complications of pregnancy, childbirth, and the puerperium compared with an estimated 270 deaths in the previous year. The maternal mortality rate was 6.9 deaths per 100,000 live births in 1980. Maternal mortality rates for 1950 and each of the last 21 years are as follows:

1980 (est.)	.6.9	1969	22.2
1979 (est.)	.7.8	1968	24.5
1978	.9.6	1967	28.0
1977	11.2	1966	29.1
1976	12.3	1965	31.6
1975	12.8	1964	33.3
1974	14.6	1963	35.8
1973	15.2	1962	35.2
1972	18.8	1961	36.9
1971	18.8	1960	37.1
1970	21.5	1950	83.3

In 1980 an estimated 45,000 infants died in the United States. The resulting infant mortality rate of 12.5 deaths per 1,000 births was the lowest annual rate ever recorded in the United States. The 1980 rate decreased nearly 4 percent from the rate of 13.0 for 1979. Both the neonatal (under 28 days) and the postneonatal (28 days to 11 months) mortality rates

decreased between 1979 and 1980 (tables G, H, and J).

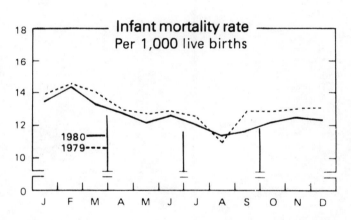

Infant mortality rate
Per 1,000 live births

1980 ——
1979 - - - -

Table J. Deaths under 1 year and infant mortality rates, by month: United States, 1979 and 1980

[Rates on an annual basis per 1,000 live births. Monthly rates adjusted for changing number of births]

Month	Number		Rate	
	1980	1979	1980	1979
Total	45,000	45,000	12.5	13.0
January	3,800	3,900	13.5	14.0
February	3,900	3,700	14.4	14.6
March	4,000	4,000	13.4	14.1
April	3,700	3,600	12.8	13.2
May	3,600	3,600	12.2	12.7
June	3,700	3,600	12.6	12.9
July	3,800	3,800	12.1	12.5
August	3,700	3,500	11.4	11.0
September	3,600	3,800	11.7	12.9
October	3,900	3,800	12.2	12.9
November	3,600	3,900	12.5	13.1
December	3,800	3,900	12.4	13.2

Deaths, infant deaths, and rates: Each reporting area, 1979 and 1980

[By place of occurrence. Rates for deaths at all ages are per 1,000 population. Infant mortality rates are deaths under 1 year per 1,000 live births]

Area	Deaths (all ages)				Infant deaths (under 1 year)			
	Number		Rate		Number		Rate	
	1980	1979	1980	1979	1980	1979	1980	1979
New England	113,639	110,061	9.2	9.0	1,614	1,706	10.3	10.8
Maine	10,857	10,367	9.9	9.5	140	152	8.7	9.6
New Hampshire	7,547	7,287	8.4	8.2	111	131	8.1	10.2
Vermont	4,312	4,364	8.6	8.9	63	57	8.2	7.7
Massachusetts	54,773	52,624	9.5	9.1	803	764	10.9	10.5
Rhode Island	9,553	9,295	10.4	10.0	150	186	12.0	15.2
Connecticut	26,597	26,124	8.5	8.4	347	416	10.2	11.3
Middle Atlantic	355,896	342,332	9.7	9.3	6,461	6,849	13.3	14.2
New York	167,769	160,937	9.5	9.1	3,210	3,661	13.8	15.8
New Jersey	64,727	64,126	8.8	8.7	1,072	1,089	11.8	11.9
Pennsylvania	123,400	117,269	10.5	10.0	2,179	2,099	13.5	13.3
East North Central	359,924	351,921	8.7	8.5	8,188	8,326	12.4	12.9
Ohio	97,779	93,197	9.1	8.7	2,020	1,966	11.9	12.0
Indiana	46,721	47,153	8.6	8.7	983	1,126	11.2	12.9
Illinois	100,450	100,218	9.0	8.9	2,696	2,750	14.4	15.2
Michigan	74,002	72,480	8.0	7.9	1,794	1,916	12.5	13.5
Wisconsin	40,972	38,873	8.6	8.2	695	568	9.3	7.8
West North Central	158,035	153,715	9.2	9.0	3,316	3,324	11.5	11.9
Minnesota	33,048	32,450	8.0	8.0	694	706	10.2	10.9
Iowa	26,714	26,237	9.2	9.0	530	476	11.0	10.1
Missouri	49,881	48,558	10.2	10.0	1,113	1,165	14.0	14.8
North Dakota	5,850	5,566	8.9	8.5	157	161	12.1	12.6
South Dakota	6,462	6,236	9.3	9.1	125	126	9.6	10.0
Nebraska	14,681	14,116	9.3	9.0	320	305	11.5	11.7
Kansas	21,399	20,552	9.0	8.7	377	385	9.6	10.4
South Atlantic	332,442	319,722	9.3	9.1	7,730	7,847	14.1	14.9
Delaware	5,201	5,048	9.0	8.7	123	144	12.9	15.8
Maryland	33,337	32,002	8.0	7.7	614	623	11.7	12.4
District of Columbia	9,165	9,042	14.4	13.8	522	392	29.3	19.3
Virginia	41,889	40,183	8.0	7.7	970	1,049	12.9	14.2
West Virginia	19,120	19,140	10.2	10.2	384	413	12.8	13.6
North Carolina	49,059	47,168	8.6	8.4	1,236	1,292	14.5	15.3
South Carolina	24,337	23,736	8.2	8.1	769	859	15.4	17.2
Georgia	43,519	42,646	8.3	8.3	1,208	1,264	12.6	14.1
Florida	106,815	100,757	11.6	11.4	1,904	1,811	14.4	15.0
East South Central	134,770	130,840	9.5	9.3	3,483	3,495	14.2	14.6
Kentucky	33,268	32,552	9.4	9.2	717	710	11.8	11.8
Tennessee	43,205	41,264	9.7	9.4	1,065	1,094	14.5	15.1
Alabama	35,386	34,304	9.4	9.1	946	872	15.1	14.4
Mississippi	22,911	22,720	9.4	9.4	755	819	15.9	17.8
West South Central	195,085	191,169	8.5	8.5	5,434	5,471	12.5	12.8
Arkansas	22,565	21,554	10.2	9.9	431	442	11.7	12.6
Louisiana	35,626	34,918	8.7	8.7	1,222	1,245	15.4	15.7
Oklahoma	28,308	27,204	9.6	9.4	555	527	11.0	11.2
Texas	108,586	107,493	7.9	8.0	3,226	3,257	12.0	12.3
Mountain	81,241	77,823	7.4	7.3	2,529	2,617	11.2	12.1
Montana	6,592	6,407	8.4	8.2	142	136	10.2	9.9
Idaho	6,431	6,061	7.0	6.7	151	155	7.7	7.9
Wyoming	3,062	2,929	6.6	6.5	63	80	6.6	8.9
Colorado	19,503	19,057	6.9	6.9	555	542	11.0	11.3
New Mexico	9,080	8,596	7.1	6.9	272	344	10.6	13.5
Arizona	21,609	20,385	8.5	8.3	684	671	13.6	14.7
Utah	8,556	8,546	6.1	6.3	505	536	11.6	12.7
Nevada	6,408	5,842	8.7	8.3	157	153	11.9	12.9
Pacific	251,417	227,288	8.1	7.5	6,247	5,456	11.5	11.2
Washington	32,495	29,496	8.1	7.5	789	599	11.6	10.9
Oregon	21,793	21,071	8.5	8.3	556	477	12.6	11.1
California	190,247	169,954	8.2	7.5	4,593	4,052	11.4	11.1
Alaska	1,692	1,639	4.1	4.0	115	137	12.3	15.4
Hawaii	5,190	5,128	5.5	5.6	194	191	10.6	11.0

Abridged life table for the total population: United States, 1980

[For explanation of the columns of the life table, see Section 5 of Vital Statistics of the United States, 1976, Volume II, Part A]

Age interval	Proportion dying	Of 100,000 born alive		Stationary population		Average remaining lifetime
Period of life between two exact ages stated in years	Proportion of persons alive at beginning of age interval dying during interval	Number living at beginning of age interval	Number dying during age interval	In the age interval	In this and all subsequent age intervals	Average number of years of life remaining at beginning of age interval
(1)	(2)	(3)	(4)	(5)	(6)	(7)
x to $x + n$	nq_x	l_x	nd_x	nL_x	T_x	$\overset{\circ}{e}_x$
0-1	0.0126	100,000	1,257	98,903	7,363,073	73.6
1-5	0.0026	98,743	257	394,375	7,264,170	73.6
5-10	0.0017	98,486	163	491,992	6,869,795	69.8
10-15	0.0015	98,323	149	491,301	6,377,803	64.9
15-20	0.0051	98,174	498	489,741	5,886,502	60.0
20-25	0.0068	97,676	665	486,739	5,396,761	55.3
25-30	0.0068	97,011	658	483,410	4,910,022	50.6
30-35	0.0073	96,353	704	480,081	4,426,612	45.9
35-40	0.0089	95,649	852	476,252	3,946,531	41.3
40-45	0.0140	94,797	1,328	470,884	3,470,279	36.6
45-50	0.0223	93,469	2,089	462,449	2,999,395	32.1
50-55	0.0356	91,380	3,254	449,271	2,536,946	27.8
55-60	0.0545	88,126	4,802	429,272	2,087,675	23.7
60-65	0.0814	83,324	6,779	400,454	1,658,403	19.9
65-70	0.1163	76,545	8,905	361,330	1,257,949	16.4
70-75	0.1668	67,640	11,285	310,881	896,619	13.3
75-80	0.2648	56,355	14,924	244,987	585,738	10.4
80-85	0.3629	41,431	15,036	168,956	340,751	8.2
85 and over	1.0000	26,395	26,395	171,795	171,795	6.5

Death rates by month: United States, 1966-80

[For 1979 and 1980, based on provisional figures; for all other years, based on final data. Rates on an annual basis per 1,000 population]

Month	1980	1979	1978	1977	1976	1975	1974	1973	1972[1]	1971	1970	1969	1968	1967	1966
Annual	8.9	8.7	8.8	8.8	8.9	8.9	9.2	9.4	9.4	9.3	9.5	9.5	9.7	9.4	9.5
January	9.2	9.1	10.6	9.5	9.3	10.1	9.6	10.8	11.0	10.0	10.6	10.9	11.6	9.8	10.1
February	10.1	9.5	9.7	9.3	10.2	9.9	9.6	10.2	10.3	10.0	10.4	9.8	10.0	9.8	10.1
March	9.6	8.8	8.9	9.1	9.9	9.1	9.6	9.3	9.3	9.6	9.5	9.8	9.6	9.6	9.9
April	9.1	8.9	8.6	8.8	9.0	8.8	9.5	9.3	9.2	9.5	9.3	9.4	9.2	9.3	9.9
May	8.6	8.4	8.6	8.6	8.5	8.6	8.9	9.2	9.1	9.2	9.1	9.3	9.1	9.3	9.4
June	8.4	8.4	8.4	8.4	8.4	8.5	8.8	9.1	8.9	9.2	9.0	9.2	9.2	9.1	9.3
July	8.6	8.5	8.4	8.6	8.3	8.5	8.9	9.0	9.3	8.9	9.1	9.2	9.1	8.9	9.6
August	8.5	8.3	8.2	8.2	8.1	8.4	8.5	8.9	8.9	8.8	8.8	8.9	9.0	8.7	8.7
September	8.2	8.1	8.3	8.2	8.2	8.4	8.7	9.0	8.8	8.8	8.8	8.8	8.8	8.9	8.8
October	8.6	8.5	8.6	8.7	8.6	8.6	9.0	9.1	9.2	9.1	9.2	9.2	9.1	9.2	9.3
November	8.7	8.8	8.7	8.7	8.9	8.6	9.0	9.4	9.4	9.4	9.5	9.6	9.7	9.5	9.3
December	9.5	8.8	9.1	9.4	9.2	9.1	9.6	9.7	10.0	9.9	9.7	10.0	11.3	10.2	9.8

[1] Based on a 50-percent sample of deaths.

Symbols

- - - Data not available

. . . Category not applicable

- Quantity zero

0.0 Quantity more than zero but less than 0.05

* Figure does not meet standards of reliability or precision

Death rates by age, race, and sex: United States, 1950, 1960, and 1970-80

[For 1979 and 1980, based on a 10-percent sample of deaths; for all other years, based on final data. Rates per 100,000 population in specified group]

Race, sex, and year	All ages[1]	Under 1 year	1-4 years	5-14 years	15-24 years	25-34 years	35-44 years	45-54 years	55-64 years	65-74 years	75-84 years	85 years and over
Total												
1980 (est.)	892.6	1,310.7	65.7	31.5	118.8	140.7	225.9	590.7	1,381.1	2,968.5	7,178.4	14,489.6
1979 (est.)	866.2	1,372.5	62.7	34.8	118.2	139.1	227.9	588.5	1,371.1	2,921.9	7,014.0	13,831.0
1978	883.4	1,434.4	69.2	33.9	117.5	135.5	238.9	609.7	1,416.3	3,027.2	7,187.8	14,700.7
1977	878.1	1,485.6	68.8	34.6	117.1	136.2	247.5	620.7	1,434.9	3,055.6	7,181.9	14,725.9
1976	889.6	1,595.0	69.9	34.7	113.5	136.2	254.1	634.8	1,475.5	3,127.6	7,331.6	15,486.9
1975	888.5	1,641.0	70.8	35.7	118.9	143.2	266.8	649.6	1,495.5	3,189.2	7,359.2	15,187.9
1974	915.1	1,755.7	73.9	38.2	121.7	146.8	278.6	675.0	1,549.2	3,327.6	7,654.8	16,532.8
1973	940.2	1,805.2	79.5	41.0	128.3	153.6	295.9	697.4	1,611.9	3,440.0	7,932.1	17,429.4
1972[2]	943.2	1,829.2	80.9	40.8	127.7	153.9	302.1	710.4	1,631.1	3,526.9	7,965.4	17,351.8
1971	934.7	1,904.8	82.6	41.1	126.6	156.5	307.5	710.2	1,622.8	3,486.2	7,866.6	17,426.4
1970	945.3	2,142.4	84.5	41.3	127.7	157.4	314.5	730.0	1,658.8	3,582.7	8,004.4	16,344.9
1960[2]	954.7	2,696.4	109.1	46.6	106.3	146.4	299.4	756.0	1,735.1	3,822.1	8,745.2	19,857.5
1950	963.8	3,299.2	139.4	60.1	128.1	178.7	358.7	853.9	[3]1,901.0	[3]4,104.3	9,331.1	20,196.9
Male												
1980 (est.)	997.0	1,454.8	74.0	37.1	179.6	205.5	301.7	778.6	1,844.9	4,064.6	9,405.1	16,901.6
1979 (est.)	974.7	1,552.4	67.8	44.2	179.9	204.6	303.4	767.1	1,855.6	4,018.2	9,127.3	16,077.8
1978	994.4	1,591.7	78.2	41.4	173.5	192.6	313.8	797.3	1,906.3	4,185.4	9,385.3	17,258.9
1977	994.1	1,659.0	76.5	42.6	172.8	193.6	323.2	814.0	1,936.0	4,230.3	9,384.8	17,299.1
1976	1,007.0	1,762.6	78.2	42.6	167.7	191.3	331.6	834.0	1,999.5	4,337.1	9,509.1	17,983.9
1975	1,013.2	1,829.3	77.8	43.9	176.8	202.7	346.9	856.3	2,034.7	4,414.5	9,519.4	17,572.6
1974	1,041.0	1,970.4	82.3	46.9	181.3	205.1	358.5	890.5	2,111.9	4,584.8	9,786.9	18,875.7
1973	1,072.9	2,032.1	88.8	50.0	189.8	214.5	380.4	916.6	2,206.6	4,731.5	10,108.1	19,809.4
1972[2]	1,080.3	2,063.6	90.0	48.9	188.1	211.8	386.6	940.0	2,245.6	4,816.6	10,124.0	19,595.8
1971	1,072.6	2,142.4	90.8	49.5	186.2	214.0	392.5	931.5	2,226.2	4,760.5	9,919.1	19,746.5
1970	1,090.3	2,410.0	93.2	50.5	188.5	215.3	402.6	958.5	2,282.7	4,873.8	10,010.2	17,821.5
1960[2]	1,104.5	3,059.3	119.5	55.7	152.1	187.9	372.8	992.2	2,309.5	4,914.4	10,178.4	21,186.3
1950	1,106.1	3,728.0	151.7	70.9	167.9	216.5	428.8	1,067.1	[3]2,395.3	[3]4,931.4	10,426.0	21,636.0
Female												
1980 (est.)	793.9	1,159.3	57.1	25.5	57.3	77.5	154.1	413.3	965.0	2,122.9	5,840.4	13,427.0
1979 (est.)	763.4	1,184.3	57.2	25.0	55.7	75.2	156.5	420.5	936.4	2,078.1	5,739.3	12,829.4
1978	778.3	1,269.6	59.9	26.1	60.9	79.7	167.8	433.2	976.3	2,137.6	5,863.1	13,541.2
1977	768.2	1,303.5	60.8	26.3	60.7	80.1	175.6	439.3	985.0	2,152.8	5,846.7	13,542.3
1976	778.3	1,419.0	61.3	26.5	58.6	82.3	180.5	448.3	1,005.5	2,198.3	6,002.5	14,312.1
1975	770.3	1,443.7	63.5	27.2	60.5	85.1	190.8	456.3	1,012.6	2,247.0	6,030.4	14,031.4
1974	795.6	1,530.7	65.2	29.1	61.7	89.9	202.7	473.7	1,045.8	2,361.0	6,329.5	15,387.6
1973	814.2	1,568.8	69.9	31.6	66.4	94.4	215.6	493.1	1,079.8	2,445.5	6,562.5	16,234.0
1972[2]	812.8	1,585.1	71.4	32.4	67.2	97.6	221.7	496.6	1,081.1	2,529.9	6,584.4	16,202.5
1971	803.8	1,656.1	74.0	32.4	67.4	100.8	226.8	504.1	1,082.4	2,498.3	6,531.5	16,215.7
1970	807.8	1,863.7	75.4	31.8	68.1	101.6	231.1	517.2	1,098.9	2,579.7	6,677.6	15,518.0
1960	809.2	2,321.3	98.4	37.3	61.3	106.6	229.4	526.7	1,196.4	2,871.8	7,633.1	19,008.4
1950	823.5	2,854.6	126.7	48.9	89.1	142.7	290.3	641.5	[3]1,404.8	[3]3,333.2	8,399.6	19,194.7
White												
1980 (est.)	905.7	1,115.9	59.9	30.5	116.0	123.0	196.5	540.2	1,301.1	2,902.3	7,095.8	15,188.8
1979 (est.)	879.3	1,160.1	57.2	33.9	115.4	120.0	198.4	538.8	1,303.3	2,865.1	6,953.1	14,474.9
1978	895.7	1,218.3	62.7	32.2	113.9	118.0	206.0	559.6	1,343.6	2,962.2	7,155.2	15,316.0
1977	888.2	1,266.2	62.5	33.1	112.8	117.6	213.2	567.9	1,361.0	2,985.3	7,164.0	15,292.2
1976	899.4	1,356.2	64.1	33.2	107.6	116.0	218.5	580.9	1,403.3	3,053.3	7,340.0	16,068.5
1975	896.8	1,413.0	64.4	33.9	111.5	121.1	229.2	597.1	1,422.8	3,107.2	7,384.0	15,707.5
1974	921.9	1,524.5	67.1	36.5	113.0	122.9	237.6	617.4	1,471.6	3,231.0	7,703.9	17,055.6
1973	944.2	1,565.1	71.4	38.8	118.5	128.2	252.0	633.6	1,529.5	3,335.2	7,976.7	17,926.6
1972[2]	946.4	1,577.5	73.4	39.1	116.2	126.5	255.1	646.2	1,550.1	3,429.1	8,017.4	17,864.5
1971	936.6	1,655.3	74.3	38.7	113.7	128.4	261.1	649.0	1,543.7	3,391.6	7,913.5	17,912.2
1970	946.3	1,869.7	75.1	39.1	115.8	129.9	267.0	666.2	1,577.1	3,490.1	8,043.3	16,889.7
1960	947.8	2,357.7	95.2	43.9	99.1	123.6	280.4	692.3	1,632.8	3,739.8	8,827.2	20,354.5
1950	945.7	2,992.6	124.1	56.4	111.7	148.3	307.6	765.0	1,799.6	4,023.1	9,416.5	20,678.6
White, male												
1980 (est.)	1,001.9	1,253.6	68.5	35.1	173.6	178.3	260.5	716.2	1,747.2	4,018.4	9,362.6	17,821.5
1979 (est.)	980.0	1,330.0	60.8	43.5	176.1	174.2	259.8	705.8	1,768.5	3,975.4	9,127.5	16,955.5
1978	999.8	1,359.6	71.7	39.2	168.5	166.7	268.1	733.8	1,819.2	4,135.6	9,414.9	18,100.3
1977	998.2	1,429.7	69.7	40.6	167.3	165.9	276.6	747.8	1,848.9	4,181.3	9,440.7	18,041.7
1976	1,010.4	1,511.8	71.9	40.7	159.4	161.7	283.7	765.9	1,915.5	4,281.1	9,595.0	18,767.6
1975	1,015.3	1,594.4	71.3	41.5	165.9	169.1	295.8	790.2	1,954.5	4,355.8	9,608.1	18,257.9
1974	1,041.6	1,727.0	75.3	44.8	168.8	170.6	305.1	820.3	2,026.1	4,509.6	9,903.1	19,543.7
1973	1,071.2	1,776.5	79.8	47.0	176.2	177.6	324.4	839.7	2,118.2	4,653.9	10,214.3	20,436.1
1972[2]	1,077.3	1,800.4	82.5	47.0	170.7	172.5	325.4	861.4	2,160.8	4,746.7	10,227.3	20,266.2
1971	1,069.8	1,876.5	81.9	46.4	167.1	174.4	334.9	860.6	2,145.1	4,696.5	10,027.1	20,420.4
1970	1,086.7	2,113.2	83.6	48.0	170.8	176.6	343.5	882.9	2,202.6	4,810.1	10,098.8	18,551.7
1960	1,098.5	2,694.1	104.9	52.7	143.7	163.2	332.6	932.2	2,225.2	4,848.4	10,299.6	21,750.0
1950	1,089.5	3,400.5	135.5	67.2	152.4	185.3	380.9	984.5	2,304.4	4,864.9	10,526.3	22,116.3

See footnotes at end of table.

Death rates by age, race, and sex: United States, 1950, 1960, and 1970-80—Con.

[For 1979 and 1980, based on a 10-percent sample of deaths; for all other years, based on final data. Rates per 100,000 population in specified group]

Race, sex, and year	All ages[1]	Under 1 year	1-4 years	5-14 years	15-24 years	25-34 years	35-44 years	45-54 years	55-64 years	65-74 years	75-84 years	85 years and over
White, female												
1980 (est.)	814.2	970.9	50.9	25.6	55.1	67.6	134.5	371.7	897.9	2,042.4	5,754.6	14,043.7
1979 (est.)	783.4	981.1	53.4	23.9	53.2	65.6	138.8	379.5	883.0	2,012.6	5,662.2	13,374.6
1978	796.5	1,069.7	53.3	25.0	58.1	69.3	145.8	393.9	914.0	2,063.8	5,810.2	14,079.0
1977	783.3	1,094.8	55.0	25.3	57.2	69.3	151.9	397.4	920.4	2,070.4	5,805.1	14,039.7
1976	793.6	1,192.1	55.9	25.4	54.7	70.3	155.4	405.9	942.0	2,114.1	5,984.6	14,823.3
1975	783.8	1,222.3	57.1	25.8	56.0	73.3	164.6	414.8	944.6	2,152.8	6,034.7	14,494.1
1974	807.6	1,312.6	58.5	27.9	56.2	75.5	172.1	426.4	973.6	2,252.5	6,354.6	15,845.4
1973	823.0	1,342.8	62.5	30.2	60.0	79.3	181.8	439.9	1,000.7	2,324.7	6,582.2	16,685.8
1972[2]	821.3	1,343.1	63.8	30.9	61.2	81.0	187.1	444.3	1,001.6	2,416.8	6,619.6	16,657.3
1971	809.7	1,422.9	66.2	30.7	60.2	83.0	189.8	450.6	1,003.3	2,386.6	6,558.8	16,629.2
1970	812.6	1,614.6	66.1	29.9	61.6	84.1	193.3	462.9	1,014.9	2,470.7	6,698.7	15,980.2
1960	800.9	2,007.7	85.2	34.7	54.9	85.0	191.1	458.8	1,078.9	2,779.3	7,696.6	19,477.7
1950	803.3	2,566.8	112.2	45.1	71.5	112.8	235.8	546.4	1,293.8	3,242.8	8,481.5	19,679.5
All other												
1980 (est.)	811.3	2,205.2	91.7	36.1	139.4	253.8	427.7	955.6	2,097.1	3,566.9	8,136.2	8,689.4
1979 (est.)	783.2	2,388.4	87.3	39.2	134.2	263.8	433.1	958.3	1,988.9	3,435.5	7,716.0	8,291.7
1978	805.1	2,456.7	99.0	41.9	137.6	250.3	466.3	990.7	2,085.5	3,620.8	7,558.2	9,228.7
1977	813.0	2,546.4	97.6	42.0	141.4	261.6	482.2	1,032.3	2,126.0	3,708.8	7,384.2	9,595.6
1976	824.8	2,781.5	96.9	42.2	147.5	273.9	499.6	1,065.5	2,153.2	3,828.7	7,238.5	10,018.5
1975	833.6	2,765.3	101.0	45.4	162.8	295.8	529.8	1,077.8	2,176.4	3,970.7	7,076.1	10,102.9
1974	869.1	2,922.9	107.8	47.3	174.1	314.4	568.4	1,153.3	2,285.1	4,266.9	7,080.8	11,245.5
1973	912.6	3,020.1	121.1	53.0	187.4	334.2	609.9	1,235.4	2,399.7	4,470.8	7,419.6	12,137.9
1972[2]	920.9	3,125.6	120.0	49.9	199.1	349.2	642.5	1,260.4	2,406.0	4,490.1	7,338.6	11,854.1
1971	921.5	3,250.7	126.4	54.3	209.0	355.0	649.4	1,242.6	2,380.8	4,414.7	7,271.7	11,990.5
1970	938.4	3,597.1	134.1	53.7	203.6	348.7	664.3	1,290.9	2,431.1	4,488.4	7,511.1	10,750.3
1960	1,008.5	4,626.4	190.8	64.3	158.2	318.6	633.4	1,342.9	2,774.6	4,784.9	7,631.1	13,907.6
1950	1,119.4	5,368.4	250.8	86.0	251.3	440.2	805.3	1,706.1	[3]3,126.6	[3]5,205.0	8,039.7	14,473.6
All other, male												
1980 (est.)	966.0	2,387.8	98.8	47.1	212.9	392.8	611.1	1,251.2	2,744.9	4,471.4	9,789.5	10,219.8
1979 (est.)	940.5	2,622.8	100.1	47.7	201.5	418.5	633.7	1,244.7	2,671.5	4,400.6	9,125.0	9,265.1
1978	959.7	2,708.5	108.1	52.3	201.9	377.2	659.3	1,305.2	2,730.1	4,632.6	8,992.4	10,678.2
1977	967.1	2,780.4	108.1	52.8	205.1	396.8	671.7	1,354.5	2,772.7	4,682.2	8,783.8	11,286.1
1976	983.5	3,012.4	107.5	52.2	217.3	410.5	692.4	1,402.5	2,812.3	4,852.8	8,652.1	11,519.1
1975	999.1	3,001.1	108.8	56.7	242.6	454.6	736.1	1,418.9	2,806.6	4,970.8	8,604.9	11,693.8
1974	1,036.3	3,212.7	117.5	58.7	259.0	467.8	768.7	1,499.7	2,942.3	5,285.0	8,555.6	12,782.5
1973	1,084.6	3,335.4	135.6	66.8	275.2	498.6	815.7	1,591.5	3,069.5	5,456.7	8,965.7	13,605.7
1972[2]	1,101.3	3,440.0	129.6	59.4	299.3	514.2	868.4	1,639.2	3,073.2	5,490.1	8,939.7	13,325.5
1971	1,094.1	3,610.0	138.9	66.7	312.0	516.1	852.8	1,572.0	3,013.1	5,377.6	8,746.0	13;351.0
1970	1,115.9	4,020.0	144.7	65.0	304.6	504.1	873.5	1,646.1	3,046.6	5,474.4	8,981.0	11,405.2
1960	1,152.0	5,189.4	207.3	75.2	213.8	386.4	729.2	1,551.0	3,151.5	5,664.0	8,662.6	15,238.7
1950	1,251.1	5,991.6	271.2	97.1	289.9	496.2	860.7	1,857.3	[3]3,480.8	[3]5,794.9	9,029.6	16,022.1
All other, female												
1980 (est.)	671.0	2,016.6	84.4	25.0	68.8	135.5	278.2	699.4	1,546.6	2,854.4	6,889.2	7,930.2
1979 (est.)	640.3	2,146.4	74.3	30.6	69.2	132.5	269.2	710.6	1,407.8	2,676.9	6,682.0	7,777.1
1978	664.5	2,206.5	89.7	31.5	75.9	142.7	308.4	718.7	1,534.6	2,821.7	6,513.6	8,449.0
1977	672.5	2,304.5	87.1	31.0	80.1	146.9	326.4	752.5	1,572.9	2,933.0	6,370.3	8,673.5
1976	680.0	2,542.2	86.1	32.0	80.6	157.8	340.8	772.3	1,590.1	3,009.4	6,217.6	9,175.2
1975	682.5	2,523.0	93.0	34.0	86.6	160.8	359.9	780.8	1,636.2	3,172.0	5,978.5	9,177.3
1974	716.3	2,614.2	98.2	35.8	93.4	184.0	402.8	852.2	1,716.3	3,442.8	6,015.4	10,342.3
1973	755.4	2,697.2	106.5	39.2	103.9	194.1	439.6	926.0	1,821.7	3,662.0	6,291.8	11,115.9
1972[2]	755.5	2,815.9	110.2	40.3	103.9	208.3	455.1	929.4	1,830.2	3,678.9	6,178.0	10,939.0
1971	763.3	2,896.7	113.9	41.8	111.9	217.8	480.1	953.8	1,829.4	3,630.0	6,195.6	11,271.1
1970	775.3	3,169.4	123.3	42.3	108.8	215.7	490.5	979.4	1,886.9	3,675.6	6,392.6	10,288.9
1960	872.6	4,067.1	174.4	53.4	106.1	260.0	547.3	1,144.9	2,409.7	3,981.4	6,708.4	12,871.2
1950	993.5	4,749.0	230.3	75.0	216.4	390.4	754.0	1,554.9	[3]2,763.0	[3]4,610.7	7,064.7	13,366.8

[1]Figures for age not stated included in "All ages" but not distributed among age groups.
[2]Based on a 50-percent sample of deaths.
[3]Based on enumerated population adjusted for age bias in the "All other" population at ages 55-69 years.

Deaths and death rates, by age, race, and sex: United States, 1980

[Based on a 10-percent sample of deaths. Rates per 100,000 population in specified group. Due to rounding estimates of deaths, figures may not add to totals]

Age	Total			White			All other		
	Both sexes	Male	Female	Both sexes	Male	Female	Both sexes	Male	Female
Number									
All ages	1,986,000	1,077,880	907,660	1,735,000	935,970	799,030	250,540	141,910	108,630
Under 1 year	45,000	25,590	19,430	31,480	18,140	13,340	13,540	7,450	6,090
1-4 years	8,270	4,760	3,510	6,160	3,610	2,550	2,110	1,150	960
5-14 years	10,680	6,440	4,240	8,520	5,020	3,500	2,160	1,420	740
15-24 years	49,100	37,350	11,770	40,120	30,610	9,510	9,000	6,740	2,260
25-34 years	50,840	36,750	14,140	38,380	27,850	10,530	12,510	8,900	3,610
35-44 years	58,210	37,860	20,380	44,190	28,840	15,350	14,050	9,020	5,030
45-54 years	134,450	86,110	48,370	107,990	70,020	37,970	26,490	16,090	10,400
55-59 years	127,260	81,020	46,240	106,150	68,030	38,120	21,110	12,990	8,120
60-64 years	166,010	104,320	61,690	142,200	90,300	51,900	23,810	14,020	9,790
65-69 years	214,810	131,390	83,420	187,190	115,820	71,370	27,620	15,570	12,050
70-74 years	247,640	144,390	103,250	219,830	129,420	90,410	27,810	14,970	12,840
75-79 years	263,780	139,720	124,060	237,360	125,730	111,630	26,420	13,990	12,430
80-84 years	252,440	114,500	137,940	231,670	104,310	127,360	20,770	10,190	10,580
85 years and over	356,010	127,100	228,930	333,090	117,800	215,290	22,940	9,300	13,640
Not stated	950	650	310	690	500	190	270	150	120
Rate									
All ages[1]	892.6	997.0	793.9	905.7	1,001.9	814.2	811.3	966.0	671.0
Under 1 year	1,310.7	1,454.8	1,159.3	1,115.9	1,253.6	970.9	2,205.2	2,387.8	2,016.6
1-4 years	65.7	74.0	57.1	59.9	68.5	50.9	91.7	98.8	84.4
5-14 years	31.5	37.1	25.5	30.5	35.1	25.6	36.1	47.1	25.0
15-24 years	118.8	179.6	57.3	115.0	173.6	55.1	139.4	212.9	68.8
25-34 years	140.7	205.5	77.5	123.0	178.3	67.6	253.8	392.8	135.5
35-44 years	225.9	301.7	154.1	196.5	260.5	134.5	427.7	611.1	278.2
45-54 years	590.7	778.6	413.3	540.2	716.2	371.7	955.6	1,251.2	699.4
55-59 years	1,116.3	1,489.1	776.0	1,037.9	1,388.9	715.3	1,799.7	2,392.3	1,288.9
60-64 years	1,688.6	2,265.4	1,180.7	1,604.8	2,168.6	1,105.0	2,457.2	3,179.1	1,854.2
65-69 years	2,458.1	3,373.3	1,722.1	2,398.6	3,320.5	1,653.6	2,954.0	3,816.2	2,282.2
70-74 years	3,621.0	4,996.2	2,614.6	3,534.2	4,949.1	2,507.9	4,492.7	5,443.6	3,732.6
75-79 years	6,073.7	8,185.1	4,708.2	5,926.6	8,070.0	4,561.9	7,839.8	9,326.7	6,611.7
80-84 years	8,863.8	11,496.0	7,452.2	8,893.3	11,602.9	7,465.4	8,547.3	10,505.2	7,246.6
85 years and over	14,489.6	16,901.6	13,427.0	15,188.8	17,821.5	14,043.7	8,689.4	10,219.8	7,930.2

[1] Figures for age not stated included in "All ages" but not distributed among age groups.

Age-specific and age-adjusted death rates for 15 leading causes and selected components: United States, 1979 and 1980

[Based on a 10-percent sample of deaths. Rates per 100,000 population in specified group]

Cause of death (Ninth Revision International Classification of Diseases, 1975)	Year	All ages	Age											Age-adjusted rate[1]
			Under 1 year	1-14 years	15-24 years	25-34 years	35-44 years	45-54 years	55-64 years	65-74 years	75-84 years	85 years and over	
All causes	1980	892.6	1,310.7	40.7	118.8	140.7	225.9	590.7	1,381.1	2,968.5	7,178.4	14,489.6	594.1
	1979	866.2	1,372.5	42.1	118.2	139.1	227.9	588.5	1,371.1	2,921.9	7,014.0	13,831.0	587.4
Diseases of heart 390-398, 402, 404-429	1980	343.0	21.8	1.4	2.6	8.6	43.4	181.9	510.8	1,210.8	3,229.7	7,134.7	205.3
	1979	331.3	18.6	0.9	2.3	7.6	46.4	183.0	514.4	1,206.6	3,151.3	6,704.5	203.0
Rheumatic fever and rheumatic heart disease 390-398	1980	3.6		0.0	0.2	0.3	1.4	4.3	8.3	16.1	21.0	24.4	2.7
	1979	3.4			0.1	0.4	1.4	3.7	7.8	15.6	21.5	24.0	2.5
Hypertensive heart disease 402	1980	9.9			0.0	0.3	1.4	6.8	17.6	35.3	88.3	181.5	6.2
	1979	9.3		0.0	0.0	0.4	1.7	6.8	16.6	34.8	85.5	152.2	6.0
Hypertensive heart and renal disease 404	1980	1.5				0.0	0.2	0.6	1.1	4.6	16.3	42.7	0.8
	1979	1.4			0.0	0.0	0.1	0.3	0.9	4.1	15.6	47.6	0.7
Ischemic heart disease 410-414	1980	254.9		0.0	0.2	3.7	29.0	132.5	383.4	924.3	2,448.1	5,139.6	152.4
	1979	249.8	1.2	0.0	0.3	3.1	30.7	138.2	393.1	934.9	2,398.2	4,918.1	153.1
Acute myocardial infarction 410	1980	135.4		0.0	0.1	2.3	19.1	92.3	254.1	564.6	1,227.4	1,798.1	87.9
	1979	137.2	0.9		0.2	2.2	21.7	97.3	268.5	585.8	1,234.8	1,734.1	91.0
Other acute and subacute forms of ischemic heart disease 411	1980	2.0				0.0	0.4	2.2	3.9	7.6	17.0	26.9	1.4
	1979	2.0	0.3			0.0	0.4	2.3	5.0	6.8	13.8	29.6	1.4
Angina pectoris 413	1980	0.2				0.0	0.0	0.0	0.5	0.4	1.7	2.4	0.1
	1979	0.2				0.0	0.0		0.2	1.0	1.0	3.9	0.1
Old myocardial infarction and other forms of chronic ischemic heart disease 412, 414	1980	117.3		0.0	0.1	1.3	9.4	37.9	124.9	351.6	1,202.1	3,312.2	63.0
	1979	110.4		0.0	0.0	0.8	8.5	38.6	119.5	341.3	1,148.7	3,150.5	60.6
Other diseases of endocardium 424	1980	3.2	0.3	0.0	0.1	0.3	0.7	1.7	4.6	11.2	31.2	52.5	2.0
	1979	2.8		0.1	0.0	0.2	0.6	1.0	4.9	10.1	29.6	43.7	1.8
All other forms of heart disease 415-423, 425-429	1980	70.0	21.5	1.2	2.0	3.9	10.7	36.0	95.8	219.3	624.9	1,693.9	41.2
	1979	64.6	17.4	0.8	1.8	3.5	12.0	33.1	91.1	207.0	600.8	1,518.9	38.9
Malignant neoplasms, including neoplasms of lymphatic and hematopoietic tissues 140-208	1980	186.3	1.5	4.7	6.6	12.6	48.8	178.9	442.5	814.8	1,331.8	1,413.1	134.2
	1979	183.5	3.0	4.7	5.9	13.3	49.3	182.9	442.1	797.5	1,300.1	1,452.8	133.4
Malignant neoplasms of lip, oral cavity, and pharynx 140-149	1980	3.8	0.0	0.0	0.1	0.1	1.2	5.2	11.8	15.4	20.7	22.0	2.9
	1979	3.6	0.0	0.0	0.0	0.2	0.8	4.9	11.6	14.9	17.9	21.9	2.7
Malignant neoplasms of digestive organs and peritoneum 150-159	1980	49.3	0.3	0.2	0.4	1.4	8.2	36.7	105.6	214.3	423.7	496.9	33.4
	1979	49.5	0.6	0.1	0.2	1.7	8.9	35.4	104.4	225.1	422.2	503.0	33.7
Malignant neoplasms of respiratory and intrathoracic organs 160-165	1980	48.6		0.0	0.1	0.8	9.5	55.4	146.6	244.3	270.5	159.5	36.7
	1979	46.7		0.0	0.2	0.7	10.6	56.2	146.5	226.1	251.1	165.5	35.8
Malignant neoplasm of breast 174-175	1980	15.7			0.0	1.9	9.1	24.7	43.1	55.4	81.4	107.0	12.3
	1979	16.0			0.0	1.6	8.9	26.6	43.4	59.1	77.7	119.6	12.7
Malignant neoplasms of genital organs 179-187	1980	20.8	0.0	0.0	0.6	1.1	4.7	13.2	36.3	88.6	194.3	239.3	13.7
	1979	20.5	0.0	0.0	0.5	1.4	5.3	14.0	35.6	88.2	188.8	243.1	13.8
Malignant neoplasms of urinary organs 188-189	1980	7.9	0.3	0.1	0.1	0.3	0.9	4.7	15.4	37.1	68.6	85.5	5.2
	1979	8.0	0.3	0.3	0.1	0.2	1.1	5.2	16.8	33.2	73.4	93.5	5.4

Age-specific and age-adjusted death rates for 15 leading causes and selected components: United States, 1979 and 1980—Con.

[Based on a 10-percent sample of deaths. Rates per 100,000 population in specified group]

Cause of death (Ninth Revision International Classification of Diseases, 1975)	Year	All ages	Under 1 year	1-14 years	15-24 years	25-34 years	35-44 years	45-54 years	55-64 years	65-74 years	75-84 years	85 years and over	Age-adjusted rate[1]
Malignant neoplasms of all other and unspecified sites ... 170-173, 190-199	1980	22.9	0.6	2.0	2.2	3.3	8.8	24.7	50.7	92.2	148.2	173.4	17.1
	1979	22.3	1.8	1.9	2.1	3.8	8.0	25.6	52.3	86.6	141.8	171.1	16.9
Leukemia ... 204-208	1980	7.7	0.3	1.9	2.1	1.9	2.9	5.9	12.8	27.0	54.5	68.0	5.7
	1979	7.4	.	1.9	1.7	1.8	2.7	6.2	11.4	26.1	55.7	71.2	5.5
Other malignant neoplasms of lymphatic and hematopoietic tissues ... 200-203	1980	9.6	.	0.5	1.1	1.9	3.3	8.4	20.1	40.6	69.9	61.5	7.0
	1979	9.3	0.3	0.4	1.1	1.7	3.0	8.8	20.0	38.1	71.6	63.9	6.9
Cerebrovascular diseases ... 430-438	1980	76.6	3.8	0.3	1.2	2.7	8.6	26.1	67.8	222.4	834.7	2,094.0	41.5
	1979	76.9	2.4	0.3	0.9	2.6	9.3	27.4	68.7	228.7	858.5	2,113.2	42.5
Accidents and adverse effects ... E800-E949	1980	47.9	34.1	18.2	62.7	49.0	36.0	40.0	46.3	58.6	126.0	275.5	43.4
	1979	47.9	28.3	20.9	63.8	47.0	37.1	38.1	44.9	57.1	133.4	265.9	43.6
Motor vehicle accidents ... E810-E825	1980	24.4	7.6	8.7	45.0	30.9	19.6	21.3	18.1	21.7	33.0	24.8	23.7
	1979	24.5	7.3	9.8	46.4	29.6	22.1	17.8	18.3	20.4	33.5	27.4	23.9
All other accidents and adverse effects ... E800-E807, E826-E949	1980	23.5	26.5	9.4	17.7	18.1	16.4	18.7	28.1	36.9	93.0	250.7	19.6
	1979	23.4	21.0	11.0	17.4	17.4	15.0	20.3	26.5	36.7	99.9	238.4	19.7
Chronic obstructive pulmonary diseases and allied conditions ... 490-496	1980	25.1	1.5	0.2	0.3	0.5	1.6	10.9	44.0	125.2	243.5	249.1	16.2
	1979	22.7	2.1	0.2	0.3	0.3	1.7	8.3	40.2	115.5	230.2	211.4	14.8
Pneumonia and influenza ... 480-487	1980	23.7	29.4	0.9	0.9	1.3	3.1	8.1	18.4	52.9	229.5	778.2	12.6
	1979	20.0	35.1	0.7	0.8	1.5	2.9	6.9	16.8	46.8	198.0	635.9	11.1
Diabetes mellitus ... 250	1980	15.4	0.3	0.2	0.3	1.7	4.0	10.0	25.9	62.7	136.6	205.5	10.1
	1979	15.0	.	0.1	0.3	1.7	4.0	8.2	25.9	60.2	142.3	204.1	9.9
Chronic liver disease and cirrhosis ... 571	1980	14.1	0.3	0.0	0.2	4.1	13.7	31.4	45.6	43.1	31.0	15.9	12.6
	1979	13.6	0.9	0.1	0.3	3.6	14.8	31.3	40.7	42.4	29.9	17.6	12.3
Atherosclerosis ... 440	1980	13.4	.	.	.	.	0.2	1.3	4.4	24.1	140.6	597.1	5.8
	1979	13.0	.	.	0.0	.	0.2	0.9	4.6	23.6	128.9	629.9	5.6
Suicide ... E950-E959	1980	12.7	...	0.2	12.8	16.8	16.7	17.1	17.4	18.8	22.0	16.3	12.2
	1979	12.6	...	0.4	12.1	17.6	14.2	17.6	18.8	18.5	22.5	14.6	12.0
Homicide and legal intervention ... E960-E978	1980	11.3	7.6	1.4	16.9	21.0	14.3	12.9	7.3	5.5	6.1	3.7	11.4
	1979	10.5	5.8	1.4	15.5	19.4	13.7	10.9	7.0	6.5	5.7	5.6	10.6
Certain conditions originating in the perinatal period ... 760-779	1980	10.1	653.0	0.2	0.0	.	.	0.1	.	.	.	.	(2)
	1979	10.4	691.9	0.2	0.1	0.0	.	0.0	.	.	.	.	(2)
Nephritis, nephrotic syndrome, and nephrosis ... 580-589	1980	7.8	7.9	0.0	0.3	0.5	1.7	3.5	9.6	25.5	77.5	162.8	4.7
	1979	7.3	7.0	0.1	0.2	0.9	1.6	3.4	8.0	25.3	73.9	146.2	4.5
Congenital anomalies ... 740-759	1980	6.2	266.4	3.3	1.8	1.1	1.2	1.6	2.2	2.7	3.2	3.3	(2)
	1979	6.1	272.8	3.2	1.4	1.2	1.3	1.8	1.9	2.5	4.3	6.0	(2)
Septicemia ... 038	1980	4.1	7.9	0.3	0.2	0.5	0.8	2.1	6.3	13.5	35.0	77.7	2.6
	1979	3.8	9.4	0.2	0.2	0.5	0.6	2.0	5.2	12.8	35.0	69.5	2.5

[1] For method of computation, see Technical notes.
[2] Since deaths from these causes occur primarily among infants, rates adjusted to the total population in 1940 are not shown. See table H.

Deaths from 72 selected causes: United States, 1970 and 1980

[For 1979 and 1980, based on a 10-percent sample of deaths; for all other years, based on final data. Data for 1979 and 1980 are based on the Ninth Revision International Classification of Diseases; for all other years, based on the Eighth Revision; see Technical notes. Comparability of causes of death between the Eighth and Ninth Revisions is described in the Technical notes. Comparability ratios are shown in table 11]

Cause of death (Ninth Revision International Classification of Diseases, 1975)	1980 (est.)	1979 (est.)	1978	1977	1976	1970
All causes	1,986,000	1,906,000	1,927,788	1,899,597	1,909,440	1,921,031
Shigellosis and amebiasis . . . 004,006	10	30	34	53	55	89
Certain other intestinal infections . . . 007-009	340	350	1,874	1,855	1,939	2,567
Tuberculosis . . . 010-018	1,770	1,980	2,914	2,968	3,130	5,217
Tuberculosis of respiratory system . . . 010-012	1,540	1,620	2,256	2,324	2,419	4,162
Other tuberculosis . . . 013-018	230	360	658	644	711	1,055
Whooping cough . . . 033	10	20	6	10	7	12
Streptococcal sore throat, scarlatina, and erysipelas . . . 034-035	10	30	5	14	14	29
Meningococcal infection . . . 036	410	390	403	338	330	550
Septicemia . . . 038	9,230	8,350	7,800	7,112	6,401	3,535
Acute poliomyelitis . . . 045	20	20	13	16	16	7
Measles . . . 055	10		11	15	12	89
Viral hepatitis . . . 070	790	650	508	508	567	1,014
Syphilis . . . 090-097	180	180	169	196	225	461
All other infectious and parasitic diseases . . . 001-003,005,020-032,037,039-041,046-054,056-066,071-088,098-139	3,730	3,320	4,305	3,845	3,857	3,079
Malignant neoplasms, including neoplasms of lymphatic and hematopoietic tissues . . . 140-208	414,320	403,780	396,992	386,686	377,312	330,730
Malignant neoplasms of lip, oral cavity, and pharynx . . . 140-149	8,500	7,890	8,341	8,454	8,114	7,612
Malignant neoplasms of digestive organs and peritoneum . . . 150-159	109,730	108,910	105,427	102,951	101,729	94,703
Malignant neoplasms of respiratory and intrathoracic organs . . . 160-165	108,000	102,740	99,898	95,182	91,131	69,517
Malignant neoplasm of breast . . . 174-175	34,940	35,290	34,609	34,762	33,403	29,917
Malignant neoplasms of genital organs . . . 179-187	46,250	45,190	45,131	44,273	44,461	41,190
Malignant neoplasms of urinary organs . . . 188-189	17,580	17,680	17,574	17,382	16,980	15,514
Malignant neoplasms of all other and unspecified sites . . . 170-173,190-199	50,990	49,180	48,943	47,276	45,975	39,068
Leukemia . . . 204-208	17,060	16,330	15,391	15,329	15,056	14,492
Other malignant neoplasms of lymphatic and hematopoietic tissues . . . 200-203	21,270	20,570	21,678	21,077	20,463	18,717
Benign neoplasms, carcinoma in situ, and neoplasms of uncertain behavior and of unspecified nature . . . 210-239	5,710	5,800	4,963	4,925	4,719	4,828
Diabetes mellitus . . . 250	34,230	33,060	33,841	32,989	34,508	38,324
Nutritional deficiencies . . . 260-269	2,300	2,250	2,855	2,606	2,619	2,470
Anemias . . . 280-285	3,420	2,940	3,300	3,121	3,182	3,427
Meningitis . . . 320-322	1,320	1,490	1,560	1,526	1,589	1,701
Major cardiovascular diseases . . . 390-448	989,690	953,100	966,120	961,539	974,429	1,007,984
Diseases of heart . . . 390-398,402,404-429	763,060	729,210	729,510	718,850	723,878	735,542
Rheumatic fever and rheumatic heart disease . . . 390-398	7,950	7,470	13,402	12,770	13,110	14,889
Hypertensive heart disease . . . 402	22,100	20,520	7,087	6,905	6,670	8,413
Hypertensive heart and renal disease . . . 404	3,340	3,150	3,249	3,530	4,020	6,578
Ischemic heart disease . . . 410-414	566,930	549,820	642,270	638,427	646,073	666,665
Acute myocardial infarction . . . 410	301,210	302,010	302,664	306,398	319,477	357,241
Other acute and subacute forms of ischemic heart disease . . . 411	4,520	4,400	4,090	3,993	4,028	4,246
Angina pectoris . . . 413	370	370	253	206	186	216
Old myocardial infarction and other forms of chronic ischemic heart disease . . . 412,414	260,830	243,040	335,263	327,830	322,382	304,962
Other diseases of endocardium . . . 424	7,030	6,160	4,072	4,024	4,195	6,705
All other forms of heart disease . . . 415-423,425-429	155,710	142,090	59,430	53,194	49,810	32,292
Hypertension with or without renal disease . . . 401,403	7,140	6,910	5,490	5,695	6,130	8,273
Cerebrovascular diseases . . . 430-438	170,420	169,350	175,629	181,934	188,623	207,166
Intracerebral and other intracranial hemorrhage . . . 431-432	20,900	22,760	22,633	23,832	24,845	41,379
Cerebral thrombosis and unspecified occlusion of cerebral arteries . . . 434.0,434.9	34,510	35,110	38,710	42,016	44,803	57,845
Cerebral embolism . . . 434.1	710	810	760	731	826	884
All other and late effects of cerebrovascular diseases . . . 430,433,435-438	114,300	110,670	113,526	115,355	118,149	107,058
Atherosclerosis . . . 440	29,830	28,650	28,940	28,754	29,366	31,682
Other diseases of arteries, arterioles, and capillaries . . . 441-448	19,240	18,980	26,551	26,306	26,432	25,321
Acute bronchitis and bronchiolitis . . . 466	590	470	756	697	854	1,310
Pneumonia and influenza . . . 480-487	52,720	44,110	58,319	51,193	61,866	62,739
Pneumonia . . . 480-486	50,130	43,520	54,267	49,889	53,989	59,032
Influenza . . . 487	2,590	590	4,052	1,304	7,877	3,707
Chronic obstructive pulmonary diseases and allied conditions . . . 490-496	55,810	49,980	21,875	22,363	24,410	30,889
Bronchitis, chronic and unspecified . . . 490-491	3,940	3,220	4,376	4,313	4,639	5,846
Emphysema . . . 492	14,130	14,070	15,627	16,376	17,796	22,721
Asthma . . . 493	2,500	2,540	1,872	1,674	1,975	2,322
Other chronic obstructive pulmonary diseases and allied conditions . . . 494-496	35,240	30,150	. . .	. . .	. . .	. . .
Ulcer of stomach and duodenum . . . 531-533	5,750	5,520	5,545	5,900	6,428	8,607
Appendicitis . . . 540-543	650	750	735	731	752	1,397
Hernia of abdominal cavity and intestinal obstruction without mention of hernia . . . 550-553, 560	5,430	5,010	5,568	115,355	5,919	7,235
Chronic liver disease and cirrhosis . . . 571	31,330	29,860	30,066	30,848	31,453	31,399
Cholelithiasis and other disorders of gallbladder . . . 574-575	3,110	2,840	2,941	2,957	2,956	3,973
Nephritis, nephrotic syndrome, and nephrosis . . . 580-589	17,390	16,080	8,868	8,519	8,541	8,877
Acute glomerulonephritis and nephrotic syndrome . . . 580-581	340	220	2,073	1,833	1,759	1,354
Chronic glomerulonephritis, nephritis and nephropathy, not specified as acute or chronic, and renal sclerosis, unspecified . . . 582-583,587	2,450	2,460	6,795	6,686	6,782	7,523
Renal failure, disorders resulting from impaired renal function, and small kidney of unknown cause . . . 584-586,588-589	14,600	13,400	6,795	6,686	6,782	7,523

Deaths from 72 selected causes: United States, 1970 and 1976-80—Con.

[For 1979 and 1980, based on a 10-percent sample of deaths; for all other years, based on final data. Data for 1979 and 1980 are based on the Ninth Revision International Classification of Diseases; for all other years, based on the Eighth Revision; see Technica. notes. Comparability of causes of death between the Eighth and Ninth Revisions is described in the Technical notes. Comparability ratios are shown in table 11]

Cause of death (Ninth Revision International Classification of Diseases, 1975)	1980 (est.)	1979 (est.)	1978	1977	1976	1970
Infections of kidney ...590	2,640	3,070	3,096	3,712	4,017	8,190
Hyperplasia of prostate ...600	810	580	854	998	1,077	2,168
Complications of pregnancy, childbirth, and the puerperium ...630-676	250	270	321	373	390	803
Pregnancy with abortive outcome ...630-638	50	60	16	20	16	128
Other complications of pregnancy, childbirth, and the puerperium ...640-676	200	210	305	353	374	675
Congenital anomalies ...740-759	13,730	13,390	12,968	12,983	13,002	16,824
Certain conditions originating in the perinatal period ...760-779	22,570	22,880	22,033	23,401	24,809	43,205
Birth trauma, intrauterine hypoxia, birth asphyxia, and respiratory distress syndrome ...767-769	7,500	8,270	11,710	12,633	13,432	22,801
Other conditions originating in the perinatal period ...760-766,770-779	15,070	14,610	10,323	10,768	11,377	20,404
Symptoms, signs, and ill-defined conditions ...780-799	29,130	28,210	31,324	32,149	30,802	25,781
All other diseases ...Residual	112,510	105,350	137,396	130,428	125,340	101,128
Accidents and adverse effects ...E800-E949	106,550	105,420	105,561	103,202	100,761	114,638
Motor vehicle accidents ...E810-E825	54,200	53,990	52,411	49,510	47,038	54,633
All other accidents and adverse effects ...E800-E807,E826-E949	52,350	51,430	53,150	53,692	53,723	60,005
Suicide ...E950-E959	28,290	27,640	27,294	28,681	26,832	23,480
Homicide and legal intervention ...E960-E978	25,090	23,040	20,432	19,968	19,554	16,848
All other external causes ...E980-E999	3,510	3,880	4,163	4,457	4,766	5,427

Death rates for 72 selected causes: United States, 1970 and 1976-80

[For 1979 and 1980, based on a 10-percent sample of deaths; for all other years, based on final data. Data for 1979 and 1980 are based on the Ninth Revision International Classification of Diseases; for all other years, based on the Eighth Revision; see Technical notes. Comparability of causes of death between the Eighth and Ninth Revisions is described in the Technical notes. Comparability ratios are shown in table 11. Rates per 100,000 population]

Cause of death (Ninth Revision International Classification of Diseases, 1975)	1980 (est.)	1979 (est.)	1978	1977	1976	1970
All causes ...	892.6	866.2	883.4	878.1	889.6	945.3
Shigellosis and amebiasis ...004,006	0.0	0.0	0.0	0.0	0.0	0.0
Certain other intestinal infections ...007-009	0.2	0.2	0.9	0.9	0.9	1.3
Tuberculosis ...010-018	0.8	0.9	1.3	1.4	1.5	2.6
Tuberculosis of respiratory system ...010-012	0.7	0.7	1.0	1.1	1.1	2.0
Other tuberculosis ...013-018	0.1	0.2	0.3	0.3	0.3	0.5
Whooping cough ...033	0.0	0.0	0.0	0.0	0.0	0.0
Streptococcal sore throat, scarlatina, and erysipelas ...034-035	0.0	0.0	0.0	0.0	0.0	0.0
Meningococcal infection ...036	0.2	0.2	0.2	0.2	0.2	0.3
Septicemia ...038	4.1	3.8	3.6	3.3	3.0	1.7
Acute poliomyelitis ...045	0.0	0.0	0.0	0.0	0.0	0.0
Measles ...055	0.0	-	0.0	0.0	0.0	0.0
Viral hepatitis ...070	0.4	0.3	0.2	0.2	0.3	0.5
Syphilis ...090-097	0.1	0.1	0.1	0.1	0.1	0.2
All other infectious and parasitic diseases ...001-003,005,020-032,037,039-041,046-054,056-066,071-088,098-139	1.7	1.5	2.0	1.8	1.8	1.5
Malignant neoplasms, including neoplasms of lymphatic and hematopoietic tissues ...140-208	186.3	183.5	181.9	178.7	175.8	162.8
Malignant neoplasms of lip, oral cavity, and pharynx ...140-149	3.8	3.6	3.8	3.9	3.8	3.7
Malignant neoplasms of digestive organs and peritoneum ...150-159	49.3	49.5	48.3	47.6	47.4	46.6
Malignant neoplasms of respiratory and intrathoracic organs ...160-165	48.6	46.7	45.8	44.0	42.5	34.2
Malignant neoplasm of breast ...174-175	15.7	16.0	15.9	16.1	15.6	14.7
Malignant neoplasms of genital organs ...179-187	20.8	20.5	20.7	20.5	20.7	20.3
Malignant neoplasms of urinary organs ...188-189	7.9	8.0	8.1	8.0	7.9	7.6
Malignant neoplasms of all other and unspecified sites ...170-173,190-199	22.9	22.3	22.4	21.9	21.4	19.2
Leukemia ...204-208	7.7	7.4	7.1	7.1	7.0	7.1
Other malignant neoplasms of lymphatic and hematopoietic tissues ...200-203	9.6	9.3	9.9	9.7	9.5	9.2
Benign neoplasms, carcinoma in situ, and neoplasms of uncertain behavior and of unspecified nature ...210-239	2.6	2.6	2.3	2.3	2.2	2.4
Diabetes mellitus ...250	15.4	15.0	15.5	15.2	16.1	18.9
Nutritional deficiencies ...260-269	1.0	1.0	1.3	1.2	1.2	1.2
Anemias ...280-285	1.5	1.3	1.5	1.4	1.5	1.7
Meningitis ...320-322	0.6	0.7	0.7	0.7	0.7	0.8
Major cardiovascular diseases ...390-448	444.9	433.0	442.7	444.5	454.0	496.0
Diseases of heart ...390-398,402,404-429	343.0	331.3	334.3	332.3	337.2	362.0
Rheumatic fever and rheumatic heart disease ...390-398	3.6	3.4	6.1	5.9	6.1	7.3
Hypertensive heart disease ...402	9.9	9.3	3.2	3.2	3.1	4.1
Hypertensive heart and renal disease ...404	1.5	1.4	1.5	1.6	1.9	3.2
Ischemic heart disease ...410-414	254.9	249.8	294.3	295.1	301.0	328.1
Acute myocardial infarction ...410	135.4	137.2	138.7	141.6	148.8	175.8
Other acute and subacute forms of ischemic heart disease ...411	2.0	2.0	1.9	1.8	1.9	2.1
Angina pectoris ...413	0.2	0.2	0.1	0.1	0.1	0.1
Old myocardial infarction and other forms of chronic ischemic heart disease ...412,414	117.3	110.4	153.6	151.5	150.2	150.1
Other diseases of endocardium ...424	3.2	2.8	1.9	1.9	2.0	3.3

Death rates for 72 selected causes: United States, 1970 and 1976-80—Con.

[For 1979 and 1980, based on a 10-percent sample of deaths; for all other years, based on final data. Data for 1979 and 1980 are based on the Ninth Revision International Classification of Diseases; for all other years, based on the Eighth Revision; see Technical notes. Comparability of causes of death between the Eighth and Ninth Revisions is described in the Technical notes. Comparability ratios are shown in table 11. Rates per 100,000 population]

Cause of death (Ninth Revision International Classification of Diseases, 1975)	1980 (est.)	1979 (est.)	1978	1977	1976	1970
All other forms of heart disease 415-423,425-429	70.0	64.6	27.2	24.6	23.2	15.9
Hypertension with or without renal disease 401-403	3.2	3.1	2.5	2.6	2.9	4.1
Cerebrovascular diseases 430-438	76.6	76.9	80.5	84.1	87.9	101.9
Intracerebral and other intracranial hemorrhage 431-432	9.4	10.3	10.4	11.0	11.6	20.4
Cerebral thrombosis and unspecified occlusion of cerebral arteries 434.0,434.9	15.5	16.0	17.7	19.4	20.9	28.5
Cerebral embolism 434.1	0.3	0.4	0.3	0.3	0.4	0.4
All other and late effects of cerebrovascular diseases 430,433,435-438	51.4	50.3	52.0	53.3	55.0	52.7
Atherosclerosis 440	13.4	13.0	13.3	13.3	13.7	15.6
Other diseases of arteries, arterioles, and capillaries 441-448	8.6	8.6	12.2	12.2	12.3	12.5
Acute bronchitis and bronchiolitis 466	0.3	0.2	0.3	0.3	0.4	0.6
Pneumonia and influenza 480-487	23.7	20.0	26.7	23.7	28.8	30.9
Pneumonia 480-486	22.5	19.8	24.9	23.1	25.2	29.0
Influenza 487	1.2	0.3	1.9	0.6	3.7	1.8
Chronic obstructive pulmonary diseases and allied conditions 490-496	25.1	22.7	10.0	10.3	11.4	15.2
Bronchitis, chronic and unspecified 490-491	1.8	1.5	2.0	2.0	2.2	2.9
Emphysema 492	6.4	6.4	7.2	7.6	8.3	11.2
Asthma 493	1.1	1.2	0.9	0.8	0.9	1.1
Other chronic obstructive pulmonary diseases and allied conditions 494-496	15.8	13.7	...	...	...	...
Ulcer of stomach and duodenum 531-533	2.6	2.5	2.5	2.7	3.0	4.2
Appendicitis 540-543	0.3	0.3	0.3	0.3	0.4	0.7
Hernia of abdominal cavity and intestinal obstruction without mention of hernia 550-553,560	2.4	2.3	2.6	2.6	2.8	3.6
Chronic liver disease and cirrhosis 571	14.1	13.6	13.8	14.3	14.7	15.5
Cholelithiasis and other disorders of gallbladder 574-575	1.4	1.3	1.3	1.4	1.4	2.0
Nephritis, nephrotic syndrome, and nephrosis 580-589	7.8	7.3	4.1	3.9	4.0	4.4
Acute glomerulonephritis and nephrotic syndrome 580-581	0.2	0.1	0.9	0.8	0.8	0.7
Chronic glomerulonephritis, nephritis and nephropathy, not specified as acute or chronic, and renal sclerosis, unspecified 582-583,587	1.1	1.1	3.1	3.1	3.2	3.7
Renal failure, disorders resulting from impaired renal function, and small kidney of unknown cause 584-586,588-589	6.6	6.1	3.1	3.1	3.2	3.7
Infections of kidney 590	1.2	1.4	1.4	1.7	1.9	4.0
Hyperplasia of prostate 600	0.4	0.3	0.4	0.5	0.5	1.1
Complications of pregnancy, childbirth, and the puerperium 630-676	0.1	0.1	0.1	0.2	0.2	0.4
Pregnancy with abortive outcome 630-638	0.0	0.0	0.0	0.0	0.0	0.1
Other complications of pregnancy, childbirth, and the puerperium 640-676	0.1	0.1	0.1	0.2	0.2	0.3
Congenital anomalies 740-759	6.2	6.1	5.9	6.0	6.1	8.3
Certain conditions originating in the perinatal period 760-779	10.1	10.4	10.1	10.8	11.6	21.3
Birth trauma, intrauterine hypoxia, birth asphyxia, and respiratory distress syndrome 767-769	3.4	3.8	5.4	5.8	6.3	11.2
Other conditions originating in the perinatal period 760-766,770-779	6.8	6.6	4.7	5.0	5.3	10.0
Symptoms, signs, and ill-defined conditions 780-799	13.1	12.8	14.4	14.9	14.3	12.7
All other diseases .... Residual	50.6	47.9	63.0	60.3	58.4	49.8
Accidents and adverse effects E800-E949	47.9	47.9	48.4	47.7	46.9	56.4
Motor vehicle accidents E810-E825	24.4	24.5	24.0	22.9	21.9	26.9
All other accidents and adverse effects E800-E807,E826-E949	23.5	23.4	24.4	24.8	25.0	29.5
Suicide E950-E959	12.7	12.6	12.5	13.3	12.5	11.6
Homicide and legal intervention E960-E978	11.3	10.5	9.4	9.2	9.1	8.3
All other external causes E980-E999	1.6	1.8	1.9	2.1	2.2	2.7

Comparable category numbers, estimated comparability ratios, and estimates of sampling variability of comparability ratios for 72 selected causes; based on a stratified random sample of 1976 deaths: United States

[For discussion of comparability ratios see Technical notes]

Cause of death (Ninth Revision International Classification of Diseases, 1975)	Category numbers according to the Eighth Revision	Estimated comparability ratio[1]	Error of the estimate of the ratio in (2)		95 percent confidence limits[2]	
			Standard error	Relative standard error	Upper	Lower
	(1)	(2)	(3)	(4)	(5)	(6)
All causes	...	1.0000	...	...	...	...
Shigellosis and amebiasis 004,006	004,006	0.9818	0.0378	3.9	1.0559	0.9077
Certain other intestinal infections 007-009	008,009	0.1821	0.0207	11.4	0.2227	0.1415
Tuberculosis 010-018	010-019	0.7668	0.0119	1.6	0.7901	0.7435
Tuberculosis of respiratory system 010-012	010-012	0.8429	0.0146	1.7	0.8715	0.8143
Other tuberculosis 013-018	013-019	0.5077	0.0167	3.3	0.5404	0.4750
Whooping cough 033	033	0.8571	0.0000	0.0	0.8571	0.8571
Streptococcal sore throat, scarlatina, and erysipelas 034-035	034	1.4286	0.0000	0.0	1.4286	1.4286
Meningococcal infection 036	036	0.9788	0.0124	1.3	1.0030	0.9546
Septicemia 038	038	0.8500	0.0180	2.1	0.8853	0.8147
Acute poliomyelitis 045	040-043	0.5000	0.0000	0.0	0.5000	0.5000
Measles 055	055	0.9167	0.0000	0.0	0.9167	0.9167
Viral hepatitis 070	070	1.3986	0.0820	5.9	1.5593	1.2379
Syphilis 090-097	090-097	1.0089	0.0259	2.6	1.0596	0.9582
All other infectious and parasitic diseases 001-003,005,020-032,037,039-041,046-054,056-066,071-088,098-139	Remainder of 000-136	1.0321	0.0634	6.1	1.1563	0.9079
Malignant neoplasms, including neoplasms of lymphatic and hematopoietic tissues 140-208	140-209	1.0026	0.0017	0.2	1.0059	0.9993
Malignant neoplasms of lip, oral cavity, and pharynx 140-149	140-149	1.0117	0.0087	0.9	1.0286	0.9948
Malignant neoplasms of digestive organs and peritoneum 150-159	150-159	1.0330	0.0035	0.3	1.0398	1.0262
Malignant neoplasms of respiratory and intrathoracic organs 160-165	160-163	1.0007	0.0033	0.3	1.0071	0.9943
Malignant neoplasm of breast 174-175	174	1.0089	0.0022	0.2	1.0131	1.0047
Malignant neoplasms of genital organs 179-187	180-187	1.0111	0.0031	0.3	1.0171	1.0051
Malignant neoplasms of urinary organs 188-189	188,189	0.9924	0.0045	0.5	1.0011	0.9837
Malignant neoplasms of all other and unspecified sites 170-173,190-199	170-173,190-199	0.9557	0.0082	0.9	0.9718	0.9396
Leukemia 204-208	204-207	1.0070	0.0056	0.6	1.0180	0.9960
Other malignant neoplasms of lymphatic and hematopoietic tissues 200-203	200-203,208,209	0.9385	0.0069	0.7	0.9519	0.9251
Benign neoplasms, carcinoma in situ, and neoplasms of uncertain behavior and of unspecified nature 210-239	210-239	1.2085	0.0261	2.2	1.2595	1.1575
Diabetes mellitus 250	250	0.9991	0.0087	0.9	1.0162	0.9820
Nutritional deficiencies 260-269	260-269	0.7167	0.0262	3.7	0.7680	0.6654
Anemias 280-285	280-285	0.9296	0.0124	1.3	0.9538	0.9054
Meningitis 320-322	320	0.9459	0.0163	1.7	0.9777	0.9141
Major cardiovascular diseases 390-448	390-448	1.0069	0.0004	0.0	1.0076	1.0062
Diseases of heart 390-398,402,404-429	390-398,402,404, 410-429	1.0126	0.0039	0.4	1.0202	1.0050
Rheumatic fever and rheumatic heart disease 390-398	390-398	0.6648	0.0080	1.2	0.6804	0.6492
Hypertensive heart disease 402	402	3.3022	0.0557	1.7	3.4114	3.1930
Hypertensive heart and renal disease 404	404	1.2119	0.0438	3.6	1.2978	1.1260
Ischemic heart disease 410-414	410-413	0.8784	0.0038	0.4	0.8859	0.8709
Acute myocardial infarction 410	410	1.0003	0.0054	0.5	1.0108	0.9898
Other acute and subacute forms of ischemic heart disease 411	411	1.2224	0.0661	5.4	1.3519	1.0929
Angina pectoris 413	413	1.0484	0.0666	6.4	1.1789	0.9179
Old myocardial infarction and other forms of chronic ischemic heart disease 412,414	412	0.7533	0.0055	0.7	0.7640	0.7426
Other diseases of endocardium 424	424,428	1.2286	0.0227	1.8	1.2731	1.1841
All other forms of heart disease 415-423,425-429	420-423,425-427,429	2.5035	0.0257	1.0	2.5539	2.4531
Hypertension with or without renal disease 401,403	400,401,403	1.2703	0.0294	2.3	1.3280	1.2126
Cerebrovascular diseases 430-438	430-438	1.0049	0.0066	0.7	1.0178	0.9920
Intracerebral and other intracranial hemorrhage 431-432	431	0.9969	0.0068	0.7	1.0102	0.9836
Cerebral thrombosis and unspecified occlusion of cerebral arteries 434.0,434.9	433	1.0340	0.0222	2.1	1.0774	0.9906
Cerebral embolism 434.1	434	1.1211	0.0924	8.2	1.3022	0.9400
All other and late effects of cerebrovascular diseases 430,433,435-438	430,432,435-438	0.9948	0.0061	0.6	1.0067	0.9829
Atherosclerosis 440	440	1.0649	0.0246	2.3	1.1130	1.0168
Other diseases of arteries, arterioles, and capillaries 441-448	441-448	0.7409	0.0098	1.3	0.7600	0.7218
Acute bronchitis and bronchiolitis 466	466	0.8888	0.0274	3.1	0.9425	0.8351
Pneumonia and influenza 480-487	470-474,480-486	0.9264	0.0067	0.7	0.9394	0.9134
Pneumonia 480-486	480-486	0.9199	0.0076	0.8	0.9347	0.9051
Influenza 487	470-474	0.9714	0.0078	0.8	0.9866	0.9562
Chronic obstructive pulmonary diseases and allied conditions 490-496	490-493	1.8846	0.0150	0.8	1.9141	1.8551
Bronchitis, chronic and unspecified 490-491	490-491	0.9383	0.0134	1.4	0.9646	0.9120
Emphysema 492	492	0.9770	0.0127	1.3	1.0018	0.9522
Asthma 493	493	1.3544	0.0636	4.7	1.4790	1.2298
Other chronic obstructive pulmonary diseases and allied conditions 494-496	.[2]	[3]...	[3]...	[3]...	[3]...	[3]...
Ulcer of stomach and duodenum 531-533	531-533	1.1192	0.0247	2.2	1.1675	1.0709
Appendicitis 540-543	540-543	1.0080	0.0264	2.6	1.0597	0.9563
Hernia of abdominal cavity and intestinal obstruction without mention of hernia 550-553,560	550-553,560	0.9432	0.0169	1.8	0.9762	0.9102

See footnotes at end of table

Comparable category numbers, estimated comparability ratios, and estimates of sampling variability of comparability ratios for 72 selected causes; based on a stratified random sample of 1976 deaths: United States—Con.

[For discussion of comparability ratios see Technical notes]

Cause of death (Ninth Revision International Classification of Diseases, 1975)	Category numbers according to the Eighth Revision	Estimated comparability ratio[1]	Error of the estimate of the ratio in (2)		95 percent confidence limits[2]	
			Standard error	Relative standard error	Upper	Lower
	(1)	(2)	(3)	(4)	(5)	(6)
Chronic liver disease and cirrhosis 571	571	1.0110	0.0069	0.7	1.0245	0.9975
Cholelithiasis and other disorders of gallbladder 574-575	574,575	1.0494	0.0445	4.2	1.1366	0.9622
Nephritis, nephrotic syndrome, and nephrosis 580-589	580-584	1.7397	0.0777	4.5	1.8920	1.5874
Acute glomerulonephritis and nephrotic syndrome 580-581	580,581	0.2422	0.0185	7.6	0.2783	0.2061
Chronic glomerulonephritis, nephritis and nephropathy, not specified as acute or chronic, and renal sclerosis, unspecified 582-583,587	582-584	0.4954	0.0195	3.9	0.5335	0.4573
Renal failure, disorders resulting from impaired renal function, and small kidney of unknown cause 584-586,588-589	582-584	1.6327	0.0958	5.9	1.8205	1.4449
Infections of kidney 590	590	0.9878	0.0091	0.9	1.0056	0.9700
Hyperplasia of prostate 600	600	1.0232	0.0226	2.2	1.0674	0.9790
Complications of pregnancy, childbirth, and the puerperium 630-676	630-678	1.1000	0.0435	4.0	1.1853	1.0147
Pregnancy with abortive outcome 630-638	640-645	3.8125	0.0000	0.0	3.8125	3.8125
Other complications of pregnancy, childbirth, and the puerperium 640-676	630-639,650-678	0.9840	0.0454	4.6	1.0729	0.8951
Congenital anomalies 740-759	740-759	0.9984	0.0100	1.0	1.0179	0.9789
Certain conditions originating in the perinatal period 760-779	760-769.2,769.4-772, 774-778	1.0765	0.0238	2.2	1.1230	1.0300
Birth trauma, intrauterine hypoxia, birth asphyxia, and respiratory distress syndrome 767-769	764-768,772,776	0.7483	0.0306	4.1	0.8083	0.6883
Other conditions originating in the perinatal period 760-766,770-779	Remainder of 760-778	1.4639	0.0371	2.5	1.5367	1.3911
Symptoms, signs, and ill-defined conditions 780-799	780-796	0.9102	0.0121	1.3	0.9338	0.8866
All other diseases . . . . Residual	Residual	0.7786	0.0082	1.1	0.7947	0.7625
Accidents and adverse effects E800-E949	E800-E949	0.9970	0.0030	0.3	1.0029	0.9911
Motor vehicle accidents E810-E825	E810-E823	1.0117	0.0027	0.3	1.0169	1.0065
All other accidents and adverse effects E800-E807,E826-E949	E800-E807,E825-E949	0.9841	0.0051	0.5	0.9941	0.9741
Suicide E950-E959	E950-E959	1.0032	0.0042	0.4	1.0114	0.9950
Homicide and legal intervention E960-E978	E960-E978	1.0057	0.0030	0.3	1.0115	0.9999
All other external causes E980-E999	E980-E999	0.9675	0.0144	1.5	0.9957	0.9393

[1] Ratio of estimated number of deaths assigned according to the Ninth Revision to deaths assigned according to the Eighth Revision.

[2] The probability is 95 percent that the true comparability ratio will have a value between the upper and lower limits shown. These limits were computed before the estimated standard error was rounded to the fourth decimal.

[3] Chronic obstructive lung disease without mention of asthma, bronchitis, or emphysema (ICDA No. *519.3), introduced by NCHS to be used with the Eighth Revision, is comparable to Other chronic obstructive pulmonary diseases and allied conditions (ICD Nos. 494-496) of the Ninth Revision. The comparability ratio for this set of titles is 1.0054, with a standard error of 0.0118, a relative error of 1.2 percent, and 95 percent confidence limits of 1.0285 and 0.9823. These data are not shown in this table because there are no sample data for ICDA No. *519.3.

Comparable category numbers, estimated comparability ratios, and estimates of sampling variability of comparable ratios for 10 selected causes of infant death; based on a stratified random sample of 1976 infant deaths: United States

[For discussion of comparability ratios see Technical notes]

Cause of death (Ninth Revision - International Classification of Diseases, 1975)	Category numbers according to the Eighth Revision	Estimated comparability ratio[1]	Error of the estimate of the ratio in (2)		95 percent confidence limits[2]	
			Standard error	Relative standard error	Upper	Lower
	(1)	(2)	(3)	(4)	(5)	(6)
All causes	. . .	1.0000	. . .	. . .	. . .	. . .
Certain gastrointestinal diseases 008-009,535,555-558	004,006-009,535, 561,563	0.4678	0.0228	4.9	0.5125	0.4231
Pneumonia and influenza 480-487	470-474,480-486	0.7471	0.0200	2.7	0.7862	0.7078
Congenital anomalies 740-759	740-759	1.0071	0.0062	0.6	1.0191	0.9949
Disorders relating to short gestation and unspecified low birthweight 765	777	0.9630	0.0107	1.1	0.9839	0.9421
Birth trauma 767	764-768(.0-.3),772	0.7154	0.0337	4.7	0.7813	0.6493
Intrauterine hypoxia and birth asphyxia 768	776.9	0.3270	0.0212	6.5	0.3684	0.2856
Respiratory distress syndrome 769	. . .	. . .	. . .	. . .	. . .	. . .
Other conditions originating in the perinatal period 760-764,766,770-779	Remainder of 760-778	0.8492	0.0098	1.1	0.8683	0.8301
Sudden infant death syndrome 798.0	. . .	. . .	. . .	. . .	. . .	. . .
All other causes . . . . Residual	Residual	0.5455	0.0061	1.1	0.5573	0.5335

[1] Ratio of estimated number of deaths assigned according to the Ninth Revision to deaths assigned according to the Eighth Revision.
[2] The probability is 95 percent that the true comparability ratio will have a value between the upper and lower limits shown. These limits were computed before the estimated standard error was rounded to the fourth decimal.

Technical notes

Nature and sources of data

All data for 1980 in this report are provisional. Data for the United States as a whole refer to events occurring within the United States; other data refer to events within the reporting areas shown.

Beginning with 1970, final birth and mortality statistics exclude data for births and deaths to nonresidents of the United States. Data for nonresidents are included in provisional data for 1979 and 1980.

Provisional or estimated figures for births, marriages, divorces, and deaths, except data estimated from the Current Mortality Sample, summarize data from monthly reports of the numbers of birth, marriage, divorce, and death certificates received in registration offices between two dates a month apart regardless of when the events occurred. Final figures are counts of events occurring in the specified year.

Mortality

All mortality figures exclude fetal deaths. Final mortality statistics for 1972 are based on a 50-percent sample of deaths. For all other years final data are based on all records received.

Current Mortality Sample

Deaths and death rates for 1979 and 1980 by cause, age, race, and sex were estimated from the Current Mortality Sample. The Current Mortality Sample is a 10-percent systematic sample of death certificates received each month in the vital statistics offices in the 50 states, the District of Columbia, and the independent registration area of New York City. The sample for each of these areas consists of one-tenth of the death certificates received in the office between a given date and the same date of the following month. All death certificates received during the 1-month period are sampled regardless of the month or year in which the death occurred. As a result, the monthly sample is not strictly comparable to a sample on a month-of-occurrence basis. The proportion of death certificates received in the samples for each month of 1980 representing deaths occurring in the current month and those occurring in other months are shown in table I.

Because of the way in which death certificates are processed in California, this State contributes a high proportion of the certificates for deaths not occurring in the sample month. For the sample exclusive of California, the percent of the sample deaths occurring in the current month constitutes about 79 percent of the total as opposed to 71 percent of the entire sample. As for the year of occurrence, 95.9 percent of the 198,038 transcripts in the 1980 sample were for deaths occurring in 1980 and 4.1 percent for deaths occurring in 1979.

Correction for bias and adjustment to provisional counts.—The Current Mortality Sample is selected at a specified time each month. Complete information concerning the underlying cause of death is sometimes not available in the State offices when the sample is drawn but is available later when copies of the final death certificates are processed. As a result, estimates based on sample counts for certain causes are recurringly biased estimates of final counts. Comparisons of sample and final counts for previous years have shown that these biases are primarily associated with certain cause-of-death groups.

Due to the introduction of the Ninth Revision in 1979, some modification was made in the rules for selection of a cause of death to be corrected for bias. An ICD-9 cause of death with a comparability ratio between 0.95 and 1.05 was considered as if there had been no discontinuity between 1978 and 1979. Final and sample data for the previous 3 years—1976, 1977, and 1978—were compared for the most nearly comparable ICDA-8 cause of death. If the sample count for these years departs from one-tenth of the final count by more than would be expected on the basis of sampling variability alone, the sample deaths for the corresponding ICD-9 causes were corrected by multiplying the sample frequency by an adjusted weight. The adjusted weight used was the ratio of the number of deaths from the given ICDA-8 cause in the final count of deaths for 1976-78 to the number of deaths from this cause in the sample returns for the same years, multiplied by 10 times the 3-year average sampling fraction for all causes.

The remaining ICD-9 causes, those with a comparability ratio less than 0.95 or greater than 1.05, were then examined to determine, empirically, if failure to correct for bias would lead to greater possible error in the provisional estimate for 1979 and 1980 than could be expected by the comparability discontinuity alone. On the basis of this examination, the following two causes were also chosen to be corrected for bias: Benign neoplasms, carcinoma in situ, and neoplasms of uncertain behavior and of unspecified nature (ICD-9 Nos. 210-239) and Symptoms, signs, and ill-defined conditions (ICD-9 Nos. 780-799). For these two causes the adjusted weights were based on data for 1976-78 for the most nearly comparable ICDA-8 categories (ICDA-8 Nos. 210-239 and ICDA-8 Nos. 780-796, respectively).

The adjusted weights which were applied to the 1979 and 1980 samples for all ages are shown in table II. Because of comparability discontinuities, no infant causes were corrected for bias.

Sampling variability.—Since the estimates of deaths and death rates presented in this report (total deaths and deaths under 1 year) are based on a sample of the death certificates, they are subject to sampling variability. The estimated percent error shown in this report is a measure of the sampling error of the estimated number of deaths (or of the estimated death rate) expressed as a percent of the estimate. The chances are about 2 out of 3 that the percent difference between an estimate and the result of a complete count is less than the percent error shown. The chances are about 19 out of 20 that the percent difference is less than twice the percent error.

Two methods are used for estimating percent errors—one for the ratio estimates for the causes of death corrected for bias and the other for estimates for the remaining causes of death or for given age-race-sex groups. The percent error of a ratio estimate for a given cause of death corrected for bias for all ages is computed as follows:

$$V = 300 \sqrt{\frac{1}{10}\left(\frac{1}{x} - \frac{1}{D}\right) + \left(\frac{1}{Y} - \frac{1}{M}\right)}$$

where

V = percent error of the estimate X

X = the estimated number of deaths (or estimated death rate) in a given cause or age-race-sex group

x = the number of deaths in the sample from the given cause

D = 198,038, the total number of death certificates in the sample for 1980

Y = the final number of deaths from the given cause in the 3 years—1976, 1977, and 1978 combined

M = 5,736,825, the final count of all deaths occurring in the 3 years—1976, 1977, and 1978 combined.

The percent errors for the remaining estimates for given causes of death not requiring a correction for bias or for a given age-race-sex group are computed as follows:

$$V = 300 \sqrt{\frac{1}{X} - \frac{1}{N}}$$

where

V = the percent error of the estimate X

X = the estimated number of deaths from a given cause or age-race-sex group

N = 1,986,000, the provisional number of registered deaths in 1980.

The percent error due to sampling may be obtained by using the above formula where X is the estimated number of deaths in a given group. For easy reference, the percent errors ascribable to sampling for estimates based on several levels in the number of deaths are shown in table III.

Cause-of-death classification

The mortality statistics presented here are compiled in accordance with the World Health Organization regulations, which specify that member nations classify causes of death in accordance with the current revision of the International Statistical Classification of Diseases, Injuries, and Causes of Death.

During the period 1968-78, causes of death were classified according to the *Eighth Revision International Classification of Diseases, Adapted for Use in the United States,* 1965 (ICDA-8).[5] Causes of death in 1979 and 1980 were classified according to the Ninth Revision (ICD-9).[6] This produces some major changes in the classification of causes of death. Cause-of-death comparisons between ICDA-8 and ICD-9 data require consideration of the comparability ratios and estimates of their standard errors, shown in tables 11 and 12. A description of the comparability ratios and how they were derived may be found in a previous report.[7]

Comparability ratios for causes of infant mortality have been computed for the List of 8 Causes of Infant Death published in the *Monthly Vital Statistics Report* for 1968-78. Because Respiratory distress syndrome (ICDA-8 No. 776.2) and Sudden infant death syndrome (ICDA-8 No. *795.0) were contained in residual categories in this list, separate comparability ratios were not computed. However, infant mortality rates for these causes based on final data for 1978 and previous years are available and are shown in table H.

Cause-of-death ranking

Cause-of-death ranking is based on the List of 72 Selected Causes of Death, adapted from one of the special lists for mortality tabulations recommended by the World Health Organization for use with the Ninth Revision of the International Classification of Diseases. Two group titles—Major cardiovascular diseases and Symptoms, signs, and ill-defined conditions—are not ranked. In addition, category titles that begin with the words "other" and "all other" are not ranked. The remaining titles are ranked according to the number of deaths for 1980 to determine the leading causes of death. When one of the titles that represents a subtotal is ranked (e.g., Tuberculosis), its component parts (in this case, Tuberculosis of respiratory system and Other tuberculosis) are not ranked.

Age-adjusted rates

The age-adjusted rates presented in this report were computed by the direct method, that is, by applying the age-specific death rates for a given cause of death to the standard population distributed by age. The total population as enumerated in 1940 was selected as the standard. The age-adjusted rates were based on 10-year age groups. Rates by cause for 1979 and 1980 were based on the same 10-year age groups except that the age group 1-14 years was used instead of 1-4 years and 5-14 years. It is important not to compare age-adjusted death rates directly with crude rates shown in other tables.

Life tables

Abridged life table values for 1967-69 have been revised using revised intercensal population estimates. Values for 1970-73 have also been revised, using the most recent U.S. decennial life tables as standard tables. In this and other recent publications these figures may differ from those initially published in *Vital Statistics of the United States.*

Seasonal adjustment

The method of seasonal adjustment used for birth, fertility, and marriage rates is described in *The*

Table I. Percent of death certificates received in the sample each month by month of occurrence: 1980

Month	Deaths occurring in—		
	Same month	Previous month	All other months
January	74.3	12.9	12.8
February	71.0	14.6	14.4
March	71.1	13.4	15.5
April	68.8	16.4	14.8
May	71.7	14.9	13.4
June	72.4	15.3	12.3
July	70.4	16.0	13.7
August	71.6	16.3	12.1
September	68.2	16.5	15.2
October	73.5	14.7	11.9
November	72.7	14.5	12.8
December	71.6	15.7	12.7

X-11 Variant of the Census Method II Seasonal Adjustment Program, Technical Paper No. 15, November 1965, published by the U.S. Bureau of the Census. Marriage rates were adjusted for monthly variation in the number of specified days of the week (Sundays, Mondays, and so forth) because marriages are more likely on some days than on others.

Population bases for computing rates

The populations used for computing rates shown in this report (furnished by the U.S. Bureau of the Census) represent the population residing in the specified area. The populations for 1980 are unpublished estimates based on the 1970 Census of Population. The rates shown here for 1980 are, therefore, comparable with the rates shown for earlier years.

Provisional rates for 1981 will be based on population estimates based on the 1980 Census of Population. Beginning with the January 1981 issue of the *Monthly Vital Statistics Report,* rates for 1980 have been recomputed using revised populations based on the 1980 enumerated population to be comparable with rates for 1981. The 1980 Census enumeration was about 4.8 million higher than the estimated population for April 1, 1980 and, therefore, rates for the total population computed using the enumerated population will be from 2 to 2.5

Table II. Causes of death corrected for bias and adjusted weights for all ages: 1980

Cause of death [1]	Adjusted weight (all ages)
Malignant neoplasms of all other and unspecified sites 170-173,190-199	9.79
Benign neoplasms, carcinoma in situ, and neoplasms of uncertain behavior and of unspecified nature 210-239	8.79
Intracerebral and other intracranial hemorrhage 431-432	10.28
Other complications of pregnancy, childbirth, and the puerperium 640-676	8.18
Symptoms, signs, and ill-defined conditions ...780-799	7.79
Motor vehicle accidents E810-E825	10.35
Suicide E950-E959	10.66
Homicide and legal intervention E960-E978	10.44
All other external causes E980-E999	11.02

[1] Causes of death eligible to have an adjusted weight were those that had 50 or more deaths based on final data for 1978.

percent lower than the rates shown here for 1980. Final rates for 1980 will be based on the enumerated population.

Infant mortality rates are based on live births. For an explanation of the method used in computing infant mortality rates adjusted for the changing numbers of births, see "Effect of Changing Birth Rates Upon Infant Mortality Rates," *Vital Statistics—Special Reports,* Vol. 19, No. 21, Nov. 1944 (U.S. Bureau of the Census).

Table III. Percent errors for estimated numbers of deaths from the Current Mortality Sample

Estimated number of deaths	Percent error	Estimated number of deaths	Percent error
10	94.9	900	10.0
20	67.1	1,000	9.5
50	42.4	2,000	6.7
100	30.0	5,000	4.2
200	21.2	10,000	3.0
300	17.3	20,000	2.1
400	15.0	50,000	1.3
500	13.4	100,000	0.9
600	12.2	200,000	0.6
700	11.3	500,000	0.4
800	10.6	1,000,000	0.2

Mortality

General

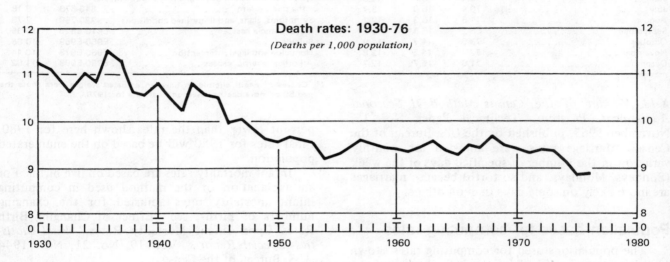

Death rates: 1930-76

(Deaths per 1,000 population)

Deaths, death rates, and age-adjusted death rates: Selected years, 1935-76

Year	Number	Rate per 1,000 population					Age-adjusted rate per 1,000 population[1]				
		Total	White		All other		Total	White		All other	
			Male	Female	Male	Female		Male	Female	Male	Female
1976[2]	1,909,440	8.9	10.1	7.9	9.8	6.8	6.3	8.0	4.4	10.7	6.4
1975[2]	1,892,879	8.9	10.2	7.8	10.0	6.8	6.4	8.1	4.5	11.0	6.5
1974[2]	1,934,388	9.2	10.4	8.1	10.4	7.2	6.7	8.4	4.7	11.5	6.9
1973[2]	1,973,003	9.4	10.7	8.2	10.8	7.6	6.9	8.7	4.8	12.1	7.4
1972[2,3]	1,963,944	9.4	10.8	8.2	11.0	7.6	7.0	8.8	4.9	12.3	7.5
1971[2]	1,927,542	9.3	10.7	8.1	10.8	7.6	7.0	8.8	4.9	12.1	7.5
1970[2]	1,921,031	9.5	10.9	8.1	11.2	7.8	7.1	8.9	5.0	12.3	7.7
1969[4]	1,921,990	9.5	11.0	8.2	11.5	8.0	7.3	9.1	5.1	12.7	8.0
1968[4]	1,930,082	9.7	11.1	8.2	11.7	8.2	7.4	9.2	5.2	12.9	8.3
1967[4]	1,851,323	9.4	10.8	8.0	11.0	7.9	7.3	9.0	5.1	12.1	8.0
1966[4]	1,863,149	9.5	11.0	8.1	11.4	8.2	7.4	9.2	5.3	12.4	8.3
1965[4]	1,828,136	9.4	10.9	8.0	11.2	8.2	7.4	9.1	5.3	12.2	8.3
1960	1,711,982	9.5	11.0	8.0	11.5	8.7	7.6	9.2	5.6	12.1	8.9
1955	1,528,717	9.3	10.7	7.8	11.3	8.8	7.6	9.1	5.7	11.9	9.1
1950	1,452,454	9.6	10.9	8.0	12.5	9.9	8.4	9.6	6.5	13.6	11.0
1945	1,401,719	10.6	12.5	8.6	13.5	10.5	9.5	10.7	7.5	14.5	11.9
1940	1,417,269	10.8	11.6	9.2	15.1	12.6	10.8	11.6	8.8	17.6	15.0
1935	1,392,752	10.9	11.6	9.5	15.6	13.0	11.6	12.3	9.8	18.5	16.1

[1] Adjusted to age distribution of U.S. population as enumerated in 1940.
[2] Excludes deaths of nonresidents of the United States.
[3] Based on a 50-percent sample.
[4] Rates are revised.

From "Facts of Life and Death," U.S. Department of Health, Education, and Welfare, Public Health Service, National Center for Health Statistics, November, 1978.

Deaths and death rates by age and sex: 1976

Age	Number			Rate per 1,000 population in specified group		
	Total	Male	Female	Total	Male	Female
All ages[1]-----------------------	1,909,440	1,051,983	857,457	8.9	10.1	7.8
Under 1 year------------------------	48,265	27,320	20,945	16.0	17.6	14.2
1-4 years--------------------------	8,606	4,915	3,691	0.7	0.8	0.6
5-9 years--------------------------	6,034	3,626	2,408	0.3	0.4	0.3
10-14 years-------------------------	6,867	4,442	2,425	0.3	0.4	0.3
15-19 years-------------------------	20,561	15,001	5,560	1.0	1.4	0.5
20-24 years-------------------------	25,520	19,252	6,268	1.3	2.0	0.6
25-29 years-------------------------	22,902	16,431	6,471	1.3	1.9	0.7
30-34 years-------------------------	20,527	13,731	6,796	1.4	2.0	0.9
35-39 years-------------------------	23,555	15,106	8,449	2.0	2.6	1.4
40-44 years-------------------------	34,914	22,054	12,860	3.1	4.1	2.3
45-49 years-------------------------	58,061	36,746	21,315	5.0	6.5	3.6
50-54 years-------------------------	91,975	58,578	33,397	7.7	10.2	5.4
55-59 years-------------------------	126,361	80,982	45,379	11.8	15.8	8.1
60-64 years-------------------------	169,699	108,713	60,986	18.2	25.0	12.3
65-69 years-------------------------	210,465	131,351	79,114	25.4	35.9	17.1
70-74 years-------------------------	233,462	136,115	97,347	39.5	54.3	28.6
75-79 years-------------------------	250,623	131,056	119,567	61.9	82.6	48.5
80-84 years-------------------------	246,096	113,137	132,959	90.3	115.2	76.3
85 years and over-------------------	304,472	113,119	191,353	154.9	179.8	143.1

[1]Includes deaths for which age was not stated.

Leading Causes

The next table shows the number of deaths and death rates for the leading causes of death in 1976 and death rates for these causes in 1900.

Figures for the 2 years show gross changes in mortality, but they are not exactly comparable in many respects. The rates for 1900 are based on deaths in 10 States and the District of Columbia, while the figures for 1976 are for the entire United States. New discoveries in medicine and new diagnostic facilities have produced an improvement in reporting causes of death. Causes of death which were not recognized as disease entities in 1900 are relatively frequent in 1976. The classification of causes of death is revised every decade to keep abreast of new information.

For 1976 deaths were classified according to the Eighth Revision International Classification of Diseases, Adapted, and for 1900 according to the First Revision of the International Lists. Also, beginning with 1949, the underlying cause of death indicated by the physician is generally the cause used in statistical tabulation. In earlier years, a fixed set of priorities was used to select the cause of death to be tabulated when more than one cause was reported.

Deaths and death rates for the 10 leading causes of death in 1976 and death rates for
these same causes in 1900

Rank, 1976	Cause of death and category numbers of the Eighth Revision International Classification of Diseases, Adapted, 1965	Number of deaths, 1976	Rate per 100,000 population	
			1976	1900
	All causes--	1,909,440	889.6	1,719.1
1	Diseases of heart----------------------390-398,402,404,410-429	723,878	337.2	137.4
2	Malignant neoplasms, including neoplasms of lymphatic and hematopoietic tissues------------------------------------140-209	377,312	175.8	64.0
3	Cerebrovascular diseases---------------------------------430-438	188,623	87.9	106.9
4	Accidents---E800-E949	100,761	46.9	72.3
5	Influenza and pneumonia------------------------470-474,480-486	61,866	28.8	202.2
6	Diabetes mellitus--250	34,508	16.1	11.0
7	Cirrhosis of liver---571	31,453	14.7	12.5
8	Arteriosclerosis---440	29,366	13.7	---
9	Suicide---E950-E959	26,832	12.5	10.2
10	Certain causes of mortality in early infancy[1]-------------------------760,769.2,769.4-772,774-778	24,809	11.6	62.6

[1]Relates to birth injuries, asphyxia, infections of newborn, ill-defined diseases, immaturity, etc.

Deaths and death rates for the 10 leading causes of death, by sex: 1976

Rank	Cause of death and category numbers of the Eighth Revision International Classification of Diseases, Adapted, 1965	Number	Rate per 100,000 population
	Male		
	All causes---	1,051,983	1,007.0
1	Diseases of heart--------------------------390-398,402,404,410-429	400,601	383.5
2	Malignant neoplasms, including neoplasms of lymphatic and hematopoietic tissues--140-209	205,406	196.6
3	Cerebrovascular diseases---------------------------------------430-438	80,597	77.1
4	Accidents--E800-E949	70,277	67.3
5	Influenza and pneumonia----------------------------470-474,480-486	32,513	31.1
6	Cirrhosis of liver---571	20,668	19.8
7	Suicide---E950-E959	19,493	18.7
8	Bronchitis, emphysema, and asthma---------------------------490-493	17,784	17.0
9	Homicide--E960-E978	15,142	14.5
10	Certain causes of mortality in early infancy----------------------------760-769.2,769.4-772,774-778	14,198	13.6
	Female		
	All causes---	857,457	778.3
1	Diseases of heart--------------------------390-398,402,404,410-429	323,277	293.4
2	Malignant neoplasms, including neoplasms of lymphatic and hematopoietic tissues--140-209	171,906	156.0
3	Cerebrovascular diseases---------------------------------------430-438	108,026	98.0
4	Accidents--E800-E949	30,484	27.7
5	Influenza and pneumonia----------------------------470-474,480-486	29,353	26.6
6	Diabetes mellitus---250	20,483	18.6
7	Arteriosclerosis---440	17,553	15.9
8	Cirrhosis of liver---571	10,785	9.8
9	Certain causes of mortality in early infancy---------------------------760-769.2,769.4-772,774-778	10,611	9.6
10	Suicide---E950-E959	7,339	6.7

Deaths and death rates for the 10 leading causes of death in specified age and sex groups: 1976

Rank	Age, sex, cause of death, and category numbers of the Eighth Revision International Classification of Diseases, Adapted, 1965	Number	Rate per 100,000 population in specified group
	1-4 years, both sexes		
	All causes---	8,606	69.9
1	Accidents---E800-E949	3,439	27.9
2	Congenital anomalies---740-759	1,114	9.0
3	Malignant neoplasms, including neoplasms of lymphatic and hematopoietic tissues--140-209	656	5.3
4	Influenza and pneumonia-------------------------------470-474,480-486	480	3.9
5	Homicide--E960-E978	306	2.5
6	Diseases of heart---------------------------390-398,402,404,410-429	227	1.8
7	Meningitis--320	220	1.8
8	Cerebrovascular diseases--------------------------------------430-438	90	0.7
8	Meningococcal infections-------------------------------------036	90	0.7
10	Enteritis and other diarrheal diseases---------------------008,009	82	0.7
	1-4 years, male		
	All causes---	4,915	78.2
1	Accidents---E800-E949	2,087	33.2
2	Congenital anomalies---740-759	550	8.7
3	Malignant neoplasms, including neoplasms of lymphatic and hematopoietic tissues--140-209	352	5.6
4	Influenza and pneumonia-------------------------------470-474,480-486	250	4.0
5	Homicide--E960-E978	154	2.4
6	Meningitis--320	152	2.4
7	Diseases of heart---------------------------390-398,402,404,410-429	133	2.1
8	Meningococcal infections-------------------------------------036	52	0.8
9	Cerebrovascular diseases--------------------------------------430-438	50	0.8
10	Enteritis and other diarrheal diseases---------------------008,009	41	0.7
	1-4 years, female		
	All causes---	3,691	61.3
1	Accidents---E800-E949	1,352	22.4
2	Congenital anomalies---740-759	564	9.4
3	Malignant neoplasms, including neoplasms of lymphatic and hematopoietic tissues--140-209	304	5.0
4	Influenza and pneumonia-------------------------------470-474,480-486	230	3.8
5	Homicide--E960-E978	152	2.5
6	Diseases of heart---------------------------390-398,402,404,410-429	94	1.6
7	Meningitis--320	68	1.1
8	Enteritis and other diarrheal diseases---------------------008,009	41	0.7
9	Cerebrovascular diseases--------------------------------------430-438	40	0.7
10	Meningococcal infections-------------------------------------036	38	0.6
10	Septicemia--038	38	0.6

Deaths and death rates for the 10 leading causes of death in specified age and sex groups: 1976—Con.

Rank	Age, sex, cause of death, and category numbers of the Eighth Revision International Classification of Diseases, Adapted, 1965	Number	Rate per 100,000 population in specified group
	5-14 years, both sexes		
	All causes --	12,901	34.7
1	Accidents---E800-E949	6,308	17.0
2	Malignant neoplasms, including neoplasms of lymphatic and hematopoietic tissues------------------------------------140-209	1,849	5.0
3	Congenital anomalies-------------------------------------740-759	745	2.0
4	Homicide---E960-E978	392	1.1
5	Influenza and pneumonia-----------------------470-474,480-486	362	1.0
6	Diseases of heart----------------------390-398,402,404,410-429	332	0.9
7	Cerebrovascular diseases----------------------------------430-438	206	0.6
8	Suicide---E950-E959	163	0.4
9	Benign neoplasms and neoplasms of unspecified nature---------210-239	112	0.3
10	Anemias---280-285	98	0.3
	5-14 years, male		
	All causes --	8,068	42.6
1	Accidents---E800-E949	4,343	22.9
2	Malignant neoplasms, including neoplasms of lymphatic and hematopoietic tissues------------------------------------140-209	1,105	5.8
3	Congenital anomalies-------------------------------------740-759	367	1.9
4	Homicide---E960-E978	240	1.3
5	Influenza and pneumonia-----------------------470-474,480-486	177	0.9
6	Diseases of heart----------------------390-398,402,404,410-429	174	0.9
7	Suicide---E950-E959	126	0.7
8	Cerebrovascular diseases----------------------------------430-438	118	0.6
9	Benign neoplasms and neoplasms of unspecified nature---------210-239	72	0.4
10	Anemias---280-285	50	0.3
	5-14 years, female		
	All causes --	4,833	26.5
1	Accidents---E800-E949	1,965	10.8
2	Malignant neoplasms, including neoplasms of lymphatic and hematopoietic tissues------------------------------------140-209	744	4.1
3	Congenital anomalies-------------------------------------740-759	378	2.1
4	Influenza and pneumonia-----------------------470-474,480-486	185	1.0
5	Diseases of heart----------------------390-398,402,404,410-429	158	0.9
6	Homicide---E960-E978	152	0.8
7	Cerebrovascular diseases----------------------------------430-438	88	0.5
8	Anemias---280-285	48	0.3
9	Meningitis--320	43	0.2
10	Benign neoplasms and neoplasms of unspecified nature---------210-239	40	0.2

Deaths and death rates for the 10 leading causes of death in specified age and sex groups: 1976—Con.

Rank	Age, sex, cause of death, and category numbers of the Eighth Revision International Classification of Diseases, Adapted, 1965	Number	Rate per 100,000 population in specified group
	15-24 years, both sexes		
	All causes---	46,081	113.5
1	Accidents---E800-E949	24,316	59.9
2	Homicide--E960-E978	5,038	12.4
3	Suicide---E950-E959	4,747	11.7
4	Malignant neoplasms, including neoplasms of lymphatic and hematopoietic tissues------------------------------------140-209	2,659	6.5
5	Diseases of heart----------------------390-398,402,404,410-429	1,072	2.6
6	Influenza and pneumonia----------------------------470-474,480-486	611	1.5
7	Congenital anomalies-----------------------------------740-759	568	1.4
8	Cerebrovascular diseases-------------------------------430-438	506	1.2
9	Diabetes mellitus---250	159	0.4
10	Anemias---280-285	138	0.3
	15-24 years, male		
	All causes---	34,253	167.7
1	Accidents---E800-E949	19,214	94.1
2	Homicide--E960-E978	3,907	19.1
3	Suicide---E950-E959	3,786	18.5
4	Malignant neoplasms, including neoplasms of lymphatic and hematopoietic tissues------------------------------------140-209	1,628	8.0
5	Diseases of heart----------------------390-398,402,404,410-429	690	3.4
6	Influenza and pneumonia----------------------------470-474,480-486	336	1.6
7	Congenital anomalies-----------------------------------740-759	329	1.6
8	Cerebrovascular diseases-------------------------------430-438	281	1.4
9	Anemias--280-285	86	0.4
10	Nephritis and nephrosis-------------------------------580-584	76	0.4
	15-24 years, female		
	All causes---	11,828	58.6
1	Accidents---E800-E949	5,102	25.3
2	Homicide--E960-E978	1,131	5.6
3	Malignant neoplasms, including neoplasms of lymphatic and hematopoietic tissues------------------------------------140-209	1,031	5.1
4	Suicide---E950-E959	961	4.8
5	Diseases of heart----------------------390-398,402,404,410-429	382	1.9
6	Influenza and pneumonia----------------------------470-474,480-486	275	1.4
7	Congenital anomalies-----------------------------------740-759	239	1.2
8	Cerebrovascular diseases-------------------------------430-438	225	1.1
9	Complications of pregnancy, childbirth, and the puerperium---630-678	137	0.7
10	Diabetes mellitus---250	85	0.4

Deaths and death rates for the 10 leading causes of death in specified age and sex groups: 1976—Con.

Rank	Age, sex, cause of death, and category numbers of the Eighth Revision International Classification of Diseases, Adapted, 1965	Number	Rate per 100,000 population in specified group
	25-44 years, both sexes		
	All causes--	101,898	185.6
1	Accidents--E800-E949	22,399	40.8
2	Malignant neoplasms, including neoplasms of lymphatic and hematopoietic tissues------------------------------------140-209	16,485	30.0
3	Diseases of heart-----------------------390-398,402,404,410-429	14,393	26.2
4	Suicide--E950-E959	8,823	16.1
5	Homicide---E960-E978	8,554	15.6
6	Cirrhosis of liver--571	5,058	9.2
7	Cerebrovascular diseases------------------------------------430-438	3,737	6.8
8	Influenza and pneumonia-----------------------------470-474,480-486	2,027	3.7
9	Diabetes mellitus--250	1,477	2.7
10	Congenital anomalies---740-759	740	1.3
	25-44 years, male		
	All causes--	67,322	249.6
1	Accidents--E800-E949	17,730	65.7
2	Diseases of heart-----------------------390-398,402,404,410-429	10,865	40.3
3	Malignant neoplasms, including neoplasms of lymphatic and hematopoietic tissues------------------------------------140-209	7,420	27.5
4	Homicide---E960-E978	6,930	25.7
5	Suicide--E950-E959	6,273	23.3
6	Cirrhosis of liver--571	3,356	12.4
7	Cerebrovascular diseases------------------------------------430-438	1,826	6.8
8	Influenza and pneumonia-----------------------------470-474,480-486	1,191	4.4
9	Diabetes mellitus--250	826	3.1
10	Congenital anomalies---740-759	400	1.5
	25-44 years, female		
	All causes--	34,576	123.8
1	Malignant neoplasms, including neoplasms of lymphatic and hematopoietic tissues------------------------------------140-209	9,065	32.5
2	Accidents--E800-E949	4,669	16.7
3	Diseases of heart-----------------------390-398,402,404,410-429	3,528	12.6
4	Suicide--E950-E959	2,550	9.1
5	Cerebrovascular diseases------------------------------------430-438	1,911	6.8
6	Cirrhosis of liver--571	1,702	6.1
7	Homicide---E960-E978	1,624	5.8
8	Influenza and pneumonia-----------------------------470-474,480-486	836	3.0
9	Diabetes mellitus--250	651	2.3
10	Congenital anomalies---740-759	340	1.2

Deaths   and death   rates   for the 10   leading causes of death   in specified   age and   sex
groups: 1976—Con.

Rank	Age, sex, cause of death, and category numbers of the Eighth Revision International Classification of Diseases, Adapted, 1965	Number	Rate per 100,000 population in specified group
	45-64 years, both sexes		
	All causes--	446,096	1,020.8
1	Diseases of heart---------------------------390-398,402,404,410-429	158,069	361.7
2	Malignant neoplasms, including neoplasms of lymphatic and hematopoietic tissues--140-209	130,993	299.8
3	Cerebrovascular diseases---------------------------------------430-438	24,630	56.4
4	Accidents--E800-E949	19,000	43.5
5	Cirrhosis of liver---571	17,821	40.8
6	Suicide--E950-E959	8,546	19.6
7	Influenza and pneumonia---------------------------470-474,480-486	8,010	18.3
8	Diabetes mellitus---250	8,006	18.3
9	Bronchitis, emphysema, and asthma-------------------------490-493	6,040	13.8
10	Homicide---E960-E978	3,837	8.8
	45-64 years, male		
	All causes---	285,019	1,362.6
1	Diseases of heart---------------------------390-398,402,404,410-429	116,062	554.9
2	Malignant neoplasms, including neoplasms of lymphatic and hematopoietic tissues--140-209	70,847	338.7
3	Accidents--E800-E949	13,595	65.0
4	Cerebrovascular diseases---------------------------------------430-438	13,196	63.1
5	Cirrhosis of liver---571	11,900	56.9
6	Suicide--E950-E959	5,816	27.8
7	Influenza and pneumonia---------------------------470-474,480-486	5,159	24.7
8	Bronchitis, emphysema, and asthma-------------------------490-493	4,089	19.5
9	Diabetes mellitus---250	3,824	18.3
10	Homicide---E960-E978	3,022	14.4
	45-64 years, female		
	All causes--	161,077	707.0
1	Malignant neoplasms, including neoplasms of lymphatic and hematopoietic tissues--140-209	60,146	264.0
2	Diseases of heart---------------------------390-398,402,404,410-429	42,007	184.4
3	Cerebrovascular diseases---------------------------------------430-438	11,434	50.2
4	Cirrhosis of liver---571	5,921	26.0
5	Accidents--E800-E949	5,405	23.7
6	Diabetes mellitus---250	4,182	18.4
7	Influenza and pneumonia---------------------------470-474,480-486	2,851	12.5
8	Suicide--E950-E959	2,730	12.0
9	Bronchitis, emphysema, and asthma-------------------------490-493	1,951	8.6
10	Nephritis and nephrosis---------------------------------------580-584	893	3.9

Deaths and death rates for the 10 leading causes of death in specified age and sex groups: 1976—Con.

Rank	Age, sex, cause of death, and category numbers of the Eighth Revision International Classification of Diseases, Adapted, 1965	Number	Rate per 100,000 population in specified group
	65 years and over, both sexes		
	All causes--	1,245,118	5,428.9
1	Diseases of heart--------------------------390-398,402,404,410-429	548,956	2,393.5
2	Malignant neoplasms, including neoplasms of lymphatic and hematopoietic tissues---------------------------------------140-209	224,543	979.0
3	Cerebrovascular diseases-------------------------------------430-438	159,304	694.6
4	Influenza and pneumonia------------------------------470-474,480-486	48,405	211.1
5	Arteriosclerosis--440	28,032	122.2
6	Diabetes mellitus---250	24,797	108.1
7	Accidents--E800-E949	23,961	104.5
8	Bronchitis, emphysema, and asthma--------------------------490-493	17,623	76.8
9	Cirrhosis of liver---571	8,378	36.5
10	Nephritis and nephrosis---------------------------------------580-584	5,732	25.0
	65 years and over, male		
	All causes--	624,778	6,672.1
1	Diseases of heart--------------------------390-398,402,404,410-429	272,205	2,906.9
2	Malignant neoplasms, including neoplasms of lymphatic and hematopoietic tissues---------------------------------------140-209	123,983	1,324.0
3	Cerebrovascular diseases-------------------------------------430-438	65,052	694.7
4	Influenza and pneumonia------------------------------470-474,480-486	24,307	259.6
5	Bronchitis, emphysema, and asthma--------------------------490-493	13,315	142.2
6	Accidents--E800-E949	12,527	133.8
7	Arteriosclerosis--440	10,963	117.1
8	Diabetes mellitus---250	9,273	99.0
9	Cirrhosis of liver---571	5,297	56.6
10	Suicide--E950-E959	3,489	37.3
	65 years and over, female		
	All causes--	620,340	4,571.1
1	Diseases of heart--------------------------390-398,402,404,410-429	276,751	2,039.3
2	Malignant neoplasms, including neoplasms of lymphatic and hematopoietic tissues---------------------------------------140-209	100,560	741.0
3	Cerebrovascular diseases-------------------------------------430-438	94,252	694.5
4	Influenza and pneumonia------------------------------470-474,480-486	24,098	177.6
5	Arteriosclerosis--440	17,069	125.8
6	Diabetes mellitus---250	15,524	114.4
7	Accidents--E800-E949	11,434	84.3
8	Bronchitis, emphysema, and asthma--------------------------490-493	4,308	31.7
9	Cirrhosis of liver---571	3,081	22.7
10	Nephritis and nephrosis---------------------------------------580-584	2,763	20.4

Marital Status

Marital Status of Persons 15 Years Old and Over, by Age, Sex, Race, Spanish Origin, and Metropolitan Residence: March 1980

[NUMBERS IN THOUSANDS.]

SUBJECT	TOTAL, 15 YEARS AND OVER	AGE (YEARS)										
		15 TO 17	18 AND 19	20 TO 24	25 TO 29	30 TO 34	35 TO 39	40 TO 44	45 TO 54	55 TO 64	65 TO 74	75 AND OVER
UNITED STATES												
ALL RACES												
BOTH SEXES	168 198	12 043	8 226	20 047	18 433	16 831	13 803	11 536	22 632	20 904	15 099	8 644
SINGLE (NEVER MARRIED)	43 236	11 825	7 273	11 869	4 887	2 108	975	657	1 251	1 069	837	487
MARRIED, SPOUSE PRESENT	97 531	151	822	7 036	11 442	12 236	10 763	9 118	17 728	15 534	9 314	3 387
MARRIED, SPOUSE ABSENT	5 269	58	100	593	792	768	613	475	841	593	314	120
SEPARATED	3 920	9	40	415	596	633	479	397	665	433	203	49
OTHER.	1 349	49	60	178	196	135	135	78	176	160	111	71
WIDOWED	12 451	-	3	25	41	114	141	196	998	2 479	4 001	4 453
DIVORCED	9 711	9	28	524	1 271	1 605	1 310	1 090	1 814	1 230	633	198
PERCENT.	100.0	100.0	100.0	100.0	100.0	100.0	100.0	100.0	100.0	100.0	100.0	100.0
SINGLE (NEVER MARRIED)	25.7	98.2	88.4	59.2	26.5	12.5	7.1	5.7	5.5	5.1	5.5	5.6
MARRIED, SPOUSE PRESENT.	58.0	1.3	10.0	35.1	62.1	72.7	78.0	79.0	78.3	74.3	61.7	39.2
MARRIED, SPOUSE ABSENT	3.1	0.5	1.2	3.0	4.3	4.6	4.4	4.1	3.7	2.8	2.1	1.4
SEPARATED	2.3	0.1	0.5	2.1	3.2	3.8	3.5	3.4	2.9	2.1	1.3	0.6
OTHER.	0.8	0.4	0.7	0.9	1.1	0.8	1.0	0.7	0.8	0.8	0.7	0.8
WIDOWED	7.4	-	-	0.1	0.2	0.7	1.0	1.7	4.4	11.9	26.5	51.5
DIVORCED	5.8	0.1	0.3	2.6	6.9	9.5	9.5	9.4	8.0	5.9	4.2	2.3
MALE	80 218	6 117	4 042	9 801	9 076	8 270	6 718	5 579	10 962	9 870	6 549	3 234
SINGLE (NEVER MARRIED)	23 512	6 078	3 808	6 721	2 940	1 298	536	368	699	565	357	142
MARRIED, WIFE PRESENT	48 765	13	207	2 730	5 366	6 008	5 395	4 548	8 979	8 130	5 200	2 190
MARRIED, WIFE ABSENT	2 093	22	25	194	284	302	237	178	368	284	146	54
SEPARATED	1 475	-	4	112	193	231	183	138	284	212	102	18
OTHER.	617	22	21	82	91	71	55	40	85	72	44	36
WIDOWED	1 972	-	-	2	8	11	19	26	176	397	557	776
DIVORCED	3 875	4	2	154	479	651	530	459	740	495	290	71
PERCENT.	100.0	100.0	100.0	100.0	100.0	100.0	100.0	100.0	100.0	100.0	100.0	100.0
SINGLE (NEVER MARRIED)	29.3	99.4	94.2	68.6	32.4	15.7	8.0	6.6	6.4	5.7	5.4	4.4
MARRIED, WIFE PRESENT.	60.8	0.2	5.1	27.9	59.1	72.6	80.3	81.5	81.9	82.4	79.4	67.7
MARRIED, WIFE ABSENT	2.6	0.4	0.6	2.0	3.1	3.6	3.5	3.2	3.4	2.9	2.2	1.7
SEPARATED	1.8	-	0.1	1.1	2.1	2.8	2.7	2.5	2.6	2.1	1.6	0.5
OTHER.	0.8	0.4	0.5	0.8	1.0	0.9	0.8	0.7	0.8	0.7	0.7	1.1
WIDOWED	2.5	-	-	-	0.1	0.1	0.3	0.5	1.6	4.0	8.5	24.0
DIVORCED	4.8	0.1	0.1	1.6	5.3	7.9	7.9	8.2	6.7	5.0	4.4	2.2
FEMALE	87 980	5 926	4 184	10 246	9 357	8 561	7 085	5 957	11 670	11 034	8 549	5 411
SINGLE (NEVER MARRIED)	19 724	5 747	3 465	5 148	1 947	810	439	289	552	504	480	344
MARRIED, HUSBAND PRESENT	48 765	138	614	4 306	6 075	6 228	5 369	4 570	8 749	7 404	4 114	1 197
MARRIED, HUSBAND ABSENT	3 176	36	75	399	509	467	376	297	473	309	168	67
SEPARATED	2 444	9	36	303	404	402	296	259	381	221	101	31
HUSBAND IN ARMED FORCES.	89	5	5	18	20	18	17	1	3	2	-	-
OTHER.	642	22	34	78	85	47	63	38	88	86	67	35
WIDOWED	10 479	-	3	23	33	102	122	170	821	2 082	3 444	3 677
DIVORCED	5 836	5	26	370	792	954	780	631	1 074	735	342	126
PERCENT.	100.0	100.0	100.0	100.0	100.0	100.0	100.0	100.0	100.0	100.0	100.0	100.0
SINGLE (NEVER MARRIED)	22.4	97.0	82.8	50.2	20.8	9.5	6.2	4.8	4.7	4.6	5.6	6.4
MARRIED, HUSBAND PRESENT	55.4	2.3	14.7	42.0	64.9	72.7	75.8	76.7	75.0	67.1	48.1	22.1
MARRIED, HUSBAND ABSENT	3.6	0.6	1.8	3.9	5.4	5.4	5.3	5.0	4.1	2.8	2.0	1.2
SEPARATED	2.8	0.2	0.9	3.0	4.3	4.7	4.2	4.3	3.3	2.0	1.2	0.6
HUSBAND IN ARMED FORCES.	0.1	0.1	0.1	0.2	0.2	0.2	0.2	-	-	-	-	-
OTHER.	0.7	0.4	0.8	0.8	0.9	0.5	0.9	0.6	0.8	0.8	0.8	0.6
WIDOWED	11.9	-	0.1	0.2	0.4	1.2	1.7	2.8	7.0	18.9	40.3	68.0
DIVORCED	6.6	0.1	0.6	3.6	8.5	11.1	11.0	10.6	9.2	6.7	4.0	2.3
WHITE												
BOTH SEXES	147 112	10 075	6 990	17 148	15 914	14 644	12 084	10 076	19 919	18 817	13 573	7 873
SINGLE (NEVER MARRIED)	35 764	9 878	6 114	9 768	3 930	1 660	728	530	1 012	936	759	449
MARRIED, SPOUSE PRESENT.	88 962	144	759	6 407	10 303	11 025	9 772	8 254	16 175	14 405	8 573	3 145
MARRIED, SPOUSE ABSENT	3 499	50	86	480	524	517	392	280	500	382	210	79
SEPARATED	2 422	6	34	314	377	405	292	225	367	260	120	22
OTHER.	1 077	43	52	165	147	112	100	55	133	122	91	57
WIDOWED	10 689	-	3	20	31	82	96	131	741	2 067	3 480	4 037
DIVORCED	8 199	4	27	474	1 126	1 358	1 095	881	1 490	1 027	551	164
PERCENT.	100.0	100.0	100.0	100.0	100.0	100.0	100.0	100.0	100.0	100.0	100.0	100.0
SINGLE (NEVER MARRIED)	24.3	98.0	87.5	57.0	24.7	11.3	6.0	5.3	5.1	5.0	5.6	5.7
MARRIED, SPOUSE PRESENT.	60.5	1.4	10.9	37.4	64.7	75.3	80.9	81.9	81.2	76.6	63.2	39.9
MARRIED, SPOUSE ABSENT	2.4	0.5	1.2	2.8	3.3	3.5	3.2	2.8	2.5	2.0	1.5	1.0
SEPARATED	1.6	0.1	0.5	1.8	2.4	2.8	2.4	2.2	1.8	1.4	0.9	0.3
OTHER.	0.7	0.4	0.7	1.0	0.9	0.8	0.8	0.5	0.7	0.6	0.7	0.7
WIDOWED	7.3	-	-	0.1	0.2	0.6	0.8	1.3	3.7	11.0	25.6	51.3
DIVORCED	5.6	-	0.4	2.8	7.1	9.3	9.1	8.7	7.5	5.5	4.1	2.1

From "Marital Status and Living Arrangements: March 1980," *Population Characteristics*, Series P–20, No. 365, U.S. Department of Commerce, Bureau of the Census, October, 1981.

Marital Status of Persons 15 Years Old and Over, by Age, Sex, Race, Spanish Origin, and Metropolitan Residence: March 1980—Continued

[NUMBERS IN THOUSANDS. FOR MEANING OF SYMBOLS, SEE TEXT]

SUBJECT	TOTAL, 15 YEARS AND OVER	15 TO 17	18 AND 19	20 TO 24	25 TO 29	30 TO 34	35 TO 39	40 TO 44	45 TO 54	55 TO 64	65 TO 74	75 AND OVER
UNITED STATES--CONTINUED												
WHITE--CONTINUED												
MALE	70 632	5 130	3 462	8 484	7 944	7 287	5 957	4 934	9 715	8 917	5 874	2 929
SINGLE (NEVER MARRIED)	19 752	5 097	3 240	5 675	2 470	1 060	405	309	561	496	312	126
MARRIED, WIFE PRESENT.	44 490	13	198	2 507	4 819	5 418	4 911	4 123	8 194	7 519	4 761	2 026
MARRIED, WIFE ABSENT	1 458	20	22	160	212	232	169	127	226	172	87	32
SEPARATED.	974	-	4	84	142	171	128	96	159	125	57	8
OTHER.	485	20	18	76	69	61	41	32	67	47	30	24
WIDOWED.	1 629	-	-	2	8	5	15	14	117	317	462	690
DIVORCED	3 303	-	2	140	435	571	457	361	616	413	252	56
PERCENT.	100.0	100.0	100.0	100.0	100.0	100.0	100.0	100.0	100.0	100.0	100.0	100.0
SINGLE (NEVER MARRIED)	28.0	99.4	93.6	66.9	31.1	14.6	6.8	6.3	5.8	5.6	5.3	4.3
MARRIED, WIFE PRESENT.	63.0	0.3	5.7	29.5	60.7	74.4	82.4	83.6	84.3	84.3	81.1	69.2
MARRIED, WIFE ABSENT	2.1	0.4	0.6	1.9	2.7	3.2	2.8	2.6	2.3	1.9	1.5	1.1
SEPARATED.	1.4	-	0.1	1.0	1.8	2.3	2.1	1.9	1.6	1.4	1.0	0.3
OTHER.	0.7	0.4	0.5	0.9	0.9	0.8	0.7	0.6	0.7	0.5	0.5	0.8
WIDOWED.	2.3	-	-	-	0.1	0.1	0.2	0.3	1.2	3.6	7.9	23.5
DIVORCED	4.7	-	-	1.7	5.5	7.8	7.7	7.3	6.3	4.6	4.3	1.9
FEMALE	76 480	4 945	3 528	8 664	7 970	7 357	6 127	5 142	10 204	9 900	7 699	4 944
SINGLE (NEVER MARRIED)	16 012	4 781	2 875	4 093	1 460	600	323	221	451	440	447	323
MARRIED, HUSBAND PRESENT.	44 472	131	561	3 900	5 484	5 607	4 861	4 131	7 981	6 886	3 812	1 119
MARRIED, HUSBAND ABSENT.	2 040	30	64	320	312	286	223	153	274	210	123	47
SEPARATED.	1 448	6	30	231	234	234	164	129	207	135	63	14
HUSBAND IN ARMED FORCES.	70	3	2	16	15	16	12	1	3	2	-	-
OTHER.	522	20	32	73	63	35	47	23	63	74	60	32
WIDOWED.	9 060	-	3	18	24	77	81	117	624	1 750	3 018	3 347
DIVORCED	4 896	4	25	334	691	787	639	521	874	614	299	108
PERCENT.	100.0	100.0	100.0	100.0	100.0	100.0	100.0	100.0	100.0	100.0	100.0	100.0
SINGLE (NEVER MARRIED)	20.9	96.7	81.5	47.2	18.3	8.2	5.3	4.3	4.4	4.4	5.8	6.5
MARRIED, HUSBAND PRESENT.	58.1	2.6	15.9	45.0	68.8	76.2	79.3	80.3	78.2	69.6	49.5	22.6
MARRIED, HUSBAND ABSENT.	2.7	0.6	1.8	3.7	3.9	3.9	3.6	3.0	2.7	2.1	1.6	0.9
SEPARATED.	1.9	0.1	0.9	2.7	2.9	3.2	2.7	2.5	2.0	1.4	0.8	0.3
HUSBAND IN ARMED FORCES.	0.1	0.1	-	0.2	0.2	0.2	0.2	-	-	-	-	-
OTHER.	0.7	0.4	0.9	0.8	0.8	0.5	0.8	0.4	0.6	0.7	0.8	0.7
WIDOWED.	11.8	-	0.1	0.2	0.3	1.1	1.3	2.3	6.1	17.7	39.2	67.7
DIVORCED	6.4	0.1	0.7	3.9	8.7	10.7	10.4	10.1	8.6	6.2	3.9	2.2
BLACK												
BOTH SEXES	17 896	1 733	1 077	2 473	2 079	1 753	1 444	1 229	2 268	1 821	1 361	658
SINGLE (NEVER MARRIED)	6 530	1 713	1 013	1 813	825	392	218	116	222	115	68	34
MARRIED, SPOUSE PRESENT.	6 753	7	50	511	877	865	774	676	1 220	932	651	190
MARRIED, SPOUSE ABSENT.	1 644	8	13	105	238	234	212	182	318	200	99	35
SEPARATED.	1 445	3	6	95	205	218	186	167	286	170	82	27
OTHER.	200	5	7	10	33	16	26	15	32	30	17	8
WIDOWED.	1 596	-	-	5	10	30	38	60	233	381	471	369
DIVORCED	1 373	5	-	38	130	231	202	195	275	192	72	31
PERCENT.	100.0	100.0	100.0	100.0	100.0	100.0	100.0	100.0	100.0	100.0	100.0	100.0
SINGLE (NEVER MARRIED)	36.5	98.9	94.1	73.3	39.7	22.4	15.1	9.5	9.8	6.3	5.0	5.2
MARRIED, SPOUSE PRESENT.	37.7	0.4	4.6	20.7	42.2	49.4	53.6	55.0	53.8	51.2	47.8	28.8
MARRIED, SPOUSE ABSENT.	9.2	0.5	1.2	4.2	11.5	13.4	14.7	14.8	14.0	11.0	7.3	5.3
SEPARATED.	8.1	0.2	0.6	3.9	9.9	12.4	12.9	13.6	12.6	9.3	6.0	4.1
OTHER.	1.1	0.3	0.7	0.4	1.6	0.9	1.8	1.2	1.4	1.6	1.3	1.2
WIDOWED.	8.9	-	-	0.2	0.5	1.7	2.6	4.9	10.3	20.9	34.6	56.1
DIVORCED	7.7	0.3	-	1.6	6.3	13.2	14.0	15.9	12.1	10.6	5.3	4.7
MALE	8 067	868	502	1 112	930	769	639	541	1 037	824	595	252
SINGLE (NEVER MARRIED)	3 244	862	491	878	397	205	119	55	128	58	36	13
MARRIED, WIFE PRESENT.	3 416	-	9	191	434	422	380	336	623	504	382	134
MARRIED, WIFE ABSENT	577	2	2	32	61	61	64	46	132	108	55	15
SEPARATED.	482	-	-	27	48	55	54	42	118	85	43	10
OTHER.	95	2	2	5	13	6	10	4	14	23	12	5
WIDOWED.	316	-	-	-	-	6	4	12	55	73	89	77
DIVORCED	515	4	-	10	38	75	72	92	99	80	33	13
PERCENT.	100.0	100.0	100.0	100.0	100.0	100.0	100.0	100.0	100.0	100.0	100.0	100.0
SINGLE (NEVER MARRIED)	40.2	99.4	97.7	79.0	42.7	26.7	18.7	10.1	12.3	7.0	6.1	5.3
MARRIED, WIFE PRESENT.	42.3	-	1.7	17.2	46.7	54.8	59.5	62.2	60.1	61.2	64.2	53.1
MARRIED, WIFE ABSENT	7.2	0.2	0.5	2.9	6.6	7.9	10.0	8.5	12.7	13.2	9.2	5.8
SEPARATED.	6.0	-	-	2.4	5.1	7.2	8.5	7.7	11.4	10.3	7.3	3.8
OTHER.	1.2	0.2	0.5	0.4	1.4	0.7	1.5	0.7	1.3	2.8	2.0	2.0
WIDOWED.	3.9	-	-	-	-	0.8	0.6	2.3	5.3	8.9	14.9	30.4
DIVORCED	6.4	0.4	0.1	0.9	4.0	9.7	11.2	16.9	9.5	9.7	5.5	5.4

Marital Status of Persons 15 Years Old and Over, by Age, Sex, Race, Spanish Origin, and Metropolitan Residence: March 1980—Continued

[NUMBERS IN THOUSANDS. FOR MEANING OF SYMBOLS, SEE TEXT]

SUBJECT	TOTAL, 15 YEARS AND OVER	15 TO 17	18 AND 19	20 TO 24	25 TO 29	30 TO 34	35 TO 39	40 TO 44	45 TO 54	55 TO 64	65 TO 74	75 AND OVER
UNITED STATES--CONTINUED												
BLACK--CONTINUED												
FEMALE	9 828	865	574	1 361	1 150	984	805	688	1 231	997	766	407
SINGLE (NEVER MARRIED)	3 286	851	522	935	428	187	98	61	94	57	32	21
MARRIED, HUSBAND PRESENT	3 337	7	41	320	443	443	394	340	597	428	269	56
MARRIED, HUSBAND ABSENT	1 067	6	11	73	177	174	148	136	187	91	44	20
SEPARATED	963	3	6	68	158	163	132	125	168	85	38	17
HUSBAND IN ARMED FORCES	16	1	4	2	4	1	4	-	-	-	-	-
OTHER	88	2	1	3	16	10	13	11	18	6	5	3
WIDOWED	1 280	-	-	5	10	24	34	47	178	308	382	292
DIVORCED	858	2	-	28	92	156	130	104	176	112	40	17
PERCENT	100.0	100.0	100.0	100.0	100.0	100.0	100.0	100.0	100.0	100.0	100.0	100.0
SINGLE (NEVER MARRIED)	33.4	98.3	90.9	68.7	37.2	19.0	12.2	8.9	7.6	5.7	4.2	5.1
MARRIED, HUSBAND PRESENT	34.0	0.8	7.2	23.5	38.5	45.1	49.0	49.4	48.5	42.9	35.1	13.8
MARRIED, HUSBAND ABSENT	10.9	0.7	1.9	5.4	15.4	17.7	18.4	19.7	15.2	9.2	5.7	4.9
SEPARATED	9.8	0.3	1.0	5.0	13.7	16.6	16.4	18.1	13.7	8.5	5.0	4.3
HUSBAND IN ARMED FORCES	0.2	0.2	0.6	0.2	0.3	0.1	0.5	-	-	-	-	-
OTHER	0.9	0.2	0.2	0.2	1.4	1.0	1.6	1.6	1.5	0.6	0.7	0.6
WIDOWED	13.0	-	-	0.4	0.8	2.4	4.2	6.9	14.5	30.9	49.9	71.9
DIVORCED	8.7	0.2	-	2.1	8.0	15.9	16.2	15.1	14.3	11.3	5.2	4.3
SPANISH ORIGIN[1]												
BOTH SEXES	8 562	780	583	1 303	1 185	1 001	750	721	1 046	631	383	180
SINGLE (NEVER MARRIED)	2 574	754	501	667	293	113	47	49	71	39	30	11
MARRIED, SPOUSE PRESENT	4 720	22	68	535	758	728	578	553	762	436	208	71
MARRIED, SPOUSE ABSENT	485	4	13	74	77	75	58	41	78	43	16	6
SEPARATED	322	1	7	48	50	47	44	28	53	30	12	2
OTHER	162	3	6	26	27	28	14	13	25	13	4	4
WIDOWED	337	-	-	6	4	9	8	11	53	62	95	89
DIVORCED	446	1	1	21	54	77	59	67	82	49	33	3
PERCENT	100.0	100.0	100.0	100.0	100.0	100.0	100.0	100.0	100.0	100.0	100.0	100.0
SINGLE (NEVER MARRIED)	30.1	96.6	85.9	51.2	24.7	11.2	6.2	6.8	6.8	6.2	7.9	5.9
MARRIED, SPOUSE PRESENT	55.1	2.8	11.7	41.1	63.9	72.7	77.1	76.7	72.9	69.2	54.4	39.8
MARRIED, SPOUSE ABSENT	5.7	0.5	2.3	5.7	6.5	7.4	7.7	5.6	7.5	6.8	4.1	3.5
SEPARATED	3.8	0.2	1.3	3.7	4.2	4.6	5.9	3.8	5.0	4.7	3.2	1.3
OTHER	1.9	0.4	1.0	2.0	2.3	2.8	1.9	1.8	2.4	2.1	1.0	2.2
WIDOWED	3.9	-	-	0.5	0.3	0.9	1.1	1.6	5.1	9.9	24.9	49.3
DIVORCED	5.2	0.1	0.1	1.6	4.6	7.7	7.8	9.3	7.8	7.8	8.7	1.6
MALE	4 224	396	299	636	599	503	369	346	517	299	176	83
SINGLE (NEVER MARRIED)	1 377	390	276	381	161	56	21	20	34	13	20	5
MARRIED, WIFE PRESENT	2 459	4	23	224	392	384	302	293	420	244	122	51
MARRIED, WIFE ABSENT	184	2	1	27	25	35	22	14	34	16	6	3
SEPARATED	89	-	-	14	11	12	14	5	15	11	6	1
OTHER	96	2	1	13	13	22	8	9	19	5	1	3
WIDOWED	58	-	-	-	2	2	1	4	7	10	11	23
DIVORCED	146	-	-	4	20	26	24	16	22	15	17	1
PERCENT	100.0	100.0	100.0	100.0	100.0	100.0	100.0	100.0	100.0	100.0	100.0	100.0
SINGLE (NEVER MARRIED)	32.6	98.5	92.2	59.9	26.9	11.2	5.7	5.7	6.5	4.4	11.4	6.2
MARRIED, WIFE PRESENT	58.2	0.9	7.6	35.2	65.4	76.4	81.7	84.5	81.3	81.8	69.5	60.9
MARRIED, WIFE ABSENT	4.4	0.5	0.2	4.2	4.1	6.9	6.0	4.1	6.6	5.3	3.6	4.0
SEPARATED	2.1	-	-	2.2	1.8	2.4	3.9	1.4	3.0	3.5	3.1	1.0
OTHER	2.3	0.5	0.2	2.0	2.3	4.4	2.2	2.7	3.6	1.8	0.5	3.0
WIDOWED	1.4	-	-	-	0.3	0.3	0.2	1.1	1.3	3.4	6.0	27.3
DIVORCED	3.5	0.1	-	0.7	3.3	5.2	6.4	4.6	4.3	5.1	9.5	1.6
FEMALE	4 338	384	284	667	586	498	380	375	529	332	207	96
SINGLE (NEVER MARRIED)	1 197	364	225	286	132	56	26	30	38	26	10	5
MARRIED, HUSBAND PRESENT	2 262	18	46	311	366	344	276	260	342	192	86	21
MARRIED, HUSBAND ABSENT	300	2	13	47	52	40	36	26	44	27	9	3
SEPARATED	234	1	7	34	39	34	30	23	37	19	7	2
HUSBAND IN ARMED FORCES	6	-	1	3	1	1	2	-	-	-	-	-
OTHER	60	1	5	11	12	5	5	4	7	8	3	1
WIDOWED	279	-	-	6	2	7	7	8	46	52	85	66
DIVORCED	300	-	1	17	34	51	35	51	59	34	16	1
PERCENT	100.0	100.0	100.0	100.0	100.0	100.0	100.0	100.0	100.0	100.0	100.0	100.0
SINGLE (NEVER MARRIED)	27.6	94.6	79.2	42.9	22.5	11.3	6.7	7.9	7.1	7.9	5.0	5.6
MARRIED, HUSBAND PRESENT	52.1	4.7	16.0	46.6	62.4	69.1	72.6	69.4	64.6	57.9	41.5	21.5
MARRIED, HUSBAND ABSENT	6.9	0.6	4.5	7.1	8.9	8.0	9.4	7.1	8.3	8.2	4.5	3.0
SEPARATED	5.4	0.3	2.6	5.1	6.7	6.9	7.8	6.1	7.1	5.8	3.2	1.6
HUSBAND IN ARMED FORCES	0.1	-	0.2	0.4	0.2	0.1	0.4	-	-	-	-	-
OTHER	1.4	0.3	1.6	1.6	2.1	1.0	1.2	0.9	1.3	2.4	1.4	1.4
WIDOWED	6.4	-	-	0.9	0.3	1.4	2.0	2.1	8.7	15.8	40.9	68.3
DIVORCED	6.9	0.1	0.3	2.5	5.8	10.3	9.3	13.6	11.2	10.3	8.0	1.5

[1] PERSONS OF SPANISH ORIGIN MAY BE OF ANY RACE.

Marital Status of Persons 15 Years Old and Over, by Age, Sex, Race, Spanish Origin, and Metropolitan Residence: March 1980—Continued

[NUMBERS IN THOUSANDS. FOR MEANING OF SYMBOLS, SEE TEXT]

SUBJECT	TOTAL, 15 YEARS AND OVER	AGE (YEARS)										
		15 TO 17	18 AND 19	20 TO 24	25 TO 29	30 TO 34	35 TO 39	40 TO 44	45 TO 54	55 TO 64	65 TO 74	75 AND OVER
METROPOLITAN												
ALL RACES												
BOTH SEXES	114 645	7 986	5 594	14 194	13 193	11 842	9 448	7 759	15 555	13 989	9 572	5 512
SINGLE (NEVER MARRIED)	31 453	7 868	5 064	8 997	3 898	1 697	785	493	934	790	576	352
MARRIED, SPOUSE PRESENT	63 831	76	449	4 416	7 764	8 240	7 087	5 954	11 899	10 179	5 708	2 061
MARRIED, SPOUSE ABSENT	3 987	34	67	441	610	597	490	365	649	453	213	66
SEPARATED.	3 023	6	29	310	466	493	392	307	522	324	149	25
OTHER.	964	28	38	131	145	104	99	58	127	129	64	41
WIDOWED.	8 221	-	-	14	35	77	96	124	676	1 666	2 647	2 887
DIVORCED	7 153	8	15	326	886	1 232	989	823	1 398	901	427	146
PERCENT.	100.0	100.0	100.0	100.0	100.0	100.0	100.0	100.0	100.0	100.0	100.0	100.0
SINGLE (NEVER MARRIED)	27.4	98.5	90.5	63.4	29.5	14.3	8.3	6.4	6.0	5.6	6.0	6.4
MARRIED, SPOUSE PRESENT	55.7	0.9	8.0	31.1	58.8	69.6	75.0	76.7	76.5	72.8	59.6	37.4
MARRIED, SPOUSE ABSENT	3.5	0.4	1.2	3.1	4.6	5.0	5.2	4.7	4.2	3.2	2.2	1.2
SEPARATED.	2.6	0.1	0.5	2.2	3.5	4.2	4.1	4.0	3.4	2.3	1.6	0.5
OTHER.	0.8	0.3	0.7	0.9	1.1	0.9	1.0	0.7	0.8	0.9	0.7	0.7
WIDOWED.	7.2	-	-	0.1	0.3	0.6	1.0	1.6	4.3	11.9	27.7	52.4
DIVORCED	6.2	0.1	0.3	2.3	6.7	10.4	10.5	10.6	9.0	6.4	4.5	2.7
MALE	54 527	4 058	2 765	6 875	6 443	5 890	4 547	3 724	7 538	6 585	4 067	2 036
SINGLE (NEVER MARRIED)	16 912	4 035	2 630	4 975	2 319	1 041	415	276	493	390	230	107
MARRIED, WIFE PRESENT.	31 916	8	114	1 673	3 591	4 114	3 525	2 952	6 082	5 341	3 189	1 326
MARRIED, WIFE ABSENT	1 567	12	19	136	213	239	186	140	268	222	100	33
SEPARATED.	1 119	-	4	76	151	183	148	106	211	160	72	8
OTHER.	448	12	15	59	61	56	39	35	57	62	28	25
WIDOWED.	1 359	-	-	1	6	8	13	22	129	281	380	520
DIVORCED	2 773	4	2	90	314	488	407	335	566	351	168	50
PERCENT.	100.0	100.0	100.0	100.0	100.0	100.0	100.0	100.0	100.0	100.0	100.0	100.0
SINGLE (NEVER MARRIED)	31.0	99.4	95.1	72.4	36.0	17.7	9.1	7.4	6.5	5.9	5.7	5.3
MARRIED, WIFE PRESENT.	58.5	0.2	4.1	24.3	55.7	69.9	77.5	79.3	80.7	81.1	78.4	65.2
MARRIED, WIFE ABSENT	2.9	0.3	0.7	2.0	3.3	4.1	4.1	3.8	3.6	3.4	2.5	1.6
SEPARATED.	2.1	-	0.1	1.1	2.4	3.1	3.2	2.8	2.8	2.4	1.8	0.4
OTHER.	0.8	0.3	0.5	0.9	0.9	0.9	0.9	0.9	0.8	0.9	0.7	1.2
WIDOWED.	2.5	-	-	-	0.1	0.1	0.3	0.6	1.7	4.3	9.4	25.5
DIVORCED	5.1	0.1	0.1	1.3	4.9	8.3	8.9	9.0	7.5	5.3	4.1	2.4
FEMALE	60 118	3 928	2 829	7 319	6 751	5 953	4 901	4 034	8 017	7 404	5 505	3 477
SINGLE (NEVER MARRIED)	14 541	3 833	2 434	4 022	1 579	656	370	217	440	399	346	245
MARRIED, HUSBAND PRESENT	31 916	67	334	2 743	4 174	4 126	3 562	3 002	5 817	4 838	2 519	734
MARRIED, HUSBAND ABSENT.	2 420	22	48	306	398	358	304	225	381	230	114	34
SEPARATED.	1 904	6	25	234	314	309	244	202	312	163	77	18
HUSBAND IN ARMED FORCES.	68	3	3	15	16	10	16	-	3	2	-	-
OTHER.	447	13	20	57	67	39	44	23	67	65	36	16
WIDOWED.	6 862	-	-	13	29	69	83	102	547	1 385	2 267	2 367
DIVORCED	4 379	5	13	236	572	744	582	488	832	551	259	97
PERCENT.	100.0	100.0	100.0	100.0	100.0	100.0	100.0	100.0	100.0	100.0	100.0	100.0
SINGLE (NEVER MARRIED)	24.2	97.6	86.0	54.9	23.4	11.0	7.5	5.4	5.5	5.4	6.3	7.0
MARRIED, HUSBAND PRESENT	53.1	1.7	11.8	37.5	61.8	69.3	72.7	74.4	72.6	65.3	45.8	21.1
MARRIED, HUSBAND ABSENT.	4.0	0.6	1.7	4.2	5.9	6.0	6.2	5.6	4.8	3.1	2.1	1.0
SEPARATED.	3.2	0.2	0.9	3.2	4.7	5.2	5.0	5.0	3.9	2.2	1.4	0.5
HUSBAND IN ARMED FORCES.	0.1	0.1	0.1	0.2	0.2	0.2	0.3	-	-	-	-	-
OTHER.	0.7	0.3	0.7	0.8	1.0	0.7	0.9	0.6	0.8	0.9	0.7	0.5
WIDOWED.	11.4	-	-	0.2	0.4	1.2	1.7	2.5	6.8	18.7	41.2	68.1
DIVORCED	7.3	0.1	0.5	3.2	8.5	12.5	11.9	12.1	10.4	7.4	4.7	2.8
WHITE												
BOTH SEXES	98 173	6 479	4 611	11 914	11 142	10 093	8 044	6 620	13 410	12 365	8 492	5 003
SINGLE (NEVER MARRIED)	25 511	6 372	4 138	7 308	3 098	1 330	596	402	741	686	517	323
MARRIED, SPOUSE PRESENT	57 295	72	401	3 947	6 871	7 293	6 275	5 301	10 704	9 303	5 217	1 909
MARRIED, SPOUSE ABSENT	2 576	31	59	358	385	399	311	205	372	273	139	45
SEPARATED.	1 819	4	24	234	284	314	238	166	282	178	85	11
OTHER.	756	28	35	124	101	85	74	40	89	94	53	34
WIDOWED.	6 950	-	-	13	27	55	62	78	478	1 375	2 257	2 607
DIVORCED	5 842	3	14	288	762	1 015	801	633	1 116	729	363	118
PERCENT.	100.0	100.0	100.0	100.0	100.0	100.0	100.0	100.0	100.0	100.0	100.0	100.0
SINGLE (NEVER MARRIED)	26.0	98.4	89.7	61.3	27.8	13.2	7.4	6.1	5.5	5.5	6.1	6.5
MARRIED, SPOUSE PRESENT	58.4	1.1	8.7	33.1	61.7	72.3	78.0	80.1	79.8	75.2	61.4	38.2
MARRIED, SPOUSE ABSENT	2.6	0.5	1.3	3.0	3.5	4.0	3.9	3.1	2.8	2.2	1.6	0.9
SEPARATED.	1.9	0.1	0.5	2.0	2.5	3.1	3.0	2.5	2.1	1.4	1.0	0.2
OTHER.	0.8	0.4	0.7	1.0	0.9	0.8	0.9	0.6	0.7	0.8	0.6	0.7
WIDOWED.	7.1	-	-	0.1	0.2	0.5	0.8	1.2	3.6	11.1	26.6	52.1
DIVORCED	6.0	-	0.3	2.4	6.8	10.1	10.0	9.6	8.3	5.9	4.3	2.4

Marital Status of Persons 15 Years Old and Over, by Age, Sex, Race, Spanish Origin, and Metropolitan Residence: March 1980—Continued

[NUMBERS IN THOUSANDS. FOR MEANING OF SYMBOLS, SEE TEXT]

SUBJECT	TOTAL, 15 YEARS AND OVER	15 TO 17	18 AND 19	20 TO 24	25 TO 29	30 TO 34	35 TO 39	40 TO 44	45 TO 54	55 TO 64	65 TO 74	75 AND OVER
METROPOLITAN--CONTINUED												
WHITE--CONTINUED												
MALE	47 067	3 291	2 310	5 869	5 534	5 084	3 937	3 223	6 548	5 852	3 587	1 832
SINGLE (NEVER MARRIED)	13 959	3 270	2 186	4 158	1 925	847	326	233	382	341	195	97
MARRIED, WIFE PRESENT	28 651	8	106	1 514	3 172	3 639	3 128	2 632	5 465	4 874	2 887	1 225
MARRIED, WIFE ABSENT	1 083	12	17	112	149	182	136	101	163	128	61	22
SEPARATED	734	-	4	56	108	136	104	73	119	91	40	3
OTHER	349	12	14	57	42	46	32	28	43	37	20	20
WIDOWED	1 094	-	-	1	6	3	9	11	81	222	307	454
DIVORCED	2 279	-	2	83	282	413	338	244	458	286	138	34
PERCENT	100.0	100.0	100.0	100.0	100.0	100.0	100.0	100.0	100.0	100.0	100.0	100.0
SINGLE (NEVER MARRIED)	29.7	99.4	94.6	70.8	34.8	16.7	8.3	7.2	5.8	5.8	5.4	5.3
MARRIED, WIFE PRESENT	60.9	0.3	4.6	25.8	57.3	71.6	79.5	81.7	83.5	83.3	80.5	66.8
MARRIED, WIFE ABSENT	2.3	0.4	0.8	1.9	2.7	3.6	3.5	3.1	2.5	2.2	1.7	1.2
SEPARATED	1.6	-	0.2	0.9	1.9	2.7	2.6	2.3	1.8	1.6	1.1	0.1
OTHER	0.7	0.4	0.6	1.0	0.8	0.9	0.8	0.9	0.7	0.6	0.6	1.1
WIDOWED	2.3	-	-	-	0.1	0.1	0.2	0.4	1.2	3.8	8.5	24.8
DIVORCED	4.8	-	0.1	1.4	5.1	8.1	8.6	7.6	7.0	4.9	3.9	1.9
FEMALE	51 106	3 188	2 301	6 045	5 608	5 008	4 107	3 397	6 862	6 514	4 905	3 171
SINGLE (NEVER MARRIED)	11 551	3 102	1 952	3 150	1 173	483	270	169	360	344	322	226
MARRIED, HUSBAND PRESENT	28 643	64	295	2 433	3 699	3 654	3 147	2 669	5 238	4 429	2 330	685
MARRIED, HUSBAND ABSENT	1 492	20	41	246	235	217	175	104	209	145	78	23
SEPARATED	1 085	4	20	179	176	177	133	93	163	87	45	8
HUSBAND IN ARMED FORCES	55	3	1	15	12	9	11	-	3	2	-	-
OTHER	352	13	20	53	47	31	31	12	43	56	33	15
WIDOWED	5 856	-	-	11	21	52	52	67	397	1 152	1 950	2 153
DIVORCED	3 563	3	12	205	480	603	463	389	658	443	224	84
PERCENT	100.0	100.0	100.0	100.0	100.0	100.0	100.0	100.0	100.0	100.0	100.0	100.0
SINGLE (NEVER MARRIED)	22.6	97.3	84.9	52.1	20.9	9.6	6.6	5.0	5.2	5.3	6.6	7.1
MARRIED, HUSBAND PRESENT	56.0	2.0	12.8	40.2	66.0	73.0	76.6	78.6	76.3	68.0	47.5	21.6
MARRIED, HUSBAND ABSENT	2.9	0.6	1.8	4.1	4.2	4.3	4.3	3.1	3.0	2.2	1.6	0.7
SEPARATED	2.1	0.1	0.9	3.0	3.1	3.5	3.2	2.7	2.4	1.3	0.9	0.3
HUSBAND IN ARMED FORCES	0.1	0.1	-	0.2	0.2	0.2	0.3	-	-	-	-	-
OTHER	0.7	0.4	0.9	0.9	0.8	0.6	0.8	0.3	0.6	0.9	0.7	0.5
WIDOWED	11.5	-	-	0.2	0.4	1.0	1.3	2.0	5.8	17.7	39.8	67.9
DIVORCED	7.0	0.1	0.5	3.4	8.6	12.0	11.3	11.4	9.6	6.8	4.6	2.7
BLACK												
BOTH SEXES	13 949	1 333	859	1 937	1 694	1 406	1 189	952	1 792	1 410	951	426
SINGLE (NEVER MARRIED)	5 177	1 322	814	1 445	683	322	166	81	179	91	50	26
MARRIED, SPOUSE PRESENT	5 106	3	38	381	690	675	643	500	929	714	423	110
MARRIED, SPOUSE ABSENT	1 320	3	8	80	200	183	174	151	257	171	71	21
SEPARATED	1 168	3	5	75	170	170	154	139	230	144	64	15
OTHER	152	-	3	5	30	13	20	12	27	27	7	6
WIDOWED	1 145	-	-	1	8	21	28	41	182	269	350	244
DIVORCED	1 201	5	-	30	114	205	178	178	245	165	57	26
PERCENT	100.0	100.0	100.0	100.0	100.0	100.0	100.0	100.0	100.0	100.0	100.0	100.0
SINGLE (NEVER MARRIED)	37.1	99.1	94.7	74.6	40.3	22.9	13.9	8.5	10.0	6.5	5.2	6.0
MARRIED, SPOUSE PRESENT	36.6	0.3	4.4	19.7	40.7	48.0	54.1	52.6	51.8	50.6	44.5	25.7
MARRIED, SPOUSE ABSENT	9.5	0.2	0.9	4.1	11.8	13.0	14.6	15.9	14.4	12.2	7.5	4.9
SEPARATED	8.4	0.2	0.5	3.9	10.0	12.1	12.9	14.6	12.8	10.2	6.7	3.4
OTHER	1.1	-	0.3	0.2	1.8	1.0	1.7	1.3	1.5	1.9	0.8	1.5
WIDOWED	8.2	-	-	0.1	0.5	1.5	2.4	4.3	10.2	19.1	36.8	57.4
DIVORCED	8.6	0.4	-	1.5	6.7	14.5	14.9	18.7	13.7	11.7	6.0	6.0
MALE	6 260	672	400	840	741	632	520	419	825	629	415	166
SINGLE (NEVER MARRIED)	2 529	668	390	673	330	167	81	39	104	42	27	7
MARRIED, WIFE PRESENT	2 588	-	9	140	328	342	319	249	487	381	257	78
MARRIED, WIFE ABSENT	446	-	1	22	53	48	50	37	96	91	37	10
SEPARATED	371	-	-	21	41	43	43	33	86	68	32	5
OTHER	75	-	1	2	12	5	7	4	10	23	5	5
WIDOWED	245	-	-	-	-	5	4	10	46	53	69	57
DIVORCED	451	4	-	4	29	71	67	84	91	62	25	13
PERCENT	100.0	100.0	100.0	100.0	100.0	100.0	100.0	100.0	100.0	100.0	100.0	100.0
SINGLE (NEVER MARRIED)	40.4	99.4	97.4	80.2	44.6	26.4	15.6	9.4	12.6	6.6	6.5	4.4
MARRIED, WIFE PRESENT	41.3	-	2.2	16.7	44.3	54.1	61.2	59.3	59.1	60.6	61.8	47.0
MARRIED, WIFE ABSENT	7.1	-	0.3	2.7	7.2	7.6	9.6	8.8	11.7	14.5	8.9	6.0
SEPARATED	5.9	-	-	2.5	5.5	6.8	8.3	7.8	10.5	10.8	7.6	3.0
OTHER	1.2	-	0.3	0.2	1.7	0.9	1.3	1.0	1.2	3.7	1.3	3.0
WIDOWED	3.9	-	-	-	-	0.8	0.8	2.4	5.6	8.4	16.7	34.5
DIVORCED	7.2	0.6	0.1	0.5	4.0	11.2	12.9	20.1	11.0	9.9	6.1	8.1

Marital Status of Persons 15 Years Old and Over, by Age, Sex, Race, Spanish Origin, and Metropolitan Residence: March 1980—Continued

[NUMBERS IN THOUSANDS. FOR MEANING OF SYMBOLS, SEE TEXT]

SUBJECT	TOTAL, 15 YEARS AND OVER	AGE (YEARS)										
		15 TO 17	18 AND 19	20 TO 24	25 TO 29	30 TO 34	35 TO 39	40 TO 44	45 TO 54	55 TO 64	65 TO 74	75 AND OVER
METROPOLITAN--CONTINUED												
BLACK--CONTINUED												
FEMALE	7 690	661	459	1 097	953	774	668	533	968	781	536	260
SINGLE (NEVER MARRIED)	2 648	653	424	772	352	155	85	42	75	49	23	18
MARRIED, HUSBAND PRESENT	2 517	3	29	241	361	333	325	252	442	333	166	31
MARRIED, HUSBAND ABSENT	874	3	6	58	147	135	124	114	161	80	34	11
SEPARATED	797	3	5	55	129	127	110	106	144	76	33	10
HUSBAND IN ARMED FORCES	11	-	2	-	4	1	4	-	-	-	-	-
OTHER	66	-	-	3	14	7	10	8	17	4	2	1
WIDOWED	900	-	-	1	8	16	24	31	136	216	281	187
DIVORCED	750	2	-	25	85	134	111	94	154	102	31	12
PERCENT	100.0	100.0	100.0	100.0	100.0	100.0	100.0	100.0	100.0	100.0	100.0	100.0
SINGLE (NEVER MARRIED)	34.4	98.8	92.3	70.3	37.0	20.1	12.7	7.8	7.7	6.3	4.2	7.1
MARRIED, HUSBAND PRESENT	32.7	0.5	6.3	22.0	37.9	43.0	48.6	47.2	45.7	42.7	31.0	12.1
MARRIED, HUSBAND ABSENT	11.4	0.4	1.4	5.3	15.4	17.5	18.6	21.5	16.6	10.3	6.4	4.2
SEPARATED	10.4	0.4	1.0	5.0	13.5	16.4	16.5	19.9	14.8	9.8	6.1	3.7
HUSBAND IN ARMED FORCES	0.1	-	0.4	-	0.4	0.2	0.6	-	-	-	-	-
OTHER	0.9	-	-	0.3	1.5	0.9	1.5	1.5	1.8	0.5	0.4	0.5
WIDOWED	11.7	-	-	0.1	0.8	2.1	3.6	5.9	14.0	27.7	52.4	72.0
DIVORCED	9.8	0.2	-	2.3	8.9	17.3	16.6	17.6	15.9	13.1	5.9	4.6
SPANISH ORIGIN[1]												
BOTH SEXES	7 200	639	485	1 114	1 010	836	639	612	878	526	320	141
SINGLE (NEVER MARRIED)	2 212	618	421	588	268	98	40	46	65	37	22	8
MARRIED, SPOUSE PRESENT	3 874	17	51	430	621	604	488	454	624	356	175	53
MARRIED, SPOUSE ABSENT	433	4	12	70	71	60	51	39	72	35	14	5
SEPARATED	293	1	7	45	47	38	40	27	49	25	10	2
OTHER	140	2	5	25	24	22	11	12	23	10	4	3
WIDOWED	284	-	-	6	4	7	6	9	45	56	80	72
DIVORCED	397	-	1	20	46	66	53	65	72	42	29	3
PERCENT	100.0	100.0	100.0	100.0	100.0	100.0	100.0	100.0	100.0	100.0	100.0	100.0
SINGLE (NEVER MARRIED)	30.7	96.7	86.9	52.7	26.5	11.8	6.2	7.5	7.5	7.0	6.9	5.4
MARRIED, SPOUSE PRESENT	53.8	2.7	10.4	38.6	61.5	72.2	76.4	74.1	71.1	67.7	54.6	37.6
MARRIED, SPOUSE ABSENT	6.0	0.6	2.5	6.3	7.0	7.2	8.0	6.4	8.2	6.7	4.4	3.9
SEPARATED	4.1	0.2	1.5	4.0	4.7	4.5	6.3	4.4	5.6	4.8	3.2	1.7
OTHER	1.9	0.4	1.0	2.2	2.4	2.6	1.7	2.0	2.6	1.9	1.2	2.2
WIDOWED	3.9	-	-	0.5	0.4	0.9	1.0	1.4	5.1	10.6	25.0	51.1
DIVORCED	5.5	-	0.2	1.8	4.6	7.9	8.3	10.6	8.2	7.9	9.1	2.0
MALE	3 531	333	247	539	506	426	310	286	434	243	144	63
SINGLE (NEVER MARRIED)	1 176	328	230	330	148	49	16	17	30	13	12	4
MARRIED, WIFE PRESENT	2 018	4	16	178	317	326	253	236	349	196	104	39
MARRIED, WIFE ABSENT	164	1	1	26	22	28	20	13	31	13	6	3
SEPARATED	81	-	-	14	10	10	14	5	15	8	5	1
OTHER	83	1	1	12	12	18	6	9	16	5	1	2
WIDOWED	47	-	-	-	2	2	1	4	6	9	7	16
DIVORCED	127	-	-	4	17	22	21	16	19	11	14	1
PERCENT	100.0	100.0	100.0	100.0	100.0	100.0	100.0	100.0	100.0	100.0	100.0	(B)
SINGLE (NEVER MARRIED)	33.3	98.5	93.3	61.2	29.2	11.5	5.1	6.1	6.8	5.3	8.4	(B)
MARRIED, WIFE PRESENT	57.1	1.1	6.4	33.1	62.7	76.4	81.5	82.5	80.3	80.7	72.5	(B)
MARRIED, WIFE ABSENT	4.6	0.4	0.3	4.9	4.4	6.6	6.4	4.6	7.1	5.5	4.1	(B)
SEPARATED	2.3	-	-	2.5	1.9	2.4	4.5	1.6	3.4	3.5	3.5	(B)
OTHER	2.3	0.4	0.3	2.3	2.5	4.2	1.9	3.0	3.7	2.0	0.6	(B)
WIDOWED	1.3	-	-	-	0.4	0.4	0.2	1.3	1.4	3.9	5.1	(B)
DIVORCED	3.6	-	-	0.8	3.4	5.2	6.8	5.4	4.4	4.6	10.0	(B)
FEMALE	3 669	306	238	575	504	409	328	326	444	283	176	78
SINGLE (NEVER MARRIED)	1 036	290	191	258	121	50	24	29	36	24	10	4
MARRIED, HUSBAND PRESENT	1 856	14	35	252	304	278	235	218	276	160	71	14
MARRIED, HUSBAND ABSENT	270	2	11	44	49	32	31	26	41	22	8	3
SEPARATED	212	1	7	31	37	28	26	22	35	17	5	2
HUSBAND IN ARMED FORCES	4	-	1	2	1	-	1	-	-	-	-	-
OTHER	53	1	4	11	11	4	4	4	7	5	3	1
WIDOWED	237	-	-	6	2	6	6	5	39	46	73	55
DIVORCED	270	-	1	16	29	44	32	49	53	30	15	1
PERCENT	100.0	100.0	100.0	100.0	100.0	100.0	100.0	100.0	100.0	100.0	100.0	100.0
SINGLE (NEVER MARRIED)	28.2	94.8	80.3	44.8	23.9	12.1	7.3	8.8	8.1	8.5	5.8	5.3
MARRIED, HUSBAND PRESENT	50.6	4.5	14.6	43.8	60.4	67.9	71.7	66.7	62.1	56.6	40.0	17.7
MARRIED, HUSBAND ABSENT	7.3	0.7	4.8	7.6	9.7	7.8	9.6	7.9	9.3	7.8	4.7	3.7
SEPARATED	5.8	0.4	3.0	5.4	7.4	6.8	8.1	6.8	7.8	6.0	3.1	2.0
HUSBAND IN ARMED FORCES	0.1	-	0.3	0.3	0.1	-	0.3	-	-	-	-	-
OTHER	1.5	0.3	1.5	1.8	2.1	1.0	1.2	1.1	1.5	1.8	1.6	1.7
WIDOWED	6.5	-	-	1.0	0.3	1.4	1.7	1.6	8.7	16.4	41.2	71.4
DIVORCED	7.4	-	0.3	2.8	5.7	10.7	9.8	15.1	11.9	10.7	8.3	1.9

[1]PERSONS OF SPANISH ORIGIN MAY BE OF ANY RACE.

Crime Index Offenses Reported

MURDER AND NONNEGLIGENT MANSLAUGHTER

DEFINITION

Murder and nonnegligent manslaughter, as defined in the Uniform Crime Reporting Program, is the willful (nonnegligent) killing of one human being by another.

The classification of this offense, as for all other Crime Index offenses, is based solely on police investigation as opposed to the determination of a court, medical examiner, coroner, jury, or other judicial body. Not included in the count for this offense classification are deaths caused by negligence, suicide, or accident; justifiable homicides, which are the killings of felons by law enforcement officers in the line of duty or by private citizens; and attempts to murder or assaults to murder, which are scored as aggravated assaults.

TREND

Year	Number of offenses	Rate per 100,000 inhabitants
1979	21,456	9.7
1980	23,044	10.2
Percent change	+7.4	+5.2

Volume

There were an estimated 23,044 murders in the United States during 1980. These offenses represented approximately 2 percent of the total violent crimes committed.

An overall view of the four regions of the Nation disclosed that the most populous, the Southern States, accounted for 42 percent of the murders. The Western States reported 21 percent; the North Central States recorded 20 percent; and the Northeastern States, 17 percent.

Murder offenses occurred more frequently during August than in any other month of 1980.

Trend

When comparing 1980 to 1979, the number of murders jumped 7 percent nationally, with the increase extending into all regions, population groups, and areas. The increase in murder volume was reflected regionally by a rise of 15 percent in the Western States; 8 percent in the Northeastern States; 5 percent in the Southern States; and

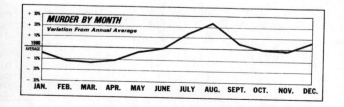

From *Crime in the United States, 1980,* U.S. Department of Justice, Federal Bureau of Investigation, September 10, 1981.

4 percent in the North Central States.

The volume of murder offenses rose in the suburban areas by 11 percent and in cities with 250,000 or more inhabitants by 8 percent. Rural areas experienced an upswing of 5 percent in the volume of murders.

The following chart reveals an increase of 23 percent nationally in the murder counts from 1976 to 1980.

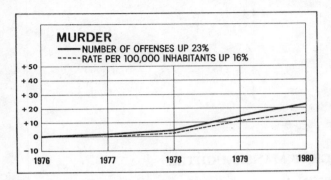

Rate

Nationally, an average of 10 of every 100,000 United States inhabitants were murder victims in 1980.

The number of murder victims in relation to population was highest in the Southern States with 13 murders per 100,000 inhabitants, a 1-percent rate increase over the previous year. The Western States' rate was 11 per 100,000, an 11-percent rise over the 1979 rate. Both the North Central and Northeastern Regions experienced rates of 8 per 100,000 population; however, the Northeast's rate represented an 8-percent increase and the North Central Region's rate a rise of 3 percent.

Collectively, the SMSAs reported a murder rate of 12 victims per 100,000 inhabitants; the rural areas recorded a rate of 7 per 100,000 inhabitants; and cities outside metropolitan areas (Other Cities) registered a murder rate of 6 per 100,000 inhabitants.

Nature

For each murder reported to the UCR Program, contributing agencies provide supplemental information which is more extensive than for the other Index crimes. Submitted monthly, the data consist of the age, sex, race, and ethnic origin of both victims and offenders; the types of weapons used; the relationships of victims to the offenders; and the circumstances surrounding the murders.

Approximately 77 percent of the murder victims in 1980 were males. An average of 53 of every 100 victims were White, 42 were Black, and 4 were persons of other races.

As depicted in the following tables, 17,559 offenders were identified in connection with murders of 15,648 victims during the year. Ninety-four percent of those killed were slain in single-victim situations; 13,028 by single offenders and 1,605 by more than one assailant. Also slain were 792 persons by 349 offenders in situations where there were multiple victims and single offenders. Concerning homicides involving multiple victims/multiple offenders, 223 persons were slain by 244 assailants.

As in recent years, firearms were the dominant weapons used in the commission of murders throughout the United States during 1980. The accompanying chart illustrates the number of murder offenses in the Nation for which the types of weapons used were reported to the UCR Program. Firearms were the weapons used in 68 percent of the murders in the Southern States; in 63 percent of

Age, Sex, Race, and Ethnic Origin of Murder Victims, 1980

Age	Number	Percent	Sex		Race				Ethnic Origin			
			Male	Female	White	Black	American Indian or Alaskan Native	Asian or Pacific Islander	Unknown	Hispanic	Non-Hispanic	Unknown
Total	21,860	....	16,896	4,964	11,646	9,267	146	164	637	1,947	11,141	8,772
Percent	....	100.0[1]	77.3	22.7	53.3	42.4	.7	.8	2.9	8.9	51.0	40.1
Infant (under 1)	211	1.0	121	90	117	88	....	3	3	13	103	95
1 to 4	324	1.5	186	138	182	131	3	4	4	22	163	139
5 to 9	146	.7	70	76	89	50	....	2	5	5	74	67
10 to 14	221	1.0	120	101	131	80	2	1	7	13	108	100
15 to 19	1,927	8.8	1,456	471	1,111	720	8	12	76	242	856	829
20 to 24	3,773	17.3	2,947	826	1,891	1,726	26	27	103	434	1,856	1,483
25 to 29	3,652	16.7	2,923	729	1,710	1,784	29	25	104	368	1,836	1,448
30 to 34	2,842	13.0	2,287	555	1,383	1,319	25	17	98	254	1,441	1,147
35 to 39	1,973	9.0	1,552	421	1,019	879	13	16	46	165	1,059	749
40 to 44	1,486	6.8	1,199	287	795	619	12	12	48	103	769	614
45 to 49	1,176	5.4	949	227	633	493	10	8	32	100	646	430
50 to 54	1,061	4.9	860	201	608	410	8	9	26	59	591	411
55 to 59	805	3.7	651	154	482	302	3	5	13	32	448	325
60 to 64	612	2.8	465	147	379	215	3	8	7	30	357	225
65 to 69	439	2.0	327	112	279	147	1	3	9	16	245	178
70 to 74	340	1.6	224	116	241	87	....	5	7	8	194	138
75 and over	497	2.3	255	242	388	97	2	5	5	14	263	220
Unknown	375	1.7	304	71	208	120	1	2	44	69	132	174

[1]Because of rounding, percentages may not add to total.

Victim/Offender Relationship by Sex, Race, and Ethnic Origin, 1980

[Single victim/Single offender]

Victim	Total victims	Total offenders	Offender										
			Race					Sex			Ethnic origin		
			White	Black	American Indian or Alaskan Native	Asian or Pacific Islander	Unknown	Male	Female	Unknown	Hispanic	Non-Hispanic	Unknown
White	6,444	6,444	5,652	670	30	19	73	5,638	733	73	954	3,302	2,188
Black	6,165	6,165	261	5,847	7	1	49	4,872	1,244	49	73	3,735	2,357
American Indian or Alaskan Native	96	96	28	8	59	1		84	12		4	54	38
Asian or Pacific Islander	78	78	18	9	2	46	3	67	8	3	6	35	37
Unknown	245	245	21	42	1		181	61	3	181	1	11	233
Male	9,811	9,811	4,433	5,150	80	50	98	7,975	1,738	98	866	5,397	3,548
Female	2,972	2,972	1,526	1,384	18	17	27	2,686	259	27	171	1,729	1,072
Unknown	245	245	21	42	1		181	61	3	181	1	11	233
Hispanic	1,001	1,001	894	100		2	5	931	65	5	849	132	20
Non-Hispanic	7,247	7,247	3,133	3,972	55	36	51	5,949	1,247	51	177	6,963	107
Unknown	4,780	4,780	1,953	2,504	44	29	250	3,842	688	250	12	42	4,726
Total	13,028	13,028	5,980	6,576	99	67	306	10,722	2,000	306	1,038	7,137	4,853

[Single victim/multiple offenders]

Victim	Total victims	Total offenders	Offender										
			Race					Sex			Ethnic origin		
			White	Black	American Indian or Alaskan Native	Asian or Pacific Islander	Unknown	Male	Female	Unknown	Hispanic	Non-Hispanic	Unknown
White	976	2,416	1,774	561	9	5	67	2,118	231	67	495	1,008	913
Black	524	1,267	146	1,063	1		57	1,088	122	57	60	527	680
American Indian or Alaskan Native	10	21	8		11		2	14	5	2		6	15
Asian or Pacific Islander	24	60	12	17		31		56	4		6	34	26
Unknown	71	174	8	66			100	73	1	100		3	171
Male	1,350	3,352	1,738	1,449	16	30	119	2,939	294	119	516	1,390	1,446
Female	184	412	202	192	5	6	7	337	68	7	39	185	188
Unknown	71	174	8	66			100	73	1	100		3	171
Hispanic	195	510	435	65	1		9	464	37	9	412	89	9
Non-Hispanic	676	1,657	867	735	10	24	21	1,446	190	21	143	1,473	41
Unknown	734	1,771	646	907	10	12	196	1,439	136	196		16	1,755
Total	1,605	3,938	1,948	1,707	21	36	226	3,349	363	226	555	1,578	1,805

Murder, Type of Weapon Used, 1980

[Percent distribution]

Region	Total all weapons used[1]	Fire-arms	Knife or other cutting instruments	Unknown or other dangerous weapons	Personal weapons
Northeastern States	100.0	54.2	24.2	13.8	7.8
North Central States	100.0	62.8	17.4	13.7	6.0
Southern States	100.0	68.4	17.0	10.4	4.2
Western States	100.0	57.8	20.8	15.0	6.4
Total	100.0	62.4	19.3	12.5	5.8

[1]Because of rounding, percentages may not add to total.

Murder, Type of Weapon Used, 1976–1980

[Percent distribution]

Year	Total		Fire-arms	Knife or other cutting instruments	Unknown or other dangerous weapons	Personal weapons
	Number	Percent[1]				
1976	16,605	100.0	63.8	17.8	12.2	6.2
1977	18,033	100.0	62.5	19.1	12.9	5.6
1978	18,714	100.0	63.6	18.8	11.8	5.7
1979	20,591	100.0	63.3	19.2	11.9	5.6
1980	21,860	100.0	62.4	19.3	12.5	5.8

[1]Because of rounding, percentages may not add to total.

those in the North Central States; in 58 percent of those in the Western States; and in 54 percent of those in the Northeastern States. Sixty-two percent of the murders nationwide were committed by the use of firearms. Of all murders, 50 percent were by handguns, 7 percent by shotguns, and 5 percent by rifles.

Of weapons other than firearms used in the commission of murders reported in 1980, 19 percent were cutting or stabbing instruments. Geographically, the Northeastern States reported the use of these instruments in 24 percent of the murders committed within that region. In the Western States, these types of weapons were employed in 21 percent of the murders, while both the Southern and North Central States reported their use in 17 percent.

Nationwide, other dangerous weapons such as blunt instruments, poison, explosives, etc., were used in 13 percent of the murders. Personal weapons (hands, fists, feet, etc.) accounted for the remaining 6 percent.

As has been noted in prior issues of this publication, criminal homicide is primarily a societal problem over which law enforcement has little or no control. Supporting this statement is the fact that 51 percent of the murders committed in 1980 were perpetrated by relatives or persons acquainted with the victims. Sixteen percent of these killings were within family relationships, one-half of which involved spouse killing spouse.

Arguments resulted in 45 percent of all murders, while 18 percent occurred as a result of felonious activities such as robbery, rape, etc. Seven percent were suspected to be the result of some felonious activity.

The accompanying table shows murder circumstances/motives for the past 5 years.

An examination of murder statistics for the past 5 years shows a slight decrease in the use of firearms as weapons. In 1976, firearms were used in 64 percent of all murders, while 62 percent of all murders in 1980 were perpetrated with these weapons. An analysis of weapons used in criminal homicides for 1976 through 1980 is shown in tabular form.

Murder Victims—Weapons Used, 1980

Age	Number	Weapons										
		Fire-arm	Cutting or stabbing instrument	Blunt object (club, hammer, etc.)	Personal weapons (hands, fists, feet, etc.)	Poison	Explosives	Arson	Narcotics	Strangu-lation	Asphyxia-tion	Other weapon or weapon not stated
Total	21,860	13,650	4,212	1,094	1,265	17	21	291	12	401	104	793
Infant (under 1)	211	10	7	16	99	1	....	13	....	3	11	51
1 to 4	324	41	20	19	153	2	....	30	....	9	13	37
5 to 9	146	39	21	7	17	2	....	26	....	13	8	13
10 to 14	221	104	40	14	19	....	2	14	....	14	3	11
15 to 19	1,927	1,232	397	82	69	....	1	14	....	45	4	83
20 to 24	3,773	2,526	797	121	111	....	2	16	2	75	6	117
25 to 29	3,652	2,513	724	121	102	2	5	31	4	51	7	92
30 to 34	2,842	1,960	524	111	95	2	2	13	4	47	5	79
35 to 39	1,973	1,349	365	85	82	....	....	23	....	12	6	51
40 to 44	1,486	1,019	263	63	69	1	4	14	....	14	2	37
45 to 49	1,176	736	230	90	60	1	1	9	....	13	4	32
50 to 54	1,061	612	230	76	67	1	1	17	....	14	6	37
55 to 59	805	452	169	70	51	1	1	9	....	19	2	31
60 to 64	612	350	116	40	47	2	....	13	....	20	3	21
65 to 69	439	226	78	46	48	1	1	15	....	10	4	10
70 to 74	340	131	70	45	47	....	....	11	1	10	5	20
75 and over	497	123	95	72	120	1	1	19	1	25	10	30
Unknown	375	227	66	16	9	....	....	4	....	7	5	41

Circumstance by Relationship, 1980

[Percent distribution]

Victim	Total	Felony type	Suspected felony type	Romantic triangle	Argument over money or property	Other arguments	Miscellaneous non-felony type	Unable to determine
Total[1]	100.0	100.0	100.0	100.0	100.0	100.0	100.0	100.0
Husband	3.6	.3	.1	4.9	1.6	7.3	3.6	.4
Wife	4.7	.2	.8	8.3	2.5	8.4	5.4	2.1
Mother	.6	.2	....	....	.7	.9	.8	.4
Father	.8	.1	.1	....	.5	1.3	1.1	.3
Daughter	.9	.2	.1	....	....	.3	3.4	.5
Son	1.2	.3	....	....	.5	1.1	3.6	.3
Brother	1.1	.2	....	....	2.9	2.1	1.1	.2
Sister	.2	.1	.1	.2	.2	.4	.3	.1
Other family	3.0	.8	.6	.6	4.5	4.7	4.4	.8
Acquaintances	26.9	16.1	3.6	58.0	57.2	37.8	32.4	7.4
Friend	3.4	1.3	.7	4.7	10.6	5.2	3.3	1.8
Boyfriend	1.3	.1	.1	3.4	.9	2.7	.9	.1
Girlfriend	1.8	.3	.2	5.9	1.3	3.2	1.7	.5
Neighbor	1.4	1.2	.1	.6	2.9	2.0	1.7	.3
Stranger	13.3	32.3	2.7	10.8	6.6	8.8	14.4	6.4
Unknown relationship	35.8	46.5	90.9	2.6	7.2	13.9	21.8	78.4

[1]Because of rounding, percentages may not add to total.

Clearances

The clearance rate for murder in 1980 was higher than for any other Crime Index offense. Nationwide, law enforcement agencies were successful in clearing 72 percent of the murders occurring in their jurisdictions.

City law enforcement agencies cleared 72 percent of the murders during the year, while those in suburban and rural areas cleared 71 and 81 percent, respectively. In 1980, persons under 18 years of age accounted for 5 percent of the willful killings cleared by law enforcement

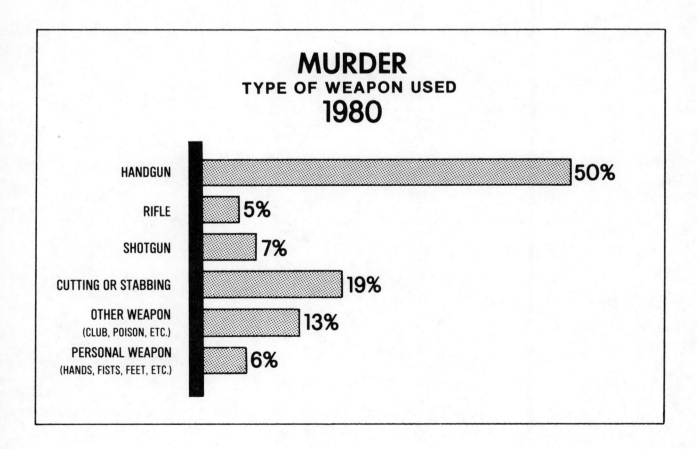

Murder Circumstances/Motives, 1976-1980

	1980	1979	1978	1977	1976
TOTAL	21,860	20,591	18,714	18,033	16,605
PERCENT[1]	100.0	100.0	100.0	100.0	100.0
FELONY TOTAL	17.7	16.9	16.7	16.7	17.7
Robbery	10.8	10.5	10.2	9.9	10.3
Narcotics	1.7	1.9	1.7	1.7	1.8
Sex Offenses	1.5	1.6	1.4	1.7	1.8
Other Felony	3.7	2.9	3.3	3.4	3.8
SUSPECTED FELONY ...	6.7	5.3	5.6	5.9	7.0
ARGUMENT TOTAL	44.6	42.9	45.5	46.6	48.3
Romantic Triangle	2.3	2.4	2.7	2.8	2.8
Influence of Alcohol and/or Narcotics[2]	4.8	4.5	5.3	5.3	5.8
Property or Money	2.6	3.0	3.5	3.3	3.9
Other Arguments	35.0	33.0	33.9	35.2	35.7
OTHER MOTIVES OR CIRCUMSTANCES	15.9	17.2	18.3	16.6	18.6
UNKNOWN MOTIVES ..	15.1	17.7	13.8	14.2	8.5

[1]Because of rounding, percentages may not add to totals.
[2]Murders committed during arguments while under influence of narcotics are not counted in felony murders.

in cities and rural areas; 6 percent of those cleared in suburban areas involved only persons in that age group.

Persons Arrested

During the period 1976-1980, murder arrests for persons under 18 years of age increased less than 1 percent, while adult arrests for this offense rose 5 percent. In 1980, of all persons arrested for murder, 45 percent were under 25 years of age, with 9 percent of the total being 17 or younger. The 18- to 24-year age group showed the greatest involvement in this offense, accounting for 35 percent of the total 1980 murder arrests.

Whites comprised 51 percent of the total arrestees for murder in 1980; Blacks made up 48 percent; and the remainder were of other races. The collection of statistics regarding ethnic origin was initiated in 1980; and according to the data reported to the UCR Program, 25 percent of the juvenile arrestees, 15 percent of the adult arrestees, and 16 percent of the total arrestees were of Hispanic ethnicity.

Accident Facts

Accidental deaths and injuries in 1980

	Deaths	Change from 1979	Disabling Injuries†
	105,000‡	0%	10,000,000‡

The death total in 1980 showed no change from 1979. Decreases in public, work and motor-vehicle deaths were offset by an increase in home. Excessive heat deaths undoubtedly contributed to the increase in home deaths. The death rate per 100,000 population was 46.2, the lowest rate on record.

	Deaths	Change from 1979	Disabling Injuries†
Motor-Vehicle	**52,600**	−*%	**2,000,000**
Public nonwork	47,900		1,800,000
Work	4,500		200,000
Home	200		10,000
Work	**13,000**	−2%	**2,200,000**
Nonmotor-vehicle	8,500		2,000,000
Motor-vehicle	4,500		200,000
Home	**23,000**	+5%	**3,400,000**
Nonmotor-vehicle	22,800		3,400,000
Motor-vehicle	200		10,000
Public††	**21,000**	−2%	**2,600,000**

Disabling Injuries† by Severity of Injury, 1980

Severity of Disabling Injury	TOTAL‡	Motor-Vehicle	Work	Home	Public††
All Disabling Injuries†	10,000,000	2,000,000	2,200,000	3,400,000	2,600,000
Permanent impairments**	360,000	150,000	80,000	90,000	60,000
Temporary total disabilities	9,600,000	1,850,000	2,100,000	3,300,000	2,500,000

Source: National Safety Council estimates (rounded) based on data from the National Center for Health Statistics, state industrial commissions, state traffic authorities, state departments of health, insurance companies, industrial establishments and other sources.

*Less than 0.5 per cent.

†**Disabling beyond the day of accident.** Injuries are not reported on a national basis, so the totals shown are approximations based on ratios of disabling injuries to deaths developed from special studies. The totals are the best estimates for the current year; however, they should not be compared with totals shown in previous editions of ACCIDENT FACTS to indicate year-to-year changes or trends.

‡Deaths and injuries above for the four separate classes total more than national figures due to rounding and because some deaths and injuries are included in more than one class. For example, 4,500 work deaths involved motor vehicles and are in both the work and motor-vehicle totals; and 200 motor-vehicle deaths occurred on home premises and are in both home and motor-vehicle. The total of such duplication amounted to about 4,700 deaths and more than 200,000 injuries in 1980.

††Excludes motor-vehicle and work accidents in public places. Includes recreation (swimming, hunting, etc.), transportation except motor-vehicle, public building accidents, etc.

**The term "permanent impairments" includes both permanent partial and permanent total disability. The above estimates thus include impairments ranging from the permanent stiffening of a joint or a finger amputation, to permanent, complete crippling.

Costs of accidents in 1980*

Accidents in which deaths or disabling injuries occurred, together with noninjury motor-vehicle accidents and fires, cost the nation in 1980, at least

$83.2 billion

(billion)

Motor-vehicle accidents $39.3

This cost figure includes wage loss, medical expense, insurance administration cost, and property damage from moving motor-vehicle accidents. Not included are the cost of public agencies such as police and fire departments, courts, indirect losses to employers of off-the-job accidents to employees, the value of cargo losses in commercial vehicles, and damages awarded in excess of direct losses. Fire damage to parked motor-vehicles is not included here but is distributed to the other classes.

Work accidents $30.2

This cost figure includes wage loss, medical expense, insurance administration cost, fire loss, and an estimate of indirect costs arising out of work accidents. Not included is the value of property damage other than fire loss, and indirect loss from fires.

Home accidents . . . . $ 8.9

This cost figure includes wage loss, medical expense, health insurance administration cost, and fire loss. Not included are the costs of property damage other than fire loss, and the indirect cost to employers of off-the-job accidents to employees.

Public accidents . . . . $ 6.4

This cost figure includes wage loss, medical expense, health insurance administration cost, and fire loss. Not included are the costs of property damage other than fire loss, and the indirect cost to employers of off-the-job accidents to employees.

Certain Costs* of Accidents by Class, 1980 ($ billions)

Cost	TOTAL**	Motor-Vehicle	Work	Home	Public Nonmotor-Vehicle
Total	$83.2	$39.3	$30.2	$8.9	$6.4
Wage loss	22.7	11.9	5.0	3.5	3.6
Medical expense	10.3	3.5	3.1	2.3	1.7
Insurance administration	16.6	10.5	5.9	0.1	0.1
Fire loss	6.2	†	2.2	3.0	1.0
Motor-veh. prop. damage	13.4	13.4	†	†	†
Indirect work loss	14.0	†	14.0	†	†

Source: National Safety Council estimates (rounded) based on information from the National Center for Health Statistics, state industrial commissions, state traffic authorities, state departments of health, insurance companies and associations, industrial establishments, and other sources.

*Cost estimates are not comparable with those of previous years. As additional or more precise data become available they are used from that year forward, but previously estimated figures are not revised.

**Duplications between work and motor-vehicle and home and motor-vehicle are eliminated in the totals.

†Not included, see comments by class of accident above.

1980 accident cost components

TOTAL—ALL ACCIDENTS** . . . . **$83.2 billion**

These costs include:
(billion)

Wage loss $22.7

Since, theoretically, a worker's contribution to the wealth of the nation is measured in terms of wages, then the total of wages lost due to accidents provides a measure of this lost productivity. For nonfatal injuries, actual wage losses are used; for fatalities and permanent disabilities, the figure used is the present value of all future earnings lost.

Medical expense $10.3

Doctor fees, hospital charges, the cost of medicines, and all other medical expenses incurred as the result of accidental injuries are included.

Insurance administration cost $16.6

This is the difference between premiums paid to insurance companies and claims paid out by them; it is their cost of doing business and is a part of the accident cost total. Claims paid by insurance companies are not identified separately, as every claim is compensation for losses such as wages, medical expenses, property damage, etc., which are included in other categories above and below.

Property damage in motor-vehicle accidents $13.4

Includes the value of property damage to vehicles from moving motor-vehicle accidents. The damage is valued at the cost to repair the vehicle or the market value of the vehicle when damage exceeds its market value. The cost of minor damage (such as scratches or dents incurred while parking) is considered part of the normal wear and tear to vehicles and is not included.

Fire loss . . . . $ 6.2

Includes losses from building fires of $5.4 billion and from nonbuilding fires, of $0.8 billion. By class of accident these totals break down as follows. Building: work $1.8 billion, home $2.9 billion, public $0.7 billion. Nonbuilding: work $0.4 billion, home $0.1 billion, public $0.3 billion.

Indirect loss from work accidents $14.0

This is the money value of time lost by noninjured workers. Includes time spent filling out accident reports, giving first aid to injured workers, and time lost due to production slowdowns. This loss is conservatively estimated as equal to the sum of lost wages, medical expenses, and insurance administration cost of work accidents.

See preceding notes.

Accidental death rates by state, 1980

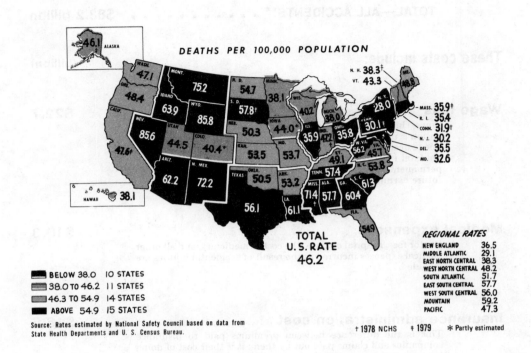

DEATHS PER 100,000 POPULATION

N. H.	38.3‡
VT.	43.3
MASS.	35.9‡
R. I.	35.4
CONN.	31.9†
N. J.	30.2
DEL.	35.5
MD.	32.6

ALASKA 46.1

WASH. 47.1
ORE. 48.4
CALIF. 85.6
NEV. 47.6†
MONT. 75.2
IDAHO 63.9
WYO. 85.8
UTAH 44.5
ARIZ. 62.2
N. MEX. 72.2
N. D. 54.7
S. D. 57.8†
NEBR. 50.3
COLO. 40.4*
KAN. 53.5
OKLA. 50.5
TEXAS 56.1
MINN. 38.1
IOWA 44.0*
MO. 53.7
ARK. 53.2
LA. 61.1
WIS. 40.2
ILL. 35.9
MICH. 38.0
IND. 47.2
KY. 49.1
TENN. 57.4
MISS. 71.4†
ALA. 57.7
GA. 60.4
OHIO 35.8
W. VA. 56.2
VA. 43.7
N. C. 53.8
S. C. 61.3
PENN. 30.1†
N. Y. 28.0

HAWAII 38.1

TOTAL U.S. RATE 46.2

REGIONAL RATES	
NEW ENGLAND	36.5
MIDDLE ATLANTIC	29.1
EAST NORTH CENTRAL	38.3
WEST NORTH CENTRAL	48.2
SOUTH ATLANTIC	51.7
EAST SOUTH CENTRAL	57.7
WEST SOUTH CENTRAL	56.0
MOUNTAIN	59.2
PACIFIC	47.3

■ BELOW 38.0   10 STATES
▨ 38.0 TO 46.2   11 STATES
▨ 46.3 TO 54.9   14 STATES
■ ABOVE 54.9   15 STATES

Source: Rates estimated by National Safety Council based on data from State Health Departments and U. S. Census Bureau.

† 1978 NCHS   ‡ 1979   * Partly estimated

Accidental Deaths by State, 1976-1978

State	Deaths† 1978	Deaths† 1977	Deaths† 1976	Death Rates 1978*	Death Rates Chg. from 1977‡	State	Deaths† 1978	Deaths† 1977	Deaths† 1976	Death Rates 1978*	Death Rates Chg. from 1977‡
U.S.†	**105,561**	**103,202**	**100,761**	**48.4**	**+ 1%**	Mo.	2,677	2,542	2,538	55.2	+ 5%
						Mont.	561	592	601	71.9	− 7%
Ala.	2,450	2,389	2,324	65.7	+ 2%	Neb.	738	776	796	47.0	− 5%
Alaska	500	463	496	121.7	+ 7%	Nev.	583	512	436	87.5	+ 8%
Ariz.	1,751	1,666	1,467	73.8	+ 2%	N. H.	332	329	317	38.2	− 1%
Ark.	1,271	1,179	1,202	58.7	+ 7%						
Calif.	11,132	10,248	10,343	49.9	+ 7%	N. J.	2,362	2,410	2,290	32.3	− 2%
						N. M.	1,062	1,026	929	87.4	+ 2%
Colo.	1,459	1,437	1,486	53.9	− 1%	N. Y.	5,808	5,544	5,606	32.7	+ 5%
Conn.	994	948	964	31.9	+ 5%	N. C.	3,247	3,148	3,164	58.3	+ 2%
Del.	247	255	240	42.3	− 3%	N. D.	403	392	419	61.7	+ 2%
D. of C.	295	355	316	44.0	−15%						
Fla.	4,614	4,246	4,186	53.3	+ 6%	Ohio	4,310	4,109	4,092	40.2	+ 5%
						Okla.	1,753	1,685	1,650	61.7	+ 3%
Ga.	3,002	3,140	2,726	59.2	− 5%	Ore.	1,472	1,403	1,320	60.0	+ 2%
Hawaii	367	311	337	40.7	+17%	Pa.	4,607	4,860	4,791	39.2	− 5%
Idaho	593	652	597	67.2	−11%	R. I.	285	361	299	30.6	−21%
Ill.	4,561	4,599	4,505	40.6	− 1%						
Ind.	2,543	2,534	2,569	47.2	0%	S. C.	1,733	1,812	1,647	59.7	− 6%
						S. D.	399	436	449	57.8	− 9%
Iowa	1,333	1,313	1,497	45.9	+ 2%	Tenn.	2,644	2,661	2,425	61.0	− 2%
Kans.	1,219	1,172	1,251	51.9	+ 3%	Texas	7,364	7,016	6,579	56.4	+ 3%
Ky.	1,896	2,259	1,983	54.3	−17%	Utah	776	713	584	58.9	+ 5%
La.	2,484	2,471	2,345	62.4	− 1%						
Maine	562	486	520	51.5	+15%	Vt.	243	240	236	49.9	0%
						Va.	2,447	2,591	2,476	47.3	− 7%
Md.	1,605	1,488	1,509	38.7	+ 8%	Wash.	2,066	2,034	1,857	54.5	− 1%
Mass.	2,274	2,100	2,133	39.4	+ 8%	W. Va.	1,071	1,094	1,086	57.5	− 3%
Mich.	3,878	3,874	3,840	42.2	0%	Wis.	2,000	1,933	2,023	42.7	+ 3%
Minn.	1,976	1,852	1,807	49.1	+ 6%	Wyo.	421	417	442	99.1	− 3%
Miss.	1,721	1,573	1,521	71.4	+ 9%						

Source: National Center for Health Statistics.
†Deaths for each state are by place of occurrence. These deaths include nonresident aliens which are excluded from the U.S. totals shown above (1978 - 530 deaths, 1977 - 444, 1976 - 455).
‡Some changes reflect disasters or revised population figures.   *Rates are deaths per 100,000 population.

Comparability of Accidental Death Totals

Beginning with 1970 data, detailed tabulations published by the National Center for Health Statistics (NCHS) no longer include deaths of nonresident aliens. In 1970, there were 438 such accidental deaths of which 212 were motor-vehicle. Also since 1970, some deaths for which a disease contributed to the occurrence of the accident are classified as disease deaths rather than as accidental deaths.

Accidental deaths are classified on the basis of a World Health Organization standard, "The International Statistical Classification of Diseases, Injuries, and Causes of Death." The ninth revision of this standard, which became effective January, 1979, provides greater detail on the agency involved, the victim's activity, and the location of the accident. Changes in the classification system include: snowmobiles specified in nontraffic motor-vehicle accidents; powered and unpowered small boats, water skier, and swimmer specified in water transport accidents; poisonings by drugs and medicaments and surgical and medical complications and misadventures are regrouped; falls categories specify escalator, ladder, scaffold, into water, etc.; source of ignition is specified in clothing fires; drownings are broken down by activity; and accidents involving machinery and cutting and piercing instruments are broken down by the general type of agent.

Accidental Deaths and Death Rates, Canadian Provinces, 1979

Province	ALL TYPES		Motor-Vehicle†	Falls	Drowning	Fires, Burns	Poison by Gas	Railroad
	Number	Rate*						
All Provinces	**11,928**	**50.4**	**5,914**	**1,902**	**613**	**644**	**120**	**66**
Alberta	1,163	57.8	698	141	38	41	21	1
British Columbia	1,716	66.8	743	324	71	104	8	8
Manitoba	497	48.2	205	83	27	36	4	5
New Brunswick	445	63.5	258	44	14	30	1	2
Newfoundland	220	38.3	106	25	22	17	1	1
Northwest Territories	52	119.8	13	3	7	12	0	0
Nova Scotia	433	51.1	208	52	20	32	14	2
Ontario	3,627	42.7	1,653	681	152	187	45	29
Prince Edward Island	55	44.7	29	4	3	3	0	1
Quebec	3,112	49.5	1,718	445	221	129	17	14
Saskatchewan	586	61.1	272	99	33	53	9	3
Yukon	22	101.9	11	1	5	0	0	0
Rate* (All Provinces)		**50.4**	**25.0**	**8.0**	**2.6**	**2.7**	**0.5**	**0.3**

Source: Vital Statistics Section, Statistics Canada.   *Per 100,000 population.
†Deaths in motor-vehicle grade crossing accidents are included in both Motor-Vehicle and Railroad.

Accidental Deaths and Death Rates by Nation

Nation	Year	Deaths	Rate†	Nation	Year	Deaths	Rate†
Hong Kong	1978	688	14.9	Costa Rica	1978	952	44.8
Dominican Republic	1978	944	18.4	Greece	1978	4,324	46.2
Singapore	1978	555	23.8	Australia	1978	6,613	46.4
Japan	1978	30,017	26.2	Scotland	1978	2,401	46.4
Nicaragua	1978	718	29.8	New Zealand	1978	1,464	46.8
Chile	1978	3,282	30.2	Norway	1979	1,906	46.8
England, Wales	1978	15,229	31.0	Canada	1977	11,182	48.0
Israel	1978	1,196	32.4	Switzerland	1979	3,054	48.4
Thailand	1978	15,647	34.8	**United States**	**1978**	**105,561**	**48.4**
Netherlands	1978	4,872	34.9	West Germany	1978	29,991	48.9
Denmark	1979	1,961	38.3	Poland	1978	19,136	54.7
Iceland	1979	93	41.2	Northern Ireland	1978	865	56.2
Argentina	1978	11,383	43.1	Luxembourg	1978	218	61.1
Bulgaria	1979	3,841	43.5	Venezuela*	1978	8,082	61.6
Sweden	1979	3,610	43.5	Austria	1979	5,073	67.6
Uruguay	1978	1,257	43.9	Hungary	1978	7,356	68.8

Source: World Health Organization.   *Excluding tribal Indians.   †Per 100,000 population.
NOTE: Differences in reporting among nations affect comparisons.

All deaths and injuries of workers

Three out of four deaths, and more than half of the injuries suffered by workers in 1980 occurred off the job. These totals, and rates per million hours exposure are shown in the table below.

Production time lost due to off-job accidents totalled nearly 70,000,000 days in 1980, compared with 45,000,000 days lost by workers injured on the job. Indirect losses of time, though, which seldom arise out of off-job accidents, totalled an estimated 200,000,000 days from accidents on the job.

Off-job accidents to workers cost the nation at least $24.7 billion in 1980, of which about one third was borne by employers.

Place	Deaths 1980	Deaths 1979	Disabling Injuries 1980	1980 Rates* Deaths	1980 Rates* Injuries
ALL ACCIDENTS	54,900	56,400	5,400,000	.10	9.6
At work	13,000	13,300	2,200,000	.07	11.4
Away from work	41,900	43,100	3,200,000	.11	8.6
Motor-vehicle	25,500	26,300	1,000,000	.72	28.3
Public nonmotor-veh. . . .	8,800	9,300	1,100,000	.07	8.3
Home	7,600	7,500	1,100,000	.04	5.4

*Per 1,000,000 hours exposure, by place.

Trends in on-job and off-job deaths and injuries

Since 1945, accidental deaths of workers on the job decreased 21 per cent and the rate per 100,000 workers decreased 61 per cent. Off the job, 1980 deaths exceeded the 1945 total by 40 per cent, but with an increase in the number of workers the *rate* was down 28 per cent. The ratio of off-job deaths to on-job deaths in 1980 was 3.22 to 1.

Year	Deaths On-Job No.	Deaths On-Job Rate*	Deaths Off-Job No.	Deaths Off-Job Rate*	Ratio Off/On	Disabling Injuries On-Job	Disabling Injuries Off-Job	Ratio Off/On
1945	16,500	33	30,000	60	1.82	2,000,000	2,750,000	1.38
1950	15,500	27	31,500	56	2.03	1,950,000	2,500,000	1.28
1955	14,200	24	31,300	53	2.20	1,950,000	2,400,000	1.23
1960	13,800	21	29,200	45	2.12	1,950,000	2,250,000	1.15
1965	14,100	20	36,500	52	2.59	2,100,000	2,700,000	1.29
1966	14,500	20	39,600	55	2.73	2,200,000	2,900,000	1.32
1967	14,200	19	40,000	54	2.82	2,200,000	3,000,000	1.36
1968	14,300	19	41,900	54	2.93	2,200,000	3,100,000	1.41
1969	14,300	18	43,300	55	3.03	2,200,000	3,200,000	1.45
1970	13,800	18	43,700	56	3.17	2,200,000	3,250,000	1.48
1971	13,700	18	41,500	53	3.03	2,300,000	3,200,000	1.39
1972	14,000	17	42,500	53	3.04	2,400,000	3,200,000	1.33
1973	14,300	17	43,700	52	3.06	2,500,000	3,300,000	1.32
1974	13,500	16	39,400	46	2.92	2,300,000	3,200,000	1.39
1975	13,000	15	37,800	45	2.91	2,200,000	3,200,000	1.45
1976	12,500	14	38,100	44	3.05	2,200,000	3,100,000	1.41
1977	12,900	14	40,200	45	3.12	2,300,000	3,200,000	1.39
1978	13,100	14	42,500	45	3.24	2,200,000	3,200,000	1.45
1979	13,300	14	43,100	45	3.24	2,300,000	3,200,000	1.39
1980	13,000	13	41,900	43	3.22	2,200,000	3,200,000	1.45
Changes								
1945-80	**−21%**	**−61%**	**+40%**	**−28%**	**+77%**	**+10%**	**+16%**	**+5%**

*Deaths per 100,000 workers.

Deaths and Death Rates from All Work Accidents, 1933-1980

Since 1933, death rates per 100,000 workers were at their highest for manufacturing in 1936 and for nonmanufacturing in 1937. Since those years, both rates decreased more than 60 per cent and reached their lowest levels in recent years. These lower rates resulted from deaths declining about one third, and increased numbers of workers.

Since 1970, deaths decreased 6 per cent while numbers of workers increased 25 per cent. This resulted in a reduction of 28 per cent in the death rate for the decade.

Year	Total				Manufacturing			Nonmanufacturing		
	Work Deaths	Work M-V‡	Workers† (000)	Rate††	Deaths	Workers† (000)	Rate††	Deaths	Workers† (000)	Rate††
1933 . . .	14,500		39,000	37	1,700	6,900	25	12,800	32,100	40
1934 . . .	16,000		41,500	39	1,900	8,100	23	14,100	33,400	42
1935 . . .	16,500		42,500	39	1,900	8,600	22	14,600	33,900	43
1936 . . .	18,500		44,000	42	2,400	9,400	26	16,100	34,600	47
1937 . . .	19,000		44,100	43	2,600	10,200	25	16,400	33,900	48
1938 . . .	16,000		42,100	38	1,900	9,000	21	14,100	33,100	43
1939 . . .	15,500		43,600	36	1,800	9,900	18	13,700	33,700	41
1940 . . .	17,000		45,200	38	2,000	10,600	19	15,000	34,600	43
1941 . . .	18,000		48,100	37	2,600	12,700	20	15,400	35,400	44
1942 . . .	18,000		51,500	35	2,900	14,700	20	15,100	36,800	41
1943 . . .	17,000		52,200	34	3,100	17,000	18	14,400	35,200	41
1944 . . .	16,000		51,800	31	2,900	16,700	17	13,100	35,100	37
1945 . . .	16,500		50,200	33	2,700	14,900	18	13,800	35,300	39
1946 . . .	16,500	§	52,400	31	2,500	14,200	18	14,000	38,200	37
1947 . . .	17,000	2,500	54,900	31	2,700	14,800	18	14,300	40,100	36
1948 . . .	16,000	2,100	56,000	29	2,600	15,000	17	13,400	41,000	33
1949 . . .	15,000	2,200	55,200	27	2,300	14,100	16	12,700	41,100	31
1950 . . .	15,500	2,700	56,400	27	2,600	15,100	17	12,900	41,300	31
1951 . . .	16,000	2,800	57,450	28	2,700	16,200	17	13,300	41,250	32
1952 . . .	15,000	2,800	57,800	26	2,400	16,400	15	12,600	41,400	30
1953 . . .	15,000	3,100	58,050	26	2,400	17,350	14	12,600	40,700	31
1954 . . .	14,000	2,800	57,500	24	2,000	16,050	12	12,000	41,450	29
1955 . . .	14,200	3,000	59,400	24	2,000	16,650	12	12,200	42,750	29
1956 . . .	14,300	3,000	61,100	23	2,000	17,000	12	12,300	44,100	28
1957 . . .	14,200	2,900	61,300	23	2,000	16,900	12	12,200	44,400	27
1958 . . .	13,300	2,600	59,900	22	1,800	15,600	12	11,500	44,300	26
1959 . . .	13,800	2,800	61,300	23	1,900	16,300	12	11,900	45,000	26
1960 . . .	13,800	2,800	64,400	21	1,800	16,600	10	12,100	47,800	25
1961 . . .	13,500	2,600	64,500	21	1,700	16,400	10	11,800	48,100	25
1962 . . .	13,700	2,700	65,200	21	1,700	16,600	11	11,900	48,600	24
1963 . . .	14,200	3,000	66,200	21	1,800	16,800	11	12,400	49,400	25
1964 . . .	14,200	3,100	67,600	21	1,700	17,000	10	12,500	50,600	25
1965 . . .	14,100	3,000	69,700	20	1,800	17,700	10	12,300	52,000	24
1966 . . .	14,500	3,200	72,600	20	1,900	18,800	10	12,600	53,800	23
1967 . . .	14,200	3,200	74,700	19	1,900	19,000	10	12,300	55,700	22
1968 . . .	14,300	3,600	76,900	19	1,800	19,400	9	12,500	57,500	22
1969 . . .	14,300	3,600	79,000	18	1,900	19,700	10	12,400	59,300	21
1970 . . .	13,800	3,700	77,700	18	1,700	19,300	9	12,100	58,400	21
1971 . . .	13,700	4,200	78,200	18	1,700	18,600	9	12,000	59,600	20
1972 . . .	14,000	4,300	80,900	17	1,700	19,100	9	12,300	61,800	20
1973 . . .	14,300	4,500	83,700	17	1,800	20,000	9	12,500	63,700	20
1974 . . .	13,500	4,000	85,400	16	1,700	19,900	9	11,800	65,500	18
1975 . . .	13,000	3,900	84,100	15	1,600	18,300	9	11,400	65,800	17
1976 . . .	12,500	4,100	86,900	14	1,700	19,000	9	10,800	67,900	16
1977 . . .	12,900	4,300	90,000	14	1,800	19,700	9	11,100	70,300	16
1978 . . .	13,100	4,500	93,800	14	1,800	20,400	9	11,300	73,400	15
1979 . . .	13,300	4,500	96,500	14	1,800	20,700	9	11,500	75,800	15
1980 . . .	13,000	4,500	96,800	13	1,600	19,900	8	11,400	76,900	15

Source: National Safety Council estimates (rounded) based on data from the National Center for Health Statistics, state departments of health, and state industrial commissions; numbers of workers are based on Bureau of Labor Statistics data.   ††Deaths per 100,000 workers.

†Workers are all persons gainfully employed, including owners, managers, other paid employees, the self-employed, and unpaid family workers, but excluding domestic servants. Due to changes in estimating procedures, the number of workers for 1970 and later years have been revised and are not comparable to those for earlier years.

‡Work deaths in motor-vehicle accidents.   §Comparable figures for prior years not available.

MOTOR-VEHICLE ACCIDENTS, 1980

Between 1912 and 1980, motor-vehicle deaths per 10,000 registered vehicles were reduced 91 per cent, from 33 to 3. (Mileage data were not available in 1912.) In 1912, there were 3,100 fatalities when the number of registered vehicles totalled only 950,000. In 1980, there were 52,600 fatalities, but registrations soared to 165 million.

Deaths	**52,600**
Disabling injuries	**2,000,000**
Costs	**$39.3 billion**
Motor-vehicle mileage	**1,511 billion**
Death rate per 100,000,000 vehicle miles	**3.48**
Registered vehicles in the U.S.	**164,900,000**
Licensed drivers in the U.S.	**146,000,000**

Accident totals

	Number of Accidents	Drivers (Vehicles) Involved
Fatal	47,400	68,300
Disabling injury	1,400,000	2,400,000
Property damage and nondisabling injury	16,500,000	27,300,000
Total (rounded)	17,900,000	29,800,000

Travel, deaths and death rates

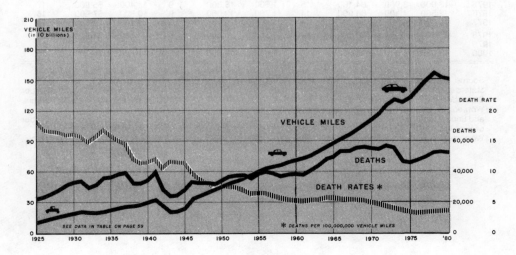

Principal classes of motor-vehicle deaths

Almost two out of three deaths in 1980 occurred in places classified as rural. In urban areas, more than one third of the victims were pedestrians; in rural areas, the victims were mostly occupants of motor vehicles. Over half of all deaths occurred in night accidents, with the proportion somewhat higher in rural areas.

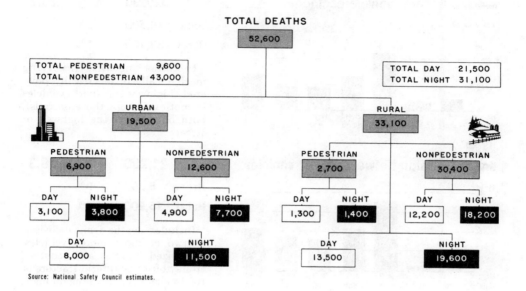

Source: National Safety Council estimates.

Trends in death rates

Motor-vehicle deaths decreased less than one half of one per cent in 1980 from 1979, vehicle mileage decreased 1 per cent, the number of vehicles increased 3 per cent, and population increased 3 per cent. The rates were as follows:

	1980	1979
Mileage death rate	3.48	3.45
Registration death rate (see chart below)	3.19	3.31
Population death rate (see chart below)	23.2	24.0

Comparing 1980 with 1979 rates, the mileage rate increased 1 per cent, the registration rate decreased 4 per cent, and the population rate decreased 3 per cent.

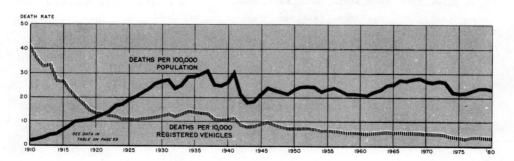

How people died in motor-vehicle accidents, 1980

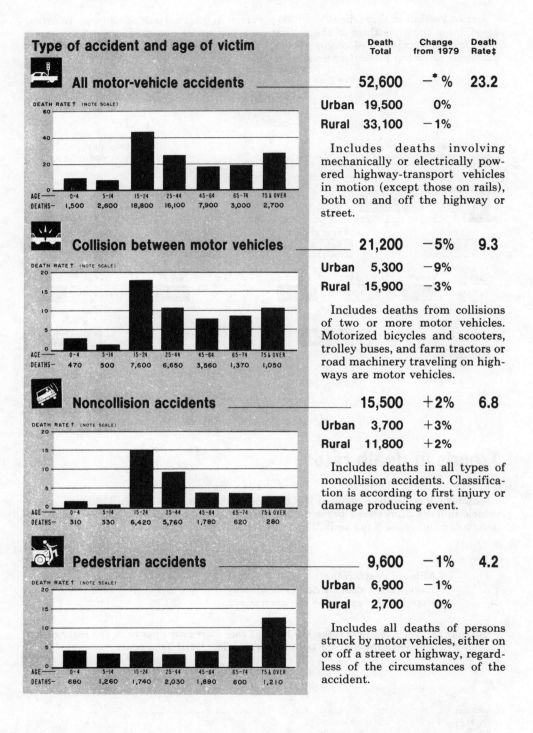

Type of accident and age of victim	Death Total	Change from 1979	Death Rate‡
All motor-vehicle accidents	**52,600**	**−*%**	**23.2**
Urban	19,500	0%	
Rural	33,100	−1%	

DEATH RATE† (NOTE SCALE)

AGE	0-4	5-14	15-24	25-44	45-64	65-74	75 & OVER
DEATHS	1,500	2,600	18,800	16,100	7,900	3,000	2,700

Includes deaths involving mechanically or electrically powered highway-transport vehicles in motion (except those on rails), both on and off the highway or street.

	Death Total	Change from 1979	Death Rate
Collision between motor vehicles	**21,200**	**−5%**	**9.3**
Urban	5,300	−9%	
Rural	15,900	−3%	

DEATH RATE† (NOTE SCALE)

AGE	0-4	5-14	15-24	25-44	45-64	65-74	75 & OVER
DEATHS	470	500	7,600	6,650	3,560	1,370	1,050

Includes deaths from collisions of two or more motor vehicles. Motorized bicycles and scooters, trolley buses, and farm tractors or road machinery traveling on highways are motor vehicles.

	Death Total	Change from 1979	Death Rate
Noncollision accidents	**15,500**	**+2%**	**6.8**
Urban	3,700	+3%	
Rural	11,800	+2%	

DEATH RATE† (NOTE SCALE)

AGE	0-4	5-14	15-24	25-44	45-64	65-74	75 & OVER
DEATHS	310	330	6,420	5,760	1,780	620	280

Includes deaths in all types of noncollision accidents. Classification is according to first injury or damage producing event.

	Death Total	Change from 1979	Death Rate
Pedestrian accidents	**9,600**	**−1%**	**4.2**
Urban	6,900	−1%	
Rural	2,700	0%	

DEATH RATE† (NOTE SCALE)

AGE	0-4	5-14	15-24	25-44	45-64	65-74	75 & OVER
DEATHS	680	1,260	1,740	2,030	1,880	800	1,210

Includes all deaths of persons struck by motor vehicles, either on or off a street or highway, regardless of the circumstances of the accident.

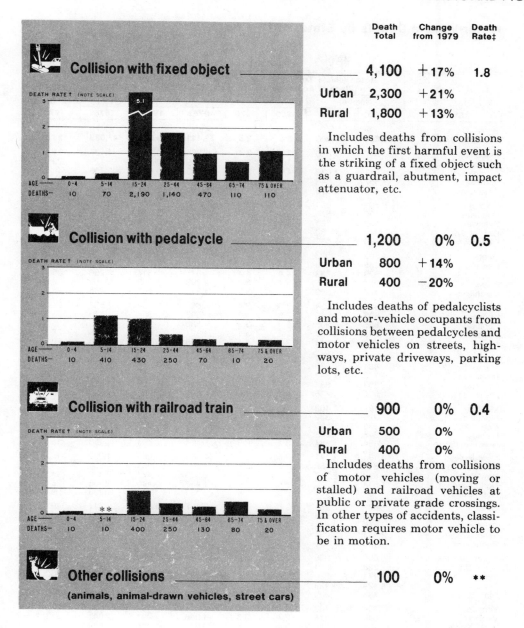

	Death Total	Change from 1979	Death Rate‡
Collision with fixed object	4,100	+17%	1.8
Urban	2,300	+21%	
Rural	1,800	+13%	

Includes deaths from collisions in which the first harmful event is the striking of a fixed object such as a guardrail, abutment, impact attenuator, etc.

DEATH RATE† (NOTE SCALE)
5.1

AGE	0-4	5-14	15-24	25-44	45-64	65-74	75 & OVER
DEATHS—	10	70	2,190	1,140	470	110	110

	Death Total	Change from 1979	Death Rate‡
Collision with pedalcycle	1,200	0%	0.5
Urban	800	+14%	
Rural	400	−20%	

Includes deaths of pedalcyclists and motor-vehicle occupants from collisions between pedalcycles and motor vehicles on streets, highways, private driveways, parking lots, etc.

DEATH RATE† (NOTE SCALE)

AGE	0-4	5-14	15-24	25-44	45-64	65-74	75 & OVER
DEATHS—	10	410	430	250	70	10	20

	Death Total	Change from 1979	Death Rate‡
Collision with railroad train	900	0%	0.4
Urban	500	0%	
Rural	400	0%	

Includes deaths from collisions of motor vehicles (moving or stalled) and railroad vehicles at public or private grade crossings. In other types of accidents, classification requires motor vehicle to be in motion.

DEATH RATE† (NOTE SCALE)
**

AGE	0-4	5-14	15-24	25-44	45-64	65-74	75 & OVER
DEATHS—	10	10	400	250	130	80	20

	Death Total	Change from 1979	Death Rate‡
Other collisions	100	0%	**

(animals, animal-drawn vehicles, street cars)

Includes deaths from motor-vehicle collisions not specified in other categories above. Most of the deaths arose out of accidents involving animals or animal-drawn vehicles. Deaths from accidents involving street cars are not yet known for 1980.

‡Deaths per 100,000 population. Rates do not add to total due to rounding.
*Less than 0.5 per cent.   **Death rate was less than 0.05.
†Deaths per 100,000 population in each age group.

Motor-Vehicle Deaths by State, 1976-1980

State	Motor-Vehicle *Traffic* Deaths (Place of Accident)				*Total* Motor-Vehicle Deaths* (Place of Residence)			
	Number		Mileage Rate†		Number			Pop. Rate†
	1980	1979	1980	1979	1978‡	1977	1976	1978
Total U.S.*	52,600	52,800	3.5	3.5	52,411	49,510	47,038	24.0
Alabama	947	1,020	3.2	3.4	1,285	1,244	1,127	34.5
Alaska	87	90	3.5	3.6	119	123	120	29.0
Arizona	947	1,030	4.9	5.3	953	894	706	40.2
Arkansas	587	548	3.6	3.4	616	549	558	28.4
California	5,489	5,503	3.5	3.4	5,754	5,275	4,766	25.8
Colorado	709	691	3.6	3.5	705	707	621	26.1
Connecticut	582	576	3.0	3.0	498	465	445	16.0
Delaware	158	121	3.9	3.0	135	115	128	23.1
Dist. of Col.	46	50	1.4	1.5	73	87	84	10.9
Florida	2,879	2,637	3.9	3.5	2,198	2,007	1,927	25.4
Georgia	1,503	1,523	3.5	3.5	1,533	1,455	1,299	30.2
Hawaii	185	205	3.9	4.3	200	143	143	22.2
Idaho	329	333	4.4	4.4	315	314	266	35.7
Illinois	1,994	2,048	3.1	3.2	2,299	2,223	2,189	20.5
Indiana	1,177	1,309	3.0	3.3	1,314	1,303	1,263	24.4
Iowa	626	654	3.3	3.4	696	659	808	24.0
Kansas	595	520	3.5	3.0	593	586	570	25.3
Kentucky	825	905	3.0	3.3	880	944	886	25.2
Louisiana	1,212	1,187	5.2	5.1	1,127	1,069	988	28.3
Maine	260	241	3.7	3.4	228	191	220	20.9
Maryland	782	700	2.8	2.5	733	682	704	17.7
Massachusetts	881	920	2.5	2.6	953	818	842	16.5
Michigan	1,772	1,847	2.8	2.8	2,153	1,999	1,982	23.4
Minnesota	863	881	3.1	3.2	983	890	826	24.4
Mississippi	697	716	4.1	4.2	868	761	690	36.0
Missouri	1,191	1,162	3.5	3.4	1,220	1,188	1,243	25.2
Montana	325	332	4.9	5.0	270	298	292	34.6
Nebraska	396	330	3.5	2.9	375	372	392	23.9
Nevada	346	365	5.9	6.2	289	219	185	43.4
New Hampshire	194	184	3.1	2.9	161	151	153	18.5
New Jersey	1,191	1,141	2.4	2.3	1,181	1,085	1,052	16.1
New Mexico	615	650	5.5	5.7	604	563	536	49.7
New York	2,619	2,377	3.4	3.1	2,628	2,471	2,310	14.8
North Carolina	1,514	1,522	3.6	3.6	1,498	1,440	1,566	26.9
North Dakota	151	127	2.9	2.4	193	191	203	29.6
Ohio	2,033	2,281	2.8	3.1	2,107	1,861	1,917	19.6
Oklahoma	972	869	3.7	3.2	970	899	871	34.1
Oregon	646	675	3.3	3.5	737	680	636	30.1
Pennsylvania	2,114	2,204	3.0	3.1	2,200	2,147	2,071	18.7
Rhode Island	128	125	2.2	2.1	127	159	144	13.6
South Carolina	859	900	3.6	3.7	911	954	809	31.4
South Dakota	228	211	4.1	3.8	196	214	238	28.4
Tennessee	1,171	1,236	3.5	3.6	1,289	1,232	1,164	29.7
Texas	4,424	4,429	4.1	3.9	3,942	3,618	3,201	30.2
Utah	335	330	3.5	3.4	385	333	286	29.2
Vermont	134	163	3.7	4.4	113	101	92	23.2
Virginia	1,045	1,014	2.7	2.6	1,086	1,191	1,041	21.0
Washington	985	1,032	3.4	3.5	1,052	988	848	27.7
West Virginia	539	532	4.7	4.6	490	503	492	26.3
Wisconsin	985	997	3.0	3.0	990	948	945	21.1
Wyoming	244	244	5.2	5.1	187	201	196	44.0

Source: Motor-Vehicle *Traffic* Deaths from state traffic authorities; *Total* Motor-Vehicle Deaths from National Center for Health Statistics.

*Includes both traffic and nontraffic motor-vehicle deaths. See definitions of traffic and nontraffic accidents on inside of back cover.

†The mileage death rate is deaths per 100,000,000 vehicle miles; the population death rate is deaths per 100,000 population. 1980 mileage death rates are National Safety Council estimates.

‡Latest year available.

Milestones in Motor-Vehicle Deaths

The first motor-vehicle death in the United States is reported to have occurred in New York City on September 14, 1899. The victim, Mr. H. H. Bliss, was struck by an electric cab when he stepped off a trolley car and turned to assist a woman to alight. The world's first motor-vehicle death probably occurred in London, England, on August 17, 1896.

Since the first motor-vehicle death in the United States, about 2,340,000 persons have died in motor-vehicle accidents through the end of 1980. Based on historical figures, the 1,000,000th motor-vehicle death occurred sometime during 1952. The 2,000,000th motor-vehicle death occurred in early 1974.

If the current annual trend in motor-vehicle deaths continues, the 3,000,000th motor-vehicle death will probably occur in the early 1990's.

Motor-Vehicle Deaths by Nation

Death totals of different nations must be compared cautiously because of differences in the volume and kinds of traffic, numbers of vehicles, population density, definitions of deaths, and other factors. (Certain definition differences are stated in the footnote.) The population rates shown provide one basis for adjustment but are not as useful as rates based on mileage, which are not available for all countries, or on vehicle registrations, which are not comparable.

The 1977 mileage death rate of 3.4 deaths per 100,000,000 vehicle miles for the United States was the lowest among twelve selected countries of the world, according to data compiled by the Motor Vehicle Manufacturers Association of the U.S., Inc. Britain recorded a death rate of 4.3 in 1977, second among leading nations. The death rate for France was 8.1 and Italy had a rate of 6.4 in 1977. Belgium's death rate of 10.0 was the highest recorded of the selected countries.

Motor-Vehicle Deaths and Death Rates by Nation

Nation	Year	Deaths	Rate*	Nation	Year	Deaths	Rate*
Egypt	1972	675	1.9	Puerto Rico	1975	509	16.3
Peru	1972	727	5.0	East Germany	1976	2,746	16.4
Paraguay	1977	161	5.4	Netherlands	1978	2,323	16.7
Nicaragua	1978	168	7.0	Ireland	1977	585	17.8
Uruguay	1978	207	7.2	Finland	1974	846	18.0
Dominican Rep.	1978	398	7.8	Czechoslovakia	1974	2,741	18.7
Guatemala	1971	437	8.3	Ecuador	1974	1,350	19.4
Japan	1978	12,030	10.5	Hungary	1978	2,111	19.8
Chile	1978	1,152	10.6	Switzerland	1979	1,260	20.0
Norway	1978	463	11.4	Greece	1978	1,960	20.9
Poland	1971	3,969	12.1	Costa Rica	1978	455	21.4
Sweden	1979	1,000	12.1	Italy	1974	12,140†	21.9
Spain	1974	4,751‡	13.6	New Zealand	1978	688	22.0
England, Wales	1978	6,720	13.7	N. Ireland	1978	345	22.4
Israel	1978	514	13.9	Canada	1977	5,255**	22.6
Denmark	1979	734	14.3	West Germany	1978	14,138	23.1
Thailand	1978	6,421	14.3	France	1976	12,307††	23.2
Bulgaria	1979	1,268	14.4	**United States**	**1978**	**52,411**	**24.0**
Argentina	1978	3,853	14.6				
Salvador	1974	568	14.6	Belgium	1976	2,463†	25.1
Cuba	1977	1,484	14.7	Australia	1978	3,840	27.0
Mexico	1974	8,887**	15.3	Austria	1979	2,099	28.0
Panama	1974	250	15.5	Portugal	1975	3,299	34.9
Scotland	1978	836	16.1	Venezuela	1978	4,822	36.7

Source: World Health Organization.   *Deaths per 100,000 population.
DEATH DEFINITION: In general, deaths are included if they occur within thirty days after the accident, but other time periods are used as follows: **one year, ††three days, ‡twenty-four hours, †at accident scene only.

Total public deaths

(Excluding motor-vehicle and persons at work)

Between 1912 and 1980, accidental public deaths per 100,000 population were reduced 70 per cent from 30 to 9. In 1912, an estimated 28,000 to 30,000 persons died in public accidents (other than motor-vehicle). In 1980, with the population more than doubled, and total recreational activity greatly increased, only 21,000 persons died in public accidents.

Year	Total Public	Transport**					Nontransport				
		Total*	Air	Water		Rail††	Total*	Falls	Drowning	Firearms	Fires, Burns
				Drowning	Other						
1950	15,000	3,950	1,050	1,000	100	1,450	11,050	2,750	3,750	1,150	500
1955	15,500	3,600	1,300	1,000	100	950	11,900	3,200	4,300	950	450
1956	16,000	3,450	1,200	1,050	100	900	12,550	3,700‡	4,100	1,000	450
1957	17,500	3,400	1,100	1,100	100	900	14,100	4,000	4,400	1,100	600
1958	16,500	3,400	1,150	1,150	100	800	13,100	3,600	4,300	1,000	750‡
1959	16,500	3,200	1,050	1,100	100	750	13,300	3,700	4,200	1,050	650
1960	17,000	3,150	1,150	1,000‡	100	700	13,850	3,700	4,350	1,100	750
1961	16,500	3,050	1,050	1,000	100	700	13,450	3,600	4,300	1,000	700
1962	17,000	3,100	1,100	1,000	100	700	13,900	3,900	4,200	1,000	750
1963	17,500	2,900	1,000	1,000	100	600	14,600	4,300	4,100	1,000	800
1964	18,500	3,200	1,200	1,000	100	700	15,300	4,800	4,400	900	800
1965	19,500	3,200	1,200	1,000	100	700	16,300	5,300	4,400	900	800
1966	20,000	3,300	1,200	1,100	100	700	16,700	5,400	4,600	1,000	800
1967	20,500	3,400	1,400	1,000	100	700	17,100	5,500	4,600	1,100	800
1968	21,500	3,500	1,500	1,100‡	100	600	18,000	5,400	4,800	900	700‡
1969	22,500	3,600	1,400	1,300	100	600	18,900	5,100	5,000	800	700
1970	23,500	3,300	1,200	1,200	100	600	20,200	5,000	5,200	900	700
1971	23,500	3,100	1,200	1,100	100	500	20,400	5,100	4,800	900	700
1972	23,500	3,200	1,200	1,200	100	500	20,300	5,100	4,900	900	700
1973	24,500	3,400	1,200	1,300		600	20,100	5,000	5,700	1,000	700
1974	23,000	3,200	1,200	1,200	100	500	19,800	5,000	5,100	900	600
1975	23,000	3,000	1,100	1,200	100	400	20,000	4,800	5,200	900	600
1976	21,500	2,800	1,100	1,000	100	400	18,700	4,800	4,400	800	600
1977	22,200	2,900	1,200	1,000	100	400	19,300	4,700	4,700	700	800
1978	22,000	3,200	1,400	1,100	100	400	18,800	4,600	4,600	700	600
1979	21,500	3,400	1,600	1,100	100	400	18,100	4,000	4,300	600	500
1980	21,000	2,800	1,200	900	100	400	18,200	3,900	4,400	600	600

Source: National Safety Council estimates based on data from National Center for Health Statistics and state health departments.
*Includes some deaths not shown separately.   ††Includes subways and elevateds.
**Transport is a primary classification but each class includes deaths from falls, drowning, burns, etc., occurring in connection with each type of transport.
‡Data for this year and subsequent years not comparable with previous years due to classification changes.

Joggers. Only a small portion of the more than 9,000 pedestrian deaths and tens of thousands of pedestrian injuries every year involve joggers. Yet the increasing popularity of the sport prompted a recent study by the Insurance Institute for Highway Safety of 60 jogger-motor vehicle collisions from mid-August 1978 to mid-August 1979. These were identified from newspaper accounts and supplemented by police reports where possible.

The 60 collisions involved 65 joggers in 28 states. Sixty-six per cent of the victims were male and 44 per cent were 15 to 24 years old. Thirty of the joggers were killed and 35 were nonfatally injured. By light condition, less than half of the collisions occurred in daylight—35 per cent of the fatals and 53 percent of the nonfatals. About half of all collisions took place between 3 p.m. and 9 p.m.

Responsibility for the collision was assigned primarily to the driver in 27 per cent of the cases and to the jogger in 31 per cent. In another 31 per cent of the cases, both driver and jogger contributed, leaving 11 per cent with undetermined responsibility. Joggers were traveling alongside the roadway "with traffic" in 53 per cent of the total, "against traffic" in 24 per cent, with the remainder running across the road (12 per cent) or other (11 per cent).

HOME ACCIDENTS, 1980

Between 1912 and 1980, accidental home deaths per 100,000 population were reduced 64 per cent from 28 to 10. In 1912, when there were 21 million homes, an estimated 26,000 to 28,000 persons were killed in home accidents. In 1980, with 79 million homes and a population more than double the earlier total, accidental home deaths were only 23,000.

	Deaths	Deaths per 100,000 Persons	Disabling Injuries‡
Total	**23,000**	**10.1**	**3,400,000†**
In urban homes*	**22,300**	**10.1**	**3,300,000**
In farm homes	**700**	**11.5**	**120,000**

*Includes rural nonfarm homes.
‡The National Health Survey indicates about 19,800,000 additional less serious injuries annually   †Rounded sum.

The injury total of 3,400,000 means that one person in 67 in the U.S. was disabled one or more days by injuries received in home accidents in 1980. About 90,000 of these injuries resulted in some permanent impairment.

The cost of home accidents in 1980 was at least $8.9 billion. This figure includes wage losses of $3.5 billion, medical expenses of $2.3 billion, fire losses of $3.0 billion and insurance administrative costs of $100 million.

Trends in home accidental deaths and standardized rates

The 1980 standardized death rate† of 8.6 was 63 per cent below the rate for 1935. Deaths from home accidents in 1980 numbered about 19 per cent below 1935, after adjusting for the 1948 change in classification. Decreases of more than 50 per cent occurred in the 0 to 4 and 5 to 14 year age groups. Deaths for those 15 to 24 years old, however, increased more than 60 per cent since 1935. The age distribution of the population has also changed since 1935, especially for the group 65 and over, who now comprise about 11 per cent of the population compared to 6 per cent in 1935. The death rate per 100,000 population for this age group has decreased about three fourths.

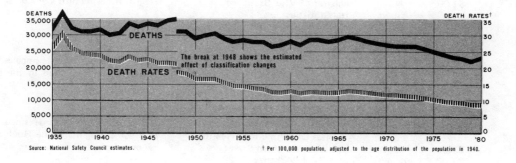

Source: National Safety Council estimates.   † Per 100,000 population, adjusted to the age distribution of the population in 1940.

Where to Write for Birth and Death Records

United States and Outlying Areas

An offical certificate of every birth and death should be on file in the locality where the event occurred. These certificates are prepared by physicians, funeral directors, other professional attendants, or hospital authorities. The Federal Government does not maintain files or indexes of these records. They are permanently filed in the central vital statistics office of the State, independent city, or outlying area where the event occurred.

To obtain a certified copy of a certificate, write or go to the vital statistics office in the State or area where the birth or death occurred. The offices are listed below.

Send a money order or certified check when writing for a certified copy because the office cannot refund cash lost in transit. Fees listed are subject to change.

Type or print all names and addresses in the letter. Give the following facts:

1. **Full name of person whose record is being requested.**
2. **Sex and race.**
3. **Parents' names, including maiden name of mother.**
4. **Month, day, and year of birth or death.**
5. **Place of birth or death (city or town, county, and State; and name of hospital, if any).**
6. **Purpose for which copy is needed.**
7. **Relationship to person whose record is being requested.**

Place of birth or death	Cost of full copy	Cost of short form	Address of vital statistics office	Remarks
Alabama	$3.00	Not issued	Division of Vital Statistics State Department of Public Health Montgomery, Alabama 36130	State office has records since January 1908. Additional copies at same time are $1.00 each. Fee for special searches is $3.00 per hour.
Alaska	$3.00	$3.00	State of Alaska Department of Health and Social Services Bureau of Vital Statistics Pouch H-02G Juneau, Alaska 99811	State office has records since 1913.
American Samoa	$1.00	Not issued	Registrar of Vital Statistics Vital Statistics Government of American Samoa Pago Pago, American Samoa 96799	Registrar has records since before 1900.
Arizona.	$2.00	$2.00	Division of Vital Records State Department of Health P.O. Box 3887 Phoenix, Arizona 85030	State office has records since July 1909 and abstracts of records filed in the counties before then.
Arkansas.			Division of Vital Records Arkansas Department of Health 4815 West Markham Street Little Rock, Arkansas 72201	State office has records since February 1914 and some original Little Rock and Fort Smith records from 1881.
Birth	$2.00	Not issued		
Death	$3.00			

NOTE: Births occurring before birth registration was required or births not registered when they occurred may have been filed as "delayed birth registrations." Keep this in mind when seeking a copy of a record.

From "Where to Write for Birth and Death Records, United States and Outlying Areas," U.S. Department of Health, Education, and Welfare, Public Health Service, National Center for Health Statistics, 1979.

Place of birth or death	Cost of full copy	Cost of short form	Address of vital statistics office	Remarks
California	$3.00	$3.00	Vital Statistics Branch Department of Health Services 410 N Street Sacramento, California 95814	State office has records since July 1905. For earlier records, write to County Recorder in county where event occurred.
Canal Zone.	Not issued	$2.00	Panama Canal Commission Vital Statistics Clerk APO Miami 34011	Records available from May 1904 to September 1979.
Colorado	$2.00	$2.00	Records and Statistics Section Colorado Department of Health 4210 East 11th Avenue Denver, Colorado 80220	State office has death records since 1900 and birth records since 1910. State office also has birth records for some counties for years before 1910. $2.00 fee is for search of files and one copy of record if found.
Connecticut	$2.00	$1.00	Public Health Statistics Section State Department of Health 79 Elm Street Hartford, Connecticut 06115	State office has records since July 1897. For earlier records, write to Registrar of Vital Statistics in town or city where event occurred.
Delaware	$2.50	$2.50	Bureau of Vital Statistics Division of Public Health Department of Health and Social Services State Health Building Dover, Delaware 19901	State office has records for 1861 to 1863 and since 1881 but no records for 1864 to 1880.
District of Columbia	$1.00	Not issued	Vital Records Section 615 Pennsylvania Avenue NW. Washington, D.C. 20004	Office has death records since 1855 and birth records since 1871, but no death records were filed during the Civil War.
Florida	$2.00	$2.00	Department of Health and Rehabilitative Services Center Operations Services Office of Vital Statistics P.O. Box 210 Jacksonville, Florida 32231	State office has some birth records since April 1865 and some death records since August 1877. The majority of records date from January 1917. (If the exact date is unknown, the fee is $2.00 for the first year searched and $1.00 for each additional year up to a maximum of $25.00. Fee includes one copy of record if found.)
Georgia.	$3.00	$3.00	Vital Records Unit State Department of Human Resources Room 217-H 47 Trinity Avenue SW. Atlanta, Georgia 30334	State office has records since January 1919. For earlier records in Atlanta or Savannah, write to County Health Department in county where event occurred. Additional copies of same record ordered at same time are $1.00 each.
Guam.	$1.00	$1.00	Office of Vital Statistics Department of Public Health and Social Services Government of Guam P.O. Box 2816 Agana, Guam, M.I. 96910	Office has records since October 26, 1901.
Hawaii	$2.00	$2.00	Research and Statistics Office State Department of Health P.O. Box 3378 Honolulu, Hawaii 96801	State office has records since 1853.

Place of birth or death	Cost of full copy	Cost of short form	Address of vital statistics office	Remarks
Idaho	$2.00	$2.00	Bureau of Vital Statistics State Department of Health and Welfare Statehouse Boise, Idaho 83720	State office has records since 1911. For records from 1907 to 1911, write to County Recorder in county where event occurred.
Illinois	$3.00	$3.00	Office of Vital Records State Department of Public Health 535 West Jefferson Street Springfield, Illinois 62761	State office has records since January 1916. For earlier records and for copies of State records since January 1916, write to County Clerk in county where event occurred. ($3.00 fee is for search of files and one copy of record if found. Additional copies of same record ordered at same time are $2.00 each.)
Indiana	$3.00	Not issued	Division of Vital Records State Board of Health 1330 West Michigan Street Indianapolis, Indiana 46206.	State office has birth records since October 1907 and death records since 1900. For earlier records, write to Health Officer in city or county where event occurred. Additional copies of same record ordered at same time are $1.00 each.
Iowa	$2.00	$2.00	Division of Records and Statistics State Department of Health Des Moines, Iowa 50319	State office has records since July 1880.
Kansas	$3.00	$3.00	Bureau of Registration and Health Statistics Kansas State Department of Health and Environment 6700 South Topeka Avenue Topeka, Kansas 66620	State office has records since July 1911. For earlier records, write to County Clerk in county were event occurred. Additional copies of same record ordered at same time are $2.00 each.
Kentucky	$4.00	$4.00	Office of Vital Statistics Department for Human Resources 275 East Main Street Frankfort, Kentucky 40621	State office has records since January 1911 and some records for the cities of Louisville, Lexington, Covington, and Newport before then.
Louisiana	$3.00	$2.00	Division of Vital Records Office of Health Services and Environmental Quality P.O. Box 60630 New Orleans, Louisiana 70160	State office has records since July 1914. Birth records for City of New Orleans available from 1790, and death records from 1803.
Maine	$2.00	$2.00	Office of Vital Records Human Services Building State House Augusta, Maine 04333	State office has records since 1892. For earlier records, write to the municipality where event occurred.
Maryland	$2.00	$2.00	Division of Vital Records State Department of Health and Mental Hygiene State Office Building P.O. Box 13146 201 West Preston Street Baltimore, Maryland 21203	State office has records since August 1898. Records for City of Baltimore are available from January 1875.

NOTE: Births occurring before birth registration was required or births not registered when they occurred may have been filed as "delayed birth registrations." Keep this in mind when seeking a copy of a record.

Place of birth or death	Cost of full copy	Cost of short form	Address of vital statistics office	Remarks
Massachusetts	$2.00	Free	Registrar of Vital Statistics Room 103 McCormack Building 1 Ashburton Place Boston, Massachusetts 02108	State office has records, except for Boston, since 1841. For earlier records, write to the City or Town Clerk in place where event occurred. Earliest Boston records available in this office are for 1848.
Michigan	$3.00	$3.00	Office of Vital and Health Statistics Michigan Department of Public Health 3500 North Logan Street Lansing, Michigan 48914	State office has records since 1867. Copies of records since 1867 may also be obtained from County Clerk in county where event occurred. Detroit records may be obtained from the City Health Department for births occurring since 1893 and for deaths since 1897.
Minnesota	$3.00	$3.00	Minnesota Department of Health Section of Vital Statistics 717 Delaware Street SE. Minneapolis, Minnesota 55440	State office has records since January 1908. Copies of earlier records may be obtained from Clerk of District Court in county where event occurred or from the Minneapolis or St. Paul City Health Department if the event occurred in either city.
Mississippi	$6.00	$3.00	Vital Records State Board of Health P.O. Box 1700 Jackson, Mississippi 39205	State office has records since 1912. Copies of death certificates and full copies of birth certificates obtained within 1 year after the event are $3.00. Additional copies of same record ordered at same time are $1.00 each.
Missouri	$1.00	$1.00	Division of Health Bureau of Vital Records State Department of Health and Welfare Jefferson City, Missouri 65101	State office has records since January 1910. If event occurred in St. Louis (city), St. Louis County, or Kansas City before 1910, write to the City or County Health Department; copies of these records are $2.00 each.
Montana	$2.00	$2.00	Bureau of Records and Statistics State Department of Health and Environmental Sciences Helena, Montana 59601	State office has records since late 1907.
Nebraska	$3.00	$3.00	Bureau of Vital Statistics State Department of Health 301 Centennial Mall South P.O. Box 95007 Lincoln, Nebraska 68509	State office has records since late 1904. If birth occurred before then, write the State office for information.
Nevada	$2.00	$1.00	Division of Health - Vital Statistics Capitol Complex Carson City, Nevada 89710	State office has records since July 1911. For earlier records, write to County Recorder in county where event occurred.
New Hampshire	$3.00	$3.00	Bureau of Vital Records Health and Welfare Building Hazen Drive Concord, New Hampshire 03301	State office has some records since 1640. Copies of records may be obtained from State office or from City or Town Clerk in place where event occurred. ($3.00 fee is for search of files and copy of record if found.)
New Jersey	$2.00	$2.00	State Department of Health Bureau of Vital Statistics P.O. Box 1540 Trenton, New Jersey 08625	State office has records since June 1878. ($2.00 fee is for search of files and one copy of record if found. Additional copies of same record ordered at same time are $1.00 each. If the exact date is unknown, the fee is an additional $0.50 per year searched.)

Place of birth or death	Cost of full copy	Cost of short form	Address of vital statistics office	Remarks
			Archives and History Bureau State Library Division State Department of Education Trenton, New Jersey 08625	For records from May 1848 to May 1878, write State Department of Education.
New Mexico	$2.00	$2.00	Vital Statistics Bureau New Mexico Health Services Division P.O. Box 968 Santa Fe, New Mexico 87503	State office has records since 1920 and delayed records since 1880. ($2.00 fee is for search of files and one copy of record if found.)
New York (except New York City) . . .	$2.00	$2.00	Bureau of Vital Records State Department of Health Empire State Plaza Tower Building Albany, New York 12237	State office has records since 1880. For records before 1914 in Albany, Buffalo, and Yonkers or before 1880 in any other city, write to Registrar of Vital Statistics in city where event occurred. For the rest of the State, except New York City, write to State office.

New York City (all boroughs) . . . .
    Birth . . . .
    Death . . . .
	
	$3.00
	$2.50
		
		$3.00
		Not issued
			Bureau of Vital Records
			Department of Health of New York City
			125 Worth Street
			New York, New York 10013
				Office has records since 1898. Additional copies of birth records ordered at same time are $1.50 each. For Old City of New York (Manhattan and part of the Bronx) birth and death records for 1865-1897, write to Municipal Archives and Records Retention Center, New York Public Library, 23 Park Row, New York, N.Y. 10038.

North Carolina	$3.00	$3.00	Department of Human Resources Division of Health Services Vital Records Branch P.O. Box 2091 Raleigh, North Carolina 27602	State office has records since October 1913 and some earlier delayed records.
North Dakota	$2.00	$2.00	Division of Vital Records State Department of Health Office of Statistical Services Bismarck, North Dakota 58505	State office has some records since July 1893; years from 1894 to 1920 are incomplete.
Ohio	$2.00	$2.00	Division of Vital Statistics Ohio Department of Health G-20 Ohio Departments Building 65 South Front Street Columbus, Ohio 43215	State office has records since December 20, 1908. For earlier records, write to Probate Court in county where event occurred.
Oklahoma	$2.00	$2.00	Vital Records Section State Department of Health Northeast 10th Street & Stonewall P.O. Box 53551 Oklahoma City, Oklahoma 73105	State office has records since October 1908.
Oregon	$5.00	$5.00	Oregon State Health Division Vital Statistics Section P.O. Box 116 Portland, Oregon 97207	State office has records since July 1903 and some earlier records for the City of Portland since approximately 1880. Additional copies of same record ordered at same time are $2.00 each.

NOTE: Births occurring before birth registration was required or births not registered when they occurred may have been filed as "delayed birth registrations." Keep this in mind when seeking a copy of a record.

Place of birth or death	Cost of full copy	Cost of short form	Address of vital statistics office	Remarks
Pennsylvania.	$2.00	$2.00	Division of Vital Statistics State Department of Health Central Building 101 South Mercer Street P.O. Box 1528 New Castle, Pennsylvania 16103	State office has records since January 1906. For earlier records, write to Register of Wills, Orphans Court, in county seat where event occurred. Persons born in Pittsburgh from 1870 to 1905 or in Allegheny City, now part of Pittsburgh, from 1882 to 1905 should write to Office of Biostatistics, Pittsburgh Health Department, City-County Building, Pittsburgh, Pa. 15219. For events occurring in City of Philadelphia from 1860 to 1915, write to Vital Statistics, Philadelphia Department of Public Health, City Hall Annex, Philadelphia, Pa. 19107.
Puerto Rico	$0.50	$0.50	Division of Demographic Registry and Vital Statistics Department of Health San Juan, Puerto Rico 00908	Central office has records since July 22, 1931. Copies of earlier records may be obtained by writing to local Registrar (Registrador Demografico) in municipality where event occurred or writing to central office for information.
Rhode Island	$2.00	$2.00	Division of Vital Statistics State Department of Health Room 101, Cannon Building 75 Davis Street Providence, Rhode Island 02908	State office had records since 1853. For earlier records, write to Town Clerk in town where event occurred.
South Carolina	$3.00	$3.00	Division of Vital Records Bureau of Health Measurement Office of Vital Records and Public Health Services Department of Health Analysis and Environmental Control 2600 Bull Street Columbia, South Carolina 29201	State office has records since January 1915. City of Charleston births from 1877 and deaths from 1821 on file at Charleston County Health Department. Ledger entries of Florence City births and deaths from 1895 to 1914 on file at Florence County Health Department. Ledger entries of Newberry City births and deaths from late 1800's on file at Newberry County Health Department. These are the only early records obtainable.
South Dakota	$2.00	$2.00	State Department of Health Health Statistics Program Joe Foss Office Building Pierre, South Dakota 57501	State office has records since July 1905 and access to other records for some events which occurred before then.
Tennessee	$3.00	$3.00	Division of Vital Records State Department of Public Health Cordell Hull Building Nashville, Tennessee 37219	State office has birth records for entire State since January 1914, for Nashville since June 1881, for Knoxville since July 1881, and for Chattanooga since January 1882. State office has death records for entire State since January 1914, for Nashville since July 1874, for Knoxville since July 1887, and for Chattanooga since March 6, 1872. Birth and death enumeration records by school district are available for July 1908-June 1912. For Memphis birth records from April 1874-December 1887 and November 1898-January 1, 1914, and for Memphis death records from May 1848- January 1, 1914, write to Memphis-Shelby County Health Department, Division of Vital Records, Memphis, Tenn. 38105.

Place of birth or death	Cost of full copy	Cost of short form	Address of vital statistics office	Remarks
Texas	$3.00	$3.00	Bureau of Vital Statistics Texas Department of Health 1100 West 49th Street Austin, Texas 78756	State office has records since 1903.
Trust Territory of the Pacific Islands	$0.25 plus $0.10 per 100 words	$0.25 plus $0.10 per 100 words	Clerk of Court in district where event occurred. (If not sure of district in which event occurred, write to Director of Medical Services, Department of Medical Services, Saipan, Mariana Islands 96950, to have inquiry referred to the correct district.)	Courts have records since November 21, 1952. Beginning 1950, a few records have been filed with the Hawaii Bureau of Vital Statistics.
Utah	$3.50	$3.00	Bureau of Vital Statistics Utah State Department of Health 150 West North Temple P.O. Box 2500 Salt Lake City, Utah 84110	State office has records since 1905. If event occurred from 1890 to 1904 in Salt Lake City or Ogden, write to City Board of Health. For records elsewhere in the State from 1898 to 1904, write to County Clerk in county where event occurred.
Vermont	$2.00	$2.00	Town or City Clerk of town where birth or death occurred.	
	$2.00	$2.00	Public Health Statistics Division Department of Health 115 Colchester Avenue Burlington, Vermont 05401	For information on vital statistics laws, how to correct a record, etc., write to Public Health Statistics Division, Department of Health.
Virginia.	$3.00	$3.00	Bureau of Vital Records and Health Statistics State Department of Health James Madison Building P.O. Box 1000 Richmond, Virginia 23208	State office has records from January 1853 to December 1896 and since June 14, 1912. For records between those dates, write to the Health Department in the city where event occurred.
Virgin Islands (U.S.) St. Croix	$2.00	Not issued	Registrar of Vital Statistics Charles Harwood Memorial Hospital St. Croix, Virgin Islands 00820	Registrar has birth and death records on file since 1840.
St. Thomas and St. John.	$2.00	Not issued	Registrar of Vital Statistics Charlotte Amalie St. Thomas, Virgin Islands 00802	Registrar has birth records on file since July 1906 and death records since January 1906.
Washington	$3.00	$3.00	Vital Records LB-11 P.O. Box 9709 Olympia, Washington 98504	State office has records since July 1907. For Seattle, Spokane, and Tacoma a copy may also be obtained from the City Health Department. For records before July 1907, write to Auditor in county where event occurred.
West Virginia	$2.00	Not issued	Divsion of Vital Statistics State Department of Health State Office Building No. 3 Charleston, West Virginia 25305	State office has records since January 1917. For earlier records, write to Clerk of County Court in county where event occurred.

NOTE: Births occurring before birth registration was required or births not registered when they occurred may have been filed as "delayed birth registrations." Keep this in mind when seeking a copy of a record.

Place of birth or death	Cost of full copy	Cost of short form	Address of vital statistics office	Remarks
Wisconsin	$4.00	$4.00	Bureau of Health Statistics Wisconsin Division of Health P.O. Box 309 Madison, Wisconsin 53701	State office has some records since 1814; early years are incomplete.
Wyoming.	$2.00	$2.00	Vital Records Services Division of Health and Medical Services Hathaway Building Cheyenne, Wyoming 82002	State office has records since July 1909.

Vital Statistics, Canada

Item / Rubrique		Canada	New-found-land / Terre-Neuve	Prince Edward Island / Île-du-Prince-Édouard	Nova Scotia / Nouvelle-Écosse	New Brunswick / Nouveau-Brunswick	Québec	Ontario	Manitoba	Saskat-chewan	Alberta	British Columbia / Colombie-Britan-nique	Yukon	Northwest Territories / Territoires du Nord-Ouest
Population ('000) June 1 – 1er juin ('000)	1978	23,483	569	122	841	695	6,283	8,445	1,033	948	1,952	2,530	22	44
	1977	23,291	562	120	835	686	6,283	8,374	1,031	937	1,900	2,498	22	43
Live births – Naissances vivantes	1978	358,852	10,480[1]	1,985	12,548	10,790	94,860[2]	120,964	16,397	16,550	35,396	37,231	447	1,204
	1977	361,400	11,110[1]	1,969	12,374	11,515	95,690[2]	122,757	16,716	16,547	34,406	36,691	433	1,192
Rates – Taux	1978	15.3	18.4[1]	16.3	14.9	15.5	15.1[2]	14.3	15.9	17.5	18.1	14.7	20.3	27.4
	1977	15.5	19.8[1]	16.4	14.8	16.8	15.2[2]	14.7	16.2	17.7	18.1	14.7	20.1	27.5
Born in hospital – Nés à l'hôpital	1978	..	..	1,980	12,525	10,764	..	120,514	16,355	16,478	35,148	36,912	447	1,181
	1977	..	..	1,965	12,347	11,494	..	122,324	16,674	16,471	34,273	36,364	428	1,172
Percentage born in hospital – Pourcentage nés à l'hôpital	1978	..	..	99.7	99.8	99.7	..	99.6	99.7	99.5	99.2	99.1	100.0	98.0
	1977	..	..	99.8	99.8	99.8	..	99.6	99.7	99.5	99.6	99.1	98.8	98.3
Deaths – Décès	1978	168,179	3,115	994	6,877	5,183	43,552	61,116	8,297	7,749	11,944	19,058	89	205
	1977	167,498	3,138	1,046	6,963	5,185	43,459	61,425	8,178	7,594	11,609	18,596	105	200
Rate – Taux	1978	7.2	5.5	8.1	8.2	7.5	6.9	7.2	8.0	8.2	6.1	7.5	4.1	4.7
	1977	7.2	5.6	8.7	8.3	7.6	6.9	7.3	7.9	8.1	6.1	7.4	4.9	4.6
Infant deaths – Mortalité infantile	1978	4,289	128	15	149	127	1,126	1,373	225	236	405	472	5	28
	1977	4,475	107	37	143	154	1,205	1,384	277	249	383	495	6	35
Rate – Taux	1978	12.0	12.2	7.6	11.9	11.8	11.9	11.3	13.7	14.3	11.4	12.7	11.2	23.3
	1977	12.4	10.3	18.8	11.6	13.4	12.4	11.3	16.6	15.0	11.1	13.5	13.9	29.4
Neonatal deaths – Mortalité néonatale	1978	2,888	94	9	112	84	805	924	152	151	244	292	4	17
	1977	2,984	70	28	95	103	859	930	183	157	245	288	3	23
Rate – Taux	1978	8.0	9.0	4.5	8.9	7.8	8.5	7.6	9.3	9.1	6.9	7.8	8.9	14.1
	1977	8.3	6.3	14.2	7.7	9.0	8.8	7.6	11.0	9.5	7.2	8.6	7.0	19.3
Post-neonatal deaths – Mortalité post-néonatale	1978	1,401	34	6	37	43	321	449	73	85	161	180	1	11
	1977	1,491	37	9	48	51	346	454	94	92	138	207	3	12
Rate – Taux	1978	3.9	3.2	3.0	2.9	4.0	3.4	3.7	4.5	5.1	4.5	4.8	2.2	9.1
	1977	4.1	3.3	4.6	3.9	4.4	3.6	3.7	5.6	5.6	4.0	5.6	6.9	10.1

From "Vital Statistics," Vol III, Mortality, Statistics Canada, Minister of Supply and Services Canada 1980, June, 1980.

Item Rubrique		Canada	New-found-land Terre-Neuve	Prince Edward Island Île-du-Prince-Édouard	Nova Scotia Nouvelle-Écosse	New Brunswick Nouveau-Brunswick	Québec	Ontario	Manitoba	Saskat-chewan	Alberta	British Columbia Colombie-Britan-nique	Yukon	Northwest Territories Territoires du Nord-Ouest
Maternal deaths – Mortalité maternelle	1978	23	–	–	1	1	7	8	–	–	1	5	–	–
	1977	18	–	–	1	–	5	7	–	–	2	3	–	–
Rate – Taux	1978	0.6	–	–	0.8	0.9	0.7	0.7	–	–	0.3	1.3	–	–
	1977	0.5	–	–	0.8	–	0.5	0.6	–	–	0.6	0.8	–	–
Percentage deaths in hospital – Pourcentage de mortalité à l'hôpital	1978	..	..	56.8	63.0	63.4	..	67.3	71.7	69.4	69.7	76.2	48.3	48.3
	1977	..	..	59.3	62.5	65.8	..	68.7	71.9	67.5	70.9	75.4	49.6	45.3
Stillbirths – Mort-nés:														
20+ weeks gestation – semaines de gestation	1978	2,884	93	14	115	84	657	971	163	139	295	331	8	14
	1977	3,116	77	21	97	85	760	1,086	170	163	307	330	2	18
Ratio – Rapport	1978	8.0	8.9	7.1	9.2	7.8	6.9	8.0	9.9	8.4	8.3	8.9	17.9	11.6
	1977	8.6	6.9	10.7	7.8	7.4	7.9	8.8	10.2	9.9	8.9	9.0	4.6	15.1
28+ weeks gestation – semaines de gestation	1978	2,236	93	12	91	78	519	767	109	104	219	227	5	12
	1977	2,437	77	14	80	70	610	850	119	126	238	237	1	15
Ratio – Rapport	1978	6.2	8.9	6.0	7.3	7.2	5.5	6.3	6.6	6.3	6.2	6.1	11.2	10.0
	1977	6.7	6.9	7.1	6.5	6.1	6.4	6.9	7.1	7.6	6.9	6.5	2.3	12.6

[1] Adjusted for expected undercount.
[2] Adjusted for estimated overcount due to duplication.

[1] On fait un ajustement, parce que le compte était censé être trop bas.
[2] On fait un ajustement, parce que le compte était censé être trop grand à cause de la duplication.

Age-specific Death Rates, by Selected Cause and Sex, Canada, 1978

No.	Cause	Category (8th Revision) / Catégorie (8e révision)	Total	0-4 years / 0-4 ans	5-9 years / 5-9 ans	10-14 years / 10-14 ans	15-19 years / 15-19 ans	20-24 years / 20-24 ans	25-29 years / 25-29 ans	30-34 years / 30-34 ans	35-39 years / 35-39 ans
	Both sexes – Les deux sexes										
			per 100,000 population – pour 100,000 habitants								
1	**All causes**	001-E999	716.2	296.2	37.7	35.6	93.2	119.3	100.3	111.5	159.3
2	All cancer	140-209	158.4	5.5	5.0	5.0	5.9	6.3	10.1	16.7	30.5
3	Lung cancer	162	34.7	0.0	0.0	0.0	0.0	0.2	0.2	1.2	2.7
4	Breast cancer	174	14.1	0.0	0.0	0.0	0.0	0.0	0.5	2.1	5.4
5	Diabetes mellitus	250	12.4	0.2	0.0	0.2	0.0	0.5	0.7	1.7	2.4
6	Diseases of the heart	393-398, 400.1, 400.9, 402, 404, 410-414, 420-429	245.2	1.5	0.4	0.7	1.2	1.8	3.3	7.5	23.8
7	Ischemic heart diseases	410-414	215.5	0.0	0.0	0.0	0.1	0.6	1.8	5.1	19.0
8	Cerebrovascular diseases	430-438	64.7	0.7	0.4	0.3	0.7	1.1	1.9	2.6	7.0
9	Respiratory diseases	460-519	47.2	17.3	1.4	1.1	1.1	1.9	2.3	2.6	3.5
10	Influenza and pneumonia	470-474	2.2	0.3	0.1	0.0	0.2	0.1	0.0	0.0	0.1
11	Bronchitis, emphysema and asthma	466, 490-493	12.8	1.9	0.3	0.4	0.3	0.3	0.3	0.4	0.6
12	Cirrhosis of liver	571	12.1	0.3	0.0	0.0	0.1	0.2	0.9	2.4	6.3
13	All accidents	E800-E999	68.5	31.7	22.6	21.6	74.1	95.3	69.7	64.6	63.6
14	Suicide	E950-E959	14.8	0.0	0.1	1.4	12.0	22.2	22.1	19.0	18.1
	Male – Masculin										
			per 100,000 population – pour 100,000 habitants								
15	**All causes**	001-E999	831.9	330.5	44.9	46.3	137.3	183.4	146.0	152.1	208.2
16	All cancer	140-209	178.6	5.9	5.1	6.6	7.1	8.6	11.5	16.8	26.9
17	Lung cancer	162	55.4	0.0	0.0	0.0	0.0	0.4	0.4	1.4	3.9
18	Breast cancer	174	0.2	0.0	0.0	0.0	0.0	0.0	0.0	0.0	0.0
19	Diabetes mellitus	250	11.6	0.2	0.0	0.3	0.0	0.4	0.9	2.3	3.3
20	Diseases of the heart	393-398, 400.1, 400.9, 402, 404, 410-414, 420-429	288.8	1.3	0.5	1.1	1.1	1.9	4.8	11.9	37.5
21	Ischemic heart diseases	410-414	259.0	0.0	0.0	0.0	0.2	0.8	3.1	8.6	30.9
22	Cerebrovascular diseases	430-438	60.0	0.8	0.4	0.5	0.4	1.1	2.0	2.5	7.6
23	Respiratory diseases	460-519	61.7	19.9	1.3	1.8	1.3	1.9	2.5	2.6	3.5
24	Influenza and pneumonia	470-474	2.0	0.3	0.1	0.0	0.2	0.0	0.2	0.0	0.1
25	Bronchitis, emphysema and asthma	466, 490-493	19.2	2.1	0.4	0.6	0.5	0.3	0.2	0.4	0.3
26	Cirrhosis of liver	571	16.6	0.1	0.0	0.0	0.2	0.4	0.6	3.1	8.8
27	All accidents	E800-E999	98.0	35.3	29.7	28.9	115.9	154.9	110.0	99.4	94.8
28	Suicide	E950-E959	22.4	0.0	0.1	2.2	19.4	37.1	34.3	29.6	26.6
	Female – Féminin										
			per 100,000 population – pour 100,000 habitants								
29	**All causes**	001-E999	601.8	260.2	30.1	24.5	47.1	54.6	54.5	70.3	109.5
30	All cancer	140-209	138.4	5.0	4.8	3.4	4.6	3.9	8.7	16.6	34.1
31	Lung cancer	162	14.3	0.1	0.0	0.0	0.0	0.0	0.0	0.9	1.5
32	Breast cancer	174	27.8	0.0	0.0	0.0	0.0	0.0	1.1	4.3	11.0
33	Diabetes mellitus	250	13.2	0.2	0.1	0.2	0.0	0.6	0.5	1.0	1.4
34	Diseases of the heart	393-398, 400.1, 400.9, 402, 404, 410-414, 420-429	202.0	1.8	0.2	0.3	1.3	1.8	1.7	3.0	9.7
35	Ischemic heart diseases	410-414	172.6	0.0	0.0	0.0	0.0	0.4	0.5	1.4	6.8
36	Cerebrovascular diseases	430-438	69.3	0.6	0.3	0.2	0.9	1.2	1.9	2.8	6.5
37	Respiratory diseases	460-519	32.8	14.7	1.6	0.5	0.9	1.8	2.1	2.6	3.5
38	Influenza and pneumonia	470-474	2.3	0.2	0.1	0.0	0.2	0.3	0.0	0.1	0.1
39	Bronchitis, emphysema and asthma	466, 490-493	6.6	1.6	0.1	0.2	0.2	0.4	0.5	0.3	0.8
40	Cirrhosis of liver	571	7.6	0.6	0.0	0.0	0.0	0.0	1.2	1.8	3.8
41	All accidents	E800-E999	39.3	28.0	15.1	13.9	30.5	35.2	29.4	29.3	31.7
42	Suicide	E950-E959	7.3	0.0	0.1	0.5	4.4	7.1	9.8	8.3	9.3

Taux de mortalité par âge, selon certaines causes et le sexe, Canada, 1978

40-44 years / ans	45-49 years / ans	50-54 years / ans	55-59 years / ans	60-64 years / ans	65-69 years / ans	70-74 years / ans	75-79 years / ans	80-84 years / ans	85+ years / ans	Cause	No
Both sexes – Les deux sexes											
per 100,000 population – pour 100,000 habitants											
241.5	**393.2**	**663.9**	**1,007.5**	**1,568.5**	**2,366.4**	**3,603.3**	**5,504.5**	**8,794.9**	**16,103.0**	Toutes les causes	1
56.6	117.4	223.4	336.1	496.3	712.8	952.2	1,244.7	1,545.0	1,810.0	Tous les cancers	2
10.0	23.8	59.6	91.4	140.0	198.3	228.1	250.1	231.6	175.2	Cancer du poumon	3
9.9	19.8	32.5	39.3	49.5	56.0	59.7	71.6	105.6	130.3	Cancer du sein	4
2.8	3.9	8.5	13.6	29.5	50.0	77.3	129.4	183.8	258.2	Diabète sucré	5
52.5	105.6	200.7	340.1	580.5	890.7	1,423.4	2,205.9	3,576.7	6,606.9	Maladies du coeur	6
45.6	94.7	177.8	304.8	516.9	800.4	1,270.8	1,957.1	3,129.5	5,650.7	Maladies ischémiques du coeur	7
9.2	18.0	28.2	47.5	89.2	164.9	334.2	652.4	1,221.2	2,889.2	Maladies cérébro-vasculaires	8
9.2	12.8	23.0	43.6	84.7	157.0	260.8	417.2	734.9	1,532.4	Maladies respiratoires	9
0.0	0.4	0.3	0.7	1.7	2.6	7.4	14.1	43.5	135.4	Grippe et pneumonie	10
2.5	4.0	8.2	17.2	34.9	64.5	89.7	122.7	159.1	221.3	Bronchite, emphysème et asthme	11
13.8	25.2	37.5	40.8	45.0	47.0	43.5	37.0	26.9	24.5	Cirrhose du foie	12
67.9	67.4	76.0	80.6	79.6	86.5	98.0	134.0	212.1	443.7	Tous les accidents	13
21.7	21.5	21.8	21.3	20.7	18.0	17.9	14.9	20.4	15.4	Suicide	14
Male – Masculin											
per 100,000 population – pour 100,000 habitants											
315.4	**512.6**	**891.1**	**1,392.9**	**2,156.2**	**3,256.3**	**4,907.8**	**7,372.8**	**11,411.4**	**18,946.2**	Toutes les causes	15
52.6	110.6	240.9	388.0	594.4	919.2	1,271.6	1,773.1	2,184.2	2,556.3	Tous les cancers	16
13.7	33.6	91.5	148.9	227.6	346.8	423.9	497.9	486.7	363.8	Cancer du poumon	17
0.0	0.0	0.0	0.6	0.9	1.4	2.4	3.1	3.5	3.3	Cancer du sein	18
3.2	4.9	10.0	16.9	32.4	55.0	84.4	124.5	197.0	265.9	Diabète sucré	19
85.0	169.7	328.2	554.3	889.8	1,312.1	1,967.0	2,914.8	4,504.1	7,246.3	Maladies du coeur	20
75.0	156.3	297.8	507.5	809.8	1,207.2	1,779.0	2,624.2	3,971.0	6,241.4	Maladies ischémiques du coeur	21
8.8	18.2	32.5	57.9	108.2	204.9	410.9	745.6	1,348.8	2,549.8	Maladies cérébro-vasculaires	22
11.8	17.1	32.3	61.1	130.0	244.7	425.4	699.6	1,235.2	2,357.3	Maladies respiratoires	23
0.2	0.2	0.5	0.9	2.1	3.3	10.2	15.9	55.6	159.9	Grippe et pneumonie	24
3.2	4.9	12.0	24.1	57.2	103.9	156.6	234.8	316.3	433.9	Bronchite, emphysème et asthme	25
19.5	37.2	55.5	57.3	64.3	67.5	63.6	54.0	41.7	45.7	Cirrhose du foie	26
97.7	100.8	109.1	118.2	112.3	117.2	142.9	182.1	279.3	507.3	Tous les accidents	27
29.3	31.7	29.8	30.3	28.7	25.5	29.0	28.8	39.4	32.6	Suicide	28
Female – Féminin											
per 100,000 population – pour 100,000 habitants											
166.0	**271.3**	**444.6**	**651.8**	**1,034.6**	**1,584.9**	**2,547.2**	**4,158.6**	**7,224.6**	**14,580.8**	Toutes les causes	29
60.5	124.3	206.6	288.2	407.3	531.5	693.7	864.0	1,161.3	1,410.5	Tous les cancers	30
6.3	13.8	28.7	38.3	60.5	67.8	69.6	71.6	78.6	74.2	Cancer du poumon	31
20.0	40.1	63.8	75.1	93.7	103.9	106.1	121.0	166.9	198.3	Cancer du sein	32
2.4	2.9	6.9	10.6	26.9	45.6	71.5	133.0	175.9	254.1	Diabète sucré	33
19.3	40.1	77.5	142.4	299.6	520.5	983.2	1,695.2	3,020.2	6,264.6	Maladies du coeur	34
15.5	31.7	62.0	117.6	250.8	443.2	859.2	1,476.6	2,624.5	5,334.5	Maladies ischémiques du coeur	35
9.5	17.8	24.1	38.0	72.0	129.8	272.0	585.2	1,144.6	2,456.8	Maladies cérébro-vasculaires	36
6.4	8.5	14.1	27.4	43.6	80.0	127.4	213.8	234.6	1,090.8	Maladies respiratoires	37
0.0	0.6	0.2	0.5	1.5	2.0	5.1	12.8	36.2	122.3	Grippe et pneumonie	38
1.8	3.0	4.5	10.9	14.6	30.0	35.6	42.0	64.7	107.4	Bronchite, emphysème et asthme	39
7.9	13.0	20.0	25.5	27.5	29.0	27.3	24.7	18.1	13.1	Cirrhose du foie	40
37.4	33.3	44.1	45.8	49.9	59.5	61.6	99.4	171.8	409.6	Tous les accidents	41
14.0	11.1	14.1	13.0	13.4	11.5	8.9	4.9	9.0	6.1	Suicide	42

Standardized Death Rates, by Selected Cause and Sex, Canada and Provinces, 1978

No.	Cause	Category (8th Revision) / Catégorie (8e révision)	Canada	New-found-land / Terre-Neuve	Prince Edward Island / Île-du-Prince-Édouard	Nova Scotia / Nouvelle-Écosse	New Brunswick / Nouveau-Brunswick	Québec
	Both sexes – Les deux sexes							
			per 100,000 population – pour 100,000 habitants					
1	**All causes**	001 - E999	**617.9**	**584.5**	**560.8**	**642.8**	**630.5**	**670.8**
2	All cancer	140 - 209	138.7	134.3	119.6	148.4	134.8	153.8
3	Lung cancer	162	32.1	23.1	19.4	37.1	29.9	37.1
4	Breast cancer	174	11.3	9.1	12.7	12.8	10.9	12.2
5	Diabetes mellitus	250	10.2	7.9	10.0	10.1	10.3	13.3
6	Diseases of the heart	393 - 398, 400.1, 400.9, 402, 404, 410 - 414, 420 - 429	202.4	207.2	191.5	214.9	210.6	217.9
7	Ischemic heart diseases	410 - 414	178.7	181.0	166.0	186.9	178.8	182.9
8	Cerebrovascular diseases	430 - 438	50.0	57.2	31.4	46.8	45.7	56.1
9	Respiratory diseases	460 - 519	40.3	35.1	36.1	43.3	44.2	43.1
10	Influenza and pneumonia	470 - 474	1.6	1.1	1.1	0.9	1.3	1.6
11	Bronchitis, emphysema and asthma	466, 490 - 493	11.6	5.3	8.9	8.2	9.0	16.1
12	Cirrhosis of liver	571	11.3	6.6	3.8	6.3	9.2	12.3
13	All accidents	E800 - E999	62.7	39.1	71.7	63.1	76.0	64.4
14	Suicide	E950 - E959	13.5	2.7	14.4	11.4	12.7	12.7
	Male – Masculin							
			per 100,000 population – pour 100,000 habitants					
15	**All causes**	001 - E999	**778.4**	**720.1**	**723.5**	**824.7**	**800.2**	**849.8**
16	All cancer	140 - 209	166.9	164.8	130.3	172.3	165.1	190.5
17	Lung cancer	162	52.1	40.7	29.9	60.0	49.7	63.0
18	Breast cancer	174	0.2	0.9	0.0	0.0	0.0	0.2
19	Diabetes mellitus	250	10.7	5.5	8.2	10.5	9.9	13.5
20	Diseases of the heart	393 - 398, 400.1, 400.9, 402, 404, 410 - 414, 420 - 429	265.2	262.0	259.9	293.1	273.0	282.3
21	Ischemic heart diseases	410 - 414	238.1	234.7	225.9	262.0	237.1	242.1
22	Cerebrovascular diseases	430 - 438	53.8	63.6	33.1	49.6	50.1	62.1
23	Respiratory diseases	460 - 519	56.7	49.2	52.2	61.2	59.2	61.9
24	Influenza and pneumonia	470 - 474	1.7	1.7	1.0	0.6	1.4	1.8
25	Bronchitis, emphysema and asthma	466, 490 - 493	17.9	9.3	16.6	11.8	10.8	25.2
26	Cirrhosis of liver	571	15.9	8.7	7.5	7.7	14.5	18.1
27	All accidents	E800 - E999	89.7	57.7	121.8	96.6	113.7	92.6
28	Suicide	E950 - E959	20.1	3.7	23.0	17.3	21.0	19.1
	Female – Féminin							
			per 100,000 population – pour 100,000 habitants					
29	**All causes**	001 - E999	**452.8**	**445.0**	**393.5**	**455.8**	**455.9**	**486.8**
30	All cancer	140 - 209	109.6	102.8	108.6	123.8	103.5	116.0
31	Lung cancer	162	11.6	4.9	8.5	13.5	9.5	10.5
32	Breast cancer	174	22.8	17.5	25.8	25.9	22.1	24.6
33	Diabetes mellitus	250	9.6	10.3	11.9	9.6	10.7	13.1
34	Diseases of the heart	393 - 398, 400.1, 400.9, 402, 404, 410 - 414, 420 - 429	137.9	150.9	121.1	134.5	146.5	151.7
35	Ischemic heart diseases	410 - 414	117.5	125.7	104.4	109.7	118.9	122.1
36	Cerebrovascular diseases	430 - 438	46.1	50.6	29.7	43.8	41.2	49.9
37	Respiratory diseases	460 - 519	23.5	20.6	19.5	25.0	28.8	23.8
38	Influenza and pneumonia	470 - 474	1.4	0.5	1.2	1.2	1.3	1.4
39	Bronchitis, emphysema and asthma	466, 490 - 493	5.0	1.2	1.0	4.5	7.1	6.8
40	Cirrhosis of liver	571	6.6	4.5	0.0	5.0	3.7	6.2
41	All accidents	E800 - E999	35.0	20.1	20.3	28.7	37.3	35.4
42	Suicide	E950 - E959	6.7	1.6	5.5	5.4	4.2	6.1

Taux comparatif de mortalité, selon certaines causes et le sexe, Canada et provinces, 1978

Ontario	Manitoba	Saskat-chewan	Alberta	British Columbia / Colombie-Britannique	Yukon	Northwest Territories / Territoires du Nord-Ouest	Cause	No
Both sexes – Les deux sexes								
per 100,000 population – pour 100,000 habitants								
609.9	**589.4**	**573.5**	**587.2**	**579.4**	**474.6**	**590.2**	Toutes les causes	1
138.2	129.9	117.5	124.2	130.6	61.4	88.2	Tous les cancers	2
32.3	29.6	24.8	25.5	30.5	15.6	22.7	Cancer du poumon	3
11.4	9.5	10.7	11.1	10.1	0.0	6.9	Cancer du sein	4
10.0	7.9	7.9	9.2	7.6	5.0	0.0	Diabète sucré	5
211.1	188.5	160.4	175.8	176.1	130.4	113.1	Maladies du coeur	6
192.3	165.3	132.6	153.0	162.9	81.6	79.5	Maladies ischémiques du coeur	7
50.1	47.2	39.0	46.7	47.6	5.8	26.3	Maladies cérébro-vasculaires	8
39.2	44.6	46.5	37.9	32.9	38.9	78.5	Maladies respiratoires	9
1.5	0.5	2.1	1.1	2.6	0.0	0.0	Grippe et pneumonie	10
8.6	7.4	8.9	10.3	17.6	0.0	8.7	Bronchite, emphysème et asthme	11
10.9	9.4	7.5	10.9	16.1	16.9	4.1	Cirrhose du foie	12
53.4	64.2	72.3	72.5	77.4	125.6	150.2	Tous les accidents	13
13.0	13.9	15.3	15.7	16.2	26.4	45.7	Suicide	14
Male – Masculin								
per 100,000 population – pour 100,000 habitants								
769.0	**744.0**	**714.4**	**732.5**	**726.5**	**630.8**	**625.1**	Toutes les causes	15
165.6	160.0	135.4	145.0	154.5	98.7	72.3	Tous les cancers	16
52.0	49.1	39.7	39.0	45.7	30.9	24.6	Cancer du poumon	17
0.3	0.1	0.5	0.1	0.0	0.0	0.0	Cancer du sein	18
10.8	7.9	10.1	9.6	8.6	9.9	0.0	Diabète sucré	19
277.3	247.1	211.6	232.8	234.0	128.9	165.3	Maladies du coeur	20
255.8	221.7	177.7	207.5	219.5	73.6	131.6	Maladies ischémiques du coeur	21
55.0	47.8	38.3	47.6	49.4	0.0	20.8	Maladies cérébro-vasculaires	22
55.1	62.7	62.5	52.3	46.4	76.6	62.1	Maladies respiratoires	23
1.7	0.5	2.2	1.5	2.5	0.0	0.0	Grippe et pneumonie	24
13.3	10.3	14.1	15.5	28.3	0.0	6.6	Bronchite, emphysème et asthme	25
15.2	13.2	10.4	14.8	21.4	33.3	8.1	Cirrhose du foie	26
75.7	92.2	102.7	104.0	106.2	205.0	203.0	Tous les accidents	27
19.1	21.8	23.0	23.8	23.4	38.7	71.9	Suicide	28
Female – Féminin								
per 100,000 population – pour 100,000 habitants								
446.4	**430.4**	**428.6**	**437.7**	**428.2**	**314.0**	**554.3**	Toutes les causes	29
110.0	98.9	99.2	102.8	106.0	23.1	104.5	Tous les cancers	30
12.2	9.6	9.5	11.6	14.7	0.0	20.8	Cancer du poumon	31
22.9	19.2	21.1	22.3	20.5	0.0	14.1	Cancer du sein	32
9.1	7.8	5.7	8.9	6.6	0.0	0.0	Diabète sucré	33
143.0	128.3	107.7	117.2	116.6	132.0	59.4	Maladies du coeur	34
127.1	107.2	86.3	97.0	104.6	89.8	25.9	Maladies ischémiques du coeur	35
45.2	46.7	39.6	45.7	45.6	11.7	31.9	Maladies cérébro-vasculaires	36
22.9	26.0	30.0	23.1	19.0	0.0	95.4	Maladies respiratoires	37
1.3	0.6	1.9	0.6	2.6	0.0	0.0	Grippe et pneumonie	38
3.8	4.4	3.5	5.0	6.6	0.0	10.9	Bronchite, emphysème et asthme	39
6.5	5.4	4.5	6.9	10.7	0.0	0.0	Cirrhose du foie	40
30.5	35.4	41.1	40.1	47.7	44.0	95.9	Tous les accidents	41
6.8	5.8	7.4	7.3	8.9	13.6	18.8	Suicide	42

Homicide Statistics, Canada

Percentage Distribution of Homicide Victims by Age and Sex, Canada, 1980

Répartition en pourcentage des victimes d'homicide selon l'âge et le sexe, Canada, 1980

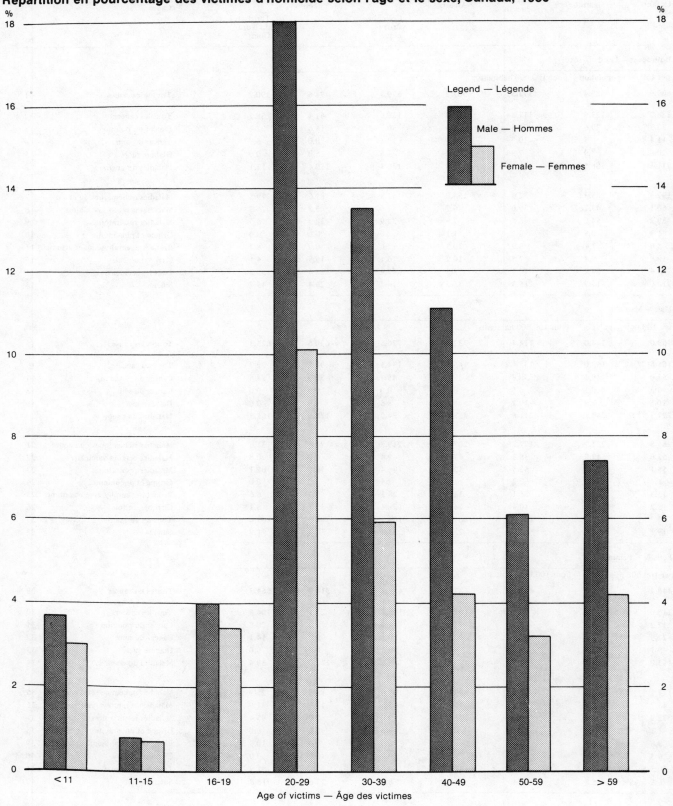

Age of victims — Âge des victimes

Legend — Légende

Male — Hommes

Female — Femmes

From "Homicide Statistics 1980," Statistics Canada, Minister of Supply and Services Canada 1982, January, 1982.

Percentage Distribution of Homicide Suspects by Age and Sex, Canada, 1980
Répartition en pourcentage des suspects d'homicide selon l'âge et le sexe, Canada, 1980

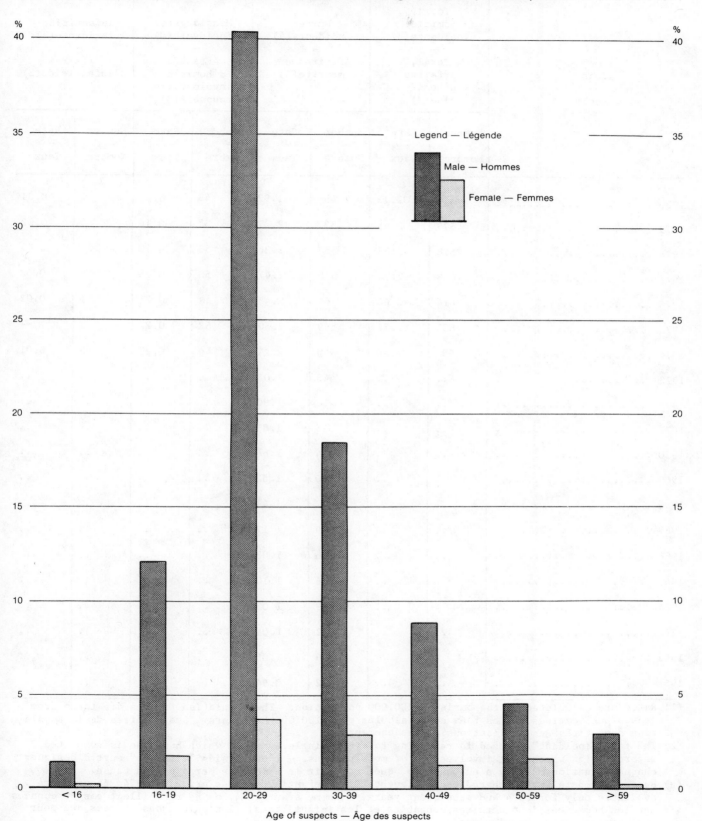

Age of suspects — Âge des suspects

Number and Rate(1) of Homicide Incidents(2) by Legal Type, Canada, 1961-1980
Nombre et taux(1) d'affaires(2) d'homicide selon le genre légal, Canada, 1961-1980

Year — Année	Total homicide incidents(3) — Total, affaires d'homicide(3)		Murder incidents(4) — Affaires de meurtre(4)		Manslaughter incidents(3) — Affaires d'homicide involontaire coupable(3)		Infanticide incidents(3) — Affaires d'infanticide(3)	
	Number — Nombre	Rate — Taux	Number — Nombre	Rate — Taux	Number — Nombre	Rate — Taux	Number — Nombre	Rate — Taux
1980	510	2.13	459	1.92	48	0.20	3	0.01
1979	579	2.45	537	2.27	37	0.16	5	0.02
1978	618	2.63	554	2.36	53	0.22	11	0.05
1977	638	2.74	575	2.47	58	0.25	5	0.02
1976	614	2.66	561	2.43	48	0.21	5	0.02
1975	632	2.77	569	2.50	62	0.27	1	--
1974	552	2.46	500	2.23	49	0.22	3	0.01
1973	..	..	448	2.03	..	..	..	..
1972	..	..	414	1.90	..	..	..	..
1971	..	..	395	1.83	..	..	..	..
1970	..	..	354	1.66	..	..	..	..
1969	..	..	320	1.52	..	..	..	..
1968	..	..	292	1.41	..	..	..	..
1967	..	..	239	1.17	..	..	..	..
1966	..	..	206	1.03	..	..	..	..
1965	..	..	216	1.10	..	..	..	..
1964	..	..	199	1.03	..	..	..	..
1963	..	..	192	1.01	..	..	..	..
1962	..	..	196	1.05	..	..	..	..
1961	..	..	172	0.94	..	..	..	..

(1) Rates are calculated on the basis of 100,000 population. The population figures are taken from census publications. — Les taux sont calculés pour 100,000 habitants. Les chiffres de la population sont tirés des publications du recensement.
(2) The term "incident" is used in referring to every single event in which homicide is committed, regardless of whether it involves one or more persons. — L'expression "affaires" sert à désigner chaque situation où il y a eu homicide, quel que soit le nombre de personnes en cause.
(3) Because no data were gathered on manslaughter and infanticide cases prior to 1974, figures are available only for 1974 and subsequent years. — Comme avant 1974, on ne recueillait pas de données sur les homicides involontaires coupables et les infanticides, il n'existe des données que pour 1974 et les années subséquentes.
(4) Murder incidents include all incidents of capital and non-capital murder and, as of July 26, 1976, first and second degree murder. — Les affaires de meurtre comprennent toutes les affaires où il y a eu meurtre qualifié et non qualifié et, à partir du 26 juillet 1976, meurtre au premier et au deuxième degré.

Number and Rate(1) of Homicide Offences(2) by Legal Type, Canada, 1961-1980
Nombre et taux(1) d'infractions(2) d'homicide selon le genre légal, Canada, 1961-1980

Year — Année	Total homicide offences — Total, infractions d'homicide		Murder offences(3) — Infractions de meurtre(3)		Manslaughter offences(4) — Infractions d'homicide involontaire coupable(4)		Infanticide offences — Infractions d'infanticide	
	Number — Nombre	Rate — Taux	Number — Nombre	Rate — Taux	Number — Nombre	Rate — Taux	Number — Nombre	Rate — Taux
1980	593	2.48	493	2.06	97	0.41	3	0.01
1979	631	2.66	587	2.48	39	0.16	5	0.02
1978	660	2.81	591	2.51	58	0.25	11	0.05
1977	711	3.05	628	2.70	78	0.33	5	0.02
1976	668	2.89	614	2.66	49	0.21	5	0.02
1975	701	3.07	636	2.79	64	0.28	1	--
1974	600	2.67	548	2.44	49	0.22	3	0.01
1973	546	2.47	480	2.17	66	0.30	..	..
1972	521	2.38	481	2.20	40	0.18	..	..
1971	473	2.19	426	1.97	47	0.22	..	..
1970	467	2.19	433	2.03	34	0.16	..	..
1969	391	1.86	347	1.65	44	0.21	..	..
1968	375	1.81	315	1.52	60	0.29	..	..
1967	338	1.66	282	1.38	56	0.28	..	..
1966	250	1.25	222	1.11	28	0.14	..	..
1965	277	1.41	243	1.24	34	0.17	..	..
1964	253	1.31	218	1.13	35	0.18	..	..
1963	249	1.32	215	1.14	34	0.18	..	..
1962	265	1.43	217	1.17	48	0.26	..	..
1961	233	1.27	185	1.01	48	0.26	..	..

(1) Rates are calculated on the basis of 100,000 population. — Les taux sont calculés pour 100,000 habitants.
(2) One offence is counted for every victim. — On compte une infraction pour chaque victime.
(3) Murder offences include all offences of capital and non-capital murder and, as of July 26, 1976, first and second degree murder. — Les infractions de meurtre comprennent toutes les infractions où il y a eu meurtre qualifié et non qualifié et, à compter du 26 juillet 1976, meurtre au premier et au deuxième degré.
(4) All manslaughter figures previous to 1974 are taken from the Uniform Crime Reporting Program and are not revised annually. — Toutes les données sur l'homicide involontaire coupable antérieures à 1974 viennent du Programme de déclaration uniforme de la criminalité et ne sont pas révisées chaque année.

Number and Rate(1) of Homicide Offences by Legal Type, Canada and Provinces, 1980

Nombre et taux(1) d'infractions d'homicide selon le genre légal, Canada et provinces, 1980

Type of offence – Genre d'infraction	Newfoundland – Terre-Neuve		Prince Edward Island – Île-du-Prince-Édouard		Nova Scotia – Nouvelle-Écosse		New Brunswick – Nouveau-Brunswick		Québec	
	Number – Nombre	Rate – Taux	Number – Nombre	Rate – Taux	Number – Nombre	Rate – Taux	Number – Nombre	Rate – Taux	Number – Nombre	Rate – Taux
Murder – Meurtre	3	0.52	1	0.80	9	1.06	9	1.27	129	2.05
Manslaughter – Homicide involontaire coupable	–	–	–	–	3	0.35	–	–	52	0.82
Infanticide	–	–	–	–	–	–	–	–	–	–
Total	3	0.52	1	0.80	12	1.41	9	1.27	181	2.87

	Ontario		Manitoba		Saskatchewan		Alberta	
	Number – Nombre	Rate – Taux	Number – Nombre	Rate – Taux	Number – Nombre	Rate – Taux	Number – Nombre	Rate – Taux
Murder – Meurtre	137	1.60	26	2.53	29	2.99	46	2.22
Manslaughter – Homicide involontaire coupable	19	0.22	5	0.49	2	0.21	9	0.43
Infanticide	3	0.04	–	–	–	–	–	–
Total	159	1.86	31	3.02	31	3.20	55	2.65

	British Columbia – Colombie-Britannique		Northwest Territories – Territoires du Nord-Ouest		Yukon		Canada	
	Number – Nombre	Rate – Taux	Number – Nombre	Rate – Taux	Number – Nombre	Rate – Taux	Number – Nombre	Rate – Taux
Murder – Meurtre	98	3.72	4	9.30	2	9.35	493	2.06
Manslaughter – Homicide involontaire coupable	7	0.26	–	–	–	–	97	0.41
Infanticide	–	–	–	–	–	–	3	0.01
Total	105	3.98	4	9.30	2	9.35	593	2.48

(1) Rates are calculated on the basis of 100,000 population. – Les taux sont calculés pour 100,000 habitants.

Distribution of Homicide Incidents(1) by Suspect-victim Relationship Type, Canada and Provinces, 1980

Répartition des affaires(1) d'homicide selon le genre de relation entre le suspect et la victime, Canada et provinces, 1980

Suspect-victim relationship type — Genre de relation entre le suspect et la victime	Newfoundland — Terre-Neuve		Prince Edward Island — Île-du-Prince-Édouard		Nova Scotia — Nouvelle-Écosse		New Brunswick — Nouveau-Brunswick		Québec	
	Number — Nombre	Per cent — Pourcentage	Number — Nombre	Per cent — Pourcentage	Number — Nombre	Per cent — Pourcentage	Number — Nombre	Per cent — Pourcentage	Number — Nombre	Per cent — Pourcentage
Domestic — Familiale	–	–	–	–	2	16.7	6	66.7	28	22.6
Social or business — Relation d'affaires ou sociale	2	66.7	–	–	4	33.3	–	–	28	22.6
No known relationship — Aucune relation connue	1	33.3	1	100.0	3	25.0	2	22.2	5	4.0
During commission of other criminal act — À l'occasion de la perpétration d'un autre acte criminel	–	–	–	–	2	16.7	–	–	15	12.1
Unsolved — Affaires non résolues	–	–	–	–	1	8.3	1	11.1	48	38.7
Total	3	100.0	1	100.0	12	100.0	9	100.0	124	100.0

	Ontario		Manitoba		Saskatchewan		Alberta	
	Number — Nombre	Per cent — Pourcentage	Number — Nombre	Per cent — Pourcentage	Number — Nombre	Per cent — Pourcentage	Number — Nombre	Per cent — Pourcentage
Domestic — Familiale	62	42.8	6	21.4	12	38.7	16	31.4
Social or business — Relation d'affaires ou sociale	38	26.2	12	42.9	8	25.8	19	37.3
No known relationship — Aucune relation connue	14	9.6	1	3.6	6	19.4	5	9.8
During commission of other criminal act — À l'occasion de la perpétration d'un autre acte criminel	12	8.3	6	21.4	5	16.1	9	17.6
Unsolved — Affaires non résolues	19	13.1	3	10.7	–	–	2	3.9
Total	145	100.0	28	100.0	31	100.0	51	100.0

	British Columbia — Colombie-Britannique		Northwest Territories — Territoires du Nord-Ouest		Yukon		Canada	
	Number — Nombre	Per cent — Pourcentage	Number — Nombre	Per cent — Pourcentage	Number — Nombre	Per cent — Pourcentage	Number — Nombre	Per cent — Pourcentage
Domestic — Familiale	24	24.0	2	50.0	–	–	158	31.0
Social or business — Relation d'affaires ou sociale	33	33.0	2	50.0	1	50.0	147	28.8
No known relationship — Aucune relation connue	15	15.0	–	–	1	50.0	54	10.6
During commission of other criminal act — À l'occasion de la perpétration d'un autre acte criminel	12	12.0	–	–	–	–	61	12.0
Unsolved — Affaires non résolues	16	16.0	–	–	–	–	90	17.6
Total	100	100.0	4	100.0	2	100.0	510	100.0

(1) Homicide incidents include all murder, manslaughter and infanticide incidents reported by police in 1980. — Les affaires d'homicide comprennent toutes les affaires de meurtre, d'homicide involontaire coupable et d'infanticide signalées par la police en 1980.

Method of Committing Homicide Offences by Suspect-victim Relationship Type
and Sex of Victim, Canada, 1980

Modalités de perpétration des infractions d'homicide selon le genre de relation entre le suspect
et la victime et le sexe de la victime, Canada, 1980

Suspect-victim relationship type and sex of victim — Genre de relation entre le suspect et la victime et sexe de la victime	Shooting — Arme à feu Number — Nombre	Per cent — Pour-centage	Stabbing — Arme pointue Number — Nombre	Per cent — Pour-centage	Beating — Coups Number — Nombre	Per cent — Pour-centage	Strangling — Strangulation Number — Nombre	Per cent — Pour-centage	Suffocation Number — Nombre	Per cent — Pour-centage
Domestic — Familiale .... M.	30	41.7	22	30.5	11	15.3	1	1.4	1	1.4
F.	41	43.2	13	13.7	18	18.9	9	9.5	3	3.2
Social or business — Relation d'affaires ou sociale .... M.	47	31.7	31	20.9	35	23.6	2	1.4	29	19.6
F.	9	16.4	10	18.2	8	14.5	4	7.3	21	38.2
Not known — Aucune relation connue .. M.	14	29.1	13	27.1	17	35.4	—	—	1	2.1
F.	2	20.0	2	20.0	—	—	—	—	—	—
During commission of other criminal act — À l'occasion de la perpétration d'un autre acte criminel ..... M.	15	30.0	17	34.0	11	22.0	4	8.0	1	2.0
F.	2	11.8	6	35.3	2	11.8	3	17.6	3	17.6
Unsolved — Affaires non résolues .... M.	32	47.7	14	20.9	8	11.9	4	6.0	3	4.5
F.	3	9.7	10	32.3	7	22.6	6	19.3	—	—
Total .... M.	138	35.8	97	25.2	82	21.3	11	2.9	35	9.1
F.	57	27.4	41	19.7	35	16.8	22	10.6	27	13.0

Suspect-victim relationship type and sex of victim	Drowning — Noyade Number — Nombre	Per cent — Pour-centage	Arson — Crime d'incendie Number — Nombre	Per cent — Pour-centage	Other — Autres Number — Nombre	Per cent — Pour-centage	Not known — Modalité non précisée Number — Nombre	Per cent — Pour-centage	Total Number — Nombre	Per cent — Pour-centage
Domestic — Familiale .... M.	2	2.8	1	1.4	4	5.5	—	—	72	100.0
F.	2	2.1	1	1.0	6	6.3	2	2.1	95	100.0
Social or business — Relation d'affaires ou sociale .... M.	1	0.7	2	1.4	1	0.7	—	—	148	100.0
F.	—	—	—	—	2	3.6	1	1.8	55	100.0
Not known — Aucune relation connue .. M.	1	2.1	1	2.1	1	2.1	—	—	48	100.0
F.	1	10.0	3	30.0	2	20.0	—	—	10	100.0
During commission of other criminal act — À l'occasion de la perpétration d'une autre acte criminel .... M.	—	—	—	—	2	4.0	—	—	50	100.0
F.	—	—	—	—	—	—	1	5.9	17	100.0
Unsolved — Affaires non résolues .... M.	1	1.5	—	—	3	4.5	2	3.0	67	100.0
F.	—	—	—	—	1	3.2	4	12.9	31	100.0
Total .... M.	5	1.3	4	1.0	11	2.9	2	0.5	385	100.0
F.	3	1.4	4	1.9	11	5.3	8	3.9	208	100.0

Age and Sex of Homicide Victims by Region, 1980

Distinction des victimes d'homicide d'après leur âge et leur sexe selon la région, 1980

Region and sex of victim — Région et sexe de la victime		10 years and under — ans et moins		11-15 years — ans		16-19 years — ans		20-29 years — ans		30-39 years — ans		40-49 years — ans		50-59 years — ans		60 years and over — ans et plus		Not known — Âge non précisé		Total	
		Number — Nombre	Per cent — Pourcentage	Number — Nombre	Per cent — Pourcentage	Number — Nombre	Per cent — Pourcentage	Number — Nombre	Per cent — Pourcentage	Number — Nombre	Per cent — Pourcentage	Number — Nombre	Per cent — Pourcentage	Number — Nombre	Per cent — Pourcentage	Number — Nombre	Per cent — Pourcentage	Number — Nombre	Per cent — Pourcentage	Number — Nombre	Per cent — Pourcentage
Atlantic provinces — Provinces de l'Atlantique	M.	2	10.0	–	–	1	5.0	5	25.0	4	20.0	3	15.0	1	5.0	4	20.0	–	–	20	100.0
	F.	–	–	–	–	–	–	1	20.0	2	40.0	–	–	–	–	2	40.0	–	–	5	100.0
Québec	M.	6	4.8	–	–	10	7.9	39	31.0	27	21.4	21	16.7	11	8.7	11	8.7	1	0.8	126	100.0
	F.	4	7.3	2	3.6	6	10.9	15	27.3	14	25.4	4	7.3	3	5.5	5	9.1	2	3.6	55	100.0
Ontario	M.	8	8.7	–	–	4	4.3	29	31.2	19	20.4	19	20.4	7	7.5	7	7.5	–	–	93	100.0
	F.	7	10.6	–	–	6	9.1	17	25.8	11	16.7	7	10.6	9	13.6	9	13.6	–	–	66	100.0
Prairie provinces — Provinces des Prairies	M.	5	6.1	3	3.7	6	7.3	23	28.0	16	19.5	10	12.2	8	9.8	11	13.4	–	–	82	100.0
	F.	4	11.4	1	2.9	3	8.6	12	34.3	3	8.6	4	11.4	4	11.4	4	11.4	–	–	35	100.0
British Columbia — Colombie-Britannique	M.	1	1.7	2	3.4	3	5.1	11	18.7	13	22.0	10	16.9	9	15.3	10	16.9	–	–	59	100.0
	F.	3	6.5	1	2.2	5	10.9	15	32.6	5	10.9	9	19.5	3	6.5	5	10.9	–	–	46	100.0
Yukon and Northwest Territories — Yukon et Territoires du Nord-Ouest	M.	–	–	–	–	–	–	–	–	1	20.0	3	60.0	–	–	1	20.0	–	–	5	100.0
	F.	–	–	–	–	–	–	–	–	–	–	1	100.0	–	–	–	–	–	–	1	100.0
Canada	M.	22	5.7	5	1.3	24	6.2	107	27.8	80	20.8	66	17.1	36	9.4	44	11.4	1	0.3	385	100.0
	F.	18	8.7	4	1.9	20	9.6	60	28.9	35	16.8	25	12.0	19	9.1	25	12.0	2	1.0	208	100.0

Age and Sex of Homicide Suspects by Region, 1980

Distinction des suspects d'homicide d'après leur âge et leur sexe selon la région, 1980

Region and sex of suspect — Région et sexe du suspect		10 years and under — ans et moins		11-15 years — ans		16-19 years — ans		20-29 years — ans		30-39 years — ans		40-49 years — ans		50-59 years — ans		60 years and over — ans et plus		Not known — Âge non précisé		Total	
		Number Nombre	Per cent Pour-centage	Number Nombre	Per cent Pour-centage	Number Nombre	Per cent Pour-centage	Number Nombre	Per cent Pour-centage	Number Nombre	Per cent Pour-centage	Number Nombre	Per cent Pour-centage	Number Nombre	Per cent Pour-centage	Number Nombre	Per cent Pour-centage	Number Nombre	Per cent Pour-centage	Number Nombre	Per cent Pour-centage
Atlantic provinces — Provinces de l'Atlantique	M.	–	–	–	–	1	4.8	11	52.4	6	28.5	–	–	1	4.8	2	9.5	–	–	21	100.0
	F.	–	–	–	–	1	25.0	2	50.0	1	25.0	–	–	–	–	–	–	–	–	4	100.0
Québec	M.	–	–	–	–	11	11.8	51	54.9	15	16.1	11	11.8	4	4.3	1	1.1	–	–	93	100.0
	F.	–	–	–	–	–	–	5	62.5	1	12.5	1	12.5	1	12.5	–	–	–	–	8	100.0
Ontario	M.	–	–	–	–	20	14.6	60	43.8	30	21.9	17	12.4	6	4.4	4	2.9	–	–	137	100.0
	F.	–	–	–	–	4	21.0	2	10.5	9	47.4	1	5.3	2	10.5	1	5.3	–	–	19	100.0
Prairie provinces — Provinces des Prairies	M.	–	–	4	3.4	22	19.0	51	44.0	20	17.2	9	7.8	6	5.2	4	3.4	–	–	116	100.0
	F.	–	–	–	–	2	14.3	7	50.0	–	–	2	14.3	3	21.4	–	–	–	–	14	100.0
British Columbia — Colombie-Britannique	M.	–	–	2	2.5	7	8.6	32	39.5	22	27.2	8	9.9	6	7.4	4	4.9	–	–	81	100.0
	F.	–	–	1	7.6	2	15.4	3	23.1	3	23.1	2	15.4	2	15.4	–	–	–	–	13	100.0
Yukon and Northwest Territories — Yukon et Territoires du Nord-Ouest	M.	–	–	1	16.7	1	16.7	2	33.3	2	33.3	–	–	–	–	–	–	–	–	6	100.0
	F.	–	–	–	–	–	–	–	–	1	100.0	–	–	–	–	–	–	–	–	1	100.0
Canada	M.	–	–	7	1.5	62	13.7	207	45.6	95	20.9	45	9.9	23	5.1	15	3.3	–	–	454	100.0
	F.	–	–	1	1.7	9	15.2	19	32.2	15	25.4	6	10.2	8	13.6	1	1.7	–	–	59	100.0

INDUSTRY STATISTICS

The Funeral:
What Determines the Cost?

It appears that funeral costs are always the subject of speculation. Are they high? Are they too high? What do you get for your money? What is included in the price the consumer pays for a funeral?

For most of us, the real mystery of funeral costs and funeral pricing is the consequence of our not buying funerals regularly enough to become familiar with funeral service costs and the way funerals are priced.

The funeral service industry, nationally and particularly in the Chicago Metropolitan area, is very aware of the sensitive aspects of funeral service pricing and so is making every effort to make this booklet on funeral costs an easy and comprehensive reference on the subject for the Chicago Metropolitan area. The funeral directors who serve Chicago and its suburbs want to provide as much information about funeral service pricing as possible before any of the families they serve are faced with the need to make funeral arrangements. The Chicagoland funeral directors are dedicated to making it as easy as possible for the consumer to understand what he is buying and receiving at the time of purchase.

Costs + Profit = Selling Price

Funeral service, like any other service oriented business that has as its major function the selling of a product or service, arrives at its selling price—the price it charges its customers for the goods and services it provides to them—by considering the following things: funeral home costs, merchandise costs, profit, and the costs of any special or optional items the family selects. There are also specific burial or cemetery costs and while the funeral director has no control over these, they need to be referenced if this review of funeral costs is to be really complete.

Let's examine each of these categories to see what they are in relationship to funeral service and how they contribute to the ultimate price the consumer pays for a funeral.

Funeral Home Costs or operating costs are often called the costs of doing business and include such items as the funeral home rent or mortgage payments, utility expenses, salaries and all of the other fixed costs which the funeral director must pay whether he handles a funeral or not. Some of these fixed costs vary from one funeral home to another just as mortgage payments and utility costs vary from one family to another and, consequently, funeral prices may also vary from one funeral home to another. The businessman takes his overhead costs and distributes them over the number of transactions he handles or estimates that he is going to handle over a period of time. In the case of the funeral director, this is an estimate of the number of funerals that he will handle . . . in a month . . . in a year or in some fixed period of time.

Merchandise Costs, the costs of goods which the family selects, are the direct costs of any funeral and relate to the specific funeral arranged by that family. Examples of such merchandise costs are the specific casket selected by the family for the funeral, the number and kind of funeral vehicles used in the funeral, and the cost of the burial vault. In short, these costs are costs which the family members arranging for the funeral control directly by their selection and their choices.

The third element that affects the funeral costs to the consumer, is the *profit* which the funeral director establishes as his target or goal. It is always in this particular area that consumers tend to become suspicious of the cost of funeral service and this is the area that is least likely to warrant their concern. Profit is the amount of money which the funeral director makes after he has paid for all of his direct and indirect costs as described above. A statistical study reveals that in 1979 the average funeral home in the Chicago Metropolitan area realized a before tax profit of $260.65 per regular adult funeral. The average annual profit of Chicago area funeral homes is 9.4% of gross sales.

There are *optional items* which families may elect to purchase in making funeral arrangements which will increase the cost of the basic funeral. Such items as death notices, flowers, clothes and music are typical expenses in this category.

Finally, there are *burial costs* associated with every funeral. Once again, these costs are neither estab-

lished nor controlled by the funeral director but are items, nevertheless, which affect the total cost of funeral service to the consumer. Included among burial costs are such items as the grave site, grave opening, grave marker or monument, or alternative forms of burial such as mausoleum entombment or cremation.

What follows is an easy-reference-chart of all the elements that affect the cost of the funeral to the consumer.

The Things That Contribute To The Cost Of A Funeral.	Overall Cost Range	Average Cost
Funeral Home Costs and Merchandise:		
These are the costs of doing business, the funeral director's overhead, if you will, some part of which is added to each funeral as part of the funeral director's charges and the costs of the goods which the family selects.		
Funeral Home. Every funeral home has fixed operating costs and these are computed into the cost of each regular adult funeral handled by that funeral home. These costs are related to the management and maintenance of the funeral home facility and include mortgage, heat, light, phone, insurance, maintenance, depreciation and taxes.	$169 to $943	$419
Funeral planning, management, supervision and embalming. These costs cover the time spent by the licensed funeral director in the removal of the remains to the funeral home and in the professional planning, management and supervision of the funeral arrangements. Embalming involves the preparation of the remains, restorative art as needed, cosmetology and simple hygienic preparations.	$137 to $422	$226
Staff and Salaries. Every funeral home, regardless of size, has people on salary, or part time, to answer phones and handle inquiries around-the-clock. Additional staff is also employed to supervise the facility and handle the ordinary business needs of bookkeeping, billing, cash disbursements, etc.	$276 to $798	$498
Funeral Vehicles. This is the cost of the vehicles used in the conduct of the funeral. Since a hearse is used in most funerals, many funeral directors include the cost of the hearse in their fee structure, while other funeral directors will itemize this cost as a separate charge. Depending upon whether the family wishes additional limousines, flower cars, etc., the funeral director will pass these costs for additional vehicles on to the family as requested.	$88 to $655	$187
Casket. Designed principally to serve the necessary function of containing the remains, caskets are purchased as well for their aesthetic and symbolic value and are available in a range of materials from simple, inexpensive woods to fabric-covered woods, steel, copper, bronze and solid hardwoods.	$65 to $7685	$556
Outer Receptacle. Most cemeteries in Chicago require a grave box or burial vault into which the casket is placed in the ground. Its primary purpose is to prevent the cave-in of the grave and the surrounding ground and to protect the casket and remains. The minimum cemetery requirement is usually an unsealed concrete box. The burial vault, used by about 80% of the families in the Chicagoland area, may be concrete or metal and some may provide the additional feature of being water-tight or water-resistant, depending on the manufacturer's warranty.	$101 to $1475	$391

	Overall Cost Range	Average Cost

Profit

The profit is the amount of money which the funeral director makes after paying all the expenses which we have talked about above. This profit helps the funeral director make sure that his service remains competitive while, at the same time, he provides for the needs of his business to earn money. In 1979, in the Chicago Metropolitan area, the average funeral home realized a before tax profit of $260.65 per regular adult funeral.

Optional Items

There are several items commonly associated with funeral service which are totally discretionary and are purchased by some families to satisfy their wishes and needs, while other families choose not to incur some of these expenses. In many cases the funeral director will advance money for these optional items on the family's behalf or arrange for their purchase as a convenience to the families he serves.

Death Notices. These can be placed or omitted, as the family wishes. The price of the death notice is established by the newspaper in which it is placed.

Flowers. The choices of floral arrangements vary widely, from fresh cut floral arrangements in vases at the head and/or the foot of the casket to intricate floral wreaths, forms and casket blankets. Funeral flowers may be ordered through any florist or through the funeral director as a convenience.

Clothes. In almost all cases now, clothing for the deceased is provided by the family. If for any reason clothing is unavailable, the funeral director can make arrangements for an appropriate burial garment.

Religious Stipend. This is a donation to a church, synagogue, rabbi or clergyman for conducting a religious funeral service. Depending upon the religious denomination or the beliefs of the deceased or his family, such service may include a church or synagogue service and grave-side service or just a service in the funeral home chapel or cemetery.

Music, Organist or Vocalist. If the family chooses to include music in the funeral service, a wide range of options are open to them regarding the kinds of music available and where in the funeral service it might be used. Traditionally, organists and/or vocalists are used at a church service while recorded music is sometimes used for services in the funeral chapel. String instruments and ensembles are also sometimes used both in the funeral chapel and in the church service. Arrangements for music at the funeral service can be made by the family directly, through their pastor or clergyman, or through the funeral director as a convenience.

Death Notices	$31 to $113	$66
Flowers	$20 to $446	$152
Clothes	$27 to $104	$68
Religious Stipend	$20 to $150	$50
Music, Organist or Vocalist	$15 to $220	$36

Burial

In its general application, burial means the final disposition of the deceased. In this sense, there are three common burial practices in the Chicago Metropolitan market: Cemetery Burial (below ground interment): Mausoleum Entombment (above ground encasement) and Cremation.

Cemetery Burial. Costs associated with this form of burial include the initial cost for the grave, the cost of opening

	Overall Cost Range	Average Cost

and closing the grave and the cost of handling the burial receptacle. Costs vary widely depending upon the cemetery, the day of service and where the grave is located in the cemetery.

Grave Memorial. Grave memorials can range from small, simple stones, flush with the ground, to an upright marker or more elaborate memorial stone. Cemeteries usually have regulations on the kind and size of grave memorials they will allow.

Mausoleum Entombment. Today, this type of burial refers to the placement of the deceased in a crypt or wall niche in a building called a mausoleum, which is usually built on cemetery property. The cost of a mausoleum crypt is determined, as was the cost of a grave, by the mausoleum in which it is located and where within the mausoleum the individual space is located. Entombment does not require the use of a burial vault or additional container other than the casket.

Cremation. The remains of the deceased are reduced to ash by direct contact with intense heat in a specially constructed furnace. Cremation normally follows a traditional funeral service.

Urn. A container used to hold the cremains (the ashes produced from cremation) after cremation. This can be simple or elaborate as the family wishes.

Columbarium. A place set aside in cemeteries, mausoleums, churches and other places for the retention of urned cremains (the ashes produced from cremation).

Overall Cost Range	Average Cost
$345 to $1065	$554
$135 to $5150	$295
$1150 to $5200	$2400
$110 to $150	$140
$30 to $1100	$152
$215 to $580	$320

Communicating the Price: How Does the Funeral Director Tell the Consumer What the Funeral Will Cost?

Chicagoland funeral directors generally use one of three methods to advise the family in advance what the funeral will cost and use this method for billing the family after the funeral. These three pricing systems are 1) single unit pricing, 2) partial itemization, and 3) full itemization.

Single unit pricing, perhaps the most common form of pricing funerals throughout the country, means that the funeral director gives the family a single dollar figure as the price of the funeral and explains that this figure includes the cost of the casket and all of the other expenses which we have identified in the chart as comprising his basic fee: the cost for the use of the funeral facility, a pro-rata portion of salaries, the cost of funeral vehicles, the costs for embalming and general preparation of the deceased. Even under this single unit pricing concept there are some incidental costs which the funeral director will itemize. Such itemized costs in this pricing system may include flowers, death notices, cemetery costs, burial vault, clothing, etc.

The partial itemization pricing system splits the price of the funeral into two specific dollar figures: the price of the casket only and the funeral director's fee, including all of the operating costs which we referenced above. In addition to these two principal itemized costs the funeral director will also itemize

costs for other monies expended on behalf of the family for things like flowers, death notices, cemetery costs, etc.

Finally, the *full itemization funeral pricing* system is exactly what you would expect, it fully itemizes every kind of expense involved in the total funeral price.

That means that the funeral director itemizes the price for the casket, the use of the facility, preparation of the remains, the funeral vehicles, and all of the attendant regular or exceptional costs which are related to the funeral in question.

Upon the completion of funeral arrangements, the funeral director will provide a written and signed confirmation to the family of all costs quoted to the family by the funeral director and accepted by them, consistent with the new Illinois Funeral Disclosure Rule.

What Else Does the Funeral Buyer Get for the Funeral Director's Charges?

In addition to their services at the time of the funeral as licensed professionals in the management of the funeral itself, Chicagoland funeral directors are very conscientious about the thoroughness of their post-interment counseling. The funeral director will provide information on the proper procedures for processing Social Security Claims, Veterans Benefit Claims and similar general obligations which the family must consider. He will work with the family, with attorneys, executors or other responsible persons whom they delegate and will often be able to recommend the most efficient means of processing claims through local government or insurance offices. The funeral director will also see that the death is properly recorded and certified and will deliver to the family certified copies of the death certificate for safe-keeping as well as keeping a complete file on the funeral and interment for future reference.

The funeral director can also provide information on pre-arrangement plans which he is licensed by the State to provide, on organ donations and the Anatomical Gift Act. He is a ready and available consultant with access to the most current information on funeral practices, prices and requirements.

Funeral Service
Facts and Figures

Map of the United States Showing the Census Bureau Divisions, Number of Firms Participating, and the Number of Funerals Reported

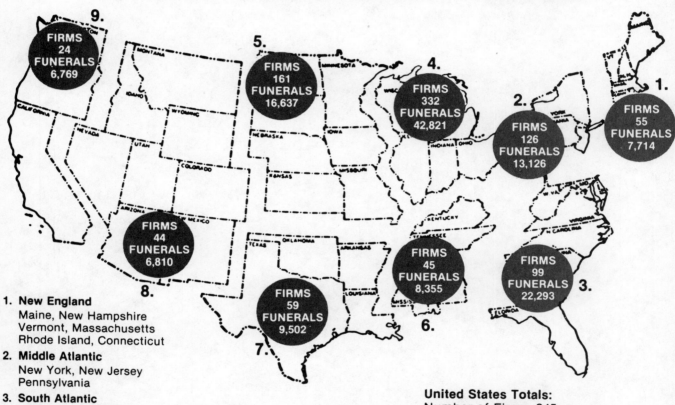

1. **New England**
   Maine, New Hampshire
   Vermont, Massachusetts
   Rhode Island, Connecticut

2. **Middle Atlantic**
   New York, New Jersey
   Pennsylvania

3. **South Atlantic**
   Delaware, Maryland
   District of Columbia
   Virginia, West Virginia
   North Carolina
   South Carolina
   Georgia, Florida

4. **East North Central**
   Ohio, Indiana
   Illinois, Michigan
   Wisconsin

5. **West North Central**
   Iowa, Minnesota, Missouri
   North Dakota
   South Dakota, Nebraska
   Kansas

6. **East South Central**
   Kentucky, Tennessee
   Alabama, Mississippi

7. **West South Central**
   Arkansas, Louisiana
   Oklahoma, Texas

8. **Mountain**
   Montana, Idaho, Wyoming
   Colorado, New Mexico
   Arizona, Utah, Nevada

9. **Pacific**
   Washington, Oregon
   California

United States Totals:
Number of Firms, 945
Number of Funerals, 134,027

Reprinted with permission from "A Statistical Abstract of Funeral Service Facts and Figures of the United States, 1981 edition," findings of a 1980 funeral service income and expense data survey conducted by Vanderlyn R. Pine, Ph.D., for the National Funeral Directors Association of the United States, Inc., Milwaukee, WI, 1981.

Number of Firms Participating and Number of Funerals Reported

	Number of Firms Reporting	Number of Funerals Reported
UNITED STATES	945	134,027
1. NEW ENGLAND	**55**	**7,714**
Connecticut	10	2,164
Maine	8	924
Massachusetts	26	3,384
New Hampshire	5	542
Rhode Island	2	431
Vermont	4	269
2. MIDDLE ATLANTIC	**126**	**13,126**
Pennsylvania	70	6,575
New Jersey	13	1,469
New York	43	5,082
3. SOUTH ATLANTIC	**99**	**22,293**
Delaware	0	0
District of Columbia	2	518
Florida	16	5,570
Georgia	17	3,705
Maryland	11	3,961
North Carolina	14	3,047
South Carolina	12	2,410
Virginia	10	1,293
West Virginia	17	1,789
4. EAST NORTH CENTRAL	**332**	**42,821**
Illinois	60	7,813
Indiana	46	5,193
Michigan	83	12,243
Ohio	73	8,997
Wisconsin	70	8,575
5. WEST NORTH CENTRAL	**161**	**16,637**
Iowa	25	1,723
Kansas	34	3,758
Minnesota	36	4,564
Missouri	24	3,042
Nebraska	21	1,644
North Dakota	7	703
South Dakota	14	1,203

	Number of Firms Reporting	Number of Funerals Reported
6. East South Central	**45**	**8,355**
Alabama	2	419
Kentucky	26	3,803
Mississippi	7	2,507
Tennessee	10	1,626
7. WEST SOUTH CENTRAL	**59**	**9,502**
Arkansas	6	1,628
Louisiana	6	1,207
Oklahoma	20	2,809
Texas	27	3,858
8. MOUNTAIN	**44**	**6,810**
Arizona	2	751
Colorado	9	1,733
Idaho	7	822
Montana	5	362
Nevada	1	159
New Mexico	6	1,153
Utah	10	1,406
Wyoming	4	424
9. PACIFIC	**24**	**6,769**
California	0	0
Oregon	11	2,215
Washington	12	4,215
Hawaii	1	339
Alaska	0	0

SOURCE OF SURVEY DATA   The Percentage of Firms Reporting and the Average Number of Services Conducted Per Firm

	VOLUME CATEGORY											
DIVISION	0-99 %	N	100-199 %	N	200-299 %	N	300-499 %	N	500 AND MORE %	N	ALL FIRMS %	N
UNITED STATES	50	62	31	140	10	233	7	382	2	764	100	142
1. NEW ENGLAND	36	63	48	141	7	239	9	365	0	0	100	140
2. MIDDLE ATLANTIC	61	61	34	137	2	217	2	431	1	689	100	104
3. SOUTH ATLANTIC	38	67	25	151	13	227	14	397	10	751	100	225
4. EAST NORTH CENTRAL	55	61	27	139	11	237	6	375	1	758	100	129
5. WEST NORTH CENTRAL	62	58	28	135	5	222	4	400	1	535	100	103
6. EAST SOUTH CENTRAL	35	69	36	141	9	217	18	377	2	1124	100	186
7. WEST SOUTH CENTRAL	36	62	42	145	10	240	10	369	2	910	100	161
8. MOUNTAIN	40	71	32	134	18	241	5	346	5	522	100	155
9. PACIFIC	13	76	29	140	25	230	25	371	8	979	100	282

FORM OF OWNERSHIP

The Percentage of Firms Reporting Their Form of Ownership

DIVISION	INDIVIDUAL PROPRIETORSHIP	PARTNERSHIP	CORPORATIONS		ALL FIRMS
			PRIVATE	PUBLIC	
UNITED STATES	27	10	62	1	100
1. NEW ENGLAND	15	4	81	0	100
2. MIDDLE ATLANTIC	43	7	49	1	100
3. SOUTH ATLANTIC	12	8	79	1	100
4. EAST NORTH CENTRAL	33	10	57	0	100
5. WEST NORTH CENTRAL	30	10	58	2	100
6. EAST SOUTH CENTRAL	13	20	67	0	100
7. WEST SOUTH CENTRAL	19	15	66	0	100
8. MOUNTAIN	18	11	71	0	100
9. PACIFIC	13	4	79	4	100

COLLECTION PROCEDURES

The Percentage of Firms Reporting That They Use Specific Collection Procedures

DIVISION	PERCENT ALLOWING CASH DISCOUNT	PERCENT CHARGING INTEREST	PERCENT USING SALES CONTRACT	PERCENT USING FINANCE PLANS
UNITED STATES	19	59	93	14
1. NEW ENGLAND	16	69	93	15
2. MIDDLE ATLANTIC	11	48	99	6
3. SOUTH ATLANTIC	33	56	93	13
4. EAST NORTH CENTRAL	17	59	93	12
5. WEST NORTH CENTRAL	23	62	92	14
6. EAST SOUTH CENTRAL	20	47	82	22
7. WEST SOUTH CENTRAL	10	63	95	22
8. MOUNTAIN	25	77	93	18
9. PACIFIC	29	75	96	29

PERSONNEL

The Percentage of Licensees Among the Full-time Personnel of the Firms Reporting and the Percentage of Firms Reporting That They Have Specific Personnel Benefit Plans

DIVISION	FULL TIME PERSONNEL		PERSONNEL BENEFITS	
	PERCENT LICENSED EMPLOYEES	PERCENT LICENSED OWNERS	PERCENT WITH EMPLOYEE RETIREMENT PLAN	PERCENT WITH PROFIT-SHARING PLAN
UNITED STATES	50	90	29	19
1. NEW ENGLAND	61	95	27	20
2. MIDDLE ATLANTIC	52	92	31	10
3. SOUTH ATLANTIC	47	87	33	19
4. EAST NORTH CENTRAL	53	91	28	18
5. WEST NORTH CENTRAL	55	93	30	19
6. EAST SOUTH CENTRAL	43	83	20	18
7. WEST SOUTH CENTRAL	41	90	17	31
8. MOUNTAIN	51	85	27	18
9. PACIFIC	51	89	50	38

MOTOR EQUIPMENT

The Percentage of Firms Reporting That They Operate an Ambulance Service and the Percentage of Firms Reporting the Way in Which They Acquire Their Motor Equipment

DIVISION	PERCENT OPERATING AMBULANCE SERVICE	PERCENT OWNING ALL OF IT	PERCENT OWNING PART OF IT AND RENTING PART OF IT	PERCENT RENTING ALL OF IT	PERCENT POOLING IT WITH OTHERS	ALL FIRMS
UNITED STATES	5	61	32	6	1	100
1. NEW ENGLAND	4	38	56	6	0	100
2. MIDDLE ATLANTIC	2	44	49	7	0	100
3. SOUTH ATLANTIC	3	77	20	2	1	100
4. EAST NORTH CENTRAL	9	53	38	8	1	100
5. WEST NORTH CENTRAL	2	75	20	4	1	100
6. EAST SOUTH CENTRAL	11	67	24	9	0	100
7. WEST SOUTH CENTRAL	3	81	14	3	2	100
8. MOUNTAIN	7	84	14	2	0	100
9. PACIFIC	0	75	21	0	4	100

INVESTMENT

The Average Investment Per Total-Adult Funeral Service

DIVISION	ACCOUNTS RECEIVABLE	MERCHANDISE INVENTORY	BUILDING	FUNERAL SERVICE EQUIPMENT	MOTOR EQUIPMENT	TOTAL INVESTMENT
UNITED STATES	351	119	891	291	277	1929
1. NEW ENGLAND	357	80	693	240	219	1589
2. MIDDLE ATLANTIC	373	94	885	318	276	1946
3. SOUTH ATLANTIC	364	101	819	233	271	1788
4. EAST NORTH CENTRAL	366	128	1039	336	274	2143
5. WEST NORTH CENTRAL	367	165	973	278	303	2087
6. EAST SOUTH CENTRAL	333	129	848	333	249	1892
7. WEST SOUTH CENTRAL	301	136	829	261	386	1912
8. MOUNTAIN	325	120	809	259	291	1804
9. PACIFIC	232	54	360	228	167	1040

CHARGES AS A PERCENT OF GROSS SALES
   FOR TOTAL-ADULT SERVICES

The Percentage of Charges for Each Category for Total-Adult Funeral Services

DIVISION	CHARGE CATEGORY				
	PERCENT FUNERAL CHARGES[a]	PERCENT INTERMENT RECEPTACLE CHARGE[b]	PERCENT OTHER FUNERAL HOME CHARGES[c]	PERCENT CASH ADVANCES	ALL CHARGES
UNITED STATES	75.9	13.0	.9	10.2	100.0
1. NEW ENGLAND	76.9	10.7	.4	12.0	100.0
2. MIDDLE ATLANTIC	74.4	12.6	.9	12.1	100.0
3. SOUTH ATLANTIC	77.1	13.7	1.2	8.0	100.0
4. EAST NORTH CENTRAL	74.2	13.9	.6	11.3	100.0
5. WEST NORTH CENTRAL	73.5	15.0	.6	10.9	100.0
6. EAST SOUTH CENTRAL	77.1	13.7	1.0	8.2	100.0
7. WEST SOUTH CENTRAL	79.5	11.9	.9	7.7	100.0
8. MOUNTAIN	82.4	7.5	1.2	8.9	100.0
9. PACIFIC	84.0	4.9	3.9	7.2	100.0

[a]The term "Funeral Charges" refers to those charges made by the funeral director for professional services, use of facilities and equipment, and the casket as selected, regardless of method of pricing and quotation. These figures do not include charges for interment receptacle, cemetery or crematory expenses, monument or marker, or miscellaneous items such as the honorarium for the clergy, flowers, additional transportation charges, burial clothing, or newspaper notices.
[b]The term "Interment Receptacle Charge" refers to the charge made for either a wooden box, concrete box, concrete grave liner, or a concrete or metal vault.
[c]The term "Other Funeral Home Charges" refers to charges made for additional items selected such as clothing, other funeral merchandise, additional automotive equipment, and other miscellaneous items.

CHARGES AND COSTS   **The Average Funeral Charges[a] and the Average Casket Cost**

DIVISION	TYPE OF SERVICE			
	TOTAL-ADULT		ALL SERVICES	
	FUNERAL CHARGES[a]	CASKET COST	FUNERAL CHARGES[a]	CASKET COST
UNITED STATES	1809	325	1561	276
1. NEW ENGLAND	1734	303	1528	263
2. MIDDLE ATLANTIC	1781	318	1533	271
3. SOUTH ATLANTIC	1766	316	1500	263
4. EAST NORTH CENTRAL	1923	343	1692	298
5. WEST NORTH CENTRAL	1830	329	1592	281
6. EAST SOUTH CENTRAL	1814	344	1593	297
7. WEST SOUTH CENTRAL	1810	335	1577	288
8. MOUNTAIN	1639	297	1310	232
9. PACIFIC	1390	244	1148	194

[a]The term "Funeral Charges" refers to those charges made by the funeral director for professional services, use of facilities and equipment, and the casket as selected, regardless of method of pricing and quotation. These figures do not include charges for interment receptacle, cemetery or crematory expenses, monument or marker, or miscellaneous items such as the honorarium for the clergy, flowers, additional transportation charges, burial clothing, or newspaper notices.

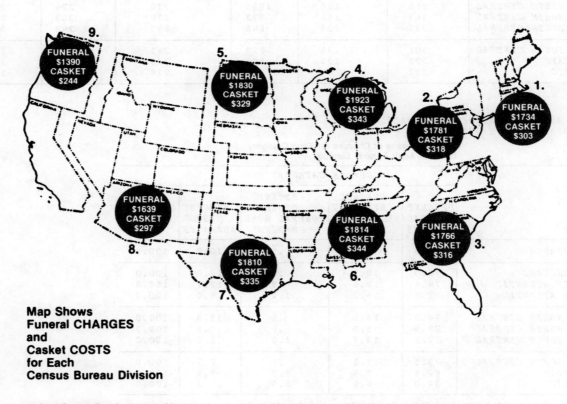

**Map Shows
Funeral CHARGES
and
Casket COSTS
for Each
Census Bureau Division**

United States Totals:
Funeral Charges, $1809 — Casket Cost, $325

AVERAGE FUNERAL CHARGES PER FIRM

Highest, Median, and Lowest Average Funeral Charges [a]
for the Total-Adult Funeral Services

DIVISION	HIGHEST	MEDIAN	LOWEST
UNITED STATES	3513	1840	650
1. NEW ENGLAND	2344	1694	1021
2. MIDDLE ATLANTIC	3513	1789	747
3. SOUTH ATLANTIC	2770	1817	650
4. EAST NORTH CENTRAL	3373	1925	863
5. WEST NORTH CENTRAL	3381	1850	1159
6. EAST SOUTH CENTRAL	2378	1841	1080
7. WEST SOUTH CENTRAL	2490	1805	1097
8. MOUNTAIN	2330	1686	1237
9. PACIFIC	2013	1504	940

[a]The average funeral charges for each firm participating in the survey was computed. This table reflects that firm which has the highest average, that firm which has the median average, and that firm which has the lowest average funeral charges for its total-adult funeral services. These figures do not include charges for interment receptacle, cemetery or crematory expenses, monument or marker, or miscellaneous items such as the honorarium for the clergy, flowers, additional transportation charges, burial clothing, or newspaper notices.

INTERMENT RECEPTACLE

The Percentage of Times an Interment Receptacle Was Used and the Average Sale and Cost of the Interment Receptacle [a]

DIVISION	PERCENT USED		AVERAGE ALL SERVICES		AVERAGE WHEN USED	
	TOTAL-ADULT	ALL SERVICES	SALE	COST	SALE	COST
UNITED STATES	83	72	263	140	365	195
1. NEW ENGLAND	82	74	209	113	283	153
2. MIDDLE ATLANTIC	81	71	263	139	372	197
3. SOUTH ATLANTIC	81	66	249	131	376	199
4. EAST NORTH CENTRAL	90	81	315	165	389	205
5. WEST NORTH CENTRAL	89	80	325	178	408	224
6. EAST SOUTH CENTRAL	92	82	278	145	341	178
7. WEST SOUTH CENTRAL	81	73	237	127	326	174
8. MOUNTAIN	57	48	117	66	242	137
9. PACIFIC	35	29	63	37	216	127

[a]The term "Interment Receptacle" refers to wooden boxes, concrete boxes, concrete grave liners, and concrete or metal vaults.

AVERAGE FUNERAL SERVICE OPERATING EXPENSES
(134027 FUNERALS)

UNITED STATES **Average Funeral Service Operating Expenses[a] by Expense Classification**

EXPENSE CLASSIFICATION	CHILD SERVICES	PARTIAL ADULT SERVICES	TOTAL ADULT SERVICES (INCLUDING WELFARE)	ALL SERVICES
1. AUTOMOBILE	26	57	134	118
2. COLLECTION	8	14	32	29
3. DIRECT FUNERAL [b]	15	33	74	65
4. FACILITIES AND EQUIPMENT	48	108	256	225
5. GENERAL [c]	30	66	144	127
6. PERSONNEL	134	290	691	605
7. PROMOTION	13	28	62	55
8. TAXES	18	38	93	81
ALL OPERATING EXPENSES	292	634	1488	1304

AVERAGE FUNERAL SERVICE OPERATING EXPENSES
(7714 FUNERALS)

NEW ENGLAND **Average Funeral Service Operating Expenses[a] by Expense Classification**

EXPENSE CLASSIFICATION	CHILD SERVICES	PARTIAL ADULT SERVICES	TOTAL ADULT SERVICES (INCLUDING WELFARE)	ALL SERVICES
1. AUTOMOBILE	31	69	143	128
2. COLLECTION	4	14	20	19
3. DIRECT FUNERAL [b]	16	33	69	62
4. FACILITIES AND EQUIPMENT	48	136	267	241
5. GENERAL [c]	30	70	144	130
6. PERSONNEL	126	308	642	577
7. PROMOTION	9	23	47	42
8. TAXES	17	44	90	81
ALL OPERATING EXPENSES	281	696	1422	1279

[a] Funeral Service Expenses were divided into the eight major classifications shown above. The average cost to the funeral director in each classification is computed as follows. The averages for all services are the total dollars of expenses divided by the total number of funerals reported. The averages for child services, partial-adult services and total-adult services are proportionately allocated dollars of expenses divided by the number of funerals reported in the category. To compute these averages, first the total expenses are allocated to each of the three main service categories — child, partial-adult and total-adult services according to the proportion of charges (income) reported. In the majority of cases, welfare-adult services are handled by funeral firms as total-adult services, the only difference being that payment for welfare services comes from one or more units of government rather than from individual funeral arrangers. Thus, the average funeral charges and casket costs shown in all tables numbered 13. indicate actual amounts for welfare services; however, the average operating expenses include welfare services with total-adult services.

[b] Embalming Supplies, Funerary Supplies (Acknowledgement cards, candles, memorial booklets, etc.). Funeral Trip Expense, Other Funeral Directors' Services.

[c] Dues-Subscriptions, Insurance (Liability, Malpractice and similar policies), Interest and Bank Charges, Laundry-Cleaning, Legal and Accounting Fees, Licenses, Postage, Printing, Stationery, Telephone-Telegraph, Travel Expense.

AVERAGE FUNERAL SERVICE OPERATING EXPENSES
  (13126 FUNERALS)

MIDDLE ATLANTIC ————— **Average Funeral Service Operating Expenses[a] by Expense Classification**

EXPENSE CLASSIFICATION	CHILD SERVICES	PARTIAL ADULT SERVICES	TOTAL ADULT SERVICES (INCLUDING WELFARE)	ALL SERVICES
1. *AUTOMOBILE*	24	56	160	140
2. *COLLECTION*	3	6	17	15
3. *DIRECT FUNERAL* [b]	15	33	89	78
4. *FACILITIES AND EQUIPMENT*	42	93	269	235
5. *GENERAL* [c]	23	53	134	119
6. *PERSONNEL*	109	212	638	557
7. *PROMOTION*	9	20	56	49
8. *TAXES*	12	27	75	66
ALL OPERATING EXPENSES	237	501	1440	1259

AVERAGE FUNERAL SERVICE OPERATING EXPENSES
  (22293 FUNERALS)

SOUTH ATLANTIC ————— **Average Funeral Service Operating Expenses[a] by Expense Classification**

EXPENSE CLASSIFICATION	CHILD SERVICES	PARTIAL ADULT SERVICES	TOTAL ADULT SERVICES (INCLUDING WELFARE)	ALL SERVICES
1. *AUTOMOBILE*	28	62	124	106
2. *COLLECTION*	12	21	44	38
3. *DIRECT FUNERAL* [b]	15	35	67	58
4. *FACILITIES AND EQUIPMENT*	50	104	224	190
5. *GENERAL* [c]	31	82	144	126
6. *PERSONNEL*	169	344	733	624
7. *PROMOTION*	13	31	56	49
8. *TAXES*	20	39	90	76
ALL OPERATING EXPENSES	338	718	1482	1268

[a]Funeral Service Expenses were divided into the eight major classifications shown above. The average cost to the funeral director in each classification is computed as follows. The averages for all services are the total dollars of expenses divided by the total number of funerals reported. The averages for child services, partial-adult services and total-adult services are proportionately allocated dollars of expenses divided by the number of funerals reported in the category. To compute these averages, first the total expenses are allocated to each of the three main service categories — child, partial-adult and total-adult services according to the proportion of charges (income) reported. In the majority of cases, welfare-adult services are handled by funeral firms as total-adult services, the only difference being that payment for welfare services comes from one or more units of government rather than from individual funeral arrangers. Thus, the average funeral charges and casket costs shown in all tables numbered 13. indicate actual amounts for welfare services; however, the average operating expenses include welfare services with total-adult services.

[b]Embalming Supplies, Funerary Supplies (Acknowledgement cards, candles, memorial booklets, etc.). Funeral Trip Expense, Other Funeral Directors' Services.

[c]Dues-Subscriptions, Insurance (Liability, Malpractice and similar policies), Interest and Bank Charges, Laundry-Cleaning, Legal and Accounting Fees, Licenses, Postage, Printing, Stationery, Telephone-Telegraph, Travel Expense.

AVERAGE FUNERAL SERVICE OPERATING EXPENSES
  (42821 FUNERALS)

EAST NORTH CENTRAL — **Average Funeral Service Operating Expenses[a] by Expense Classification**

EXPENSE CLASSIFICATION	CHILD SERVICES	PARTIAL ADULT SERVICES	TOTAL ADULT SERVICES (INCLUDING WELFARE)	ALL SERVICES
1. AUTOMOBILE	27	65	141	126
2. COLLECTION	5	12	26	23
3. DIRECT FUNERAL[b]	13	34	70	63
4. FACILITIES AND EQUIPMENT	55	138	297	267
5. GENERAL[c]	30	67	143	129
6. PERSONNEL	135	329	730	654
7. PROMOTION	13	35	72	65
8. TAXES	22	53	119	107
ALL OPERATING EXPENSES	300	732	1598	1433

AVERAGE FUNERAL SERVICE OPERATING EXPENSES
  (16637 FUNERALS)

WEST NORTH CENTRAL — **Average Funeral Service Operating Expenses[a] by Expense Classification**

EXPENSE CLASSIFICATION	CHILD SERVICES	PARTIAL ADULT SERVICES	TOTAL ADULT SERVICES (INCLUDING WELFARE)	ALL SERVICES
1. AUTOMOBILE	24	43	128	113
2. COLLECTION	7	12	34	30
3. DIRECT FUNERAL[b]	14	31	80	71
4. FACILITIES AND EQUIPMENT	43	99	250	222
5. GENERAL[c]	26	51	146	129
6. PERSONNEL	128	256	753	661
7. PROMOTION	11	21	61	54
8. TAXES	14	28	85	74
ALL OPERATING EXPENSES	267	541	1538	1354

[a] Funeral Service Expenses were divided into the eight major classifications shown above. The average cost to the funeral director in each classification is computed as follows. The averages for all services are the total dollars of expenses divided by the total number of funerals reported. The averages for child services, partial-adult services and total-adult services are proportionately allocated dollars of expenses divided by the number of funerals reported in the category. To compute these averages, first the total expenses are allocated to each of the three main service categories — child, partial-adult and total-adult services according to the proportion of charges (income) reported. In the majority of cases, welfare-adult services are handled by funeral firms as total-adult services, the only difference being that payment for welfare services comes from one or more units of government rather than from individual funeral arrangers. Thus, the average funeral charges and casket costs shown in all tables numbered 13. indicate actual amounts for welfare services; however, the average operating expenses include welfare services with total-adult services.

[b] Embalming Supplies, Funerary Supplies (Acknowledgement cards, candles, memorial booklets, etc.). Funeral Trip Expense, Other Funeral Directors' Services.

[c] Dues-Subscriptions, Insurance (Liability, Malpractice and similar policies), Interest and Bank Charges, Laundry-Cleaning, Legal and Accounting Fees, Licenses, Postage, Printing, Stationery, Telephone-Telegraph, Travel Expense.

AVERAGE FUNERAL SERVICE OPERATING EXPENSES
  (8355 FUNERALS)

EAST SOUTH CENTRAL

Average Funeral Service Operating Expenses[a] by Expense Classification

EXPENSE CLASSIFICATION	CHILD SERVICES	PARTIAL ADULT SERVICES	TOTAL ADULT SERVICES (INCLUDING WELFARE)	ALL SERVICES
1. AUTOMOBILE	30	65	138	124
2. COLLECTION	11	16	44	39
3. DIRECT FUNERAL[b]	16	37	74	67
4. FACILITIES AND EQUIPMENT	62	113	253	227
5. GENERAL[c]	32	65	153	136
6. PERSONNEL	184	278	736	652
7. PROMOTION	9	28	52	47
8. TAXES	18	32	74	66
ALL OPERATING EXPENSES	362	633	1524	1358

AVERAGE FUNERAL SERVICE OPERATING EXPENSES
  (9502 FUNERALS)

WEST SOUTH CENTRAL

Average Funeral Service Operating Expenses[a] by Expense Classification

EXPENSE CLASSIFICATION	CHILD SERVICES	PARTIAL ADULT SERVICES	TOTAL ADULT SERVICES (INCLUDING WELFARE)	ALL SERVICES
1. AUTOMOBILE	33	49	146	129
2. COLLECTION	19	17	66	57
3. DIRECT FUNERAL[b]	16	25	78	68
4. FACILITIES AND EQUIPMENT	53	81	251	220
5. GENERAL[c]	37	55	171	150
6. PERSONNEL	122	194	583	511
7. PROMOTION	18	22	71	62
8. TAXES	16	25	70	62
ALL OPERATING EXPENSES	314	468	1435	1258

[a] Funeral Service Expenses were divided into the eight major classifications shown above. The average cost to the funeral director in each classification is computed as follows. The averages for all services are the total dollars of expenses divided by the total number of funerals reported. The averages for child services, partial-adult services and total-adult services are proportionately allocated dollars of expenses divided by the number of funerals reported in the category. To compute these averages, first the total expenses are allocated to each of the three main service categories — child, partial-adult and total-adult services according to the proportion of charges (income) reported. In the majority of cases, welfare-adult services are handled by funeral firms as total-adult services, the only difference being that payment for welfare services comes from one or more units of government rather than from individual funeral arrangers. Thus, the average funeral charges and casket costs shown in all tables numbered 13. indicate actual amounts for welfare services; however, the average operating expenses include welfare services with total-adult services.

[b] Embalming Supplies, Funerary Supplies (Acknowledgment cards, candles, memorial booklets, etc.). Funeral Trip Expense, Other Funeral Directors' Services.

[c] Dues-Subscriptions, Insurance (Liability, Malpractice and similar policies), Interest and Bank Charges, Laundry-Cleaning, Legal and Accounting Fees, Licenses, Postage, Printing, Stationery, Telephone-Telegraph, Travel Expense.

AVERAGE FUNERAL SERVICE OPERATING EXPENSES
  (6810 FUNERALS)

<u>MOUNTAIN</u>   **Average Funeral Service Operating Expensesa by Expense Classification**

EXPENSE CLASSIFICATION	CHILD SERVICES	PARTIAL ADULT SERVICES	TOTAL ADULT SERVICES (INCLUDING WELFARE)	ALL SERVICES
1. AUTOMOBILE	23	49	116	94
2. COLLECTION	6	12	29	24
3. DIRECT FUNERAL [b]	19	31	93	74
4. FACILITIES AND EQUIPMENT	39	72	182	147
5. GENERAL [c]	31	56	145	117
6. PERSONNEL	117	237	575	465
7. PROMOTION	14	26	59	48
8. TAXES	17	28	71	57
ALL OPERATING EXPENSES	266	511	1270	1025

AVERAGE FUNERAL SERVICE OPERATING EXPENSES
  (6769 FUNERALS)

<u>PACIFIC</u>   **Average Funeral Service Operating Expensesa by Expense Classification**

EXPENSE CLASSIFICATION	CHILD SERVICES	PARTIAL ADULT SERVICES	TOTAL ADULT SERVICES (INCLUDING WELFARE)	ALL SERVICES
1. AUTOMOBILE	14	34	68	58
2. COLLECTION	4	10	20	17
3. DIRECT FUNERAL [b]	12	25	53	45
4. FACILITIES AND EQUIPMENT	30	72	139	121
5. GENERAL [c]	27	58	117	101
6. PERSONNEL	104	235	508	434
7. PROMOTION	10	26	50	43
8. TAXES	12	27	62	53
ALL OPERATING EXPENSES	213	488	1017	872

[a]Funeral Service Expenses were divided into the eight major classifications shown above. The average cost to the funeral director in each classification is computed as follows. The averages for all services are the total dollars of expenses divided by the total number of funerals reported. The averages for child services, partial-adult services and total-adult services are proportionately allocated dollars of expenses divided by the number of funerals reported in the category. To compute these averages, first the total expenses are allocated to each of the three main service categories — child, partial-adult and total-adult services according to the proportion of charges (income) reported. In the majority of cases, welfare-adult services are handled by funeral firms as total-adult services, the only difference being that payment for welfare services comes from one or more units of government rather than from individual funeral arrangers. Thus, the average funeral charges and casket costs shown in all tables numbered 13. indicate actual amounts for welfare services; however, the average operating expenses include welfare services with total-adult services.

[b]Embalming Supplies, Funerary Supplies (Acknowledgment cards, candles, memorial booklets, etc.). Funeral Trip Expense, Other Funeral Directors' Services.

[c]Dues-Subscriptions, Insurance (Liability, Malpractice and similar policies), Interest and Bank Charges, Laundry-Cleaning, Legal and Accounting Fees, Licenses, Postage, Printing, Stationery, Telephone-Telegraph, Travel Expense.

SELECTED EXPENSES
(AVERAGE PER TOTAL-ADULT FUNERAL SERVICE)

DIVISION	PERSONNEL		AUTOMOBILE	BUILDING
	EMPLOYEES' COMPENSATION	OWNERS' COMPENSATION		
UNITED STATES	304	387	134	256
1. NEW ENGLAND	288	354	143	267
2. MIDDLE ATLANTIC	218	421	160	269
3. SOUTH ATLANTIC	401	332	124	224
4. EAST NORTH CENTRAL	310	419	141	297
5. WEST NORTH CENTRAL	247	506	128	250
6. EAST SOUTH CENTRAL	354	382	138	253
7. WEST SOUTH CENTRAL	318	265	146	251
8. MOUNTAIN	231	344	116	182
9. PACIFIC	288	220	68	139

AVERAGE AND PERCENTAGE PER SERVICE INCOME AND EXPENSE STATEMENT FOR ALL SERVICES
  (134027 FUNERALS, 945 FIRMS)

UNITED STATES

OPERATING INCOME		AVERAGE		PERCENTAGE
FUNERAL CHARGES		1561		75.4
INTERMENT RECEPTACLE CHARGE		263		12.7
OTHER FUNERAL HOME CHARGES		19		.9
CASH ADVANCES		228		11.0
ALL OPERATING INCOME		2071		100.0
MERCHANDISE COSTS AND CASH ADVANCES				
CASKET COST	276		13.3	
INTERMENT RECEPTACLE COST	140		6.8	
OTHER FUNERAL HOME COSTS	11		.5	
CASH ADVANCES	219		10.6	
ALL MERCHANDISE COSTS AND CASH ADVANCES	646	646	31.2	31.2
OPERATING MARGIN		1425		68.8
OPERATING EXPENSES				
AUTOMOBILE	118		5.7	
COLLECTION	29		1.4	
DIRECT FUNERAL	65		3.1	
FACILITIES AND EQUIPMENT	225		10.8	
GENERAL	127		6.1	
PERSONNEL	605		29.3	
PROMOTION	55		2.6	
TAXES	81		3.9	
ALL OPERATING EXPENSES	1305	1305	62.9	62.9
NET MARGIN BEFORE INCOME TAXES		120		5.9

AVERAGE AND PERCENTAGE PER SERVICE INCOME AND EXPENSE STATEMENT FOR ALL SERVICES
(7714 FUNERALS, 55 FIRMS)

NEW ENGLAND

OPERATING INCOME		AVERAGE		PERCENTAGE
FUNERAL CHARGES		1528		76.4
INTERMENT RECEPTACLE CHARGE		209		10.5
OTHER FUNERAL HOME CHARGES		8		.4
CASH ADVANCES		254		12.7
ALL OPERATING INCOME		1999		100.0
MERCHANDISE COSTS AND CASH ADVANCES				
CASKET COST	263		13.2	
INTERMENT RECEPTACLE COST	113		5.6	
OTHER FUNERAL HOME COSTS	5		.2	
CASH ADVANCES	237		11.9	
ALL MERCHANDISE COSTS AND				
CASH ADVANCES	618	618	30.9	30.9
OPERATING MARGIN		1381		69.1
OPERATING EXPENSES				
AUTOMOBILE	128		6.4	
COLLECTION	19		.9	
DIRECT FUNERAL	62		3.1	
FACILITIES AND EQUIPMENT	241		12.1	
GENERAL	130		6.5	
PERSONNEL	577		28.9	
PROMOTION	42		2.1	
TAXES	81		4.0	
ALL OPERATING EXPENSES	1280	1280	64.0	64.0
NET MARGIN BEFORE INCOME TAXES		101		5.1

AVERAGE AND PERCENTAGE PER SERVICE INCOME AND EXPENSE STATEMENT FOR ALL SERVICES
(13126 FUNERALS, 126 FIRMS)

MIDDLE ATLANTIC

OPERATING INCOME		AVERAGE		PERCENTAGE
FUNERAL CHARGES		1533		73.8
INTERMENT RECEPTACLE CHARGE		263		12.6
OTHER FUNERAL HOME CHARGES		22		1.1
CASH ADVANCES		261		12.5
ALL OPERATING INCOME		2079		100.0
MERCHANDISE COSTS AND CASH ADVANCES				
CASKET COST	271		13.0	
INTERMENT RECEPTACLE COST	139		6.7	
OTHER FUNERAL HOME COSTS	17		.8	
CASH ADVANCES	233		11.2	
ALL MERCHANDISE COSTS AND				
CASH ADVANCES	660	660	31.7	31.7
OPERATING MARGIN		1419		68.3
OPERATING EXPENSES				
AUTOMOBILE	140		6.7	
COLLECTION	15		.7	
DIRECT FUNERAL	78		3.8	
FACILITIES AND EQUIPMENT	235		11.3	
GENERAL	119		5.7	
PERSONNEL	557		26.8	
PROMOTION	49		2.4	
TAXES	66		3.2	
ALL OPERATING EXPENSES	1259	1259	60.6	60.6
NET MARGIN BEFORE INCOME TAXES		160		7.7

AVERAGE AND PERCENTAGE PER SERVICE INCOME AND EXPENSE STATEMENT FOR ALL SERVICES
 (22293 FUNERALS, 99 FIRMS)

SOUTH ATLANTIC

OPERATING INCOME		AVERAGE		PERCENTAGE
FUNERAL CHARGES		1500		76.8
INTERMENT RECEPTACLE CHARGE		249		12.7
OTHER FUNERAL HOME CHARGES		28		1.4
CASH ADVANCES		179		9.1
ALL OPERATING INCOME		1956		100.0
MERCHANDISE COSTS AND CASH ADVANCES				
CASKET COST	263		13.5	
INTERMENT RECEPTACLE COST	131		6.7	
OTHER FUNERAL HOME COSTS	14		.7	
CASH ADVANCES	172		8.8	
ALL MERCHANDISE COSTS AND				
CASH ADVANCES	580	580	29.7	29.7
OPERATING MARGIN		1376		70.3
OPERATING EXPENSES				
AUTOMOBILE	106		5.4	
COLLECTION	38		1.9	
DIRECT FUNERAL	58		3.0	
FACILITIES AND EQUIPMENT	190		9.7	
GENERAL	126		6.5	
PERSONNEL	624		31.9	
PROMOTION	49		2.5	
TAXES	76		3.9	
ALL OPERATING EXPENSES	1267	1267	64.8	64.8
NET MARGIN BEFORE INCOME TAXES		109		5.5

AVERAGE AND PERCENTAGE PER SERVICE INCOME AND EXPENSE STATEMENT FOR ALL SERVICES
 (42821 FUNERALS, 332 FIRMS)

EAST NORTH CENTRAL

OPERATING INCOME		AVERAGE		PERCENTAGE
FUNERAL CHARGES		1692		73.6
INTERMENT RECEPTACLE CHARGE		315		13.7
OTHER FUNERAL HOME CHARGES		13		.6
CASH ADVANCES		278		12.1
ALL OPERATING INCOME		2298		100.0
MERCHANDISE COSTS AND CASH ADVANCES				
CASKET COST	298		12.9	
INTERMENT RECEPTACLE COST	165		7.2	
OTHER FUNERAL HOME COSTS	8		.4	
CASH ADVANCES	259		11.3	
ALL MERCHANDISE COSTS AND				
CASH ADVANCES	730	730	31.8	31.8
OPERATING MARGIN		1568		68.2
OPERATING EXPENSES				
AUTOMOBILE	126		5.5	
COLLECTION	23		1.0	
DIRECT FUNERAL	63		2.8	
FACILITIES AND EQUIPMENT	267		11.6	
GENERAL	129		5.6	
PERSONNEL	654		28.5	
PROMOTION	65		2.8	
TAXES	107		4.6	
ALL OPERATING EXPENSES	1434	1434	62.4	62.4
NET MARGIN BEFORE INCOME TAXES		134		5.8

AVERAGE AND PERCENTAGE PER SERVICE INCOME AND EXPENSE STATEMENT FOR ALL SERVICES
(16637 FUNERALS, 161 FIRMS)

WEST NORTH CENTRAL

OPERATING INCOME		AVERAGE		PERCENTAGE	
FUNERAL CHARGES		1592		73.0	
INTERMENT RECEPTACLE CHARGE		325		14.9	
OTHER FUNERAL HOME CHARGES		13		.6	
CASH ADVANCES		250		11.5	
ALL OPERATING INCOME		2180		100.0	
MERCHANDISE COSTS AND CASH ADVANCES					
CASKET COST	281		12.9		
INTERMENT RECEPTACLE COST	178		8.2		
OTHER FUNERAL HOME COSTS	8		.4		
CASH ADVANCES	273		12.5		
ALL MERCHANDISE COSTS AND					
CASH ADVANCES	740	740	34.0	34.0	
OPERATING MARGIN		1440		66.0	
OPERATING EXPENSES					
AUTOMOBILE	113		5.2		
COLLECTION	30		1.4		
DIRECT FUNERAL	71		3.2		
FACILITIES AND EQUIPMENT	222		10.2		
GENERAL	129		5.9		
PERSONNEL	661		30.3		
PROMOTION	54		2.5		
TAXES	74		3.4		
ALL OPERATING EXPENSES	1354	1354	62.1	62.1	
NET MARGIN BEFORE INCOME TAXES		86		3.9	

AVERAGE AND PERCENTAGE PER SERVICE INCOME AND EXPENSE STATEMENT FOR ALL SERVICES
(8355 FUNERALS, 45 FIRMS)

EAST SOUTH CENTRAL

OPERATING INCOME		AVERAGE		PERCENTAGE	
FUNERAL CHARGES		1593		76.9	
INTERMENT RECEPTACLE CHARGE		278		13.4	
OTHER FUNERAL HOME CHARGES		20		1.0	
CASH ADVANCES		180		8.7	
ALL OPERATING INCOME		2071		100.0	
MERCHANDISE COSTS AND CASH ADVANCES					
CASKET COST	297		14.4		
INTERMENT RECEPTACLE COST	145		7.0		
OTHER FUNERAL HOME COSTS	11		.5		
CASH ADVANCES	176		8.5		
ALL MERCHANDISE COSTS AND					
CASH ADVANCES	629	629	30.4	30.4	
OPERATING MARGIN		1442		69.6	
OPERATING EXPENSES					
AUTOMOBILE	124		6.0		
COLLECTION	39		1.9		
DIRECT FUNERAL	67		3.2		
FACILITIES AND EQUIPMENT	227		11.0		
GENERAL	136		6.6		
PERSONNEL	652		31.4		
PROMOTION	47		2.3		
TAXES	66		3.2		
ALL OPERATING EXPENSES	1358	1358	65.6	65.6	
NET MARGIN BEFORE INCOME TAXES		84		4.0	

AVERAGE AND PERCENTAGE PER SERVICE INCOME AND EXPENSE STATEMENT FOR ALL SERVICES
    (9502 FUNERALS, 59 FIRMS)

WEST SOUTH CENTRAL

OPERATING INCOME		AVERAGE		PERCENTAGE	
FUNERAL CHARGES		1577		78.9	
INTERMENT RECEPTACLE CHARGE		237		11.9	
OTHER FUNERAL HOME CHARGES		17		.9	
CASH ADVANCES		167		8.3	
ALL OPERATING INCOME		1998		100.0	
MERCHANDISE COSTS AND CASH ADVANCES					
CASKET COST	288			14.4	
INTERMENT RECEPTACLE COST	127			6.3	
OTHER FUNERAL HOME COSTS	8			.4	
CASH ADVANCES	159			8.0	
ALL MERCHANDISE COSTS AND					
CASH ADVANCES	582	582		29.1	29.1
OPERATING MARGIN		1416			70.9
OPERATING EXPENSES					
AUTOMOBILE	129			6.4	
COLLECTION	57			2.9	
DIRECT FUNERAL	68			3.4	
FACILITIES AND EQUIPMENT	220			11.0	
GENERAL	150			7.5	
PERSONNEL	511			25.6	
PROMOTION	62			3.1	
TAXES	62			3.1	
ALL OPERATING EXPENSES	1259	1259		63.0	63.0
NET MARGIN BEFORE INCOME TAXES		157			7.9

AVERAGE AND PERCENTAGE PER SERVICE INCOME AND EXPENSE STATEMENT FOR ALL SERVICES
    (6810 FUNERALS, 44 FIRMS)

MOUNTAIN

OPERATING INCOME		AVERAGE		PERCENTAGE	
FUNERAL CHARGES		1310		80.7	
INTERMENT RECEPTACLE CHARGE		117		7.2	
OTHER FUNERAL HOME CHARGES		21		1.3	
CASH ADVANCES		175		10.8	
ALL OPERATING INCOME		1623		100.0	
MERCHANDISE COSTS AND CASH ADVANCES					
CASKET COST	232			14.3	
INTERMENT RECEPTACLE COST	66			4.1	
OTHER FUNERAL HOME COSTS	13			.8	
CASH ADVANCES	174			10.8	
ALL MERCHANDISE COSTS AND					
CASH ADVANCES	485	485		30.0	30.0
OPERATING MARGIN		1138			70.0
OPERATING EXPENSES					
AUTOMOBILE	94			5.8	
COLLECTION	24			1.4	
DIRECT FUNERAL	74			4.5	
FACILITIES AND EQUIPMENT	147			9.0	
GENERAL	117			7.2	
PERSONNEL	465			28.7	
PROMOTION	48			3.0	
TAXES	57			3.5	
ALL OPERATING EXPENSES	1026	1026		63.1	63.1
NET MARGIN BEFORE INCOME TAXES		112			6.9

AVERAGE AND PERCENTAGE PER SERVICE INCOME AND EXPENSE STATEMENT FOR ALL SERVICES
(6769 FUNERALS, 24 FIRMS)

PACIFIC

	AVERAGE		PERCENTAGE	
OPERATING INCOME				
FUNERAL CHARGES	1148		83.0	
INTERMENT RECEPTACLE CHARGE	63		4.6	
OTHER FUNERAL HOME CHARGES	56		4.0	
CASH ADVANCES	116		8.4	
ALL OPERATING INCOME	1383		100.0	
MERCHANDISE COSTS AND CASH ADVANCES				
CASKET COST	194		14.0	
INTERMENT RECEPTACLE COST	37		2.7	
OTHER FUNERAL HOME COSTS	26		1.9	
CASH ADVANCES	113		8.1	
ALL MERCHANDISE COSTS AND CASH ADVANCES	370	370	26.7	26.7
OPERATING MARGIN		1013		73.3
OPERATING EXPENSES				
AUTOMOBILE	58		4.2	
COLLECTION	17		1.2	
DIRECT FUNERAL	45		3.3	
FACILITIES AND EQUIPMENT	121		8.7	
GENERAL	101		7.3	
PERSONNEL	434		31.5	
PROMOTION	43		3.1	
TAXES	53		3.8	
ALL OPERATING EXPENSES	872	872	63.1	63.1
NET MARGIN BEFORE INCOME TAXES		141		10.2

RANGES IN PRICES OF SERVICES OFFERED

UNITED STATES	**Lowest, Median and Highest Prices for the Three Lowest (Funerals A, B, C) and the Three Highest (Funerals X, Y, Z) Total-Adult Services Offered.[a] The Median was computed.**		
	LOWEST	*MEDIAN*	*HIGHEST*
FUNERAL A (FIRST LOWEST PRICED)	125	1185	2158
FUNERAL B (SECOND LOWEST PRICED)	204	1365	2207
FUNERAL C (THIRD LOWEST PRICED)	416	1495	2445
• • •			
FUNERAL X (THIRD HIGHEST PRICED)	1105	2890	8985
FUNERAL Y (SECOND HIGHEST PRICED)	1150	3333	12780
FUNERAL Z (FIRST HIGHEST PRICED)	1255	4003	25000

[a]*The Definition of a "Standard" funeral differs from firm to firm and locale to locale. Using the reporting firm's own definition for adult funerals in which it provides all of the customary professional services, necessary facilities and equipment, and the casket as selected, the values in this table reflect the current prices for each of the three (3) lowest and the three (3) highest total-adult funeral services offered by that firm to anyone who desires them and which are within sight of all those who use its selection room.*

CHARGES AND COSTS FOR FIRMS USING SINGLE UNIT PRICING (49123 FUNERALS, 373 FIRMS)

	TYPE OF SERVICE			
	TOTAL-ADULT		ALL SERVICES	
DIVISION	FUNERAL CHARGES[a]	CASKET COST	FUNERAL CHARGES[a]	CASKET COST
UNITED STATES	1840	334	1636	293
1. NEW ENGLAND	1555	286	1443	267
2. MIDDLE ATLANTIC	1647	310	1511	281
3. SOUTH ATLANTIC	1823	323	1603	276
4. EAST NORTH CENTRAL	1925	349	1706	305
5. WEST NORTH CENTRAL	1800	315	1603	276
6. EAST SOUTH CENTRAL	1820	354	1617	310
7. WEST SOUTH CENTRAL	1760	312	1592	279
8. MOUNTAIN	1593	310	1408	268
9. PACIFIC	1595	303	1293	233

CHARGES AND COSTS FOR FIRMS USING BI-UNIT PRICING (18550 FUNERALS, 133 FIRMS)

	TYPE OF SERVICE					
	TOTAL-ADULT			ALL SERVICES		
DIVISION	FUNERAL CHARGES[a]	CASKET CHARGES	CASKET COST	FUNERAL CHARGES[a]	CASKET CHARGES	CASKET COST
UNITED STATES	1183	565	316	1026	474	266
1. NEW ENGLAND	1049	616	325	962	552	294
2. MIDDLE ATLANTIC	1205	562	299	1105	497	267
3. SOUTH ATLANTIC	1178	636	324	1020	541	276
4. EAST NORTH CENTRAL	1172	721	346	1056	629	303
5. WEST NORTH CENTRAL	1167	798	351	1042	689	304
6. EAST SOUTH CENTRAL	1787	78	320	1472	57	259
7. WEST SOUTH CENTRAL	1418	296	315	1231	260	272
8. MOUNTAIN	1047	597	297	830	439	223
9. PACIFIC	740	517	226	658	426	188

[a]*These figures do not include charges for interment receptacle, cemetery or crematory expenses, monument or marker, or miscellaneous items such as the honorarium for the clergy, flowers, additional transportation charges, burial clothing, or newspaper notices.*

CHARGES AND COSTS FOR FIRMS USING TRI-UNIT PRICING
   (18866 FUNERALS, 136 FIRMS)

TYPE OF SERVICE

TOTAL-ADULT

DIVISION	FUNERAL CHARGES[a]	FACILITIES AND EQUIPMENT	CASKET CHARGES	CASKET COST
UNITED STATES	791	367	693	334
1. NEW ENGLAND	646	461	607	298
2. MIDDLE ATLANTIC	558	542	889	336
3. SOUTH ATLANTIC	655	335	720	334
4. EAST NORTH CENTRAL	924	344	649	333
5. WEST NORTH CENTRAL	666	380	830	344
6. EAST SOUTH CENTRAL	0	0	0	0
7. WEST SOUTH CENTRAL	1179	274	664	433
8. MOUNTAIN	463	430	810	325
9. PACIFIC	1355	157	273	317

ALL SERVICES

DIVISION	FUNERAL CHARGES[a]	FACILITIES AND EQUIPMENT	CASKET CHARGES	CASKET COST
UNITED STATES	694	319	589	285
1. NEW ENGLAND	593	407	518	258
2. MIDDLE ATLANTIC	456	430	700	265
3. SOUTH ATLANTIC	579	295	620	289
4. EAST NORTH CENTRAL	818	305	563	289
5. WEST NORTH CENTRAL	597	339	722	302
6. EAST SOUTH CENTRAL	0	0	0	0
7. WEST SOUTH CENTRAL	1000	231	554	357
8. MOUNTAIN	396	349	633	258
9. PACIFIC	1109	131	215	255

[a]These figures do not include charges for interment receptacle, cemetery or crematory expenses, monument or marker, or miscellaneous items such as the honorarium for the clergy, flowers, additional transportation charges, burial clothing, or newspaper notices.

CHARGES AND COSTS FOR FIRMS USING MULTI-UNIT PRICING
   (47488 FUNERALS, 303 FIRMS)

TYPE OF SERVICE

TOTAL-ADULT

DIVISION	FUNERAL CHARGES[a]	FACILITIES AND EQUIPMENT	MOTOR EQUIPMENT	CASKET CHARGES	CASKET COST
UNITED STATES	773	212	103	693	315
1. NEW ENGLAND	668	347	152	698	309
2. MIDDLE ATLANTIC	903	193	97	602	321
3. SOUTH ATLANTIC	755	184	94	682	299
4. EAST NORTH CENTRAL	735	262	130	812	337
5. WEST NORTH CENTRAL	791	203	99	699	328
6. EAST SOUTH CENTRAL	684	266	143	629	308
7. WEST SOUTH CENTRAL	968	132	84	695	354
8. MOUNTAIN	461	242	80	824	281
9. PACIFIC	672	122	48	530	236

ALL SERVICES

DIVISION	FUNERAL CHARGES[a]	FACILITIES AND EQUIPMENT	MOTOR EQUIPMENT	CASKET CHARGES	CASKET COST
UNITED STATES	663	174	90	564	259
1. NEW ENGLAND	584	289	137	574	257
2. MIDDLE ATLANTIC	780	160	91	492	269
3. SOUTH ATLANTIC	630	141	79	543	240
4. EAST NORTH CENTRAL	651	222	115	681	287
5. WEST NORTH CENTRAL	691	169	86	563	269
6. EAST SOUTH CENTRAL	608	235	133	550	269
7. WEST SOUTH CENTRAL	829	111	73	586	297
8. MOUNTAIN	396	196	64	654	225
9. PACIFIC	564	102	43	402	182

[a]These figures do not include charges for interment receptacle, cemetery or crematory expenses, monument or marker, or miscellaneous items such as the honorarium for the clergy, flowers, additional transportation charges, burial clothing, or newspaper notices.

OPERATING SERVICE INCOME BY ARRANGEMENT STATUS

UNITED STATES		The Percentage of Funeral Services and the Average Funeral Charges by Arrangement Status				
		CHILD	*WELFARE ADULT*	*PARTIAL ADULT*	*TOTAL ADULT*	*ALL SERVICES*
NUMBER OF FUNERALS		4111	2419	23075	104422	134027
NON-PREARRANGED SERVICES	*PERCENTAGE*	99.66	98.80	97.90	96.59	96.95
	AVERAGE FUNERAL CHARGES	353	556	760	1821	1567
PREARRANGED SERVICES	*PERCENTAGE*	.34	1.20	2.10	3.41	3.05
	AVERAGE FUNERAL CHARGES	306	596	800	1477	1387
ALL SERVICES	*PERCENTAGE*	100.00	100.00	100.00	100.00	100.00
	AVERAGE FUNERAL CHARGES	352	556	761	1809	1561

AVERAGE VALUES BY COMPETITION CATEGORY (ALL SERVICES)
(134027 FUNERALS, 945 FIRMS)

UNITED STATES

	0 FIRMS	1 FIRM	2-3 FIRMS	4 OR MORE
NUMBER OF COMPETING FIRMS				
PERCENTAGE OF FIRMS	24	21	26	29
AVERAGE SERVICES PER FIRM	87	101	141	215
OPERATING INCOME PER SERVICE				
FUNERAL CHARGES	1624	1634	1600	1493
INTERMENT RECEPTACLE CHARGE	312	326	270	223
OTHER FUNERAL HOME CHARGES	16	16	21	21
CASH ADVANCES	222	231	228	228
ALL OPERATING INCOME	2174	2207	2119	1965
MERCHANDISE COSTS				
CASKET COSTS	293	292	288	258
INTERMENT RECEPTACLE COSTS	167	173	144	118
OTHER FUNERAL HOME COSTS	9	8	12	12
CASH ADVANCES	209	224	231	212
ALL MERCHANDISE COSTS	678	697	675	601
OPERATING MARGIN	1496	1510	1444	1364
OPERATING EXPENSES				
AUTOMOBILE	127	123	120	112
COLLECTION	30	23	30	29
DIRECT FUNERAL	59	70	61	67
FACILITIES AND EQUIPMENT	231	226	231	218
GENERAL	141	137	133	116
PERSONNEL	596	663	595	594
PROMOTION	43	50	56	59
TAXES	79	90	78	81
ALL OPERATING EXPENSES	1306	1382	1304	1276
NET MARGIN	190	128	140	88
INVESTMENT DATA				
ACCOUNTS RECEIVABLE	24837	33375	44894	62313
MERCHANDISE INVENTORY	13291	14042	14818	15451
BUILDING	81449	85808	105909	150326
FUNERAL SERVICE EQUIPMENT	24963	28005	33941	51157
MOTOR EQUIPMENT	27001	28514	33520	42418
ALL INVESTMENTS	171541	189744	233082	321664
AVERAGE PER TOTAL-ADULT FUNERAL				
FUNERAL CHARGES	1853	1880	1842	1747
CASKET COST	340	341	335	308

Facts and Figures on the Burial Casket Industry

What Is a Casket?

The word "casket" comes from a French word meaning a receptacle for something precious. In its contemporary meaning, a casket is a container used to display, transport and bury the deceased. It is an integral part of traditional funeral service in American society, and has been a part of social customs for most of the world's civilizations.

What Are Caskets Made Of?

More than 99% of all caskets manufactured in the United States are made of metal or wood. Roughly 71% are steel. Another 13% are hardwood, such as oak, poplar, willow, cottonwood, cherry, maple, walnut, birch, and mahogany. Wood caskets are made very much like fine furniture.

Less than 10% are cloth covered—usually inexpensive caskets made of softwood such as fir, pine, redwood, plywood or particle board, with a textile fabric glued to the surface in place of paint or lacquer. More than 3% are copper, bronze, or stainless steel, which—along with some of the hardwoods—tend to be the finest and most expensive caskets.

The balance is made up of such minor categories as plastic or fiberglass, zinc, aluminum and cultured marble (less than 1%), and children's caskets (less than 2%).

Casket interiors come in a wide variety, but most are either velvet, crepe or taffeta. Caskets are available in a great range of colors, interiors, styles, sizes and ornamentation. There are even units available with built-in lighting, adjustable inner springs, and with denim interiors. While the vast majority of caskets are still "traditional" in appearance, a consumer can find many nontraditional styles and features to meet his needs and preferences.

What Do Caskets Cost?

Most caskets are sold as part of a funeral service package rather than itemized separately. However, where the casket alone is separately priced by the funeral director, the average price is somewhere in the range of $700-$800, though at the extremes the price can vary from less than $200 to more than $5,000.

The cost of the casket is only a fraction of the total price of a complete funeral service. The average adult funeral currently costs $1,500 to $1,700, not counting cemetery expenses or such possible additional items as a burial vault, burial garments, flowers, clergy honorarium, etc. When these additional expenses are included, the total funeral cost probably averages $2,200-$2,400. However, a complete funeral, including casket, can still be purchased in most places for less than $1,000.

In late 1979, the *wholesale* price of the average adult casket ranged between $300 and $350. By category, the average wholesale prices were as follows: steel, slightly more than $300; hardwood, just under $450; copper or bronze, around $950; stainless steel, approximately $650; cloth covered, about $130; and children's, just over $80. In terms of the cost to the funeral director, the wholesale cost of the casket represents about 18%-19% of the total cost of the funeral.

Although the wholesale price of the average casket has increased for four years, the increase is less than the increase in the Consumer Price Index. Consumer prices have risen more than 35%. During the same time, the average wholesale price of caskets increased about 30%. Copper and bronze caskets actually declined in price, while stainless steel caskets went up less than 20%. Steel caskets, the most frequently sold, have increased in price by less than 30% over the same four years.

What Is A "Sealer" Casket?

Some metal units are called "sealer" or protective caskets. They are equipped with a gasket and locking mechanism which provides added protection against underground water and other elements. A gasketed protective casket is not designed to provide a permanent airtight seal; nor (like any man-made object) can it be expected to last forever after underground burial. However, a fine protective casket, manufactured to exacting specifications and with careful testing before leaving the factory, can provide an added measure of protection and security after burial.

How Many Caskets Are Used Each Year?

Americans use nearly two million caskets annually. Twenty years ago, the number of caskets sold coincided almost exactly with total mortality. Today, however, casket sales are nearly 5% lower than total deaths, primarily because of cremations and other "direct disposals" which do not make use of a casket. The following chart shows total mortality and estimated casket sales since 1968, with a projection for 1980.

YEAR	TOTAL MORTALITY	CASKETS SOLD
1968	1,930,082	1,880,286
1970	1,921,031	1,868,011
1972	1,963,944	1,905,026
1974	1,934,388	1,863,589
1976	1,909,440	1,827,354
1978	1,918,000	1,827,854
1980	1,930,000	1,830,000

The number of cremations in the U.S. has been inching up slowly for many years. The percentage of total deaths resulting in cremation was as follows for the last three years for which data are available: 1976, 7.33%; 1977, 7.66%; 1978, 8.58%. However, it is estimated that nearly 40% of all cremations involve a more or less traditional funeral utilizing a casket. (In other words, cremations are not synonymous with "direct disposal.") It is expected that the downward trend in mortality will be reversed in the 1980's, due to the steady growth in the number of elderly people.

Is It Possible To Rent A Casket?

Yes, a few funeral homes (probably fewer than 5%) do offer caskets on a rental basis. Following the service utilizing the rented casket, the body is placed in a cardboard, wooden or plastic receptacle and then usually cremated. The savings in cost range from nothing to several hundred dollars.

Who Makes Burial Caskets?

In the mid-1960's there were nearly 600 casket companies in the U.S. By 1979, the number had dropped to approximately 450 scattered through some 46 states. However, not all of these are manufacturers. A substantial minority do no manufacturing at all but simply act as distributors or middlemen between the manufacturer and funeral director.

The "typical" casket company is small (in the neighborhood of $1 million a year in sales), family—owned, has been in business for two or three generations, and offers no other products or services. However, there are great deviations from the average. In dollar sales volume, for instance, casket companies range from more than $100 million to less than $100,000 annually.

This is a mature industry, highly competitive, with little growth potential. The average profit (sales margin) of all U.S. casket companies is about 3%, based on surveys taken annually by the Casket Manufacturers Association. The number of caskets sold annually is rigidly limited by the mortality rate, which declined substantially from 1973 to 1979, due to improvements in health care for the aged, sharp reductions in infant mortality, and fewer accidental deaths. The low profits and highly competitive conditions in the industry have steadily reduced the number of firms in business through the 1960's and 1970's, amounting to a 20%-25% attrition over a 10 year period.

How Large Is The Casket Industry?

The total wholesale value of all the caskets sold each year by manufacturers and suppliers to funeral homes is well over a half-billion dollars. The industry uses more than 200 million pounds (100,000 tons) of steel, and more than seven million pounds of copper and bronze annually, in addition to the lumber, textiles and other materials used in the manufacture of caskets. In terms of employment, nearly 20,000 people draw their livelihood from the casket business, including factory and office workers, managers and sales people.

While these statistics may sound impressive, especially the total dollar figures, the truth is that by American industrial standards, casket manufacturing is very much a small business.

Is A Burial Vault Another Kind Of Casket?

No, a burial vault is an outer receptacle designed to encase and protect the casket—much as the casket itself holds the body of the deceased. The great majority of vaults are made of concrete or metal (steel, copper, bronze, stainless steel, etc.), but there are a few plastic and fiberglass units available also.

As with caskets, burial vaults cover a considerable price range and come in many styles and colors. There are nearly a thousand mnaufacturers of concrete burial vaults scattered all over the United States, most of them quite small and many of them engaged in the manufacture of other concrete products.

Funeral Service— Meeting Needs ... Serving People

Funeral Service/Retrospect

In the history of mankind, to all people in all ages and cultures the disposition of the dead has seemed an act of such solemnity as to require group concern for its fitting ceremonial observation. Out of a sense of loss, grief, mystery, or terror, men of all times have slowly developed patterns of conduct to provide for their behavior during the death cycle. Chief among the many factors setting such patterns have been religious beliefs. Thus funeral and burial customs have been created and developed.

Disposition of the dead is a process rooted in the very nature of mortality. The evidence of earth burial emerges from the remains of the paleolithic or "Old Stone" period, although undoubtedly it was a custom practiced for thousands of years before.

Although early Judeo-Christian burials were simple, little by little the Western world developed ceremonies surrounding the funeral. Medieval Europe witnessed great funeral pageantry. The Protestant Reformation reintroduced some of the earlier concepts, but by the 17th and 18th Century the English "undertaker" was becoming a recognized occupation.

These early English practices found their way into Colonial America and in the late 18th Century, undertakers began to offer goods and services in America. The earliest persons so engaged were often cabinet makers, sextons, nurses or livery men whose prime occupation made for a natural relationship to funeral service.

The first half of the 20th Century saw an intensification and development of the forces making for such change.

Funeral Service/Contemporary

Funeral service has accomplished a shift in emphasis from preoccupation with death and the dead to a genuine concern for life and the living, from safe-guarding the physical health of the survivors to safeguarding their mental and emotional health.

There has emerged a distinct vocation, in which an occupational group, motivated by professional-ization, is legally required to possess certain training and other qualifications in order to carry out specific tasks, which are assigned exclusively to it by both law and custom. The persons so serving are not merely preserving the dead but are also taking care of many funeral details and arrangements. Thus they are serving both sanitation and humanitarian needs. Changing funeral customs have opened new areas of social service to them. An emerging professional consciousness continues to take funeral operations out of the category of trade and business and into the category of professional service to people.

The young people today who select funeral service as their profession will find it necessary to be adequately trained and socially sensitive to the professional responsibility required for licensure and social service.

Funeral Service/Educational

Funeral service personnel, like pharmacists, doctors, lawyers and nurses, must meet certain requirements to get a license from the state in which they want to practice. Each state sets up its own requirements, which you can learn by writing the licensing agency in that state or any college offering training in funeral service.

These requirements generally include: (1) The minimum of a high school graduation; (2) In five states one year of college, in 21 states two years of college; (3) In every state at least a year in a professional curriculum; (4) Passing a state board licensing examination and (5) In every state a period of "internship" or apprenticeship ranging from one to three years with the norm being one year.

In most instances the professional curriculum is of four quarters duration or the equivalent thereof.

It encompasses courses in the areas of: Basic and Health Science
Including Anatomy, chemistry, bacteriology, pathology, hygiene and public health.
Funeral service arts and sciences
Including: Embalming and restorative art
Funeral service administration
Including: Accounting, funeral law, psychology, funeral principles, directing and management.

The cost of education in the professional curriculum varies depending on the type of school selected. The range for tuition for a year in the professional curriculum is $450 to $3,000. The cost of the professional training is one of the many criteria which should be evaluated in the final selection of a college.

The Commissioner of the U.S. Office of Education, Department of Health Education and Welfare has granted recognition to the American Board of Funeral Service Education as the sole accrediting agency in the United States for funeral service education. The schools and colleges so accredited are listed herein.

Funeral Service/Motivation

Young people today as they seek out and evaluate those vocational goals and objectives which will give them fulfillment and committment often ask, "is Funeral Service for me?" Affirmative answers to the questions below would most times indicate to such a person that they have the qualities possessed by a majority of the successful funeral service practitioners.

- [ ] Do you believe in and recognize the inherent dignity of man?

- [ ] Do you recognize the importance of ceremony as a means of expressing the feelings and needs of people?

- [ ] Do you have a sincere desire to serve people, especially when they are unable to meet their own needs for service?

- [ ] Do you realize the need for each individual to express his personal feelings as best fits his emotional reactions?

- [ ] Do you possess tolerance and understanding as each person expresses and uses his religious faith and practice?

- [ ] Do you desire, in return for deep personal satisfaction, to dedicate your life to a service profession which demands your sensitivity to the needs and desires of persons in bereavement?

- [ ] Do you desire to learn and become adept in those skills which enable persons in bereavement to face the reality of death?

Funeral Service/Care Giving

Approximately 1600 young people matriculate in funeral service education curriculums each year having chosen funeral service as a vocation. They find in it an opportunity for self-actualization that will permit them to be care-givers in their communities while meeting the needs of those who face dying, death and bereavement. These persons who choose to make Funeral Service a Career do so knowing that their major concern will be with the living and helping them work through the grief process. They will find themselves involved in hours of counseling—time spent with families in anticipation of the death of a family member, time spent in making decisions for the many arrangements and details when the death has occurred and time spent in post funeral counseling when their attention will be given to helping the family return to the mainstream of normal living. Throughout the counseling period these persons will also give attention to the respectful care and disposition of the person who has died. While this is the major emphasis of a funeral directors practice, he also attends to all of the related duties of routine daily tasks including maintenance of the funeral home

facility and other day-to-day operations that are important to community as well as the families being served. Legal requirements, community customs and mores as well as religious practices will be carefully observed and implemented. Beyond the family that survives the death, the funeral service practitioner will also make provisions for the community to recognize the fact that a death has occurred as it gives testimony to the fact that a life has been lived. Funeral Service exists in any given community with the sanction of citizens, as evidenced by proper licensure for the individual, as a way to provide proper care of the dead, give social support to the survivors and permit ceremonial recognition to mark the rite of passage.

Funeral Service/Service and Facility

Throughout recorded time men everywhere have sought by funeral ceremonies to honor their dead, and to aid the bereaved to return to normal activity. The rites they have used to accomplish these ends were as various as the cultures and religious beliefs in which they found root. Today, funerals in the United States are implanted in a fairly stable culture, and manifest a rather uniform pattern. But, whatever their forms, funeral can never be casual matters. The solemnity of the fact of death itself mitigates against mere fashion and whim; and the desire to show reverence for the dead, and respect and sympathy for the living, arises out of the deepest needs and the highest motives of human nature.

A funeral is the only ceremony to which none is formally invited but all may come. When the remains are present and viewable, at least while in state, the reality and finality of death are confirmed for the survivors.

The period of the funeral provides a proper climate for the natural and therapeutic expression of grief by those who have suffered loss. The bereaved may lessen their sorrow by sharing it, and confirm the love and sympathy of friends and relatives at a time when no love is asked in return. In addition, where a religious service is held, the profound consolations of the supernatural are added to these natural benefits.

The modern funeral home has been established as an appropriate place for making arrangements for the funeral, for the "in state" period and for conducting the funeral rites in whole or part. It has been especially planned to permit efficiency in the performance of the functions of funeral service, including preservation and preparation. It is so designed and equipped as to play its part in relieving the burden of sorrow of death through comfortable and convenient surroundings.

Funeral Service/Duties and Responsibilities

Service Details—After being selected by a family to serve them, the funeral director arranges for the removal of the deceased to the funeral home. Information for the death certificate and obituary notice is secured. The funeral director is responsible for the proper completion and filing of the death certificate, at which time the burial or transit permit is issued.

The funeral director makes an appointment to discuss the various phases of the service. These phases include: the place of service—church or funeral home; the time of service; the clergyman who will officiate at the funeral—always contacting him before the time and place are finally determined; selecting cemetery space—which may mean the purchase of a cemetery lot, or arranging for the opening of a grave in the family plot; music for the service, including organist, singer, and selection of titles; contacting fraternal officials (if any); notifying casket bearers; selecting the clothing necessary; and choosing the casket and outside receptacle. These preliminary arrangements are usually subject to subsequent checking and organization of details. Additional arrangements are considered in event the deceased is to be transferred to some other city for interment.

On the day of the services, which may be one day or two, three or more days from the time of death, the funeral director attends to floral arrangements, arranges for the physical facilities, provides cars for the family and casket bearers, receives and ushers friends to their seats, assists with the clergyman, organizes the funeral cortege, and has a car available to send flowers to the cemetery. The many separate details in the funeral service require the careful attention of the funeral director and his assistants.

Usually there will be a few further items that will be dictated by the particular service, appearing only as that service is planned and arranged. The family's wishes and desires will modify some of the details, for each entire funeral must be in keeping with the preferences of each family.

After the service the funeral director assists the family in filing necessary claims for social security, veteran's and union benefits, and insurance. Often a funeral director serves a family for several months following a funeral until all matters and details are satisfactorily completed for the family.

Funeral Service/Definitions

Funeral Director—This term is used commonly to designate that person who serves the public in all aspects of funeral service. Approximately 75% of all persons licensed in funeral service hold both a funeral director's and an embalmer's license or a combination thereof.

Embalmer—This term designates that person who by virtue of his education and training is licensed to prepare human remains for the purpose of a funeral and burial. Every state requires such persons to be licensed before practicing embalming.

Single License—some states grant a combined or single license covering the activity of both the embalmer and funeral director.

Intern or Resident Trainee (Apprentice)—All states require of prospective licensees a period of training under a licensee already engaged in funeral service. This period of training is known as resident training or apprenticeship. The length of this period varies from one to three years with the most common duration being one year.

Funeral Home—That place set aside for the practice of funeral service. The funeral home usually contains a room or rooms for funeral services, reception areas, visitation rooms and preparation areas. Such terms as mortuary and funeral parlor are used less frequently. In some instances the funeral home is licensed by either the state or community in which it is located.

Licensing Agency—Presently licenses to practice in funeral services are issued by state agencies so empowered.

Funeral Service/Statistical Data

Funeral Service, like all other professions, should be evaluated properly as to its potential for employment. Although the personnel turnover in funeral service is low, contrary to popular opinion it is not a closed field. Presently less than half of the persons entering funeral service have any prior or family connections in the profession. This is evidence that those seeking a funeral service vocation are motivated by other factors than merely family background.

Statistics recently gathered indicate there are approximately 22,500 funeral homes in the United States. The current number of deaths per year approximates 1.9 million making for a ratio of approximately 85 funerals per funeral home per year. This must be recognized simply as a statistical average. The ratio of funeral homes to population indicates that there is one funeral home for about every 9,300 persons.

In 1978, the average annual cash salary per employee was $18,224 plus additional personnel expenses for medical and hospital insurance and retirement and/or profit sharing. 31% of the firms have an employee retirement program, in addition to other fringe benefits. The average annual compensation for an owner was $30,273. In addition to this compensation owners had an average return of approximately $93 per funeral with an average total of 142 funerals per firm, including all services conducted and all merchandise provided, such as interment receptacles, clothing and net margin before income taxes.

Funeral homes are a stable organization. The average firm has been in the community 45 years. It is becoming common for funeral homes to have a history of 75-100 years of service. Some of these funeral homes are in the fourth generation of the family. This is evidence of both the stability of the funeral home within the community it serves and of the personnel serving the firm.

Funeral Service/Professional and Business Relationships

The direction and conduct of funerals brings the funeral director into close working association with practitioners in other service health care professions, and with a variety of businessmen. He has frequent contacts with physicians, health officers, medical examiners and coroners in the legal and medical aspects of post-mortem examinations. In cooperating with these officials, he is alert to conditions surrounding death, and to any other evidence which may create suspicion of criminal action.

He has frequent associations with the clergy of all denominations in planning funeral services in cooperation with ministers, priests, or rabbis, according to the religious preferences of the families he serves. In these contacts he displays his understanding of the faiths represented. Legal, tax and business problems bring him into contact with lawyers and accountants. He deals on a limited basis with newspaper reporters and editors. His work closely associates him with cemetery, crematory, and mausoleum officials.

Responding to a growing consciousness of common professional problems, most funeral directors are members of their state and national professional associations. Such membership not only provides pleasant social relationships among persons with a community of interests, tastes, backgrounds, and duties, but more important, the membership has value in supplying in-service training, through institutes, periodicals, conventions and other programs. Professional associations represent an occupational group before boards, legislatures and regulatory agencies, to stimulate and undertake research, and to evaluate and work for the improvement of professional standards and public relations.

In addition to membership in professional groups, the majority of funeral directors hold memberships in one, several, or many service clubs, such as Rotary, Lions, Kiwanis, or fraternal lodges, religious societies, or trade or business organizations. Many funeral directors are leaders and workers in community service events, campaigns, or governing bodies. One of the most satisfying compensations their profession brings is the time and opportunity of serving with the best elements of the community in such worthwhile community services.

Funeral Service/The Opportunity for Women

Throughout the history of Funeral Service, women have played an important role in the profession. They have served in fully licensed capacities and have adequately practiced in all phases of the profession. As funeral directors and embalmers, women can often add a special dimension to those they are serving as they determine their needs to work through and resolve their grief.

An even greater number of women are involved in funeral service in a non-licensed capacity. They serve as consultants, assistants, office managers, receptionists and secretaries. In these functions they have a great deal of contact with the families being served and the general public.

Though there are no statistics available based on recent emperical research there appears to be an ever increasing interest of women in funeral service both in licensed and non-licensed status.

Funeral Service/Literature

A Bibliography of Significant Books Dealing with Death, Grief, and Bereavement in Our Culture

Feifel, Herman; *The New Meaning of Death*, McGraw-Hill, N.Y., 1977
Gorer, Geoffrey; *Death, Grief, and Mourning*, Doubleday, N.Y., 1965
Grollman, Earl; *Explaining Death to Children*, Beacon, Boston, 1967
   Talking About Death, Beacon, Boston, 1970
   Concerning Death, A Practical Guide to Living, Beacon, Boston, 1974
Habenstein and Lamers; *The History of American Funeral Directing*, Bulfin Press, Milwaukee, 1955
   Funeral Customs the World Over, Bulfin Press, Milwaukee, 1963
Irion, Paul; *The Funeral — Vestige or Value?*, Abingdon. N.Y., 1966
   Cremation, Fortress Press, Philadelphia, 1968
Jackson, Edgar N.; *Understanding Grief*, Abingdon, N.Y., 1957
   You and Your Grief, Channel, N.Y., 1961
   The Christian Funeral, Channel N.Y., 1967
Kubler-Ross, Elizabeth; *On Death and Dying*, Macmillan, N.Y., 1969
Pine, *Caretaker of the Dead*, Halstead Press, N.Y., 1975
Raether, Howard C.; *Successful Funeral Service Practice*, Prentice-Hall, N.J., 1971
Raether, Howard C. Slater, Robert C.; *The Funeral Director And His Role As A Counselor*, Bulfin Press, Milwaukee, 1975
Sudnow, David; *Passing On*, Prentice-Hall, N.J., 1967
Westberg, Granger E.; *Good Grief*, Augustana Press, 1962
Monographs and Brochures available from:
   National Funeral Directors Association, 135 West Wells Street, Milwaukee, Wisconsin 53203
Fulton, *A Compilation of Studies of Attitudes toward Death, Funerals Funeral Directors*
Irion, *The Funeral an Experience of Value*
Jackson, *The Significance of the Christian Funeral*
Lamers, *Death, Grief, Mourning, The Funeral and the Child*

Brochure Series:
Facts About: Funerals . . . Disposition . . . Memorialization . . . Other Post Death Expenses . . . Sources of Information (NFDA Publication)
Why Do We Have Funerals Anyway? (NFDA Publication)
But I Never Made Funeral Arrangements Before! (NFDA Publication)
How Would You Tell Your Son His Grandpa Died? (NFDA Publication)
Should I Go To The Funeral? What Do I Say? (NFDA Publication)
Should The Body Be Present At The Funeral? (NFDA Publication)
Questions and Answers on Anatomical Gifts (NFDA Publication)
When A Death Occurs: . . . Needs . . . Concerns . . . Decisions (NFDA Publication)
Considerations Concerning Cremation (NFDA Publication)
Facts About Embalming (NFDA Publication)
Preparing Today For The Eventual Tomorrow — A Brief Review of Information Relating to the Funeral and Alternatives to it, Forms of Final Disposition, Planning in Advance and Helping Others
Preparing Today for the Eventual Tomorrow — Data and Preferences for Consideration Following the Death of _____

Changing Role of the Funeral Director

Some funeral service practitioners are apprehensive of paying visits to the sick because of a stigma on this practice in the past. However, that is changing with the impetus coming from outside of funeral service, primarily within the hospice movement. There are people who want to plan their funeral/alternatives while alive. Most times they want this done in the presence of a member(s) of their family. Either or both (terminally ill person—family member(s)) feel a funeral director should be present. This falls in line with the trend of many persons wanting to prearrange/pre-finance their funeral. Prearranging is prearranging whether done by an apparently healthy person or one who is fatally ill. The stigma which previously existed is lessening. However, the situation is sensitive and should be dealt with in a discreet manner. Regardless, the fact that it is happening signifies a change, although small, in the role of the funeral director.

Time of and Attitude During Arrangement

In the early 1950s there was a move to prearrange and pre-finance funerals as part of a package plan unlike the providing of funds for a funeral service through burial or funeral insurance. The trend to pre-arrange or to prearrange and pre-finance has grown. In 1980 approx-imately 2% of the services conducted had been prearranged by the deceased/survivors. This percentage will grow as the individuals who have prearranged their services get older and die. It is estimated that the number of services which will be prearranged and pre-financed will increase at a rate of at least 20% per year for the next 5 years. Most persons who prearrange and often pre-finance a funeral or an alternative do it more deliberately unless they are pressured by a salesperson anxious to get a name on the dotted line. If they feel a mystique about post-death activities they try to compensate with many more questions than when arrangements are made at the time of death. However, the mystique is not nearly as great as it once was even for those arranging immediately after death. The mystique coupled with "let's do what's right" is often being replaced by a person who is skeptical. A funeral director who does not eliminate the skepticism could build a feeling of suspicion hard to adapt to.

The Removal

Funeral service is witnessing somewhat of a reversion to practices of the early 20th Century. The hospice movement could result in more persons dying at home. Because of the closeness that hospice care creates and embellishes between the dying person and those in the same household, the survivors present sometimes assist in the "removal" to the extent of cleaning the body, wrapping it and help-ing to place it on the cot. Even if they do none of this, they are present while the removal is made, not shunted off to another room out of sight.

There are also some medical facilities where death occurs which now allow the family to be present at the time of death or see the deceased immediately following it. The significance of this is it per-mits those persons to view the body and confront the reality of what has taken place. This does not negate the value of further viewing during the visitation. It may enhance it depending on the condition of the body at the time of death. But it is a "happening" to be considered if and when the value of viewing is discussed sub-sequently with those who saw the deceased.

Embalming

There was a time in the United States when embalming was felt necessary for public health. Laws and regulations stated that if death occurred from any one of a number of diseases the body would have to be embalmed under any one of a number of circum-stances. There even were laws and regulations or emergency edicts that if death occurred from a stipulated disease, there could not be a public funeral.

That has changed. There seldom is an instance of a person get-ting one of the diseases previously listed as requiring embalming. And, authorities have denied and even attacked the public health claims for embalming. One of the most supportive facts for those who question the health value of embalming is the health of the persons in nations where embalming is a rarity.

However, embalming does have an undeniable public welfare consideration. An unembalmed body becomes a public nuisance un-less refrigerated or unless the temperature of the area is low enough where the body is to delay putrefaction. It could continue to be such unless there is final disposition within a rather limited period or the body is dry iced. Many times an unembalmed body is un-pleasant to see especially if mutilated or devastated by a lengthy illness.

If there is to be any delay in disposition of the body and/or the body is to be present for any rites or ceremonies, embalming is important as to the condition of the body per se and for the pur-pose of recall if there is to be visiting whether or not the dead body had been viewed before being embalmed.

A funeral director who says or implies anything different than these facts is guilty of outright or implied misrepresentation.

Disclosure

Mandated or volunteered disclosures are also somewhat a reversion to the past when the undertaker was an order taker—he would have a list of merchandise, livery and services available, find out what the family wanted and proceed to provide it on an itemized basis.

Reprinted from "Tradition in Transition," The Report of the 21st Century Committee of the National Funeral Directors Association, October 26, 1981.

Then there was a long period of time when the role of the funeral director changed from an order taker to a provider of standard or complete services. Persons wanted the "package" desiring total dollar costs.

Today the funeral director is not an order taker nor a provider of packaged offerings. Rather, the funeral director is a provider of service, facilities, equipment and an access to merchandise available for selection to allow for adaptation by those responsible for the arrangements.

In most instances, while making funeral arrangements for a widow of 85 the funeral director does not suggest as a starting point what the widow selected for her husband who died 20 years previously. Nor is the arrangement session following the death of a teenage suicide victim similar to that for an octogenarian or of a middle-aged husband and father who died suddenly.

While there are some funeral directors who offer a package(s) there must be adaptability regarding what is wanted or not wanted in the package. The future of funeral service hinges to an extent on those who made funeral arrangements saying they had options available to them, that they got what they wanted and paid for what they got, understanding that they must share the cost of making choices available to them.

Funeral, Disposition, Merchandise and Goods

Funeral, disposition, merchandise and goods have some value for everyone if only to transport the body and be a receptacle for final disposition.

The casket has value for most people for aesthetic reasons in association with the post-death rites and ceremonies as well as providing "protection" for the body.

In the latter instance body image of those making arrangements comes into play. "Protection" is also the basis for the purchase of a vault or grave liner when there is earth interment—"protection" which ranges from keeping the grave from caving in to protection against the elements of the grave.

Conversely, there are a growing number of people who see little or no value in a casket and want an alternative container or a rental unit. Among them are those who feel if there is earth burial that the casket or alternative should be bio-degradable. This is not to say that this attitude symbolizes a person who is anti-funeral. On the contrary some who want a minimum casket seek the best in services and facilities.

"The casket is not the funeral and the funeral is not the casket" is an adage of some years but its philosophy is not ingrained in many funeral directors. Those wanting to continue to practice funeral service must approach those selecting a funeral or alternative and price services and facilities in a manner which diminishes the over-reliance on the casket to "make ends meet."

Religious Facets of Post-Death Activities

There is increasing evidence that the public perceives the clergy-person as being less influential in the arrangement of and conduct of a funeral service. This is not to say that the clergyperson does not continue to be important. Funeral directors in the future will have to discreetly inquire about the religious background of the deceased and those who survived to ascertain to what extent, if at all, they wish a religious service with some of the service being at a church and if they are anxious to have a particular clergyperson. In this re-gard there are a growing number of instances where because of the shortage of clergypersons, especially in large metropolitan areas, the clergyperson shows up late or is unable to be in attendance. This is especially true when the service is not being held in church.

Extended Post-Death Activities

For many years it was said that the funeral director serves the living as the dead are cared for in a manner which maintains the dignity of man. Currently a proper statement is that the funeral director serves the living as the dead are cared for in a manner which maintains the dignity of humankind. The services of the funeral director are avail-able prior to need, at-need and long after the period of the funeral has ended. Not only is the funeral director involved in arranging for immediate post-death activities prior to and at-need but also should be attuned to and assist with extended post-death activities. It will almost become axiomatic that the American funeral service practi-tioner no longer can restrict activities to those which are of a pre-death and immediate post-death nature. There must be an interest in extended post-death activities. There are concerned widows looking for adjustment and advice. There are parents about to be divorced because of a death of an infant or a child. There are chil-dren having difficulty facing life because they lost a parent or sib-ling. These people need help. They seek a place where they can get it and meet with others in the same predicament as they are. This must become the role of funeral service licensees because they are involved daily with death and can be better catalysts to help iden-tify those who need help and provide some vehicle for giving it. This is an extension of care-giving. There are many self-help groups throughout the United States available to bereaved persons. These social support groups are growing. They are a recreation of the ex-tended family. It is within these self-help groups that the bereaved can find empathetic understanding both expressed and shared.

It is also with these groups that funeral directors should liaison and become a part of their programming not only as a group(s) of reference but also as a group to be assisted with literature, audio-visual aids and if need be a place to meet. Steps in this direction will help remove some of the image of the funeral home being a house of death with the funeral director a merchant selling the "products" available at that house.

Multi-Disciplinary Relations

There is no discipline which is involved with death and its immedi-ate and long range aftermath as much as are those in funeral service.

There are members of no profession or service trade which have the knowledge and experience to relate pre-death, at-death and post-death human behavior than that acquired by funeral service estab-lishments. There is perhaps no discipline which is the subject of more attacks than are funeral directors, most of which is because of their relationship to death.

There is no better way for individuals to become aware of what the funeral director does and why than the funeral director becom-ing and staying involved in multi-disciplinary activities. Funeral ser-vice can benefit in understanding by creating relationships with social workers, mental health workers, nurses and other health care professionals. It may take time but those in other care-giving professions do realize the tremendous task of the funeral director and the more than adequate manner in which the funeral director fulfills that task. Funeral directors who say nothing about what they know when pertinent are being conversation dropouts. For funeral directors not to initiate or become involved in multi-disciplinary proceedings borders on dereliction of responsibility.

The role of the funeral director goes beyond defending when derogatory charges are made. The role is to change those negative attitudes by relating the facts and being able to document the source of such facts by experience and/or by that which has been written and said.

Funeral Directors and Embalmers

Nature of the Work

Few occupations require the tact, discretion, and compassion called for in the work of funeral directors and embalmers. The family and friends of the deceased may be under considerable emotional stress and may be bewildered by the many details of the occasion. The *funeral director* (D.O.T. 187.167-30) helps them to make the personal and business arrangements necessary for the service and burial. The *embalmer* (D.O.T. 338.-371-014) prepares the body for viewing and burial. In many instances, one person performs both functions.

The director's duties begin when a call is received from a family requesting services. After arranging for the deceased to be removed to the funeral home, the director obtains the information needed for the death certificate, such as date and place of birth and cause of death. The director makes an appointment with the family to discuss the details of the funeral. These include time and place of service, clergy and organist, selection of casket and clothing, and provision for burial or cremation. Directors also make arrangements with the cemetery, place obituary notices in newspapers, and take care of other details as necessary. Directors must be familiar with the funeral and burial customs of various religious faiths and fraternal organizations.

Embalming is a sanitary, preservative and cosmetic measure. Embalmers, perhaps with the help of resident trainees (apprentices), first wash the body with germicidal soap. The embalming process itself replaces the blood with a preservative fluid. Embalmers apply cosmetics to give the body a natural appearance and, if necessary, restore disfigured features. Finally, they dress the body and place it in the casket selected by the family.

On the day of the funeral, directors provide cars for the family and casketbearers,

receive and usher guests to their seats, and organize the funeral procession. After the service they may help the family file claims for social security, insurance, and other benefits. Directors may serve a family for several months following the funeral until such matters are satisfactorily completed.

Working Conditions

Funeral directors and embalmers often work long hours and may be required to be "on call" and within quick traveling distance of the funeral home. Some employees work shifts; for example, nights 1 week, and days the next.

Occasionally embalmers may come into contact with contagious diseases, but the possibility of their becoming ill is remote, even less likely than for a doctor or nurse.

Places of Employment

About 45,000 persons were licensed as funeral directors and embalmers in 1978. A substantial number of the directors were funeral home owners.

Most of the 22,000 funeral homes in 1978 had 1 to 3 directors and embalmers, including the owner. Many large homes, however, had 20 or more. Besides the embalmers employed by funeral homes, several hundred worked for morgues and hospitals.

Training, Other Qualifications, and Advancement

A license is needed to practice embalming. State licensing standards vary, but generally an embalmer must be 21 years old, have a high school diploma or its equivalent, graduate from a funeral service college, serve a 1- or 2-year resident traineeship, and pass a State board examination. One-half of the States require a year or more of college in addition to training in mortuary science.

All but six States also require funeral directors to be licensed. Qualifications are similar to those for embalmers, but directors may have to take special apprenticeship training and board examinations. Most people entering the field obtain both licenses, however some States issue a single license to embalmer/funeral directors. Information on licensing requirements is available from the State office of occupational licensing.

High school students can start preparing for a career in this field by taking courses in biology, chemistry, and speech. Students may find a part-time or summer job in a funeral home. Although these jobs consist mostly of maintenance and clean-up tasks, such as washing and polishing funeral coaches, they can be helpful in gaining familiarity with the operation of funeral homes.

In 1978, 35 schools had mortuary science programs accredited by the American Board of Funeral Service Education. About one-half were private vocational schools that offer 1-year programs emphasizing basic subjects such as anatomy and physiology as well as practical skills such as embalming techniques and restorative art. Community colleges offer 2-year programs, and a small number of colleges and universities offer 2- and 4-year programs in funeral service. These programs included liberal arts and management courses as well as mortuary science. All programs offered courses in psychology, accounting, and funeral law.

State board examinations consist of written and oral tests and actual demonstration of skills. After passing the examination and meeting other requirements, resident trainees receive a license to practice. If they want to work in another State, they may have to pass its examination, although many States have mutual agreements that make this unnecessary.

Important personal traits for funeral direc-

Reprinted from *Occupational Outlook Handbook,* 1980–81 Edition, U.S. Department of Labor, Bureau of Labor Statistics, Bulletin 2075, March 1980.

tors are composure, tact, and the ability to communicate easily with the public. They also should have the desire and ability to comfort people in their time of sorrow.

Advancement opportunities are best in large funeral homes where directors and embalmers may earn promotion to higher paying positions such as personnel manager or general manager. Some workers eventually acquire enough money and experience to establish their own businesses.

Employment Outlook

Little change in the employment of funeral directors and embalmers is expected through the 1980's. Demand for funeral services will rise as the population grows and deaths in-, crease. Most funeral homes, however, will be able to meet the demand without expanding their employment. The average funeral home conducts only one or two funerals each week and is capable of handling several more without hiring additional employees.

In recent years, the number of funeral service college graduates has approximately equaled the number of jobs available due to retirements, deaths, and transfers to other occupations. Because there are a limited number of employers in any geographical area, many students should secure a promise of employment before entering a program. However, barring any significant growth in enrollments, future graduates should find job opportunities available.

Earnings

In 1978, funeral directors and embalmers generally earned from $11,000 to $17,000 a year. Resident trainees earned between $135 and $220 a week. Managers generally earned between $13,000 and $24,500 a year, and many owners and officers of homes earned more than $35,000. In addition, the majority of funeral homes have health or life insurance programs, and many homes provide directors with clothing allowances.

In large funeral homes, employees usually have a regular work schedule. Typically they put in 8 hours a day, 5 or 6 days a week. Occasionally, however, overtime may be necessary.

Mortuary Operation as a Career

Charles H. Nichols, Ph.D.
Director and Trustee Emeritus
National Foundation of Funeral Service
Evanston, Illinois

Introduction

It's wonderful to be young—but sometimes a bit bewildering, too! The high school senior or young college freshman has most of his life stretching before him, with thousands of fascinating vocational possibilities. How to invest that life, however, in a manner that will be rich and rewarding—not only to himself, but to his fellow man as well—is a momentous decision to make! It is not a decision to be made lightly, or to have forced upon one. It must be done wisely, after a careful consideration of all the different possibilities, and not without a considerable amount of thought about one's capabilities, one's own interests and aptitudes. To aim too low may result in frustration. To aim too high, beyond one's capabilities, may lead to heartbreak. To aim outside the scope of one's interests may result in a dronish life of boredom and failure. So take your time and don't rush in where angels fear to tread!

Scope of This Monograph. Now funeral service is one, but just one, of the countless occupations from which you might choose. A wise choice is necessarily based upon information and understanding—of yourself, and of the vocational possibilities open to you. Your teacher or the vocational guidance counselor at your school will be able to help you discover the facts about yourself: where your vocational interests lie, what special aptitudes you may have, your personality strengths and weaknesses and similar important information. That is half of the picture; the other half is information about the vocations from which you might choose. It is the purpose of this monograph to give you an overall picture of one of these vocations—mortuary operation. Now, obviously, in a booklet the length of this one, it is not possible to treat each and every phase of mortuary operation in great detail, but we shall talk just enough about each important aspect of the field to give you a good idea of everything that's involved. We shall

discuss the terms and ideals of the field, consider its history and development, investigate its importance, describe the place in which the work is actually done, take a look at the work itself—its attractions and disadvantages, its demands and remunerations. Most important, we shall look into the matter of preparation for the field, the means of breaking into it, the kind of jobs you might expect to find and sources of further information about it—organizations and books and magazines.*

Definitions. Perhaps you were a bit surprised at the title of this monograph—"Mortuary Operation As A Career." There is a good reason for speaking of "mortuary operation" rather than some other term you might have expected. The field is a broader one than you might have realized and it includes a number of different kinds of workers—and of work.

Most important of these workers is the funeral director or mortician, whichever you prefer. Both terms are in fairly common usage within the field, although "funeral director" seems to be the vocational name that has widest acceptance. A number of years ago he was referred to as an "undertaker"—one who undertook the task of caring for the dead—and this term is still used by some of the public at large. However, the new terminology is not only more accurate in its description of the worker involved, but it also gives due recognition to the vast amount of professional progress that has been made in the field since the turn of the century.

The embalmer is another important worker in mortuary operation. It is he who devotes his skill, not only to the disinfection and relative preservation of the dead human body, but, in cases of emaciating illness or mutilating accidents, to restoration of the dead human body to acceptable appearance so important to creation of a lasting "memory picture" of the deceased. It is this part of his job, with its emphasis upon consideration for survivors, that has contributed

---

*See the **Associations** and **Publications** sections of this book.

Reprinted from "Mortuary Operation as a Career," National Foundation of Funeral Service, The Foundation Press, Evanston, IL, 1979.

much toward making modern funeral service a service for the living. All too often, funeral service is starkly defined as "care and disposal of the dead." That definition lacks a great deal insofar as the modern concept is concerned. First of all, it makes no mention of religious sentiment or humanist concern for the individual dignity of man, so important to U.S. funeral service. Secondly, it omits the fact that, as has been said, funeral service is largely a service to the living—those who are left behind. After all, there is precious little, if anything, that can be done for the dead; they are beyond human help. But there is much that the funeral director can and does do to help the living, to ease their grief, to aid them in meeting the problems that death leaves in its wake. This service, through a long development, has become so complete that the bereaved family usually needs do no more than call the funeral director and, if religiously oriented, their clergyman.

It is important to recognize that funeral director and embalmer are performing two separate functions and, by many states, separate licenses are issued to these practitioners. Very often an individual will hold both licenses—but not necessarily. Nor are these the only workers in funeral service or in mortuary operation: there are, particularly in the larger funeral firms, many other types to be found—receptionists, clerical workers, housekeepers, gardeners and maintenance men, chauffeurs and others who will be mentioned later in their proper place.

But it won't do to mislead you! The average funeral director is a small operator, not likely to have more than several assistants at the most, perhaps part-time assistants at that. Population concentration, more than any other factor, determines the kind of funeral operation you are likely to find. In the large metropolitan areas, where population is highly concentrated, you will find both large and small establishments, in varying degrees of completeness; but here you will also find the funeral broker—a type of operator frowned upon by the more ethical group in the field. He possesses only a license to operate. He arranges to have the embalming done in another establishment, either by himself (if he is a licensed embalmer) or by a trade embalmer (who sells his services on a "per case" basis). He takes his clients to the display room of the manufacturer to select a casket. He conducts the funeral either from the home, or the church, or both. In short, he has no establishment except possibly an office, but, more likely, even this is in his home. In order to exist, he must operate on a margin—and too often it is more than it should be. This type of operator has done altogether too much to create public misunderstanding and bad feeling toward funeral service, and the associations in the field work constantly to combat his ill effects.

In more sparsely inhabited areas, where the population is not sufficiently large to support a full time funeral director, you will find the combination director or multiple business operator. He really works at two occupations at the same time—one of which is funeral service. The most traditional combination is that of funeral service and furniture; there are still many smaller towns throughout the West and Northwest where the funeral director sells furniture on the side.

Ideals. Mention was made, in the preceding section, of ethics. Practically every vocational group has ideals by which it works and, particularly at the professional level, these ideals are embodied in codes of ethics. Funeral service, too, has its ethical codes—those of the national associations, of the state groups, and often of local groups as well. In spite of the fact that there are a number of codes, there is a recurrence of the same principles in these codes—principles that you must be prepared to work by if you choose funeral service as your occupation.

Foremost among these principles is that of public service. The welfare of the community is placed above that of the individual and no ethical practitioner will engage in activities that conflict with the public interest, however much they might enhance his selfish advantage. The ethical funeral director pledges full support of the laws of his city, his state and nation, with special obligations toward those involving public health and the recording of vital statistics.

Observance of a high level of morality is another recurrent principle in these various codes. This is usually spelled out in terms of fitting conduct, strict honesty, just dealings, and fair competitive practices. In earlier codes, prescribed action for specific situations was sometimes to be found—but the modern codes have recognized that it is impossible to cover every situation that might arise; as a result they are now framed in general terms with reliance upon the conscience of the ethical man to interpret the spirit of the code in terms of the situation he faces at any given moment.

The obligation of the funeral director to the family he serves is also paramount among the ethical principles of the profession. The funeral director pledges understanding and respect for all religious creeds and customs. Particularly, he pledges to maintain a strictly confidential relationship with his clients—for he often comes into possession of information which would be highly embarrassing, even damaging, to the welfare and reputations of his clients, should he violate their trust.

Another principle frequently found in the codes is advancement of the profession itself. Mention will be found of suitable educational standards, of proper licensing laws, of research and scientific progress, of professional competency, dignity and cooperation, interchange of ideas and knowledge, and similar considerations. This principle is indirectly in the public interest, for the realization of such ideals ensures an even higher level of service.

When everything is said and done, the spirit of all these codes has been expressed beyond improvement by Jesus of Nazareth when he admonished: "Whatsoever ye would that men should do unto you, do ye also unto them." As a matter of fact, the Golden Rule is embodied in at least one ethical code of funeral service.

History of the Vocation

Every member of an occupational group looks with pride upon the background of that group. Should you choose mortuary operation as *your* career, you will undoubtedly wish to examine in some detail the history of this vocational field. However, for our purposes here, we are interested only in those phases of such history which shed some light upon the problem at hand—examination of the field from the point of view of possible vocational choice.

Origins of Burial Customs. Human death is almost as old as man himself, so it would be difficult to trace funeral service to its earliest beginnings. It *is* possible, however, to consider some of the origins of burial customs, restricting ourselves to those which seem to have left an imprint upon the customs of our own place, in our own day.

"Show me the manner in which a nation cares for its dead," said the great English statesman, Gladstone, "and I will measure with mathematical exactness its respect for the laws of order and society." Respectful care of the dead has characterized every great civilization, albeit the expression of that care has taken many forms. Interestingly, some of this variety is reflected in the burial customs of our own people today.

The early Egyptians introduced the practice of embalming—in an effort to preserve the body, which they believed would be reinhabited by the departed spirit at some future time. The practice, after a lapse of many centuries, has been revived today—though the purpose and the methods are far different. Embalming in our country today is largely a public health measure, which also makes possible a more pleasant final "memory picture" of the deceased for survivors. The Egyptian method was essentially a crude disemboweling and pickling process; today's method is a simple replacement of the body's blood with disinfectant and preservative chemical fluids. "Preservation" is a relative term, for time stretches ahead endlessly, and embalming is intended to prevent putrefaction and postpone for an indefinite period that time when the body will ultimately be reduced to its elements.

Jewish customs, among the orthodox, have been preserved to the present day. To them, the body, as the dwelling place of the spirit, must be absolutely inviolate: so they oppose cremation and, in some instances, embalming. Normally, burial takes place before sundown of the same day on which death occurs—but if temporary preservation is necessary, ice is still used among the very orthodox. The burial receptacle is either a shroud or a very simple, and very plain, unfinished wooden casket.

To the ancient Greeks and Romans we owe another current custom—that of cremation, the practice of burning the dead. While the Greeks and Romans normally used huge funeral pyres for the purpose, modern technology has devised electric furnaces capable of generating intense heat, so that the process is much more quick and complete. The orthodox Jews, as has been said, object to cremation; so, generally, do certain denominational groups of the Christian faith—most often for religious reasons. Some, with strong feelings about the body as the temple of the soul, feel that cremation is a desecration of God's handiwork; others are equally strong in their conviction that cremation is a way of utilizing natural forces, equally God-given, to reduce the body more cleanly and more quickly to its irreducible components. In either case, the ethical funeral director will serve the family as it wishes to be served.

Cremation does not usually form a part of the mortuary operator's work: it is done in specially designed and constructed crematories and whether the family chooses earth burial, entombment, or cremation for final disposition, the service rendered by the funeral director is essentially the same. Hence, cremation will receive no further discussion, except as it may be incidentally involved, in this monograph.

To the Romans, also, we owe the derivation of our modern term, "funeral." It comes from the Latin word, "funeralis," meaning "torchlight." It derives its current meaning, in English, from the fact that so many Roman funerals were held at night, by torchlight.

To the Jews and early Christians we are indebted for the use of tombs or sepulchres. The principle involved is placement of the dead in prepared burial chambers, either above or below ground: above ground as in the case of the cave-tomb used for the body of Jesus, below ground as in the case of the catacombs, where the early Christians buried their dead—and where they were safe from the Romans, who had superstitious fears of the places of the dead. The modern counterpart of such prepared burial chambers is the mausoleum. It has limited use over the country at large, but there are sections of the country, such as in the New Orleans area, where the subterranean water level is so high that either *very* shallow graves must be dug or, as is common practice, mausoleums are used.

Importance of National and Denominational Customs. One of the great strengths of our American heritage is the intermingling of many different cultural backgrounds, many different racial and national customs, many different denominational points of view. In the large metropolitan areas of the nation, as you well know, there are dozens and dozens of such different groups, all living together in one city. This is not so true of rural areas, yet even here it is possible to find sections of the country that have been populated by some one particular group with social customs peculiar to itself—as the Mormons, Mennonites, or, for that matter, concentrated nationality groups.

While the process of assimilation into what might eventually be called an American type goes on all the time, yet it is desirable, for the enrichment of our own culture, that the mores of these groups be recognized and fostered. For the funeral director, it is more than desirable; it is mandatory! These groups, or many of them, do have funeral customs distinctly their own. There is not space to treat them here, but we *are* pointing out their importance! Fortunately, a funeral director seldom has to be acquainted with them all—but he must know thoroughly any peculiarity of custom among those groups that comprise his own clientele.

Development of Funeral Service in the United States. In our early history, when society itself was relatively simple as compared to modern complexities, the family and friends of the deceased usually handled the details of the funeral. The local cabinet maker was called in to build a coffin—literally, a wedge-shaped box to hold the body. Homes were usually clustered around the village church, and the churchyard was usually the burial place, so that transportation was no great problem. There were no means of preservation, so burial took place as soon as practicable after death.

The nation grew and developed. It changed from a predominantly simple agrarian or rural economy to a much more complicated industrial one. We fought several wars, and during the Civil War an army surgeon conducted some of the early work in embalming—in this country—in order to return the remains of certain war dead to their homes. People began to congregate in cities and towns. Their smaller living quarters did not often lend themselves to funerals when death occurred in a family. Moreover, churchyards became inadequate as burial grounds and it became less desirable to have such places within the confines of the city or town. Accordingly, they were moved to the outskirts—and the livery man entered the funeral picture, to provide the necessary transportation.

During the first quarter of the Twentieth Century, roughly, a new pattern of funeral service emerged. Funerals were moved from private homes to specially designed, or remodelled, funeral establishments. At first these establishments were more or less confined to metropolitan areas, but they have gradually spread throughout the rural areas of the nation. Embalming techniques, now vastly improved, came into wider usage. Motorized equipment replaced horse-drawn vehicles in funeral service. Marching with time came new developments in funeral merchandise and equipment, a new conception of service to the living replacing mere disposal of the dead. In this process, the "undertaker" gave way to the "funeral director" or "mortician." Funeral service became more professional in the rendering of a highly specialized service to the living, such as counsel and guidance in making the adjustment to great personal loss, help and advice, not only in matters of the funeral, but in matters of insurance, estate, government benefits (such as social security, veterans' benefits, old age pension benefits from the state, etc.), and similar considerations. Obviously, the funeral director did not replace the lawyer, the banker, or the insurance broker in these matters, but he was expected to be familiar enough with the problems and procedures involved to guide the family in taking the right initial steps.

A serious effort was made to "degloom" funeral service and transform it into a genuinely helpful service for survivors. Religious aspects were by no means lost in the process, but reenforced through close cooperation with church and clergy. This significant change in professional point of view is reflected in the very terminology of the field. "Undertaker," as has been pointed out, is no longer well used; it has been replaced by "funeral director" or "mortician." What once was baldly called the "morgue" is now called the "preparation room." The "grave yard" is now a "cemetery." The "coffin" has been replaced by a "casket," differently designed and signifying a receptacle for something precious—as the remains usually are to the family and friends. A "tombstone" has become a "monument" or "memorial tablet." The "hearse" is now a "casket

coach." These changes represent something far more fundamental than mere alterations in the verbal tags; they are signs of the underlying change that has occurred in actual philosophy; they are keys to understanding the modern concept of funeral service as contrasted to what it was a half-century ago.

Importance of the Vocation

Perhaps before all others, the American people recognize the dignity of labor. All value, in a broad sense, stems from one sort of labor or another—whether it be manual or mental, creative or routine, administrative or productive, distributive, professional, service, or what. The world and all that is within it has its source of human values in human labor, conceived in this broad sense. So no work is without importance, but each, perhaps, has its special importance—and to consider the special importance of mortuary operation is our purpose now.

When death strikes a family, then, if ever, that family needs a friend—a friend who is capable, through background and experience, of rendering all the specialized services and furnishing all the specialized merchandise needed for a funeral; a friend who will help tide them over a trying period of grief and dislocation of family affairs. Such a friend is the funeral director. Ideally, the ethical practitioner attempts to anticipate every need, every desire, of the bereaved family, so that this difficult time is made as easy as possible for them.

Scope. It is easy to form a mental picture of the geographical scope of funeral service if you keep in mind that it is essentially a community service. A funeral home should be within reasonable reach of everyone in the community, just, for example, as a high school should be. Where people are scattered over a broad territory, then they may have to travel a bit farther to reach a funeral home; but, again, this is true of some high schools when they represent, for purposes of economy and efficiency, consolidated districts. According to the 1978 *Statistical Abstract of the United States,* there are about 25,000 public high schools in the United States. This figure should be compared to approximately 22,000 funeral homes in the nation. (The government reports 20,900 funeral service establishments and crematories, but this figure does not include many smaller combination businesses.)

Perhaps the scope of mortuary operation will be somewhat clarified if we consider a few additional statistics. According to 1970 Census figures, total population of the United States was then 203,211,926. A quick rule of thumb for death rate is ten per thousand people per year. The actual death rate for the census year, 1970, was 9.4 deaths per thousand of population, and actual mortality totalled 1,921,000. By 1977, the death rate dropped to 8.8 and mortality declined to 1,898,000. Government figures from the 1978 *Statistical Abstract* (but actually covering the year 1972) indicate there were 70,200 paid employees with 15,400 payroll establishments—plus 5,500 non-payroll establishments—to handle this mortality.

Using government figures from the 1978 *Abstract* (for 1972), there was an average of 94 deaths per year per funeral establishment. W. M. Krieger, in his book, *Successful Funeral Service Management,* stipulated that a funeral director who is contemplating his own business must be able to count upon at least sixty cases per year if he hopes to operate efficiently and with a decent return to himself. Public interest is very directly involved in this consideration, for if a firm must spread its operating costs plus a profit over too few cases, then prices become unjustifiably high, from a socio-economic point of view. Yet, considering that the average cited above was 94 deaths per firm, it is well to keep in mind that the typical establishment, in funeral service, is a small establishment.

Impressions of Young Practitioners. Don't you find it helpful, very often, when you are facing a particularly knotty problem, to get the thinking of your own age group? Of course the oldsters are always ready to lend a few well-chosen words of advice, but it is sometimes more to the point to get your pal's slant, or your girl friend's or at least someone's not too much older than yourself. With this thought in mind, I am reproducing here excerpts from three prize-winning essays, written by young people on the topic, "Funeral Service as a Career." I give them to you without comment, for I think you will find them thought-provoking.

"Few careers present a young man the challenges of funeral service. In this profession, he is constantly working with people who are under deep emotional strain. These people must be helped and guided in a manner requiring tact, courtesy, and a sympathetic understanding. One must also sacrifice some of his personal and family life in order to serve others. This requires understanding by his family. The close relationship with people offers constant variety in one's daily work, the inner satisfaction of helping in time of need, and the pride of a job well-done."

"Funeral Service has come to mean the successful execution of all details necessary in the preparation, display and burial of a deceased person, to the complete satisfaction of the survivors. It has become so complete and intricate that it has risen to a professional level. What finer career could a man select than to serve his fellow man by offering his life as a bulwark to soften the griefs which will inevitably be thrust upon them by the passing of their loved ones? In this career there is an open field for improvement. The measure of success will be decided by the completeness of this service and its faultless execution."

"Funeral Service is a profession dealing not with the dead, as is the common thought, but with the living. Factual thinking proves this point. The funeral director acts entirely for the survivors, doing all within his means to make those shattered hours a little more peaceful and bearable. Through his service and attention, the sense of loss and shock is greatly reduced. In the utmost confidence he is called upon to care for the remains of the deceased, the most precious possession of that family. From the embalming procedure to the funeral service itself he is concerned with but one object—the alleviation of grief and sorrow of the living by assuring them every comfort, consideration, and service possible. Rendering a service to the living, in tribute to their dead, is the funeral director's aim."

The Funeral Home

In considering this field, you will naturally be interested in the place of work. Any absolutely true answer would have to be given in terms of a specific firm, for there is much variation. Generally speaking, a funeral service firm conducts its operation from a mortuary constructed or remodelled specially for its purpose. If there is a preparation room on the premises where the embalming is done, and if an actual selection of funeral merchandise, chiefly caskets, is made available on the premises—in addition to the other rooms required for normal service—then the mortuary is spoken of as a "complete establishment." This is a major distinction, you will recall, between funeral directors and funeral brokers.

A Typical Funeral Home. The remarks which follow, let it be understood, apply to the complete establishment. These are rooms you will normally find in a good physical plant: a Preparation Room where the body is cleaned, shaved, embalmed, groomed, restored when necessary, dressed, cosmetized and casketed—very much like a modern operating room in a hospital; a Selection Room or Display Room where a balanced selection of caskets is shown, often with the addition of vaults, burial garments, cremation urns; several State or Reception Rooms, where the deceased is kept prior to the funeral service; a Chapel or Service Room, where the funeral service itself is normally conducted, often with a private Family Room off to one side. In addition, you will frequently find all the normal rooms and conveniences of a regular home. Very often, too, where personnel are required to live at the home, or to remain at the home for set periods, a recreation room, bedrooms, sometimes an apartment, will be provided for their use. Generally speaking, the owners of funeral establishments realize that their personnel must spend a considerable amount of time in the funeral home, both waiting and on duty, so they make every effort to provide pleasant and comfortable surroundings for them.

Facilities and Equipment. Apart from the physical plant, the funeral director has a considerable investment in furnishings and equipment. No attempt will be made here—although we shall consider overall investment later—to itemize the costs of furnishing and equipping each type of room; obviously, even as in furnishing a regular home, a considerable amount of variation will be found, depending upon the levels of quality selected, the degree of lavishness, and similar factors. In the Preparation Room you will normally find an operating table—possibly several—with special water supply and drainage facilities, embalming equipment and supplies, wheeled tables for moving the deceased, and casket trucks. In the Selection Room, which is usually a beautifully decorated, carpeted and lighted room, you will frequently find simple furniture groupings in addition to the actual funeral merchandise shown. The Chapel or Service Room is normally furnished with fixed pews, as in a church, or in drawing room fashion with appropriately styled furniture; in the latter instance, folding chairs are usually available to increase seating capacity to the desired number. In the Chapel or Service Room, too, you will find either a regular pipe organ, an electric organ, a record player with amplifying equipment, or a piano—possibly all these things. Custom varies, so that in some few sections of the country the State or Reception Room is furnished as a regular bedroom, while in most others it is like a miniature drawing room with special provision for the casketed remains of the deceased—a lighted alcove or niche.

The average funeral director has a big investment, too, in his motor equipment—what is often called his "rolling stock"—though sometimes, in the metropolitan areas, such equipment can be largely rented from special livery companies or secured from association owned or cooperative pools. Even where such automotive equipment is rented, however, the funeral director must have some kind of vehicle for making what is professionally known as "the first call." In addition, a casket coach is necessary for operation, as well as a flower car, limousines and, possibly, utility or service cars. As if this weren't enough, those funeral directors who offer an ambulance service (as many of them do) will require an ambulance, possibly several, and this is a very expensive piece of automotive equipment indeed!

It is impossible to mention all of the smaller items of specialized equipment needed throughout the funeral home. Catafalques or casket standards (upon which the casket rests) can be quite expensive, particularly when you consider that he will require at least as many as the number of caskets he displays in his Selection Room—anywhere from ten to fifty—plus those he normally uses in his State Rooms and Chapel. Special religious equipment is sometimes needed—as prayer rails, candelabra, a display crucifix, a rostrum for the clergyman, etc. Sometimes special equipment is needed in connection with interment at the cemetery, such as a lowering device, a tent to protect the funeral assemblage from inclement weather, and simulated grass matting for decoration of the grave; these may or may not be provided by the cemetery—though usually they are.

No mention has been made of the necessity for providing ample off-the-street parking facilities, a garage for any automotive equipment the funeral director might himself own, or, in many instances, beautifully landscaped areas to enhance the appearance and public appeal of the mortuary. Enough has been said, however, to make it clear that the complete establishment represents a very substantial investment in terms of money, work and careful planning.

It must be recognized that mortuary operation is undertaken in all degrees of completeness of establishment—from the broker who has absolutely none to the large firm that has simply everything. The kind of physical surroundings in which you work, therefore, should you choose to follow this career, will be largely determined by the specific operation with which you become associated, or, if you go into business for yourself, the kind which you establish. There is probably as much variation in this field, from the point of view of working conditions, as you will find in any other area of occupational endeavor.

Jobs in Funeral Service

There is some disagreement among funeral directors themselves as to whether their occupation is a profession, a business or an industry. When emphasis is placed upon service to the living, the occupation is decidedly professional. It must be admitted that the sale of funeral merchandise—a casket, perhaps a vault, clothing, urns, etc.—is also involved, which introduces business elements. There are other undeniable business aspects to the work, such as the growing tendency of firms in the field to incorporate, the invasion of unionism, some reliance upon purely commercial techniques such as advertising and funeral insurance. If one takes the broad view, from initial manufacturing to final use of funeral merchandise, including the casket manufacturers, the vault manufacturers, chemical manufacturers, manufacturers of special automotive equipment, funeral directors, the cemetery group, and a host of others, then we are not altogether wrong in thinking of "the burial industry." When we remember that roughly ten out of every thousand people in the United States die each year, we can get some impression of the vast scope of this occupation—from the industrial point of view. Looking at the broad picture, the "burial industry" if you please, we must recognize that funeral service is just one element of the total. All the other groups mentioned above must also be considered. But it is with the funeral director that most of these other groups culminate. It is the funeral director who maintains the most complete contact with the public, and it is largely through him that these other groups make their contribution.

To be just as objective as possible, perhaps we must compromise on the statement that funeral service, at its present level of development is semi-professional, but striving toward full professionalism. I believe we can also, with objectivity, speak of "the burial industry"—when we are taking the overall view, from production to final disposition of funeral merchandise.

Classification of Jobs. Jobs in funeral service have been classified by National Selected Morticians with the caution that while not every firm, depending upon the size, will actually have all of the positions listed, yet they will have classifications which include a number of the positions shown. The list is revealing—and will probably be surprising to that reader who thinks of the field solely in terms of the funeral director. This, then, is their list:

Managerial or Supervisory:
    Manager
    Branch Manager
    Supervisor

Professional:
  Funeral Director
  Assistant Funeral Director
  Funeral Director—Embalmer
  Embalmer
  Assistant Embalmer
  Apprentice

Clerical:
  Lady Assistant
  Office Manager
  Sales—Arrangement
  Sales—Insurance
  Credit Manager
  Bookkeeper
  Bookkeeper—Stenographer
  Stenographer
  Secretary
  Office Clerk
  Telephone Operator
  Hostess—Receptionist

Utility:
  Porter—Janitor
  Yard Man—Gardener
  Houseman
  Housekeeper—Matron

Miscellaneous:
  Chauffeur
  Garage—Mechanic Attendant
  Ambulance Attendant
  Night Man
  Stock (Merchandise) Man
  Cemetery Man
  Organist
  Vocalist

Typical Duties. Most of the jobs included in this list are just about what their titles indicate them to be. Perhaps, however, some of them, particularly in the professional category, would be clarified by a brief word of explanation.

The manager is charged with overall responsibility for the operation of the firm, both professional and business-wise. He is faced by all of the problems which face any type of business operation—problems of accounting and taxation, advertising and public relations, legal problems, sales problems, credit and collection problems, insurance, merchandising and management—to mention but a few of the more obvious. To meet the special needs of the owner and manager of funeral service firms, the National Foundation of Funeral Service at Evanston, Illinois has established The School of Funeral Service Management—about which more will be said later.

The branch manager is faced with these same problems, but on a lesser scale. Only the large operations, and not all of them by any means, have branch operations, but when they do it is necessary to have someone, comparable to the regular manager, at the branch. Most of the large operations, too, have large staffs of personnel; some few firms in the nation have personnel in excess of a hundred. These larger firms, obviously, are departmentalized—and here the work of a supervisor becomes important.

The funeral director, necessarily licensed in most states, has, perhaps, the most direct contact with the public. Literally, he directs the funeral—but this comprises much more than just the funeral. Particularly in the smaller establishment, it probably involves: making the first call upon the family; securing necessary information about the deceased for death certificates, obituaries, burial permits and similar reports; making the removal of the remains from the home to the funeral home; completing all necessary arrangements with the family, including the selection of appropriate funeral merchandise; making the necessary contacts with the clergyman and the cemetery or crematory; seeing to it that the funeral service is conducted exactly in accordance with the expressed wishes of the next of kin and the clergyman; helping the survivors to file any necessary forms for insurance payment, veteran or social security benefits; and a host of similar duties. Sometimes there are special problems in connection with transportation, telegrams and long-distance arrangements; the securing of necessary rail or airplane tickets; records of flowers or visitors—hundreds and hundreds of details, no one of which can be neglected or overlooked.

The embalmer, on the other hand, is charged with the responsibility of proper hygienic preparation and restoration of the deceased. His goal is to prepare the body in such a way as to achieve a natural, serene appearance which will be a comforting final "memory picture" for survivors. The circumstances of the death largely determine the ease or difficulty of his task, but regardless of the obstacles, the task is rich in its own rewards. The embalmer must always be licensed to practice by the state.

It is very common practice in the field to prepare for and secure both the embalmer's and funeral director's license. That is the reason for the classification, "Funeral Director—Embalmer" in the list. As you will learn in greater detail later, a period of apprenticeship is required for the embalmer's license—and that is the reason for the classification, "Apprentice."

The "Lady Assistant," listed in the clerical group, primarily performs clerical duties in the funeral home; but she is very often a hair dresser as well—to care for the hair of lady patients. She may be called upon to play the organ or piano, or to sing, or to double as receptionist. Hers is most typically a combination job. The classification, "Sales—Insurance," has particular reference to the sale and administration of funeral insurance, which is typically handled in some degree by more and more funeral firms in the South and West. The "Night Man" is very frequently a student by day who lives at the mortuary by night, taking care of night calls and emergency situations. The other classifications are more or less self-explanatory.

One final word on duties! Only in the very large firms will you find such a high degree of specialization that all of these classifications are represented on a full-time basis. As you might surmise, therefore, a very few individuals—possibly only one—handle ALL these classifications in a small operation. So what you might expect to do, should you choose this field, would be largely determined by the size of the firm with which you become associated.

The Vocational Function

We have been talking about specific jobs within the mortuary operation. Perhaps it would prove enlightening to consider what happens in handling the details of a single funeral service.

A Typical Funeral Service. Any description of a "typical" funeral service must necessarily slight the multiplicity of variations that exist; actually, I suppose there is no such thing as a "typical" service. But it is possible to describe some of the operations that might normally be involved.

The service usually begins with the ringing of the telephone: someone is in need of the services of the funeral director. This call might come at any hour of the night or day, for funeral service, like the services of the police department or the fire department, is essentially an emergency service. Thus the funeral director must be equipped and staffed to receive these calls at any time. The individual receiving the call notes the essential information—usually the name of the deceased, the name of the person making the call, the address and the telephone number, in case it is necessary to call back for any reason.

Immediately a car is sent to the address given, with at least two attendants. If the deceased happens to be a woman or a girl, a lady assistant sometimes goes on this "first call" in addition. The attendants transport the body from the residence to the mortuary—but, before they leave the residence, they verify the essential information about the deceased and secure, or make arrangements to secure, a signed death certificate from the attending physician. If medical attendance has not preceded the death, the coroner must be notified and he provides the proper cause of death entry, requiring or waiving an autopsy at his own discretion. The death certificate, properly executed, is presented to the local Board of Health, which in turn issues a burial or cremation permit, bearing the same number as that on the death certificate. The funeral director is then free to proceed.

In order to complete arrangements with the cemetery, the funeral director presents the burial permit to cemetery officials: they, in turn, report the burial back to the Board of Health, so that a complete and necessary control is maintained by the Board of Health at all times. Even in the case of out-of-state shipment, the Board of Health of the state in which death occurred must issue a transportation permit, which affords them the opportunity of making sure that all requirements of the sanitary code have been met. Transportation regulations vary from state to state so that it is necessary for organizations in the field to maintain up-to-date digests of current regulations at all times.

Now, obviously, not all of these details can be handled on the "first call"—but at least the necessary information to set the procedure in motion must be secured. The body, once returned to the mortuary with the necessary authority of the next-of-kin, is embalmed as soon as practical after death; not only is the embalming easier and more successful, but you must not lose sight of the fact that it is essentially a sanitary measure.

As soon as possible after this first call has been made, the funeral director arranges to meet the family and work out the details of the funeral to their satisfaction. This is usually called the "arrangement conference." Sometimes the funeral director goes to the home of the family involved, but, more often, he sends a car to bring the family to his establishment. The reason for this is simply that there is also the matter of selecting a casket and such other funeral merchandise as the family might desire, possibly a vault—which the funeral director normally sells—or suitable garments for burial—if the family does not wish to use other clothing of the deceased. All the details of service—time, place, clergyman, obituaries, cemetery plot, music selection, handling of flowers, pall-bearers, limousine requirements, etc.—are worked out with the family. It is at this time, too, that the progressive funeral director usually presents a contract or memorandum of agreement for the signature of the responsible party or parties—a very normal business requirement, particularly considering the funeral director's investment in merchandise, personnel, overhead and, frequently, actual cash outlays for cemetery lots, transportation, newspaper space or similar items. He should have some knowledge of where responsibility for his payment lies. The family should also have a record of the arrangement and financial obligation.

Most often, the actual funeral service is conducted on the third day following death. In the meantime, the remains of the deceased, properly dressed and casketed, are placed in one of the state or reception rooms, where they may be viewed by family and friends who call at the funeral home to pay their last respects. The funeral director usually maintains a careful record of those who call and he also sees to it that any flowers sent are artistically grouped about the casket and that the family receives a complete record on each floral piece sent.

The actual service may be held in the home, or in the church, or in the funeral home chapel. Sometimes both funeral home and church are used. There is a growing tendency to use the funeral home for this purpose, but the ethical funeral director is completely responsive to the wishes of the family in this matter. The religious ceremony, of course, is under the jurisdiction of the clergyman; it is the funeral director's obligation to see that all aspects of the service are smooth and dignified—not necessarily morbid or solemn—and in keeping with the family's wishes.

Following the actual service, he forms the funeral cortege, supervises the movement of the mourners and friends to their cars and of the cars to the cemetery. There a brief, final committal service is held, whereupon the funeral director sees to the safe return of the family to their homes. Service does not, as you might expect, end here. The ethical practitioner will continue to do all he can to help the family adjust to its loss—to execute necessary insurance forms, social security or other governmental benefit forms, to recommend legal or financial counsel if necessary, in short, to do everything he reasonably can!

Multiplicity of Tasks. From what has been said, you can readily see that funeral service is what its name implies—SERVICE! Unfortunately, some of the general public still think in terms of buying a casket, and they fail to realize that most of what they pay for is not merchandise, by any means, but a huge accumulation of various services that must be performed in connection with the funeral. This was the main point of a prize-winning funeral service advertisement, which I should like to paraphrase in an effort to demonstrate to you the multiplicity of tasks involved.

The entire ad is designed to answer the question, "What does a funeral service include?" First it makes mention of some eleven building facilities which are made available for proper rendition of the service: use of all mortuary facilities, services in either the chapel or private drawing rooms, air conditioning, ample selection of funeral merchandise, fair pricing policies, discount service, covered drives, family rooms, pipe organ and organist, and elevator. Then, referring to staff, the ad goes on to emphasize the number of personnel required to render service, their religious and fraternal associations, their continuous availability, and the fact that a lady attendant is available if required. The next section deals with facilities: it points out such features as proper casket setting, veils or covers for the casket, fans, suites for visiting family members, slumber rooms, religious paraphernalia, special lighting equipment, sanitary linen service and special rooms for the use of lodges or fraternal groups. Professional and detail services comprises the next section. They included: removal, bathing, sterilization, preservation, shampooing and waving of hair, trimming, shaving, manicuring, derma surgery when necessary, dressing, casketing, securing statistical information, death certificate, burial permit, arranging for pallbearers, soloists, etc., obituary notices, ordering grave space, vault, tent, grass coverings, lowering device, etc., direction of service, recording of visitors. Then transportation facilities were listed, including limousine, casket coach, flower car, car lists for funeral service, arrangement of funeral cortege, securing police escort when necessary. Clergyman arrangements included the provision of a study for his use at the funeral home, arrangement for time of service, furnishing necessary data—and even robes—for the use of minister, priest, reader or rabbi. In connection with flowers, mention was made of floral arrangement and maintenance, record of donors, the supplying of cards for acknowledging floral tributes and, in some instances, the arrangement for post-funeral donation of flowers to hospitals or charitable organizations. Legal, governmental and statistical services included the securing of an American Flag for honorably discharged veterans, processing of applications for veterans benefits, execution of insurance forms, pre-arrangement of funeral services, Notary Public service, maintenance of a permanent biographical file for legal reference, provision of budget payment plans, filing of Social Security reports. Under "out-of-city" arrangements were listed membership in several national associations, procurement of plane or train tickets, packing and transporting of casket to depot in a shipping case. In a final section on other facilities, available at extra charge, were included the provision of crypts for delayed burials, a crematory, columbarium—where cremation urns are placed, a selection of cremation urns, 24-hour ambulance service and airplane ambulance service.

Now certainly not every funeral home offers all these services; on the other hand, some mortuaries may offer services which are not specifically detailed in this advertisement. The point is that this vocation has a complicated service pattern—and there is little room in it for the young man or young woman who is not service-minded.

Attractive Features of the Vocation

There are definite attractions that mortuary operation holds for the service minded young person. No other calling will give you the same measure of personal satisfaction which comes from rendering a needed service to your fellow man. Because this service has its professional nature, moreover, you will enjoy a high degree of prestige and status in your community. You should be able to count on a comfortable living, perhaps upon some measure of affluence if, eventually, you were to succeed in business for yourself. Your opportunity for real social contribution would be almost unlimited and, at the same time, the opportunity for personal development would be ever-present. More than most, you would have an opportunity to develop worthwhile values in life, for your constant association with death would show the futility of so many purely materialistic ends. If you are endowed with an artistic sense, you would have ample opportunity for exercising it in the matters of restoration, funeral settings, floral arrangements, interior decoration, and similar considerations. In time of local or even national emergency, such as fire, flood, mine casualties, transportation accidents, or enemy attacks, yours would be the chance to perform outstanding public service. You would find variety in this work, for both the problems of a profession and of a business would face you. If you enjoy association with people, again the opportunities would be numerous, for funeral directors are necessarily great "joiners"—participating actively in civic, social, community and organizational activities. And, with a large measure of success, you might eventually become your own boss—one of the great American dreams—with all the privileges and rewards, as well as responsibilities, that fall to the boss's lot! Incidentally, if you did eventually find yourself in business, funeral service has one distinct advantage—steadiness. Only a few business failures are reported annually. It is a necessary service regardless of prevailing economic conditions and also, it should be noted, the death rate operates inevitably: death takes no holidays!

Disadvantages of the Vocation

Objectivity is our aim in this monograph, so let's frankly consider some of the disadvantages of funeral service work: we already looked at the silver lining, so now let's take a look at the cloud itself.

Hours are generally long and often uncertain. It has already been said that death takes no holidays. But if this is an advantage in one sense, it is a disadvantage in another—for death is willfully capricious in its choice of times. You will be called upon to get up and go at any and all hours of the day or night.

As you become known in your work, you become in ever greater personal demand—providing you are doing the kind of a job that attracts clients to you. But this means that even as the head of a large firm, you might be called upon by your clients to handle personally those details which you might normally have delegated to another. The client simply will not accept a substitute for you!

If your firm is your own, then your investment is high and your costs of maintenance likewise high. The field is by no means easy to enter and competition is keen. Competition is bad enough even when ethical conditions prevail—and there is no point in denying that the field has its fringe of unethical operators who make practice difficult for everybody else. The death rate is fairly constant, so usually your only means of increasing volume is by winning business from your competitors.

Like the fire department, yours is largely an emergency service, so that there are bound to be fluctuations in volume and long periods of waiting. Finally, there is always the incipient danger of contagious disease—but, as a funeral director, you would be ethically bound to face this danger as one of your vocational hazards. It must be frankly admitted that with the advance in modern medicine, this danger is not too great—but it certainly is not one that has been entirely eliminated!

Qualifications for the Career

In considering any occupational field, it is well to raise the question, "What personal characteristics must I have for success in this field?" Well, what are the ones you should have for success in mortuary operation?

Most people in funeral service are in constant contact with the public, and this fact will give you an important clue to the qualities required for success. Obvious ones would include attractiveness of appearance, neatness and discrimination in dress, a personality which draws people to you, honesty and straight-forwardness, an inborn courtesy that won't crack under strain, alert intelligence, ease and correctness of expression, and a self confidence that steers midway between abashed shyness and offensive brashness. Of course such qualities as industriousness, the willingness to apply yourself to get ahead, loyalty to your employer and to your firm, consideration for others, a spirit of cooperation, and similar traits are stepping-stones to success in any vocation, and they apply equally here.

You must be certain, too, that you have a genuine interest in this work. Ask your instructor or your vocational counselor to administer to you, if possible, the *Strong Vocational Interest Inventory,* and have it scored on the funeral director's scale. This will give you objective information on how closely your own personal interests parallel those of successful funeral directors.

Undoubtedly most important of all, you must have a very genuine interest in the welfare of people and a desire to help them. Funeral service, contrary to some popular misconceptions, is not a vocation at which you will become enormously rich, but it should afford a good living, and it should enable the sincerely altruistic person to make a contribution to society.

Be sure to raise the question with yourself, "Will I be happy, spending my life in this field?" Consider this question carefully. No one can answer it for you, but it must be answered for yourself before you make any decision. One spends most of the rest of his life at his vocation—particularly the young men and boys. Girls may marry and leave their vocations for new careers of housewife and mother, but boys will usually work at something until the day that they take leave of this world. Weigh and evaluate the information being given to you in this monograph and then try to answer the $64.00 question for yourself! Remember—"all the rest of your life" is, for most of us, rather a long time!

In addition to personal qualifications, of course, there are vocational qualifications to be met. These, however, will be more fully dealt with in the sections to follow dealing with preparation for mortuary operation as a career.

Preparing for the Vocation

As with many vocations today, the requirements are constantly rising. What is important to you—they vary from state to state. Make absolutely certain, therefore, that you write directly to the Board of Funeral Directors and Embalmers, or a comparable agency, in the state where you hope to work, and determine precisely what their requirements are. Most states now issue a single license for both funeral directors and embalmers, but many of them issue separate licenses, and some of them require mortuary college credit prerequisites for the funeral director's license. As a kind of general average, the requirements for an embalmer's license are these: minimum age of 18; good moral character; references from several embalmers already licensed by the state; one to two year college prerequisites (but high school is sufficient in many states); residency in the state; one year of apprenticeship; a 12 month course of instruction in an approved college of mortuary science; passing of an examination given by the State's Board of Embalming Examiners; and payment of such examination fees as might be required by such a board.

State Licensing Requirements. Each year one of the journals of the field, *The Southern Funeral Director,* compiles and publishes the current "Licensing Rules and Regulations." . . .

Careful perusal of the "Licensing Rules and Regulations" will disclose that primary requirements are in two major categories, education and apprenticeship. There is little uniformity from state to state, so the only safe procedure for the individual contemplating mortuary operation as his or her career is to study and conform to those requirements of the one state where he hopes to work. The table also indicates that most—but not all—of the states maintain reciprocity with one another; where such reciprocity agreements exist it is possible to move from state to state in your employment or your operation, but otherwise you are confined in your practice to the particular state in which you secure your license.

Desirable High School Preparation. There are no prerequisites of secondary education established by the licensing boards, but if it is not too late in your high school career, it would prove desirable to concentrate in certain subject areas. Certainly some emphasis should be placed upon the sciences, particularly the natural sciences such as biology, zoology, physiology—if these subjects are taught in your school. In the area of physical science, include chemistry. Try, if you can, to include a course in First Aid. Take all the work you can in Art and Music, for both these subjects find direct expression in funeral service. If you have any thought of eventually going into business for yourself, or if you aspire to management level in funeral service, don't neglect commercial subjects, for they may eventually find more direct application than you now think.

Please bear in mind, too, that some of the states require college prerequisites, up to two years, in fulfillment of licensing requirements. Very often specific subjects are stipulated, particularly in English, Chemistry, and Biology. Again, it is wise to check the particular requirements of the state in which you might be interested.

Typical Course in the College of Mortuary Science. Every state requires the completion of a course in mortuary science, varying in length from nine to twelve months. You might be interested in knowing the kind of curriculum to expect in such a school.

Normally, something in the following subject areas is included.

Anatomy instruction includes lectures, demonstrations and dissection. Charts, models, photo slides, motion pictures, anatomical specimens, manikins and cadavers are used as visual aids. Histology is studied so the student may learn some of the important aspects of cell structure and organ architecture. Embryology is approached from the standpoint of developmental anatomy.

Physiology correlates the subjects just mentioned, and explains the functions of the various organs of the body and the changes which take place at death.

Pathology covers the cause, course, results and effects of disease processes in the human body, as well as anatomical and functional changes caused by disease processes.

Bacteriology deals with bacteria, protozoa and fungi, and their relation to pathology and, particularly, to infections and contagious diseases. It is related to embalming by studying the effects of disinfectants and embalming fluid on bacteria.

Hygiene instruction provides practical information on public health, disease, and the precautions necessary to prevent and overcome the spread of disease.

First aid, taught according to accepted American Red Cross technique and standards, is important because some funeral directors and embalmers serve as emergency ambulance personnel.

Embalming is, of course, the basic subject. The history of embalming, tests of death, physical and chemical postmortem changes, diagnosis, and the relationship of other curricular subjects are given attention in both classroom and laboratory. Each student is made personally familiar with all embalming techniques.

Restorative art teaches the student to restore a normal appearance to bodies mutilated by physical or pathological agents.

Cosmetology classes are correlated with studies in embalming and restorative art. The student is made familiar with hair dressing, barbering, the application of cosmetics, and the use of lighting effects.

Chemistry lectures and laboratory work take up that broad subject from its inorganic, organic and physiological aspects. Toxicology and the chemistry of disinfectants and embalming fluids are covered.

Mortuary administration is a title used to cover several related subjects, including the fundamentals of funeral procedure, of sound accounting principles and practices, of professional and business ethics, and of psychology as related to grief. This latter is frequently given separate and enlarged emphasis.

Mortuary Law teaches the principles of law and applies them to such subjects as legislation, contracts, negotiable instruments, personal property, wills, estates, and the laws pertaining to the dead human body, funeral conduct, interment, cremation, exhumation, transportation, and quarantine.

For this concise information on the curriculum of the mortuary colleges, we are indebted to the studies of National Selected Morticians. Remember, however, that these descriptions are necessarily generalized, so be sure to investigate for yourself the particular curriculum of the mortuary colleges in which you are interested.

Colleges of Mortuary Science. You should know that there are a number of colleges of mortuary science distributed over the United States. The accrediting agency for these schools is the American Board of Funeral Service Education, Inc., with headquarters at 201 Columbia Street, Fairmont, West Virginia. The accredited mortuary schools, as listed by this Board, are contained in the same *Southern Funeral Director* reprint accompanying this monograph.*

You should also know that graduate training in the administrative aspects of mortuary operation is given, in brief intensive courses, by the School of Management, conducted periodically throughout the year by the National Foundation of Funeral Service, 1614 Central Street, Evanston, Illinois. This training is essentially for those who have completed all preliminary work, and the majority of those in attendance are licensed personnel—owners, managers and key employees of funeral firms who are primarily interested in the business success of their operations.

Perhaps this is the place to mention an important function of the Conference of Funeral Service Examining Boards, located at 9 Jackson Avenue, Naperville, Illinois 60540. One task of the colleges of mortuary science is to prepare their graduates to take their state license examinations successfully. There used to be considerable variation in examinations from state to state. Usually the examination is threefold—a written examination, an oral examination, and a practical demonstration of embalming skill. The Conference has done much good work in making available to the various state boards comprehensive, objective examination material in the subject matter of the college of

---

*The reprint is not included in this volume.

mortuary science. A number of boards have adopted these materials in lieu of the old written examination requirements, with the result that the candidates are not only more thoroughly examined, but there is greater uniformity among states that use the Conference service. The Conference also administers a National Board Examination, the results of which are accepted by many state boards.

Apprenticeship. The table on licensing requirements of the various states clearly indicates what the apprenticeship requirements are in terms of time. However, a word should be said about the general nature of apprenticeship.

Often young people are attracted to mortuary operation because they think the field will offer them a fat salary check and the opportunity to dress "to kill," as the saying goes. Get both ideas out of your head! It is perfectly true that, with conscientious work over a period of time, mortuary operation will offer, in most instances, a good living; it is equally true that those in funeral service must dress presentably at all times that they are in contact with the public. But, there are many jobs, particularly in the smaller firm, that the apprentice and young licensee may be called upon to do—jobs pertaining to maintenance and cleanliness of the funeral home itself, and to automotive equipment. You may be doing such things as washing cars, handling and caring for floral pieces, moving chairs and other furniture, etc. Of course, the main purpose of any apprenticeship is to learn, by first-hand experience, the various requirements of your job—and in such a learning situation, your remuneration will not be great, and your duties will be many and varied.

Remuneration

Everyone, be he ever so altruistic, must be concerned to some extent about this basic question: "What's in it for me?" He has to be, for we do not live on love alone in the practical world of daily affairs. No one can give you hard, fast answers, particularly to this one, for the answers are always changing.

Salaries and Wages. National Selected Morticians reported median weekly salaries paid in 1977 for various positions, by size of firm. To give a simpler, generalized idea of salaries and wages for each position, we have averaged the medians reported for the several size categories.

Owners/Officers	$515
Managers	328
Assistant Managers	295
Funeral Director—Embalmer	251
Funeral Director	218
Embalmer	218
Apprentice	158
Lady Assistant—Receptionist	126
Office Personnel	152
Maintenance Personnel	138
Other	147

Bear in mind that these are averages. As such, as one columnist put it, they include "the best of the worst, and the worst of the best." Moreover, these figures represent salary averages for workers with various degrees of experience—not beginners, for the most part! Remember, too, that many variable factors have a bearing upon a specific firm's wage levels. Such factors might include: the location of the funeral home and economic levels prevailing there; the type (urban or rural) and population of its service area; case volume; total number of employees; the existence or non-existence of a union; the "business health" of the firm; and others.

Hours. Closely linked to the matter of wages is the question of hours. A serious effort is being made by some funeral firms to approach the forty-hour week; however, this is an ideal difficult of attainment in this field—for death observes no time schedules, making it necessary for the funeral firm to be able to render service at any hour of the day or night. This means, at best, a longer than average working week for funeral service personnel, plus certain periods when they are necessarily "on call" in case of need. This being "on call" simply means that you are free to go where you will, or do what you will—except that you must be within reaching distance in case you are needed, and you must leave word as to exactly where you will be at what hours.

Actual working hours are determined largely by the size of the firm and the volume of calls, both of which factors tend to determine staff size. You would have to get a specific answer to this question from the firm with which you contemplated a connection. General information is contained in the following excerpt from the 1974–75 Labor Dept. *Occupational Outlook Handbook;* still true:

"In large funeral homes, employees usually have a regular work schedule. Typically they put in 8 hours a day, 5 or 6 days a week. Overtime, however, may be necessary when emergencies arise. Some employees work shifts; for example, nights one week, and days the next."

Benefits. It is well known today that not all remuneration comes in the form of direct salary or wages. Employee benefits, too, are a kind of remuneration. Again, there is much variation from firm to firm. The larger firms, and the more progressive of the smaller firms, make an effort to provide benefits which are comparable to those afforded by any other line of vocational endeavor. These might include: bonuses; pensions; sick benefits; paid vacations; hospitalization insurance; group life insurance; etc. Under governmental legislation the employees of funeral service firms are also covered by Social Security.

Mobility. You might well raise the question, "If I choose mortuary operation as a career, will I be able to work anywhere I choose?" It cannot be denied that mobility is an important consideration. The answer is a qualified "yes." Yes—but only if your employment falls into a category not requiring a state license. If you are a licensed employee, that is, a funeral director or an embalmer, you are legally permitted to work only in those states where you are licensed. Some states, it was previously noted, have entered into what are called "reciprocity agreements" whereby the licensees of one state are permitted to work in the other states becoming a party to the agreement. You would have to check directly with your own State Board of Funeral Directors and Embalmers to determine what reciprocity agreements, if any, may exist. . . .

Employment Trends

Job Opportunities. What are the chances of placement? There is no point in fooling ourselves about a question as important as this. We had better be realistic in our approach. Many, many funeral firms in the United States have remained in the same family for a number of generations. When these firms are not large, job opportunities in them may be restricted to members and friends of the family. There are also, however, many larger firms which do have jobs to offer. The safe thing to do is to make absolutely certain of an apprenticeship connection *before* you commit yourself to a long program of training for this field. Better still, if possible, assure yourself of a job opportunity in addition to apprenticeship.

An old adage has it, "There is always room at the top." In other words, a person who is genuinely interested and highly qualified, with the will to persevere, can carve a place for himself in any field, mortuary operation not excluded. Nevertheless, discretion is the better part of valor!

Expansion into Rural Areas. When the modern funeral home first appeared on the American scene, it was strictly a phenomenon of the city—where there was sufficient population concentration to support it. The past decade or two has brought about a definite expansion into rural areas throughout the country. Improved transportation facilities have played their part in this development.

This is a trend which young people who might be interested in setting themselves up in mortuary operation should not overlook. Many a young person has completed his preparation in this field, taken a job with a good firm for a number of years—for the sake of acquiring experience, and then established himself in business in some smaller community, rural or semi-rural, where the need for a funeral home definitely existed.

Self-Employment. Americans are the greatest exponents of private enterprise on the face of the earth today! It is perfectly natural, therefore, to hope that you will one day be able to go into business for yourself. Many young people in funeral service have this ambition. But it is no easy road! For one thing, you will often be competing with old, established firms, and the going will be tough. For another thing, the profit level is not nearly as high as many people outside the field might suppose; a firm averaging from ten to fifteen percent net profit, before taxes, is doing exceptionally well! The idea of high profit in funeral service is a misconception. The average selling price of a funeral in 1978—all services considered—was $1,402; match this with the service pattern that has been outlined and you will realize that this is no field for "easy money."

Success on your own does not come easily. You will need all of the qualifications that have been mentioned in an earlier section plus sound business sense and the will to work slavishly for a while. You will need a minimum population of 6,000* to support your operation at a reasonable level—so that a town of 18,000 could support, at the very outside, no more than three funeral homes—and even this is a fairly close ratio. Most of all, you will need capital. You have already been given some conception of what's needed for a complete establishment, and just how much of an investment might be required would depend largely upon property values, construction costs, salary levels, and similar factors at the place where you contemplated going into business. Figures reported by the National Funeral Directors Association indicate that the average 1977 investment range was from $185,674 (for firms in the Middle Atlantic census area) to $635,564 (for firms in the Pacific area). They reported an average of $233,534 for all firms.

Avenues of Entry

From my observations as Director of the National Foundation of Funeral Service, these, in decreasing order of frequency, are the means by which funeral directors came into possession of their own businesses: inheritance—for this is largely a generational business, as has been said; marriage—to the widows or daughters of funeral firm owners, where there is no other logical successor; movement up the employment ladder until eventually you are permitted to buy an interest in the business with your accumulated savings; outright purchase of an already existing business; establishment of a new business from scratch, in a promising location, and usually only after you have acquired reasonable experience with some other firm.

Getting the First Job. From what has been said, it becomes obvious that mortuary operation isn't exactly the easiest field in the world to enter. It is possible to get jobs in the field—but those jobs should be carefully scrutinized for their future potential. The best possible means of getting that first job is through personal acquaintance with a practicing funeral director. During high school years, you can perhaps get a job as handy man around the establishment, or, if you are a college student, as night man or ambulance assistant. This trial work experience will be highly beneficial, for only by sampling the actual flavor of the work can you intelligently decide whether or not you will be interested in continuing with it. If you are interested, that is the time to find out whether the funeral director would be willing to sponsor your apprenticeship and possibly even hire you as a regular employee when you have succeeded in getting your license from the state.

Safeguards to be Taken. Be extremely cautious of undertaking the long period of preparation and training that is required for a license until you have reasonable assurance of

---

*8,500 at the national level, i.e. population per funeral home.

a place at which to serve your apprenticeship and a first working opportunity. Many colleges of mortuary science will attempt to help their graduates secure such openings, but there are no guarantees. Some of the schools will actually insist that the apprenticeship opening be certified before they will admit you.

Also take note of the fact that some states stipulate whether apprenticeship be served before or after the period of training in the college of mortuary science. If the proper sequence is not followed, it might prove necessary to serve the apprenticeship a second time.

"What," you might ask, "does a licensed individual do if he finds himself in need of a job at some later time in his career?" There are a number of possibilities. First of all, he might keep a close eye on the journals of the field, for such openings are usually advertised in these publications. Secondly, he might himself place a "situation wanted" ad in such a journal. Third, he might register with one or more of the associations that maintain an employment or personnel exchange service. In the fourth place, he might contact his college of mortuary science on the possibility that the school could line him up with a prospective employer. Finally, he would maintain his active participation in the professional associations so that by personal investigation, asking and seeking, he would become aware of any openings that might exist. Another possibility that is not without merit is to maintain close contact with the salesmen of funeral merchandise, particularly those who travel a territory calling upon funeral homes, for they are in a good position to know what employment opportunities exist—and where.

Related Jobs—Outside of Funeral Service

It is always well to consider what jobs are related sufficiently to the one for which you prepare so that, if necessary or desirable, you could switch over. Usually, the more highly specialized a particular occupation is, the more difficult it is to relate it to other jobs. That is true, it must be admitted, of mortuary operation.

However, there are some possibilities. There are quite a few licensed embalmers and/or funeral directors who are engaged in sales work for funeral supply manufacturers, such as casket manufacturers, chemical companies (that manufacture embalming fluids, cosmetics and similar items), vault companies, etc. Some licensed personnel are also to be found among the associations of the field, doing straight trade association work. Other licensed people have turned their major attention to teaching in the colleges of mortuary science. In a limited sense, some few research opportunities exist, usually with the larger manufacturers, occasionally with the national associations; frankly, these are too few to count upon. The journals of the field may offer a few opportunities to individuals interested in journalistic application of the work. Similarly, there are a few advertising and public relations agencies that specialize in work for funeral service firms. Generally speaking, it is wiser not to choose the career unless you are planning to enter the field directly.

Opportunities for Women in Funeral Service

The ministry of women at times of great importance in the family—marriage and birth, illness and death—is too well known to require emphasis here. It is both logical and fitting that they be represented in the field of mortuary operation—and they are represented!

Practically no state is without some licensed women funeral directors and licensed women embalmers; not many, but some! Particularly where a firm is handling the death of a wife, a mother or a daughter, some families will prefer that a licensed woman practitioner be in attendance.

Apart from the licensed positions, however, there are a number of jobs in mortuary operation for which women are actually more fittingly qualified than men. The dressing of hair, the arrangement and handling of flowers, the receiving of callers, the supervision of cleaning and even maintenance operations in the funeral home, the handling of the telephone and many clerical jobs in the office, all these represent jobs in the field that are definitely open to women. There is no one job classification (given earlier in this monograph) for which some women incumbents cannot be found in the field.

Organizations Within the Field

Funeral service is a much more highly organized field than most laymen realize. It might almost be said that wherever you can find enough funeral directors to support an organization, you will find them organized. Many counties, for example, and many cities or metropolitan areas throughout the nation, will have their own local associations. In addition, you will always find a state association and, at the top level, national—even international—associations.

The association, then, is the typical form of organization that has been employed, characteristic of professional and semi-professional groups. It should, perhaps, be mentioned here that unionism has invaded the field of mortuary operation, not to any great extent, but with some success in areas of population concentration. There is a possibility that this trend, especially unionization of drivers and of embalmers, will continue throughout future years.

National Foundation of Funeral Service. In 1945, an educational foundation, The National Foundation of Funeral Service, was organized by a group of leaders in the field. It is a non-profit, tax-exempt, educational trust, located at 1614 Central Street, Evanston, Illinois 60201, with a five-fold educational program for funeral service and the public: (1) operation of a School of Management designed to raise the level of funeral service by reaching, influencing and educating key management and ownership personnel of the field; (2) compilation of the literature of funeral service and preservation of that literature in the foundation's library; (3) public information and education on all phases of funeral service; (4) the display of old, American funeral service items in a Museum of Funeral Service Artifacts; (5) maintenance of demonstration-display rooms, currently including: The Selection Room for

Merchandising Research, The Burial Vault Selection Room, The NCBVA Room, and The Burial Garment Selection Room. The foundation is unlike an association in that it has no membership. It is supported by donations, pledges, bequests from all segments of the funeral service industry and it is open to anyone who is in any way interested in the field. The operation of the foundation is directed by Dr. Joe A. Adams.

The Code of Good Funeral Practice

National Selected Morticians

As funeral directors, our calling imposes upon us special responsibilities to those we serve and to the public at large. Chief among them is the obligation to inform the public so that everyone can make knowledgeable decisions about funerals and funeral directors.

In acceptance of our responsibilities, and as a condition of our membership in National Selected Morticians, we affirm the following standards of good funeral practice and hereby pledge:

1. To provide the public with information about funerals, including prices, and about the functions, services and responsibilities of funeral directors.

2. To afford a continuing opportunity to all persons to discuss or arrange funerals in advance.

3. To make funerals available in as wide a range of price categories as necessary to meet the need of all segments of the community, and affirmatively to extend to everyone the right of inspecting and freely considering all of them.

4. To quote conspicuously in writing the charges for every funeral offered; to identify clearly the services, facilities, equipment and merchandise included in such quotations; and to follow a policy of reasonable adjustment when less than the quoted offering is utilized.

5. To furnish to each family at the time funeral arrangements are made, a written memorandum of charges and to make no additional charge without the approval of the purchaser.

6. To make no presentation, written or oral, which may be false or misleading, and to apply a standard of total honesty in all dealings.

7. To respect all faiths, creeds and customs, and to give full effect to the role of the clergy.

8. To maintain a qualified and competent staff, complete facilities and suitable equipment required for comprehensive funeral service.

9. To assure those we serve the right of personal choice and decision in making funeral arrangements.

10. To be responsive to the needs of the poor, serving them within their means.

We pledge to conduct ourselves in every way and at all times in such a manner as to deserve the public trust, and to place a copy of this Code of Good Funeral Practice in the possession of a representative of all parties with whom we arrange funerals.

Reprinted with permission from "The Code of Good Funeral Practice," National Selected Morticians, Evanston, IL 60201.

Voluntary Certification Program

Academy of Professional Funeral Service Practice

ELIGIBILITY

A. Each applicant must be currently licensed to practice funeral service by a state licensing authority.
B. The formal application and payment of prescribed fees must be accepted by the Academy.

FEES

To offset part of the cost of administering the certification program, a fee of $40.00 will be payable with the filing of the application, which covers the first three years of registration. Each succeeding year will require a $15.00 renewal fee while completing or maintaining original registration. Candidates who successfully complete the requirements for original certification will pay an additional fee of $50.00.

Fees for seminars, symposia, home study courses and special activities will be determined by the sponsoring organizations and are payable by the registrant.

QUALIFYING ACTIVITIES FOR PROFESSIONAL CERTIFICATION

The following activities are examples rather than an exhaustive list of those programs approved for credit leading to certification by the Academy of Professional Funeral Service Practice. Appropriate credit for specific or innovative activities will be determined through application to the Academy.

- Attendance at conferences, conventions, seminars and workshops sponsored by:
  1. National Funeral Directors Association
  2. National Selected Morticians
  3. National Funeral Directors and Morticians Association
  4. Jewish Funeral Directors Association
  5. National Foundation of Funeral Service
  6. Order of the Golden Rule
  7. Preferred Funeral Directors International
  8. State, district or local funeral director associations
  9. Schools, colleges and universities
  10. Funeral service suppliers
- Completion of related courses offered by associations and accredited institutions of higher learning.

- Credit of variable degree may be awarded for participating as an instructor in school (elementary and secondary) and college or university presentations and other related conferences, institutes, seminars and workshops. Examples are:
  1. **Understanding Death**, Berg and Daugherty
  2. **Perspectives on Death**, Berg and Daugherty
  3. **Dimensions of Death**, Berg and Daugherty
  4. Programs for the widowed
  5. Career days
  6. Death and life studies with religious and civic groups

Appropriate credit for certification will be awarded upon receipt of a format of the program, notification of its completion and evaluations as requested.

- Credit may be awarded for completion of home study courses from accredited institutions offering such courses or home study courses prepared by the Academy.

- Appropriate credit may be awarded toward certification for speeches on funeral service before funeral, religious or civic organizations; published articles, papers or other literary contributions; and research studies and questionnaires to better understand the many facets of funeral service. Evidence of these activities or sample materials as requested must be submitted to the Academy for credit.

- Appropriate credit toward certification may be awarded upon submission to the Academy of a format of an in-service training period prior to its inception, requirements, personnel and tasks involved, a notification of successful completion of the training period and evaluations as requested.

- Limited credit toward certification may be awarded by the Academy for membership in local, district, state, regional and national associations and regular attendance at meetings of these associations. Evidence of participation must be submitted to the Academy for appropriate credit. For persons serving as a board member or officer of these associations and on standing and ad hoc committees, evidence of the extent of participation therein will again serve as criteria for determining credit.

Reprinted with permission from Academy of Professional Funeral Service Practice, Minneapolis, MN 55455, 1980.

- Appropriate credit of a limited nature may be awarded by the Academy upon submission of evidence of service in civic organizations.
- Career Review. A registrant may be given credit within guidelines established by the Academy for professional and community activity completed prior to registration in the Academy.

DESIGNATED CREDIT EVALUATION

Credit toward professional certification shall be granted in terms of CONTINUING EDUCATION UNITS.

One C.E.U. consists of ten (10) contact hours of participation in an **approved** continuing education experience. A contact hour shall consist of fifty (50) minutes of academic instruction or its **rated equivalent**. The following formula may be used to determine an "acceptable" total of C.E.U.'s for certification:

60 hours per year = 6 C.E.U.'s per year

6 C.E.U.'s per year × 3 years* = 18 C.E.U.'s required for basic certification or

180 contact hours required for basic certification

*NOTE: This formula is based upon the ability of the practitioner to devote five (5) hours monthly toward activities leading to certification.

The Evaluation Committee has suggested the following proportionate value for various activities leading to professional certification and renewal.

A. Academic activities — 60% or 10.8 C.E.U.'s (108 contact hours)
   1. Earned academic credit from accredited institutions of higher learning.
   2. Completion of APFSP approved home study courses.
   3. Published articles, papers and other literary contributions in scholarly journals.

B. Professional activities — 40% or 7.2 C.E.U.'s (72 contact hours)
   1. Attendance at workshops, conferences, seminars and institutes of approved funeral service educational opportunities (annual conventions, annual seminars, professional conferences).
   2. Published articles, papers and other literary contributions in professional journals and others that have literary merit and enjoy a broad readership.
   3. In-service training programs for funeral service personnel.

C. Career review — 30% or 5.4 C.E.U.'s (54 contact hours)
   1. The career review must be basically related to funeral service.

   2. A narrative of five hundred words or less on the career of the applicant must be submitted to the Academy for review. Included in the narrative should be:
      a. Evidence of self-improvement as a licensee.
      b. The contribution of the applicant to funeral service.
      c. The contribution as a licensee to the community through community service.
   3. Following review of the application and narrative, the Academy will award appropriate credit.

D. Public education and service — 10% or 1.8 C.E.U.'s (18 contact hours)
   1. Participating as an instructor in school presentations (elementary, secondary, college) and other related workshops, conferences, seminars and institutes.
   2. Speeches on funeral service before funeral, religious or civic organizations.
   3. Service on recognized civic organizations. Service on public boards and/or committees (hospital, school, municipalities).

It should be noted that the percentages as expressed represent the maximum that may be accumulated in each respective area.

MAINTAINING CERTIFICATION

In order to be recertified annually, a member of the Academy shall earn a minimum of 2.0 C.E.U.'s in Section A or B, with at least 1.0 C.E.U. to be in Section A.

The annual fee for recertification is $15.00.

USE OF PROFESSIONAL CERTIFICATION DESIGNATION

Successful candidates for certification in the Academy of Professional Funeral Service Practice may use the CFSP (Certified Funeral Service Practitioner) designation with their names on their business letterheads and business cards.

Certification is for individuals only and may not be used to imply that a firm is certified.

MANDATED CONTINUING EDUCATION

Those registrants who reside in states which require continuing education for annual license renewal will find the services of the Academy useful and helpful in completing such requirements.

Members of the Academy, upon request, may have their transcript certified to any state requiring continuing education.

Accredited Colleges of Funeral Service Education

The following list of colleges of funeral service education are accredited by the American Board of Funeral Service Education, Inc., an agency recognized by the United States Commissioner of Education. Effective October 23, 1981 for a one year period.

AMERICAN ACADEMY McALLISTER INSTITUTE OF FUNERAL SERVICE, INC.

229 Park Avenue South
New York, New York 10003
Patrick J. O'Connor, President
Programs offered: Diploma (1 yr.)
Associate in Occupational Studies
Phone: (212) 260-2900

CATONSVILLE COMMUNITY COLLEGE MORTUARY SCIENCE PROGRAM

800 South Rolling Road
Catonsville, Maryland 21228
William C. Gonce, Coordinator
Programs offered: Certificate (15 months)
   Associate in Arts (2 yrs.)
Phone: (301) 455-4276

CENTRAL STATE UNIVERSITY DEPARTMENT OF FUNERAL SERVICE EDUCATION

Edmond, Oklahoma 73034
John H. Cage, Chairman
Programs offered: Certificate (2 yrs.)
   Bachelor of Science (4 yrs.)
Phone: (405) 341-2980   Ext. 377

CINCINNATI COLLEGE OF MORTUARY SCIENCE

2220 Victory Parkway
Cincinnati, Ohio 45206
David FitzSimmons, Director
Programs offered: Diploma (1 yr.)
Associate in Applied Science (2 yrs.)
Phone: (513) 861-3240

COMMONWEALTH COLLEGE OF FUNERAL SERVICE

215 Dennis at Baldwin
Houston, Texas 77006
John Rice, President
Program offered: Diploma (1 yr.)
Phone: (713) 529-3471

CYPRESS COLLEGE MORTUARY SCIENCE DEPARTMENT

9200 Valley View Street
Cypress, California 90630
Robert A. Baughman, Director
Programs offered: Certificate (1 yr.)
   Associate in Arts (2 yrs.)
Phone: (714) 826-2220   Ext. 240

DALLAS INSTITUTE OF FUNERAL SERVICE

3906 Worth Street
Dallas, Texas 75246
Robert P. Kite, President
Program offered: Diploma (1 yr.)
Phone: (214) 823-6159

DELGADO COMMUNITY COLLEGE DEPARTMENT OF FUNERAL SERVICE EDUCATION

City Park Campus
615 City Park Avenue
New Orleans, Louisiana 70119
Boyd G. Simmons, Chairman
Programs offered: Certificate (1 yr.)
   Associate in Science (2 yrs.)
Phone: (504) 486-4393

EAST MISSISSIPPI JUNIOR COLLEGE MORTUARY SCIENCE PROGRAM

Scooba, Mississippi 39358
John M. Mitchell, Chairman
Program offered: Associate in Science (2 yrs.)
Phone: (601) 476-8189

FAYETTEVILLE TECHNICAL INSTITUTE FUNERAL SERVICE EDUCATION DEPARTMENT

Post Office Box 35236
Fayetteville, North Carolina 28303
John R. Lifsey, Chairman
Program offered Associate in Applied Science (2 yrs.)
Phone: (919) 323-1961

Reprinted with permission of American Board of Funeral Service Education, Inc., Fairmont, WV 26554, 1981.

GUPTON-JONES COLLEGE OF FUNERAL SERVICE

280 Mt. Zion Road
Atlanta, Georgia 30354
Russell M. Millison, President
Programs offered: Diploma (1 yr.)
Associate of Science Degree (2 yrs.)
Phone: (404) 761-3118

**HUDSON VALLEY COMMUNITY COLLEGE
MORTUARY SCIENCE DEPARTMENT**

80 Vandenburgh Avenue
Troy, New York 12180
Deborah H. Orecki, Chairman
Program offered: Associate in Applied Science (2 yrs.)
Phone: (518) 283-1100

**JEFFERSON STATE JUNIOR COLLEGE
FUNERAL SERVICE EDUCATION PROGRAM**

2601 Carson Road
Birmingham, Alabama 35215
James D. Townson, Director
Programs offered:
Associate in Applied Science
Phone: (205) 853-1200

JOHN A. GUPTON COLLEGE

2507 West End Avenue
Nashville, Tennessee 37203
John A. Gupton, President
Program offered: Associate of Arts (2 yrs.)
Phone: (615) 327-3927

**JOHN TYLER COMMUNITY COLLEGE
FUNERAL SERVICE PROGRAM**

Chester, Virginia 23831
Agnes S. Hairston, Program Head
Program offered: Associate in Applied Science (2 yrs.)
Phone: (804) 748-5481

KANSAS CITY KANSAS COMMUNITY COLLEGE

7250 State Ave.
Kansas City, Kansas 66112
Robert O. Todd, Director
Program offered: Associate in Arts (2 yrs.)
Phone: (913) 334-1100   Ext. 79

**McNEESE STATE UNIVERSITY
MORTUARY SCIENCE CURRICULUM**

Lake Charles, Louisiana 70609
William F. Matthews, Coordinator
Program offered: Associate in Mortuary Science (2 yrs.)
Phone: (318) 477-2520   Ext. 558

**MERCER COUNTY COMMUNITY COLLEGE
FUNERAL SERVICE CURRICULUM**

1200 Old Trenton Road — P. O. Box B
Trenton, New Jersey 08690
Frank X. Mulligan, Jr., Coordinator
Program offered: Certificate (1 yr.)
Phone: (609) 586-4800

**MIAMI-DADE COMMUNITY COLLEGE
DEPT. OF FUNERAL SERVICE EDUCATION**

11380 N.W. 27th Avenue
Miami, Florida 33167
Darwin E. Gearhart, Coordinator
Program offered: Associate in Science (2 yrs.)
Phone: (305) 685-4481

MID-AMERICA COLLEGE OF FUNERAL SERVICE

3111 Hamburg Pike
Jeffersonville, Indiana 47130
John R. Braboy, President
Programs offered: Diploma (1 yr.)
Associate in Applied Science (2 yrs.)
Phone: (812) 288-8878

**MILWAUKEE AREA TECHNICAL COLLEGE
FUNERAL SERVICE DEPARTMENT**

1015 N. Sixth Street
Milwaukee, Wisconsin 53203
Mrs. Mildred J. Gau, Dean Business Div.
Program offered: Associate in Applied Science (2 yrs.)
Phone: (414) 278-6600

**MT. HOOD COMMUNITY COLLEGE
DEPT. OF FUNERAL SERVICE EDUCATION**

26000 S.E. Stark Street
Gresham, Oregon 97030
Walter K. Thorsell, Director
Program offered: Associate in Funeral Service Education (2 yrs.)
Phone: (503) 667-7363

**NEW ENGLAND INSTITUTE OF APPLIED
ARTS AND SCIENCES**

656 Beacon Street
Boston, Massachusetts 02215
Victor F. Scalise, Jr., President
Programs offered: Diploma (1 yr.)
Associate of Science in Funeral Service (2 yrs.)
Certificate of Advanced Study in Funeral Service (3 yrs.)
Phone: (617) 536-6970

**NORTHHAMPTON COUNTY AREA COMMUNITY COLLEGE
DEPARTMENT OF FUNERAL EDUCATION**

3835 Green Pond Road
Bethlehem, Pennsylvania 18017
Richard D. Trexler, Director
Program offered: Associate in Applied Science (3 yrs.)
Phone: (215) 865-5351

**NORTHWEST MISSISSIPPI JUNIOR COLLEGE
MORTUARY SCIENCE PROGRAM**

Desoto Center
Southaven, Mississippi 38671
Joe Broadway, Director
Program Offered: Associate in Applied Science, (2 yrs.)
Phone: (601) 342-1570

PITTSBURGH INSTITUTE OF MORTUARY SCIENCE

3337 Forbes Avenue
Pittsburgh, Pennsylvania 15213
Dr. Emory S. James, President
Program offered: Diploma (1 yr.)
Phone: (412) 682-0334

**ST. LOUIS COMMUNITY COLLEGE AT FOREST PARK
DEPARTMENT OF FUNERAL SERVICE EDUCATION**

5600 Oakland Avenue
St. Louis, Missouri 63110
Steven B. Koosman, Chairman
Program offered: Associate in Applied Science (2 yrs.)
Phone: (314) 644-9327

**SAN ANTONIO COLLEGE
DEPARTMENT OF MORTUARY SCIENCE**

1300 San Pedro Avenue
San Antonio, Texas 78284
J. Byron Starr, Chairman
Program offered: Associate in Mortuary Science (2 yrs.)
Phone: (512) 733-2905

SAN FRANCISCO COLLEGE OF MORTUARY SCIENCE

1450 Post Street
San Francisco, California 94109
Dale W. Sly, President
Programs offered: Diploma (1 yr.)
Associate in Arts (2 yrs.)
Phone: (415) 567-0674

SIMMONS SCHOOL OF MORTUARY SCIENCE, INC.

1828 South Avenue
Syracuse, New York 13207
William R. Vaughan, Dean
Program offered: Diploma (1 yr.)
Phone: (315) 475-5142

SOUTHERN ILLINOIS UNIVERSITY
MORTUARY SCIENCE AND FUNERAL SERVICE

Carbondale, Illinois 62901
Donald Hertz, Coordinator
Program offered: Associate in Applied Science (2 yrs.)
Phone: (618) 536-6682 Ext. 254

STATE UNIVERSITY OF NEW YORK
AGRICULTURAL AND TECHNICAL COLLEGE
MORTUARY SCIENCE PROGRAM

Canton, New York 13617
Ralph Klicker, Director
Program offered: Associate in Applied Science (2 yrs.)
Phone: (315) 386-7407

STATE UNIVERSITY OF NEW YORK
AGRICULTURAL AND TECHNICAL COLLEGE
**   AT FARMINGDALE**

Mortuary Science Department
Farmingdale, New York 11735
John M. Lieblang, Chairman
Program offered: Associate in Applied Science (2 yrs.)
Phone: (516) 420-2295

UNIVERSITY OF DISTRICT OF COLUMBIA
VAN NESS CAMPUS
MORTUARY SCIENCE DEPARTMENT

4200 Connecticut Ave., N.W.
Washington, D.C. 20008
Leander M. Coles, Department Chairman
Program offered: Associate in Applied Science (2 yrs.)
Phone: (202) 282-7733

UNIVERSITY OF MINNESOTA
DEPARTMENT OF MORTUARY SCIENCE

114 Vincent Hall
Minneapolis, Minnesota 55455
Robert C. Slater, Director
Program offered: Bachelor of Science (4 yrs.)
Phone: (612) 373-3870

VINCENNES UNIVERSITY JUNIOR COLLEGE
FUNERAL SERVICE EDUCATION PROGRAM

Vincennes, Indiana 47591
John Kroshus, Coordinator
Program offered: Associate in Science (2 and 3 yrs.)
Phone: (812) 885-4211

WAYNE STATE UNIVERSITY
DEPARTMENT OF MORTUARY SCIENCE

627 West Alexandrine
Detroit, Michigan 48201
Walter D. Pool, Director
Program offered: Certificate (3 yrs.)
Phone: (313) 577-2050

WORSHAM COLLEGE OF MORTUARY SCIENCE

3701 Davis Street
Skokie, Illinois 60203
Frederick C. Cappetta, Chief Administrator
Program offered: Diploma (1 yr.)
Phone: (312) 673-4330

Funeral Service/ Educational and Licensure

Indicates cities in which accredited colleges of Funeral Service education are located (as of June 1980)

States requiring only high school graduation and a one-year professional curriculum: Alabama, Arizona, Arkansas, California, Connecticut, Florida, Georgia, Kentucky, Louisiana, Maryland, Massachusetts, Mississippi, Missouri, New Hampshire, North Carolina, Oregon, Rhode Island, South Carolina, Tennessee, Texas, Virginia, Wyoming, District of Columbia

States requiring one year of college and one year in a professional curriculum: Illinois, Indiana, Maine, New York and Vermont

States requiring two years of college and one year in a professional curriculum: Colorado, Delaware, Idaho, Iowa, Kansas, Michigan, Minnesota, Montana, Nebraska, Nevada, New Jersey, New Mexico, North Dakota, Ohio, Oklahoma, Pennsylvania, South Dakota, Utah, Washington, West Virginia, Wisconsin

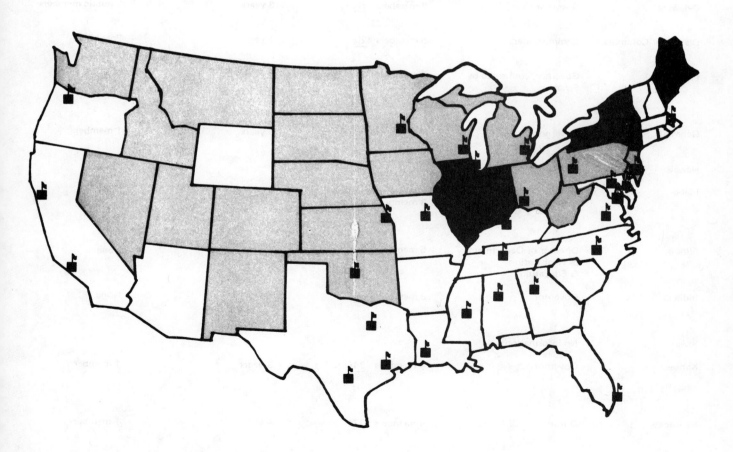

Licensing Boards—Those Appointed Details as to Numbers, Meetings and Honoraria

State	Who Appoints	Members (No.)	Term of Office	Public Member
Alaska	Department of Commerce and Economic Development has jurisdiction over the practice of mortuary science			
Alabama	Governor	7 members 1/	2 years 2/	None
Arizona	Governor	6 members 5/	2 years	2 lay members
Arkansas	Governor	6 members	5 years	1 public member
California	Governor	8 members 8/	4 years	5 public members
Colorado	Governor except Director of Health	5 members 11/	5 years	1 clergy 2 public
Connecticut	Governor	5 members 14/	5 years	None (subject to change)
Delaware	Governor	7 members 16/	3 years	2 public members
District of Columbia	Commissioners	5 members 20/	1 year	Possibly 3
Florida	Governor, confirmed by Senate	7 members 21/	4 years 22/	Two
Georgia	Governor	7 members 25/	6 years	1 member
Hawaii	No board 28/			
Idaho	Governor	Board of Morticians 3 members 29/	3 years	None
Illinois	Director of Department of Registration & Education	5 members 30/	5 years	None
Indiana	Governor	6 members 32/	4 years	None
Iowa	No information			
Kansas	Governor	4 members 34/	3 years	1 member
Kentucky	Governor 36/	4 members 37/	4 years	1 member

Reprinted with permission from "Digest of State Licensing Laws," National Funeral Directors Association of the United States, Inc., Milwaukee, WI 53203, 1978.

Full or Part-time	Officers	Frequency of Meetings	Powers: Independent Subj. to Review	Compensation Honorarium and/or Per Diem
Part-time	Chairman, Vice-Chairman, Secretary, Treasurer 3/	Not less than 1 meeting quarterly	Yes. Legislature 4/	No compensation except expenses
Part-time	President, Secretary, Treasurer 6/	At once each quarter year	Not subject to review 7/	Compensation pursuant to 38–611
Part-time	President, Vice-President, Secretary, Treasurer	3 a year or at call of President	Independent, power to adopt rules, give exams, revoke license	Per diem plus expenses
Part-time	President, Vice President, Secretary 9/	Annually and when needed	Not subject to review 10/	$25 per diem while in meetings + expenses
Part-time	President, Vice-President, Secretary 12/	At least 6 times a year 13/	Under Department of Regulatory Agencies	Per diem of $35 actual services and expenses
Part-time	President, Secretary 15/	At least once a year	Adopt regulations. Review by Lesiglative Review Committee	Rates established by Personnel Board
Part-time	President, Vice-President, Secretary 17/	Not less than once annually	Not subject to review 18/	No compensation. Only expenses 19/
Part-time	No provision		To conduct exam of application for license	$10 per day
Part-time	President, Vice-President, Secretary, Treasurer 23/	At least one each year	Independent. May adopt reasonable rules and regulations not inconsistent with law	$25 per day 24/
Part-time	President 26/	Not less than one annually	Full power and authority to regulate profession	$25 per day 27/
Part-time	Chairman, Vice-Chairman, Secretary	Not less than annually	Make recommendations to Governor on enforcement of provisions of act Recommendations to Director 31/	$35 per day plus expenses spent on duties
Part-time	Chairman, Chairman Pro Tem, Secretary-Treasurer 33/	1st Tuesday of every month	Independent	$25 per day for Board business, travel expenses
Part-time	President, Vice-President 35/	Annual meeting in May. Meeting in January, April, July & October	Independent power to carry out act and make reasonable rules and regulations	$35 per day plus expenses
Part-time	President, Secretary (optional), Treasurer	Not less than once a year	Adopt regulations subject to Legislative Research Committee	$25 a day 38/

State	Who Appoints	Members (No.)	Term of Office	Public Member
Louisiana	Governor	7 members 39/	5 years	None
Maine	Governor 41/	8 members 42/	4 years	1 member
Maryland	Governor	11 members 45/	4 years	None
Massachusetts	Governor 47/	5 members 48/	5 years	None
Michigan	Governor 49/	7 members 50/	4 years	1 public member
Minnesota	Commissioner of Health— no licensing	4 examiners 52/	4 years	None
Mississippi	Governor	7 members 53/	4 years	None
Missouri	Governor	5 members 57/	5 years	None
Montana	Governor	6 members 59/	5 years	1 public member
Nebraska	Board of Health	4 members	3 years	One
Nevada	Governor	3 members 60/	3 years	None
New Hampshire	Governor	5 members 62/	4 years	None
New Jersey	Governor	8 members 65/	3 years 66/	Two
New Mexico	Governor	5 members 68/	4 years	One
New York	Commissioner of Health	7 members 70/	3 years	Possibly one
North Carolina	Elected by vote of all licensed funeral directors and funeral service licensees & embalmers	9 members 73/	5 members—5 years 2 members—2 years 1 public—4 years	One
North Dakota	Governor	4 members 74/	4 years	None
Ohio	Governor	5 members 78/	5 years	None
Oklahoma	Governor	7 members 80/	5 years	Two

Full or Part-time	Officers	Frequency of Meetings	Powers: Independent Subj. to Review	Compensation Honorarium and/or Per Diem
Part-time	President, Vice-President, Secretary, Treasurer 40/	At least once a year	Independent power for administering and enforcing chapter	Expenses and $50 per day
Part-time	Chairman, Secretary	Regular meeting, 4 times a year 43/	Adoption of rules subject to Attorney General 44/	$20 a day and expenses while engaging in Board business
Part-time	President, Vice-President, Treasurer 46/	At least once a year	Prescribed by Department of Health & Mental Hygiene	$15 a meeting plus expenses
Part-time	Chairman, Secretary	At least once a month		Salary—$1,250 plus expenses
Part-time	Chairman (Board has authority to select from its members)	At least once a month	Not subject to review 51/	$35 per day plus expenses
Part-time		12 a year	Adopt rules subject to Attorney General	$35 per diem plus expenses
Part-time	President, Secretary-Treasurer 54/	At least once a year	Adopt rules not inconsistent with Board of Health, State or U.S. law 55/	Expenses 56/
Part-time	Chairman, Vice-Chairman, Secretary 58/	At least two regular meetings		$25 for each day on Board business and expenses
Part-time	Chairman, Secretary-Treasurer from its members	Such meetings as necessary	Independent. May adopt rules and regulations to carry out act	$25 a day for meetings and expenses
Part-time	Chairman, Vice-Chairman, Secretary	Held at discretion of Department of Health	Embalmers subject to review. Funeral directors independent	$15 per diem for meeting and expenses
Part-time	President, Secretary and Treasurer from members	At least once a year	Independent 61/	No salary but get expenses
Part-time	Chairman, Secretary-Treasurer 63/	When necessary	Independent 64/	$25 a day on Board business and expenses
Part-time	President, Secretary	1st Tuesday of month and any time necessary	Subject to review by Attorney General 67/	$25 a day on board business and expenses
Part-time	Shall elect from members Chairman, Vice-Chairman, Secretary and Treasurer	Not less than 2 meetings annually	Not subject to review 69/	Per diem and mileage—no other compensation Secretary may be part-time salaried employee
Part-time	Chairman and Vice-Chairman 71/	At least once every 3 months	Under control of Commissioner 72/	No compensation but get reasonable expenses
Part-time	President, Vice-President, Secretary elected from board members for 1 year	At least 2 each year	Independent	Per diem plus expenses. No other compensation
Part-time	President, Secretary-Treasurer 75/	At least 1 each year	Independent 76/	Traveling expenses 77/
Part-time	Select from own members—President, Secretary, Treasurer	Not less than one annually	Independent 79/	
Part-time	President, Secretary, Executive Secretary-Treasurer 81/	At least 2 each year	Independent	$25 per day, plus necessary travel

State	Who Appoints	Members (No.)	Term of Office	Public Member
Oregon	Governor	5 members 82/	2 years	None
Pennsylvania	Departmental Adm.	5 members 84/	5 years	None
Rhode Island	Governor	3 members 87/	3 years	None
South Carolina	Governor	9 members 88/	3 years	None
South Dakota	Governor	8 members	5 years	2 lay members
Tennessee	Governor	5 members 91/	5 years	None
Texas	Governor 93/	6 members 94/	6 years 95/	Four
Utah	Director of Registration 98/	3 members 99/	3 years	None
Vermont	Governor	3 members 100/	6 years	None
Virginia	Governor	7 members 101/	7 years	None
Washington	Governor	5 members	5 years	One
West Virginia	Board of Embalmers and Funeral Directors of West Virginia. No other information given.			
Wisconsin	Governor	5 members	3 years	1 member
Wyoming	Governor 102/	5 members 103/	3 years	None

Full or Part-time	Officers	Frequency of Meetings	Powers: Independent Subj. to Review	Compensation Honorarium and/or Per Diem
Part-time	President, Vice-President, Secretary, Treasurer 83/	Semi-annually and when needed	Independent—power to adopt and enforce laws	Compensation and expenses
Part-time	Chairman, Secretary 85/		Independent 86/	$30 per day on business and expenses
Part-time	Chairman	At least twice a year	Subject to Director of Health	$20 per meeting
Part-time	President 89/	At least once a year	Independent, power to make rules	$35 per day and necessary expenses 90/
Part-time	President, Vice-President, Secretary, Treasurer	At least once a year		
Part-time	President, Secretary, Treasurer from members		Independent. Adopt and enforce rules	$25 per day 92/
Part-time	President, Vice-President, Secretary 96/	At least two a year	Independent. Licensing power. Make annual report to Governor	$50 per day 97/
Part-time		At least four a year	Subject to Department of Registration	$5 for every day spent in performance
Part-time	President, Secretary, Treasurer	Monthly	Adopt rules and regulations for its business	$30 per diem and expenses when doing Board work
Part-time	President, Vice-President, Secretary, Treasurer	At least 2 regular meetings	Member of Department of Health Regulatory Board	$50 a day on business and and expenses
Part-time	Chairman, Vice-Chairman, Secretary	At least once	Subject to Director of Licensing	$25 for each board meeting and expenses
Part-time	Chairman, Vice-Chairman, Secretary	At least once a year	Independent. Make and enforce rules	$25 per diem plus expenses
Part-time	President and Secretary-Treasurer	At least once a year	Independent	$5 per day and expenses

Licensure—Funeral Director—

State	Citizenship	Accredited (funeral director) Diploma Required	Length of Course
Alaska		No	
Alabama	U.S.	No	
Arizona	Single license required. See embalmer's qualifications		
Arkansas		No	
California		No	
Colorado	As of December 31, 1967, no separate license for embalmer and funeral director.		
Connecticut	U.S.		
Delaware	U.S.	Yes	
District of Columbia	No separate licenses. One undertaker's license		
Florida	Meet all embalming qualifications and be a practicing licensed embalmer in Florida for at least 1 year. Shall have 1 year of practical training an an intern funeral director, Assoc. of Arts degree in mortuary science, passed exam prepared by Dept. of Regulation		
Georgia	U.S.	No	
Hawaii	License funeral homes, not funeral directors. Embalmer's license is only other license given.		
Idaho	One license—mortician's license issued		
Illinois	U.S.	Yes	1 year
Indiana	U.S. Must hold an Indiana License as an embalmer.		
Iowa		Yes	1 year
Kansas	U.S.		
Kentucky		No	
Louisiana		Yes	
Maine	U.S.	Yes	
Maryland	Combination license issued covering both embalmers and funeral directors. Requirements given in embalming section.		
Massachusetts	U.S.	Yes	9 months
Michigan	Practitioner of Mortuary Science license—only license issued.		
Minnesota	Combined license issued. (117/). Requirements under embalmers		
Mississippi	No funeral director's license required.		
Missouri		No	
Montana	Use mono-license. (118/). Requirements given in embalmer's section.		
Nebraska	2-year course in an accredited college consisting of 60 semester hours. One school year in an accredited college or mortuary science or hold a Nebraska embalmer's license.		
Nevada		No	
New Hampshire	Applicant for a funeral director's license must hold an embalmer's license.		

Reprinted with permission from "Digest of State Licensing Laws," National Funeral Directors Association of the United States, Inc., Milwaukee, WI 53203, 1978.

Basic Requirements

Pre-Funeral Director School Education	Apprenticeship Required	Must Apprentice Register w/Board	Apprenticeship Before or After School
1 year college	Yes		Optional
	Yes		Before
High school	No		
	No		
2-yr. post-secondary school approved by Board	Yes	Yes	After
2 years college	Yes	One license—funeral service license	
	Yes	Yes	
High school	No		
1 year college	Yes 225/	Yes	After
	Yes		
2 years college	Yes	Yes	After
2 years college	Yes	Yes	
High school	Yes	Yes	
1 year college	Yes		
	Yes		
High school	No		
	No		
	No		

State	Citizenship	Accredited (funeral director) Diploma Required	Length of Course
New Jersey	Combination license issued—requirements in embalmer's section		
New York	Combination license issued—requirements in embalmer's section		
New Mexico	Single license as "Funeral Service Practitioner" required. See qualifications under Embalmers.		
North Carolina	U.S.	Yes	or
North Dakota			
Ohio	U.S.	No (Optional) 119/	12 months (Op.) 119/
Oklahoma	Must be a licensed embalmer or have available a licensed embalmer		
Oregon			
Pennsylvania	Combination license issued—see requirements in embalmer's section		
Rhode Island	U.S.	Must hold an embalmer's certificate	
South Carolina	U.S.	1 year college or mortuary school	
South Dakota	Combination license—see embalmer's requirements		
Tennessee	U.S.	Yes	
Texas		Yes	1 year
Utah	Combination license (Funeral Service License)—see embalmer's requirements		
Vermont			
Virginia	No longer issue separate funeral director and embalmer licenses. See embalming requirements		
Washington		No	
West Virginia	Must hold an embalmer's license.		
Wisconsin		No	
Wyoming		No	

Pre-Funeral Director School Education	Apprenticeship Required	Must Apprentice Register w/Board	Apprenticeship Before or After School
32 hours in an accredited college	Yes		Optional
2 years college	Yes	Yes	Optional
	Yes	Yes	
High school	Yes	Yes	Optional
High school	Yes	Yes	Optional
High school	Yes	Yes	Optional
2 years college	Yes	Yes	Optional
	Yes	Yes	
	No	Yes	Optional
	No		

State	Apprenticeship Must Precede Exam	Must Apprenticeship be Served in this State	Required Years of Apprenticeship	No. of Funerals to Assist	Examination Required
Alaska		Yes			Yes
Alabama			2 years within period of 3 consecutive years		Yes
Arizona					
Arkansas					
California					Yes
Colorado					
Connecticut	After		2 years		
Delaware			1 year		
District of Columbia					
Florida	Yes	Yes	1 year		Yes
Georgia					
Hawaii					
Idaho					
Illinois		Yes	1 year		Yes
Indiana	Yes	Yes	1 year (internship) 225/		Yes
Iowa	After	Yes	1 year	25 funerals	
Kansas					
Kentucky	Optional	Yes	3 years		
Louisiana					
Maine			1 year		
Maryland				20 funerals	
Massachusetts	Must be a duly registered embalmer.				No
Michigan					
Mississippi					
Missouri					
Montana			None		
Nebraska	Applicant for a Funeral Director license must have been a full time employee of a licensed Nebraska F.D. for not less than 6 mo. prior to making application for licensure.			25 funerals	Yes
Nevada					Yes
New Hampshire					
New Jersey					
New York					
New Mexico				50 funerals	
North Carolina	Yes		12 months		Yes

State	Apprenticeship Must Precede Exam	Must Apprenticeship be Served in this State	Required Years of Apprenticeship	No. of Funerals to Assist	Examination Required
North Dakota					
Ohio	Yes		2 years. 119/	25 funerals	Yes
Oklahoma					
Oregon	Yes, but not more than 2 yrs. prior		2 years		Yes
Pennsylvania					
Rhode Island					
South Carolina	Yes	Yes	1 year		Yes
South Dakota					
Tennessee	No	Yes	1 year		Yes
Texas	Optional	Yes	1 year	60 funerals	Yes
Utah				50 funerals	
Vermont					
Virginia					
Washington	No	Yes	1 year		Yes
West Virginia	Yes	Yes	1 year		Yes
Wisconsin	Optional	Yes	1 year		Yes
Wyoming					Yes

Licensure—Funeral Director—

State	Funeral Director Professional License Required	Fee for Funeral Director Exam	Funeral Director Renewal License Fee
Alaska			
Alabama	Yes	$50.00	$15.00
Arizona	Yes	$25.00	$25.00
Arkansas	Yes		$10.00
California	No	$50.00 121/	$150.00
Colorado	Yes	$50.00	$15.00
Connecticut	Yes	$40.00	$100.00
Delaware	Yes (single license)		
District of Columbia	Yes	None	
Florida	Yes		Set by board. Not to exceed $250.00 biennially
Georgia	Yes	$50.00	$10.00 biennially
Hawaii	No		
Idaho	Yes	127/	$25.00
Illinois	Yes	$25.00	$6.00
Indiana	Yes	$25.00 set by Board—not less than $5.00 or more than $25.00	$5.00 set by Board—not to exceed $10.00
Iowa	Yes	$10.00	$5.00
Kansas	Yes	$40.00	$35.00
Kentucky	Yes	$25.00	$10.00
Louisiana	Yes	$100.00	$20.00
Maine	Yes	$20.00	$15.00
Maryland	Yes 129/	$100.00	$50.00
Massachusetts	Yes	$10.00	$10.00
Michigan	Yes 130/	$22.00 131/ $50.00 proposed	$10.00 $25.00 proposed
Minnesota	Yes 117/	$50.00	$25.00
Mississippi	No		
Missouri	Yes	$40.00	$10.00
Montana	Yes 118/	118/	$10.00 132/
Nebraska	Yes		
Nevada	Yes	$100.00	$35.00

Reprinted with permission from "Digest of State Licensing Laws," National Funeral Directors Association of the United States, Inc., Milwaukee, WI 53203, 1978.

Specific Requirements

Minimum Age Funeral Director License	Is Single Funeral Director Embalmers License Now Required?	Must Funeral Director Applicant be Resident of State?	Is Funeral Home License Required?
18	No	Yes	Yes
	Yes	Yes	Yes
18	Yes	Yes	Yes
18	No	No	Yes
21	Yes but 122/	Yes	Yes
18	No	Yes	Yes 123/
124/	Yes	Yes	Yes
21	Yes	No	No
18 125/	Yes	Yes	Yes
21	Yes 126/	Yes	Yes
	No		Yes
127/	Yes	127/	Yes
21	No	Yes	No
18	Yes 128/	Yes	Yes
21	Yes	Yes	No
21	No	Yes	Yes
18	No	Yes	No
18	No	Yes	Yes
18	Yes	Yes	Yes
21	Yes 129/	No	No
21	Yes	Yes	Yes
18 130/	Yes	No 130/	Yes
18	Yes		Yes
	No		No
21	No	Yes	Yes
18	Yes		Yes
21	No	No	Yes
18	No		No 133/

State	Funeral Director Professional License Required	Fee for Funeral Director Exam	Funeral Director Renewal License Fee
New Hampshire	Yes 134/	$20.00 + license $20.00 135/	$40.00–$50.00 for '78 & '79
New Jersey	Yes 136/	$50.00 practitioner's exam	$50.00 biennial 136/
New Mexico	Yes		$50.00
New York	Yes	$35.00 137/	$15.00 138/
North Carolina	Yes		$15.00
Ohio	Yes	$32.50	$22.50
Oklahoma	Yes	$20.00	$17.50
Oregon	Yes	$35.00 140/	$15.00
Pennsylvania	Yes 141/	$25.00 141/	
Rhode Island	Yes	$50.00	$20.00
South Carolina	Yes	$50.00	$20.00
South Dakota	Yes 141/	$25.00	$25.00
Tennessee	Yes	$25.00	$10.00
Texas	Yes	$50.00	$40.00 biennially
Utah	Yes 141/		
Vermont	Yes	$15.00, $10.00 orig. license	$10.00
Virginia	Yes 143/	$35.00 143/	$20.00 143/
Washington	Yes	$45.00	$18.00
West Virginia	Yes	$50.00	$5.00
Wisconsin	Yes	$50.00	$30.00 biennially odd no. years
Wyoming	Yes	$25.00	$50.00

Minimum Age Funeral Director License	Is Single Funeral Director Embalmers License Now Required?	Must Funeral Director Applicant be Resident of State?	Is Funeral Home License Required?
18	No	No	No, but must be inspected & registered
18	Yes. Practitioners include embalm. & fun. dir.	No	Yes
21	Yes—funeral service practitioner license	Yes	Yes
	Yes 137/	No	Yes 138/
18	No	Yes	Yes
21	Yes	No 139/	No
21	No. Can obtain either license	Yes	Yes
21	No	No	Yes
21	Yes 141/	No	No
18	Yes	No	No
21	No	Yes	Yes
18	Yes 141/		Yes
18	No	Yes	Yes
18	Yes	Yes	Yes
18	Yes 141/	Yes	No 142/
21	No	Yes	Yes
18	Yes	Yes	Yes
18	No	No	Yes
21	No	Yes	Yes
18	Yes	No	Yes
21	No	Yes	No—funeral dir. license

Licensure— Embalmer—

State	Type of License	Minimum Age Embalmers	Citizenship
Alaska	Funeral Director and/or embalmer	18	
Alabama	Funeral director and/or embalmer	18	U.S.
Arizona	Cert. of qualification for embalming & funeral directing		
Arkansas	Funeral Director and Embalmer	18	U.S.
California	Funeral director and/or Embalmer	18	
Colorado	To practice mortuary science	18	
Connecticut	Funeral director and/or embalmer	18	U.S.
Delaware	For practice of funeral service	124/	U.S.
District of Columbia		21	U.S.
Florida	Funeral director and/or embalmer	18	
Georgia	Funeral director and/or embalmer	21	U.S.
Hawaii	Embalmer, undertaker or funeral director	over 20	
Idaho	Mortician and/or funeral director	21	
Illinois	Funeral director and/or embalmer	21	U.S.
Indiana	Funeral director and/or embalmer	18	U.S.
Iowa	Funeral director and/or embalmer	21	
Kansas	Funeral director and/or embalmer		U.S.
Kentucky	Funeral director & embalmer	18	
Louisiana	Funeral director & embalmer	18	U.S.
Maine	Funeral director & embalmer and funeral service combination	18	U.S.
Maryland	Funeral director & embalmer	18	
Massachusetts	Embalmers registered by Board of Embalming. Funeral directors licensed by Board of Health	21	U.S.
Michigan	Mortuary Science	18	U.S.
Minnesota	Funeral director & embalmer	18	
Mississippi	Embalmer	21	
Missouri	Funeral director & embalmer	21	
Montana	Mortician's license	18	
Nebraska	Funeral director & embalmer	21	
Nevada	Embalmer's license	18	
New Hampshire	Funeral director & embalmer	18	U.S.

Reprinted with permission from "Digest of State Licensing Laws," National Funeral Directors Association of the United States, Inc., Milwaukee, WI 53203, 1978.

Basic Requirements

Resident	Accredited School Diploma Required	Length of (Emb.) Professional School Course	Pre-Embalming School Education
	Yes		
Yes	Yes	12 months	High school
Yes	Yes	12 months	High school
Yes	Yes	12 months	High school
	No	9 months 144/	High school
Yes	Yes	9 months	2 years college
Yes	Yes	12 months	High school
Yes for 6 months prior to application	Yes	12 months	2 years college
	Yes	9 months	High school
	Yes	145/	High school
Resident of Ga.	Yes	12 months	High school
For at least 2 yrs.	No	159/	159/
	Yes	12 months	2 years college
Yes	No 146/	12 months	1 year college
Yes 147/	Yes 148/	12 months 148/	1 year college
	Yes	12 months	2 years college
Yes	Yes	12 months	2 years college
	Yes	12 months	High school
Yes	Yes	12 months	High school
Yes	Yes	12 months	1 year college
	Yes	12 months 149/	
	Yes	9 months	High school
Yes	Yes	1 year	2 years college
	Yes	9 months	2 years college
	Yes	12 months	High school
Yes except bordering counties	Yes	12 months	High school
	Yes	9 months	2 years college
	Yes	9 months	2 years college 150/
	Yes	12 months	2 years college
	Yes	12 months	High school

State	Type of License	Minimum Age Embalmers	Citizenship
New Jersey	Funeral director & embalmer Single license, practitioner of mortuary science	18	
New Mexico	Funeral service license	18	
New York	Combined license, funeral director's license		U.S.
North Carolina	Funeral director & embalmer Funeral service license	18	U.S.
North Dakota	Embalmer's license	21	
Ohio	Funeral director & embalmer	21	U.S.
Oklahoma	Funeral director & embalmer	21	U.S.
Oregon	Funeral director	21	
Pennsylvania	Funeral director	21	U.S.
Rhode Island	Funeral director's & embalmer's certificates	18	U.S.
South Carolina	Funeral director & embalmer	21	U.S.
South Dakota	License to practice funeral service	18	U.S.
Tennessee	Funeral director & embalmer	18	U.S.
Texas	Funeral director & embalmer	18	
Utah	Funeral director & embalmer	18	U.S.
Vermont	Funeral director & embalmer	18	U.S.
Virginia	Funeral Service License	18	
Washington	Funeral director & embalmer	18	
West Virginia	Funeral director & embalmer	21	U.S.
Wisconsin	Funeral director & embalmer	18	U.S.
Wyoming	Funeral director & embalmer	21—adult citizen	U.S.

Resident	Accredited School Diploma Required	Length of (Emb.) Professional School Course	Pre-Embalming School Education
	Yes	12 months	2 years college
Yes	Yes	12 months	2 years college
	Yes	12 months	1 year college
Yes	Yes	151/	High school
	Yes	9 months	2 years college
	Yes	12 months	2 years college
Yes	Yes	12 months	60 credit hours
	Yes	12 months	High school
	No	12 months	2 years college
	Yes	12 months	High school
Yes, 1 yr.	Yes	12 months	High school
Yes	Yes	12 months	2 years college
	Yes	12 months	High school
Yes	Yes	Not less than 4 academic quarters	High school
Yes	Yes	12 months	2 years college
Yes	Yes	12 months	30 college credit hours
	152/	152/	High school
	Yes	Full course of instruction	2 years college
	Yes	12 months	2 years college
	Yes	9 months	2 years college 153/
	Yes	9 months	High school

State	Apprenticeship Required	Apprenticeship Before or After School	Must Apprenticeship Precede Exam
Alaska	Yes	Optional	Optional
Alabama	Yes	Optional	Yes
Arizona	Yes	Optional	Yes
Arkansas	Yes	Optional	No
California	Yes	Optional	No
Colorado	Yes	Optional	Yes
Connecticut	Yes	After	No
Delaware	Yes	After 157/	Yes
District of Columbia	Yes	Optional 158/	Yes
Florida	Yes	After	Yes
Georgia	Yes	Optional	Yes
Hawaii	159/	Optional	Yes
Idaho	Yes	Optional	Yes
Illinois	Yes	After	
Indiana	Yes	After	160/
Iowa	Yes	After	No
Kansas	Yes	After	
Kentucky	Yes	Optional	Yes
Louisiana	Yes	Optional	No
Maine	Yes	Optional	No
Maryland	Yes	Optional	Yes
Massachusetts	Yes	Optional	Yes
Michigan	Yes	Optional	Yes
Minnesota	Yes	After	Yes
Mississippi	Yes	Optional	Optional
Missouri	Yes	After	No
Montana	Yes	After	No, comes after
Nebraska	Yes	After	No (can follow written portion of exam)
Nevada	Yes	Optional	No
New Hampshire	Yes	Optional	Yes
New Jersey	Yes	Optional	Optional
New Mexico	Yes	After	Yes
New York	Yes	Optional	No, comes after
North Carolina	Yes	Optional	No
North Dakota	Yes	After	No

Must Apprenticeship Be Served in This State	Required Years of Apprenticeship	Must Apprentice Register with Board	No. of Bodies to Be Embalmed
	1		
Yes	2 154/	Yes	
No	2 155/	Yes	25
Yes	2	Yes	50
Yes	2 156/	Yes	100
Yes	1	Yes	25
Yes (exceptions can be made)	2	Yes	100
Yes	1	Yes	25
Yes	2	Yes	25
Yes	1	Yes	
Yes	2 years	Yes	50
Yes	159/	Yes	25
Yes	1	Yes	25
Yes	1	Yes	25
Yes	1 225/	Yes	
Yes	1	Yes 161/	25
Yes	1	Yes	25
Yes	3 226/	Yes	
Yes	1	Yes	25
Yes	1	Yes	25
Yes	2 149/	Yes	20
Yes	2	Yes	50
Yes	1	Yes	25
No	1	Yes	25
Yes	1	Yes	25
No	1	Yes	25
Yes	1	Yes	25
Yes	1	Yes	25
Yes	1	Yes	50
Yes	2	Yes	50
Yes	2 162/	Yes	75
Yes	1	Yes	50
Yes	1	Yes	
Yes	1	Yes	25
No	9 months	Yes	25

State	Apprenticeship Required	Apprenticeship Before or After School	Must Apprenticeship Precede Exam
Ohio	Yes	After	No
Oklahoma	Yes	Optional	No
Oregon	Yes	Optional	Optional
Pennsylvania	Yes	After	Yes
Rhode Island	Yes	Optional	Yes
South Carolina	Yes	Optional	Yes
South Dakota	Yes	Optional	No
Tennessee	Yes	Optional	No
Texas	Yes	Optional	No
Utah	Yes	Optional 163/	Yes
Vermont	Yes	Optional	Yes
Virginia	Yes	Optional but prefer before	Yes
Washington	Yes	Optional	No
West Virginia	Yes	Before	Yes
Wisconsin	Yes	Optional	Optional
Wyoming	Yes	Optional	Yes

Must Apprenticeship Be Served in This State	Required Years of Apprenticeship	Must Apprentice Register with Board	No. of Bodies to Be Embalmed
Yes	1	Yes	25
Yes	1	Yes	25
Yes	1 (plus mortuary college)	Yes	60
Yes	1	Yes	At least 25 (Set by Board)
Yes	2	Yes	50
Yes	2	Yes	
No	1	Yes	25
Yes	1	Yes	
Yes	1	Yes	60
Yes	1	Yes	50
Yes	1	Yes	30
Yes	2	Yes	25
Yes	2	Yes	50
Yes	1	Yes	25
Yes	1	Yes	25
Yes	2 164/	Yes	25

Licensure—Embalmers—

State	When Held	Given By	Accept Conference Natl. Board Exam
Alaska		Department	
Alabama	Quarterly 164A/	Board	Yes
Arizona	January & July	Board	166/ No
Arkansas	March, May & September	Board	Yes
California	June & December 168/	Board	169/ No
Colorado	January & July	Board	Yes
Connecticut	April & October	Board	Yes
Delaware	Not specified 172/	Board	Yes
District of Columbia	April	Committee	Yes
Florida	June & December	Dept. of Professional Regulation	Yes
Georgia	June & December	Board	173/ No
Hawaii	April & October	Board of Health	174/ No
Idaho	January & July	Board of Morticians	175/ No
Illinois	April & October	Board of Examiners	No
Indiana	Annually	Board of funeral directors	Yes
Iowa	April & October	Board	Yes
Kansas	Quarterly	Board of Embalmers	No
Kentucky	June & December	State Board of Embalmers & Funeral Directors	Yes
Louisiana	March & September	State Board of Embalmers and Funeral Directors	No
Maine	May & November	Board of Funeral Directors	Yes
Maryland	March	Board of Funeral Directors and Embalmers	Yes
Massachusetts	March & October	Board of Embalmers	No
Michigan	January & July	Examiners in Mortuary Science	Yes
Minnesota	January & June	Comm. of Health	Yes
Mississippi	April & October	Embalming Board	Yes
Missouri	Annually—By June 30	Board of Embalmers and Funeral Directors	Yes
Montana	January & July	Board of Morticians	Yes
Nebraska	January & July	Board of Examiners in Embalming	No
Nevada		Board of Funeral Directors & Embalmers	No
New Hampshire	Optional	Board of Registered Funeral Directors and Embalmers	Yes

Reprinted with permission from "Digest of State Licensing Laws," National Funeral Directors Association of the United States, Inc., Milwaukee, WI 53203, 1978.

Examinations and Renewal

Fee for Embalming License Exam	Embalmer's Renewal How Often?	Embalmer's Renewal Fee
	Biennially	
$50.00	Every year 165/	$15.00
$50.00	Every year 167/	$15.00
$25.00	Every year	$10.00
$50.00	Every year 170/	$50.00
$50.00	Every year	$15.00
$40.00	Every year 171/	$10.00
$75.00	Biennially	$20.00
$10.00	Every year	$15.00
Not to exceed $250.00	Biennial renewal	Not to exceed $250.00
$50.00	Biennially	$10.00
$25.00	Every year—August 1	$10.00
$25.00	Every year	$25.00
$25.00	Every year	$6.00
$25.00	Every 2 yrs.—expires December 31	$5.00—Board sets not to exceed $10.00
$10.00	Annually	$10.00
$40.00	Every year—July 1	$20.00
$25.00	Annually—Expires July 31	$10.00
$100.00	Annually—expires December 31	$20.00
$20.00	Annually—expires December 31	$15.00
$100.00	Annually	$50.00
$10.00	Annually—November 1	$5.00
$11.00	Annually	$25.00
$50.00	Annually	$25.00
$50.00	Annually—expires June 30	$5.00
$40.00	Annually—by June 15	$10.00
$50.00	Annually—before July 1	$15.00
$30.00	Annually—February 1	$10.00
$100.00	Annually	$35.00
written $20.00 176/ oral and practical $20.00	Annually—expires December 31	$40.00 except 1978 & 1979 $50.00

State	When Held	Given By	Accept Conference Natl. Board Exam
New Jersey	June & October	Board of Mortuary Science	No
New Mexico	Quarterly	State Board of Thantopractice	Yes
New York	Twice a year	Comm. of Health	Yes
North Carolina	April & November	Board	Yes
North Dakota	January & July	Board of Embalmers	Yes
Ohio	April & October	Board of Embalmers	Yes 177/
Oklahoma	March & September	Board of Embalmers & Funeral Directors	Yes, if given in Okla. & monitored by Bd. Reps.
Oregon	January & August	Board of Embalmers & Funeral Directors	No
Pennsylvania	June & December	Board of Funeral Directors	No
Rhode Island	2 per year	Div. of Prof. Reg.	Yes
South Carolina	Annually	Board of Funeral Serv.	Yes
South Dakota	April & July	Board of Funeral Serv.	Yes
Tennessee	April & November	Board of Funeral Directors & Embalmers	Yes
Texas	March & September	Board of Morticians	No
Utah	Quarterly	Dept. of Registration	Yes
Vermont	Semi-annually	Bd. of Funeral Services	Yes
Virginia	May, August, November	Board of Funeral Directors & Embalmers	Yes
Washington	May & November	Board of Funeral Directors & Embalmers	Yes
West Virginia	April & November	Board of Embalmers & Funeral Directors	Yes
Wisconsin	Annually	Board of Funeral Directors	No
Wyoming	Twice each year at discretion of Board. Provision for spec. exams.	Board of Embalmers	Yes

Fee for Embalming License Exam	Embalmer's Renewal How Often?	Embalmer's Renewal Fee
$50.00 (practitioner exam)	Biennially	$50.00
$75.00	Annually	$60.00
$35.00 137/	Biennially	$7.50
	Annually—expires December 31	$15.00
$15.00	Annually	$15.00
$32.50	Annually	$22.50
$20.00	Annually	$15.00
$35.00	Annually—Renewals due 1 yr. from date of issuance	$15.00
$25.00	Biennially	
$25.00 each	Annually	$20.00
$50.00	Annually	$20.00
$25.00	Annually	$25.00
$25.00	Annually	$10.00
$50.00	Biennially	$40.00
	Every 3 years 228/	
$15.00	Annually	$10.00
$.00	Annually	$20.00
$45.00	Annually	$18.00
$50.00	Annually—expires June 30	$5.00
$50.00	Biennially—odd years	$30.00
$25.00	Annually	$30.00 178/

Direct Disposers

State	Minimum Age	Citizenship	Resident	Educational Requirement	Examination Requirement
Florida (Permit)	18			High school	Yes
New Mexico (License)	18		Yes	High school	Yes

Reprinted with permission from "Digest of State Licensing Laws," National Funeral Directors Association of the United States, Inc., Milwaukee, WI 53203, 1978.

Fee for Direct Disposer Exam	Renewal How Often	Renewal Fee	Direct Disposer Est. Permit
Not to exceed $250 as provided by dept.	Biennially	Not to exceed $250.00	Yes
$75.00	Annually	$60.00	Yes

Footnotes and Addendum

1. There shall be one member appointed from each of seven geographical districts, which shall be identical with the seven Congressional Districts as fixed by Title 17, Sec. 425 of 194 Code of Ala., as amended by Act No. 120 of the 3rd Special Session of 1971 approved June 19, 1972 and as thereafter be amended. Four members serving on Board must be practicing and licensed embalmers in Ala. for the last ten (10) consecutive years immediately preceding their appointment, and shall be licensed embalmers and funeral directors in Ala. Three of said members shall have been actively engaged in funeral directing in Ala. for the last ten (10) consecutive years preceding their appointment, and shall be licensed funeral directors and at the time of their appointment to the Board be *operators* of funeral establishments in Ala.

2. Each member may be reappointed for one (1) additional two-year term. No person shall serve more than four years as a member of the board.

3. No two offices to be held by same person. Chairman and Vice Chairman cannot be of same race. Board may employ an Executive Secretary and Assistant Executive Secretary who are on salary.

4. The Alabama Board of Funeral Directors is subject to review by the Sunset Review Committee of the Alabama Legislature every four (4) years.

5. Four members shall be qualified practicing funeral directors or embalmers in Arizona, one of whom shall be a non-owner of a funeral establishment, and two lay members. All members shall be residents of Arizona.

6. Choose from among its membership.

7. Adopt rules and regulations consistent with provisions of this chapter. Members of board sign all certificates of qualification.

8. The three licentiates of the board shall be licensed funeral directors or embalmers with a minimum of five consecutive years experience immediately preceding their appointment. Members including the five public shall not be financially interested in or faculty members of funeral directing or embalming schools. Board members may serve only two four year terms (eight years maximum).

9. Elected by and from board members for one year terms.

10. The Board may, pursuant to the provisions of the Adm. Procedure Act (1) adopt rules and regulations concerning the practice of embalming, (2) business of funeral directing, (3) sanitary condition of funeral homes, (4) condition for approval of funeral establishments and embalming schools, (5) scope of exams.

11. Two of the members so appointed shall be licensed practitioners actively engaged in mortuary science who have been licensed for five years or have had five years consecutive experience as funeral directors or embalmers. Three members shall be public members having no relation to the mortuary science business, one of whom shall have been duly ordained or otherwise officially designated as a member of the clergy. At least one member shall be from west of the continental divide.

12. From its members for a term of one year.

13. Special meetings may be called whenever necessary by the secretary or shall be called by the secretary upon the request of the president or upon written request of any two members of the Board.

14. The examining board members shall be residents of Connecticut, shall be practical arterial embalmers who have had at least five years' experience in this state in the practice of embalming and the preparation and disposal of dead bodies, shall be actively engaged in the practice of embalming at the time of their respective appointments and shall be licensed embalmers.

15. Each will serve for one year and be elected by board from its number.

16. Members must be citizens of the U.S. and residents of the State. Five of the members must have been licensed to practice funeral directing for 10 consecutive years in the state preceding appointment. Two members from general public and not connected with funeral directing.

17. Board selects officers from its own membership. No two offices may be held by same person.

18. Board may adopt and promulgate rules and regulations for the transaction of its business and for betterment of promotion of standards of service and practice to be followed by the funeral service profession in the state. Board shall determine qualifications necessary to engage in funeral service profession and examine all applicants for licenses and shall issue licenses to all persons who successfully pass an examination.

19. With the exception of the Secretary.

20. Two persons shall have been actually and continually engaged in discharging the duties of an undertaker or embalmer for at least five years next preceding their appointment in D.C. The Health Officer of D.C. or a member of the personnel of the Health Department designated by him shall serve as an ex officio member of the committee.

21. Five members of the board shall be chosen from licensees. The remaining two members shall be Florida residents who have never been licensed, embalmer or funeral director and are in no way connected with practice of embalming or funeral directing. Actual licensing is done by the Department of Professional Regulation.

22. Appointment to fill unexpired terms shall be for the remainder of such terms only.

23. Officers shall serve for one year and until successors are elected by the board and qualified. President and Secretary-Treasurer shall receive a just and fair salary for services required and rendered, to be fixed by the board.

24. $25 a day while attending the official board meetings not to exceed 12 meetings per year.

25. Members shall be licensed and practicing funeral directors and embalmers with a minimum of five consecutive years as such in Georgia immediately preceding appointment.

26. Shall elect from its members a President for a term of one year.

27. Each member shall receive not more than $25 per diem, not to exceed 30 days per year, for time actually spent on business of Board and necessary expenses.

28. Hawaii has no Licensing Board. All duties with respect to licensing funeral directors in Hawaii lie with the Director of Health.

29. Each member shall be a duly licensed mortician under laws of Idaho and resident of Idaho for at least 5 years next preceding his appointment, during which time he shall have been continuously engaged in the practice as a mortician as defined in this act. Names of prospective members shall be given to the Governor by Idaho Funeral Service Association.

30. Must be engaged in practice of funeral directing for 5 years prior to appointment to board, and in no way connected with or interested in any school or college where funeral directing is taught.

31. Board shall make recommendations to the Director of Rules and Regulations for his determination; conduct all examinations for license of funeral directors and embalmers; for and at the direction of the Director conduct hearings upon all complaints for revocation or suspension of license and return records of the hearing and their recommendations and report to him.

32. Five members shall be both practical and practicing licensed embalmers and also practicing licensed funeral directors and who shall then be practicing their profession and business in the state of Indiana. The sixth man shall be secretary of the State Board of Health ex officio.

33. Chairman is appointed by the Governor. The Board shall elect one of its members as chairman pro-tempore to serve in chairman's absence. The Board, by Governor's approval, elects a Secretary-Treasurer, who need not be a member of the Board but must be a licensed embalmer and licensed funeral director. His compensation shall not exceed $6,000 per annum.

34. Members of State Board of Embalming shall be residents of Kansas. Three members shall hold embalmers license issued by the State Board, have five consecutive years experience, and be currently engaged in the practice of embalming and care and disposition of dead human bodies in Kansas. The fourth member of the Board shall be a representative of the public in general and shall not hold any license issued by the Board.

35. President and Vice President from the Board and shall serve for one year.
A secretary shall be elected by the Board who shall serve for four years and be the executive officer of the Board but not a member thereof.

36. The Governor shall make appointments from a list of three (3) names furnished him each year by the members of the Funeral Directors Association of Kentucky. The Governor shall appoint one member of the board each year and every fourth year appoint two members.

37. Three members shall be residents of Kentucky and shall be licensed embalmers and licensed funeral directors of Kentucky with an established funeral home there, and one shall be a member of the public.

38. Every member except the Secretary-Treasurer shall receive $25.00 per day, not to exceed 60 days per year actually spent by him on the business of the board. The Secretary-Treasurer shall receive an annual salary to be fixed by the board.

39. Three licensed embalmers and four licensed funeral directors, all of whom shall be residents of Louisiana for at least five years and have experience in their respective professions for at least five years.

40. Elected from its members for a period of one year.

41. Other than the Director of Health.

42. One of the members of the State Board of Funeral Service shall be the Director of Health, six shall be persons licensed for the practice of funeral service for 10 consecutive years or who have had 10 consecutive years experience as an embalmer or funeral director in the state immediately preceding their appointment; and one shall be a member of the public.

43. Regular meetings shall be held on the 2nd Tuesday of January, April, July and October. If second Tuesday falls on a legal holiday, the meeting shall be held the next day. Special meetings shall be called by Chairman or Secretary on request of any two members.

44. Adoption, amendment or repeal of a rule shall not become effective until approved as to form and legality by Attorney General. Approval presumed if Attorney General takes no action within 30 days.

45. Members shall be eleven licensed funeral directors and embalmers, residents of Maryland, who shall have been actively engaged in their profession for the last five years immediately preceding their appointment. The Commissioner of Health or some person designated by him shall be an ex officio member.

46. From among its members.

47. Massachusetts Board of Registration in Embalming and Funeral Directing. This is a Board of Registration not licensing. Licensing of applicant is done by the appropriate Board of Health.

48. Each member of the Board must be a citizen and resident of Massachusetts and have at least five years practical experience in embalming dead human bodies and funeral directing.

49. Governor selects from a list of five names proposed annually by Michigan Funeral Directors Association. At least one member must be from upper peninsula.

50. Six members shall be citizens of U.S. licensed in mortuary science with a minimum of seven consecutive years' experience in Michigan immediately preceding their appointment and one member who is representative of the general public.

51. Board has the authority to adopt and promulgate such rules and regulations for the transaction of its business and the betterment and promotion of the standards of service and practice to be followed in the profession of mortuary science in the state of Michigan, as it may deem expedient and consistent with the laws of the state.

52. To assist in the holding of the examination and enforcement of the provisions of this chapter the Commission shall establish a committee of examiners. Two examiners shall be licensed in mortuary science and shall have five years experience immediately preceding their appointment in the preparation and disposition of dead human bodies and in the practice of mortuary science. A third shall be a representative of the Commissioner, and the fourth shall be a full time academic staff member of the course in mortuary science at the University of Minnesota.

53. The State Embalming Board shall consist of seven members, one to the Executive Office of the State Board of Health and one to the Director of the Bureau of Vital Statistics and the other five to be appointed by the Governor. All members shall be residents of Mississippi and licensed by the State Embalming Board for at least five years and who, for at least five years prior to such appointment shall have been a practicing embalmer.

54. From among members to serve for one year.

55. Shall not pass any rules or regulations pertaining to the handling of dead bodies in any manner, or requiring them to be embalmed.

56. Each member shall be allowed a reasonable amount for service, hotel bills, traveling and incidental expenses.

57. Each member must have a license to practice embalming or funeral directing in this state or both said licenses and have been actively engaged in embalming or funeral directing for five years next before his appointment. Each member must be a citizen and a qualified voter of Missouri, be of good moral character. Not more than three members may be from same political party.

58. Elected from among members for a term fixed by regulation of the board.

59. Five members shall be licensed morticians. One member shall be a representative of the public who is not engaged in mortuary science of funeral directing. The public member may not participate in administering, license examination and mortuary inspection.

60. Members of the State Board of Funeral Directors and Embalmers shall be practical and practicing funeral directors and embalmers.

61. May adopt reasonable rules and regulations for purpose of carrying out Chapter 642 NRS and adopt and enforce reasonable rules and regulations relating to business of funeral directors and to sanitary conditions of such establishments.

62. The State Board of Registration of Funeral Directors and Embalmers shall be composed of the Director, Division of Public Health Services of the Department of Health & Welfare, or his designated alternate, ex officio, and four members to be appointed by the governor with the advice and consent of the council. Appointees shall be funeral directors, shall be citizens and residents of the state who have had at least five years of practical experience in funeral directing and embalming and shall have been engaged therein in this state for a period of at least five years. Appointees shall be chosen from a list of three names annually submitted to the governor and council by the New Hampshire Funeral Directors Association.

63. The Chairman and a Treasurer are elected by the board within 30 days after appointment and qualification of a member. The Director, Division of Public Health Services of the Department of Health and Welfare shall be secretary of the board. The office of secretary and treasurer may be held by one member.

64. Board has the power to adopt rules and regulations for the transaction of its business, for betterment and promotion of educational and other standards and for the regulation, etc., of the profession of funeral directing and embalming.

65. Five members of the *State Board of Mortuary Science of New Jersey* shall be a citizen of the U.S. and a resident of the state of N.J., and duly licensed as a practitioner of mortuary science and shall have a minimum of five consecutive years of experience as a practitioner of mortuary science in N.J. immediately preceding his appointment, plus two public members and one state government member.

66. Board member may not serve more than two consecutive terms.

67. Board is empowered to adopt such rules and regulations as shall be reasonably proper and advisable, but they are subject to review by Attorney General.

68. Three of the members of the board shall be licensed for the practice of funeral service under the Thantopractice License Law for 5 consecutive years immediately preceding his appointment. One member shall not be a funeral service licensee or a direct disposer and shall be a public representative. One member shall be a direct disposer or have practical experience in the health care field.

69. Duties and Powers—The board shall investigate violations of Thantopractice License Law and discipline violators. It shall examine and determine qualifications for applicants for licenses, registrations and permits under the Thantopractice License Law. Administer and enforce said law, including adopting, amending and repealing such reasonable rules as necessary to carry out its provisions.

70. At least six shall be licensed funeral directors, undertakers or embalmers for at least five years prior to appointment and shall be citizens of U.S.

71. Funeral Directing Advisory Board shall annually from its members elect a chairman and vice-chairman. The Commissioner shall designate an officer or employee of the department of health to act as secretary of Board. He shall not be a member of the Board.

72. The advisory board shall have no executive administrative or appointive powers or duties.

73. Consists of five funeral service licensees who are licensed to practice funeral service in N.C. and are actually engaged in the practice of funeral service in N.C. Must have had above license for not less than five consecutive years prior thereto. Two members shall be either two funeral directors or two more funeral service licensees. The funeral directors must be licensed in N.C. and have been licensed for not less than five consecutive years prior thereto. Chairman of the Commission of Health Services shall be an ex officio member. One public (voting) member shall be appointed by Governor for four year term.

74. The Board shall consist of the state health officer and three persons appointed by Governor who are persons practicing embalming in North Dakota.

75. Officers elected by board from their number. The Treasurer shall be bonded in the penal sum of $500.

76. Board has power to adopt rule for the transaction of its business, promulgate regulations protecting funeral home customers, and adopt rules to prevent the spread of contagious diseases.

77. Members receive traveling expenses and other necessary expenses and in addition the secretary receives $100 a year for his services.

78. The members of the Board of Embalmers and Funeral Directors must be licensed embalmers and practicing funeral directors with a minimum of 10 consecutive years experience in Ohio immediately preceding their appointment.

79. Board may adopt, promulgate and enforce such rules and regulations for the transaction of its business, its betterment and promotions for the transaction of its business, its betterment and promotion of the educational standards of the profession and the standards of service and practice to be followed in the profession as it may deem expedient.

80. Members must be residents of Oklahoma. Five shall be actively engaged in embalming and funeral directing in Oklahoma for not less than 10 consecutive years immediately prior to appointment and have an active license and keep it effective and remain in state during term. Two shall be from general public with no ties to funeral business. One of the general public members should, if possible, be actively engaged in and licensed in health care.

81. Appointment by and from members of board. The board may employ an executive-secretary for a salary set by the board.

82. All members shall have a minimum of five consecutive years of experience immediately preceding their appointment in the preparation and disposition of dead human bodies and the practicing of embalming within the State of Oregon.

83. Board shall elect from its members for a term of one year.

84. The members of the State Board of Funeral Directors shall be licensed funeral directors of good moral character and who shall also have been actively engaged in the practice of funeral directing for at least 10 years immediately preceding their appointment. The Commissioner of Professional & Occupational Affairs shall be an ex officio member of the said board, acting on behalf of the secretary of state.

85. The board selects a Chairman from among its number and a secretary who need not be a member of the board.

86. Duties of board—(1) empowered to formulate necessary rules and regulations for proper conduct of the profession of funeral directing and enforce Act 16. (2) appoint an inspector, empowered to serve all processes and papers of the board, and have the right to enter and inspect any place where business of funeral directing is carried on. (3) Board shall keep record of its proceedings and a register of names and addresses of all persons applying for and receiving licenses.

87. Members of the Board of Examiners in embalming shall be citizens and residents of this state and shall have had at least 5 years practical experience in embalming and funeral directing, and engaged therein on their own account in this state.

88. Members must be a holder of both a current license as a funeral director and a current license as an embalmer with a minimum of five years uninterrupted experience as a funeral director and embalmer within South Carolina immediately preceding the date of appointment. All members must be bona fide residents of South Carolina and have been for five years preceding the date of appointment.

89. Shall elect a president from its members for a one year term. The Board shall employ a secretary.

90. The $35 per diem is for time spent actually on business of the Board not to exceed 30 days per year.

91. Must be licensed funeral directors or embalmers with a minimum of ten consecutive years experience in Tennessee immediately preceding their appointment. At least three shall be licensed embalmers.

92. Member serves without compensation but shall be reimbursed for expenses and receive $25 per diem for time spent on business of board not to exceed 60 days per year.

93. By and with the consent of the Senate.

94. Members shall be citizens of the United States and residents of Texas. 5 members must be licensed embalmers or funeral directors in the state and each of these members must have a minimum of 5 consecutive years' experience in Texas immediately preceding appointment. At least 3 such licensed members shall be embalmers; 4 members must be representative of general public.

95. Cannot be appointed for more than two terms of service.

96. Shall be elected from Board's members and shall serve for two years. May appoint an Executive Secretary who will be bonded but if no Executive Secretary is appointed the Secretary must be bonded.

97. $25 per diem for each day actually spent on board business not to exceed 50 days a year. Membership shall be reimbursed by traveling expenses. The Secretary, in absence of Executive Secretary, shall receive a salary as compensation and traveling expenses to be set by board.

98. The Director of the Department of Registration, who is appointed by the Commission of Business Regulation, shall appoint a committee of three licensed funeral directors or embalmers. His appointments are subject to the confirmation or rejection of the governor. The committee shall be known as the "State Board of Funeral Service."

99. Each member must have had an embalmer's or funeral director's license to practice in Utah for a period of five years immediately prior to his appointment and five years experience in the preparation and disposition of dead human bodies and in the practice of embalming.

100. Three licensed embalmers who have had five years experience as such.

101. Must be citizens of U.S. (Attorney General rules this provision is unconstitutional), residents of Virginia, and licensed for the practice of funeral service for five consecutive years and five consecutive years experience as a funeral service licensee and funeral director or embalmer in Virginia immediately preceding appointment.

102. With consent of Senate. (State Board of Embalming)

103. Secretary of State Board of Health shall be a member and other members shall be licensed embalmers, residents of Wyoming with at least three years experience in practice of embalming and unexpired license.

104. The notice shall include: (1) a statement of the time, place and nature of the hearing; (2) a statement of the legal authority and jurisdiction under which the hearing is to be held; (3) a reference to the particular sections of the statutes and regulations involved; and (4) a short and plain statement of the matters asserted.

105. After the Board conducts an investigation into the complaint they, after finding reasonable grounds for belief that the accused may have been guilty, file a statement or complaint with the Administrative Hearing Commissioner. Then a hearing will be held by the Administrative Court Judge.

106. If a hearing is requested a written notice shall be sent by the Secretary of the Board to all interested parties at least thirty (30) days prior thereto. Notice shall state issues or charges involved and the date, time and place of the hearing.

107. The Commissioner of Health may refuse to grant, refuse to renew, or may suspend or revoke a license of any applicant or licensee for any of the enumerated causes or acts. A hearing required by Minnesota Administrative Procedure Act.

108. After investigation, if board feels there is a reasonable ground, it may institute administrative disciplinary action or commence criminal prosecution or an action for judicial relief.

109. This power is given to Commissioner of Health, not Board.

110. Inform party that he is entitled to a hearing if he requests it within thirty (30) days of time of mailing the notice. Hearing shall be set up within fifteen (15) days but not earlier than seven (7) days after request.

111. Board has no authority to suspend or revoke the license of the accused except when accused admits a violation and agrees in writing to a judgment of the board. Board may initiate a civil action in the district court of accused's residence.

112. For the purpose of investigation of a complaint the Director of Motor Vehicles may administer oaths and affirmations, subpoena witnesses duces tecum, compel their attendance. The director may refer above evidence to the attorney general or the prosecuting attorney of the county wherein the alleged violation arose, who may, in their discretion bring an action in the name of the state.

113. Hearing conducted by and said powers given to the Department of Registration and Education.

114. Upon appeal court shall be limited to a determination as to whether the board has acted in excess of its powers or fraudulently or arbitrarily.

115. Any action by the Commissioner in revoking or suspending a license may be subject to review by a writ of certiorari issued by the district court of any county.

116. Must file notice in writing of such appeal with the Clerk of district and pay a docket fee of twenty (20.00) Dollars, and by mailing a copy of such notice of appeal, registered, to the Secretary of the Board, all within thirty (30) days of receipt of Board's decision.

117. One combined license is issued in Minnesota as a mortuary science license. Funeral Director licenses as such are not issued except to those persons whose custom, rites, or religious beliefs forbid the practice of embalming.

118. Montana will issue no separate Funeral Director license in the future. Returned to a mono-license called a Morticians license effected June 1, 1963.

119. An applicant for a funeral director's license in Ohio must serve *one* year of apprenticeship under a funeral director licensed in the State of Ohio after having completed twelve (12) months instruction in a college of mortuary science recognized by the Board, or show evidence of having completed a three-year academic instruction or mortuary science program in a college or university approved by the Board, or in lieu of mortuary college training, must satisfactorily complete *two* years of apprenticeship under a funeral director licensed in Ohio.

120. In lieu of study in such funeral director's school, an applicant must have not less than 2 years of practical training and experience.

121. The application fee for a funeral director's license shall be $150.00, while the application fee for a funeral director's examination shall be $50.00.

122. No new license issued but funeral director's license may be renewed.

123. An application shall be submitted in writing for an inspection certificate for each place of business with a fee of $50.00. An inspection must be renewed annually.

124. There is no minimum age stated for the granting of a license in the State of Delaware; however, a person must be 18 years of age to register as a resident trainee (apprentice).

125. Shall meet all requirements as qualifications for embalmers, shall be a practicing licensed embalmer of Florida for 1 year and shall have 1 year practical training as an intern funeral director in an approved training agency under a funeral director licensed in Florida. Must have an Associate of Arts degree in mortuary science. Must pass an exam prepared by the Department of Regulations.

126. An applicant for a funeral director's license shall have a valid embalmer's license approved by Georgia.

127. Persons currently licensed as only funeral directors may continue to renew but no new licenses will be issued.

128. Must be an embalmer to be eligible to receive funeral director's license.

129. Combination license is issued covering both embalmer and funeral director.

130. Funeral directors licenses as such are no longer issued in Michigan. The two licenses issued are the embalmers license and the Practitioner of Mortuary Science license. To qualify for the latter license an applicant must be a resident trainee for 1 year and graduated from a 3 year course in mortuary science from an accredited institution. At the Board's discretion another year (4th year) of instruction in an accredited institution may be substituted for the one year of resident training.

131. Fee to take mortuary science examination. $50 proposed to 1968 leg. and probably will pass as recommended.

132. Persons licensed to practice funeral directing prior to June 1, 1963, are entitled to an annual renewal of his license on payment of fee to department on July 1, each year.

133. An applicant for a funeral establishment license shall be a licensed funeral director. The applicant shall be named on the license as manager of the funeral establishment, and shall be responsible for all transactions conducted therein.

134. Applicant for a Funeral Director license must hold an Embalmer's License.

135. Special license Funeral Director and/or Embalmer (RSA325:22) $50.00.

136. Combination license is issued covering both embalmers and funeral directors.

137. Combination license.

138. An undertaker or embalmer shall pay to the department: a) biennial registration fee of $7.50; b) a funeral director shall pay $15.00 biennially; c) owner of a funeral establishment shall pay a registration fee of $25.00 for the first registration of a funeral home and a biennial registration fee thereafter of $15.00 per establishment.

139. But funeral director apprenticeship must be served in the state.

140. Plus initial license fee of $15.00 for both embalming license and funeral director license.

141. Combined license.

142. A license for the practice of funeral service is issued for a fixed place of establishment.

143. Virginia now issues a combined funeral service license. The Board continues to issue $20.00 renewals for the separate funeral director and embalmer licenses.

144. Applicants must have 9 months' transcript received from an accredited school.

145. Must complete a course in mortuary science approved by board. Must include *at least* the following subjects: theory and practice of embalming, restorative art, pathology, anatomy, microbiology, chemistry, hygiene, public health & sanitation.

146. School must be accredited by the Illinois Department of Registration and Education.

147. For at least one year prior to application.

148. Applicant can either complete: a) 1 year of college then spend 12 months in a college school or department of funeral service education approved by the Board, or b) 21 month program in a college school, or dept. of funeral service education approved by the Board, consisting of two semesters of college type courses and two semesters of funeral service type courses. Needs a diploma from the funeral service education program in either option a) or option b).

149. If two year course in embalming taken then only one year apprenticeship required.

150. Must have completed specific course in English, Chemistry, Biology and Accounting.

151. Applicant must be a graduate of a state approved mortuary science college.

152. Graduation from a Mortuary College approved by the Board.

153. Second year of college may be before or after mortuary school.

154. Apprenticeship must be completed within a period of three (3) consecutive years under an embalmer or embalmers licensed and engaged in practice as an embalmer in this state.

155. And upon payment of the $50.00 license fee for the embalming and/or funeral directing license.

156. Two year apprenticeship under an embalmer licensed and engaged in practice as embalmer in this state in funeral establishment approved for apprentices by Board.

157. A person desiring to become a resident trainee shall be over 18 years of age, of good moral character and shall have successfully completed the educational requirements.

158. Must secure apprentice license. $10.00 a year.

159. Must meet one of three qualifications: One year of practical experience and graduation from a recognized school of embalming; two years practical experience under registered embalmer or undertaker in Hawaii and completion of four years of high school; or five years practical experience under a registered embalmer or undertaker in Hawaii.

160. Follows examination.

161. Prior to entering mortuary school.

162. The required years of apprenticeship is one year for a person who has satisfactorily completed three academic years of instruction in such a college or university, and one year of instruction in such an approved school of mortuary science.

163. Apprenticeship must be served continuously. Only break allowed is for purpose of attending embalming school.

164. One year of the two years of apprenticeship must be served in this state.

164A. Examination held at least once a quarter at such time and place as Board may determine.

165. Expires October 1 of every year.

166. 70 written questions on the subjects of anatomy, embalming and subject taught by a recognized school of embalming and 30 oral questions on above subjects and if possible demonstrative in nature conducted upon a cadaver.

167. Expires June 30 of every year.

168. Examinations shall be held at such times and place as determined by Board.

169. The examination shall include: a) Theory and Practice of Embalming b) Anatomy c) Pathology and Bacteriology d) Hygiene e) Chemistry f) Restorative Art g) Law, Rules and Regulations of Board.

170. Expires 12:00 P.M. on January 31 of each year.

171. Embalming license expires July 1 each year.

172. Annually—the Board shall hold not less than one meeting annually for the purpose of examining applicants for licenses, at such time and place as the Board may determine.

173. Examination for an embalmer's license shall consist of in writing 150 questions on subjects Board deems necessary in the practice of

embalming. Shall be not more than 100 oral questions and a practical examination with a cadaver. Written counts for 50% and oral and practical 25% each.

174. Conducted in writing and supplemented by practical demonstration upon subjects as prescribed by department of health.

175. Board of morticians has sole power of determining the nature, type and extent of examination.

176. Embalmer fees—Applicant fee $10; Written examination $20; Practical-Oral Examination $20; License $20.

177. Accepted, but the embalmer's examination on the Ohio laws and the complete funeral director's examination given by the Board must be taken.

178. Board sets yearly renewal fee not to exceed $100.00. The 1978 fee was $30.00 for embalmers and $50.00 for funeral directors.

179. A permit from the Board shall be obtained by the Funeral Director desiring to change the location or name of the business. Application shall be accompanied by a $50.00 fee. A Funeral Director proposing to engage in or conduct more than one funeral establishment shall procure a certificate of qualification for each establishment.

180. Upon application for inspection certificate, an inspection of each building shall be conducted by the Board or department of health.

181. Permit from Board needed for each establishment and must be displayed. Permit not required for service held in private residence, church or lodge hall. Fee of $20.00 for permit. Must be renewed biennially.

182. No person shall conduct, maintain, manage or operate a funeral establishment unless an establishment operating license has been issued by the department for that funeral establishment.

183. Reciprocity applies only to embalmers. Applicant must have been licensed and practicing for at least five (5) years and furnish proof that he has complied with requirement substantially equal to Oregon's.

184. Permission before embalming is required from the coroner or medical examiner if death is of a nature subject to their examination.

185. No person shall embalm the body of someone who has died from an unknown cause, except with the permission of the coroner.

186. No specific waiting period before body can be cremated, but these requirements must be met: (i) Authorization in writing by the next of kin; (ii) signed death certificate by attending physician and funeral director; (iii) authorizing signature by the State Medical Examiner; (iv) authorizing signature by the State Attorney General.

187. Any human remains held 24 hours beyond death, shall be embalmed or sealed in a hermetically sealed container. Any human remains kept under refrigeration over the 24-hour period beyond death must be maintained at a temperature level not to exceed a maximum of 31 degrees F., and must be buried, cremated or entombed within 5 hours of removal from refrigeration.

188. . . . or must make a documented reasonable effort over a period of at least 2 hours to obtain such permission.

189. No licensee shall assume control of any dead body without having first obtained permission from the person or persons lawfully entitled thereto, being the next of kin, or, in a proper case, a coroner, health officer or other public official lawfully entitled to such control.

190. Any person who has died of smallpox, plague, anthrax, or other disease which the state Board of Health may specify must comply with the following regulations:

    (a) Wash body with an approved germicidal solution;
    (b) Effectively plug all body orifices immediately;
    (c) *Embalm* arterially and by cavity injection with an approved disinfectant fluid.

191. The body of any person dead of a non-contagious disease must be embalmed if the remains cannot reach its destination within 24 hours after death. If shipped by common carrier, an unembalmed body must be in a casket and a shipping case.

192. The contagious diseases referred to are: smallpox, bubonic plague, Asiatic cholera, glanders, or anthrax.

193. In Hawaii a body may not be embalmed if death was from plague, Asiatic cholera, smallpox, epidemic typhus fever, yellow fever, or louse-borne relapsing fever without permission from the Director of Health.

194. The body shall be embalmed with a disinfectant fluid when a body dead of smallpox, plague, Asiatic cholera, leprosy, typhus fever, diphtheria, membranous croup, diphtheritic sore throat, scarlet fever, epidemic meningitis is to be transported.

195. A body dead of a disease or cause not dangerous to public health shall not be transported or shipped unless (1) embalmed and encased in a sound casket and outside box; (2) if not embalmed it shall be prepared by washing body with disinfectant, closing orifices and wrapping with inch thick cotton, placing in a sheet, bandaging it, and encasing it in an air-tight casket or box properly sealed.

196. A body dead of a disease dangerous to public health shall not be transported unless the body is encased in a hermetically sealed casket or box and embalmed.

197. A body shall not be transported unless embalmed. If not transported it still must be embalmed unless buried or cremated within twenty-four (24) hours.

198. Destination on common carrier must be able to be reached in twenty-four (24) hours from time of death or body must be embalmed.

199. The body must reach its destination within twenty-four (24) hours following death, provided, however, that an unembalmed body may be retained in storage at a constant temperature of less than forty (40) degrees Fahrenheit for not more than seventy-two (72) hours. When said body is removed from storage and transported, it must reach its destination within twenty-four (24) hours following removal from storage.

200. Exception—In the event the body is placed in a metal or metal lined hermetically sealed container immediately after death it may be considered for the purpose of transporting same as an embalmed body.

201. If body cannot reach its destination in twenty-four (24) hours, it must be embalmed.

202. Funeral Director or Embalmer shall conspicuously display the price on each casket available. Each shall be priced individually, irrespective of the type of service purchased.

203. Prohibition on the reuse of a casket shall not apply to exterior casket hardware which is not sold to the customer or where same is reserved by contract.

204. Each funeral home shall have a card or brochure in (or for) each casket stating the price of the funeral service using said casket and listing the services and other merchandise included in the price. Where there are separate prices for the casket, professional services, the use of the facilities and equipment, the above card shall indicate price of each item (except in those instances such as unknown transportation costs and similar items which services must be stated with price fixed upon billing).

205. Where a funeral service establishment does not have a casket selection room, but uses the facilities of a manufacturer, jobber, or other place where caskets are displayed for selection, the requirements of a card or brochure are the same as in footnote No. 204.

206. Cremation without a burial or funeral casket is specifically authorized, though a simple container adequate for the purpose may be required. Any representation to the contrary by licensee, or his agents, or employees is prohibited.

207. The following must appear on the cost statement when cremation is involved, "Minnesota law does not require that remains be placed in a casket before or at the time of cremation.

208. The re-use of a receptacle which is commonly known as a shipping case when the service and receptacle is paid for from public funds is permitted.

209. It is unlawful to require a casket be purchased, furnished, rented or charged for when a dead human body is cremated.

210. Each casket and service or supplemental item of merchandise shall have the price clearly marked thereon.

211. . . . the least expensive casket offered for sale by a funeral establishment must be displayed in the same general manner as other caskets are displayed. A commercial embalmer (with commercial embalming establishment permit) shall not be required to display caskets.

212. The card referred to in footnote 204 shall also contain a statement that the separate price of the casket and other merchandise, facilities, equipment, and personal services will be provided upon request. Only the price of the casket need be displayed in the casket if the other separately priced items are given in writing prior to selection of the casket.

213. Funeral directors, embalmer or mortuary science practitioner must inform the person making arrangements at the time they are made that he may have, at that time, if he wishes, a written statement which includes an itemized listing of the services and merchandise to be provided, together with the accompanying prices for each such service and article of merchandise, insofar as the same can be specified at that time.

214. Particularly removal, embalming, other care of body, use of facilities for visitation and/or services, personal services of staff, transportation.

215. Must furnish for retention to anyone who inquires in person about the arrangement of merchandise and services, before any discussion of selection, a list of retail prices for at least the following items:

   a. Transfer of body to establishment
   b. Embalming—with statement not required by law
   c. Use of facilities for viewing
   d. Use of facilities for funeral service
   e. Use of hearse
   f. Use of limousine
   g. Other transportation
   h. Casket price range—with statement complete price list available
   i. Alternate container price
   j. Outer burial container price range
   k. Other professional services

216. Must furnish for retention of each customer listing at least the following categories of services and merchandise, if selected by the customer, together with the price of each item:

   a. Embalming
   b. Other preparation of the body

216. Cont.

   c. Use of facilities for viewing
   d. Use of facilities for ceremony
   e. Services of funeral director and staff
   f. Casket or alternate container as selected
   g. Other specifically itemized charges
   h. Specifically itemized cash advances, if estimates. A written statement of actual charges must be provided before the final bill is paid.

217. Every person licensed including funeral directors and funeral establishments shall furnish at the time funeral arrangements are made for the care and disposition of the body of a deceased person, an itemized statement in compliance with rules adopted by the Commissioner of Health pursuant to Minnesota Statute Chapter 18. The rule shall require a separate listing of cost in the following categories: casket, burial vault, use of facilities for funeral services, use of facilities for revival, specifically itemized transportation costs, specifically itemized funeral service merchandise, embalming, preparation of the body, other professional services, and a statement of all anticipated cash advances and expenditures.

218. At the time funeral arrangements are made, a written statement showing thereon the price of the funeral, including an itemized list of services and merchandise to be furnished for such price, with the price of each item of such services and merchandise set forth opposite every such item and a statement of the cash advances and expenditures to be advanced, shall be furnished to the person or persons making such arrangements. Such statement shall include the following:

   (1) Name of deceased together with place and date of death.

   (2) The price of the funeral together with a list of the following significant items, where furnished, for such price, whether such items be known under the following titles, designations or otherwise, with the price for item being set forth opposite each such item:

   (i) Merchandise:

   (a) Casket
   (b) Outer receptacle
   (c) Clothing or burial garments
   (d) Memorial and/or acknowledgement cards

   (ii) Services:

   (a) Transfer of remains to funeral establishment
   (b) Embalming
   (c) Other preparation of remains
   (d) Arrangements and supervision

   (iii) Rental or use of equipment and/or facilities:

   (a) Livery:

   (1) Hearse
   (2) Other specified funeral coach
   (3) Flower car
   (4) Passenger cars (specify number)

   (i) If additional cars should be needed, specify price per car.

   (b) Facilities:

   (1) Funeral establishment other than (2) below
   (2) Operating or preparation room

   (3) An itemized statement of the cash advances and expenditures to be advanced.

219. (1) A word description of the type and material of the casket, the name of the immediate supplier thereof, the kind and gauge or weight of metal or species of wood and, where supplied, model name or number.

   (2) A word description of the material of the interior of the casket.

   (3) A word description of the material of the outer receptacle, the name of the outer receptacle, the name of the immediate supplier thereof, and in the case of a metal or concrete vault the model name or number where supplied.

   (4) The signature of the licensed funeral director or undertaker making arrangements, whose name, as well as the name of the firm, shall also be legibly printed or typed, and the date the statement was furnished.

   (5) Charges for merchandise, services or facilities shall not be estimates and the term "estimate" shall not appear on a statement in reference to such items.

   (6) True copies of all such statements shall be consecutively numbered and maintained in numerical order at the funeral establishment for a period of not less than two years following the funeral and shall during normal business hours within such period be open to inspection by the commissioner or his representatives.

   (7) Itemization of social services and other governmental cases shall be in compliance with the rules of the department or agency having jurisdiction. True copies of documents pertaining to all such cases shall be consecutively numbered and maintained at the funeral establishment for a period of not less than two years following the funeral and shall during normal business hours within such period be open to inspection by the commissioner or his representatives. Where any portion of the payment for such cases is not provided for by such department or agency, itemization shall be governed by this Part.

220. At the time funeral arrangements are made, a specific itemization of the charges which will be made for such arrangements shall be compiled and a copy given to the person making those arrangements. Such itemization is to include the categories as listed below. Each category must be itemized at least to the extent listed below:

   (a) Professional Services—Facilities and transportation.
   (b) Casket.
   (c) The supplemental items of service and/or merchandise requested and the price of each such item.
   (d) Insofar as it can be specified at that time, the items for which the funeral director will advance his money as an accommodation; and
   (e) The terms or method of payment.

221. . . . must make available to customer at the time of discussion or selection of funeral services and merchandise a list of at least the following items:

   (a) Transferring deceased to funeral home
   (b) Embalming
   (c) Use of facilities for viewing
   (d) Use of facilities for ceremonies
   (e) Hearses
   (f) Limousines
   (g) Itemized services of staff
   (h) Casket
   (i) Outer enclosure

222. Must provide customer a written memorandum itemizing the cost of funeral services and merchandise selected by the customer. May satisfy the itemization requirements of this section by providing prices to the purchaser on a component or unit pricing basis that provides a discount to the purchaser if any component or unit is declined or if all components or units are selected.

223. . . . must include but not limited to the following charges: casket, other funeral merchandise, vault or other burial receptacle, facilities used, transportation costs, embalming and preparation of the body and other professional services used.

224. ". . . a written, itemized statement showing to the extent then known the price of merchandise and service that such person making such arrangements has selected."

225. The required one year internship required for either an embalmer or funeral director license can be served simultaneously.

226. Year spent in embalming college counts as 1 year of apprenticeship. In effect, apprenticeship requirement is 2 years if the requirement of 1 year of embalming college is completed before apprenticeship program.

227. Exception—bodies addressed for demonstration of anatomy at a medical college or for other demonstration purposes, or which will arrive at destination within forty-eight (48) hours may be transported when encased in a sound shipping case.

228. As of January, 1981, applicants for renewal of their funeral service license shall furnish evidence of having completed ten (10) contact hours of continuing education in the previous calendar year in subjects approved by the board. Any applicant who has been licensed for forty (40) years or more, or who has attained the age of 65 years shall not be required to fulfill the continuing education requirement. The board, at its discretion, may require an examination to assess continuing competency.

229. A licensed person may be in charge of more than one funeral establishment of a multi-unit enterprise within Utah if the person is stationed within one hundred (100) miles of the other establishments. Establishment must contain a preparation room, the necessary instruments and supplies and an area where the public can gather or meet. Only one preparation room required for a multi-unit enterprise if other establishments are within one hundred (100) miles of the establishment with the preparation room.

230. Before arrangement, full disclosure of all available services is required. The funeral establishment shall identify all services and the prices thereof included in the arrangement and alternative arrangements under consideration and shall also identify as far as possible the related services and expenses of others such as cemeteries and florists.

BODY/ORGAN DONATIONS

Uniform Anatomical Gift Act

PREFATORY NOTE

Human bodies and parts thereof are used in many aspects of medical science, including teaching, research, therapy and transplantation. It is a rapidly expanding branch of medical technology. Transplantation of parts may involve skin grafts, bones, blood, corneas, kidneys, livers, arteries and even hearts. It is said that 6,000 to 10,000 lives could be saved each year by renal transplants if a sufficient supply of kidneys were available.

Transplantation may be effected within narrow limits from one living person to another living person. In such case, all that is required is an appropriate "informed consent" authorizing the surgical removal on the one hand, and the implantation on the other. Tissues and organs from the dead can also be used to bring health and years of life to the living. From this source the potential supply is very great. But, if utilization of bodies and parts of bodies is to be effectuated, a number of competing interests in a dead body must be harmonized, and several troublesome legal questions must be answered.

The principal competing interests are: (1) the wishes of the deceased during his lifetime concerning the disposition of his body; (2) the desires of the surviving spouse or next of kin; (3) the interest of the state in determining by autopsy, the cause of death in cases involving crime or violence; (4) the need of autopsy to determine the cause of death when private legal rights are dependent upon such cause; and (5) the need of society for bodies, tissues, and organs for medical education, research, therapy, and transplantation. These interests compete with one another to a greater or lesser extent and this creates problems.

The principal legal questions arising from these various interests are: (1) who may during his lifetime make a legally effective gift of his body or a part thereof; (2) what is the right of the next of kin, either to set aside the decedent's expressed wishes, or themselves to make the anatomical gifts from the dead body; (3) who may legally become donees of anatomical gifts; (4) for what purposes may such gifts be

Reprinted with permission from the National Conference of Commissioners on Uniform State Laws, 645 North Michigan Avenue, Chicago, IL 60611, 1968.

made; (5) how may gifts be made, can it be done by will, by writing, by a card carried on the person, or by telegraphic or recorded telephonic communication; (6) how may a gift be revoked by the donor during his liftetime; (7) what are the rights of survivors in the body after removal of donated parts; (8) what protection from legal liability should be afforded to surgeons and others involved in carrying out anatomical gifts; (9) should such protection be afforded regardless of the state in which the document of gift is executed; (10) what should the effect of an anatomical gift be in case of conflict with laws concerning autopsies; (11) should the time of death be defined by law in any way; (12) should the interest in preserving life by the physician in charge of a decedent preclude him from participating in the transplant procedure by which donated tissues or organs are transferred to a new host. These are the principal legal questions that should be covered in an anatomical gift act. The Uniform Anatomical Gift Act covers them.

The laws now on the statute books do not, in general, deal with these legal questions in a complete or adequate manner. The laws are a confusing mixture of old common law dating back to the seventeenth century and state statutes that have been enacted from time to time. Some 39 states and the District of Columbia have donation statutes that deal in a variety of ways with some, but by no means all, of the above listed legal questions. Four other states have statutes providing for the gift of eyes only.

These statutes differ from each other in a variety of respects, both as to content and coverage. They differ in their enumeration of permissible donees (some require that donees be specified, others permit gifts to be made to any hospital or physician in charge at death); they vary as to acceptable purposes for anatomical gifts (some, for example, do not include licensed tissue banks); they prescribe a variety of minimum ages for the donors; others differ as to the manner of execution of gifts and the manner of revocation. Some require delivery of the instrument of gift or filing in a public office, or both, as a condition of validity; others make no such provision. Since the statutes differ in important respects, a gift adequate in one state may or may not protect the surgeon in another state who relies upon the law in effect where the transplant takes place. In short, both the common law and the preseent statutory picture is one of confusion, diversity, and inadequacy. This tends to discourage anatomical gifts and to create difficulties for physicians, especially for transplant surgeons.

In view of the foregoing, the need for a comprehensive act and an act applicable in all states is apparent. The Uniform Anatomical Gift Act herewith presented by the National Conference of Commissioners on Uniform State Laws carefully weighs the numerous conflicting interests and legal problems. Wherever adopted it will encourage the making of anatomical gifts, thus facilitating therapy involving such procedures. When generally adopted, even if the place of death, or the residence of the donor, or the place of use of the gift occurs in a state other than that of the execution of the gift, uncertainty as to the applicable law will be eliminated and all parties will be protected. At the same time the Act will serve the needs of the several conflicting interests in a manner consistent with prevailing customs and desires in this country respecting dignified disposition of dead bodies. It will provide a useful and uniform legal environment throughout the country for this new frontier of modern medicine.

UNIFORM ANATOMICAL GIFT ACT

AN ACT authorizing the gift of all or part of a human body after death for specified purposes.

1 SECTION 1. [*Definitions.*]
2 (a) "Bank or storage facility" means a facility licensed, ac-
3 credited, or approved under the laws of any state for storage of
4 human bodies or parts thereof.
5 (b) "Decedent" means a deceased individual and includes a
6 stillborn infant or fetus.
7 (c) "Donor" means an individual who makes a gift of all or
8 part of his body.
9 (d) "Hospital" means a hospital licensed, accredited, or ap-
10 proved under the laws of any state; includes a hospital operated
11 by the United States government, a state, or a subdivision thereof,
12 although not required to be licensed under state laws.
13 (e) "Part" means organs, tissues, eyes, bones, arteries, blood,
14 other fluids and any other portions of a human body.
15 (f) "Person" means an individual, corporation, government or
16 governmental subdivision or agency, business trust, estate, trust,
17 partnership or association, or any other legal entity.
18 (g) "Physician" or "surgeon" means a physician or surgeon
19 licensed or authorized to practice under the laws of any state.
20 (h) "State" includes any state, district, commonwealth, terri-
21 tory, insular possession, and any other area subject to the legisla-
22 tive authority of the United States of America.

COMMENT

Subsection (f) is taken verbatim from the Uniform Statutory Construction Act, section 26 (4). In any state that has adopted the Uniform Act or its equivalent, this subsection will be unnecessary.

Subsection (h) is taken from section 26 (9) of the Uniform Statutory Construction Act.

1 SECTION 2. [*Persons Who May Execute an Anatomical Gift.*]
2 (a) Any individual of sound mind and 18 years of age or more
3 may give all or any part of his body for any purpose specified in
4 section 3, the gift to take effect upon death.
5 (b) Any of the following persons, in order of priority stated,
6 when persons in prior classes are not available at the time of death,
7 and in the absence of actual notice of contrary indications by the
8 decedent or actual notice of opposition by a member of the same
9 or a prior class, may give all or any part of the decedent's body
10 for any purpose specified in section 3:
11 (1) the spouse,
12 (2) an adult son or daughter,
13 (3) either parent,
14 (4) an adult brother or sister,
15 (5) a guardian of the person of the decedent at the time of
16 his death,
17 (6) any other person authorized or under obligation to dis-
18 pose of the body.
19 (c) If the donee has actual notice of contrary indications by
20 the decedent or that a gift by a member of a class is opposed by a
21 member of the same or a prior class, the donee shall not accept the

22   gift. The persons authorized by subsection (b) may make the gift
23   after or immediately before death.
24   (d) A gift of all or part of a body authorizes any examination
25   necessary to assure medical acceptability of the gift for the pur-
26   poses intended.
27   (e) The rights of the donee created by the gift are paramount
28   to the rights of others except as provided by Section 7 (d).

COMMENT

Existing state statutes differ in their respective standards establishing the donor's competence to execute an anatomical gift.

"Competence to execute a will" is used as the standard in 10 states. "Legal age" and sound mind is required in 5 states. "Twenty-one years and sound mind" is the stated standard in the statutes of 10 states. In 4 states a person who is 18 years of age or older may make the gift, and in 6 states "any person" may do so. One state requires 21 years accompanied by a certificate of a physician that the donor is "of sound mind and not under the influence of narcotic drugs."

To minimize confusion there is merit in having a uniform provision throughout the country. Also it is desirable to enlarge the class of possible donors as much as possible. Subsection (a) of Section 2, providing that any person of sound mind and 18 years or more of age may execute a gift, will afford both nation-wide uniformity and a desirable enlargement of the class of donors. Persons 18 years of age or more are of sufficient maturity to make the required decisions and the Uniform Act takes advantage of this fact.

Subsection (b) spells out the right of survivors to make the gift. Taking into account the very limited time available following death for the successful re-moval of such critical tissues as the kidney, the liver, and the heart, it seems desirable to eliminate all possible question by specifically stating the rights of and the priorities among the survivors.

Also, Section 2 (b) provides for the effect of indicated objections by the decedent, and differences of view among the survivors. Finally it authorizes the survivors to execute the necessary documents even prior to death. In view of the fact that persons under 18 years of age are excluded from subsection (a), it is especially desirable to cover with care the status of survivors, so younger decedents may be included.

Subsection (d) is added at the suggestion of members of the medical profession who regard a post mortem examination, to the extent necessary to ascertain freedom from disease that might cause injury to the new host for transplanted parts, as essential to good medical practice.

Subsection (e) recognizes and gives legal effect to the right of the individual to dispose of his own body without subsequent veto by others.

1   SECTION 3. [*Persons Who May Become Donees; Purposes for*
2   *Which Anatomical Gifts May be Made.*] The following persons
3   may become donees of gifts of bodies or parts thereof for the pur-
4   poses stated:
5   (1) any hospital, surgeon, or physician, for medical or dental
6   education, research, advancement of medical or dental science,
7   therapy, or transplantation; or
8   (2) any accredited medical or dental school, college or uni-
9   versity for education, research, advancement of medical or
10   dental science, or therapy; or
11   (3) any bank or storage facility, for medical or dental educa-
12   tion, research, advancement of medical or dental science, ther-
13   apy, or transplantation; or
14   (4) any specified individual for therapy or transplantation
15   needed by him.

COMMENT

Existing state statutes reveal great diversity of provisions concerning possible donees and the purposes for which anatomical gifts may be made.

As to donees, the lists include licensed hospitals, storage banks, teaching institutions, universities, colleges, medical schools, state public health and anatomy boards, and institutions approved by the state department of health. Some of the statutes are detailed and comprehensive. Others are limited, brief, and general. A few do not seek in any way to name or limit the donees. The Uniform Act attempts to achieve a maximum of clarity and precision by carefully naming the permissible donees.

The statutes in a few states specify that no donor shall ask compensation and no donee shall receive it. Several statutes provide that storage banks shall be non-profit organizations. On the other hand, most of the states have chosen not to deal with this question. The Uniform Act follows the latter course in this regard.

As to purposes, again there is great diversity among the statutes. The list of purposes includes teaching, research, advancement of medical science, therapy, transplantation, rehabilitation, and scientific uses. Again some of the statutes are detailed, and others are brief and general. A few statutes contain no limitation whatsoever—merely naming the donees, thus assuring that gifts will not be made to undesirable persons or organizations, and then they are inclusive in naming the purposes in broad terms, thus assuring flexibility. The Uniform Act follows this course.

1   SECTION 4. [*Manner of Executing Anatomical Gifts.*]
2   (a) A gift of all or part of the body under Section 2 (a) may be
3   made by will. The gift becomes effective upon the death of the
4   testator without waiting for probate. If the will is not probated,
5   or if it is declared invalid for testamentary purposes, the gift, to
6   the extent that it has been acted upon in good faith, is nevertheless
7   valid and effective.
8   (b) A gift of all or part of the body under Section 2 (a) may
9   also be made by document other than a will. The gift becomes
10   effective upon the death of the donor. The document, which may
11   be a card designed to be carried on the person, must be signed by
12   the donor in the presence of 2 witnesses who must sign the docu-
13   ment in his presence. If the donor cannot sign, the document may
14   be signed for him at his direction and in his presence in the pres-
15   ence of 2 witnesses who must sign the document in his presence.
16   Delivery of the document of gift during the donor's lifetime is not
17   necessary to make the gift valid.
18   (c) The gift may be made to a specified donee or without
19   specifying a donee. If the latter, the gift may be accepted by the
20   attending physician as donee upon or following death. If the gift
21   is made to a specified donee who is not available at the time and
22   place of death, the attending physician upon or following death,
23   in the absence of any expressed indication that the donor desired
24   otherwise, may accept the gift as donee. The physician who
25   becomes a donee under this subsection shall not participate in the
26   procedures for removing or transplanting a part.
27   (d) Notwithstanding Section 7 (b), the donor may designate
28   in his will, card, or other document of gift the surgeon or physician
29   to carry out the appropriate procedures. In the absence of a desig-
30   nation or if the designee is not available, the donee or other person
31   authorized to accept the gift may employ or authorize any sur-
32   geon or physician for the purpose.
33   (e) Any gift by a person designated in Section 2 (b) shall

34   be made by a document signed by him or made by his telegraphic,
35   recorded telephonic, or other recorded message.

COMMENT

Most existing state statutes authorizing anatomical gifts provide for doing so either by will or by other document in writing. The number of witnesses varies from state to state, but the majority require two witnesses. The Uniform Act requires two witnesses to validate a gift during the donor's lifetime, but witnesses are relatively unnecessary in the case of a gift by next of kin since they are available in person. Hence, none are required in such cases. To facilitate availability of evidence of the gift, a card may be carried on the person, a practice commonly and successfully followed in connection with gifts of eyes. This is an important provision, for we are a peripatetic people and the advantages of a card carried on the person stating the donor's intention to donate is apparent.

Also important are the provisions of subsection (c) that permit the attending physician upon or following death to be the donee when no donee is named or when the named donee is not available. The donee physician cannot participate personally in removing or transplanting a part, but he can, of course, make a further gift to another person for any authorized purpose.

Attention should also be called to subsection (e) authorizing the next of kin to make gifts by "telegraphic, recorded telephonic, or other recorded message." Frequently the next of kin are far away, and this provision, not found in any existing statute, has the advantage of expediting the procedures where time for effective action is short.

As the Uniform Act becomes widely accepted it will prove helpful if the forms by which gifts are made are similar in each of the participating states. Such forms should be as simple and understandable as possible. The following forms are suggested for the purpose:

Anatomical Gift by a Living Donor

I am of sound mind and 18 years or more of age.

I hereby make this anatomical gift to take effect upon my death. The marks in the appropriate squares and words filled into the blanks below indicate my desires.

I give: ☐ my body; ☐ any needed organs or parts; ☐ the following organs or parts _____ ;

To the following person (or institution): ☐ the physician in attendance at my death; ☐ the hospital in which I die; ☐ the following named physician, hospital, storage bank or other medical institution_____ _____ ; ☐ the following individual for treatment _____ _____ ;

for the following purposes: ☐ any purpose authorized by law; ☐ transplantation; ☐ therapy; ☐ research; ☐ medical education.

Dated _____City and State _____
Signed by the Donor in the
presence of the following
who sign as witnesses: _____
                                               Signature of Donor

_____   _____
Witness   Address of Donor

_____
Witness

Anatomical Gift by Next of Kin
or Other Authorized Person

I hereby make this anatomical gift of or from the body of_____ _____ who died on _____ at the _____ _____ in _____ . The marks in the appropriate squares and the words filled into the blanks below indicate my relationship to the deceased and my desires respecting the gift.

I am the surviving: ☐ spouse; ☐ adult son or daughter; ☐ parent; ☐ adult brother or sister; ☐ guardian; ☐ _____, authorized to dispose of the body;

I give ☐ the body of deceased; ☐ any needed organs or parts; ☐ the following organs or parts _____ ;

To the following person (or institution) _____
(insert the name of a physician, hospital, research or educational institution, storage bank, or individual),

for the following purposes: ☐ any purpose authorized by law; ☐ transplantation; ☐ therapy; ☐ research; ☐ medical education.

Dated _____ City and State _____

_____
Signature of Survivor

_____
Address of Survivor

1   SECTION 5. [*Delivery of Document of Gift.*] If the gift is made
2   by the donor to a specified donee, the will, card, or other document,
3   or an executed copy thereof, may be delivered to the donee to
4   expedite the appropriate procedures immediately after death. De-
5   livery is not necessary to the validity of the gift. The will, card,
6   or other document, or an executed copy thereof, may be deposited
7   in any hospital, bank or storage facility or registry office that
8   accepts it for safekeeping or for facilitation of procedures after
9   death. On request of any interested party upon or after the donor's
10 death, the person in possession shall produce the document for
11 examination.

COMMENT

Some of the statutes make rather formal mandatory provisions for filing of documents of gift. Thus in two states the gift must be "filed for record in the office of the judge of probate." In another the document must be filed either before death or within 60 hours after death with the State Department of Health. In another the instrument must be filed for record "in the office of the clerk of the district court of the parish wherein the person making the gift resides." In still another the instrument must be filed in the probate court. In two states it is provided that the instrument shall be delivered by the donor to the donee. On the other hand, in the great majority of the states, no provision is made for filing, recording, or delivery to the donee. The gift is by implication effective without such formality. Section 5 of the Uniform Act follows the majority permissive practice, but includes permissive filing provisions to expedite postmortem procedures.

1   SECTION 6. [*Amendment or Revocation of the Gift.*]
2   (a) If the will, card, or other document or executed copy
3   thereof, has been delivered to a specified donee, the donor may
4   amend or revoke the gift by:
5   (1) the execution and delivery to the donee of a signed
6   statement, or
7   (2) an oral statement made in the presence of 2 persons
8   and communicated to the donee, or
9   (3) a statement during a terminal illness or injury addressed
10 to an attending physician and communicated to the donee, or
11   (4) a signed card or document found on his person or in
12 his effects.
13 (b) Any document of gift which has not been delivered to the

14 donee may be revoked by the donor in the manner set out in
15 subsection (a), or by destruction, cancellation, or mutilation of
16 the document and all executed copies thereof.
17   (c) Any gift made by a will may also be amended or revoked
18 in the manner provided for amendment or revocation of wills, or
19 as provided in subsection (a).

COMMENT

In about one half of the states no provision is made for revocation. However, in the interest of carrying out the ultimate desires of the donor, there is good reason for facilitating revocation. Accordingly, about half of the states make affirmative provisions concerning the matter. Usually it is provided that revocation may be accomplished by executing a "like instrument" filed in the manner provided for the instrument of gift and delivered to the donee. In a few states revocation is accomplished by demanding return of the document of gift. There is merit in making revocation both simple and easy to accomplish. Prospective donors are more likely to look with favor on making anatomical gifts if they realize that revocation is readily possible. The Uniform Act makes careful and complete provision for revocation under various contingencies. However, if a donor has deposited an executed copy of an undelivered document of gift as authorized by Section 5, and if the donor desires to revoke the gift, he must see to it that the executed copy which has been deposited is destroyed.

1   SECTION 7. [*Rights and Duties at Death.*]
2   (a) The donee may accept or reject the gift. If the donee ac-
3   cepts a gift of the entire body, he may, subject to the terms of
4   the gift, authorize embalming and the use of the body in funeral
5   services. If the gift is of a part of the body, the donee, upon the
6   death of the donor and prior to embalming, shall cause the part
7   to be removed without unnecessary mutilation. After removal
8   of the part, custody of the remainder of the body vests in the
9   surviving spouse, next of kin, or other persons under obligation
10 to dispose of the body.
11   (b) The time of death shall be determined by a physician who
12 tends the donor at his death, or, if none, the physician who certi-
13 fies the death. The physician shall not participate in the proce-
14 dures for removing or transplanting a part.
15   (c) A person who acts in good faith in accord with the terms
16 of this Act or with the anatomical gift laws of another state
17 [or a foreign country] is not liable for damages in any civil action
18 or subject to prosecution in any criminal proceeding for his act.
19   (d) The provisions of this Act are subject to the laws of this
20 state prescribing powers and duties with respect to autopsies.

COMMENT

Section 7 contains several important provisions. The donee may of course, reject the gift if he deems it best to do so. If he accepts the gift, all possible provision is made for taking account of the interests of the survivors in dignified memorial ceremonies. Also if the donee accepts the gift, absolute ownership vests in him. He may, if he so desires, transfer his ownership to another person, whether the gift be of the whole body or merely a part. He may "cause the part to be removed" either by himself or by another person. The only restrictions are that the part must be removed without mutilation and the remainder of the body vests in the next of kin.

Subsection (b) leaves the determination of the time of death to the attending or certifying physician. No attempt is made to define the uncertain point in time when life terminates. This point is not subject to clear cut definition and medical authorities are currently working toward a consensus on the matter.

Modern methods of cardiac pacing, artificial respiration, artificial blood circulation and cardiac stimulation can continue certain bodily systems and metabolism far beyond spontaneous limits. The real question is when have irreversible changes taken place that preclude return to normal brain activity and self sustaining bodily functions. No reasonable statutory definition is possible. The answer depends upon many variables, differing from case to case. Reliance must be placed upon the judgment of the physician in attendance. The Uniform Act so provides.

However, because time is short following death for a transplant to be successful, the transplant team needs to remove the critical organ as soon as possible. Hence there is a possible conflict of interest between the attending physician and the transplant team, and accordingly subsection (b) excludes the attending physician from any part in the transplant procedures. Such a provision isolates the conflict of interest and is eminently desirable. However, the language of the provision does not prevent the donor's attending physician from communicating with the transplant team or other relevant donees. This communication is essential to permit the transfer of important knowledge concerning the donor, for example, the nature of the disease processes affecting the donor or the results of studies carried out for tissue matching and other immunological data.

Subsection (d) is necessary to preclude the frustration of the important medical examiners' duties in cases of death by suspected crime or violence. However, since such cases often can provide transplants of value to living persons, it may prove desirable in many if not most states to reexamine and amend, the medical examiner statutes to authorize and direct medical examiners to expedite their autopsy procedures in cases in which the public interest will not suffer.

The entire section 7 merits genuinely liberal interpretation to effectuate the purpose and intent of the Uniform Act, that is, to encourage and facilitate the important and ever increasing need for human tissue and organs for medical research, education and therapy, including transplantation.

1   SECTION 8. [*Uniformity of Interpretation.*] This Act shall be
2 so construed as to effectuate its general purpose to make uniform
3 the law of those states which enact it.

1   SECTION 9. [*Short Title.*] This Act may be cited as the Uniform
2 Anatomical Gift Act.

1   SECTION 10. [*Repeal.*] The following acts and parts of acts
2 are repealed:
3   (1)
4   (2)
5   (3)

1   SECTION 11. [*Time of Taking Effect.*] This Act shall take
2 effect . . . . .

Uniform Determination of Death Act

The Committee which acted for the National Conference of Commissioners on Uniform State Laws in preparing the Uniform Determination of Death Act was as follows:

GEORGE C. KEELY, 1600 Colorado National Building, 950 Seventeenth Street, Denver, CO 80202, *Chairman*

ANNE McGILL GORSUCH, 243 South Fairfax, Denver, CO 80222

JOHN M. McCABE, Room 510, 645 North Michigan Avenue, Chicago, IL 60611, *Legal Counsel*

WILLIAM H. WOOD, 208 Walnut Street, Harrisburg, PA 17108

JOHN C. DEACON, P.O. Box 1245, Jonesboro, AR 72401, *President, Ex Officio*

M. KING HILL, JR., 6th Floor, 100 Light Street, Baltimore, MD 21202, *Chairman, Executive Committee, Ex Officio*

WILLIAM J. PIERCE, University of Michigan, School of Law, Ann Arbor, MI 48109, *Executive Director, Ex Officio*

PETER F. LANGROCK, P.O. Drawer 351, Middlebury, VT 05753, *Chairman, Division E, Ex Officio*

This Act provides comprehensive bases for determining death in all situations. It is based on a ten-year evolution of statutory language on this subject. The first statute passed in Kansas in 1970. In 1972, Professor Alexander Capron and Dr. Leon Kass refined the concept further in "A Statutory Definition of the Standards for Determining Human Death: An Appraisal and a Proposal," 121 Pa. L. Rev. 87. In 1975, the Law and Medicine Committee of the American Bar Association (ABA) drafted a Model Definition of Death Act. In 1978, the National Conference of Commissioners on Uniform State Laws (NCCUSL) completed the Uniform Brain Death Act. It was based on the prior work of the ABA. In 1979, the American Medical Association (AMA) created its own Model Determination of Death statute. In the meantime, some twenty-five state legislatures adopted statutes based on one or another of the existing models.

The interest in these statutes arises from modern advances in life-saving technology. A person may be artificially supported for respiration and circulation after all brain functions cease irreversibly.

The medical profession, also, has developed techniques for determining loss of brain functions while cardiorespiratory support is administered. At the same time, the common law definition of death cannot assure recognition of these techniques. The common law standard for determining death is the cessation of all vital functions, traditionally demonstrated by "an absence of spontaneous respiratory and cardiac functions." There is, then, a potential disparity between current and accepted biomedical practice and the common law.

The proliferation of model acts and uniform acts, while indicating a legislative need, also may be confusing. All existing acts have the same principal goal—extension of the common law to include the new techniques for determination of death. With no essential disagreement on policy, the associations which have drafted statutes met to find common language. This Act contains that common language, and is the result of agreement between the ABA, AMA, and NCCUSL.

Part (1) codifies the existing common law basis for determining death—total failure of the cardiorespiratory system. Part (2) extends the common law to include the new procedures for determination of death based upon irreversible loss of all brain functions. The overwhelming majority of cases will continue to be determined according to part (1). When artificial means of support preclude a determination under part (1), the Act recognizes that death can be determined by the alternative procedures.

Under part (2), the entire brain must cease to function, irreversibly. The "entire brain" includes the brain stem, as well as the neocortex. The concept of "entire brain" distinguishes determination of death under this Act from "neocortical death" or "persistent vegetative state." These are not deemed valid medical or legal bases for determining death.

This Act also does not concern itself with living wills, death with dignity, euthanasia, rules on death certificates, maintaining life support beyond brain death in cases of pregnant women or of organ donors, and protection for the dead body. These subjects are left to other law.

This Act is silent on acceptable diagnostic tests and medical procedures. It sets the general legal standard for determining death, but not the medical criteria for doing so. The medical profession remains free to formulate acceptable medical practices and to utilize new biomedical knowledge, diagnostic tests, and equipment.

It is unnecessary for the Act to address specifically the liability of persons who make determinations. No person authorized by law to determine death, who makes such a determination in accordance with the Act, should, or will be, liable for damages in any civil action or subject to prosecution in any criminal proceeding for his acts or the acts of others based on that determination. No person who acts in good faith, in reliance on a determination of death, should, or will be, liable for damages in any civil action or subject to prosecution in any criminal proceeding for his acts. There is no need to deal with these issues in the text of this Act.

Time of death, also, is not specifically addressed. In those instances in which time of death affects legal rights, this Act states the bases for determining death. Time of death is a fact to be determined with all others in each individual case, and may be resolved, when in doubt, upon expert testimony before the appropriate court.

Finally, since this Act should apply to all situations, it should not be joined with the Uniform Anatomical Gift Act so that its application is limited to cases of organ donation.

UNIFORM DETERMINATION OF DEATH ACT

1 §1. [*Determination of Death.*] An individual who has sus-
2 tained either (1) irreversible cessation of circulatory and res-
3 piratory functions, or (2) irreversible cessation of all functions
4 of the entire brain, including the brain stem, is dead. A de-
5 termination of death must be made in accordance with ac-
6 cepted medical standards.

1 §2. [*Uniformity of Construction and Application.*] This Act
2 shall be applied and construed to effectuate its general purpose
3 to make uniform the law with respect to the subject of this Act
4 among states enacting it.

1 §3. [*Short Title.*] This Act may be cited as the Uniform
2 Determination of Death Act.

The Human Tissue Gift Act, 1971

Her Majesty, by and with the advice and consent of the Legislative Assembly of the Province of Ontario, enacts as follows:

Interpretation
The R.S.O. 1960, c. 234

1. In this Act,

    (a) "consent" means a consent given under this Act;
    (b) "physician" means a person registered under The Medical Act;
    (c) "tissue" includes an organ, but does not include any skin, bone, blood, blood constituent or other tissue that is replaceable by natural processes of repair;
    (d) "transplant" as a noun means the removal of tissue from a human body, whether living or dead, and its implantation in a living human body, and in its other forms it has corresponding meanings;
    (e) "writing" for the purposes of Part II includes a will and any other testamentary instrument whether or not probate has been applied for or granted and whether or not the will or other testamentary instrument is valid.

PART I
INTER-VIVOS GIFTS FOR TRANSPLANTS

Transplants under Act
are lawful

2. A transplant from one living human body to another living human body may be done in accordance with this Act, but not otherwise.

Consent for transplant

3. (1) Any person who has attained the age of majority, is mentally competent to consent, and is able to make a free and informed decision may in a writing signed by him consent to the removal forthwith from his body of the tissue specified in the consent and its implantation in the body of another living person.

Consent of person under
age, etc.

(2) Notwithstanding subsection 1, a consent given thereunder by a person who had not attained the age of majority, was not mentally competent to consent, or was not able to make a free and informed decision is valid for the purposes of this Act if the person who acted upon it had no reason to believe that the person who gave it had not attained the age of majority, was not mentally competent to consent, and was not able to make a free and informed decision, as the case may be.

Consent is full authority
to proceed

(3) A consent given under this section is full authority for any physician,

(a) to make any examination necessary to assure medical acceptability of the tissue specified therein; and
(b) to remove forthwith such tissue from the body of the person who gave the consent.

Stale consent void

(4) If for any reason the tissue specified in the consent is not removed in the circumstances to which the consent relates, the consent is void.

PART II
POST MORTEM GIFTS FOR TRANSPLANTS
AND OTHER USES

Consent by person for use
of his body after death

4. (1) Any person who has attained the age of majority may consent,

(a) in a writing signed by him at any time; or
(b) orally in the presence of at least two witnesses during his last illness,

that his body or the part or parts thereof specified in the consent be used after his death for therapeutic purposes, medical education or scientific research.

Where donor under age

(2) Notwithstanding subsection 1, a consent given by a person who had not attained the age of majority is valid for the purposes of this Act if the person who acted upon it had no reason to believe that the person who gave it had not attained the age of majority.

Reprinted with permission from the Uniform Law Conference of Canada, Fredericton, New Brunswick.

Consent is full authority exception

(3) Upon the death of a person who has given a consent under this section, the consent is binding and is full authority for the use of the body or the removal and use of the specified part or parts for the purpose specified, except that no person shall act upon a consent given under this section if he has reason to believe that it was subsequently withdrawn.

Consent by spouse, etc. for use of body after death

5. (1) Where a person of any age who has not given a consent under section 4 dies, or in the opinion of a physician is incapable of giving a consent by reason of injury or disease and his death is imminent,

(a) his spouse of any age; or

(b) if none or if his spouse is not readily available, any one of his children who has attained the age of majority; or

(c) if none or if none is readily available, either of his parents; or

(d) if none or if neither is readily available, any one of his brothers or sisters who has attained the age of majority; or

(e) if none or if none is readily available, any other of his next of kin who has attained the age of majority; or

(f) if none or if none is readily available, the person lawfully in possession of the body other than where he died in hospital, the administrative head of the hospital,

may consent,

(g) in a writing signed by the spouse, relative or other person, or

(h) orally by the spouse, relative or other person in the presence of at least two witnesses; or

(i) by the telegraphic, recorded telephonic, or other recorded message of the spouse, relative or other person,

to the body or the part or parts thereof specified in the consent being used after death for therapeutic purposes, medical education or scientific research.

Prohibition

(2) No person shall give a consent under this section if he has reason to believe that the person who died or whose death is imminent would have objected thereto.

Consent is full authority, exceptions

(3) Upon the death of a person in respect of whom a consent was given under this section the consent is binding and is, subject to section 6, full authority for the use of the body or for the removal and use of the specified part or parts for the purpose specified except that no person shall act on a consent given under this section if he has actual knowledge of an objection thereto by the person in respect of whom the consent was given or by a person of the same or closer relationship to person in respect of whom the consent was given than the person who gave the consent.

Person lawfully in possession of body, exceptions

R.S.O. 1960, c. 69

R.S.O. 1960, c. 80

(4) In subsection 1, "person lawfully in possession of the body" does not include,

(a) the supervising coroner or a coroner in possession of the body for the purposes of the Coroners Act;

(b) the Public Trustee in possession of the body for the purpose of its burial under The Crown Administration of Estates Act;

(c) an embalmer or funeral director in possession of the body for the purpose of its burial, cremation or other disposition; or

(d) the superintendent of a crematorium in possession of the body for the purpose of its cremation.

Coroner's direction

6. Where in the opinion of a physician, the death of a person is imminent by reason of injury or disease and the physician has reason to believe that section 7, 21 or 22 of The Coroners Act may apply when death does occur and a consent under this part has been obtained for a post-mortem transplant of tissue from the body, a coroner having jurisdiction, notwithstanding that death has not yet occurred, may give such directions as he thinks proper respecting the removal of such tissue after the death of the person, and every such direction has the same force and effect as if it had been made after death under section 8 of The Coroners Act.

Determination of death

7. (1) For the purposes of a post-mortem transplant, the fact of death shall be determined by at least two physicians in accordance with accepted medical practice.

Prohibition

(2) No physician who has had any association with the proposed recipient that might influence his judgment shall take any part in the determination of the fact of death of the donor.

Idem

(3) No physician who took any part in the determination of the fact of death of the donor shall participate in any way in the transplant procedures.

Exception

(4) Nothing in this section in any way affects a physician in the removal of eyes for cornea transplants.

Where specified use fails

8. Where a gift under this Part cannot for any reason be used for any of the purposes specified in the consent, the subject matter of the gift and the body to which it belongs shall be dealt with and disposed of as if no consent had been given.

PART III
GENERAL

Civil liability

9. No action or other proceeding for damages lies against any person for any act done in good faith and without negligence in the exercise or intended exercise of any authority conferred by this Act.

Sale, etc. of tissue prohibited

10. No person shall buy, sell or otherwise deal in, directly or indirectly, for a valuable consideration, any tissue for a transplant, or any body or part or parts thereof other than blood or a blood constituent, for therapeutic purposes, medical education or scientific research, and any such dealing is invalid as being contrary to public policy.

Disclosure of information

11. (1) Except where legally required, no person shall disclose or give to any other person any information or document whereby the identity of any person,

    (a) who has given or refused to give a consent;
    (b) with respect to whom a consent has been given; or
    (c) into whose body tissue has been, is being or may be transplanted,

may become known publicly.

Exception

(2) Where the information or document disclosed or given pertains only to the person who disclosed or gave the information or document, subsection 1 does not apply.

Lawful dealings not affected exception

12. Any dealing with a body or part or parts thereof that was lawful before this Act came into force shall, except as provided in this Act, continue to be lawful.

Offence

13. Every person who knowingly contravenes any provision of this Act is guilty of an offence and on summary conviction is liable to a fine of no more than $1,000 or to imprisonment for a term of not more than six months, or to both.

R.S.O. 1960, c. 69 not affected

14. Except as provided in section 6, nothing in this Act affects the operation of The Coroners Act.

Transitional provision 1962-63, c. 59

15. A request made or an authorization given under The Human Tissue Act, 1962-63 before this Act came into force may be acted upon in accordance with that Act notwithstanding the repeal of that Act.

PART IV
MISCELLANEOUS

1962-63, c. 59 1967, c. 38 repealed

16. The Human Tissue Act, 1962-63 and the Human Tissue Amendment Act, 1967 are repealed.

Commencement

17. This Act comes into force on the day it receives Royal Assent.

Short title

18. This Act may be cited as The Human Tissue Gift Act, 1971.

Uniform Donor Card

<table>
<tr>
<td>

UNIFORM DONOR CARD

OF_____
                Print or type name of donor
In the hope that I may help others, I hereby make this anatomical gift, if medically acceptable, to take effect upon my death. The words and marks below indicate my desires.

I give: (a) _____ any needed organs or parts
           (b) _____ only the following organs or parts

_____
          Specify the organ(s) or part(s)
for the purposes of transplantation, therapy, medical research or education;
           (c) _____ my body for anatomical study if needed.

Limitations or
special wishes, if any :_____

</td>
<td>

Signed by the donor and the following two witnesses in the presence of each other:

_____   _____
Signature of Donor   Date of Birth of Donor

_____   _____
Date Signed   City & State

_____   _____
Witness   Witness

This is a legal document under the Uniform Anatomical Gift Act or similar laws.

For further information consult your local memorial society or:

Continental Association of Funeral & Memorial Societies
1828 L Street, N.W., Washington, D.C. 20036

</td>
</tr>
</table>

Reprinted with permission from Continental Association of Funeral Memorial Societies, Washington, DC 20036.

Medic Alert Foundation International

MedicAlert Foundation International
P.O. Box 1009
Turlock, California 95380
209/668-3333

Medic Alert Foundation/Chicago
840 North Lake Shore Drive
Chicago, IL 60611
312/280-6366
Joyce Drake, Regional Director

Medic Alert Foundation/Florida
600 Courtland Street
Orlando, FL 32804
305/647-2497
Marybeth Harvey, Acting Regional Director

Medic Alert Foundation/New York
777 United Nations Plaza
New York, NY 10017
212/697-7470
Carolyn Twiname, Regional Director

Medic Alert Foundation/Utah
965 East 4800 South
Salt Lake City, UT 84117
801/261-2058
Bruce Hanks, Regional Director

Organ Donations

Organ recovery procedures vary from hospital to hospital. Usually there is either an organ recovery unit and/or a transplant coordinator within a hospital to make all the arrangements. Sometimes a hospital works with or "harvests" organs from a separate organ bank or a regional organ procurement agency.

In general, procedure for donation of organs usually includes the following:

- Hospital staff identifies the potential donor.
- Organ recovery program or transplant coordinator is notified.
- Consent of next of kin is obtained.
- Declaration is made that the donor is brain dead. (The definition of *brain death* may vary some from hospital to hospital. Generally, a person who is brain dead has suffered total cessation of brain function and his respirations are completely supported by a respirator.
- Perspective donor's medical history is evaluated to determine donor suitability.
- Maintenance of donor until surgical procedure is performed.
- Medical-examiner consent obtained, if necessary.

U.S.A.

Arizona

**UNIVERSITY OF ARIZONA HOSPITAL
DIVISION OF CARDIOTHORACIC SURGERY**
Karen Siroky, R.N.
1501 N. Campbell Ave.
Tucson, AZ 85712
602/626-6339
Accepting: Hearts; eyes and kidneys (through associated program).
Restrictions: *Hearts*—brain-dead, heart-beating donors under thirty-five years with no history of cardiac disease.
Transportation Fees: Paid by University of Arizona Hospital.

California

**REGIONAL ORGAN PROCUREMENT AGENCY
OF SOUTHERN CALIFORNIA**
1000 Veteran Ave.
Los Angeles, CA 90024
Accepting: All organs.
Restrictions: Variable according to organ.
Transportation Fees: Paid by Medicare (for kidneys).

**NORTHERN CALIFORNIA TRANSPLANT BANK
AT PACIFIC MEDICAL CENTER**
P.O. Box 7999
San Francisco, CA 94120
415/563-4321 (Ext. 2401); 415/922-3100 (24-hour hotline)
Accepting: Hearts; kidneys; lungs; bones; cartilage; dura mater, fascia lata; middle ears; eyes (cornea and sclera); pituitary glands.
Restrictions: *Hearts*—donors thirty-five years or younger; *kidneys*—donors usually under sixty years; *tissues*—donors often sixty-five years or older. [*Note:* In California, donors under eighteen years must have formal approval of a parent or legal guardian.]

WESTERN MEDICAL CENTER
Beverly Parr, Director, Orange County Eye Bank
1001 N. Tustin Ave.
Santa Ana, CA 92705
714/835-3555
Accepting: Eyes (cornea).
Restrictions: Donors with no transferable diseases (i.e., hepatitis); six-hour time limit for removal.
Transportation Fees: Paid by accepting physician.

Colorado

**UNIVERSITY OF COLORADO
HEALTH SCIENCES CENTER**
Paul D. Taylor, Transplant Coordinator
4200 E. Ninth Ave.
Denver, CO 80262
303/399-1211

Prepared by Marquis editorial staff.

Accepting: Multiple organs and tissues.
Restrictions: Variable according to organ or tissue.
Transportation Fees: Variable according to organ or tissue.

Connecticut

HARTFORD TRANSPLANT SERVICE
HARTFORD HOSPITAL
SURGICAL RESEARCH DEPARTMENT
80 Seymour St.
Hartford, CT 06115
203-524-2256
Accepting: Kidneys.
Transportation Fees: Paid by Hartford Transplant Service.

District of Columbia

WASHINGTON HOSPITAL CENTER
TRANSPLANT OFFICE
Charles B. Currier, M.D., Director
110 Irving St.
Washington, DC 20010
202/541-6058
Accepting: Eyes; kidneys; skin.
Restrictions: *Eyes*—six-hour time limit for removal following cardiac arrest; *kidneys*—brain-dead donors between one and sixty-five years; *skin*—eighteen-hour time limit for removal following cardiac arrest.
Transportation Fees: Paid by Washington Hospital Center (with permission).

Florida

UNIVERSITY OF MIAMI SCHOOL OF MEDICINE
DEPARTMENT OF SURGERY (R-310)
Les Olson, Director, Organ Bank
Miami, FL 33136
305/547-6315
Accepting: Kidneys; pancreas.
Restrictions: Brain-dead donors under sixty-five years with good health.
Transportation Fees: Paid by University of Miami School of Medicine.

Illinois

RUSH-PRESBYTERIAN-ST. LUKE'S MEDICAL CENTER
ORGAN & TISSUE PROCUREMENT PROGRAM
Amy S. Peele, R.N., Senior Coordinator
1753 W. Congress Pkwy.
Chicago, IL 60612
312/942-6242
Accepting: Kidney; cornea; skin; bone; other organs and tissues as needed.
Transportation Fees: Organs and tissues are generally received from patients within hospital.

Indiana

RENAL TRANSPLANT CENTER
INDIANA UNIVERSITY HOSPITALS
David Mainous, Transplant Coordinator
1100 W. Michigan St.
Indianapolis, IN 46223
317/264-4370
Transportation Fees: Paid by Southeastern Organ Procurement Foundation.

Iowa

UNIVERISTY OF IOWA
HOSPITALS & CLINICS
Robert J. Corry, M.D., Director, Transplant Service
Iowa City, IA 52242
319/356-1616
Accepting: Kidneys; pancreas; liver; heart.

Massachusetts

MASSACHUSETTS EYE & EAR INFIRMARY
NEW ENGLAND EYE BANK
Valerie P. Belcher, Executive Director
243 Charles St.
Boston, MA 02114
617/525-2900
Accepting: Eyes.
Transportation Fees: Paid by eye bank.

Michigan

TRANSPLANTATION SOCIETY OF MICHIGAN
3374 Washtenaw Ave.
Ann Arbor, MI 48104

UNIVERSITY OF MICHIGAN HOSPITALS
Richard Fuller, Manager, Eye Bank
Norm Williams, Manager, Skin Bank
1405 E. Ann St.
Ann Arbor, MI 48109
313/764-3262; 313/764-0512
Accepting: Eyes; skin.
Transportation Fees: None.

MOUNT CARMEL MERCY HOSPITAL
6701 W. Outer Dr.
Detroit, MI 48235
313/927-7000
Accepting: Kidneys; pancreas.
Transportation Fees: Paid by the Transplantation Society.

Minnesota

UNIVERSITY OF MINNESOTA
TRANSPLANT PROGRAM
Jane Van Hack, R.N., C.C.R.N., Transplant Coordinator
Box 166, Mayo
Minneapolis, MN 55455
612/373-8322
Accepting: Kidneys; pancreas; heart; liver.
Transportation Fees: Paid by transplant program.

Missouri

MIDWEST ORGAN BANK
Donald Cross, M.D.
305 W. Forty-third
Kansas City, MO 64111
816/931-6353 (24 hours)

SAINT LUKE'S HOSPITAL OF KANSAS CITY
P.O. Box 1647
Kansas City, MO 64141
816/932-2000
Accepting: Kidneys; corneas; coordinate with liver donation.
Transportation Fees: Paid by Midwest Organ Bank.

PRESIDENT'S OFFICE
BARNES HOSPITAL
St. Louis, MO 63110
314/454-2000
Accepting: Multiple organs and tissues.
Transportation Fees: N/a.

VETERANS ADMINISTRATION MEDICAL CENTER
RENAL TRANSPLANT CENTER
St. Louis, MO 63106
314/652-4100
Accepting: Kidneys.
Transportation Fees: Paid by recovery agency involved.

New Jersey

NEW JERSEY EYE BANK
EYE INSTITUTE OF NEW JERSEY
Marshall S. Klein, Director
15 S. Ninth St.
Newark, NJ 07107
201/456-4626
Accepting: Eyes.
Transportation Fees: No fee; state police provide transportation.

New Mexico

PRESBYTERIAN HOSPITAL
Robert Shafer, Assistant Administrator
1100 Central Ave. SE
Albuquerque, NM 87102
505/844-1444

Accepting: Kidneys; corneas.
Transportation Fees: Donee pays fee.

New York

ALBANY MEDICAL CENTER HOSPITAL
DEPARTMENT OF SURGERY
DEPARTMENT OF OPHTHALMOLOGY
Frank Taft, Transplant Coordinator
43 New Scotland Ave.
Albany, NY 12208
518/445-5614
Accepting: Kidneys; eyes.
Transportation Fees: There usually are none.

THE GIFT OF LIFE PROGRAM
DOWNSTATE MEDICAL CENTER
Lea Emmett, R.N., and William Cantirino,
Transplant Coordinators
450 Clarkson Ave.
P.O. Box 98
Brooklyn, NY 11203
212/270-2120
Accepting: Primarily kidneys. Also acquire hearts, liver, pancreas, eyes and skin when necessary.
Transportation Fees: Through The Gift of Life Program via Medicare.

ST. LUKE'S-ROOSEVELT HOSPITAL CENTER
Patricia Manning, Transplant Coordinator
113th St. & Amsterdam Ave.
New York, NY 10025
212/870-1773 (24 hours)
Accepting: Kidneys.
Transportation Fees: Paid by the hospital.

North Carolina

DURHAM VA & DUKE UNIVERSITY
MEDICAL CENTERS
Corbin Peterson
508 Fulton St.
Durham, NC 27705
919/648-8111
Accepting: Kidneys and corneas for transplantation; all others for research.
Transportation Fees: Usually paid by donor institution.

Ohio

OHIO VALLEY ORGAN PROCUREMENT CENTER
UNIVERSITY OF CINCINNATI MEDICAL CENTER
J. Wesley Alexander, M.D., Director; Ronald Dreffer, Coordinator
231 Bethesda Ave.
Cincinnati, OH 45267
513/872-5000 (Transplant hotline); 513/872-4156 (Office)
Transportation Fees: Paid by center.

Oregon

OREGON LIONS EYE BANK
GOOD SAMARITAN HOSPITAL & MEDICAL CENTER
Kristi Voth, Executive Director
1015 N.W. Twenty-second
Portland, OR 97210
503/229-7523 (24-hour hotline)
Accepting: Corneas
Transportation Fees: Paid by eye bank.

Pennsylvania

ALBERT EINSTEIN MEDICAL CENTER
Diane Kaschak, R.N., Transplant Nurse Clinician
York & Tabor Rds.
Philadelphia, PA 19141
215/456-6933
Accepting: Kidneys.
Transportation Fees: Paid by regional organ procurement agency or Medicare.

ST. AGNES MEDICAL CENTER, SKIN BANK
1900 S. Broad St.
Philadelphia, PA 19145
215/339-4323
Accepting: Skin.
Transportation Fees: None; skin bank staff will travel to wherever necessary to perform procedure.

Texas

CORPUS CHRISTI LIONS EYE BANK
512/881-4788

MEMORIAL MEDICAL CENTER
Susan Daniel, R.N., M.S.
2606 Hospital Blvd.
P.O. Box 5280
Corpus Christi, TX 78405
713/762-2560
Accepting: All.
Transportation Fees: Paid by organ bank.

EYE BANK, BAPTIST MEMORIAL HOSPITAL
Mary Jane Bullock, Coordinator
111 Dallas
San Antonio, TX 78286
512/222-8431
Accepting: Eyes.
Transportation Fees: Paid by eye bank.

SOUTH TEXAS ORGAN BANK
Robert J. Gosnell, Executive Director
Lamar Building
Koger Executive Center
4553 Piedras Drive
Suite 101
San Antonio, TX 78228
Accepting: Primarily kidneys; but will take any usable organ.
Transportation Fees: Paid by organ bank.

Utah

INTERMOUNTAIN ORGAN BANK
UNIVERSITY OF UTAH MEDICAL CENTER
Janet MacCalman, R.N., Transplant Coordinator
50 N. Medical Dr.
Salt Lake City, UT 84132
Accepting: Kidneys; eyes; skin (heart, liver—also work with other transplant centers).
Transportation Fees: N/a. Transplant team travels to procure organs.

Wisconsin

ST. MARY'S HOSPITAL
Ralph M. Guttman, M.S., Director, Skin Bank
P.O. Box 503
Milwaukee, WI 53217
414/289-7143
Accepting: Skin.
Transportation Fees: Use local donors only (within a 50 mile radius of Milwaukee).

Organ Banks

Eye Banks

Corneal transplant operations are now effective in restoring sight in ninety percent of the most common corneal diseases. The Lions Clubs support sixty-five eye banks in the U.S. During 1979 their efforts made 10,176 corneal transplants possible. According to the Eye Bank Association of America, approximately 25,000 cornea transplants were performed in 1981; 50,000 could have been done if corneal tissue had been available.

Eye Bank Association of America
1111 Tulane Ave.
New Orleans, LA 70112
504/523-6343

The Eye Bank for Sight Restoration, Inc.
210 E. Sixty-fourth St.
New York, NY 10021
212/838-9200

Kidneys

National Kidney Foundation, Inc.
2 Park Ave.
New York, NY 10016

According to figures from the Health Care Finance Administration, approximately 16,000 people were waiting in 1980 for a kidney transplant; the number of transplants actually performed was 4,697. There are approximately 1,000 kidney centers in the U.S., including outpatient centers for dialysis.

American Kidney Foundation
7315 Wisconsin Ave.
Washington, DC 20014
202/387-8730

National Association of Patients
on Hemodialysis & Transplantation
P.O. Box 60
Brooklyn, NY 11203

Pituitary Glands

National Pituitary Agency
Richard J. Barth, Administrator
210 W. Fayette St.
Baltimore, MD 21201
301/837-2552

Approximately 10,000 children in the U.S. suffer from a serious pituitary gland deficiency. In order to attain normal growth for one year, each of these children needs the growth hormone extracted from about 200 pituitary glands. Only 1,400 to 1,500 children now receive it. An additional estimated 50,000 children with partial deficiencies could be helped by the growth hormone.

Temporal Bone Banks

The Deafness Research Foundation
342 Madison Ave.
New York, NY 10002
212/684-6556

Over 18,000,000 people in the U.S. are partially or totally deaf. The inner ear structure is needed for research. The removal of the ear structures is a specialized task for which arrangements are made by the National Temporal Bone Banks Center of the Deaf Research Foundation at the time of death.

National Temporal Bone Banks
Center of the Deaf Research Foundation
550 N. Broadway
Room 103
Johns Hopkins University
School of Medicine
Baltimore, MD 21205

Prepared by Marquis editorial staff.

Tissue

For persons suffering from serious burns, human skin is a very effective dressing. Sometimes successful grafts are possible.

The American Association of Tissue Banks
Harold T. Meryman, M.D., President
12111 Parkinson Dr.
Rockville, MD 20852

A private association (including physicians, nurses, lawyers, technicians and laymen) which is planning to conduct a national survey on resources in transplantable organs and tissues.

The Tissue Bank
The Naval Medical Research Institute
NNMC, Bethesda, MD 20014
202/295-1121

The Tissue Bank accepts anatomical donations (particularly from persons thirty-five and under) who die within the National Medical Center or at San Diego Naval Hospital. The bodies must be cremated or buried at the family's expense.

The Northern California Transplant Bank
751 S. Bascom Ave.
San Jose, CA 95128
408/289-8200

A regional approach to procuring, processing, storing, and distributing tissues for transplant. Transplant units within the organization are concerned with bone, ear, eye, heart, heart valve, artery, cartilage renewal and skin.

General

MEDICAL DATA BANC
7920 Ward Parkway
Kansas City, MO 64114
816/333-2080

Medical Data Banc is a for-profit organization that keeps microfilm chips, providing a person's complete medical history and anatomical gift instructions. Individual membership is $18.00 a year; family membership is $36.00.

THE LIVING BANK
Sandra Tucker, Director
Hermann Professional Building
P.O. Box 6725
Houston, Texas 77005
713/528-2971

The Living Bank is a nonprofit organization that acts as a clearinghouse between a donor and a donee, explaining the procedure and providing a legal donor card to persons interested in donating any part or all of their bodies for transplantation or anatomical studies at their death. The Living Bank serves Texas and all other states with a twenty-four-hour referral service. Donor cards are kept on file as a permanent record. In addition, the donor's pertinent information and donation are placed on computer and microfiche for instant referral at the time of death. After being notified of a death by a next of kin, the trained staff will contact the nearest organ bank, hospital or medical school, according to the donor's specifications.

Anatomical Gifts

A prospective donor may donate individual organs and tissues for transplantation or a prospective donor may donate his or her body to a medical or dental school for education and research.

For Transplantation

Blood (transfusions)
Bone marrow (aplastic anemia)
Cornea
Heart
Kidney
Liver
Pituitary gland (growth hormone)
Skin (grafts and burn dressings)

For Study and Research

Brain
Cadaver
Ear bones (temporal bones)
Heart muscle
Kidneys
Liver
Long leg bone
Lungs
Ovaries

Recycling of Non-organic Materials

New Eyes for the Needy, Inc.
Short Hills, NJ 07078

Will recycle glasses left by the dead to benefit the needy.

Inland Empire Human Resources Center
c/o Congregational Church
2 W. Olive Ave.
Redlands, CA 92373

Will accept old eyeglasses and tooth fillings (gold) to benefit the needy.

DEATH/SURVIVOR BENEFITS

Survivor Benefits

Dale R. Detlefs, A.B., B.S.C., M.B.A., J.D.

The amount of the survivor benefits paid is based on your P.I.A. at the date of your death.

EASY-REFERENCE TABLE

Again, here is an easy-reference table showing the approximate monthly benefit amounts payable to your family members if you should die in 1982. The figures are based on the assumption that you have worked steadily and received average pay raises throughout your working career. Only by going through the steps described can you make a completely accurate calculation.

The figures shown are subject to increases by the cost-of-living percentage effective each June.

Lump-Sum Death Benefit

At the time of your death, whether you are still working or retired, there is a one-time lump-sum amount of $255 payable towards your funeral expenses.

The benefit is payable to a surviving spouse who is living with you at the time of death. If you don't have a spouse, then payment may be made to children who are eligible for monthly benefits in the month of death; otherwise the benefit is not payable.

Qualifications For Survivors Benefits

For your dependents to receive monthly survivor benefits or the lump-sum death benefit, you must be either
• Fully Insured . . . or
• Currently Insured. (For some benefits but not all)

Fully Insured

The following table shows how many quarters of coverage you need to be fully insured. To use the table, find your year of birth. Next to it is a column showing the number of quarters you must have if you die in 1982. For example, if you were born in 1940, you need 20 quarters of coverage to be fully insured.

Currently Insured

If you are currently insured, the following survivors qualify for monthly benefits:
• spouse caring for an eligible child under age 16
• divorced wife caring for an eligible child under age 16
• eligible child
   To be "currently insured," you need six quarters of coverage. You must have earned them during the last 13 calendar quarters ending with the quarter in which you die.

Monthly Benefits If You Should Die

YOUR PRESENT AGE	WHO RECEIVES BENEFITS	$10,000-15,000	YOUR PRESENT ANNUAL EARNINGS			
			$15,000-28,000	$20,000-25,000	$25,000-30,000	$30,000 & UP
63-65	Spouse, age 65	446	568	626	640	646
	Spouse, age 60	318	406	447	457	461
	Child; spouse caring for Child	334	426	469	480	484
	Maximum family benefit	789	994	1,095	1,120	1,130
53-62	Spouse, age 65	410	521	576	588	593
	Spouse, age 60	293	372	411	420	423
	Child; spouse caring for Child	307	390	432	441	444
	Maximum family benefits	756	925	1,008	1,029	1,038
48-52	Spouse, age 65	411	521	579	592	597
	Spouse, age 60	293	372	413	423	426
	Child; spouse caring for Child	308	390	434	444	447
	Maximum family benefit	759	925	1,013	1,036	1,045
43-47	Spouse, age 65	411	522	586	602	609
	Spouse, age 60	293	373	418	430	435
	Child; spouse caring for Child	308	391	439	451	456
	Maximum family benefit	759	927	1,026	1,054	1,066
38-42	Spouse, age 65	411	523	596	618	627
	Spouse, age 60	293	373	426	441	448
	Child; spouse caring for Child	308	392	447	463	470
	Maximum family benefit	759	928	1,043	1,082	1,097
30-37	Spouse, age 65	413	526	606	645	664
	Spouse, age 60	295	376	433	461	474
	Child; spouse caring for Child	309	394	454	483	498
	Maximum family benefits	764	932	1,061	1,129	1,162
Under 30	Spouse, age 65	423	539	614	668	715
	Spouse, age 60	302	385	439	477	511
	Child; spouse caring for Child	317	404	460	501	536
	Maximum family benefit	791	950	1,075	1,169	1,251

Reprinted with permission from *Meidinger Guide to Social Security*, 1982 (Tenth) Edition, Meidinger, Inc., Louisville, KY 40204, 1981.

Family Members

Here are the surviving dependents who may receive benefits based on your P.I.A. The table also shows the percentage of your P.I.A. payable to each member:

Who Receives Benefits If You Die

BENEFITS PAID TO	% OF P.I.A. PAYABLE
Spouse, age 65	100%
Spouse, age 62	82.9%
Spouse, age 60	71.5%
Disabled Spouse, age 50-59	50%-71.5%
Spouse under age 61 caring for eligible child under age 16	75%
Each child	75%

Eligibility

Unless otherwise noted, your SPOUSE qualifies if he or she was
- married to you for nine months before your death (If death is due to an accident or military duty, nine months of marriage is not required)...or
- the parent of your child (natural or adopted).

Surviving Spouse, Age 60 or over

The benefit is 100% of your P.I.A. if the spouse is age 65. If you had retired early and had a reduced benefit, your spouse at age 65 will receive the reduced benefit that you were receiving (but not less than 82.5% of your P.I.A.).

Your DIVORCED SPOUSE qualifies for a benefit if married to you for 10 years. The benefit is the same as that payable to a spouse.

Surviving Spouse, Age 50-59

Your DISABLED SPOUSE whose disability is so severe (mental or physical) that he or she can't work for a living will qualify for benefits as early as age 50. At that age, your spouse is entitled to 50% of your P.I.A. There will be a "Waiting Period" of five months before the disabled spouse benefit begins.

Your DISABLED DIVORCED SPOUSE qualifies the same as a Disabled Spouse except the marriage must have lasted 10 years before the divorce.

Benefits payable to a surviving spouse, age 50-59, will stop on remarriage. However, if the remarriage is to someone entitled to Social Security benefits as a *parent, widow, widower,* or *disabled child,* the benefit will not stop.

Surviving Spouse Caring for Child

Your SPOUSE CARING FOR AN ELIGIBLE CHILD under age 16 receives 75% of your P.I.A. The benefit stops when the youngest child reaches age 16 unless the parent is caring for a disabled child.

Your SURVIVING DIVORCED SPOUSE CARING FOR YOUR ELIGIBLE CHILD under age 16 is eligible to receive 75% of your P.I.A.

Your SURVIVING DIVORCED SPOUSE CARING FOR YOUR DISABLED CHILD qualifies on the same basis as a parent. The child must be disabled before age 22. Your divorced spouse is not required to have been married to you for any specified length of time. The benefit is 75% of your P.I.A.

Eligible Child

An eligible child qualifies for a benefit of 75% of the deceased parent's P.I.A. If both parents are dead, a child can qualify for benefits on either the earnings record of the mother or father, whichever gives the larger benefit.

Dependent Parents

YOUR PARENT qualifies if
- he or she is at least age 62,
- was receiving at least one-half of his or her support from you, and
- has not remarried since your death.

The benefit is 82.5% of your P.I.A. However, if both parents are entitled to benefits, each will receive 75%. "Parent" means your father or mother (not your spouse's parents). This also includes a parent who adopted you before age 16 and a step-parent who married your father or mother before you were age 16. Benefits will stop if the parent remarries. (In some cases the benefit will continue if the parent marries someone entitled to Social Security benefits.)

Maximum Family Benefit

The Maximum Family Benefit applies.

Non-Duplication Of Benefits

A person eligible for more than one Social Security benefit may receive the larger of the two benefits. For example, a wife of a deceased worker may receive a retirement benefit based on her own work record or a widow's benefit, but not both.

Earnings Limitation

Anyone receiving survivor benefits is subject to the Earnings Limitation. Any earnings in excess of this limitation will reduce the benefit of the person earning the excess.

How To Figure Survivor Benefits

Survivor benefits are based on your Primary Insurance Amount, or P.I.A., when you die. To find out your P.I.A., you need to know your earnings history since your P.I.A. is based on your Average Indexed Monthly Earnings (AIME). By following the steps below, you can figure your own AIME. This, in turn, will give you a good estimate of your P.I.A. if you die in 1982. The following discussion does not apply to persons who attained age 62 before 1982; also persons who attain age 62 in 1979-83 and die later have an alternative method of computation available

Here's how to figure your AIME:

1. In column C of the Calculation Table below, enter your earnings

QUARTERS OF COVERAGE REQUIRED TO BE FULLY INSURED IF YOU SHOULD DIE IN 1982

Year of Birth	Quarters	Year of Birth	Quarters
1912*	23	1938	22
1913	24	1939	21
1914	25	1940	20
1915	26	1941	19
1916	27	1942	18
1917	28	1943	17
1918	29	1944	16
1919	30	1945	15
1920-1929	31	1946	14
1930	30	1947	13
1931	29	1948	12
1932	28	1949	11
1933	27	1950	10
1934	26	1951	9
1935	25	1952	8
1936	24	1953	7
1937	23	1954 and later	6

*Add 1 quarter for men.

for each year. **You can get some of this information from the Report of Earnings** you receive when you send in the card. You will also need income tax returns or some other records to be able to fill in each year.

IMPORTANT: If your earnings for any year were greater than the Maximum Taxable Amount shown for that year, use **only** the Maximum for that year. **Always** fill in column C with the **lesser** of your earnings or the Maximum Taxable Amount from column B. If you have worked very little since 1950, but did before 1951, ask your local Social Security office about using the alternate "old start" method not described here.

2. If you die anytime in 1982, earnings for most calendar years are multiplied by an "Index Factor" in column D. The index factor makes past earnings comparable to the same level of earnings today. Enter the results of your multiplication in column E, entitled, "Indexed Earnings."

3. Not all of the indexed earnings in column E are used to figure your average indexed monthly earnings. Here is a Table for determining how many years of earnings to use for death in 1982. Find your year of birth. Beside it is the number of years of earnings that must be used.

Number of Years You Must Use To Figure Average Indexed Monthly Earnings (AIME)

Year of Birth	Years	Year of Birth	Years
1920-29	26	1941	14
1930	25	1942	13
1931	24	1943	12
1932	23	1944	11
1933	22	1945	10
1934	21	1946	9
1935	20	1947	8
1936	19	1948	7
1937	18	1949	6
1938	17	1950	5
1939	16	1951	4
1940	15	1952	3
		After 1952	2

Enter the number of years you use............._____

4. On the Calculation Table, put a check mark in column F, "High Years," by the years of your highest indexed earnings in column E until you have checked the number of years you must use from (3).

5. Add up all the indexed earnings

Calculation Table For Figuring Your Indexed Earnings

A Calendar Year	B Taxable Amount	C Enter Your Taxable Earnings	× D Index Factor	= E Indexed Earnings	F High Years
1951	$ 3,600		4.4704		
1952	3,600		4.2086		
1953	3,600		3.9859		
1954	3,600		3.9654		
1955	4,200		3.7903		
1956	4,200		3.5425		
1957	4,200		3.4361		
1958	4,200		3.4061		
1959	4,800		3.2454		
1960	4,800		3.1228		
1961	4,800		3.0620		
1962	4,800		2.9159		
1963	4,800		2.8461		
1964	4,800		2.7344		
1965	4,800		2.6860		
1966	6,600		2.5339		
1967	6,600		2.4002		
1968	7,800		2.2459		
1969	7,800		2.1232		
1970	7,800		2.0228		
1971	7,800		1.9260		
1972	9,000		1.7541		
1973	10,800		1.6508		
1974	13,200		1.5582		
1975	14,100		1.4498		
1976	15,300		1.3563		
1977	16,500		1.2796		
1978	17,700		1.1854		
1979	22,900		1.0901		
1980	25,900		1.0000		
1981	29,700		1.0000		
1982	32,400		1.0000		

NOTE: The "average earnings," which is the basis for new index factors, is determined by the Social Security Administration and changes each year.

in column E for the years you have checked in column F.
.... _____

6. Multiply the number of years in (3) by 12 to get months
.... _____

7. Divide the total earnings shown in (5) by the months shown in (6) to get your Average Indexed Monthly Earnings. (Drop cents) _____

Now, to find your P.I.A.:

8. Find your Average Indexed Monthly Earnings from (7) in the first column of the table. The numbers beside your Average Indexed Monthly Earnings show your P.I.A. and the survivor benefits based on it.

Bob gets a job

Bob gets a full-time job. He earns $9,440 for the year. This is $5,000 more than the Earnings Limitation maximum of $4,440.

Bob's entire benefit is reduced by $1 for every $2 he earns over the limit: $5,000 annual earnings over the Earnings Limitation ÷ 2 = $2,500 benefit reduction.

Since Bob's annual Social Security benefit is only $2,256, the $2,500 benefit reduction totally eliminates his benefit. However, the rest of the family continues to receive the same total benefit. From the total original entitlement of $2,295, subtract $450 for Bob leaving $1,845, divided into the maximum family benefit of $1,050, this provides each remaining beneficiary with 56.9% of the original entitlement amount, as follows:

READJUSTED BENEFITS AFTER BOB STARTS JOB

Mary	$256
Bob	-0-
Larry	$256
Suzanne	$256
Gwendolyn	$282
Total	$1,050

Suzanne reaches age 16

Mary's benefit as a mother caring for an eligible child stops when Suzanne reaches age 16. However, Suzanne remains entitled to a benefit until she is 18 (or 19 if in high school). Gwendolyn's benefit also continues. The family's total benefit becomes:

Suzanne	$450
Gwendolyn	495
Total	$945

Suzanne reaches age 18

When the youngest child reaches age 18 and has completed high school, all of the children's benefits have been stopped. Gwendolyn has died. No further benefits are payable until Mary reaches age 60 unless she becomes disabled and qualifies as a Disabled Surviving Spouse.

Mary reaches age 60

Mary can elect to receive a surviving spouse's benefit of $429 a month for the rest of her life, which is 71.5% of Sam's P.I.A. of $600. Or, she can wait until she is age 65 to start her benefit.

Mary at age 65

If Mary waits until she is 65 before receiving benefits, she is entitled to 100% of Sam's P.I.A., or $600 a month. If she starts working after her benefits begin, she is subject to the Earnings Limitation.

EXAMPLE
Survivor Benefits

Sam's P.I.A. at age 50	$600

Sam's Dependents	Age
Mary—spouse	50
Bob—son, in high school	18
Larry—son	15
Suzanne—daughter	13
Gwendolyn—Sam's mother	70

In 1982, Sam dies at age 50, leaving five survivors

Each dependent is entitled to a monthly benefit based on Sam's P.I.A.:

	QUALIFICATION FOR BENEFIT	PERCENTAGE OF SAM'S P.I.A.	UNADJUSTED MONTHLY BENEFIT AMOUNT
Mary	spouse caring for eligible child	75%	$450
Bob	eligible child	75%	$450
Larry	eligible child	75%	$450
Suzanne	eligible child	75%	$450
Gwendolyn	dependent mother of Sam	82.5%	$495
	Total		$2,295

There is a limit on the amount payable to a single family based on the worker's P.I.A. In the case of Sam's family, the Maximum Family Benefit is $1,050. This means that everyone's benefit must be reduced proportionately so that the total doesn't go over $960. ($960 ÷ $2,295 = 45.75% which is the portion of each person's benefit entitlement actually paid.)

ADJUSTED MAXIMUM MONTHLY FAMILY BENEFIT

Mary	$206
Bob	$206
Larry	$206
Suzanne	$206
Gwendolyn	$226
Total	$1,050

Social Security Rules
Retirement

1. Quarters of coverage needed to be fully insured:
Count one quarter for each year **after** 1950 (or after the year that you become 21, if later) up through the year before you reach age 62. That's how many quarters of coverage you need to be "fully insured."

2. Number of years of earnings needed to figure your Average Indexed Monthly Earnings: Subtract five from the number of quarters of coverage you need to be fully insured. That's how many years of earnings you must use to find your Average Indexed Monthly Earnings.

Disability

3. Quarters of coverage needed to qualify for benefits:

   a) if you become disabled after reaching age 31:

      i) You must be "fully insured." Count the number of years after 1950 (or after the year you become 21, if later) up through the year before you become disabled or before age 62, if earlier. That's how many quarters of coverage you need to be "fully insured."

      ALSO

      ii) You must have 20 quarters of coverage during the 40 calendar quarter period ending with the calendar quarter in which you become disabled.

   b) if you become disabled between ages 24 and 31:

      You must have one quarter of coverage for each two calendar quarters between the time you reached age 21 and the time you became disabled. You must have at least six quarters of covered work.

   c) if you become disabled before age 24:

      you must have six quarters of coverage in the 12-quarter period before you became disabled.

4. Number of years of earnings needed to figure your Average Indexed Monthly Earnings: Subtract five from the number of quarters of coverage you need to be fully insured for disability, if you are age 47 or older in the year of disablement. The remainder is the number of years of earnings you must use to find your Average Indexed Monthly Earnings. No

drop-out years are allowed for disability under age 27; 1 year for ages 27-31; 2 years for ages 32-36; 3 years for ages 37-41; 4 years for ages 42-46. However, such drop-out years can be increased for persons disabled before age 37 — but only up to 2 years — for persons who have "child care years" — by one year for each child-care year. In any event you must have at least two years of earnings in the computation.

Death

5. Quarters of coverage needed to be fully insured:
   The number of years **after** 1950 (or after the year you turn 21, if later) will be counted up through the year before death occurs (or up **through** the year you become age 61 if earlier). That's how many quarters of coverage you need.

6. Number of years of earnings needed to figure your average indexed monthly earnings:
   Subtract five from the number of quarters of coverage you need to be fully insured for survivor benefits. That's how many years of earnings you must use to find your average indexed monthly earnings.

NOTE: You must use **at least** two years in figuring your average.

Benefit amount formula

7. For persons attaining age 62 or dying, or becoming disabled before attaining age 62 in 1982, the benefit formula is 90% of the first $230 of Average Indexed Monthly Earnings (AIME), plus 32% of the next $1,158 of AIME, plus 15% of the AIME in excess of $1,388. The **formula** itself, as it applies to deaths and disabilities before age 62 and to attainment of age 62 after 1982, will be adjusted in its dollar amounts in the formula by changes in average wage levels. The **amounts** resulting from the formula are subject to cost-of-living increases.

Maximum family benefit

8. For persons reaching age 62 or dying before age 62 in 1982, (or later), the maximum family benefit is 150% of the first $294 of the Primary Insurance Amount (P.I.A.), 272% of the next $131, 134% of the next $129 and 175% of the excess of the P.I.A. over $554. For persons becoming **disabled** in 1982 or later, it is the smaller of (a) 150% of PIA or (b) 85% of Average Indexed Monthly Earnings (AIME) but not less than the P.I.A. Any family affected by these maximums will be eligible for increases in it on the basis of increases in the cost-of-living as measured by the Consumer Price Index (CPI).

Reduction factors for early retirement

If you claim your benefit before 65, for each month that the benefit will be received before the month in which you reach age 65, reduce the P.I.A. (benefit at age 65) as follows:

Workers between ages 62 and 65 .... 5/9th of 1%
Spouse between ages 62 and 65 .... 25/36ths of 1%
Surviving Spouse between ages 60 and 65 .... 19/40ths of 1%
Disabled Surviving Spouse between
ages 50 and 59 .... 28.5% plus 43/240ths of 1%
for each month under age 60

Social Security Benefits

Your Social Security

Social Security is the Nation's basic method of providing a continuing income when family earnings are reduced or stop because of retirement, disability, or death.

Social Security payments are not intended to replace all lost earnings. People should try to supplement Social Security payments with savings, pensions, investments, or other insurance.
○ Nine out of 10 workers in the United States are earning protection under Social Security.
○ About 1 out of every 6 persons in this country receives monthly Social Security checks.
○ Over 24 million people 65 and over, nearly all of the Nation's older population, have health insurance under Medicare. Another 3 million disabled people under 65 also have Medicare.

Nearly every family, then, has a stake in Social Security.

This booklet is about your Social Security. It tells how you earn protection under Social Security, the kinds of benefits you and your family can get, how Social Security is financed, and other information that can help you in planning for the future.

Serving you

Social Security offices
The Social Security Administration has over 1,300 offices conveniently located throughout the country. Represent-atives of these offices also make regular stops in neighboring communities.

When you should contact us
Before you or your family can get any Social Security checks, you must apply for them.

Get in touch with any Social Security office if:
○ You're unable to work because of an illness or injury that is expected to last a year or longer.
○ You're 62 or older and plan to retire.
○ You're within 3 months of 65 even if you don't plan to retire.
○ Someone in your family dies.
○ You, your wife or husband, or your dependent children suffer permanent kidney failure.

It's important for you to call, visit, or write any Social Security office before you reach 65, not only about retirement checks, but also about Medicare, which is available whether or not you retire. You may find it easier to conduct your business with Social Security by telephone. Look in your telephone directory under "Social Security Administration" for the number of the nearest office.

Who gets checks?

Monthly Social Security checks may go to workers and their dependents when the worker retires, becomes severely disabled, or dies. Then, there's Medicare, which helps pay the cost of health care for eligible people who are 65 or over or disabled.

Monthly Social Security benefits include:
Retirement checks—When you retire, you can start getting retirement checks as early as 62.
Disability checks—A worker who becomes severely disabled before 65 can get disability checks.

Under Social Security, you're considered disabled if you have a severe physical or mental condition which:
○ Prevents you from working, and
○ Is expected to last (or has lasted) for at least 12 months, or is expected to result in death.

Your checks can start for the 6th full month of your disability. Once checks start, they'll continue as long as you are disabled and unable to perform substantial gainful work. Most cases are reviewed periodically to make sure the person remains disabled. If you are severely disabled, you could get benefits even though you manage to work a little.

Survivors checks—If the worker dies, survivors checks can go to certain members of the worker's family. A lump-sum payment also can be made when a worker dies. It is generally $255. This payment can only be made if there is an eligible surviving widow, widower, or entitled child.

Checks for a worker's family
Monthly Social Security checks also are paid to certain dependents of a worker who has retired, become disabled, or died.
Retirement or disability—If a worker is receiving retirement or disability

Reprinted from "Your Social Security," U.S. Department of Health and Human Services, Social Security Administration, Publication No. 05–10035, September, 1981.

benefits, monthly benefits also can be made to his or her:

○ Unmarried children under 18 (or under 19 if full-time high school students).

○ Unmarried children 18 or over who were severely disabled before 22 and who continue to be disabled.

○ Wife or husband 62 or over.

○ Wife or husband under 62 if she or he is caring for a child under 16 (or disabled) who's getting a benefit based on the retired or disabled worker's earnings.

Survivors—Monthly payments can be made to a deceased worker's:

○ Unmarried children under 18 (or under 19 if full-time high school students).

○ Unmarried son or daughter 18 or over who was severely disabled before 22 and who continues to be disabled.

○ Widow or widower 60 or older.

○ Widow, widower, or surviving divorced mother or father if caring for worker's child under 16 (or disabled) who is getting a benefit based on the earnings of the deceased worker.

○ Widow or widower 50 or older who becomes disabled not later than 7 years after the worker's death, or within 7 years after mother's or father's benefits end.

○ Dependent parents 62 or older.

Checks also can go to a divorced spouse at 62 or over, or a surviving divorced spouse at 60, or to a disabled surviving divorced spouse 50 or older if the marriage lasted 10 years or more. Under certain conditions, children may be eligible for Social Security benefits based on a grandparent's earnings.

Generally, a marriage must have lasted at least 1 year before dependents of a retired or disabled worker can get monthly benefits; survivors can get benefits in most cases if the marriage lasted at least 9 months.

Generally, benefits can be paid only for months the person is eligible throughout the entire month.

Medicare

The two parts of Medicare—hospital insurance and medical insurance—help protect people 65 and over from the high costs of health care. Disabled people under 65 who have been entitled to Social Security disability benefits for 24 or more months are also eligible for Medicare. Insured workers and their dependents who need dialysis treatment or a kidney transplant because of permanent kidney failure also have Medicare protection.

If you are disabled by blindness, you do not have to meet the requirement of recent work. But, you do need credit for ¼ year of work for each year since 1950 (or the year you reached 21 if later), up to the year you become blind. A minimum of 1½ years of credit is needed.

Work credit for survivors and disability benefits

Born after 1929, die or become diabled at	Born before 1930, die or become disabled before 62 in	Years you need
28 or younger		1½
30		2
32		2½
34		3
36		3½
38		4
40		4½
42		5
44		5½
46		6
48		6½
50		7
52	1981	7½
54	1983	8
56	1985	8½
58	1987	9
60	1989	9½
62 or older	1991 or later	10

Financing

The basic idea

The basic idea of Social Security is simple: During working years, employees, their employers, and self-employed people pay Social Security taxes. This money is used only to pay benefits to the 36 million people getting benefits and to pay administrative costs of the program.

Then, when today's workers' earnings stop or are reduced because of retirement, death, or disability, benefits will be paid to them from taxes paid by people in covered work and self-employment at that time.

Part of the taxes goes for hospital insurance under Medicare so workers and their dependents will have help in paying their hospital bills when they become eligible for Medicare. The medical insurance part of Medicare is financed by premiums paid by the people who have enrolled for this protection and amounts from the Federal Government.

The Government's share of the cost for the medical insurance part of Medicare and certain other Social

Security costs comes from general revenues of the U.S. Treasury, not from Social Security taxes.

Funds not required for current benefit payments and expenses are invested in interest-bearing U.S. Government securities.

Tax rates

If you're employed, you and your employer each pay an equal share of Social Security taxes. If you're self-employed, you pay taxes for retirement, survivors, and disability insurance at a rate about 1½ times the employee rate. The hospital insurance tax rate is the same for the employer, the employee, and the self-employed person.

As long as you have earnings that are covered by the law, you continue to pay Social Security taxes regardless of your age and even if you are receiving Social Security benefits.

This table shows the present and future Social Security tax rates now scheduled in the law.

Tax rate for employees and employers (each)

	Percent of covered earnings		
Years	For cash benefits	For hospital insurance	Total
1981	5.35	1.30	6.65
1982-84	5.40	1.30	6.70
1985	5.70	1.35	7.05
1986-89	5.70	1.45	7.15
1990 and after	6.20	1.45	7.65

Tax rate for self-employed people

	Percent of covered earnings		
Years	For cash benefits	For hospital insurance	Total
1981	8.00	1.30	9.30
1982-84	8.05	1.30	9.35
1985	8.55	1.35	9.90
1986-89	8.55	1.45	10.00
1990 and after	9.30	1 45	10.75

Automatic increases in the earnings base

The maximum amount of annual earnings that counts for Social Security is $29,700 for 1981. After 1981, the maximum will rise automatically in future years as earnings levels rise. Every year the increase in average covered wages will be figured; and if wage levels have increased since the base was set last, the base will be raised—but only if there is an automatic benefit increase the same year.

How taxes are paid

If you're employed, your Social Security tax is deducted from your wages each payday. Your employer matches your payment and sends the combined amount to the Internal Revenue Service.

If you're self-employed and your net earnings are $400 or more in a year, you must report your earnings and pay your self-employment tax each year when you file your income tax return. This is true even if you owe no income tax.

Your wages and self-employment income are entered on your Social Security record throughout your working years. This record of your earnings will be used to determine your eligibility for benefits and the amount of cash benefits you and your dependents will receive.

Excess earnings, taxes

When you work for more than one employer in a year and pay Social Security taxes on wages over the maximum amount, you may claim a refund of the excess amount on your income tax return for that year. If you work for only one employer who deducts too much in taxes, you should apply to the employer for a refund. A refund is made only when more than the required amount has been paid. Questions about taxes or refunds should be directed to the Internal Revenue Service.

Earnings over the maximum may appear on your Social Security earnings record, but they cannot be used to figure your benefit rate.

Right of appeal

If you feel that a decision made on your claim is not correct, you may ask the Social Security Administration to reconsider it. If, after this reconsideration, you still disagree with the decision, you may ask for a hearing by an administrative law judge of the Office of Hearings and Appeals. And, if you're not satisfied with the hearing decision, you may request a review by the Appeals Council. If you're still not satisfied, you may take your case to the Federal courts.

The Social Security Administration makes no charge for any of the appeals before the administration. You may, however, choose to be represented by a person of your own choice, and he or she may charge you a fee. The amount of such a fee is limited and must be approved by the Social Security Administration.

Someone in any Social Security office will explain how you may appeal and will help you get your claim reconsidered or request a hearing.

Supplemental security income

In addition to the benefits mentioned in this booklet, there is a Federal program called supplemental security income (SSI). It assures a minimum monthly income to needy people with limited income and resources who are 65 or older or blind or disabled. Eligiblity is based on income and assets. Payments of up to $264.70 a month ($397 for a couple), can be made. Although the program is administered by the Social Security Administration, it is financed from general revenues, not from Social Security taxes.

Life Insurance and Annuity Benefit Payments

American Council of Life Insurance

Americans received $38.0 billion in payments from life insurance policies and annuities during 1980, a 17.5% increase over 1979.

These payments, increasing steadily for many years, reflect the growing use of life insurance, not only in providing funds for the family whose breadwinner dies but for family financial needs during the policyholder's lifetime.

Since the majority of payments to beneficiaries, as well as payments to policyholders and annuitants, are made well after the time of purchase, life insurance benefit payments have not yet fully reflected the increase in life insurance and annuity purchases of the past two decades.

Several factors affect the pattern of life insurance benefit payments. Primary among them are the changes in the death rate among policyholders and the growth of group life insurance and other term insurance policies which do not incorporate a cash value.

These figures do not include $2.1 billion of benefits paid by other organizations issuing legal reserve life insurance, including fraternal societies, and by the Federal government.

Life Insurance and Annuity Benefit Payments
In the United States (000,000 Omitted)

| Year | Life Policyholders and Beneficiaries | | | | | | Annuity Payments | Grand Total |
	Death Payments	Matured Endowments	Disability Payments	Surrender Values	Policy Dividends	Total		
1940 ...	$ 995	$ 269	$104	$ 652	$ 468	$ 2,488	$ 176	$ 2,664
1945 ...	1,279	407	88	211	466	2,451	216	2,667
1950 ...	1,590	495	100	592	627	3,404	327	3,731
1955 ...	2,241	614	110	896	1,021	4,882	501	5,383
1960 ...	3,346	673	124	1,633	1,512	7,288	830	8,118
1965 ...	4,832	931	163	1,932	2,259	10,117	1,300	11,417
1966 ...	5,218	982	169	2,120	2,416	10,905	1,437	12,342
1967 ...	5,665	1,017	175	2,243	2,596	11,696	1,598	13,294
1968 ...	6,209	967	196	2,456	2,803	12,631	1,754	14,385
1969 ...	6,758	953	205	2,722	2,967	13,605	1,920	15,525
1970 ...	7,017	978	233	2,887	3,214	14,329	2,120	16,449
1971 ...	7,423	990	257	2,882	3,300	14,852	2,325	17,177
1972 ...	8,007	1,001	271	3,027	3,640	15,946	2,628	18,574
1973 ...	8,572	1,025	317	3,418	3,948	17,280	3,033	20,313
1974 ...	8,885	991	375	3,642	4,208	18,101	3,351	21,452
1975 ...	9,192	946	426	3,763	4,544	18,871	3,665	22,536
1976 ...	9,593	976	458	4,148	5,017	20,192	4,419	24,611
1977 ...	10,196	932	495	4,309	5,263	21,195	5,267	26,462
1978 ...	11,108	916	533	4,520	5,674	22,751	5,863	28,614
1979 ...	11,766	913	554	5,473	6,131	24,837	7,548	32,385
1980 ...	12,884	908	592	6,678	6,785	27,847	10,195	38,042

Note: Figures represent benefit payments under original policy contracts, including benefits that are left with the companies for future payment under supplementary contracts, but excluding payments from existing supplementary contracts.

Source: American Council of Life Insurance.

Reprinted with permission from 1981 Life Insurance Fact Book, American Council of Life Insurance, Washington, DC 20006.

Life Insurance and Annuity Benefit Payments

In the United States by State 1980 *(000 Omitted)*

State	Death Payments	Matured Endowments	Annuity Payments	Disability Payments	Surrender Values	Policy and Contract Dividends	Total
Alabama	$ 218,700	$ 9,000	$ 69,100	$ 8,400	$ 88,500	$ 91,500	$ 485,200
Alaska	21,200	600	9,200	500	7,300	8,900	47,700
Arizona	136,100	8,400	127,300	6,800	79,300	84,600	442,500
Arkansas	83,600	5,000	39,300	5,300	40,000	45,500	218,700
California	1,188,600	69,000	1,286,500	58,200	637,700	684,000	3,924,000
Colorado	153,700	8,800	88,500	5,500	93,500	108,800	458,800
Connecticut	220,300	18,000	243,200	8,400	141,100	148,900	779,900
Delaware	51,000	3,200	21,700	2,400	18,200	25,200	121,700
D. C.	69,700	3,300	36,200	2,000	18,500	24,500	154,200
Florida	542,300	40,000	522,900	27,200	330,600	306,200	1,769,200
Georgia	316,400	14,500	93,400	14,600	156,600	142,200	737,700
Hawaii	47,700	4,100	56,300	2,400	27,500	40,800	178,800
Idaho	36,700	2,600	26,100	1,500	22,800	27,500	117,200
Illinois	778,800	64,000	490,700	32,200	390,900	542,200	2,298,800
Indiana	310,800	24,400	194,200	15,800	155,800	196,800	897,800
Iowa	157,700	15,700	130,500	12,200	87,000	142,000	545,100
Kansas	127,800	10,200	76,500	7,700	66,100	89,700	378,000
Kentucky	159,600	12,000	65,700	7,300	68,000	85,700	398,300
Louisiana	225,700	9,900	89,600	10,000	84,400	108,500	528,100
Maine	52,700	6,800	37,100	2,500	35,800	43,500	178,400
Maryland	262,700	19,400	152,300	7,600	119,400	147,600	709,000
Massachusetts	312,000	26,800	336,500	10,700	193,900	217,900	1,097,800
Michigan	590,000	38,900	357,300	38,800	264,700	290,100	1,579,800
Minnesota	190,600	16,300	163,700	9,000	116,500	165,600	661,700
Mississippi	89,500	4,000	22,600	4,200	39,600	45,400	205,300
Missouri	270,200	20,000	154,500	12,300	132,500	163,000	752,500
Montana	37,300	2,800	21,600	1,200	20,500	23,700	107,100
Nebraska	84,800	7,500	65,100	3,300	49,200	78,100	288,000
Nevada	45,000	1,600	24,100	1,100	18,200	19,300	109,300
New Hampshire	43,000	5,400	34,900	1,600	27,600	33,900	146,400
New Jersey	565,000	42,800	479,100	24,800	309,200	334,400	1,755,300
New Mexico	58,000	2,700	36,700	2,100	26,000	30,400	155,900
New York	1,157,900	88,500	826,700	55,100	659,000	850,500	3,637,700
North Carolina	291,300	17,900	128,700	10,300	142,100	148,800	739,100
North Dakota	33,100	2,500	15,100	1,100	18,900	20,700	91,400
Ohio	708,200	56,700	538,100	36,700	357,300	424,000	2,121,000
Oklahoma	155,500	8,300	91,200	6,300	68,600	83,900	413,800
Oregon	121,800	9,300	115,100	5,300	75,400	78,600	405,500
Pennsylvania	767,300	75,600	513,700	38,500	396,800	468,600	2,260,500
Rhode Island	58,900	4,500	47,300	1,900	36,400	41,100	190,100
South Carolina	157,600	8,600	51,900	6,500	69,100	61,600	355,300
South Dakota	31,400	2,500	14,100	1,400	16,900	23,900	90,200
Tennessee	230,700	11,600	118,400	11,600	118,400	122,100	612,800
Texas	786,900	33,100	582,900	28,300	366,100	321,700	2,119,000
Utah	57,300	3,800	35,400	3,000	35,700	35,400	170,600
Vermont	23,000	2,800	27,200	1,100	15,600	18,100	87,800
Virginia	308,100	19,300	149,800	9,500	137,700	141,300	765,700
Washington	187,500	12,200	165,200	9,100	109,800	128,500	612,300
West Virginia	99,200	8,000	74,000	7,600	31,900	50,100	270,800
Wisconsin	240,200	23,700	184,400	10,600	145,100	206,000	810,000
Wyoming	21,300	1,500	11,900	600	10,400	14,600	60,300
Total U. S.	$12,884,400	$908,100	$9,243,500	$592,100	$6,678,100	$7,735,900	$38,042,100

Note: annuity dividends in this table are included with policy dividends rather than with annuity payments.

Source: American Council of Life Insurance.

Payments to Beneficiaries

The main reason people buy life insurance is to protect their dependents against financial hardship when the policyholder dies. The extent to which American families depend upon life insurance to provide this economic protection was documented in a survey of widows several years ago, which showed that life insurance of some type was owned by 92% of the husbands. Individually purchased policies bought from legal reserve companies were owned by 7 out of 10 husbands.

Nationally, the growth in the level of life insurance ownership has been the primary reason for the almost uninterrupted rise in life insurance death payments over the years, despite a generally downward trend in death rates among life insurance policyholders, as evidenced by a decline in recent years in the number of death claims.

During 1980, life insurance companies paid $12.9 billion to beneficiaries of policyholders who died. Of this total, ordinary life insurance policies accounted for 47.3% of the payments and provided $6.1 billion. Group life insurance payments to beneficiaries totaled $5.7 billion. Group life insurance has grown as a proportion of total death payments, accounting for 44.0% of death payments in 1980, compared to 41.4% in 1975. Payments to beneficiaries from industrial life insurance came to some $493 million in 1980. Benefits paid under short-term individual and group credit life insurance policies (life insurance on loans of 10 years' or less duration) were $626 million in 1980.

The largest amount of death payments in 1980 by state was made in California—$1,189 million. New York ranked second with $1,158 million.

Relative Growth in Average Size Life Insurance Death Benefit Payments in the United States

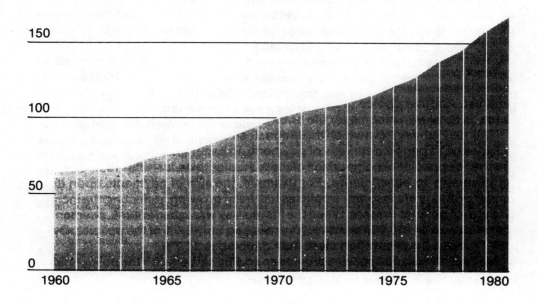

200 Index   1970 = 100

Payments to Life Insurance Beneficiaries in the United States

(No. in Thousands, Amount in Millions)

Year	Ordinary No.	Ordinary Amount	Group No.	Group Amount	Industrial No.	Industrial Amount	Credit* No.	Credit* Amount	Total No.	Total Amount
1940	267	$ 729	50	$ 104	707	$162	–	–	1,024	$ 995
1945	370	897	92	171	856	212	–	–	1,318	1,280
1950	403	1,090	133	283	843	217	–	–	1,379	1,590
1955	489	1,380	243	591	929	270	–	–	1,661	2,241
1960	630	1,904	394	1,115	1,014	327	–	–	2,038	3,346
1961	649	2,001	481	1,246	1,010	334	–	–	2,140	3,581
1962	684	2,138	535	1,382	1,045	358	–	–	2,264	3,878
1963	730	2,311	580	1,521	1,074	377	–	–	2,384	4,209
1964	763	2,485	608	1,664	1,057	385	–	–	2,428	4,534
1965	784	2,604	636	1,824	1,082	403	–	–	2,502	4,831
1966	815	2,750	683	2,058	1,079	410	–	–	2,577	5,218
1967	832	2,961	721	2,288	1,060	416	–	–	2,613	5,665
1968	930	3,210	746	2,578	1,039	421	–	–	2,715	6,209
1969	955	3,424	769	2,898	1,025	436	–	–	2,749	6,758
1970	960	3,545	767	3,027	1,014	445	–	–	2,741	7,017
1971	987	3,699	761	3,267	1,017	457	–	–	2,765	7,423
1972	1,036	4,004	810	3,537	1,040	466	–	–	2,886	8,007
1973	1,057	4,222	541	3,377	1,018	477	398	$496	3,014	8,572
1974	1,068	4,340	590	3,580	974	472	377	493	3,009	8,885
1975	1,076	4,439	591	3,807	922	462	337	484	2,926	9,192
1976	1,090	4,635	580	3,991	933	475	322	492	2,925	9,593
1977	1,081	4,879	571	4,334	911	475	307	508	2,870	10,196
1978	1,123	5,312	592	4,738	928	488	318	570	2,961	11,108
1979	1,103	5,548	601	5,127	881	480	309	611	2,894	11,766
1980	1,172	6,094	637	5,671	873	493	285	626	2,967	12,884

*Prior to 1973 death payments under Credit Life Insurance are included with Ordinary and Group.
Source: American Council of Life Insurance.

Analyses of death payments indicate that members of policyholders' immediate families are the beneficiaries of most of the proceeds from all types of life insurance. Most other payments go to relatives outside the immediate family, with smaller proportions going to estates and trusts, business firms and partners, and to educational, charitable and other institutions.

The most recent study of benefit payments showed that in April 1977, 25% of all death payments from ordinary life insurance were on the lives of policyholders under the age of 50, 57% were on policyholders aged 50 to 74, and 18% were on the lives of persons 75 years old or older.

Most payments to beneficiaries are taken in a lump sum. However, some beneficiaries elect to leave the proceeds with the insurance companies at interest. Another choice of settlement, under both group and ordinary insurance, is to take an income for life or for a specified period.

The 1977 survey from which these conclusions are drawn is the most recent in a series of 11 periodic surveys of payments to beneficiaries under ordinary life insurance policies. A comparison of these studies reveals shifts in some aspects of payments to beneficiaries. For example, the size of payments upon death under ordinary life insurance policies has been growing, reflecting the increasing size of policies in force. When the first survey was taken in 1948, payments to beneficiaries of $10,000 or more were made on only 5.6% of the policies. By the 1977 survey, the proportion more than doubled to 11.7%.

Many life insurance policies provide an additional benefit if the policyholder's death is accidental. During 1980, life insurance companies' payments under accidental death clauses totaled $280 million.

Payments to Life Insurance Beneficiaries In the United States by State 1980

State	Ordinary* No.	Ordinary* Amount (000 Omitted)	Group** No.	Group** Amount (000 Omitted)	Industrial No.	Industrial Amount (000 Omitted)	Total No.	Total Amount (000 Omitted)
Alabama	14,400	$ 96,000	15,500	$ 96,800	62,500	$25,900	92,400	$ 218,700
Alaska	600	9,200	1,500	12,000	—	—	2,100	21,200
Arizona	13,000	78,300	9,000	56,000	2,800	1,800	24,800	136,100
Arkansas	7,900	43,600	5,500	37,800	3,900	2,200	17,300	83,600
California	82,800	566,400	87,900	600,900	30,900	21,300	201,600	1,188,600
Colorado	11,800	76,900	10,900	74,300	3,500	2,500	26,200	153,700
Connecticut	21,300	95,600	15,600	120,700	6,600	4,000	43,500	220,300
Delaware	3,300	20,900	3,100	28,300	3,400	1,800	9,800	51,000
D. C.	2,800	17,100	7,000	49,900	5,100	2,700	14,900	69,700
Florida	58,000	309,800	30,600	201,200	57,600	31,300	146,200	542,300
Georgia	27,300	145,300	20,900	143,500	52,400	27,600	100,600	316,400
Hawaii	2,600	23,700	4,000	23,900	100	100	6,700	47, 00
Idaho	3,200	19,200	3,100	17,300	200	200	6,500	36,700
Illinois	77,600	386,200	55,200	361,400	47,300	31,200	180,100	778,800
Indiana	29,800	138,600	22,000	157,700	24,600	14,500	76,400	310,800
Iowa	18,200	91,000	10,600	64,300	3,500	2,400	32,300	157,700
Kansas	13,800	73,300	8,100	51,700	4,300	2,800	26,200	127,800
Kentucky	18,100	75,600	10,700	74,000	20,200	10,000	49,000	159,600
Louisiana	15,900	102,000	14,400	104,800	38,300	18,900	68,600	225,700
Maine	5,800	28,100	4,600	23,500	2,000	1,100	12,400	52,700
Maryland	20,900	111,200	19,500	139,200	23,800	12,300	64,200	262,700
Massachusetts	42,600	147,000	23,200	156,000	18,700	9,000	84,500	312,000
Michigan	42,300	202,700	48,600	370,800	25,400	16,500	116,300	590,000
Minnesota	19,600	93,200	16,600	94,300	4,700	3,100	40,900	190,600
Mississippi	6,700	44,700	6,900	41,300	6,900	3,500	20,500	89,500
Missouri	32,100	130,700	20,000	128,100	19,800	11,400	71,900	270,200
Montana	3,200	21,100	2,800	16,000	300	200	6,300	37,300
Nebraska	9,900	52,800	4,800	30,900	1,700	1,100	16,400	84,800
Nevada	2,200	15,800	4,400	29,000	300	200	6,900	45,000
New Hampshire	5,000	21,400	3,300	20,500	2,200	1,100	10,500	43,000
New Jersey	53,100	251,700	32,500	292,400	33,400	20,900	119,000	565,000
New Mexico	3,900	29,200	4,300	28,100	1,300	700	9,500	58,000
New York	114,500	568,900	72,700	556,800	50,100	32,200	237,300	1,157,900
North Carolina	28,500	145,900	20,300	128,600	31,400	16,800	80,200	291,300
North Dakota	3,200	20,400	2,000	12,600	100	100	5,300	33,100
Ohio	65,100	316,300	52,100	359,000	53,100	32,900	170,300	708,200
Oklahoma	13,200	86,300	8,900	66,600	4,400	2,600	26,500	155,500
Oregon	8,900	54,300	10,000	66,300	1,600	1,200	20,500	121,800
Pennsylvania	93,200	353,900	57,200	367,400	77,100	46,000	227,500	767,300
Rhode Island	9,100	30,600	4,400	26,500	3,900	1,800	17,400	58,900
South Carolina	18,500	73,700	11,100	68,300	27,200	15,600	56,800	157,600
South Dakota	3,700	19,600	2,200	11,700	100	100	6,000	31,400
Tennessee	19,700	106,500	18,000	110,500	28,400	13,700	66,100	230,700
Texas	59,300	393,500	50,700	374,300	36,500	19,100	146,500	786,900
Utah	4,500	28,000	5,100	28,600	1,000	700	10,600	57,300
Vermont	2,700	12,200	1,800	10,400	900	400	5,400	23,000
Virginia	22,100	126,200	23,100	165,800	30,300	16,100	75,500	308,100
Washington	13,100	89,200	15,200	96,800	2,200	1,500	30,500	187,500
West Virginia	7,900	41,800	8,200	53,000	7,700	4,400	23,800	99,200
Wisconsin	25,500	123,900	18,000	110,300	9,500	6,000	53,000	240,200
Wyoming	1,800	10,300	1,600	10,900	100	100	3,500	21,300
Total U. S.	1,184,200	$6,119,800	909,700	$6,271,000	873,300	$493,600	2,967,200	$12,884,400

*Includes $26 million in payments to beneficiaries under individual credit life insurance policies on loans of 10 years' or less duration.

**Includes $600 million in payments to beneficiaries under group credit life insurance on loans of 10 years' or less duration.

Source: American Council of Life Insurance.

Analysis of Payments to Beneficiaries Under Ordinary Life Insurance in the United States

	Percent of Policies			Percent of Amount		
	May 1969	May 1973	April 1977	May 1969	May 1973	April 1977
SEX OF INSURED						
Male	78.8	77.0	75.4	91.1	89.2	88.6
Female	21.2	23.0	24.6	8.9	10.8	11.4
Total	100.0	100.0	100.0	100.0	100.0	100.0
AGE OF INSURED AT DEATH						
Under 25	4.0	3.4	3.0	4.1	3.4	3.2
25-34	2.0	2.5	2.5	4.2	5.5	6.0
35-44	4.7	4.3	3.7	8.4	9.2	8.7
45-54	12.2	11.8	10.5	18.7	18.2	17.5
55-64	24.4	23.3	21.7	25.5	24.5	25.1
65-74	26.9	27.2	28.0	19.8	21.7	21.4
75 or Older	25.8	27.5	30.6	19.3	17.5	18.1
Total	100.0	100.0	100.0	100.0	100.0	100.0
RELATIONSHIP OF BENEFICIARY TO INSURED						
Husband	8.2	8.6	9.1	3.2	3.9	4.4
Wife	54.1	51.5	52.0	57.9	54.1	58.2
Child or Children	16.1	17.7	18.0	9.5	11.0	10.6
Other Relatives	12.0	11.6	10.9	9.4	7.8	8.3
Estate or Trust	5.9	6.9	6.3	9.7	9.7	9.0
Institution	.6	.6	.6	1.4	1.7	1.4
All Other	3.1	3.1	3.1	8.9	11.8	8.1
Total	100.0	100.0	100.0	100.0	100.0	100.0
DURATION OF POLICY WHEN IT BECAME A CLAIM						
Less Than 1 Year	1.8	1.9	1.5	3.4	4.2	3.8
1 to 5 Years	7.4	7.0	6.2	13.6	14.2	15.2
5 to 10 Years	9.7	9.0	8.5	14.7	15.2	16.2
10 to 20 Years	18.2	20.1	21.1	22.4	23.2	24.1
20 to 30 Years	20.3	17.0	16.6	16.6	15.3	15.5
30 Years or More	42.6	45.0	46.1	29.3	27.9	25.2
Total	100.0	100.0	100.0	100.0	100.0	100.0
SEX OF BENEFICIARY						
Male	19.3	20.3	19.4	12.2	12.1	11.4
Female	68.7	67.3	66.7	66.3	65.1	67.6
Both Sexes Represented ..	4.4	4.6	6.0	4.6	6.2	6.0
All Other	7.6	7.8	7.9	16.9	16.6	15.0
Total	100.0	100.0	100.0	100.0	100.0	100.0
METHOD OF PAYING PROCEEDS						
Lump Sum	94.5	95.8	97.2	89.7	93.0	93.9
Life Income	1.0	.8	.3	1.6	1.0	.5
Annuity Certain	1.8	1.1	.9	3.5	2.0	1.3
Held at Interest	2.2	1.8	1.4	4.4	3.3	4.0
All Other	.5	.5	.2	.8	.7	.3
Total	100.0	100.0	100.0	100.0	100.0	100.0

Note: Figures exclude individual credit life insurance on loans of 10 years' or less duration.

Source: American Council of Life Insurance.

LIFE EXPECTANCY

The average length of a person's life in the United States has increased by more than 50% during this century.

Most of the improvement in life expectancy took place during the first half of the century. Little change has occurred since the mid-1950s. Between 1900 and 1955, life expectancy increased by 22.3 years, but since 1955, it has increased by only 4.2 years to 73.8 years in 1979 (the latest year for which data are available).

But while this century's advances in medicine, public health and safety have added to people's lives, the benefits have not been distributed equally. By far the largest increase in life expectancy has been among the newborn as a result of sharp reductions in mortality among infants and young children. Increases in life expectancy have been progressively smaller at older ages, and smaller for men than for women at all ages.

The measure of life expectancy results from the calculation of the average number of years of life that remain to a group of persons now at the same age, based on a particular mortality table. The measurement refers to the entire group and cannot be taken to indicate how long a particular individual may expect to live.

The gain in life expectancy for women since the turn of the century has been greater than for men at nearly all ages. Female life expectancy at birth has increased by 29.5 years since 1900, while male life expectancy has increased by 23.6 years. The difference in the average length of life between men and women has increased. Life expectancy at age 40 was about 1.4 years longer for a woman than for a man at the turn of the century; it is now 7.9 years longer.

Expectation of Life
At Birth in the United States (Years)

Year	White			All Other			Total		
	Male	Female	Total	Male	Female	Total	Male	Female	Total
1900	46.6	48.7	47.6	32.5	33.5	33.0	46.3	48.3	47.3
1910	48.6	52.0	50.3	33.8	37.5	35.6	48.4	51.8	50.0
1920	54.4	55.6	54.9	45.5	45.2	45.3	53.6	54.6	54.1
1930	59.7	63.5	61.4	47.3	49.2	48.1	58.1	61.6	59.7
1940	62.1	66.6	64.2	51.5	54.9	53.1	60.8	65.2	62.9
1950	66.5	72.2	69.1	59.1	62.9	60.8	65.6	71.1	68.2
1960	67.4	74.1	70.6	61.1	66.3	63.6	66.6	73.1	69.7
1961	67.8	74.5	71.0	61.9	67.0	64.4	67.0	73.6	70.2
1962	67.6	74.4	70.9	61.5	66.8	64.1	66.8	73.4	70.0
1963	67.5	74.4	70.8	60.9	66.5	63.6	66.6	73.4	69.9
1964	67.7	74.6	71.0	61.1	67.2	64.1	66.9	73.7	70.2
1965	67.6	74.7	71.0	61.1	67.4	64.1	66.8	73.7	70.2
1966	67.6	74.7	71.0	60.7	67.4	64.0	66.7	73.8	70.1
1967	67.8	75.1	71.3	61.1	68.2	64.6	67.0	74.2	70.5
1968	67.5	74.9	71.1	60.1	67.5	63.7	66.6	74.0	70.2
1969	67.8	75.1	71.3	60.5	68.4	64.3	66.8	74.3	70.4
1970	68.0	75.6	71.7	61.3	69.4	65.3	67.1	74.8	70.9
1971	68.3	75.8	72.0	61.6	69.7	65.6	67.4	75.0	71.1
1972	68.3	75.9	72.0	61.5	69.9	65.6	67.4	75.1	71.1
1973	68.4	76.1	72.2	61.9	70.1	65.9	67.6	75.3	71.3
1974	68.9	76.6	72.7	62.9	71.2	67.0	68.2	75.9	71.9
1975	69.4	77.2	73.2	63.6	72.3	67.9	68.7	76.5	72.5
1976	69.7	77.3	73.5	64.1	72.6	68.3	69.0	76.7	72.8
1977	70.0	77.7	73.8	64.6	73.1	68.8	69.3	77.1	73.2
1978	70.2	77.8	74.0	65.0	73.6	69.2	69.5	77.2	73.3
1979*	70.6	78.3	74.4	65.5	74.5	69.9	69.9	77.8	73.8

*Provisional data.

Source: National Center for Health Statistics, U.S. Department of Health and Human Services.

In contrast, the difference in life expectancy between white and nonwhite Americans has been greatly reduced in this century. Generally, the gain for nonwhite males has exceeded that for white males at all ages. Nonwhite females showed the greatest gains at the younger and older ages. For white females, life expectancy improved most between the ages of about 45 and 65.

In 1979, the difference in life expectancy between white and nonwhite persons at birth was 3.8 years for females and 5.1 years for males, and this difference decreased with age.

Expectation of Life at Various Ages In the United States 1979

	White			All Other			Total		
Age	Male	Female	Total	Male	Female	Total	Male	Female	Total
0	70.6	78.3	74.4	65.5	74.5	69.9	69.9	77.8	73.8
1	70.5	78.1	74.3	66.0	74.9	70.4	69.9	77.6	73.8
5	66.6	74.2	70.4	62.2	71.1	66.6	66.1	73.8	69.9
10	61.8	69.3	65.5	57.4	66.2	61.8	61.2	68.9	65.0
15	56.9	64.4	60.6	52.5	61.3	56.9	56.4	64.0	60.2
20	52.3	59.6	55.9	47.8	56.4	52.1	51.8	59.1	55.5
25	47.8	54.7	51.3	43.5	51.7	47.6	47.3	54.3	50.8
30	43.2	49.9	46.6	39.3	47.0	43.1	42.8	49.5	46.2
35	38.6	45.0	41.8	35.1	42.3	38.7	38.2	44.7	41.5
40	34.0	40.3	37.2	31.0	37.7	34.4	33.6	39.9	36.8
45	29.5	35.6	32.6	27.1	33.3	30.2	29.2	35.3	32.3
50	25.2	31.1	28.2	23.3	29.2	26.2	25.0	30.8	28.0
55	21.2	26.8	24.1	20.0	25.4	22.7	21.1	26.6	23.9
60	17.5	22.6	20.2	17.1	21.7	19.5	17.5	22.5	20.1
65	14.3	18.7	16.7	14.6	18.5	16.6	14.3	18.7	16.7
70	11.4	15.1	13.4	12.0	15.2	13.7	11.4	15.1	13.5
75	8.9	11.8	10.6	10.1	12.8	11.6	9.0	11.8	10.6
80	7.0	9.1	8.3	9.7	11.8	11.0	7.2	9.3	8.5
85 and Over ..	5.6	7.1	6.6	8.9	10.7	10.0	5.9	7.3	6.8

Note: Data are provisional.

Source: National Center for Health Statistics, U.S. Department of Health and Human Services.

Expectation of Life at Various Ages In the United States 1979

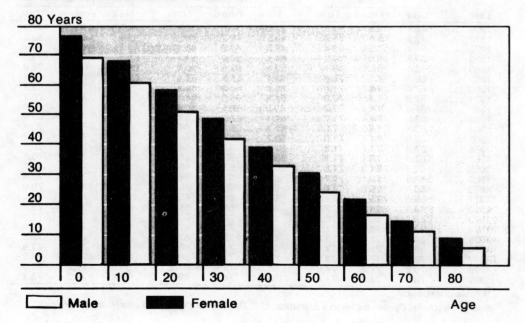

CAUSES OF DEATH

In recent decades, the overall death rate of the U.S. population has decreased due to medical developments, improvements in public health and job safety, and rising standards of living. The crude death rate in 1980 rose slightly over 1979, to 8.9 per 1,000 population, up from 8.7 in 1979.

Medical improvements and environmental changes have been more effective in reducing deaths from some causes than others. There has been increasing success in identifying and controlling contagious diseases, but there has been less success in controlling deaths from accidental causes.

In 1980, the deaths of 7 out of 10 ordinary life insurance policyholders with U.S. life companies were due to two principal causes: cardiovascular-renal diseases and cancer.

Since the 1950s, deaths attributable to cardiovascular-renal diseases have decreased slightly, whereas cancer has been an increasing cause of death. These trends have followed those of the general population of the United States.

The percentage of deaths due to cardiovascular-renal diseases declined to 47.9% of all deaths in 1980. Deaths due to ischemic heart disease and chronic disease of endocardium and other myocardial insufficiencies were 29.2% in 1980. Cerebrovascular diseases also declined, to 5.6%. The decline in these latter causes of death in recent years has accounted for most of the decline in the percentage of deaths due to cardiovascular-renal disease. Heart disease has decreased significantly in recent years and has affected the overall declining death rate.

The proportion of deaths due to cancer continued to increase; 23.2% of policyholder deaths were attributed to this cause.

Motor vehicle accidents are another major cause of death. Between 1965 and 1973, motor vehicle deaths annually accounted for about 3.5% of policyholder deaths. In 1974 motor vehicle accidents accounted for 3.0% of policyholder deaths, but in 1975 the percentage began rising, to 3.3% in 1978, 1979 and 1980.

Bronchitis and other respiratory diseases accounted for 3.2% of policyholder deaths. Pneumonia and influenza combined were responsible for 2.6% of deaths, while cirrhosis of the liver represented 1.1%.

The percentage of deaths attributable to accidents, other than those involving motor vehicles, amounted to 2.6% of policyholder deaths in 1980. Two other external causes of death, suicide and homicide, represented 2.5% of deaths.

Over the years, the nation's life insurance companies have made significant contributions to basic research relating to causes of death. The recent focus of individual company contributions and research grants has been in the areas of delivery of health care services and preventive medicine. The Insurance Medical Scientist Scholarship Fund, supported by insurance company contributions, provides scholarships for students planning careers in medical research and teaching.

Distribution of Ordinary
Policyholder Deaths by Cause U.S. Life Insurance Companies

Cause of Death	1945	1950	1955	1960	1965	1970
NATURAL CAUSES						
Cardiovascular-renal Disease	49.3%	57.0%	57.2%	55.7%	53.9%	52.1%
Cancer	14.8	17.3	18.6	18.7	19.2	20.1
Pneumonia and Influenza	3.1	1.9	2.0	3.2	3.1	3.3
Tuberculosis (all forms)	2.8	1.3	.5	.3	.2	.1
Diabetes	1.5	1.3	.9	1.0	1.1	1.0
Other Diseases*	18.2	12.0	12.3	13.1	13.6	14.5
Total Natural Causes	89.7	90.8	91.5	92.0	91.1	91.1
EXTERNAL CAUSES						
Motor Vehicle Accidents	2.3	3.1	3.1	2.9	3.6	3.5
Other Accidents	5.9	3.6	3.2	3.1	3.2	3.1
Suicide	1.9	2.2	2.0	1.8	1.8	1.7
Homicide	.2	.3	.2	.2	.3	.6
Total External Causes	10.3	9.2	8.5	8.0	8.9	8.9
Total All Causes	100.0%	100.0%	100.0%	100.0%	100.0%	100.0%

Cause of Death	1975	1976	1977	1978	1979	1980
NATURAL CAUSES						
Cardiovascular-renal Disease						
Diseases of the Heart						
and Hypertension						
Ischemic Heart Disease and Other						
Myocardial Insufficiencies	32.3%	32.0%	31.6%	31.7%	30.7%	29.2%
Hypertensive Heart Disease						
and Hypertension	1.3	1.3	1.2	1.2	1.3	1.5
Other Diseases of the Heart	4.6	5.3	5.7	5.4	6.0	7.3
Total Diseases of the Heart	38.2	38.6	38.5	38.3	38.0	38.0
Cerebrovascular Disease	6.7	6.5	6.4	6.1	6.0	5.6
Arteriosclerosis and Other						
Diseases of Arteries, Arteriolas						
and Capillaries	3.3	2.9	2.9	2.9	2.9	2.9
Other	1.6	1.5	1.5	1.5	1.3	1.4
Total Cardiovascular-renal	49.8	49.5	49.3	48.8	48.2	47.9
Cancer	21.4	21.9	22.3	22.4	23.1	23.2
Pneumonia and Influenza	2.8	2.9	2.6	2.7	2.5	2.6
Diabetes	1.0	1.0	.9	.9	.9	.9
Other Diseases						
Bronchitis and Other						
Respiratory Diseases	2.9	3.0	3.0	3.1	3.1	3.2
Cirrhosis	1.3	1.3	1.2	1.2	1.2	1.1
Other*	12.0	11.8	12.1	12.4	12.4	12.7
Total Other Diseases	16.2	16.1	16.3	16.7	16.7	17.0
Total Natural Causes	91.2	91.4	91.4	91.5	91.4	91.6
EXTERNAL CAUSES						
Motor Vehicle Accidents	3.0	3.1	3.1	3.3	3.3	3.3
Other Accidents	3.1	2.9	2.9	2.7	2.7	2.6
Suicide	1.8	1.8	1.8	1.7	1.7	1.6
Homicide	.9	.8	.8	.8	.9	.9
Total External Causes	8.8	8.6	8.6	8.5	8.6	8.4
Total All Causes	100.0%	100.0%	100.0%	100.0%	100.0%	100.0%

Note: A small number classified as "War Deaths" is included in "Other Diseases" in the data for 1960 and 1965; in other years the category is excluded. If "War Deaths" were included in the 1980 data, this category would be .01% of the resulting distribution.

*Includes those causes not specified.

Source: American Council of Life Insurance.

Death Rate

Mortality among Americans, as measured by the death rate, has decreased in recent years, after remaining at about the same level for more than a decade.

The age-adjusted death rate (technically adjusted for the changing proportion of people at each age in the U.S. population) was 5.9 per thousand in 1979 (the latest year for which data are available), the lowest rate ever recorded. In 1967, the age-adjusted rate was 7.3. From 1967 to 1972 there was a 4.1% drop to 7.0. The drop from 1972 to 1979 was even more significant — a decrease of 15.7%.

The decrease in mortality reflects continuing downtrends for two causes of death: diseases of the heart and cerebrovascular diseases. The age-adjusted mortality rates for these two causes, which accounted for 41.8% of the 1979 age-adjusted mortality rate, have decreased 21.9% from 1972 to 1979, compared to 6.9% from 1967 to 1972.

For 1979 the age-adjusted death rate for the male population was 7.8 per thousand, compared with the female rate of 4.3 per thousand. Similarly, the rate

Age-Adjusted Death Rate in the United States

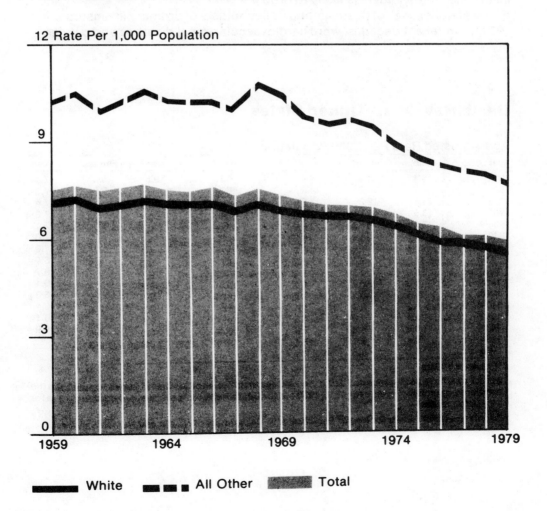

12 Rate Per 1,000 Population

White   All Other   Total

for persons of races other than white was 7.7 per thousand, compared with a rate of 5.6 per thousand for white persons.

During the first half of this century there was a sharp decline in the death rate due to advances in medicine. This decline resulted in a reduction of deaths at young and middle ages, so that many more people now live into their seventies and eighties.

Between 1950 and 1970, however, there was relatively little change in the age-adjusted death rate for the total population. As the seventies began, the death rate began to decline more noticeably, falling from 7.3 per thousand in 1969 to 5.9 per thousand in 1979. During the same period, the death rate for nonwhites declined even more significantly, from 10.2 per thousand to 7.7 per thousand. Since 1969, the overall death rate for women has dropped more significantly than the death rate for men. The rate per thousand for men declined from 9.5 per thousand to 7.8, a decrease of 17.9%; for women the change was from 5.4 per thousand in 1969 to 4.3 per thousand in 1979, a decrease of 20.4%.

Because life insurance policyholders as a group represent a large proportion of the total population, their overall mortality rates are likely to parallel those for the nation as a whole. Even though the actual experience of a particular life company may differ from the general pattern, long-term population mortality trends are a useful indicator of the probable experience of most life companies. If the general death rate in the United States declines, the rate among life insurance policyholders is likely to drop.

The major causes of death among policyholders of ordinary life insurance in 1979, as in recent decades, were cardiovascular-renal diseases and cancer.

Death Rate in the United States

Age-Adjusted Rate Per 1,000 Population

Year	Male	Female	Total	Year	Male	Female	Total
1915	15.4	13.4	14.4	1966	9.5	5.6	7.4
1920	14.7	13.8	14.2	1967	9.4	5.5	7.3
1925	13.8	12.2	13.0	1968	9.7	5.6	7.4
1930	13.5	11.3	12.5	1969	9.5	5.4	7.3
1935	12.9	10.4	11.6	1970	9.3	5.3	7.1
1940	12.1	9.4	10.8	1971	9.2	5.2	7.0
1945	11.1	8.0	9.5	1972	9.2	5.2	7.0
1950	10.0	6.9	8.4	1973	9.1	5.1	6.9
1955	9.3	6.1	7.7	1974	8.8	4.9	6.7
1960	9.5	5.9	7.6	1975	8.5	4.7	6.4
1961	9.2	5.7	7.4	1976	8.3	4.6	6.3
1962	9.4	5.8	7.5	1977	8.1	4.5	6.1
1963	9.6	5.8	7.6	1978	8.0	4.5	6.1
1964	9.4	5.7	7.4	1979*	7.8	4.3	5.9
1965	9.5	5.6	7.4				

*Provisional data.

Note: Rates have been computed using the 1940 age distribution of the United States population as the standard population. Figures for 1915-1930 are for Death Registration States only; 1935-1979 are for the United States.

Source: National Center for Health Statistics, U.S. Department of Health and Human Services.

Analysis of Workers' Compensation Laws

U.S. Chamber of Commerce

BENEFITS PROVIDED

Since workers' compensation imposes an absolute (but limited) liability upon the employer for employee disabilities caused by the employment, the benefits payable to the injured employee attempt to cover most of the worker's economic loss. This loss includes both loss of earnings and extra expenses associated with the injury.

Specifically, the benefits provided are:

● **Cash benefits,** which include both impairment benefits and disability benefits. The former are paid for certain specific physical impairments, while the latter are available whenever there is an impairment *and* a wage loss.

● **Medical benefits,** which are usually provided without dollar or time limits. In the case of most workplace injuries, only medical benefits are provided since substantial impairment or wage loss is not involved.

● **Rehabilitation benefits,** which include both medical rehabilitation and vocational rehabilitation for those cases involving severe disabilities.

CASH BENEFITS

In considering workers' compensation income or cash benefits—which replace employee loss of income or earning capacity due to occupational injury or disease—*four classifications of disability* are used: (1) temporary total, (2) permanent total, (3) temporary partial, and (4) permanent partial. Permanent partial is divided into "non-scheduled" and "scheduled" disabilities.

Most cases involve *temporary total disability*. That is, the employee—although totally disabled during the period when benefits are payable—is expected to recover and return to employment. *Permanent total disability* generally indicates that the employee is regarded as totally and permanently unable to perform gainful employment.

SURVIVOR BENEFITS FOR FATAL INJURIES: CHART VII

Benefits payable in the event of fatal injuries—comprising more than 14 percent of all total income benefits—are shown in Chart VII. The benefits provided include a burial allowance as well as a proportion of the worker's former weekly wages.

Although death is the ultimate work-related tragedy, the economic loss associated with death cases is often less than that of a permanent total disability. Because of these considerations, death benefits are generally paid to the spouse until remarriage and to the children until a specified age. In addition, some laws provide a maximum benefit total expressed as a maximum period for the payment of benefits.

CHART VII   FATALITIES—INCOME BENEFITS FOR SPOUSE AND CHILDREN   January 1, 1982

JURISDICTION	PERCENT OF WAGES			MAXIMUM WEEKLY PAYMENT		MINIMUM PER WEEK SPOUSE ONLY	TIME LIMIT	AMOUNT LIMIT[1]		MAXIMUM BURIAL ALLOWANCE
	SPOUSE PLUS CHILDREN	SPOUSE ONLY	ONE CHILD ONLY	SPOUSE PLUS CHILDREN	SPOUSE ONLY			SPOUSE PLUS CHILDREN	SPOUSE ONLY	
ALABAMA	66-2/3	50	50	$161.00*	$161.00*	$60.00*	500 weeks [2,6]	$80,500	$80,500	$1,000
ALASKA	66-2/3	66-2/3	66-2/3	942.00*	942.00*	45.00	(2,4,**)			1,000
AMERICAN SAMOA	66-2/3	35	35	70.00	36.75	5.25[8]	(2,4)			1,000
ARIZONA	66-2/3	35	25	203.64	107.00	107.00	(2,4)			1,000
ARKANSAS	66-2/3	35	50	140.00*	140.00*	15.00	(2,4)	(..)	(..)	750
CALIFORNIA	(-)	(-)	(-)	175.00	175.00	(-)	(2)	75,000	75,000	1,500
COLORADO	66-2/3	66-2/3	66-2/3	261.80*	261.80*	65.45*	(2,4)			1,000
CONNECTICUT	66-2/3	66-2/3	66-2/3	310.00*	310.00*	20.00	(2,3,**)			1,500
DELAWARE	80	66-2/3	66-2/3	292.22*	194.81*	64.94*	(2,4)			700**
DISTRICT OF COLUMBIA	66-2/3	50	50	396.78*	396.78*	99.20*	(2,4)			1,000
FLORIDA	66-2/3	50	33-1/3	253.00*	253.00*	20.00[8]	(2,3)	50,000	50,000	1,000
GEORGIA	66-2/3	66-2/3	66-2/3	115.00	115.00	25.00[8]	400 weeks[2,3]	46,000	32,500	750
GUAM	66-2/3	35	35	50.00	29.40	29.40	(2,4)			600
HAWAII	66-2/3	50	40	252.00*	189.00*	63.00*	(2,4)	(..)	(..)	1,500***
IDAHO				145.20*	108.90*	108.90*	500 weeks[2]	72,600	54,450	1,500[7]
ILLINOIS	66-2/3	66-2/3	66-2/3	403.12*	403.12*	151.17*	20 years[2,4,**]	250,000	250,000	1,750
INDIANA	66-2/3	66-2/3	66-2/3	140.00	140.00	50.00[8]	500 weeks[2,4]	70,000	70,000	1,500
IOWA	80% of spendable earnings	80% of spendable earnings	80% of spendable earnings	501.00*	501.00*	(..)	(2,4)			1,000
KANSAS	66-2/3	66-2/3	66-2/3	187.00*	187.00*	25.00	(2,6)	100,000	100,000	2,000
KENTUCKY	75	50	50	190.75*	127.17*	50.87*	(2,4)			1,500[7]
LOUISIANA	65	32-1/2	32-1/2	183.00*	183.00*	55.00*	(2,4)			3,000
MAINE[9]	66-2/3	66-2/3	66-2/3	367.25*	367.25*	25.00	(2,3)			1,000
MARYLAND	66-2/3	66-2/3	66-2/3	267.00*	267.00*	25.00[8]	(2,4)			1,200**
MASSACHUSETTS	80% of spendable earnings	80% of spendable earnings	80% of spendable earnings	(-)	110.00*	110.00*	(2,4,**)	(..)	(..)	2,000
MICHIGAN	80% of spendable earnings	80% of spendable earnings	80% of spendable earnings	307.00*	307.00*	170.00*	500 weeks[2,6,***]	153,500	85,000	1,500
MINNESOTA	66-2/3	50	55	267.00*	267.00*	267.00*	(2,**)			1,000
MISSISSIPPI[9]	66-2/3	35	25	112.00	112.00	25.00	450 weeks[2]	44,100	44,100	1,000
MISSOURI	66-2/3	66-2/3	66-2/3	174.00*	174.00*		(2,4,**)	195,000	195,000	2,000
MONTANA	66-2/3	66-2/3	66-2/3	241.00*	241.00*	120.50*	(2,4)			1,400
NEBRASKA	75	66-2/3	66-2/3	180.00	180.00	49.00[8]	(2,4)			2,000
NEVADA	66-2/3	66-2/3	66-2/3	269.99*	269.99	30.00*	(2,4)			2,500[7]
NEW HAMPSHIRE	66-2/3*	66-2/3*	66-2/3*	234.00**	234.00*	30.00*	(2,***)			1,200
NEW JERSEY	70	50	50	217.00*	217.00*	58.00*	(2,3,**)			2,000
NEW MEXICO	66-2/3	66-2/3	66-2/3	246.44*	246.44*	36.00	600 weeks[2,4]	147,864	147,864	1,500
NEW YORK	66-2/3	66-2/3	66-2/3	215.00	215.00	30.00	(2,4,*)			1,250

¹Amount limits have been computed where not stipulated by law and are shown in italics. Disability payments deducted in all laws, except those of Arizona, Arkansas, California, Delaware, District of Columbia, Florida, Michigan, Mississippi, Missouri, Nevada, New York, North Dakota, Oregon, Washington, West Virginia, Wisconsin, Wyoming, F.E.C.A., and Longshore Act.

²To child until age 18 (16 in Manitoba, Newfoundland, Northwest Territories, Ontario, Saskatchewan, and Yukon; 19 in Alaska and Wyoming; 21 in Michigan and—if in school—New Brunswick). If invalid, for duration of invalidity (for 15 years in Wisconsin; for period decedent would have supported child in Alberta, Newfoundland, Prince Edward Island, and Yukon). If student, to age 21 in Colorado, British Columbia, New Brunswick, Nova Scotia, Newfoundland, Prince Edward Island, Saskatchewan, and C.M.S.C.A.; 22 in Connecticut, Florida, Kentucky, Missouri, Nevada, South Dakota, Tennessee, and Virgin Islands; 23 in D.C., Kansas, Louisiana, Maine, Maryland, Mississippi, New Mexico, New York, Oklahoma, Oregon, Pennsylvania, Rhode Island, South Carolina, Virginia, Washington, F.E.C.A., and Longshore Act; 25 in America Samoa, Arkansas, Delaware, Hawaii, Illinois, Iowa, Minnesota, Montana, Nebraska, New Hampshire, Ohio, Puerto Rico, Texas, West Virginia, and Alberta; no age limit in Alaska (4 years only), Massachusetts, Vermont, Manitoba, Northwest Territories, Ontario, and Quebec.

³To spouse for life; compensation ceases on remarriage.

⁴To spouse for life; 2 years' lump sum upon remarriage (but only if no children in Colorado, Illinois, Indiana, and Iowa) or balance of compensation if less (Indiana, New Mexico, South Carolina, and Saskatchewan).

⁵To spouse for life; 1 year's lump sum upon remarriage.

⁶To spouse for life; cash lump sum on remarriage: Alabama—500 weeks or balance if less; Kansas—100 weeks or balance if less; Michigan—$500 or balance if less; Oregon—$5,000; Washington—$7,500 or 50% of remaining annuity value if less; Manitoba—$3,600; Nova Scotia—$2,443; Prince Edward Island—$1,200; Yukon—$4,902.

⁷Additional allowance for transportation of body; no maximum except: Virginia—$500; Alberta—$700; British Columbia—$423.24 and $423.24 for incidental death expenses; Nova Scotia—$300; Prince Edward Island—$100; Yukon—$198 for 1981; C.M.S.C.A.—$125.

⁸Actual wage if less.

⁹Spouse receives cash lump sum in addition to other benefits: Maine—$1,000; Mississippi—$250; North Dakota—$300 plus $100 per child; Oklahoma—$10,000 plus $2,500 per dependent (maximum $15,000); Washington—$800; British Columbia—$1,058.05; Manitoba—$1,050; New Brunswick—$500; Newfoundland—$1,000; Northwest Territories—$928; Nova Scotia—$1,000; Ontario—$1,200; Prince Edward Island—$500; Quebec—$500; Yukon—$979; C.M.S.C.A.—$750.

¹⁰If no dependents.

Alab. *Maximum is 66-2/3% of SAWW for spouse and children, 50% of SAWW for spouse only. Minimum is 25% of SAWW, actual wage if less.

Alaska *Maximum is 200% of SAWW.
**Spousal benefit reduced by 1/3 as of 5 years after worker's death, by 1/2 as of 8 years, and ceases after 10 years; reductions do not apply if spouse is over 52 or permanently and totally disabled. Limited Social Security offset.

Ark. *Maximum death benefit is $140 effective 3/1/81 and $154 effective 3/1/82.
**Benefits in excess of $75,000 payable from Death and Permanent Disability Bank Fund.

Calif. *Statutory benefit is 66-2/3% of wages, but Appeals Board has authority to award benefits up to the maximum regardless of wage.

Colo. *Maximum is 80% of SAWW; minimum is 25% of maximum.
**Social Security offset.

Conn. *Maximum is 100% of SAWW. Employer-funded cost of living increase payable each October.

Del. *Maximum is 80% of SAWW for spouse and children, 66-2/3% of SAWW for spouse only. Minimum for spouse only is 1/3 of maximum for spouse only.
**Additional burial allowance payable on Board approval.

D.C. Entries for D.C. effective July 27, 1982. Maximum is 100% of SAWW (but no less than $396.78); minimum is 25% of SAWW (but no less than $99.20).

Fla. *Maximum is 100% of SAWW.

Hawaii *Maximum is 100% of SAWW for spouse and children, 75% of SAWW for spouse only. Minimum is 25% of SAWW.
**Maximum amount for persons other than spouse and children is the maximum benefit times 312.
***Includes $500 for cemetery.

Idaho *Death benefit is fixed at 45% of SAWW for spouse plus 5% of SAWW per dependent child up to 3; 30% of SAWW for one child if no dependent spouse.

Ill. *Maximum is 133-1/3% of SAWW; minimum is 50% of SAWW.
**Child under 18 is entitled to at least 6 years' benefits.

Iowa *Maximum is 200% of SAWW, effective 7/1/81.
**Minimum weekly wage is 35% of SAWW (= $87.68); benefits determined by worker's tax status.

Kans. *Maximum is 75% of SAWW, effective 7/1/80.

Ky. *Maximum is 75% of SAWW for spouse and children, 50% of SAWW for spouse only. Minimum is 20% of SAWW.

La. *Maximum is 66-2/3% of SAWW. Minimum is 20% of SAWW, actual wage if less.

Maine *Maximum is 166-2/3% of SAWW.

Md. *Maximum is 100% of SAWW.
**Additional burial allowance payable on Commission approval.

Mass. *Death benefit is fixed at $110 weekly for spouse, plus $6 per child.
**After 400 weeks or $32,000, spouse must prove actual dependence; time and amount limits do not apply to children's benefits.

Mich. *Maximum is 90% of SAWW, minimum is 50% of SAWW.
**500-week limit does not apply to children.

Minn. *Maximum is 100% of SAWW.
**Social Security survivors' benefits offset. 10 years' benefits if no dependent children or after last child ceases to be dependent; 2 years' benefits (or balance if less) if spouse elected to receive benefits weekly rather than in lump sum settlement.

Mo. *Maximum is 66-2/3% of SAWW effective 8/13/81.
**4 years' benefits payable to child on active duty in armed forces at age 18 who enrolls in school prior to age 23.

Mont. *Maximum is 100% of SAWW; minimum is 50% of SAWW, actual wage if less.

Nev. *Maximum is 100% of SAWW.

N.H. *If wage is less than $30, benefit is actual wage; if wage $30-$35, benefit is $30; if wage $35-$40, benefit is $32; benefit increases in $3 increments per $5 increase in wage, up to $135; if wage $135-138, benefit is $92; if wage is over $138, benefit is 66-2/3% of wage up to maximum.
**Maximum is 100% of SAWW.
***After 400 weeks, spousal benefits cease unless spouse is permanently and totally disabled. Spousal benefits are payable for 400 weeks and thereafter while a child is eligible for benefits (no time limit if spouse is totally disabled). On remarriage, the unpaid balance otherwise payable for dependent children is payable to parent or guardian for the children's benefit.

N.J. *Maximum is 75% of SAWW; minimum is 20% of SAWW.
**After 450 weeks, spouse's earnings are deducted.

N.M. *Maximum is 100% of SAWW.

N.Y. *Social Security offset.

FATALITIES—INCOME BENEFITS FOR SPOUSE AND CHILDREN □ January 1, 1982 (continued)

JURISDICTION	PERCENT OF WAGES			MAXIMUM WEEKLY PAYMENT		MINIMUM PER WEEK SPOUSE ONLY	TIME LIMIT	AMOUNT LIMIT[1]		MAXIMUM BURIAL ALLOWANCE
	SPOUSE PLUS CHILDREN	SPOUSE ONLY	ONE CHILD ONLY	SPOUSE PLUS CHILDREN	SPOUSE ONLY			SPOUSE PLUS CHILDREN	SPOUSE ONLY	
NORTH CAROLINA	66-2/3	66-2/3	66-2/3	$228.00*	$228.00*	$30.00	(2,3,**)			$1,000
NORTH DAKOTA[9]	66-2/3	66-2/3	66-2/3	(-)	100.00	10.00	(2,4)			2,000
OHIO[9]	66-2/3	66-2/3	66-2/3	298.00*	298.00*	149.00*	(2,4)			1,200
OKLAHOMA[9]	75	50	35	175.00*	175.00*	30.00[8]	(2,4)			1,000[11]
OREGON				286.88*	143.44*	143.44*	(2,6,**)			3,000
PENNSYLVANIA	66-2/3	51	32	284.00*	284.00*	142.00*	(2,4)			1,500
PUERTO RICO	85	50	60	28.85*	23.08*	11.54*	(2,4,**)			300[11]
RHODE ISLAND	80	66-2/3	66-2/3	285.60*	238.00*	30.00	(2,3)			1,800
SOUTH CAROLINA	66-2/3	66-2/3	66-2/3	235.00*	235.00*	25.00	500 weeks[2,4]	117,500	117,500	400
SOUTH DAKOTA	66-2/3	66-2/3	66-2/3	(-)	208.00*	104.00*	(2,4)			2,000[7]
TENNESSEE	66-2/3	50	50	126.00	126.00	15.00	(2,3)			1,250*
TEXAS	66-2/3	66-2/3	66-2/3	154.00	154.00	25.00	(2,4)	50,400	50,400	1,250
UTAH	66-2/3*	66-2/3	66-2/3	218.00*	218.00*	45.00[8]	(2,**)			1,000
VERMONT	76-2/3	66-2/3	71-2/3	225.00*	225.00*	112.50*	(2,**)			1,000
VIRGIN ISLANDS	66-2/3	66-2/3		(-)	(-)	(-)	(2)	16,500*	16,500*	800[11]
VIRGINIA	66-2/3	66-2/3	66-2/3	231.00*	231.00*	57.75*	500 weeks[2,**]	115,500	115,500	2,000[7]
WASHINGTON[9]	70	60	35	223.11*	223.11*	42.69	(2,6,**)			1,000
WEST VIRGINIA	66-2/3	66-2/3	66-2/3	276.29*	276.29*	92.10*	(2,3)			1,500
WISCONSIN	66-2/3	66-2/3	66-2/3	269.00*	269.00*	30.00	(-,**)	80,700***	80,700***	1,000
WYOMING				(-)	277.12*	277.12*	(-)	(-)	(-)	1,100**
F.E.C.A.	75*	50	40	829.33	829.33	90.20	(2,4,**)			800[7,***]
LONGSHORE ACT	66-2/3	50	50	(-)	(-)	165.57*	(2,4)			1,000
ALBERTA[10]	75	75		(-)	(-)	(-)	5 years[2]			1,200[7]
BRITISH COLUMBIA[10]				(-)	(-)	(-)	(2,4)			1,269.66[7]
MANITOBA[10]	75	75	30	331.73*	331.73*	109.62*	(2,6)			300[7,***]
NEW BRUNSWICK[10]				(-)	83.08*	83.08*	(2,5)			600[7]
NEWFOUNDLAND[10]				(-)	94.62*	94.62*	(2)			1,000[7]
NORTHWEST TERRITORIES[10]				(-)	147.23*	147.23*	(2,5)			928[7]
NOVA SCOTIA[10]	(-)	(-)		(-)	109.85*	109.85*	(2,6)			750[7]
ONTARIO[10]				(-)	113.23*	113.23*	(2,4)			1,200[7]
PRINCE EDWARD ISLAND[10]	(-)	(-)		(-)	69.23*	69.23*	(2,6)			500[7]
QUEBEC[10]	72	49-1/2 (weighted net income)	49-1/2	277.65*	277.65*	76.89*	(2,3,**)			600[7]
SASKATCHEWAN	75	75		375.00	375.00	133.86	5 years[2,4]			1,000[7]
YUKON TERRITORY[10]		75		(-)	89.52*	89.52*	(2,6)			1,121[7,*]
CANADIAN MERCHANT SEAMEN'S ACT[10]				216.35*	83.08*	83.08[8]	(2,4)			700[7]

N.C. *Maximum is 100% of SAWW.
**After 400 weeks, spouse must be dependent or disabled.

N.D. *Maximum $100 plus $7 per dependent child under 18.

Ohio *Maximum is 100% of SAWW; minimum is 50% of SAWW.

Okla. *Maximum is 66-2/3% of SAWW.

Oregon *Monthly spousal benefit is fixed at 50% of SAWW times 4.35 (= $623.96 for 1981-82); an additional $150 each is payable monthly for the first and second children, plus $50 monthly per additional child, up to monthly maximum. Maximum is 100% of SAWW times 4.35 (= $1,247.93 for 1981-82).
**Child's benefit payable to age 19 if in high school.

Pa. *Maximum is 100% of SAWW; minimum is 50% of SAWW.

P.R. *Maximum for spouse and children is $125 monthly; for spouse only, $100 monthly. Minimum is $50 monthly. Maximum advance payment is $500 to widow plus $50 per child, up to $1,100 total.
**540-week limit inapplicable to spouse and children.

R.I. *Maximum is 100% of SAWW plus $6 per dependent child, up to 80% of pre-injury wages.

S.C. *Maximum is 100% of SAWW.

S.D. *Maximum is 100% of SAWW; minimum is 50% of SAWW, actual wage if less. Additional $50 monthly is payable for each dependent child.

Tenn. *Employer must pay $10,000 lump sum into estate if worker had no dependents.

Utah *Additional allowance for dependents is $5 for spouse plus $5 for dependent child (up to 4). Maximum (including dependents' allowance) is 85% of SAWW.
**After 312 weeks payments are continued only after annual review, minimum $85. Balance of 312 weeks up to 52 weeks is payable to spouse upon remarriage. Social Security death benefits partially offset.

Vt. *Maximum is 100% of SAWW; minimum is 50% of SAWW, actual wage if less.
**To spouse until age 62 or when entitled to Social Security; balance of 330 weeks, if any, is payable on remarriage. Maximum 330 weeks payable to or for any child.

V.I. *Death benefit is $12,500 to $16,500, payable in installments or lump sum; 60% is payable to children, if any. Amount limit includes amounts paid for disability.

Va. *Maximum is 100% of SAWW; minimum is 25% of SAWW, actual wage if less.
**Social Security offset.

Wash. *Maximum monthly benefit is 75% of state average monthly wage.
**Social Security offset.

W. Va. *Maximum is 100% of SAWW; minimum is 33-1/3% of SAWW.

Wis. *Maximum is 100% of SAWW.
**If death follows disability, total time limit for disability plus death is 1,000 weeks.
***Amount limit is 300 times SAWW. When primary benefit expires, a supplementary monthly benefit continues for children at 10% of the spouse's monthly benefit, payable from the Children's Fund, to age 18 or for 15 years if invalid.

Wyo. *Monthly benefit is fixed at 66-2/3% of state average monthly wage plus lump sum computed at $60 monthly per child until age 19 (21 if invalid). After 231 weeks, court may continue payments at 33-1/3% of state average monthly wage. PT benefits in excess of $4,000 are deducted.
**Employer may make other arrangements.

F.E.C.A. *3 or more children.
**Spouse who remarries after age 60 continues to receive monthly benefits.
***Additional $200 lump sum payable for cost of terminating status as U.S. employee.

Longshore *No maximum for death benefits. Director of OWCP v. Rasmussen, 440 U.S. 29 (1979). Minimum is 66-2/3 of NAWW, actual wages if less.

Alta. *5 years' declining payment, effective 1/1/82.

B.C. *Maximum monthly benefit for spouse with 2 children is $1,563.02, plus $137.51 for each additional child. Childless widow under 40 receives capital sum of $21,161.43. Benefits for childless widow age 40 or older vary by age. Canada pension is offset.

Man. *Maximum is $1,437.50 monthly; minimum is $475 monthly. Allowance for 1 dependent is additional $107 monthly if under 16 or $119 monthly if over 16 and in school; allowance for 2 or more dependents is amount payable for 2 oldest children; total monthly benefit may not exceed maximum.
**Plus up to $50 for plot or urn.

N.B. *Fixed monthly benefit is $360 plus $75 monthly per child.

Nfld. *Fixed monthly benefit is $410 plus $95 monthly per child. Board may pay additional $10 monthly per child on account of illness.

N.W.T. *Fixed monthly benefit is $638 plus $145 monthly per child.

N.S. *Fixed monthly benefit is $476 plus $124 monthly per child.

Ont. *Fixed monthly benefit is $492 plus $136 monthly per child.

P.E.I. *Fixed monthly benefit is $300 plus $60 monthly per child. If decedent was corporate officer and shareholder, benefit is 75% of maximum earnings of $15,000.

Quebec *Maximum is 80% of maximum PT disability benefit.
**Benefits stop after 5 years if spouse was under 35. Five years' benefits are payable to any spouse regardless of marital status.

Yukon *Fixed monthly benefit is $389 plus $128 monthly per child (1982 figures not available at publication).

C.M.S.C.A. *Fixed monthly benefit is $360 for spouse only, actual weekly wage if less. Monthly benefit for spouse and children is $360 plus $75 per child, up to $937.50 monthly.

ADMINISTRATION

Since workers' compensation grew out of a public dissatisfaction with the manner in which job-related disabilities were handled, it is not surprising that the system was designed with an eye toward prompt and effective disposition of disability cases. Without an effective delivery system, many of the problems associated with the common law and employer liability statutes would remain.

This requirement for an effective delivery system remains valid today. Indeed the National Commission on State Workmen's Compensation Laws, in listing this as a major objective for a modern workers' compensation system, made special note that the achievement of the system's objectives for protecting against workplace disabilities was dependent upon an effective system for delivery of the benefits and services. This observation was reaffirmed by a second federal report on workers' compensation delivery in 1977 (**see Special Report in 1977 edition**) which emphasized the importance of efficient program administration.

As originally envisioned, the system would be self-administering. Over time, the complexities of the system proved too much for a laissez-faire approach, and states moved to take a more affirmative role in the administration of their laws.

Generally, the states have moved either to administer their laws through their court system, a special commission or board, or a combination of both. In Canada, administrative activities are carried out by a board. The principal areas of administration include—

• Supervision of compliance with statutory requirements for employers, employees, carriers, and medical and legal personnel.

• Investigation and decision on disputed claims and the supervision of medical and vocational rehabilitation.

• Management of second-injury funds, special assessment requirements.

• Collection of data and evaluation of program performance.

ADMINISTRATION—NOTICE TO EMPLOYER—CLAIMS: CHART X

Workers' compensation laws generally are administered by commissions or boards created by law. A few states provide for court administration.

Chart X shows statutory provisions relating to administration. These include (1) time limits in which employers must be advised of injury, (2) time in which claims must be filed, (3) claims settlement conditions, and (4) regulation of attorney fees.

EMPLOYER'S REPORT OF ACCIDENTS: CHART XI

All employers are interested in requirements legally imposed on them to report injuries, and the penalty—if any—imposed for failure to report. In many jurisdictions, except for preliminary reports, the insured's company relieves an employer of this burden. Provisions for employers' reports of accidents are summarized in Chart XI.

APPEAL PROVISIONS: CHART XIV

Appeal provisions—including designation of the court of appeal and nature of the procedures—are summarized in Chart XIV. Most Canadian jurisdictions use the inquiry system and do not provide for judicial appeals.

DIRECTORY: CHART XV

The names and addresses of the administrators, boards, and commissioners for all jurisdictions reported upon by the *Analysis* are furnished.

Chart X

ADMINISTRATION—NOTICE TO EMPLOYER—CLAIMS January 1, 1982

JURISDICTION	ADMINISTRATION	NOTICE TO EMPLOYER	CLAIM FILING	HOW CLAIMS ARE SETTLED	AWARD EFFECT	REVIEW BY AGENCY	MODIFICATIONS	ATTORNEY'S FEES
ALABAMA	Courts	In writing within 5 days; excusable up to 90 days.	Within 1 year after accident, last payment, or removal of incapacity.	By agreement, which must conform substantially to terms of act unless court approves lesser sum. Disputed cases settled by courts.	Lien when registered with probate judge.		Award for more than 6 months at any time by agreement of parties with court approval.	Fixed by Circuit Court judge up to 15% of award.
ALASKA	Workmen's Compensation Board	In writing to Board and employer within 30 days; excusable.	Within 2 years after knowledge of disability. Within one year after death or 2 years after last payment.	By Board	Lien; recording required in 1 year. Interest and penalties accrue.	By Board	Within 1 year after last payment of compensation or after rejection of claim.	Fixed by Board
AMERICAN SAMOA	Workmen's Compensation Commission	In writing within 30 days; excusable.	Disability—within 1 year after injury or last payment. Death—within 1 year after death or claimant should know relation to employment.	Compensation payable without award except in disputed cases. Disputed cases settled by Commission.	Award is effective upon filing, enforceable by High Court.		By Commissioner on application or own motion within 1 year after last payment or rejection of claim. At any time in case of fraud.	Subject to approval of Commissioner or High Court. Court may assess costs against party that proceeds without reasonable grounds.
ARIZONA	Industrial Commission	Forthwith; excusable	Within 1 year after injury or accrual of right; excusable.* Claim not barred if compensation has commenced.	By Commission	Lien upon filing	By administrative law judge within 30 days	By administrative law judge on application	Commission may regulate; maximum 25% of award.
ARKANSAS	Workers' Compensation Commission	Within 60 days; excusable	Within 2 years after injury or death	Compensation is payable without award except in contested claims. Disputed claims heard by Commission, member, or administrative law judge, upon application.	Preference rights of unpaid wage claims	By Commission from decision of member of administrative law judge within 30 days	By Commission with 6 months of end of compensation period except in "joint settlements."*	Sliding scale subject to approval by Commission; fees awarded in addition to compensation. Maximum $100 on appeal to full Commission; $250 on appeal to Court.
CALIFORNIA	Division of Industrial Accidents handles administration. Appeals Board handles judicial functions.	In writing within 30 days; excusable	Disability—within 1 year from date of injury or last payment. Death—within 1 year after death to 240 weeks after injury.	By agreement on approval of Appeals Board which may order hearing. Disputed cases settled by Appeals Board on application.	Judgment on filing in Superior Court	By Appeals Board from referee's findings	Reconsideration within 20 days; no modification after 5 years.	Reasonable fee fixed by Appeals Board. If Court finds no reasonable basis for appeal, Appeals Board may award fees as supplementary award.
COLORADO	Director, Division of Labor	Within 2 days; excusable (claimant loses one day's compensation for each day's delay).	Within 3 years after injury or death. Does not apply if compensation paid or if reasonable excuse in 5 years.	By agreement approved by Division of Labor. Disputed claims settled by referee.	Judgment on filing copy of award against uninsured employer in District Court.	By Industrial Commission from referee's decision	By Division of Labor within 6 years from date of accident or 2 years after last payment (whichever is later).	Upon request, director may approve reasonableness of fee; 25% in contested case, more in difficult case on appeal.
CONNECTICUT	Workers' Compensation Commissioners (one for each of 7 districts plus chairman and one at large).	Forthwith; excusable	Within 1 year after accident. If death results within 2 years after accident or disease—within 2 years from accident or disease, or within 1 year from death (whichever is later).*	By agreement, on approval of Commission. Disputed cases settled by Commission.	Judgment on filing in Superior Court. Award has preference rights of unpaid wages.	By Compensation Review Division within 10 days.**	By Commissioner during compensation period.	Subject to approval of Board
DELAWARE	Industrial Accident Board	If notice not given in 90 days no compensation due until notice or knowledge of injury.	Within 2 years after injury, death, or 5 years from last payment	By agreement, on approval of Board. Disputed cases settled by Board after hearing.	Preference rights of unpaid claims		By Board at any time, but no more than once each 6 months.	30% of award or $2,250, whichever is less. Reasonable fee on appeals.
DISTRICT OF COLUMBIA	D.C. Office of Workers' Compensation.	In writing within 30 days; excusable.	Within 1 year after accident or last payment.	By Mayor.	Award is effective upon filing.	By Mayor on application or own motion.	By Mayor within 1 year after last payment or denial of claim.	Approval by Mayor.

Jurisdiction	Agency	Notice	Limit on filing	Compensation settlement	Award enforcement	By administrator upon own motion or application at any time	By administrator	Fees subject to approval
DISTRICT OF COLUMBIA GOVERNMENT WORKERS	D.C. Office of Workers' Compensation	48 hours; extended for cause.	Within 60 days after injury or 1 year after death; extended for cause.					Subject to approval by administrator.
FLORIDA	Division of Workers' Compensation	In writing within 30 days; excusable.	Within 2 years after injury, death, or last payment.	By agreement, but Division may investigate. Upon application Division must order hearing conducted by deputy commissioner.	May be filed in proper court; execution or other process in Circuit Court.		By deputy commissioner on application or own motion within 2 years after last payment or claim rejection.	Subject to approval of Division, deputy commissioner, or court; claimant pays own fee.
GEORGIA	Board of Workers' Compensation	Within 30 days; excusable	Within 1 year after injury, death, or medical care; or within 2 years after last payment.	Compensation is payable without award except in contested claims. Disputed claims settled by Board, Director, or administrative law judge.	Judgment in Superior Court on certified copy of award.*	By Board on application within 30 days.	By Board on application or own motion within 2 years after final payment. Final settlement may not be modified.	Fees in excess of $100 subject to Board approval. Board may assess attorney's fees against any party who proceeds without reasonable grounds or fails to provide income benefits as required.
GUAM	Director of Labor and Personnel	In writing within 30 days; excusable.	Within 1 year after injury, death, or last payment.	Compensation is payable without award within 14 days after knowledge of injury or death. Controverted claims are settled by the Commission.	Lien against assets of carrier or employer. Enforcement of final order by Island Court.		By Commissioner within 1 year after last payment or rejection of claim, on own motion or application.	Subject to approval of Commissioner or Court on review. Costs assessed against party who proceeds without reasonable grounds.
HAWAII	Director of Labor and Industrial Relations	Forthwith; excusable	2 years after date on which effects of injury become manifest, but within 5 years after date of accident causing injury.	Agreements must be prepared by Director in accord with law. If not agreed, Director makes award.	Judgment on filing in Circuit Court.	By Appellate Board within 20 days.	By Director on own motion or on application of any party within 20 days.	Subject to approval of Director. Maximum 10% of average benefit duration multiplied by claimant's weekly benefit amount.
IDAHO	Industrial Commission	In writing within 60 days after accident; excusable.	Within 1 year after accident or death.	By agreement, subject to approval of Commission. Disputed cases settled by Commission or member after hearing.	Judgment in District Court on filing certified copy of award.	By Commission within 20 days	By Commission within 5 years of accident, but no more often than once in 6 months.	Subject to approval of Commission

Ariz. *Limit on filing runs from when injury is manifest or when claimant knows/should know relation to employment; tolled during incapacity.

Ark. A "joint settlement" is authorized where all parties petition an immediate final settlement by the Commission. In such cases, an order of the Commission is final except as to appeals to the courts, but an order of the Commission allowing or denying such petition is not appealable.

Conn. *Within 3 years after first symptom of disease. Lack of notice excused if voluntary agreement, or medical treatment within 1 year after accident.
**The 9 Commissioners comprise the Review Division.

Ga. *7 percent interest on all accrued amounts of awards. Interest runs on Superior Court judgment in event of appeal.

ADMINISTRATION—NOTICE TO EMPLOYER—CLAIMS ☐ January 1, 1982 (continued)

JURISDICTION	ADMINISTRATION	NOTICE TO EMPLOYER	CLAIM FILING	HOW CLAIMS ARE SETTLED	AWARD EFFECT	REVIEW BY AGENCY	MODIFICATIONS	ATTORNEY'S FEES
ILLINOIS	Industrial Commission	Within 45 days. For radiological injury, within 90 days after employee knows or suspects that he has received an excessive dose of radiation.	Barred after 3 years from injury or death, or 2 years after last payment, whichever is later. Radiation—within 25 years after last exposure for injury; within 1 year after death.*	By agreement, subject to approval of Commission, after 7 days from injury. Disputed cases settled by arbitrator or arbitration committee.	Judgment in Circuit Court on filing certified copy of award.	By Commission from decision of arbitrator or arbitration committee within 15 days	By Commission within 30 months of agreement or award.	Maximum 20% of compensation paid, up to 364 weeks of permanent total disability. Unreasonable or vexatious delay by employer or carrier in payment of compensation may be penalized by payment of attorney's fees.
INDIANA	Industrial Board	In writing as soon as practicable; excusable. Compensation accrues from date of notice if given after 30 days.	Within 2 years after injury or death. Radiation—2 years after worker knows/should know relation to employment.	By agreement, after 7 days from injury or at any time after death, subject to approval of Board. Disputed cases settled by Board or member on application.	Judgment in Circuit or Superior Court on certified copy of agreement or award. Preference rights of unpaid wages.	By full Board within 20 days after award	By Board on application or own motion, within 2 years after last day for which compensation is paid.	Subject to approval of Board. Paid out of award unless bad faith by employer or lack of diligence, in which case minimum fee is $150.
IOWA	Industrial Commissioner	Within 90 days after injury unless employer has actual knowledge.	Within 2 years after injury	By agreement, subject to approval of Industrial Commissioner.	Judgment in District Court on filing certified copy of agreement or decision.	By Commissioner from decision of Deputy Commissioner within 20 days	By Commissioner within 3 years from last payment, award, or noncommuted settlement.	Subject to Commissioner's approval
KANSAS	Division of Workers' Compensation	Within 10 days; excusable.	Claim must be served on employer within 200 days after accident or last payment, or within 1 year after death for death within 5 years after accident. Application for hearing must be filed with Division within 3 years after accident or within 2 years after last payment, whichever is later.*	By agreement, subject to approval of Director. Disputed cases settled by administrative law judge after hearing, subject to an appeal to the Director.	Judgment in district court on filing certified copy of award.	By Director at any time before final payment, on application	By Director, before final payment and within 1 year of prior approval, on application.	Maximum 25% of recovery in matters before Director or district court, subject to approval of Director pursuant to written contract which must be filed.
KENTUCKY	Workers' Compensation Board	In writing as soon as practicable; excusable.	Within 2 years after accident or death. If paid voluntarily—claim submitted to employer within 1 year after suspension, or 2 years after accident, whichever is later. Limits tolled during minority or incapacity.	By agreement, subject to approval of Board. Disputed cases settled by full Board.	Judgment in Circuit Court on filing certified copy of award or approved agreement.	By Board	By Board at any time, on application or own motion.	Subject to Board's approval. Maximum $6,500, except $750 maximum in uncontested occupational disease case.
LOUISIANA	Courts	In writing within 6 months (12 if employer fails to post requirements); excusable.	Within 1 year after accident, death, or last payment; 2 years for delayed development of injury; 3 years from last payment in cases of partial disability.	By agreement, subject to approval of court. Disputed cases settled by the courts.	Settlement approved by court entered as judgment.		By court after 6 months or any time by agreement.	Subject to court approval; maximum 20% of award on first $10,000 and 10 percent of any additional amount.
MAINE	Workers' Compensation Commission	Within 30 days after injury; within 3 months after death; excusable.	Within 2 years after accident or last payment, or within 1 year after death. If mistake of fact, within a reasonable time; but no more than 10 years after last payment in any case.	By agreement, subject to approval of Commission. Disputed cases determined by commissioner after hearing.	Award is judgement.	By single commissioner, then by Appellate Division*	On application; approved lump sum is final.	Commission may assess against employer if services were necessary.

State	Agency	Notice to Employer	Time to File Claim	Settlement	Enforcement	Appeal	Reopening	Attorney Fees
MARYLAND	Workmen's Compensation Commission	Within 10 days after injury (30 days for hernia); within 30 days after death; excusable.	Within 60 days after disability begins; excusable to 2 years. Within 18 months after death. Not barred for 3 years if treated by physician acting for employer.*	By agreement, subject to approval of Commission. Disputed cases settled by Commission or arbitration committee; hearing required on application.		By Commission from arbitration committee on application	From final award, on application or own motion within 5 years.	Subject to approval of Commission
MASSACHUSETTS	Division of Industrial Accidents, under supervision of Industrial Accidents Board	In writing as soon as practicable; excusable.	Within one year after injury or death; excusable.	By agreement, subject to approval of Division. Disputed cases settled by member of Division after preliminary conference prior to hearing.	Decree in Superior Court on certified copy of agreement or decision.	By reviewing Board from decision of member	On application at any time; limited in death cases.	Subject to approval of Division
MICHIGAN	Bureau of Workers' Disability Compensation	Within 90 days after injury, excusable.	Within 2 years after injury, death, recovery from incapacity, or after worker knows/should know relation of disease to employment.*	Compensation without award except in contested cases. Disputed cases settled by administrative law judge (by Bureau if "small dispute").	Judgment in Circuit Court on filing certified copy of award.	By Appeal Board within 15 days from decision of administrative law judge		Subject to approval of Bureau based on administrative rules and schedules.
MINNESOTA	Commissioner, Department of Labor and Industry as head of Workers' Compensation Division	In writing within 14 days; excusable up to 180 days (later if mental or physical incapacity).	Within 3 years after employer's report; no more than 6 years from date of injury.*	By hearing process or agreement prior to hearing.	Judgment in District Court on filing certified copy of award.	By Court of Appeals within 30 days from decision of compensation judge.	By petition to Court of Appeals to vacate.	Sliding scale, subject to approval by compensation judge or district court judge.**
MISSISSIPPI	Workmen's Compensation Commission	Within 30 days; excusable.	Within 2 years after injury or death	Compensation is payable without award except in contested claims. Disputed claims heard by Commission member or referee on application.	Lien against assets and has preference rights of unpaid wages.	By Commission from decision of administrative judge within 20 days.	By Commission on application or own motion within 1 year from last payment or claim rejection	Subject to approval of Commission or court.
MISSOURI	Industrial Commission through Division of Workers' Compensation	In writing within 30 days unless employer has actual knowledge. Division notifies worker of rights.	Within 2 years after injury or death, or last payment (3 years if no report filed).	By agreement, after 7 days from injury or death, subject to approval of administrative law judge or Commission. Disputed cases settled by administrative law judge.	Judgment in Circuit Court on certified copy of memorandum of agreement, order, decision, or award of Division or Commission.	By Industrial Commission within 20 days.	By Commission on application or own motion, after notice and hearing	Commission or Division may allow reasonable fee.

Ill. *Death from radiation must occur within 2 years from last exposure if not compensation or Bureau within 2 years after injury, death, paid.

Kans. *If employer fails to report accident within 28 days, claim must be served on employer within 1 year after accident, and application must be filed with Division within 3 years after employer reports accident. *Childress v. Childress Painting Co.*, 597 P.2d 637 (Kansas S. Ct. 1979).

Maine *Overpayments are made pending review and may be recovered in lawsuit by employer if employee resumes work. Any award or agreement may be reopened within 30 days on grounds of newly discovered evidence.

Md. *Employer or insurer who receives completed claim form must send it to Commission immediately and may not advise claimant that claim is denied.

Mich. *No claim valid unless made within 2 years after injury, manifestation of disability, or last employment, whichever is later. Deadline suspended if worker receives any disability benefits.

Minn. *Employer who threatens to discharge claimant for filing claim is subject to civil suit for treble damages, costs, and attorney fees.
**In controversy with insurer, successful claimant is awarded 25% of fee in excess of $250.

ADMINISTRATION—NOTICE TO EMPLOYER—CLAIMS ☐ January 1, 1982 (continued)

JURISDICTION	ADMINISTRATION	NOTICE TO EMPLOYER	CLAIM FILING	HOW CLAIMS ARE SETTLED	AWARD EFFECT	REVIEW BY AGENCY	MODIFICATIONS	ATTORNEY'S FEES
MONTANA	Division of Workers' Compensation	For injuries not resulting in death, within 60 days unless employer has actual knowledge.	Verified claim within 12 months after accident; Commission may grant additional 24 months.	By agreement subject to approval of Division. Disputed cases settled by Workers' Compensation Judge.	Lien on deposit of employer or insurer.	By W.C. Judge. 10 days to disapprove final compromise settlement.	By W. C. judge within 4 years after final award. Final compromise settlement not reviewable.	May be fixed by Division or W. C. judge. Added to successful claimant's award on appeals.
NEBRASKA	Workmen's Compensation Court	In writing as soon as practicable; excusable.	Within 2 years after injury, death, removal of incapacity, or last payment. For minors within 2 years after becoming 19.	By agreement with consent of insurer, but must be in accordance with Act. Disputed claims submitted to Compensation Court for hearing. Lump sums approved by Compensation Court and district court.	Judgment in District Court on filing certified copy of order or award.	By Compensation Court within 14 days after order or award of Judge.	By agreement, subject to approval of Compensation Court; or on application after 6 months by Compensation Court.	Subject to approval of judge of Compensation Court or Supreme Court (for lien purposes).
NEVADA	Industrial Commission*	Immediately; excusable within 30 days from accident 60 days after death.	Within 90 days after accident, 1 year after death	By agreement, in conformity with Act, subject to approval of Commission.		By Dept. of Administration Hearing Officer, then to Appeals Officer	On application within 1 year after injury or accrual of right. Medical investigation may be conducted at any time based on changed circumstances.	District Court may assess costs and attorney's fees if appeal is frivolous.
NEW HAMPSHIRE	Department of Labor	In writing as soon as practicable and before voluntarily leaving employment.	Within 90 days after injury, death, removal of incapacity, or last payment. Claims barred unless notice given within 2 years from date of accident.	Compensation payable without award except in contested cases.		By Commissioner. Special review board for state employees.	Commissioner of Labor may modify no later than 4 years after last payment, award, or last medical payment.	Subject to approval of Labor Commissioner or court. Attorney's fees and interest to successful claimant on appeal.
NEW JERSEY	Division of Workers' Compensation	Within 14 days; excusable up to 90 days. Separate provisions for occupational diseases.	Within 2 years after accident, death, last payment, or default. Separate provisions for occupational diseases.	By agreement, subject to approval of Division. Disputed cases settled by Division.	On filing with county clerk has effect of County Court judgment; may be docketed in Superior Court.		By agreement or on application for review within 2 years of last payment. Settlement approved by compensation judge is final and conclusive.	Not over 20 percent before Division. Court may fix reasonable fee on appeal.*
NEW MEXICO	Courts*	In writing within 30 days; excusable up to 60 days, and for knowledge.	Within 1 year after notice, death, or failure to pay. Time limit tolled while in same employment.	By agreement, subject to approval of District Court. Disputed cases settled by court.	Award is judgment.		Provision only for decrease or termination.	10 percent except on successful contest. Court may allow additional fee payable by employer.
NEW YORK	Workers' Compensation Board	In writing 30 days; excusable.	Within 2 years after accident or death. When advance payment is made, claim is not barred.	Compensation is payable without award within 18 days after disability, except in contested claims. Disputed claims settled by referee or Board. Hearing is mandatory upon application.	Payment within 10 days after decision, except in event of appeal. Judgment on filing certified copy of award in default.	By Board on application or own motion.	By Board at any time. Subject to special conditions.	As a lien on award if approved by Board.
NORTH CAROLINA	Industrial Commission	In writing within 30 days; excusable.	Within 24 months after accident	By agreement, after 7 days from injury, or at any time in case of death, subject to approval of Commission. Disputed cases settled by Commission or member.	Judgment in Superior Court on filing certified copy of agreement or decision.	By Commission upon application within 15 days after award.	By Commission on application or own motion, within 2 years.	Subject to approval of Commission. Commission may assess attorney's fees and court costs against party who proceeds without reasonable ground.
NORTH DAKOTA	Workmen's Compensation Bureau	None required.	Within 1 year after injury or 2 years after death	By Bureau	Fund pays award and has liquidated claim against defaulting uninsured employers.		By Bureau at any time on application or own motion	Determined by schedule adopted by Bureau; trial judge fixes on appeal but must give consideration to amount allowed by Bureau.

State	Administered by	Notice of injury	Time limit for claim	Agreement/settlement	Award payment	First appeal	Reopening/second appeal	Attorney fees
OHIO	Bureau of Workers' Compensation and Industrial Commission	None required except to self-insurers.	Within 2 years after accident, injury, or death	By Industrial Commission after hearing	Fund or self insurer pays award after judgment.	By regional review board or Comm. within 20 days of decision of district hearing officer.	By Commission or by Bureau within 6 years after injury or 10 years from last payment or death	Court fixes on appeals and in disputes. Maximum 20% for awards up to $3,000. 10% for awards over $3,000. Maximum $1,500.*
OKLAHOMA	Workers' Compensation Court and an Administrator	In writing within 30 days; excusable.*	Within 1 year after injury or last payment. Death claims within 1 year after death or last payment.**	By agreement, after 3-day disability, subject to approval of Workers' Compensation Court. Disputed cases settled by Court.	Judgment in District Court on certified copy after 10-day default.	By Workers' Compensation Court within 10 days	By W.C. Court on application or own motion at any time. May reopen case within maximum number of weeks for which award is possible.	W.C. Court must approve and direct payment; 10% maximum for temporary disability; 20% maximum for permanent disability or death.
OREGON	Workers' Compensation Department	In writing within 30 days; excusable.	Within 1 year after accident, last payment, or last date of medical services.	Insurer must either accept or reject claim within 60 days.*		By referee on application within 60 days; further appeal to Board within 30 days.	By Board on own motion or on application of employee within 5 years.	Subject to approval of hearing officer, Board, or Court. Board establishes fee schedule.
PENNSYLVANIA	Bureau of Workers' Compensation*	Within 21 days; excusable to 120 days. No compensation due until notice is given.	Within 3 years after injury, death, or last payment.	By agreement, after 7 days from injury, subject to approval of Department. Disputed cases determined by Appeal Board after hearing. Claim may be assigned to referee for hearing.	Judgment in court on filing award or agreement.	By Appeal Board from referee's decision within 20 days	By Department on application within 3 years.	Subject to approval of referee, Appeal Board, or court.
PUERTO RICO	Manager of the State Insurance Fund and Industrial Commission	None required.	As soon as possible.	By the Manager under rules he makes.	Fund pays award.	By Manager at any time	By Commission, within 30 days after copy of Manager's decision is served on the employee. Reconsideration on own motion or upon petition of interested party within 10 days.	No attorneys required in hearings, but if requested by employee, they are paid a percentage of the award fixed by the Commission, court, or Fund.
RHODE ISLAND	Workers' Compensation Commission	In writing within 30 days; excusable.	Within 3 years after injury, manifestation, knowledge of injury, death, or removal of incapacity.	By agreement approved by Director. By Commissioner with appeal to full Commission.	Director's order enforceable by Commission and Superior Court.	By Commission within 48 hours	By Commission during compensation period or within 10 years after compensation period has ceased, on own motion or on petition of either party.	Subject to approval of Commission. Commission to issue fee schedules following legislative review.

Nev. *Effective July 1, 1982, Commission is replaced by Department of Industrial Relations, and State Insurance Fund is replaced by State Industrial Insurance System.

N.J. *Based on excess over amount of award tendered in good faith a reasonable time before a hearing.

N.M. *Occupational Disease Act administered by Superintendent of Insurance.

Ohio Insurance.

Ohio *Commission must fix attorney's fees in controversies, approve method of payment, and allow a reasonable fee upon application for review.

Okla. *If employer has actual notice of injury, statute of limitations is tolled until employer informs worker of right to file a claim.

**Employer that discriminates against claimant is liable for damages.

Pa. *Workers' Compensation Advisory Council recommends changes in administration of law.

ADMINISTRATION—NOTICE TO EMPLOYER—CLAIMS ☐ January 1, 1982 (continued)

JURISDICTION	ADMINISTRATION	NOTICE TO EMPLOYER	CLAIM FILING	HOW CLAIMS ARE SETTLED	AWARD EFFECT	REVIEW BY AGENCY	MODIFICATIONS	ATTORNEY'S FEES
SOUTH CAROLINA	Industrial Commission—2 divisions: Judicial Division and Administration Department	In writing as soon as practicable or within 90 days; excusable.	Within 2 years after accident or 1 year after death.	By agreement, after 7 days from date of injury or any time in case of death, subject to approval of Commission or member, after hearing, upon application.	Judgment in Common Pleas Court on certified copy of agreement or award.	By 3-member panel within 14 days after award.	To Commission on application or own motion within 12 months from last payment.	Subject to approval of Commission.
SOUTH DAKOTA	Division of Labor and Management	In writing as soon as practicable within 30 days; excusable.	Within 2 years after notice of intention to deny coverage.	By agreement, if not disapproved by Commissioner within 20 days. Disputed cases settled by Commissioner after hearing, upon application.	Judgment in Circuit Court on certified copy of agreement or decision.	By Commissioner within 10 days	By Commissioner on application.	Subject to approval of Commissioner.
TENNESSEE	Courts and Workers' Compensation Division	In writing within 30 days; excusable up to 1 year.	Within 1 year after accident. Dependents—within 1 year after employer's notice accepting liability.	By agreement, subject to approval of County Court. Disputed cases determined by Circuit Court.	Judgment in Circuit Court on approved agreement.		By court, on application after 6 months. Award payable for more than 6 months may be modified by agreement approved by court.	Subject to approval of court; maximum 20% of recovery or award.
TEXAS	Industrial Accident Board	Within 30 days; excusable.	Within 6 months after injury, death, or removal of incapacity; excusable.*	By agreement, in conformity to Act, subject to approval of Board (compromise agreements may be approved). Disputed cases settled by Board.	Collectible by suit.		By Board at any time during compensation period, on application or own motion.	Subject to approval of Board or court but not to exceed 25% of recovery. No attorney fees in uncontested permanent total disability cases.
UTAH	Industrial Commission	Within 48 hours; excusable up to 1 year.	Within 1 year after death; within 3 years after disability or last payment. Payment of benefits after filing injury report tolls limitation on claim filing until denial of liability.*	By Industrial Commission.	Lien from time of docketing in District Court.	By Commission within 15 days	By Commission at any time. Award may be reviewed upon showing change within 2 years for silicosis—if complicated, 5 years.	Fixed by Commission.
VERMONT	Commissioner of Labor and Industry	In writing as soon as practicable; excusable.	Within 6 months after injury, death, loss of damage suit, or removal of incapacity; excusable.	By agreement, in conformity to Act, subject to approval of Commissioner (compromise agreements may be approved). Disputed cases settled by Commissioner.	Judgment in county court on certified copy of agreement or award.	By Commissioner on application within 6 months	By Commissioner on own motion or application at any time.	Commissioner may award to successful claimant, and on appeal, 6% interest on contested part of award.
VIRGIN ISLANDS	Commissioner of Labor	In writing within 48 hours; extendable up to 30 days. Occupational disease—within 30 days from first manifestation; extendable to 90 days.	Within 60 days after injury.		First priority lien on employer's assets.	By Deputy Commissioner	By Deputy Commissioner	Subject to approval of Commissioner.
VIRGINIA	Industrial Commission	In writing within 30 days.	Within 2 years after accident or 1 year after death.	By agreement, after 10 days from injury, or at any time after death, subject to approval of Commission. Disputed cases settled by Commission or member after hearing upon application.	Judgment in Circuit Court on certified copy of agreement or award.	By full Commission within 20 days after opinion	By Commission on own motion or application within 2 years of last payment, or 3 years for scheduled injuries.	Subject to approval of Commission.

WASHINGTON	Department of Labor and Industries	Immediately	Within 1 year after injury, death, or notice of occupational disease.	By Department of Labor and Industries[1]		By Board of Industrial Insurance Appeals within 60 days on application.	By Department within 7 years, on application or own motion, 10 years for loss of vision claims.	By Appeals Board upon application; reviewable by Superior Court.
WEST VIRGINIA	Workmen's Compensation Commissioner	Immediately	Within 2 years after injury or death	By Commissioner; hearing upon application.		By Appeal Board within 30 days, or 60 days without notice.	By Commissioner within set time limits, on written application; subject to review by Appeal Board.[*]	Maximum fees established; limited to 20% of total award.
WISCONSIN	Workers' Compensation Division	Within 30 days; excusable.	Within 2 years after injury or death. Excusable if employer knew of disability. All rights barred after 12 years from injury, death, or last payment.	By agreement, or compromise subject to review by Commission within 1 year. Disputed cases settled by Commission.	Judgment in Circuit Court on certified copy of award.	By Commission within 21 days from examiner.	By Commission on its own motion within 21 days; compromises may be modified within 1 year. If occupational disease, subject to review within 6 years.	Limited to 20% of amount in dispute. If admitted liability, not to exceed 10% or $100.
WYOMING	Courts and Division of Worker's Compensation	Within 24 hours (also within 20 days to the court); excusable.	Within 1 year after injury or discovery of injury not readily apparent.	By District Court with right of jury trial in certain cases			By court within 2 years or during time payments are made on application.	Limited to 10% of recovery. If unusual, complex case, may get a reasonable fee.
F.E.C.A.	Division of Federal Employees' Compensation, O.W.C.P., U.S. Department of Labor	48 hours; extended for cause.	Within 60 days after injury or 1 year after death; extended for cause.	By Division	Fund pays award.	By Administrator upon own motion or application at any time.	By Administrator or Employees' Compensation Appeals Board on review.	Subject to approval by Division or Appeals Board.
LONGSHORE ACT	Division of Longshore and Harbor Workers' Compensation, O.W.C.P., U.S. Department of Labor	Within 30 days	Within 1 year after injury or death.	By Deputy Commissioner (by agreement) or administrative law judge (formal hearing).	Award is effective on filing.	By Deputy Commissioner upon own motion or application and by Benefits Review Board on Appeal.	By Deputy Commissioner or court on review	Approval by Deputy Commissioner, court, or Review Board where service given.

[1]Modification of award due to aggravation or recurrence of injury may be based on earnings and benefits in effect at that time.

Texas [*]Employer who discriminates against claimant is liable for damages.

Utah [*]Claim must be filed within 8 years after injury.

Man. [*]Government-appointed advisor injury.

Wash. [*]Provision is made for recoupment of benefits paid through mistake or fraud.

W. Va. [*]Within 2 years for fatal or non-fatal cases, 5 years for temporary total disability or in cases of no awards.

ADMINISTRATION—NOTICE TO EMPLOYER—CLAIMS ☐ January 1, 1982 (continued)

JURISDICTION	ADMINISTRATION	NOTICE TO EMPLOYER	CLAIM FILING	HOW CLAIMS ARE SETTLED	AWARD EFFECT	REVIEW BY AGENCY	MODIFICATIONS	ATTORNEY'S FEES
ALBERTA	Workers' Compensation Board	As soon as practicable	Within 1 year after injury or death; 3 years after death if worker filed for injury; excusable.	By claims officer.	Fund pays award.	By review committee on request, then by full Board, at any time.	By Board at any time on application or own motion	
BRITISH COLUMBIA	Workers' Compensation Board	As soon as practicable	Within 1 year after injury, death, or disablement by disease; excusable within 3 years.*	By Board	Fund pays award.	By Board of Review within 90 days. From Board of Review to commissioners of the Board within 60 days (30 days if at request of Chairman of Board of Review).	By Board at any time.	Board may award expenses of proceeding to successful party.**
MANITOBA	Workers' Compensation Board	In writing as soon as practicable but no later than 30 days; excusable.	Within 12 months after accident or death; excusable.	By Board	Fund pays award.	At any time.	By Board	(·)
NEW BRUNSWICK	Workmen's Compensation Board	As soon as practicable	Within 1 year after injury or 6 months after death; excusable.	By Board	Fund pays award.	At any time.	By Board[1]	
NEWFOUNDLAND	Workers' Compensation Board	As soon as practicable	Within 6 months after injury or death.	By Board	Fund pays award.	At any time.	By Board	
NORTHWEST TERRITORIES	Workers' Compensation Board	As soon as practicable	Within 1 year after injury or death; excusable if as soon as practicable; maximum 3 years after death.	By Board	Fund pays award.	At any time.	By Board	
NOVA SCOTIA	Workers' Compensation Board	As soon as practicable	Within 6 months after injury or death; excusable.	By Board	Fund pays award.	At any time.	By Board at any time or Workers' Compensation Appeal Board within 90 days.	(·)
ONTARIO	Workmen's Compensation Board	As soon as practicable	Within 6 months after injury or death.	By Board	Fund pays award.	At any time.	By Board	
PRINCE EDWARD ISLAND	Workers' Compensation Board	As soon as practicable	Within 6 months after injury or death.	By Board	Fund pays award.	At any time.	By Board[1]	
QUEBEC	Commission de la Santé et de la Sécurité du Travail	As soon as practicable	Within 6 months after injury or death.	By Commission	Fund pays award.	At any time.*	By Commission[1]	
SASKATCHEWAN	Workers' Compensation Board	As soon as practicable; excusable.	Within 6 months after injury or death; excusable.	By Board	Fund pays award.	At any time.	By Board	(·)
YUKON TERRITORY	Workers' Compensation Board	As soon as practicable	Within 1 year after injury or death; excusable if proof of disability or death is furnished within 3 years after accident and claim is a just one.	By Board	Fund pays award.	By Board at any time.	By Board	

CANADIAN MERCHANT SEAMEN'S ACT	Merchant Seamen Compensation Board	As soon as practicable	Within 6 months after injury or death; excusable.	By Board	Judgment in county district, or Quebec Superior Court on certified copy of award.	At any time.	By Board	Board may award "expenses of proceeding" to successful party.

[1] Modification of award due to aggravation or recurrence of injury may be based on earnings and benefits in effect at that time.

B.C. *After 3 years, compensation is payable only from date of filing.
**Government-appointed advisors handle workers' and employers' claims.

Man. *Government-appointed advisor handles workers workers' claims.

N.S. *Gov.-in-Council may appoint counselor to assist claimants.

Quebec *Claimant may appeal from Commission to Social Affairs Commission.

Sask. *Government-appointed advisor handles workers' claims.

Chart XI

EMPLOYER'S REPORT OF ACCIDENTS

January 1, 1982

JURISDICTION	KEEPING OF ACCIDENT RECORDS BY EMPLOYER[1]	REPORTING REQUIREMENTS[1]		PENALTIES FOR FAILURE TO REPORT		
		INJURIES COVERED	TIME LIMIT	FINES		IMPRISONMENT
				MAXIMUM	MINIMUM	
ALABAMA	Required	Death or disability exceeding 3 days	Within 15 days	$500	$12	Up to 12 months
ALASKA	Required	Death or injury or disease or infection	Within 10 days	(-)		
AMERICAN SAMOA	Required	Injury or death	Within 10 days*	500		
ARIZONA	Not required	All injuries	Immediately and as required			Petty offense
ARKANSAS	Required	Injury or death	Within 10 days and as required	100		
CALIFORNIA	Required	Death cases or serious injuries	Immediately*	100	25	
		1 day or more than first aid	As prescribed			
		Occupational diseases or pesticide poisoning	Within 5 days			
COLORADO	Required	Death cases	Immediately	100 per day		
		All injuries causing lost time of 3 days or more*	Within 10 days*			
CONNECTICUT	Required	Disability of 1 day or more	7 days, or as directed	250		
DELAWARE	Required	Death cases or injuries requiring hospitalization	Within 48 hours*	100	25	Up to 20 days
		Other injuries	Within 10 days*			
DISTRICT OF COLUMBIA	Required	All injuries	Within 10 days	1,000		
FLORIDA	Required	Death cases	Within 24 hours*	100		
		All injuries	Within 7 days and as required*			
GEORGIA	Required	All injuries requiring medical or surgical treatment or causing over 7 days' absence	Within 10 days*	100**		
GUAM	Required	Injury or death	Within 10 days*	500**		Up to 90 days
HAWAII	Required	Death cases	Within 48 hours	100		
		1 day of absence	Within 7 days			
IDAHO	Required	All injuries requiring medical treatment or causing 1 day's absence	As soon as practicable but not later than 10 days after the accident[2]	300		Up to 6 months
ILLINOIS	Required*	Death cases or serious injuries	Within 2 working days	200	100	Misdemeanor
		Disability of over 1 day	Between 15th and 25th of month			
		Permanent disability	Soon as determinable			
INDIANA	Required	Disability of 1 day or more	Within 7 days*	500		
IOWA	Required	Disability of more than 3 days	Within 4 days	100	100	
KANSAS	Not required	Death cases	Within 28 days	(-)		
		Disability of 1 day or more	Within 28 days			
KENTUCKY	Required	Disability of more than 1 day	Within 7 days[2]	25		
LOUISIANA	Not required		No statutory provision			

State	Report required	Reports required for	Time limit	Fine	Fine	Penalty
MAINE	Not required	All injuries	Within 7 days	100		
MARYLAND	Not required	Disability of more than 3 days	Within 10 days	50		
MASSACHUSETTS	Required	All injuries	Within 48 hours[2]	100		
MICHIGAN	Required	Death cases, disabilities of 7 days or more, and specific losses	Immediately			
MINNESOTA	Not required	Death or serious injury	Within 48 hours		50	
		Disability of 3 days or more	Within 15 days			
MISSISSIPPI	Required	Disability of one day or working shift	Within 10 days	100*		
MISSOURI	Not required	Death or disability of more than 3 days	Within 10 days*	500	50	1 week to 1 year
MONTANA	Required	All injuries	Within 6 days*	500–1,000		Misdemeanor
NEBRASKA	Required	Death cases*	Within 48 hours*	1,000*		Up to 6 months
		All injuries*	Within 7 days*			
NEVADA	Required	All injuries	Within 6 working days	100, each failure		
NEW HAMPSHIRE	Required	All injuries	Within 48 hours	25		
NEW JERSEY	Required	All injuries*	Immediately	50	10	

[1] Federal Occupational Safety and Health Act of 1970 established uniform requirements and forms to meet its criteria for all businesses affecting interstate commerce to be used for statistical purposes and compliance with the Act. 12 U.S.C. §651.

[2] Supplemental report required after 60 days, or upon termination of disability.

[3] Attending physician also required to make periodic reports to Board.

[4] Supplemental report within 24 hours after returning to work or knowledge that worker is able to return.

Alaska *20% of unpaid amounts due. Supplemental report due within 1 year after injury, then annually, or after final payment.

Am. Samoa *Employer must also notify Commissioner upon first payment and suspension of payment, and within 16 days after final payment.

Calif. *To Safety Division, in form required by federal Occupational Safety and Health Act.

Colo. *Failure to report tolls time limit for claims. Disability of less than 3 days must be reported to insurer.

Del. *Supplemental report disability.

Fla. *Supplemental report within 30 days after final payment.

Ga. *Supplemental report on first payment and suspension of payment, and within 30 days after final payment.
**For each refusal or willful neglect to report.

Guam *Failure to report tolls limits for claims.
**For each refusal or willful neglect to report.

Ill. *To Safety Division, in form required by federal Occupational Safety and Health Act.

Ind. *Supplemental report within 10 days after termination of compensation period.

Kans. *Failure to report tolls time limit for claims. Childress v. Childress Painting Co. (Kans. App. 1979).

Miss. *Added to compensation.

Mo. *Supplemental report within 1 month after original notice to Division.

Mont. *Insurance carrier also required to report (by rule).

Neb. *Report may be made by insurance carrier or employer. Failure to report tolls time limits.

Nev. *Self-insured employers must report as required by Commissioner of Insurance.

N.J. *Uninsured employers are required to report compensable injuries only. If insured, carrier is also required to make report.

EMPLOYER'S REPORT OF ACCIDENTS □ January 1, 1982 (continued)

JURISDICTION	KEEPING OF ACCIDENT RECORDS BY EMPLOYER[1]	REPORTING REQUIREMENTS[1]		PENALTIES FOR FAILURE TO REPORT		
		INJURIES COVERED	TIME LIMIT	FINES		IMPRISONMENT
				MAXIMUM	MINIMUM	
NEW MEXICO	Required	Compensable injuries*	Within 10 days	$100	$ 25	
		All injuries**	Within 30 days			
NEW YORK	Required	Disability of 1 day or more or requiring medical care beyond two first aid treatments	Within 10 days	500		
		All injuries	As required			
NORTH CAROLINA	Required	Disability of more than 1 day	Within 5 days[2]	25	5	
NORTH DAKOTA	Required	All injuries	Within 1 week	500		
OHIO	Required	Injuries causing 7 days total disability or more	Within 1 week	500	500	
OKLAHOMA	Required	All injuries	Within 10 days or a reasonable time	500		
OREGON	Required	All serious injuries	Within 5 days.	(-)		
PENNSYLVANIA	Not required	Death cases	Within 48 hours			Up to 30 days
		Disability of 1 day or more	After 7 days but not later than 10 days	100		
PUERTO RICO	Required	All injuries	Within 5 days	100		
RHODE ISLAND	Not required	Death cases	Within 48 hours	50		
		Disability of 3 days or more	Within 10 days*			
SOUTH CAROLINA	Required	All injuries requiring medical attention	Within 10 days[2]	50	10	
SOUTH DAKOTA	Required	All injuries	Within 10 days	100		Or 30 days
TENNESSEE	Not required	Disability of 7 days or more	Within 14 days	100	50	
TEXAS	Required	Disability of more than 1 day	Within 8 days[2]	1,000		
UTAH	Required	All injuries	Within 1 week	500		
VERMONT	Required	Disability of 1 day or more or requiring medical care	Within 72 hours[2]	25		
VIRGIN ISLANDS	Required	Injury or disease	Within 8 days	500		Up to 6 months
VIRGINIA	Required	All injuries	Within 10 days[2]	250		
WASHINGTON	Not required	All injuries requiring medical attention	Immediately	100		
WEST VIRGINIA	Not required	All injuries	Within 5 days			
WISCONSIN	Required	Disability beyond 3-day waiting period	Within 4 days	100	10	
WYOMING	Required	All injuries	Within 10 days	100		Up to 6 months
F.E.C.A.	No provision	Death or probable disability	Immediately			
LONGSHORE ACT	Required	All accidents	10 days	500		
ALBERTA	Required	Disability of 1 day or more or requiring medical aid not covered by Alberta Health Care Insurance.	24 hours[3,4]	50	10 per day	

		Death cases	Immediately	(·)		
BRITISH COLUMBIA	No provision	All injuries	3 days[3]			
MANITOBA	No provision	All injuries	3 days[3,4]	500*	50	
NEW BRUNSWICK	No provision	All injuries that disable or require medical aid.	3 days[3,4]	50		
NEWFOUNDLAND	No provision	All accidents that disable or require medical aid.	3 days	150		
NORTHWEST TERRITORIES	No provision	All accidents and deaths.	3 days[3,*]	250		
NOVA SCOTIA	No provision	All accidents that disable or require medical aid.	3 days[3]	50		
ONTARIO	Required	All accidents that disable or require medical aid.	3 days[3,4]	250	25	
PRINCE EDWARD ISLAND	No provision	All accidents that disable or require medical aid.	3 days	100	10 per day	
QUEBEC	Required for minor injuries.	All accidents that disable or require medical aid.	2 working days	600 plus fees	300 plus fees	
SASKATCHEWAN	No provision	All accidents	3 days[3]	500*		
YUKON TERRITORY	First aid cases	All accidents in which workman is injured	3 days*	1,000		Failure to pay penalty, imprisonment of 6 months to 1 year in aggregate.
CANADIAN MERCHANT SEAMEN'S ACT	No provision	All accidents that disable or require medical aid.	60 days	500		Up to 12 months

N.M. *To the State Labor Commissioner.
**To the Insurance Department of the State Corporation Commission.
Oregon *25% additional compensation plus attorneys' fees.
R.I. *Supplemental report upon termination of disability.

B.C. *Employer may be liable for full cost of claim.
Man. *Plus 50% of compensation payable.
N.W.T. *Supplemental report within 3 days after return to work or knowledge that worker is able to return.
Sask. *Plus percentage of assessment.

Chart XIV

APPEAL PROVISIONS

January 1, 1982

JURISDICTION	ADMINISTRATION	TIME FOR APPEAL	TO WHAT COURT	PROCESS AND PROCEDURE	QUESTIONS REVIEWED — LAW ONLY	QUESTIONS REVIEWED — LAW AND FACT	BASIS FOR REVIEW[1]	JURY TRIAL[1]
ALABAMA	Courts	30 days	Supreme Court	Certiorari	Yes		Record	No
ALASKA	Workmen's Compensation Board	30 days	Superior Court	Injunction	Yes		Record	No
AMERICAN SAMOA	Workmen's Compensation Commission	30 days	High Court	As in civil actions	Yes		Record	No
ARIZONA	Industrial Commission	30 days	Supreme Court of Appeals	Certiorari		Yes	Record	No
ARKANSAS	Workers' Compensation Commission	30 days	Court of Appeals	As in civil actions, with precedence over all other civil cases	Yes		Record	No
		No provision	Supreme Court	As in civil actions	Yes			
CALIFORNIA	Appeals Board	45 days	Supreme Court, or District Court of Appeals	Writ of review	Yes		Record	No
COLORADO	Industrial Commission	20 days	District Court	Action to modify or vacate	Yes		Record	No
		No provision	Supreme Court	Writ of error	Yes		Record	
CONNECTICUT	9 commissioners	20 days	Appellate session of Superior Court* Supreme Court	Notice of appeal**	Yes		Record	No
DELAWARE	Industrial Accident Board	20 days	Superior Court	As prescribed by the court		Yes	Record	No
DISTRICT OF COLUMBIA	D.C. Office of Workers' Compensation.	30 days	Review board	Petition		Yes	Record	No
		60 days	D.C. Court of Appeals	Petition	Yes		Record	
DISTRICT OF COLUMBIA GOVT. WORKERS	Office of Workers' Compensation	90 days to a year	Superior Court	Application for review		Yes	Record	No
FLORIDA	Division of Workers' Compensation	20 days	District Court of Appeals, First District	Notice of appeal	Yes		Record	No
GEORGIA	State Board of Workers' Compensation	30 days	Superior Court / Court of Appeals	Notice of appeal	Yes		Record	No
GUAM	Workmen's Compensation Commission	30 days	Island Court	Injunction proceedings	Yes			No
HAWAII	Disability Compensation Division	30 days	Supreme Court	Notice of appeal*	Yes		Record	Yes, if claimed within 10 days from the date case is docketed.
IDAHO	Industrial Commission	42 days	Supreme Court	Notice of appeal	Yes		Record and transcript of evidence	No
ILLINOIS	Industrial Commission	20 days	Circuit Court, or City Court in cities over 25,000*	Certiorari		Yes	Record; no additional evidence	No
		30 days	Supreme Court	Writ of error	Yes			
INDIANA	Industrial Board	30 days	Court of Appeals	As in civil action*	Yes		Assignment of errors	No
IOWA	Industrial Commissioner	30 days	District Court	Petition for judicial review	Yes		Certified transcript of documents and evidence	Only when employee has right to sue uninsured employer.
KANSAS	Division of Workers' Compensation	20 days	District Court*	Notice of appeal		Yes	Transcript of evidence and proceedings	No
		30 days	Court of Appeals	Notice of appeal	Yes			
KENTUCKY	Workers' Compensation Board	20 days	Circuit Court	Petition, summons, answer	Yes		Certified record	No
		No provision	Court of Appeals / Supreme Court	As in civil actions			Certified record or scheduled portions	
LOUISIANA	Courts	30 days*	Appellate Court	As in civil actions		Yes	Transcript of proceedings	No
			Supreme Court	As in civil actions		Yes	Certified record	No

State	Administering agency	Time to appeal	Law Court	As in equity procedure*	(review)	(certify)	Certified record	No
MAINE	Workers' Compensation Commission	20 days		As in equity procedure*	Yes	Yes, except in occupational disease cases	Certified record	No
MARYLAND	Workmen's Compensation Commission	30 days	County Circuit Courts or Baltimore Common Law Courts	Notice, followed by informal and summary trial	Yes, in occupational disease cases	Yes, except in occupational disease cases	Trial de novo	Yes, on demand
		No provision	Court of Special Appeals Court of Appeals	As in civil cases				
MASSACHUSETTS	Industrial Accidents Board	10 days	Superior Court	As in civil cases	Yes		Agreed statement of facts and findings and decision	No
		No provision	Supreme Judicial Court	As in civil cases	Yes			
MICHIGAN	Workers' Compensation Appeal Board	30 days	Court of Appeals	Certiorari, mandamus, or other permissible method	Yes			No
		30 days	Supreme Court					
MINNESOTA	Workers' Compensation Court of Appeals	30 days*	Supreme Court	Certiorari		Yes	Certified record**	No
MISSISSIPPI	Workmen's Compensation Commission	30 days	Circuit Court	Notice of appeal	Yes		Record	No
			Supreme Court	As in civil cases				
MISSOURI	Division of Workers' Compensation*	30 days	Appellate Court	Notice of appeal	Yes		Record	No
MONTANA	Division of Workers' Compensation	30 days	Supreme Court	Notice of appeal		Yes	Certified record	No
NEBRASKA	Workmen's Compensation Court*	1 month	Supreme Court	Notice of appeal and bill of exceptions (under general laws)	Yes		Certified record	No
NEVADA	Department of Administration Appeals Officer	No provision	District Court		Yes		Record	No
NEW HAMPSHIRE	Commissioner of Labor	30 days	Superior Court Supreme Court	Petition for a hearing		Yes	Trial de novo	No

NOTE—Other Canadian jurisdictions do not provide for judicial appeal.

[1] Generally courts may set aside an award on one of the following grounds: (1) that the Commission acted in excess of its powers, (2) that the award was procured by fraud, (3) that the facts found by the Commission did not support the award, and (4) that there was not sufficient competent evidence in the record to warrant the finding.

[2] Board may request opinion on question of law or jurisdiction on its own motion.

[3] Court has power to pass only upon question of law or jurisdiction of the Board

Conn. *Claimant may appeal commissioner's decision to Compensation Review Division (panel of all 8 commissioners), then to appellate session of Superior Court.
**Division may certify question of law on its own motion.

Hawaii *Appellate Board may certify questions of law to Supreme Court.

Ill. *If defendants cannot be found in state, then in Circuit Court of county where accident occurred.

Ind. *Board may also certify questions of law on its own motion.

Kansas *If court fails to appeal within 60 days, Director must request decision; if no decision is issued within 30 days after request, Director must advise Supreme Court.

La. *60 days for devolutive appeal.

Maine *First level of appeal is Appellate Division. Denial of review by Law Court is final. No appeal from decree based on memorandum of agreement.

Minn. *Compensation paid under mistake of law or fact need not be refunded.
**Appeal based on error of law or fraud may be heard de novo.

Mo. *Administrative Law Judge's award may be appealed to Industrial Commission.

Neb. *The Court is constituted the same as the boards and commissions in other states.

APPEAL PROVISIONS □ January 1, 1982 (continued)

JURISDICTION	ADMINISTRATION	TIME FOR APPEAL	TO WHAT COURT	PROCESS AND PROCEDURE	QUESTIONS REVIEWED — LAW ONLY	QUESTIONS REVIEWED — LAW AND FACT	BASIS FOR REVIEW[1]	JURY TRIAL
NEW JERSEY	Division of Workers' Compensation	No provision	Appellate Division of Superior Court	Notice of appeal		Yes	Trial de novo on the record	No
NEW MEXICO	Courts	No provision	Court of Appeals Supreme Court	Writ of error or appeal, or certiorari	Yes		Certified record	No
NEW YORK	Workers' Compensation Board	30 days after decision on review*	Appellate Division, Supreme Court, Third Department	As in civil actions, with precedence over all other civil cases.	Yes			No
		No provision	Court of Appeals	Regular appeal			Record	No
NORTH CAROLINA	Industrial Commission	30 days	Court of Appeals	As in civil actions*	Yes		Record	No
NORTH DAKOTA	Workmen's Compensation Bureau	30 days	District Court	Appeal		Yes	Record	No
		No provision	Supreme Court	Writ of error			Record	No
OHIO	Industrial Commission	60 days (no appeal in occupational disease cases)	Court of Common Pleas	Notice of appeal and petition by claimant		Yes	Trial de novo	Yes, on demand
		No provision	Supreme Court					
OKLAHOMA	Workers' Compensation Court	20 days	Supreme Court	Petition	Yes		Certified record and specifications of error	No
OREGON	Workers' Compensation Board	30 days	Court of Appeals	Notice of appeal		Yes	Record*	No
PENNSYLVANIA	Workers' Compensation Bureau*	20 days	Commonwealth Court	Notice of appeal	Yes		Certified record	No
		30 days	Supreme Court	As in civil actions	Yes			
PUERTO RICO	Manager of the State Insurance Fund	30 days	Industrial Commission or a single Commissioner	Appeal		Yes	Record	No
		15 days	Supreme Court	Petition for review	Yes	(·)	Certified record	No
RHODE ISLAND	Director of Labor and Commission	5 days	3 members of appellate commission	Claim of appeal		Yes	Certified documents and testimony	No
SOUTH CAROLINA	Industrial Commission—Judicial Division	10 days	Court of Common Pleas	Claim of appeal	Yes		Record	No
SOUTH DAKOTA	Division of Labor and Management	30 days*	Circuit Court	Notice of appeal	Yes		Certified record	No
		120 days	Supreme Court	As in civil actions				
TENNESSEE	Courts	10 days	Circuit Courts	As in civil actions		Yes	Trial de novo	No
		No provision	Supreme Court	Writ of error				
TEXAS	Industrial Accident Board	20 days	Court of county of injury or worker's residence	Suit to set aside decision of Board		Yes	Trial de novo	Yes
UTAH	Industrial Commission	30 days	Supreme Court	Certiorari	Yes		Certified record	No
VERMONT	Commissioner of Labor and Industry	30 days	County Court*	As prescribed by Court	Yes		Certified record	Yes, on demand
		After 30 days	Supreme Court	As prescribed by Court	Yes			
VIRGIN ISLANDS	Commissioner of Labor	30 days	Court of competent jurisdiction	As in civil actions	Yes		Record	No
VIRGINIA	Industrial Commission	30 days	Supreme Court	As in equity	Yes		Certified record	No
WASHINGTON	Board of Industrial Insurance Appeals	60 days	Superior Court	Notice of Appeal		Yes	Trial de novo, but on testimony before the Board	Yes, on demand
		30 days	Further appeal	As in civil actions				
WEST VIRGINIA	Compensation Commissioner	30 days	Supreme Court of Appeals	Petition		Yes	Record of proceedings	No

Jurisdiction	Administrative agency	Time	Court	Action against Commission			Type of review	
WISCONSIN	Department of Industry, Labor, and Human Relations	30 days	Circuit Court, Dane County	As from orders	Yes		Record	No
WYOMING	Courts	70 days	Supreme Court	Petition and bill of exceptions		Yes	Record	No
F.E.C.A.	Division of Federal Employees' Compensation, O.W.C.P.	90 days to a year	Federal Employees' Compensation Board*	Application for review		Yes	Record	No
LONGSHORE ACT	Division of Longshore and Harbor Workers' Compensation, O.W.C.P.	30 days	Benefits Review Board*	Petition		Yes	Record	No
		60 days	U.S. Court of Appeals	Petition	Yes		Record	No
BRITISH COLUMBIA	Ministry of Labour	90 days	Board of Review	Appeal	Yes		Record and written or oral testimony	No
		90 days	Medical Review Panel	Appeal (medical facts only)			Diagnosis from file and examination	No
NEW BRUNSWICK	Workers' Compensation Board	10 days	Appeal Division, Supreme Court	Under Judicature Act[2]	Yes[3]		Record	No
NEWFOUNDLAND	Workers' Compensation Board	30 days	Supreme Court	Petition[2]		Yes	Trial de novo unless Court directs otherwise	No
NOVA SCOTIA	Workers' Compensation Board	90 days	Workers' Compensation Appeal Board	Appeal		Yes	De novo	No
		30 days	Appeal Division, Supreme Court	Petition to judge for permission*	Yes[3]		Record	No
PRINCE EDWARD ISLAND	Workers' Compensation Board	15 days	Supreme Court in banco	Petition to judge for permission	Yes[3]		Record	No
QUEBEC	Commission	30 to 90 days	Board of Review*	Notice of appeal		Yes	Trial de novo	No

N.Y. *Compensation is paid pending appeal; if reversed, carrier is reimbursed from Administration Fund.

N.C. *Commission may certify questions of law to Court of Appeals. Commission may order payment of portion of award not in dispute.

Oregon *Court may take additional evidence on disability not available at hearing.

Pa. *Decisions of referees are subject to appeal to the Workers' Compensation Appeal Board.

P.R. *On weight of expert testimony.

S. Dak. *Commission may order payment of portion of award not in dispute.

Vt. *Then to Supreme Court on exception.

F.E.C.A. *There is no court appeal; Board has authority to make final decision on appeals.

Longshore *First level of appeal is to Benefits Review Board within the U.S. Department of Labor.

N.S. *Board may request opinion on question of law on its own motion.

Quebec *Further appeal to Social Affairs Commission.

Chart XV
DIRECTORY OF WORKERS' COMPENSATION ADMINISTRATORS
January 1, 1982

ALABAMA

Workmen's Compensation Division
Department of Industrial Relations
Industrial Relations Building
Montgomery, Alabama 36130
(205) 832-5040
    Mr. Marcus A. Davis, Examiner

ALASKA

Workmen's Compensation Division
Department of Labor
P.O. Box 1149
Juneau, Alaska 99811
(907) 465-2790
    Ms. Jacquelyn McClintock, Director

Workmen's Compensation Board
Same address as Division
    Mr. Edmund Orbeck, Chairman
    Mr. Thomas Chandler, Member
    Mrs. Ann Pittinger, Member
    Mr. Jim Robison, Member
    Mr. David Richards, Member
    Mr. Jan Baughman, Member
    Mr. M. M. Langberg, Member

AMERICAN SAMOA

Workmen's Compensation Commission
Office of the Governor
American Samoa Government
Pago Pago, American Samoa 96799
    Mr. Morris Scanlan, Chairman

ARIZONA

Industrial Commission
1601 West Jefferson
P.O. Box 19070
Phoenix, Arizona 85005
(602) 255-4661
    Mr. Charles W. Pine, Chairman
    Mr. Duane D. Pell, Commissioner
    Mr. G. Vernon McCracken, Commissioner
    Mr. Daniel R. Ortega, Commissioner
    Mr. Eugene J. Lane, Commissioner
    Mr. Harry G. Kelley, Director

State Compensation Fund
1616 West Adams
Phoenix, Arizona 85007
    Mr. William L. Finley, Manager

ARKANSAS

Workers' Compensation Commission
Justice Building
State Capitol Grounds
Little Rock, Arkansas 72201
(501) 372-3930
    Mr. Berl Rotenberry, Chairman
    Mr. Jimmie D. Clark, Commissioner
    Mr. Allyn C. Tatum, Commissioner

CALIFORNIA

Division of Industrial Accidents
P.O. Box 603, Room 617
San Francisco, California 94101
(415) 557-3542
    Mr. Franklin O. Grady, Administrative Director

Workers' Compensation Appeals Board
455 Golden Gate Avenue
San Francisco, California 94102
    Mr. Jack Fenton, Chairman
    Mr. John F. Dunlap, Commissioner
    Mr. Gordon R. Gaines, Commissioner
    Mr. Hubert J. Martin, Commissioner
    Mr. Charles L. Swezey, Commissioner
    Mr. Robert E. Burton, Commissioner

State Compensation Insurance Fund
1275 Market Street
San Francisco, California 94103
    Mr. E.A. Sandberg, President

COLORADO

Division of Labor
1313 Sherman Street, Room 314
Denver, Colorado 80203
(303) 866-2446
    Mr. Charles J. McGrath, Director

Industrial Commission
State Services Building, 5th Floor
1525 Sherman Street
Denver, Colorado 80203
    Mr. Miguel Baca, Chairman
    Mr. Richard Wise, Commissioner
    Mr. Peter D. Nims, Commissioner

State Compensation Insurance Fund
950 Broadway
Denver, Colorado 80203
    Mr. Glenn Adams, Manager

CONNECTICUT

Workers' Compensation Commission
295 Treadwell Street
Hamden, Connecticut 06514
(203) 789-7783
    Mr. John A. Arcudi, Chairman
    Mr. A. Paul Berte, Commissioner
    Mr. Gerald Kolinsky, Commissioner
    Mrs. Rhoda L. Loeb, Commissioner
    Mr. Andrew P. Denuzze, Commissioner
    Mr. Edward F. Bradley, Commissioner
    Mr. Varius J. Spain, Commissioner
    Mr. Robin W. Waller, Commissioner
    Mr. Vincent Tisi, Commissioner

DELAWARE

Industrial Accident Board
State Office Building, 6th Floor
820 North French Street
Wilmington, Delaware 19801
(302) 571-2885
    Mr. Thomas E. Hickman, Chairman
    Mr. Irving H. Garton, Member
    Mr. Warren T. Foraker, Member
    Mr. Ellsworth Jackson, Member
    Mr. Edward T. Campbell, Member
    Mrs. Kathryn D. Ribynski, Administrator

DISTRICT OF COLUMBIA

Government of the District of Columbia
Office of Workers' Compensation
950 Upshur Street, N.W.
Washington, D.C. 20011
(202) 576-7088
    Mr. Robert M. Duvall, Associate Director

United States Department of Labor
Office of Workers' Compensation Programs
District 40
P.O. Box 19421
Washington, D.C. 20036
(202) 254-3470
    Ms. Janice Bryant, Deputy Commissioner

FLORIDA

Division of Workers' Compensation
Department of Labor and Employment Security
1321 Executive Center Drive-East
Tallahassee, Florida 32301
(904) 488-2548
    Mr. J. Baxter Swing, Director

GEORGIA

Board of Workers' Compensation
1800 Peachtree Street, N.W.
Suite 400
Atlanta, Georgia 30309
(404) 894-3082
    Mr. Herbert T. Greenholtz, Jr., Chairman
    Mr. Don K. Knowles, Director
    Mr. James W. Paris, Director

GUAM

Director of Labor and Personnel
Government of Guam
P.O. Box 367
Agana, Guam 96910
    Mr. José R. Rivera

HAWAII

Disability Compensation Division
Department of Labor and Industrial Relations
825 Mililani Street
Honolulu, Hawaii 96813
(808) 548-4131
    Dr. Joshua C. Agsalud, Director
    Mr. Orlando K. Watanabe, Administrator

Labor and Industrial Relations Appeals Board
888 Mililani Street
Room 400
Honolulu, Hawaii 96813
    Mr. E. John McConnell, Chairman
    Mr. James H. Takushi, Member
    Mr. Yukio Takemoto, Member

IDAHO

Industrial Commission
317 Main Street
Boise, Idaho 83720
(208) 334-2193
    Mr. L. G. Sirhall, Chairman
    Mr. Will S. Defenbach, Member
    Mr. Gerald A. Geddes, Member
    Mr. Lawrence J. Spjute, Administrator

State Insurance Fund
P.O. Box 1038
Boise, Idaho 83704
    Ms. Diane Plastino, Manager

ILLINOIS

Industrial Commission
160 North LaSalle Street
Chicago, Illinois 60601
(312) 793-6611
    Ms. Rebecca Schneiderman, Chairman
    Mr. Ralph W. Miller, Jr., Commissioner
    Mr. Theodies Black, Jr., Commissioner
    Mr. Calvin F. Tansor, Commissioner
    Mr. James A. Thomas, Commissioner
    Mrs. Elsie Kurasch, Secretary

INDIANA

Industrial Board
601 State Office Building
100 North Senate Avenue
Indianapolis, Indiana 46204
(317) 232-3808
    Mr. Robert W. McNevin, Chairman
    Mr. R.J. Noel, Member
    Mr. J.J. McDonagh, Member
    Mr. R.J. Cronin, Member
    Mr. John A. Rader, Member
    Mr. Everett N. Lucas
    Mr. G. Terance Coriden, Member

IOWA

Industrial Commissioner's Office
507 10th Street
Des Moines, Iowa 50319
(515) 281-5935
    Mr. Robert C. Landess, Industrial
    Commissioner

KANSAS

Division of Workers' Compensation
Department of Human Resources
6th Floor
535 Kansas Avenue
Topeka, Kansas 66603
(913) 296-3441
    Mr. Bryce B. Moore, Director

KENTUCKY

Workers' Compensation Board
127 Building
U.S. 127 South
Frankfort, Kentucky 40601
(502) 564-5550
    Mr. Glenn L. Schilling, Chairman
    Mr. Darryl T. Owens, Member
    Mr. Lanny Holbrook, Member
    Mr. William Brooks, Member
    Mr. Larry Creathouse, Member
    Mr. Gerald V. Roberts, Director

LOUISIANA

Department of Labor
1045 State Land and Natural Resources
    Building
Box 44094
Baton Rouge, Louisiana 70804
(504) 925-4298
    Mr. J.T. Armatta, Commissioner

MAINE

Workers' Compensation Commission
State Office Building
Augusta, Maine 04333
(207) 289-3751
    Mr. Charles D. Devoe, Chairman
    Mr. Ronald D. Russell, Commissioner
    Mr. James M. Coyne, Commissioner
    Mr. David C. Pomeroy, Commissioner
    Mr. Edward F. Gaulin, Commissioner
    Mr. Joseph M. Jabar, Sr., Commissioner
    Mrs. Suzanne E.K. Smith, Commissioner
    Mr. Ralph Tucker, Commissioner

MARYLAND

Workmen's Compensation Commission
108 East Lexington Street
Baltimore, Maryland 21202
(301) 383-4700
    Mr. Charles J. Krysiak, Chairman
    Mr. Clement R. Mercaldo, Commissioner
    Mr. Harold Lee Frankel, Commissioner
    Mr. Sidney W. Albert, Commissioner
    Mr. Edward A. Palamara, Commissioner
    Mr. G. Joseph Sills, Jr., Commissioner
    Ms. Carmel J. Snow, Commissioner
    Mr. Francis J. Valle, Commissioner

State Accident Fund
8722 Loch Raven Boulevard
Towson, Maryland 21204
    Mr. Donald Potter, Superintendent

MASSACHUSETTS

Industrial Accidents Board
Leverett Saltonstall Office Building
100 Cambridge Street
Boston, Massachusetts 02202
(617) 727-3400
    Mr. William A. Pickett, Chairman
    Mr. Louis C. Gallo, Commissioner
    Mr. Harry Demeter, Jr., Commissioner
    Mr. William McCarthy, Commissioner
    Mr. Salvatore Musco, Commissioner
    Mr. Wallace B. Crawford, Commissioner

Ms. Dorothy A. Antonnelli, Commissioner
Mr. R. A. Roberts, Commissioner
Mr. John McKinnon, Commissioner
Mr. Richard A. Rogers, Commissioner
Mr. Nicholas J. Vergados, Commissioner
Mr. John G. Martin, Commissioner

MICHIGAN

Bureau of Workers' Disability Compensation
Department of Labor
309 North Washington Square
Lansing, Michigan 48909
(517) 373-3480
    Mr. James M. Brakora, Director
    Mr. John P. Miron, Chief Deputy

Workers' Compensation Appeal Board
309 North Washington Square
Leonard Plaza Building
Lansing, Michigan 48909
    Mr. Michael J. Gillman, Chairman
    Mr. Ferris Arnold, Member
    Ms. Nancy Day, Member
    Mr. Robert Kehres, Member
    Mr. K. Michael Miller, Member
    Mr. John Hays, Member
    Mr. Arpo Yemen, Member
    Ms. Eleanor Powell, Member
    Mrs. Molly Beitner, Member
    Mr. William C. Marshall, Member
    Mr. Robert J. Hostetler, Member
    Mrs. Janet H. Phelps, Member
    Mr. Karl N. Benghauser, Member
    Mr. Stephen C. Oldstrom, Member
    Mr. Robert L. Richardson, Member

State Accident Fund
232 South Capitol Street
Lansing, Michigan 48914
    Mr. Floyd Luginbill, Manager

MINNESOTA

Workers' Compensation Division
Department of Labor and Industry
444 Layafette Road
St. Paul, Minnesota 55101
(612) 296-2258
    Mr. Bruce Swanson, Commissioner
    Mr. B. James Berg, Administrator

Workers' Compensation Court of Appeals
Second Floor
MEA Building
55 Sherburne Avenue
St. Paul, Minnesota 55103
    Hon. Raymond O. Adel, Chief Judge
    Hon. Robert B. McCarthy, Judge
    Hon. Leigh Gard, Judge
    Hon. John Wallraff, Judge
    Hon. Paul V. Rieke, Judge

MISSISSIPPI

Workmen's Compensation Commission
1404 Walter Sillers State Office Building
P.O. Box 987
Jackson, Mississippi 39205
(601) 354-7496
    Mr. Marshall G. Bennett, Chairman
    Mr. J. Tillis Hill, Commissioner
    Mr. Walter M. O'Barr, Commissioner
    Mrs. Mildred Morrison, Secretary

MISSOURI

Division of Workers' Compensation
Department of Labor and Industrial Relations
P.O. Box 58
Jefferson City, Missouri 65102
(314) 751-4231
    Mr. Richard R. Rousselot, Director

Labor and Industrial Relations Commission
1904 Missouri Boulevard
P.O. Box 599
Jefferson City, Missouri 65102
    Mr. Terry C. Allen, Chairman
    Mr. Herbert L. Ford, Member

MONTANA

Division of Workers' Compensation
815 Front Street
Helena, Montana 59601
(406) 449-2047
    Mr. Laury M. Lewis, Administrator

Workers' Compensation Court
1422 Cedar-Airport Way
P.O. Box 4127
Helena, Montana 59601
    Judge Timothy W. Reardon

State Compensation Insurance Fund
Same address as Division
    Mr. A.G. Pillen, Bureau Chief

NEBRASKA

Workmen's Compensation Court
State House, 12th Floor
Lincoln, Nebraska 68509
(402) 471-2568
    Hon. Mark A. Buchholz, Presiding Judge
    Hon. Paul E. LeClair, Judge
    Hon. Ben Novicoff, Judge
    Hon. James P. Monen, Judge
    Hon. Theodore W. Vrana, Judge
    Mrs. Yvonne Leung, Administrator

NEVADA

Industrial Commission
515 East Musser Street
Carson City, Nevada 89714
(702) 885-5284
    Mr. Joe E. Nusbaum, Chairman
    Mr. James S. Lorigan, Commissioner
    Mr. Hal G. Curtis, Commissioner

State Insurance Fund
Same address as Commission

NEW HAMPSHIRE

Department of Labor
19 Pillsbury Street
Concord, New Hampshire 03301
(603) 271-3171
    Dennis E. Murphy, Jr., Commissioner

NEW JERSEY

Division of Workers' Compensation
Department of Labor and Industry
P.O. Box CN 381
John Fitch Plaza
Trenton, New Jersey 08625
(609) 292-2414
    Hon. A.J. Napier, Chief Judge and
    Acting Director

NEW MEXICO

Labor and Industrial Commission
509 Camino De Los Marquez
Suite 2
Santa Fe, New Mexico 87501
(505) 827-2756
    Mr. R.C. Brooks, Labor Commissioner
    Ms. Consuelo C. Smith, Manager V

NEW YORK

Workers' Compensation Board
Two World Trade Center
New York, New York 10047
(212) 488-3033
    Mr. William Kroeger, Chairman
    Mr. Francis J. Griffin, Vice Chairman
    Mr. Daniel J. Higgins, Commissioner
    Mr. Walter Shields, Commissioner
    Ms. Ilene Slater, Commissioner
    Ms. Monica Gollub, Commissioner
    Mr. Donald Vass, Commissioner
    Mr. Henry M. Christman, Commissioner
    Mr. Ferdinand Tremiti, Commissioner
    Mr. Seymour Posner, Commissioner
    Mr. Ernest R. Latham, Commissioner
    Mr. Joseph Tauriello, Commissioner

State Insurance Fund
199 Church Street
New York, New York 10007
   Mr. Arnold Kideckel, Executive Director

NORTH CAROLINA

Industrial Commission
Dobbs Building
430 North Salisbury Street
Raleigh, North Carolina 27611
(919) 733-4820
   Mr. William H. Stephenson, Chairman
   Mr. Coy Vance, Commissioner
   Mr. Charles Clay, Commissioner

NORTH DAKOTA

Workmen's Compensation Bureau
Russell Building
Highway 83 North
Bismarck, North Dakota 58505
(701) 224-2700
   Mr. Bronald Thompson, Chairman
   Mr. Quentin Retterath, Commissioner
   Mrs. Loretta Jennings, Commissioner

Workmen's Compensation Fund
Same address as Bureau

OHIO

Bureau of Workers' Compensation
246 North High Street
Columbus, Ohio 43215
(614) 466-2950
   Mr. Raymond A. Connor, Administrator

Industrial Commission
Same address as Bureau
   Mr. William W. Johnson, Chairman
   Mr. W. Craig Zimpher, Vice Chairman
   Mr. Leonard T. Lancaster, Member

State Insurance Fund
Same address as Bureau

OKLAHOMA

Oklahoma Workers' Compensation Court
Jim Thorpe Building
2101 North Lincoln
Oklahoma City, Oklahoma 73105
(405) 521-8025
   Hon. Patrick C. Ryan, Presiding Judge
   Hon. Charles L. Cashion, Judge
   Hon. Larry C. Brawner, Judge
   Hon. Victor Seagle, Judge
   Hon. Bill Cross, Judge
   Hon. Dick Lynn, Judge
   Hon. Mary Elizabeth Cox, Judge

State Insurance Fund
5th and Walnut
Oklahoma City, Oklahoma 73105
   Mr. David Gillogly, Manager

OREGON

Workers' Compensation Department
Labor and Industries Building
Salem, Oregon 97310
(503) 378-3304
   Mr. Roy G. Green, Director

Workers' Compensation Board
Mill Creek Office Park
555 13th Street, N.E.
Salem, Oregon 97310
   Mr. Kendall M. Barnes, Chairman
   Mr. George E. Lewis, Member
   Mr. Robert L. McCallister, Member

SAIF Corporation
400 High Street, S.E.
Salem, Oregon 97312
   Mr. Charles B. Gill, Jr., General Manager

PENNSYLVANIA

Bureau of Workers' Compensation
Department of Labor and Industry
3607 Derry Street

Harrisburg, Pennsylvania 17111
(717) 783-5421
   Mr. Bruce Hockman, Director

Workers' Compensation Appeal Board
2601 Herr Street
3rd Floor
Harrisburg, Pennsylvania 17103
   Mr. Harold Fergus, Chairman
   Mr. Anthony R. Cognetti, Commissioner
   Mr. William R. Hagner, Commissioner

State Workmen's Insurance Fund
100 Lackawanna Avenue
Scranton, Pennsylvania 18503
   Mr. Wilbert Scheuer, Acting Manager

PUERTO RICO

Industrial Commissioner's Office
G.P.O. Box 4466
San Juan, Puerto Rico 00936
(809) 783-4455
   Ms. Jeannette Tomasini de Ramos, Chairman

RHODE ISLAND

Workers' Compensation Commission
25 Canal Street
Providence, Rhode Island 02903
(401) 277-3097
   Mr. Eugene J. Laferriere, Chairman
   Mr. John A. Notte, Jr., Vice Chairman
   Mr. Robert F. Arrigan, Commissioner
   Mr. William G. Gilroy, Commissioner
   Mr. Moses Kando, Commissioner
   Mr. Dennis Revens, Administrator

SOUTH CAROLINA

Industrial Commission
Middleburg Office Park
1800 St. Julian Place
Columbia, South Carolina 29202
(803) 758-2556
   Mr. T.M. Nelson, Chairman
   Mr. Paul M. Macmillan, Jr., Commissioner
   Mr. James J. Reid, Commissioner
   Mr. J. Dawson Addis, Commissioner
   Mr. Holmes C. Dreher, Commissioner
   Mr. Frederick Zeigler, Commissioner
   Mr. Samuel E. Kirven, Administrative Director

SOUTH DAKOTA

Division of Labor and Management
Department of Labor
Kneip Building, Second Floor
Pierre, South Dakota 57501
(605) 773-3681
   Mr. Peter de Hueck, Director

TENNESSEE

Workers' Compensation Division
Department of Labor
501 Union Building
Nashville, Tennessee 37219
(615) 741-2395
   Director to be appointed

TEXAS

Industrial Accident Board
200 East Riverside, First Floor
Austin, Texas 78704
(512) 475-3126
   Mr. H.S. Harris, Chairman
   Mr. Bobby Barnes, Commissioner
   Mr. Sid E. McKinney, Commissioner
   Mr. William Treacy, Executive Director

UTAH

Industrial Commission
350 East 500 South
Salt Lake City, Utah 84111
(801) 533-6411
   Mr. Walter T. Axelgard, Chairman
   Mr. Stephen M. Hadley, Commissioner
   Mr. Milton E. Saathoff, Commissioner

State Insurance Fund
Same address as Commission
   Mr. Dale Williams, Manager

VERMONT

Department of Labor and Industry
Montpelier, Vermont 05602
(802) 828-2286
   Mr. Dean B. Pinelas, Commissioner

VIRGIN ISLANDS

Commissioner of Labor's Office
Government of the Virgin Islands
St. Thomas, Virgin Islands 00801
(809) 773-6200
   Mr. Richard Upson, Commissioner

VIRGINIA

Industrial Commission
Blanton Building
P.O. Box 1794
Richmond, Virginia 23214
(804) 786-3644
   Mr. Robert P. Joyner, Chairman
   Mr. Charles G. James, Commissioner
   Mr. Thomas M. Miller, Commissioner

WASHINGTON

Department of Labor and Industries
General Administration Building
AX-31
Olympia, Washington 98504
(206) 753-6308
   Mr. Sam Kinville, Director

Board of Industrial Insurance Appeals
410 West 5th
Capitol Center Building
Olympia, Washington 98504
   Mr. Michael L. Hall, Chairman
   Mr. Frank Fennerty, Jr., Member
   Mr. Phillip T. Bork, Member

Industrial Insurance Division (State Fund)
Same address as Department
   Mr. Richard Slunaker, Supervisor

WEST VIRGINIA

Workmen's Compensation Commissioner's Office
P.O. Box 3151
Charleston, West Virginia 25332
(304) 384-2580
   Ms. Gretchen O. Lewis, Commissioner

Workmen's Compensation Appeal Board
112 California Avenue
Room 115
Charleston, West Virginia 25305
   Mr. John Hankins, Chairman
   Mr. Louis J. John, Member
   Mrs. R. Sue Core, Member

Workmen's Compensation Fund
Same address as Commissioner's Office

WISCONSIN

Workers' Compensation Division
Department of Industry, Labor, and Human Relations
P.O. Box 7901
Room 152
201 East Washington Avenue
Madison, Wisconsin 53707
(608) 266-1340
   Mrs. K. Sue Mattka, Administrator

Labor and Industry Review Commission
P.O. Box 8126
Madison, Wisconsin 53708
   Ms. Virginia B. Hart, Chairman

WYOMING

Worker's Compensation Division
State Treasurer's Office
2305 Carey Avenue
Cheyenne, Wyoming 82002

(307) 777-7441
Mr. Kirk F. Jensen, Director

Industrial Accident Fund
Same address as Division

UNITED STATES
Department of Labor
Employment Standards Administration
Washington, D.C. 20210
(202) 523-6191
Mr. Robert Collyer, Deputy Under Secretary

Office of Workers' Compensation Programs
(202) 523-6579
Mr. Ralph Hartman, Director

Division of Coal Mine Workers' Compensation
(202) 523-6692
Mr. James R. Yocom, Associate Director

Division of Federal Employees' Compensation
(202) 523-8463
Mr. John D. McLellan, Associate Director

Division of Longshore and Harbor Workers'
Compensation
(202) 523-8721
Mr. Neil A. Montone, Associate Director

Division of State Workers' Compensation
Standards
(202) 523-7391
Mrs. June Robinson, Associate Director

Benefits Review Board
1111 20th Street, N.W.
Suite 757
Vanguard Building
Washington, D.C. 20036
Mr. Robert Ramsey, Chairman
Mr. Julius Miller, Member
Mrs. Ismene Kalaris, Member

Employees' Compensation Appeals Board
300 Reporters Building
7th & D Streets, S.W.
Room 300
Washington, D.C. 20210
Mr. Gerald Lamboley, Chairman
Mr. George E. Rivers, Member
Ms. Margaret Pallansch, Member

ALBERTA
Workers' Compensation Board
P.O. Box 2415
9912 107th Street.
Edmonton, Alberta T5J 2S5
(403) 427-1100
Mr. Roy H. Jamha, Chairman
Mr. Peter Kolba, Member
Dr. A.E. Hohol, Member
Mr. T.P. Griffin, Executive Director-
Administration
Mr. John Wisocky, Executive Director-Claims
Services
Mr. J.R. Thomson, Executive Director-Finance

BRITISH COLUMBIA
Workers' Compensation Board
5255 Heather Street
Vancouver, British Columbia V5Z 3L8
(604) 266-0211
Mr. Art Gibbons, Chairman
Mr. Bob Bucher, Commissioner
Mr. Michael Parr, Commissioner

MANITOBA
Workers' Compensation Board
333 Maryland Street
Winnipeg, Manitoba R3G 1M2
(204) 786-5471
Mr. R. G. Jones, Chairman
Mr. D. Proctor, Commissioner
Mr. W. F. Kennedy, Commissioner
Mr. Ralph A. Boyes, Executive Director

NEW BRUNSWICK
Workers' Compensation Board
P.O. Box 160
Saint John, New Brunswick E2L 3X9
(506) 652-2250
Mr. Robert G. Jones, Chairman
Mr. Roland C. Boudreau, Vice Chairman
Mr. M.P. Fisher, Commissioner
Mr. Bryan Baxter, Executive Director

NEWFOUNDLAND
Workers' Compensation Board
P.O. Box 9000
Station B
St. John's, Newfoundland A1A 3B8
(709) 754-2940
Mr. Edward Maynard, Chairman
Mr. Gordon F. Woodford, Commissioner
Mr. Andrew G. Rose, Commissioner
Mr. Roland H. Baggs, Executive Director

NORTHWEST TERRITORIES
Workers' Compensation Board
P.O. Box 8888
Yellowknife, Northwest Territories X1A 2R3
(403) 873-7484
Mr. J.D.C. MacLean, Chairman
Mr. Bill Berezowski, Member
Mr. Colin Adjun, Member
Mr. W. Hettrick, Member
Mr. D. Johnston, Member
Mr. W. Maduke, Member
Mr. W.R. Hargrave, Member
Mr. W. Adams, Member
Mr. J. Todd, Member
Mr. B. Roberts, Member

NOVA SCOTIA
Workers' Compensation Board
5668 South Street
P.O. Box 1150
Halifax, Nova Scotia B3J 2Y2
(902) 424-8081
Mr. J.R. Lynk, Chairman
Mr. Burt Coutts, Vice Chairman
Mr. James Vaughan, Commissioner
Mr. J.H. Cottenden, Executive Director

Workers' Compensation Appeal Board
3rd Floor, Lord Nelson Arcade
Spring Garden Road
P.O. Box 3311
Halifax, Nova Scotia B3J 3J1
Mr. Hugh J. MacLeod, Chairman
Mr. H. Maxwell Pierce, Member
Mr. Donald Hutchinson, Member
Mr. Lawrence F. Scaravelli, Member
Mr. George Beckwith, Member
Mr. John J. O'Brien, Executive Officer

ONTARIO
Workmen's Compensation Board
2 Bloor Street East

Toronto, Ontario M4W 3C3
(416) 965-8884
Hon. Lincoln M. Alexander, Chairman
Mr. A.G. MacDonald, Vice Chairman-
Administration
Mr. T.D. Warrington, Vice Chairman-Appeals
Mr. D.F. Hamilton, Commissioner-Appeals
Dr. W.F. Jacobs, Commissioner-Appeals
Mr. Thomas A. McEwan, Commissioner-
Appeals
Mr. William R. Kerr, Senior Executive Director
Mr. Alex Joma, Secretary

PRINCE EDWARD ISLAND
Workers' Compensation Board
60 Belvedere Avenue
P.O. Box 757
Charlottetown, Prince Edward Island C1A 7L7
(902) 894-8555
Mr. Leo Rossiter, Chairman
Mr. Arthur Brown, Member
Mr. Raymond Livingstone, Member
Mr. C.E. Ready, Executive Secretary

QUEBEC
Commission de la Sante et de la Securite du Travail
524 Bourdages Street
Quebec, Quebec G1K 7E2
(418) 643-5973
Hon. Robert Sauvé, President
Mr. Jean-Louis Bertrand, Vice President
Mr. Lionel Bernier, Vice President
Mr. J. Gilles Massé, Vice President
Mr. Gilles Néron, Vice President

SASKATCHEWAN
Workers' Compensation Board
1840 Lorne Street
Regina, Saskatchewan S4P 2L8
(306) 565-4370
Mr. Brian N. King, Chairman
Mr. M.G. Bourne, Member
Mr. H.S. Elkin, Member
Mr. J.A. McLean, Executive Director

YUKON
Workers' Compensation Board
4110 4th Avenue
Suite 300
Whitehorse, Yukon Y1A 4N7
(403) 667-5645
Chairman to be appointed
Mrs. Jean Banks, Member
Mr. Gerry Dobson, Member
Mr. Charles Friday, Member
Mr. Brian Booth, Executive Director

CANADA
Labour Canada
Occupational Safety and Health Branch
Injury Compensation Division
Ottawa, Ontario K1A 0J3
(613) 997-2281
Mr. J.F. Ellsworth, Chief

Merchant Seamen Compensation Board
Labour Canada
Ottawa, Ontario K1A 0J2
Mr. André Déom, Chairman
Capt. J.G. Daniels, Vice Chairman
Mr. F. Bodie, Member
Mr. J.F. Ellsworth, Secretary

Workers' Compensation Insurance: Recent Trends in Employer Costs

Martin W. Elson and John F. Burton, Jr.

*Costs of insuring against work-related injuries
and diseases have escalated rapidly since 1972;
growing variation in premiums among States
over the same period may indicate unequal rates
of improvement in workers' compensation laws*

The workers' compensation program provides cash benefits, medical care, and rehabilitation services for persons who experience job-related injuries and diseases. Because each State operates its own compensation program, the levels of protection for workers and the associated costs of the plan to employers differ considerably among jurisdictions. Variations among jurisdictions in the insurance arrangements available to employers may also affect premiums: 32 States and the District of Columbia allow employers to purchase insurance from private carriers; six States only allow purchase from a State fund; and 12 States permit a choice between private carriers and State funds. In addition, all but four States allow employers with sufficient financial ability and satisfactory records for paying past claims to self-insure.[1]

The existence of interstate differences in the cost of workers' compensation insurance raises certain questions with policy implications. Are the variations in premiums great enough to influence employers' decisions to locate their establishments? And, do recent trends in premium levels indicate any reluctance by States to boost program benefits and costs, for fear of losing employers to lower cost jurisdictions?

As a first step toward answering such questions, this article presents estimates of employers' costs of insurance purchased from private carriers or State funds in 47 jurisdictions[2] as of July 1, 1978. Historical information since 1950 is also provided for a smaller number of jurisdictions. The following discussion is a condensed

and updated version of a more comprehensive report[3] that details the methodology used to derive the cost estimates.

Measuring insurance costs

Employers' costs of workers' compensation insurance may be measured in several ways. For purposes of this study, three combinations of employers that account for substantial percentages of national payroll were selected, and the costs of workers' compensation insurance for these groups of employers were determined for each State. This procedure makes possible an estimate of the differences in insurance costs which employers would encounter by moving among the States.[4]

The first combination consists of 45 types of employers for which workers' compensation insurance rates are available since 1950. This group includes 13 manufacturing, seven contracting, and 25 other types of firms, and accounts for almost 57 percent of the payroll covered by workers' compensation insurance.[5] The second combination represents 25 types of manufacturing employers which comprise 10 percent of covered payroll; rates for this groups are available since 1958. The third combination, for which rates are only available since 1972, includes 30 manufacturing, 13 contracting, and 36 other types of employers; these 79 types of firms account for 72 percent of covered payroll.[6]

Insurance rates for each type of employer may be obtained from a State manual. These manual rates are given in dollars per $100 of weekly earnings for each employee. Table 1 shows the average July 1, 1978, manual rates for the three combinations of employers in 47 jurisdictions. As indicated, the average manual rate for the 45 types of employers was $1.043 per $100 of pay-

Martin W. Elson is a law student at Case Western Reserve University. John F. Burton, Jr. is a professor of industrial and labor relations at Cornell University.

Reprinted from *Monthly Labor Review*, March, 1981, vol. 104, no. 3, U.S. Department of Labor, Bureau of Labor Statistics, Washington, DC 20212, 1981.

roll in Alabama, while the same group of employers in Alaska had a mean rate of $2.149.

However, estimates of average manual rates provide only a beginning toward accurate interstate comparisons of workers' compensation costs. For many employers, the weekly premium is not simply the product of the manual rate and the weekly payroll. Rather, their insurance costs are influenced by premium discounts for quantity purchases, dividends received from mutual companies and participating stock companies, modifications of the manual rate resulting from the employer's own accident experience, and other factors.

Consequently, the average employer in the 45 States with private insurance carriers pays an adjusted manual rate that is 18 percent less than the published manual rate.[7] In Ohio and West Virginia—States with State insurance funds and no private carriers—manual rates are reduced, on average, 7.5 percent and 31.4 percent respectively to arrive at adjusted manual rates.[8]

The average adjusted manual rates for the three combinations of employers as of July 1, 1978, are also found in table 1. Although the average manual rate for the 45 types of employers in Alabama was $1.043 per $100 of payroll, the average *adjusted* manual rate for

Table 1. Employers' average weekly costs of workers' compensation insurance in 47 jurisdictions, July 1, 1978

Jurisdiction	Manual rates (per $100 of payroll)			Adjusted manual rates (per $100 of payroll)			Net costs of insurance (per employee)		
	45 types of employers	25 types of manufacturing employers	79 types of employers	45 types of employers	25 types of manufacturing employers	79 types of employers	45 types of employers	25 types of manufacturing employers	79 types of employers
Alabama	$1.043	$2.041	$1.295	$0.855	$1.674	$1.062	$1.544	$3.022	$1,918
Alaska	2.149	3.484	2.524	1.762	2.857	2.070	4.879	7.910	5.731
Arizona	3.055	5.546	3.686	2.505	4.548	3.023	5.294	9.610	6.387
Arkansas	1.576	3.023	1.903	1.292	2.479	1.560	2.078	3.986	2.509
California	2.604	5.173	3.238	2.135	4.241	2.655	4.816	9.567	5.989
Colorado	1.475	3.159	1.812	1.210	2.590	1.486	2.554	5.469	3.137
Connecticut	1.650	3.434	2.140	1.353	2.816	1.755	2.768	5.762	3.590
Delaware	1.742	3.544	(¹)	1.428	2.906	(¹)	2.922	5.944	(¹)
District of Columbia	4.271	8.063	5.098	3.502	6.612	4.181	8.199	15.480	9.788
Florida	3.221	5.733	3.764	2.641	4.701	3.086	4.793	8.531	5.600
Georgia	1.313	2.886	1.634	1.077	2.366	1.340	1.912	4.202	2.380
Hawaii	2.508	5.060	3.232	2.057	4.149	2.650	3.964	7.996	5.108
Idaho	1.569	2.813	1.961	1.287	2.307	1.608	2.238	4.013	2.797
Illinois	1.685	2.965	2.012	1.382	2.431	1.649	3.063	5.390	3.657
Indiana	.585	1.109	.713	.480	.910	.585	1.015	1.927	1.239
Iowa	1.322	2.114	1.569	1.084	1.734	1.286	2.190	3.502	2.599
Kansas	1.072	2.061	1.297	.879	1.690	1.064	1.659	3.190	2.008
Kentucky	1.685	3.737	2.215	1.382	3.064	1.816	2.781	6.166	3.655
Louisiana	1.844	4.027	2.359	1.512	3.302	1.934	2.909	6.354	3.721
Maine	1.684	3.571	2.038	1.380	2.929	1.671	2.581	5.476	3.125
Maryland	1.539	3.019	1.861	1.262	2.476	1.526	2.526	4.955	3.055
Massachusetts	1.674	3.934	2.166	1.373	3.226	1.776	2.757	6.479	3.567
Michigan	2.305	6.140	3.040	1.890	5.035	2.493	4.370	11.641	5.764
Minnesota	2.220	5.081	2.800	1.821	4.167	2.296	3.733	8.543	4.709
Mississippi	1.100	1.903	1.336	.902	1.561	1.096	1.457	2.521	1.770
Missouri	.903	1.771	1.136	.740	1.452	.932	1.196	2.345	1.505
Montana	1.712	2.781	2.064	1.404	2.280	1.692	2.795	4.539	3.368
Nebraska	.865	1.573	1.015	.710	1.290	.834	1.484	2.698	1.744
New Hampshire	1.422	2.883	1.850	1.166	2.364	1.517	2.128	4.314	2.769
New Jersey	2.057	4.249	2.418	1.687	3.484	1.983	3.651	7.541	4.292
New Mexico	1.757	3.827	2.165	1.441	3.138	1.775	2.479	5.400	3.054
New York	2.158	4.678	2.639	1.770	3.836	2.164	3.844	8.332	4.701
North Carolina	.649	1.314	.830	.532	1.077	.680	.899	1.820	1.149
Ohio	1.664	2.904	1.977	1.550	2.697	1.839	3.352	5.834	3.979
Oklahoma	1.763	4.320	2.293	1.446	3.542	1.880	2.654	6.503	3.451
Oregon	3.558	7.841	4.600	2.918	6.430	3.772	6.288	13.858	8.130
Pennsylvania	1.431	3.125	(¹)	1.173	2.563	(¹)	2.382	5.202	(¹)
Rhode Island	1.589	3.978	2.002	1.303	3.262	1.641	2.387	5.975	3.007
South Carolina	1.020	2.094	1.286	.836	1.717	1.055	1.360	2.794	1.716
South Dakota	1.027	1.725	1.222	.842	1.414	1.002	1.649	2.769	1.962
Tennessee	1.101	2.339	1.435	.903	1.918	1.177	1.666	3.538	2.171
Texas	2.137	4.338	2.708	1.753	3.557	2.220	3.293	6.683	4.172
Utah	1.087	2.000	1.320	.892	1.640	1.083	1.701	3.130	2.066
Vermont	1.067	1.996	1.267	.875	1.637	1.039	1.646	3.079	1.955
Virginia	1.074	1.645	1.283	.880	1.349	1.052	1.525	2.337	1.824
West Virginia	.962	1.914	(¹)	.660	1.313	(¹)	1.229	2.444	(¹)
Wisconsin	.917	1.852	1.174	.752	1.519	.963	1.582	3.198	2.027

¹ Data are not available.

the group was $0.855, reflecting the 18-percent reduction. Adjusted manual rates may be interpreted as the cost of workers' compensation insurance as a percentage of payroll; thus, for the 45 types of Alabama employers, premiums were the equivalent of 0.855 percent of payroll.

The average weekly insurance premium per worker provides another measure of employers' costs of workers' compensation. The adjusted manual rate multiplied by the State's average weekly wage yields the approximate net cost of insurance to policyholders.[9] Again according to table 1, the average weekly net cost of insurance as of July 1, 1978, for the 45 types of employers in Alabama was $1.544 per employee.

Historical data

Information on employers' costs of workers' compensation insurance is available for the 45 types of employers for selected years since 1950. Data for 20 States are available for 8 years between 1950 and 1978; data for eight more States are available for 6 years between 1958 and 1978; 42 jurisdictions have data for 1972, 1975, and 1978; and by 1978, 47 jurisdictions may be compared.

The average adjusted manual rates for the 45-employer group are shown in table 2. As indicated, Alabama employers expended, on average, the equivalent of 0.282 percent of payroll on workers' compensation premiums in 1950, compared with 0.855 percent in 1978. Table 3 presents the approximate net cost to the same group of policyholders for several years between 1950 and 1978. These results show, for example, that the employers in Alabama expended a weekly average of $0.136 per worker on premiums in 1950, and $1.544 in 1978.

The data in tables 2 and 3 are valuable for tracing changes in workers' compensation costs over time in a particular State, but the volume of information makes it difficult to comprehend general developments. Tables 4 and 5 provide a compact summary of these data, permitting evaluation of interstate trends.

Table 4, for example, illustrates the changes over time in the average adjusted manual rates for the various combinations of States. Each State's observation was weighted by the size of the State's labor force in 1970 to provide results which are representative of the national experience.

The mean adjusted manual rate in the 20 States was the equivalent of 0.471 percent of payroll in 1950, 0.651 percent in 1972, and 1.185 percent in 1978. Of particular interest is the rise in cost between 1972 and 1978, which was more than double the 1950–72 increase. The average employer in the 28- and 42-jurisdiction comparisons also experienced large increases in premiums between 1972 and 1978. Data for the latter combination of jurisdictions indicate that the average employer spent

an amount equal to 1.461 percent of payroll on workers' compensation premiums in 1978.[10]

The average adjusted manual rate for any year obviously reflects some State data which are higher than the mean and some which are lower. For example, the mean adjusted rate for the 20 States was 0.471 percent of payroll in 1950, but the average employer in Alabama paid only 0.282 percent of payroll for workers' compensation insurance while his or her counterpart in Rhode Island paid 0.829 percent. A statistic providing a convenient summary of the extent of variation among the States around the mean cost is the standard deviation.[11] The larger the standard deviation, the greater the variation among the States in the percentage equivalent

Table 2. Average weekly adjusted manual rates per $100 of payroll for 45 types of employers in 47 jurisdictions, selected years, 1950 to 1978

Jurisdiction	Year							
	1950	1954	1958	1962	1965	1972	1975	1978
Alabama	$0.282	$0.310	$0.348	$0.364	$0.437	$0.479	$0.599	$0.855
Alaska	....	....	....	....	....	.832	1.721	1.762
Arizona	....	....	....	....	....	1.385	2.178	2.505
Arkansas	....	....	....	....	....	.915	1.038	1.292
California	....	....	.707	.858	1.183	1.102	1.406	2.135
Colorado	....	....	....	....	....	.649	.654	1.210
Connecticut	.660	.838	.812	.762	.689	.697	.827	1.353
Delaware	....	....	....	....	....	.578	.736	1.428
District of Columbia	....	....	....	....	....	.737	1.404	3.502
Florida	....	....	....	....	....	....	....	2.641
Georgia	....	....	....	....	....	.501	.760	1.077
Hawaii	....	....	....	....	....	.960	1.335	2.057
Idaho	.519	.664	.581	.582	.667	.865	1.283	1.287
Illinois	.437	.497	.514	.609	.624	.657	1.002	1.382
Indiana	.358	.363	.410	.398	.430	.385	.417	.480
Iowa	....	....	....	....	....	.451	.662	1.084
Kansas	....	....	....	....	....	.575	.766	.879
Kentucky	.390	.369	.394	.448	.558	.668	1.065	1.382
Louisiana	....	....	....	....	....	....	....	1.512
Maine	.415	.398	.340	.370	.337	.520	.981	1.380
Maryland	.501	.600	.661	.747	.854	.816	1.009	1.262
Massachusetts	....	....	.859	1.034	1.141	1.106	1.171	1.373
Michigan	.476	.416	.450	.694	.715	.914	1.238	1.890
Minnesota	....	....	.653	.692	.738	.854	1.240	1.821
Mississippi	.638	.727	.758	.988	.980	.751	.902	.902
Missouri	....	....	....	....	....	....	....	.740
Montana	.590	.644	.792	.721	.845	.948	1.565	1.404
Nebraska	.572	.474	.437	.527	.447	.529	.789	.710
New Hampshire	.528	.586	.531	.495	.560	.534	.746	1.166
New Jersey	....	....	.911	1.054	1.039	1.224	1.233	1.687
New Mexico	.463	.858	.838	.863	.945	.787	1.069	1.441
New York	....	....	....	....	....	.864	.973	1.770
North Carolina	.392	.512	.473	.492	.474	.420	.433	.532
Ohio	....	....	.627	.813	.820	.885	1.109	1.550
Oklahoma	....	....	....	....	....	....	1.052	1.446
Oregon	....	....	.630	1.007	....	1.491	2.074	2.918
Pennsylvania	....	....	.355	.396	.386	.387	.776	1.173
Rhode Island	.829	.930	.831	.834	.842	.767	.899	1.393
South Carolina	.658	.607	.567	.690	.696	.609	.590	.836
South Dakota	.537	.400	.315	.392	.389	.511	.635	.842
Tennessee	....	....	....	....	....	.664	.710	.903
Texas	....	....	....	....	....	....	....	1.753
Utah	.524	.545	.502	.422	.531	.503	.766	.892
Vermont	.398	.457	.524	.505	.595	.514	.588	.875
Virginia	....	....	....	....	....	.391	.539	.880
West Virginia	....	....	.268	.345	.404	.428	.671	.660
Wisconsin	....	....	.523	.556	.603	.505	.581	.752

NOTE: Dashes indicate data not available.

of payroll expended on workers' compensation insurance. The data in table 4 indicate that over time the magnitude of such variation has increased.

Table 5 traces the net cost to policyholders for the 45 types of employers between 1950 and 1978. The average employer in the 20 States spent $0.249 per week on workers' compensation premiums for each worker in 1950, $0.945 in 1972, and $2.468 in 1978. Again, the sharp increase in costs after 1972 is evident from data for each combination of jurisdictions. In 1978, the mean weekly premium for employers in the 42 jurisdictions was just over $3.09 per worker.[12]

Table 5 also shows the extent of variation among the States around the net cost to policyholders. In 1950,

Table 4. Means and standard deviations[1] of adjusted manual rates for 45 types of employers in various combinations of jurisdictions, selected years, 1950 to 1978

[Percent of total payroll]

Year	20 jurisdictions[2]		28 jurisdictions[3]		42 jurisdictions[4]	
	Mean	Standard deviation	Mean	Standard deviation	Mean	Standard deviation
1950	0.471	0.108	...	...	...	...
1954	.512	.145	...	...	...	...
1958	.521	.133	0.587	0.172	...	...
1962	.599	.150	.689	.212	...	...
1965	.623	.150	.760	.277	...	...
1972	.651	.171	.776	.276	0.774	0.271
1975	.871	.284	1.006	.302	.995	.328
1978	1.185	.446	1.409	.488	1.461	.543

[1] Results are based on data in table 2. Weights are each jurisdiction's total nonagricultural employment from *Employment and Earnings Statistics for States and Areas, 1939–70*, Bulletin 1370–8, (Bureau of Labor Statistics, 1971).
The weighted standard deviations were calculated using a formula provided by Cornell University Professors Paul F. Velleman and Philip J. McCarthy, to whom we express our appreciation.
[2] The 20-jurisdiction combination consists of: Alabama, Connecticut, Idaho, Illinois, Indiana, Kentucky, Maine, Maryland, Michigan, Mississippi, Montana, Nebraska, New Hampshire, New Mexico, North Carolina, Rhode Island, South Dakota, Utah, and Vermont.
[3] The 28-jurisdiction combination includes the 20 States listed in footnote 2 plus California, Massachusetts, Minnesota, New Jersey, Ohio, Pennsylvania, West Virginia, and Wisconsin.
[4] The 42-jurisdiction combination includes the 28 States in footnote 3 plus Alaska, Arizona, Arkansas, Colorado, Delaware, District of Columbia, Georgia, Hawaii, Iowa, Kansas, New York, Oregon, Tennessee, and Virginia.
NOTE: Dashes indicate data not available.

when the average cost was $0.249 per worker per week in the 20 States, the standard deviation among the States was $0.056. By 1978, however, the mean weekly cost per worker was $2.468—up almost 10-fold since 1950—while the standard deviation ($1.113 in 1978) had grown nearly 20-fold over the same period.

The adjusted manual rate is probably the most useful and comprehensive measure of cost because, as previously noted, it may be interpreted as the percentage equivalent of payroll expended on workers' compensation insurance premiums. Chart 1 shows the trend in the average adjusted manual rates for the 45 types of employers in the 20 States for which there are comparable data since 1950.

The solid line in chart 1 tracks the weighted mean of the rates for the eight observations (years) available. The surrounding light area delineates the values of the

Table 3. Average weekly net costs of insurance per employee for 45 types of employers in 47 jurisdictions, selected years, 1950 to 1978

Jurisdiction	1950	1954	1958	1962	1965	1972	1975	1978
Alabama	$0.136	$0.183	$0.242	$0.281	$0.369	$0.611	$0.938	$1.544
Alaska	....	....	....	....	....	1.627	4.127	4.879
Arizona	....	....	....	....	....	2.066	3.985	5.293
Arkansas	....	....	....	....	....	1.040	1.447	2.078
California	....	....	.631	.858	1.296	1.755	2.746	4.816
Colorado	....	....	....	....	....	.968	1.196	2.554
Connecticut	.353	.548	.627	.669	.663	1.008	1.467	2.768
Delaware	....	....	....	....	....	.835	1.304	2.922
District of Columbia	....	....	....	....	....	1.219	2.847	8.199
Florida	....	....	....	....	....	....	....	4.793
Georgia	....	....	....	....	....	.629	1.169	1.912
Hawaii	....	....	....	....	....	1.306	2.229	3.964
Idaho	.253	.396	.409	.447	.561	1.063	1.933	2.238
Illinois	.261	.363	.443	.588	.660	1.029	1.925	3.063
Indiana	.197	.245	.326	.357	.422	.576	.766	1.016
Iowa	....	....	....	....	....	.644	1.159	2.190
Kansas	....	....	....	....	....	.767	1.253	1.659
Kentucky	.205	.237	.299	.380	.518	.949	1.856	2.781
Louisiana	....	....	....	....	....	....	....	2.909
Maine	.195	.229	.230	.286	.286	.687	1.588	2.581
Maryland	.266	.390	.507	.639	.800	1.154	1.750	2.526
Massachusetts	....	....	.660	.888	1.073	1.569	2.037	2.757
Michigan	.271	.290	.370	.655	.740	1.493	2.480	4.370
Minnesota	....	....	.519	.620	.724	1.237	2.203	3.733
Mississippi	.273	.382	.469	.671	.729	.856	1.261	1.457
Missouri	....	....	....	....	....	....	....	1.196
Montana	.310	.414	.600	.584	.750	1.330	2.695	2.795
Nebraska	.303	.308	.335	.468	.435	.782	1.430	1.484
New Hampshire	.250	.339	.363	.385	.477	.689	1.179	2.128
New Jersey	....	....	.759	.993	1.072	1.872	2.312	3.651
New Mexico	.249	.565	.650	.722	.866	.957	1.594	2.479
New York	....	....	....	....	....	1.326	1.830	3.844
North Carolina	.167	.267	.291	.335	.354	.501	.634	.899
Ohio	....	....	.509	.755	.834	1.352	2.077	3.352
Oklahoma	....	....	....	....	....	....	1.673	2.654
Oregon	....	....	.541	.949	....	2.269	3.872	6.288
Pennsylvania	....	....	.280	.346	.369	.554	1.365	2.382
Rhode Island	.404	.555	.586	.656	.726	.993	1.427	2.387
South Carolina	.284	.321	.353	.500	.553	.700	.832	1.360
South Dakota	.274	.250	.233	.330	.358	.706	1.077	1.649
Tennessee	....	....	....	....	....	.866	1.134	1.666
Texas	....	....	....	....	....	....	....	3.293
Utah	.283	.361	.392	.365	.504	.678	1.267	1.701
Vermont	.192	.270	.365	.396	.511	.684	.963	1.646
Virginia	....	....	....	....	....	.478	.808	1.525
West Virginia	....	....	.200	.279	.358	.563	1.069	1.229
Wisconsin	....	....	.412	.494	.587	.751	1.060	1.582

NOTE: Dashes indicate data not available.

Table 5. Means and standard deviations[1] of net weekly costs of insurance for 45 types of employers in various combinations of jurisdictions, selected years, 1950 to 1978

Year	20 jurisdictions		28 jurisdictions		42 jurisdictions	
	Mean	Standard deviation	Mean	Standard deviation	Mean	Standard deviation
1950	$0.249	$0.056	....	....	....	....
1954	.330	.092	....	....	....	....
1958	.399	.104	$0.472	$0.153	....	....
1962	.518	.139	.625	.215	....	....
1965	.590	.154	.760	.317	....	....
1972	.945	.311	1.160	.461	$1.150	$0.454
1975	1.563	.610	1.848	.643	1.817	.689
1978	2.468	1.113	3.000	1.197	3.093	1.328

[1] Results are based on data in table 3. See footnotes to table 4 for other information pertaining to this tabulation.
NOTE: Dashes indicate data not available.

Chart 1. Means and standard deviations of adjusted manual rates for employers in 20 States, selected years, 1950 to 1978

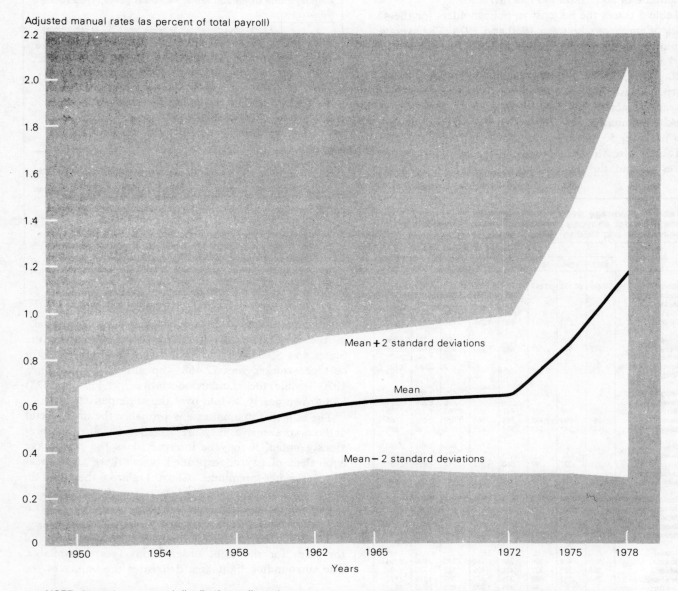

Adjusted manual rates (as percent of total payroll)

NOTE: Assuming a normal distribution, adjusted manual rates for approximately 95 percent of the States should fall within ± 2 standard deviations of the mean.

adjusted manual rates that are within 2 standard deviations of the mean. This range (mean ± 2 standard deviations) is a useful statistical measure because, assuming a normal distribution, approximately 95 percent of the individual State averages will fall within the interval.

Chart 1 and tables 3 and 4 tell a consistent story: on average, employers' premiums for workers' compensation insurance have increased sharply since 1972, and at the same time, cost differences among jurisdictions have widened considerably.

MANY FACTORS outside the purview of this article influence the level of and trend in workers' compensation insurance premiums, including the extent of litigation, differing legal interpretations of statutory provisions, the local cost of medical and rehabilitation services for victims of job-related injuries and diseases, and the approach used by the State to compensate permanent partial disabilities.[13] However, recent increases in the multistate premium averages may also be explained in part by the States' modifications of their programs in response to recommendations contained in the 1972 Report of the National Commission on State Workmen's Compensation Laws.[14] Similarly, there are several possible reasons for the growth of interstate variations in costs, the most controversial being differences among States in the extent of improvement in their laws since 1972.[15]

The National Commission unanimously advised that Federal workers' compensation standards be enacted in 1975 if States had not adopted its 19 essential recommendations by that time. An underlying rationale for mandated standards was to reduce interstate differences in employers' insurance premiums. The Commission considered these variations a likely impediment to State reform of workers' compensation programs; State legislatures might perceive the higher costs of better insurance plans as an incentive for employers to locate in other, lower cost jurisdictions. If the growth in interstate cost differentials since 1972 is related to unequal rates of improvement in State statutes,[16] the case for Federal minimum standards for workers' compensation is considerably strengthened.

———— FOOTNOTES ————

ACKNOWLEDGMENT: The authors thank John Bickerman, Robert Hutchens, and John Worrall for helpful comments as well as other assistance.

[1] The enumerated insurance arrangements pertain to private sector employers which are the focus of this article. These data are from C. Arthur Williams, Jr., and Peter S. Barth, *Compendium on Workmen's Compensation* (Washington, Government Printing Office, 1973). Because information on self-insurers is limited, and such employers account for a small percentage of benefit payments, these firms are excluded from the analysis.

[2] Programs in Nevada, North Dakota, Washington, and Wyoming allowed insurance only through a State fund, and the insurance classifications were not comparable with those in the remaining 47 jurisdictions. Therefore, these States were excluded from the analysis.

[3] John F. Burton, Jr., "Workers' Compensation Costs for Employers," *Research Report of the Interdepartmental Workers' Compensation Task Force*, Vol. 3 (Washington, Government Printing Office, 1979), pp. 9–32. An errata sheet for this study is available from the author.

[4] Some employers provide benefits in addition to workers' compensation to their employees who are disabled by work-related injuries or diseases. To the extent that these benefits are integrated with workers' compensation benefits, the changes in total costs for work-related disability benefits resulting from interstate movements by employers may vary from the cost differences examined in this article. There are insufficient data to make an estimate of the interstate differences in the costs of these additional benefits.

[5] In five States included in this study, employers' liability for workers' compensation premiums is limited to a maximum amount of an employee's weekly earnings ("covered pay"). In Massachusetts, for example, premiums are based on only the first $300 of weekly pay. Thus, in some States, payroll covered by workers' compensation insurance is less than total payroll.

[6] Table 3 in *Research Report of the Task Force* provides a detailed description of each of the 79 types of employers and information on the percent of payroll in 28 States accounted for by the various combinations of employers. Examples of manufacturing employers are bakeries, foundries, and furniture mills. Contracting employers include firms doing plumbing, concrete work, and street construction. "Other" establishments include retail stores, hospitals, and general employers of sales and clerical workers.

[7] The derivation of the 18-percent difference between manual rates and adjusted manual rates is provided in Section D of *Research Report of the Task Force*. The 18-percent figure is a national average based on experience in 34 jurisdictions. The actual difference will vary somewhat among States, depending on such factors as the relative importance of mutual companies, participating stock companies, and nonparticipating stock companies.

[8] Section D of *Research Report of the Task Force* explains the derivation of the percentages used to reduce manual rates in order to calculate adjusted manual rates in Ohio and West Virginia.

[9] As explained in Section F of *Research Report of the Task Force*, the net cost to policyholders in a State (or other jurisdiction) is calculated by multiplying the product of the adjusted manual rate and the State's index number (which measures the State's earnings relative to U.S. earnings in 1970) by the national average of weekly earnings for workers covered by the unemployment insurance program. For 1976 (the latest year for which data were available when the tables for this article were prepared), the latter figure was $203.88.

[10] The text indicates that in the 42 jurisdictions, the 45 types of employers spent, on average, 1.461 percent of payroll on workers' compensation premiums in 1978. This combination of jurisdictions and employers was chosen to provide historically comparable data. For the largest combination of employers (79) and jurisdictions (44) shown in table 1, the average employer spent the equivalent of 1.843 percent of payroll on workers' compensation premiums in 1978, based on weighted observations.

The 1.843-percent figure is close to Daniel Price's estimate that premium costs nationally (including Federal and self-insurance, but excluding programs financed by general revenue, such as the black lung program) were 1.85 percent of payroll in 1978. Price's estimate is included in "Workers' Compensation: 1978 Program Update," *Social Security Bulletin*, October 1980, pp. 3–10.

For a comparison of the estimating procedures used by Price and Burton, involving 1975 data, see *Research Report of the Task Force*, footnote 35.

[11] For an elementary discussion of the standard deviation, see Daniel B. Suits, *Statistics: An Introduction to Quantitative Economic Research* (Chicago, Rand McNally and Co., 1963), pp. 38–52.

[12] For the largest combination of employers (79) and jurisdictions (44) shown in table 1, the average employer spent $3.915 per week per worker on workers' compensation insurance in 1978, based on weighted observations.

[13] For a discussion of some of these factors, see John F. Burton, Jr., *The Significance and Causes of the Interstate Variations in the Employers' Costs of Workmen's Compensation* (Ph.D. diss., University of Michigan, 1965). The results of a study of interstate cost differences associated with various approaches to permanent partial disability benefits may be found in John F. Burton, Jr. and Wayne Vroman, "A Report on Permanent Partial Disabilities under Workers' Compensation," *Research Report of the Interdepartmental Workers' Compensation Task Force*, Vol. 6 (Washington, Government Printing Office, forthcoming).

[14] (Washington, Government Printing Office, 1972).

[15] Laws in effect on January 1, 1980, in 52 jurisdictions (including the District of Columbia and Puerto Rico) were on average in compliance with 12.03 of the 19 essential recommendations of the National Commission, according to information provided in January 1980 by the Division of State Workers' Compensation Standards of the Employment Standards Administration, U.S. Department of Labor. The range among the jurisdictions in 1980 was considerable, with Montana, New Hampshire, and Ohio in compliance with at least 15.5 of the essential recommendations, while Arkansas, Mississippi, and Tennessee were in compliance with 8.5 or fewer of the recommendations.

[16] The assumed relationship between cost increases and improvements in State laws from 1972 to 1978 are being examined in an ongoing study by John F. Burton, Jr.

Workers' Compensation Laws—Key Amendments of 1979

LaVerne C. Tinsley

*All but three of the States increased
temporary total disability benefits;
some also sought to cut costs by investigating
medical bills, offsetting benefits by other
transfer payments, and reducing the effect
of disabilities through rehabilitation programs*

The legislatures of 49 States and Puerto Rico enacted 220 amendments to workers' compensation laws during 1979. A review of these amendments indicates that States are continuing to improve benefits for covered workers, while seeking to control costs through better administration. Many States have shifted their focus from meeting the essential recommendations of the National Commission on State Workmen's Compensation Laws to dealing with other issues addressed by the commission, including rehabilitation and administration.

All but three States and Puerto Rico increased weekly payments for temporary total disability. Connecticut and Florida increased benefits across the board up to 100 percent of the State average weekly wage. (See table 1.)

Half a dozen States revised provisions for handling medical expenses. Maine and Texas strengthened disclosure requirements for health care providers, and Minnesota will establish criteria for excessive medical costs. Seven States updated rehabilitation provisions for injured workers. Minnesota and Montana now withhold benefits in whole or in part for failure to participate

in such programs; Arkansas prohibited such withholding.

Florida approved a major revision of its law by incorporating a "wage loss" system for compensating permanent partial disability. In addition, watts telephone lines were authorized Statewide to facilitate communication among all parties involved in workers' compensation matters. Michigan provided that certain State employees, if victims of workplace assaults, will receive supplemental benefits that, combined with workers' compensation, could equal their full salaries.

Twenty-one States were concerned with revising coverage provisions. Ten legislatures approved amendments which exempt or provide for elective coverage of sole proprietors, partners, and corporate officers. Idaho exempted members of volunteer ski patrols; North Carolina exempted members of the Civil Air Patrol and reduced numerical exemptions from fewer than five employees to fewer than four. The remaining States primarily expanded coverage for State and emergency service personnel.

Among other jurisdictions that amended benefit provisions, Kansas raised maximum weekly benefits from 66 2/3 percent to 72 percent of the State average weekly wage. Arkansas established a three-step monetary increase from a weekly maximum of $87.50 to $112 (currently payable) to $126 by March of 1980. Arkansas, Indiana, Mississippi, Missouri, Nebraska, New

LaVerne C. Tinsley is a workers' compensation specialist in the Division of State Workers' Compensation Standards, Employment Standards Administration. U.S. Department of Labor.

Reprinted from *Monthly Labor Review,* February, 1980, vol. 103, no. 2, U.S. Department of Labor, Bureau of Labor Statistics, Washington, DC 20212, 1980.

Table 1. Jurisdictions that increased maximum weekly temporary total disability benefits during 1979[1]

Jurisdiction	Former maximum	New maximum
Alabama	$128.00	$136.00
Alaska	$607.85	$654.30
Arkansas	$ 87.50	$112.00
Colorado	$173.60	$222.74
Connecticut	$204.00, plus $10 for each dependent under 18 years of age not to exceed 75 percent of employee's wage	$222.00, plus $10 for each dependent under 18 years of age not to exceed 75 percent of employee's wage
Delaware	$154.50	$164.71
District of Columbia	$396.78	$426.26
Florida	$130.00	$195.00
Hawaii	$189.00	$200.00
Idaho	$109.80 to $164.70 according to number of dependents, plus 7 percent of SAWW for each child up to 5	$115.80 to $173.70 according to number of dependents plus 7 percent of SAWW for each child up to 5
Illinois	$329.82	$342.19
Indiana	$120.00	$130.00
Iowa	$265.00	$352.00
Kansas	$129.06	$148.00
Kentucky	$112.00	$121.00
Louisiana	$141.00	$149.00
Maine	$231.72	$306.23
Maryland	$202.00	$220.00
Massachusetts	$211.37, plus $6 for each dependent; aggregate not to exceed worker's average weekly wage	$227.31, plus $6 for each dependent; aggregate not to exceed worker's average weekly wage
Michigan	$142.00 to $171.00, according to number of dependents	$156.00 to $185.00, according to number of dependents
Minnesota	$209.00	$226.00
Mississippi	$ 91.00	$ 98.00
Missouri	$115.00	$125.00
Montana	$188.00	$198.00
Nebraska	$155.00	$180.00
Nevada	$212.02	$229.71
New Hampshire	$180.00	$195.00
New Jersey	$146.00	$156.00
New Mexico	$172.46	$186.38
New York	$180.00	$215.00
North Carolina	$178.00	$194.00
North Dakota	$180.00, plus $5 for each dependent child; aggregate not to exceed worker's net wage after taxes and social security	$196.00, plus $5 for each dependent child; aggregate not to exceed worker's net wage after taxes and social security
Ohio	$216.00	$241.00
Oklahoma	$132.00	$141.00
Oregon	$224.16	$241.70
Pennsylvania	$213.00	$227.00
Rhode Island	$183.00, plus $6 for each dependent; aggregate not to exceed 80 percent of worker's average weekly wage	$199.00, plus $6 for each dependent; aggregate not to exceed 80 percent of worker's average weekly wage
South Carolina	$172.00	$185.00
South Dakota	$155.00	$175.00
Tennessee	$100.00	$107.00
Texas	$105.00	$119.00
Utah	$197.00, plus $5 for dependent spouse and each dependent child up to 4, but not to exceed 100 percent of SAWW	$210.00, plus $5 for dependent spouse and each dependent child up to 4, but not to exceed 100 percent of SAWW
Vermont	$181.00, plus $5 for each dependent under 21 years of age	$192.00, plus $5 for each dependent under 21 years of age
Virginia	$187.00	$199.00
Washington	$175.30	$186.88
West Virginia	$224.00	$237.00
Wisconsin	$202.00	$218.00
Wyoming	$224.98	$239.59

[1] Benefit increases are based on the applicable State's average weekly wage, and for the District of Columbia, the national average weekly wage. However, 10 States (Arizona, Arkansas, California, Georgia, Indiana, Mississippi, Missouri, Nebraska, New York, and Tennessee) and Puerto Rico prescribe statutory amounts; three States (Arizona, California, and Georgia) and Puerto Rico are not listed since no increases for temporary total disability were legislated during 1979.

York, North Dakota, Tennessee, and Washington increased statutory amounts for both disability and death. Offset provisions were created or revised in Florida, Maine, North Dakota, Ohio, Oregon, Utah, and Washington. Burial allowances were increased in Nevada. Colorado equalized entitlement to compensation for residents and nonresidents; and New York and Tennessee established the same rights for widowers as those existing for widows.

Long-term recipients of workers' compensation were given increases in Nevada, North Dakota, Pennsylvania (occupational disease cases), Utah, and West Virginia.

Following is a summary of 1979 enactments by State pertaining to coverage and benefits, as well as rehabilitation, administration, and other aspects of State workers' compensation.

Alabama

Sole proprietors and partners are now permitted to elect coverage for themselves. Previously, such employers could not elect coverage for themselves for benefit purposes.

Alaska

Political subdivisions may now elect coverage for their volunteer ambulance attendants and volunteer police.

Arizona

Coverage for volunteer firefighters now includes those in both private protection squads and fire departments in unincorporated communities.

Arkansas

For coverage purposes, the definition of employee now includes full-time sole proprietors and partners. A three-step increase retroactive to March 2, 1978, will raise the maximum weekly benefits for all disabilities and for death from $87.50 to $126.00 by March 1, 1980. The maximum awards for other than both permanent total disability and death will also increase to $56,700 on March 1, 1980. The discount rate in computing lump sum settlements was increased from 4 to 7 percent. An employer's obligation for additional vocational rehabilitation expenses was limited to 60 weeks; but no employee is required to participate in a vocational rehabilitation program without his or her consent. Employers cannot be held responsible for unauthorized medical expenses.

A claimant's failure to give notice within the required 60 days does not bar a claim if the employee had no knowledge that the disability arose out of and in the course of employment. A lump sum payment of attorney fees is now permitted even if the award is to be paid in installments.

Various rules, regulations, and procedures regarding Second Injury Funds and appeals were established or revised. The employer will only be liable for the specific disability resulting from the last injury in both permanent partial and permanent total disability claims. Any principal officer, director, stockholder, or partner acting in the capacity of an employer assumes employers' exemption from liability under common law; the negligent acts of an employee cannot be imputed to the employer.

Self-insured employers are allowed to enter into pooling agreements with other employers in the same type of business. When established that failure to file a claim for compensation was induced by fraud, the claim may be filed within 1 year from the date of discovery of the fraud.

All authority related to the filing, processing, and payment of public employee claims has been transferred from the Workers' Compensation Commission to the Public Employee Claims Division of the Arkansas Insurance Department.

California

Volunteer workers for public agencies or nonprofit organizations who receive no remuneration other than meals, transportation, lodging, or reimbursement for incidental expenses are excluded from coverage, provided such persons are included under Title II of the Domestic Volunteer Service Act of 1973.

The revolving Compensation Insurance Fund was changed to a Public Enterprise Fund, which is exempt from certain State provisions. References to "widow" have been changed to "spouse" throughout the law.

Colorado

Death benefits for nonresident dependents are now the same as for resident dependents in deaths that occurred on or after July 1, 1979.

Under nonmedical treatment, chiropractic care must now be paid by self-insured employers.

A penalty of $500 or 60 days imprisonment, or both, may be assessed against any person, company, or corporation who fails to provide or maintain insurance coverage for the term of the contract when performing services on a farm or ranching operation.

Connecticut

The law was redesignated as the Workers' Compensation Act, and references to "workmen's" were changed to "workers'" throughout the law.

Elective coverage was extended to sole proprietors and business partners.

Benefits for both disability and death were increased from 85 to 100 percent of the State average weekly wage.

A 12-percent interest rate, formerly 6 percent, will be applied as additional compensation in cases where benefit payments are unduly delayed.

The number of compensation commissioners was increased from seven to eight. Appellate procedures were revised with the creation of the Compensation Review Division to hear appeals, testimony, or evidence. The Division's decision may be appealed to Superior Court.

Delaware

A Workmen's Compensation Commission was established to study workers' compensation insurance and to make recommendations for improving the law. A sum of $50,000 was appropriated to the commissioner for administrative use.

Florida

The law was renamed the Workers' Compensation Act, and references to "workmen's" were replaced by "workers'" throughout the law.

Officers of a corporation who elect to be exempt from coverage are excluded from the definition of employee. The definition of independent contractor now includes musicians and other entertainers who are not otherwise covered.

Maximum weekly benefits for both disability and death were increased from 66 2/3 percent to 100 percent of the State average weekly wage. The percentage of the employee's wage upon which benefits are based was increased from 60 to 66 2/3 percent for both temporary and permanent total disability. Payment for temporary partial disability was increased from 60 percent to 66 2/3 percent of the difference between preinjury and postinjury income. A wage loss approach for payment of permanent partial disability was established, and the scheduled payment periods for such disability eliminated.

Compensation for dependents will now be offset by the amount of any social security benefits received. The law also was changed to bar compensation for both temporary and permanent total disability when unemployment compensation is being received.

All attorney fees are now to be paid out of the claimant's award except under certain circumstances. Medical and hospital fees will be closely regulated, and peer review of medical care has been established.

The reporting procedures regarding an injury were changed. When an injury occurs, the employer is required to notify both the Division of Workers' Compensation and the employee, as well as the insurance carrier.

The penalty for a late payment of compensation was reduced from 20 to 10 percent of that payment.

Compromise and release of future medical benefits are now prohibited. Lump sum settlements cannot be considered until 6 months after the worker has reached maximum medical improvement.

The full responsibility for rehabilitation of injured workers rests with both the employer and the carrier.

The Bureau of Workmen's Compensation has been abolished and the Division of Workers' Compensation created to assume an active and forceful role in the administration of the act. Watts lines have been set up in the State to assist the resolution of workers' compensation matters.

Hawaii

A corporate officer who performs voluntary services in a corporation in which he or she is at least a 25-percent stockholder is excluded from coverage.

The State Department of Labor and Industrial Relations is authorized to set maximum employer liability for medical care and supplies using the Consumer Price Index for the Honolulu region.

A 2-year filing limit was set for benefit claims involving asbestosis or other mineral substance with carcinogenic properties. Initial judicial review of claims was changed from the State Supreme Court to the Appellate Court.

Idaho

Members of volunteer ski patrols were exempted from compulsory coverage.

Illinois

Any employee receiving compensation for work-related injuries now must be notified of his or her rights to rehabilitation care and services.

By amendment, "workmen's" was changed to "workers'" in the title and throughout the act.

Indiana

Coverage was extended to volunteer firefighters and to sole proprietors and partners actually engaged in a business.

The maximum weekly benefit for both total disability and death was raised in two steps: effective July 1, 1979, it was raised to $195; on July 1, 1980, it will increase to $210. On the same two dates, the maximum aggregate amount first changed from $60,000 to $65,000 and will increase to $70,000. The maximum number of weeks for payment of temporary total disability in conjunction with permanent partial disability was increased from 26 to 52 weeks. Replacement of prosthodontic devices is now permitted for employees with a compensable mouth injury.

Iowa

Elective coverage for police and firefighters in municipalities with populations of 8,000 or more will be permitted after December 31, 1979.

Employers are required to repair or replace artificial appliances when damaged or no longer usable as a result of work-related circumstances (other than normal wear and tear).

Kansas

The maximum weekly benefit for disability and death was raised from 66 2/3 percent to 72 percent of the State average weekly wage; the minimum weekly benefit increased from $7 to $25. The maximums for total benefits also increased: both permanent total disability and death went from $50,000 to $100,000; temporary total disability and permanent or temporary partial disability increased from $50,000 to $75,000.

Claimants are entitled to 8 percent interest on the amount of benefits found by the workers' compensation examiner or director or State court to be due and unpaid.

Louisiana

Sole proprietors and partners are now permitted to waive coverage.

The law now authorizes group self-insurance funds. Five or more employers of the same trade or business with a minimum combined net worth of $500,000 are now permitted to pool their potential liabilities.

Joint self-insurance programs are now permitted for local government employers through the formation of an interlocal risk management agency.

Maine

Coverage now includes all fire personnel whether or not they perform administrative duties.

Injured employees are now permitted to receive podiatric services from licensed podiatrists in Maine.

Occupational hearing loss is now measured in accordance with the National Standards Institute (Standard S3.22, 1976) rather than the American Standards Association (Standard Z24.5, 1951).

The Workers' Compensation Commission was authorized to enforce the provisions pertaining to interest on awards. Attorneys are prohibited from receiving payments directly from clients. The Second Injury Fund is no longer liable for any claim that exceeds its assets.

Workers' "average weekly wage, earnings or salary" was redefined to exclude any allowance given to the employee to purchase chainsaws or skidders used on the job.

All benefits, except for scheduled permanent partial disabilities and lump sum settlements, will now be offset by the amount of any concurrently received unemployment benefits.

There are new procedures to regulate the disclosure of relevant information in the insurance rate filing system.

Massachusetts

The Industrial Accident Board was newly authorized to order payment of medical and hospital bills, and reports prepared by physicians who have since died are now permitted at hearings before the Board.

Michigan

Supplemental benefits (up to full salary) are now provided to certain State employees injured as a result of workplace assaults. Carriers who pay benefits for disability or death caused by exposure to polybrominated biphenyl will now be reimbursed from the Silicosis and Dust Disease Fund.

Minnesota

Many changes were made in the workers' compensation law this year. Major changes include the following.

Business partners who own a business or farm are now permitted to elect coverage for themselves and their immediate relatives.

Death benefits can now be awarded to either surviving spouse, rather than to the widow only. Eligibility for these benefits by children has been extended to full-time students up to age 25. The 104-week limit on total disability payments has been removed. Supplementary benefit payments are increased from 60 to 65 percent of the State average weekly wage. A Reopened Case Fund has been created to assume liability for all new claims filed 7 years from the date of injury or death or 3 years from the last payment of compensation, whichever is later. The Commissioner of Labor and Industry must establish procedures for determining whether health care charges are excessive. An employee who has been mentally and physically incapacitated is now allowed to file a claim for compensation within 180 days of the incapacity. The responsibility for administration of employers' self-insurance was transferred from the Commissioner of Labor and Industry to the Commissioner of Insurance.

Employers are required to provide for both podiatric and orthodontic treatment for claimants.

A worker permanently transferred to another State is no longer covered by the extraterritoriality provision if he or she travels extensively outside that State.

The liability of an employee who intentionally or grossly caused injury to another employee was limited.

Comprehensive procedures were established for rehabilitation, emphasizing the need for comparable employment and on-the-job training. Retraining to a higher status was permitted when employability would be increased by doing so. The director of rehabilitation services, appointed by the Commissioner of Labor and Industry from persons in the Classified Service, will oversee this new program.

Mississippi

Maximum weekly compensation for disability and death was increased from $91 to $98; the total maximum was raised from $40,950 to $44,100.

Missouri

Elective coverage was allowed when an employer files notice with the Division of Workmen's Compensation. The maximum weekly benefit for temporary partial and temporary total disability was increased from $115 to $125, and the weekly compensation for both permanent total disability and death was increased from $115 to $120.

Montana

The law was redesignated the Workers' Compensation Act, and references to "workmen's" were changed to "workers'" throughout the law. The Occupational Disease Disability Act was retitled the Occupational Disease Act. The Vocational Rehabilitation Division has been renamed the Department of Social Aid Rehabilitation Services.

Municipalities must now pay the difference between a law enforcement officer's full salary and the amount of workers' compensation benefits.

The division is now authorized to require that a claimant pursue a vocational rehabilitation program, if feasible and appropriate, for continuation of benefits. Refusal to participate in the program may lead to the termination of benefits.

Full medical care without time or dollar limits was provided. Under previous law, medical treatment was restricted to a maximum of $2,500 for a nondisabling occupational disease.

Several pneumoconiosis provisions were repealed, thereby making no practical distinction between pneumoconiosis and other occupational diseases. A fine of not more than $500, up from $100, may now be assessed against an employer who fails to provide information (from books, records, and payrolls) at the request of the division. Uninsured employers are now required to pay into the Uninsured Employer's Fund either double the premium amount the employer would have paid if insured by the State fund or $200, whichever is greater. Third-party suits are no longer permitted against an employer covered by the act. State agencies are now required to be insured under the State fund. The penalty assessed against an insurer for delayed benefit payments was increased from 10 percent to 20 percent.

A provision providing employer nonliability for work contracted to an independent party was eliminated. Benefit payments are due after 15 days of an entitlement notice by the insurer.

Nebraska

The maximum weekly benefit for both disability and death was increased from $155 to $180.

Nevada

Coverage was extended to off-duty regular firefighters who perform voluntary services both within the jurisdiction served by their departments and in jurisdictions with reciprocal aid agreements.

Benefits were increased to 35 percent above the initial benefit amount for permanent total disabilities incurred prior to April 9, 1971, and for deaths prior to July 1, 1973. The burial expense allowance was increased from $1,200 to $2,500.

Cooperative agreements for rehabilitation services were authorized for the Industrial Commission, the Rehabilitation Division of the Department of Human Resources, and other agencies to provide the necessary rehabilitation services for disabled workers to return to gainful employment.

Employers are now permitted to self-insure their potential liabilities. In addition, an administrative fund was created to defray all costs and expenses of administering self-insurance programs.

New Hampshire

Death benefits for dependent and totally disabled widows or widowers will now extend for the duration of such total disability. A totally disabled widow or widower with dependent children will continue to receive supplemental compensation for their dependents according to the weekly benefit amounts until the children are no longer entitled. Lump sum agreements, except for medical care, may now be permitted at the discretion of the labor commissioner.

New Jersey

Injuries to fingers and toes will no longer be compensated unless a permanent loss of function occurs. A disfiguring injury, with scars less than three inches, will also no longer be compensable except when involving the face.

New Mexico

The definition of "workmen" was broadened to include public employees and salaried public officers.

New York

Coverage is extended to film inspection assistants, school safety supervisors, and instructors of addiction employed by school districts in a city with a population of 1 million or more.

Death benefits for either surviving spouse were equalized.

The authority of the chairman of the Workers' Compensation Board to approve rates for medical services charged to employers was extended until December 31, 1980. The board was also authorized to impose a 1½-percent monthly interest penalty for overdue payments of physician fees.

North Carolina

The law was retitled the Workers' Compensation Law, and references to "workmen's" were changed to "workers'" throughout the law.

The numerical exemption was reduced from five to four employees. Sole proprietors or partners are now permitted to elect coverage; senior members of the Civil Air Patrol were exempted.

When a totally disabled employee dies of asbestosis or silicosis, the compensation will now be the unpaid portion of the 104 weeks of disability compensation plus an additional 300 weeks of benefits.

Attorney fees in third party subrogation actions now must be approved by the Industrial Commission. Two or more employers are now permitted to pool their potential liabilities. Employers can no longer discharge or demote an employee for filing a compensation claim. When a medical bill remains unpaid after 60 days, a 10-percent penalty will now be added. The commission was also authorized to assess the costs of proceedings against any person who has brought, prosecuted, or defended such proceedings without reasonable grounds.

North Dakota

The maximum weekly benefit for death was increased from $75 to $90.

Persons on the compensation rolls as of July 1, 1975, who are continuing to receive benefits as of July 1, 1979, are now entitled to supplementary benefits. A claim for death benefits can now be filed up to 2 years (previously 1 year) following the worker's death. Court fees for cases that are being appealed are now determined by the Appellate Court, rather than by the trial judge. Temporary total and permanent total disability benefits will now be offset by the amount of any social security benefits.

Ohio

Temporary total disability benefits for the first 12 weeks of compensation will now be based on 72 percent of the employee's last full weekly wage instead of the employee's average weekly wage.

A Rehabilitation Division was established in the Industrial Commission to provide a comprehensive system designed to rehabilitate the injured worker. In the event of a concurrent and duplicative benefit under an employer-funded, non-occupational benefits plan, temporary total disability benefits will now be reduced.

The time limit for premium defaults was changed from 6 to 8 weeks. Premium rates are now set by the Industrial Commission to assure the solvency of the State Insurance Fund.

Oregon

Upon election by a municipality, coverage can now be extended to all municipal volunteer personnel as well as to subcontractors and their employees. Mentally disabled persons in special educational training programs and participants in work training programs are now covered, except that the trainees are not entitled to temporary total disability benefits.

Compensation for permanent disability was changed from $85 to $100 for each degree of injury based on a fixed scale. Where the rating is based on permanent loss of earning capacity, the benefit value per degree is now $85.

The law was amended to limit an injured worker to four changes of his or her attending physician (following the initial choice) without approval from the director.

Self-insured employers must now have certain excess insurance to cover their potential liabilities.

The State Accident Insurance Fund was made an independent public corporation governed by five directors appointed by the Governor.

An assessment of six cents per day will now be charged to every subject employer for each worker employed each day or part of a day. Permanent total disability benefits will now be offset by the amount of social security benefits received.

Rhode Island

The Workmen's Compensation Commission was retitled the Workers' Compensation Commission.

Determinations for the reasonableness of disputed medical charges will now be made by the Workers' Compensation Commissioner.

The time period for filing occupational disease claims was extended from 24 to 36 months.

South Carolina

The amount of compensation a minor dependent may receive without the appointment of a guardian was increased from $1,000 to $2,500.

Tennessee

Maximum weekly benefits for disability or death were increased from $100 to $107, and the total maximum was raised from $40,000 to $42,800. The $15 weekly minimum remained unchanged. Death benefits payable to a widower are now the same as those payable to a widow. Lump sum payments may be commuted upon motion by any party involved in the court proceeding.

Texas

The definition of State employee was broadened to include persons paid from State funds and working for and receiving supervision from a political subdivision of the State.

Dependency no longer applies to parents who abandoned or failed to support the disabled or deceased worker during preadult years. When no claim for death benefits has been filed within 8 months of death, it will now be presumed that there are no dependents entitled to benefits; thus payments will be made into the Second Injury Fund. However, this presumption does not apply to minor beneficiaries or to beneficiaries of unsound mind for whom no guardian has been appointed. A written report must now be filed by an employer within 8 days after an employee's absence from work because of a work-related injury.

The law now requires hospitals to furnish relevant records upon request. Physicians and chiropractors were already covered by this provision.

A Workers' Compensation Advisory Committee was appointed by the Governor to study the law and to formulate possible ways to improve the system.

Utah

Minimum weekly compensation was increased from $75 to $85 for persons permanently and totally disabled and entitled to benefits from the Special Fund. References in the law to either "Special" or "Combined" Injury Fund were deemed to concern the Second Injury Fund.

Employer liability in no-dependency cases was increased from $15,600 to $18,720, payable into the Second Injury Fund. All death benefits formerly paid from the fund will now be paid by the carrier. After the first 6 years of dependency, death benefits will be subject to a 50-percent offset based on Federal social security death benefits.

The minimum weekly benefit for an employee undergoing rehabilitation was increased from $35 to $45.

Virginia

The 2-year limit for filing first or second stage pneumoconiosis claims was removed. Only in cases of pneumoconiosis or silicosis, where x-ray evidence has demonstrated a positive diagnosis of the disease, will waivers from coverage be permitted.

Requirements for group self-insurance were strengthened, with new payroll reporting procedures and the adoption of uniform rules on compliance and certification of insurance. Other insurance changes were also made.

Washington

Corporate officers were excluded from compulsory coverage; elective coverage is now permitted.

Permanent partial disability benefits (thus all disability benefits) will now be offset by any Federal social security benefits. A new provision also allows recovery of overpayment based on this offset.

Weekly compensation for scheduled injuries (where benefit amounts have been precalculated) was doubled, and total compensation for impairment to the whole body was increased from $30,000 to $60,000.

A $45,000 maximum was placed on compensation for unscheduled permanent partial disability to the back when no objective clinical findings are available.

The annual cost-of-living adjustment for both total disability and death benefits for claimants on the rolls since July 1, 1971, was extended to July 1, 1980.

West Virginia

The commissioner must now establish guidelines for determining anticipated periods of disability. Eligibility requirements under the Disabled Workmen's Relief Fund will now extend coverage to persons who receive less than 33 1/3 percent of the State average weekly wage. Payment of reasonable medical expenses is now permitted without prior authorization under certain circumstances.

A Workers' Compensation Advisory Board consisting of 10 members was created to advise the commissioner on compensation administration and make long-range plans for improvements in the Disabled Workmen's Relief Fund.

Wyoming

The presumed pay of volunteer emergency personnel was increased from $50 per month to $100 per month. Thus, they will now be entitled to maximum benefits for temporary total disability.

The dollar limits on attorney fees were eliminated.

The cost of safety incentives

The pain and suffering of a serious disability represent a substantial portion of the costs of an injury. It would be desirable for the legal system to assign liability for such losses so that the full cost of injuries is borne by the party in the best position to prevent the accident. The dilemma, however, is that if the awards routinely made in a workers' compensation system were to be so generous as to include pain and suffering there would be a strong incentive for employees to act with less than an optimal amount of care. . . .

There is some evidence that even the more generous States within the current system may fail to encourage an appropriate amount of careful employee behavior. Only a system that provides the opportunity for detailed examination of the circumstances and consequences of the injury could avoid such a distortion of incentives; but again, this would be very costly.

—JAMES ROBERT CHELIUS
Workplace Safety and Health: The Role of Workers' Compensation (Washington, American Enterprise Institute for Public Policy Research, 1978), p. 62.

State Labor Legislation Enacted in 1978

Richard R. Nelson

Although it was a light legislative year, 17 States revised minimum wage rates; other action included anti-discrimination laws, easing of mandatory retirement rules, and new programs to help displaced homemakers

The volume of labor legislation enacted by State legislatures was less in 1978 than in recent years;[1] however, significant activity took place both in traditional standards fields, including minimum wage rates, child labor, and job discrimination, and in more recently emerging fields, including mandatory retirement, sunset laws, and help for displaced homemakers.

Much legislative activity concerned minimum wage rates, as increases provided for in the 1977 amendments to the Fair Labor Standards Act (FLSA) spurred State action. New legislation was enacted in 1978 or late 1977 in 17 jurisdictions. Also, minimum wage rates in several States were increased by prior law, wage order, or administrative action.

Twelve jurisdictions now have a minimum rate equal to the $2.65-an-hour Federal standard, and 11 of these will match the Federal increase to $2.90 on January 1, 1979, or later in the year. Alaska, Connecticut, and certain industries in the District of Columbia now have minimums higher than the Federal rate. In addition, in almost half the jurisdictions, the minimum wage for tipped employees was set higher than that payable under the FLSA.

Several States altered provisions of their wage laws. Michigan extended coverage of its law from employers of four or more to employers of two or more and removed the exemption for persons 65 years of age and over. The Oklahoma tripartite Wage and Hour Commission, formerly responsible for administering the minimum wage law, was abolished, and its powers were vested exclusively in the labor commissioner. In Kentucky, the wage payment sections of several laws were amended to enlarge the definition of wages for purposes of the minimum wage, prevailing wage, equal pay, and wage payment laws to include vested vacation pay, overtime, severance pay, bonuses, and other payments.

Wage garnishment or assignment continued to attract legislative attention, with laws enacted in 12 States. Most of these dealt with the amount of a person's earnings that may be garnished. Laws in six States specifically mentioned child support payments. Maryland required employers to honor multiple garnishments against the same employee in the order they are received.

Child labor legislation continued recent patterns of amendments to ease employment restrictions. Restrictions concerning nightwork and maximum hours were eliminated for 16- and 17-year-old minors in Ohio and Tennessee. Certificate requirements were eased in New York, Pennsylvania, and Virginia and were replaced in Tennessee by an employer obligation to require proof of age.

Richard R. Nelson is a labor standards adviser in the Division of State Employment Standards, Employment Standards Administration, U.S. Department of Labor.

This article appears here to make information on state laws pertaining to "displaced homemakers" available to widows.

Reprinted from *Monthly Labor Review*, January, 1979, with corrections, U.S. Department of Labor, Bureau of Labor Statistics, Washington, DC 20212.

Employment of minors in theatrical or other performances was the subject of legislation in Georgia, Louisiana, New Jersey, New York, and Oklahoma. Michigan's new child labor law retained most of the previous law's standards, but it eliminated a requirement that employers have occupational approval numbers, changed the farm work exemption from a total exemption to an exemption only for employment not in violation of department standards, and expanded the high school graduate exemption. Pennsylvania removed provisions that were more restrictive for female than for male workers.

Laws concerning arbitrary compulsory retirement based upon age were enacted in 10 States, some perhaps as a result of the 1978 amendments to the Federal Age Discrimination in Employment Act. Among other States, Arizona and Delaware raised the mandatory retirement age from 65 to 70 for State employees, and, effective June 1, 1980, Minnesota raised the retirement age similarly for most private and public sector employees. In Louisiana, administrative officers were asked to waive the 65-year mandatory retirement age of State and local employees prior to the effective date of the Federal law (Jan. 1, 1979), and an executive order, effective in November 1977, abolished mandatory retirement of State employees in Kansas.

Various forms of employment discrimination were addressed by legislation in 29 jurisdictions. Most notable were new comprehensive human rights laws for public employees in Georgia and for both public and private sector workers in Tennessee. Sex discrimination was addressed by legislation in 12 jurisdictions, including Alaska, which created a commission on the status of women, and the District of Columbia, which gave statutory status to a commission which previously existed by executive order. Legislation to aid handicapped workers was enacted in 12 States. The primary purpose of these laws was to prohibit employment discrimination on the basis of a handicap that is unrelated to ability to perform the job. In Ohio, any qualified person between 40 and 65 who is refused a job interview or discharged without cause may bring a civil action against the employer on the basis of age discrimination. Discrimination in the employment or occupational licensing of persons with arrest or conviction records was prohibited in Kentucky and Minnesota. As a result of legislative action in Iowa, employers who discriminate on any basis may lose public contracts.

Help for displaced homemakers has attracted considerable attention over the last few years, with the passage of several laws. During 1978, eight additional States—Delaware, Iowa, Kentucky, Massachusetts, New Mexico, Oklahoma, Rhode Island, and Wisconsin—passed legislation to help homemakers displaced because of dissolution of marriage or other loss of family income. Because of their age or lack of paid work experience, displaced homemakers often face difficulty in getting jobs and are frequently ineligible for financial assistance from public sources. Almost all of the new laws provide for the establishment of multipurpose centers to provide employment services and other aids.

A comprehensive law in Pennsylvania grants seasonal farmworkers important new protection. These workers now must be paid the State minimum wage, may not work in excess of specified hours, and are afforded numerous other or stronger protections governing child labor, equal pay, wage payment, the registration of farm labor contractors, and the certification of labor camps. In other legislation affecting agricultural workers, California required that unloaders of farm products in produce markets in three counties be registered by the State labor commissioner, who may investigate complaints and mediate disputes on the scale of charges. Virginia created a farmworkers commission.

Various other areas of labor standards were subjects of legislation in 1978. Kansas modified its illegal alien law to exempt from the ban on employment those aliens who are permitted to remain in the United States by Federal law, and Louisiana appointed a committee to study the relationship between unemployment and the employment of illegal aliens. Independent labor departments were established through the consolidation of previously separate boards in the District of Columbia and by the transfer of various divisions from other departments in Florida. "Sunset laws" requiring periodic reexamination of State agencies, rules, and regulations were enacted or amended in Florida, Georgia, and Kansas.

In Maryland, the labor commissioner was authorized to enter into reciprocal agreements with other States to collect unpaid wages due from out-of-State employers and employers who leave the State without making payment. An intergovernmental relations council was established in Rhode Island to study the relationship between and among the local, State, and Federal governments and to consider methods of fostering better relations; and, in South Carolina, a law was enacted permitting the exchange of employees between and among Federal, State, and local governments.

Labor relations issues were the subject of statutes, court action, and referenda. Collective bargaining was authorized by law for teachers in Tennessee and for employees of the California State Universities and Colleges and by a constitutional amendment for Michigan State Police. In Utah, the State supreme court held that the Labor Disputes Act, which recognizes labor's right to collective bargaining, does not apply to municipal employees. A "right-to-work" constitutional amendment was rejected by Missouri voters in the November general election.

No additional States ratified the proposed Equal Rights Amendment to the U.S. Constitution, but Congress extended the deadline for securing approval by the three additional States necessary for ratification to June 30, 1982. States will not be permitted to rescind prior ratification.

The following is a summary by jurisdiction of labor legislation during 1978:

Alaska

Wages. By prior law, which sets the minimum wage at 50 cents above the Federal rate, the State rate rose to $3.15 an hour in 1978 and will increase each year, reaching $3.85 on January 1, 1981.

Equal employment opportunity. The Commission on the Status of Women was created with authority to examine such issues as education, homemaking, civil and legal rights, and labor and employment. The commission, which will be terminated on June 30, 1983, is to make annual reports to the governor on its proceedings and recommendations.

The State personnel act was amended so that persons certified as severely handicapped may be granted employment preference without taking a competitive examination.

A resolution was adopted that urges the U.S. Department of Labor to conduct, with the State department of labor, an investigation of the labor certification of nonimmigrant aliens working in Alaska's fish processing industry and to consult the State about the availability of Alaskan workers for certain jobs before issuing work permits to nonimmigrant aliens.

Other laws. The name of the Governor's Committee on Employment of the Physically Handicapped was changed to the Governor's Committee on Employment of the Handicapped, and publicly-financed vocational rehabilitation services now are to be provided to all handicapped individuals, not just to those who require public assistance.

The U.S. Supreme Court held unconstitutional the "Alaska Hire" Act, which required hiring preference for State residents in all oil and gas leases, easements, right-of-way permits, and unitization agreements on the basis that it violated the privileges and immunities clause. This clause bars discrimination against citizens of other States.

Arizona

Wages. Prisoners under the prison industries program may now receive wages up to 50 cents per hour, instead of 35 cents; if the director of the Department of Corrections contracts with private parties to provide services or labor, prisoners may receive higher wages, not to exceed the minimum wage prescribed by law.

Equal employment opportunity. The mandatory retirement age was raised from 65 to 70 for State employees; provisions were made for continued employment after age 70 by annual requests if performance and other standards are met.

Discrimination based on race, color, religion, national origin, or sex was prohibited in all phases of apprenticeship employment and training.

Occupational safety and health. A new provision provides for inspection of boilers and heaters by the Industrial Commission and establishes safety conditions for elevators and similar conveyances.

Other laws. The number of hours required on-the-job work experience in apprenticeship programs was reduced from 4,000 to 2,000, and criteria were established for determining apprenticeable occupations.

California

Wages. A wage order increased the minimum wage rate from $2.50 an hour to $2.65 effective April 1, 1978, with a further increase to $2.90 scheduled on January 1, 1979.

An employee may designate in writing a representative to act for him in filing specified wage and other monetary claims with the labor commissioner for collection.

Retaliation against employees for filing bona fide complaints or claims under any of the provisions of the labor code within the jurisdiction of the labor commissioner was prohibited as was retaliation against an employee who has filed or intends to file a claim against an employer alleging an occupational injury.

An exemption from garnishment or attachment in bankruptcy proceedings for monies held in private retirement or profit-sharing plans was expanded to provide a total exemption from any garnishment or attachment of such funds.

An employee's earnings protection law was enacted to govern the procedures for wage garnishment. The Judicial Council was authorized to do all that is required by the U.S. Department of Labor to exempt the State from the earnings garnishment provisions of the Federal Consumer Credit Protection Act.

Child labor. The law permitting minors between 16 and 18 years old enrolled in approved work experience education programs to work as late as 12:30 a.m. was extended to minors in similar programs conducted by private schools.

Agriculture. All employees of the Agricultural Labor Relations Board now are specifically required to perform their duties in an objective and impartial manner without prejudice toward any party subject to the board's jurisdiction.

Separate provisions on regulating unloaders of farm products in produce markets were enacted for Alameda, San Francisco, and San Mateo counties. The labor commissioner will register unloaders, investigate complaints, and mediate disputes involving the establishment of a scale of charges.

Equal employment opportunity. To conform to the Federal Age Discrimination in Employment Act amendments of 1978, changes were made in State and local retirement systems to extend prohibitions against mandatory retirement prior to the age of 70 for public employees.

Inquiries into the physical condition or medical history of job applicants is permissible if directly related to the position.

The review authority of the Division of Fair Employment Practices, previously limited to public works contracts, was changed to a general authority to review and investigate employment policies and practices of all State contractors and subcontractors and to recommend appropriate sanctions.

State licensing boards, agencies, and authorities in the Department of Consumer Affairs were included within the coverage of the Fair Employment Practice Act, which states that it is unlawful to require an examination or qualification that is not job related and that discriminates because of an applicant's race, creed, color, national origin or ancestry, sex, age, medical condition, or physical handicap.

The ban on employment discrimination against pregnant women by district school boards was expanded to apply to all employers. Among other prohibitions, an employer may not refuse to promote or to select a pregnant employee for training if the training program can be completed at least 3 months before beginning maternity leave, nor can an employee be discharged for pregnancy. A pregnant employee must receive the same benefits as other employees, except that an employer is not required to grant disability leave for more than 6 weeks.

Labor relations. An employer-employee relations act, applicable to employees of the State college and university systems, was enacted, to be administered by the public employment relations board. Provision was made for mediation and factfinding in cases of impasses, and authority was given for agreements providing for binding arbitration.

Up to three representatives from each employee organization representing State college and university system employees are to be given reasonable time off during working hours to attend and make presentations at trustees meetings if a matter affecting conditions of employment is scheduled for consideration.

The name of the State Conciliation Service was changed to the State Mediation and Conciliation Service. The service is within the Department of Industrial Relations.

An employee organization alleging, in a petition to the public employment relations board, that the employees in an appropriate unit no longer wish to be represented by another employee organization may no longer use current dues deduction authorizations as evidence of support.

Private employment agencies. The requirement that agency counselors register with the Bureau of Employment Agencies was repealed, but agencies now must provide approved training for all new counselors. The exemption for management consultants now applies if they do not recommend individuals to positions having a starting salary of less than $25,000 per year, rather than the previous $20,000.

Regulation of musician booking agencies was transferred from the Department of Consumer Affairs to the labor department, where they, along with artists' managers, will be included within the provisions governing talent agencies.

Occupational safety and health. An employer cited for a first-instance occupational safety and health violation, resulting from an onsite inspection, will not be assessed a civil penalty unless the inspection finds 10 violations or more. This policy has been implemented by administrative regulations in effect since January 1, 1977.

The Department of Industrial Relations will be responsible for developing a long-range program for upgrading and expanding the State's resources in occupational health and medicine, including the creation of health centers that will train occupational health specialists, serve as referral centers for occupational illnesses, and engage in research on the causes, diagnosis, and prevention of occupational illnesses. The department is also to develop and maintain a repository of research information and data relating to toxic materials and harmful physical agents in use in places of employment.

A limited jurisdiction of the Division of Industrial Safety over workers employed in the construction and repair of railroad equipment was expanded to include jurisdiction over occupational safety and health problems of railroad employees.

Resolutions urged the Congress to amend the Occupational Safety and Health Act to allow the State program the administrative flexibility it needs to operate more effectively and to amend the Federal Mine Safety and Health Act to avoid duplication of efforts and conflicting laws, regulations, and penalties and to permit the State's Division of Industrial Safety to be the sole safety enforcement agency in the State.

Other laws. Discrimination against or discharge of an employee who is required to serve as a witness in court is prohibited provided reasonable notice is given to the employer. Discrimination of any type, rather than the previous discharge only, against an employee who serves as an inquest or trial juror is now unlawful.

The use of private investigators to provide employers with information concerning their employees was regulated. Among other provisions, employees now must receive copies of investigation reports prior to discipline or discharge, and the payment of bonuses to private investigators for discovering unfavorable information is prohibited.

A resolution urges the State and local governments, charitable and service organizations, and private employers to take volunteer work experience into account in job announcements, in application forms, and in the consideration of applicants for employment.

Connecticut

Wages. The hourly minimum wage increased to $2.66 on July 1, with further increases on January 1 of each year, to $2.91 in 1979, $3.12 in 1980, and $3.37 in 1981. The former wage differential was eliminated for farmworkers, who now are entitled to the same rate as others.

Employers' civil liability for unpaid wages was doubled to twice the amount of wages due along with costs and reasonable attorney fees, and the maximum fine for violation was increased from $200 to $1,000.

If an employer policy or collective bargaining agreement provides for payment of accrued fringe benefits to a discharged employee, the employer must pay for them in the form of wages.

The amount of wages exempt from garnishment for support payments was increased from $50 a week to the first $70 of disposable weekly earnings.

Equal employment opportunity. Provisions affecting involuntary retirement under the antidiscrimination law were conformed to the 1978 amendments to the Federal age discrimination act; however, termination of employment is now specifically permissible where age is a bona fide occupational qualification, such as in police work or firefighting.

It is now unlawful for an employer, employment agency, or labor organization to discriminate against mentally retarded persons, unless the disability prevents performance of the particular work involved.

Labor relations. The municipal collective bargaining law was amended to prohibit the inclusion of both supervisory and other employees in any new collective bargaining units.

Other laws. The number of hours of required training in approved apprenticeship programs was reduced from 4,000 to 2,000.

The Department of Corrections may contract with private nonprofit agencies to help prior offenders obtain employment, housing, transportation, and counseling.

Delaware

Wages. The State tax commissioner is now specifically authorized to issue a warrant to garnish wages of delinquent taxpayers after obtaining a judgment.

Child labor. The Alcoholic Beverage Control Act, which has a 20-year age minimum for liquor possession, was amended to permit liquor importers to employ persons 18 and 19 years old in occupations other than sales, and catering businesses and bowling alleys to employ 16-year-olds and over, provided the minors do not sell or serve liquor. Prior exemptions permit the employment of 16-year-olds in hotels, clubs, restaurants, and racetracks which have liquor licenses.

Equal employment opportunity. The mandatory retirement age for State employees was raised from 65 to 70 years.

A public employee will be guilty of a misdemeanor, if, in performing his official functions, he knowingly practices discrimination on the basis of race, creed, color, sex, or national origin.

Resolutions were adopted urging the congressional delegation to work for an extension of the deadline for ratification of the proposed Federal Equal Rights Amendment and to support legislation to establish a national office of the handicapped.

Displaced homemakers. A displaced homemakers act directs the State secretary of labor to establish and coordinate multipurpose service programs for displaced homemakers to provide job counseling, training, and placement as well as information on subjects such as financial management and health services.

District of Columbia

Wages. A revised wage order, effective April 15, 1978, increases the minimum wage for laundry and drycleaning industry employees from $2.40 to $3 an hour.

Equal employment opportunity. A new enactment gives statutory status to the Commission on Women, which previously existed by executive order of the mayor, and new procedures were adopted for the selection of future members and the appointment of a chairperson.

Other laws. The previously separate Minimum Wage and Industrial Safety Board, Unemployment Compensation Board, and Department of Manpower were abolished and their functions consolidated into a newly created Department of Labor.

Florida

Wages. The courts were authorized to award costs and reasonable attorney's fees in a civil action for unpaid wages. A continuing writ of garnishment, formerly issuable for child support payments, may now be issued also for periodic alimony payments.

Equal employment opportunity. The Human Rights Act was amended to conform provisions concerning involuntary retirement under seniority systems or employee benefit plans to the 1978 amendments to the Federal Age Discrimination in Employment Act.

Veterans' preference provisions in public employment were clarified to include certain spouses and unmarried widows and widowers under the privilege of preference in promotion or appointment to noncompetitive positions, formerly available only to veterans themselves.

Private employment agencies. The maximum period of employment during which employees are entitled to a refund of 75 percent of the fee they paid the agency, if they are discharged through no fault of their own, was increased from 14 to 30 days.

Other laws. The Divisions of Labor and of Employment Security were removed from the Department of Commerce and combined into a new Department of Labor and Employment Security. This department also includes commmissions on public employee relations, industrial relations, and unemployment appeals.

A sunset law was enacted to abolish certain statutory boards, committees, commissions, and councils that have not met since January 1, 1975, including the Employment Service Council, and setting an October 1, 1981, termination date for several others, unless reviewed and reestablished by the legislature. Some of those slated for review are the Private Employment Agencies Advisory Committee, State Apprenticeship Council, Industry Advisory Council, and Small Business Advisory Council.

Georgia

Child labor. Minors now may work in motion picture, theatrical, radio, or television productions or as photographic or advertising models with written consent of the labor commissioner. Employment of any minor for pornographic purposes is a felony.

Equal employment opportunity. A comprehensive fair employment practices law was enacted which prohibits employment discrimination against public employees on the basis of race, color, religion, national origin, sex, handicap, or age (between 40 and 65) and establishes an office of fair employment practices and a fair employment practices advisory board.

A resolution sustains the study committee on services for the aged and directs it to study recommendations of the 1977 committee, including employment and mandatory retirement, and to report its findings and legislative proposals to the general assembly by January 1, 1979.

Private employment agencies. The scheduled termination date of the employment agency regulatory law and advisory council under the sunset law was extended from July 1, 1978, to July 1, 1984.

Guam

Wages. The minimum wage rose to $2.65 an hour and will continue to increase each year to match Federal rates under a prior law which adopted the FLSA rates by reference.

Hawaii

Wages. The minimum wage rate was raised from $2.40

to $2.65 an hour effective July 1, 1978, with future increases to $2.90 on July 1, 1979, $3.10 on July 1, 1980, and $3.35 on July 1, 1981. These increases are identical to those under the Federal law.

The amount of wages subject to garnishment is computed on wages remaining after the withholding of deductions required by law.

Equal employment opportunity. It is now unlawful to discharge or suspend an employee for receiving or responding to a summons to serve as a witness or prospective witness. In case of violation, the employee may bring a civil action for reinstatement and for reimbursement for up to 6 weeks of lost wages and a reasonable attorney's fee.

Labor relations. The Public Employment Relations Board will help resolve bargaining impasses between firefighters and public employers by implementing special mediation and arbitration procedures.

The mandatory adjustment of compensation, hours, terms and conditions of employment, and other benefits applicable to public employees who are excluded from collective bargaining was extended to most court officers and employees.

Private employment agencies. All applicants for employment agency licenses are required to pass a certified employment consultant examination as designated by the director of the labor department.

Occupational safety and health. Several resolutions related to safety and health were adopted. The State's congressional delegation was requested to support efforts to gain Federal certification of its State occupational safety and health plan; labor unions and employers were urged to cooperate in the development and implementation of occupational safety and health programs with help from the legislature; and the State labor department was requested to cooperate with workers' compensation insurers to start employer safety consultation services.

Other laws. Hours of training required under apprenticeship agreements were changed from 4,000 hours to 2,000 hours or 12 months of reasonably continuous employment.

A 1-year residency requirement for public employment was replaced with a hiring preference for applicants who have filed resident income tax returns or who have been claimed as dependents on such returns.

A resolution urged the State's congressional delegation to work for passage of the Humphrey-Hawkins Full Employment and Balanced Growth Act.

Idaho

Wages. An exemption from the minimum wage law was added for seasonal employees of a nonprofit camping program.

Equal employment opportunity. A resolution was adopted delaying from February 2, 1978, to February 2, 1979, the effective date of amendments to the rules of the Human Rights Commission pertaining to the filing of discriminatory complaints, postfiling procedures, and orders issued by the commission.

Illinois

Agriculture. The effective date of the surety bond requirement for farm labor contractors was delayed until July 1, 1979. During this time, the director of the Deparment of Labor is to study the availability of surety bonds and other sources of financial assurance for such contractors and recommend continuance or discontinuance of the requirement.

Equal employment opportunity. The Department of Equal Employment Opportunity and the Equal Employment Opportunity Advisory Council were created to implement equal employment opportunity and affirmative action programs in State agencies.

Within 120 days after the filing of an unfair employment practices charge, the Fair Employment Practices Commission is to convene a factfinding conference to obtain evidence, identify issues in dispute, and explore the feasibility of negotiating a settlement prior to taking further action.

It was resolved that a special House Committee on equal employment opportunity be created to study and investigate discrimination in State employment against women, minorities, the handicapped, elderly, and persons with disabilities, to review the operations of the Department of Personnel and the EEO officer, and to determine the need for revisions in State law or additional financial aid and manpower to improve the State EEO program.

Private employment agencies. Administration of the private employment agencies act was strengthened by authorizing the labor director to issue orders to cease violating the law and to obtain court orders commanding agencies to comply, under penalty of contempt of court. Agency negligence, not only misconduct, will now be a basis for action against the surety bond.

Iowa

Wages. Court-ordered wage assignments for child support were made binding upon employers. "Disposable earnings" for purposes of garnishment limitation was redefined to mean earnings remaining after deductions required by law to be withheld or assigned instead of only withheld.

Equal employment opportunity. Several changes were made in the civil rights law including authorizing complainants to file court action if their complaints are not resolved by the Civil Rights Commission within 120 days and permitting the commission to designate local agencies as referral agencies for the disposition of complaints.

Other changes specifically exempt from the age discrimination provisions bona fide apprenticeship programs if the employee involved is more than 45 years old,

persons under 18 not legally considered adults, and State or Federal programs designed to benefit a specific age group. Also, employers may now lose public contracts if they discriminate on any basis.

A resolution proposes that an equal rights amendment to the State constitution be considered by the next general assembly.

Labor relations. The exemption from the open meetings law of public employer and employee negotiating sessions, strategy meetings, mediation, and arbitration deliberations was amended to require public meetings when parties present their initial bargaining positions.

Occupational safety and health. The position of State boiler inspector was eliminated and the labor commissioner was made responsible for inspections and enforcement of safety provisions for all boilers and unfired steam pressure vessels.

Displaced homemakers. Money was designated from the appropriation for adult and children services to fund displaced homemaker projects.

Kansas

Wages. Wage deductions were authorized for State employee organization membership dues at the employee's written request.

Limits were placed on the percentage of earnings which may be garnished to satisfy support payment orders.

Equal employment opportunity. Administrative regulations of the Commission on Civil Rights, pertaining to discrimination on public works contracts, were amended to reduce compliance requirements. For example, the commission may no longer require affirmative action programs but now must negotiate for their preparation and implementation, and contractors must no longer solicit bids from minority and female contractors but instead are prohibited from discriminatorily excluding such contractors from bidding.

An executive order effective November 23, 1977, abolished mandatory retirement at age 65 of State agency employees if they remain able to perform acceptable work.

Several changes were made in the civil service act, including the addition of a requirement that all personnel actions be made without regard to race, national origin or ancestry, religion, political affiliation, or other factors not relating to merit and shall not be based on sex, age, or physical disability except where sex, age, and physical requirements constitute a bona fide occupational qualification. Retaliation against an employee for using the appeals procedure is prohibited.

Occupational safety and health. Amendments to the law included extending coverage to State agencies and public works, broadening the scope of investigations to include additional factors such as job-related illness and occupant capacity, and prohibiting retaliation against employees for filing complaints or furnishing information.

Undocumented workers. The existing ban on employment of illegal aliens will not apply to the employment of aliens who have illegally entered the United States but who are permitted by Federal law to remain.

Other laws. A sunset law abolishes several regulatory agencies and boards on various dates. For example, the Commission on Civil Rights is scheduled for termination on July 1, 1981. The law also provides for public hearings to determine the need for continued existence with legislative action required to continue or reestablish these agencies.

Kentucky

Wages. The minimum wage rate was raised from $1.60 to $2 an hour, with a future increase to $2.15 on July 1, 1979.

Changes were made affecting the wage payment sections of several laws. The definition of wages for purposes of the minimum wage, prevailing wage, equal pay, and wage payment laws was enlarged to specifically include vested vacation pay, overtime, severance pay, bonuses, and other payments. The wage payment law was extended to include all employers instead of only corporations, and most State employees were exempted from the minimum wage law. Under the wage payment law, the labor commissioner was authorized to take assignment for collection of unpaid wages rather than for minimum wage and overtime only and to enforce the prevailing wage law, including collecting of wages due and taking action against employers in violation. Employers may be barred from future public works contracts until they comply with the law's provisions.

It is now unlawful for any employer to withhold from an employee any part of an agreed upon wage (formerly the prohibition applied only to collectively bargained wage agreements). The exception for withholdings authorized by State or Federal law was extended to include local laws.

The definition of public authority in the prevailing wage law was amended to include any nonprofit corporation funded to act as a government agency in connection with the construction of public buildings.

Hours of work. Employers using continuous work scheduling are now exempt from the Sunday closing law, provided each employee receives 1 day of rest in each calendar week.

Equal employment opportunity. With the exception of those who practice law and of nonelective peace officers, it is now unlawful to deny public employment or an occupational license because of a prior conviction of a crime, except for crimes involving moral turpitude or relating directly to the employment or license sought.

Labor relations. Use of an injunction without a preliminary hearing is prohibited during a strike, picketing, or assembly, except when violence has occurred.

An 18-member labor-management advisory council composed of 8 management and 8 labor members was created. The commissioners of labor and commerce will be ex officio nonvoting members, with the commissioner of labor serving as chairman.

Occupational safety and health. Most safety legislation related to mining. Mine inspectors were authorized to enter and inspect any coal or clay mine at any reasonable time. It was made a felony to operate a validly closed mine. Procedures were expanded for corrective action when miners are deemed to be in imminent danger of bodily harm. Also, educational, training, and certification requirements for miners were strengthened.

Displaced homemakers. A new law permits the secretary of the Department for Human Resources to establish multipurpose service centers to provide job training and counseling, placement, health education, and financial and educational services to displaced homemakers. Whenever possible, staff positions will be filled by displaced homemakers.

Louisiana

Wages. The minimum amount of disposable income exempt from garnishment was increased from $70 per week to 30 times the Federal minimum hourly wage.

Child labor. An exemption from the law of any minor 14 or over in a concert or theatrical performance, with a permit granted by the commissioner of labor, was repealed. A new exemption was enacted permitting the participation by any minor, with written parental consent, in any theatrical or musical performance sponsored by a nonprofit private organization or public body, or in a commercial motion picture being produced or filmed in the State, with the written consent of the director of the film commission.

Equal employment opportunity. Age discrimination in employment against persons at least 40 but less than 70 years of age by employers of 20 employees or more, employment agencies, and labor organizations is now prohibited. The law previously prohibited such discrimination against persons under 50 by employers of at least 25 employees. Age discrimination in employment practices is prohibited by any State or local agency or political subdivision.

The Governor was authorized to establish an Office of Civil Rights to perform such duties as investigate and act on equal employment opportunity and discrimination complaints in State services.

A resolution requested administrative officers to waive mandatory retirement of State and local employees who reach age 65 before January 1, 1979, the effective date of the Federal law raising the mandatory retirement age to 70.

A bureau for handicapped persons was created within the Department of Health and Human Resources to administer and expand responsibilities formerly exercised by the Governor's Committee on Employment of the Physically Handicapped. Duties will include conducting programs to educate employers on the advantages of hiring the handicapped, Federal tax incentives, and Federal laws pertaining to employment, training, and advancement of handicapped persons.

Civil service entrance or promotion tests in cities with populations of more than 100,000 will be adapted for applicants with impaired sensory, manual, or speaking skills, unless such skills are a bona fide occupational qualification. Public notice will be given of the availability of such tests.

Undocumented workers. A joint legislative committee was created to study the relationship between unemployment in the State and the employment of illegal aliens. A report of findings and any proposed legislation are due prior to the 1979 regular session of the legislature.

Other laws. A work opportunity program was established which includes training, job placement, and public service employment, with participation mandatory for most welfare and unemployment insurance recipients.

The number of hours of required training in approved apprenticeship programs was reduced from 4,000 to 2,000.

Maine

Wages. The minimum wage was increased to $2.65 on January 1, 1978, and will increase to $2.90 a year later, under a prior law which mandated matching State increases to the Federal rate, up to a maximum $3 rate.

Labor relations. Attorneys employed in the office of the attorney general were excluded from coverage under the State Employees Labor Relations Act. Classified employees were removed as 1 of the 3 occupational bargaining units permitted for vocational-technical institutes and State schools under the University of Maine Labor Relations Act. The two other groups, faculty and instructors, and administrative staff remain covered.

Maryland

Wages. The minimum wage rose to $2.65 an hour and will continue to increase each year to match the Federal rate under a prior State law which adopted the FLSA rates by reference.

Farm machinery salesmen and employees of nonprofit organizations that furnish temporary home care services for the sick, aged, mentally ill, handicapped, or disabled are now exempt from overtime pay requirements.

The labor commissioner was authorized to enter into reciprocal agreements with other States to collect unpaid wages from out-of-State employers.

The time limit for bringing action under the equal pay law was extended from 1 to 3 years after the date of the alleged violation.

Employers must now honor garnishments against the same employee in the order they are received and must remit amounts withheld within 15 days of the close of the last pay period each month. Creditors are to furnish monthly statements of payments credited, and garnishment orders now lapse upon dismissal or resignation, unless the employee is reinstated within 90 days.

Child labor. The minimum consecutive hours of time off outside of school that minors of 16 and 17 must have in each 24-hour day were reduced from 9 to 8. The nightwork prohibition between 7 p.m. and 8 a.m. for those under 16 was retained.

Persons 18 or older now may be employed to stock alcoholic beverages in Anne Arundel County; however, persons under 21 continue to be prohibited from employment by the holder of a class D liquor license in the sale of alcoholic beverages.

Equal employment opportunity. The prohibition against the use of lie detector tests as a condition of employment was extended to State, county, and local government employment, except for employees of law enforcement agencies.

An employer cannot require an applicant to answer any question pertaining to a physical, psychological, or psychiatric illness, disability, handicap, or treatment that is not material to his fitness or capacity to perform the job. Previously, employers could not ask about any psychological or psychiatric condition or treatment.

Labor relations. State departments now are prohibited from awarding public contracts to persons found in contempt of court by a Federal Court of Appeals for failure to correct an unfair labor practice.

A formal five-step grievance procedure was established for classified employees of the University of Maryland.

Private employment agencies. Agencies knowingly charging or attempting to collect a higher fee than specified in the schedule previously filed with the administrator now forfeit their rights to any fee and must refund in full any previously collected fees. Agencies are no longer required to publish their address in all advertisements. The bond that they must deposit with the labor commissioner was increased from $5,000 to $7,000.

Occupational safety and health. Labor department investigators or inspectors who are authorized or required by law to inspect certain premises or property for occupational safety or health purposes may now apply to the District Court for administrative search warrants when, having made a proper request for entry, they are denied access.

The labor commissioner is authorized to issue regulations governing working conditions of employees working with high-voltage electrical lines.

Massachusetts

Wages. By an amendment adopted in late 1977, the minimum wage rate was increased to $2.65 an hour on

January 1, 1978, and will increase to $2.90 on January 1, 1979, $3.10 on January 1, 1980, and $3.35 on January 1, 1981. An administrative regulation established subminimum rates for full-time students.

Equal employment opportunity. Age discrimination by dismissal or refusal to employ any person between 45 and 65 years of age is now subject to a fine of up to $500. A fine was not previously specified.

Labor relations. Advance notice must be posted alerting affected public employees to hearings being held by the labor relations commission to determine the exclusive representative for collective bargaining and for all elections.

Displaced homemakers. A new law directs the secretary of the Office of Economic Development and Manpower Affairs to establish multipurpose centers to provide displaced homemakers with counseling, training, education, and placement services to help them find employment. Whenever possible, the centers will be staffed by displaced homemakers.

Michigan

Wages. By an amendment adopted in late 1977, the minimum wage increased to $2.65 an hour on January 1, 1978, with future increases to $2.90 on January 1, 1979, $3.10 on January 1, 1980, and $3.35 on January 1, 1981. These increases equal those under the Federal law.

Coverage of the minimum wage law was extended from employers of four employees or more to employers of two or more at any time within a calendar year. The exemption for persons 65 years of age and over was removed.

Several changes were made in the wage payment law, including the following: authorizing the labor department rather than the county prosecutor to initiate action to enforce final agency orders; requiring written employee authorization for wage deductions; setting a time limit of 12 months after an alleged violation for filing a complaint; and establishing recordkeeping requirements. Other changes prohibit the kickback of wages as a condition of employment, prohibit retaliation against an employee for filing a complaint, and increase the penalties for violation.

The prevailing wage law now also applies to school construction.

Child labor. A revised child labor law made several changes: elimination of a requirement that employers have occupational approval numbers; a change from a total farmwork exemption to an exemption only for employment not in violation of department standards; and exemption from the law for 16-year-olds who have completed the requirements for graduation from high school and for 17-year-olds who have passed a general educational development test. Previously only 17-year-olds with high school diplomas were exempt.

A youth employment clearinghouse was created within the Department of Labor to assemble data on unemployed persons 14 through 23 years of age and to monitor, evaluate, and make recommendations concerning youth employment programs.

Equal employment opportunity. The prohibition against sex discrimination was expanded to include discrimination by reason of pregnancy, childbirth, or related conditions, exclusive of abortion not intended to save the life of the mother.

Labor relations. The right to petition the court for relief from an unfair labor practice, under the public employee collective bargaining law, was extended to any party with a complaint, rather than limited only to the Employment Relations Commission.

Special strike notice provisions for hospitals and public utilities were eliminated from the Labor Mediation Act. The same notice as for other employees is now required.

A constitutional amendment, passed in the 1978 general election, authorizes collective bargaining for the State police. As civil service employees, they did not previously have this right under the Public Employment Relations Act.

Private employment agencies. Applicants for employment agency licenses who are not of good moral character will be subject to rejection, suspension, revocation, or refusal to renew the license.

Occupational safety and health. The Fire Safety Board was authorized to issue rules for the storage, transportation, and handling of hazardous materials, and the State fire marshal is now required to inspect and certify each establishment and vehicle of firms engaged in transporting hazardous materials.

The Occupational Safety Standards Commission is no longer required to consult with an advisory committee that represents employee and employer interests in farm operations on the impact of any proposed safety regulations applicable to agriculture.

Any occupational safety and health board, commission, and committee is to conduct business at public meetings and is specifically required to give public notice of the time, date, and place of each meeting.

Other laws. A "right-to-know" law gives public and private employees the right to review their personnel files. It also establishes criteria both for the nature of material permitted to be kept on file or divulged to third parties and for procedures for correction or removal of false information.

The law governing occupational licensing of former offenders was amended to require the head of the licensing agency to screen criminal records prior to their use by the licensing board to insure that no prohibited information is included. The agency head is to set regulations for licensing boards to govern how they prescribe offenses that indicate an applicant is not likely to serve in the public interest.

Minnesota

Wages. Workers under 18 in corn detasseling work are now protected by overtime pay and all other provisions of minimum wage law, except for the minimum rate itself. Before, minors in all types of farmwork were exempt from the law.

For employees of residential buildings who receive housing as full or partial payment, the minimum wage entitlement is to be computed for time actually worked and to exclude on-call time on the premises.

Under an explicit wage deduction, employees may agree in advance to deductions, either at regular intervals or upon termination, for purchases from the employer.

Equal employment opportunity. Effective June 1, 1980, mandatory retirement before age 70 will be prohibited for most private and public sector employees. The compulsory retirement age for most State employees is currently 65.

The Commissioner of Personnel was directed to institute an affirmative action program in the State civil service to eliminate underutilization of qualified women, handicapped persons, blacks, Hispanics, Asian or Pacific Islanders, American Indians, or Alaskan natives. A Council on Affairs of Spanish-Speaking People was created to advise the Governor and legislature on problems such as education, employment, human rights, health, housing, and social welfare and to serve as a liaison with the Spanish-speaking community. Retaliatory employment discrimination by employers or unions against present or former members of the legislature for comments made or beliefs held while serving was prohibited.

Labor relations. The public employee labor relations act was amended to clarify the definition of a public employee to include, in addition to the State and the board of regents of the University of Minnesota, the governing bodies of political subdivisions that have final budgetary approval authority with respect to employees. Also, physical and occupational therapists were added to the definition of teacher. Public employees covered by both union grievance procedures and civil service appeals procedures are now authorized to pursue redress through either, but not both, means.

Occupational safety and health. Corn detasselers who leave the worksite because of injury, illness, or discharge must be furnished transportation to the pick-up point and be paid for the time returning there. Employers of corn detasselers must provide an accessible water supply in the field and sanitary equipment for its use.

Other laws. Employers are prohibited from stopping or threatening to stop employee insurance coverage or pension benefits because of job performance, unless the employee has the opportunity to continue coverage by making the same contribution the employer would have made.

Missouri

Equal employment opportunity. Discrimination in employment based on a handicap that is unrelated to ability to perform the job was prohibited.

Labor relations. An attempt to enact a "right-to-work" constitutional amendment was rejected by voters in the November general election.

Nebraska

Equal employment opportunity. The authority of cities and villages to enact antidiscrimination ordinances was expanded to authorize discrimination bans on the basis of marital status, age, and disability.

Resolutions were adopted that authorize various studies: to investigate and propose legislation on such topics as job sharing, part-time employment, flexible hours, parental leave, and upward mobility; to facilitate the entrance of women into the job market; to determine actions that might be taken to identify and correct salary disparities in comparable jobs performed by men and women; and to examine and propose specific legislation dealing with the State's affirmative action efforts. The study committees are to report to the next regular session of the Legislature.

Occupational safety and health. The Department of Health was given authority to adopt regulations for the issuance of licenses to persons manufacturing, using, transporting, or possessing any source of radiation and to establish qualifications pertaining to the education and knowledge of radiation safety procedures for all users of radioactive materials. Penalties for violation include suspension, revocation, or limitation of a license.

Nevada

Wages. The labor commissioner, exercising specific authority given him in 1977, increased the minimum wage by regulation to $2.50 an hour on January 1, 1978, $2.65 on July 1, 1978, and $2.75 on January 1, 1979.

New Hampshire

Wages. The minimum wage rose to $2.65 an hour and will continue to increase each year to match Federal rates, under a prior State law which adopted the FLSA rates by reference.

New Jersey

Child labor. An 8-year minimum age for the professional employment of minors in theatrical productions was removed. Permit requirements now specify that minors not be endangered by the working conditions and that physical examinations of minors under age 8 include vision screening if practicable. The department of labor is to prescribe safeguards for the working conditions, supervision, and education of workers under 16 with special attention to those under 6. It will be unlawful to employ persons under 16 to perform an indecent or immoral exhibition.

Equal employment opportunity. It was made an unlawful employment practice to deny any blind person a job or promotion unless the blindness would prevent performance of the job.

A commission, composed of four legislative members, four public members, and the director of the Division on Women, was created to study sex discriminatory provisions in the statutes and to recommend necessary revisions to the Governor and legislature.

New Mexico

Displaced homemakers. The Office for Displaced Homemakers was created, within the Commission on the Status of Women, to research the problems of displaced homemakers and to plan job counseling, training, placement, and other programs for them.

Other laws. The apprenticeship council was placed in the Employment Services Division of the newly created Human Services Department, and a reduction from 4,000 to 2,000 was made in the required hours for an apprenticeship agreement in any given trade.

New York

Wages. The minimum wage rate for nonagricultural workers was increased from $2.30 to $2.65 an hour with additional increases to $2.90 on January 1, 1979, $3.10 on January 1, 1980, and $3.35 on January 1, 1981. Corresponding proportionate increases were made in allowances for tips, meals, lodging, and other specified rates in existing wage orders.

Procedures were clarified to establish that a hearing is not required before prevailing rates are determined or redetermined for public works but is necessary in an investigation of failure to pay prevailing rates.

Child labor. A minor applying for an employment certificate will now be issued a certificate of physical fitness if a physical examination has been made within 12 rather than 6 months. If a known health problem exists at the time of application, another examination may be required by the issuing authority.

The employment or exhibition of a person under 16 years of age as a rope walker, wire walker, horse rider, gymnast, or acrobat now will be permitted if the minor is protected by safety devices or protective equipment and has a child performer permit. The liquor authority may now issue permits to persons under age 18 to appear as entertainers on premises licensed for retail sales. Among other requirements, a parent or guardian must be present during the minor's appearance.

Equal employment opportunity. The industrial commissioner is to submit to the Governor and legislature an annual report on the status of older workers, including those over age 65. The report will include the employment needs of older workers, ability of the State employment service to deal with their problems, economic impact of unemployment among them, and need for affirmative action. It also will make recommendations for improved programs or changes in laws or regulations.

Labor relations. Public employees who violate the strike prohibition are no longer subject to the penalty of 1-year's probation with loss of tenure; other penalties were retained.

Jurisdiction over improper public employer and employee organization practices in New York City was transferred from the Public Employment Relations Board to the New York City Board of Collective Bargaining.

The civil service law was amended to permit employees to be represented by a union representative or counsel at disciplinary hearings, instead of only by counsel.

Police officers may not be penalized for failure to meet an established quota of traffic violations, other than parking, standing, or stopping.

State employees subject to agency shop deductions may now, in addition to demanding a refund of any portion of the deduction used for activities not directly related to terms and conditions of employment, also demand a refund for expenditures of a political or ideological nature.

Occupational safety and health. The industrial commissioner is to survey political subdivisions to determine the extent of capital expenditures required to conform to Federal OSHA standards and the availability of Federal funding for such projects. Findings are to be submitted to the Governor and legislature by February 15, 1979.

Work on an unsafe machine or in a dangerous area tagged as such by the industrial commissioner may not be resumed under any circumstances until reinspection by the commissioner and removal of the tag.

The Department of Environmental Conservation was given authority to regulate the transfer, storage, and disposal of hazardous wastes.

The time for municipalities to elect to enforce safety and health standards for places of public assembly, instead of the State labor department, was extended until July 1, 1979.

Other laws. The Administrative Regulations Review Commission, composed of eight legislators, was established to review the rules and regulations of State agencies for compliance with their legislative intent, their impact on the economy, on operations of the State and local governments, and on affected parties.

It is unlawful for an employer to conduct or require any employee or job applicant to submit to an examination to evaluate psychological stress. An employee discriminated against for filing a complaint or testifying in a proceeding relating to the use of such an examination may recover double the wages and benefits lost.

The Department of Correctional Services is to maintain a list of prison inmates who are eligible for release or parole and the vocational and training programs completed by them and to supply this list to approved prospective employers.

Promotion of business expansion for job creation and other purposes was the objective of three enactments. One enlarged the scope of financial assistance available under the economic development program of the Job Development Authority, another expanded the job incentive program through tax incentives to additional types of firms, and the third authorized the New York/New Jersey Port Authority to prepare and adopt a master development plan for the port district, taking such matters as unemployment into account.

North Carolina

Wages. An increase in the minimum wage to $2.50 an hour took effect January, 1, 1978. The State wage law authorized an increase to this amount when equaled or exceeded by the Federal rate.

Ohio

Wages. Calculation of time-and-one-half overtime pay for county employees who work over 40 hours is to be based on all "active-pay-status" hours, rather than hours actually worked, and county employees now may elect to receive compensatory time off on a time-and-one-half basis in lieu of overtime pay.

Minors participating in programs established under the Federal Young Adult Conservation Act of 1977 are to be paid in accordance with the State and Federal minimum wage laws.

Public works contractors are now required to furnish, on the first pay date, to each employee not covered by a collective bargaining agreement individual written notification of his or her job classification assignment and its prevailing hourly rate and fringe benefits as well as the identity of the prevailing wage coordinator. Other contractors and unions now may file complaints with the director of industrial relations alleging prevailing wage violations.

Child labor. Changes in the law included elimination of maximum hours and nightwork restrictions for 16- and 17-year-olds and conformance of restrictions for minors under age 16 to the Federal standards.

Equal employment opportunity. Any qualified person between the ages of 40 and 65 who is refused a job interview or is discharged without cause may bring a civil action against the employer on the basis of age discrimination, except where arbitration is available.

Labor relations. Use of successor employer clauses in private sector collective bargaining agreements will be permitted for employers not covered under the National Labor Relations Act or Railway Labor Act.

Private employment agencies. The required surety bond for employment agencies was increased from $1,000 to $5,000, and temporary help services meeting certain requirements were specifically exempted from the entire law.

Oklahoma

Wages. The tripartite Wage and Hour Commission, formerly responsible for rulemaking and administration of the minimum wage law, was abolished and its powers vested exclusively in the labor commissioner.

Prejudgment garnishment is now specifically permitted for support in divorce proceedings, and court-ordered garnishment of up to one-third of earnings for child support was authorized, with a 25-percent maximum otherwise applicable.

Child labor. A prohibition against work in theaters and bowling alleys by persons under age 14 was eliminated; any performer under age 15 must be accompanied by a parent who remains on stage during the performance.

Labor relations. The law establishing procedures for the recognition of professional organizations representing teachers was amended: separate petition and election procedures were established for school districts with an average daily attendance of 35,000 or more. Principals and assistant principals of school districts of this size will constitute separate collective bargaining units.

Occupational safety and health. A mining safety law, which specifies safety standards for miners, was enacted and will be administered by the State mining board. Standards included governing storage, transportation, and use of explosives; mine inspection; first aid; and certification of general managers, superintendents, mine foremen, shot firers, electricians, and repairmen. Certain provisions that required fire escapes on public and private buildings were repealed.

Displaced homemakers. A displaced homemakers act authorizes the Board of Vocational and Technical Education to establish a pilot multipurpose service center to provide job counseling, training, support, and educational services. The center will be operated in an area vocational-technical school and staffed whenever possible by displaced homemakers.

Other laws. Discharge of an employee because of jury service was made a misdemeanor punishable by a fine of up to $5,000, and the employer was made subject to civil action by the employee for damages.

Pennsylvania

Wages. The minimum wage rate was increased from $2.30 to $2.65 an hour, with future increases to $2.90 on January 1, 1979, $3.10 on January 1, 1980, and $3.35 on January 1, 1981. These increases are identical to those under the Federal law. The maximum tip credit was reduced to 45 percent of the minimum rate, with a further reduction to 40 percent on January 1, 1980. Hotel, motel, and restaurant employees will now receive overtime pay for work in excess of 44 hours a week, rather than 48, with a reduction to 40 hours scheduled for January 1, 1979.

When employees are paid, railroads must furnish each with a separate listing of daily wages and how they were computed or be subject to a monthly penalty of up to $200 per employee.

Child labor. A new physical examination to obtain each reissuance of an employment certificate is no longer required. Minors now need present only a promise of employment.

Constraints for girls, formerly more restrictive than for boys, were removed in street trades employment, in certain messenger work, and as caddies: all minors in such jobs are now subject to the same laws.

Agriculture. A new comprehensive, seasonal farm labor act was enacted. It establishes permissible hours of work, assures the payment of wages, provides for equal pay, and requires payment of the State minimum wage. Persons under 14 may not work as seasonal farmworkers, and those age 14 to 17 were made subject to the child labor law, including a prohibition against working during school hours. Other provisions require annual registration of farm labor contractors, set forth such contractor's duties and prohibited activities, establish requirements for the certification of labor camps, mandate visitation rights, and prescribe penalties for violation.

Equal employment opportunity. Sex-designated language was eliminated from numerous laws, such as those governing public appointments, entitlement to employment benefits, and employment rights.

Other laws. An employer may not dismiss or threaten to dismiss any employee because of required jury duty. In case of violation, the employee may sue for damages and may seek injunctive relief to secure reinstatement.

Rhode Island

Wages. The minimum wage law was amended to exempt from the overtime pay requirement any salaried employee of a nonprofit, national, voluntary health agency who chooses compensatory time off rather than overtime pay. A special legislative commission was established to study the feasibility of a special minimum wage for handicapped workers and to report to the general assembly by March 1, 1979.

Labor relations. The State labor relations board was expanded from 3 to 5 members by adding additional union and industry representatives.

Employers who willfully fail to make payments within 60 days to a health, welfare, or pension fund, as provided by a union contract, now are subject to a fine, imprisonment, or both. Prior law provided for a fine only with no time limit specified.

Displaced homemakers. A displaced homemakers act authorizes the director of community affairs to establish a pilot multipurpose service center to provide displaced homemakers with counseling, training, education, and placement services to help them find employment. The center is authorized until January 31, 1980.

Other laws. An intergovernmental relations council was established to study the relationships between and among the local, State, and Federal governments and to consider methods of fostering better relations among these three levels and among local governments.

A legislative commission will study the feasibility of creating and expanding flexible time, part-time, and job-sharing employment in State employment positions and of developing a program to encourage such job opportunities in the private sector.

South Carolina

Equal employment opportunity. The name of the Commission on the Status of Women was changed to the Commission on Women. Among other duties, the commission was empowered to receive and disburse State and Federal funds.

Private employment agencies. Agencies are now required to guarantee placed applicants a job lasting 90 days, with fees prorated over the 90-day period, if employment terminates for any reason. Applicants not reporting for work for any reason owe no fee.

Other laws. A law was enacted permitting the exchange of employees between and among Federal, State, and local governments with their consent and for a period of up to 4 years.

South Dakota

Wages. The minimum wage was increased from $2 to $2.30 an hour.

Labor relations. The public employee bargaining law was amended to exclude the following from all but the grievance provisions: elected officials, members of any board or commission, most administrators, students employed part time, temporary employees, the State National Guard, and judges and court employees.

Other laws. A resolution was adopted requesting the Legislative Research Council to study the feasibility of developing and financing a comprehensive vocational rehabilitation referral center.

Tennessee

Wages. The prevailing wage law was amended to require *annual* wage determinations for highway construction, but biennial determinations were retained for building construction. Also, the Prevailing Wage Commission is now authorized to make an adjustment of up to 6 percent in the determined wage to reflect changing economic conditions.

Withholdings from employee's pay for private pension and retirement plans are to be deposited into a separate trust fund which can be used only for providing benefits and administrative costs.

The amount of wages exempt from garnishment was increased from 50 percent of weekly earnings up to $50 for heads of household and 40 percent weekly up to $40 for other persons to 75 percent of disposable weekly earnings or 30 times the Federal minimum wage, whichever is greater, for all debtors.

Members of the general assembly will now be subject to wage garnishment in the same manner as are other public employees.

Child labor. Several significant changes were made in the child labor law, including replacement of employment certificate requirements with an employer obligation to require proof of age, elimination of maximum hours and nightwork restrictions for 16- and 17-year-olds, and easing nightwork restrictions for 14- and 15-year-olds.

Equal employment opportunity. A comprehensive antidiscrimination act was enacted covering both public employers and private employers of eight workers or more. The new law prohibits discrimination in employment by employers, labor organizations, employment agencies, and joint apprenticeship committees on the basis of race, creed, color, religion, sex, or national origin. The Commission for Human Development was given enforcement authority, including authority to order hiring, reinstatement, and back pay.

Labor relations. A new law provides for collective bargaining between boards of education and professional school employees. Good-faith bargaining is required by both parties, and strikes are prohibited. Negotiable items include wages, fringe benefits, grievance procedures, and working conditions. Impasse procedures consist of mediation, factfinding, and advisory arbitration.

Other laws. Employers of five employees or more now will be required to excuse from work any employees summoned to jury duty and to pay them their usual wages less any jury fees received. The Institute for Labor Studies within the labor department, and a Labor Educational Advisory Committee were established to develop an association between labor and higher education and to provide educational services to workers throughout the State.

Utah

Wages. By administrative action, minimum wage rates were increased for the retail trade, public housekeeping, restaurant, laundry, cleaning, dyeing and pressing industries, and the geographic rate zones were reduced in number. The new minimum in Salt Lake, Weber, Utah, and Davis counties and in all cities with a population of 5,000 or more was set for $2.30 an hour on April 1, 1978, with further increases to $2.45 on January 1, 1979, $2.60 on January 1, 1980, and $2.75 on January 1, 1981. The minimum for other areas was raised to $2.05 on April 1, 1978, with further increases scheduled on the above dates to $2.20, $2.35, and $2.50. The tip credit was increased from 25 to 30 percent of the minimum rate on April 1, 1978. The credit will return to 25 percent on January 1, 1980.

Labor relations. The State supreme court held that the Utah Labor Disputes Act, which recognizes labor's right to collective bargaining, was not intended to and does not, vest collective bargaining rights in municipal employees.

Vermont

Wages. The minimum wage rate was raised from $2.30 to $2.65 an hour, with future increases to $2.90 on January 1, 1979, $3.10 on January 1, 1980, and $3.35 on January 1, 1981. By wage order action, the maximum tip credits were also increased.

The wage payment law was amended: employer liability to employees for actual damages caused by failure to pay benefits required by a written agreement was established; any action for lack of payment of wages is required to be brought within 2 years of the cause of action; employers must pay discharged employees within 72 hours rather than immediately; and employees are permitted to authorize the deposit of their wages through electronic transfer to a bank of their choice.

Equal employment opportunity. The State commissioner of personnel is required to adopt rules and procedures to facilitate employment of the handicapped. He may waive certain requirements which exclude an otherwise qualified person to give him equal access to employment and may require certification that the applicant is physically qualified to do the work without hazard to himself or to others.

Other laws. To enhance employment opportunities in the State, the secretary of development and community affairs is authorized to contract with employers who, under specified conditions, will employ qualified State residents, recruited and trained by the secretary.

Elected municipal employees may now continue to serve and be elected to new terms of office after age 70 and will receive benefits accrued to the effective date of retirement.

Virginia

Wages. The minimum wage rate was increased from $2.20 per hour to $2.35 effective January 1, 1979.

Limits were placed on the percentage of earnings which may be garnished to satisfy support payment orders; previously there was no limit.

Child labor. Amendments to the child labor law eliminate time limits on the validity of employment and physical fitness certificates and exempt from the law, except for the certificate of physical fitness requirement, persons between ages 12 and 18 who are employed as pages or clerks in the State legislature.

A resolution requested that a joint legislative subcommittee be created to study and report on conflicts in State and Federal child labor laws and to recommend ways to resolve such conflicts and to end unnecessary employment restrictions.

Agriculture. A 15-member migrant and seasonal farm-workers commission was created as an advisory body to the Governor and general assembly. Membership will include representatives of growers, migrant and seasonal farmworkers, and crew leaders; government, public, and private agencies; and interest groups or citizens concerned with migrant and seasonal farmworkers.

Labor relations. Minimum criteria for State employees grievance procedures are to be established by the Department of Personnel and Training, and the Office of Employee Relations Counselors was created to furnish employees with information on grievance procedures and to investigate allegations of reprisal as a result of their use. Political subdivisions with more than 15 employees must conform their mandatory grievance procedures to standards established for State workers.

Private employment agencies. Administration of the act was transferred from the labor department to the newly created Department of Commerce, and the composition of the advisory board was changed from all agency representatives to include also representatives from consumer protection interest groups and a State official familiar with employment agency regulation. Rulemaking authority was delegated to the Board of Commerce, composed of nine citizens appointed by the Governor. Agency action against an applicant for a fee which the employer agreed to pay was barred, and agencies are prohibited from charging fees without a bona fide job order or without having made an appointment with the employer.

Occupational safety and health. Several changes were made in the mine safety law, including amendments to clarify required onsite emergency medical care, to provide for first aid training programs for mine employees, and to strengthen various provisions, including work assignments of inexperienced miners, use of cranes and hoists, storage and use of explosives, and noise levels. Other changes strengthened standards for safety lamps, roof supports, gas detection, two-way communications, and fire safety. In addition, ventilation and dust control requirements were expanded, and the employment of fire bosses is now required in all mines rather than only in those classed as "gaseous" or "gassy."

Other laws. The required period of on-the-job work experience for apprentices was reduced from 4,000 to 2,000 hours, "apprenticeable occupation" was defined, and the apprenticeship council was given authority to review decisions of local and State committees adjusting apprenticeship disputes and to initiate deregistration proceedings in appropriate instances.

The Department of Welfare was authorized to establish projects through any governmental unit or private, nonprofit agency to provide work experience for welfare recipients. Refusal to accept work experience will be grounds for denial of public assistance.

Both the Department and Board of Vocational Rehabilitation were reconstituted as the Department and Board of Rehabilitative Services, and the duties, responsibilities, and services of each were expanded.

West Virginia

Wages. As a result of pending litigation on the question of wage and hour law coverage of public safety department members, a law was passed explicitly exempting such members from the law but providing for supplemental payments to them in lieu of overtime pay. A similar law was enacted exempting State conservation officers following a State supreme court decision which deemed them subject to the wage and hour law.

Wisconsin

Wages. By administrative action, minimum hourly wage rates were increased from $2.10 to $2.55 effective August 1, 1978, with further increases on January 1 to $2.80 in 1979, $3 in 1980, and $3.25 in 1981. Differential minimums in farmwork and for workers under age 18 also were raised. Permissible tip credits, formerly set at 25 percent of the minimum wage, were converted to a rising scale of dollar amounts, reaching in 1981 the equivalent of a 40-percent credit, as in the Federal FLSA.

The wage payment law was amended to exempt from the frequency of payment provision school district employees who voluntarily request payment over a 12-month period and employees covered by collective bargaining agreements that establish different payment periods.

Equal employment opportunity. An employee who quits work because the employer made employment, compensation, promotion, or job assignments contingent upon consent to sexual contact or intercourse will not suffer loss of benefits. In addition, such activity by any employer, labor organization, or licensing agency now may be the basis for a complaint of sex discrimination.

Pilot grants are to be given to nonprofit employment facilities that employ the developmentally disabled in the manufacture of marketable products.

Displaced homemakers. A displaced homemakers act provides for the creation of a multipurpose center to provide counseling, training, education, and placement services to help displaced homemakers seeking employment. Whenever possible, the center will be staffed by displaced homemakers.

Other laws. An effort is to be made to place persons who are recipients of Aid to Families with Dependent Children (AFDC) and are registered with the work incentive program in part-time jobs that will provide training that may help them become self-supporting or where the earnings combined with child support payments will result in removal from the AFDC program. A mandatory work experience program was established for Indians receiving public assistance.

Employers now are required to grant employees a leave of absence without loss of time in service, seniority, or pay advancement while on jury duty. Public and private employers must grant employees serving as election officials time off without penalty, except deduction for time lost, for the entire 24-hour period on election day, if such employees give 7 days notice of application for such leave.

FOOTNOTES

[1] The legislatures did not meet this year in Arkansas, Montana, Nevada, North Dakota, Oregon, and Washington. Sessions were held in Alabama, Colorado, Indiana, Mississippi, New Hampshire, North Carolina, Texas, Utah, and Wyoming; but no significant labor legislation was enacted. Puerto Rico and the Virgin Islands were not included in the study.

Veterans Administration Benefits

Compensation and Pension

Comparative Highlights

	FY 1980	FY 1979	Percent Change
Cost (billions)	$11.3	$10.5	+ 7.6
Disability cases on rolls	3,195,395	3,240,283	− 1.4
Service connected	2,273,589	2,266,243	+ 0.3
Non-service connected	921,602	973,813	− 5.4
Special acts and retired officers	204	227	− 10.1
Death cases on rolls	1,450,785	1,529,206	− 5.1
Service connected	357,971	360,688	− 0.7
Non-service connected	1,092,797	1,168,499	− 6.5
Special acts	17	19	− 10.5

Summary

Compensation and pension programs administered by the VA fall into five broad categories:

1. *Disability Compensation* - A veteran is entitled to compensation for disability incurred or aggravated while on active duty. The amount of compensation is based on the degree of disability.

2. *DIC and Death Compensation* - Dependents of a veteran who died of service connected causes on or after January 1, 1957 are entitled to dependency and indemnity compensation (DIC). Dependents of veterans who died before that date are entitled to death compensation, or may elect to receive DIC.

3. *Disability Pension* - Veterans who served in time of war are eligible for pension benefits for non-service connected disabilities. The veteran must either be permanently and totally disabled or age 65 or older, and meet specific income limitations. Spanish-American War veterans are entitled to a pension on the basis of their service.

4. *Death Pension* - The surviving spouse and children of a war veteran who died of non-service connected causes are eligible for death pension benefits, subject to specific income limitations.

5. *Burial Allowances* - These benefits include a burial allowance, a burial plot allowance, and a flag to drape the casket of a deceased veteran. All benefits require separation from the armed service under other than dishonorable conditions. A plot allowance is available in the case of veterans who die of non-service connected disabilities and are not buried in a national cemetery. An award of $1,100 in lieu of basic burial and plot allowances is payable for veterans who die of a service connected disability.

During FY 1980 the cost of compensation and pension benefits continued to rise, reaching $11.3 billion in FY 1980, an increase of $718 million from last fiscal year. This increased cost is primarily attributable to new legislation which granted cost of living increases.

Public Law 96-128 increased the rates of disability and dependency and indemnity compensation for disabled veterans and their survivors by 9.9 percent. This law also resulted in the following changes:

• A 9.9 percent increase in allowances for dependents, and in benefits for housebound, and aid and attendance.

• An increase in the annual clothing allowance from $218 to $240.

Compensation

As shown in the accompanying chart, the number of veterans receiving compensation for service connected disabilities increased slightly during FY 1980, despite declines among World War I, World War II, and Korean con-

Reprinted from *1980 Annual Report,* Veterans Administration, Administrator of Veterans Affairs, Washington, DC 20420, May, 1981.

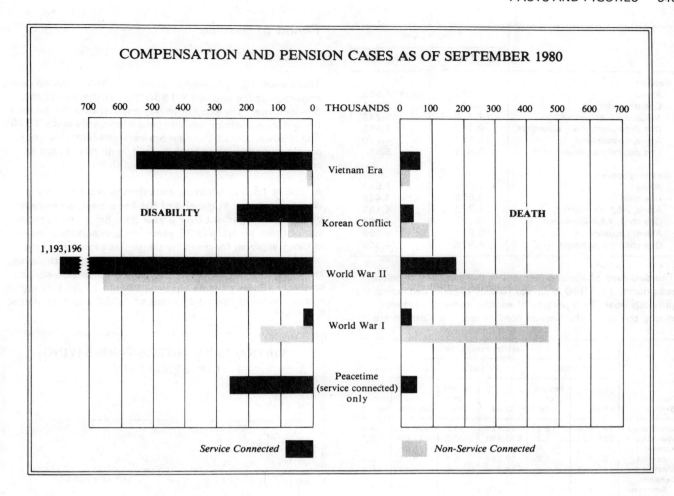

COMPENSATION AND PENSION CASES AS OF SEPTEMBER 1980

		Disability Compensation Cases					
		FY 1980		FY 1979		Change	
Period of Service	Cases	Percent of Total	Cases	Percent of Total	Number	Percent	
World War I	29,720	1.3	34,217	1.5	− 4,497	− 13.1	
World War II	1,193,196	52.5	1,217,522	53.7	− 24,326	− 2.0	
Korean conflict	235,654	10.4	237,102	10.5	− 1,448	− 0.6	
Vietnam era	553,326	24.3	537,208	23.7	+ 16,118	+ 3.0	
Peacetime	261,685	11.5	240,186	10.6	+ 21,499	+ 8.9	
Spanish-American	3	*	3	*	0	0	
Mexican Border	5	*	5	*	0	0	
Total	2,273,589	100.0	2,266,243	100.0	+ 7,346	+ 0.3	

*Less than 0.1 percent

		Service Connected Death Cases					
		FY 1980		FY 1979		Change	
Period of Service	Cases	Percent of Total	Cases	Percent of Total	Number	Percent	
World War I	30,128	8.4	31,284	8.7	− 1,156	− 3.7	
World War II	173,286	48.4	176,742	49.0	− 3,456	− 2.0	
Korean conflict	39,186	10.9	39,237	10.9	− 51	− 0.1	
Vietnam era	65,284	18.2	64,076	17.7	+ 1,208	+ 1.9	
Peacetime	49,943	13.9	49,188	13.6	+ 755	+ 1.5	
Spanish-American	137	*	151	*	− 14	− 9.3	
Mexican Border	2	*	3	*	− 1	− 33.3	
Indian War	0	*	1	*	− 1	− 100.0	
Civil War	5	*	6	*	− 1	− 16.7	
Total	357,971	100.0	360,688	100.0	− 2,717	− 0.7	

*Less than 0.1 percent

flict cases. The overall increase recorded in FY 1980 was 107 below the increase in FY 1979.

For the fourth straight year there has been a decline in the number of service connected death cases for which payments are made to dependents of deceased veterans. Like the previous year, the overall decline was less than 1 percent. Only Vietnam era and peacetime cases showed an increase from FY 1979.

Pension

Effective June 1, 1980, pension rates under the improved pension program were increased by 14.3 percent simultaneously with social security rates. The maximum annual rate of pension payable is shown in the accompanying table.

	Effective Date	
	June 1980	June 1979
Veteran		
Alone	$ 4,460	$ 3,902
One dependent	5,844	5,112
Alone, A&A allowance	7,136	6,243
One dependent, A&A allowance	8,519	7,453
Alone, housebound	5,453	4,770
One dependent, housebound	6,836	5,980
Surviving spouse		
Alone	$ 2,989	$ 2,615
One child	3,915	3,425
Alone, A&A allowance	4,782	4,183
One child, A&A allowance	5,707	4,993
Alone, housebound	3,654	3,196
One child, housebound	4,579	4,006

The decrease of about 5 percent in the disability pension rolls during FY 1980 is similar to that experienced during the previous year. Two periods of service showed increases during the year - the Korean conflict and the Vietnam era.

Disability Pension Cases						
	FY 1980		FY 1979		Change	
Period of Service	Cases	Percent of Total	Cases	Percent of Total	Number	Percent
World War I	167,808	18.2	196,423	20.2	−28,615	−14.6
World War II	656,401	71.2	681,493	70.0	−25,092	−3.7
Korean conflict	81,018	8.8	80,266	8.2	+752	+0.9
Vietnam era	16,049	1.7	15,210	1.6	+839	+5.5
Spanish-American	135	*	206	*	−71	−34.5
Mexican Border	191	*	215	*	−24	−11.2
Total	921,602	100.0	973,813	100.0	−52,211	−5.4

*Less than 0.1 percent

The following table shows that for the second year in a row the number of death pension cases decreased in all eight periods of service. The overall decrease of 6.5 percent is a smaller decline than that recorded during the previous fiscal year (7.3 percent).

Death Pension Cases						
	FY 1980		FY 1979		Change	
Period of Service	Cases	Percent of Total	Cases	Percent of Total	Number	Percent
World War I	464,327	42.5	493,171	42.2	−28,844	−5.8
World War II	497,073	45.5	531,716	45.5	−34,643	−6.5
Korean conflict	89,753	8.2	99,113	8.5	−9,360	−9.4
Vietnam era	27,861	2.6	28,891	2.5	−1,030	−3.6
Spanish-American	13,027	1.2	14,786	1.3	−1,759	−11.9
Mexican Border	527	*	560	*	−33	−5.9
Indian War	45	*	48	*	−3	−6.2
Civil War	184	*	214	*	−30	−14.0
Total	1,092,797	100.0	1,168,499	100.0	−75,702	−6.5

*Less than 0.1 percent

Period of Service

Vietnam Era

There were 16,118 more Vietnam veterans receiving compensation at the end of FY 1980 than at the end of the previous year. The accompanying chart shows the general trend in new Vietnam era compensation cases since 1970. The total number of Vietnam era veterans receiving compensation continues to increase and, with new cases exceeding losses, this trend is expected to continue.

A total of 16,049 Vietnam era veterans were receiving disability pension at the end of the fiscal year, an increase of 839 or 5.5 percent over a year ago. Since the average age of these veterans is 33 years, no appreciable increase in those applying for disability pension is expected in the near future. The number of service connected death cases increased by nearly 2 percent to 65,284. The non-service connected death pension cases numbered 27,861 at the end of the fiscal year, a decrease of 1,030 cases or almost 4 percent.

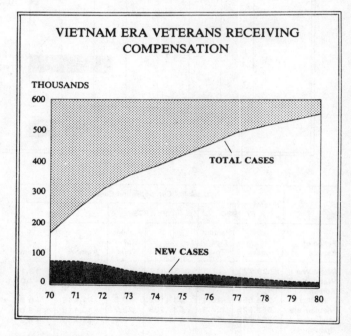

VIETNAM ERA VETERANS RECEIVING COMPENSATION

Korean Conflict

The number of Korean conflict veterans receiving compensation decreased to 235,654 during FY 1980, the seventh consecutive drop in that figure. The high mark on the rolls (240,765) was reached in June 1973, 18 years after that conflict ended. For comparison, the highest number of World War II veterans receiving compensation was reached in FY 1953, only 8 years after the end of that war.

In contrast to compensation, the number of Korean conflict veterans receiving pension continues to rise. At the end of the fiscal year there were 81,018 Korean conflict veterans on the pension rolls, nearly a 1 percent increase over FY 1979. As this group grows older the number on the pension rolls can be expected to increase.

The number of service connected death cases remained virtually the same at the end of the fiscal year, and the number of death pension cases decreased 9 percent to 89,753.

World War II

Veterans of World War II still constitute the largest single group receiving compensation for service connected disabilities, although their numbers continued to decline in FY 1980. Non-service connected pension showed a decrease of nearly 4 percent to 656,401. Service connected death cases declined by 3,456 cases or about 2 percent in FY 1980. The non-service connected death pension caseload decreased 34,643 to 497,073 or 6.5 percent in FY 1980.

World War I

The number of World War I veterans receiving disability compensation declined during the past fiscal year, about 13 percent. World War I disability pension also decreased (nearly 15 percent in the past fiscal year). The advanced age of this group of veterans will accelerate these decreases in the next few years. Decreases were also recorded for service connected death cases (about 4 percent) and death pension cases (almost 6 percent).

Other Periods

In addition to the recipients of disability compensation and pension payments from the wars and armed conflicts cited above, there were three veterans of the Spanish-American War receiving disability compensation as of September 30, 1980, and 135 were receiving disability pension in FY 1980, a decline of nearly 34 percent. The service connected death and death pension caseloads were 137 and 13,027 respectively. There were 5 veterans of the Mexican Border service receiving disability compensation. Disability pensioners totaled 191 in FY 1980, down 24 from last fiscal year. There were two service connected death cases while the death pension cases decreased 6 percent to

527. Although there are no living veterans of the Indian Wars and the Civil War, 36 widows and nine helpless children are receiving death pension benefits based on service in those periods. There are two widows and three helpless children receiving service connected death benefits with Civil War entitlement and 64 widows and 121 helpless children receiving death pension. There are 261,685 peacetime veterans receiving compensation as of September 30, 1980, an increase of about 9 percent over the previous year. Beneficiaries of deceased peacetime veterans increased 755 to 49,943 in FY 1980.

Burial Allowance

Statutory burial allowances are designed to assist in providing a respectable burial for deceased veterans separated from the armed service under other than dishonorable conditions. The allowance is payable for a veteran who was separated from wartime service. It is also payable in the case of a peacetime veteran discharged or retired for a disability incurred in or aggravated by service in line of duty or a veteran who was in receipt of compensation for a service connected disability.

Generally the VA will pay a sum not exceeding $300 (plus transportation charges when death occurs while the veteran is under VA care or entitled to disability compensation) to help cover burial and funeral expenses. An additional allowance of $150 for a burial plot when a veteran is not buried in a national cemetery is also payable. An award of $1,100 in lieu of these basic allowances is authorized for an eligible veteran who died of a service connected disability.

In FY 1980 basic burial allowance was paid for 324,033 claims in an amount in excess of $101 million. Cemetery plot allowances amounting to over $42.8 million were paid to 293,245 claimants; service connected burial benefits amounting to $9.3 million were paid to 10,083 claimants. This year a total of 272,743 burial flags were issued, a decrease of 7.9 percent from FY 1979. The cost of each flag was $17.95, making a total of $4.9 million.

National Cemetery System

Comparative Highlights

	FY 1980	FY 1979	Percent Change
Interments in national cemeteries	41,120	39,248	+4.8
Applications for headstone/ markers	274,235	254,833	+7.6
Canceled	37,352	24,212	+54.3
Headstones/markers ordered	230,703	230,600	---
National cemeteries	51,973	42,800	+21.4
Private cemeteries	178,730	187,800	-4.8
Replacement headstones/ markers	13,058	6,838	+91.0

Summary

The Department of Memorial Affairs (DMA) is responsible for the National Cemetery program, the Headstone and Marker program, the Memorial Marker and Plot program, and the State Cemetery Grants program.

In FY 1980, DMA accomplished over 41,000 interments and ordered nearly 231,000 headstones and markers for the unmarked gravesites of eligible persons. Applications totaling $2 million were submitted by four states for grant assistance and two grants were awarded. Among the other significant events that took place during the year were the following:

• Completion of the initial phase of construction at the Massachusetts National Cemetery. Interments will commence in early FY 1981.

• Completion of an in-depth study evaluating alternative interment methods for national cemeteries.

• The beginning of negotiations with the Department of the Army to transfer responsibility for the post cemetery at Fort Richardson, Alaska, to the VA.

• Transferred responsibility for Perryville National Cemetery to the State of Kentucky.

At the end of FY 1980, the National Cemetery System consisted of 107 cemeteries totaling over 8,200 acres, two tentative regional sites, and 33 soldiers' lots and plots totaling 20 acres. Nearly 3,000 acres of land have been developed for burials, with gravesites available in 57 national cemeteries. There were approximately 148,000 gravesites available for burials in existing cemeteries, and 72,000 reserved gravesites. Potential gravesites, including undeveloped acreage in five cemeteries not yet open for interments, totaled over two million.

Construction Projects

The FY 1980 construction program included five major and three minor construction or development projects at eight national cemeteries, as shown in the accompanying table.

National Cemetery	Project	Cost (In thousands)
Region IV	Develop 50 acres for interments and administration and service buildings (Phase I)	$3,385
Region V	Develop 11.5 acres for interments and administration and service buildings (Phase I)	4,000
Riverside	Develop 45 acres and first unit of columbarium	2,570
Fort Sam Houston	Design and develop 31 acres and relocate utilities	1,832
Jefferson Barracks	Design and develop 40 acres (Phase II)	775
Fort Gibson	Design and develop 5 acres	270
Lebanon	Design and develop 2 acres	80
Biloxi	Design and develop 4 acres	186
		$13,098

The first phase of a three-year project to provide barrier-free access to public buildings in existing cemeteries was completed during FY 1980. Design criteria and directives have been established to provide barrier-free access in all new cemetery design and construction. The conceptual approach is to omit barriers by design rather than to make special adaptations to overcome them.

During FY 1980, the Department of Memorial Affairs initiated surveys to evaluate the energy efficiency of all structures within the national cemetery system. These studies will result in modifications to existing structures and systems to enhance fossil fuel efficiency. Presently in the design stage are passive solar heating and cooling systems which will be installed at Leavenworth National Cemetery. Energy conservation continues to be a prime consideration in the design of all new structures.

Headstones and Markers

The VA administers the largest program of its kind in the issuance of government headstones and markers for the graves of eligible veterans and their dependents. Of the monuments distributed this fiscal year, 77 percent were shipped for placement in private cemeteries in the U.S. The remainder were placed in VA national cemeteries, Department of Defense cemeteries, and private overseas cemeteries.

The Quality Assurance Activity in the Monument Service assured that government monuments conform to strict standards. Inspectors look at all headstones and markers and reject approximately 10 percent for inscription errors. This practice not only saves money but also avoids many complaints.

During the past fiscal year, 274, 235 original applications were received. Of this number, 37,352 were canceled either for ineligibility or for duplicate applications; 230,703 resulted in orders placed with nine contractors. Replacement orders showed a significant increase (91 percent) as a result of a program of upgrading illegible and damaged markers in the National Cemetery System.

The total cost, including shipping charges, of the headstones and markers ordered during FY 1980, was $11,306,596. The average cost per monument was $49. There were 118,861 bronze markers cast and 111,842 stone headstones and markers manufactured. There were

Type Headstone/Marker	Number Ordered	
	FY 1980	FY 1979
Total	230,703	230,600
Upright marble	44,821	39,668
Flat marble	8,056	9,544
Flat granite	58,661	64,972
Flat bronze	118,861	116,342
Niche covers	200	--
Special purchase orders	104	74

also 104 special purchase orders which represent commemorative bronze plaques for various sites in national cemeteries. During recent years, there has been an increasing demand for bronze markers over marble and granite. This trend is illustrated in the accompanying table which shows orders for the last two fiscal years.

The past fiscal year saw over 2,400 markers shipped to destinations outside the continental U.S. The accompanying table shows these overseas destinations. Each such shipment requires complicated transportation arrangements often made through embassy offices.

Destination	Number	Destination	Number
Alaska	87	Hawaii	324
American Samoa	7	Ireland	9
Australia	1	Italy	3
Guyana	1	Jamaica	1
British West Indies	2	Japan	3
Canada	29	Mexico	4
Canal Zone	5	Norway	2
Central America	1	Philippines	786
Costa Rica	1	Puerto Rico	1,083
Cuba	31	Virgin Islands	15
England	2	Yugoslavia	1
France	1		
Germany	10		
Guam	20	TOTAL	2,429

Two major events affected the processing of headstones and markers during fiscal year 1980.

• VA is now providing niche markers for Arlington National Cemetery, where a new 5000-niche columbarium section was recently opened. This is the first section of what will eventually be 50,000 niches.

• An on-line visual display terminal (Target) is being used in Central Office to speed up inquiries concerning eligibility and to supply information omitted from application forms. Prior to installation of this terminal, a much slower teletype was relied upon.

State Cemetery Grants Program

The VA's relationship to state veterans' cemeteries is based on a Federal assistance program to aid any state in establishing, expanding, or improving veterans' cemeteries owned by it. In FY 1980, the VA received five applications totaling $2 million from four states; two grants were awarded. The accompanying table provides details on these applications.

Location	Project	Grant (Thousands) Request	Award
Illinois Quincy	Construct roadway	$ 60	$ 60[1]
Maine Augusta	Cemetery improvement/ expansion	330	
Maryland Cheltenham	Construct admin. bldg. and chapel	402	
Crownsville	Site development; construct admin. bldg.	593	
Eastern Shore	Construct chapel and storm drainage system	163[2]	163
Rocky Gap	Construct admin. bldg. and chapel; repair drainage	277[2]	277
Rhode Island Exeter	Cemetery improvement/ expansion	600	

[1] Conditional approval
[2] Request made in FY 1979

Government Life Insurance Programs for Veterans and Members of the Service

INSURANCE FACTS
(As of December 31, 1981)

	Policy Prefix	Program Began	Ending Date New Issues	No. Policies In Force	Average Attained Age	Deaths Per 1000
U.S. Government Life Insurance (USGLI) (Established to handle the conversion of World War I War Risk Term insurance.)	K	1-1-19	4-24-51	89,551	77.5	87.9
National Service Life Insurance (NSLI) (Issued to World War II servicemen.)	V	10-8-40	4-24-51	3,450,823	59.1	15.0
National Service Life Insurance (NSLI) (Issued to World War II veterans with Service-incurred disabilities.)	H	8-1-46	12-31-49	3,697	62.6	25.7
Veterans Special Life Insurance (VSLI) (Post service government life insurance for Korean veterans, without a service-connected disability.)	RS,W	4-25-51	12-31-56	520,140	49.5	4.5
Service-Disabled Veterans Insurance(SDVI) (Open to veterans separated from service on or after April 25, 1951, who received a service-connected disability rating for which compensation would be payable if 10% or more in degree.)	RH	4-25-51	OPEN	191,087	41.0	10.8
Veterans Reopened Insurance (VRI) (A limited reopening of National Service Life Insurance for certain disabled World War II and Korean veterans.)	J,JR,JS	5-1-65	5-2-66	163,334	58.8	13.8

TOTAL
Total Face Amount of Insurance $30,054,648,646   4,418,632

*Excludes $1,655,318,774 Paid-up additions

Reprinted from "Government Life Insurance Programs for Veterans and Members of the Services," Veterans Administration Regional Office and Insurance Center, Philadelph, PA, January, 1982.

GENERAL INFORMATION

The Insurance programs are administered by the Veterans Administration Regional Office and Insurance Center in Philadelphia with a field operating office at the VA Regional Office and Insurance Center, St. Paul, Minnesota.

The St. Paul office which basically services 28 states west of the Mississippi River maintains 1,607,251 policies. The Philadelphia office maintains the balance, 2,811,381 policies. The Philadelphia office, in addition to handling the 22 eastern states, has jurisdiction over:

```
All USGLI ("K") accounts . . . . . .  89,551 accounts
All accounts paid by allotment
    from service or retired pay . . . 373,207 accounts
All accounts paid by deduction
    from VA benefit payments. . . . . 207,854 accounts
All employer payroll deduction
    accounts. . . . . . . . . . . . .  11,252 accounts
```

In addition to the above, all actuarial functions are performed in the Philadelphia office.

The Insurance Program Management Division which has the responsibility of formulating policy, plans and procedures affecting the underwriting, accounts, death and disability claims function is also located in the Philadelphia Center. In addition to its functions for the Government Life Insurance programs, the Division is responsible for supervising the Servicemen's Group Life Insurance, Veterans' Group Life Insurance and Veterans Mortgage Life Insurance programs.

UNITED STATES GOVERNMENT LIFE INSURANCE

(Policy numbers prefixed with "K")

This program was established in 1919 to handle the insurance converted from the War Risk Term Insurance of World War I. A total of approximately 1,150,000 policies were issued under this class of insurance, of which 89,551 remain in force. Since this program was closed to new issues in 1951, the insurance is decreasing at an accelerating pace, now in the neighborhood of 8.9 percent per year.

In addition to the death benefit, all USGLI policies except Special Endowment at Age 96 provide a permanent total disability benefit without terminal age. This disability benefit matures the policy and pays monthly installments of $5.75 per $1,000 of insurance over 20 years with such installments continuing for life if disability continues. An optional total disability income benefit providing a monthly income of $5.75 per $1,000 of insurance is available at an extra premium.

This program is self-supporting except for administrative expenses and except for claim losses traceable to the extra occupational hazard of service in the Armed Forces. Dividends are paid annually based on the experience in this Fund.

The following statistical information is of interest:

    No. of 5-Year Term Policies in Force 464

    No. of Permanent Plan Policies in Force. . . . 89,087

    Average Amount Per Policy. $4,030

    Average Attained Age in 1981. . . . . 77.5 Years

    Average Annual Death Rate. . . . . 87.9 per 1,000

NATIONAL SERVICE LIFE INSURANCE

(Policy numbers prefixed with "V" or "H")

This program was established in 1940 to handle the insurance needs of World War II. Considerations of equity made it desirable to separate this insurance operation from the earlier group of World War I. Over 22 million policies were issued under this program, of which 3,454,520 policies remain in force for a total amount of approximately $22,318,269,241 of insurance in force.

The lapses were, of course, the heaviest at demobilization after the close of World War II. This was followed by heavy reinstatements and lapses in the intervening years until the Korean Conflict when a large influx of new issues was recorded. In April 1951 the program was closed to new issues and only reinstatements now add to the in-force total.

All NSLI policies provide for a death benefit and a disability premium waiver benefit without a stated extra premium. An optional total disability income benefit covering disability occurring before age 65, providing a monthly income of $10 per $1,000 of insurance, is available at an extra premium.

This program like USGLI is self-supporting except for administrative expenses and except for claim losses traceable to the extra occupational hazard of service in the Armed Forces. Dividends are paid annually based on this Fund's own experience.

Included in the 3,454,520 total accounts in this program are 3,697 "H" accounts. This insurance was issued between August 1, 1946, and December 31, 1949, to certain veterans with service-incurred disabilities. This insurance has the same premium rates and policy provisions as "V" insurance except that it is not participating.

The following statistical information is of interest:

No. of 5-Year Term Policies in Force 1,101,249

No. of Permanent Plan Policies in Force. . . . 2,353,271

Average Amount Per Policy. $6,461

Average Attained Age in 1981. . . . . .59.1 Years

Average Annual Death Rate. . . . . 15.0 per 1,000

VETERANS SPECIAL LIFE INSURANCE

(Policy numbers prefixed with "RS" or "W")

This insurance was available, without medical examination, to veterans separated from service on or after April 25, 1951, and before January 1, 1957. Application for insurance had to be made within 120 days after separation from service. Approximately 800,000 policies were issued, of which 520,140 remain in force.

Until 1959, only 5-Year Level Premium Term indefinitely renewable, was available. Legislation enacted in 1958 provided for an exchange to a lower priced term, not renewable after age 50, and for conversion to permanent plans. An optional total disability income benefit covering disability occurring before age 65, providing a monthly income of $10 per $1,000 of insurance, is available at an extra premium.

This program was set up by law on a nonparticipating basis (no dividends), with the Government underwriting the entire program. The Insurance Act of 1974, PL 93-289, effective May 24, 1974, made this insurance participating. The first dividend of $6.1 million was paid in 1975. In 1982 the dividend amounted to $35.0 million.

The following statistical information is of interest:

No. of 5-Year Term Policies in Force 284,626

No. of Permanent Plan Policies in Force. . . . 235,514

Average Amount Per Policy. $8,697

Average Attained Age in 1981. . . . . .49.5 Years

Average Annual Death Rate. . . . . 4.5 per 1,000

SERVICE-DISABLED VETERANS INSURANCE

(Policy numbers prefixed with "RH")

This insurance is available to veterans separated from service after April 24, 1951, who are suffering from a service connected disability but who are otherwise insurable. Generally, the insurance must be applied for within one year from the date of notice of rating of disability by the Veterans Administration.

If the veteran is totally disabled at the time of application, the endowment plans are not available; but all the others are. This program provides for premium waiver from the effective date of issuance of the policy if caused by service-connected disabilities.

This program insures medically substandard lives at standard rates of premium. Hence, the program is not self-supporting and the losses are met by periodic Congressional appropriations. The Fund is operated on virtually a pay-as-you-go basis.

The following statistical information is of interest:

No. of 5-Year Term Policies in Force 87,893

No. of Permanent Plan Policies in Force. . . . 103,194

No. of Policies Issued in 1981. 8,282

Average Amount Per Policy. $9,059

Average Attained Age in 1981. . . . . 41.0 Years

Average Annual Death Rate. . . . . 10.8 per 1,000

VETERANS REOPENED INSURANCE

(Policy numbers prefixed with "J," "JR" and "JS")

In 1964 Congress enacted legislation which provided for a limited reopening of National Service Life Insurance for a period of one year beginning May 1, 1965, to veterans who qualified under the following conditions:

1. They must have been eligible to buy National Service Life Insurance between October 8, 1940 and January 1, 1957, but must not have been on active duty at date of issue of the policy.

and

2. They must have had either:

    a. A service-connected disability which was compensable, or would have been compensable if it were rated 10% or more in degree - without any serious nonservice disability which would have disqualified them for standard insurance (prefixed with "J" OR "JR"), or

    b. A nonservice disability, or a combination of service and nonservice disabilities, so serious that they could not obtain commercial insurance at the highest rates (prefixed with "JS").

The premium rates for this insurance depend on the nature and severity of the disability. For those with service disabilities only, the rates vary from standard to a maximum of some two to three times the standard. For those with serious nonservice disabilities, the rates vary from two to three times the standard to a maximum of $50 a month plus the standard monthly rate per $1,000 of insurance.

Term insurance is not available in this program.

The administrative cost of this program is added to the premium paid by the insured. The policy charge for this cost has been set at 42 cents per month per policy.

Favorable claim rates and rising interest levels made possible a reduction, effective October 1970, in premiums for all policies with "J" prefixes, i.e., those policies issued at standard rates (85% of all the policies in the Veterans Reopened Insurance program). The reduction averaged about 18% of the premiums. In October of 1976 a further reduction of 22% was made on standard "J" policies and for the first time a reduction of 34% on "JR" policies.

In 1977 it was determined that with the present monies in the fund and the future interest earnings, there were sufficient funds available to pay all future claims for those insureds with a "JS" policy. As a result of this determination all policies were declared paid up as of the anniversary date in October 1977. All policyholders were notified and any premiums paid beyond September 1977 were refunded.

In order to insure more equitable treatment to each insured, all segments of this program were made participating by a change in the law in November, 1979. The initial dividends were paid on the policy anniversary dates in 1980.

The following statistical information is of interest:

No. of Policies in Force 163,334

Average Amount Per Policy. $6,861

Average Attained Age in 1981. . . . . .58.8 Years

Average Annual Death Rate. . . . . 13.8 per 1,000

PLANS OF INSURANCE

5-YEAR LEVEL PREMIUM TERM

This is a term policy that is renewed every 5 years at the then attained age of the insured. It may be converted to a permanent plan. Premiums are very low at the younger ages but increase very much at the older ages. This insurance provides for protection only and has no cash or loan values. When premiums are not paid, the protection stops. This plan is available on all programs except J-JR-JS.

5-YEAR LIMITED CONVERTIBLE TERM

This plan is similar to the 5-Year Level Term plan described above, except that the premium rates are lower. The policy may not be renewed after the insured's 50th birthday. If not converted before the end of the term period which expires on or after the insured's 50th birthday, all insurance protection ceases. This plan is available on W policies only.

MODIFIED LIFE AT AGE 65

This plan can only be purchased prior to the insured attaining insurance age 61. It affords a permanent plan of insurance at the lowest possible premium payment. The face amount of the insurance is automatically decreased by one-half on the day before the insured's 65th birthday, but the premium is not reduced and must be paid for life. The decreased amount may, without medical examination, be replaced with an Ordinary Life policy by making application prior to and no later than the day before the insured's 65th birthday.

MODIFIED LIFE AT AGE 70

This plan of insurance was made available in July 1972. It has the same provision as the Modified Life Age 65, except that reduction takes place on the day before the insured's 70th birthday. Conversion to this plan can be made through insurance age 69.

ORDINARY LIFE

Ordinary Life is frequently called "Straight Life." The premiums remain constant and are payable for the lifetime of the insured.

30-PAYMENT LIFE

Premiums on this plan are slightly higher than on Ordinary Life and are payable for 30 years from the effective date of the policy.

20-PAYMENT LIFE

Premiums on this plan are higher than on the 30-Payment Life and are payable for a period of 20 years.

20-YEAR ENDOWMENT

Premiums on this plan of insurance are payable for 20 years from the effective date of the policy. At the end of the 20 years, the face amount of the policy less any indebtedness, will be paid to the policyholder. He

or she may select to receive the proceeds in a lump sum
or on an installment basis.

ENDOWMENT AT AGE 60

This is also an endowment policy on which the face
amount less any indebtedness, is payable on the anniversary
date nearest the insured's 60th birthday.

ENDOWMENT AT AGE 65

Same as endowment at Age 60 except that proceeds are
payable on the anniversary date nearest the insured's 65th
birthday.

ENDOWMENT AT AGE 96

This is a special policy which was made available to
WWI veterans who were still carrying their USGLI under the
term plan. It is a regular endowment plan maturing at age
96 with a level premium from the date of issue. The plan
does not include permanent and total disability benefits,
nor waiver of premiums. However, a waiver of premium provision
may be purchased for an additional premium and only at the
time the term is exchanged for this plan.

DIVIDENDS

The United States Government Life Insurance Program (policies
prefixed with the letter "K"), National Service Life Insurance
Program (policies prefixed with the letter "V"), Veterans
Special Life Insurance Program (policies prefixed with
letters "RS" or "W") and the Veterans Reopened Insurance
(policies prefixed with letters "J," "JR" and "JS") are
all participating - meaning that dividends are payable on
these policies.

Dividends for 1982 for each of these programs were declared
in December 1981 in the following amounts:

        USGLI . . . . $23.9 million
        NSLI . . . . $590.0 million
        VSLI . . . . $35.0 million
        VRI   . . . . $15.69 million

The following dividend options are available for all programs:

Cash . . . . . . Paid to policyholder by Treasury check.
Credit . . . . . Held by the VA in an account for the insured
                 with interest. The VA can use this money
                 to prevent lapse, should the insured fail
                 to pay a premium.
Deposit. . . . . Held by the VA in an account for the insured
                 with interest. Amount can be used to automati-
                 cally purchase extended insurance, increase
                 the cash value or as the insured directs.
                 This option is available on permanent plan
                 policies only.
Premium. . . . . Dividend automatically applied to pay premiums
                 in advance.
Indebtedness . . Dividend automatically applied toward an
                 indebtedness on a policy - normally a loan.

In July 1972, legislation was enacted which made a new option
available for "V" policyholders which permitted dividends
to be used to purchase paid-up additions. This new option
is also available for "RS" and "W" policyholders. As of
December 31, 1981, 862,343 policies have this option of
record. Paid-up additions on these accounts totaled
$1,655,318,744. This option became available to "J," "JR"
and "JS" policyholders for the first time on January 1,
1980.

WAIVER OF PREMIUMS

All NSLI policies include a waiver of premium provision.
The cost for this provision is included in the regular premium.
This provision provides for the waiver of premiums for an
insured who has a mental or physical disability which prevents
him or her from pursuing gainful employment. The disability
must commence before the insured's 65th birthday and must
be continuous for at least six consecutive months.

The proper form for filing a claim is VA Form 29-357. Any
writing which expresses a desire to apply for this benefit
will be accepted as an informal claim.

As the waiver benefit, in most cases, can only be granted
one year prior to receipt of claim, it is important to
notify the VA as quickly as possible.

We currently have 224,070 accounts on which premiums are
being waived. This represents slightly more than 5.07%
of the total accounts.

TOTAL DISABILITY INCOME PROVISION

All policies, except Service-Disabled Veterans Insurance
(RH), Veterans Service-Disabled Rated Insurance (JR) and
Veterans Nonservice-Disabled Insurance (JS), provide for
the addition of a Total Disability Income Provision to the
basic policy. Applicant must be in good health and application
must be made before the insured's 55th birthday. The provision
provides for a monthly income if disabled for at least six
consecutive months. Payments commence on the first day
of the seventh month of continuous total disability. Payments
continue as long as the total disability continues. To
obtain benefits the insured must submit proof of total disability.
If there is a delay in submitting proof, no payment will
be made for any month earlier than six months before the
submission of such proof, unless failure to do so was due
to circumstances beyond the insured's control.

There are three types of Total Disability Income Provisions
currently in force. They are:

a. $5 Age 60 provision.

This plan was issued during the period August 1,
1946 to November 1, 1958. It provides for a monthly payment
of $5 for each $1000 of insurance, provided disability commenced
before the insured's 60th birthday or the policy anniversary
date nearest the 60th birthday, whichever is later.

b. $10 Age 60 provision.

This plan was issued from November 1, 1958 to
January 1, 1965 and provides for a monthly income of $10
for each $1000 insurance in force, provided total disability
commenced before the insured's 60th birthday.

c. $10 Age 65 provision.

This plan became available on January 1, 1965
and is still available to those insureds who can meet good
health requirements and have not reached their 55th birthday.
This provision provides for a monthly income of $10 per
$1000 insurance in force, provided total disability commenced
before the insured's 65th birthday.

As of December 31, 1981, there were 524,734 accounts which
included the Total Disability Income Provision. Total
Disability Income benefits are currently being paid on
28,900 accounts.

BENEFICIARY AND OPTION DESIGNATION

Under the terms of a Government Life Insurance contract, an insured has the right to designate a beneficiary or make an optional settlement selection at any time. This can be done without the knowledge or consent of the designated beneficiary or beneficiaries.

The proceeds of a Government Life Insurance policy will be paid to the last named beneficiary of record according to the settlement option selected by the insured. Public Law 97-66, effective October 1, 1981, permits a beneficiary to select any settlement option if the insured failed to select one.

We have several ongoing programs to notify those insureds who have not updated their designation of beneficiary and optional settlement selection within the past 20 years.

SERVICEMEN'S GROUP LIFE INSURANCE

The Servicemen's Group Life Insurance (SGLI) program provides life insurance coverage for individuals currently in the military service and for certain specified periods after separation or release from periods of reserve duty. With the passage of Public Law 97-66, the maximum available SGLI coverage was increased from $20,000 to $35,000, effective December 1, 1981.

The program is supervised by the Veterans Administration but is administered by the Office of Servicemen's Group Life Insurance (OSGLI) under the terms as specified in a group insurance contract.

Full-time coverage is available for commissioned, warrant and enlisted members of the Army, Navy, Air Force, Marine Corps and Coast Guard; and commissioned members of the National Oceanic and Atmospheric Administration and the Public Health Service. Cadets or midshipmen of the four United States Service Academies are also provided full-time coverage.

Full-time coverage is also available to Ready Reservists who are scheduled to perform at least 12 periods of inactive training per year. Persons assigned to, or who upon application would be eligible for assignment to the Retired Reserve, and have not yet received their retirement pay and have not reached 61 years of age, are also eligible for full-time coverage.

Part-time coverage is provided to eligible members of the Reserves who do not qualify for full-time coverage. Part-time coverage is in effect while such members are performing periods of active duty training.

At the present time there are about 3 million members covered by the insurance.

Coverage is automatic (with the exception of Retired Reservists who must apply for coverage) upon entry into a period of active duty or reserve status. If the member does not wish the coverage or desires coverage in an amount less than $35,000, he or she must make such an election in writing.

Full-time coverage is in effect throughout a member's period of active duty or reserve status and for a 120-day free period following separation or release from active duty or reserve status. In addition, members who are totally disabled at the time of separation may also apply for up to a one-year period of free coverage.

Retired Reservists' coverage ceases when a member receives his or her first increment of retired pay, attains age 61 or fails to pay premiums.

Part-time coverage is in effect only on the days of active duty or active duty for training and for periods of travel to and from such duty. Coverage may be extended for a free period of 120 days if a member under part-time coverage incurs a disability or aggravates a preexisting disability while performing a period of duty.

The premium rate for active duty members and Ready Reservists is $5.25 for $35,000 or 75 cents per $5,000 insurance if lesser amounts of insurance are elected. The premium rate for part-time coverage is $3.50 per year for $35,000 coverage.

Monthly premium rate for Retired Reservists are as follows:

AGE	$35,000	$30,000	$25,000	$20,000
Through 39	$10.50	$ 9.00	$ 7.50	$ 6.00
40 through 49	14.00	12.00	10.00	8.00
50 through 59	17.50	15.00	12.50	10.00

AGE	$15,000	$10,000	$5,000
Through 39	$ 4.50	$ 3.00	$ 1.50
40 through 49	6.00	4.00	2.00
50 through 59	7.50	5.00	2.50

The proceeds of this insurance can be paid in a lump sum or over a 36-month period, depending on which option the insured selected. Any beneficiary can be named, but in the event none is selected, the insurance devolves by law in the following order: (1) spouse, or (2) children, or (3) parents, or (4) executor of estate, or (5) other next of kin.

VETERANS' GROUP LIFE INSURANCE

Veterans' Group Life Insurance (VGLI) is a program of post-separation insurance which provides for the conversion of SGLI to a 5-year nonrenewable term policy at reasonable rates. This program, like Servicemen's Group Life Insurance (SGLI), is supervised by the Veterans Administration but administered by the Office of Servicemen's Group Life Insurance (OSGLI).

At the end of the term period, a member has the right to convert the insurance to an individual commercial life insurance policy with any one of approximately 360 participating commercial insurance companies.

This insurance is not available to Retired Reservists. Eligible Retired Reservists who do not desire continued SGLI coverage may, however, elect to exercise the commercial conversion privilege if they do so within a 120-day period following separation or release from reserve status.

Persons who are eligible to be covered are members being released from active duty for periods not specified as less than 31 days and Reservists who are performing training periods of less than 31 days who suffer an injury or disability which renders them uninsurable at standard premium rates.

To apply for coverage, an eligible member must submit an application with the required premium during the 120 days following separation. If a member fails to make application during this period, he or she may still do so for up to one year after SGLI coverage terminates, providing he or she submits evidence of insurability.

If a member is totally disabled at the time of separation and is granted extended free SGLI coverage, he or she may apply for the VGLI anytime during the one year period of extension.

VGLI is issued in amounts of $5,000, $10,000, $15,000, $20,000, $25,000, $30,000 or $35,000, but not for more than the amount of SGLI the member had in force at the time of separation. With the passage of Public Law 97-66, maximum available VGLI coverage was increased from $20,000 to $35,000, effective December 1, 1981, for members separated after that date.

Premium payments are made directly to the Office of Servicemen's Group Life Insurance. Upon approval of the VGLI application, OSGLI will send the insured a certificate and a supply of monthly premium payment coupons. Premiums may also be paid on a quarterly, semiannual or annual basis, provided the appropriate number of payment coupons are submitted with the remittance. There are no provisions for having premiums deducted from VA compensation or military retirement pay.

Premiums are based on the amount of insurance issued and on the insured's age at the time of issue.

Premium rates are as follows:

AGE	$35,000	$30,000	$25,000	$20,000
Through 34	$ 5.95	$ 5.10	$4.25	$3.40
35 and over	11.90	10.20	8.50	6.80

AGE	$15,000	$10,000	$5,000
Through 34	$ 2.55	$ 1.70	$ .85
35 and over	5.10	3.40	1.70

An application for an incompetent member may be made by a guardian, committee, conservator or curator. In the absence of a court appointed representative, the application may be submitted by a family member or anyone acting in the member's behalf.

The beneficiary and the method of payment of the insurance proceeds for VGLI are the same as those for SGLI.

In order to alert members to the availability of this coverage, the VA mails an application and explanatory pamphlet to eligible members 30 days after separation. The packet is mailed to the address shown on the member's DD Form 214 or equivalent separation orders.

VETERANS MORTGAGE LIFE INSURANCE

Veterans Mortgage Life Insurance is designed to provide financial protection to cover an eligible veteran's outstanding home mortgage in the event of his or her death. The insurance is provided under a group policy issued to the Administrator of Veterans Affairs. The Office of Veterans Mortgage Life Insurance, P. O. Box 81497, Lincoln, Nebraska 68501, has been established to administer the mortgage protection program under the supervision of the Veterans Administration.

The insurance is restricted to those disabled veterans who have received grants for the purchase of specially-adapted housing under the authority of Title 38, United States Code, Chapter 21. Such grants are available to those veterans who are entitled to compensation for service-connected permanent and total disability due to one or more of the following conditions:

    1. Loss, or loss of use, of both legs, which precludes locomotion without the aid of braces, crutches, canes, or a wheelchair; or

2.   Blindness in both eyes, having only light perception, plus the loss, or loss of use, of one leg; or

3.   Loss, or loss of use, of one leg together with residuals of organic disease or injury which so affect the functions of balance or propulsion as to preclude locomotion without resort to a wheelchair.

4.   Loss, or loss of use, of one lower extremity together with the loss, or loss of use, of one upper extremity, which so affect functions of balance or propulsion as to preclude, or render medically inadvisable, locomotion without specific aids.

Public Law 96-385, effective October 7, 1980, enlarged the class of veterans entitled to a housing grant under Chapter 21 of Title 38. It provides a grant of up to $5,000 for veterans (other than those eligible for assistance as described above) who are entitled to compensation for service-connected permanent and total disability due to:

1.   blindness in both eyes with 5/200 visual acuity or less, or

2.   the anatomical loss or loss of use of both hands.

The grant is for the purpose of acquiring adaptions needed for the eligible veteran's residence because of his or her disabilities.

The grant is conditioned upon residence in a home owned by the veteran or family member.

The lifetime maximum amount of VMLI allowed an eligible veteran may not exceed $40,000. The maximum amount is permanently reduced at the same time the principal of the mortgage loan is reduced below $40,000.

The maximum amount of insurance available at one time may not exceed the lesser of the following amounts:

1. $40,000

2.   The reduced remaining coverage available if the veteran has already used a portion of his or her mortgage insurance protection on an earlier loan. This reduced maximum respresents $40,000, less any amount paid on a prior loan of $40,000 or less.

3.   The total mortgage loan if it is less than $40,000.

The insurance is not available to veterans who have reached their 70th birthday.

The insurance is payable at the death of the veteran only to the holder of the mortgage loan. No insurance is payable if the mortgage is paid off prior to the veteran's death.

If title to the mortgaged property is shared with anyone other than the veteran's spouse, the insurance coverage is only for the percentage of the title that is in the veteran's name.

A veteran is automatically insured upon receipt of a grant and the securing of a mortgage on the property.

Insurance contracted for under this law will terminate under any of the following conditions:

1. Veteran's 70th birthday;
2. Mortgage paid in full;
3. Termination of veteran's ownership of the property securing the loan;
4. Payment of premiums discontinued by the veteran;
5. Entire contract or agreement discontinued;
6. Request of the veteran;
7. Failure of the veteran to submit timely statement or other required information.

The premiums for this protection are based only on the mortality costs of insuring standard lives and should, therefore, be lower than any commercial insurance premiums for similar coverage.

The Government bears the administrative costs of the insurance and all costs for claims in excess of the premiums paid by the insured veteran.

Premiums are determined by the insurance age of the veteran, the outstanding balance of the mortgage at the time of application and the remaining length of time the mortgage has to run.

Premiums are payable on a monthly basis. Veterans who desire the insurance will be advised of the correct premium when it is determined. If a veteran is receiving compensation or pension payments from the VA, he or she must have the premiums automatically deducted from his or her monthly benefit check. If a veteran is not receiving VA benefit payments, it is his or her responsibility to pay the monthly premiums directly to the insurance company. If there is a delay in initiating deductions, the amount needed to make up for earlier premiums will be included in the initial deduction.

Federal Benefits for Veterans and Dependents

An insured under VGLI has the right to convert to an individual commercial policy at standard premium rates, regardless of health, with any of the participating companies licensed to do business in the veteran's state. The individual policy will be effective the date after the insured's VGLI terminates at the end of the five-year term period. The OSGLI will advise the insured of the impending date of termination and additional information regarding the conversion of VGLI to an individual policy.

Veterans wanting further information may contact their nearest VA office, or write to the Office of Servicemen's Group Life Insurance.

VETERANS MORTGAGE LIFE INSURANCE
For Totally Disabled Veterans with Special Adapted Housing Grants

Effective August 11, 1971, PL 92-95 established a program of group type mortgage life insurance for those who have been granted or will be granted a specially adapted housing grant. Public Law 94-433 increased the maximum amount of this insurance to $40,000 effective October 1, 1976. Protection is automatic unless eligible veterans decline in writing or fail to respond to a final request for information on which their premium can be based. Premiums are automatically deducted from VA benefit payments or paid direct, if the veteran does not draw compensation, and will continue until the mortgage (up to the maximum amount of insurance) has been liquidated, or the home is sold, or until the veteran reaches age 70, or dies. If a mortgage is disposed of through liquidation or sale of the property, any unused portion of the life insurance coverage may be used on the mortgage of a second or subsequent home.

SOLDIERS' AND SAILORS' CIVIL RELIEF ACT
Guaranty of Premiums on Commercial Life Insurance

Commercial life insurance purchased by service personnel must be purchased and in force on a premium paying basis for 180 days before the insured enters into active duty. The premiums and interest due on eligible commercial life insurance policies, not exceeding $10,000 in any individual case, may be guaranteed by the government while the policyholder is on active military duty and for two years

Reprinted from "Federal Benefits for Veterans and Dependents," Veterans Administration, Washington, DC 20420, January, 1982.

thereafter. Repayment must be made to the government for any amount paid insurers due to the protected policy.

DEPENDENCY AND INDEMNITY COMPENSATION (DIC)
(May be selected in lieu of death compensation for service-connected deaths before January 1, 1957)
For Survivors of Deceased Veterans of Spanish-American War, Mexican Border Campaign, World War I, World War II, Korean Conflict Period, Vietnam Era, and Peacetime Service

Coverage
(a) Death Due to Service-Connected Disability—DIC payments are authorized for surviving spouses, unmarried children under 18 (as well as certain helpless children and those between 18 and 23 if attending a VA-approved school), and certain parents of service personnel or veterans who die on or after January 1, 1957, from: (1) a disease or injury incurred or aggravated in line of duty while on active duty or active duty for training; or (2) an injury incurred or aggravated in line of duty while on inactive duty training; or (3) a disability otherwise compensable under laws administered by VA.

(b) Death Due to Nonservice-Connected Cause—DIC payments are also authorized for surviving spouses, unmarried children under 18 (as well as certain helpless children and those between 18 and 23 if attending a VA-approved school) of certain veterans who were totally service-connected disabled at time of death and whose deaths were not the result of their service-connected disability, if: (1) the veteran was continuously rated totally disabled for a period of 10 or more years or (2) if so rated for less than 10 years, was so rated for a period of not less than five years from the date of discharge from military service. Payments under this provision are subject to offset by the amount received from judicial proceedings brought on account of the veteran's death.

Definition of Surviving Spouse
(a) Date of Marriage—Generally to qualify a surviving spouse must have married the veteran at least one year prior to his or her death unless a child resulted from the union. A surviving spouse of a Vietnam Era veteran is eligible regardless of when she or he married the veteran provided such marriage occurs prior to May 8, 1985. Marriage for a period of at least two years immediately preceding the veteran's death is required to establish eligibility to DIC payments under paragraph (b) above.

(b) Residence With Veteran—The surviving spouse must have lived continuously with the veteran from the time of marriage until the veteran's death, except where there was a separation due to the misconduct of, or procured by, the veteran without fault on the spouse's part.

(c) Surviving Spouse Remarriage—Remarriage makes a surviving spouse ineligible based on the death of that veteran unless the purported remarriage was void, has been annulled, or terminates in death or divorce. A surviving spouse may also be ineligible if, after the death of the veteran, she or he has lived with another man or woman and held herself or himself out openly to the public to be the spouse. Should such relationship terminate, she or he may re-apply for benefits.

(d) Purported Marriage—If she or he meets the other qualifications, a person who married a veteran without knowing that a legal impediment to the marriage existed may be eligible for compensation under certain conditions.

DIC SURVIVING SPOUSE RATES

Pay grade	Monthly rate	Pay grade	Monthly rate
E—1	$415	W—4	$ 595
E—2	428	O—1	525
E—3	438	O—2	542
E—4	466	O—3	580
E—5	479	O—4	613
E—6	490	O—5	676
E—7	514	O—6	761
E—8	542	O—7	824
E—9*	567	O—8	903
W—1	525	O—9	970
W—2	546	O—10*	1,061
W—3	562		

There are special rates for certain individuals in these categories.

There are additional payments for children.

The monthly rates of DIC for parents range from $5 to $230 based upon the income of the parents and whether there is only 1 parent, 2 parents not living together or 2 parents together or remarried with spouse. The income limit for 2 parents together or remarried and with spouse is $7,587, that for 1 parent or 2 parents not together is $5,642.

Aid and Attendance

Surviving spouses qualified for either death compensation or DIC, and parents receiving death compensation or DIC, may be granted a special allowance for aid and attendance if they are: patients in a nursing home; helpless or blind, or so nearly helpless or blind as to require the regular aid and attendance of another person. The allowance is $125 monthly payable in addition to the DIC rate for a surviving spouse and $121 monthly additional for a parent receiving DIC.

Housebound

Surviving spouses qualified for DIC who are not so disabled as to require the regular aid and attendance of another person but who due to disability are permanently housebound may be granted a special allowance of $62 monthly in addition to the DIC rate otherwise payable.

Where to Apply.   Any VA office.

DEATH COMPENSATION RELATING TO DEATHS
BEFORE JANUARY 1, 1957
For Survivors of Deceased Veterans of Spanish-American War,
Mexican Border Period, World War I, World War II,
Korean Conflict Period, and Peacetime Service

Coverage

Death compensation payments are authorized for surviving spouses, unmarried children under 18 (or until 23 if attending a VA-approved school), helpless children, and dependent parents of servicepersons or veterans who died before January 1, 1957, from a service-connected cause not the result of willful misconduct.

If service-connected death occurred after service, the veteran's discharge must have been under conditions other than dishonorable.

Surviving spouses, children, and parents eligible for death compensation under this section may elect to receive DIC payments instead. They may not thereafter choose death compensation. For surviving spouses and children, DIC is the greater benefit. For dependent parents, it may or may not be depending on annual income.

Definition of Surviving Spouse

(a) **Date of Marriage**—Generally, to qualify, a surviving spouse must have married the veteran at least one year prior to his or her death unless a child resulted from the union.

(b) **Residence with Veteran**—The surviving spouse must have lived continuously with the veteran from the time of marriage until the veteran's death, except where there was a separation due to the misconduct of, or procured by, the veteran without fault on the part of the spouse.

(c) **Surviving Spouse's Remarriage**—The surviving spouse's remarriage following the death of the veteran makes her or him permanently ineligible for compensation based on the death of that veteran unless the purported remarriage is void, has been annulled or ends in death or divorce. A surviving spouse may also be ineligible if she or he has lived with another man or woman openly as the spouse. Should such relationship end, she or he may re-apply for benefits.

(d) **Purported Marriages**—If she or he meets the other qualifications, a person who married a veteran without knowing that a legal impediment to the marriage existed may be eligible for compensation in certain cases.

Helpless Children

Children who become permanently incapable of self-support because of a mental or physical defect before reaching age 18 may receive death compensation as long as the condition exists or until they marry.

Definition of Dependent Parents

Parents are held to be dependent for death compensation if their income is insufficient to provide reasonable maintenance for themselves and for members of their family under legal age. Proof of dependency must be submitted to VA upon application for death compensation under this section.

Nature of Benefit

Monthly payments to eligible survivors are at rates of $87 for surviving spouse, only with higher amounts if there are eligible children: children only $67, $94 and $122 for one, two or three children respectively with $23 for each additional child; and $75 for one dependent parent or $40 each for two dependent parents.

Additional Allowance for Surviving Spouses in Need of Aid and Attendance

A surviving spouse who qualified for death compensation may be granted a special allowance for aid and attendance if she or he is: a patient in a nursing home; helpless or blind; or, so nearly helpless or blind as to need or require the regular aid and attendance of another person. The additional allowance is $79 monthly, which is payable in addition to the basic death compensation rate for which the surviving spouse otherwise qualifies.

Where To Apply. Any VA office.

NONSERVICE-CONNECTED DEATH PENSION
For Surviving Spouses and Children of Deceased Spanish-American War, Mexican Border Period, World War I, World War II, Korean Conflict Period and Vietnam Era Veterans who have died of nonservice-connected causes.

Conditions of Veteran's Service
The veteran must have had 90 days' service, unless discharged or retired sooner for service-connected disability, and was discharged under conditions other than dishonorable. If the veteran died in service not in line of duty, benefits may be payable if the veteran had completed at least two years of honorable active service.

Definition of Surviving Spouse
(a) **Date of Marriage**—Generally, to qualify, a surviving spouse must have married the veteran at least one year prior to his or her death unless a child resulted from the union; or, in the case of Vietnam Era veterans; the marriage occurs prior to May 8, 1985.

(b) **Residence with Veteran**—A surviving spouse must have lived continuously with the veteran from time of marriage until veteran's death, except while there was a separation due to the misconduct of or procured by the veteran without fault on the part of the spouse.

(c) **Remarriage**—Remarriage following the death of the veteran makes the surviving spouse ineligible for pension based on the death of that veteran unless the purported remarriage is void or has been annulled or is terminated by death or divorce. A surviving spouse may also be ineligible if after the death of the veteran she or he has lived with another man or woman and held herself or himself out openly to the public to be the spouse. Should such relationship terminate, she or he may reapply for benefits.

(d) **Purported Marriages**—If she or he meets the other qualifications, a person who married a veteran without knowing that a legal impediment to the marriage existed, may be eligible for pension in certain cases.

Eligibility Requirements for Surviving Spouses
Surviving spouses and unmarried children under age 18 (or until age 23 if attending a VA-approved school) of deceased veterans of these wars or conflicts may be eligible for pension based on need if they meet the applicable income standards.

Otherwise qualified children who became permanently incapable of self-support because of a mental or physical defect before reaching age 18 may receive a pension as long as the condition exists or until they marry.

Pension is not payable to those whose estates are so large that it is reasonable they look to the estates for maintenance.

Aid and Attendance
Surviving spouses qualified for death pension may be granted a special

allowance for aid and attendance if they are: a patient in a nursing home; helpless or blind, or so nearly helpless or blind as to require the regular aid and attendance of another person.

IMPROVED PENSION

Effective June 1, 1981, the improved pension program provides for the following annual rates, generally payable monthly, reduced by the amount of the annual countable income of the surviving spouse and/or dependent children.

Pension Rates for Surviving Spouse:
Surviving spouse without dependent children	$3,324
Surviving spouse with one dependent child	$4,354
Surviving spouse in need of regular aid and attendance without dependent child	$5,318
Surviving spouse in need of regular aid and attendance with one dependent child	$6,347
Surviving spouse permanently housebound without dependent child	$4,064
Surviving spouse permanently housebound with one dependent child	$5,092
Increase for each additional dependent child	$ 840

Pension Rates for Surviving Children:
Child alone	$ 840
Each additional child	$ 840

PRIOR LAWS

Section 306 (formerly 86-211) and Old Law
All surviving spouses and children (except those of Spanish-American War veterans who have the right to elect under the prior law) who were on the rolls December 31, 1978, who do not elect improved pension, may continue receiving pension under the prior law at the rate they were receiving on that date. Monthly payments shall continue as long as their income does not exceed the applicable income limitation or they do not lose a dependent.

Income Limitations for Section 306 Survivors:
Surviving Spouse without dependent child(ren)	$5,642
Child(ren) alone	$4,610
Surviving Spouse with child(ren)	$7,587

Income Limitations for Old Law Survivors:
Surviving spouse without dependent child(ren)	$4,938
Child(ren) alone	$4,938
Surviving spouse with child(ren)	$7,123

Spanish-American War Death Pension
A surviving spouse of a Spanish-American War veteran receives a death pension of $70 a month, or $75 if she or he was the spouse during service. An additional $8.13 is paid for each child. An additional $79 is payable to a surviving spouse who is in need of the aid and attendance of another person or is a patient in a nursing home.

Death pension of $73.13 per month is paid for one child where there is no surviving spouse, plus $8.13 for each additional child.

REIMBURSEMENT OF BURIAL EXPENSES
For Veterans of Spanish-American War, Mexican Border Period,
World War I, World War II, Korean Conflict Period,
Vietnam Era, and Certain Peacetime Service

Eligibility (Deaths prior to October 1, 1981)

The deceased veteran must have been discharged under conditions other than dishonorable and have been either a wartime or Korean Conflict or
Vietnam veteran; or a peacetime veteran entitled to service-connected compensation at time of death or discharge or retired for disability incurred in line of duty. Applications filed under these eligibility criteria must be received by the VA within two years of the date of death.

Eligibility (Deaths on or after October 1, 1981)

For the burial allowance benefit the deceased veteran must have been discharged under conditions other than dishonorable and have been
entitled to receive compensation or pension at the time of death, or would have been entitled to receive compensation but for the receipt of military retired pay. Eligibility may also be established when death occurs in a Veterans Administration facility to which the deceased was properly admitted for hospital, nursing home, or domiciliary care.

Eligibility for the plot or interment allowance is established if the requirements for the burial allowance are met. Eligibility may also be established if the deceased was a veteran of any war, or was discharged from active duty because of a disability which was incurred or aggravated in line of duty.

Who May Claim Reimbursement

Funeral director, if unpaid, otherwise person who bore veteran's burial expenses.

Nature of Benefit

Payment, not to exceed $300, toward veteran's burial expenses. Claim must be filed within two years after permanent burial or cremation. Additional costs of transportation of the remains may be allowed if the veteran died while hospitalized or domiciled in a VA hospital or domiciliary or at VA's expense or died in transit at VA's expense to or from a hospital, domiciliary or VA regional office.

Payment of an amount not exceeding $150 as a plot or interment allowance in addition to the $300 basic burial allowance when the veteran is not buried in a National Cemetery or other cemetery under the jurisdiction of the United States Government.

Burial or plot allowances may not be paid to the extent that they were paid by the deceased's employer or by a State agency or a political subdivision of a State. However, when a veteran is interred in a cemetery or a section of a cemetery owned by a State or a political subdivision of a State which is reserved solely for veteran burials, the plot allowance of up to $150 may be payable to the State or the political subdivision thereof.

Payment of an amount not exceeding $1,100 or the Federal Death Benefit, whichever is greater, as a burial allowance if the veteran's death is service-connected. This payment is in lieu of the $300 basic burial allowance and the $150 plot-interment allowance.

The VA will pay the cost of transporting the remains of deceased, service-disabled veterans to the national cemetery nearest their home having available grave space.

Where To Apply.   Any VA office.

BURIAL FLAGS
For Veterans of Spanish-American War, Mexican Border Period, World War I, World War II, Korean Conflict Period, Vietnam Era and of Certain Peacetime Service

Eligibility
The deceased veteran must have been discharged under conditions other than dishonorable and must have been either a wartime veteran or one who served after Jan. 31, 1955, or a veteran who served at least one enlistment during peacetime, unless discharged or released sooner for disability incurred in line of duty. VA may also issue a flag for a veteran who is missing in action and is later presumed dead.

Nature of Benefit
American flag to drape casket of veteran, after which it may be given to next of kin, close friend or associate of the deceased.

Where To Apply.   Any VA office or most local post offices.

BURIAL IN NATIONAL CEMETERIES
For Veterans of Spanish-American War, Mexican Border Period, World War I, World War II, Korean Conflict Period, Vietnam Era, Peacetime Service, and Certain Members of Their Families

Eligibility
Burial is available to any deceased veteran of wartime or peacetime service (other than for training) who was discharged under conditions other than dishonorable at all Veterans Administration national cemeteries.
Members of the Reserve and the Army and Air National Guard who die while performing or as a result of performing active duty for training may also be eligible.
Burial is also available to eligible veteran's wife, husband, widow, widower, minor children and, under certain conditions, to unmarried adult children.
Headstones and markers are provided for the gravesites of those interred in national cemeteries. No application is required.
Detailed information regarding eligibility and interments is contained in VA pamphlet titled, "Interments in National Cemeteries." Copies may be obtained from any VA office.

Arlington National Cemetery (Department of the Army)
This Cemetery is under the jurisdiction of the Department of the Army and

burial is limited to specific categories of military personnel and veterans except in the case of cremated remains to be placed in the columbarium. For information you should write to the Superintendent, Arlington National Cemetery, Arlington, Va. 22211 or telephone (202) 695-3253 or 3250.

Where to Apply

Any VA office will provide information and other assistance in filing burial request applications. Applications should be made only at the time of death of the veteran or that of an eligible dependent by contacting the Director of the National Cemetery desired. Ordinarily this is done by the attending funeral director.

HEADSTONE OR GRAVE MARKER
For Veterans of Spanish-American War, Mexican Border, World War I, World War II, Korean Conflict Period, Vietnam Era, and Peacetime Service

Headstones and markers are provided for the gravesites of those interred in national cemeteries. No application is required.

Eligibility

Headstone or grave marker is available for any deceased veteran of wartime or peacetime service (other than for training) who was discharged under conditions other than dishonorable and is buried in a private cemetery.

Members of the Reserve and the Army and Air National Guard who die while performing or as a result of performing active duty for training may also be eligible.

Nature of Benefit

A headstone or grave marker is provided without charge and shipped at Government expense to the consignee designated. The cost of placing the marker in a private cemetery must be borne by the applicant. Applicants are cautioned to ensure the correctness of all information.

The benefit does not apply to members of a veteran's family who are buried in a private cemetery but does apply to the family members buried in a veteran's cemetery owned by a State.

(See below for Headstone or Grave Marker Monetary Allowance.)

Where to Apply

Forward applications (VA Form 40-1330) to the Director, Monument Service (42), Department of Memorial Affairs, Veterans Administration, Washington, D.C. 20420. Any VA office will provide information, and other assistance in filing applications.

Inquiries

Information regarding the status of a headstone/marker application for placement in a private cemetery can be obtained by writing to the Director, Monument Service (42), Department of Memorial Affairs, Veterans Administration, Washington, D.C. 20420 or by calling (202) 275-1494 or 1495.

Inquiries regarding the headstone/marker for a gravesite in a national cemetery can be obtained from the Director of the National Cemetery involved.

HEADSTONE OR GRAVE MARKER
MONETARY ALLOWANCE

Eligibility and Nature of Benefit

See above, "Headstone or grave marker" section.

The VA may pay an amount not to exceed the average actual cost of a Government headstone or marker as partial reimbursement for the cost incurred by the person acquiring a non-Government headstone or marker *for placement in a cemetery other than a national cemetery*. The amount normally changes from year to year. Effective October 1, 1981, it was $63.

Where to Apply.   Any VA Regional Office. Ask for VA Form 21-8834.

PRESIDENTIAL MEMORIAL CERTIFICATES
For the Next of Kin of Deceased Eligible Veterans
or of Persons Who Were Members of the Armed Forces
at Time of Death

Eligibility

Eligibility for a deceased veteran is based on having a discharge other than dishonorable.

Eligible recipients include the next of kin (widow, widower, oldest child, parent or oldest sibling), a relative or friend upon request, or an authorized representative acting on behalf of such relative or friend.

Nature of Benefit

The certificate expresses the country's grateful recognition of the person's service in the Armed Forces and bears the signature of the President.

Where to Apply

Notice of a veteran's death is normally received in one of VA's regional offices and that facility identifies the next of kin from the veteran's records and requests the certificate from Washington, D.C. Next of kin of veterans need not apply. Others should apply to a VA regional office.

MEMORIAL MARKERS AND MEMORIAL PLOTS
For Certain Veterans Whose Remains are Nonrecoverable,
Not Identified, Buried at Sea, Donated to Science,
or Cremated and Ashes Scattered

Eligibility

A memorial headstone or marker may be furnished on application of a close relative recognized as the next of kin to commemorate any eligible veteran (including a person who died in the active military, naval, or air service) whose remains have not been recovered or identified, or were buried at sea (whether by the veteran's own choice or otherwise); were donated to science, or were cremated and the ashes scattered without interment of any portion of the ashes. The memorial may be erected in a private cemetery in a plot provided by the applicant or in a memorial section of a national cemetery.

Where to Apply

Forward applications (VA Form 40-1330) for memorial markers to Director,

Monument Service, (42), Department of Memorial Affairs, Veterans Administration, Washington, D.C. 20420. Any VA office will provide information and other assistance in filing applications.

OVERSEAS BENEFITS

Medical Benefits

Veterans with service-connected disabilities should obtain a statement of the disabilities from the VA office that maintains their medical records before going overseas.

The statement will enable the veteran to obtain emergency treatment or hospitalization—paid for by VA—when proper application for medical benefits and the statement are presented to a U.S. Embassy or Consulate in a foreign country. Application for treatment should be made in advance or within 72 hours of need for emergency care.

The Veterans Memorial Medical Center in Manila is the only overseas hospital where VA-paid care is available to veterans with nonservice-connected disabilities. Veterans may be admitted on a space-available basis and then only if they cannot afford other hospitalization.

Other Overseas Benefits

Certain VA educational benefits are available overseas to eligible veterans, their spouses and children. Details on the availability of these benefits should be obtained from VA when planning an extended trip or permanent move overseas.

VA will mail compensation and pension checks to most overseas locations, but GI home loans are not available for overseas properties.

Veterans residing in foreign countries should contact the nearest American Embassy or Consulate for information or assistance.

APPEALS
All Veterans

Eligibility

Veterans have the right to appeal determinations made by a VA regional office or hospital which they believe are unfavorable to them. Not all field determinations are appealable but those dealing with compensation or pension benefits, education benefits, waiver of recovery of overpayments, and reimbursement of unauthorized medical services are typical issues which may be appealed to the Board of Veterans Appeals.

Time Limits; Where to File

A veteran has one year from the date stamped on the notification of the determination within which to file an appeal. An appeal is initiated by filing a "Notice of Disagreement" in which the veteran expresses his dissatisfaction and requests appellate review. This Notice of Disagreement should be filed with the VA regional office responsible for making the determination.

Following receipt of a Notice of Disagreement, the VA office will furnish the veteran a "Statement of the Case" setting forth the issue, facts, applicable law and regulations, and the reasons for the determination.

In order to complete the request for appeal, the veteran must file a "Substantive Appeal" within 60 days after the date stamped on the Statement of the Case.

Board of Veterans Appeals

The Board of Veterans Appeals is responsible for rendering all final decisions. A personal hearing on appeal may be arranged any time following the filing of a Notice of Disagreement. The personal hearing may be held in Washington, D.C., before a traveling section of the Board at a nearby VA office, or before a Rating Board of the VA office acting as agents for the Board of Veterans Appeals.

Additional information on appeals may be found in VA pamphlet 1-1, "Board of Veterans Appeals, Rules of Practice," available from VA (01C1), Board of Veterans Appeals, Washington, D.C. 20420.

NON-VA BENEFITS

There are various benefits available to veterans and their dependents which are not administered by the Veterans Administration. These are summarized below with information as to how to contact the proper agency.

REEMPLOYMENT RIGHTS
For Veterans of World War II, Korean Conflict Period, Post-Korean Period, Vietnam Era and Peacetime Service

Administered by

(1) **For private employment and State or local government employment.** Office of Veteran's Reemployment Rights, Labor-Management Services Administration, U.S. Department of Labor. Contact any field office of the Labor-Management Services Administration.

(2) **For Federal employment.** U.S. Office of Personnel Management. Contact any of its regional offices or any Federal Job Information Center.

Eligibility

(1) **Private employment and State or local government employment.** Veteran must have left other than temporary employment to enter military service; must have served not more than 5 years after August 1, 1961, after leaving the employment to which he or she claims restoration, provided that any service over four years was at the request and for the convenience of the Government; must have been separated honorably or under honorable conditions; and must be qualified to perform the duties of that job or, if disabled while in military service, some other job in employer's organization of comparable seniority, status, and pay. Veterans returning to state or local government employment are protected if released from military training or service on or after Dec. 3, 1974. The time limits on active duty are extended, in the case of a member of the Selected Reserve called up for active duty (other than for training) for not more than 90 days, by the length of such active duty.

(2) **Federal employment, including employment by the U.S. Postal Service.** Generally the same as for private employment.

Nature of Benefit

Restoration in the position the veteran would have attained had he or she not been absent, or in another position of like seniority, status, and pay, including all benefits falling due after reemployment which would have accrued by seniority. Protection against discharge without cause for 1 year (6 months in the case of a Reservist or Guardsman returning from initial active duty for training, or a member of the Selected Reserve returning from a call-up to active duty, other than for training, for not more than 90 days).

Applying for Reemployment

A veteran must apply to his preservice employer *within 90 days* after separation from active duty or release from hospitalization continuing for not more than a year immediately after active duty. For Reservists and National Guardsmen returning from initial active duty for training of 3 consecutive months or more, and for members of the Selected Reserve returning from active duty (other than for training) for not more than 90 days, the application period is 31 days instead of 90. Reservists and National Guardsmen returning from other types of military training duty must report back to their employer for the next scheduled work period after their return home, allowing for hospitization and necessary travel time.

UNEMPLOYMENT COMPENSATION

The purpose of unemployment compensation for veterans is to provide a weekly income for a limited period of time to help veterans meet basic needs while searching for employment. The amount and duration of payments are governed by State laws and vary considerably. Benefits are paid from Federal funds.

The veteran must have 365 days or more of continuous active service or be discharged because of a service-connected disability.

Federal law passed in 1981 requires that the servicemember must be discharged or released under honorable conditions, must not resign or voluntarily leave the service, and must not be released or discharged for cause. He/she must be able to work and be available for work.

Generally benefits are not paid to persons receiving certain educational assistance or vocational subsistence allowances from VA.

Veterans should apply immediately after leaving service at their nearest local State employment service/job service office (NOT at the VA) and present copy 4 of their DD Form 214 to establish their type of separation from service.

JOB-FINDING ASSISTANCE

The U.S. Department of Labor is the Federal agency responsible for assuring that employment assistance is provided to veterans through State employment/ job service local offices throughout the country. The local Veterans Employment Representatives provide functional supervision of job counseling, testing and employment placement services provided to veterans. Priority in referral to job openings and training programs is given to eligible veterans, with preferential treatment for the disabled veterans. In addition, the job service assists veterans who are seeking employment by providing information about job marts, on-the-job and apprenticeship training opportunities, etc., in cooperation with VA Regional Offices, U.S. Veterans Assistance Centers, and Veterans Outreach Centers.

EMPLOYMENT IN THE FEDERAL GOVERNMENT

As a result of the Vietnam Era Veterans' Readjustment Assistance Act of 1974, the United States has a policy of promoting maximum job opportunities within the Federal government for qualified disabled veterans and Vietnam era veterans.

Under the law, all Federal agencies are required to establish affirmative action plans to facilitate employment and advancement of disabled veterans and other handicapped persons.

All veterans may be eligible to receive helpful advantages in Federal employment such as additional points added to passing scores in job examinations, waivers of certain physical requirements, first consideration for certain jobs, and preference for retention in layoffs.

Similar benefits are provided for: (1) unremarried widows or widowers and mothers of certain deceased veterans or military personnel; (2) spouses of service-connected disabled veterans who are no longer able to work in their usual occupations; and (3) mothers of permanently and totally service-connected disabled veterans.

Under the expanded Veterans Readjustment Appointment (VRA) authority, a nondisabled Vietnam Era veteran who has completed no more than 14 years of education may be hired by a Federal agency without requiring competition in a regular civil service examination, provided that the veteran agrees to participate in a program of education or training. This 14 years of education restriction does not apply to compensably disabled Vietnam era veterans nor Vietnam era veterans discharged because of service-connected disabilities.

Under the noncompetitive appointment authority for 30 percent disabled veterans, a disabled veteran with a compensable service-connected disability of 30 percent or more may be given by a Federal agency a non-competitive appointment which may lead to conversion to career or career-conditional employment.

More specific information concerning these benefits and other Federal job information may be obtained by contacting the Federal Job Information Centers of the U.S. Office of Personnel Managment. The Centers are listed in telephone books under United States Government. Or veterans may obtain a nationwide listing of the Federal Job Information Centers by writing the U.S. Office of Personnel Management, Federal Job Information Center, 1900 E Steet, N.W., Washington, D.C. 20415.

Veterans may also inquire at any Veterans Administration facility for information about employment in the Federal government.

AFFIRMATIVE ACTION IN EMPLOYMENT

Section 402 of the Vietnam Era Veterans' Readjustment Assistance Act of 1974 prohibits employers with federal contracts or subcontracts of $10,000 or more from discriminating in employment against Vietnam-era and all disabled veterans. It also requires these contractors to take affirmative action — or positive steps — to employ and advance in employment Vietnam-era and all disabled veterans.

Vietnam-era veterans are covered by this program during the first four years after their discharge. Disabled veterans, covered throughout their working life, are those with a 30 cent or more disability and those whose discharge or release from active duty resulted from a disability incurred or aggravated in the line of duty.

Section 402 is administered by the U.S. Labor Department's Office of Federal Contract Compliance Programs. Complaints may be filed with this office or the local Veterans' Employment Representative at the local State employment service office.

CORRECTION OF MILITARY RECORDS

The Secretary of a military department, acting through a Board for Correction of Military Records, has authority to correct any military record when he considers it necessary to correct an error or remove an injustice.

Some veterans may encounter situations in which they feel they have been victims of error or injustice related to their military service. Applications for correction of a military record, including review of discharges granted by courts martial, may be considered by a correction board.

Generally, a request for correction must be filed by the veteran, survivor or legal representative within three years after discovery of the alleged error or injustice. However, the board may excuse failure to file within the prescribed time if it finds it would be in the interest of justice to do so. In order to justify correction, it is necessary to show to the satisfaction of the board that the alleged entry or omission in the records was in error or unjust. Applications should include all evidence which may be available such as signed statements of witnesses or a brief of arguments supporting the requested correction. Application must be made on DD Form 149, which may be obtained at any VA office.

MEDALS

Medals awarded while in active service will be issued upon individual request to the appropriate service: ARMY — Commander, U.S. Army Reserve Components, Personnel and Administration Center. ATTN: AGUS-PSE-A, 9700 Page Blvd., St. Louis, Mo. 63132. NAVY — Chief of Naval Personnel, Department of the Navy, Washington, D.C. 20370. AIR FORCE — Commander, U.S. Air Force Military Personnel Center, ATTN: AFPM-PE, Randolph Air Force Base, Texas 78148. MARINES — Commandant, U.S. Marine Corps, Code: DL, Washington, D.C. 20380, COAST GUARD — Commandant, U.S. Coast Guard, 13th and E Streets N.W., Washington, D.C. 20226.

COMMISSARY AND EXCHANGE PRIVILEGES

Honorably discharged veterans with a service-connected disability rated at 100 percent, unmarried surviving spouses of members or retired members of the Armed Forces, recipients of the Medal of Honor, eligible dependents of the foregoing categories, and eligible orphans are entitled to unlimited exchange and commissary store privileges in the United States. Certain reservists and dependents also are eligible. (Entitlement to these privileges overseas is governed by international law, and privileges are available only to the extent agreed upon by the foreign governments concerned.) Certification of total disability will be given by the Veterans Administration. Assistance in completing DD Form 1172 (Application for Uniformed Services Identification and Privilege Card) may be provided by the VA.

CREDIT FOR FARMS, HOMES, COMMUNITY DEVELOPMENT

Credit and management advice can be provided by Farmers Home Administration (FmHA) to qualify individuals to buy, improve or operate farms. Loans for housing in towns principally up to 10,000 population are available as are loans to communities to install water and waste disposal systems and other community facilities.

For individual loans, applications from eligible veterans have preference for processing. For further information contact FmHA, U.S. Department of Agriculture, Washington, D.C. 20250, or apply at local FmHA offices, usually located in county seat towns.

FEDERAL HOUSING ADMINISTRATION (FHA) HOME MORTGAGE INSURANCE

HUD administers the FHA Home Mortgage Insurance Program for veterans. These home loans require less downpayment than under other FHA programs and are available to eligible veterans. Veterans discharged under other than dishonorable conditions with at least 90 days' service which began before September 8, 1980, are eligible. Veterans with enlisted service after September 7, 1980, must have served at least 24 months unless discharged for hardship or disability. Active duty for training is qualifying service. Submit VA Form 26-8261a (from any VA office) to VA for a Certificate of Veterans Status. This certificate is submitted by the lender to FHA.

COMPREHENSIVE EMPLOYMENT AND TRAINING ACT

The Labor Department administers through the Employment and Training Administration employment and training programs authorized by the Comprehensive Employment and Training Act (CETA). Under this act funds are provided to fund sponsors which are generally States and local government bodies, for comprehensive employment and training assistance to economically disadvantaged, unemployed,and underemployed individuals, including veterans. CETA regulations specify that prime sponsors as recipients of funds must take appropriate steps to provide for the increased participation of qualified disabled veterans and Vietnam Era veterans in their programs. Veterans may inquire directly about CETA programs through the local prime sponsor or the Veterans Employment Representative of the local state employment service office.

DISABLED VETERANS OUTREACH PROGRAM

The Department of Labor provides funds for State employment/job services offices to locate and inform jobless disabled veterans about job training and employment opportunities. This staff works with the VA, veterans organizations, and other community groups to locate disabled and Vietnam Era veterans in need of employment and training assistance and has available the resources of the State employment/job service office, including the job bank for referral to job openings.

NATURALIZATION PREFERENCE

Aliens with service in the U.S. Armed Forces during periods in which the United States was engaged in conflicts or hostilities, who have either been lawfully admitted to the United States for permanent residence or who, not having been so admitted, were inducted, enlisted, re-enlisted or extended an enlistment in the Armed Fores while within the United States, Puerto Rico, Guam, the Virgin Islands of the United States, the Canal Zone, American Samoa or Swains Island, may be naturalized without having to comply with some of the general requirements for naturalization. Apply at the nearest office of the Immigration and Naturalization Service.

Aliens with honorable service in the U.S. Armed Forces for three years or more during periods not considered a conflict or hostility by Executive Order may be naturalized provided they have been lawfully admitted to the United States for permanent residence. Applications must be made within six months of discharge for eligibility.

REVIEW OF DISCHARGES

Each of the services maintains a Discharge Review Board with authority to change, correct or modify discharges or dismissals that are NOT issued by a sentence of a general court-martial. The Board has NO authority to address medical discharges. The veteran (or, if deceased or incompetent, the surviving spouse, next of kin or legal representative) may apply for a review of discharge by writing to the Military Department concerned using Department of Defense Form 293 (DD-293), which may be obtained at any VA office. If more than 15 years have passed since discharge, DD Form 149 should be used.

Service discharge review boards conduct hearings by established boards in Washington, D.C. Also traveling review boards visit selected cities to hear cases based on demand as evidenced by the number of applicants who have submitted DD Forms 293. In addition, the Army sends teams to other locations to video tape applicant's testimony. This tape is reviewed by a regularly constituted board in Washington, D.C.

Under Public Law 95-126, discharges awarded as a result of unauthorized absence in excess of 180 days make persons ineligible for receipt of VA benefits regardless of action taken by discharge review boards unless the VA determines there were "compelling circumstances" for the absences. Boards for the Correction of Military Records may assist eligible veterans to overcome this restriction. Applications to the boards are made on DD Form 149.

Veterans with disabilities incurred or aggravated during active military, naval, or air-service in line of duty may qualify for medical or related benefits regardless of the type of administrative separation and characterization of service.

Veterans separated administratively under other than honorable conditions solely for the personal use and possession of drugs prior to July 1971 may request that their discharges be reviewed for possible recharacterization to "under honorable conditions." Additionally veterans with discharges under other than honorable conditions based solely on alcoholism will be reviewed upon application for possible recharacterization.

Questions regarding discharge review may be addressed to the "Senior Member of the Discharge Review Board" at the following addresses:

Army—Washington, D.C. 20310
Navy and USMC—Washington, D.C. 20370
Coast Guard—Washington, D.C. 20591
Air Force—Randolph AFB, Texas 78148

DEATH GRATUITY

Military services provide death gratuities to surviving spouses and dependents.

A sum, equal to 6-months pay of the deceased but not less than $800 nor more than $3,000, is paid to the deceased veteran's spouse, children, or if designated by the deceased, parents, brothers, or sisters. This is paid as soon as possible by the command to which the deceased was attached. If not received within a reasonable time, application should be made to the service concerned. The death gratuity is payable in case of any death in active service, or any death within 120 days thereafter from specified causes related to active service.

SMALL BUSINESS ADMINISTRATION

SBA has a number of progams designed to help foster and encourage small business enterprise, including businesses owned or operated by veterans. SBA also assists veterans to become the owners of their own small businesses. Help available from SBA includes advocacy in addition to financial and management assistance. Most SBA loans are made under its Loan Guaranty Program. The money is advanced by the bank or other lending institution, with SBA guaranteeing up to 90 percent of the total amount. Information on any of SBA's programs is available without charge from any of its national network of about 100 field offices. Veterans should check the U.S. Government section of the local phone book for addresses of the nearest SBA office.

SOCIAL SECURITY CREDITS

Monthly retirement, disability, and survivors benefits under Social Security are payable to a veteran and dependents if he or she has earned enough work credits under the program. A lump sum death payment of $255 also is made upon the veteran's death and can be paid only to the veteran's eligible spouse or child entitled to benefits. In addition, the veteran may qualify at 65 for Medicare's hospital insurance and medical insurance. Medicare protection also is available to people who have received Social Security disability benefits for 24 months and to insured people and their dependents with permanent kidney failure who need dialysis or kidney transplants.

Active duty (or active duty for training) in the United States uniformed services has counted toward Social Security, since January 1957, when taxes were first withheld from a serviceperson's basic pay. Service personnel and veterans receive an extra $300 credit for each quarter in which he or she received any basic pay for active duty or active duty for training after 1956 and before 1978. After 1977, a credit of $100 is granted for each $300 of reported wages up to a maximum credit of $1,200 if reported wages are $3,600 or more. No additional Social Security taxes are withheld from pay for these extra credits. Also, noncontributory Social Security credits of $160 a month may be granted to veterans who served after September 15, 1940, and before 1957.

Further information about Social Security credits and benefits is available from any of the more than 1,300 Social Security offices. For the address and phone number, look in the telephone directory under Social Security Administration, or ask at the post office.

ATTENTION VETERANS, VETERANS' FAMILIES

The VA Administers benefits for certain veterans, children, and parents of veterans. All are described in this pamphlet.

To file a claim, it will be necessary to identify the veteran. If the veteran, in turn, had ever filed a VA claim and the veteran's file number ("C" number) is known, there will be no problem.

Otherwise, it will be necessary to establish the veteran's identity by submitting the veteran's full name and a copy of discharge from service (or military service number, branch of service, and dates served).

The VA advises keeping the above information, and the veteran's government insurance number, in a safe, convenient location. Also, a statement regarding burial preference (location and type of burial should be included in the veteran's personal papers.

If not already on record in VA files, the following documents will be required for claims.

(a) The veteran's death certificate for all claims where the veteran died outside of service or outside of a VA hospital.

(b) The veteran's marriage certificate where the claim is made by the surviving spouse or by or for her or his children.

(c) The children's birth certificates, whether claim is made in the child's own right or by the widow or widower.

(d) The veteran's birth certificate if the parents of the veteran wish to establish eligibility.

Immediate Death Benefits

The immediate benefits following the death of the veteran—a burial flag and burial in national cemeteries   can be secured with the aid of the funeral director handling the veteran's funeral. The funeral director's requests are usually sufficient to alert the VA insurance division so that an insurance claims form is automatically sent to the veteran's beneficiary without inquiry on the beneficiary's part.

GI Insurance

If the funeral director has not alerted the VA at the time of the veteran's death, families in the eastern half of the United States should send their insurance claim to the VA Center, 5000 Wissahickon Ave., Philadelphia, Pa. 19101. Families in the western half of the nation should address the VA Center, Fort Snelling, St. Paul, Minn. 55111. Be sure to send the complete name of the veteran and number of the policy or, if the number is unknown, identify the veteran by file number, military serial number or the branch and dates of military service, and date of birth.

Servicemen's Group Life Insurance (SGLI)
Veterans Group Life Insurance (VGLI)

Designated beneficiaries of those deceased persons covered by SGLI or VGLI may submit their claim to the Office of Servicemen's Group Life Insurance, 212 Washington St., Newark, N.J. 07102. They should be sure to send the full name of the insured member together with other identifying information such as military serial number, branch of service, dates of military service, Social Security number and dates of birth and death. Claim forms may be secured from the nearest VA office, or by writing to the Office of Servicemen's Group Life Insurance at the above address.

Burial Expense Reimbursement
The funeral director will also assist in filing for *Reimbursement of Burial Expenses*.

Compensation
If the veteran's death was service-connected, the surviving spouse and minor children may be eligible for *Dependency and Indemnity Compensation*.

Pension
Nonservice-connected death may entitle the surviving spouse and veteran's minor children to *Pension* payments.

Parent's Compensation
In certain cases, parents may be eligible for *Dependency and Indemnity Compensation*.

Children's Benefits — Restoration or Entitlement to, Upon Termination of Child's Marriage.
Entitlement to benefits payable to or on behalf of a child which has been denied or terminated by reason of the child's marriage may be restored if the marriage is terminated by death or dissolved by a court decree.

Children's Education
Children of veterans who die or become permanently and totally disabled because of service-connected disabilities or of service personnel who are missing in action or prisoners of war may be eligible for *Dependents' Educational Assistance*.

Surviving Spouse's Education
Surviving spouses of veterans who died as the result of service-connected disabilities are eligible for educational assistance.

Spouse's Education
Spouses of veterans who are permanently and totally disabled because of a service-connected disability and spouses of servicepersons who are missing in action or prisoners of war are eligible for educational assistance.

Home Loans for Surviving Spouses
Unmarried surviving spouses of veterans of any period of service occurring since September 16, 1940, whose deaths were service-connected, are eligible for a GI *home loan*.

Home Loans for Spouses
Spouses of service personnel who are missing in action or prisoners of war are

eligible for a GI *home loan*.

Death Gratuity

Paid by the Armed Services to surviving spouses, children—and if designated by the deceased—to parents, brothers or sisters.

Notice

Veterans should acquaint their families with the location of their military records, their file number and the insurance numbers to save delay.

"VA — May I Help You?"

For information or assistance in applying for veterans' benefits, write, call, or visit a Veterans Benefits Counselor at your nearest VA regional office or VA office listed on the following pages, or a local veterans service organization representative. Application for medical benefits may be made at a VA medical center (see H—Hospital Care) or any VA station with medical facilities.

To help VA provide prompt service, callers are advised to have full identifying information on hand when they call VA.

All 50 states have toll-free telephone services to VA regional offices. The telephone numbers listed after each regional office are the toll-free benefits information numbers to that office for the areas shown. Local telephone numbers are also listed for VA hospitals and clinics.

Please note: Telephone numbers are subject to change. If you are unable to reach VA at the number listed for your area or if you are unsure which number to call, consult the white pages of your local telephone directory under U.S. Government, Veterans Administration, for the benefits information number. The directory assistance operator can also assist you.

To assure that accurate information and courteous responses are given to the public, VA supervisory personnel occasionally monitor telephone calls. No record is kept of the caller's name, address, claim or telephone number.

GI life insurance is administered at the VA Regional Office and Insurance Center in St. Paul or Philadelphia. For any information concerning a policy, write directly to the VA Center administering it. Give the insured's policy number, if known. The insured's full name, date of birth, and service number should be given if the policy number is not known.

VA FACILITIES—WHERE TO GO FOR HELP

VA installations are listed below by state. Information on VA benefits may be obtained from the following installations: Regional Offices (RO); other offices (O); Regional Office and Insurance Centers in Philadelphia and St. Paul, and United States Veterans Assistance Centers (USVAC) listed immediately following the state listing below. Abbreviations of other installations are as follows: H—Hospital Care; D—Domiciliary Care; NHC—Nursing Home Care; OC—Outpatient Clinic (independent); OCH—Outpatient Clinic (physically separated from hospital); OCS—Outpatient Clinic Substation.

Beneficiaries residing or traveling overseas requiring information or assistance relative to VA benefits should contact the nearest American Embassy or Consulate.

ALABAMA

Birmingham (H) 35233
700 S. 19th St.
(205) 933-8101

Mobile (OCS) 36617
2451 Fillingim St.
(205) 690-2875

Montgomery (H) 36109
215 Perry Hill Rd.
(205) 272-4670

Montgomery (RO) 36104
474 S. Court St.

If you reside in the local
telephone area of:

Birmingham — 322-2492
Huntsville — 539-7742
Mobile — 432-8645
Montgomery — 262-7781
All other areas in Alabama
(800) 392-8054

Tuscaloosa (H&NHC) 35404
Loop Rd.
(205) 553-3760

Tuskegee (H&NHC) 36083
(205) 727-0550

ALASKA

Anchorage (RO&OC) 99501
235 E. 8th Avenue

If you live in the local
telephone area of:
Anchorage 271-4053
All other Alaska communities
ask operator for Zenith 2500

ARIZONA

Phoenix (H) 85012
7th St. & Indian School Rd.
(602) 277-5551

Phoenix (RO) 85012
3225 N. Central Ave.
If you live in the local
telephone area of:
Phoenix — 263-5411
Tucson — 622-6424
All other Arizona areas
(800) 352-0451

Prescott (H&D) 86313
(602) 445-4860

Tucson (H&NHC) 85723
3601 S. 6th Ave.
(602) 792-1450

ARKANSAS

Fayetteville (H) 72701
1100 N. College Ave.
(501) 443-4301

Little Rock (RO) 72201
1200 W. 3rd St.
If you live in the local
telephone area of:
Fort Smith — 785-2637
Little Rock — 378-5971
Pine Bluff — 536-8100
Texarkana — 774-2166
All other Arkansas areas
(800) 482-5434

Little Rock (H&NHC) 72206
300 E. Roosevelt Rd.
(501) 372-8361

CALIFORNIA

Compton (USVAC) 90220
322 West Compton Blvd.
Suite 104
(213) 537-3203

East Los Angeles
  (USVAC) 90063
East L.A. Service Center
915 N. Bonnie Beach Pl.
(213) 264-1068

Fresno (H) 93703
2615 E. Clinton Ave.
(209) 225-6100

Livermore (H) 94550
(415) 447-2560

Loma Linda (H) 92357
11201 Benton St.
(714) 825-7084

Long Beach (H&NHC) 90822
5901 E. 7th St.
(213) 498-1313

Los Angeles (RO) 90024
Federal Building
11000 Wilshire Blvd.
West Los Angeles

Counties of Inyo, Kern, Los
Angeles, Orange, San
Bernardino, San Luis
Obispo, Santa Barbara
and Ventura:

If you live in the local
telephone area of:
Central LA — 879-1303
Inglewood — 645-5420
La Crescenta — 248-0450
Malibu/Santa Monica—451-0672

San Fernando/
    Van Nuys — 997-6401
San Pedro/
    Long Beach — 833-5241
Sierra Madre — 355-3305
West Los Angeles — 479-4011
Whittier — 945-3841

Outside LA
Anaheim — 821-1020
Bakersfield — 834-3142
Huntington Beach — 848-1500
Ontario — 983-9784
Oxnard — 487-3977
San Bernardino — 884-4874
Santa Ana — 543-8403
Santa Barbara — 963-0643

All other areas of the above
counties — (800) 352-6592

Counties of Alpine, Lassen,
Modoc and Mono served by:
Reno, NV (RO) 89520
1201 Terminal Way

If you live in the above
California counties —
(800) 648-5406

Los Angeles (H&D) 90073
11301 Wilshire Blvd.
(213) 478-3711

Los Angeles (OC) 90013
425 S. Hill St.
(213) 688-2000

Martinez (H) 94553
150 Muir Rd.
(415) 228-6800

Oakland (OCS) 94612
1515 Clay St.
(415) 273-7125

Palo Alto (H&NHC) 94304
3801 Miranda Ave.
(415) 493-5000

Sacramento (OCS) 95820
4600 Broadway
(916) 440-2625

San Diego (RO) 92108
2022 Camino Del Rio North
Counties of Imperial,
Riverside, and San Diego:
If you live in the local
telephone area of:
Riverside — 686-1132
San Diego — 297-8220

All other areas of the above
counties (800) 532-3811

San Diego (H&NHC) 92161
3350 LaJolla Village Dr.
(714) 453-7500

San Diego (OCH) 92108
Palomar Building
2022 Camino Del Rio North

San Francisco (RO) 94105
211 Main St.
If you live in the local
telephone area of:
Fremont — 796-9212
Fresno — (800) 652-1296
Modesto — 521-9260
Monterey — 649-3550
Oakland — 893-0405
Palo Alto — 321-5615
Sacramento — 929-5863
San Francisco — 495-8900
San Jose — 998-7373
Santa Rosa — 544-3520
Stockton — 948-8860
Vallejo — 552-1556
All other areas of
Northern California—
(800) 652-1240

San Francisco (H) 94121
4150 Clement St.
(415) 221-4810

Santa Barbara (OCS) 93105
315 Camino Del Remedio
(805) 683-1491

Sepulveda (H&NHC) 91343
16111 Plummer St.
(213) 894-8271

COLORADO

Denver (RO) 80225
Building 20
Denver Federal Center
If you live in the local
telephone area of:
Colorado Springs — 475-9911
Denver — 233-6300
Pueblo — 545-1764
All other Colorado areas —
(800) 332-6742

Denver (H) 80220
1055 Clermont St.
(303) 399-8020

Fort Lyon (H&NHC) 81038
(303) 456-1260

Grand Junction (H&NHC)
 81501
2121 North Ave.
(303) 242-0731

CONNECTICUT

Hartford (RO) 06103
450 Main St.
If you live in the local
telephone area of:
Bridgeport — 384-9861
Danbury — 743-2791
Hartford — 278-3230
New Haven — 562-2113
New London — 447-0377
Norwalk — 853-8141
Stamford — 325-4039
Waterbury — 757-0347
All other Connecticut areas
— (800) 842-4315/4317

Newington (H) 06111
55 Willard Ave.
(203) 666-6951

West Haven (H&NHC) 06516
W. Spring St.
(203) 932-5711

DELAWARE

Wilmington (RO) 19805
1601 Kirkwood Highway
If you live in the local
telephone area of:
Wilmington — 998--0191
All other Delaware areas —
(800) 292-7855

Wilmington (H) 19805
1601 Kirkwood Highway
(302) 994-2511

DISTRICT OF COLUMBIA

Washington, D.C. (RO) 20421
941 N. Capitol St., N.E.
(202) 872-1151

Washington, D.C. (H) 20422
50 Irving St., N.W.
(202) 745-8000

FLORIDA

Bay Pines (H, D, NHC, & OCH)
 33504
1000 Bay Pines Blvd., N
(813) 391-9644

Fort Myers (OCS) 33901
2070 Carrell Road
(813) 893-3528

Gainsville (H) 32602
Archer Rd.
(904) 376-1611

Jacksonville (O) 32201
Post Office & Courthouse Bldg.
311 W. Monroe St.
(904) 356-1581

Jacksonville (OCS) 32206
1833 Boulevard
(904) 791-2751

Lake City (H&NHC) 32055
S. Marion St.
(904) 752-1400

Miami (H&NHC) 33125
1201 N.W. 16th St.
(305) 324-4455

Miami (O) 33130
Federal Building, Rm. 100
51 S.W. 1st Ave.
(305) 358-0669

Orlando (OCS) 32806
83 W. Columbia St.
(305) 425-7521

Riviera Beach (OPC) 33404
Exec. Plaza, 301 Broadway
(305) 845-2800

St. Petersburg (OCH) 33701
144 First Ave., S.
(813) 893-3706

St. Petersburg (RO) 33731
144 1st Ave. S.
If you live in the local
telephone area of:
Cocoa/Cocoa Beach —
 783-8930
Daytona Beach — 255-8351
Ft. Lauderdale/Hollywood
 — 522-4725
Ft. Myers — 334-0900
Gainesville — 376-5266
Jacksonville — 356-1581
Lakeland/Winter Haven
 — 683-7481
Melbourne — 724-5600
Miami — 358-0669
Orlando — 425-2626
Pensacola — 434-3537
Sarasota — 366-2939
Tallahassee — 224-6872
Tampa — 229-0451
West Palm Beach — 833-5734
St. Petersburg — 898-2121
All other Florida areas —
(800) 282-8821
Tampa (H) 33612
13000 N. 30th St.
(813) 971-4500

GEORGIA

Atlanta (RO) 30365
730 Peachtree St., N.E.
If you live in the local
telephone area of:
Albany — 439-2331
Atlanta — 881-1776
Augusta — 738-5403
Columbus — 324-6646
Macon — 745-6517
Savannah — 232-3365
All other Georgia areas
— (800) 282-0232

Augusta (H&NHC) 30904
(404) 724-5116

Decatur (H) 30033
1670 Clairmont Rd.
(404) 321-6111

Dublin (H, D & NHC) 31021
(912) 272-1210

HAWAII

Honolulu (RO) 96813
PJKK Federal Bldg.
300 Ala Moana Blvd.
If you live in the local
telephone area of:
Is. of Hawaii — Ask operator
 for Enterprise 5308
Is. of Kauai — Ask operator
 for Enterprise 5310
Is. of Maui/Lanai/Molokai —
 Ask operator Enterprise
 5309
Is. of Oahu — 546-8962

Honolulu Clinic 96850
P.O. Box 50188
300 Ala. Moana Blvd.
(808) 546-2146

IDAHO

Boise (RO) 83724
Federal Bldg. and
U.S. Courthouse

550 W. Fort St.
If you live in the local
telephone area of:
Boise — 334-1010
All other Idaho areas —
(800) 632-2003

Boise (H) 83702
5th and Fort St.
(208) 336-5100

ILLINOIS

Chicago (H) 60611
333 E. Huron St. (Lakeside)
(312) 943-6600

Chicago (H) 60680
(West Side)
820 S. Damen Ave.
(312) 666-6500

Chicago (RO) 60680
536 S. Clark St.
If you live in the local
telephone area of:
Bloomington/Normal —
  829-4374
Carbondale — 457-8161
Champaign-Urbana —
  344-7505
Chicago — 663-5510
Decatur — 429-9445
E. St. Louis — 274-5444
Peoria — 674-0901
Rockford — 968-0538
Springfield — 789-1246

All other Illinois areas —
(800) 972-5327

Danville (H&NHC) 61832
(217) 442-8000

Hines (H) 60141
(312) 343-7200

Marion (H) 62959
(618) 997-5311

North Chicago (H&NHC)
  60064
Downey
(312) 689-1900

Peoria (OCS) 61605
411 West Seventh St.
(309) 371-7327

INDIANA

Evansville (OCS) 47708
214 S.E. 6th St.
(812) 423-6871 Ext. 316

Fort Wayne (H&NHC) 46805
1600 Randalia Dr.
(219) 743-5431

Indianapolis (RO) 46204
575 N. Pennsylvania St.
If you live in the local
telephone area of:
Anderson/Muncie — 289-9377
Evansville — 426-1403
Ft. Wayne — 422-9189
Gary/Hammond/E. Chicago —
  886-9184
Indianapolis — 269-5566
Lafayette/W. Lafayette —
  742-0084

South Bend — 232-3011
Terre Haute — 232-1030
All other Indiana areas —
(800) 382-4540

Indianapolis (H&NHC) 46202
1481 W. 10th St.
(317) 635-7401

Marion (H&NHC) 46952
E. 38th St.
(317) 674-3321

IOWA

Des Moines (RO) 50309
210 Walnut St.
If you live in the local
telephone area of:
Cedar Rapids — 366-7681
Davenport/Rock Is./Moline, IL
  — 326-4051
Des Moines — 280-7220
Sioux City — 252-3291
Waterloo — 235-6721
All other Iowa areas —
(800) 362-2222

Des Moines (H) 50310
30th & Euclid Ave.
(515) 255-2173

Iowa City (H) 52240
(319) 338-0581

Knoxville (H&NHC) 50138
1515 W. Pleasant St.
(515) 842-3101

KANSAS

Leavenworth (H, D & NHC)
  66048
4201 S. 4th St., Trafficway
(913) 682-2000

Topeka (H&NHC) 66622
2200 Gage Blvd.
(913) 272-3111

Wichita (RO) 67211
Blvd. Office Park
901 George Washington Blvd.
If you live in the local
telephone area of:
Kansas City — 432-1650
Topeka — 357-5301
Wichita — 264-9123

All other Kansas areas
  (800) 362-2444

Wichita (H) 67218
5500 E. Kellogg
(316) 685-2221

KENTUCKY

Lexington (H&NHC) 40507
(606) 233-4511

Louisville (RO) 40202
600 Federal Place
If you live in the local
telephone area of:
Lexington — 253-0566
Louisville — 584-2231
All other areas — (800) 292-4562

Louisville (H) 40202
800 Zorn Ave.
(502) 895-3401

LOUISIANA

Alexandria (H&NHC) 71301
(318) 473-0010

New Orleans (RO) 70113
701 Loyola Ave.
If you live in the local
telephone area of:
Baton Rouge — 343-5539
New Orleans — 561-0121
Shreveport — 424-8442

All other Louisiana areas
— (800) 462-9510

New Orleans (H) 70146
1601 Perdido St.
(504) 568-0811

Shreveport (H&O) 71130
510 E. Stoner Ave.
(318) 424-8442 (Office)
(318) 221-8411 (Hospital)

MAINE

Portland (O) 04111
One Maine Savings Plaza
Congress St.
(207) 775-6391

Togus (RO) 04330
If you live in the local
telephone area of:
Portland — 775-6391
Togus — 623-8411 ext. 498

All other Maine areas —
(800) 452-1935

Togus (H&NHC) 04330
(207) 623-8411

MARYLAND

Counties of Montgomery
and Prince Georges:
Washington, DC (RO) 20421
941 N. Capitol St., N.E.
If you live in the above
Maryland counties — 872-1151

All other Maryland counties:
Baltimore (RO) 21201
31 Hopkins Plaza
Federal Building
If you live in the local
telephone area of:
Baltimore — 685-5454
All other Maryland areas:
(800) 492-9503

Baltimore (OCH) 21201
31 Hopkins Plaza
Federal Building
(301) 962-4610

Baltimore (H) 21218
3900 Loch Raven Blvd.
(301) 467-9932

Fort Howard (H&NHC) 21052
(301) 477-1800

Perry Point (H&NHC) 21902
(301) 642-2411

MASSACHUSETTS

Bedford (H&NHC) 01730
200 Spring Rd.
(617) 275-7500

Boston (H) 02130
150 S. Huntington Ave.
(617) 232-9500

Towns of Fall River and
New Bedford and counties of
Barnstable, Dukes, Nantucket,
part of Plymouth, and Bristol
are served by
Providence, R.I. (RO) 02903
321 S. Main St.
(800) 556-3893

Remaining Massachusetts
counties served by:

Boston (RO) 02203
John Fitzgerald Kennedy
Federal Bldg.
Government Center

If you live in the local
telephone area of:
Boston — 227-4600
Brockton — 588-0764
Fitchburg/Leominster —
    342-8927
Lawrence — 687-3332
Lowell — 454-5463
Springfield — 785-5343
Worcester — 791-3595
All other Massachusetts areas
— (800) 392-6015

Boston (OC) 02108
17 Court St.
(617) 223-2021

Brockton (H&NHC) 02401
945 Belmont St.
(617) 583-4500

Lowell (OCS) 01852
Old Post Office Bldg.
50 Kearney Square
(617) 453-1746

New Bedford (OCS) 02740
53 N. Sixth St.
(617) 997-8721

Northampton (H&NHC) 01060
N. Main St.
(413) 584-4040

Springfield (O) 01103
1200 Main St.
(413) 785-5343

Springfield (OCS) 01103
101 State St.
(413) 781-2420

West Roxbury (H) 02132
1400 VFW Parkway
(617) 323-7700

Worcester (OCS) 01609
575 Main St.
(617) 791-2251

MICHIGAN

Allen Park (H&NHC) 48101
Southfield & Outer Drive
(313) 562-6000

Ann Arbor (H) 48105
2215 Fuller Rd.
(313) 769-7100

Battle Creek (H&NHC) 49016
(616) 965-3281

Detroit (RO) 48226
Patrick V. McNamara
    Federal Bldg.
477 Michigan Ave.
If you live in the local
telephone area of:
Ann Arbor — 662-2506
Battle Creek — 962-7568
Bay City — 894-4556
Detroit — 964-5110
Flint — 234-8646
Grand Rapids — 456-8511
Jackson — 787-7030
Kalamazoo — 344-0156
Lansing/E. Lansing —
    484-7713
Muskegon — 726-4895
Saginaw — 754-7475
All other Michigan areas —
(800) 482-0740

Grand Rapids (OCS) 49503
260 Jefferson St., S.E.
(616) 459-2200

Iron Mountain (H&NHC) 49801
(906) 774-3300

Saginaw (H) 48602
1500 Weiss St.
(517) 793-2340

MINNESOTA

Minneapolis (H) 55417
54th St. & 48th Ave., South
(612) 725-6767

St. Cloud (H&NHC) 56301
(612) 252-1670

St. Paul (RO & Insurance Center)
55111
Federal Bldg., Fort Snelling
If you live in the local
telephone area of:
Duluth — 722-4467
Minneapolis — 726-1454
Rochester — 288-5888
St. Cloud — 253-9300
St. Paul — 726-1454

Counties of Becker, Beltrami, Clay,
Clearwater, Kittson, Lake of the
Woods, Mahnomen, Marshall, Norman, Otter Tail, Pennington, Polk,
Red Lake, Roseau, and Wilkin are
served by Fargo, ND (RO) —
(800) 437-4668
All other Minnesota areas —
(800) 692-2121

St. Paul (OCH) 55111
Fort Snelling
(612) 725-6767

MISSISSIPPI

Biloxi (H, D & NHC) 39531
(601) 388-5541

Jackson (H&NHC) 39216
1500 E. Woodrow Wilson Dr.
(601) 362-4471

Jackson (RO) 39201
100 W. Capitol St.

If you live in the local
telephone area of:
Biloxi/Gulfport — 432-5996
Jackson — 960-4873
Meridian — 693-6166
All other Mississippi areas —
(800) 682-5270

MISSOURI

Columbia (H&NHC) 65201
800 Stadium Road
(314) 443-2511

Kansas City (H) 64128
4801 Linwood Blvd.
(816) 861-4700

Kansas City (O) 64106
Federal Office Bldg.
601 E. 12th St.
(816) 861-3761

Poplar Bluff (H&NHC) 63901
(314) 686-4151

St. Louis (RO) 63103
Federal Bldg.
1520 Market St.

If you live in the local
telephone area of:
Columbia — 449-1276
Kansas City — 861-3761
St. Joseph — 364-1171
St. Louis — 342-1171
Springfield — 883-7470
All other Missouri areas —
(800) 392-3761

St. Louis (H&NHC) 63106
915 N. Grand Blvd.
(314) 652-4100

MONTANA

Fort Harrison (RO) 59636
If you live in the local
telephone area of:
Fort Harrison/Helena —
    442-6839
Great Falls — 761-3215
All other Montana areas —
(800) 332-6125

Fort Harrison (H) 59636
(406) 442-6410

Miles City (H&NHC) 59301
210 S. Winchester
(406) 232-3060

NEBRASKA

Grand Island (H&NHC) 68801
2201 N. Broadway
(308) 382-3660

Lincoln (RO) 68508
Federal Bldg.
100 Centennial Mall North
If you live in the local
telephone area of:
Lincoln — 471-5001
Omaha/Council Bluff —
  221-3291

All other Nebraska areas —
(800) 742-7554

Lincoln (H) 68510
600 S. 70th St.
(402) 489-3802

Omaha (H) 68105
4101 Woolworth Ave.
(402) 346-8800

NEVADA

Las Vegas (OCS) 89102
1703 W. Charleston
(702) 385-3700

Reno (H&NHC) 89520
1000 Locust St.
(702) 329-1051

Reno (RO) 89520
245 East Liberty Street
If you live in the local
telephone area of:
Las Vegas — 386-2921
Reno — 329-9244
All other Nevada areas —
(800) 992-5740

NEW HAMPSHIRE

Manchester (RO) 03101
Norris Cotton Federal Bldg.
275 Chestnut St.
If you live in the local
telephone area of:
Manchester — 666-7785
All other New Hampshire areas
— (800) 562-5260

Manchester (H&NHC) 03104
718 Smyth Rd.
(603) 624-4366

NEW JERSEY

East Orange (H&NHC) 07019
Tremont Ave. & S. Center
(201) 676-1000

Lyons (H&NHC) 07939
(201) 647-0180

Newark (RO) 07102
20 Washington Place
If you live in the local
telephone area of:
Atlantic City — 348-8550
Camden — 541-8650
Clifton/Paterson/Passaic—
  472-9632
Long Branch/Asbury Park —
  870-2550
New Brunswick/Sayreville —
  828-5600
Newark — 645-2150
Perth Amboy — 442-5300
Trenton — 989-8116
All other New Jersey areas —
(800) 242-5867

Newark (OCH) 07102
20 Washington Place
(201) 645-3491

NEW MEXICO

Albuquerque (RO) 87102
Dennis Chavez Federal Bldg.
U.S. Courthouse
500 Gold Ave., S.W.
If you live in the local
telephone area of:
Albuquerque — 766-3361
All other New Mexico areas —
(800) 432-6853

Albuquerque (H&NHC) 87108
2100 Ridgecrest Dr., S.E.
(505) 265-1711

NEW YORK

Albany (H&NHC) 12208
113 Holland Ave.
(518) 462-3311

Albany (O) 12207
Leo W. O'Brien Federal Bldg.
Clinton Ave. & N. Pearl St.
(800) 442-5882

Batavia (H) 14020
Redfield Pkwy.
(716) 343-7500

Bath (H,D&NHC) 14810
(607) 776-2111

Bronx (H) 10468
130 W.Kingsbridge Rd.
(212) 584-9000

Brooklyn (H&NHC) 11209
800 Poly Place
(212) 836-6600

Brooklyn (OC) 11205
35 Ryerson St.
(212) 330-7785,86

Buffalo (RO) 14202
Federal Bldg.
111 W. Huron St.
If you live in the local
telephone area of:
Binghamton — 772-0856
Buffalo — 846-5191
Rochester — 232-5290
Syracuse — 476-5544
Utica — 735-6431

All other areas of Western New
York State — (800) 462-1130

Buffalo (H&NHC) 14215
3495 Bailey Ave.
(716) 834-9200

Canandaigua (H&NHC) 14424
Ft. Hill Ave.
(716) 394-2000

Castle Point (H&NHC) 12511
(914) 831-2000

Montrose (H&NHC) 10548
(914) 737-4400

New York City (H) 10010
1st Ave. at E. 24th St.
(212) 686-7500

New York City (RO) 10001
252 Seventh Ave. at 24th St.
Counties of Albany, Bronx,
Clinton, Columbia, Delaware,
Dutchess, Essex, Franklin,
Fulton, Greene, Hamilton,
Kings, Montgomery, Nassau,
New York, Orange, Otsego,
Putnam, Queens, Rensselaer,
Richmond, Rockland,
Saratoga, Schenectady,
Schoharie, Suffolk, Sullivan,
Ulster, Warren, Washington,
Westchester:
If you live in the local
telephone area of:
Nassau — 483-6188
New York — 620-6901
Poughkeepsie — 452-5330
Westchester — 723-7476
All other areas in the above
counties — (800) 442-5882

New York City (OCH) 10001
252 7th Ave. at 24th St.
(212) 620-6776

New York City (Prosthetic
  Center) 10001
252 7th Ave.
(212) 620-6636

Northport (H) 11768
Long Island — Middleville Rd.
(516) 261-4400

Rochester (O&OCS) 14614
Federal Office Bldg. and
Courthouse
100 State St.
(716) 232-5290 (O)
(716) 263-5734 (OCS)

Syracuse (O) 13260
U.S. Courthouse and
Federal Building
100 S. Clinton St.
(315) 476-5544

Syracuse (Mental Hygiene
  Clinic) 13202
Gateway Bldg.
803 S. Salina St.
(315) 473-2619

Syracuse (H&NHC) 13210
Irving Ave. & University Pl.
(315) 476-7641

NORTH CAROLINA

Asheville (H&NHC) 28805
(704) 298-7911

Durham (H) 27705
508 Fulton St.
(919) 286-0411

Fayetteville (H&NHC) 28301
2300 Ramsey St.
(919) 488-2120

Salisbury (H&NHC) 28144
1601 Brenner Ave.
(704) 636-2351

Winston-Salem (OCH) 27102
Federal Bldg.
251 N. Main St.
(919) 761-3562

Winston-Salem (RO) 27102
Federal Bldg.
251 N. Main St.
If you live in the local
telephone area of:
Asheville — 253-6861
Charlotte — 375-9351
Durham — 683-1367
Fayetteville — 323-1242
Greensboro — 274-1994
High Point — 887-1202
Raleigh — 821-1166
Winston-Salem — 748-1800

All other North Carolina
areas — (800) 642-0841

NORTH DAKOTA

Fargo (RO) 58102
21st Ave. & Elm St.

If you live in the local
telephone area of:
Fargo — 293-3656

All other North Dakota areas
(800) 342-4790

Fargo (H&NHC) 58102
2101 Elm St.
(701) 232-3241

OHIO

Brecksville (H&NHC) 44141
10000 Brecksville Rd.
(216) 526-3030

Chillicothe (H&NHC) 45601
(614) 773-1141

Cincinnati (H&NHC) 45220
3200 Vine St.
(513) 861-3100

Cincinnati (O) 45202
Rm. 1024 Federal Off. Bldg.
550 Main St.
(513) 579-0505

Cleveland (H) 44106
10701 E. Boulevard
(216) 791-3800

Cleveland (RO) 44199
Anthony J. Celebrezze
  Federal Bldg.
1240 E. 9th St.
If you live in the local
telephone area of:
Akron — 535-3327
Canton — 453-8113
Cincinnati — 579-0505
Cleveland — 621-5050
Columbus — 224-8872
Dayton — 223-1394
Springfield — 322-4907
Toledo — 241-6223
Warren — 399-8985
Youngstown — 744-4383

All other Ohio areas —
(800) 362-9024

Columbus (O) 43215
Rm. 309 Fed. Bldg.
200 N. High St.
(614) 224-8872

Columbus (OC) 43210
456 Clinic Drive
(614) 469-5664

Dayton (H,D&NHC) 45428
4100 W. 3rd St.
(513) 268-6511

Toledo (OCS) 43614
3333 Glendale Ave.
(419) 259-2000

OKLAHOMA

Muskogee (H) 74401
Memorial Station
Honor Heights Dr.
(918) 683-3261

Muskogee (RO) 74401
Federal Bldg.
125 S. Main St.
If you live in the local
telephone area of:

Lawton — 357-2400
Muskogee — 687-2500
Oklahoma City — 235-2641
Stillwater — 377-1770
Tulsa — 583-5891

All other Oklahoma areas —
(800) 482-2800

Oklahoma City (O) 73102
200 N.W. 4th St.
(405) 235-2641

Oklahoma City (H) 73104
921 N.E. 13th St.
(405) 272-9876

Tulsa (OCS) 74101
635 W. 11th St.
(918) 581-7152

OREGON

Portland (H) 97207
3710 SW. U.S. Veterans Rd.
(503) 222-9221

Portland (RO) 97204
Federal Bldg.
1220 SW. 3rd Avenue
If you live in the local
telephone area of:
Eugene/Springfield —
  342-8274
Portland — 221-2431
Salem — 581-9343

All other Oregon areas —
(800) 452-7276

Portland (OCH) 97204
426 S.W. Stark St.
(503) 221-2575

Rosenburg (H&NHC) 97470
(503) 672-4411

White City (D) 97501
(503) 424-3796

PENNSYLVANIA

Allentown (OCS) 18104
2937 Hamilton Blvd.
(215) 776-4304

Altoona (H&NHC) 16603
Pleasant Valley Blvd.
(814) 943-8164

Butler (H&NHC) 16001
(412) 287-4781

Coatesville (H&NHC) 19320
Black Horse Rd.
(215) 384-7711

Erie (H&NHC) 16501
135 E. 38th St.
(814) 868-8661

Harrisburg (OCS) 17108
Federal Bldg.
228 Walnut St.
(717) 782-4590

Lebanon (H&NHC) 17042
(717) 272-6621

Philadelphia (H) 19104
University & Woodland Aves.
(215) 382-2400

Philadelphia (OCH) 19102
1421 Cherry St.
(215) 597--3311
Ask for OCH

Philadelphia (RO & Insurance
  Center)
P.O. Box 8079
5000 Wissahickon Ave.

Counties of Adams, Berks,
Bradford, Bucks, Cameron,
Carbon, Centre, Chester,
Clinton, Columbia, Cumberland,
Dauphin, Delaware, Franklin,
Juniata, Lackawanna,
Lancaster, Lebanon, Lehigh,
Luzerne, Lycoming, Mifflin,
Monroe, Montgomery,
Montour, Northampton,
Northumberland, Perry,
Philadelphia, Pike, Potter,
Schuylkill, Snyder, Sullivan,
Susquehanna, Tioga, Union,
Wayne, Wyoming, and York:
If you live in the local
telephone area of:
Allentown/Bethlehem/
  Easton — 821-6823
Harrisburg — 232-6677
Lancaster — 394-0596
Philadelphia — 438-5225
Reading — 376-6548
Scranton — 961-3883
Wilkes-Barre — 824-4636
Williamsport — 322-4649
York — 845-6686
All other areas in the above
counties — (800) 822-3920

Pittsburgh (RO) 15222
1000 Liberty Ave.
If you live in the local
telephone area of:
Altoona — 944-7101
Johnstown — 535-8625
Pittsburgh — 281-4233
All other areas in Western
Pennsylvania — (800) 242-0233

Pittsburgh (OCH) 15222
1000 Liberty Ave.
(412) 644-6750

Pittsburgh (H&NHC) 15240
University Drive C.
(412) 683-3000

Pittsburgh (H) 15206
Highland Drive
(412) 363-4900

Wilkes-Barre (O) 18701
19-27 N. Main St.
(717) 824-4636

Wilkes-Barre (H) 18711
1111 E. End Blvd.
(717) 824-3521

PHILLIPPINES

Manila (RO&OC) 96528
1131 Roxas Blvd. (Manila)
APO San Francisco (Air Mail)

PUERTO RICO

Mayaguez (OCS) 00708
Road Number 2
(809) 833-4600
Ask for Ext. 204

Ponce (OCS) 00731
Calle Isabel No. 60
(809) 843-5151

San Juan (H) 00921
Barrio Monacillos
Rio Piedras GPO Box 4867
(809) 843-5151

San Juan (RO) 00918
U.S. Courthouse & Fed. Bldg.
Carlos E. Chardon St.
Hato Rey
(809) 753-4141

RHODE ISLAND

Providence (RO) 02903
321 S. Main St.
If you live in the local
telephone area of:
Providence — 273-4910
All other Rhode Island areas —
(800) 322-0230

Providence (H) 02908
Davis Park
(401) 273-7100

SOUTH CAROLINA

Charleston (H) 29403
109 Bee St.
(803) 577-5011

Columbia (RO) 29201
1801 Assembly St.
If you live in the local
telephone area of:
Charleston — 723-5581
Columbia — 765-5861
Greenville — 232-2457
All other South Carolina
areas — (800) 922-1000

Columbia (H&NHC) 29201
Garners Ferry Rd.
(803) 776-4000

Greenville (OCS) 29607
Piedmont East Bldg.
37 Villa Road
(803) 232-7303

SOUTH DAKOTA

Fort Meade (H) 57741
(605) 347-2511

Hot Springs (H&D) 57747
(605) 745-4101

Sioux Falls (H&NHC) 57101
2501 W. 22nd St.
(605) 336-3230

Sioux Falls (RO) 57101
Courthouse Plaza Bldg.
300 North Dakota Ave.
If you live in the local
telephone area of:
Sioux Falls — 336-3496

All other South Dakota areas
— (800) 952-3550

TENNESSEE

Chattanooga (OCS) 37411
Bldg. 6300 East Gate Center
(615) 266-3151

Knoxville (OCS) 37919
9047 Executive Park Dr.
Suite 100
(615) 637-9300

Memphis (H) 38104
1030 Jefferson Ave.
(901) 523-8990

Mountain Home (H,D&NHC)
37684
Johnson City
(615) 926-1171

Murfreesboro (H&NHC) 37130
(615) 893-1360

Nashville (RO) 37203
110 9th Ave., S.
If you live in the local
telephone area of:
Chattanooga — 267-6587
Knoxville — 546-5700
Memphis — 527-4583
Nashville — 254-5411

All other Tennessee areas —
(800) 342-8330

Nashville (H) 37203
1310 24th Ave., S.
(615) 327-4751

TEXAS

Amarillo (H) 79106
6010 Amarillo Blvd., W.
(806) 355-9703

Beaumont (OCS) 77701
3385 Fannin St.
(713) 838-0271

Big Spring (H&NHC) 79720
2400 S. Gregg St.
(915) 263-7361

Bonham (H,D&NHC) 75418
Ninth & Lipscomb
(214) 583-2111

Corpus Christi (OCS) 78404
1502 S. Brownlee Blvd.
(512) 888-3251

Dallas (O) 75202
U.S. Courthouse and
Fed. Office Bldg.
1100 Commerce St.
(214) 824-5440

Dallas (H) 75216
4500 S. Lancaster Rd.
(214) 376-5451

El Paso (OC) 79925
5919 Brook Hollow Dr.
(915) 543-7890

Houston (RO) 77054
2515 Murworth Dr.

Counties of Angelina, Aransas,
Atascosa, Austin, Bandera, Bee,
Bexar, Blanco, Brazoria,
Brewster, Brooks, Caldwell,
Calhoun, Cameron, Chambers,
Colorado, Comal, Crockett,
DeWitt, Dimmitt, Duval,
Edwards, Fort Bend, Frio,
Galveston, Gillispie, Goliad,
Gonzales, Grimes, Guadalupe,
Hardin, Harris, Hays, Hidalgo,
Houston, Jackson, Jasper,
Jefferson, Jim Hogg, Jim
Wells, Karnes, Kendall,
Kenedy, Kerr, Kimble,
Kinney, Kleberg, LaSalle,
Lavaca, Liberty, Live Oak,
McCulloch, McMullen, Mason,
Matagorda, Maverick, Medina,
Menard, Montgomery,
Nacogdoches, Newton,
Nueces, Orange, Pecos, Polk,
Real, Refugio, Sabine, San
Augustine, San Jacinto, San
Patricio, Schleicher, Shelby,
Starr, Sutton, Terrell, Trinity,
Tyler, Uvalde, Val Verde,
Victoria, Walker, Waller,
Washington, Webb, Wharton,
Willacy, Wilson, Zapata,
Zavala:

If you live in the local
telephone area of:

Beaumont — 838-6222
Corpus Christi — 884-1994
Edinburg/McAllen/Pharr —
383-8168
Houston — 664-4664
San Antonio — 226-7661
Texas City/Galveston — 948-3011

All other areas in the above
counties — (800) 392-2200

Houston (H&NHC) 77211
2002 Holcombe Blvd.
(713) 795-4411

Kerrville (H&NHC) 78028
(512) 896-2020

Lubbock (O&OC) 79401
Federal Building
1205 Texas Ave.
(806) 762-7219 (OC)
(806) 747-5256 (O)

Marlin (H) 76661
1016 Ward St.
(817) 883-3511

McAllen (OCS) 78501
1220 Jackson Ave.
(512) 682-4581

San Antonio (H) 78284
7400 Merton Minter Blvd.
(512) 696-9660

San Antonio (O) 78285
307 Dwyer Ave.
(512) 226-7661

San Antonio (OC) 78285
307 Dwyer Ave.
(512) 225-5511

Temple (H&D) 76501
1901 S. First
(817) 778-4811

Waco (RO) 76799
1400 N. Valley Mills Dr.
If you live in the local
telephone area of:
Abilene — 673-5286
Amarillo — 376-7202
Austin — 477-5831
Dallas — 824-5440
El Paso — 545-2500
Ft. Worth — 336-1641
Killeen — 699-2351
Lubbock — 747-5256
Midland/Odessa/Terminal —
    563-0324
Waco — 772-3060
Wichita Falls — 723-7103

All other areas in Texas —
(800) 792-3271

Waco (H&NHC) 76703
Memorial Drive
(817) 752-6581

Waco (OCH) 76710
1400 N. Valley Mills Dr.
(817) 756-6511

UTAH

Salt Lake City (RO) 84138
Federal Bldg.
125 S. State St.
If you live in the local
telephone area of:
Ogden — 399-4433
Provo/Orem — 375-2902
Salt Lake City — 524-5960

All other Utah areas —
(800) 662-9163

Salt Lake City (H&NHC) 84148
500 Foothill Blvd.
(801) 582-1565

VERMONT

White River Junction   RO)
    05001
If you live in the local
telephone area of:
White River Junction —
    295-9363
All other Vermont areas —
(800) 622-4134

White River Junction (H,NHC)
    05001
(802) 295-9363

VIRGINIA

Hampton (H,D&NHC) 23667
(804) 722-9961

Richmond (H) 23249
1201 Broad Rock Rd.
(804) 231-9011

Northern Virginia
Counties of Arlington and
Fairfax and the cities of
Alexandria, Fairfax, and
Falls Church:

Washington, DC (RO) 20421
941 N. Capitol St., N.E.
If you live in the above
Virginia counties or cities —
872-1151

Roanoke (RO) 24011
210 Franklin Rd., SW.
If you live in the local
telephone area of:
Hampton — 722-7477
Norfolk — 627-0441
Richmond — 648-1621
Roanoke — 982-6440
All other Virginia areas —
(800) 542-5826

Salem (H&NHC) 24153
(703) 982-2463

WASHINGTON

Seattle (RO) 98174
Federal Bldg.
915 2nd Ave.
If you live in the local
telephone area of:
Everett — 259-9232
Seattle — 624-7200
Spokane — 747-3041
Tacoma — 383-3851
Yakima — 248-7970
All other Washington areas —
(800) 552-7480

Seattle (H) 98108
4435 Beacon Ave., S.
(206) 762-1010

Seattle (OCH) 98104
Smith Tower, 2nd & Yesler
(206) 442-5030

Spokane (H) 99208
N. 4815 Assembly St.
(509) 328-4521

Tacoma (H&NHC) 98493
American Lake
(206) 588-2185

Vancouver (H) 98661
(503) 222-9221

Walla Walla (H) 99362
77 Wainwright Dr.
(509) 525-5200

WEST VIRGINIA

Beckley (H&NHC) 25801
200 Veterans Ave.
(304) 255-2121

Clarksburg (H) 26301
(304) 623-3461

Counties of Brooke, Hancock,
Marshall and Ohio:
Pittsburgh, PA (RO) 15222
1000 Liberty Ave.

If you live in the local
telephone area of:
Wheeling — 232-1431
Other: (800) 642-3520
(Huntington, WV RO)

Remaining counties in
West Virginia served by:

Huntington, (RO) 25701
640 Fourth Avenue
If you live in the local
telephone area of:
Charleston — 344-3531
Huntington — 529-5720

All other areas in West
Virginia — (800) 642-3520

Huntington (H) 25704
1540 Spring Valley Dr.
(304) 429-1381

Martinsburg (H&D) 25401
(304) 263-0811

Wheeling (OCS) 26003
11th & Chapline St.
(304) 234-0123

WISCONSIN

Madison (H) 53705
2500 Overlook Terrace
(608) 256-1901

Milwaukee (RO) 53202
342 N. Water St.
If you live in the local
telephone area of:
Green Bay — 437-9001

Madison — 257-5467
Milwaukee — 278-8680
Racine — 637-6743

All other Wisconsin areas —
(800) 242-9025

Tomah (H&NHC) 54660
(608) 372-3971

Wood (H,D&NHC) 53193
5000 W. National Ave.
(414) 384-2000

WYOMING

Cheyenne (RO) 82001
2360 E. Pershing Blvd.
If you live in the local
telephone area of:
Cheyenne — 632-6426

All other Wyoming areas —
(800) 442-2761

Cheyenne (H&NHC) 82001
2360 E. Pershing Blvd.
(307) 778-7550

Sheridan (H) 82801
(307) 672-3473

Where To Apply for Alcohol or Drug Dependence Treatment

Patients may be admitted to any VA medical center for inpatient care. However, there are specialized VA Alcohol Dependence Treatment Programs and Drug Dependence Treatment Programs for inpatient and/or outpatient care in the following cities:

Both Alcohol and Drug Dependence Treatment Programs: Albany, N.Y.; Allen Park, Mich.; American Lake (Tacoma), Wash.; Baltimore, Md.; Battle Creek, Mich.; Bedford, Mass.; Boston (OC), Mass.; Bronx, N.Y.; Brooklyn, N.Y.; Buffalo, N.Y.; Chicago (West Side), Ill.; Cincinnati, Ohio; Cleveland (Brecksville), Ohio; Coatesville, Pa.; Dallas, Tex.; Decatur, Ga.; Denver, Colo.; East Orange, N.J.; Hines, Ill.; Houston, Tex.; Indianapolis (10th St.), Ind.; Little Rock, Ark.; Long Beach, Calif.; Los Angeles (Brentwood), Calif.; Martinez, Calif.; Memphis, Tenn.; Miami, Fla.; Milwaukee (Wood), Wis.; Minneapolis, Minn.; Montrose, N.Y.; New Orleans, La.; New York (Bronx and Brooklyn), N.Y.; North Chicago, Ill.; Oklahoma City, Okla.; Palo Alto (Miranda Ave.), Calif.; Philadelphia, Pa.; Providence, R.I.; Salt Lake City, Utah; San Diego, Calif.; San Francisco, Calif.; San Juan, P.R.; Seattle, Wash.; Sepulveda, Calif.; St. Louis (Jefferson Barracks), Mo.; Tucson, Ariz.; Washington, D.C.; Wood, Wis.

Alcohol Dependence Treatment Programs only: Albuquerque, N.M.; Anchorage, Alaska; Augusta (Lenwood Div.), Ga.; Bay Pines, Fla.; Big Spring, Tex.; Biloxi, Miss.; Birmingham, Ala.; Brockton, Mass.; Canadaigua, N.Y.; Charleston, S.C.; Cleveland (Wade Park), Ohio; Columbia, S.C.; Danville, Ill.; Des Moines, Ia.; Ft. Howard, Md.; Ft. Lyon, Colo.; Ft. Meade, S.D.; Fresno, Calif.; Gainesville, Fla.; Hampton, Va.; Hot Springs, S.D.; Jackson, Miss.; Kansas City, Mo.; Knoxville, Ia.; Leavenworth, Kans.; Lexington, Ky.; Lincoln, Neb.; Loma Linda, Calif.; Lyons, N.J.; Manchester, N.H.; Marion, Ind.; Martinsburg, W.V.; Mountain Home, Tenn.; Murfreesboro, Tenn.; Nashville, Tenn.; Northampton, Mass.; Omaha, Neb.; Phoenix, Ariz.; Pittsburgh, (Highland Drive), Pa.; Prescott, Ariz.; Roseburg, Ore., Salem, Va.; St. Cloud, Minn.; Temple, Tex.; Togus, Me.; Tomah, Wis.; Topeka, Kans.; Tuscaloosa, Ala.; Waco, Tex.; West Haven, Conn.; White City, Ore.; White River Junction, Vt.

Drug Dependence Treatment Programs only: Boston, Mass.; Los Angeles (OC), Calif.; New York, N.Y.; Pittsburgh (University Drive), Pa.; Richmond, Va.; Tulsa, Okla.; Vancouver, Wash.

VETERANS ADMINISTRATION VET CENTERS

If the address and/or phone number listed below has changed for any Vet Center, please contact your local telephone operator, the nearest VA office, or (202) 389-3317 or 3303 in Washington, D.C. 20420

ALABAMA

2145 Highland Ave., Suite 250
Birmingham 35205
(205) 933-0500

ALASKA

550 West 8th Ave. Rm. 101
Anchorage 99501
(907) 277-1501

ARIZONA

807 N. 3rd St.
Phoenix 85004
(602) 261-4769

727 N. Swan
Tucson 85711
(602) 323-3271

ARKANSAS

811 West 3rd St.
Little Rock 72206
(501) 378-6395

CALIFORNIA

859 S. Harbor Blvd.
Anaheim 92805
(714) 776-0161

251 W. 85th Place
Los Angeles 90003
(213) 753-1391/2/3

2449 W. Beverly Blvd.
Montebello 90640
(213) 728-9984/9999
(213) 728-9966/7

616 16th St.
Oakland 94612
(415) 763-3904

1520 State St., Suite 110
San Diego 92101
(714) 235-9728

1708 Waller St.
San Francisco 94117
(415) 386-6726/7/8

2989 Mission St.
San Francisco 94110
(415) 824-5111/2

1648 E. Santa Clara
San Jose 95116
(408) 258-5600

361 S. Monroe St., Suite 5
San Jose 95128
(408) 249-1643

7222 Van Nuys Blvd. Suite E
Van Nuys 91406
(213) 988-6904/5

1406 Pacific Ave.
Venice 90291
(213) 392-4124/5/6

COLORADO

875 W. Moreno Ave.
Colorado Springs 80905
(303) 633-2902

1820 Gilpin St.
Denver 80218
(303) 861-9281/7521

CONNECTICUT

370 Market St.
Hartford 06120
(203) 278-1290

363 Whalley Ave.
New Haven 06510
(203) 624-7234/0355

DELAWARE

Van Buren Medical Center
1411 N. Van Buren St.
Wilmington 19806
(302) 571-8277

DISTRICT OF COLUMBIA

1101 Pennsylvania Ave., S.E.
Washington 20003
(202) 543-4701/2/3

402 H St. N.E.
Washington 20002
(202) 543-5225/1555

FLORIDA

400 N.E. 44th St.
Ft. Lauderdale 33444
(305) 563-2992/3

228 Pearl St.
Jacksonville 32202
(904) 358-1232

2615 Biscayne Blvd.
Miami 33137
(305) 573-8830/1/2

250 31st St., South
St. Petersburg 33712
(813) 821-3344

1507 W. Sligh Ave.
Tampa 33610
(813) 821-3355

GEORGIA

43 14th St., N.E.
Atlanta 30309
(404) 872-4614

HAWAII

1291 Kapiolani Blvd.
Honolulu 96814
(808) 546-3743

IDAHO

103 W. State St.
Boise 83702
(208) 342-3612

ILLINOIS

547 W. Roosevelt Rd.
Chicago 60607
(312) 829-4400

1100 W. Garfield Ave.
Oak Park 60304
(312) 383-3225

411 W. 7th St.
Peoria 61605
(309) 671-7359

INDIANA

101 N. Kentucky Ave.
Evansville 47711
(812) 425-6496

528 W. Berry St.
Fort Wayne 46802
(219) 423-9456

811 Massachusetts Ave.
Indianapolis 46204
(317) 269-2838

IOWA

2001 Cottage Grove Ave.
Des Moines 50312
(515) 282-4476

KANSAS

310 S. Laura St.
Wichita 67211
(316) 265-3260

KENTUCKY

821 S. 2nd St.
Louisville 40203
(502) 589-1981

LOUISIANA

1529 N. Claiborne
New Orleans 70116
(504) 943-8386

MAINE

175 Lancaster St. Rm. 213
Portland 04101
(207) 780-3584

MARYLAND

1420 W. Patapsco Ave.
Patapsco Plaza Shopping Ctr.
Baltimore 21230
(301) 355-8592

1153 Mondawmin Concourse
Mondawmin Shopping Ctr.
Baltimore 21215
(301) 728-8924

7 Elkton Commercial Plaza
Elkton 21921
(301) 398-0171

MASSACHUSETTS

480 Tremont St.
Boston 02116
(617) 451-0171/2/3

362 Washington St.
Brighton 02135
(617) 783-1343/4

15 Bolton Place
Brockton 02401
(617) 580-2720

MICHIGAN

5514 Woodward Ave.
Detroit 48202
(313) 871-3233

18411 W. Seven Mile Rd.
Detroit 48219
(313) 535-3333/4

MINNESOTA

3338 University Ave., S.E.
Minneapolis 55414
(612) 623-1970

MISSISSIPPI

522 North State St.
Jackson 39201
(601) 353-4912

MISSOURI

3600 Broadway, Suite 19
Kansas City 64111
(816) 753-1866/1974

2345 Pine St.
St. Louis 63103
(314) 231-1260/1/2

MONTANA

2708 Montana Ave.
Billings 59101
(406) 657-6071

NEBRASKA

1240 N. 10th St.
Lincoln 68508
(402) 476-9736

2510 Harney St.
Omaha 68131
(402) 344-8181

NEVADA

214 S. 8th St.
Las Vegas 89101
(702) 385-2212/3

341 S. Arlington St.
Reno 89501
(702) 323-1294

NEW HAMPSHIRE

14 Pearl St.
Manchester 03104
(603) 668-7060

NEW JERSEY

626 Newark Ave.
Jersey City 07306
(201) 656-6986/7484

601 Broad St.
Newark 07102
(201) 622-6940

NEW MEXICO

4603 4th St., N.W.
Albuquerque 87107
(505) 345-8366/8877

NEW YORK

226 E. Fordham Rd.
Rooms 216,217
Bronx, N.Y. 10458
(212) 367-3500

165 Cadman Plaza, East
Brooklyn 11201
(212) 330-2825

114 Elmwood Ave.
Buffalo 14201
(716) 882-0505

166 W. 75th St.
Manhattan 10023
(212) 944-2917

148-43 Hillside Ave.
Queens, New York 11435
(212) 658-6767/8

NORTH CAROLINA

#4 Market Square
Fayetteville 28301
(919) 323-4908

NORTH DAKOTA

1300 S. 13½ St.
Fargo 58103
(701) 237-0942

OHIO

31 E. 12th St., 4th Floor
Cincinnati 45202
(513) 241-9420

11511 Lorain Ave.
Cleveland 44111
(216) 671-8530/1/2

4959 N. High St.
Columbus 43214
(614) 436-0300

438 Wayne Ave.
Dayton 45410
(513) 461-9150

14206 Euclid Ave.
East Cleveland 44112
(216) 451-3200

OKLAHOMA

4111 North Lincoln Blvd., #10
Oklahoma City 73105
(405) 521-9308

OREGON

2450 S.E. Belmont
Portland 97214
(503) 231-1586

PENNSYLVANIA

1107 Arch St.
Philadelphia 19107
(215) 627-0238

954 Penn. Ave.
Pittsburgh 15222
(412) 765-1193

PUERTO RICO

Suite LC 8-A/9
Medical Center Plaza
La Riviera Rio Piedras
San Juan 00921
(809) 783-8269

RHODE ISLAND

172 Pine St.
Pawtucket 02860
(401) 728-9501

SOUTH DAKOTA

100 W. 6th St., Suite 101
Sioux Falls 57102
(605) 332-0856

SOUTH CAROLINA

3366 Rivers Ave.
No. Charleston 29405
(803) 747-8387

TENNESSEE

Sterick Bldg.
8 North 3rd St.
Memphis 38103
(901) 521-3506

TEXAS

500-A Lancaster-Kiest Ctr.
Dallas 75216
(214) 371-0490

2121 Wyoming St.
El Paso 79903
(915) 542-2851/2/3

3121 San Jacinto St.
Suite 106
Houston 77004
(713) 522-5354/5376

717 Corpus Christi
Laredo 78040
(512) 723-4680

107 Lexington Ave.
San Antonio 78205
(512) 229-4025

UTAH

216 E. 5th St., South
Salt Lake City 84102
(801) 584-1294

VERMONT

75 Woodstock Rd.
White River Junction 05001
(802) 295-2908

RFD #2, Tafts Corners
Williston 05495
(802) 878-3371

VIRGIN ISLANDS

Room 140-A, Federal Bldg.
U.S. Courthouse, Veterans Dr.
St. Thomas 00801
(809) 774-2769

VIRGINIA

7450½ Tidewater Dr.
Norfolk 23505
(804) 587-1338

WASHINGTON

1322 E. Pike St.
Seattle 98122
(206) 442-2706

North 1611 Division
Spokane 99208
(509) 326-6970

3591 South D. St.
Tacoma 98408
(206) 473-0731/2

WEST VIRGINIA

1014 6th Ave.
Huntington 25701
(304) 523-8387

WISCONSIN

1610 N. Water St.
Milwaukee 53202
(414) 271-6557/6387

WYOMING

1810 Pioneer St.
Cheyenne 82001
(307) 778-2660

U.S. Railroad Retirement Board

The U.S. Railroad Retirement Board is an independent agency in the executive branch of the Federal Government. The Board's primary function is to administer comprehensive retirement-survivor and unemployment-sickness benefit programs for the nation's railroad workers and their families, under the Railroad Retirement and Railroad Unemployment Insurance Acts. In connection with the retirement program, the Board has administrative responsibilities under the Social Security Act for certain benefit payments and railroad workers' Medicare coverage.

During the 1981 fiscal year, retirement-survivor benefits were running about $5 billion a year to over one million annuitants. Unemployment-sickness benefits were running approximately $260 million a year to over 200,000 beneficiaries.

Because of its experience with railroad benefit plans, the Board has been given, in recent years, administrative responsibility for certain employee protection measures provided by other Federal railroad legislation, such as the Regional Rail Reorganization Act, the Northeast Rail Service Act, the Milwaukee Railroad Restructuring Act, and the Rock Island Railroad Transition and Employee Assistance Act.

Development of the Railroad Retirement and Unemployment Insurance Systems

The Board was created in the 1930's by legislation establishing a retirement benefit program for the nation's railroad workers. Private industrial pension plans had been pioneered in the railroad industry; the first industrial pension plan in the United States was established on a railroad in 1874. By the 1930's, pension plans were far more developed in the rail industry than in most other businesses or industries; but these plans had serious defects which were magnified by the great depression.

The economic conditions of the 1930's demonstrated the need for retirement plans on a national basis, because few of the nation's elderly were covered under any type of retirement program. While the social security system was in the planning stage, railroad workers sought a separate railroad retirement system which would continue and broaden the existing railroad programs under a uniform national plan. The proposed social security system was not scheduled to begin monthly benefit payments for several years and would not give credit for service performed prior to 1937, while conditions in the railroad industry called for immediate benefit payments based on prior service.

Legislation was enacted in 1934, 1935, and 1937 to establish a railroad retirement system separate from the social security program legislated in 1935. Such legislation, taking into account particular circumstances of the rail industry, was not without precedent. Numerous laws pertaining to rail operations and safety had already been enacted since the Interstate Commerce Act of 1887. Since passage of the Railroad Retirement Acts of the 1930's, numerous other railroad laws have subsequently been enacted.

While the railroad retirement system has remained separate from the social security system, the two systems are closely coordinated with regard to earnings credits, benefit payments, and taxes. The financing of the two systems is linked through a financial interchange under which, in effect, the portion of railroad retirement annuities that is equivalent to social security benefits is reinsured through the social security system. The purpose of this financial coordination is to place the social security trust funds in the same position they would be in if railroad service were covered by the social security program instead of the railroad retirement program.

Following the recommendations of a Federal Commission on Railroad Retirement, legislation enacted in 1974 restructured railroad retirement benefits into two tiers, so as to coordinate them more fully with social security benefits. The first tier is based on combined railroad retirement and social security credits, using social security benefit formulas. The second tier is based on railroad service only and is comparable to the private pensions paid

Reprinted from "U.S. Railroad Retirement Board" [Information Sheet], U.S. Railroad Retirement Board, Chicago, IL 60611.

workers in other heavy industries.

The Board's unemployment insurance system was also established in the 1930's. The great depression demonstrated the need for unemployment compensation programs, and State unemployment programs had been established under the Social Security Act in 1935. While the State unemployment programs generally covered railroad workers, railroad operations which crossed State lines caused special problems. Because of differences in State laws, railroad employees working in the same jobs on the same railroad, but in different States, received different treatment and different benefit amounts when they became unemployed. Employees whose jobs required that they cross State lines sometimes found that they weren't eligible for benefits in any of the States in which they worked.

The National Security Commission, which reported on the nationwide State plans for unemployment insurance, recommended that railroad workers be covered by a separate plan because of the complications their coverage had caused the State plans. Congress subsequently enacted the Railroad Unemployment Insurance Act in June 1938. The Act established a system of benefits for unemployed railroaders, financed entirely by railroad employers and administered by the Board. Sickness benefits were added in 1946.

Railroad Retirement Act

Under the Railroad Retirement Act, the Board pays retirement and disability annuities to railroad workers with at least ten years of service. Benefits are also paid to spouses of retired workers and to survivors (widows, widowers, children, and parents) of deceased workers. Qualified railroad retirement beneficiaries are covered by Medicare in the same way as social security beneficiaries.

Jurisdiction over the payment of retirement and survivor benefits is shared by the Board and the Social Security Administration. The Board has jurisdiction over the payment of retirement benefits if the employee had at least ten years of railroad service; for survivor benefits, there is an additional requirement that the employee's last regular employment before retirement or death was in the railroad industry. If a railroad employee or his survivors do not qualify for railroad retirement benefits, the Board transfers the employee's railroad retirement credits to the Social Security Administration, where they are treated as social security credits.

The primary source of income for the railroad retirement-survivor benefit program is payroll taxes paid by railroad employers and their employees. By law, railroad retirement taxes are coordinated with social security taxes. Employees and employers pay tier I taxes at the same rate as social security taxes. In addition, both employees and employers pay tier II taxes which are used to finance railroad retirement benefit payments over and above social security levels. Historically, railroad retirement taxes have been considerably higher than social security taxes. On top of the regular retirement taxes, railroad employers also pay a cents per work-hour tax, determined quarterly by the Board, to finance a supplemental annuity program for career employees.

Other sources of income include the financial interchange with the social security trust funds, interest on investments, and appropriations from general treasury revenues provided after 1974 as part of a phase-out of certain dual benefits.

Railroad Unemployment Insurance Act

Under the Railroad Unemployment Insurance Act, the Board pays (1) unemployment benefits to railroad workers who are unemployed but ready, willing, and able to work and (2) sickness benefits to railroad workers who are unable to work because of illness or injury. The Board also operates a placement service to assist unemployed railroaders in securing employment.

A new unemployment-sickness benefit year begins every July 1, with eligibility generally based on railroad service and earnings in the preceding calendar year. Up to 26 weeks of normal unemployment or sickness benefits are payable to an individual in a benefit year. Additional extended benefits are payable for up to 13 weeks to persons with ten years of service and 26 weeks to those with 15 years of service.

The railroad unemployment-sickness benefit program is financed solely by taxes on railroad employers. The unemployment insurance tax rate fluctuates from year to year, depending on the balance of the account in the previous year.

Rail Reorganization Act of 1973
Northeast Rail Service Act of 1981
Milwaukee Railroad Restructuring Act
Rock Island Railroad Transition and Employee Assistance Act

In general, these Federal laws concern the restructuring of certain railroad operations in the northeast and midwest regions of the U.S. In addition to provisions concerning railroad operations in those areas, these laws include various protective measures for the employees of railroads affected by the legislation. The Board assists in the administration of the various employee protection measures, which can include subsistence allowances, supplemental unemployment benefits, new career training assistance payments, moving expense reimbursements, and special hiring rights.

Funding of the employee protection measures administered by the Board under the Rail Reorganization Act, Northeast Rail Service Act, Milwaukee Railroad Restructuring Act, and the Rock Island Railroad Transition and Employee Assistance Act is provided by Congressional appropriations.

Board Organization and Functions

The Board is headed by three members appointed by the President of the United States, with the advice and consent of the Senate. One member is appointed upon recommendation of railroad employers, one is appointed upon recommendation of railroad labor organizations and the third, who is the Chairman, is appointed to represent the public interest. The Board members' terms of office are five years and are scheduled to expire in different years.

The primary function of the Board is the determination and payment of benefits under the retirement-survivor and unemployment-sickness programs. To this end, the Board must maintain lifetime earnings records for covered employees, field representatives to assist railroad personnel and their families in filing claims for benefits, examiners to adjudicate the claims, and extensive electronic data processing equipment and technicians to process payments.

The Board also employs actuaries to predict the future income and outlays of the Railroad Retirement Account, statisticians and economists to provide statistics and other vital data necessary to conduct and maintain financial and claims operations, and attorneys to draft and interpret legislation and to represent the Board in litigation. Internal administration requires an audit and management analysis staff, a budget and accounting staff, and personnel specialists.

The Board's headquarters are located at 844 Rush Street in Chicago, Illinois.

The Board and the Federal Government

As an independent agency in the executive branch of the Federal Government, the Board reports to the President on its operations and to the Congress. Officials of the Board frequently testify at Congressional hearings on proposed legislation to amend the Railroad Retirement and Railroad Unemployment Insurance Acts. Congress has jurisdiction over the amounts available for benefit payments and for administration under the railroad retirement system.

The Board works closely with other Federal agencies and with some State agencies. Its dealings with some of these agencies, such as the President's Office of Management and Budget, the Office of Personnel Management, the General Accounting Office, and the Department of the Treasury, are similar to the dealings of other executive branch agencies with these units. The Board's relations with certain others—principally, the Social Security Administration, the Veterans Administration, the State employment security departments and, on a smaller scale, the Interstate Commerce Commission and the Department of Labor—are related directly or indirectly to the various benefit programs.

The Board and the Railroad Industry

The administrative organization of the Board fosters close relations with railroad employers, employees and their representatives. Two of the Board's three members are, by law, appointed on the recommendations of representatives of railroad employers and employees, respectively. In addition, representatives of railroad employers and employees, at the direction of Congress, have been active in the development of the Board's programs since the Board's inception.

The Board relies on railroad employers and labor groups for assistance in keeping railroad personnel informed about the Board's benefit programs. The Board conducts informational programs for railroad management and labor officials to acquaint them with the details of the benefit programs. These officials, in turn, educate railroad workers as to their benefit rights and responsibilities.

Railroad employers and railway labor groups also cooperate with the Board in a joint placement program to find jobs for unemployed personnel. These joint placement efforts help to reduce the costs of the unemployment benefit program. Railroad employers also provide claims agents, who assist those applying for unemployment benefits.

The Board has direct contact with railroad employees through its field offices. Board personnel in these offices explain benefit rights and responsibilities on an individual basis, assist employees in applying for benefits and answer any questions related to the Board's programs.

Major Differences Between Railroad Retirement and Social Security

U.S. Railroad Retirement Board

Annuities awarded under the Railroad Retirement Act are for substantially greater amounts than the benefits awarded under the Social Security Act. Railroad retirement annuities include a portion, called tier I, which is the equivalent of a social security benefit, and a second portion, tier II, which is comparable to the private industrial pensions payable over and above social security benefits. In addition, there are differences between some of the age requirements, the benefits available under the 2 systems and work restrictions.

Some of these basic differences are described in the following questions and answers.

1. What is the approximate difference in retirement benefit amounts awarded recent retirees under the Railroad Retirement and Social Security Acts?

For career railroad employees retiring directly from the railroad industry in fiscal year 1981, regular annuities, including 1981 cost-of-living increases, averaged about $920 a month. Monthly benefits awarded at the end of fiscal year 1981 to regularly employed workers covered under social security averaged about $530. If benefits for their spouses are added in this example, the combined benefits for the employee and spouse would approximate $1,450 under railroad retirement coverage compared to about $700 under social security coverage.

The Railroad Retirement Act also provides supplemental railroad retirement annuities of between $23 and $43, which are payable to employees who retire directly from the industry with 25 or more years of service. Adding a supplemental annuity to the railroad family's benefit increases total benefits to over $1,475 a month.

2. Are the benefits awarded to recent retirees generally greater than the benefits payable to those who retired years ago?

Yes. Under both railroad retirement and social security, the benefits awarded recent retirees are generally greater than the benefits payable to those who retired years ago, primarily because recent awards are based on higher average earnings. The average age retirement benefit paid at the end

of fiscal year 1981 to retired employees on the Board's rolls was $580 compared to $385 under social security. Spouse benefit payments averaged $250 under railroad retirement compared to $185 under social security.

3. How do disability awards to employees compare?

Disabled railroad workers retiring directly from the railroad industry in fiscal year 1981 received about $810 a month on the average, including the July 1981 cost-of-living increase, compared to about $430 a month for disabled workers under social security.

Under both railroad retirement and social security coverage, benefits are payable to workers who are totally disabled. The Railroad Retirement Act also provides disability benefits to career employees who are disabled for work in their regular railroad occupation, even though not totally disabled. The Social Security Act requires a 5-month waiting period before benefits are payable, while disability benefit payments under railroad retirement can be effective with the first month an employee is disabled.

4. What are the highest amounts recent retirees could receive?

The maximum monthly amount payable to an employee and spouse at the end of calendar year 1981 was about $1,660 under the Railroad Retirement Act, compared to about $1,100 under the Social Security Act. This example is based on a rail employee who began work in 1937 and continuously earned the maximum creditable toward retirement benefits each year through 1981. For example, under both systems, annual earnings up to $3,600 were creditable in 1951, while annual earnings up to $29,700 were creditable for 1981. Very few employees earn the maximum amount creditable each year throughout their careers, so these maximum benefits are payable to relatively few families.

5. Can railroaders retire at earlier ages than workers under social security?

Railroad employees with less than 30 years of service, and their spouses, can receive annuities at age 65, or at age 62 with an early retirement reduction. These age require-

Reprinted from "Major Differences Between Railroad Retirement and Social Security," U.S. Railroad Retirement Board, Chicago, IL 60611, February, 1982.

ments are the same as under social security. But, railroad employees with 30 or more years of service, and their spouses, can receive railroad retirement annuities at age 60, without an early retirement reduction.

6. Does social security offer any benefits which are not available under railroad retirement?

Social security does pay certain types of benefits which are not available under railroad retirement. For example, if an employee is disabled before retirement age and his wife is caring for minor or disabled children, social security pays additional benefits to the family members. However, the Railroad Retirement Act includes a special minimum guarantee provision, which insures that an employee's benefits will at least equal the amount that would be payable to the family under social security. Therefore, if a retired rail employee's family includes persons who would otherwise qualify under social security, the retired rail employee's annuity would be increased to reflect what social security would pay the family, unless the annuity is already greater than that amount.

7. How do railroad retirement and social security survivor benefits differ?

Survivor benefits are generally higher if payable by the Board rather than social security. Survivor benefits awarded by the Board to widows and widowers of railroaders in fiscal year 1981 averaged $470 a month, compared to about $340 under social security.

Both the railroad retirement and social security systems provide a lump-sum death benefit to help pay burial expenses. But, the railroad retirement lump-sum benefit is generally payable only if survivor annuities are not immediately due upon an employee's death, while the social security lump-sum benefit may be payable regardless of whether monthly benefits are also due. Under social security law, the lump-sum benefit is $255, while under railroad retirement the lump sum can be over $1,100 if the employee had completed 10 years of service before 1975.

The railroad retirement system also provides a residual lump-sum death payment which, in effect, insures that the railroad family receives at least as much in benefits as the employee paid in railroad retirement taxes before 1975. Reductions are made for any retirement benefit paid based on the deceased employee's railroad credits and for any survivor benefits paid by either the Board or the Social Security Administration. In general, if an employee had received railroad retirement benefits for a few years before death, the benefit payments would be greater than the railroad retirement taxes the employee paid; consequently,

a residual benefit would not be payable.

8. How do work restrictions differ between the 2 systems?

Under both railroad retirement and social security, retirement benefits may be reduced if an employee works after retirement. In 1982, a reduction of $1 in retirement benefits is made for every $2 earned over $6,000 for those age 65–71 and over $4,440 for those under age 65. Under social security, the entire benefit is subject to reduction; under railroad retirement, only a portion of employee and spouse annuities is subject to work reduction. Under both systems, the entire amount of survivor benefits is subject to work reductions. Special restrictions apply under both systems to any earnings by disabled workers.

The railroad retirement system requires that an employee or spouse actually retire, that is, stop working for the last employer before retirement. Railroad retirement benefits are not payable for any month an annuitant works for a railroad, and employee and spouse annuities are not payable for any month the annuitant works for the last pre-retirement employer. Under social security, an individual is not required to stop working for the last pre-retirement employer to receive benefits.

9. How do railroad retirement and social security taxes compare?

Historically, railroad retirement taxes have been considerably higher than social security taxes. In 1969 and 1970, they were almost twice as high as social security taxes. These higher railroad retirement taxes were required to finance the higher benefits payable under railroad retirement. While railroad retirement taxes on employees were reduced to the same rate paid by workers under social security in 1973, the taxes on railroad employers were increased to pick up the difference, so that the combined rate remained much higher than the combined rate on social security covered work.

The 1981 amendments to the Railroad Retirement Act substantially increased railroad retirement taxes on both employers and employees. In 1982, workers under both railroad retirement and social security pay retirement taxes of 6.7% on earnings up to $32,400 a year. Both railroad and social security covered employers match these retirement taxes. However, railroad employees also pay an additional 2% tax on earnings up to $24,300 a year, while their employers pay additional retirement taxes of 11.75% on earnings up to $24,300 a year. Railroad employers also currently pay a separate 17¢ per work-hour tax to finance the railroad retirement supplemental annuity program.

Retirement Tax on Sickness Benefits

U.S. Railroad Retirement Board

Recent legislation (Public Law 97-123) extended social security taxes to the first 6 months of sick pay. This law also amended the Railroad Retirement Tax Act so that the railroad retirement tier I tax (the social security level tax) will apply to both privately paid sickness benefits in the railroad industry and to sickness benefits paid under the Railroad Unemployment Insurance Act. In other words, these benefits are now considered to be "compensation" for purposes of the Railroad Retirement Tax Act, and thus subject to the tier I tax.

Although certain items of this legislation will require clarification, the following questions and answers outline its basic provisions as they apply to Railroad Retirement Board sickness payments.

1. Specifically, what sickness benefits will be subject to this tier I tax?

Under the new law, compensation subject to the railroad retirement tier I tax shall, effective January 1, 1982, include all payments made to an employee or his dependents on account of sickness or accident disability during the first 6 months the employee is off work. Excluded from this tax are payments which are made under a workmen's compensation law, payments under the Railroad Retirement Act, or payments under the Railroad Unemployment Insurance Act for days of sickness resulting from on-the-job injuries. Sickness benefits paid by the Railroad Retirement Board will, therefore, be subject to the tier I railroad retirement tax, unless the benefits are claimed because of on-the-job injuries.

2. If sickness benefits are now subject to the railroad retirement tier I tax will they also be considered as compensation for purposes of the Railroad Retirement Act?

No. The legislation, as currently written, makes no provision to credit these taxable benefits as compensation under either the Railroad Retirement or Railroad Unemployment Insurance Acts.

3. Will the Railroad Retirement Board withhold these taxes from sickness benefit payments?

Yes. The Board is required to deduct the employee's portion of the tier I taxes from the payment of taxable sickness benefits. The taxes the Board withholds then will be deposited with the Internal Revenue Service.

4. How much will this tax amount to?

The tier I railroad retirement tax rate is 6.7%. This means that if sickness benefits of $250.00 are otherwise payable for a 14-day claim period, $16.75 would be withheld for the tier I tax.

5. Will railroad employers also be subject to this tax?

Yes. In addition to withholding the employee's portion, the Board is to notify the employee's normal railroad employer of the sickness benefits paid. Upon notification by the Board, employers of the employees who receive these benefits will have to make matching tier I tax contributions.

6. Will the monthly maximum that applies to railroad retirement taxation be considered in the withholding of this tier I tax?

No. The taxes will be withheld without regard to the maximum amount taxable each month. In the event that an employee determines that taxes in excess of the maximum have been withheld, it will be up to the employee to seek a refund of these excess taxes when filing his or her Federal income tax return.

7. Will the Board notify those individuals who received these taxable benefits as to the amount received and the tax withheld?

Yes. At the end of calendar year 1982, and each succeeding year, the Board will send statements to sickness claimants showing the amount of sickness benefits paid which was subject to the tier I railroad retirement tax and the amount of tier I tax withheld.

Reprinted from "Retirement Tax on Sickness Benefits," U.S. Railroad Retirement Board, Chicago, IL 60611, March, 1982.

Changes in Student Benefits

U.S. Railroad Retirement Board

The 1981 amendments to the Social Security Act made major changes in the social security students benefit program. Because of coordination between the railroad retirement and social security systems, this legislation will affect payments of student benefits under the Railroad Retirement Act.

While this legislation is rather complex, the following questions and answers will outline its basic provisions and general effects on railroad retirement student survivor benefits.

1. How did the law change?

Under prior social security law, a student was defined as an individual 18–21 in full-time attendance at a qualified educational institution. A qualified educational institution could be a high school, college, junior college, trade or vocational school, and certain other institutions. Such student benefits ended at age 22 or with the end of the school term after attainment of age 22.

The social security amendments changed the definitions of a student and an educational institution. Beginning August 1982, a student is defined as a child under age 19 (changed from 22) in full-time attendance or deemed attendance at an elementary school or a secondary school (high school). Phase-out provisions will govern student benefits already in the process of payment.

Because railroad retirement laws concerning student benefits are cross-referenced with the social security laws, the Railroad Retirement Board will have to make certain corresponding changes in the benefits which it pays students. Beginning August 1982, the Board will be paying many student benefits to individuals, who have attained age 18, only until they complete high school or they attain age 19, whichever is earlier. However, benefits currently being paid by the Board to post-secondary school students, age 18–21, such as college students, can, under certain conditions, be continued under the phase-out provisions between now and 1985. And, some benefits will be paid on a limited basis, beyond age 19, under certain provisions of the railroad retirement laws not cross-referenced with social security laws.

These amendments do not affect benefits paid by the Board to minor children under age 18, or disabled children over age 18 receiving benefits on the basis of having become permanently disabled before age 22.

2. What requirements have to be met in order for an individual's student benefits to come under the phase-out provisions?

To qualify under the phase-out provisions, students, age 18–21, must have been attending a *post-secondary* school during a month prior to May 1982, and have been entitled to some kind of railroad retirement benefit, such as a minor child's benefit, as of August 1981. Post-secondary schools include colleges, junior colleges, universities and trade or vocational schools. The entitlement of these students can continue until they are age 22, provided entitlement does not terminate earlier because of death, marriage, or ceasing full-time attendance. If these students cease full-time attendance after July 1982, they cannot become re-entitled as students at a later date.

3. Will the phase-out payments be the same as those provided under previous law?

No. Beginning in 1982, benefits will no longer be payable for the months of May, June, July, and August. Benefits payable for September 1982 through April 1983 will be 25% less than the amount of the student's original benefit in effect for August 1981. Benefits payable for September 1983 through April 1984 will be 50% less than the original amount, and benefits payable for September 1984 through April 1985 will be 75% less.

In addition, future cost-of-living increases cannot be applied to whatever benefit rate these students are receiving between 1982 and 1985.

No benefits can be paid to such students after April 1985.

4. How will students who do not fall into the phase-out category be affected?

Generally, survivors attaining age 18 can now be paid benefits only until they complete high school or they reach age 19, whichever is earlier. But, benefits can be continued beyond age 19 until the student completes a course in

Reprinted from "Changes in Student Benefits," U.S. Railroad Retirement Board, Chicago, IL 60611, April, 1982.

progress, or for 2 months, whichever is earlier. Unlike phase-out students, they are entitled to cost-of-living increases and can be paid for the summer months if they are in actual or deemed attendance at an elementary or secondary school.

The benefits of those already in college or other post-secondary schools who do not meet the phase-out requirements will end after July 1982.

However, in some cases where the family's railroad retirement benefit entitlement first began after September 1981, student benefits may continue on a partial payment basis beyond age 19, until the student attains age 22 or completes requirements for a post-secondary school diploma, whichever is earlier. These exceptions are not phase-out students; the benefit payable would be limited to the amount by which a railroad retirement student benefit exceeds a social security student benefit.

5. **Do these changes affect any railroad employee retirement annuities?**

While student benefits are not payable to the children of retired employees who are still living, the existence of a student may, in some cases, serve to increase the retired employee's annuity.

These employee annuities will be adjusted accordingly, depending on the status of the student. Any change in the annuity would depend on the number of other family members included in the annuity computation. The annuity rate may decrease or the annuity may no longer be computed under the special formula that applies in these cases.

6. **What steps is the Railroad Retirement Board taking to implement this legislation?**

The Board's field offices are contacting individual students in their areas to compile information required for determinations regarding the status of their benefits. If students or retirees have questions about the effects of this new legislation they should contact the local Board office closest to them.

A Review of Fiscal Year 1980

U.S. Railroad Retirement Board

Benefit Operations

Retirement and survivor benefit payments totaled $4,731 million in fiscal year 1980, representing an increase of $456 million over the prior fiscal year. An estimated $230 million of this rise was attributable to the June 1979 cost-of-living increases, while an additional $125 million was due to the June 1980 increases. Cost-of-living increases of 9.9 percent in 1979 and 14.3 percent in 1980 were applied to the tier I component of employee and spouse annuities and to both tier I and tier II of survivor annuities. The tier I component is determined according to social security formulas and is automatically increased by the same cost-of-living percentage applicable to social security benefits. Cost-of-living increases were also applied to certain portions of the tier II component of employee and spouse annuities. Under the Railroad Retirement Act, the tier II increase is determined to be equal to 32.5 percent of the rise in the unadjusted Consumer Price Index between the first calendar quarter of one year and the corresponding period a year earlier. The employee and spouse tier II increases were 3.2 percent in 1979 and 4.6 percent in 1980. The following table presents benefit payment totals for fiscal years 1980 and 1979 and the percentage changes between years, by type of benefit:

Type of benefit	Amount (in millions)		Percent change
	Fiscal year 1980	Fiscal year 1979	
Retirement benefits:			
Employee annuities			
Regular	$2,633.3	$2,372.3	11.0
Supplemental	121.6	120.1	1.2
Spouse annuities	634.9	572.1	11.0
Total	3,389.8	3,064.5	10.6
Survivor benefits:			
Annuities	1,327.2	1,194.9	11.1
Lump-sum benefits	13.6	15.5	−12.6
Total	1,340.8	1,210.4	10.8
Total	4,730.6	4,274.9	10.7

At the end of the 1980 fiscal year, 1,203,000 monthly benefits were being paid, approximately 2,000 fewer than one year earlier. The number of monthly beneficiaries declined by almost 8,000 during the year to 1,006,000

Reprinted from *1980 Annual Report for Fiscal Year Ending September 30,* U.S. Railroad Retirement Board, Chicago, IL 60611.

as of September 30, 1980. The number of benefits is larger than the number of beneficiaries because some retired employees receive more than one type of benefit. The second benefit is usually a supplemental employee annuity, but in some cases it is a spouse or widow(er)'s annuity. Regular employee age annuities being paid totaled 356,000, almost 3,000 fewer than a year earlier. An increase of 11,000 in the number who had retired between the ages of 60–64 with 30 or more years of service (60/30 annuitants) was more than offset by a decline of 13,000 in the number of normal age annuitants. At the end of the fiscal year, 94,000 60/30 annuities and 195,000 normal age annuities were being paid. The number who had retired at ages 62–64 with a reduced annuity remained at 67,000. The number of disability annuities declined by nearly 2,000 to a total of 95,000 at the end of the fiscal year. Spouse annuities numbered 234,000, nearly the same as a year earlier. Supplemental annuities being paid increased by over 5,000 to 188,000 by the end of the year. Survivor annuities declined by over 3,000 to 330,000, primarily due to a decrease in the number of aged widow(er)s and children being paid.

Chart 2 compares benefit payments for fiscal year 1980 and for the same 12-month period five years earlier. Over the five-year interval, total benefit payments increased by $1,541 million, or 48 percent, largely as a result of the higher average benefit amounts being paid. The overall cost-of-living increase in 1980 averaged 10.9 percent for all annuities, contributing to a 36 percent cumulative cost-of-living increase during the five-year period. Awards during the five years were generally based on longer service and higher compensation than those which were terminated. Charts 3 and 4 present the changes over the five-year interval in the number of beneficiaries on the rolls and the average amounts being paid. Despite an overall decline in the number of beneficiaries during the five-year period, the dramatic increases in average annuity amounts paid over the same period resulted in increased benefit payments.

Retirement

Regular employee annuities.—During fiscal year 1980, the number of regular annuity awards increased, albeit slightly, for the first time in five years. All of the increase was in the number of full age annuities awarded; the number of reduced age and disability annuity awards continued to decline. Data on regular employee annuity awards for fiscal year 1980 are compared, by type of annuity, in the following table:

Type of annuity	Number	Percent	Average		
			Annuity amount	Years of service	Age at retirement
Age:					
Beginning at age 65 or over	4,600	17	$562	24.3	66.0
Full, beginning at ages 60–64	13,100	50	898	35.9	61.7
Reduced, beginning before age 65	3,100	12	308	17.6	62.9
Disability	5,600	21	620	25.0	55.7
Total	26,400	100	711	29.5	61.3

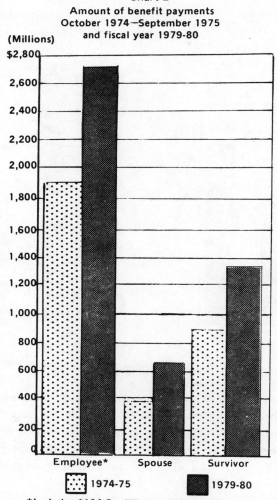

Chart 2
Amount of benefit payments
October 1974—September 1975
and fiscal year 1979-80

(Millions)

1974-75   1979-80

*Includes $104.5 million in 1974-75 and $121.6 million in 1979-80 for supplemental annuities.

Full age annuities were awarded in the fiscal year to 4,600 employees who retired at age 65 or over and 13,100 employees who retired at ages 60-64 with 30 or more years of service. The average length of service for the 60/30 retirees was 36 years. Approximately 3,100 reduced age annuities were awarded to employees ages 62-64 with less than 30 years of service. Reduced age retirees, whose annuities are reduced by 1/180 for each full month they are under age 65 when their annuities begin, had an average of 18 years of railroad service. Award averages varied considerably depending on the basis of retirement. Reduced age retirees were awarded an average annuity of $308, while normal age and 60/30 retirees were awarded annuities averaging $562 and $898, respectively.

Disability annuity awards numbered 5,600 during the fiscal year and averaged $620. Employees may be granted a disability annuity based either on total disability precluding all employment or on disability only in their regular occupation. Awards for the year included 1,800, averaging $344, based on total disability and 3,800, averaging $752, based on occupational disability. The number of occupational disability awards is somewhat over-

Chart 3

Number of monthly beneficiaries
September 30, 1975 and 1980

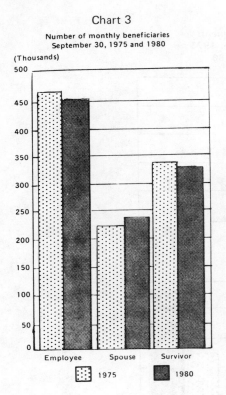

1975   1980

Chart 4

Average annuity amounts
September 30, 1975 and 1980

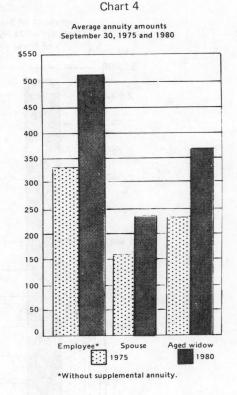

1975   1980

*Without supplemental annuity.

stated, however, as many employees who were totally disabled were initially awarded occupational disability annuities. In order to expedite payment, totally disabled employees initially are awarded an occupational disability annuity if they meet the age and service requirements, since the medical standards for occupational disability are less stringent than those for total disability.

Approximately 75 percent of the employees awarded disability annuities during the fiscal year will meet the medical standards for a "disability freeze" determination. The standards for the freeze are determined according to social security law and are comparable to criteria used by the Board in determining total disability. If a freeze is granted, months within the freeze period may be excluded from the computation of the tier I benefit, which generally results in higher annuity amounts. In addition, the employee can qualify for Medicare before age 65 if the freeze beginning date is 30 or more months before attainment of that age.

Survivor

Monthly benefits. — Annuity awards to survivors of deceased employees numbered 20,700 in fiscal year 1980. Awards to widow(er)s included 16,800 to aged widow(er)s, 600 to disabled widow(er)s, and 800 to widowed mothers (fathers). Children's awards included 1,600 to minor children (under age 18), 600 to full-time students ages 18-21, and 300 to disabled children ages 18 and older who became permanently disabled before age 22.

Over 330,000 survivor annuities were being paid at the end of the fiscal year, including over 2,000 to widow(er)s temporarily being paid a spouse annuity pending conversion to a survivor annuity. Aged widow(er)s numbered 290,000, accounting for 88 percent of all survivor annuitants on the rolls at the end of fiscal year 1980. Other survivor annuitants on the rolls included 7,000 disabled widow(er)s, 5,000 widowed mothers (fathers), and over 27,000 children. About 200 parents' annuities and 300 survivor option annuities were also being paid. A parent at age 60, dependent for at least one-half of his or her support on a railroad employee, may be paid a survivor annuity if the employee leaves no other survivors who can qualify for an annuity. Survivor option annuities are paid to the surviving spouse of an employee who made an election before August 1946 to receive a reduced retirement annuity in order to provide an annuity for the spouse after the employee's death. The following table shows numbers and average amounts of survivor annuities, by type of annuity, for annuities awarded during the fiscal year and for those being paid at the end of the year:

Type of annuity	Awarded in fiscal year 1980		In current-payment status on September 30, 1980	
	Number	Average amount	Number	Average amount
Aged widow(er)s'	16,800	$424	290,200	$361
Disabled widow(er)s'	600	317	7,000	302
Widowed mothers' (fathers')	800	416	5,000	392
Children's:				
Under age 18	1,600	381	11,200	373
Student	600	420	5,600	396
Disabled	300	358	10,500	298
Parents'	1	327	200	310
Survivor option	1	281	300	98
Total	20,700	. . . .	330,000	. . . .

[1] Fewer than 50.

Survivor annuities, like regular employee and spouse annuities, consist of up to three components. The survivor tier I component is computed according to social security formulas and is based on the deceased employee's combined railroad and social security earnings. This amount is subject to reduction for receipt of a social security benefit, railroad retirement annuity, government pension, or for early retirement. The tier II component of a survivor annuity is equal to 30 percent of the survivor tier I amount, prior to reduction for the survivor's own railroad retirement or social security benefits, but after any other reductions. A dual benefit windfall may be payable to widows or certain widowers who were fully insured under social security law based on their own earnings as of December 31, 1974, provided the deceased employee had at least 10 years of railroad service prior to 1975.

If aged widow(er)s elect to receive benefits between the ages of 60 and 64, both the tier I and tier II components are reduced by 19/40 of one percent for each month they are under age 65 when the annuity begins, with a maximum reduction of 36 months, or about 17 percent. The 94,000 aged widow(er)s receiving reduced annuities were being paid an average monthly amount of $345 at the end of the fiscal year, while the annuities of aged widow(er)s receiving full rates averaged $368. The average net tier I amount paid to aged widow(er)s as of September 30, 1980, was $268, but in 24,000 cases the tier I amount was wholly offset by reductions. The average tier I offset due to social security entitlement was $225. Tier II benefits paid to aged widow(er)s averaged $107. A total of 135,000 aged widow(er)s were receiving social security benefits, averaging $237. In addition, approximately 58,000 aged widow(er)s were being paid windfall benefits, averaging $45.

The tier I and tier II components of disabled widow(er)s ages 50–59 are reduced by 28-1/2 percent, plus 43/240 of one percent of the full annuity amount for each month they are under age 60 when their annuities begin. At age 50, this is equal to a 50 percent reduction. Disabled widow(er)s on the rolls at the end of the fiscal year were paid tier I amounts averaging $230 and tier II amounts averaging $82. Nearly 2,100 disabled widow(er)s received social security benefits, averaging $245. The average tier I reduction for these benefits was $219. Windfall benefits, averaging $66, were being paid to nearly 1,700 disabled widow(er)s.

Widowed mothers (fathers) under age 60, whose eligibility is based on having a minor or disabled child in their care, are paid a tier I benefit similar to a social security benefit. This survivor tier I amount is generally equal to 75 percent of the full tier I amount payable to aged widow(er)s, prior to any reductions. Eligible children and grandchildren are paid the same tier I amount. The tier II amount paid these beneficiaries is 30 percent of the tier I amount prior to reduction for social security entitlement. However, if the sum of the tier I amounts for all family members exceeds the social security family maximum, then all tier I benefits are reduced proportionately to total that maximum, with corresponding reductions of the tier II amounts. A reduction for the family maximum generally occurs when three or more family members are eligible to receive survivor benefits. The average net tier I amounts being paid to widowed mothers (fathers) and children at the end of the fiscal year were $301 and $268, respectively. The corresponding tier II amounts were $92 and $84. Social security benefits were paid to 100 widowed mothers (fathers) and 2,900 children, averaging $247 and $163, respectively. Average tier I reductions for social security benefits were $218 and $155, respectively. Windfall benefits, averaging $73, were paid to 100 widowed mothers (fathers). Children and dependent parents are not eligible for windfall benefits.

The average age of aged widow(er)s on the rolls at the end of fiscal year 1980 was 78 years. The average age of 63 years for disabled widow(er)s was considerably lower since this type of benefit is awarded at ages 50–59 and has been in effect only since 1968. The average age for widowed mothers (fathers) was 52; this type of benefit terminates when the youngest child attains age 18, unless the child is disabled. Average ages for minor and student children were 15 and 20 years, respectively. The average age of 49 years for disabled children was relatively high, as this type of annuity begins after age 18 and is usually payable for life.

Lump-sum benefits. — Two types of lump-sum benefits are payable to survivors of deceased railroad employees — an insurance lump sum and a residual payment.

An insurance lump-sum benefit is payable at the time of the employee's death only if there are no survivors immediately eligible for monthly benefits. When an insurance lump sum is not payable at death, a deferred lump sum can be paid 12 months later, if the total of monthly benefits paid to a widow(er) during the year is less than the full insurance lump-sum amount would have been. For survivors of employees with 10 years of railroad service prior to 1975, the insurance lump sum is based on earnings through 1974, with a maximum benefit of nearly $1,200. Insurance lump sums to survivors of employees with less than 10 years of service prior to 1975 are limited to $255, the same as social security lump-sum payments.

Insurance lump sums awarded during the fiscal year numbered 11,800 and averaged $785. About 11,700 of these awards were regular insurance lump sums, averaging $785, while the remaining 100 were deferred lump sums, averaging $804. The regular lump sums included 2,000 to widow(er)s and 9,700 to the individuals, usually the employee's adult children, who paid the employee's funeral expenses. The deferred payments were to widow(er)s who worked for most or all of the year following the employee's death.

Residual payments guarantee that railroad employees and their survivors will receive at least as much in benefits as the employee paid in railroad retirement taxes for the years 1937-74. A residual payment, which includes an allowance in lieu of interest, can only be made if no other benefits based wholly or in part on railroad service will be payable in the future. It is reduced for any retirement benefits that have been paid on the basis of the employee's railroad service, and for any survivor benefits previously paid by either the Railroad Retirement Board or the Social Security Administration. Widow(er)s and parents under age 60 can elect to waive their rights to future benefits based on the employee's railroad service in order to receive the residual payment. Awards of residual payments during the fiscal year totaled 1,000 and averaged $5,760. Widow(er)s received almost 500 of these payments based on an election to waive future benefits. The balance of the residual payments were made to other relatives, designated beneficiaries, or the employee's estate.

Administrative Rulings

The following administrative rulings which were rendered during the 1980 fiscal year have been selected for inclusion in this report because of their special significance or interest.

Railroad Retirement and Survivor Benefits

1. The amount of a supplemental annuity which is subject to reduction for an employee's entitlement to an employer pension under Section 2(h)(2) of the Railroad Retirement Act was determined to be the net supplemental annuity after reduction for the railroad retirement maximum required by Section 3(f)(1).

2. The General Counsel held that, in determining the work deduction component of an individual's annuity, the amount subject to work deductions should first be adjusted for any military service reduction pursuant to Section 2(h)(1) of the Act.

3. The General Counsel's opinion L-80-122 discussed the application of Section 3(f)(3) of the Act in determining whether a child is to be included in the computation of the amount payable under the social security minimum provision. This opinion held that, in order for a child to be included in the computation under this section, the child must have attained the status of "child" as defined in the Social Security Act at the time the employee's annuity begins or at the termination of a period of disability, whichever comes later.

4. Section 6(c)(1) of the Railroad Retirement Act provides that a residual lump sum may be paid, under certain circumstances, when it appears that no benefits or further benefits will be payable. The General Counsel ruled that a residual lump sum may be paid in a case where, due to a reduction for receipt of a public pension, the annuity rate is zero.

5. The Board's Bureau of Law reviewed Section 867.03 of the Wisconsin statutes, which provides for administration of small estates, and determined that the Board may pay a lump-sum death benefit pursuant to that section. That section requires that an affidavit be filed showing a description and the total value of the decedent's property within the State of Wisconsin. Thus, when the amount of the Board's lump-sum death benefit is shown on the affidavit, the Board may pay the lump-sum death payment to the affiant.

6. It was held that the Courts of New York would recognize a valid common law marriage arising between the parties during a brief vacation in Michigan in 1953, where the parties, domiciled in New York, were free to marry and subsequently cohabited as husband and wife, and the existence of an agreement to marry could be inferred or be said to have continued from day to day.

7. It was held that to rebut a presumption in favor of the validity of a subsequent marriage under Arkansas law where one party to such a subsequent marriage is deceased, the person challenging the validity of that marriage must provide conclusive proof that no divorce from the prior marriage was obtained by either party to such marriage.

8. The General Counsel held that a long-term disability plan established by an employer may be considered a supplemental pension plan under Section 2(h)(2) of the Railroad Retirement Act.

Beneficiaries and benefit payments under the Railroad Retirement and Railroad
Unemployment Insurance Acts, by fiscal year, 1971-80

Fiscal year	Total	Retirement	Survivor	Unem-ployment	Sickness
BENEFICIARIES (in thousands)					
1970-71..........................	1,373	718	372	249	86
1971-72..........................	1,426	714	380	317	82
1972-73..........................	1,232	712	377	105	74
1973-74..........................	1,177	708	381	48	71
1974-75..........................	1,225	733	380	78	67
1975-76..........................	1,265	740	377	105	77
July-September 1976..............	1,119	700	350	42	34
1976-77..........................	1,258	743	378	86	83
1977-78..........................	1,268	742	374	108	82
1978-79..........................	1,251	737	370	101	79
1979-80..........................	1,254	731	367	118	76
BENEFIT PAYMENTS (in millions)					
1970-71..........................	$ 2,004.8	$ 1,435.0	$ 474.8	$ 45.0	$ 50.1
1971-72..........................	2,242.0	1,603.4	518.5	80.7	39.4
1972-73..........................	2,529.6	1,831.3	625.5	41.2	31.6
1973-74..........................	2,721.0	1,961.3	709.3	22.4	28.1
1974-75..........................	3,127.5	2,222.4	837.9	37.5	29.6
1975-76..........................	3,687.4	2,481.3	987.8	143.0	74.9
July-September 1976..............	963.5	652.9	264.0	25.7	20.9
1976-77..........................	3,966.6	2,712.0	1,074.9	101.7	78.0
1977-78..........................	4,185.4	2,853.1	1,134.9	128.0	69.3
1978-79..........................	4,416.8	3,064.5	1,210.4	81.1	60.8
1979-80..........................	4,942.9	3,389.8	1,340.8	148.5	63.7
Cumulative through September 1980.............	[1]58,297.0	[2]39,929.7	13,791.4	[3]3,056.0	1,518.9

1/   Includes a small amount of payments for hospital insurance benefits for services in Canada.
2/   Includes supplemental annuity payments.
3/   Includes extended benefits paid under temporary emergency programs spanning 1957-62 period.

NOTE.—Number of beneficiaries represents all individuals paid benefits in year or in transition
quarter. In total number for each year, beneficiaries are counted only once, even though they may have
received more than one type of benefit; in total count for transition quarter, the small number of
duplications resulting from individuals being paid benefits under both the Railroad Retirement Act and
the Railroad Unemployment Insurance Act was not removed because precise data were not available. In
1979-80, some 14,000 individuals received both retirement and survivor benefits, 15,000 employees
received both unemployment and sickness benefits, and 9,000 employees received benefits under both the
Railroad Retirement Act and the Railroad Unemployment Insurance Act. These figures are partly
estimated, and totals for earlier years are similarly adjusted.

Retirement, survivor, unemployment and sickness benefit payments, by class of benefit and state of residence of beneficiary, fiscal year 1980
(In thousands)

State	Total	Retirement benefits	Survivor benefits	Unemployment benefits	Sickness benefits
Alabama	$ 72,546	$ 47,436	$23,164	$ 1,158	$ 788
Alaska	588	331	185	61	11
Arizona	65,579	49,764	13,378	2,063	374
Arkansas	68,018	46,201	18,039	2,918	860
California	339,078	245,480	84,918	4,917	3,763
Colorado	67,567	47,323	18,014	1,610	619
Connecticut	30,525	21,225	8,415	494	391
Delaware	14,955	10,118	4,310	302	225
District of Columbia	13,639	9,658	3,621	223	137
Florida	219,492	163,764	53,022	1,385	1,320
Georgia	101,073	69,203	28,988	1,305	1,577
Hawaii	1,960	1,435	519	3	3
Idaho	32,383	24,837	6,154	919	472
Illinois	346,970	233,306	90,733	17,038	5,893
Indiana	134,396	87,867	38,266	5,931	2,332
Iowa	83,480	53,916	23,365	5,226	974
Kansas	112,680	79,432	28,853	3,162	1,232
Kentucky	112,389	71,962	34,970	3,438	2,020
Louisiana	64,377	42,498	20,160	848	871
Maine	25,349	17,264	6,840	885	361
Maryland	86,989	60,318	23,852	1,352	1,467
Massachusetts	62,362	42,477	17,903	1,472	510
Michigan	115,704	73,702	30,172	9,260	2,570
Minnesota	137,780	96,816	36,091	3,375	1,498
Mississippi	44,164	28,575	14,059	971	559
Missouri	171,501	118,218	45,591	5,723	1,969
Montana	43,939	31,561	9,605	1,998	775
Nebraska	74,215	51,841	17,902	3,145	1,327
Nevada	16,737	12,472	3,828	295	143
New Hampshire	9,776	6,369	3,223	120	64
New Jersey	117,270	80,151	33,536	2,192	1,391
New Mexico	35,854	25,718	8,069	1,736	331
New York	284,388	193,581	78,979	8,439	3,389
North Carolina	67,947	46,243	20,313	733	659
North Dakota	23,366	16,589	5,603	871	303
Ohio	284,419	185,388	79,106	15,540	4,385
Oklahoma	46,219	30,007	12,980	2,854	378
Oregon	68,242	51,345	14,829	1,290	778
Pennsylvania	423,483	286,363	117,642	13,364	6,113
Rhode Island	7,692	5,266	2,121	239	65
South Carolina	37,453	24,952	11,305	773	423
South Dakota	12,187	7,938	3,343	756	149
Tennessee	97,420	63,402	31,211	1,722	1,086
Texas	251,872	175,231	69,608	3,821	3,212
Utah	48,477	37,090	10,182	744	460
Vermont	10,826	7,249	3,253	265	59
Virginia	139,827	94,377	41,640	2,202	1,609
Washington	82,420	58,788	19,759	2,772	1,100
West Virginia	84,621	54,947	25,941	2,486	1,246
Wisconsin	89,261	60,345	24,669	3,166	1,082
Wyoming	25,315	18,690	5,555	745	326
Outside United States:					
Canada[1]	21,921	13,928	7,702	217	73
Mexico	4,023	2,708	1,315	2/	2/
All others	7,899	3,943	3,949	7	1
Total	[1] 4,942,853	[3] 3,389,789	[3] 1,340,756	148,534	63,720

1/ Includes $54,000 in hospital insurance benefits for services in Canada.
2/ Less than $500.
3/ Includes $183,000 in retirement and $4,000 in survivor tax refund payments.

NOTE.—Data partly estimated.

Number and average amount of retirement and survivor annuities in current payment status on September 30, 1980, by type of annuity and status of annuitant under Social Security Act

Type of annuity	Total		Annuitants receiving social security benefits				Annuitants not receiving social security benefits	
	Number	Average railroad retirement annuity	Number	Percent of total	Average railroad retirement annuity	Average social security benefit	Number	Average railroad retirement annuity
EMPLOYEE ANNUITIES								
All retirements:								
Full age.............	288,800	$575	106,000	37	$384	$251	182,800	$687
Reduced age.........	67,200	315	46,300	69	244	268	20,800	474
Disability..........	[1]95,200	477	32,000	34	290	242	63,200	571
Total.............	451,200	516	184,300	41	332	254	266,900	643
Immediate retirements[2]:								
Full age.............	245,800	633	71,700	29	480	198	174,100	696
Reduced age.........	27,800	468	13,500	49	395	205	14,300	537
Disability..........	70,300	547	16,600	24	384	181	53,700	597
Total.............	343,900	602	101,900	30	453	196	242,000	664
Deferred retirements[2]:								
Full age.............	43,000	248	34,300	80	183	363	8,700	505
Reduced age.........	39,400	208	32,800	83	182	295	6,600	337
Disability..........	24,900	278	15,400	62	188	308	9,500	423
Total.............	107,300	240	82,500	77	183	326	24,800	429
SPOUSE ANNUITIES								
Full rate............	125,900	$287	70,400	56	$212	$232	55,500	$382
Reduced rate........	108,000	177	77,200	72	147	192	30,800	253
Total.............	233,900	236	147,600	63	178	211	86,300	336
SURVIVOR ANNUITIES[3]								
Aged widow(er)s......	287,900	361	135,100	47	250	237	152,800	459
Disabled widow(er)s..	[4]7,000	302	2,100	29	189	245	4,900	348
Widowed mothers (fathers)..........	5,000	392	100	2	216	247	4,800	396
Children:								
Under age 18.......	11,200	373	500	4	236	161	10,700	379
Full-time students, ages 18-22.......	5,600	396	400	7	237	172	5,200	408
Disabled, over age 18..............	10,500	298	2,000	19	179	162	8,500	326
Total.........	327,100	359	140,100	43	248	236	187,000	442

1/ Includes 53,300 annuities now payable as age annuities.
2/ Retirement is considered immediate if the annuity began in the calendar year of employee's last railroad service or in the following year; all others are considered deferred.
3/ Excludes interim widows', survivor (option), and parents' annuities.
4/ Includes 4,900 annuities now payable as aged widows' annuities.

Insurance lump-sum benefits and residual payments awarded, fiscal years 1971-80

Fiscal year	Total		Status of employee at death			
			Nonretired		Retired	
	Number	Average amount	Number	Average amount	Number	Average amount
INSURANCE LUMP SUMS[1]						
1970-71..................	15,277	$705	2,498	$860	12,779	$674
1971-72..................	16,150	714	2,452	873	13,698	686
1972-73..................	14,348	728	1,991	902	12,357	700
1973-74..................	15,128	734	1,903	928	13,225	706
1974-75..................	13,902	743	1,613	962	12,289	715
1975-76..................	12,353	753	1,293	987	11,060	726
July-September 1976.....	4,150	755	411	995	3,739	728
1976-77..................	12,995	764	1,266	987	11,729	740
1977-78..................	12,346	772	1,192	991	11,154	748
1978-79..................	11,980	781	1,155	990	10,825	758
1979-80..................	11,657	785	1,050	980	10,607	766
Cumulative 1947-80....	550,707	...	150,935	...	399,772	...
RESIDUAL PAYMENTS						
1970-71..................	3,702	$4,050	2,762	$4,265	940	$3,418
1971-72..................	4,112	4,475	3,068	4,779	1,044	3,583
1972-73..................	3,229	4,865	2,428	5,361	801	3,360
1973-74..................	2,871	5,395	2,141	5,965	730	3,722
1974-75..................	2,347	5,820	1,812	6,306	535	4,175
1975-76..................	1,931	6,033	1,450	6,485	481	4,664
July-September 1976.....	463	6,118	353	6,740	110	4,123
1976-77..................	1,668	6,171	1,269	6,674	399	4,571
1977-78..................	1,374	5,863	1,079	6,189	295	4,671
1978-79..................	1,212	6,237	946	6,670	266	4,699
1979-80..................	1,002	5,760	852	6,075	150	3,970
Cumulative 1938-80....	300,996	.....	275,885	.....	25,111	.....

1/ Excludes 14,952 deferred lump-sum benefits, of which 112 averaging $804 were awarded in 1979-80.

NOTE.—There have been 32,925 tax refund awards, of which 3,033 averaging $62 were made in 1979-80.

Survivor annuities in current-payment status on September 30, 1980, by type and component

Component	Total		Aged widows and widowers		Disabled widows and widowers		Widowed mothers and fathers	
	Number	Average	Number	Average	Number	Average	Number	Average
Total, railroad..........................	327,300	$359	287,900	$361	7,000	$302	5,000	$392
Tier I, net.................................	301,800	267	263,500	268	6,200	230	4,900	301
Gross tier I............................	327,300	360	287,900	368	7,000	399	5,000	305
Offset for social security benefit[1]......	143,200	226	138,000	228	2,100	221	100	224
Age reduction...........................	100,800	46	93,800	40	7,000	127	.....	....
Tier II, total.............................	327,300	104	287,900	107	7,000	82	5,000	92
Regular tier II........................	327,300	104	287,900	106	7,000	81	5,000	91
Additional tier II[2].....................	3,600	72	3,200	76	100	106	100	51
Dual railroad retirement-social security windfall.................................	59,300	46	57,600	45	1,700	66	100	73
Social security benefit.....................	140,200	236	135,100	237	2,100	245	100	247

	Children—							
	Under age 18		Students ages 18-22		Ages 18 and over and disabled		Parents	
	Number	Average	Number	Average	Number	Average	Number	Average
Total, railroad..........................	11,200	$373	5,600	$396	10,500	$298	200	$310
Tier I, net.................................	11,100	287	5,600	305	10,200	228	200	218
Gross tier I............................	11,200	292	5,600	314	10,500	252	200	337
Offset for social security benefit[1]......	500	151	400	163	2,000	154	100	211
Tier II, total.............................	11,200	88	5,600	94	10,500	76	200	102
Regular tier II........................	11,200	88	5,600	94	10,500	76	200	102
Additional tier II[2].....................	3/	55	3/	20	300	13	3/	5
Social security benefit.....................	500	161	400	172	2,000	162	100	215

1/   Includes offset for tier I portion of employee annuity.
2/   Includes spouse minimum increases, conversion from 1937 Act increases, and restorations of tier I reduction for receipt of employee annuity.
3/   Fewer than 50.

NOTE.—Detail will not produce overall average annuity amounts as deductions for work and other adjustments are not reflected. Component data based on cases where record is available. Data exclude 300 survivor (option) annuities and 2,500 annuities to widow(er)s temporarily being paid at spouse rates pending final adjudication of survivor annuities.

Survivor annuities in current-payment status on September 30, 1980, and awarded in fiscal year 1980, by type and amount

Amount of annuity	Total[1]		Aged widows and widowers		Disabled widows and widowers		Widowed mothers and fathers		Children— Under age 18 or students ages 18-22		Children— Ages 18 and over and disabled	
	Number	Percent	Number	Percent	Number	Percent	Number	Percent	Number	Percent	Number	Percent
IN CURRENT-PAYMENT STATUS ON SEPTEMBER 30, 1980												
Less than $100	3,100	1	2,300	1	100	2	2/	2/	200	1	500	5
$100 to $149.99	16,800	5	15,500	5	500	7	100	1	300	2	500	4
$150 to $199.99	33,500	10	31,000	11	800	12	100	3	600	4	1,000	9
$200 to $249.99	34,300	10	30,700	11	900	12	300	5	1,100	7	1,400	13
$250 to $299.99	30,400	9	25,800	9	900	14	400	8	1,600	10	1,600	15
$300 to $349.99	32,900	10	27,400	10	1,300	18	500	10	1,700	10	1,900	18
$350 to $399.99	37,300	11	28,800	10	1,300	19	1,100	23	3,500	21	2,500	24
$400 to $449.99	34,100	10	27,800	10	900	13	1,100	22	3,400	21	800	8
$450 to $499.99	41,100	13	37,900	13	300	4	600	13	2,100	8	200	2
$500 to $549.99	47,400	14	45,500	16	2/	2/	400	9	1,300	4	100	1
$550 to $599.99	10,900	3	9,900	3	2/	..	200	4	700	1	2/	2/
$600 to $649.99	4,000	1	3,800	1	...	..	2/	2/	100	2/	2/	2/
$650 to $699.99	1,100	2/	1,000	2/	...	..	2/	2/	100	2/	....	..
$700 and over	500	2/	400	2/	...		2/	2/	2/		....	..
Total	327,300	100	287,900	100	[3] 7,000	100	5,000	100	16,800	100	10,500	100
Average annuity	.....		$361		$302		$392		$381		$298	

See footnotes at end of table.

Survivor annuities in current-payment status on September 30, 1980, and awarded in fiscal year 1980, by type and amount—Continued

Amount of annuity	Total[1]		Aged widows and widowers		Disabled widows and widowers		Widowed mothers and fathers		Children—Under age 18 or students ages 18-22		Children—Ages 18 and over and disabled	
	Number	Percent	Number	Percent	Number	Percent	Number	Percent	Number	Percent	Number	Percent
AWARDED IN FISCAL YEAR 1980												
Less than $100	200	1	100	1	2/	2	2/	1	2/	1	2/	3
$100 to $149.99	300	1	200	1	2/	2	2/	2/	100	2	2/	4
$150 to $199.99	800	4	600	4	2/	8	2/	2	100	4	2/	5
$200 to $249.99	1,700	8	1,400	9	100	15	2/	4	200	8	2/	6
$250 to $299.99	1,800	8	1,400	8	100	19	100	7	200	8	2/	8
$300 to $349.99	1,800	9	1,400	8	100	16	100	10	300	12	2/	11
$350 to $399.99	2,200	10	1,700	10	100	16	100	13	200	10	100	25
$400 to $449.99	2,500	12	1,800	11	100	13	200	21	400	19	100	18
$450 to $499.99	2,600	12	2,100	12	2/	7	100	17	300	13	2/	9
$500 to $549.99	3,600	17	3,100	19	2/	2	100	16	300	14	2/	5
$550 to $599.99	1,800	9	1,600	9	2/	2/	100	7	200	8	2/	3
$600 to $649.99	900	4	900	5	...	...	2/	1	2/	1	2/	1
$650 to $699.99	400	2	400	2	...	...	2/	2/	2/	2/	...	...
$700 and over	100	1	100	1	...	...	...	...	...	...	...	...
Total	20,700	100	16,800	100	600	100	800	100	2,200	100	300	100
Average annuity	....		$424		$317		$416		$392		$358	

1/ Includes annuities to dependent parents.
2/ Fewer than 50 or less than 0.5 percent.
3/ Includes 4,900 annuities now payable as aged widow(er)s' annuities.

NOTE.—Data exclude 300 survivor (option) annuities averaging $98 and 2,500 annuities to widow(er)s temporarily being paid at spouse rates pending final adjudication of survivor annuities.

Survivor annuities in current-payment status on September 30, 1980, and awarded in fiscal year 1980, by type and age of annuitant

Age of annuitant[1]	Total[2]		Aged widows and widowers		Disabled widows and widowers		Widowed mothers and fathers		Children— Under age 18 or students ages 18-22		Children— Ages 18 and over and disabled	
	Number	Percent	Number	Percent	Number	Percent	Number	Percent	Number	Percent	Number	Percent
IN CURRENT-PAYMENT STATUS ON SEPTEMBER 30, 1980												
Under 10	1,000	3/	...	...	...	...	...	...	1,000	6	...	...
10 to 17	10,100	3	...	...	...	...	...	...	10,100	60	...	...
18 to 21	5,800	2	...	...	...	...	...	...	5,600	33	200	2
22 to 29	1,100	3/	...	...	...	...	3/	1	[4]100	1	1,000	9
30 to 39	2,300	1	...	...	...	...	400	7	...	...	1,900	18
40 to 49	3,700	1	...	...	2,100	30	1,500	29	...	...	2,300	21
50 to 59	7,400	2	...	...	4,500	64	2,500	50	...	...	2,800	26
60 to 69	57,700	18	50,800	18	400	6	600	12	...	...	1,800	17
70 to 79	119,300	36	118,400	41	...	...	3/	3/	...	...	500	5
80 to 89	99,900	31	99,700	35	...	...	...	...	...	...	100	1
90 and over	19,000	6	19,000	7	...	...	...	...	...	...	3/	3/
Total	327,300	100	287,900	100	[5]7,000	100	5,000	100	16,800	100	10,500	100
Average age	....		77.8		62.6		51.5		16.3		48.5	

See footnotes at end of table.

Survivor annuities in current-payment status on September 30, 1980, and awarded in fiscal year 1980, by type and age of annuitant—Continued

Age of annuitant[1]	Total[2]		Aged widows and widowers		Disabled widows and widowers		Widowed mothers and fathers		Children— Under age 18 or students ages 18-22		Children— Ages 18 and over and disabled	
	Number	Percent	Number	Percent	Number	Percent	Number	Percent	Number	Percent	Number	Percent
AWARDED IN FISCAL YEAR 1980												
Under 10	300	2	...	...	...	...	...	...	300	15	...	...
10 to 17	1,200	6	...	...	...	...	...	...	1,200	56	...	...
18 to 21	700	3	...	...	...	...	...	...	600	29	3/	9
22 to 29	100	3/	...	...	...	...	3/	3	3/ 4/	3/	100	18
30 to 39	200	1	...	...	...	...	100	13	...	...	100	31
40 to 49	300	2	...	...	...	...	300	34	...	...	100	20
50 to 59	1,000	5	...	...	600	100	400	45	...	...	100	17
60 to 69	8,300	40	8,200	49	...	...	3/	6	...	...	3/	4
70 to 79	5,900	29	5,900	35	...	...	...	...	...	...	...	...
80 to 89	2,400	12	2,400	15	...	...	...	...	...	...	...	...
90 and over	300	1	200	1	...	...	...	...	...	...	...	...
Total	20,700	100	16,800	100	600	100	800	100	2,200	100	300	100
Average age	.....		70.4		54.4		47.4		15.1		38.5	

1/ Age on birthday in fiscal year 1980 for annuities in current-payment status at end of year and age on beginning date for annuities awarded in year.

2/ Includes annuities to dependent parents.

3/ Fewer than 50 or less than 0.5 percent.

4/ Students eligible until end of semester following 22nd birthday.

5/ Includes 4,900 annuities now payable as aged widow(er)s' annuities.

NOTE.—Data exclude 300 survivor (option) annuities and 2,500 annuities to widow(er)s temporarily being paid at spouse rates pending final adjudication of survivor annuities.

Railroad Retirement Board Benefits

Annuities are payable to surviving widows and widowers, children and certain other dependents. Insurance lump-sum benefits are payable after the death of a railroad employee only if there are no qualified survivors of the employee immediately eligible for annuities. With the exception of a lump-sum residual death benefit, eligibility for survivor benefits depends on whether or not the employee was "insured" under the Railroad Retirement Act at the time of death.

An employee is insured if he or she has at least 10 years of railroad service and a "current connection" with the railroad industry at the time of retirement or death. The current connection requirement is described at the beginning of this pamphlet.

If a deceased employee was not so insured, jurisdiction of any survivor benefits payable is transferred to the Social Security Administration and survivor benefits are paid by that agency instead of the Board. Regardless of which agency has jurisdiction, the deceased employee's railroad retirement and social security credits will both be used for the purpose of benefit computations.

Types of Survivor Benefits

Annuities are payable to widows, widowers, parents and unmarried children; in certain cases, benefits

Reprinted from "Railroad Retirement and Survivor Benefits," U.S. Railroad Retirement Board, Chicago, IL 60611, January, 1982.

are also payable to surviving divorced wives
(husbands) and mothers (fathers), remarried
widow(er)s and grandchildren.

WIDOWS' and WIDOWERS' ANNUITIES are payable at:

- Age 60 or over.

- At any age if the widow(er) is caring for
  a child under age 18 (16 in some cases),
  or a child over age 18 who was disabled
  before age 22.

- At ages 50-59 if the widow(er) is permanently disabled and unable to work in any
  regular employment. The disability must
  have begun within 7 years after the
  employee's death or within 7 years after
  the termination of an annuity based on
  caring for a child.

Survivor annuities may also be payable to a
surviving divorced wife (husband), surviving
divorced mother (father) or remarried widow(er),
but the amounts payable are limited to what social
security would pay.

To be eligible a surviving divorced wife (husband)
must have been married to the employee for at
least 10 years, have attained age 60 (or be
between ages 50-59 and totally disabled) and not
be married. A surviving divorced mother (father)
must not be married, must be under age 60 and must
be caring for children of the employee who are
under age 16 or disabled.

If a widow(er) has remarried, she or he must, to
be eligible, have remarried after age 60 or the
remarriage must have ended; and she or he must
have attained age 60 (or be between ages 50-59 and
totally disabled) or be under age 60 and have in
her or his care a child of the employee under age
16 or disabled.

OTHER SURVIVOR ANNUITIES are payable to:

- A child under age 18.

- A child over age 18 if the child became permanently disabled before age 22.

- A child age 18-21 attending school full-time. Such student benefits end at age 22 or with the end of the school term after attainment of age 22.

- A dependent grandchild meeting any of the requirements described above for a child, if both the grandchild's parents are deceased or disabled.

- A parent at age 60 who was dependent on the employee for at least half of the parent's support provided the employee did not leave a widow, widower, or child who can qualify for an annuity.

Survivor Annuity Estimates

The best way for survivors to obtain an annuity estimate is to visit the nearest Board district office. Active or retired employees who are concerned about the amount of benefits which would be payable to their survivors may also receive estimates from the nearest Board district office. The following information may be helpful in providing an idea of the amount of potential survivor benefits:

- The average annuity awarded to widow(er)s in 1981 was $460 a month. Children received $430 a month, on the average. Total family benefits for widows or widowers with children averaged $1,050 a month.

- If the spouse of a retired employee is receiving an annuity from the Board, the survivor annuity will be at least as much as the spouse annuity.

Survivor Annuity Tiers

Survivor annuities, like retirement annuities, consist of tier I and tier II components.

Tier I is based on the deceased employee's combined railroad retirement and social security credits, and is equivalent to the amount that would have been payable under social security.

Tier II amounts under new formulas are percentages of the deceased employee's tier II amount, as described in the section on formulas at the back of this pamphlet. However, until October of 1986, most survivor tier II amounts awarded will be paid under the previous formula, which yielded 30% of the survivor tier I amount.

Survivor Annuitants Also Receiving Social Security Benefits

The tier I annuity portion is reduced by the amount of any social security benefits received by a survivor annuitant, even if the social security benefit is based on the survivor's own earnings. This reduction follows the principles of social security law under which only the higher of a retirement or survivor benefit is, in effect, payable to a beneficiary. The tier II amount, however, is not reduced for social security benefits.

When dual benefits are payable, the railroad retirement and social security payments are generally combined into a single check issued through the Board.

Widows or Widowers Also Entitled to Public Pensions

The tier I annuity portion of a widow's or widower's annuity may be reduced by the amount of any Federal, State or local government pension based on the annuitant's earnings. The reduction does not apply if the employment on which the public pension is based was covered under social security as of the last day of the individual's employment.

The tier II amount is not affected by any tier I reduction for a public pension.

Widows or Widowers Also Receiving Railroad Retirement Employee Annuities

If a widow or widower is qualified for a railroad retirement employee annuity as well as a survivor annuity, a special guarantee applies if either the deceased employee or the survivor annuitant completed 120 months of railroad service before 1975. In effect, the widow or widower would receive both an employee annuity and a survivor annuity, without a full dual benefit reduction.

If either the deceased employee or the survivor annuitant had some service before 1975 but had not completed 120 months of railroad service before 1975, the employee annuity and the tier II portion of the survivor annuity would be payable. The tier I portion of the survivor annuity would be payable only to the extent that it exceeds the tier I portion of the employee annuity.

If both the widow or widower and the deceased employee started railroad employment after 1974, only the railroad retirement employee annuity or the survivor annuity, whichever is larger, is, in effect, payable to the widow or widower.

Cost-Of-Living Increases in Survivor Annuities

Tier I benefits are increased automatically for the cost of living, based on increases in the Consumer Price Index (CPI). Tier I increases are made at the same time, July 1, and by the same percentage, 100% of the CPI increase, as increases in social security benefits. Tier II increases are based on 32.5% of the CPI increase and are payable at the same time as the tier I increase.

If a survivor annuitant is receiving both railroad retirement and social security benefits, the

increased tier I portion is reduced by the
increased social security benefit.

Certain guarantee amounts payable in addition to
tiers I and II are not subject to cost-of-living
increases.

Work and Earnings Limitations

- A survivor annuity is not payable for
  any month the survivor works for a
  railroad or railroad union.

- Except for annuities based on disability, the annuities of survivors
  under age 72 in 1982 (70 in 1983) are
  reduced $1 for every $2 of earnings over
  $6,000 in 1982, or $4,440 if the survivor
  is under age 65.

In the first year benefits are payable, work
deductions apply only if monthly earnings are
greater than 1/12 of the annual exempt amount.

These earnings restrictions do not apply to
disabled widows or widowers under age 60 or to
disabled children. However, any work or earnings
by a disability annuitant is reviewed to determine
whether it indicates recovery from the disability.

When Survivor Payments Stop

- Payment stops upon death, and no annuity
  is payable for the month of death.

- A widow's or widower's annuity will
  stop if (1) she or he remarries, but a
  widow(er) may, under certain conditions,
  qualify for a remarried widow(er)'s benefit
  as previously described, (2) the annuity was
  based on caring for a minor or disabled child
  and the child is no longer under age 18 (16
  in some cases) or disabled (the annuity can
  resume when the widow or widower becomes age
  60), or (3) the annuity was based on
  disability and the widow or widower recovers

from the disability before age 60. A
disabled widow's or widower's annuity can be
reinstated if the disability recurs within 7
years.

- A child's or grandchild's annuity will stop
if he or she (1) marries, (2) reaches age 18
(if the child is a full-time student, it
stops at age 22, or at the end of the first
school semester after attainment of age 22),
or (3) recovers from the disability on which
his or her annuity was based.

- A parent's survivor annuity will stop upon
remarriage.

Insurance Lump-Sum Benefit

An insurance lump-sum benefit is payable to
survivors of an employee with 10 or more years of
railroad service and a current connection with the
railroad industry if there is no one in the family
immediately eligible for an annuity upon the
employee's death.

The amount payable depends primarily on whether
the deceased employee (1) was credited with 10
years of service before January 1, 1975, in which
case the maximum insurance lump-sum benefit
payable is close to $1,200, or (2) completed 10
years of railroad service after 1974, in which
case the lump-sum benefit is almost always $255.

The insurance lump-sum benefit is first payable to
the widow or widower either living with the
employee or supported by such employee at the time
of death. If the employee had 10 years of service
prior to 1975, and was not survived by a qualified
widow or widower, the lump sum may be paid to the
funeral home or the payer of the funeral expenses
but the amount paid cannot exceed the actual costs
involved.

If a widow or widower is eligible for monthly
benefits at the time of the employee's death, but
the survivor had excess earnings deductions which

prevented annuity payments or for any other reason did not receive the equivalent of 12 months of benefits, the difference between the lump-sum benefit and monthly benefits actually paid, if any, is payable in the form of a deferred lump-sum benefit.

Residual Lump-Sum Payment

There is one type of death benefit--a residual payment--for which an insured status is not required. The residual lump sum is, in effect, a refund of a deceased employee's pre-1975 railroad retirement taxes plus an allowance in lieu of interest. The maximum residual payable is almost $14,000. However, the residual is reduced for any retirement benefits that have been paid on the basis of the employee's railroad service, and for any survivor benefits previously paid by either the Railroad Retirement Board or the Social Security Administration. Therefore, if an employee received an annuity for 2 or more years, there is little chance that a residual would be payable to his or her survivors.

A residual cannot be paid if there are immediate or future monthly survivor benefits payable. However, a widow, widower or parent who would be eligible in the future can, before attaining age 60, elect to waive future rights to monthly benefits in order to receive the residual payment. Before such an election, a widow(er) or parent is required to consult with personnel in one of the Board's district offices since future monthly benefits are generally more valuable than the lump-sum payment.

Once a residual is paid, no future benefits payable by either the Social Security Administration or the Board will reflect credit for the employee's railroad earnings.

Furthermore, the widow(er) or parent electing a residual also gives up rights to Medicare based on the deceased employee's railroad service. While such a widow(er) could qualify for Medicare as an uninsured person, she or he would have to pay substantial premiums for hospital insurance coverage, in addition to the normally required medical insurance premiums.

The residual payment is made to the employee's widow or widower, children, grandchildren, parents, brothers and sisters, or estate, in that order of precedence. If an employee wishes any residual payment that may become due to be made differently, he or she can file a designation of beneficiary with the Board. Such forms are available at any district office. Once such a designation is made, the employee must file a new one if he or she ever wants to change the beneficiary.

LEGAL INFORMATION/ TAXES AND LAWS

Legal Information/ Taxes and Laws

This section provides data on some legal aspects of the subjects covered elsewhere in this sourcebook.

While it is not possible here to sum up the current status of state and federal tax law for the United States, one can locate current information on tax law with the aid of a good law library. Following is a brief review of the methods and materials for conducting legal research pertaining to death and dying.

Legal Research

Although there are no shortcuts to becoming a lawyer or tax expert, it is possible to learn to use large portions of any law library's maze of materials. The key is understanding that most law libraries are organized in the same way. An expert is able to pick out the precise volume of interest from among thousands of books because he or she understands this country's system of citation.

The system of citation has two major functions. First, it enables the lawyer or judge to determine at a glance the degree of authority behind whatever principle, rule, or interpretation is being cited. For example, West Publishing Company's *Federal Reporter* series contains opinions written by judges in appellate courts only. If the case hadn't been appealed, it would not have been included in any of the hundreds of volumes of this series.

The second, and probably more important, function of the citation is its role in providing the precise page number of the exact volume that contains the piece of information sought. For example, to find 526 F.2d 35 the researcher would go to the shelf containing the *Federal Reporter* (F.), second series (2d), look for volume number 526, and turn to page 35. Any law library will contain books and pamphlets explaining precisely how these abbreviations and numbers translate into names of books and page numbers. The best of these sources is entitled *A Uniform System of Citation* (usually referred to as the "Blue Book"), published by the Harvard Law Review Association.

Other volumes that will introduce the researcher to citation and to law library materials include:

Cohen, Morris. *Legal Research in a Nutshell.* St. Paul, MN: West Publishing Co., 1968 (updated every few years).

The Living Law. Rochester, NY: The Lawyers Cooperative Publishing Co., 1978. Of particular interest to researchers on death and dying are the federal tax volumes discussed in this guide. Rewritten annually, they are also supplemented during the year when the tax law changes.

West's Law Finder. St. Paul, MN: West Publishing Co., 1978. This volume gives information on using West Publishing Company's law books, including the on-line computer retrieval system WESTLAW and an ultrafiche edition of the *National Reporter* system.

Finally, for those who seek information on state laws pertaining to death, dying, and taxes, *Legal Research in a Nutshell* provides a list of state research guides.

Note that many other more comprehensive books on legal research are also available, but they would require lengthier study to be of use to the layperson.

Legal Periodicals

The next step in finding information on death-related taxes or any other legal subject would be to consult the large number of legal periodicals. Those periodicals fall into the general categories of law school reviews, bar association journals, newspapers on law, specialized commercial journals, and specialized scholarly journals. A selection of all of these can be found in any law library.

The key to using the legal periodicals lies in the various indexes available. Your local law library should contain one or more of the following indexes.

Index to Legal Periodicals. Covering almost 400 periodicals, this index is particularly useful because it is arranged by subject as well as by other categories. One could, for example, look up the Uniform Anatomical Gift Act or the subject of dying confessions in the index, find numerous law review articles dealing with either topic, and with the aid of the citator, then find and read the article listed in the index. The law review article itself will contain many citations for other sources of information, specific areas of tax law (for example), case law, or even other articles.

Harvard Current and Annual Legal Bibliography. This index includes 2,500 periodicals and 8,000 monographs per year. It is arranged by subject as well as legal system and country.

Index to Periodical Articles Related to Law. Includes journals not indexed in *Index to Legal Periodicals* or in the foreign edition of that index.

Current Index to Legal Periodicals (University of Washington Law Library and *Washington Law Review*). This index covers law school reviews and other major periodicals.

Index to Canadian Periodical Literature. With more than 60 periodicals represented, this index is arranged by subject as well as other headings.

Readers may also be interested in a periodical digest published by Commerce Clearing House, *Federal Tax Articles,* which comes with monthly supplements.

Tax experts and law firms usually receive the regularly published *Internal Revenue Bulletins,* as well as the Treasury Department's *Cumulative Bulletins* (which are also available in bound form at the end of each year), but the casual researcher would not necessarily be able to find anything important concerning the area of tax law in which he is interested in an isolated bulletin.

The Treasury Department bulletins are just one of the looseleaf services published in the legal field. The following list includes other such services.

Looseleaf Services
Taxes
Published by Commerce Clearing House:
Federal Taxes—IRS Letter Rulings

Standard Federal Tax Reporter
State Tax Guide
State Tax Reporter
Tax Court Reporter
Published by Prentice-Hall:
Federal Taxes Citator
Federal Taxes—Private Letter Rulings
Federal Taxes Service
Property Tax Service
State and Local Taxes
State Income Taxes Service
Tax Court Service
Tax Ideas
Published by Research Institute of America:
Tax Coordinator
Tax Guide
Published by Bureau of National Affairs:
Tax Management—U.S. Income
Tax Management—Primary Sources
Published by Institute for Business Planning:
Tax Planning

Estate Planning/Wills
Published by Commerce Clearing House:
Inheritance, Estate and Gift Taxes
Published by Institute for Business Planning:
Estate Planning
Published by Prentice-Hall:
Inheritance Taxes
Successful Estate Planning Ideas and Methods
Wills, Estates and Trusts
Published by Bureau of National Affairs:
Tax Management—Estates, Gifts, and Trusts

Insurance
Published by Commerce Clearing House:
Insurance Law Reporter
Published by Matthew Bender & Company:
Benefits Review Board Service
Published by Prentice-Hall:
Insurance Guide

To gain access to a law library, check with local universities. Many cities also have law libraries that are open to the public. In addition, national or state bar associations may be able to steer researchers to nearby law libraries. Check the following list of bar associations in the United States for groups in your area.

Bar Associations

American Bar Association

PREFACE

This is the latest edition of our annual Directory of Bar Associations. The Directory contains the name, address and telephone number of the president, president-elect or vice president and executive director or executive secretary of every listed bar association; the year when the bar association was founded; the approximate number of members in each association; and the date of the association's next annual meeting. The survey was conducted in the fall of 1981. Wherever possible, the information has been updated through November, 1981.

Features include American Bar Association information, rankings of the bar associations by size of membership and a map illustrating the location of states with unified bars. We hope that all who receive the Directory will find it a valuable reference source. To those people who supplied the information, we offer our sincere thanks. Corrections and update information should be sent to the Division of Bar Services.

AMERICAN BAR ASSOCIATION

	President	President-Elect	Executive Director
American Bar Association Founded 1878 282,210 Members A/M: August, 1982	David R. Brink 2200 First Bk. Plc. East Minneapolis, MN 55402 612/340-2704	Morris Harrell 4200 Republic Nat'l Bk. Twr. Dallas, TX 75201 214/742-1021	Thomas H. Gonser 1155 E. 60th Street Chicago, IL 60637 312/947-4020

Division of Bar Services Staff

77 South Wacker Drive, 6th Floor
Chicago, IL 60606

ALAN E. KURLAND, Director - (312) 621-9285
BRAD G. CARR, Staff Director - (312) 621-9286
JOHN J. SWEENEY, Staff Director - (312) 621-9287
ROSEANNE THEIS, MAP Program Coordinator - (312) 621-9284
KATHI SCHACHINGER, Field Service Representative - (312) 621-9281
LORRAYNE J. COMER, Staff Assistant - (312) 621-9289
SHARON E. PALMER, Administrator - (312) 621-9288
CALLIE R. LACY, Clerk-Analyst - (312) 621-9288
ELLA WILLIS, Clerk-Analyst - (312) 621-9284

CANADIAN BAR ASSOCIATION

	President	President-Elect	Executive Director
Canadian Bar Association Founded 1896 28,124 Members A/M: August, 1982	Paul D. K. Fraser 1570 Avord Bldg. 777 Hornby St. Vancouver, BC V6Z 1T3 604/687-3216	L. Yves Fortier, c.r. 700-Place Ville Marie Montreal, Quebec H3B 1Z7 514/875-5424	Bernard Blanchard 130 Albert St. Suite 1700 Ottawa, Ontario K1P 5G4 613/237-2925

STATE BAR ASSOCIATIONS

Association	President	President-Elect or Vice President	Executive Director or Executive Secretary
*Alabama State Bar Founded 1879 6,208 members A/M: July, 1982	Broox G. Garrett P.O. Box 387 Brewton 36424 205/869-6063	Norborne C. Stone, Jr. P.O. Box 1109 Bay Minette 36507 205/937-2417	Reginald T. Hamner P.O. Box 671 Montgomery 36101 205/269-1515
*Alaska Bar Assn. Founded 1955 1,615 members A/M: May, 1982	Karen L. Hunt 1007 West Third Ave. Suite 400 Anchorage 99501 907/279-3581	Andrew J. Kleinfeld 200 N. Cushman St., Ste. 201 Fairbanks 99701 907/452-1305	Randall P. Burns P.O. Box 279 Anchorage 99510 907/272-7469
*State Bar of Arizona Founded 1933 6,828 members A/M: May, 1982	Jack Redhair 234 N. Central Ave., #858 Phoenix 85004 602/252-4804	William F. Haug 111 W. Monroe, Ste. 800 Phoenix 85003 602/258-6292	Eldon L. Husted 234 N. Central, Ste. 858 Phoenix 85004 602/252-4804
Arkansas Bar Assn. Founded 1899 2,724 Members A/M: June, 1982	James D. Cypert Box 869 Springdale 72764 501/751-5222	James L. Shaver Box 592 Wynne 72396 501/238-2317	C. E. Ransick 400 W. Markham Little Rock 72201 501/375-4605
*State Bar of California Founded 1927 75,000 Members A/M: October, 1982	Samuel L. Williams 611 West Sixth Street, #2220 Los Angeles 90017 213/626-0671	Dale I. Stoops 266 Grand Ave., #200 Oakland 94610 415/893-5040	555 Franklin St. San Francisco 94102 415/561-8200
Colorado Bar Assn. Founded 1897 7,028 A/M: September, 1982	David L. Wood P.O. Box 2003 Ft. Collins 80521 303/484-2928	Katherine Tamblyn 718 17th St., Ste. 1220 Denver 80202 303/534-1580	Charles C. Turner 205 W. 14th St., Ste. 800 Denver 80204 303/629-6873
Connecticut Bar Assn. Founded 1875 6,800 Members A/M: June, 1982	Maxwell Heiman 43 Bellevue Ave. Bristol 06010 203/589-4343	Jack H. Evans 261 Bradley St. New Haven 06507 203/772-4900	Daniel Hovey 15 Lewis St. Hartford 06103 203/249-9141
Delaware State Bar Assn. Founded 1923 946 Members A/M: June, 1982	Bruce M. Stargatt P.O. Box 391 Wilmington 19899 302/571-6615	E. Norman Veasey P.O. Box 551 Wilmington 19899 302/658-6541	Charles R. Harris 25 Public Bldg. Wilmington 19801 302/658-5278
*The District of Columbia Bar Founded 1972 35,471 Members A/M: June, 1982	James J. Bierbower 1426 H St., N.W., 8th Fl. Washington 20005 202/638-1500	Jacob A. Stein 1426 H St., N.W., 8th Fl. Washington 20005 202/638-1500	J. David Ellwanger 1426 H St., N.W., 8th Fl. Washington 20005 202/638-1500
Bar Assn. of the District of Columbia Founded 1871 4,600 Members A/M: June, 1982	Frank J. Martell 1215 - 19th St., N.W., #1215 Washington 20036 202/331-8330	Thomas P. Jackson 1120 - 20th St., N.W., #1120 Washington 20036 202/457-1600	Marie J. Rivera 1819 H St., N.W., #300 Washington 20006 202/223-1480
*The Florida Bar Founded 1950 28,429 Members A/M: June, 1982	Samuel S. Smith 1111 Lincoln Rd. Mall Miami Beach 33139 305/673-1100	James C. Rinaman P.O. Box 447 Jacksonville 32201 904/335-6681	John F. Harkness, Jr. The Florida Bar Center Tallahassee 32301 904/222-5286

---

*Unified Bar
A/M: Date of Annual Meeting

State Bar Associations (Cont.)

Association	President	President-Elect or Vice President	Executive Director or Executive Secretary
*State Bar of Georgia Founded 1964 14,000 Members A/M: June, 1982	J. Douglas Stewart P.O. Box 430 Gainesville 30503 404/536-0101	Frank Love, Jr. 1100 C & S Bank Bldg. Atlanta 30335 404/572-6608	Allan Kirwan 84 Peachtree St. 11th Fl. Atlanta 30303 404/522-6255
Hawaii State Bar Assn. Founded 1899 1,930 Members A/M: November, 1982	James E. Duffy, Jr. P.O. Box 26 Honolulu 96810 808/536-0802	B. Martin Luna P.O. Box 26 Honolulu 96810 808/244-7914	Eleanor I. Pierce P.O. Box 26 Honolulu 96810 808/537-1868
*Idaho State Bar Founded 1923 1,610 Members A/M: July, 1982	Donald L. Burnett, Jr. P.O. Box 4645 Pocatello 83201 208/233-0780	Richard C. Fields P.O. Box 829 Boise 83701 208/345-2334	Leta Dally P.O. Box 895 Boise 83701 208/342-8958
Illinois State Bar Assn. Founded 1877 25,800 Members A/M: June, 1982	Michel A. Coccia 130 E. Randolph St., #2700 Chicago 60601 312/861-2810	John E. Feirich 2001 W. Main St. P.O. Box 2408 Carbondale 62901 618/529-3000	John H. Dickason Illinois Bar Center Springfield 62701 217/525-1760 800/252-8908
Indiana State Bar Founded 1896 7,580 Members A/M: October, 1982	Frank W. Campbell 198 South 9th St. P.O. Box E Noblesville 46060 317/773-2090	Leon R. Kaminski 916 Lincolnway Ste. 202, P.O. Box 516 LaPorte 46350 219/362-1577	Jack Lyle 230 E. Ohio, 6th Fl. Indianapolis 46204 317/639-5465
Iowa State Bar Assn. Founded 1874 5,900 Members A/M: June, 1982	Roger L. Lande P.O. Box 619 300 First National Building Muscatine 52761 319/263-8771	John A. McClintock 803 Fleming Bldg. Des Moines 50309 515/244-2141	Edward H. Jones 1101 Fleming Bldg. Des Moines 50309 515/243-3179
Kansas Bar Assn. Founded 1882 3,600 Members A/M: May, 1982	Charles E. Henshall P.O. Box 667 Chanute 66720 316/431-2600	John J. Gardner P.O. Box 548 Olathe 66061 913/782-2350	Ken Klein 1200 Harrison St. P.O. Box 1037 Topeka 66601 913/234-5696
*Kentucky Bar Assn. Founded 1871 7,513 Members A/M: May, 1982	William W. Lawrence 1916 Ky. Home Life Bldg. Louisville 40202 502/583-4484	Charles Landrum, Jr. 210 Security Trust Bldg. Lexington 40507 606/255-2424	Leslie G. Whitmer West Main at Kentucky River Frankfort 40601 502/564-3795
*Louisiana State Bar Assn. Founded 1941 10,500 Members A/M: April, 1982	Edward F. Glusman P.O. Box 2630 Baton Rouge 70821 504/387-5551	Henry B. Alsobrook, Jr. 4500 One Shell Sq. New Orleans 70139 504/581-3234	Thomas O. Collins, Jr. 225 Baronne St., Ste. 210 New Orleans 70112 504/566-1600
Maine State Bar Assn. Founded 1891 1,596 Members A/M: January, 1982	John N. Kelly 53 Exchange St. Portland 04101 207/775-1020	Ralph I. Lancaster 1 Monument Sq. Portland 04111 207/773-6411	Edward M. Bonney 124 State St. P.O. Box 788 Augusta 04330 207/622-7523
Maryland State Bar Assn. Founded 1896 8,400 Members A/M: June, 1982	J. Michael McWilliams 201 N. Charles St. Ste. 2300 Baltimore 21201 301/752-6100	James C. Chapin Capitol Office Park 6301 Ivy Lane, Ste. 808 Greenbelt 20770 301/345-4300	William J. Smith, Jr. Suite 905 207 E. Redwood St. Baltimore 21202 301/685-7878

_____
*Unified Bar
A/M: Date of Annual Meeting

State Bar Associations (Cont.)

Association	President	President-Elect or Vice President	Executive Director or Executive Secretary
Massachusetts Bar Assn. Founded 1911 10,964 Members A/M: June, 1982	Thomas J. Wynn One Taunton Green Taunton 02780 617/823-4567	Daniel O. Mahoney 1 Beacon St., 22nd Fl. Boston 02108 617/227-4400	Carl A. Modecki One Center Plaza Boston 02108 617/523-4529
*State Bar of **Michigan** Founded 1936 20,243 Members A/M: September, 1982	Patrick J. Keating 1910 Fisher Bldg. Detroit 48202 313/872-4620	John A. Krsul, Jr. 800 1st Nat'l Bldg. Detroit 48226 313/223-3586	Michael Franck 306 Townsend St. Lansing 48933 517/372-9030
Minnesota State Bar Assn. Founded 1883 7,900 Members A/M: June, 1982	Clinton A. Schroeder 300 Roanoke Building Minneapolis 55402 612/339-9501	Theodore J. Collins W-1177 First Nat'l Bk. Bldg. St. Paul 55402 612/227-0611	Celene Greene 100 Minnesota Fed. Bldg. Minneapolis 55402 612/335-1183
*Mississippi State Bar Founded 1905 4,700 Members A/M: June, 1982	Leonard B. Melvin, Jr. P.O. Box 142 Laurel 39440 601/426-6306	Curtis Coker P.O. Box 1084 Jackson 39205 601/969-7607	Larry Houchins P.O. Box 2168 Jackson 39205 610/948-4471
*The **Missouri** Bar Founded 1944 12,500 Members A/M: September, 1982	Stephen N. Limbaugh 2027 Broadway Cape Giradeau 63701 314/335-3316	James E. McDaniel 818 Olive St. #1400 St. Louis 63101 314/241-5500	Wade F. Baker P.O. Box 119 Jefferson City 65102 314/635-4128
*State Bar of **Montana** Founded 1975 2,010 Members A/M: July, 1982	Alexander A. George 510 Glacier Bldg. Missoula 59801 406/728-4310	Ward A. Shanahan P.O. Box 1686 Helena 59601 406/442-8560	Kent M. Parcell P.O. Box 4669 Helena 55901 406/442-7660
*Nebraska State Bar Assn. Founded 1877 5,429 Members A/M: October, 1982	Richard M. Spire 525 Farm Credit Bldg. Omaha 68102 402/341-4133	Theodore L. Kessner 400 Lincoln Benefit Life Bldg. Lincoln 68508 402/475-5131	Ted E. Dillow 1019 Sharp Bldg. Lincoln 68508 402/475-7091
*State Bar of **Nevada** Founded 1928 1,840 Members A/M: June, 1982	Paul C. Parraquirre 302 E. Carson Suite 1104 Las Vegas 89101 702/382-5921	F. DeArmond Sharp 1 E. Liberty Suite 416 Reno 89504 702/786-4646	J. Roger Detweiler 300 E. First St. Reno 89501 702/329-4100
*New Hampshire Bar Assn. Founded 1873 1,901 Members A/M: June, 1982	Paul McEachern 25 Maplewood Ave. Portsmouth 03801 603/436-3110	Richard E. Galway, Jr. 1850 Elm St. Box 719 Manchester 03105 603/668-3737	Gail Kinney 18 Centre St. Concord 03301 603/224-6942
New Jersey State Bar Assn. Founded 1899 12,000 Members A/M: May, 1982	Octavius A. Orbe 40 W. Ridgewood Ridgewood 07450 201/445-6722	Marie L. Garibaldi 744 Broad St. Newark 07102 201/622-7700	Dalton W. Menhall 172 W. State St. Trenton 08608 609/394-1101
*State Bar of **New Mexico** Founded 1886 3,200 Members A/M: October, 1982	John F. McCarthy, Jr. P.O. Box 787 Santa Fe 87501 505/982-4374	William W. Bivins P.O. Drawer O Las Cruces 87001 505/524-8624	Judy A. Zanotti P.O. Box 25883 Albuquerque 87125 505/842-6132
New York State Bar Founded 1876 32,200 Members A/M: May, 1982	David S. Williams 75 State Street Albany 12201 518/434-3136	Bernard J. Reilly 200 West Main St. Babylon 11702 516/669-3000	William J. Carroll One Elk St. Albany 12207 518/445-1211

---

*Unified Bar
A/M: Date of Annual Meeting

State Bar Associations (Cont.)

Association	President	President-Elect or Vice President	Executive Director or Executive Secretary
*North Carolina State Bar Founded 1933 8,802 Members A/M: October, 1982	John Campbell P.O. Box 1424 Lumberton 919/738-8534	George R. Kornegay, Jr. P.O. Box 646 Mount Olive 919/658-9436	B. E. James P.O. Box 25908 Raleigh 27611 919/828-4620
North Carolina Bar Assn. Founded 1899 5,800 Members A/M: June, 1982	James E. Walker 2700 Wachovia Center Charlotte 28285 704/377-5700	Robert F. Baker P.O. Box 270 Durham 27702 919/682-5721	Allan B. Head 1025 Wade Ave. Raleigh 27605 919/828-0561
*State Bar Assn. of North Dakota Founded 1921 1,214 Members A/M: June, 1982	Paul G. Kloster P.O. Box 1097 Dickinson 58601 701/227-1841	H. F. Gierke III P.O. Box 528 Watford 58854 701/842-3621	Michael Rost P.O. Box 2136 Bismark 58502 701/255-1404
Ohio State Bar Assn. Founded 1880 16,700 Members A/M: May, 1982	John A. Howard 201 Loomis Bldg. Elyria 44035 216/456-8341	Norman W. Shibley 1500 Nat'l Cty. Bk. Bldg. Cleveland 44114 216/696-3232	Joseph B. Miller 33 W. Eleventh Ave. Columbus 43201 614/421-2121
*Oklahoma Bar Assn. Founded 1939 9,625 Members A/M: December, 1982	Ben T. Owens P.O. Box 1168 Miami 74354 918/542-5501	John L. Boyd 800 Grantson Blvd. 111 W. 5th St. Tulsa 74103 405/524-2365	Marvin C. Emerson P.O. Box 53036 Oklahoma City 73152 405/524-2365
*Oregon State Bar Founded 1935 7,327 Members A/M: September, 1982	Art C. Johnson 101 E. Broadway #400 Eugene 97401 503/485-0220	David J. Krieger 1300 S.W. Fifth Ave. Portland 97204 503/221-0550	Robert J. Elfers 1776 S.W. Madison St. Portland 97205 503/224-4280
Pennsylvania Bar Assn. Founded 1895 19,757 Members A/M: May, 1982	Robert M. Landis 3400 Centre Square S. Philadelphia 19102 215/927-3765	Charles C. Keller 70 E. Beau St. Washington 15301 412/222-4520	Peter P. Roper P.O. Box 186 Harrisburg 17108 717/238-6715
*Puerto Rico Bar Assn. Founded 1840 5,314 Members A/M: September, 1982	Louis F. Camacho P.O. Box 1900 San Juan 00903 809/724-3358	Mario Rodriguez-Matias P.O. Box 10 114 Bayamon San Juan 00619 809/724-3358	Catherine Torres P.O. Box 1900 San Juan 00903 809/724-3358
*Rhode Island Bar Assn. Founded 1898 2,410 Members A/M: June, 1982	Beverly Glenn Long 2700 Hospital Trust Tower Providence 02903 401/274-9200	Melvin A. Chernick 1114 Industrial Bank Bldg. Providence 02903 401/421-6333	Edward P. Smith 1804 Industrial Bk. Bldg. Providence 02903 401/421-5740
*South Carolina Bar Founded 1975 4,798 Members A/M: June, 1982	Thomas S. Tisdale P.O. Box 993 Charleston 29402 803/577-4000	Terrell L. Glenn P.O. Box 11390 Columbia 29211 803/799-9800	Robert N. DuRant P.O. Box 11039 Columbia 29211 803/799-6653
*State Bar of South Dakota Founded 1931 1,505 Members A/M: June, 1982	Robert D. Hofer P.O. Box 280 Pierre 57501 605/224-5826	Thomas H. Foye P.O. Box 2670 Rapid City 57709 605/343-1040	William K. Sahr 222 E. Capitol Pierre 57501 605/224-7554
Tennessee Bar Assn. Founded 1881 5,146 Members A/M: June, 1982	Richard Allen, Sr. 1900 One Commerce Sq. Memphis 38103 901/523-8211	John C. Tune 26th Fl., 1st America Cntr. Nashville 37238 615/244-2770	Billie Bethel 3622 West End Ave. Nashville 37205 615/383-7421

*Unified Bar
A/M: Date of Annual Meeting

State Bar Associations (Cont.)

Association	President	President-Elect or Vice President	Executive Director or Executive Secretary
*State Bar of Texas Founded 1939 35,300 Members A/M: June, 1982	Wayne Fisher 2600 Two Houston Center Houston 77002 713/654-4433	Orrin Johnson 402 E. Van Buren Harlingen 78550 512/423-0213	W. Reed Quilliam, Jr. P.O. Box 12487 Austin 78711 512/475-4200
*Utah State Bar Founded 1931 3,672 Members A/M: July, 1982	Duane A. Frandsen 90 W. 100 North Price 84501 801/637-1245	O. Wood Woyle III 600 Deseret Plaza Salt Lake City 8411 801/521-0250	Dean W. Sheffield 425 E. First South Salt Lake City 84111 801/531-9077
Vermont Bar Assn. Founded 1878 1,034 Members A/M: September, 1982	Wynn Underwood 12 Red Rock, Austin Dr. Burlington 05401 802/863-5705	Donald H. Hackel P.O. Box 890 Rutland 05701 802/775-2361	Lawrence J. Turgeon P.O. Box 100 Montpelier 05602 802/223-2020
*Virginia State Bar Founded 1938 16,000 Members A/M: June, 1982	William B. Poff P.O. Box 720 Roanoke 24004 703/982-4200	Waller H. Horsley P.O. Box 1535 Richmond 23212 804/788-8416	N. Samuel Clifton Ste. 1622, 700 Bldg. Richmond 23219 804/786-2061
Virginia Bar Assn. Founded 1888 3,639 Members A/M: January, 1982	Hugh L. Patterson 1800 Va. Nat'l Bk. Bldg. Norfolk 23510 804/627-0611	John F. Kay, Jr. P.O. Box 1122 Richmond 23208 804/644-6011	A. Ward Sims P.O. Box 1029 Charlottesville 22902 804/977-1396
*Washington State Bar Assn. Founded 1890 11,000 Members A/M: April, 1982	David A. Welts 505 Madison Seattle 98104 206/622-6054		John Michalik 505 Madison Seattle 98104 206/622-6054
*West Virginia State Bar Founded 1947 2,931 Members A/M: May, 1982	John E. Busch One Randoph Ave. Elkins 26241 304/636-3560	David H. Daugherty 1202 First Huntington Bldg. Huntginton 25701 304/523-0131	Mark P. Smith E-40 State Capitol Charleston 25305 304/346-8414
West Virginia Bar Assn. Founded 1886 1,226 Members A/M: September, 1982	Frederick P. Stamp, Jr. 816 Central Union Bldg. Wheeling 26003 304/233-3390	E. Glenn Robinson P.O. Box 951 Charleston 25323 304/343-4841	F. Wichter McCullough P.O. Box 346 Charleston 25322 304/342-1474
*State Bar of Wisconsin Founded 1957 11,929 Members A/M: June, 1982	Myron E. LaRowe 110 Main St. Reedsburg 53959 608/524-6444	Edward A. Dudek 825 N. Jefferson Milwaukee 53202 414/273-4000	Stephen L. Smay P.O. Box 7158 Madison 53707 608/257-3838
*Wyoming State Bar Founded 1915 1,099 Members A/M: September, 1982	Howell C. McDaniel, Jr. Ste. 500 Wyoming Bldg. Casper 82601 307/234-9345	William R. Jones P.O. Drawer 189 Wheatland 82201 307/322-2882	Daniel E. White P.O. Box 109 Cheyenne 82001 307/632-9061

*Unified Bar
A/M: Date of Annual Meeting

LOCAL BAR ASSOCIATIONS REPRESENTED IN THE
ABA HOUSE OF DELEGATES

Association	President	President-Elect or Vice President	Executive Director or Executive Secretary
ALABAMA			
Birmingham Bar Assn. Founded 1885 1,507 Members A/M: December, 1982	Charles J. Najjar 1030 Brown Marx Bldg. Birmingham 35203 205/252-2116		Beth Carmichael 900 Jefferson County Court House Birmingham 35263 205/251-8006
ARIZONA			
Maricopa County Bar Assn. Founded 1914 2,150 Members A/M: June, 1982	Ralph E. Mahowald 3003 N. Central Ave., #1800 Phoenix 85012 602/263-3900	Christopher A. Combs 2202 E. Camelback, #114 Phoenix 85016 602/957-9810	Nan Wilder 3033 N. Central Ave. Suite 604 Phoenix 85012 602/277-2366
CALIFORNIA			
Alameda County Bar Assn. Founded 1877 2,133 Members A/M: November, 1982	Wm. McKinstry 1225 Fallon Street Oakland 94612 415/874-6565	Robin M. Edwards 415 20th St., 4th Fl. Oakland 94612 415/451-0544	Harold C. Norton 405-14th Street, Ste. 208 Oakland 94612 415/893-7155
Beverly Hills Bar Assn. Founded 1931 2,700 Members A/M: September, 1982	Herman S. Palarz 9100 Wilshire Blvd., Ste. 250 Beverly Hills 90212 213/278-9100	Sol Rosenthal 1900 Ave. of the Stars, #1780 Los Angeles 90067 213/990-2165	Linda R. Davis 300 S. Beverly Dr. #201 Beverly Hills 90212 213-553-6644
Lawyers' Club of Los Angeles Founded 1930 1,500 Members A/M: November, 1982	Robert D. Bannon 611 W. 6th St., #3320 Los Angeles 90017 213/624-6253	Richard R. Clements 611 W. 6th St., #3000 Los Angeles 90017 213/624-9774	Comm. Hyman Danoff 6340 W. 5th St. Los Angeles 90212 213/933-8185
Los Angeles County Bar Founded 1878 16,714 Members A/M: June, 1982	Richard M. Coleman P.O. Box 55020 Los Angeles 90055 213/627-2727	Roy H. Aaron P.O. Box 55020 Los Angeles 90055 213/627-2727	Georgia Franklin P.O. Box 55020 Los Angeles 90055 213/627-2727
Orange County Bar Assn. Founded 1901 3,100 Members A/M: November, 1982	Eugene C. Andres 505 City Parkway West, #900 Orange 92668 714/634-1612	James B. Bear 610 Newport Cntr. Dr., #1600 Newport Beach 92660 714/760-0404	Adele Elliott 17291 Irvine Blvd. Suite 309 Tustin 92680 714/838-9200
San Diego County Bar Assn. Founded 1920 3,600 Members A/M: June, 1982	Daniel J. Tobin 1434 Fifth Ave. San Diego 92101 714/462-9225	Thomas H. Ault 1434 Fifth Ave. San Diego 92101 714/295-1202	Julie A. Hegg 1434 Fifth Ave. San Diego 92101 714/231-0781
Bar Assn. of San Francisco Founded 1872 5,200 Members A/M: December, 1982	Joanne Garvey 1400 Alcoa Bldg. San Francisco 94111 415/397-4600	Stanley Friedman 407 Sansome St., Ste. 400 San Francisco 94111 415/788-2200	Irving F. Reichert, Jr. 220 Bush St., 21st Fl. San Francisco 94104 415/392-3960
Lawyers Club of San Francisco Founded 1946 1,800 Members A/M: August, 1982	Richard J. Wall 1 Embarcadero Cntr., #2201 San Francisco 94111 415/434-3323	Frank D. Winston 601 California St., #704 San Francisco 94108 415/398-2500	Marti Lockridge 870 Market, #1115 San Francisco 94102 415/433-2133

A/M: Date of Annual Meeting

Locals Represented in House of Delegates (Cont.)

Association	President	President-Elect or Vice President	Executive Director or Executive Secretary
Santa Clara County Bar Assn. Founded 1917 1,850 Members A/M: January, 1982	John M. Collins 38 W. Santa Clara St., 2nd Fl. San Jose 95113 408/287-3518	Phillip M. Sims 84 W. Santa Clara St., #660 San Jose 95113 408/998-3400	Gretchen G. Blood 111 N. Market St. Suite #712 San Jose 95113 408/288-8840

COLORADO

Denver Bar Assn. Founded 1891 3,384 Members A/M: June, 1982	Donald P. MacDonald 1600 Broadway, #1900 Denver 80202 303/861-7070	Miles C. Cortez, Jr. 1700 Broadway, #1100 Denver 80290 303/861-8013	Charles C. Turner 200 West 14th Ave., #800 Denver 80204 303/629-6873

FLORIDA

Dade County Bar Assn. Founded 1918 3,000 Members A/M: May, 1982	Joe N. Unger 111 N.W. 1st Ave., #214 Miami 33128 304/374-5500	Richard P. Cole 111 N.W. 1st Ave., #214 Miami 33128 305/379-6411	Mrs. Johnnie M. Ridgely 111 N.W. First Ave., #214 Miami 33128 305/379-0641

GEORGIA

Atlanta Bar Assn. Founded 1888 3,825 Members A/M: April, 1982	C. David Butler 1100 Peach Tree Harris Tower Atlanta 30303 404/521-0781	Jack S. Schroder Haas-Howell Bldg. Atlanta 30303 404/522-2508	Robert C. Mitchell Ste. 606 Equitable Bldg. 100 Peachtree St., N.W. Atlanta 30303 404/521-0781

ILLINOIS

The Chicago Bar Assn. Founded 1874 16,300 Members A/M: June, 1982	Kevin M. Forde 111 W. Washington, #2025 Chicago 60602 312/726-5015	David C. Hilliard Prudential Plaza, #3500 Chicago 60601 312/642-9518	John F. McBride 29 S. LaSalle St. Ste. 1040 Chicago 60603 312/782-7348
Chicago Council of Lawyers Founded 1969 1,500 Members A/M: October, 1982	Gary T. Johnson 213 S. LaSalle St. Chicago 60604 312/782-0600	Douglas W. Cassel, Jr. 109 N. Dearborn Chicago 60602 312/641-5570	Lois Weisberg 220 S. State St., Rm. 800 Chicago 60604 312/427-0710

INDIANA

Indianapolis Bar Assn. Founded 1878 2,300 Members A/M: January, 1982	Donald L. Jackson One Indiana Sq. Suite 2700 Indianapolia 46204 317/635-8900	G. Weldon Johnson 8900 Keystone Crossing Suite 1240 Indianapolis 46240 317/848-5808	Rosalie F. Felton One Indiana Sq. Suite 2550 Indianapolis 46204 317/632-8240

KENTUCKY

Louisville Bar Assn. Founded 1900 1,725 Members A/M: November, 1982	Paul G. Tobin 701 W. Jefferson St. Louisville 40202 502/426-1615	George Schuhman 1234 United Ky. Bk. Bldg. Louisville 40202 502/583-5314	Jane F. Hopson 200 S. 5th St. Louisville 40202 502/583-5314

MARYLAND

Bar Assn. of Baltimore City Founded 1880 2,750 Members A/M: June, 1982	Herbert J. Belgrad Sun Life Bldg., 10th Fl. Blatimore 21201 301/539-6967	John E. Sandbower III 100 Light St., 6th Fl. Baltimore 21202 301/727-1164	Paul Carlin 627 Civil Courts Bldg. Baltimore 21202 301/539-5936

A/M: Date of Annual Meeting

Locals Represented in House of Delegates (Cont.)

Association	President	President-Elect or Vice President	Executive Director or Executive Secretary
MASSACHUSETTS			
Boston Bar Assn. Founded 1961 5,000 Members A/M: May, 1982	Raymond H. Young 60 State Street Boston 02109 617/227-9490	John A. Perkins One Beacon St. Boston 02108 617/227-4400	Frederick H. Norton, Jr. 16 Beacon St. Boston 02108 617/742-0615
MICHIGAN			
Detroit Bar Assn. Founded 1836 3,875 Members A/M: May, 1982	Robert G. Russell 2100 Detroit Bank & Trust Bldg. Detroit 48226 313/961-0200	Carole L. Chiamp 515 E. Larned St. Detroit 48226 313/237-0811	Roger S. Lennert 600 Woodward Ave. Detroit 48226 313/961-6120
Oakland County Bar Assn. Founded 1934 2,350 Members A/M: May, 1982	Thomas G. Sawyer 4086 Rochester Rd. Troy 48098 313/689-5700	Hanley M. Gurwin 17117 W. 9 Mile Rd., Ste. 1600 Southfield 48075 313/559-7500	Nancy A. Galloway 2101 S. Telegraph Rd. Bloomfield Hills 48013 313/338-2100 or 313/398-3937
MINNESOTA			
Hennepin County Bar Assn. Founded 1919 3,846 Members A/M: May, 1982	Helen I. Kelly 777 Nicollet Mall Minneapolis 55402 612/370-6426	Roger V. Stageberg 1600 TCF Tower Minneapolis 55402 612/333-1341	R. Patrick Maxwell 700 Cargill Bldg. Minneapolis 55402 612/335-0921
MISSOURI			
Kansas City Bar Assn. Founded 1884 2,400 Members A/M: December, 1982	Willard B. Bunch 1612 Traders Bk. Bldg. 1125 Grand Ave. Kansas City 46106 816/221-2211	R. Lawrence Ward 900 Commerce Bank Bldg. P.O. Box 13007 Kansas City 64199 816/421-3355	Bobbie Lou Hunsperger P.O. Box 26276 Kansas City 64196 816/474-4322
Bar Assn. of Metropolitan St. Louis Founded 1874 3,767 Members A/M: April, 1982	Anthony Sestric 1015 Locust, Ste. 601 St. Louis 63101 314/241-8600	Charles Todt 212 S. Meramec Clayton 63105 314/862-5520	Terry Brummer One Mercantile Cntr. Suite 3600 St. Louis 63101 314/421-4134
NEW JERSEY			
Essex County Bar Assn. Founded 1898 2,700 Members A/M: April, 1982	George J. Kenny Gateway 1, Suite 1600 Newark 07102 201/643-2060	Waldron Kraemer 1180 Raymond Blvd. Newark 07102 201/624-5701	Maureen E. McCully 24 Commerce St. Newark 07102 201/622-6207
NEW YORK			
Assn. of the Bar of the City of New York Founded 1871 13,000 Members A/M: May, 1982	Oscar M. Ruebhausen 42 West 44th St. New York 10036 212/840-3550, Ext. 717	Louis A. Craco 1 City Corp. Center New York 10022 212/935-8000	42 West 44th St. New York 10036 212/840-3550
New York County Lawyers Assn. Founded 1908 10,400 Members A/M: May, 1982	James W. Lamberton 1 State St. Plaza New York 10004 212/344-0600	Denis McInerney 80 Pine St. New York 10005 212/825-0100	William J. Greene III 14 Vesey St. New York 10007 212/267-6646

A/M: Date of Annual Meeting

Locals Represented in House of Delegates (Cont.)

Association	President	President-Elect or Vice President	Executive Director or Executive Secretary
OHIO			
The Bar Assn. of Greater Cleveland Founded 1873 4,128 Members A/M: May, 1982	Louis Paisley 2500 Terminal Tower Cleveland 44113 216/241-6602	Gerald S. Gold 1100 Investment Plaza Cleveland 44114 216/696-6122	Thomas J. Brady 118 St. Clair Ave. Second Fl. Cleveland 44114 216/696-3525
Cincinnati Bar Assn. Founded 1873 2,528 Members A/M: April, 1982	John S. Wirthlin 2912 Carew Twr. 441 Vine St. Cincinnati 45202 513/621-5370	Alan Vogeler 2500 Central Tr. Cntr. 201 E. 5th St. Cincinnati 45202 513/651-6829	Martha H. Perin Suite 400 26 East Sixth St. Cincinnati 45202 513/381-8213
Columbus Bar Assn. Founded 1869 2,700 Members A/M: May, 1982	Robert J. Perry 150 E. Broad St. Columbus 43215 614/464-2111	Gerald L. Draper 100 E. Broad Columbus 43215 614/227-2300	Alexander Lagusch 66 S. Third St. Columbus 43115 614/221-4112
Cuyahoga County Bar Assn. Founded 1928 2,062 Members A/M: May, 1982	Thomas L. Dettelbach 1300 Bond Court Bldg. Cleveland 44114 216/696-3311	William L. Summers 1040 Standard Bldg. Cleveland 44113 216/696-0727	Sam L. Lazzaro 305 Women's Federal Bldg. Cleveland 44114 216/621-5112
OKLAHOMA			
Oklahoma County Bar Assn. Founded 1902 1,700 Members A/M: September, 1982	Jerry Tubb 306 Fidelity Plaza Oklahoma 73102 405/235-2575	D. Kent Meyers 20 N. Broadway Oklahoma 73102 405/235-7700	John B. Berry 311 N. Harvey Oklahoma City 73102 405/236-8421
Tulsa County Bar Assn. Founded 1903 2,008 Members A/M: November, 1982	James R. Eagleton 1606 1st Nat'l Bank Tower Tulsa 74103 918/587-0021	C. B. Savage 201 W. 5th St., Ste. 500 Tulsa 74103 918/584-4716	Lois M. McIlroy 619 So. Main Street Tulsa 74119 918/584-5243
OREGON			
Multnomah Bar Assn. Founded 1951 1,843 Members A/M: December, 1982	Leonard A. Girard 2300 G-P Bldg. 900 S.W. Fifth Portland 97204 503/224-3380	Douglass M. Hamilton 1000 Williamette Ctr. 121 S.W. Salmon Portland 97204 503/228-6351	Mary Ann Carter 1126 SW 13th Street Portland 97205 503/222-3275
PENNSYLVANIA			
Allegheny County Bar Assn. Founded 1870 5,013 Members A/M: October, 1982	Jack W. Plowman 3400 Grant Bldg. Pittsburgh 15219 412/471-8521	George M. Weis 920 Grant Bldg. Pittsburgh 15219 412/261-1848	James I. Smith III 920 City County Bldg. Pittsburgh 15219 412/216-0518
Philadelphia Bar Assn. Founded 1802 7,630 Members A/M: December, 1982	Robert C. Daniels 211 S. Broad Street, 17th Fl. Philadelphia 19107 215/568-8282	Howard Gittis 1339 Chestnut, 2nd Fl. Philadelphia 19107 215/686-5686	Kenneth Shear 1339 Chestnut St. 2nd Floor Philadelphia 19107 215/686-5686
TEXAS			
Dallas Bar Assn. Founded 1873 4,019 Members A/M: November, 1982	Darrell E. Jordan 2001 Bryan Twr., #2800 Dallas 75201 214/651-1919	Jerry Lastelick P.O. Box 59105 Dallas 75229 214/620-8050	Jo Anna Moreland 2101 Ross Ave. Dallas 75201 214/742-4675

A/M: Date of Annual Meeting

Locals Represented in House of Delegates (Cont.)

Association	President	President-Elect or Vice President	Executive Director or Executive Secretary
Houston Bar Assn. Founded 1870 5,700 Members A/M: May, 1982	Joe L. Draughn P.O. Box 22285 Municipal Court #2 Houston 77027 713/222-3362	William K. Wilde 2900 S. Tower Pennzoil Place Houston 77002 713/223-2900	Kay Sim 707 Travis #1300 Houston 77002 713/222-1441

WASHINGTON

Seattle-King County Bar Assn. Founded 1906 3,404 Members A/M: June, 1982	Stephen E. DeForest 4400 Seattle-First Nat'l Bk. Bldg. Seattle 98154 206/624-3600	Harold F. Vhugen 1600 Seattle Twr. Seattle 98101 206/624-8844	Helen K. Pulsifer 320 Central Bldg. Seattle 98104 206-624-9365

WISCONSIN

Milwaukee Bar Assn. Founded 1858 1,676 Members A/M: June, 1982	Wayne E. Babler 780 N. Water St. Milwaukee 53202 414/277-5000	David J. Cannon 250 E. Wisconsin Ave. Ste. 2000 Milwaukee 53202 414/271-6560	Thomas W. Nedwek 610 N. Jackson St. Milwaukee 53202 414/271-3833

A/M: Date of Annual Meeting

LOCAL BAR ASSOCIATIONS WITH MEMBERSHIPS OVER 300
WHICH ARE NOT REPRESENTED IN THE ABA HOUSE OF DELEGATES

Association	President	President-Elect or Vice President	Executive Director or Executive Secretary
ALABAMA			
The Mobile Bar Assn. Founded 1869 620 Members A/M: December, 1982	Mylan R. Engel P.O. Box 1045 Mobile 36633 205/438-3625	James J. Duffy, Jr. P.O. Box 1109 Mobile 36633 205/433-5441	Ruth Norris P.O. Drawer 2005 Mobile 36652 205/433-9790
Montgomery County Bar Assn. Founded 1900 481 Members A/M: January, 1982	Lawrence H. Kloess 474 S. Court St. Montgomery 36104 205/832-7048	Richard M. Jordan P.O. Box 1946 Montgomery 36103 205/265-4561	James R. Seale P.O. Box 2069 Montgomery 36103 205/262-1671
ARIZONA			
Pima County Bar Assn. Founded 1900 870 Members A/M: May, 1982	Michael Lacagnina P.O. Box 871 Tucson 85702 602/792-4800	Carol Wilson 177 N. Church, #905 Tucson 85701 602/884-8930	Elizabeth F. Beck 177 N. Church Tucson 85701 602/623-8258
ARKANSAS			
Pulaski County Bar Assn. Founded: 1950 677 Members A/M: May, 1982	Vincent Foster, Jr. 120 E. Fourth St. Little Rock 72201 501/375-9151	W. Russell Meeks III 1151 First Nat'l Bank Bldg. Little Rock 72201 501/376-4660	Frank B. Sewall P.O. Box 2900 Little Rock 72203 501/372-5000
CALIFORNIA			
Century City Bar Assn. Founded 675 Members A/M: January, 1982	Arthur R. Chenen 1801 Century Pk. E., 25th Fl. Los Angeles 90067 213/556-2000	Jerald M. Lackowicz 1900 Ave. of the Stars Los Angeles 90067 213/879-1222	Michael D. Harris 1888 Century Park East Los Angeles 90067 213/277-8141
Contra Costa County Bar Assn. Founded 1957 600 Members A/M: January, 1982	William E. Cagen, Jr. P.O. Box 218 Danville 94526 415/837-0585	Rodney Marraccini 1280 Boulevard Way, #202 Walnut Creek 94596 415/943-1850	Lillian F. Galvin 706 Main Street, #B Martinez 94553 415/372-8100
Eastern Bar Assn. of Los Angeles County Founded 310 Members A/M: July, 1982	Paul Mahoney 100 Pomona Mall W. Suite 506 Pomona 91766 714/623-2411	H. George Taylor 401 S. Main St. P.O. Box 1216 Pomona 91769 714/623-1678	Mary Robutz 426 San Gabriel Ave. P.O. Box 776 Azusa 91702 213/334-9384
Fresno County Bar Assn. Founded 1890 750 Members A/M: December, 1982	Robert H. Oliver 2300 Civic Center Square, #300 Fresno 93721 209/485-2131	Douglass B. Jensen 6th Fl., Security Bk. Bldg. Fresno 93721 209/442-0550	Val Weston 420 T. W. Patterson Bldg. Fresno 93721 209/264-0137
Hollywood Bar Assn. Founded 1931 310 Members A/M: December, 1982	Toxey H. Smith 6255 Sunset Blvd., 20th Fl. Hollywood 90028 213/463-4861	Bertha Rapaport 7060 Franklin Ave. Hollywood 90028 213/876-1293	Fred Woessner 952 N. Hudson Ave., #2 Los Angeles 90038 213/462-8566
Lawyers' Club of Alameda County Founded 752 Members A/M: June, 1982	Harvey Hamel Public Defender 420 3rd St. Oakland 94607 415/874-7141	William Strickland 436 14th St. Oakland 94612 415/763-2324	Peter Rugh 405 14th St. Oakland 94612 415/763-3000

A/M: Date of Annual Meeting

Other Local Associations (Cont.)

Association	President	President-Elect or Vice President	Executive Director or Executive Secretary
Long Beach Bar Assn. Founded 1917 623 Members A/M: January, 1982	R. J. Kilpherick 444 W. Ocean #500 Long Beach 90802 213/421-9354	Richard G. Wilson 444 W. Ocean #500 Long Beach 90802 213/435-6565	Nila Carney 444 W. Ocean Blvd. Suite 500 Long Beach 90802 213/432-5913
Marin County Bar Assn. Founded 1959 575 Members A/M: November, 1982	Beverly B. Savitt 828 Mission Ave. San Rafael 94901 415/454-8980	Gary Ragghianti 1534 Fifth Ave. San Rafael 94901 415/453-9433	Jeannette C. Stewart 1010 B St. #419 San Rafael 94901 415/453-5505
Monterey County Bar Assn. Founded 1969 333 Members A/M: December, 1982	Jack Arancio 232 Madison Monterey 93940 408/373-1005	Sam Lavorato 310 Capitol Salinas 93901 408/758-2786	Michael Newman 539 Hartnell Monterey 93940 408/649-0957
Palo Alto Area Assn. Founded 1975 327 Members A/M: June, 1982	George C. Fisher 321 Lytton Ave. Palo Alto 94301 415/327-6700	William I. Cohen 385 Sheiman Ave. Palo Alto 94306 415/321-3555	Betty J. Schindler 405 Sherman Ave. Palo Alto 94306 415/326-8322
Pasadena Bar Assn. Founded 1930 387 Members A/M: October, 1982	Leonard Maranci 301 E. Colorado Blvd., #900 Pasadena 91101 213/796-9123	Clifford R. Anderson, Jr. 301 E. Colorado, Ste. 704 Pasadena 91101 213/449-4812	Jean Moore 127 N. Madison, Rm. 201 Pasadena 91101 213/795-5641
Riverside County Bar Assn. Founded 1892 501 Members A/M: June, 1982	Stephen D. Cunnison 4000 Tenth St. Riverside 92501 714/686-3092	Dallas Holmes 4200 Orange St. Riverside 92501 714/686-1450	William Cunningham 3765 Tenth St. Riverside 92501 714/682-1015
Sacramento County Bar Assn. Founded 1925 1,665 Members A/M: November, 1982	Thomas W. Eres 555 Capitol Mall, #900 Sacramento 95814 916/444-8920	Joe S. Gray 555 Capitol Mall, #1100 Sacramento 95814 916/441-2430	Robert M. Stone 910 H St., Ste. 101 Sacramento 95814 916/448-1087
San Bernardino County Bar Assn. Founded 1875 516 Members A/M: June, 1982	Phillip M. Savage III 398 West Fourth St. San Bernardino 92401 714/884-2171	Brian J. Simpson 150 West 5th St., Ste. 104 San Bernardino 92401 714/889-3565	Lowell R. Jameson 150 W. 5th St., Ste. 108 San Bernardino 92401 714/885-1986
San Fernando Valley Bar Assn. Founded 1926 850 Members A/M: October, 1982	Herbert F. Blanck 16633 Ventura Blvd., #903 Encino 91436 213/783-5777	Herman J. Isman 15915 Ventura Blvd. Encino 91436 213/990-9040	Susan Keating 6454 Van Nuys Blvd., #151 Van Nuys 91411 213/786-5055
San Joaquin County Bar Assn. Founded 1940 390 Members A/M: September, 1982	Patricia M. Frederick 301 East Weber Ave. Stockton 95202 209/948-0125	Donald O. Geiger 404 Bk. of Stockton Bldg. Stockton 95202 209/948-0434	Adelle Barrette 301 E. Weber Ave. Stockton 95202 209/948-0125
San Mateo County Bar Assn. Founded 1931 813 Members A/M: September, 1982	Gordon W. Hackett P.O. Box 279 San Bruno 94066 415/588-0367	P. Terry Anderlini 600 S. El Camino Real, #700 San Mateo 94402 415/348-0102	Shirley W. Masters 333 Bradford St. Redwood 94064 415/369-4149

A/M: Date of Annual Meeting

Other Local Associations (Cont.)

Association	President	President-Elect or Vice President	Executive Director or Executive Secretary
Santa Barbara County Bar Assn. Founded 325 Members A/M: December, 1982	Malvin D. Dohrman 210 E. Figueroa St. Santa Barbara 93101 805/963-1941	Harry Lober 118 E. Figueroa St. Santa Barbara 93101 805/963-6158	Thomas P. Anderle 1114 State St. Suite 300 Santa Barbara 93101 805/963-3826
Santa Monica Bay District Bar Assn. Founded 1928 432 Members A/M: September, 1982	Lee Petillon 9841 Airport Blvd., #820 Los Angeles 90045 213/346-8480	Nijole V. Treciokas 600 Wilshire Blvd., #702 Santa Monica 90401 213/393-0239	Ingrid L. Andren 225 Santa Monica Blvd. Santa Monica 90401 213/451-5633
South Bay Bar Founded 1953 510 Members A/M: October, 1982	William P. Powell, Jr. 23150 Crenshaw Blvd., Ste. 200 Torrance 90505 213/530-5105	Mervin I. Tarlow 3812 Sepalveda Blvd., Ste. 400 Torrance 90505 213/373-6821	Ann Gonzales 825 Maple Ave. Torrance 90503 213/320-4295
Southeast District Bar Assn. Founded 1956 304 Members A/M: August, 1982	Richard La Pan 8050 E. Florence Ave., #16 Downey 90240 213/923-7206	Edwin P. Ratcliffe 9701 Lakewood BLvd. Downing 90240 213/862-1961	Connie Garcia 12720 Norwalk Blvd. Rm. 104-E Norwalk 90650 213/868-6787
Ventura County Bar Assn. Founded 1934 515 Members A/M: October, 1982	Frederick Bysshe, Jr. P.O. Drawer 1417 Ventura 93002 805/648-3224	James D. Loebl 2580 E. Main St., Ste. 101 Ventura 93003 805/648-3303	Vivian Stephenson 3200 Telegraph Rd., #207 Ventura 93003 805/656-1306
Women's Lawyers Assn. of Los Angeles Founded 1,000 Members A/M: September, 1982	Carol Frederick 3580 Wilshire Blvd., Ste. 700 Los Angeles 90010 213/736-2194	Joan Patsy Ostroy 10960 Wilshire Blvd. Los Angeles 90024 213/478-2514	Ellie Schneir P.O. Box 480197 Los Angeles 90048 213/653-3322

COLORADO

Association	President	President-Elect or Vice President	Executive Director or Executive Secretary
Arapahoe County Bar Assn. Founded 1950 333 Members A/M: June, 1982	Edward B. Lee 3470 S. Sherman St., #2 Englewood 80110 303/761-5910	Thomas C. Levi 15400 E. 14th Pl., #211 Aurora 80011 303/344-1010	John E. Berglund 5601 S. Broadway, #347 Littleton 80120 303/795-2211
Boulder County Bar Assn. Founded 1907 465 Members A/M: June, 1982	William R. Gray 2305 Broadway Boulder 80302 303/449-2830	John Gaddis 521 Main St. Longmont 80501 303/442-8830	Midge A. Korczak 3023 7th St. Boulder 80302 303/440-4758

CONNECTICUT

Association	President	President-Elect or Vice President	Executive Director or Executive Secretary
Greater Bridgeport Bar Founded 1880 625 Members A/M: May, 1982	William P. Gumpper 114 State St. Bridgeport 06604 203/384-1385	Martin F. Wolf 10 Middle St. Bridgeport 06604 203/368-0211	Barbara D. Quinn 955 Main St. Bridgeport 06604 203/334-6539
Hartford County Bar Assn. Founded 1783 1,900 Members A/M: March, 1982	Gary A. Friedle One Prospect St. New Britain 06050 203/225-8636	Joseph Lorenzo 40 Russ St. Hartford 06106 203/521-7200	Mary E. St. Clair 266 Pearl St., Ste. 402 Hartford 06103 203/525-8106
New Haven County Bar Assn. Founded 1907 800 Members A/M: October, 1982	Lawrence M. Liebman 2405 Whitney Ave. Hamden 06518 203/288-6293	Brian Murphy 215 Church St. New Haven 06510 203/865-2133	Joan Margolis P.O. Box 1441 New Haven 06506 203/562-9652

A/M: Date of Annual Meeting

Other Local Associations (Cont.)

Association	President	President-Elect or Vice President	Executive Director or Executive Secretary
DISTRICT OF COLUMBIA			
Washington Bar Assn. Founded 1,000 Members A/M: June, 1982	Thomas A. Duckenbield 1415 Whittier St., N.W. Washington 20011 202/727-1660	Iverson Mitchell 1660 K St., N.W. #600 Washington 20006 202/457-7822	Wendell Bardner 1320 Somerset St., N.W. Washington 20011 202/233-5840
The Women's Bar Assn. of D.C. Founded 1,200 Members A/M: May, 1982	Susan A. Low 100 H St., N.W. Washington 20080 202/624-2096	Elizabeth Medaglia 1511 N. Wakefield St. Arlington, VA 22207 202/632-6280	Marie J. Rivera 1819 H St., N.W., #300 Washington 20006 202/775-0420
FLORIDA			
Broward County Bar Assn. Founded 1956 1,315 Members A/M: May, 1982	Russell E. Carlisle 415 S.E. 12th St. Ft. Lauderdale 33316 305/764-4000	Hugh T. Maloney 790 E. Broward Blvd., Ste. 200 Ft. Lauderdale 33301 305/522-1700	Norma B. Howard 735 N.E. Third Ave. Ft. Lauderdale 33304 305/764-8040
Clearwater Bar Assn. Founded 1960 305 Members A/M: May, 1982	Bruce M. Harlan 110 Turner St. Clearwater 33516 813/441-9991	C. Richard Nail 114 Turner St. Clearwater 33516 813/461-4546	Dee Croker P.O. Box 1609 Clearwater 33517 813/461-4849
Hillsborough County Bar Assn. Founded 1937 1,112 Members A/M: May, 1982	Benjamin H. Hill P.O. Box 3324 Tampa 33601 813/273-5000	C. Timothy Corcoran III P.O. Box 3239 Tampa 33601 813/223-5366	Dorothy D. Vines P.O. Box 26 Tampa 33601 813/226-6431
Jacksonville Bar Assn. Founded 1897 961 Members A/M: May, 1982	Stephen D. Busey 1102 Barnett Bk. Bldg. Jacksonville 32202 904/354-2144	A. Hamilton Cooke 1102 Barnett Bk. Bldg. Jacksonville 32202 904/354-2144	Diane Bounds 1102 Barnett Bk. Bldg. Jacksonville 32202 904/354-2144
Orange County Bar Assn. Founded 1933 1,297 Members A/M: May, 1982	Patricia C. Fawsett P.O. Box 231 Orlando 32802 305/843-7860	Darryl M. Bloodworth P.O. Box 2346 Orlando 32802 305/841-1200	Eloise O. Fox P.O. Box 1466 Orlando 32802 305/422-4551
Palm Beach County Bar Founded 1922 1,073 Members A/M: May, 1982	David L. Roth P.O. Box 3466 W. Palm Beach 33402 305/655-8100	D. Culver Smith III P.O. Box 2096 W. Palm Beach 33402 305/659-7200	Catherine S. Royce 105 S. Narcissus Ave. 505 Citizens Bldg. W. Palm Beach 33401
St. Petersburg Bar Assn. Founded 1925 600 Members A/M: June, 1982	William F. Blews 666 First Ave. North St. Petersburg 33701 813/822-8322	E. Thomas Fisher 275 4th St. North St. Petersburg 33701 813/898-1181	Patricia M. Hicks 30 6th St., N.W. P.O. Box 262 St. Petersburg 33731 813/823-7474
Tallahassee Bar Assn. Founded 1976 555 Members A/M: March, 1982	C. Edwin Rude, Jr. P.O. Box 1170 Tallahassee 32302 904/224-9135	Edwin A. Green II P.O. Box 938 Tallahassee 32302 904/222-7770	Mary Lou Santry P.O. Box 1833 Tallahassee 32302 904/222-7206
Volusia County Bar Assn. Founded 1940 372 Members A/M: July, 1982	W. M. Chanfrau P.O. Box 3156 645 N. Peninsula Dr. Daytona Beach 32014 904/254-7313	Paul A. Bernardini P.O. Drawer 2200 424 S. Ridgewood Ave. Daytona Beach 32014 904/258-3453	Rae Mastropierro Courthouse Annex, Rm. 207 125 E. Orange Ave. Daytona Beach 32014 904/255-3434

A/M: Date of Annual Meeting

Other Local Associations (Cont.)

Association	President	President-Elect or Vice President	Executive Director or Executive Secretary
GEORGIA			
Lawyers' Club of Atlanta, Inc. Founded 1922 1,500 Members A/M: May, 1982	Robert D. Feagin 3900 First Atlanta Twr. Atlanta 30383 404/658-1620	J. O. Humphries 1000 Grant Bldg. Atlanta 30303 404/522-2020	Betsy K. Walsh 14th Fl. Commerce Bldg. Atlanta 30303 404/668-9627
IDAHO			
Boise Bar Assn. Founded 1925 615 Members A/M: May, 1982	Merrily Munther P.O. Box 1559 Boise 83701 208/343-5454	James A. Bevis P.O. Box 522 Boise 83701 208/345-1040	David W. Hyde 1 Capital Cntr., #800 Boise 83702 208/345-6485
ILLINOIS			
Cook County Bar Assn. Founded 1914 500 Members A/M: June, 1982	Ronald S. Sammuels 2600 S. Michigan Ave. Chicago 60616 312/782-1151	Anne L. Fredd 111 W. Washington Chicago 60602 312/641-7144	Ellen E. Douglas 219 S. Dearborn Chicago 60604 312/353-7413
DuPage County Bar Assn. Founded 1879 1,058 Members A/M: June, 1982	Ralph A. Gabric 201 Naperville Road Wheaton 60187 312/653-3110	William J. Wylie 416 E. Roosevelt Wheaton 60187 312/653-9300	Sara J. Schmitz 571 W. Liberty Dr. Wheaton 60187 312/663-7779
Kane County Bar Assn. Founded 1858 440 Members A/M: May, 1982	Lawrence I. Crisanti 707 Davis Rd. Elgin 60120 312/695-7200	Michael J. Colwell 900 N. Lake St. Aurora 60506 312/897-8764	Barbara S. Wertz P.O. Box 571 Geneva 60134 312/232-6416
Lake County Bar Assn. Founded 1912 512 Members A/M: May, 1982	Paul L. Bartolian 15 S. County St. Waukegan 60085 312/662-8000	Ted C. Larson P.O. Box O 388 Lake St. Antioch 60002 312/395-0799	Jo Ann D. Osmond 7 N. County St. Waukegan 60085 312/244-3140
Northwest Suburban Bar Assn. Founded 580 Members A/M: June, 1982	John B. Clarke 120 W. Eastman, #304 Arlington Hgts. 60004 312/392-4450	Robert M. Hoenig Westmoreland Bldg. 5029 Old Orchard Skokie 60077 312/676-4880	Nancy Hughes 1350 W. Northwest Hwy. Mt. Prospect 60056 312/253-2562
Peoria County Bar Assn. Founded 1879 467 Members A/M: July, 1982	Paul C. Cation 309 Security Savings Bldg. Peoria 61602 309/676-8986	Lyle W. Allen 600 Jefferson Bk. Bldg. Peoria 61602 309/646-0400	Kent A. Noble 1900 Sav. Centr. Twr. Peoria 61602 309/673-0741
Sangamon County Bar Assn. Founded 1862 400 Members A/M: November, 1982	Charles Gramlich 918 E. Capitol Springfield 62701 217/525-0520	Robert T. Lawley Reisch Bldg. Springfield 62701 217/544-5468	Paul Brown One N. Old St. Capitol INB Bldg., Ste. 575 Springfield 62701 217/522-8822
West Suburban Bar Assn. Founded 1943 377 Members A/M: December, 1982	Robert M. Ransom 711 S. Blvd. Oak Park 60302 312/383-4649	Edward A. Matuga 1651 Westchester Blvd. Westchester 60153 312/345-5768	James Groat 104 N. Oak Park Oak Park 60302 312/383-3000
Winnebago County Bar Assn. Founded 1906 373 Members A/M: June, 1982	Keith H. Hyzer 414 Y Blvd. Rockford 61107 815/963-0149	Bradner C. Riggs 400 W. State St. Rockford 61101 815/987-3062	Patricia S. Peterson 1201 Talcott Bldg. Rockford 61101 815/964-5152

A/M: Date of Annual Meeting

Other Local Associations (Cont.)

Association	President	President-Elect or Vice President	Executive Director or Executive Secretary
Women's Bar Assn. of Illinois Founded 1914 550 Members A/M: June, 1982	Loretta C. Douglas One N. LaSalle St., Ste. 4220 Chicago 60602 312/372-4220	Hon. Marilyn R. Komosa 2909 N. Hamlin Chicago 60618 312/235-4919	Hon. Susan Snow Ruffolo 9552 S. Bell Chicago 60620 312/881-0010

INDIANA

Allen County Indiana Bar Assn. Founded 1901 493 Members A/M: October, 1982	Donald D. Doxsee 323 W. Berry Ft. Wayne 46802 219/422-4363	Walter P. Helmke 309 Standard Bldg. Ft. Wayne 46802 219/422-7422	Barbara Carto 1904 Fort Wayne Nat'l Bank Bldg. Fort Wayne 46802 219/423-2358
St. Joseph County Bar Assn. Founded 340 Members A/M: September, 1982	James H. Pankow 1800 Amer. Nat'l Bk. Bldg. South Bend 46601 219/233-1194	Thomas H. Singer 101 Lafayette Bld. South Bend 46601 219/233-9341	Robert M. Parker 1100 LaSalle West Bldg. South Bend 46601 219/234-4149

IOWA

Linn County Bar Assn. Founded 316 Members A/M: June, 1982	Harry R. Terpstra 830 Higley Bldg. Cedar Rapids 52401 319/364-2467	Minor Barnes 1010 American Bldg. Cedar Rapids 52401 319/366-7621	David S. Good Amer. Fed. Savings & Loan Bldg. Cedar Rapids 52401 319/398-3449
Polk County Bar Assn. Founded 695 Members A/M: April, 1982	William J. Lillis 820 Liberty Bldg. Des Moines 50309 515/243-8157	Terrence A. Hopkins 1040 5th St. Des Moines 50314 515/244-0111	Richard W. Lazier, Jr. 902 Liberty Bldg. Des moines 50309 515/244-8325

KANSAS

Johnson County Bar Assn. Founded 1938 435 Members A/M: June, 1982	Lawrence E. Sheppard 9400 Mission Rd., Ste. 205 Prairie Village 66206 913/381-5220	Thomas A. Hamill P.O. Box 1146 Mission 66222 913/384-5111	Lewis R. Lewis Court House Olathe 66061 913/782-5000
S.W. Kansas Bar Assn. Founded 1938 450 Members A/M: September, 1982	Gordon Penny P.O. Box 148 Medicine Lodge 67104 316/886-5611		Max E. Estes P.O. Box 39 Dodge City 67801 316/225-4168
Topeka Bar Assn. Founded 1906 528 Members A/M: April, 1982	Glenn Cogswell Columbian Title Topeka 66603 913/232-5409	Myron Listrom Capitol Federal Bldg. Topeka 66603 913/357-6311	Linda Elrod School of Law 1700 College Topeka 66604
Wichita Bar Assn. Founded 1915 940 Members A/M: March, 1982	Robert Arnold 305 Century Plaza Bldg. Wichita 67202 316/262-3796	Roger Sherwood P.O. Box 830 Wichita 67202 316/267-1281	Mrs. Jonalou M. Pinell 700 Century Plaza Wichita 67202 316/263-2251
Wyandotte County Bar Assn. Founded 1893 343 Members A/M: January, 1982	Joseph H. McDowell 600 Security Nat'l Bk. Bldg. Kansas City 66101 913/371-7750	J. Paul Maurin III Box "F", 9th & Armstrong Kansas City 66101 913/371-8383	Rita Kancel 710 N. 7th Street Kansas City 66101 913/573-2899

LOUISIANA

Baton Rouge Bar Assn., Inc. Founded 1949 750 Members A/M: May, 1982	Fred H. Belcher, Jr. 8281 Goodwood Blvd., Ste. K Baton Rouge 70806 504/925-8136	Anthony J. Clesi, Jr. 435 Louisiana Ave. Baton Rouge 70802 504/387-0241	W. Shelby McKenzie P.O. Box 2471 Baton Rouge 70821 504/387-3221

A/M: Date of Annual Meeting

Other Local Associations (Cont.)

Association	President	President-Elect or Vice President	Executive Director or Executive Secretary
New Orleans Bar Assn. Founded 1924 1,379 Members A/M: November, 1982	Albert J. Flettrich 505 Hibernia Bldg. New Orleans 70112 504/586-1323	A. R. Christovich 1900 Amer. Bk. Bldg. New Orleans 70130 504/561-5700	Gloria Phares 703 Maritime Bldg. New Orleans 70130 504/525-7453
Shreveport Bar Assn. Founded 1964 446 Members A/M: September, 1982	Jacques L. Wiener, Jr. Commercial Nat'l Bk., Rm. 411 Shreveport 71101 318/226-9100	Robert E. Mayo 200 Ray P. Oden Bldg. Shreveport 71101 318/222-3292	Richard S. Schmidt 717 Commercial Nat'l Bank Bldg. Shreveport 71101 318/227-1990

MAINE

Cumberland Bar Assn. Founded 1918 550 Members A/M: January, 1982	Bruce A. Coggeshall One Monument Sq. Portland 04101 207/773-6411	Caroline D. Glassman 80 Exchange St. Portland 04101 207/773-1751	Owen W. Wells One Canal Plaza Portland 04112 207/774-2635

MARYLAND

Baltimore County Bar Assn. Founded 1920 535 Members A/M: January, 1982	Ernest C. Trimble 305 W. Pennsylvania Towson 21204 301/825-5512	Alfred L. Brennan 825 Eastern Ave. Essex 21221 301/687-3434	Sheri Bonner 100 County Courts Bldg. Towson 21204 301/296-6237
Bar Assn. of Montgomery County Founded 1894 1,094 Members A/M: June, 1982	James J. Cromwell 17 W. Jefferson St. Rockville 20850 301/424-3454	Charles E. Wilson 17 W. Jefferson St. Rockville 20850 301/424-3454	Beverly C. Mondin 17 W. Jefferson St. Suite 105 Rockville 20850 301/424-3454
Prince George's County Bar Assn. Founded 1905 720 Members A/M: June, 1982	George A. Brugger 10210 Greenbelt Rd., Ste. 720 Seabrook 20801 301/794-6900	Karl G. Feissner 7676 New Hampshire Ave. Ste. 406 Langley Park 20783	Mildred E. Windley 4333 Gallatin St. Hyattsville 20781 301/277-1183

MASSACHUSETTS

Hampden County Bar Assn. Founded 1864 783 Members A/M: November, 1982	Richard T. Egan 36 Court St. Springfield 01103 413/787-6085	Michael S. Ratner 95 State St. Springfield 01103 413/781-0560	Judith K. Potter 50 State St. Springfield 01103 413/732-4648
Middlesex County Bar Assn. Founded 1895 982 Members A/M: January, 1982	Anthony R. Rizzo 44 Park Street Somerville 02143 617/623-7723	John F. Zamparelli 100 G. P. Hassett Dr. Medford 02155 617/395-6630	William Highgas 422 Washington Street Woburn 01801 617/494-4150
Bar Assn. of Norfolk County Founded 1886 980 Members A/M: May, 1982	Harold B. Nash 4 Pearl St. Dedham 02026 617/326-0933	Paul B. Carroll 742 Washington St. Canton 02021 617/828-2250	Charles J. Hely 614 High St. Dedham 02026 617/326-1600
Worcester County Bar Assn. Founded 1887 800 Members A/M: October, 1982	Joseph Lian, Jr. 34 Mechanics St. Worcester 01608 617/798-4461	Philip L. Berkeley 370 Main St., #600 Worcester 01608 617/791-8621	John J. Moynihan 390 Main St., Ste. 600 Worcester 01608 617/791-8181

A/M: Date of Annual Meeting

Other Local Associations (Cont.)

Association	President	President-Elect or Vice President	Executive Director or Executive Secretary
MICHIGAN			
Genesee County Bar Assn. Founded 1934 412 Members A/M: June, 1982	Carl L. Bekofske 352 S. Saginaw St. Suite 706 Flint 48502 313/234-8000	Edward G. Henneke G-4413 Corruna Rd. Flint 48504 313/733-2050	Bethany L. Borey 706 Genesee Bk. Bldg. Flint 48502 313/232-6000
Grand Rapids Bar Assn. Founded 1902 934 Members A/M: April, 1982	Charles E. Day 580 Old Kent Bldg. Grand Rapids 49509 616-774-8121	Robert J. Eleveld 666 Old Kent Bldg. Grand Rapids 49509 616/459-4186	Marjorie C. Wilcox 1010 Old Kent Bldg. Grand Rapids 49509 616/454-9493
Ingham County Bar Assn. Founded 650 Members A/M: June, 1982	James Burren Brown 115 W. Allegan, 10th Fl. Lansing 48933 517/372-6031	Judson M. Werbelow 121 East Allegan Lansing 48933 517/371-1730	Donald A. Hines 1018 Michigan Nat'l Twr. Lansing 48933 517/372-0235
Kalamazoo County Bar Assn. Founded 400 Members A/M: May, 1982	William H. Culver 615 S. Burdick P.O. Box 191 Kalamazoo 49007	Joseph J. Burgie 119 N. Church St. Kalamazoo 49006 616/349-6691	C. Giles Smith 615 S. Burdick P.O. Box 191 Kalamazoo 49007 616/345-6117
Macomb County Bar Assn. Founded 1920 700 Members A/M: April, 1982	Robert J. Hribar 22417 Gratiot Ave. East Detroit 480 313/776-2010	Daniel T. Stepek One S. Gratiot Mt. Clemens 48043 313/469-2633	Kevin Lee Macomb County Court Bldg. Room 437 Mt. Clemens 48043 313/468-2940
Washtenaw County Bar Assn. Founded 330 Members A/M: April, 1982	William F. Anhut 105 Pearl St. Ypsilanti 48197 313/481-1234	Peter Flintoft 121 S. Main St. Chelsea 48118 313/475-8671	Robert L. Henry, Jr. 211 E. Huron St., Ste. 1 Ann Arbor 48104 313/663-2100
MINNESOTA			
11th District Bar Assn. Founded 323 Members A/M: April, 1982	John J. Killen 811 1st Nat. Bk. Bldg. Duluth 55802 218/722-6331	Leo M. McDonnell 720 1st Fed. Sav. Bldg. Duluth 55802 218/727-8451	R. Craft Dryer 720 1st Fed. Sav. Bldg. Duluth 55802 218/727-8451
7th District Bar Assn. Founded 1930 325 Members A/M: Spring, 1982	Richard L. Pemberton 110 N. Mill St. Fergus Falls 56537 218/736-5493	Lynn Hummel P.O. Box 743 Detroit Lakes 56501 218/847-3155	James O. Ramstad P.O. Box 683 Detroit Lakes 56501 218/847-5653
Ramsey County Bar Assn. Founded 1883 1,760 Members A/M: April, 1982	Gordon W. Shumaker 430 Minn. Bldg. St. Paul 55101 612/226-8844	A. Patrick Leighton 1400 Northwestern Nat'l Bk. Bldg. St. Paul 55101 612/227-7683	Jane L. Harens 40 North Milton St. St. Paul 55104 612/222-0846
MISSISSIPPI			
Hinds County Bar Assn. Founded 1932 722 Members A/M: June, 1982	James P. Cothren 425 Tombigbee St. Jackson 39201 601/948-6151	Lauch M. Magruder, Jr. 1800 Deposit Guaranty Plaza Jackson 39201 601/354-5504	Richard T. Bennett 162 Amite St. Jackson 39201 601/354-5504
MISSOURI			
Greene County Bar Assn. Founded 305 Members A/M: January, 1982	William A. R. Dalton P.O. Box 1397 SSS Springfield 65805 417/865-6641	Harold S. Fisher P.O. Box 1245 SSS Springfield 65805 417/869-0581	York Johnson 426 Woodruff Bldg. Springfield 65806 417/831-2783

A/M: Date of Annual Meeting

Other Local Associations (Cont.)

Association	President	President-Elect or Vice President	Executive Director or Executive Secretary
The Lawyers Assn. of Kansas City Founded 1936 957 Members A/M: May, 1982	Stanley P. Weiner 1900 City Cntr. Sq. 1100 Main St. Kansas City 64105 816/471-8650	Kent E. Whittaker 2715 Commerce Twr. Kansas City 64105 816/221-0355	Betty Bergstresser 8003 E. 88th Terrace Kansas City 64138 816/765-3036
The Lawyers Assn. of St. Louis Founded 1933 500 Members A/M: June, 1982	George L. Fitzsimmons 111 S. Bemiston Clayton 63105 314/727-9266	Michael P. Gunn 1015 Locust St. St. Louis 63101 314/421-6565	Oliver P. Dulle 722 Chestnut St. Suite 1018 St. Louis 63101 314/231-9567
St. Louis County Bar Assn. Founded 1931 600 Members A/M: May, 1982	Mary Fiser 7546 York Drive Clayton 63105 314/863-4100	A. Wimmer Carr 120 S. Central, Suite 540 Clayton 63105 314/863-4151	Eric Tremayne 120 S. Central Clayton 63105 314/863-4151

NEBRASKA

Lincoln Bar Assn. Founded 1900 450 Members A/M: April, 1982	Richard M. Duxbury 1811 1st Nat'l Bk. Bldg. Lincoln 68508 402/475-8433	Edwin C. Perry 1806 1st Nat'l Bk. Bldg. Lincoln 68508 402/475-2856	Douglas Duchek 1900 1st Nat'l Bk. Bldg. Lincoln 68508 402/474-6900
Omaha Bar Assn. Founded 1889 1,083 Members A/M: September, 1982	Tyler B. Gaines 10050 Regency Circle Omaha 68114 402/397-5500	Joseph B. Cashen 1900 One First Nat'l Center Omaha 68102 402/342-8200	Mardee Korinek 2133 California Omaha 68178 402/342-3786

NEVADA

Clark County Bar Assn. Founded 1947 750 Members A/M: December, 1982	Robert M. Buckalew 300 S. Fourth St., #1700 Las Vegas 89101 702/385-2188	Paul H. Schofield 516 S. Third St. Las Vegas 89101 702/382-2211	William S. Skupa 600 S. Seventh St. Las Vegas 89101 702/385-2557
Washoe County Bar Assn. Founded 850 Members A/M: June, 1982	Larry D. Struve Heroes Memorial Bldg. Carson 89710 702/747-3152	Thomas J. Hall P.O. Box 2838 Reno 89505 702/786-2366	Ruth E. Wheeler 834 Willow St., Ste. 2 Reno 89505 702/323-7631

NEW JERSEY

Atlantic County Bar Assn. Founded 1880 350 Members A/M: June, 1982	Edwin J. Jacobs, Jr. 1 S. South Carolina Ave. Atlantic 08401 609/348-1125	Mark Biel 3201 Atlantic Ave. Atlantic 08401 609/344-1173	Pasquale Cardone 535 Tilton Rd. Northfield 08225 609/645-1111
Bergen County Bar Assn. Founded 1898 1,381 Members A/M: April, 1982	David A. Pressler 222 Bridge Plaza S. Fort Lee 07024 201/947-7500	Vincent P. Rigolosi 75 Essex St. Hackensack 07601 201/646-1600	Elisabeth C. Thompson 61 Hudson St. Hackensack 07601 201/488-0032
Camden County Bar Assn. Founded 1881 1,010 Members A/M: May, 1982	William B. Scatchard Jr. 304 Harper Dr. Moorestown 08057 609/234-6800	M. Gene Haberle 130 N. Broadway Camden 08102 609/936-6026	Jay A. Strassberg P.O. Box 1027 Heritage Bk. Bldg Camden 80101 609/964-3420
Hudson County Bar Assn. Founded 1887 686 Members A/M: January, 1982	Jay Liebman 26 Journal Square Jersey City 07306 201/434-8777	Jack P. Doran 617 Pazonia Ave. Jersey City 07306 201/332-5303	Maurice Gallipoli 70 Sip Ave. Jersey City 07306 201/798-0400

A/M: Date of Annual Meeting

Other Local Associations (Cont.)

Association	President	President-Elect or Vice President	Executive Director or Executive Secretary
Mercer County Bar Assn. Founded 1901 650 Members A/M: January, 1982	Lemuel H. Blackburn, Jr. 849 W. State St. Trenton 08618 609/393-2325	Charles J. Casale 1072 Parkway Ave. Trenton 08628 609/883-8200	Roxanne E. Foster Mercer County Courthouse Trenton 08650 609/989-8880
Middlesex County Bar Assn. Founded 1948 752 Members A/M: June, 1982	William H. Gazi 1430 Oak Tree Rd. Iselin 08830 201/283-0900	Ishmael Sklarew 47 Paterson St. New Brunswick 08901 201/247-6230	Suzanne Jablonski Courthouse, Fl. 2 JFK Square New Brunswick 08901 201/494-2929 or 828-0053
Monmouth Bar Assn. Founded 1908 1,000 Members A/M: April, 1982	David K. Ansell Court House Freehold 07728 201/431-5544	H. Frank Carpentier Court House Freehold 07728 201/431-5544	Patricia A. Grignard Court House Freehold 07728 201/431-5544
Morris County Bar Assn. Founded 1900 656 Members A/M: June, 1982	Edward J. Farrell 43 Maple Ave. Morristown 07960 201/267-8130	Martin Newmark 10 Park Place Morristown 07960 201/267-8130	Nancy G. Gardner 10 Park Place, Rm. 329 Morristown 07960 201/267-5882
Ocean County Bar Assn. Founded 1924 370 Members A/M: September, 1982	James J. Barry 1433 Hooper Ave. Toms River 08753 201/349-7234	Daniel J. Carluccio 214 Washington St. Toms River 08753 201/240-3666	Sherie M. Blumenthal P.O. Box 381 Tom River 08753 201/240-3666
Passaic County Bar Assn. Founded 1899 770 Members A/M: July, 1982	Charles E. Miller 1033 Clifton Ave. Clifton 07013 201/777-8311	William F. Rabbat 205 Route 46 West Totowa 07512 201/785-1156	Anita Hoogstra District Court House Hamilton St. Paterson 07505 201/345-4585
Union County Bar Founded 1902 792 Members A/M: October, 1982	Charles N. Winetsky 401 N. Wood Ave. P.O. Box 67 Linden 07036 201/486-2761	Leo Kaplowitz 923 N. Wood Ave. Linden 07036 201/925-2468	Grace T. Nail Union County Courthouse Annex, Room 307 Elizabeth 07207 201/527-4769

NEW MEXICO

Association	President	President-Elect or Vice President	Executive Director or Executive Secretary
Albuquerque Bar Assn. Founded 1954 800 Members A/M: December, 1982	Rex D. Trockmorton P.O. Box 1888 Albuquerque 87103 505/765-5900	William W. Deaton, Jr. 20 First Plaza, #417 Albuquerque 87103 505/247-0717	Olive G. Brinkman 1210 First Enter State Bldg. Fourth & Gold S.W. Albuquerque 87103 505/243-2615

NEW YORK

Association	President	President-Elect or Vice President	Executive Director or Executive Secretary
Albany County Bar Assn. Founded 1900 850 Members A/M: January, 1982	Thomas E. Dolin 60 State St. Albany 12207 518/434-2163	E. David Duncan 100 State St. Albany 12207 518/463-2195	Pamela E. Bixby Albany County Court House Albany 12207 518/445-7691
Bronx County Bar Assn. Founded 1902 1,242 Members A/M: June, 1982	Joseph P. Garrozza Upper Mall Cross County Center Yonkers 10704 914/423-1100	Carl Radin 860 Grand Concourse Bronx 10451 212/LU5-7576	Francis G. Beck 851 Grand Concourse Bronx 10451 212/293-5600
Brooklyn Bar Assn. Founded 1872 2,000 Members A/M: May, 1982	John E. Murphy 123 Rensen St. Brooklyn 11201 212/624-0675	Marshall G. Kaplan 123 Rensen St. Brooklyn 11201 212/624-0675	John A. Pannone, Jr. 123 Remsen St. Brooklyn 11201 212/624-0675

A/M: Date of Annual Meeting

Other Local Associations (Cont.)

Association	President	President-Elect or Vice President	Executive Director or Executive Secretary
Broome County Bar Assn. Founded 1906 441 Members A/M: May, 1982	Dwight R. Ball P.O. Box 1740, 8th Floor Center Plaza Binghamton 13902 607/772-6070	Philip J. Kramer P.O. Box 1865 Binghamton 13902 607/723-6321	Sandra M. Hian 74 Front Street Binghamton 13905 607/723-6331
Dutchess County Bar Assn. Founded 340 Members A/M: May, 1982	John A. Wolf P.O. Box 4865 Poughkeepsie 12602 914/454-4141	Charlotte McCambridge Frank 54 Market St. Poughkeepsie 12601 914/454-4141	Roger M. Dunwell 54 Market St. Poughkeepsie 12601 914/454-4141
Erie County Bar Assn. Founded 1887 2,300 Members A/M: June, 1982	Maryann S. Freedman 1758 Statler Bldg. Buffalo 14202 716/852-8687	James L. Magazers 1758 Statler Bldg. Buffalo 14202 716/852-8687	Carol J. Seal 1758 Statler Bldg. Buffalo 14202 716/852-8687
Monroe County Bar Assn. Founded 1892 1,446 Members A/M: December, 1982	Robert A. Feldman 1025 Times Square Bldg. Rochester 14614 716/232-1980	David L. Hoffberg 2200 Lincoln First Tower Rochester 14614 716/546-8000	Beth H. Neiger 1125 First Fed. Plaza Rochester 14614 716/546-1817
Bar Assn. of Nassau County Founded 1899 3,589 Members A/M: May, 1982	Edward T. O'Brien 1050 Franklin Ave. Garden City 11530 516/747-3300	Robert W. Corcoran 1565 Franklin Ave. Mineola 11501 516/746-2626	Fred E. Merrell 15th & West Sts. P.O. Box 431 Mineola 11501 516/747-4070
Nassau Lawyers Assn. of Long Island Founded 1947 900 Members A/M: January, 1982	Anthony J. DeGregorio P.O. Box 614 Mineola 11501 516/742-8340	Stanley Amelkin 380 N. Broadway Gericho 11753 516/433-2424	Richard McGill 600 Old Country Rd. Garden City 11530 516/742-3666
New York Women's Bar Assn. Founded 1934 500 Members A/M: April, 1982	Diane S. Wilner 919 Third Ave., 35th Fl. New York 10022 212/371-6000	Karla Moskowitz 171 West 12th St. New York 10011 212/889-7111	Miriam Adelman 7 W. 145h St. New York 10011 212/593-4557
Oneida County Bar Assn. Founded 1898 336 Members A/M: December, 1982	Samuel D. Hester 124 Bleecker St. Utica 13501 315/724-8101	Robert A. Bankert 231 Genesee St. Utica 13501 315/724-4151	Frank J. NeBush, Jr. 505 Mayro Bldg. Utica 13501 315/724-3785
Onondaga County Bar Assn. Founded 1875 1,011 Members A/M: November, 1982	Raymond J. DeSilva 811 Kemper Bldg. Syracuse 13202 315/422-4179	James Dwyer 505 State Twr. Bldg. Syracuse 13202 315/478-2131	Donna Supper 505 State Twr. Bldg. Syracuse 13202 315/471-2667
Orange County Bar Assn. Founded 1910 375 Members A/M: April, 1982	Harry V. Lynch 1 Jersey Ave. Greenwood Lake 10925 914/477-2444	James J. McMahon 22 James St. Middletown 10940 914/343-1044	Edward D. Kaplan 436 Robinson Ave. Newburgh 12550 914/562-0203
Queens County Bar Assn. Founded 1876 2,453 Members A/M: March, 1982	Douglas H. Krieger 39-01 Main St. Flushing 11354 212/539-4422	Howard D. Stave 108-18 Queen Blvd. Forest Hills 11375 212/261-2121	Fred A. Brue 90-35 148th St. Jamaica 11435 212/291-4500

A/M: Date of Annual Meeting

Other Local Associations (Cont.)

Association	President	President-Elect or Vice President	Executive Director or Executive Secretary
Richmond County Bar Assn. Founded 1907 500 Members A/M: 1982	Frederic R. Grae 1058 Forest Ave. Staten Island 10310 212/720-7000	Charles Kuffner 1010 Forest Ave. Staten Island 10310 212/442-0900	Richard Lasher 2012 Victory Blvd. Staten Island 10314 212/447-5353
Rockland County Bar Assn. Founded 1941 364 Members A/M: May, 1982	Gerard M. Damiani 455 Route 304 Bardonia 10954 914/623-7711	Martin Hurwitz 450 S. Main New City 10956 914/634-4966	Marian De Gennaro P.O. Box 371 60 S. Main St. New City 10956 914/634-2149
Suffolk County Bar Assn. Founded 1908 1,463 Members A/M: May, 1982	Richard C. Cahn 4175 Veterans Memorial Hwy. Ronkonkoma 11779 516/981-1600	Gustave Fishell 300 John St. P.O. Box 490 Babylon 11702 516/669-0894	Marjorie Dion 4175 Veterans Mem. Hwy. Ronkonkoma 11779 516/981-1600
Westchester County Bar Assn. Founded 1896 2,031 Members A/M: March, 1982	Martin Drazen 175 Main St. White Plains 10601 914/946-3700	H. Glen Hall 351 Manville Rd. Pleasantville 10570 914/769-4635	Ellen M. Cherry 65 Court St. White Plains 10601 914/761-3707

NORTH CAROLINA

Association	President	President-Elect or Vice President	Executive Director or Executive Secretary
Greensboro Bar Assn. Founded 1927 457 Members A/M: April, 1982	Jordan Frassineti Gate City Bldg., #304 Greensboro 27401 919/273-9794	Percy Wall P.O. Box 3485 Greensboro 27402 919/288-2607	P.O. Box 1825 Greensboro 27402 919/288-7393
Mecklenburg County Bar Founded 1912 945 Members A/M: May, 1982	Francis O. Clarkson 3250 NCNB Plaza Charlotte 28280 704/374-1550	Hamlin A. Wade 2100 First Union Plaza Charlotte 28282 704/377-1634	Laura A. Kratt 600 E. Trade Street Charlotte 28202 704/374-2254
Wake County Bar Assn. Founded 1910 548 Members A/M: November, 1982	Carl P. Hollerman Drawer M. Apex 27502 919/362-8873	Samuel R. Leager Box 2417 Raleigh 27602 919/821-7052	Dan M. Hartzog P.O. Box 310 Raleigh 27602 919/821-7052

OHIO

Association	President	President-Elect or Vice President	Executive Director or Executive Secretary
Akron Bar Assn. Founded 1875 1,150 Members A/M: June, 1982	William R. Ferguson 430 Centran Bldg. Akron 44308 216/762-6281	Robert F. Orth 300 Centran Bldg. Akron 44308 216/384-9560	Susan Lengal 90 S. High St. Akron 44308 216/253-5007
Dayton Bar Assn. Founded 1925 988 Members A/M: May, 1982	David C. Greer 400 Gem Plaza, Third & Main St. Dayton 45402 513/223-3277	Peter J. Donahue P.O. Box 1817 Dayton 45401 513/226-6565	Sharron S. Cowley 120 W. Second St. Ste. 1700 Dayton 45402 513/222-7902
Lucas County Bar Assn. Founded 300 Members A/M: January, 1982	James M. Markwood 905 Spitzer Bldg. Toledo 43604 419/248-3561	Warren Rayman 937 Spitzer Bldg. Toledo 43604 419/243-2265	William M. Culbert 609 Security Bldg. Toledo 43604 419/248-4494
Mahoning County Bar Assn. Founded 1912 490 Members A/M: May, 1982	Robert J. Kalafut 206 Legal Arts Center Youngstown 44503 216/746-6591	Lou A. O'Apolito 204 Stambaugh Bld. Youngstown 44503 216/744-5151	Mrs. Mary Beth Williamson 3rd Fl., Court House Youngstown 44503 216/746-2933

_____
A/M: Date of Annual Meeting

Other Local Associations (Cont.)

Association	President	President-Elect or Vice President	Executive Director or Executive Secretary
Stark County Bar Assn. Founded 1900 543 Members A/M: October, 1982	John R. Werren 800 Cleve-Tusc Bldg. Canton 44702 216/455-0173	Ronald W. Dougerty 526 Citizen Savings Bldg. Canton 44702 216/456-2421	Mary L. Holland 309 Ameritrust Bldg. Canton 44702 216/453-0686
The Toledo Bar Assn. Founded 1878 1,400 Members A/M: June, 1982	Robert W. Rowley 1010 United Savings Bldg. Toledo 43604 419/248-3561	James P. Silk 1st Nat'l Bank Toledo 43603 419/259-6991	Marjorie S. Hunter Commodore Perry Arcade 505 Jefferson Ave. 419/242-9363

OREGON

Association	President	President-Elect or Vice President	Executive Director or Executive Secretary
Lane County Bar Assn. Founded 1929 490 Members A/M: June, 1982	Laurie Smith 303 Centre Court 44 W. Broadway Eugene 97401 505/345-3333	Larry D. Thomson 975 Oak St., Suite 620 Eugene 97401 503/686-2321	James Anderson 777 High Street Eugene 97401 503/686-2321

PENNSYLVANIA

Association	President	President-Elect or Vice President	Executive Director or Executive Secretary
Berks County Bar Assn. Founded 1888 329 Members A/M: October, 1982	Robert K. Boland 44 N. Sixth St. P.O. Box 8521 Reading 19603 215/374-8211	William R. Forry 529 Court St. Reading 19601 215/373-4291	Barbara Kittrell 544 Court St. P.O. Box 1058 Reading 19603 215/375-4591
Bucks County Bar Assn. Founded 1883 385 Members A/M: May, 1982	Robert W. Valimont 102 N. Main St. Doylestown 18901 215/355-7500	Frank N. Gallagher 60 E. Court St. Doylestown 18901 215/345-7000	Elizabeth G. Lawfer 135 E. State St. Doylestown 18901 215/348-9413
Chester County Bar Assn. Founded 1929 372 Members A/M: November, 1980	Albert P. Massey 30 Darby Road Westchester 19380 215/436-4140	C. Robert Elicker, Jr. 218 W. Miner St. West Chester 19380 215/436-4140	Deborah L. Ceribelli Wilmont Mews West Chester 19380 215/692-1889
Dauphin County Bar Assn. Founded 1895 540 Members A/M: January, 1982	Lee C. Swartz P.O. Box 889 Harrisburg 17108 717/234-4121	Richard W. Cleckner 31 N. Second St. Harrisburg 17101 717/238-1731	Allen Levinthal 213 N. Front St. Harrisburg 17101 717/232-7536
Delaware County Bar Assn. Founded 1872 650 Members A/M: January, 1982	George J. Giunta Second & Jackson P.O. Box 257 Media 19063 215/566-9525	Esther F. Clark 204 E. Chester Pike Ridley Park 19078 215/521-0600	Elizabeth C. Price Front & Lemon Sts. P.O. Box 466 Media 19063 215/566-6627
Erie County Bar Assn. Founded 315 Members A/M: December, 1982	Irving Aldo Murphy 700 First Nat'l Bank Erie 16501 814/453-4691	James D. McDonald 1400 Baldwin Bldg. Erie 16501 814/454-3821	Dolores M. Alex 501 Sassafras St. Erie 16507 814/459-3111
Lackawanna Bar Assn. Founded 1890 387 Members A/M: January, 1982	Henry C. McGrath 1000 Bank Twrs. Bldg. Scranton 18503 717/346-7651	John A. Morano Penn Security Bk. Bldg. Scranton 18503 717/961-5824	William Warren, Jr. Penn Security Bk. Bldg. Scranton 18503 717/346-7569
Lancaster Bar Assn. Founded 1945 335 Members A/M: January, 1982	William C. Storb 53 N. Duke St., 3rd Fl. Lancaster 17602 717/394-7182	David R. Eaby 3 Central Plaza Lancaster 17602 717/397-7747	Maureen E. Cullen 44 E. Orange St. Lancaster 17602 717/393-0737

A/M: Date of Annual Meeting

Other Local Associations (Cont.)

Association	President	President-Elect or Vice President	Executive Director or Executive Secretary
Bar Assn. of Lehigh County Founded 1905 324 Members A/M: January, 1982	Robert K. Young 512 Hamilton St., Ste. 200 Allentown 18101 215/434-6197	E. Keller Kline 517 Hamilton St. Allentown 18101 215/439-0461	Lehigh County Bar Assn. Old Lehigh Cnty. Ct. Hse. Allentown 18105
Luzerne County Bar Assn. Founded 1866 409 Members A/M: January, 1982	Arthur L. Piccone 700 United Penn Bk. Bldg. Wilkes-Barre 18701 717/825-9401	John L. Bigelow 1100 Northeastern Bldg. Hazleton 18201 717/455-6355	Lawrence H. Sindaco Law Library Court House, Room 23 Wilkes-Barre 18711 717/822-6029
Montgomery Bar Assn. Founded 1930 1,332 Members A/M: January, 1982	Thomas E. Waters, Jr. Ste. 701, One Montgomery Plaza Norristown 19401 215/279-7600	Frederic M. Wentz Ste. Square P.O. Box 268 115 W. Germantown Pike Norristown 19401 215/279-2480	Joseph F. Gallo P.O. Box 268 Norristown 19404 215/279-9660
Northampton County Bar Assn. Founded 1874 328 Members A/M: January, 1982	Robert B. Taylor 561 E. Market St. Bethlehem 18018 215/865-2644	Elwood M. Molos First Nat'l Bank Bldg. Easton 18042 215/253-4251	June A. Vial 201 S. 7th St. Easton 18042 215/258-6333
Westmoreland Bar Assn. Founded 1886 355 Members A/M: April, 1982	Leslie J. Mlakar First National Bk. Bldg. Greensburg 15601 412/834-6040	Dante G. Bertani 100 N. Main St. Greensburg 15601 412/837-1212	David W. Cook 11 N. Main St. Greensburg 15601 412/834-5610
York County Bar Assn. Founded 1888 304 Members A/M: December, 1982	Gary M. Gilbert 139 E. Market St. York 17401 717/845-8602	Richard H. Horn 137 E. Mark St. York 17401 717/845-7577	Diane Kearney York County Court House York 17401 717/848-3301, Ext. 361

SOUTH CAROLINA

Association	President	President-Elect or Vice President	Executive Director or Executive Secretary
Charleston County Bar Assn. Founded 412 Members A/M: February, 1982	A. Arthur Rosenblum 42 Broad St. Charleston 29401 803/577-3353	Joseph W. Cabaniss P.O. Box 816 Charleston 29402 803/577-9440	Lucas C. Padgett, Jr. 141 E. Bay St. Charleston 29401 803/723-7831
Richland County Bar Assn. Founded 1930 750 Members A/M: December, 1982	Robert J. Thomas 1000 Security Fed. Bldg. Columbia 29201 803/799-9360	Michael H. Quinn P.O. Box 73 Columbia 29202 803/779-6365	James H. Quackenbush, Jr. P.O. Box 11252 Columbia 29211 803/799-9222

TENNESSEE

Association	President	President-Elect or Vice President	Executive Director or Executive Secretary
Chattanooga Bar Assn. Founded 1897 564 Members A/M: April, 1982	Arthur C. Grisham, Jr. 1114 First Tenn. Bldg. Chattanooga 37402 615/267-1158	David B. Kesler 1200 Maclellan Bldg. Chatanooga 37402 615/266-2721	Mrs. Sheila Kaufman 62 Maclellian Bldg. Chatanooga 37402 615/266-5950
Knoxville Bar Assn. Founded 1900 649 Members A/M: December, 1982	Fred G. Musick 2121 United Amer. Plaza Knoxville 37929 615/524-1873		Marguerite McCampbell P.O. Box 2027 Knoxville 37901 615/522-7501
Memphis & Shelby County Bar Assn. Founded 1921 1,600 Members A/M: December, 1982	Donn A. Southern 100 N. Main Bldg., #3201 Memphis 38103 901/523-7111	Henry Klein 2108 First Twr. Bk. Bldg. Memphis 38103 901/523-2363	De Anne Downing Shelby Courthouse #200 Memphis 38103 901/527-3573

A/M: Date of Annual Meeting

Other Local Associations (Cont.)

Association	President	President-Elect or Vice President	Executive Director or Executive Secretary
Nashville Bar Assn. Founded 1831 1,233 Members A/M: December, 1982	Robert J. Walker 2700 First Amer. Ctr. Nashville 37238 615/244-5370		Nashville Bar Assn. 316 Stahlman Blvd. Nashville 37238 615/254-9272

TEXAS

El Paso Bar Founded 1913 460 Members A/M: September, 1982	Ray Caballero 521 Taxas Avenue El Paso 79902 915/542-4222	Royal Furgeson 20th Fl. State Natl. Plaza El Paso 79901 915/533-4424	Joan Coleman 800 Montana, #208 El Paso 79902 915/532-7052
Ft. Worth-Tarrant Bar Assn. Founded 1928 831 Members A/M: June, 1982	Morgan K. Williams 2012 Continental Life Bldg. Ft. Worth 76102 817/332-3211	Bill Bowers 2700 Continental Nat'l Bk. Ft. Worth 76102 817/336-9333	Nancy Madsen 2015 Continental Nat'l Bk. Bldg. Fort Worth 76102 817/338-4092
Jefferson County Bar Assn. Founded 1950 327 Members A/M: May, 1982	James M. Black P.O. Box 3286 Port Arthur 77640 713/982-9433	Everett Lord 85 IH 10 N. Suite 201 Beaumont 77707 713/835-8647	Gail Heiman 4th Fl., 1149 Pearl St. Beaumont 77701 713/835-8647
Northeast Texas Bar Assn. Founded 360 Members A/M: June, 1982	Jimmy L. White P.O. Box 710 Mt. Pleasant 75455	Tom Wells 41 First St., N.W. Paris 75460	Sam Williams P.O. Box 7 Mt. Pleasant 75455 214/572-8131
Nueces County Bar Assn. Founded 1929 447 Members A/M: June, 1982	Philip M. Hall 140 Guaranty Bank Plaza Corpus Christi 78475 512/883-6223	Shirley Selz P.O. Box 371 Corpus Christi 78403 512/884-1961	Irene C. Canales Nueces County Courthouse Suite 312, 901 Leopard Corpus Christi 78401 512/883-4022
San Antonio Bar Assn. Founded 1916 1,540 Members A/M: August, 1982	James N. Martin 615 Soledad, Ste. 300 San Antonio 78205 512/227-7591	James A. Branton San Antonio Bank & Trust Bldg. Ste. 255 San Antonio 78205 512/222-2271	Jimmy Allison Bexar County Courthouse, 5th Floor San Antonio 78205 512/227-8822
Travis County Bar Assn. Founded 1914 826 Members A/M: May, 1982	Gaylord Armstrong 900 Congress Austin 78701 512/476-6982	Robert D. Jones 710 W. Ave. Austin 78701 512/478-2518	Carol Leggett 507 W. 11th Street Austin 78701 512/472-0279

UTAH

Salt Lake County Bar Assn. Founded 1930 990 Members A/M: May, 1982	Kent M. Kasting 1000 Boston Bldg. Salt Lake City 84111 801/532-6996	H. James Clegg P.O. Box 3000 Salt Lake City 84110 801/521-9000	Lawrence E. Stevens 79 South State Salt Lake City 84111 801/532-1234

VIRGINIA

Alexandria Bar Assn. Founded 305 Members A/M: February, 1982	H. Bradley Evans 122 S. Royal Street P.O. Box 701 Alexandria 22314 703/549-7510	W. Curtis Sewell 510 King Street Suite 200 Alexandria 22314 703/836-8400	Pat Shea P.O. Box 1233 Alexandria 22313 703/548-8800

A/M: Date of Annual Meeting

Other Local Associations (Cont.)

Association	President	President-Elect or Vice President	Executive Director or Executive Secretary
Arlington County Bar Assn. Founded 1926 412 Members A/M: May, 1982	James W. Korman 2007 15th Street Arlington 22216 703/525-4000	Joanne F. Alper 1400 N. Uhle Street Arlington 22201 703/525-2260	Betty J. Waldow 1400 N. Courthouse Rd #501 Arlington 22201 703/558-2243
Fairfax Bar Assn. Founded 1935 785 Members A/M: May, 1982	Arthur L. Moshos 10521 Judicial Dr., Ste. 20 Fairfax 22030 703/691-1200	Charles F. Geschickter, Jr. 10533 Main St. Fairfax 22030 703/273-6400	Rosalie A. Small 4000 Chain Bridge Road Room 68 Fairfax 22030 703/273-6860 703/273-6800
Norfolk and Portsmouth Bar Assn. Founded 1900 807 Members A/M: December, 1982	William B. Eley 1500 United Vir. Bank Bldg. Norfolk 23514 804/622-6655	Charles R. Waters II 2030 Vir. Nat'l Bank Bldg. Norfolk 23510 804/625-7611	William J. Davis 1105 Virginia Nat'l Bank Bldg. Norfolk 23510 804/622-3152
Bar Assn. of the City of Richmond Founded 1885 1,288 Members A/M: May, 1982	Murray J. Janus 7th & Franklin Bldg. #1500 Richmond 23219 804/644-0721	Joseph M. Spivey P.O. Box 1535 Richmond 23212 804/788-8451	Hunter W. Martin 1002 Mutual Bldg. Richmond 23219 804/643-8616
Roanoke Bar Assn. Founded 1925 360 Members A/M: June, 1982	Evans B. Jessee 4th Fl. Shenandoah Bldg. Roanoke 24011 703/345-1420	William J. Lemon Boxley Bldg. Roanoke 24011 703/982-1000	James N. Kincanon 720 Shenandoah Bldg. Roanoke 24011 703/344-8722
Virginia Beach Bar Assn. Founded 1969 296 Members A/M: January, 1982	Henery C. Morgan, Jr. Ste. 400 Beach Twr. 3330 Pacific Ave. Virginia Beach 23451 804/425-7801	Donald H. Clark 211 Pembroke Three Bldg. Virginia Beach 23454 804/490-1281	William A. Cox III 12020 First & Merchants Norfolk 804/627-8365
WASHINGTON			
Spokane County Bar Assn. Founded 1908 650 Members A/M: June, 1982	John M. Klobucher 631 Lincoln Building Spokane 99201 509/838-8364	Wm. Frem Nielsen 1212 Washington Mutual Spokane 99201 509/455-6000	Maryjon Endicott North 721 Monroe, #401 Spokane 99201 509/456-6032
Tacoma-Pierce County Bar Assn. Founded 1852 480 Members A/M: January, 1982	Edwin J. Wheeler 401 Tacoma Mall Office Bldg. Tacoma 98409 206/475-2700	Edward Haarman 621 Amer. Fed. Svgs. Tacoma 98402 206/383-4808	Beth A. Jensen 930 Tacoma Ave. S. Room 240 Tacoma 98402 206/383-3432
WISCONSIN			
Dane County Bar Assn. Founded 962 Members A/M: February, 1982	Earl Munson Jr. 222 W. Washington Madison 53703 608/257-3911	Donald Heaney 122 W. Washington Madison 53703 608/257-7766	Dane Cnty. Bar Assn. 131 W. Wilson Street Madison 53703 608/257-2866

A/M: Date of Annual Meeting

OTHER ORGANIZATIONS REPRESENTED IN THE ABA HOUSE OF DELEGATES

Association	President	President-Elect or Vice President	Executive Director or Executive Secretary
American Judicature Society 36,000 Members A/M: August, 1982	E. N. Carpenter One Rondy Square P.O. Box 551 Wilmington, DE 19899 302/658-6541	Talbot D'Alemberte 1400 S.E. First Nat'l Bldg. Miami 33130 305/577-2816	George H. Williams 200 W. Monroe, Ste. 1606 Chicago, IL 60606 312/558-6900
American Law Institute 2,443 Members A/M: May, 1982	Roswell B. Perkins 299 Park Ave., 31st Fl. New York, NY 10017 212/752-6400	Bernard G. Segal 1719 Packard Bldg. Philadelphia, PA 19102 215/988-2222	Paul A. Wolkin 4025 Chestnut, 5th Fl. Philadelphia, PA 19104 215/243-1611
Assn. of American Law Schools 138 Schools A/M: January, 1982	Albert M. Sacks Law School Harvard University Cambridge, MA 02138 617/495-4601	Sanford H. Kadish University of California At Berkeley School of Law Berkeley, CA 94720 415/642-1741	John A. Bauman Suite 370 One DuPont Circle, N.W. Washington, DC 20036 202/296-8851
Assn. of Life Insurance Counsel 922 Members A/M: May, 1982	John B. Stoddart Prudential Insurance Prudential Plaza Newark, NJ 07101 201/877-6000	Herman T. Bailey Bankers Life Co. 711 High Street Des Moines, IA 50307 515/247-5111	Paul E. Klein 51 Madison Avenue New York, NY 10010 212/679-1110
Conference of Chief Justices 55 Members A/M: July, 1982	Albert W. Barney 111 State Street Montpelier, VT 05602 802/828-3281	Lawrence H. Cooke Monticellos Courthouse Monticello, NY 12701 914/794-4068	Edward B. McConnell 300 Newport Avenue Williamsburg, VA 23158 804/253-2000
The Federal Bar Assn. 15,000 Members A/M: October, 1982	W. Edwin Youngblood 4117 Ranier Ct. Ft. Worth, TX 76109 817/926-9628	Paul Denbling 1111 19 Street, N.W. Washington, DC 20036 202/463-2920	J. Thomas Rouland 1815 H St., NW, Ste. 408 Washington, DC 20006 202/638-0252
Federal Communications Bar Association 1,005 Members A/M: June, 1982	Earl R. Stanley 1225 Connecticut Ave. Washington, DC 20036 202/862-8044	Herbert E. Forrest 1250 Connecticut Ave., NW Washington, DC 20036 202/862-2219	Margot S. Humphrey 1150 Connecticut Ave., NW Washington, DC 20036
Judge Advocates Assn. 1,623 Members A/M: August, 1982	Alexander P. White 1300 River Drive Des Plaines, IL 60018 312/296-2288	William H. Gibbes 1518 Washington St. Columbia, SC 29201 803/799-9706	Richard A. Buddeke 4031 University Dr., #201 Fairfax, VA 22030 703/273-6564
Maritime Law Assn. of the United States 2,694 Members A/M: May, 1982	John W. Sims Hibernia Bank Bldg. New Orleans, LA 70112 504/566-1311	Gordon W. Paulsen One State St. Plaza New York, NY 10004 212/344-6800	MacDonald Deming One State St. Plaza New York, NY 10004 212/344-6800
National Assn. of Attorneys General 50 Members A/M: November, 1982	John D. Ashcroft P.O. Box 899 Jefferson City, MO 65102 314/751-3321	William J. Guste 2-3-4 Loyola Ave. New Orleans, LA 70122 504/568-5575	C. Raymond Marvin 444 N. Captiol St. Ste. 177 Washington, DC 20001 202/624-5454
National Assn. of Bar Executives 404 Members A/M: August, 1982	Robert N. DuRant P.O. Box 11038 Colombia, SC 29211 206/622-6054		Lorrayne J. Comer American Bar Association 77 S. Wacker Dr., 6th Fl. 312/621-9289

A/M: Date of Annual Meeting

Other Organizations Represented in House of Delegates (Cont.)

Association	President	President-Elect or Vice President	Executive Director or Executive Secretary
National Assn. of College and University Attorneys 2,147 Members A/M: June, 1982	Marvin E. Wright 609 E. Walnut St. Columbia, SC 65201 314/449-2613	William H. Oswald 820 North Michigan Ave. Chicago, IL 60611 312/670-2815	Phillip M. Grier One DuPont Circle, #650 Washington, DC 20036 202/296-0207
National Assn. of Criminal Defense Lawyers 2,043 Members A/M: August, 1982	Murray Janus 701 E. Franklin Richmond, VA 23219 804/644-0721	John E. Ackerman Nat'l College for Criminal Defense College of Law Univ. Houston, TX 77004 713/749-2283	Louis F. Linden 2600 South Loop W. #320 Houston, TX 77054 713/666-2777
National Assn. of Women Lawyers 1,060 Members A/M: August, 1982	Meredith Sparks 370 Minorca Avenue Coral Gables, FL 33134 305/443-2552	Claire E. Morrison 1415 Parker Avenue Detroit, MI 48214 313/964-6950	Patricia O'Mahoney 1155 E. 60th St. Chicago, IL 60637 312/947-3549
National Bar Assn. 8,000 Members A/M: August, 1982	Arnette R. Hubbard 134 North LaSalle, Ste. 300 Chicago, IL 60602 312/332-1168	Warren H. Dawson 3556 North 29th Street Tampa, FL 33605 813/248-1173	John Crump 1900 L Street, NW, #203 Washington, DC 20036 202/463-4210
National Conference of Bar Examiners 650 Members A/M: August, 1982	Francis D. Morrisey Baker & McKenzie Prudential Plaza Chicago, IL 312/861-2819	John F. O'Hara Parker, Milliken, Clark & O'Hara 333 South Hope St. Los Angeles, CA 90071 213/683-6500	Allan Ashman 333 N. Michigan Avenue Chicago, IL 60601 312/641-0968
National Conference of Commissioners on Uniform State Laws 294 Members A/M: August, 1982	M. King Hill, Jr. 100 Light, 6th Fl. Baltimore, MD 21202 301/727-1164	Carlyle C. Ring, Jr. 308 Monticello Blvd. Alexandria, VA 22305 703/548-7454	William J. Pierce University of Michigan School of Law Ann Arbor, MI 48109 313/764-9336
National District Attorneys Assn. 7,680 Members A/M: July, 1982	David L. Armstrong 30th Judicial District Jefferson Hall of Justice Louisville, KY 40202 502/581-6040	Gene Orlando Dist. Attrny. Shawneee Cnty. 200 E. 7th Square Topeka, KS 66603 913/295-4330	Jack Yuerton 708 Pondelton St. Alexandria, VA 22314 703/549-9222
National Legal Aid and Defender Assn. 1,924 Members A/M: December, 1982	C. Lyonel Jones Cleveland Legal Aid Soc. 1223 W. 6th Street Cleveland, OH 44113 216/566-7999	Jerrold R. Becker Park Nat'l Bk. Bldg. Suite #604 Knoxville, TN 37902 615/522-4194	Howard B. Eisenberg 1625 K Street, NW 8th Floor Washington, DC 20006 202/452-0620

A/M: Date of Annual Meeting

BAR ASSOCIATION RANKINGS BY

SIZE OF MEMBERSHIP

The following tables are based on the responses to the mid-1981 survey of geographically based, general purpose bars that produced the roster information in the preceeding sections. The results of a separate, more detailed survey conducted in 1980 are contained in Directory of Bar Activities, a listing of program activities and membership, staff and budget data on 234 state and local bars. Copies of this 64-page report, published in August 1980, by the Division of Bar Services, are available at $5.00 each from the ABA's Order Billing Department, 1155 E. 60th St., Chicago, IL 60637. Specify Product Code Number 171-0006.

State Bars. This group includes 47 states and Puerto Rico, each of which has one jurisdiction-wide bar association, whether unified or voluntary, and four jurisdictions (District of Columbia, North Carolina, Virginia and West Virginia) which have both unified and voluntary bars. The 56 state bars have a collective (and somewhat overlapping) membership of 555,193. The average (mean) size is 9,914 members. The median size (with about half the bars in the category larger and half smaller) is 6,000.

Locals in the House. There are 41 local bar associations represented in the ABA House of Delegates. They have a collective membership of 168,787. The average is 4,116 and the median is 2,750.

Others over 300. Responding to the survey were 170 other local bar associations which are not represented in the ABA's House of Delegates. Virtually all such associations are listed. They have a collective membership of 101,341. The average size is 591. This section includes some special purpose bar associations.

State Bar Associations

Rank	Name	Members	Rank	Name	Members
* 1.	State Bar of California	75,000	29.	Iowa State Bar Assn.	5,900
* 2.	The District of Columbia Bar (M)	35,471	30.	North Carolina Bar Assn. (M)	5,800
* 3.	State Bar of Texas	35,300	*31.	Nebraska State Bar Assn.	5,429
4.	New York State Bar Assn.	32,200	*32.	Puerto Rico Bar Assn.	5,314
* 5.	The Florida Bar	28,429	33.	Tennessee Bar Assn.	5,146
6.	Illinois State Bar Assn.	25,800	*34.	South Carolina Bar	4,798
* 7.	State Bar of Michigan	20,243	*35.	Mississippi State Bar	4,700
8.	Pennsylvania Bar Assn.	19,757	36.	Bar Assn. of the Dist. of Col. (M)	4,600
9.	Ohio State Bar Assn.	16,700	*37.	Utah State Bar	3,672
*10.	Virginia State Bar (M)	16,000	38.	Virginia Bar Assn. (M)	3,639
*11.	State Bar of Georgia	14,000	39.	Kansas Bar Assn.	3,600
*12.	The Missouri Bar	12,500	*40.	State Bar of New Mexico	3,200
13.	New Jersey State Bar Assn.	12,000	*41.	West Virginia State Bar (M)	2,931
*14.	State Bar of Wisconsin	11,929	42.	Arkansas Bar Assn.	2,724
*15.	Washington State Bar Assn.	11,000	*43.	Rhode Island Bar Assn.	2,410
16.	Massachusetts Bar Assn.	10,964	*44.	State Bar of Montana	2,010
*17.	Louisiana State Bar Assn.	10,500	45.	Hawaii State Bar Assn.	1,930
*18.	Oklahoma Bar Assn.	9,625	46.	New Hampshire Bar Assn.	1,901
*19.	North Carolina State Bar (M)	8,802	*47.	State Bar of Nevada	1,840
20.	Maryland State Bar Assn.	8,400	*48.	Alaksa Bar Assn.	1,615
21.	Minnesota State Bar Assn.	7,900	*49.	Idaho State Bar	1,610
22.	Indiana State Bar	7,580	50.	Maine State Bar Assn.	1,596
*23.	Kentucky Bar Assn.	7,513	*51.	State Bar of South Dakota	1,505
*24.	Oregon State Bar	7,327	52.	West Virginia Bar Assn. (M)	1,226
25.	Colorado Bar Assn.	7,028	*53.	State Bar Assn. of North Dakota	1,214
*26.	State Bar of Arizona	6,828	*54.	Wyoming State Bar	1,099
27.	Connecticut Bar Assn.	6,800	55.	Vermont Bar Assn.	1,034
*28.	Alabama State Bar	6,208	56.	Delaware State Bar Assn.	946

TOTAL: 555,193

(56 Associations)

* Indicates unified (mandatory membership) bars.
M Indicates jurisdiction with both unified and voluntary bars.

Local Bar Associations Represented in
the ABA House of Delegates

Rank	Name	Members	Rank	Name	Members
1.	Los Angeles County Bar Assn. (CA)	16,714	21.	Bar Assn. of Baltimore City (MD)	2,750
2.	The Chicago Bar Assn. (IL)	16,300	22.	Beverly Hills Bar Assn. (CA)	2,700
3.	Assn. of the Bar of the City		22.	Essex County Bar Assn. (NJ)	2,700
	of New York (NY)	13,000	22.	Columbus Bar Assn. (OH)	2,700
4.	New York County Lawyers Assn. (NY)	10,400	23.	Cincinnati Bar Assn. (OH)	2,528
5.	Philadelphia Bar Assn. (PA)	7,630	24.	Kansas City Bar Assn. (MO)	2,400
6.	Houston Bar Assn. (TX)	5,700	25.	Oakland County Bar Assn. (MI)	2,350
7.	Bar Assn. of San Francisco (CA)	5,200	26.	Indianapolis Bar Assn. (IN)	2,300
8.	Allegheny County Bar Assn. (PA)	5,013	27.	Maricopa County Bar Assn. (AZ)	2,150
9.	Boston Bar Assn. (MA)	5,000	28.	Alameda County Bar Assn. (CA)	2,133
10.	The Bar Assn. of Greater Cleveland (OH) . . .	4,128	29.	Cuyahoga County Bar Assn. (OH)	2,062
11.	Dallas Bar Assn. (TX)	4,019	30.	Tulsa County Bar Assn. (OK)	1,500
12.	Detroit Bar Assn. (MI)	3,875	31.	Santa Clara County Bar Assn. (CA)	1,850
13.	Hennepin County Bar Assn. (MN)	3,846	32.	Multnomah Bar Assn. (OR)	1,843
14.	Atlanta Bar Assn. (GA)	3,825	33.	Lawyers Club of San Francisco (CA)	1,800
15.	Bar Assn. of Metropolitan St. Louis (MO) . . .	3,767	34.	Louisville Bar Assn. (KY)	1,725
16.	San Diego County Bar Assn. (CA)	3,600	35.	Oklahoma County Bar Assn. (OK)	1,700
17.	Seattle-King County Bar Assn. (WA)	3,404	36.	Milwaukee Bar Assn. (WI)	1,676
18.	Denver Bar Assn. (CO)	3,384	37.	Birmingham Bar Assn. (AL)	1,507
19.	Orange County Bar Assn. (CA)	3,100	38.	Lawyers' Club of Los Angeles (CA)	1,500
20.	Dade County Bar Assn. (FL)	3,000	38.	Chicago Council of Lawyers (IL)	1,500

TOTAL 168,787

(41 Associations)

Local Bar Associations with Memberships Over 300
Which Are Not Represented in
the ABA House of Delegates

Rank	Name	Members	Rank	Name	Members
1.	Bar Assn. of Nassau County (NY)	3,589	35.	Middlesex County Bar Assn. (MA)	982
2.	Queens County Bar Assn. (NY)	2,453	36.	Bar Assn. of Norfolk County (MA)	980
3.	Erie County Bar Assn. (NY)	2,300	37.	Dane County Bar Assn. (WI)	962
4.	Westchester County Bar Assn. (NY)	2,031	38.	Jacksonville Bar Assn. (FL)	961
5.	Brooklyn Bar Assn. (NY)	2,000	39.	The Lawyers Assn. of Kansas City (MO)	957
6.	Hartford County Bar Assn. (CT)	1,900	40.	Mecklenburg County Bar (NC)	945
7.	Ramsey County Bar Assn. (MN)	1,760	41.	Wichita Bar Assn. (KS)	940
8.	Sacramento County Bar Assn. (CA)	1,665	42.	Grand Rapids Bar Assn. (MI)	934
9.	Memphis & Shelby County Bar Assn. (TN) . . .	1,600	43.	Nassau Lawyers Assn. of Long Island (NY) . .	900
10.	San Antonio Bar Assn. (TX)	1,540	44.	Pima County Bar Assn. (AZ)	870
11.	Lawyers' Club of Atlanta, Inc. (GA)	1,500	45.	San Fernando Valley Bar Assn. (CA)	850
12.	Suffolk County Bar Assn. (NY)	1,463	45.	Washoe County Bar Assn. (NB)	850
13.	Monroe County Bar Assn. (NY)	1,446	45.	Albany County Bar Assn. (NY)	850
14.	The Toledo Bar Assn. (OH)	1,400	46.	Ft. Worth-Tarrant Bar Assn. (TX)	831
15.	Bergen County Bar Assn. (NJ)	1,381	47.	Travis County Bar Assn. (TX)	826
16.	New Orleans Bar Assn. (LA)	1,379	48.	San Mateo County Bar Assn. (CA)	813
17.	Montgomery Bar Assn. (PA)	1,332	49.	Norfolk and Portsmouth Bar Assn. (VA)	807
18.	Broward County Bar Assn. (FL)	1,315	50.	New Haven County Bar Assn. (CT)	800
19.	Orange County Bar Assn. (FL)	1,297	50.	Worcester County Bar Assn. (MA)	800
20.	Bar Assn. of the City of Richmond (VA) . . .	1,288	50.	Albuquerque Bar Assn. (NM)	800
21.	Bronx County Bar Assn. (NY)	1,242	51.	Union County Bar (NJ)	792
22.	Nashville Bar Assn. (TN)	1,233	52.	Fairfax Bar Assn.	785
23.	The Women's Bar Assn. of D.C. (DC)	1,200	53.	Hampden County Bar Assn. (MA)	783
24.	Akron Bar Assn. (OH)	1,150	54.	Passaic County Bar Assn. (NJ)	770
25.	Hillsborough County Bar Assn. (FL)	1,112	55.	Lawyers' Club of Alameda County (CA)	752
26.	Bar Assn. of Montgomery County (MD)	1,094	55.	Middlesex County Bar Assn. (NJ)	752
27.	Omaha Bar Assn. (NB)	1,083	56.	Fresno County Bar Assn. (CA)	750
28.	Palm Beach County Bar (FL)	1,073	56.	Baton Rouge Bar Assn., Inc. (LA)	750
29.	DuPage County Bar Assn. (IL)	1,058	56.	Clark County Bar Assn. NB)	750
30.	Onondaga County Bar Assn. (NY)	1,011	56.	Richland County Bar Assn. (SC)	750
31.	Camden County Bar Assn. (NJ)	1,010	57.	Hinds County Bar Assn. (MS)	722
32.	Women's Lawyers Assn. of Los Angeles (CA) . .	1,000	58.	Prince George's County Bar Assn. (MD)	720
32.	Washington Bar (DC)	1,000	59.	Macomb County Bar Assn. (MI)	700
32.	Monmouth Bar Assn. (NJ)	1,000	60.	Polk County (IN)	695
33.	Salt Lake County Bar Assn. (UT)	990	61.	Hudson County Bar Assn. (NJ)	686
34.	Dayton Bar Assn. (OH)	988	62.	Pulaski County Bar Assn. (AR)	677

Rank	Name	Members	Rank	Name	Members
63.	Century City Bar Assn. (CA)	675	101.	Johnson County Bar Assn. (KS)	435
64.	Morris County Bar Assn. (NJ)	656	102.	Santa Monica Bay District Bar Assn. (CA)	432
65.	Indham County Bar Assn. (MI)	650	103.	Genessee County Bar Assn. (MI)	412
65.	Mercer County Bar Assn. (NJ)	650	103.	Charleston County Bar Assn. (SC)	412
65.	Delaware County Bar Assn. (PA)	650	103.	Arlington County Bar Assn. (VA)	412
65.	Spokane County Bar Assn. (WA)	650	104.	Luzerne County Bar Assn. (PA)	409
66.	Knoxville Bar Assn. (TN)	649	105.	Sangamon County Bar Assn. (IL)	400
67.	Greater Bridgeport Bar (CT)	625	105.	Kalamazoo County Bar Assn. (MI)	400
68.	Long Beach Bar Assn. (CA)	623	106.	San Joaquin County Bar Assn. (CA)	390
69.	The Mobile Bar Assn. (AL)	620	107.	Pasadena Bar Assn. (CA)	387
70.	Boise Bar Assn. (ID)	615	107.	Lackawanna Bar Assn. (PA)	387
71.	Contra Costa County Bar Assn. (CA)	600	108.	Bucks County Bar Assn. (PA)	385
71.	St. Petersburg Bar Assn. (FL)	600	109.	West Suburban Bar Assn. (IL)	377
71.	St. Louis County Bar Assn. (MO)	600	110.	Orange County Bar Assn. (NY)	375
72.	Northwest Suburban (IL)	580	111.	Winnebago County Bar Assn. (IL)	373
73.	Marin County Bar Assn. (CA)	575	112.	Volusia County Bar Assn. (FL)	372
74.	Chatanooga Bar Assn. (TN)	564	112.	Chester County Bar Assn. (PA)	372
75.	Tallahassee Bar Assn. (FL)	555	113.	Ocean County Bar Assn. (NJ)	370
76.	Women's Bar Assn. of Illinois (IL)	550	114.	Rockland County Bar Assn. (NY)	364
76.	Cumberland Bar Assn. (ME)	550	115.	Dutchess County Bar Assn. (NY)	360
77.	Wake County Bar Assn. (NC)	548	115.	Northeast Texas Bar Assn. (TX)	360
78.	Stark County Bar Assn. (OH)	543	115.	Roanoke Bar Assn. (VA)	360
79.	Dauphin County Bar Assn. (PA)	540	116.	Westmoreland Bar Assn. (PA)	355
80.	Baltimore County Bar Assn. (MD)	535	117.	Atlantic County Bar Assn. (NJ)	350
81.	Topeka Bar Assn. (KS)	528	118.	Wyandotte County Bar Assn. (KS)	343
82.	San Bernardino County Bar Assn. (CA)	516	119.	St. Joseph County Bar Assn. (IN)	340
83.	Ventura County Bar Assn. (CA)	515	120.	Oneida County Bar Assn. (NY)	336
84.	Lake County Bar Assn. (IL)	512	121.	Lancaster Bar Assn. (PA)	335
85.	South Bay Bar (CA)	510	122.	Monterey County Bar Assn. (CA)	333
86.	Riverside County Bar Assn. (CA)	501	122.	Arapahoe County Bar Assn. (CO)	333
87.	Cook County Bar Assn. (IL)	500	123.	Berks County Bar Assn. (PA)	329
87.	The Lawyers Assn. of St. Louis (MO)	500	124.	Northampton County Bar Assn. (PA)	328
87.	New York Women's Bar Assn. (NY)	500	125.	Palo Alto Area Assn. (CA)	327
87.	Richmond County Bar Assn. (NY)	500	125.	Jefferson County Bar Assn. (TX)	327
88.	Allen County Indiana Bar Assn. (IN)	493	126.	Santa Barbara County Bar Assn. (CA)	325
89.	Mahoning County Bar Assn. (OH)	490	126.	7th District Bar Assn. (MN)	325
89.	Lane County Bar Assn. (OR)	490	127.	Bar Assn. of Lehigh County (PA)	324
90.	Montgomery County Bar Assn. (AL)	481	128.	11th District Bar Assn. (MN)	323
91.	Tacoma-Pierce County Bar Assn. (WA)	480	129.	Linn County Bar Assn. (IA)	316
92.	Peoria County Bar Assn. (IL)	467	130.	Erie County Bar Assn. (PA)	315
93.	Boulder County Bar Assn. (CO)	465	131.	Eastern Bar Assn. of Los Angeles County (CA)	310
94.	El Paso Bar (TX)	460	131.	Hollywood Bar Assn. (CA)	310
95.	Greensboro Bar Assn. (NC)	457	132.	Clearwater Bar Assn. (FL)	305
96.	S.W. Kansas Bar Assn. (KS)	450	132.	Greene County Bar Assn. (MO)	305
96.	Lincoln Bar Assn. (NB)	450	132.	Alexandria Bar Assn. (CA)	305
97.	Nueces County Bar Assn. (TX)	447	133.	Southeast District Bart Assn. (CA)	304
98.	Shreveport Bar Assn. (LA)	446	133.	York County Bar Assn. (PA)	304
99.	Broome County Bar Assn. (NY)	441	134.	Lucas County Bar Assn. (OH)	300
100.	Kane County Bar Assn. (IL)	440	135.	Virginia Beach Bar Assn. (VA)	296

TOTAL   101,341

A Legal Guide to the Living Will

Concern for Dying

> ### To My Family, My Physician, My Lawyer
> ### and All Others Whom It May Concern
>
> Death is as much a reality as birth, growth, maturity and old age—it is the one certainty of life. If the time comes when I can no longer take part in decisions for my own future, let this statement stand as an expression of my wishes and directions, while I am still of sound mind.
>
> If at such a time the situation should arise in which there is no reasonable expectation of my recovery from extreme physical or mental disability, I direct that I be allowed to die and not be kept alive by medications, artificial means or "heroic measures". I do, however, ask that medication be mercifully administered to me to alleviate suffering even though this may shorten my remaining life.
>
> This statement is made after careful consideration and is in accordance with my strong convictions and beliefs. I want the wishes and directions here expressed carried out to the extent permitted by law. Insofar as they are not legally enforceable, I hope that those to whom this Will is addressed will regard themselves as morally bound by these provisions.
>
> Signed _____
>
> Date _____
>
> Witness _____
>
> Witness _____
>
> Copies of this request have been given to _____
> _____
> _____
> _____

Introduction

It is not a novel proposition that terminally ill and incompetent people should be permitted to die without the administration of extraordinary remedies that might prolong their lives for more than a few days or even indefinitely. It is and has long been generally understood among the medical profession that acquiescence in natural death is a proper procedure. Two factors have apparently combined in recent years to cause a few physicians and hospital authorities to hesitate to permit the patient to die a natural death: the development of more sophisticated techniques to prolong life; and the substantial increase in the number of malpractice suits. Because of such suits, physicians have become reluctant to fail to take action when such failure might conceivably expose them to any civil or criminal penalty. As we later observe there have not been, however, any malpractice actions in natural death cases nor is the fear of such actions a reasonable one.

The result has been that a number of terminally ill, incompetent and often comatose people have had their lives prolonged for considerable and even extended periods of time, affording them no satisfaction, causing suffering both to them and to their relatives and necessitating great expense, sometimes borne by the patients themselves, often to the complete exhaustion of their resources, sometimes by their families and sometimes by various public agencies at great expense to the state.

In view of the long and categorical recognition by the courts of the right of a competent person to control the disposition of his own body by virtue of his constitutional right of privacy, it is logical that the same right of privacy should continue to be available to a person who has become incompetent, although necessarily the right must be exercised by someone else. The Living Will form circulated by Concern for Dying provides a space in which the declarant appoints a specific person chosen by him to make medical decisions on his behalf. Although the validity of such appointments has not been determined by the courts, such an appointment might well be accepted at least to the extent that the court would give special weight to the recommendations of a person so designated. What is most imporant, however, is the recognition of the right of privacy; such recognition means that the terminally ill incompetent does not become the victim of well-intentioned health care professionals and the prey of unscrupulous ones.

C. DICKERMAN WILLIAMS, ESQ.

Reprinted with permission from "A Legal Guide to the Living Will," Concern for Dying, 250 W. 57th Street, New York, New York 10107, 1979.

The Living Will

The Living Will is a document through which a person, *while still competent,* directs that certain so-called "heroic medical measures" not be used to prolong life and suffering should that person become terminally ill with no reasonable expectation of recovery.

Its purposes are: (1) to assure patient autonomy in regard to treatment during terminal illness, even after the patient has become comatose or incompetent; and (2) to offer a measure of protection against liability to physicians, health care professionals and institutions by providing documented, informed consent by the patient to the withholding or withdrawing of available life-prolonging technology.

More than three million copies of the Living Will have been distributed by Concern for Dying throughout the United States since 1968. Similar documents have been distributed by the Catholic Hospital Association, the Protestant Hospital Association and several other organizations.

It is not possible to tell how many have been used. It also is impossible to determine how many have been honored by physicians, family and institutions . . . or, for that matter, in how many instances an incompetent patient's prior expression of wishes through a Living Will was disregarded.

Because there have been no legal challenges to a Living Will between 1968 and 1979, only analogous case law is available.

This pamphlet has been prepared in response to numerous inquiries from:

attorneys who have been asked to draft and execute a Living Will for a client;

attorneys for physicians who have been asked to cooperate with the patient's wishes as expressed in a Living Will; and

counsel for hospitals and other health care institutions.

It is an attempt to summarize existing law and authoritative commentary on the questions that bear upon whether a Living Will is legally *binding and enforceable* (our legal counsel believes that it is), and whether family, guardians, physicians, health care professionals or institutions may incur *civil or criminal liability* through acting in conformity with the patient's expressed desires. (Our advisors believe that the Living Will offers such a forceful and compelling defense as to make such actions highly improbable, as the absence of any such actions has demonstrated during the decade that such documents have been used.)

Each year thousands of terminally-ill persons are spared unwarranted and unwanted life-support measures and permitted to die with a maximum of dignity and a minimum of pain . . . and no litigation ensues. This is only because all concerned are in agreement — family, physician, institution and the all important patient.

Every major faith has affirmed the ethical principles upon which the Living Will is based.

This summary addresses the situations which may arise when one or another of the parties whose cooperation is needed to comply with a Living Will may choose to oppose it.

Rights of the Competent Patient

Federal and state courts generally have viewed the right to self-determination as encompasssing the right of a competent patient to refuse treatment in most cases, even when such refusal appears foolhardy, reckless, or irrational. In the early and leading case of UNION PACIFIC RY. V. BOTSFORD,[1] the Court said at p. 10001:

> "No right is held more sacred, or is more carefully guarded by the common law, than the right of every individual to the possession and control of his own person, free from all restraint or interference by others, unless by clear and unquestionable authority of law."

Indeed, a physician or institution may be liable for damages for assault and battery if treatment is imposed without the patient's consent or that of someone legally authorized to give it for him/her.

In another early case, SCHLOENDORF V. SOCIETY OF NEW YORK HOSPITAL,[2] the Court said:

> "Every human being of adult years has a right to determine what shall be done with his own body; and a surgeon who performs an operation without his patient's consent, commits an assault for which he is liable in damages."

In the more recent case of WINTERS V. MILLER,[3] the Court held that hospital authorities have no right to impose compulsory medical treatment against the patient's will and that to do so constitutes common-law assault and battery.

In the case of ERICKSON V. DILGARD,[4] the superintendent of a hospital applied to the Court for an order authorizing administration of a blood transfusion. In the absence of such a transfusion, the superintendent alleged, the patient would die. The application was denied, the Court saying at p. 28:

> "In this case, however, there is no question that the patient has been completely competent at all times while being presented with the decision to be made and in the making of the decision that he did. That being so, the court declines to make any order that blood be administered."

A multitude of cases have upheld the right of a competent person to refuse treatment such as radical surgery when that person understands that such refusal may lead to death. (Lawyers who have available case digests published by the West Publishing Company will find such cases listed under the category of "Assault 2" of these digests.)

The interests of the state may be compelling enough to override this under some circumstances. State interests that frequently have been asserted are the preservation and sanctity of human life, the prevention of suicide, the protection of innocent third parties (especially children), and the integrity of the medical decision-making process.

When treatment serves only to prolong life with no hope of recovery "the state can *never* demonstrate an interest compelling enough to outweigh the patient's constitutional right to refuse treatment as exercised either by himself or a legal guardian."[5]

The Incompetent Patient

Only two state supreme courts have spoken on the matter of refusing treatment for the terminally ill incompetent: the QUINLAN[6] court in New Jersey and the SAIKEWICZ[7] court in Massachusetts. Both courts agreed that competent individuals have a constitutional right to refuse treatment and that this right may be exercised for them by others under certain circumstances. Equally important for our discussion, however, is that both courts approved, without explicitly discussing it, the fundamental principle of the living will — i.e. both agreed that the most important factor to consider when granting an incompetent the right to refuse treatment is the wishes and desires of the incompetent himself, i.e. what would the incompetent decide if he could decide? The living will, of course, would be the *best* evidence of the prior intent or wishes of the now incompetent patient and had it been present it would probably have been determinative. (For detailed discussion of these cases, see [5] op. cit.)

When treatment poses a minimal bodily intrusion (such as a blood transfusion) and the prognosis for return to a normal life is good, it is likely that courts will order treatment for a child or incompetent, even over the objections of parents or relatives — and probably even over the presumed objections of the incompetent himself as in some of the Jehovah's Witness cases.

Medical Decision-Making and the Terminally-Ill

Courts hearing medicolegal cases generally give considerable weight to testimony regarding "standard medical practice." Standard medical practice in treating terminal patients, however, varies widely among physicians and hospitals. In addition, ten states which now have "Right to Die"

or "Living Will" Acts place limitations upon the decision not to treat. Only a judicial decision can confer *absolute immunity* from civil or criminal liability upon a physician or institution for refusal to use every available "heroic measure" of medical technology to keep a patient alive.

Therefore, if the patient's wishes are to be respected and litigation avoided, the prudent course is to consult with the physician and hospital to make certain that each is willing to respect the terms of the Living Will. Litigation not only is expensive, but it is time consuming, and the time consumed thwarts the patient's intent in executing the document.

Emergencies, a sudden onset of illness or other circumstances sometimes make it impossible for a patient to choose his physician or hospital. It is important, in case such situations arise, that the family and the attorney have copies of the Living Will to present to the attending physician and the hospital. Should the doctor and/or the hospital administration insist upon using heroic measures, the alternatives are either to change physicians and/or hospitals or to seek a summary judgment.

Even the best-intended efforts of physicians and institutions to give compassionate care to terminal patients have led to many instances of extreme and often cruel treatment. Glantz and Swazey[8] contend that misinterpretation of *Saikewicz* among Massachusetts lawyers and physicians has led to incidents such as the implantation of a cardiac pacemaker in a brain-dead "patient" and the defibrillation of a terminally-ill woman 70 times in the 24 hours before she finally died of her disease.

In RE DINNERSTEIN[9] brought some clarity to those who had been confused by the Saikewicz court. The patient suffered from a degenerative disease of the brain which results in destruction of brain tissue, typically leading to a vegetative condition and death. In this case, the action was brought by the physician with the concurrence of the patient's son (a physician) and daughter. The court held simply that prior court approval was not needed before a physician could write a "no code" order on a *hopeless* patient.

A recent Florida case, PERLMUTTER V. FLORIDA MEDICAL CENTER[10], highlights the importance of determining in advance, whenever possible, that the medical decisions will respect the patient's constitutional right.

Before Mr. Perlmutter's illness had progressed to an agonizing state, he had consented to use of a respirator that involved the insertion of an air tube into his trachea. As his condition deteriorated, he asked to have the respirator removed, knowing that death would occur within hours rather than months. When this request was denied, he removed the respirator himself, forcibly with great difficulty, only to have it replaced. His attorney sought a summary judgment, the lower court found him competent but stayed the order to remove the respirator pending an appeal by the state. The appellate court affirmed and the respirator finally was removed — five painful months after his initial decision.

Liability

Even some of the best intentioned doctors and hospitals fear liability. (The appellate court in *Perlmutter* noted that they were "not insensitive to this tragedy".) The attorney for the signer of a Living Will can do much to assuage these fears by acquainting doctors with the preponderant weight of the applicable law as described in this pamphlet. The absence of wrongful death actions in natural death cases suggests the difficulty of envisioning a scenario in which substantial damages could be claimed. There are three elements of damages in a wrongful death action:

1) Loss of earnings; as a terminally ill, incompetent person cannot be earning anything, his death cannot cause a loss of earnings.
2) Pain and suffering; a natural death shortens the patient's pain and suffering.
3) Out-of-pocket medical expenses; after a natural death there are no such expenses.

Additionally, a malpractice plaintiff would be on inherently weak ground in complaining that the defendant followed the wishes of the patient so far as they could be ascertained. There cannot reasonably be fear of malpractice actions from permitting the patient to die a natural death.

Homicide? Suicide?

The decision not to consent to medical treatment never has been, so far as our research has been able to determine, considered as suicide either by courts or by insurance companies. In fact, in several "natural death" statutes and in the *Perlmutter* case, it has been clearly stated that death of a terminally ill person which follows the withholding or withdrawing of treatment is a natural death and may not be considered a suicide.

Similarly, decisions not to treat or to cease treatment of the terminal patient have not been considered as questions of murder or manslaughter, under applicable state statutes, but rather as matters of private and medical decision-making. In the QUINLAN decision, the Court stated that:

"Under the statutes of this State, the unlawful killing of another human being

is criminal homicide…But we believe that the ensuing death would not be homicide but the expiration from existing natural causes. Secondly, even if it were to be regarded as homicide, it would not be unlawful. These conclusions rest on definitional and constitutional bases. The termination of treatment pursuant to the right to privacy is, within the limitations of this case, *ipso facto* lawful… There is a real, and in this case, determinative distinction between the unlawful taking of the life of another and the ending of artificial life-support systems as a matter of self-determination."

The distinction between the actions called for by a Living Will and either suicide or "mercy killing" is that the latter involve forms of active intervention to hasten death, whereas the Living Will asks only that death be permitted to occur naturally without the intervention of unwarranted and unwanted medical technology.

State Laws: Living Will, Natural Death, Right to Die Acts

Ten states have enacted statutes, with varying provisions, for the enforcement of documents such as the Living Will: Arkansas, California, Idaho, Kansas, Nevada, New Mexico, North Carolina, Oregon, Texas and Washington. Similar legislation is being considered in a number of other states.

A Living Will is advisable for residents of these states, both to clarify the person's wishes and as protection in the event that the person is stricken in another state.

Attorneys are advised to consult the applicable state law. Concern for Dying will furnish the appropriate document for use in the states which have such legislation.

Executing and Updating A Living Will and Supporting Documents

It is recommended that the Living Will be notarized and witnessed by two persons who are not blood relatives or beneficiaries of the estate. (A number of states require this.)

It is also recommended that the Living Will be updated periodically, either by initialling with a new date or, preferably, by a new document or a notarized and witnessed codicil. This should be done at no more than five-year intervals. Since the Living Will is invoked only when the signer is incompetent, in case of a dispute it is important that the document unquestionably reflect the present wishes of the individual.

Another reason for updating is that it enables the person to designate the individuals to represent him/her in the making of medical decisions, with a reasonable certainty that those designated will be both available and willing to support the dying person's intent.

Powers of Attorney

In states where a power of attorney may be exercised on behalf of an incompetent person, it may also be advisable for the signer of a Living Will to confer a limited power of attorney upon the person(s) designated to make medical decisions for him/her. Suggested forms for such powers of attorney are available upon request from Concern for Dying.

Hospitals and attending physicians, when providing care to a terminal patient who has expressed an oral desire not to have life-prolonging heroic measures used, may consider having him/her execute a Living Will while the patient still is competent to do so. Concern for Dying also has available a sample release form for hospitals and attending physicians as a supplement to the standard consent forms.

Such documentation can be important for the providers of health care, especially when the patient's family is divided and when treatment in the early stages of a terminal illness become contra-indicated in the final stages for reasons of patient well-being and expense. It also can obviate the need (whether real or perceived) to go to court for the appointment of an ad litem guardian.

The Issue of Incompetence

Absent case law on the enforceability of a Living Will, it is possible only to speculate on situations in which the document might be challenged on the grounds that the person was not competent at the time of signing.

The case most directly in point as regards the Living Will is IN RE YETTER.[11] Here the Court enforced prior oral expression of wishes made by a patient who subsequently became delusional and was found to have a malignant tumor. Upon an application of a relative for appointment as guardian to give consent to surgery on the patient's behalf, the Court denied the application, saying at p. 623:

> "In our opinion, the *constitutional right of privacy* (emphasis supplied) includes the right of a mature competent adult to refuse to accept medical recommendations that may prolong one's life and which, to a third person at least, appear to be in his best interests; in short, that the right of privacy includes a right

to die with which the State should not interfere where there are no minor children and no clear and present danger to public health, welfare or morals. If the person was competent while being presented with the decision and in making the decision which she did, the court should not interfere even though her decision might be considered unwise, foolish or ridiculous."

An analogous case is that of LANE V. CANDURA.[12] A 77 year old woman suffering from diabetic gangrene refused a leg amputation, after having signed a consent form one day earlier. She had previously lost a toe and then part of a foot. She subsequently told a number of people that she preferred to die rather than live incapacitated in a nursing home and undergo additional amputations. Her daughter then petitioned to be appointed guardian for the purpose of consenting to the operation.

Mrs. Candura was in a state of senility, depression and occasional confusion. The lower court found that she was not competent to make a rational decision. The appellate court reversed, finding that, while her decision was not a rational *medical* decision, it had been made when she was lucid and fully aware that the alternative was death. The court made a precatory statement that she might change her mind, but ruled that she had the constitutional right to refuse treatment no matter how irrational that refusal might appear to others.

Cases involving the same issue as *Yetter* and *Candura* have resulted in findings both of competence and incompetence, depending upon the circumstances. The key issue has generally been the patient's understanding of the nature and consequences of the decision to refuse treatment.

These cases suggest that, when a Living Will is executed under extreme conditions, it is advisable that the attorney for the patient also have witnesses attest that it was an informed act with full knowledge of the consequences. It may also be advisable, depending upon the dying person's circumstances, to have an attending physician or another medical expert attest to the signer's competence. Allegations of senility, mental illness and other causes for opposing the patient's wishes — unlikely as they are to be made — are best dealt with before they are made.

SUMMARY

The foregoing discussion should, we believe, persuade an attorney that there is reason to believe from the *Quinlan, Yetter* and analogous cases that a Living Will is enforceable in that a court would either uphold the patient's right to refuse treatment or would appoint a guardian or conservator authorized to direct the withholding or withdrawal of life-sustaining procedures.

Further, that if a patient has a signed, witnessed Living Will a physician may withhold or discontinue life-sustaining procedures without fear of legal action.

One possible course remains if a physician or hospital persists in life-sustaining procedures despite a patient's Living Will: an action for assault and battery. The courts have repeatedly said that "informed consent" is a necessary condition precedent to medical treatment. Although no case of assault and battery for overtreatment of a terminally ill patient has been found, the conclusion is readily drawn that such an action could be taken.

Footnotes

1. *Union Pac. Ry. v. Botsford,* 141 U.S. 250, 11 Sup. CT. 1000, (1891).
   Doctrines of informed consent and the right to bodily integrity.

2. *Schloendorf v. Society of New York Hospital,* 211 N.Y. 125, 129 (1914).
   "Every human being of adult years has a right to determine what shall be done with his own body; and a surgeon who performs an operation without his patient's consent, commits an assault for which he is liable in damages."

3. *Winters v. Miller,* 446 F.2d 65 (2d, cir. 1971).
   Court held that hospital authorities have no right to impose compulsory medical treatment against the patient's will and to do so constitutes common-law assault and battery.

4. *Erickson v. Dilgard,* 44 Misc. 2d 27 (N.Y. Sup. Ct. Nassau Cty. 1962).
   Order authorizing administration of a blood transfusion refused.

5. Annas, G. J., Reconciling *Quinlan* and *Saikewicz:* Decision Making for the Terminally Ill Incompetent, 4 American J. of Law & Medicine 367, 383 (1979).

6. *Matter of Quinlan,* 70, N.J. 10, 355A 2d 647 (1976).
   Guardianship for purpose of discontinuing respirator granted.

7. *Superintendent of Belchertown State Hospital v. Saikewicz,* 370 N.E. 2d 417 (1977).
   Petition for guardianship to refuse treatment in the case of an incompetent patient granted.

8. Glantz, L. H., and Swazey, J. P., "Decisions Not to Treat: The Saikewicz Case and Its Aftermath", 2 *Forum on Medicine* 22 (1979).

9. *Matter of Dinnerstein,* 380 N.E. 2d 134 (1978).
   Physician attending an incompetent terminally ill person may lawfully direct that resuscitation measures be withheld in the event of cardiac or respiratory arrest where such direction is approved by the patient's family and the patient's condition is hopeless.

10. *Perlmutter v. Fla. Med. Ctr.,* Florida, (Broward County Court, 78-1486, 1978).
    Patient sought declaratory judgement permitting the removal of his respirator. Permission granted. Ensuing death defined as from "natural" causes and not to constitute self-murder.

11. *In re Yetter,* 62 Pa. D. & C. 2d 619 (1973).
    Guardianship to consent to biopsy and surgical removal of possible breast cancer denied, notwithstanding patient's delusions on some subjects.

12. *Lane v. Candura,* Mass. Appeals Court, (Middlesex Cty., 1978).
    Guardianship to consent to amputation refused notwithstanding patient's confusion on some subjects.

Other Relevant Cases

13. *In re Osborne,* 294 A. 2d 372 (D.C. 1972).
    Guardianship to consent to blood transfusion denied.

14. *Roe v. Wade,* 93 S. Ct. 705 (1973).
    The right of personal privacy.

15. *In re Melideo,* 88 Misc. 2d 974 (N.Y. Sup. Ct., 1976).
    Court permission for blood transfusion denied.

16. *F. Dockery v. D. Dockery,* Tenn., (Hamilton County Court, 1977).
    Declaratory judgement action seeking determination of rights and liabilities. Request for appointment of guardian with power to terminate treatment granted. Treating physician declared to be without authority to continue use of respirator unless with consent of family once he has made the determination that:
    (1) There is no reasonable possibility of the patient ever emerging from the comatose condition; and
    (2) There is no reasonable possibility that the medical treatment that requires the invasion of the incompetent's body will cure the patient, who is otherwise terminally ill.

17. *In the Matter of Quackenbush,* N.J. Sup., (Morris County Court, 1978).
    Court declared patient competent to refuse amputation despite fluctuations in lucidity because he was capable of appreciating the nature and consequences of his decision.

18. *In the Matter of Vincent M. Young,* California Superior Court, (Orange County, 1979).
    Court affirms right of conservator to exercise the right to accept or refuse medical treatment, including the right to terminate life support systems on behalf of a conservatee.

Highlights of Right-to-Die Movement

Society for the Right to Die

1938: Euthanasia Society of America, predecessor of the Society for the Right to Die, founded to legalize the right of incurable sufferers to a "good death."

1957: Address by Pope Piux XII distinguished between use of "ordinary" and "extraordinary" means to prolong the life of a dying patient.

1967: "Living Will" proposed at a meeting of the Euthanasia Society by Luis Kutner, president of World Habeas Corpus.

1973: American Hospital Association approved "Patient's Bill of Rights" which included right of informed consent and right to refuse treatment.

1975: Publication of first *Legislative Manual* by Society for the Right to Die containing a Model Bill to make the Living Will a legally binding document. *Manual* included "death with dignity" bills introduced in ten state legislatures.

1976: New Jersey Supreme Court upholds individual's right to die in *Quinlan* decision.
>   **Enactment of California Natural Death Act, the nation's first right-to-die law.**

1977: Enactment of right-to-die laws in Arkansas, Idaho, Nevada, New Mexico, North Carolina, Oregon and Texas.

1978: YLS Model Bill drafted in Yale Legislative Services Project, in cooperation with Society for the Right to Die.

1979: Kansas and Washington enact right-to-die laws.

1980: Society for the Right to Die revises charter to work as an educational, legislative and judicial organization for the individual's right to die.

1980: Society initiates Awareness Campaigns in ten states with right-to-die laws.

1980: Florida Supreme Court joins New Jersey and Massachusetts high courts in upholding the individual's right to die.

1980: Vatican's "Declaration on Euthanasia" reaffirms that dying need not be prolonged by "burdensome" life-support systems.

1981:   Alabama enacts right-to-die law.

Reprinted with permission from *1981 Handbook,* published by Society for the Right to Die, 250 W. 57th Street, New York, New York 10019.

THE SOCIETY . . .

- Believes that the basic rights of self-determination and of privacy include the right to control decisions relating to one's own medical care.

- Opposes the use of medical procedures which serve to prolong the dying process needlessly, thereby causing unnecessary pain and suffering and loss of dignity. At the same time we support the use of medications and medical procedures which will provide comfort care to the dying.

- Recognizes that a terminally ill patient may become unable to take part in medical care decisions and that a patient's previously expressed wishes may not be observed by physician and/or hospital.

- Seeks to: 1) protect the rights of a dying patient, and 2) protect physicians, hospitals and health care providers from the threat of liability for complying with the mandated desires of those who wish to die with medical intervention limited to the provision of comfort care.

A Living Will

Persons wishing to not be kept "alive" with extraordinary measures when there is no serious hope of recovery should make an advance decision to this effect to assure their wishes being carried out, to protect their doctors from legal action and to avoid leaving their survivors with a sense of guilt. To help do this the Society for the Right to Die, 250 W. 57th St., New York, N.Y. 10019 has prepared a "Living Will" which reads:

A LIVING WILL

To my family, my physician, my lawyer, my clergyman
To any medical facility in whose care I happen to be
To anyone who may become responsible for my health, welfare or affairs

Death is as much a reality as birth, growth, maturity and old age—it is the one certainty of life. If the time comes when I, _____ can no longer take part in decisions for my own future, let this statement stand as an expression of my wishes, while I am still of sound mind.

If the situation should arise in which there is no reasonable expectation of my recovery from physical or mental disability, I request that I be allowed to die and not be kept alive by artificial means or "heroic measures." I do not fear death itself as much as the indignities or deterioration, dependence and hopeless pain. I, therefore, ask that medication be mercifully administered to me to alleviate suffering even though this may hasten the moment of death.

This request is made after careful consideration. I hope you who care for me will feel morally bound to follow its mandate. I recognize that this appears to place a heavy responsibility upon you, but it is with the intention of relieving you of such responsibility and of placing it upon myself in accordance with my strong convictions, that this statement is made.

Signed _____

Date _____

Witnessed by:

_____   _____

TO MAKE BEST USE OF YOUR LIVING WILL: 1) Sign and date before two witnesses. This is to insure that you signed of your own free will and not under any pressure. 2) Give your doctor a copy for your medical file and make sure he is in agreement. Bear in mind that the Living Will is not a legal document. 3) Give copies to those most likely to be concerned. Note their names at the bottom of your copy. Keep the original readily available. 4) Discuss your intentions with those closest to you NOW. This is very important. 5) Glance over your Living Will once a year; re-date it and initial the new date to make it clear that you have not changed your mind.

"RIGHT TO DIE" LEGISLATION, giving official status to the above type of instrument, has been adopted by Arkansas, California, Idaho, Kansas, Nevada, New Mexico, North Carolina, Oregon, Texas and Washington and is pending in some two dozen other states.

From *A Manual of Death Education and Simple Burial* by Ernest Morgan. Reprinted with the permission of Celo Press. If you wish to have a copy of the Manual, it can be obtained for $3.50 (ppd.) from Celo Press, Route 5, Burnsville, NC 28714.

"Living Will" Legislation

Concern for Dying

State	Became law	Time after which directive must be reexecuted	Form provided	Hospital and physician legally protected unless negligent	Binding on physician	Can be executed by adult in good health	In order to be binding, must be reexecuted after patient becomes terminal
Arkansas (Act 879)	July 1977	None	No	Yes	Same as New Mexico	Yes	No
California (A.B. 3060)	Jan. 1977	5 years	Yes	Yes	Yes, if directive signed 14 days after patient becomes terminal	Yes, but not binding unless patient is terminal	Yes
Idaho (S.B. 1164)	July 1977	5 years	Yes	Yes	Same as New Mexico (if patient is terminal and cannot communicate)	Same as California	Yes
Kansas (S 99)	April 1979	None	Suggested form	Yes	Yes	Yes	No
Nevada (A.B. 8)	July 1977	None	Yes	Yes	No	Yes	No (but directive is not binding at any time)
New Mexico (S.B. 16)	June 1977	None	No	Yes, but physician must show "reasonable care and judgment"	Yes, but no penalty if physician does not comply	Yes	No
North Carolina (S.B. 504)	July 1977	None	Yes	Physicians are protected; hospitals not specifically protected	No	Yes	Same as Nevada

Void while patient is pregnant	Provides for an agent to act on behalf of a minor	Provides for "ombudsman" for a patient in a skilled nursing facility	Provision for revocation	Penalties for hiding destroying, or falsifiying directive or revocation	Other provisions
No	Yes	No	No	No	Physician need not determine validity. Physician need not certify illness as terminal except for minors and incompetent patients. Proxy may act for incompetent patient. Signer may request life-sustaining procedures.
Yes	No	Yes	Yes	Yes	Physician must determine validity of directive and witnesses. Concealing evidence of revocation constitutes murder. Directive must be placed in patient's medical record.
No	No	No	Yes	No	Physician need not determine validity. Only operative if patient is comatose or unable to communicate with physician. Specifically does not cover persons not signing directives.
Yes	No	No	Yes	Yes	Physician need not determine validity. Patient has responsibility of notifying physician of existence of document.
Yes	No	No	Yes	Yes	Physician need not determine validity. Directive must be placed in patient's medical record. Similar documents executed before law went into effect "have same effect" as directives executed under the law.
No	Yes	No	Yes	Yes	Physician need not determine validity. Court must certify agent's decision when minor is involved. Minor may counter agent's decision. Directive must be placed in patient's medical record or physician's case file.
No	No	No	Yes	No	Physician need not determine validity. Hospitals not specifically protected but can cite law as a defense. Clerk of court must validate directive. No age provisions. Brain death defined.

State	Became law	Time after which directive must be reexecuted	Form provided	Hospital and physician legally protected unless negligent	Binding on physician	Can be executed by adult in good health	In order to be binding, must be re-executed after patient becomes terminal
Oregon (S.B. 438)	June 1977	5 years	Yes	Yes	Same as California	Same as California	Yes
Texas (S.B. 148)	Aug. 1977	5 years	Yes	Yes	Same as California	Same as California	Yes
Washington (H 264)	March 1979	None	Suggested form	Yes	No	Yes	No

Note: Alabama (Act 772) became law May, 1981.

Void while patient is pregnant	Provides for an agent to act on behalf of a minor	Provides for "ombudsman" for a patient in a skilled nursing facility	Provision for revocation	Penalties for hiding destroying, or falsifiying directive or revocation	Other provisions
No	No	Yes	Yes	Yes	Physician need not determine validity. Directive must be placed in patient's medical record.
Yes	No	No	Yes	Yes	Basically the same as the California law except (1) physician need not determine validity and (2) no provision for ombudsman for patients in skilled nursing facilities.
Yes	No	No	Yes	Yes	Physician need not determine validity. Patient has responsibility of notifying physician of existence of document.

Comparison of Right to Die Laws

Society for the Right to Die

	Arkansas ACT 879 March, 1977	California A.B. 3060 September, 1976	Idaho S.B. 1164 March, 1977	Kansas S.B. 99 April, 1979	Nevada A.B. 8 May, 1977
Title		Natural Death Act	Natural Death Act		
Purpose	Permits an individual to "request or refuse in writing . . . procedures calculated to prolong his life."	To recognize the right of adult person to make a written directive instructing physician to withhold or withdraw life-sustaining procedures in event of terminal condition.	To recognize right to execute written directive instructing physician to withhold or withdraw life-sustaining procedures when such a person is in a terminal condition.	To recognize an adult's right to make a written declaration instructing the physician to withhold or withdraw life-sustaining procedures in the event of a terminal condition.	To protect the terminal, comatose patient by means of an advance directive which is advisory only to physician.
Who May Elect?	Any adult. Also permits a proxy to execute document on behalf of minor or incompetent.	Any adult person.	Adult persons diagnosed as terminal.	Any adult person.	Any adult person.
How to Elect	Voluntary execution of a document requiring two witnesses and notarization. For minors and incompetents, document can be executed by specified family members.	Voluntary execution of Directive to Physician, legally binding when executed 14 days after diagnosis of terminal condition; otherwise it is advisory.	Voluntary execution of a document which is legally binding if executed after diagnosis of a terminal condition.	Voluntary execution at any time of a written document directing the withholding or withdrawing of life-sustaining procedures in the event of a terminal illness.	Voluntary execution of "Directive to Physicians."
Is Form Included?	No.	Yes.	Yes.	Yes, but may include other specific directions.	Yes, but need only be followed "substantially."
Formalities of Execution	As with a will of property, two witnesses and notarization of document.	Directive requires 2 witnesses not related, nor entitled to estate nor in employ of physician. Must be made part of patient's medical record.	Signed, written directive, two witnesses with same exclusions as California. Requires notarization.	Signed, written, witnessed directive, same witness exclusions as California. Permits signing by another on behalf of declarant, incapable of so doing, in his/her presence and under his/her direction.	Directive requires two witnesses, same exclusions as California. Must be made part of patient's record.
How Long is Document Effective?	In force unless revoked.	5 years.	5 years.	In effect unless revoked.	In force unless revoked.
When Does Document Become Controlling?	Law is imprecise except to state person's right to "die with dignity."	1) Certification of terminal condition by 2 physicians; 2) attending physician must determine validity of directive; 3) death must be "imminent" in judgment of physician.	After determination by attending physician that death is imminent if patient is unable to communicate instructions.	Upon certification of terminal condition by two physicians.	Advisory only.
Revocation Procedures Specified?	No.	Yes.	Yes.	Yes.	Yes.
Is Document Binding on Physicians?	No penalty for non-compliance.	Yes. Unprofessional conduct for failure to comply unless arrangements made to transfer patients.	No penalty for noncompliance.	Yes. Failure to comply or effect the transfer of a qualified patient constitutes unprofessional conduct.	No. Physician shall give weight to declaration but may consider other factors.
Are There Immunity Provisions?	Yes, for "person, hospital or other medical institution."	Yes, for physician, health facility and health professionals.	Yes, for physicians and health facilities.	Yes, for physician, health-care professionals, medical care facilities.	Yes, for physician, hospital, health professional.
Penalties for Destruction, Concealment, Falsification Of Directive or Revocation	No.	Yes.	No.	Yes.	Yes.

	New Mexico S.B. 16 April, 1977	North Carolina S.B. 504 June, 1977	Oregon S.B. 438 June, 1977	Texas S.B. 148 August, 1977	Washington H.B. 264 March, 1979
Title	Right to Die Act.	Right to a Natural Death; Brain Death.	Act Relating to the Right to Die.	Natural Death Act	Natural Death Act
Purpose	To allow an adult of sound mind to execute a document directing withholding of maintenance medical treatment when certified as terminal; also has provisions for terminally-ill minor.	To provide a procedure for the individual's right to a peaceful and natural death.	To allow an individual to execute or re-execute a directive directing the withholding or withdrawal of life-sustaining procedures should declarant become a qualified patient.	To establish a procedure for a person to provide in advance for the withdrawal or withholding of life-sustaining procedures in event of a terminal condition.	To allow adults to control decisions relating to their own medical care, including decision to have life-sustaining procedures withheld or withdrawn in event of terminal condition.
Who May Elect?	1) Adult of sound mind. 2) On behalf of a terminally-ill minor by specified family members with court certification.	Competent individual. No age provision specified. Also on behalf of terminal, comatose patients by specified family members.	Adult of sound mind.	Any adult person	Any person at least 18 years old, of sound mind.
How to Elect	Voluntary execution of document with same formalities as will. On behalf of minor by family member after certification of terminal condition by two physicians and requiring court certification of document.	Voluntary execution of an advisory document directing the withholding or discontinuance of extraordinary means.	Directive must be signed 14 days after diagnosis and certification of terminal illness to be legally binding.	Voluntary execution of Directive to Physicians legally binding when executed after the diagnosis of a terminal condition; otherwise it is advisory.	Voluntary execution of advance directive directing the withholding or withdrawal of life-sustaining procedures in a terminal condition.
Is Form Included?	No.	Yes, a suggested form to meet requirements of law: "Declaration of a Desire for a Natural Death."	Yes.	Yes.	Yes, but may include other specific directions.
Formalities of Execution	Requires two witnesses and notarization.	Signed declaration with 2 witnesses, same exclusions as California. Must be "Proved" before notary or clerk of court.	Directive requires 2 witnesses not related, nor entitled to estate nor in employ of physician. Directive must be placed in patient's medical record.	Directive requires 2 witnesses not related, nor entitled to estate nor in employ of physician. Must be made part of patient's medical record.	Signed declaration, requiring two witnesses with same exclusions as California. To be made part of patient's medical record.
How Long is Document Effective?	In effect unless revoked.	Valid until revoked.	Five years.	In force until revoked.	In force unless revoked.
When Does Document Become Controlling?	After certification of terminal illness by two physicians.	Upon certification of terminal condition by 2 physicians.	When attending physician determines "death is imminent" and when life-prolonging procedures would only prolong dying. Physician need not determine validity of directive.	Upon diagnosis and certification of terminal condition by two physicians (one the attending). Physician must determine validity of directive.	Upon written verification of terminal condition by two physicians when life-sustaining procedures would only prolong "moment of death."
Revocation Procedures Specified?	Yes.	Yes.	Yes.	Yes.	Yes.
Is Document Binding on Physicians?	Yes, but no penalty for noncompliance.	No. Only advisory.	No. Shall make "reasonable effort" to transfer patient.	Yes. Unprofessional conduct for failure to comply unless arrangements made to transfer patient.	No. Must make a "good faith effort" to transfer patient.
Are There Immunity Provisions?	Yes.	Yes.	Yes.	Yes.	Yes. Physician, health personnel and facility.
Penalties for Destruction, Concealment, Falsification Of Directive or Revocation	Yes.	No.	Yes.	Yes	Yes.

Basic Data on State Pre-Need Trust Laws

Howard C. Raether and Thomas H. Clark

STATE	PRE-NEED STATUTE	STATE CONTROL AGENCY	PERMIT REQUIRED	AMOUNT OF PAYMENTS PUT IN TRUST	AMOUNT OF INCOME PART OF TRUST	AMOUNT BUYER CAN WITHDRAW
1. ALABAMA	no law					
2. ALASKA	yes	yes	no	100%	100%	100%
3. ARIZONA	yes	yes	no	100%	100%	100%
4. ARKANSAS	yes	yes	yes	100%	100%	none
5. CALIFORNIA	Funeral directors only	yes	no	100%	Use to pay expenses and forfeitures	100% of payments
6. COLORADO	yes	yes	yes	85%	Up to 15% of contract	85% of payments & interest accrued.
7. CONNECTICUT	Insurance law governs	yes	yes			
8. DELAWARE	yes	yes	yes	100%	100%	100%
9. DISTRICT OF COLUMBIA	no law					
10. FLORIDA	yes	yes	yes (only licensees can arrange)	100%	NONE	100%
11. GEORGIA	yes	yes	yes	100%	100%	100%
12. HAWAII	yes	yes	yes	*	NONE	CONTRACTUAL REFUND
13. IDAHO	yes	no	no	100%	100%	100% less cost of operating trust
14. ILLINOIS	yes	yes	yes	95%	95%	Amount in trust account less 25% or $35.00 whichever is greater.
15. INDIANA	yes	yes	yes	100% less trustee's expense	100% less trustee's expense	Amount in trust account less 10% or $35.00 whichever is greater
16. IOWA	yes	no	no	80%	100%	Amount in trust account on mutual consent

*all payments after recovery of acquisition costs.

Printed with permission of Howard C. Raether and Thomas H. Clark, 1982.

STATE	PRE-NEED STATUTE	STATE CONTROL AGENCY	PERMIT REQUIRED	AMOUNT OF PAYMENTS PUT IN TRUST	AMOUNT OF INCOME PART OF TRUST	AMOUNT BUYER CAN WITHDRAW
17. KANSAS	yes	no	no	100%	100%	100%
18. KENTUCKY	yes	yes	yes	100%	100%	100%
19. LOUISIANA	yes	yes	*	100%	100%	100%
20. MAINE	yes	no	no	100%	100%	100%
21. MARYLAND	yes	yes	Licensed funeral director and embalmer only	100%	100%	100%
22. MASSACHUSETTS	no law					
23. MICHIGAN	yes	no	no	100%	100%	100%
24. MINNESOTA	yes	no	no	100%	100%	100%
25. MISSISSIPPI	Pre-need contracts limited severely and controlled by Insurance Commissioner					
26. MISSOURI	yes	yes	no	80%	none	80%
27. MONTANA	yes	yes	no	100%	100%	100% on mutual consent
28. NEBRASKA	yes	yes	no	100%	100%	100%
29. NEVADA	yes	yes	yes	75%	25%	net purchase price of contract
30. NEW HAMPSHIRE	yes	yes	no	100%	100%	100%
31. NEW JERSEY	yes	no	no	100%	100%	100%
32. NEW MEXICO	yes	yes	yes	100%	100%	100% less cost of operating trust
33. NEW YORK	yes	yes	no	100%	100%	100%
34. NORTH CAROLINA	yes	yes	yes	100%	100%	100%
35. NORTH DAKOTA	yes	yes	Can be engaged in only by operators of licensed funeral establishments	100%	100%	100%

*Licensed funeral director and embalmer only.

STATE	PRE-NEED STATUTE	STATE CONTROL AGENCY	PERMIT REQUIRED	AMOUNT OF PAYMENTS PUT IN TRUST	AMOUNT OF INCOME PART OF TRUST	AMOUNT BUYER CAN WITHDRAW
36. OHIO	yes	no	no	100%	100%	100%
37. OKLAHOMA	yes	yes	yes	90%	100%	100% of amount paid into trust fund
38. OREGON	yes	no	no	100%	100%	100%
39. PENNSYLVANIA	yes	yes	no	last 70%	100% on deposit	last 70% of payments
40. RHODE ISLAND	no law—Pre-need arrangements may be grounds for suspension or revocation of license					
41. SOUTH CAROLINA	yes	yes	yes	100%	100%	100%
42. SOUTH DAKOTA	yes	yes	*	100%	100%	100%
43. TENNESSEE	yes	yes	no	100%	100%	100%
44. TEXAS	yes	yes	yes	90%	100% less trust expenses	All of payments held in trust—no interest
45. UTAH	yes	yes	yes	at least 75%	100% of trust	90% of the amount placed in trust
46. VERMONT	no law					
47. VIRGINIA	yes	no	no	100%	100%	Mutual consent
48. WASHINGTON	yes	yes	yes	85%	100%	100% of amount in trust
49. WEST VIRGINIA	yes	yes	no	95%	95%	Amount in trust less 25% or $35.00 whichever is greater
50. WISCONSIN	yes	no	no	100%	100%	100%
51. WYOMING	Commissioner of Insurance sets out rules and regulations.					

* Licensed funeral director or operator of funeral establishment.

State Legislation and Regulations Proposed And Enacted Relative To Hospice

CALIFORNIA: Assembly Bill 1586 (law 1978).

CONNECTICUT: Public Act 78-76, Substitute Senate Bill 289 (law 1978).

CONNECTICUT: Regulations of the State Department of Health Section 19-13-D46, (effective January 18, 1979).

FLORIDA: Senate Bill 1255 (law 1978).

FLORIDA: Senate Bill 628 (amending 1978 Senate Bill 1255 above, law 1980).

FLORIDA: House Bill 1257, House Bill 1815, and House Bill 1255 (all were defeated or included in Senate Bill 628 that passed in 1980).

HAWAII: Senate Bill 135 and 136 (Failed 1979).

HAWAII: Senate Resolution 40 (law 1980).

ILLINOIS: To establish a study commission on hospice (Failed 1979).

ILLINOIS: Senate Bill 1815 (In Process, July 1980).

IOWA: House Bill 618 (Failed 1979).

IOWA: House File 2178 and Senate File 2135 (Both Failed, 1980).

KANSAS: House Bill 3114 (In Process, July 1980).

MARYLAND: House Joint Resolution 38 (law 1979).

MARYLAND: House Bill 133 (Failed 1979).

MICHIGAN: On Licensure of Hospice (Failed 1979).

MICHIGAN: House Bill 4909 (In Process, July 1980).

NEVADA: Senate Bill 466 (law 1979).

NEW JERSEY: Senate Bills 43 and 358 (Failed 1979).

NEW JERSEY: Senate Bill 394 (In Process, July 1980).

NEW JERSEY: Proposed MANUAL OF STANDARDS FOR LICENSURE OF HOSPICES (June 1980).

NEW YORK: Chapter 718 (law 1978).

OHIO: House Bill 1103 and Senate Bill 360 (In Process, July 1980).

OREGON: House Bill 2807 (law 1979).

VIRGINIA: House Joint Resolution 252 (law 1979).

WEST VIRGINIA: House Bill 1400 (Failed 1979).

PART 3

SOURCES OF INFORMATION AND ASSISTANCE

ASSOCIATIONS

Associations

AGE/AGING

U.S.A.

AMERICAN AGING ASSOCIATION
D. Harman, M.D.
College of Medicine
University of Nebraska
Omaha, NE 68105
402/559-4416

AMERICAN FOUNDATION FOR AGING RESEARCH
Dr. Paul F. Agris, President
117 Tucker Hall
University of Missouri
Columbia, MO 65211
314/882-6426
Founded: 1979.
Purpose: To support research in the biology of aging and of age-related diseases by awarding grants; to engage in such research.

INTERNATIONAL FEDERATION ON AGEING
Richard E. Johnson, General Secretary
1909 K St. NW
Washington, DC 20049
202/872-4886
Founded: 1973.
Membership: 55 associations.
Purpose: To act as a clearinghouse for information with practical application to the needs of the aged; to serve as an international advocate for the elderly.
Publication: "Social Services for the Aged, Dying and Bereaved in International Perspective, 1978."

LEGAL COUNSEL FOR THE ELDERLY (*See* **LEGAL/ MEDICAL** listing.)

NATIONAL ASSOCIATION OF OLDER AMERICANS
Charles M. Musick, President
129 N. Cherry St.
Eaton, OH 45381
513/228-0108
Founded: 1972.
Purpose: To provide assistance and information to members on the subjects of aging and retirement.
Services: Offers counseling for widows and widowers and for spouses of the terminally ill.
Publication: "Heartline Almanac for Older Americans."

WESTERN GERONTOLOGICAL ASSOCIATION
Gloria Cavanaugh, Director
833 Market St.
Fifth Floor
San Francisco, CA 94103
415/543-2617
Founded: 1954.
Purpose: To provide information on aging; to train students in the art of dealing with aging.
Publication: Magazine (quarterly).

WIDOWED PERSONS SERVICE
Leo E. Baldwin, Sr., Coordinator
1909 K St. NW
Washington, DC 20049
202/872-4922
Founded: 1973.
Affiliation: A national program of the American Association of Retired Persons.
Purpose: To provide technical assistance in developing outreach programs to the newly widowed using widowed volunteers and a broad organizational base. [*Note:* Currently, WPS co-sponsors 135 programs in the United States for both men and women of all ages.]
Publications: Bibliography on widowhood (revised annually); directory of service to widowed in U.S. and Canada; report—*WPS Insights* (quarterly).

CONSUMER GROUPS

U.S.A.

AMERICAN COUNCIL ON CONSUMER INTERESTS
Mel Zelenak, Executive Director
162 Stanley Hall
University of Missouri
Columbia, MO 65201
Publications: Occasional book reviews.

CEMETERY CONSUMER SERVICE COUNCIL, INC.
(*See* **FUNERAL INDUSTRY** listing.)

CENTER FOR CONSUMER AFFAIRS
UNIVERSITY OF WISCONSIN—EXTENSION
James L. Brown, Director
929 N. Sixth St.
Milwaukee, WI 53203
414/224-4177
Purpose: To serve consumer interests.
Services: Offers workshops, seminars and classes; conducts research; testifies on pending state and national legislation; provides speakers for community groups and media broadcasts; consults with business and government leaders; advises consumer organizations in state; maintains a library; researches bibliographies on specific consumer topics.
Publication: Booklet—"Wisconsin Funeral Service—A Consumer Guide."

CONSUMERS UNION
Rhoda H. Karpatkin, Executive Director
256 Washington St.
Mount Vernon, NY 10550
914/664-6400
Founded: 1936.
Purpose: To provide consumers with information and counsel on consumer goods and services.
Publications: Book—*Funerals: Consumers' Last Rights—The Consumers Union Report on Conventional Funerals and Burial . . . and Some Alternatives, including Cremation, Direct Cremation, Direct Burial, and Body Donation;* magazine—*Consumer Reports* (monthly).

CONTINENTAL ASSOCIATION OF FUNERAL &
MEMORIAL SOCIETIES
Elizabeth C. Clemmer, Executive Director
1828 L St. NW
Suite 1100
Washington, DC 20036
202/293-4821
Founded: 1963.
Membership: 175 memorial societies.
Affiliation: Memorial Society Association of Canada.
Purpose: Through its local memorial societies, to assist members in preplanning simple, dignified and inexpensive funerals; to coordinate the activities of the more than 175 memorial societies in the United States.

Services: Works exclusively on funeral industry consumer issues; provides expert testimony; offers consumer education programs; lobbies for funeral reform.
Publications: Books—*A Manual of Death Education and Simple Burial* and *Handbook for Funeral & Memorial Societies;* chart—"Funeral Practices: Survey of State Laws and Regulations"; numerous other booklets, pamphlets, charts, handouts, etc.

CONSUMER AFFAIRS COMMITTEE
Ann Brown, Chairperson
3005 Audubon Terrace NW
Washington, DC 20008
202/244-4080
Membership: 40.
Affiliation: Americans for Democratic Action.
Purpose: To participate in consumer investigation and advocacy.
Services: Have entered into hearings at the FTC; chairperson has sat on the mayor's funeral-regulations committee in Washington, DC.
Publication: Survey—"Survey of Cemetery Prices and Policies."

OFFICE OF CONSUMER AFFAIRS (*See* **GOVERNMENT AGENCIES** listing.)

CANADA

CONSUMERS' ASSOCIATION OF CANADA
Janice Kerr, National President
703-251 Laurier Ave. W
Ottawa, Ontario K1S 5J3 Canada
613/232-9661
Founded: 1947.
Membership: 150,000.
Purpose: To act as consumer advocate for Canadians; to solve consumer problems; to gather information and to provide counsel on consumer goods and services.
Publications: Address—"Notes for an Address to the Funeral Service Association of Canada"; magazine—*Canadian Consumer.*

EDUCATION

U.S.A.

AMERICAN BOARD OF FUNERAL SERVICE EDUCA—
TION (*See* **FUNERAL INDUSTRY** listing.)

ASSOCIATION FOR GERONTOLOGY IN HIGHER
EDUCATION
Elizabeth B. Douglass, Executive Director
600 Maryland Ave. SW
WW 204
Washington, DC 20024
202/484-7505

Founded: 1974.
Membership: 220 institutions.
Affiliation: Leadership Council of Aging Organizations.
Purpose: To develop and expand gerontology programs in academic institutions; to improve the capacity of such institutions to serve the nation's elderly; to advocate the interests of gerontology in higher education and of education in the field of aging.

CENTER FOR BIOETHICS
Doris Goldstein, Director; Judith Mistichelli,
Senior Librarian
Kennedy Institute
Georgetown University
Washington, DC 20057
202/625-2383
Founded: 1973.
Affiliations: Kennedy Institute; Georgetown University.
Purpose: To sponsor research and to collect and disseminate information relating to ethical issues in biomedicine.
Publications: *Encyclopedia of Bioethics, 1978; Bibliography of Bioethics* (annually); *New Titles in Bioethics* (monthly); computer data base—*Bioethicsline;* various materials by resident and visiting scholars on ethical values in death and dying.

CENTER FOR DEATH EDUCATION AND RESEARCH
Dr. Robert Fulton, Director
University of Minnesota
1167 Social Sciences Building
Minneapolis, MN 55455
612/376-3641
Founded: 1969.
Affiliations: French Thanatological Association; International Work Group for Death, Grief and Bereavement.
Purpose: To gather information and engage in research.

FORUM FOR DEATH EDUCATION AND COUNSELING, INC.
Bruce Bowman, Acting President
P.O. Box 1226
Arlington, VA 22210
301/434-3468
Founded: 1976.
Membership: 800.
Purpose: To raise professional standards for death educators and counselors; to provide a forum for professional and lay discussion of issues in the field.
Services: Distributes educational materials; sponsors conferences, meetings and workshops.
Publications: Essay anthology—*New Directions in Death Education and Counseling: Enhancing the Quality of Life in the Nuclear Age;* newsletter—*Forum Newsletter* (ten issues per year).

GRIEF EDUCATION INSTITUTE
Irene Meier, Administrative Assistant
2422 S. Downing
Denver, CO 80210
303/777-9234

Founded: 1976.
Membership: 150.
Purpose: To promote the healthy resolution of grief following bereavement; to teach laymen and professionals how to cope with grief in themselves and in others.
Services: Provides comprehensive services to the bereaved; offers educational programs for laymen and professionals; engages in research; maintains a speakers bureau and a lending library.
Publications: *Bereavement Support Groups: Leadership Manual;* newsletter—"GEI Newsletter" (quarterly).

HOLISTIC LIFE INSTITUTE
Allen Klein, Coordinator, Life/Death Transition Program
1627 Tenth Ave.
San Francisco, CA 94117
415/664-4900
Founded: 1976.
Affiliation: Holistic Life Foundation.
Purpose: To present workshops and classes on the life/death transition process.
Publication: Newspaper/catalog—"Holistic Life" (quarterly).

INSTITUTE OF GERONTOLOGY
Willie M. Edwards, Head Librarian
520 E. Liberty St.
University of Michigan
Ann Arbor, MI 48109
Founded: 1965.
Purpose: To engage in research, training and service on the topic of aging.
Services: Disseminates information on the subject of death and dying; provides a referral service; maintains a library.

NATIONAL RESEARCH & INFORMATION CENTER
Joe A. Adams, Ph.D., Director
1614 Central St.
Evanston, IL 60201
312/328-6545
Founded: 1978.
Purpose: To serve as an independent organization for research concerning death, grief and funeral service.
Services: Grants awards for research; conducts original research.
Publication: Newsletter—*The National Reporter* (monthly).

EUTHANASIA

U.S.A.

AMERICAN EUTHANASIA ASSOCIATION
Vincent F. Sullivan, Executive Director
95 N. Birch Rd.
Ft. Lauderdale, FL 33304
305/467-8080
Founded: 1972.
Membership: 40,000.
Purpose: To persuade doctors to reevaluate their belief in prolonging life at all costs; to publicize the argument for

euthanasia; to provide the public with a means for declaring the wish to die rather than to be kept alive by extraordinary means—"The Mercy Will."
Publications: Pamphlet—"The Will to Die"; "The Mercy Will."

CONCERN FOR DYING (*See* **PATIENT RIGHTS** listing).

NATIONAL EUTHANASIA COUNCIL
A. J. Levinson, Director
250 W. Fifty-seventh St.
New York, NY 10019
212/246-6962
Founded: 1967.
Services: Distributes films on euthanasia; provides students with training weekends.
Publications: Book—*Euthanasia: A Decade of Change;* ten pamphlets.

SOCIETY FOR THE RIGHT TO DIE (*See* **PATIENT RIGHTS** listing.)

FUNERAL INDUSTRY

U.S.A.

AMERICAN BOARD OF FUNERAL SERVICE EDUCATION
William H. Ford, Administrator
201 Columbia St.
P.O. Box 2098
Fairmont, WV 26554
Purpose: To accredit colleges of funeral service education.
Services: Provides a list of colleges offering one-, two-, three- and four-year programs in mortuary science.

AMERICAN CEMETERY ASSOCIATION
Stephen L. Morgan, Executive Vice-President
5201 Leesburg Pike
Suite 1111
Falls Church, VA 22041
703/379-5838
Founded: 1887.
Membership: 2,504.
Purpose: To promote association among owners and operators of cemeteries, mausoleums and columbariums; to encourage good business practices; to encourage building of modern interment places and provide for their care and maintenance; to elevate ethical standards and foster greater respect for the industry; to encourage pre-arrangement of cemetery needs.
Services: Disseminates information relating to the operation of cemeteries, mausoleums and columbariums.
Publication: *Cemetery Management* (monthly).

AMERICAN INSTITUTE OF COMMEMORATIVE ART
H. J. Sehaller, Executive Director
P.O. Box 145
Valhalla, NY 10595
212/753-8181

Purpose: To provide members with a forum for the exchange of ideas on monument design, etc.

AMERICAN MONUMENT ASSOCIATION
Pennie L. Sabel, Executive Director
6902 N. High St.
Worthington, OH 43085
614/885-2713
Founded: 1904.
Membership: 178.
Purpose: As the national trade association of granite manufacturers, to promote the use of granite monuments; to serve as a central organization for the three granite manufacturing areas in the United States; to provide credit and collection services.
Publication: Brochure—"Choosing a Monument"; magazine—*Stone in America* (monthly); newsletter (monthly).

CASKET MANUFACTURERS ASSOCIATION OF AMERICA
708 Church St.
Evanston, IL 60601
312/866-8383
Founded: 1913.
Purpose: To function as a trade association.

CEMETERIES ASSOCIATION OF GREATER CHICAGO
7600 Cermak Rd.
Forest Park, IL 60130
312/443-8500

CEMETERY CONSUMER SERVICE COUNCIL, INC.
R. B. Gray, Jr., Secretary
P.O. Box 3574
Washington, DC 20007
703/379-6426
Founded: 1979.
Affiliations: American Cemetery Association; Cremation Association of North America; Pre-Arrangement Interment Association of North America.
Purpose: To provide a mechanism for informally resolving consumer complaints and inquiries about cemetery services.

THE CONFERENCE OF FUNERAL SERVICE EXAMINING BOARDS
Richard R. Poindexter, Executive Director
520 E. Van Trees St.
P.O. Box 497
Washington, IN 47501
812/254-7887
Purpose: To administer national and state board examinations for funeral directors and embalmers.

CREMATION ASSOCIATION OF NORTH AMERICA
Paul G. Bryan, Secretary; Jean M. Scribner, Editorial Consultant
P.O. Box 7047
Incline Village, NV 89450
702/831-3848
Founded: 1913.

Membership: 400.
Purpose: To serve as a trade association for crematory operators.
Services: Supplies promotional material; provides legal advice.
Publication: *Cremationist* (quarterly).

FEDERATED FUNERAL DIRECTORS OF AMERICA
Wendell W. Hahn, President
1622 S. MacArthur Blvd.
Springfield, IL 62708
217/525-1712
Founded: 1925.
Purposes: To provided financial and business information to funeral homes.

INTERNATIONAL CEMETERY SUPPLY ASSOCIATION
Robert F. Loffer, Secretary-Treasurer
P.O. Box 7779
Columbus, OH 43207
614/443-4675

INTERNATIONAL ORDER OF THE GOLDEN RULE
Dale L. Rollings, Executive Director
929 S. Second St.
Springfield, IL 62704
217/544-7428
Founded: 1928.
Membership: By invitation.
Purpose: To provide consultation to managers of public relations in the funeral home industry.
Publications: Newsletters—"Knight Letter" and "Trend Line."

JEWISH FUNERAL DIRECTORS OF AMERICA
Judith L. Weiss, Director
122 E. Forty-second St.
New York, NY 10168
212/370-0024
Founded: 1928.
Purpose: To preserve finest traditions of Jewish funeral services; to promote highest principles of Jewish funeral professionals.
Publication: Magazine (quarterly).

MONUMENT BUILDERS OF NORTH AMERICA
John E. Dianis, CAE, Executive Vice-President
1612 Central
Evanston, IL 60201
312/869-2031
Founded: 1906.
Purpose: To promote ideals of monuments throughout the world; to serve as a clearinghouse for the industry and the public.
Publication: "Living With an Empty Chair."

NATIONAL CATHOLIC CEMETERY CONFERENCE
James R. Mulvaney, Executive Secretary
710 N. River Rd.
Des Plaines, IL 60016
312/824-8131

Founded: 1949.
Affiliation: National Welfare Conference, Washington, DC.
Purpose: To bury Catholic dead according to canon law established by Catholic Church.

NATIONAL CONCRETE BURIAL VAULT ASSOCIATION
Earl J. Brutsche, Executive Director
P.O. Box 1031
Battle Creek, MI 49016
Founded: 1929.
Purpose: To make funeral vaults to sell to funeral directors.

NATIONAL FOUNDATION OF FUNERAL SERVICE
Dr. Joe Adams, Director
1614 Central St.
Evanston, IL 60201
312/328-6545
Founded: 1950s.
Purpose: To promote continuing education for funeral directors.
Services: Provides a management school.

NATIONAL FUNERAL DIRECTORS AND
MORTICIANS ASSOCIATION
Gertrude Roberts Moore, Acting Executive Secretary
C/O Miller & Major Funeral Home
734 W. Seventy-ninth St.
Chicago, IL 60620
312/752-7419; 312/487-3600

NATIONAL FUNERAL DIRECTORS &
MORTICIANS ASSOCIATION, INC.
Larry C. Williams, Sr.
Williams and Brown
733 Fifteenth St. NW
Suite 620
Woodward Building
Washington, DC 20005
202/347-6464 (Law firm)

NATIONAL SELECTED MORTICIANS
Frank W. Miller, Executive Director
1616 Central St.
Evanston, IL 60201
312/475-3413
Founded: 1917.
Membership: 950.
Purpose: To assist in developing sound business and professional practices in the funeral industry by gathering data and by providing a forum for the exchange of information and ideas; to oversee compliance with the NSM Code of Good Funeral Practice.
Services: Conducts educational meetings; provides speakers and films.
Publications: Bulletins—*NSM Bulletin* (quarterly) and special service bulletins; newsletter—"NSMailgram" (biweekly); rosters—"NSM Personal Roster" (annually) and "NSM Official Membership Roster" (annually).

CANADA

BOARD OF FUNERAL SERVICES
D. B. Steenson, Registrar
24 Grosvenor St.
First Floor
George Drew Building
Toronto, Ontario M4Y 1A9 Canada
416/921-5164
Purpose: To act as a licensing and disciplinary board to administer the Funeral Services Act under the Ontario Ministry of Health.
Publication: Brochure—"Facts About Funerals."

CANADIAN FUNERAL SUPPLY ASSOCIATION
159 Bay St.
Suite 207
Toronto, Ontario M5I 1J7 Canada
416/366-1495

GOVERNMENT AGENCIES

U.S.A.

OFFICE OF CONSUMER AFFAIRS
Virginia H. Knauer, Director
1009 Premier Building
Washington, DC 20201
202/634-4329
Founded: 1964.
Purpose: Executive Order 11583 (February 24, 1971) directs OCA "to encourage and assist in the development and implementation of consumer programs, coordinate and review those policies and programs, seek resolution of conflicts, and advise agencies on the effectiveness of their consumer programs." [Note: Mrs. Knauer, as Special Assistant to President Reagan, has responsibilities for consumer affairs, health care, aging, disabled, and safety concerns.]
Services: Functions as an advisor for ThanaCap, the funeral complaint mechanism sponsored by the National Funeral Directors Association.
Publication: Newsletter—"Consumer News" (bimonthly).

UNITED STATES SOCIAL SECURITY ADMINISTRATION
John A. Svahn, Commissioner of Social Security
Office of Information
4J10 West Highrise
Baltimore, MD 21235
301/594-2883
Founded: 1935.
Affiliation: Agency of U.S. Department of Health and Human Resources.
Purpose: To administer the Social Security, Supplemental Security Income, Aid to Families with Dependent Children and Child Support Enforcement programs; to take applications for and provide information about Medicare.
Publication: Booklet—"Your Social Security" (updated annually).

CANADA

HEALTH RESOURCES DIRECTORATE
DEPARTMENT OF NATIONAL HEALTH AND WELFARE
R. Lachaine, Director General, Health Resources Directorate, Health Services and Promotion Branch
Room 620
Jeanne Mance Building
Ottawa, Ontario K1A 1B4 Canada
613/593-6509; 613/996-3211
Affiliation: Department of National Health and Welfare.
Purpose: At the federal level, to administer the national health insurance programs under which virtually all Canadians are insured through the corresponding provincial hospital and medical care insurance plans. [Note: The publicly-financed health insurance programs in Canada include prepaid coverage for medically-necessary care, including terminal care, but do not include death benefits.]

HEALTH

U.S.A.

AMERICAN CANCER SOCIETY
777 Third Ave.
New York, NY 10017
212/371-2900
Founded: 1913. (Reorganized: 1945.)
Purpose: To serve as a nonprofit organization dedicated to the elimination of cancer.
Services: Provides sick-room equipment for the home use of dying patients; supplies reference material to doctors.

AMERICAN LUNG ASSOCIATION
James A. Swomley, Managing Director
1740 Broadway
New York, NY 10019
212/245-8000
Founded: 1904.
Affiliation: Approximately 200 associations in the United States.
Purpose: To help Americans prevent lung disease through public and professional education.
Services: Conducts seminars and courses; sponsors professional and technical publications and films; makes numerous printed materials, films and other resources available to the public.

THE AMERICAN RED CROSS
George M. Elsey, President
Seventeenth and D Sts. NW
Washington, DC 20006
202/737-8300
Founded: 1881.
Membership: Millions.
Affiliation: League of Red Cross Societies (Geneva, Switzerland).
Publication: "Basic Information for Prospective Kidney Donors."

Purpose: To improve the quality of human life and enhance individual self-reliance and concern for others; to help people avoid emergencies, prepare for emergencies and cope with emergencies.

Services: Provides volunteer blood services; serves as a medium of relief and communication between the public and the armed forces; maintains a system of local, national and international disaster relief; assists the government in meeting humanitarian treaty commitments.

Publication: Textbook—*Family Health and Home Nursing.*

ASSOCIATION FOR THE CARE OF CHILDREN'S HEALTH

Beverley H. Johnson, Executive Director
3615 Wisconsin Ave.
Washington, DC 20016
202/244-1801
Founded: 1965.
Membership: 3,200.
Purpose: To promote the emotional and social well-being of children and their families in all types of health care settings.
Services: Holds regional meetings and an annual conference; sponsors a public education campaign.
Publications: Annotated bibliographies; journal (quarterly); newsletter (bimonthly); pamphlets.

CENTER FOR MEDICAL CONSUMERS AND HEALTH CARE INFORMATION

Arthur Levin, Director
237 Thompson St.
New York, NY 10012
212/674-7105
Founded: 1976.
Purpose: To provide information to the public through its newsletter and its library.
Publication: Newletter—"Health Facts."

CONSUMER COALITION FOR HEALTH

1751 N St. NW
Washington, DC 20036
202/546-5800

NATIONAL KIDNEY FOUNDATION, INC.

Dolph Chianchiano, Acting Executive Director
2 Park Ave.
New York, NY 10016
212/889-2210
Founded: 1950.
Membership: 11,000; over 1,000,000 volunteers.
Affiliations: American Blood Commission; National Health Agencies for the Combined Federal Campaign; National Health Council; National High Blood Pressure Education Program.
Purpose: To serve as the only voluntary health agency seeking the prevention, treatment and cure for diseases of the kidney.
Services: Engages in research; provides a nationwide organ donor program; sponsors professional education; disseminates information to the public.

CANADA

BRITISH COLUMBIA HEALTH ASSOCIATION

Mrs. P. Wadsworth, Executive Director
440 Cambie St.
Vancouver, British Columbia V6B 2N6 Canada
604/683-7421
Founded: 1917.
Membership: 162 health care facilities.
Affiliation: Canadian Hospital Association.
Purpose: To offer education, consultation and service to its member facilities; to lobby on their behalf.
Services: Sponsors education conferences and maintains a library loan collection on the subject of death and dying.
Publication: Newsletter.

CANADIAN HOSPITAL ASSOCIATION

Jean-Claude Martin, President
410 Laurier Ave. W
Suite 800
Ottawa, Ontario K1R 7T6 Canada
613/238-8005
Founded: 1928.
Purpose: To promote the welfare of the Canadian public through its leadership and assistance to member health care facilities.
Services: Publishes periodicals and books for health professionals; offers educational extension services; maintains a resource library.

CANADIAN LUNG ASSOCIATION

Dr. Earl Hershfield, Executive Director
75 Albert St.
Suite 908
Ottawa, Ontario K1P 5E7 Canada
613/237-1208
Founded: Ca. 1900.
Purpose: To provide health education, information and service; to engage in research.

CANADIAN MENTAL HEALTH ASSOCIATION

George Rohn, General Director
2160 Yonge St.
Third Floor
Toronto, Ontario M5S SZ3 Canada
416/484-7750
Founded: 1926.
Membership: 25,000.
Purpose: To promote the concept of positive mental health.
Services: Focuses attention on special educational needs of children; promotes research; provides help for hospitalized patients; provides rehabilitation and employment opportunities; mobilizes community volunteers.
Publication: Pamphlet—"Coping with Bereavement."

KIDNEY FOUNDATION OF CANADA

Winston Evans, Executive Director
1650 de Maisonneuve W
Suite 400
Montreal, Quebec H3H 2P3 Canada
514/934-4806

Founded: 1964.
Membership: 10,000.
Purpose: To sponsor research on the causes, prevention and cure for kidney disease and related disorders; to administer public and professional education and patient services.
Publication: Newsletter (quarterly).

NATIONAL CANCER INSTITUTE OF CANADA; CANADIAN CANCER SOCIETY
Dr. R. A. Macbeth, Executive Vice-President
77 Bloor St. W
Suite 401
Toronto, Ontario M5S 2V7 Canada
416/961-7223
Founded: 1938.
Affiliations: Each other.

NOVA SCOTIA ASSOCIATION OF HEALTH ORGANIZATIONS
J. F. Ingram, Executive Director
5991 Spring Garden Rd.
Suite 600
Halifax, Nova Scotia B3H 1Y6 Canada
902/429-4020
Founded: 1960.
Membership: 65 institutions.
Affiliation: Member—Canadian Hospital Association.
Purpose: To assist member institutions in providing quality health care to the residents of Nova Scotia.

ONTARIO HOSPITAL ASSOCIATION
G. R. Cunningham, Executive Director
150 Ferrand Dr.
Don Mills, Ontario M3C 1H6 Canada
416/429-2661
Founded: 1924.
Membership: 375 (individuals and institutions).
Affiliations: Canadian Hospital Association; American Hospital Association.
Purpose: To stimulate, encourage and assist in the provision of the highest affordable standard of hospital care and related health services.
Services: Has cosponsored two conferences on palliative care; plans to expand library acquisitions on death and dying; has published reports in various OHA publications on hospital initiatives to develop palliative care sections.

HOSPICE

U.S.A.

BAY AREA HOSPICE ASSOCIATION
830 Market St.
San Francisco, CA 94102
415/392-2626

CONNECTICUT HOSPICE INSTITUTE FOR EDUCATION, TRAINING AND RESEARCH
R. Johnson-Hurzeler, Executive Director; John W. Abbott, Project Coordinator
61 Burban Dr.
Branford, CT 06405
203/481-6231
Founded: 1978.
Purpose: To weave the hospice concept and philosophy into the fabric of the health-care system; to enhance the skills and awareness of caregivers working with terminally-ill patients and families.
Services: Conducts continuing education courses for physicians, nurses, social workers, clergy, volunteer directors and administrators; produces films and video tapes.

HOSPICE INSTITUTE FOR EDUCATION, TRAINING AND RESEARCH
765 Prospect St.
New Haven, CT 05611
203/787-9946
Services: Information and education.
Publication: Newsletter.

NATIONAL HOSPICE ORGANIZATION
Josefina B. Magno, M.D., Director
1311A Dolley Madison Blvd.
McLean, VA 22101
703/356-6770
Founded: June 1978.
Purpose: To promote the hospice concept of care and to ensure quality of care for patients and families by working on areas of concern to local hospices (standards criteria, legislation, reimbursement, licensing, education, training, ethics, fund development, research, evaluation, public relations, etc.); to provide a referral resource for hospice programs in the United States.
Publications: Hospice bibliographies.

LEGAL/MEDICAL

U.S.A.

AMERICAN COLLEGE OF LEGAL MEDICINE
Edgar A. Reed, M.D., J.D., FCLM, President
213 W. Institute Pl.
Suite 412
Chicago, IL 60610
312/440-0080
Founded: 1955.
Membership: 670.
Purpose: To address problems at the interface of law and medicine, especially medical jurisprudence and forensic medicine.
Publications: *Journal of Legal Medicine; Legal Aspects of Medical Practice.*

AMERICAN SOCIETY OF LAW & MEDICINE
A. Edward Doudera, J.D., Executive Director
765 Commonwealth Ave.
Sixteenth Floor
Boston, MA 02215
617/262-4990
Founded: 1971.
Membership: 2,700.
Purpose: To advance continuing medicolegal education.
Services: Publishes journals; conducts conferences on issues such as treatment of critically- or terminally-ill patients.
Publications: Journals—*American Journal of Law & Medicine* (quarterly) and *Law, Medicine & Health Care* (six issues per year); textbook—*Legal & Ethical Aspects of Treatment for Critically and Terminally III Patients.*

LEGAL COUNSEL FOR THE ELDERLY
Wayne Moore, Project Director; Terre Poppe,
Office Manager
1331 H St. NW
LL120
Washington, DC 20005
202/234-0970
Founded: 1976.
Affiliation: The American Association of Retired Persons.
Purpose: To provide free legal service to DC residents sixty years and older.
Services: Specializes in protective services (conservatorships, etc.), nursing home reform and estate planning.

NATIONAL HEALTH LAWYERS ASSOCIATION
David J. Greenburg, Esq., Executive Director
522 Twenty-first St. NW
Washington, DC 20006
202/393-3050
Founded: 1971.
Membership: 2,100.
Purpose: To provide a forum on health law.
Services: Sponsors educational conferences on health law.
Publications: Newsletters—"Health Law Digest" (monthly) and "Health Lawyers News Report" (monthly).

**PRE-ARRANGEMENT INTERMENT ASSOCIATION
OF AMERICA**
E. Augusta Parks, Executive Vice-President
6849 Old Dominion Dr.
Suite 223
McLean, VA 22101
703/790-5822
Founded: 1956.
Publications: "I Don't Want to Think About It"; magazine (bimonthly).

CANADA

CANADIAN MEDICAL PROTECTIVE ASSOCIATION
P.O. Box 8225
Ottawa, Ontario K1G 3H7 Canada
613/236-2100
Purpose: To protect Canadian doctors in legal matters.

ORGAN DONATION

U.S.A.

DEMONSTRATORS ASSOCIATION OF ILLINOIS
Robert W. North, Curator
2240 W. Fillmore St.
Chicago, IL 60612
312/733-5140
Founded: 1885.
Membership: 9 Illinois medical schools.
Affiliation: Owned and operated by the nine medical schools located in Illinois.
Purpose: To receive, prepare and deliver to nine Illinois medical schools human remains donated to scientific study.

EYE BANK ASSOCIATION OF AMERICA
Emile J. Farge, Ph.D., Executive Director
6560 Fannin
Level Nine
Houston, TX 77030
713/790-6126
Founded: 1961.
Membership: 81.
Purpose: To certify eye banks and to train and certify technicians; to work for upgrading of organ donation legislation; to engage in fund raising on behalf of member eye banks; to encourage eye donation.
Services: Participates in regional and national meetings on donor procurement.

NATIONAL TEMPORAL BONE BANKS
Charles T. Wood, Director
Massachusetts Eye and Ear Infirmary
243 Charles St.
Boston, MA 02114
617/523-7900
Founded: 1827.
Affiliation: Harvard Medical School.
Purpose: To engage in preventive medicine (eyes, ears, nose and throat); to participate in research; to teach doctors in those fields.

ORGAN RECOVERY, INC.
Marcia Blech, Executive Director
1991 Lee Rd.
Cleveland, OH 44118
216/371-8455
Founded: 1969.
Purpose: To facilitate the recovery and transplant of cadaveric organs; to encourage organ donation through public and professional education; to involve the families of terminally-ill patients in the donor process.

TRANSPLANTATION SOCIETY
The State University of New York at Stony Brook
Stony Brook, NY 11794
516/444-2209

CANADA

ORGAN DONORS CANADA

Mae Cox, Executive Director
5326 Ada Blvd.
Edmonton, Alberta T5W 4N7 Canada
403/479-9363
Founded: 1974.
Purpose: To encourage and facilitate the process of anatomical gift giving in Canada.
Publications: Newsletter—"Transplant News" (quarterly); "Human Transplants in Canada: The Problems, The Challenge."

PATIENT RIGHTS

U.S.A.

AMERICAN EUTHANASIA ASSOCIATION (*See* EUTHANASIA listing.)

CONCERN FOR DYING

Mrs. A. J. Levinson, Executive Director
250 W. Fifty-seventh St.
Room 831
New York, NY 10107
212/246-6962
Founded: 1967.

Purpose: To assure patient autonomy in regard to treatment during terminal illness; to prevent futile prolongation of the dying process and needless suffering by the dying.
Services: Distributes living will and advises on its effective use; sponsors conferences, workshops, lectures and study groups; develops and distributes educational materials on death, dying and euthanasia.
Publication: "Euthanasia—A Decade of Change"; "A Legal Guide to the Living Will"; newsletter (quarterly).

NATIONAL EUTHANASIA COUNCIL (*See* EUTHANASIA listing.)

PATIENTS' AID SOCIETY

505 Fifth Ave.
Eighteenth Floor
New York, NY 10017
212/687-0890

SOCIETY FOR THE RIGHT TO DIE

Sidney D. Rosoff, President; Alice Mehling,
Executive Director
250 W. Fifty-seventh St.
New York, NY 10019
212/246-6973
Founded: 1938.
Purpose: To work for the recognition of the individual's right to die with dignity.
Publications: Fact sheets on right-to-die court cases; handbook (annual); newsletter (semiannual).

MEMORIAL SOCIETIES

Introduction

Most memorial societies are small, nonprofit organizations dedicated to making simple, dignified, economical burial and cremation available to the public. Memorial societies see their purpose as twofold: to educate the public about death and to act as consumer watchdogs of the funeral industry. The societies disseminate literature and provide speakers, sponsor legislation and lobby for funeral reform, and work with local funeral directors to provide low-cost services for the society's members in time of need.

The following listing includes memorial societies that belong to the two national associations of memorial societies (the Continental Association of Funeral and Memorial Societies in Washington, D.C. and the Memorial Society Association of Canada in Weston, Ontario) and a few organizations that for various reasons have not complied with the national associations' standards and codes. Not listed are the for-profit direct disposition firms, many of which use the words "memorial society" in their name but which are not a recognized part of the consumer movement represented by the memorial societies and their parent associations.

Because new societies are formed regularly, please check with the national associations for new listings.

Prices included in this list represent those available as of late 1981, unless otherwise indicated. The fees generally include the mortician's basic charges for direct burial or cremation. In general, cemetery costs and the costs of vaults and liners are not included. Most of the quotes include the cost of a casket and of a memorial service to take place after the burial or cremation. "Traditional" funeral services can also be arranged with the cooperating mortician or through arrangement with a memorial society.

Memorial Societies

U.S.A.

ALABAMA

THE AZALEA FUNERAL & MEMORIAL COUNCIL
302 Bay Shore Ave.
P.O. Box 92
Mobile, Al 36607
205/653-9092
Membership: 207.

ALASKA

COOK INLET MEMORIAL SOCIETY
P.O. Box 2414
Anchorage, AK 99501
907/277-6001
Founded: 1973.
Area: Municipal Anchorage.
Membership: 310.
Fees: Lifetime individual—$10.00; lifetime family—$20.00.
Services: One area mortuary provides: cremation—$565.00; burial—$800.00.

ARIZONA

VALLEY MEMORIAL SOCIETY
1446 E. Second Pl.
Mesa, AZ 85023
602/969-7801
Founded: 1959.
Area: Maricopa and northern Pima counties.
Membership: 3,600.
Fees: Lifetime individual and family—$20.00; records fee—$5.00 (remitted by mortician at time of services).

MEMORIAL SOCIETY OF PRESCOTT
335 Aubrey St.
Prescott, AZ 86301
602/778-3000
Founded: 1974.
Area: CoConin, Mohave and Vavapai counties.
Membership: Individual—62; family—168.
Fees: Lifetime membership—$20.00; incoming transfer fee—$4.00.
Services: Nine area mortuaries provide: cremation—$365.00 to $700.00; burial—$375.00 to $725.00.

TUCSON MEMORIAL SOCIETY
P.O. Box 12661
Tucson, AZ 85732
602/884-5099
Founded: 1960.
Area: Arizona (mainly Pima County).

Membership: Individual—5,000; family—2,500.
Fees: Lifetime membership—$20.00; incoming transfer fee—$3.00.
Services: One mortuary provides: cremation—$360.00 and up; simple burial—$400.00 and up.
Donors referred to: Lions Club Eye Bank; University of Arizona Medical School.

MEMORIAL SOCIETY OF YUMA
P.O. Box 4314
Yuma, AZ 85364
602/783-2339

ARKANSAS

NORTHWEST ARKANSAS MEMORIAL SOCIETY
1227 S. Maxwell
Fayetteville, AK 72701
501/442-5580

MEMORIAL SOCIETY OF CENTRAL ARKANSAS
12213 Rivercrest Dr.
Little Rock, AK 72207
501/225-7276

CALIFORNIA

HUMBOLDT FUNERAL SOCIETY
666 Eleventh St.
Arcata, CA 95521
707/822-1321
Founded: 1965.
Area: Del Norte, Humboldt, Mendocino and Siskiyou counties.
Membership: Individual—333; family—237.
Fees: Lifetime individual—$5.00; lifetime family—$10.00.
Services: Two mortuaries provide: cremation—$500.00 and up (not including casket and cemetery charges); burial—$300.00 and up (not including casket and cemetery charges).

BAY AREA FUNERAL SOCIETY
P.O. Box 264
Berkeley, CA 94701
415/841-6653
Founded: 1956/7.
Area: Alameda, Contra Costa, Lake, Marin, Napa, San Francisco, Solano and Sonoma counties.
Membership: 18,900.
Fees: Lifetime individual—$15.00; lifetime family—$25.00.
Services: Fourteen mortuaries provide: complete cremation—$295.00 to $350.00; immediate burial—$250.00 to $400.00.
Donors referred to: Northern California Transfer Bank; University of California at San Francisco Medical School.

Prepared by Marquis editorial staff.

VALLEY MEMORIAL SOCIETY
P.O. Box 101
Fresno, CA 93707
209/224-9580
Founded: 1962.
Area: Central California.
Membership: 542.
Fees: Lifetime individual—$15.00; lifetime family—$25.00; incoming transfer fee—$5.00.
Services: One mortuary provides: immediate cremation—$290.00; immediate burial—$208.00; modified funeral—$665.00.
Donors referred to: Northern California Transplant Bank.

TRI-COUNTY MEMORIAL-FUNERAL SOCIETY
P.O. Box 114
Midway City, CA 92655

STANISLAUS MEMORIAL SOCIETY
P.O. Box 4252
Modesto, CA 95352
209/523-0316
Founded: 1960.
Area: Mercede, Stanislaus and Tuolumne counties.
Membership: Over 400 families.
Fees: Lifetime membership—$10.00; incoming transfer fee—$2.00.
Services: One mortuary provides economical cremation.

PENINSULA FUNERAL SOCIETY
P.O. Box 11356A
Palo Alto, CA 94306
412/321-2109
Founded: 1952.
Area: San Francisco, San Mateo and Santa Clara counties.
Membership: 10,000.
Fees: Lifetime individual—$25.00 (includes records fee—$10.00); incoming transfer fee—$15.00 (includes records fee—$10.00).
Services: Four mortuaries and one limited service firm provide: direct cremation—$295.00 to $450.00; direct burial—$300.00 to $500.00; simplest funeral—$450.00 to $720.00; full funeral—$825.00 to $1,000.00.
Donors referred to: State Curator, University of California School of Medicine; Stanford University Medical School; Northern California Transplant Bank.

LOS ANGELES FUNERAL SOCIETY, INC.
P.O. Box 44188
Panorama City, CA 91412
213/786-6845
Founded: 1957.
Area: Los Angeles County.
Membership: 25,000 (individual and family).
Fees: Lifetime individual—$15.00; lifetime family—$25.00; records fee—$7.50 (remitted by mortician at time of death); incoming transfer fees—$3.00 (individual) and $5.00 (family).
Services: By referral to cooperating morticians.
Donors referred to: University of Southern California; University of California at Los Angeles; Los Angeles College of Chiropractry.

KERN MEMORIAL SOCIETY
P.O. Box 2122
Ridgecrest, CA 93555
Membership: 588.
Fees: Incoming transfer fee.

SACRAMENTO VALLEY MEMORIAL SOCIETY
P.O. Box 161688
3720 Folsom Blvd.
Sacramento, CA 95816
916/451-4641
Founded: 1959.
Area: Nineteen counties in northern California.
Fees: Lifetime individual—$15.00; lifetime family—$25.00; records fee—$2.00; incoming transfer fee—$5.00.

SAN DIEGO MEMORIAL SOCIETY
P.O. Box 16336
San Diego, CA 92116
714/284-1465
Founded: 1958.
Area: Imperial and San Diego counties.
Membership: 11,000.
Fees: Lifetime individual—$15.00; incoming transfer fee—$7.50.
Services: One mortuary provides: cremation—$248.00; burial—$168.00; funeral—$595.00.
Donors referred to: University of California at San Diego, Organ Donor Program.

CENTRAL COAST MEMORIAL SOCIETY
P.O. Box 679
San Luis Obispo, CA 93406
805/543-6133
Founded: 1960.
Area: San Luis Obispo and northern Santa Barbara counties.
Membership: 1,850.
Fees: Lifetime individual—$15.00; lifetime family—$25.00.
Services: One mortuary provides: cremation—$200.00 and up; direct burial—$170.00 and up.

CHANNEL CITIES MEMORIAL SOCIETY
P.O. Box 424
Santa Barbara, CA 93102
805/962-4794
Membership: 11,036.
Fees: Incoming transfer fee.
Services: By written agreement with two mortuaries.

FUNERAL & MEMORIAL SOCIETY OF MONTEREY BAY, INC.
P.O. Box 2900
Santa Cruz, CA 95063
408/462-1333
Membership: 826.
Fees: Records fee; incoming transfer fee.
Services: By contract with at least one mortuary.

SAN JOAQUIN MEMORIAL SOCIETY
P.O. Box 4832
Stockton, CA 95204
209/462-8739
Membership: 833.
Services: By written agreement with one mortuary.

COLORADO

ROCKY MOUNTAIN MEMORIAL SOCIETY
1400 Lafayette St.
Denver, CO 80218
303/830-0502
Membership: 7,022.
Fees: Incoming transfer fee.
Services: By contract with at least one mortuary.

CONNECTICUT

MEMORIAL SOCIETY OF SOUTHEAST CONNECTICUT
P.O. Box 825
Groton, CT 06340
203/445-8348

MEMORIAL SOCIETY OF GREATER NEW HAVEN
60 Connelly Parkway
C/O Co-op
Hamden, CT 06514
203/288-6463
Membership: 1,870.
Fees: Incoming transfer fee.

MEMORIAL SOCIETY OF GREATER HARTFORD
6 Sagamore Dr.
R.D. 1
Simsbury, CT 06070
203/728-6609
Founded: 1975.
Area: Northern Connecticut.
Membership: 548.
Fees: Lifetime individual—$10.00; incoming transfer fee—$3.00.
Services: Advisory.
Donors referred to: Yale School of Medicine; University of Connecticut School of Medicine; Connecticut Eye Bank; Kidney Foundation; Human Growth Foundation.

GREATER NEW HAVEN MEMORIAL SOCIETY
SOUTHBURY BRANCH
974-A Heritage Village
Southbury, CT 06488
203/264-7564

MEMORIAL SOCIETY OF SOUTHWEST CONNECTICUT
71 Hillendale Rd.
Westport, CT 06880
203/227-8705

DISTRICT OF COLUMBIA

MEMORIAL SOCIETY OF METROPOLITAN WASHINGTON
1500 Harvard St. NW
Washington, DC 20009
202/234-7777
Founded: 1965.
Area: Metropolitan Washington.
Fees: Lifetime individual—$10.00; lifetime family—$15.00.
Services: Advisory.
Donors referred to: University of Georgetown Medical School; Howard University Medical School.

FLORIDA

MEMORIAL SOCIETY OF BREVARD COUNTY
P.O. Box 276
Cocoa, FL 32922
305/783-8699
Membership: 493.
Services: By written agreement with seven mortuaries.

FUNERAL SOCIETY OF MID-FLORIDA
P.O. Box 262
DeBary, FL 32713
305/668-6587
Membership: 814.
Services: By written agreement with two mortuaries.

MEMORIAL SOCIETY OF ALACHUA COUNTY
P.O. Box 13195
Gainesville, FL 32604
904/376-7073

JACKSONVILLE MEMORIAL SOCIETY
6915 Holiday Rd. N
Jacksonville, FL 32216
904/724-3766

MIAMI MEMORIAL SOCIETY
P.O. Box 557422
Ludlam Branch
Miami, FL 33155
305/667-3697

FUNERAL & MEMORIAL SOCIETY OF SOUTHWEST FLORIDA
6 E. First St.

P.O. Box 6
Windmill Village
North Ft. Myers, FL 33903
813/995-1596
Founded: 1968.
Area: Fifty mile radius (including Charlotte and Collier counties).
Membership: Individual—698; family—1,152.
Fees: Lifetime membership—$25.00.
Services: One mortuary provides: cremation—$350.00; burial—$350.00; funeral—$350.00.
Donors referred to: State of Florida, Anatomical Board; University of Miami School of Medicine; Department of Biological Structures, Miami.

ORANGE COUNTY MEMORIAL SOCIETY
C/O First Unitarian Church
1815 E. Robinson St.
Orlando, FL 32803
305/893-3621

FUNERAL & MEMORIAL SOCIETY OF PENSACOLA & NORTHWEST FLORIDA
P.O. Box 4778
Pensacola, FL 32507
904/456-7028

SUNCOAST-TAMPA BAY MEMORIAL SOCIETY
719 Arlington Ave. N
St. Petersburg, FL 33701
813/953-3740

MEMORIAL SOCIETY OF SARASOTA
P.O. Box 5683
Sarasota, FL 33579
813/953-3740
Membership: 4,105.
Fees: Records fee; incoming transfer fee.
Services: By verbal agreement with three mortuaries.

FUNERAL & MEMORIAL SOCIETY OF LEON COUNTY
P.O. Box 20189
Tallahassee, FL 32304
Founded: 1972.
Area: One hundred fifty mile radius in northern Florida.
Membership: Individual—50; family—125.
Fees: Lifetime individual—$10.00; lifetime family—$15.00; records fee—$10.00 (individual) and $15.00 (family) (remitted to society by mortician at time of services).
Services: Advisory.
Donors referred to: North Florida Eye Bank; Tallahassee Regional Medical Center; Lions Club; University of Florida.

TAMPA MEMORIAL SOCIETY
3915 N. A St.
Tampa, FL 33609
813/877-4604
Founded: 1962.
Area: One hundred mile radius of Tampa.
Membership: 1,146 (including 325 families).
Fees: Lifetime individual—$15.00; lifetime family—$30.00.
Services: One mortuary provides: cremation—about $400.00; simple burial—$450.00.
Donors referred to: Eye banks; University of Florida Medical School.

PALM BEACH FUNERAL SOCIETY
P.O. Box 2065
West Palm Beach, FL 33402
305/833-8936
Membership: 11,671.
Fees: Records fee; incoming transfer fee.
Services: By contract or written agreement with three mortuaries.

GEORGIA

MEMORIAL SOCIETY OF GEORGIA
1911 Cliff Valley Way NE
Atlanta, GA 30329
404/634-2896
Membership: 2,358.
Fees: Records fee.
Services: By written agreement with two mortuaries.

HAWAII

FUNERAL & MEMORIAL SOCIETY OF HAWAII
200 N. Vineyard Blvd.
Suite 403
Honolulu, HI 96817
808/538-1282
Membership: 2,351.
Fees: Records fee; incoming transfer fee.
Services: By written agreement with six mortuaries.

IDAHO

IDAHO MEMORIAL ASSOCIATION
P.O. Box 2622
Boise, ID 83705
208/466-7311
Founded: 1972.
Area: One hundred fifty mile radius of Boise; *branch*—The Pioneer Burial Society.
Membership: Individual—40; family—24.
Fees: Lifetime membership—$15.00.
Services: Advisory.

ILLINOIS

CHICAGO MEMORIAL SOCIETY
McLEAN COUNTY BRANCH
1612 E. Emerson
Bloomington, IL 61701
309/828-0235

MEMORIAL SOCIETY OF CARBONDALE AREA
905 Carter St.
Carbondale, IL 62901
618/457-6240
Membership: 65.
Services: Advisory.

CHICAGO MEMORIAL ASSOCIATION
59 E. Van Buren St.
Chicago, IL 60605
312/939-0678
Founded: 1959.
Area: Metropolitan Chicago; *branch*—Bloomington (McLean County).
Membership: 10,000.
Fees: Lifetime individual—$20.00; lifetime family—$25.00.
Services: Advisory.

FOX VALLEY FUNERAL ASSOCIATION
783 Highland Ave.
Elgin, IL 60120
312/695-5265
Membership: 144.
Services: By verbal agreement with at least one mortuary.

MEMORIAL SOCIETY OF GREATER PEORIA
908 Hamilton Blvd.
Peoria, IL 61603
309/673-5391
Membership: 134.

MEMORIAL SOCIETY OF NORTHERN ILLINOIS
P.O. Box 6131
Rockford, IL 61125
815/964-7697
Membership: 220.

CHAMPAIGN COUNTY MEMORIAL SOCIETY
309 W. Green St.
Urbana, IL 61801
217/384-8862
Membership: 378.
Services: By written agreement with at least one mortuary.

INDIANA

BLOOMINGTON MEMORIAL SOCIETY
2120 N. Fee Ln.
Bloomington, IN 47401
812/332-3695
Founded: 1967.
Membership: 405 (including 175 families).
Fees: Lifetimes individual—$5.00; lifetime family—$10.00; records fee.
Services: Two mortuaries provide: cremation—$225.00 to $485.00; burial—$225.00 to $250.00; funeral—$350.00 to $400.00.
Donors referred to: Indiana University at Indianapolis Medical School.

MEMORIAL SOCIETY OF NORTHEAST INDIANA
306 W. Rudsill Blvd.
Ft. Wayne, IN 46807
219/745-4756; 219/637-6478

INDIANAPOLIS MEMORIAL SOCIETY
5805 E. Fifty-sixth St.
Indianapolis, IN 46226
317/545-6005
Area: Marion County.
Fees: Lifetime individual—$5.00; lifetime family—$10.00; records fee—$5.00 to $10.00.
Services: Advisory; by cooperation with two mortuaries.
Donors referred to: Kidney Foundation; Eye Bank of Indianapolis.

MEMORIAL SOCIETY OF MUNCIE AREA
1900 N. Morrison Rd.
Muncie, IN 47304
317/289-1500

MEMORIAL SOCIETY OF NORTHWEST INDIANA
356 McIntyre Ct.
Valparaiso, IN 46383
219/462-5701
Membership: 268.
Services: By written agreement with two mortuaries.

GREATER LAFAYETTE MEMORIAL SOCIETY
P.O. Box 2155
West Lafayette, IN 47906
317/463-9645
Founded: 1964.
Area: Tippecanoe County.
Membership: 250 (including 150 families).
Fees: Lifetime membership—$15.00.
Services: By agreement with one mortuary.
Donors referred to: Indiana University, Indianapolis.

IOWA

CENTRAL IOWA MEMORIAL SOCIETY
1015 Hyland Ave.
Ames, IA 50010
515/239-2314

Founded: 1976.
Fees: Lifetime membership—$5.00.
Services: Advisory.
Donors referred to: College of Osteopathic Medicine, Des Moines; College of Medicine, Iowa City.

MEMORIAL OPTION SERVICES OF CEDAR RAPIDS
203 Twenty-third Ave. NE
Cedar Rapids, IA 52402
319/363-3927 (evenings)

BLACKHAWK MEMORIAL SOCIETY
3707 Eastern Ave.
Davenport, IA 52807
319/359-0816
Membership: 179.
Services: Advisory.

MEMORIAL SOCIETY OF IOWA RIVER VALLEY
120 Dubuque St.
Iowa City, IA 52240
319/337-3019; 319/359-0816
Membership: 172.
Services: By verbal agreement with at least one mortuary.

KANSAS

MID-KANSAS MEMORIAL SOCIETY
Woolcott Building
Room 310
Hutchinson, KS 67501

KENTUCKY

MEMORIAL SOCIETY OF LEXINGTON, INC.
P.O. Box 22351
Lexington, KY 40522
606/269-7788

MEMORIAL SOCIETY OF GREATER LOUISVILLE
322 York St.
Louisville, KY 40203
502/585-5119

LOUISIANA

MEMORIAL SOCIETY OF GREATER BATON ROUGE
8470 Goodwood Ave.
Baton Rouge, LA 70806
504/926-2291

MEMORIAL SOCIETY OF GREATER NEW ORLEANS
1800 Jefferson Ave.
New Orleans, LA 70115
504/891-4055

MAINE

MEMORIAL SOCIETY OF MAINE
425 Congress St.
Portland, ME 04111
207/773-5747
Membership: 1,164.
Fees: Records fee; incoming transfer fee.

MARYLAND

MEMORIAL SOCIETY OF GREATER BALTIMORE
3 Ruxview Ct.
Apartment 101
Baltimore, MD 21204
301/296-4657; 301/488-6532
Founded: 1962.
Area: Maryland (areas not served by other memorial societies).

Membership: Individual—672; family—462.
Fees: Lifetime membership—$15.00.
Services: One mortuary provides: cremation—$270.00; burial—$590.00.
Donors referred to: Anatomy Board of Maryland.

HOWARD COUNTY MEMORIAL FOUNDATION
10451 Twin Rivers Rd.
Wilde Lake Village
Columbia, MD 21044
301/730-7920; 301/997-1188
Membership: 490.
Services: By written agreement with at least two mortuaries.

MARYLAND SUBURBAN MEMORIAL SOCIETY
1423 Laurell Hill
Greenbelt, MD 20770
301/474-6468
Founded: 1961.
Area: Montgomery and Prince George's counties.
Membership: 1,800.
Fees: Lifetime individual—$5.00 (each additional adult—$2.50).
Services: Eight mortuaries provide: cremation—$380.00 to $440.00; simple burial—$500.00 to $600.00; funeral—about $750.00 (not including cemetery charges).
Donors referred to: Area medical schools; Eye Bank and Research Foundation, Washington, DC.

MEMORIAL SOCIETY OF TRI-STATE AREA
15 S. Mulberry
Hagerstown, MD 21740
301/733-3565
Founded: 1977.
Area: Forty to sixty mile radius of Hagerstown in western Maryland.
Membership: Individual—140; family—85.
Fees: Lifetime individual—$10.00; lifetime family—$15.00; records fee—$7.50 (remitted to society by mortician at time of services).
Services: Three mortuaries provide: cremation—$295.00 to $315.00; immediate burial—$350.00 to $400.00 (not including cemetery charges).
Donors referred to: Anatomy Board of Maryland.

MASSACHUSETTS

MEMORIAL SOCIETY OF NEW ENGLAND
25 Monmouth St.
Brookline, MA 02146
617/731-2073
Founded: 1962.
Area: New England.
Membership: 4,000.
Fees: Lifetime family—$20.00.
Services: Advisory; by referral to cooperating morticians.

MEMORIAL SOCIETY OF GREATER NEW BEDFORD, INC.
71 Eighth St.
New Bedford, MA 02740
617/994-9686
Founded: 1977.
Area: Fall River, greater New Bedford and Tauton.
Membership: 262 (including 70 families).
Fees: Lifetime individual—$15.00; lifetime family—$20.00.
Services: Six mortuaries quote prices on services: cremation—$475.00 to $750.00; burial—$300.00 to $850.00; funeral—$525.00 to $1,570.00.
Donors referred to: Coordinator of Anatomical Gifts for donation to Massachusetts medical schools.

MEMORIAL SOCIETY OF CAPE COD
P.O. Box 1346
Orleans, MA 02653
617/255-3841
Membership: 1,223.
Fees: Incoming transfer fee.

SPRINGFIELD MEMORIAL SOCIETY
P.O. Box 2821
Springfield, MA 01101
413/733-7874
Membership: 3,858.

MICHIGAN

MEMORIAL SOCIETY & PLANNING SERVICE
P.O. Box 7325
Ann Arbor, MI 48107
313/663-2697

MEMORIAL SOCIETY OF BATTLE CREEK
C/O Art Center
265 E. Emmet St.
Battle Creek, MI 49017
616/962-5362
Membership: 112.

GREATER DETROIT MEMORIAL SOCIETY
4605 Cass Ave.
Detroit, MI 48201
313/833-9107
Founded: 1961.
Area: Macomb, Oakland and Wayne counties.
Membership: 5,675.
Fees: Lifetime membership—$10.00.
Services: Advisory.
Donors referred to: Wayne State University, Department of Anatomy.

LANSING AREA MEMORIAL PLANNING SOCIETY
855 Grove St.
East Lansing, MI 48823
517/351-4081

MEMORIAL SOCIETY OF FLINT
G-2474 S. Ballenger Hwy.
Flint, MI 48507
313/232-4023

MEMORIAL SOCIETY OF GREATER GRAND VALLEY
P.O. Box 1426
Grand Rapids, MI 49501
Founded: 1978.
Area: Western Michigan.
Membership: 275.
Fees: Lifetime individual—$12.00; lifetime family—$20.00.
Services: Advisory.
Donors referred to: University of Michigan; Michigan State University; Wayne State University (not presently accepting donations).

MEMORIAL SOCIETY OF GREATER KALAMAZOO
315 W. Michigan
Kalamazoo, MI 49006

MEMORIAL SOCIETY OF MID-MICHIGAN
P.O. Box 172
Mt. Pleasant, MI 48858
517/773-9548

MINNESOTA

MINNESOTA FUNERAL & MEMORIAL SOCIETY
900 Mt. Curve Ave.
Minneapolis, MN 55403
612/824-2440
Membership: 5,579.
Services: By contract with at least one mortuary.

MISSISSIPPI

FUNERAL & MEMORIAL SOCIETY OF MISSISSIPPI
GULF COAST
P.O. Box 7406
Gulfport, MS 39501
601/435-2284
Founded: 1977.
Area: Southern Mississippi.
Membership: 208 (including 90 families).
Fees: Lifetime membership—$7.50.
Donors referred to: Tulane University Medical School; Lions Eye Bank; Kidney Foundation.

MISSOURI

GREATER KANSAS CITY MEMORIAL SOCIETY
4500 Warwick Blvd.
Kansas City, MO 64111
816/561-6322

MEMORIAL & PLANNED FUNERAL SOCIETY
5007 Waterman Blvd.
St. Louis, MO 63108
314/361-0595
Membership: 1,130 (in 1980).
Services: By verbal agreement with at least one mortuary.

MONTANA

MEMORIAL SOCIETY OF MONTANA
1024 Princeton Ave.
Billings, MT 59102
406/252-5065
Founded: 1972.
Area: Eastern Montana and northern Wyoming.
Membership: 172.
Fees: Lifetime membership—$10.00.
Services: Advisory.

FIVE VALLEYS BURIAL MEMORIAL ASSOCIATION
401 University Ave.
Missoula, MT 59801
406/543-6952
Membership: 1,651.
Fees: Records fee; incoming transfer fee.
Services: By contract with at least one mortuary.

NEBRASKA

MIDLAND MEMORIAL SOCIETY
3114 Harney St.
Omaha, NE 68131
402/345-3039
Membership: 319.
Services: By verbal agreement with five mortuaries.

NEVADA

FUNERAL & MEMORIAL SOCIETY OF SOUTH NEVADA, INC.
P.O. Box 1324
Las Vegas, NV 89125
702/739-6979
Membership: 449.

MEMORIAL SOCIETY OF WEST NEVADA
P.O. Box 8413
University Station
Reno, NV 89507
702/322-0688
Founded: 1966.
Area: Northwestern Nevada and California (adjacent parts).

Membership: 530.
Fees: Lifetime individual—$10.00; lifetime family—$15.00; incoming transfer fee—$1.00.
Services: One mortuary provides: cremation—about $450.00; low-cost funeral—$550.00; traditional adult funeral—$1,400.00.
Donors referred to: University of Nevada Medical School, Reno, NV.

NEW HAMPSHIRE

MEMORIAL SOCIETY OF NEW HAMPSHIRE
P.O. Box 702
Concord, NH 03301
603/224-8913
Membership: 759.
Fees: Incoming transfer fee.

NEW JERSEY

MEMORIAL SOCIETY OF SOUTH JERSEY
P.O. Box 592
Cape May, NJ 08204
609/884-8852
Founded: 1975.
Area: Atlantic, Cape May, Cumberland, Gloucester and Salem counties.
Membership: 400.
Fees: Lifetime individual—$5.00; lifetime family—$10.00; incoming transfer fee—$2.00.
Services: Thirteen mortuaries quote prices on services: cremation—about $500.00; direct burial—about $600.00.
Donors referred to: Rutgers University; The Living Bank, Texas; Humanities Gift Registry, Pennsylvania.

RARITAN VALLEY MEMORIAL SOCIETY
176 Tices Ln.
East Brunswick, NJ 08816
201/246-9620; 201/572-1470
Founded: 1971.
Area: Middlesex County.
Membership: 373.
Fees: Lifetime membership—$20.00.
Services: A group of funeral homes provides: cremation—$530.25; direct burial—$450.25.
Donors referred to: New Jersey College of Medicine and Dentistry.

MEMORIAL ASSOCIATION OF MONMOUTH COUNTY
1475 W. Front St.
Lincroft, NJ 07738
201/741-8092
Membership: 1,256.
Fees: Records fee; incoming transfer fee.
Services: By verbal agreement with at least one mortuary.

MORRIS MEMORIAL SOCIETY
P.O. Box 156
Madison, NJ 07940
201/540-1177
Membership: 360.
Fees: Records fee.
Services: By written agreement with five mortuaries.

MEMORIAL SOCIETY OF ESSEX
67 Church St.
Montclair, NJ 07042
201/338-9510
Membership: 970.
Services: By contract with at least one mortuary.

CENTRAL MEMORIAL SOCIETY
156 Forest Ave.
Paramus, NJ 07652
201/445-6008

MEMORIAL SOCIETY OF PLAINFIELD
P.O. Box 307
Plainfield, NJ 07061

PRINCETON MEMORIAL ASSOCIATION
P.O. Box 1154
Princeton, NJ 08753
609/924-1604
Founded: 1956.
Area: Burlington, Gloucester, Huntington and Mercer counties.
Membership: Individual—288; family—595.
Fees: Lifetime individual—$15.00.
Services: Three mortuaries provide: traditional adult funeral—$500.00 (average).
Donors referred to: Farleigh Dickinson University; Rutgers University.

MEMORIAL ASSOCIATION OF OCEAN COUNTY
P.O. Box 1329
Toms River, NJ 08753
201/350-0228
Membership: 464.
Fees: Records fee; incoming transfer fee.
Services: By verbal agreement with at least one mortuary.

NEW MEXICO

MEMORIAL ASSOCIATION OF CENTRAL NEW MEXICO
P.O. Box 3251
Albuquerque, NM 87190
505/299-5384
Founded: 1964.
Area: Albuquerque and Bernalillo counties.
Membership: 1,052.
Fees: Lifetime individual—$5.00; lifetime family—$10.00.
Services: Advisory.
Donors referred to: University of New Mexico Medical School.

FOUR CORNERS MEMORIAL & FUNERAL SOCIETY
P.O. Box 1254
Farmington, NM 87410
Founded: 1980.
Membership: 14.
Services: By contract with at least one mortuary.

MEMORIAL & FUNERAL SOCIETY OF
SOUTHERN NEW MEXICO
P.O. Box 2563
Las Cruces, NM 88001
Services: By verbal agreement with at least one mortuary.

MEMORIAL & FUNERAL SOCIETY OF SOUTHERN
NEW MEXICO
P.O. Box 178
Los Alamos, NM 87544
505/662-2346
Membership: 565.
Services: By verbal agreement with two mortuaries.

NEW YORK

ALBANY AREA MEMORIAL SOCIETY
405 Washington Ave.
Albany, NY 12206
518/465-9664
Founded: 1964.
Area: Albany, Columbia, Greene, Renesselaer, Saratoga and Schenectady counties.
Membership: 1,600.
Fees: Individual—$10.00; family—$20.00; records fee—$5.00 (remitted to society by mortician at time of services).
Services: Six mortuaries provide: cremation—$315.00 (not including cemetery charges); simple earth burial—$315.00 (not including grave-opening charge).
Donors referred to: Albany Medical College.

SOUTHERN TIER MEMORIAL SOCIETY
183 Riverside
Binghamton, NY 13905
607/729-1641
Membership: 558.
Fees: Incoming transfer fee.
Services: Advisory.

GREATER BUFFALO MEMORIAL SOCIETY
695 Elmwood
Buffalo, NY 14222
726/885-2136
Membership: 1,316.
Services: By written agreement with at least one mortuary.

MEMORIAL SOCIETY OF NORTHERN NEW YORK
R.D. 2
P.O. Box 321
Clayton, NY 13624
315/788-5340

MEMORIAL SOCIETY OF GREATER CORNING
P.O. Box 23
Painted Post
Corning, NY 14870
607/962-2690
Membership: 112 (in 1980).
Services: By verbal agreement with two mortuaries.

SYRACUSE MEMORIAL SOCIETY
P.O. Box 67
Dewitt, NY 13214
315/474-4580

ITHACA MEMORIAL SOCIETY
P.O. Box 134
Ithaca, NY 14850
607/272-5476
Membership: 900.
Services: By contract with three mortuaries and verbal agreement with one mortuary.

MOHAWK VALLEY MEMORIAL SOCIETY
28 Oxford Rd.
New Hartford, NY 13413
315/797-1955
Membership: 131 (in 1980).
Fees: Records fee.
Services By verbal agreement with at least one mortuary.

NEW YORK CITY COMMUNITY FUNERAL SOCIETY
40 E. Thirty-fifth St.
New York, NY 10003
212/674-5400

NEW YORK CITY CONSUMERS MEMORIAL SOCIETY
C/O Urban Church
770 Broadway
New York, NY 10003
212/674-5400
Membership: 902 (in 1980).
Services: By verbal agreement with at least one mortuary.

NEW YORK CITY MEMORIAL SOCIETY
OF RIVERSIDE CHURCH
490 Riverside
New York, NY 10027
212/749-7000

MEMORIAL SOCIETY OF GREATER ONEONTA
12 Ford
Oneonta, NY 13820
607/432-3491

ROCKLAND COUNTY MEMORIAL SOCIETY
P.O. Box 461
Pomona, NY 10970
914/354-2917

MEMORIAL SOCIETY OF LONG ISLAND
P.O. Box 303
Port Washington, NY 11050
516/627-6590; 516/767-0926
Founded: 1963.
Area: Long Island, Nassau and Suffolk counties; Queens; Brooklyn.
Membership: 1,500.
Fees: Lifetime membership—$15.00.
Services: Twenty-one mortuaries provide: immediate cremation; cremation after viewing; immediate burial; burial after viewing.
Donors referred to: Downtown Medical Center, Brooklyn; Stony Brook State University; Eye Bank for Sight Restoration; Kidney Foundation; tissue banks.

MID-HUDSON MEMORIAL SOCIETY
249 Hooker
Poughkeepsie, NY 12603
914/471-5078
Membership: 1,014.
Fees: Incoming transfer fee.
Services: By written agreement with seven mortuaries.

ROCHESTER MEMORIAL SOCIETY
220 Winton Rd. S
Rochester, NY 14610
716/461-1620
Founded: 1957.
Area: Seventy-five mile radius of Rochester.
Membership: 1,800.
Fees: Lifetime membership—$15.00.
Services: Advisory.
Donors referred to: University of Rochester School of Medicine; Rochester Human Parts Bank.

UPPER GENESEE MEMORIAL SOCIETY
P.O. Box 274
Wellsville, NY 14895
716/593-1060

FUNERAL PLANNING ASSOCIATION OF WESTCHESTER
Rosedale Ave. & Sycamore Ln.
White Plains, NY 10605
914/946-1660

NORTH CAROLINA

BLUE RIDGE MEMORIAL SOCIETY
P.O. Box 2601
Asheville, NC 28801
Membership: 469.
Services: By verbal agreement with at least one mortuary.

TRIANGLE MEMORIAL & FUNERAL SOCIETY
P.O. Box 1223
Chapel Hill, NC 27514
919/942-4427
Founded: 1965.
Area: Chapel Hill and Raleigh-Durham.
Fees: Lifetime membership—$15.00; records fee—$5.00; incoming transfer fee.
Services: Local service provides cremation.
Donors referred to: North Carolina medical schools; North Carolina Eye & Human Tissue Bank.

PIEDMONT MEMORIAL & FUNERAL SOCIETY
P.O. Box 16192
Greensboro, NC 17406
919/674-5501

Membership: 861.
Fees: Incoming transfer fee.
Services: By verbal agreement with at least one mortuary.

SCOTLAND COUNTY FUNERAL & MEMORIAL SOCIETY
P.O. Box 192
Laurinburg, NC 28352
Membership: 80.

OHIO

CANTON-AKRON MEMORIAL SOCIETY
3300 Morewood Rd.
Akron, OH 44313
216/836-8094
Founded: 1969.
Area: Holmes, Medina, Portage, Stark and Summit counties.
Membership: 1,400 (700 families).
Fees: Individual—$8.00; family—$15.00.
Services: All three area mortuaries provide: cremation—$330.00; burial—$430.00 (not including cemetery charges).
Donors referred to: Northeast Ohio Medical School; Ohio State University Medical School.

MEMORIAL SOCIETY OF GREATER YOUNGSTOWN
75 Jackson Dr.
Campbell, OH 44405
216/755-8696

MEMORIAL SOCIETY OF GREATER CINCINNATI, INC.
536 Linton St.
Cincinnati, OH 45219
513/281-1564
Founded: 1963.
Area: Three states.
Membership: 800.
Fees: Lifetime membership—$20.00.
Services: Three mortuaries provide two types of economical services.

CLEVELAND MEMORIAL SOCIETY
21600 Shaker Blvd.
Cleveland, OH 44122
216/751-5515

MEMORIAL SOCIETY OF THE COLUMBUS AREA
P.O. Box 14103
Columbus, OH 43214
614/267-4696
Founded: 1953.
Area: Fifty mile radius of Columbus; *branches*—Waverly and Yellow Springs.
Membership: 2,058.
Fees: Lifetime membership—$10.00; records fee—$15.00 (remitted to society by cooperating mortician).
Donors referred to: Ohio State University, Department of Anatomy; National Kidney Foundation; Lions Eye Bank.

DAYTON MEMORIAL SOCIETY
665 Salem Ave.
Dayton, OH 45406
513/274-5890
Founded: 1958.
Area: Dayton; Montgomery County.
Membership: 350.
Fees: Lifetime membership—$10.00; records fee—$15.00 (collected by mortician at time of services).
Services: Two mortuaries provide five types of services.
Donors referred to: Wright State University.

MEMORIAL SOCIETY OF NORTHWEST OHIO
2210 Collingwood Blvd.
Toledo, OH 43620
419/475-4812

Founded: 1964 (in Bowling Green).
Area: Forty mile radius in northwest Ohio; fourteen counties.
Membership: 624 (including 184 families).
Fees: Lifetime individual (adult)—$15.00; records fee—$15.00 (collected by mortician at time of services).
Services: Eight mortuaries provide: cremation without embalming—$200.00 (not including cemetery charges) to $500.00; immediate burial without embalming—$200.00 to $450.00 (not including cemetery and vault charges); cremation with embalming and memorial service—$560.00 to $1,000.00 (not including crematory charges); burial with embalming—$560.00 to $1,150.00 (not including cemetery and vault charges).
Donors referred to: Nearby medical schools; cornea and kidney banks.

FUNERAL & MEMORIAL SOCIETY OF SOUTHWEST OHIO
66 N. Mulberry St.
Wilmington, OH 45177
513/382-2349
Founded: 1971.
Area: Southwest Ohio (areas not served by other memorial societies).
Membership: Individual—13; family—36.
Fees: Lifetime individual—$15.00; lifetime family—$20.00.
Services: Three mortuaries provide: cremation (with and without embalming)—$300.00 to $795.00; immediate burial (with and without embalming)—$629.00 to $1,100.00; cremation after standard adult service—$1,737.00.
Donors referred to: University of Cincinnati; Ohio State University; Wright State University.

MEMORIAL SOCIETY OF COLUMBUS AREA
YELLOW SPRINGS BRANCH
317 Dayton St.
Yellow Springs, OH 45387
513/767-2011

OKLAHOMA

MEMORIAL SOCIETY OF CENTRAL OKLAHOMA
600 N.W. Thirteenth St.
Oklahoma City, OK 73103
415/232-9224
Founded: 1975.
Area: Metropolitan Oklahoma City.
Membership: 200.
Fees: Lifetime membership—$10.00; incoming transfer fee—$2.00.
Services: Advisory.
Donors referred to: Oklahoma University Medical School; McGee Eye Bank.

MEMORIAL SOCIETY OF EAST OKLAHOMA
2942 S. Peoria
Tulsa, OK 74114
918/743-2363

OREGON

THE EMERALD MEMORIAL ASSOCIATION
P.O. Box 667
Pleasant Hill, OR 97401

OREGON MEMORIAL ASSOCIATION
6220 S.W. 130th St., 17
Beaverton
Portland, OR 97005
503/283-5500

PENNSYLVANIA

LEHIGH VALLEY MEMORIAL SOCIETY
701 Lechauweki Ave.
Bethlehem, PA 18105
215/866-7652

THANATOPSIS SOCIETY OF ERIE
P.O. Box 3495
Erie, PA 16508
814/864-9300

MEMORIAL SOCIETY OF GREATER HARRISBURG
1280 Clover Ln.
Harrisburg, PA 17113
717/564-4761
Founded: 1965.
Area: One hundred mile radius of Harrisburg.
Fees: Lifetime membership—$20.00; incoming transfer fee—$3.00.
Donors referred to: Pennsylvania Humanity Gifts Registry; Lions Club Eye Bank; Kidney Foundation.

MEMORIAL SOCIETY OF GREATER PHILADELPHIA
2125 Chestnut St.
Philadelphia, PA 19103
215/567-1065
Branch: Pottstown.
Membership: 2,402 (in 1980).
Services: By verbal agreement with at least one mortuary.

PITTSBURGH MEMORIAL SOCIETY
605 Morewood
Pittsburgh, PA 15213
412/621-8008

MEMORIAL SOCIETY OF GREATER PHILADELPHIA
POTTSTOWN BRANCH
1409 N. State St.
Pottstown, PA 19464
215/323-5561

MEMORIAL SOCIETY OF SCRANTON/WILKES-BARRE AREA
P.O. Box 212
R.D. 6
Clarks Summit
Scranton, PA 18411
717/586-5255

RHODE ISLAND

MEMORIAL SOCIETY OF RHODE ISLAND
119 Kenyon Ave.
East Greenwich, RI 02818
401/884-5933; 401/884-5451
Founded: 1979.
Area: Rhode Island; Maine (adjacent part).
Membership: 159 (including 54 families).
Fees: Lifetime individual—$15.00; lifetime family—$20.00; incoming transfer fee—$8.00.
Services: Three mortuaries provide: cremation—$600.00; burial—$575.00 to $765.00; funeral—$1,000.00 to $1,350.00.
Donors referred to: Brown University Medical School.

SOUTH CAROLINA

MEMORIAL SOCIETY OF CHARLESTON
1340 Honeysuckle Ln.
Charleston, SC 29412
803/449-3064

MEMORIAL SOCIETY OF EASTERN CAROLINA
P.O . Box 712
Myrtle Beach, SC 29577
803/449-6526; 803/449-3064
Membership: 237.
Fees: Records fee; incoming transfer fee.
Services: By verbal agreement with at least one mortuary.

TENNESSEE

MEMORIAL SOCIETY OF CHATTANOOGA
3224 Navajo Dr.
Chattanooga, TN 37411
615/899-9315
Membership: 85.
Services: By verbal agreement with one mortuary.

EAST TENNESSEE MEMORIAL SOCIETY
P.O. Box 10507
Knoxville, TN 37919
615/523-4176
Branches: Cumberland (Pleasant Hill).
Membership: 1,093.
Services: Advisory.

MIDDLE TENNESSEE MEMORIAL SOCIETY
1808 Woodmont
Nashville, TN 37215
615/383-5760

EAST TENNESSEE MEMORIAL SOCIETY
CUMBERLAND BRANCH
P.O. Box 246
Pleasant Hill, TN 38578
615/277-3795

TEXAS

AUSTIN MEMORIAL & BURIAL INFORMATION SOCIETY
P.O. Box 4382
Austin, TX 78765
Membership: 338.
Fees: Incoming transfer fee.
Services: By verbal agreement with at least one mortuary.

GOLDEN TRIANGLE MEMORIAL SOCIETY
P.O. Box 6136
Beaumont, TX 77705
713/833-6883
Membership: 39.
Services: By written agreement with at least one mortuary.

MEMORIAL SOCIETY OF BRYAN/COLLEGE STATION
P.O. Box 9078
College Station, TX 77840
713/696-6944
Membership: 56 (in 1980).

DALLAS AREA MEMORIAL SOCIETY
4015 Normandy
Dallas, TX 75205
214/528-3990

MEMORIAL SOCIETY OF EL PASO
P.O. Box 4951
El Paso, TX 79914
515/824-4565
Membership: 46 (in 1980).
Services: By contract with at least one mortuary.

HOUSTON AREA MEMORIAL SOCIETY
5210 Fannin St.
Houston, TX 77004
713/526-1571

LUBBOCK AREA MEMORIAL SOCIETY
P.O. Box 6562
Lubbock, TX 79413
806/792-0367

SAN ANTONIO MEMORIAL SOCIETY
777 San Antonio Bank & Trust Building
771 Navarro
San Antonio, TX 78205

UTAH

UTAH MEMORIAL ASSOCIATION
569 S. Thirteenth E
Salt Lake City, UT 84102
801/582-8687

VERMONT

VERMONT MEMORIAL SOCIETY
P.O. Box 67
Burlington, VT 05401
802/863-4701
Founded: 1967.
Area: Vermont.
Membership: 350 (individual and family).
Fees: Lifetime individual—$10.00; lifetime family—$15.00; records fee—$10.00 (remitted to society by mortician at time of services).
Services: Two mortuaries provide: cremation—about $300.00 (not including urn).

VIRGINIA

MT. VERNON MEMORIAL SOCIETY
1909 Windmill Ln.
Alexandria, VA 22307
703/765-5950
Services: Advisory.
Donors referred to: Georgetown University Medical School; George Washington University Medical School; Howard University Medical School.

MEMORIAL SOCIETY OF ARLINGTON
4444 Arlington
Arlington, VA 22204
703/892-2565
Membership: 1,011.
Fees: Records fee; incoming transfer fee.

MEMORIAL PLANNING SOCIETY OF THE PIEDMONT
Edgewood Ln. at Rugby Rd.
Charlottesville, VA 22903
804/293-8179; 804/293-3133
Fees: Incoming transfer fee.
Services: Advisory.

FAIRFAX MEMORIAL SOCIETY
P.O. Box 130
Oakton, VA 22124
703/281-4230
Founded: 1960.
Area: Fairfax, Fauquier, Loudoun and northern Prince William counties.
Membership: 1,100 (including 378 families).
Fees: Lifetime individual and family—$5.00.
Donors referred to: Area (Washington, DC) medical schools; organ and tissue programs.

MEMORIAL SOCIETY OF GREATER RICHMOND
P.O. Box 180
Richmond, VA 23202
804/355-0777

MEMORIAL SOCIETY OF ROANOKE VALLEY, INC.
P.O. Box 8001
Roanoke, VA 24014-0001
703/774-9314
Founded: 1972.
Area: Fifty mile radius of Roanoke.
Membership: Adults—164; children—36.
Fees: Lifetime individual—$10.00; lifetime family—$15.00.
Services: By agreement with two mortuaries.

Donors referred to: University of Virginia, Charlottesville; Medical College of Virginia, Richmond.

MEMORIAL SOCIETY OF TIDEWATER
P.O. Box 4621
Virginia Beach, VA 23454
804/428-1804
Membership: 238.
Services: By written agreement with at least one mortuary.

WASHINGTON

PEOPLE'S MEMORIAL ASSOCIATION
2366 Eastlake Ave. E
Seattle, WA 98102
206/325-0489
Founded: 1939. (*Note:* People's Memorial Association is the oldest memorial society in the United States. It's exclusive contract with one area mortician began the memorial society movement.)
Area: Western Washington.
Membership: 65,120.
Fees: Lifetime individual—$5.00; records fee—$15.00 (remitted to society by mortician at time of services).
Services: One mortuary provides: cremation—$350.00; burial—$531.00; funeral—$406.00.
Donors referred to: University of Washington Medical School; Organ Donation Information Center.

SPOKANE MEMORIAL ASSOCIATION
P.O. Box 13613
Spokane, WA 99213
509/838-5000
Membership: 3,086.
Fees: Records fee.
Services: By written contract with at least one mortuary.

MEMORIAL SOCIETY OF CENTRAL WASHINGTON
P.O. Box 379
Yakima, WA 98907
Membership: 132.
Services: By written agreement with at least one mortuary.

WISCONSIN

FUNERAL & MEMORIAL SOCIETY
OF GREATER MILWAUKEE
2618 Hackett Ave.
Milwaukee, WI 52311
414/332-0400
Founded: 1978.
Area: Milwaukee area.
Membership: Individual—300.
Fees: Lifetime individual—$10.00
Services: Advisory.
Donors referred to: Marquette University; University of Wisconsin Medical School.

FUNERAL & MEMORIAL SOCIETY OF RACINE & KENOSHA
625 College Ave.
Racine, WI 53403
414/634-0659

WESTERN WISCONSIN FUNERAL SOCIETY
110 N. Third
River Falls, WI 54022
715/425-2052

MEMORIAL SOCIETY OF DOOR COUNTY
C/O Hope United Church of Christ
Sturgeon Bay, WI 54235
414/743-2701

CANADA

ALBERTA

CALGARY CO-OP MEMORIAL SOCIETY
28 Norsemen Pl. NW
Calgary, Alberta T2K 5M6 Canada
403/243-5088

MEMORIAL SOCIETY OF EDMONTON & DISTRICT
11447 Forty-third Ave.
Edmonton, Alberta T6J 0Y2 Canada
403/484-1845

MEMORIAL SOCIETY OF GRANDE PRAIRIE
P.O. Box 471
Grande Prairie, Alberta T8V 3A7 Canada

MEMORIAL SOCIETY OF SOUTHERN ALBERTA
924 20th St. S
Lethbridge, Alberta T1J 3J7 Canada

MEMORIAL SOCIETY OF RED DEER & DISTRICT
P.O. Box 817
Red Deer, Alberta T4N 5H2 Canada
Founded: 1978.
Area: Fifty mile radius in central Alberta.
Membership: Individual—163; family—272.
Fees: Lifetime individual—$10.00; lifetime family—$20.00; incoming transfer fee—$3.00.
Services: One mortuary provides: cremation—about $590.00; burial—about $700.00; funeral—about $1,000.00.
Donors referred to: University of Calgary Faculty of Medicine; Red Deer Regional Hospital Center; Canadian National Institute for the Blind.

BRITISH COLUMBIA

MEMORIAL SOCIETY OF BRITISH COLUMBIA
NANAIMO BRANCH
P.O. Box 177
Nanaimo, British Columbia V9R 5K9 Canada

MEMORIAL SOCIETY OF BRITISH COLUMBIA
410, 207 W. Hastings St.
Vancouver, British Columbia V6B 1J3 Canada
Branches: Nanaimo and Victoria.

MEMORIAL SOCIETY OF BRITISH COLUMBIA
VICTORIA BRANCH
P.O. Box 685
Victoria, British Columbia V8W 2P9 Canada

MANITOBA

FUNERAL PLANNING & MEMORIAL SOCIETY
790 Banning St.
Winnepeg, Manitoba R3E 2H9 Canada
Founded: 1956.
Area: Province of Manitoba.
Membership: 4,300.
Fees: Lifetime individual—$12.00; lifetime family—$20.00.
Services: Morticians belonging to the Funeral Services Association provide: minimum-services funeral—$200.00.
Donors referred to: University of Manitoba, Department of Anatomy.

NEW BRUNSWICK

MEMORIAL SOCIETY OF NEW BRUNSWICK
P.O. Box 662
Fredericton, New Brunswick E38 5A6 Canada

NEWFOUNDLAND

MEMORIAL & FUNERAL PLANNING ASSOCIATION
OF NEWFOUNDLAND
P.O. Box 291
St. John's, Newfoundland A1A 2X9 Canada

NOVA SCOTIA

GREATER HALIFAX MEMORIAL SOCIETY
P.O. Box 291
Armdale
Halifax, Nova Scotia B3L 4K1 Canada

MEMORIAL SOCIETY OF CAPE BRETON
P.O. Box 934
Sydney, Nova Scotia B1P 6J4 Canada

ONTARIO

MEMORIAL SOCIETY OF GUELPH
P.O. Box 1784
Guelph, Ontario N1H 7A1 Canada
519/822-7430

HAMILTON MEMORIAL SOCIETY
P.O. Box 164
Hamilton, Ontario L8N 3A2 Canada
416/549-6385
Founded: 1971.
Area: Forty mile radius of Hamilton/Wentworth.
Membership: Individual—4,170.
Fees: Lifetime individual—$10.00.
Services: Seven mortuaries provide: cremation—$110.00; funeral—$250.00 to $395.00.
Donors referred to: McMasters University, Department of Anatomy; Canadian National Institute for the Blind; Banting Institute, Temporal Bone Bank; Kidney Foundation of Canada.

MEMORIAL SOCIETY OF KINGSTON
P.O. Box 1081
Kingston, Ontario K7L 4Y5 Canada
613/542-7271

KITCHENER-WATERLOO MEMORIAL SOCIETY
P.O. Box 113
Kitchener, Ontario N2G 3W9 Canada
519/743-5481

MEMORIAL SOCIETY OF LONDON
P.O. Box 1729
Station A
London, Ontario N6A 5H9 Canada

NIAGARA PENINSULA MEMORIAL SOCIETY
P.O. Box 2102
4500 Queen St.
Niagara Peninsula, Ontario L2E 6Z2 Canada

MEMORIAL SOCIETY OF NORTHERN ONTARIO
P.O. Box 2563
Station A
Sudbury, Northern Ontario P3A 4S9 Canada
Founded: 1979.
Area: One hundred mile radius of Sudbury.
Membership: 470.
Fees: Lifetime individual and family—$7.00; records fee—$10.00 (collected and remitted to society by mortician at time of services).
Services: Two mortuaries provide: simple funeral—$255.54 to $325.00; $398.58 to $525.00.
Donors referred to: Area hospitals and medical schools.

OTTAWA MEMORIAL SOCIETY
R.R. 7
62 Steeple Hill Crescent
Nepean
Ottawa, Ontario K2H 7V2 Canada
613/836-5630

MEMORIAL SOCIETY OF PETERBOROUGH & DISTRICT
P.O. Box 1795
Peterborough, Ontario K9J 7X6 Canada

MEMORIAL SOCIETY OF THUNDER BAY
P.O. Box 501
Station F
Thunder Bay, Ontario P7C 4W4 Canada
807/683-3051

TORONTO MEMORIAL SOCIETY
P.O. Box 96
Station A
Weston, Ontario M9N 3M6 Canada
416/241-6274
Founded: 1956.
Area: Greater metropolitan Toronto.
Membership: 24,000.
Fees: Lifetime individual—$10.00; records fee—$10.00 (remitted to society by estate of deceased at time of death).
Services: Eight mortuaries provide: burial—$300.00 and up; traditional funeral—$850.00 to $1,100.00.
Donors referred to: University of Toronto Eye Bank; Kidney Foundation; Metro Organ Retrieval Exchange.

MEMORIAL SOCIETY OF WINDSOR
P.O. Box 481
Windsor, Ontario N9A 6M6 Canada
519/969-2252

QUEBEC

L'ASSOCIATION FUNERAIRE DE MONTREAL
P.O. Box 400
Station C
Montreal, Quebec H2L 4K3 Canada
514/521-2815
Founded: 1955.
Area: Province of Quebec.
Membership: 4,000.
Fees: Lifetime individual—$20.00; lifetime family—$30.00.
Services: One mortuary provides: cremation—$110.00; burial—$500.00; funeral—$450.00.
Donors referred to: Local universities.

SASKATCHEWAN

LLOYDMINSTER, VERMILLION & DISTRICTS
MEMORIAL SOCIETY
4729 Forty-fifth St.
Lloydminster, Saskatchewan S9V 0H6 Canada

MEMORIAL SOCIETY OF SASKATCHEWAN
P.O. Box 1846
Saskatoon, Saskatchewan S7K 3S2 Canada
306/374-5190

SELF-HELP GROUPS

Introduction

Jared Hermalin, Ph.D. *

More than 15 million people are estimated to belong to more than 500,000 "self-help" community groups (Evans, 1979). The attraction of such groups to individuals at all socioeconomic levels can best be understood by gaining an appreciation of the nature and process of the self-help phenomenon:

Self-help groups are voluntary, small group structures for mutual aid and the accomplishment of a special purpose. They are usually formed by peers who have come together for mutual assistance in satisfying a common need, overcoming a common handicap or life-disrupting problem, and bringing about desired and/or personal change. . . . Self-help groups emphasize face-to-face social interactions and the assumption of personal responsibility by members. They often provide material assistance, as well as emotional support, they are frequently "cause"-orientated, and promulgate an ideology or values through which members may attain an enhanced sense of personal identity (Katz & Bender, 1976, p. 9).

While these groups are not friendship cliques or family networks, they do provide extremely high levels of support, feedback, and assistance to individuals undergoing stressful periods. Because self-help groups tend not to be hierarchically-based, group members are treated as equals, each having the same rights and responsibilities. Everyone's opinions are listened to; everyone's concerns are attended to by fellow group members. In short, self-help groups are local, community organizations, not affiliated with the more formal, health/mental health/social service agencies. They are comprised of individuals sharing common needs, working together toward solution of those needs. It is for this reason that they are often referred to as "mutual aid" groups.

These groups cover a wide spectrum of human involvement. There are self-help groups devised around issues of health, mental health, community development, drugs, alcoholism, hospitalization, and rehabilitation. There are also groups created to deal with problems related to families, youth, older adults, divorce, separation, and widowhood, to cite but a few parameters of concern. A more inclusive listing can be obtained from the various self-help clearinghouses located across the country or by reference to a Gartner & Riessman publication, *Help: A Working Guide to Self-Help Groups* (1980).

For individuals, their families, and friends facing the stresses and strains associated with "death and dying," there may be some comfort in knowing that self-help groups exist in these important areas as well. Such persons need not undergo the turmoil, the unhappiness, the tragedy alone. By talking and interacting with others undergoing the same hard times, support, encouragement, hope, and the will to go on can be obtained, coping and management skills can be heightened, and grief and guilt may be expressed within a positive, receptive atmosphere.

For professionals working with family and friends as well as for the victim, it is important to add that while counseling, therapy, or guidance can be most advantageous, people sometimes also need more than individual, group, or family sessions. They need to get together with others sharing the same feelings and the same tribulations. They need to hear firsthand how others in similar situations are managing or adjusting to their new lifestyles. They need to hear how others have gotten over their loss and what they did to accomplish this. Thus, self-help groups are not seen as a substitute for anyone requiring professional care or advice. Rather, they provide yet another recourse for those experiencing the anguish of the death and dying process.

Self-help groups, in general, are most amenable to receiving referrals from professionals and service delivery agencies. People wishing to join a group can usually do so quite easily—either by calling or writing to the relevant contact person or group (if no contact person is listed), or by simply coming to group meetings or functions. Where self-help groups do not already exist, they can often be started

---

*Dr. Hermalin is Director of the Philadelphia Self-Help Clearinghouse, John F. Kennedy Community Mental Health/Mental Retardation Center, Philadelphia.

quite quickly either in one's own community or nearby. Membership dues or donations tend to be quite low, if group membership is not free, and should not present an economic hardship to those motivated to join. The group meets as often as the members decide, pursuing activities aimed at solving or ameliorating the problems/concerns for which the group was devised.

But how does one find a self-help group? How does one learn of the group's philosophy and goals? Or if no group exists, how can concerned individuals start a group of their own? The network of self-help clearinghouses in the United States is extremely valuable in these regards. The national clearinghouse in New York City and the regional clearinghouses located in various states (see the following list of clearinghouses) are largely publicly-funded, multi-purpose organizations designed to assist individuals, family members, friends, and professionals. The clearinghouses were established by individuals who saw a need for centralized sources of information about self-help groups and they offer help in the following ways:

1. By publication of self-help directories listing relevant groups, objectives, contact persons, and meeting times.

2. By responding to telephone and mail inquiries regarding self-help groups or the movement in general.

3. By promoting or helping to organize self-help groups where needs are expressed.

4. By training and consulting with self-help groups to promote leadership skills, group dynamics, publicity, fund-raising, and other necessities related to group viability and maintenance.

5. By providing a resource listing of other groups, organizations, or agencies that can provide information or assistance to self-help groups (e.g. on matters related to incorporation, developing by-laws, collecting monies).

6. By assisting in the referral process between professional care providers and self-help groups.

7. By educating the public and human service providers about the importance and nature of the self-help movement.

8. By researching or evaluating the process, effectiveness, member satisfaction, and needs of self-help groups.

9. By maintaining a library of self-help publications, newsletters, and relevant subject matter disseminated by the various self-help groups.

10. By publishing articles and books and by participating in workshops, fairs, symposiums, and conferences.

For further background information about the organization and functioning of the various self-help clearinghouses, the reader is referred to Borck's article, "The Role of the Self-Help Clearinghouse," listed in "References" following this section.

To avoid invading the privacy of any individual whose name and address are used as contacts for local self-help groups, we have included in this list only information pertaining to self-help groups affiliated with institutions, national organizations with large memberships, or clearinghouses. However, to be of greatest assistance to users of this book, the names of cities and towns with self-help groups not itemized here are included after the name of their states. To obtain information about specific groups, contact the nearest regional clearinghouse.

Please note that there may be self-help groups in your state for which information was not available at the time of publication. For additional information, contact the nearest regional clearinghouse.

Entries preceded by an asterisk (*) are national offices.

References

Borck, Leslie and Aronowitz, Eugene. "The Role of the Self-Help Clearinghouse." *Prevention and Human Services* 1(3), Spring, 1982.

Gartner, Alan and Riessman, Frank. *Help: A Working Guide to Self-Help Groups* (N.Y.: New Viewpoints/Vision Books, 1980).

Katz, Alfred and Bender, Eugene (eds.). *The Strength in Us: Self-Help Groups In The Modern World* (N.Y.: New Viewpoints, 1976).

Self-help Clearinghouse

A detailed listing of U.S. self-help clearinghouses and centers is provided below to facilitate awareness of and access to self-help groups located across the country. The National Self-help Clearinghouse is presented first. The others are arranged in alphabetical order by state.

National Self-help Clearinghouses

Graduate School & University Center
Frank Riessman and Alan Gartner, Co-Directors
City University of New York
33 W. Forty-second St.
New York, NY 10036
212/840-7606

Schools of Public Health & Social Welfare
Alfred Katz, Director
UCLA
Los Angeles, CA 90024
213/825-5333

S. F. SH Clearinghouse
Mental Health Association of San Francisco
Sharon J. George, Director
2398 Pine St.
San Francisco, CA 94115
415/921-4401

Hamden Mental Health Service
Marvin A. Steinberg, Director
3000 Dixwell Ave.
Hamden, CT 06518
203/288-6253

The Consultation Center
Sophie Tworkowski, Director
19 Howe St.
New Haven, CT 06511
203/789-7645

Self-Help Center
Len Borman, Director
1600 Dodge Ave.
Evanston, IL 60201
312/328-0470

Mental Health Association of Minnesota
Doug Freeman, Director
6715 Minnetonka Blvd.
Minneapolis, MN 55426

Self-Help Information Services
Barbara R. Fox, Director
1601 Euclid Ave.
Lincoln, NE 68502
402/476-9668

New Jersey Self-Help Clearinghouse
Ed Madara, Director
St. Clare's Community Mental Health Center
Denville, NJ 07834
From within NJ: 800/452-9790
Outside NY: 201/625-6215

Heights Hills Mental Health Service
Robert L. Evans, Director
South Beach Psych.
50 Court St.
Brooklyn, NY 11201
212/834-7304

Long Island Self-Help Clearinghouse
Audrey Leif, Director

New York Institute of Technology
6350 Jericho Turnpike
Commack, NY 11725
516/499-8800

New York City Self-Help Clearinghouse
Carol Eisman, Associate Director
240 E. Sixty-fourth St.
New York, NY 10021
212/840-0860

Westchester Community College
Leslie Borck, Director
Academic/Arts Bldg.
75 Grasslands Rd.
Valhalla, NY 10595
914/347-3620

C&E/R&E Services
Jared Hermalin, Director
John F. Kennedy CMH/MR Center
Hahnemann Medical College & Hospital
112 N. Broad St.
Philadelphia, PA 19102
214/568-0860 (Ext. 276)

University of Texas at Arlington
Shirley W. King, Director
P.O. Box 19129
Arlington, TX 76019
817/273-2707

Dallas Community Mental Health Association
Self-Help Clearinghouse
Carol Madison, Director
2500 Maple Ave.
Dallas, TX 75206
214/748-7825

Tarrent Community Mental Health Association
Self-Help Clearinghouse
Karen Hale, Director
804 W. Seventh St.
Fort Worth, TX 76102
817/335-5405

Continuing Education in Mental Health
Patrick W. Prindle, Director
University of Wisconsin-Extension
415 Lowell Hall
610 Langdon St.
Madison, WI 53706

Self-help Groups

U.S.A.

CALIFORNIA

In addition to the following list of self-help groups in this state, these cities and towns also have self-help groups: Calabasas, San Diego, Tiburon. For further information, contact the closest regional clearinghouse.

Berkeley

*SHANTI PROJECT
1314 Addison St.
Berkeley, CA 94702
415/849-4980
Purpose: To provide volunteer counseling for patients and families experiencing the problems associated with life-threatening illness.
Chapters: 1 group serving the Bay Area. 50 similar groups throughout the country.

La Mesa

*SOCIETY OF MILITARY WIDOWS
P.O. Box 1714
La Mesa, CA 92041
714/461-1154
Purpose: To provide self-help for widows (and widowers) of career military personnel.

Los Angeles

SCHOOLS OF PUBLIC HEALTH & SOCIAL WELFARE
Alfred Katz, Director
UCLA
Los Angeles, CA 90024
213/825-5333

San Francisco

COMPASSIONATE FRIENDS
c/o San Francisco Bay Self-Help Clearinghouse
Mental Health Association of San Francisco
2398 Pine St.
San Francisco, CA 94115
415/921-4401 (Clearinghouse)
Purpose: To provide support for parents of deceased children.

PARENTS WITHOUT PARTNERS
595 Buckingham Way
San Francisco, CA 94132
415/566-8600
Purpose: To provide a support network for single parents who are widowed, separated, divorced, or never married.

SAN FRANCISCO SELF-HELP CLEARINGHOUSE
Sharon J. George, Director
Mental Health Association of San Francisco
2398 Pine St.
San Francisco, CA 94115
415/921-4401

SEPARATED-DIVORCED-WIDOWED GROUP
OF ST. ELIZABETH'S
St. Elizabeth's Parish Center
449 Holyoke St.
San Francisco, CA 94134
415/468-5024
Purpose: To provide support for people, especially Catholics, in adjusting to marriage separation, divorce, or death of a spouse.

WIDOW-WIDOWER OUTREACH PROGRAM
Jewish Family & Children's Service
1600 Scott St.
San Francisco, CA 94115
415/567-8860 (Ext. 28)

---

*Entries preceded by an asterisk (*) are national offices.

Purpose: To provide support for helping the newly widowed adjust to death of a spouse.

PARENTS OF MURDERED CHILDREN
c/o Crises and Suicide Intervention
P.O. Box 4852
Walnut Creek, CA 94569
415/939-1916
Purpose: To provide self-help for parents whose child has been a victim of homicide.

COLORADO

Englewood

GRIEF EDUCATION INSTITUTE
P.O. Box 623
Englewood, CO 80151
303/777-9234
Purpose: To provide support for the bereaved.
Services: Offers seminars and workshops for helping professionals; engages in public education; promotes research.

CONNECTICUT

Hamden

HAMDEN MENTAL HEALTH SERVICE
Marvin A. Steinberg, Director
3000 Dixwell Ave.
Hamden, CT 06518
203/288-6253

New Haven

THE CONSULTATION CENTER
Sophie Tworkowski, Director
19 Howe St.
New Haven, CT 06511
203/789-7645

DISTRICT OF COLUMBIA

For further information on self-help groups in Washington, DC, contact the closest regional clearinghouse.

* AMERICAN NATIONAL RED CROSS
National Headquarters
Washington, DC 20006
Services: May offer programs of interest to the widowed at local level. (Contact the Red Cross Office of Community Volunteer Programs for further information.)

NAIM CONFERENCE
Family Life Division
U.S. Catholic Conference
1312 Massachusetts Ave. NW
Washington, DC 25550
Purpose: To provide support for widowed Catholics and the spouses of deceased Catholics.

* THE WIDOWED PERSONS SERVICE
American Association of Retired Persons (AARP)
Leo Baldwin, Senior Coordinator; Ruth Loewinshon,
Senior Program Specialist
1909 K St. NW
Washington, DC 20049
202/872-4700
Purpose: To put widowed persons in contact with programs in their communities; to provide manuals for starting a program.

FLORIDA

In addition to the following list of self-help groups in this state, the Hillsborough County area also has self-help groups. For further information, contact the closest regional clearinghouse.

Lutz

NEONATAL HOPES, INC. (HELPING OTHER PARENTS EXPERIENCE SORROW)
P.O. Box 1143
Lutz, FL 33549
Purpose: To provide support for parents experiencing the loss of a newborn (infants never released from the hospital, stillbirths, and miscarriages).
Services: Holds monthly meetings.

Tampa

AMEND (AIDING A MOTHER EXPERIENCING A NEONATAL DEATH)
5104 127th Ave.
Tampa, FL 33617
813/988-7996 (24 hours)
Purpose: To provide support for parents who have lost newborns (not restricted to babies who have not left the hospital).
Services: Holds monthly meetings; educates health professionals and clergy.
Chapters: Several groups with loose links.

FLORIDA SELF-HELP PROJECT
Florida Mental Health Institute
University of Southern Florida
13301 N. Thirtieth St.
Tampa, FL 33612
813/974-4672

MAKE TODAY COUNT
P.O. Box 15392
Tampa, FL 33684
Purpose: As a grief support group affiliate, to provide aid for persons with life-threatening illnesses and their families.
Services: Offers meetings (open to the public).

PARENTS WITHOUT PARTNERS, INC.
P.O. Box 23243
Tampa, FL 33622
813/935-1111 (24-hour answering service)

Purpose: As an international, nonprofit, nonsectarian, educational organization, to provide support for single parents (widowed, separated, divorced, or never married).
Services: Offers family activities, adult parties and discussion groups.

SURVIVORS OF SUICIDE
Suicide and Crisis Center
2214 E. Henry St.
Tampa, FL 33610
813/238-8821 (24-hour hotline)
Purpose: To provide support for friends and relatives of suicide victims (or attempted suicides).

ILLINOIS

In addition to the following list of self-help groups in this state, these cities and towns also have self-help groups: Arlington Heights, Aurora, Danville, Glen Ellyn-Wheaton area, Hinsdale, Joliet, Matteson, Mount Prospect, Skokie, Vernon Hills, Wilmette, and Winfield. The Chicago area also has groups in addition to those listed. For further information, contact the closest regional clearinghouse.

Chicago

LOSS (LOVING OUTREACH TO SURVIVORS OF SUICIDE)
Father Charles T. Rubey, Director of Mental Health Services
Catholic Charities
126 N. Des Plaines St.
Chicago, IL 60606
312/236-5172 (Ext. 360)
Purpose: To provide aid for people who have lost a loved one by suicide.
Services: Offers group meetings; has occasional guest speakers; makes initial contact by phone.
Chapters: 2 chapters.

* NATIONAL SUDDEN INFANT DEATH SYNDROME FOUNDATION
310 S. Michigan Ave.
Chicago, IL 60604
301/459-3388; 312/663-0650
Purpose: To provide support for those experiencing the trauma of SIDS death.
Chapters: 43 chapters.

* NAIM CONFERENCE—U.S. CATHOLIC CONFERENCE, FAMILY LIFE DIVISION
Charles Stuk, President
721 N. LaSalle St.
Chicago, IL 60610
312/944-1286
Purpose: To provide support for widowed Catholics and spouses of deceased Catholics.
Chapters: 26 chapters in Illinois—including Chicago, Wilmette, Arlington Heights, Mundelein, Mt. Prospect, Hins-

dale, Clarendon Hills, Forest Park, Bolingbrook, Elmhurst, Glendale Heights, Berwyn, Riverside, Riverdale, Niles, Elgin, and Aurora.

RAP GROUP
Ravenswood Hospital
4545 N. Damen Ave.
Chicago, IL 60625
312/878-4300 (Ext. 1455)
Purpose: To share feelings about grief.

SOLOS
Ravenswood Hospital
Nurses' Residence
4500 N. Winchester
Chicago, IL 60640
312/878-4300 (Ext. 1455)
Purpose: To offer social support (organization of widowed programs).

WIDOW-WIDOWER OUTREACH
Ravenswood Hospital—Community Mental Health Center
4550 N. Winchester
Chicago, IL 60625
312/878-4300 (Ext. 1590)
Purpose: Through widows (trained at Ravenswood) to provide phone contact for widowers and widows.

WOW (WIDOWS OR WIDOWERS)
St. Viator's
4140 W. Addison
Chicago, IL 60641
312/286-4040 (Church office)
Purpose: To provide social, psychological and religious support for widowed individuals.

Crystal Lake

THEOS
Congregational Church
611 Pierson St.
Crystal Lake, IL 60014
815/459-4494
Purpose: As a nondenominational Christian self-help group for the young and middle-aged widowed and their families, to provide shared grief experiences.
Services: Holds monthly meetings.

Elmhurst

THEOS
Yorkfield United Presbyterian Church
1099 S. York St.
Elmhurst, IL 60126
312/543-3481
Purpose: As a nondenominational Christian self-help group for the young and middle-aged widowed and their families, to provide shared grief experiences.
Services: Holds monthly meetings.

Evanston

SELF-HELP CENTER
Len Borman, Director
1600 Dodge Ave.
Evanston, IL 60201
312/328-0470

Harvey

GRIEF AND LOSS GROUP
Ingalls Memorial Hospital
Ingalls Dr.
Harvey, IL 60426
312/333-2300 (Ext. 5380)
Purpose: To provide bereavement support.

Highland Park

CONGREGATION SOLEL'S SELF-HELP GROUP
Rabbi Robert Marx
1301 Clavey Rd.
Highland Park, IL. 60035
312/433-3555
Purpose: To provide emotional support for parents (of all faiths) who have lost a child.

Mattoon

THEOS
Broadway Christian Church
1205 S. Ninth St.
Mattoon, IL 61938
217/234-7696
Purpose: As a nondenominational Christian self-help group for the young and middle-aged widowed and their families, to provide shared grief experiences.
Services: Holds monthly meetings.

Maywood

SUDDEN INFANT DEATH SYNDROME
Dr. Goldberg
Loyola Medical Center
2160 S. First Ave.
Maywood, IL 60153
312/531-3210
Purpose: To provide help for newly-bereaved parents (from parents who have experienced SIDS).
Services: Offers speakers and films.

Mount Prospect

NEW OPTIONS—PHOENIX GROUP
Pastoral Ministry Center
301 S. I-Oka
Mount Prospect, IL 60056
312/253-8600
Purpose: To provide support for separated, divorced and widowed persons.
Services: Holds weekly meetings.

Oak Brook

*THE COMPASSIONATE FRIENDS
Reverend Donald Dalsteer, President
800 Enterprise Dr.
P.O. Box 1347
Oak Brook, IL 60521
312/323-5010
Purpose: To provide support and understanding by and for parents who have lost a child.
Chapters: 105 groups.

Oak Lawn

REMEMBRANCE SERVICES
Christ Hospital
Chaplaincy Office
4440 W. Ninety-fifth St.
Oak Lawn, II 60453
312/425-8000 (Ext. 5175)
Purpose: To provide aid for persons having difficulty accepting a loved one's death.
Services: Chaplain conducts memorial service and open group therapy session.

Orland Park

WOW (WIDOWS OR WIDOWERS)
St. Michael's
14327 S. Highland
Orland Park, IL 60462
312/349-0903
Purpose: To provide social, psychological and religious support for widowed persons.

Park Ridge

GRIEF AND GROWTH GROUP
Chaplain Jim Arnold
Lutheran General Hospital
1775 Dempster St.
Park Ridge, IL 60068
312/696-2210
Purpose: To provide support for bereaved parents.
Services: Offers bimonthly meetings.

GRIEF SUPPORT GROUPS
Pastoral Care Department
Lutheran General Hospital
1775 Dempster St.
Park Ridge, IL 60068
312/696-6395
Purpose: To provide support for bereaved adolescents and adults.

Skokie

INFORMAL WIDOWS LUNCHEON SUPPORT GROUP
Peggy Gilmour, Director
Skokie Office on Aging
Smith Activities Center

Lincoln & Galitz
Skokie, IL 60076
312/673-0500
Purpose: To provide social support for widows.

WIDOWS SUPPORT GROUP
Jewish Community Center
5050 Church St.
Skokie, IL 60076
312/675-2200
Purpose: To provide support for widows (focusing on grieving stage).

Springfield

*SHARE (SOURCE OF HELP IN AIRING AND RESOLVING EXPERIENCES)
St. John's Hospital
800 E. Carpenter St.
Springfield, IL 62702
Purpose: To provide support for parents experiencing miscarriage or newborn death (prior to dismissal from hospital nursery).
Chapters: Chapters in Belleville, Effingham, Carbondale, Jacksonville, Litchfield, Melrose Park, Peoria, Quincy, Rockford, and Urbana.

Sycamore

THEOS
Sycamore United Methodist Church
Sycamore, IL 61078
815/895-5001
Purpose: As a nondenominational Christian self-help group for the young and middle-aged widowed and their families, to provide shared grief experiences.

Wilmette

COMPASSIONATE FRIENDS—WILMETTE
c/o Beth Hillel Congregation
3220 Big Tree Ln.
Wilmette, IL 60091
312/251-4390
Purpose: To provide support and understanding by and for bereaved parents.

Winnetka

THEOS
Reverend Richard Agusperger
Institute of Living
Winnetka, IL 60093
312/446-6955
Purpose: As a nondenominational Christian self-help group for the young and middle-aged widowed and their families, to provide shared grief experiences.

IOWA

Burlington

*MAKE TODAY COUNT
P.O. Box 303
Burlington, IA 52601
319/754-7266
Purpose: To provide a positive approach for dealing with cancer (designed for those who have cancer and their families); to facilitate learning to live with dying.
Chapters: 208 groups.

MARYLAND

Bethesda

*PARENTS WITHOUT PARTNERS
7910 Woodmont Ave.
Suite 1008
Bethesda, MD 20014
301/654-8850
Purpose: To provide support for single parents (separated, divorced, widowed and never married).
Chapters: 1,000 chapters (local chapters in most areas).

Clarksville

SUICIDERS ANONYMOUS
P.O. Box 15
Clarksville, MD 21029
Purpose: Relying on the same concepts as Alcoholics Anonymous, to provide help for suicidal individuals (no therapy, no counseling, etc.).

MASSACHUSETTS

In addition to the following list of self-help groups in this state, these cities and towns also have self-help groups: East Falmouth, Longmeadow, Needham, North Reading, Waltham, and West Bolyston. For further information, contact the closest regional clearinghouse.

Boston

*THE SAMARITANS
802 Boylston St.
Boston, MA 02199
617/247-0220
Purpose: As a telephone and befriending service, to provide suicidal people with someone to talk to; to provide further support (through Safe Place) for those bereaved by suicide.
Chapters: 4 branches.

Hingham

THE COMPASSIONATE FRIENDS, INC.
Hingham Chapter
Sister Rose Marie
St. Paul's Church
Hingham, Massachusetts 02043
617/749-5568
Purpose: To provide mutual aid and support for bereaved parents.

MICHIGAN

Livonia has a self-help group. For specific information, contact the closest regional clearinghouse.

MINNESOTA

Minneapolis

GRIEF THERAPY GROUPS
Minnesota Age & Opportunity Center, Inc.
1801 Nicollet Ave.
Minneapolis, MN 55403
612/874-5525
Purpose: To provide support and trained counselors for bereaved older people.

MENTAL HEALTH ASSOCIATION OF MINNESOTA
Doug Freeman, Director
6715 Minnetonka Blvd.
Minneapolis, MN 55426

MISSOURI

Cities including St. Louis have self-help groups. For specific information, contact the closest regional clearinghouse.

NEBRASKA

In addition to the following list of self-help groups in this state, these cities and towns also have self-help groups: Aurora, Bellevue, Elwood, Fremont, Grand Island, Hastings, Kearney, Kimball, Lincoln, McCook, Omaha, and Waverly. For further information, contact the closest regional clearinghouse.

Beatrice

THEOS
First Presbyterian Church
Fifth and Ella
Beatrice, NE 68310
Purpose: As a nondenominational self-help group for the young and middle-aged widowed and their families, to help rebuild their lives through mutual self-help.
Services: Holds group meetings.

Grand Island

THEOS
First Christian Church
2400 W. Fourteenth
Grand Island, NE 68801
Purpose: As a nondenominational self-help group for the young and middle-aged widowed and their families, to help rebuild their lives through mutual self-help.
Services: Holds group meetings.

Holdrege

THEOS
First Presbyterian Church
1103 Sheridan St.
Holdrege, NE 68949
Purpose: As a nondenominational self-help group for the young and middle-aged widowed and their families, to rebuild their lives through mutual self-help.
Services: Holds group meetings.

Kearney

THEOS
First Presbyterian Church
115 W. Twenty-second
Kearney, NE 68847
Purpose: As a nondenominational self-help group for the young and middle-aged widowed and their families, to rebuild their lives through mutual self-help.
Services: Holds group meetings.

Lincoln

GRIEF CENTER
Reverend Otto Schulz; Reverend Dennis Rock
Lincoln General Hospital
Independence Center
2300 S. Sixteenth
Lincoln, NE 68502
402/473-5268
Services: Holds two weekly group sessions.

MAKE TODAY COUNT
2942 Clinton St.
Lincoln, NE 68503
Purpose: To provide support for those with cancer or other life-threatening illness and their families. [Note: Send a stamped, self-addressed envelope for free brochures; provides information for starting a group.]
Chapters: State chapter.

SELF-HELP INFORMATION SERVICES
Barbara R. Fox, Director
1601 Euclid Ave.
Lincoln, NE 68502
402/476-9668

THEOS
3400 Randolph St.
Lincoln, NE 68510
402/474-5683
Purpose: To serve as a nondenominational, self-help group for the young and middle-aged widowed and their families.
Services: Holds group meetings.
Chapters: State chapter. [Note: Send a stamped, self-addressed envelope for free brochures; provides information for starting a group.]

Omaha

THEOS
Church of Cross
114th and Pacific
Omaha, NE 68154
402/592-0385
Purpose: As a nondenominational self-help group for the young and middle-aged widowed and their families, to rebuild their lives through mutual self-help.
Services: Holds group meetings.

NEW JERSEY

In addition to the regional clearinghouse, these cities and towns have self-help groups: Camden, Mountain Lakes, Princeton, and Willingboro. For further information, contact the New Jersey regional clearinghouse.

Denville

NEW JERSEY SELF-HELP CLEARINGHOUSE
Ed Madara, Director
St. Clare's Community Mental Health Center
Denville, NJ 07834
From within NJ: 800/452-9790
Outside NY: 201/625-6215

NEW YORK

In addition to the following list of self-help groups in this state, these areas also have self-help groups: Brooklyn, Commack, Floral Park, Flushing, Huntington Station, North Bellmore, North Salem, Peeksill, Plainview, Searingtown, Syosset, and Westchester County. The New York City area also has additional groups. For further information, contact the closest regional clearinghouse.

Bedford Hills

WORDS—WIDOWED AND DIVORCED SINGLES
Northern Westchester YM-YWHA
129 Plainfield Ave.
Bedford Hills, NY 10507
914/241-2064

Purpose: To provide mutual support and social opportunities for widowed and divorced persons over forty-five.
Services: Holds bimonthly meetings.
Membership: Y members—free; non-members—$3.00 per session.

Bronx

BRONX BEREAVED PARENTS
Holy Rosary Church
Father Winter's Hall
Eastchester and Gun Hill Rds.
Bronx, New York 10469
212/881-3852
Purpose: To provide support for grieving parents and other family members.
Services: Holds monthly meetings.

WIDOWS SELF HELP GROUPS
Sherry Narodick, S.W.
Geriatric Division
Jacobi Hospital
Bronx, New York 10461
212/430-0618 (Weekdays 9-5)
Purpose: To provide support for women fifty-five and over, widowed two years, and men (through referral).
Fees: Sliding scale; Medicare; Medicaid.

Brooklyn

HEIGHTS HILLS MENTAL HEALTH SERVICE
Robert L. Evans, Director
South Beach Psych.
50 Court St.
Brooklyn, NY 11201
212/834-7304

METROPOLITAN WIDOWED PERSONS SERVICE
Ellen Gorman, S.W., Chairperson
2061 Voorhees Ave.
Brooklyn, NY 11235
or
3087 Ocean Ave.
Brooklyn, NY 11235
212/891-6264 (Hotline)
Services: Has monthly newsletter, some social activities, and weekly meetings.
Fee: $10.00.

Commack

LONG ISLAND SELF-HELP CLEARINGHOUSE
Audrey Leif, Director
New York Institute of Technology
6350 Jericho Turnpike
Commack, NY 11725
516/499-8800

Far Rockaway

WIDOWED PERSONS SERVICE
Cyndie McQuade, S.W., Coordinator
Gustave Hartman YM-YWHA
710 Hartman Ln.
Far Rockaway, NY 11691
212/471-0200
Purpose: As a trained volunteer group of widows organized under the Hartman Senior Preventive Health Center, to offer support to newly widowed men and women.
Services: Trains additional volunteers.

Hempstead

FAMILY SERVICE ASSOCIATION—BEREAVEMENT CENTER
129 Jackson St.
Hempstead, NY 11550
516/485-4600
Purpose: To provide mutual aid for widowed persons and bereaved parents.

Hicksville

LEVITTOWN WIDOWS' AND WIDOWERS' CLUB
Ann Zappulla, President
V.F.W. Hall
320 S. Broadway
Hicksville, NY 11801
516/334-4975
Purpose: As a social group, to provide support for widowed individuals during readjustment period.
Services: Has monthly meetings, speakers and social activities.

PARENTS WITHOUT PARTNERS
P.O. Box 495
Hicksville, NY 11802
Purpose: An international organization of single parents—widowed, divorced, separated, never married—to provide discussion groups, family activities, social and recreational opportunities, educational programs.
Services: Has a newsletter and a professional advisory board.

Huntington

ST. PATRICK'S WIDOWS' AND WIDOWERS' CLUB
St. Patrick's Church
400 Main St.
Huntington, NY 11743
516/271-9360
Purpose: To provide a nonsectarian support group for widowed persons of all ages.
Services: Has monthly meetings and social events.

Lake Ronkonkoma

PARENTS WITHOUT PARTNERS
P.O. Box 806
Lake Ronkonkoma, NY 11779

Purpose: An international organization of single parents—widowed, divorced, separated, never married—to provide discussion groups, family activities, social and recreational opportunities, educational programs.
Services: Has a newsletter and a professional advisory board.

Levittown

DISPLACED HOMEMAKER MULTISERVICE CENTER
Action Council of Central Nassau
Farmedge Rd.
Levittown, NY 11756
516/579-7617
Purpose: To provide assistance for women changing from homemakers to working women due to widowhood, divorce, separation, through counseling, support groups, workshops, preemployment and employment advice, and socializing.

Long Beach

LONG BEACH MENTAL HEALTH CLINIC
450 E. Bay Dr.
Long Beach, NY 11561
516/432-8000 (Ext. 292)
Services: Offers multiple services including mutual support groups for widowhood and bereavement.

Manhasset

ATTITUDINAL HEALING CENTER OF LONG ISLAND
1691 Northern Blvd.
Manhasset, NY 11030
516/869-8118
Purpose: To provide support for patients facing life-threatening illness and their families.
Services: Has adults' and children's groups, parents', siblings' and peers' groups.

Mineola

THE FIRST STEP
Helen Miles, R.N., Director of Nursing and Health Services
American Red Cross
264 Old Country Rd.
Mineola, NY 11501
516/747-3500
Purpose: To provide support for the newly bereaved.
Services: Offers a preventive mental health program, weekly meetings, and crisis intervention.

New Hyde Park

WIDOWED PERSONS SERVICE
OF NASSAU AND QUEENS
Leonard Tazman, S.W.
Long Island Jewish-Hillside Medical Center
Room O-102
Lakeville Rd.
New Hyde Park, NY 11040

212/470-4249 (Weekdays 9-5); 516/352-1711 (Leave message.)
Purpose: To serve as a group of widowed persons helping the newly bereaved adjust to loss of a spouse through telephone contact, public education, and referral.

New York

BEREAVEMENT AND LOSS CENTER
Mrs. Ann Rosberger; Dr. Henry Rosberger, Medical Director
170 E. Eighty-third St.
New York, NY 10028
212/879-5655
Purpose: As a professional counseling and consultation service, to provide three counselors, a financial advisor, and a career counselor, individual and group sessions of eight to ten men or women, and (after initial period) five workshop sessions for combined groups of men and women.
Fees: Intake—$35.00; individual session—$35.00; group sessions—$20.00; workshop series—$50.00.

BEREAVEMENT GROUP
New York City Self-Help Clearinghouse
240 E. Sixty-fourth St.
New York, NY 10021
212/421-3133 (Weekdays 9:30-5)
Purpose: To provide a self-help discussion group for persons experiencing the loss of a parent.

BROTHERS AND SISTERS OF HOMICIDE VICTIMS
Victims Service Agency
2 Lafayette St.
New York, NY 10007
212/577-7700 (Weekdays 9-5)
Purpose: To provide self-help and support for siblings of homicide victims.

*COMMITTEE TO COMBAT HUNTINGTON'S DISEASE
250 W. Fifty-seventh St.
New York, NY 10019
212/757-0443
Purpose: To aid persons with Huntington's disease and their families.
Chapters: 28 chapters.

THE FAMILIES OF HOMICIDE VICTIMS PROJECT
Rosemary Masters, M.S.W.
Victims Service Agency
2 Lafayette St.
New York, NY 10007
212/577-7754 (9:30-5:30); 212/577-7777 (Hotline)
Purpose: In the Brooklyn borough, to help families needing financial services, psychological support, and education in the criminal justice system when a loved one is victim of homicide.
Services: Offers family and individual counseling, reassurance, and telephone calls.

FOUNDATION OF THANATOLOGY
Dr. Austin Kutscher, President
630 W. 168th St.
New York, NY 10032
Purpose: To assist professional personnel or scholars of thanatology.

*NATIONAL FOUNDATION FOR SUDDEN INFANT DEATH, INC.
1501 Broadway
New York, NY 10036
Purpose: To offer support for parents whose infants are victims of SIDS.
Chapters: 23 affiliates.

*NATIONAL SELF-HELP CLEARINGHOUSE
Frank Riessman, Co-Director; Alan Gartner, Co-Director
Graduate School & University Center
City University of New York
33 W. Forty-second St.
New York, NY 10036
Clearinghouse: 212/840-7606

NEW YORK CITY SELF-HELP CLEARINGHOUSE
Carol Eisman, Associate Director
240 E. Sixty-fourth St.
New York, NY 10021
212/840-0860

PARENTS OF MURDERED CHILDREN
Victims Service Agency
2 Lafayette St.
New York, NY 10007
212/577-7700 (Weekdays 9-5)
Purpose: To provide support for parents whose children are homicide victims.
Services: Holds monthly meeting.

PARENTS WITHOUT PARTNERS, MANHATTAN
P.O. Box 1002 GPO
New York, NY 10001
212/523-1313 (24-hour, 7-day, answering service)
Purpose: As an international organization, to support the single parent—separated, divorced, widowed, or never married.
Services: Publishes a newsletter.
Fee: $18.00.

SERVICES TO THE WIDOWED
Jewish Board of Family and Children Services
33 W. Sixtieth St.
New York, NY 10023
212/586-2900
Purpose: To provide counseling and support services for individuals, groups (fifteen weekly sessions), and families.
Chapters: 10 additional locations in New York area.
Fees: Groups—$10.00 per session; sliding scale (financial hardship); Medicaid; Medicare (for psychiatric counseling).

SUDDEN INFANT DEATH INFORMATION AND COUNSELING
New York City area
212/686-8854 (Weekdays 9-5)
Purpose: To provide counseling for families of SIDS victims and educational programs for emergency room and ambulance personnel.

Pelham

W.I.S.E.R. (WIDOWED IN SEARCH OF EFFECTIVE RECOVERY)
Huguenot Church
Pelham, NY 10803
914/738-3488
Purpose: To provide self-help for any widowed person.

Queens

LIFE SKILLS FOR ADULTS (OVER 60)
Flushing YM-YWHA
45-35 Kissena Blvd.
Queens, NY 11355
212/461-3030 (Weekdays 9-5)
Purpose: Sponsored by Flushing Y Senior Center and Self Help, to teach life skills to all adults over sixty (cooking, nutrition, consumerism, banking, etc.).
Services: Holds weekly meetings; is especially helpful for widowed persons.
Membership: Participants must be members of either the Flushing Y Senior Center (sixty-five and up) or of Self Help (sixty and up); an interview and registration are necessary.

WIDOWED OR DIVORCED SINGLES GROUP
Flushing YM-YWHA
45-35 Kissena Blvd.
Queens, NY 11355
212/461-3030 (Weekdays 9-5)
Purpose: To provide support for singles, widowed or divorced, between the ages of forty-five and sixty.

Scarsdale

WOMAN TO WOMAN—MID-WESTCHESTER YM-YWHA
Mid-Westchester YM-YWHA
999 Wilmot Rd.
Scarsdale, NY 10583
914/472-3300
Purpose: To provide support for divorced, separated and widowed women.
Services: Holds two monthly meetings.
Fee: Annual membership—$15.00.

Smithtown

SINGLE SET
West Suffolk YM-YWHA
22 Lawrence Ave.
Smithtown, NY 11787
516/979-8000
Purpose: To offer a social and recreation group for single adults, thirty-five and over, including the newly widowed, separated, and divorced.
Services: Has discussion groups and social activities.

WEST SUFFOLK YM—YWHA
22 Lawrence Ave.
Smithtown, NY 11787
516/979-8000
Purpose: To provide many community services including support groups for the newly-widowed.

St. James

SHARING
c/o St. James Methodist Church
Moriches Rd.
St. James, NY 11780
516/979-9422; 516/724-3647
Purpose: To provide a social and recreation group for widowed, divorced, and separated persons thirty-five and over—music, films, speakers, outings, etc.
Services: Has weekly meetings.

Valhalla

WESTCHESTER COMMUNITY COLLEGE
Leslie Borck, Director
Academic/Arts Building
75 Grasslands Rd.
Valhalla, NY 10595
914/347-3620

White Plains

THE BEREAVED CHILDREN'S PROGRAM
Dr. Barbara Kaplan
Westchester Jewish Community Services
172 S. Broadway
White Plains, NY 10605
914/949-6761
Purpose: To provide support for children who have lost parents.
Services: Holds weekly meetings.

WIDOWS AND WIDOWERS GROUP
YWCA
North St.
White Plains, NY 10605
914/948-8004 (Linda Gilberto)
Purpose: To offer mutual support, education and social opportunities for widowed persons.
Services: Meets periodically at YWCA.
Fee: Activity fee (some programs).

YOUNG WIDOWS AND WIDOWERS OF WESTCHESTER
Temple Israel Center
White Plains, NY
and
Greenburgh Hebrew Center

Dobbs Ferry, NY 10522
Purpose: To offer mutual support and programs to meet the emotional, cultural, and social needs of members
Services: Holds bimonthly meetings.
Fees: Annual membership—$10.00; fees per meeting—$2.00 (members); $4.00 (nonmembers).

NORTH DAKOTA

Fargo has a self-help group. For specific information, contact the closest regional clearinghouse.

OHIO

In addition to the following list of self-help groups in this state, Beachwood also has a self-help group. For further information, contact the closest regional clearinghouse.

Cincinnati

*PARENTS OF MURDERED CHILDREN
1739 Bella Vista
Cincinnati, OH 45237
513/242-8025
Purpose: To provide support for parents who have lost a child through homicide.

Cleveland

*SURVIVORS OF SUICIDE VICTIMS
2675 Warrensville Center Rd.
Cleveland, OH 44122
216/321-3058
Purpose: To provide help and encouragement for friends and relatives of suicide victims.
Services: Holds monthly formal meetings with speakers dealing with the grief of suicide and informal discussion groups with parents; publishes a monthly newsletter.
Chapters: 1 group.

University Heights

PARENTS WHO HAVE EXPERIENCED NEO-NATAL
DEATH (PEND)
3837 Favershun St.
University Heights, OH 44118
216/371-8353
Purpose: To provide support to parents experiencing stillborn or neo-natal death.
Services: Holds informal monthly meetings with group leaders.
Chapters: 1 group.

PENNSYLVANIA

In addition to the following list of self-help groups in this state, these cities and towns also have self-help groups: Jenkintown, Lansdale, Lauderdale, Pudley Park, and West-

chester. The Philadelphia area has additional groups. For further information, contact the closest regional clearinghouse.

Bala Cynwyd

COMPASSIONATE FRIENDS, INC.
PENN-WYNNE CHAPTER
George Steinberg, Site Manager
Two Bala Cynwyd Plaza
Suite 614
Bala Cynwyd, PA 19004
215/667-2240
Purpose: To provide self-help for parents who have lost a child (from infancy to adulthood).
Services: Maintains a library of books and tapes; has occasional guest speakers.

Philadelphia

C&E/R&E SERVICES
Jared Hermalin, Director
John F. Kennedy CMH/MR Center
Hahnemann Medical College & Hospital
112 N. Broad St.
Philadelphia, PA 19102
215/568-0860 (Ext. 276)

COPING WITH LOSS
Northeastern Community Mental Health/
Mental Retardation Center
Roosevelt Blvd./Evans Ave.
Philadelphia, PA
215/831-2945
Purpose: To provide support for families who have lost a child.

MAKE TODAY COUNT
JoAnn Funches, R.T.
Germantown Dispensary and Hospital
E. Penn and E. Wister Sts.
Germantown
Philadelphia, PA 19144
215/248-3917
Purpose: To help those with cancer and other life-threatening diseases and their families live life to the fullest.

MAKE TODAY COUNT
MARSHA SLAVIN CHAPTER
P.O. Box 25043
Philadelphia, PA 19147
215/879-4402 (Philadelphia hotline)
Purpose: To provide support to help those with cancer and other life-threatening illnesses, their families, and other interested persons learn to live life to the fullest.

WIDOW AND WIDOWER COUNSELING AND
REFERRAL SERVICE
8001 Roosevelt Blvd.
Philadelphia, PA 19152
215/338-9934

Purpose: To provide support for those who have experienced the death of a spouse.
Services: Offers counseling and information; holds regular meetings.

Pittsburgh

*THEOS FOUNDATION
(THEY HELP EACH OTHER SPIRITUALLY)
The Penn Hills Mall Office Building
Room 306
Pittsburgh, PA 15235
412/243-4299
Purpose: To provide a nondenominational Christian self-help group for the young and middle-aged widowed and their families.
Services: Holds meetings once or twice a month. (Each chapter institutes its own program.)
Chapters: Chapters throughout U.S. and Canada.

Pottstown

MAKE TODAY COUNT
Pottstown Memorial Medical Center
Firestone Blvd. and High St.
Pottstown, PA 19464
215/327-7058
Purpose: To provide support to assist those with cancer and other life-threatening diseases and their families live life to the fullest.

Scranton

COMPASSIONATE FRIENDS
Community Medical Center Nursing School
1822 Mulberry St.
Scranton, PA 18510
Purpose: To provide support and understanding by and for parents who have lost a child.

F.I.R.S.T. (FREE INFORMATION REFERRAL SERVICE TELEPHONE)
Arlene Hopkins, Program Director
200 Adams Ave.
Scranton, PA 18503
717/961-1234
Purpose: To provide a referral service and other related information for self-help groups.

Sellersville

MAKE TODAY COUNT
Grand View Hospital
700 Lawn Ave.
Sellersville, PA 18960
215/257-3611 (Ext. 605)
Purpose: To provide support to assist those with cancer and other life-threatening diseases and their families live life to the fullest.

Westchester

T.L.A., INC. (TO LIVE AGAIN)
Elizabeth Schroeder, President
P.O. Box 103
Westchester, PA 19380
215/839-1433; 215/242-3286
Purpose: Based on the book *To Live Again.*
Chapters: Regional group (chapters in Pennsylvania, Wilmington, Delaware, and eastern New Jersey).

Yardley

SUICIDERS ANONYMOUS
Thomas Dana Bond, Site Manager
Yardley Historical Association Building
Yardley, PA 19067
215/245-1442 (24-hour service)
Purpose: To aid suicidal individuals, their families and friends.

TEXAS

Arlington

UNIVERSITY OF TEXAS AT ARLINGTON
Shirley W. King, Director
P.O. Box 19129
Arlington, TX 76019
817/273-2707

Dallas

COMPASSIONATE FRIENDS
3000 Turtle Creek Plaza
Suite 201
Dallas, TX 75219
214/521-7420
Purpose: To provide support and understanding by and for parents who have lost a child.

DALLAS COMMUNITY MENTAL HEALTH
ASSOCIATION SELF-HELP CLEARINGHOUSE
Carol Madison, Director
2500 Maple Ave.
Dallas, TX 75206
214/748-7825

Fort Worth

TARRENT COMMUNITY MENTAL HEALTH
ASSOCIATION SELF-HELP CLEARINGHOUSE
Karen Hale, Director
804 W. Seventh St.
Fort Worth, TX 76102
817/335-5405

VIRGINIA

Arlington

FORUM FOR DEATH EDUCATION AND COUNSELING
P.O. Box 1226
Arlington, VA 22210
Purpose: As an international organization, to provide support and information for the death educator/counselor.

McLean

NATIONAL HOSPICE ORGANIZATION
1750 Old Meadow Rd.
McLean, VA 22102
Purpose: To provide care, support, and bereavement counseling for the terminally ill and their families.

WASHINGTON

Kennewick has a self-help group. For specific information, contact the closest regional clearinghouse.

WISCONSIN

In addition to the following list of self-help groups in this state, Milwaukee has other self-help groups. For further information, contact the closest regional clearinghouse.

Madison

CONTINUING EDUCATION IN MENTAL HEALTH
Patrick W. Prindle, Director
University of Wisconsin-Extension
415 Lowell Hall
610 Langdon St.
Madison, WI 53706

Milwaukee

AIID—AID IN INFANT DEATH
St. Joseph's Hospital
5000 W. Chambers St.
Milwaukee, WI 53210
414/774-4103
Purpose: To provide support and mutual aid for parents who have lost an infant through miscarriage, stillbirth, prematurity, congenital defects or other reasons.
Services: Monthly meetings and discussion groups.

BEREAVEMENT SUPPORT GROUP
Father Arnold Pangrazzi
Pentecost Lutheran Church
5226 West Burleigh
Milwaukee, WI 53210
414/782-6312; 414/447-2190
Purpose: To provide mutual aid for individuals of different ages experiencing grief.

Services: Uses group discussion and speakers; meets twice monthly.

COMPASSIONATE FRIENDS
Mt. Zion Lutheran Church
120th and North
Milwaukee, WI 53226
414/546-3390 (Hotline number)
Purpose: To provide mutual support, socializing, and education to aid parents who have lost a child.
Services: Offers a speakers bureau.

**CRISIS, CHANGE, RECOVERY
FOR MIDDLE AGED ADULTS**
Concordia College
3201 W. Highland Blvd.
Milwaukee, WI 53208
414/344-3400
Purpose: To provide mutual aid and education for widows, widowers, and divorced people.
Services: Holds weekly meetings; has speakers available; prefers phone contact first.

NAIM
Family Life Center
2021 N. Sixtieth St.
Milwaukee, WI 53208

Our Lady of Good Hope
7125 N. Forty-first St.
Milwaukee, WI 53209

St. Paul
3945 S. Kansas Ave.
Milwaukee, WI 53207
414/771-6968; 414/445-9582
Purpose: To provide mutual aid and support for widows and widowers.
Services: Offers socializing and education; holds monthly meetings (open to members, visitors interested in becoming members, and guests of members).
Chapters: 3 Milwaukee area chapters (other chapters in southeast Wisconsin).

**NATIONAL SUDDEN INFANT DEATH SYNDROME—
SIDS**
Wisconsin SIDS Center
Milwaukee Children's Hospital
1700 W. Wisconsin Ave.
Milwaukee, WI 53233
414/931-4049; 414/257-5884
Purpose: To provide mutual support for parents of SIDS victims.
Services: Holds dicussion groups; counsels; conducts SIDS research studies; has quarterly meetings (open to all).

ON OUR OWN
South Community Organization Office
2324 S. Thirteenth St.
Milwaukee, WI 53215
414/643-7913

Purpose: To provide support for widows under fifty-six years of age.
Services: Offers socializing and education; has monthly meetings (open to visitors interested in becoming members and guests of members, but prefers prior phone contact).

PARENTS WITHOUT PARTNERS
Milwaukee, WI
414/481-2050 (Activity center); 414/258-5616 (Answering service)
Purpose: To provide support for single parents (widowed, divorced, separated and never married).
Services: Offers discussions, speakers, a newsletter, and a library; has many activities.
Membership: Annual fee—$20.00.

S.O.S.—SURVIVORS OF SUICIDE
First Wisconsin National Bank
Thirty-seventh and Villard
Milwaukee, WI 53209
414/442-4638
Purpose: To provide mutual aid and discussion for family and friends of suicide victims.
Services: Holds monthly meetings (open to interested individuals).

WIDOWS & WIDOWERS
Memorial Lutheran Church
7701 N. Green Bay Rd.
Milwaukee, WI 53209
414/449-5010; 414/352-1160
Purpose: To provide mutual support and socialization for widowed persons.
Services: Holds monthly meetings (open to individuals interested in membership and guests of members, but prefers phone contact before attending).

WIDOW TO WIDOW
Jewish Community Center
1400 N. Prospect
Milwaukee, WI 53202
414/276-0716; 414/352-2921
Purpose: To provide support for widows of any age.
Services: Offers socialization and education; has monthly meetings (open to any interested person, but prefers phone contact before coming).

New Berlin

LOSS OF A LOVED ONE
Forest Park Presbyterian Church
2300 S. Sunnyslope Rd.
New Berlin, WI 53151
414/425-1842; 414/548-5566
Purpose: To provide mutual support and socializing for anyone experiencing the death of a loved one.
Services: Has weekly meetings (open to any bereaved person).

Waukesha

COMPASSIONATE FRIENDS
WCTI Commons Building
Waukesha, WI 53186
414/546-3390 (Hotline number)
Purpose: To provide mutual support, socializing and education for parents who have lost a child.
Services: Has a speakers bureau.

West Allis

FRIENDLY WIDOWS & WIDOWERS
Mt. Hope Lutheran Church
8633 W. Becher
West Allis, WI 53227
414/321-6064
Services: Provides socializing and educational programs; aids in adjustment to being alone; has monthly meetings (open to those interested in becoming members and guests of members).

CANADA

In addition to the following self-help groups in Canada, these towns also have groups: Abbotsford, British Columbia; North Bay, Ontario. For further information, contact the National Self-Help Clearinghouse in New York.

ONTARIO

Hamilton

WIDOW TO WIDOW
Anne Stewart, Adult Education Director
75 MacNab Street S.
Hamilton, Ontario L8P 3C1 Canada
416/529-8121

Toronto

COMMUNITY CONTACTS FOR THE WIDOWED
Barbara Scott, Coordinator
1643 Yonge St.
Toronto, Ontario M4T 2A1 Canada
416/486-9945

Windsor

BEREAVEMENT RESOURCES
Louise Allen, Bereavement Resource Worker
1226 Ovellette Ave.
Windsor, Ontario N8X 1J5 Canada
519/254-2556

Hospices

The hospice movement reflects the growing concern for offering a humane environment in which dying people can spend the last period of life. Hospice offers an alternative to traditional hospital settings and nursing homes and provides an opportunity for people to die with or near their families and in familiar surroundings.

U.S.A.

ALABAMA

Birmingham

HOSPICE, BAPTIST MEDICAL CENTER—PRINCETON
Bette R. Janes, R.N., Nursing Coordinator
701 Princeton Ave.
Birmingham, AL 35211
205/783-3022
Scope of care: Patient prognosis six months or less.
Type of care: Home care; inpatient.
Fee: None; Medicare; insurance-carrier reimbursement.
Bereavement counseling: Hospice chaplain, staff.

HOSPICE OF THE BAPTIST MEDICAL CENTERS—MONTCLAIR
Chaplain Robert L. Ross, Administrative Director
800 Montclair Rd.
Birmingham, AL 35213
205/592-1059
Scope of care: Cancer patients; prognosis weeks or months.
Type of care: Home care; inpatient.
Fee: None.
Bereavement counseling: Professional, volunteer; follow-up (one year).

Montgomery

HOSPICE OF MONTGOMERY, INC.
Wanda Ruffin, Education/Volunteer Coordinator
P.O. Box 1882
Montgomery, AL 36103
205/262-6596
Scope of care: Patient prognosis one year or less.
Type of care: Home care; volunteers stay with patient in hospital.
Fee: None.
Bereavement counseling: Follow-up.

ARIZONA

Tucson

HILLHAVEN HOSPICE
Daniel M. McDonnell, Hospice Director
5504 E. Pima
Tucson, AZ 85712
602/622-5833
Scope of care: Patient prognosis weeks or months.
Type of care: Home care; inpatient; outreach to nursing homes.
Fee: Sliding scale.
Bereavement counseling: Professional staff, volunteers; education, contact, survivors' group, additional counseling (as needed).

ARKANSAS

Fayetteville

NORTHWEST ARKANSAS HOSPICE ASSOCIATION
Donald S. Amussen, Executive Director
P.O. Box 817
Fayetteville, AR 72701
501/521-7429
Scope of care: Patient prognosis limited.
Type of care: Home care.
Fee: None.
Bereavement counseling: Individual, group.

Jonesboro

HOSPICE OF NORTHEAST ARKANSAS, INC.
Elizabeth French King, Executive Director
P.O. Box 725
Jonesboro, AR 72401
501/972-6270
Scope of care: Patient prognosis poor or terminal.
Type of care: Home care.
Fee: None.
Bereavement counseling: Volunteer; follow-up (one year).

Mountain Home

HOSPICE OF THE OZARKS, INC.
M. Carolyn Wilson, M.D., Executive Director
906 Baker St.
Mountain Home, AR 72653
501/425-2797
Scope of care: Patient prognosis limited.
Type of care: Home care; follow patients to hospitals and nursing homes.
Fee: None.
Bereavement counseling: Staff, volunteer; follow-up.

Prepared by Marquis editorial staff.

CALIFORNIA

Anaheim

MARTIN LUTHER HOSPITAL MEDICAL CENTER
Pastor Harry Stief, Coordinator
1830 W. Romneya Dr.
P.O. Box 3304
Anaheim, CA 92803
714/520-5456
Scope of care: Patient needs palliative only.
Type of care: Home care.
Fee: Sliding scale.
Bereavement counseling: Professionals, volunteers; visits, meetings.

Berkeley

ALTA BATES HOSPICE—
CENTER FOR FAMILY HOSPICE CARE
Robin Heath, R.N., B.S.N., Hospice Patient Care Coordinator
3030 Telegraph Ave.
Berkeley, CA 94705
415/540-8166
Scope of care: Patients eighteen or older; prognosis six months or less.
Type of care: Home care; inpatient.
Fee: Set fee.
Bereavement counseling: Visits, telephone, one-to-one (if necessary).

Burlingame

MISSION HOSPICE, INC. OF SAN MATEO COUNTY
Marilyn Stone, Executive Director
530 El Camino Rd.
Suite B
Burlingame, CA 94010
415/347-1218
Scope of care: Patient prognosis six months or less.
Type of care: Home care; visit clients in institutions.
Fee: Set fee.
Bereavement counseling: Individual, group (monthly).

Carmel

HOSPICE OF THE MONTEREY PENINSULA
Raymond G. Decker, Executive Director
8900 Carmel Valley Rd.
Carmel, CA 93923
408/625-0666
Scope of care: Patient prognosis terminal.
Type of care: Home care; inpatient.
Fee: Sliding scale.
Bereavement counseling: Professional, paraprofessional; follow-up, cancer support group, resource center.

Cupertino

SOUTH BAY HOSPICE
Linda Appleton, Program Manager
20863 Stevens Creek Blvd.
Cupertino, CA 95014
408/252-3110
Scope of care: Patient prognosis weeks or months.
Type of care: Home care.
Fee: Set fee; third-party reimbursement.
Bereavement counseling: Volunteers; contact, family support group.

Escondido

THE ELIZABETH HOSPICE, INC.
Betty Bulen, Executive Director
336 S. Kalmia St.
P.O. Box 891
Escondido, CA 92025
714/741-2092
Scope of care: Patient prognosis six months or less.
Type of care: Home care; inpatient.
Fee: None.
Bereavement counseling: Intern, volunteers.

Eureka

HOSPICE OF HUMBOLDT
Margaret A. Gainer, Executive Director
2427 Harrison Ave.
P.O. Box 3811
Eureka, CA 95501
707/445-1221
Scope of care: Patient prognosis one year or less.
Type of care: Home care; inpatient.
Fee: None.
Bereavement counseling: Trained volunteers; visits, two support groups (weekly).

Granada Hills

HOSPICE-GRANADA HILLS
GRANADA HILLS COMMUNITY HOSPITAL
Charlene Gillette, Hospice Coordinator
10445 Balboa Blvd.
Granada Hills, CA 91344
213/360-1021
Scope of care: Patient prognosis one year or less.
Type of care: Inpatient; contract for home care.
Fee: Set fee.
Bereavement counseling: Social worker, psychiatric nurse, nurses; widowed program, make-today-count program.

Hayward

KAISER/PERMANENTE
HAYWARD HOSPICE PROGRAM
Richard Brett, Hospice Coordinator
27400 Hesperian Blvd.
Hayward, CA 94545
415/784-5730
Scope of care: Adult patients; prognosis six months or less.
Type of care: Home care; inpatient.
Fee: Kaiser/Permanente health-plan membership mandatory.
Bereavement counseling: Social worker, psychologist, coordinator; telephone, individual.

Laguna Hills

HOSPICE ORANGE COUNTY, INC.
Paula Cariker, Director of Volunteers
24953 Paseo de Valencia
Suite 16B
Laguna Hills, CA 92653
714/837-6500
Scope of care: Patient prognosis six months or less.
Type of care: Volunteers work with ten local home health agencies.
Fee: None.
Bereavement counseling: Individual, ongoing groups.

Long Beach

LONG BEACH COMMUNITY HOSPITAL
Norman Tardy, P.H.N., Director
1720 Termino Ave.
P.O. Box 2587
Long Beach, CA 90801
213/597-6655
Scope of care: Life-threatening-condition patients.
Type of care: Home care.
Fee: Set fee; no patient refused care because of inability to pay.
Bereavement counseling: Staff; new-directions group for widows/widowers.

Los Angeles

VA WADSWORTH MEDICAL CENTER
PALLIATIVE TREATMENT PROGRAM
Robert W. Krasnow, M.D., Director
Wilshire & Sawtelle Blvds. (691/11H)
Los Angeles, CA 90073
213/824-4305
Scope of care: Cancer patients; prognosis one year or less.
Type of care: Home care; inpatient.

Fee: (Veterans hospital.)
Bereavement counseling: Individual, groups, widow to widow.

THE VISITING NURSE ASSOCIATION OF LOS ANGELES, INC.
Yvette Luque, Director of Hospice
2530 W. Eighth St.
Los Angeles, CA 90057
213/380-3965
Scope of care: Patient prognosis less than six months.
Type of care: Home care.
Fee: Set fee; third-party reimbursement.
Bereavement counseling: Professionals, volunteers; telephone, visits.

Modesto

MODESTO COMMUNITY HOSPICE
Mary Jean Coeur-Barron, Executive Director
1320 L St.
Modesto, CA 95354
209/577-0615
Scope of care: Cancer patients; prognosis less than six months.
Type of care: Home care; contact maintained with patients in hospitals or other facilities.
Fee: Set fee.
Bereavement counseling: Volunteers, professional bereavement counselor; bereavement education programs (monthly) open to all.

Northridge

HEALTHWEST HOME HEALTH CARE
NORTHRIDGE HOSPITAL
Jeneane Braun, Director
18300 Roscoe Blvd.
Northridge, CA 91328
213/885-5359
Scope of care: Patient prognosis terminal.
Type of care: Home care.
Fee: Set fee.
Bereavement counseling: Telephone, visits.

Oxnard

MERCY HOSPICE OF ST. JOHN'S HOSPITAL
Richard P. Ames, Hospice Coordinator
333 N. F St.
Oxnard, CA 93030
805/487-7861
Scope of care: Patients of physicians on hospital staff; prognosis terminal. (*Note:* Ninety percent are cancer patients; prognosis six months to one year.)
Type of care: Home care; inpatient.
Fee: None.
Bereavement counseling: Bereavement coordinator, professional team.

Palo Alto

MIDPENINSULA HEALTH SERVICE, INC.
Debbie Stinchfield
385 Homer Ave.
Palo Alto, CA 94301
415/324-1964
Scope of care: Patient prognosis terminal.
Type of care: Home care.
Fee: Sliding scale.
Bereavement counseling: Individual, group.

Redwood City

SEQUOIA HOSPITAL DISTRICT
PATIENT SUPPORT PROGRAM
Sheila Kennedy, Hospice Program Director
Whipple/Alameda
Redwood City, CA 94063
415/367-5556
Scope of care: Mostly adult cancer patients; prognosis six months or less.
Type of care: Home care; inpatient.

Fee: Insurance-carrier reimbursement for nursing visits; Medicare.
Bereavement counseling: Social worker, volunteers; follow-up, individual (available).

Sacramento

HOSPICE OF MERCY
Sister M. Cornelius, R.N., M.S.W.
4001 J St.
Sacramento, CA 95819
916/453-4545
Scope of care: Patient prognosis limited.
Type of care: Home care; inpatient.
Fee: None; donations.
Bereavement counseling: Visits, family nights.

San Diego

SAN DIEGO COUNTY HOSPICE CORPORATION
Donna A. Spaulding, Executive Director
3134 El Cajon Blvd.
San Diego, CA 92104
714/283-6335
Scope of care: Mostly cancer patients; prognosis six months or less.
Type of care: Home care.
Fee: None; insurance-carrier reimbursement.
Bereavement counseling: Staff, volunteer; individual, group (monthly).

San Jose

HOSPICE OF THE VALLEY
Barbara Noggle, R.N., B.S., Program Director
349 S. Monroe
Suite 2
San Jose, CA 95128
408/947-1233
Scope of care: Cancer patients; prognosis terminal.
Type of care: Home care.
Fee: None.
Bereavement counseling: Individual, small support groups, social gatherings.

San Leandro

VESPER HOSPICE
Vivian Schutte, Director
311 MacArthur Blvd.
San Leandro, CA 94577
415/351-8686
Scope of care: Cancer patients; prognosis terminal.
Type of care: Home care.
Fee: None; contributions encouraged; some insurance reimbursement.
Bereavement counseling: Individual, new-beginnings support group, referral (as necessary).

San Luis Obispo

HOSPICE OF SAN LUIS OBISPO COUNTY, INC.
Elsie Hill, Program Director
P.O. Box 1342
San Luis Obispo, CA 93406
805/544-2266
Scope of care: Patient prognosis one year or less.
Type of care: Home care.
Fee: None.
Bereavement counseling: Hospice counselor, volunteers; individual, group.

San Pedro

SAN PEDRO PENINSULA HOSPITAL
Mary Dete, R.N., P.H.N., Director
1300 Seventh St.
San Pedro, CA 90732
213/832-3311
Scope of care: Patient prognosis six months to one year.
Type of care: Home care; inpatient.
Fee: Set fee.

Bereavement counseling: Telephone, support group (bi-monthly), widow to widow, widower to widower.

San Rafael

HOSPICE OF MARIN
Mary Taverna, R.N., Executive Director
77 Mark Drive, 17
San Rafael, CA 94903
415/472-6240
Scope of care: Cancer patients; prognosis terminal.
Type of care: Home care.
Fee: Sliding scale; insurance-carrier reimbursement; donations.
Bereavement counseling: Individual; group.

Santa Barbara

HOSPICE OF SANTA BARBARA, INC.
Charles E. Zimmer, Executive Director
330 E. Carrillo St.
Santa Barbara, CA 93101
805/963-8608
Scope of care: Patient prognosis six months or less.
Type of care: Home care.
Fee: Donations requested.
Bereavement counseling: Professional, volunteer; individual, make-today-count support group.

Santa Clara

THE VISITING NURSE ASSOCIATION
Cappe Eudy, R.N., and Sharron Miller, R.N., Nursing Supervisors
2216 The Alameda
Santa Clara, CA 95050
408/244-1280
Scope of care: Patient prognosis weeks or months.
Type of care: Home care.
Fee: Set fee; sliding scale.
Bereavement counseling: Nurse, therapist, volunteer.

Santa Cruz

HOSPICE OF SANTA CRUZ COUNTY, INC.
Marilyn Young, President
115 Maple St.
P.O. Box 61248
Santa Cruz, CA 95061
408/426-1993
Scope of care: Patient prognosis terminal.
Type of care: Home care.
Fee: None.
Bereavement counseling: Individual (as needed), potluck gathering (monthly).

Santa Rosa

HOME HOSPICE OF SONOMA COUNTY
Jan Francis-Brown, Office Manager
P.O. Box 11546
Santa Rosa, CA 95406
707/542-5045
Scope of care: Life-threatening-condition patients; prognosis three to six months.
Type of care: Home care.
Fee: None.
Bereavement counseling: Trained bereavement team; individual, peer-group support, follow-up.

Sonoma

VALLEY OF THE MOON HOSPICE
SONOMA VALLEY HOSPITAL DISTRICT
Carole Bridges, R.N., Hospice Coordinator
347 Andrieux St.
P.O. Box 600
Sonoma, CA 95476
707/938-4545
Scope of care: Primarily advanced cancer patients; prognosis limited.
Type of care: Home care; in-hospital (acute care and convalescent).
Fee: None; donations encouraged.

Bereavement counseling: Anticipatory (from admission), individual and group (after death), telephone, referrals, social group, education.

Thousand Oaks

CONEJO HOSPICE, INC.
O.B.A.—HOSPICE OF THE CONEJO
Harriet Hughes, Patient Care Coordinator; Dolores Groom, Administrative Coordinator
199 E. Thousand Oaks Blvd.
Suite 3
Thousand Oaks, CA 91360
805/495-2145
Scope of care: Patient prognosis six months or less.
Type of care: Home care; patient followed to hospital.
Fee: None; support from United Way and donations.
Bereavement counseling: Follow-up (at least one year) by counselor, support group (weekly), children's group (as needed), crisis counseling (by specialist).

Van Nuys

CONTINUITY OF LIFE PROGRAM
NATIONAL IN-HOME HEALTH SERVICES
Barbara Friedman, Director
6850 Van Nuys Blvd., 208
Van Nuys, CA 91405
213/988-7575
Scope of care: Patient prognosis six months or less.
Type of care: Home care.
Fee: Set fee.
Bereavement counseling: Staff, volunteers; visit, telephone.

Walnut Creek

HOSPICE OF CONTRA COSTA
P.O. Box 4608
Walnut Creek, CA 94596
415/932-8229
Scope of care: Cancer patients; prognosis terminal.
Type of care: Home care; inpatient.
Fee: None; donations; memorials; fund raising.
Bereavement counseling: Nurse (pre-terminal), volunteers (post-terminal).

COLORADO

Colorado Springs

PIKES PEAK HOSPICE, INC.
Moira Reinhardt, Administrator
601 N. Tejon St.
Colorado Springs, CO 80903
303/633-3400
Scope of care: Patient prognosis terminal.
Type of care: Home care.
Fee: Sliding scale.
Bereavement counseling: Individual, groups.

Denver

HOSPICE OF METRO DENVER
M. Elaine Graves, R.N., Director
1719 E. Nineteenth Ave.
Denver, CO 80218
303/839-6256
Scope of care: Patients over eighteen; prognosis days, weeks or months. (Will soon admit children.)
Type of care: Home care.
Fee: Sliding scale; third-party insurance.
Bereavement counseling: Bereavement team; visits, telephone, group.

Lakewood

HOSPICE OF ST. JOHN
Father Paul von Lobkowitz, O.S.J., Director
1625 Carr St.
Lakewood, CO 80215
303/399-6078

Scope of care: Cancer and black lung patients; prognosis six months or less.
Type of care: Home care; inpatient.
Fee: Set fee; Medicare; Medicaid; insurance-carrier reimbursement.
Bereavement counseling: Individualized.

New Castle

GRAND RIVER HOSPICE
Sheila Y. Liston, R.N., Executive Director
P.O. Box 351
New Castle, CO 81647
303/984-2004
Scope of care: Patient prognosis terminal.
Type of care: Home care; inpatient.
Fee: Third-party reimbursement for professional services.
Bereavement counseling: Trained counselors, volunteers; counseling (sudden and accidental death), support group.

DISTRICT OF COLUMBIA

HOSPICE CARE OF THE DISTRICT OF COLUMBIA
Joan Hoover, Executive Director
1828 L St. NW, 505
Washington, DC 20036
202/347-1700
Scope of care: Adult patients; prognosis six months or less.
Type of care: Home care.
Fee: Sliding scale; no patient refused care because of inability to pay.
Bereavement counseling: Social worker, trained volunteers; visits, follow-up (one year).

THE WASHINGTON HOME HOSPICE
Kristin K. Spector, Hospice Director
3720 Upton St. NW
Washington, DC 20016
202/966-3720
Scope of care: Cancer patients over sixteen; prognosis three months or less.
Type of care: Inpatient (nursing home).
Fee: Set fee.
Bereavement counseling: Staff; follow-up (one year), telephone, visits, social gatherings.

FLORIDA

Boca Raton

HOSPICE OF BOCA RATON
Adelaide M. Getty, Patient Care Coordinator
1840 N. Dixie Hwy.
Boca Raton, FL 33432
305/395-5031
Scope of care: Patient prognosis six months or less.
Type of care: Home care; inpatient (planned).
Fee: None.
Bereavement counseling: Staff counselor, trained volunteers; individual, group.

Daytona Beach

HOSPICE OF VOLUSIA
HALIFAX HOSPITAL MEDICAL CENTER
Fran Solenson, R.N., Hospice Coordinator
P.O. Box 1990
Daytona Beach, FL 32015
904/258-2038
Scope of care: Patients recommended by attending physicians; prognosis limited.
Fee: None.
Bereavement counseling: Hospice chaplain, volunteers.

Ft. Lauderdale

HOSPICE CARE OF BROWARD COUNTY, INC.
Mary Bymel, Executive Director
3625 N. Andrews Ave.
Ft. Lauderdale, FL 33309
305/467-7423

Scope of care: Patient prognosis one year or less.
Type of care: Home care; inpatient (planned).
Fee: None; sliding scale (based on need).
Bereavement counseling: Trained volunteers, psychotherapist; support groups, bereavement crisis line.

Jacksonville

HOSPICE OF NORTHEAST FLORIDA
Dorothy S. Dorion, Director
3599 University Blvd. S
Suite 3
Jacksonville, FL 32216
904/398-4724
Scope of care: Congenital-defect, ALS, COPD and cancer patients; prognosis one year or less.
Type of care: Home care; inpatient.
Fee: None.
Bereavement counseling: Individual, group, workshops, social functions, telephone.

METHODIST HOSPICE
Michael P. Rosen, Administrator
580 W. Eighth St.
Jacksonville, FL 32209
904/356-7008
Scope of care: Patient prognosis one year or less.
Type of care: Home care; inpatient; outpatient.
Fee: Sliding scale.
Bereavement counseling: Staff, volunteers; individual, group, referrals to community agencies.

Lauderdale Lakes

HOSPICE, INC.
Donald J. Gaetz, Area Administrator
3085 N.W. Thirtieth St.
Lauderdale Lakes, FL 33311
305/486-4085
Scope of care: Patient prognosis one year or less.
Type of care: Home care; inpatient; outpatient.
Fee: Sliding scale; Medicare; Medicaid; no patient refused care because of inability to pay.
Bereavement counseling: Visits, group, formal.

Miami

HOSPICE, INC. OF MIAMI, FT. LAUDERDALE
Hugh A. Westbrook, Executive Director
111 N.W. Tenth Ave.
Miami, FL 33128
305/325-0245
Scope of care: Patient prognosis one year or less.
Type of care: Home care; inpatient; outpatient.
Fee: Sliding scale; Medicare; Medicaid; no patient refused care because of inability to pay.
Bereavement counseling: Visits, group, formal.

Pompano Beach

GOLD COAST HOME HEALTH SERVICES HOSPICE TEAM
Ella Charland, R.N., Patient/Family Coordinator
4699 N. Federal Hwy.
Suite 205
Pompano Beach, FL 33064
305/785-2990
Scope of care: Patient prognosis one year or less.
Type of care: Home care; inpatient.
Fee: Sliding scale; set fee; none.
Bereavement counseling: Group (weekly), individual, follow-up (as needed).

Sarasota

HOSPICE OF SARASOTA COUNTY, INC.
Constance C. Hurd, Administrative Associate
P.O. Box 15225
Sarasota, FL 33579
813/953-5737

Scope of care: Patient prognosis six months or less.
Type of care: Home care.
Fee: None.
Bereavement counseling: Individual, trained volunteer.

Seminole

HOSPICE CARE, INC.
Sparky Clark, Administrator
8891 Seventy-eighth Ave.
Seminole, FL 33534
813/397-0474
Scope of care: Patient prognosis less than six months.
Type of care: Home care; inpatient; outpatient.
Fee: Set fee (waived, as applicable); no patient refused care because of inability to pay.
Bereavement counseling: Social workers, volunteers.

Winter Haven

GOOD SHEPHERD HOSPICE, INC.
Susan Morgan, Patient Care Coordinator; Pat Dilley, Office Manager
110 Third St. NW (Office)
P.O. Box 1183
Winter Haven, FL 33880
813/293-6737
Scope of care: Patient prognosis limited.
Type of care: Home care.
Fee: None.
Bereavement counseling: Individual, group.

Winter Park

HOSPICE ORLANDO, INC.
Anne Van Landingham, Patient Care Coordinator
P.O. Box 449
Winter Park, FL 32790
Scope of care: Patient prognosis limited.
Type of care: Home care; inpatient (planned).
Fee: None.
Bereavement counseling: Professionals, paraprofessional volunteers; individual, group (planned).

GEORGIA

Atlanta

GRADY HOSPICE
GRADY MEMORIAL HOSPITAL
Vernon R. Gramling, Director
80 Butler St. SE
Atlanta, GA 30303
404/588-4885
Scope of care: Cancer patients; prognosis three months.
Type of care: Home care; inpatient.
Fee: None.
Bereavement counseling: Volunteer; follow-up.

ILLINOIS

Chicago

HORIZON HOSPICE, INC.
Sally Owen-Still
541 W. Diversey Ave.
Chicago, IL 60618
312/871-3658
Scope of care: Patient prognosis six months or less.
Type of care: Home care; inpatient (planned).
Fee: None; some third-party insurance and/or Medicare.
Bereavement counseling: Volunteers; follow-up (at least one year).

ILLINOIS MASONIC MEDICAL CENTER HOSPICE SERVICES
Kathleen Woods, A.C.S.W., Hospice Coordinator
836 W. Wellington St.
Chicago, IL 60657
312/975-1600
Scope of care: Patient prognosis six months or less.
Type of care: Home care; inpatient.

Fee: Not available.
Bereavement counseling: Available.

Glen Ellyn

HOSPICE VOLUNTEERS OF DUPAGE
Jane Gallaher, Executive Director
588 Williamsburgh
Glen Ellyn, IL 60137
312/790-1460
Scope of care: Patient prognosis limited.
Type of care: Home care (non-physical).
Fee: None; educational training fees only.
Bereavement counseling: Trained volunteers.

Granite City

HOSPICE OF MADISON COUNTY
Nina Millett, R.N., M.S.W., Program Director
2120 Madison Ave.
Granite City, IL 62040
618/798-3220
Scope of care: Patients over sixteen; prognosis six months or less.
Type of care: Home care; inpatient (planned).
Fee: Third-party reimbursement.
Bereavement counseling: Trained volunteers; social group.

Highland Park

HOSPICE OF HIGHLAND PARK HOSPITAL
Elizabeth McWilliams, S.L., M.A., Hospice Coordinator
718 Glenview Ave.
Highland Park, IL 60035
312/432-8000
Scope of care: Patient prognosis three to six months.
Type of care: Home care; inpatient.
Fee: None.
Bereavement counseling: Individual, referrals to support groups (as needed).

Rockford

NORTHERN ILLINOIS HOSPICE ASSOCIATION
Judith A. Carra, Executive Director
106 N. Main St.
Rockford, IL 61101
815/964-0230
Scope of care: Patient prognosis six months or less.
Type of care: Home care.
Fee: Sliding scale.
Bereavement counseling: Trained staff, professional volunteers; speakers, groups, referrals to intensive therapy (as needed).

Urbana

MERCY HOSPICE CARE PROGRAM
Sister Bette Maniatis, A.C.S.W., Director
1400 W. Park
Urbana, IL 61801
217/337-2470
Scope of care: Patient prognosis limited.
Type of care: Home care; inpatient.
Fee: Routine acute-care costs and home health visits mostly reimbursed; no patient refused care because of inability to pay.
Bereavement counseling: Coordinator, volunteer; follow-up.

INDIANA

Fort Wayne

PARKVIEW HOSPICE
Hazel E. Etzler, R.N., Hospice Nurse Coordinator
2200 Randalia Dr.
Fort Wayne, IN 46805
219/484-6636
Scope of care: Cancer patients; prognosis one year or less.
Type of care: Home care.
Fee: Set fee.
Bereavement counseling: Bereavement committee; telephone, personal contact.

Indianapolis

METHODIST HOSPITAL OF INDIANA, INC.
HOSPICE UNIT
Dr. Mwalimu Imara, Director
1604 N. Capitol Ave.
Indianapolis, IN 46206
317/927-3510
Scope of care: Patients over eighteen; prognosis six months to one year.
Type of care: Home care; inpatient.
Fee: Set fee.
Bereavement counseling: Trained lay and professional staff.

New Albany

HOSPICE OF SOUTHERN INDIANA
Vicki M. Runnion, Executive Director
702 E. Market St.
New Albany, IN 47150
812/945-4596
Scope of care: Patient prognosis weeks or months (flexible).
Type of care: Home care; inpatient; patients followed to hospitals and nursing homes.
Fee: None.
Bereavement counseling: Trained volunteers; follow-up, annual memorial service, support groups.

IOWA

Sioux City

MARIAN HEALTH CENTER HOSPICE
HOME HEALTH SERVICE
2101 Court St.
Sioux City, IA 51104
712/279-2514
Scope of care: Patient prognosis limited.
Type of care: Home care; inpatient (planned).
Fee: Set fee; some memorial reimbursement.
Bereavement counseling: Individual, group (planned).

KANSAS

Hays

HOSPICE OF THE PLAINS, INC.
Lois LaCoss, R.N., Clinical Director; S. Michaeleen Frahm, R.N., Associate Clinical Director
507 Elm St.
Hays, KS 67601
913/625-1139
Scope of care: Patient prognosis six months to one year.
Type of care: Home care.
Fee: Sliding scale; some Medicare reimbursement.
Bereavement counseling: Follow-up (to one year).

Salina

HOSPICE OF SALINA
Kaye Proque, R.N., Hospice Coordinator
P.O. Box 1448
Salina, KS 67401
913/827-5591
Scope of care: Patients eighteen and over; usual prognosis six months or less.
Type of care: Home care; inpatient.
Fee: None; sliding scale; third-party reimbursement.
Bereavement counseling: Support group (monthly), follow-up by nurses.

MAINE

Portland

HOSPICE OF MAINE, INC.
Mary Spencer, Coordinator of Services
32 Thomas St.
Portland, ME 04102
207/774-4417
Scope of care: Patient prognosis six months or less.
Type of care: Home care.
Fee: None.
Bereavement counseling: Not available.

MARYLAND

Baltimore

CHURCH HOSPITAL CORPORATION
Kathleen A. Roche, R.N., M.A., Director Home Health/Hospice
100 N. Broadway
Baltimore, MD 21231
301/732-4730
Scope of care: Patient prognosis five days to six months.
Type of care: Home care; inpatient.
Fee: Based on service needs.
Bereavement counseling: Visits, telephone, annual memorial service.

Silver Spring

HOLY CROSS HOSPITAL OF SILVER SPRING,
MARYLAND HOME HEALTH AGENCY
JoAnne E. Bayles, R.N., Director of Home Care
1500 Forest Glen Rd.
Silver Spring, MD 20901
301/565-1171
Scope of care: Patient prognosis six months or less.
Type of care: Home care.
Fee: Set fee.
Bereavement counseling: Thanatologist, staff, volunteers; widows/widowers group, follow-up (planned).

MASSACHUSETTS

Beverly

HOSPICE OF THE NORTH SHORE, INC.
Sister Betty Murtaugh, Program Coordinator
283 Cabot St.
Beverly, MA 21915
617/927-7075
Scope of care: Patient prognosis terminal.
Type of care: Not available.
Fee: None.
Bereavement counseling: Not available.

Fitchburg

BURBANK HOSPITAL HOSPICE HOME CARE PROGRAM
Myra CaCace, Hospice Coordinator
Nichols Rd.
Fitchburg, MA 01420
617/345-4311
Scope of care: Patient prognosis limited.
Type of care: Home care; case management in hospitals and skilled nursing facilities.
Fee: Set fee; sliding scale.
Bereavement counseling: Trained staff, clergy, medical social worker, volunteers; follow-up (one year).

Waban

HOSPICE OF THE GOOD SHEPHERD, INC.
NEWTON-WELLESLEY HOSPITAL
Linda Kilburn, Executive Director
P.O. Box 144
Waban, MA 02162
617/969-6130
Scope of care: Newton and Wellesley area patients; prognosis terminal.
Type of care: Home care; inpatient (planned).
Fee: None.
Bereavement counseling: Social worker; individual, support groups.

Worcester

PALLIATIVE CARE SERVICES
UNIVERSITY OF MASSACHUSETTS MEDICAL CENTER

Ann Kaye, Administrator
55 Lake Ave. N
Worcester, MA 01605
617/856-3931
Scope of care: Cancer patients eighteen and over; prognosis six months.
Type of care: Home care; inpatient.
Fee: Third-party reimbursement.
Bereavement counseling: Counselor; follow-up (one year).

MICHIGAN

Battle Creek

GOOD SAMARITAN HOSPICE CARE
KELLOGG COMMUNITY COLLEGE
Carolyn Fitzpatrick, Director
450 North Ave.
Battle Creek, MI 49017
616/965-1391
Scope of care: Patient prognosis six months (physician certified).
Type of care: Home care.
Fee: Set fee.
Bereavement counseling: Bereavement coordinator; follow-up (eighteen months).

Flint

COMMUNITY HOSPICE, INC.
Peter A. Levine, M.P.H.
806 W. Sixth Ave.
Flint, MI 48503
313/238-1230
Scope of care: Patient prognosis six months or less.
Type of care: Home care; inpatient.
Fee: Not available.
Bereavement counseling: Professional staff, volunteers.

Grand Rapids

HOSPICE OF GREATER GRAND RAPIDS, INC.
Mary Ann Finn, R.N., Nurse Administrator
1715 E. Fulton
Grand Rapids, MI 49503
616/454-1426
Scope of care: Cancer patients; prognosis six months or less.
Type of care: Home care.
Fee: None.
Bereavement counseling: Available.

Saginaw

HOSPICE OF SAGINAW, INC.
David B. Naylor, Executive Director
803 S. Washington
Suite 100
Saginaw, MI 48601
517/754-1446
Scope of care: Patient prognosis six months or less.
Type of care: Home care.
Fee: Set fee.
Bereavement counseling: Hospice home care team, volunteers.

MINNESOTA

Duluth

HOSPICE DULUTH
ST. LUKE'S HOSPITAL
Lynette A. Hohn, Director
915 E. First St.
Duluth, MN 55805
218/726-5632
Scope of care: Patient prognosis less than one year.
Type of care: Home care; inpatient.
Fee: Sliding scale.
Bereavement counseling: Medical social worker, volunteer; individual, group, telephone, memorial services.

Minneapolis

ABBOTT-NORTHWESTERN HOSPITAL

Howard K. Bell, M.Div., Coordinator for Hospice Care
2727 Chicago Ave. S
Minneapolis, MN 55407
612/874-5959
Scope of care: Patient prognosis weeks or months.
Type of care: Home care; inpatient.
Fee: Set fee.
Bereavement counseling: Individual, support groups (weekly).

FAIRVIEW-SOUTHDALE HOSPITAL HOSPICE PROGRAM
Paula Welford, Program Coordinator
6401 France Ave. S
Minneapolis, MN 55435
612/924-5000
Scope of care: Patient prognosis one to six months.
Type of care: Home care; inpatient.
Fee: None.
Bereavement counseling: Time-to-mourn group (eight weeks).

METHODIST HOSPITAL HOSPICE PROJECT
Peggy Martinson, Coordinator Cancer Care Program
6500 Excelsior Blvd.
P.O. Box 650
Minneapolis, MN 55440
612/932-5138
Scope of care: Cancer patients over sixteen; prognosis weeks to months.
Type of care: Home care; inpatient.
Fee: Sliding scale.
Bereavement counseling: Individual, educational class.

NORTH MEMORIAL MEDICAL CENTER HOSPICE
Kitty Kotchion Smith, Hospice Coordinator
3220 Lowry Ave. N
Minneapolis, MN 55422
612/520-5770
Scope of care: Patient prognosis weeks or months.
Type of care: Home care; inpatient.
Fee: Set fee.
Bereavement counseling: Staff, volunteer team; support group (weekly), telephone, visits.

ST. MARY'S HOSPITAL HOSPICE PROGRAM
Dr. Bruce Agneberg, Medical Director
2414 S. Seventh St.
Minneapolis, MN 55454
612/338-2229
Scope of care: Patient prognosis terminal (no further treatment available).
Type of care: Home care; inpatient.
Fee: Sliding scale.
Bereavement counseling: Individual, support groups.

MISSOURI

Columbia

JOHN H. WALTER'S HOSPICE OF CENTRAL MISSOURI, INC.
Mary Kaye Doyle, R.N., M.S.P.H., Executive Director
P.O. Box 451
Columbia, MO 65205
314/875-2215
Scope of care: Patient prognosis less than six months.
Type of care: Home care; follow patients to hospitals and nursing homes.
Fee: None.
Bereavement counseling: Individual, group.

Joplin

ST. JOHN'S HOSPICE
Sister Mary Del Rey, R.S.M., Director
2732 Picher
Joplin, MO 64801
417/781-2727
Scope of care: Patient prognosis days, weeks or months.
Type of care: Home care; inpatient.
Fee: None.
Bereavement counseling: Staff, volunteers, clergy; telephone, visits.

Kansas City

HOSPICE CARE OF MID-AMERICA
Kevin Flattery, Executive Director
1005 Grand Ave.
Suite 743
Kansas City, MO 64106
816/221-1044
Scope of care: Patient prognosis six months or less.
Type of care: Home care.
Fee: None.
Bereavement counseling: Individual (if needed), six group sessions.

St. Louis

CONTINUING CARE UNIT
LUTHERAN MEDICAL CENTER
Maxine Stein, M.S.W., Hospice Coordinator
2639 Miami
St. Louis, MO 63118
314/772-1456
Scope of care: Patient prognosis six months or less.
Type of care: Home care; inpatient.
Fee: Sliding scale.
Bereavement counseling: Individual, group (monthly), telephone.

ST. LUKE'S HOSPITALS HOSPICE
Ricki O'Meara, Coordinator
5535 Delmar Blvd.
St. Louis, MO 63112
314/361-1212
Scope of care: Patient prognosis limited.
Type of care: Home care; inpatient.
Fee: None.
Bereavement counseling: Group (monthly), telephone, individual (as needed).

NEVADA

Las Vegas

NATHAN ADELSON HOSPICE
Ernest W. Libman, Administrator
3201 S. Maryland Pkwy.
Suite 330
Las Vegas, NV 89109
702/733-0320
Scope of care: Patient prognosis six months or less.
Type of care: Home care; inpatient (planned).
Fee: Set fee (negotiable); none (if no payment source exists).
Bereavement counseling: Individual (when needed), group, social gatherings.

NEW HAMPSHIRE

Exeter

SEACOAST HOSPICE
Elizabeth G. Feuer, Coordinator of Volunteers
P.O. Box 237
Exeter, NH 03833
603/778-7391
Scope of care: Mostly referred cancer patients; prognosis six months or less.
Type of care: Home care; non-medical visits to local hospitals and nursing homes.
Fee: None.
Bereavement counseling: Individual, group, outreach.

Lebanon

HOSPICE OF THE UPPER VALLEY
Doreen Schweizer, Program Coordinator
1 School St.
P.O. Box 225
Lebanon, NH 03766
603/448-5182
Scope of care: Life-threatening-disease patients; prognosis terminal patients.

Type of care: Volunteer visits to homes, hospitals and nursing homes.
Bereavement counseling: Staff, volunteers; follow-up, support group, individual.

Littleton

NORTH COUNTRY HOME HEALTH AGENCY
Roberta Daycock, R.N.
60 High St.
Littleton, NH 03561
603/444-5317
Scope of care: Patient prognosis limited.
Type of care: Home care; inpatient (planned).
Fee: None (volunteers); insurance reimbursement (R.N. visits).
Bereavement counseling: Nurses, volunteers; follow-up (one year), visits.

Manchester

VISITING NURSE ASSOCIATION—HOME HEALTH AGENCY OF GR. MANCHESTER, INC.
Therese Steckowych, R.N., Coordinator
194 Concord St.
Manchester, NJ 03104
603/622-3781
Scope of care: Patient prognosis limited.
Type of care: Home care.
Fee: Variable; sliding scale and funds available.
Bereavement counseling: Nurse, social worker; visits, support.

NEW JERSEY

Collingswood

COMMUNITY HEALTH AND NURSING SERVICES OF GREATER CAMDEN COUNTY, INC.
Ann Callaghan, A.C.S.W., CHANS/Hospice Administrator
28 W. Collings Ave.
Collingswood, NJ 08108
609/854-0040
Scope of care: Patient prognosis six months or less.
Type of care: Home care.
Fee: Set fee; sliding scale; no patient refused care because of inability to pay.
Bereavement counseling: Nurses, medical social workers, volunteers.

Hackensack

HOSPICE PROGRAM—HACKENSACK MEDICAL CENTER
Shelley Van Kempen, R.N., M.S., Patient Care Coordinator
Hackensack, NJ 07601
201/441-2050
Scope of care: Mostly Bergen County cancer patients; prognosis weeks to months.
Type of care: Home care.
Fee: Sliding scale.
Bereavement counseling: Volunteers; individual (as needed), group (weekly).

Summit

OVERLOOK HOSPITAL HOSPICE HOME CARE
Judith Geller
193 Morris Ave.
Summit, NJ 07901
201/522-2846
Scope of care: Patient prognosis less than one year.
Type of care: Home care.
Fee: Set fee; sliding scale (as needed).
Bereavement counseling: Individual, small support group.

NEW MEXICO

Albuquerque

HOSPICE HOME HEALTH CARE—HOSPICE CARE
Kathleen Hart, M.A., Director of Hospice Care; Ann Chaffee, R.N., M.S.N., Patient Care Coordinator
500 Walter NE

Suite 316
Albuquerque, NM 87102
505/842-5967
Scope of care: Patients over eighteen; prognosis less than one year.
Type of care: Home care.
Fee: Set fee; sliding scale (by arrangement); no patient refused care because of inability to pay.
Bereavement counseling: Counselor, clinical staff; individual, groups, open houses, social.

NEW YORK

Binghamton

LOURDES HOSPITAL HOSPICE
Andrew B. Adams, M.D., Director of Hospice
169 Riverside Dr.
Binghamton, NY 13905
607/798-5697
Scope of care: Mostly end-stage cancer patients; prognosis limited.
Type of care: Home care; inpatient.
Fee: Some third-party reimbursement.
Bereavement counseling: Professional, volunteer.

Brooklyn

THE BROOKLYN HOSPICE
METROPOLITAN JEWISH GERIATRIC CENTER
Dr. William Liss-Levinson, Director
4915 Tenth Ave.
Brooklyn, NY 11219
212/853-2800
Scope of care: Patient prognosis six months or less.
Type of care: Home care.
Fee: Set fee (counseling); sliding scale (home care).
Bereavement counseling: Social worker, psychologist, volunteers; individual, family, group, visits, workshops.

Buffalo

HOSPICE BUFFALO, INC.
Charlotte N. Shedd, Executive Director
2929 Main St.
Buffalo, NY 14214
716/838-4438
Scope of care: Advanced cancer patients eighteen or over; prognosis six months or less.
Type of care: Home care; inpatient.
Fee: Set fee.
Bereavement counseling: Social worker, trained volunteers (lay and professional); support groups.

Elmira Heights

SOUTHERN TIER HOSPICE
Martin D. Schaefer, Director
416 E. Fourteenth St.
Elmira Heights, NY 14903
607/734-1570
Scope of care: Patient prognosis weeks or months.
Type of care: Home care; inpatient.
Fee: None.
Bereavement counseling: Individual, group, telephone, social.

Long Island

MERCY HOSPITAL HOSPICE
Sister Dolores Castillano, Hospice Director
1000 N. Village Ave.
Rockville Centre
Long Island, NY 11570
516/255-2360
Scope of care: Cancer patients eighteen or over; prognosis one year or less.
Type of care: Home care; inpatient.
Fee: Third-party reimbursement.
Bereavement counseling: Available.

New Hartford

HOSPICE CARE, INC.
Sandra S. Huegel, R.N., Patient Care Coordinator
Middle Settlement Rd.
New Hartford, NY 13413
315/798-6160
Scope of care: Patient prognosis six months or less.
Type of care: Home care; acute-care-unit work.
Fee: None.
Bereavement counseling: Volunteers; follow-up (one year).

New York City

CABRINI HOSPICE
Kevin Corridan, Administrator
227 E. Nineteenth St.
New York, NY 10003
212/725-6480
Scope of care: Cancer patients sixteen or over; prognosis six months or less.
Type of care: Home care; inpatient.
Fee: Medicare and Medicaid reimbursement.
Bereavement counseling: Pastoral care coordinator, psychiatrist, staff.

HOSPICE OF ST. LUKE'S
ST. LUKE'S-ROOSEVELT HOSPITAL CENTER
Sister Patrice O'Connor, Coordinator
Amsterdam Ave. & 114th St.
New York, NY 10025
212/870-1732
Scope of care: Cancer patients; prognosis six months.
Type of care: Home care; inpatient.
Fee: None.
Bereavement counseling: Individual.

Pomona

HOSPICE OF ROCKLAND, INC.
ROCKLAND COUNTY HEALTH COMPLEX
Pomona, NY 10970
914/354-0200
Scope of care: Patient prognosis less than six months.
Type of care: Home care; inpatient; volunteers visit patients in county hospitals and nursing homes.
Fee: None.
Bereavement counseling: Volunteers; contact (one year).

Port Chester

UNITED HOSPITAL HOSPICE
Andrée deLisser, Hospice Nurse Coordinator
406 Boston Post Rd.
Port Chester, NY 10573
914/939-7000
Scope of care: Cancer patients; prognosis six months or less.
Type of care: Home care; inpatient.
Fee: Sliding scale; all possibilities exhausted before patient asked to pay anything.
Bereavement counseling: Social workers, nurses, trained volunteers; individual, groups (monthly).

NORTH CAROLINA

Asheboro

THORNTON R. CLEEK MEMORIAL HOSPICE
OF RANDOLPH COUNTY
Fred Graham, M.D., Hospice Vice-President
125 Taft St.
Asheboro, NC 27203
919/625-4215
Scope of care: Patient prognosis six months or less.
Type of care: Home care; inpatient.
Fee: None; donations encouraged.
Bereavement counseling: Social workers, clergy, medical personnel, volunteers; individual, referral to cancer support groups (as needed).

Asheville

MOUNTAIN AREA HOSPICE, INC.
Melford E. Howard, Jr., Executive Director; Judith L. Noth, Nurse Director
P.O. Box 8784
Asheville, NC 28814
704/255-0231
Scope of care: Mostly advanced cancer patients (case-by-case exceptions); prognosis six months or less.
Type of care: Home care.
Fee: None.
Bereavement counseling: Bereavement team; early involvement, bereavement training/education, workshops (planned.).

Boone

HOSPICE OF BOONE AREA, INC.
Stella Singleton, R.N., Nurse Coordinator
P.O. Box 2392
Boone, NC 28607
704/264-8782
Scope of care: Patient prognosis six months or less.
Type of care: Home care.
Fee: None.
Bereavement counseling: Volunteer team; individualized, referrals (as needed).

Carrboro

TRIANGLE HOSPICE, INC.
Carr Mill
Suite 218
Carrboro, NC 27510
919/942-8597; 919/688-8503
Scope of care: Patient prognosis six months or less.
Type of care: Home care; follow patients to institutions.
Fee: None.
Bereavement counseling: Chaplain, social worker, volunteers; conversations, follow-up, psychiatric counseling (by referral, as needed).

Durham

HOSPICE OF NORTH CAROLINA, INC.
Judi Lund, Executive Director
P.O. Box 2858
Durham, NC 27705
919/286-1134
Scope of care: Patient prognosis one year or less.
Type of care: Home care.
Fee: None.
Bereavement counseling: Staff.

Fayetteville

VA MEDICAL CENTER HOSPICE
FAYETTEVILLE MEDICAL CENTER
VETERANS ADMINISTRATION
Minnie S. Howie, Chairman, Hospice Committee
Fayetteville, NC 28301
919/488-2120
Scope of care: Mostly cancer patients (veterans); prognosis six months or less.
Type of care: Inpatient; referral to community hospices.
Fee: (Veterans hospital.)
Bereavement counseling: By request.

Lenoir

CALDWELL COUNTY HOSPICE
Gibbie Harris, R.N., Nurse Coordinator
1002 Kirkwood St. NW
Lenoir, NC 28645
704/754-0101
Scope of care: Patient prognosis six months or less.
Type of care: Home care; follow patients to hospitals.
Fee: None.
Bereavement counseling: Volunteers (lay and professional); one-to-one.

New Bern

CRAVEN COUNTY HOME HEALTH HOSPICE
Carol Pullen, M.E.D., Hospice Coordinator
P.O. Box 1390
New Bern, NC 28560
919/633-2605
Scope of care: Patients referred by physicians; prognosis terminal.
Type of care: Home care; follow patients to institutions.
Fee: None.
Bereavement counseling: Clergy, lay counselor, volunteers; follow-up (one year).

Winston-Salem

HOSPICE OF WINSTON-SALEM/FORSYTH COUNTY, INC.
Linda Scherl, Hospice Care Coordinator
3333 Silas Creek Pkwy.
Winston-Salem, NC 27103
919/768-3972
Scope of care: Patient prognosis six months or less.
Type of care: Home care.
Fee: Sliding scale.
Bereavement counseling: Trained volunteers; visit, telephone, support group (monthly).

OHIO

Akron

VISITING NURSE SERVICE, INC.
Melinda Otto, Hospice Team Leader
1200 McArthur Dr.
Akron, OH 44313
216/745-1601
Scope of care: Patient prognosis six months or less.
Type of care: Home care.
Fee: United Way; third-party reimbursement.
Bereavement counseling: Trained staff.

Cincinnati

HOSPICE OF CINCINNATI, INC.
Leigh Gerdsen, Assistant Director
2710 Reading Rd.
Cincinnati, OH 45206
513/559-3100
Scope of care: Patient prognosis six months.
Type of care: Home care; inpatient.
Fee: Set fee.
Bereavement counseling: Trained volunteers (lay and clergy); as needed.

Dayton

HOSPICE OF DAYTON, INC.
Betty Schmoll, Executive Director
908 S. Main St.
Dayton, OH 45402
513/223-0759
Scope of care: Patient prognosis six months.
Type of care: Home care; inpatient consultation.
Fee: Insurance reimbursement.
Bereavement counseling: Staff, volunteer; follow-up, individual, group.

Springfield

HOSPICE OF SPRINGFIELD & CLARK COUNTY
Joanne Smith, Director
2615 E. High St.
Springfield, OH 45501
513/325-0531
Scope of care: Patient prognosis limited.
Type of care: Home care.
Fee: Set fee.
Bereavement counseling: Trained clergy, volunteers.

OREGON

Portland

PROVIDENCE HOSPICE
Shirley Buxton, R.C.S.W., Director of Social Work
700 N.E. Forty-seventh Ave.
Portland, OR 97213
503/230-6161
Scope of care: Adult patients; prognosis six months or less.
Type of care: Home care; inpatient.
Fee: Third-party reimbursement.
Bereavement counseling: Individual, group.

PENNSYLVANIA

Bryn Mawr

BRYN MAWR HOSPITAL HOSPICE PROGRAM
BRYN MAWR HOSPITAL
Joan Rollins Frazier, Program Coordinator
Bryn Mawr, PA 19010
215/896-3265
Scope of care: Patient prognosis six months.
Type of care: Home care; inpatient.
Fee: None.
Bereavement counseling: Trained volunteers; follow-up (one year).

Franklin

HOSPICE—VENAGO COUNTY VISITING NURSES
ASSOCIATION, INC.
Ronald R. Bickel, Hospice Program Director
P.O. Box 231
Franklin, PA 16323
814/437-7826
Scope of care: Patient prognosis months or less.
Type of care: Home care.
Fee: None; third-party reimbursement.
Bereavement counseling: Staff, volunteers; one year (maximum).

Kingston

HOSPICE SAINT JOHN
DIVISION: LUTHERAN WELFARE SERVICES
Philip Decker, Director
383 Wyoming Ave.
Kingston, PA 18704
717/288-5428
Scope of care: Patient prognosis poor.
Type of care: Home care.
Fee: Sliding scale.
Bereavement counseling: Chaplain (bereavement coordinator).

Paoli

PAOLI MEMORIAL HOSPITAL
Dolores J. Ferron, Director
Lancaster Pike
Paoli, PA 19301
717/648-1205
Scope of care: Patient prognosis limited.
Type of care: Home care; inpatient.
Fee: Insurance reimbursement.
Bereavement counseling: Individual, open-ended groups.

Philadelphia

PRESBYTERIAN UNIVERSITY OF PENNSYLVANIA
MEDICAL CENTER
Susanne Palmer, R.N., M.S., Hospice Coordinator
51 N. Thirty-ninth St.
Philadelphia, PA 19104
215/662-8996
Scope of care: Cancer patients; prognosis six months or less.
Type of care: Home care; inpatient.
Fee: Set fee (waived, if necessary).
Bereavement counseling: One-to-one, visits (quarterly for one year).

Pittsburgh

FORBES HEALTH SYSTEM
FORBES HOSPICE
Maryanne Fello, Director
500 Finley St.
Pittsburgh, PA 15206
412/665-3301
Scope of care: Patient prognosis limited.
Type of care: Home care; inpatient.
Fee: Sliding scale; third-party insurance.
Bereavement counseling: Group, individual, follow-up.

Waynesburg

HOSPICE OF GREENE COUNTY, INC.
Denise Harris, Executive Director
P.O. Box 168
93 E. High St.
Waynesburg, PA 15370
412/627-8118
Scope of care: Patient prognosis limited.
Type of care: Home care.
Fee: Sliding scale; Medicare; Medicaid.
Bereavement counseling: Social workers, volunteers; individual, support group (widows/family members).

SOUTH CAROLINA

Columbia

BAPTIST MEDICAL CENTER HOSPICE
Youna E. Ruff, Hospice Coordinator
Taylor at Marion St.
Columbia, SC 29220
803/771-5002
Scope of care: Patient prognosis limited.
Type of care: Home care.
Fee: Set fee; financial assistance available though hospice fund.
Bereavement counseling: Chaplain, ministers, trained volunteers.

TENNESSEE

Memphis

MID-SOUTH COMPREHENSIVE HOME & HOSPICE, INC.
Russell F. Vizzi, Executive Director
5705 Stage Rd.
Suite 201
Memphis, TN 38134
901/372-2500
Scope of care: Patient prognosis limited.
Type of care: Home care.
Fee: Set fee; none (charity patients).
Bereavement counseling: Social workers.

TEXAS

Austin

GIRLING & ASSOCIATES HOME HEALTH SERVICES, INC.
Bettie J. Girling, Coordinator Professional Services
4000 Medical Pkwy.
Austin, TX 78756
512/459-3291
Scope of care: Patient prognosis limited.
Type of care: Home care.
Fee: Set fee; some charity patients.
Bereavement counseling: One-to-one, group.

Brenham

HOME HEALTH-HOME CARE, INC.
BRENHAM SUB-UNIT
Melvin Q. Thorne, M.S.W., Director
511 W. Alamo
Brenham, TX 77833
713/836-6134

Scope of care: Patient prognosis limited.
Type of care: Home care.
Fee: Set fee; no patient refused care because of inability to pay.
Bereavement counseling: Medical social worker, volunteers.

Dallas

VISITING NURSE ASSOCIATION OF DALLAS/HOME HOSPICE
Sanford J. Mann, M.P.H., L.N.H.A., Director of Home Hospice
2818 Maple Ave.
Suite 103
Dallas, TX 75201
214/741-6400
Scope of care: Patient prognosis six months or less.
Type of care: Home care.
Fee: Sliding scale; set fee; none (United Way and donations).
Bereavement counseling: Trained staff, volunteers.

Denton

ANN'S HAVEN: HOSPICE OF DENTON COUNTY
Mary Walling, Assistant Administrator
P.O. Box 856
Denton, TX 76201
817/566-3387
Scope of care: Cancer patients; prognosis six months.
Type of care: Home care.
Fee: Set fee; sliding scale; no patient refused care because of inability to pay.
Bereavement counseling: Professional staff, volunteers; follow-up (one year).

Fort Worth

COMMUNITY HOSPICE OF ST. JOSEPH
Martha Jo Trostel, Program Director
1401 S. Main
Fort Worth, TX 76104
817/336-9371
Scope of care: Cancer patients; prognosis six months or less.
Type of care: Home care.
Fee: None; sliding scale; Medicare; Medicaid; insurance-carrier reimbursement; charitable funds available.
Bereavement counseling: Visits, support groups (by request).

Houston

VNA HOUSTON HOSPICE
Maggie Kao, M.S.W., Director
2100 Timmons, 200
Houston, TX 77027
713/840-7744
Scope of care: Patient prognosis six months or less.
Type of care: Home care.
Fee: Sliding scale.
Bereavement counseling: Social worker, nurse; visits.

Orange

HOME HEALTH-HOME CARE, INC.
Ann Manuel, R.N., Director
3118 Edgar Brown Dr.
Orange, TX 77630
800/392-1346 or 800/886-2283
Scope of care: Life-threatening-condition patients.
Type of care: Home care.
Fee: None.
Bereavement counseling: Hospice team.

THE SOUTHEAST TEXAS HOSPICE, INC.
Mary McKenna, Administrator
712 W. Park
P.O. Box 2385
Orange, TX 77630
713/886-0622
Scope of care: Patient prognosis six months to one year.
Type of care: Home care.
Fee: Set fee; no patient refused care because of inability to pay.
Bereavement counseling: Professionals, volunteers; visits, support groups (quarterly).

San Antonio

HOME HEALTH-HOME CARE, INC.
SAN ANTONIO SUB-UNIT
Billie Cook, Director
6017 Rittiman Pl.
San Antonio, TX 78218
512/821-6904
Scope of care: Patient prognosis limited.
Type of care: Home care.
Fee: Set fee; insurance-carrier reimbursement.
Bereavement counseling: Volunteer pastors.

SAINT BENEDICT'S HOSPICE
H. Rosen, Director
323 E. Johnson St.
San Antonio, TX 78204
512/222-0171
Scope of care: Patients over twenty-one; prognosis six months or less.
Type of care: Home care; respite care (two-week limit).
Fee: Set fee; charity funds available.
Bereavement counseling: Referrals to community agencies.

UTAH

Salt Lake City

HOSPICE OF SALT LAKE
Byron T. Okutsu, M.S.P.H., Executive Director
610 E. South Temple
Salt Lake City, UT 84102
801/355-8112
Scope of care: Cancer patients; prognosis six months or less.
Type of care: Home care; inpatient (planned).
Fee: Third-party reimbursement.
Bereavement counseling: Visits, telephone.

VERMONT

Burlington

VISITING NURSE ASSOCIATION, INC.
Sara P. Thompson, Associate Director
260 College St.
Burlington, VT 05401
802/658-1900
Scope of care: Patient prognosis six months or less.
Type of care: Home care.
Fee: Sliding scale.
Bereavement counseling: R.N. assesses referral needs.

VIRGINIA

Arlington

HOSPICE OF NORTHERN VIRGINIA, INC.
Dorothy Moga, Executive Director
4715 N. Fifteenth St.
Arlington, VA 22205
703/525-7070
Scope of care: Northern Virginia patients finished with therapeutic treatment; prognosis six months or less.
Type of care: Home care; inpatient.
Fee: Set fee; no patient refused care because of inability to pay.
Bereavement counseling: Bereavement coordinator, trained volunteers.

Charlottesville

HOSPICE OF THE PIEDMONT
Dinah Ansley, Executive Director
P.O. Box 507
Charlottesville, VA 22902
804/296-6238
Scope of care: Patient prognosis four to six months.
Type of care: Home care.
Fee: None.

Bereavement counseling: Multidisciplinary team, social worker; follow-up (one year).

Roanoke

ROANOKE MEMORIAL HOSPITALS
Kitty Fisher, Hospice Clinical Team Leader
Belleview at Jefferson St.
P.O. Box 13367
Roanoke, VA 24033
703/981-7453
Scope of care: Patient prognosis six months or less.
Type of care: Home care; inpatient.
Fee: Set fee.
Bereavement counseling: Individual, group.

Suffolk

EDMARC HOSPICE FOR CHILDREN, INC.
Reverend Barbara S. Mease, Director of Professional Services
410 N. Broad St.
P.O. Box 1684
Suffolk, VA 23434
804/539-2041
Scope of care: Children sixteen or under; prognosis six months or less.
Type of care: Home care.
Fee: Sliding scale.
Bereavement counseling: Staff, professional volunteers.

WASHINGTON

Port Angeles

HOSPICE OF CLALLAM COUNTY
Rose Crumb, R.N., Executive Director
416 S. Peabody
P.O. Box 2014
Port Angeles, WA 98362
206/452-2956
Scope of care: Mostly cancer patients; prognosis months.
Type of care: Home care.
Fee: None.
Bereavement counseling: Follow-up visits, contact (one year).

Seattle

HOSPICE OF COMMUNITY HOME HEALTH CARE
M. Greenstein, Director of Hospice
200 W. Thomas
Seattle, WA 98119
206/282-5048
Scope of care: Patients over sixteen; prognosis less than six months.
Type of care: Home care; inpatient coordination.
Fee: Sliding scale; Medicare; Medicaid; insurance-carrier reimbursement.
Bereavement counseling: Individual, groups.

HOSPICE OF SEATTLE
Elaine G. McIntosh, Administrator
7814 Greenwood Ave. N
Seattle, WA 98104
206/784-9221
Scope of care: Patients eighteen and over; prognosis limited.
Type of care: Home care.
Fee: Sliding scale.
Bereavement counseling: Individual, support.

Spokane

HOSPICE MARAN ATHA
Willa Johns, Executive Director
N. 1620 Monroe
P.O. Box 1724
Spokane, WA 99210
509/325-2536
Scope of care: Patient prognosis one year or less.
Type of care: Home care.
Fee: None; memorials; donations.

Bereavement Counseling: Professional staff, volunteers; individual, group, counseling for non-home-care clients, education.

Tacoma

HOSPICE OF TACOMA
Anne Katterhagen, R.N., B.S.N., Executive Director
742 Market St.
Tacoma, WA 98402
206/383-1788
Scope of care: End-stage, advanced-disease patients.
Type of care: Home care; inpatient (planned).
Fee: Set fee; sliding scale.
Bereavement counseling: Volunteers; individual, support groups.

WEST VIRGINIA

Wheeling

CLARA WELTY HOSPICE
Lawrence Papi, Executive Director
109 Main St.
Wheeling, WV 26003
304/232-3370
Scope of care: Cancer patients; prognosis limited.
Type of care: Home care.
Fee: Case-by-case; fee schedule (planned).
Bereavement counseling: Visits, telephone, letters.

WISCONSIN

Eau Claire

SACRED HEART HOSPITAL HOSPICE
Cheryl Johnson, R.N., Nurse Coordinator
900 W. Clairemont Ave.
Eau Claire, WI 54701
715/839-4113
Scope of care: Patient prognosis six months or less (flexible).
Type of care: Home care; inpatient.
Fee: Set fee.
Bereavement counseling: Bereavement counselor; good-grieving sessions (weekly), visits.

Fond du Lac

HOSPICE HOPE—ST. AGNES HOSPITAL
Sister Mary Agreda Touchett, C.S.A., R.N., Director of Hospice Hope
430 E. Division St.
Fond du Lac, WI 54935
414/921-2300
Scope of care: Patient needs palliative only.
Type of care: Home care; inpatient.
Fee: Set fee.
Bereavement counseling: Trained social worker, follow-up person.

Green Bay

BELLIN HOSPICE
BELLIN MEMORIAL HOSPITAL
Mary Lou Stradthoff, R.N., B.S., Manager
744 S. Webster Ave.
P.O. Box 1700
Green Bay, WI 54305
414/433-3683
Scope of care: End-stage cancer, organ-disease or neuromuscular disease patients; prognosis one year or less.
Type of care: Home care; inpatient.
Fee: Set fee; no patient refused care because of inability to pay.
Bereavement counseling: Telephone, memorial services, gatherings, referrals (where necessary), grief booklet.

Madison

HOSPICECARE, INC.
Sarah Gorodezky, Executive Director
1504 Madison St.
Madison, WI 53711
608/255-0915

Scope of care: Patient prognosis six months or less.
Type of care: Home care; services to inpatient facilities.
Fee: None.
Bereavement counseling: Staff, volunteers; one-to-one (by request).

Milwaukee

MILWAUKEE HOSPICE, HOME CARE
James J. Ewens, Director
1022 N. Ninth St.
Milwaukee, WI 53233
414/271-3686
Scope of care: Patient prognosis three to six months.
Type of care: Home care.
Fee: Variable.
Bereavement counseling: Available.

MOUNT SINAI HOSPICE
James C. Platten, Administrative Director
6925 N. Port Washington Rd.
Milwaukee, WI 53217
414/352-3300
Scope of care: End-stage disseminated-carcinoma, neuromuscular or organ-disease patients; patient needs palliative only.
Type of care: Home care; inpatient; day care.
Fee: Set fee.
Bereavement counseling: Telephone, visits, referrals, socials (quarterly).

ST. MARY'S HOSPICE
Jeanne Clear, R.N., Administrative Director
2323 N. Lake Dr.
Milwaukee, WI 53211
414/289-7199
Scope of care: Adult patients; prognosis less than six months.
Type of care: Home care; inpatient.
Fee: Set fee; third-party reimbursement.
Bereavement counseling: Available.

Oconomowoc

ROGERS MEMORIAL HOSPITAL HOSPICE
Social Services Department
34810 Pabst Rd.
Oconomowoc, WI 53066
414/567-5535
Scope of care: Patient prognosis limited.
Type of care: Home care (VNA); inpatient.
Fee: Set fee.
Bereavement counseling: Staff; follow-up, further counseling (as needed).

Wausau

WAUSAU HOSPICE PROGRAM
Carole C. Bibeau, R.N., Director
933 Pine Ridge Blvd.
Wausau, WI 54401
715/847-2620
Scope of care: Patient prognosis weeks or months.
Type of care: Home care; inpatient.
Fee: Set fee (for services covered by third-party reimbursement).
Bereavement counseling: Individual, group, professional (optional), memorial services.

CANADA

MANITOBA

Winnipeg

ST. BONIFACE GENE HOSPITAL
PALLIATIVE CARE UNIT
Dr. Paul Henteleff
409 Tache Ave.
Winnipeg, Manitoba R2M 2A6 Canada
204/237-2409
Scope of care: Hospital patients over sixteen; prognosis limited.
Type of care: Home care.
Fee: Third-party reimbursement.
Bereavement counseling: Individual.

NEWFOUNDLAND

St. John's

ST. CLARE'S MERCY HOSPITAL
PALLIATIVE CARE SECTION
Sister M. Lucy Power, Executive Director
St. John's, Newfoundland, Canada
709/778-3111
Scope of care: Cancer patients over sixteen; prognosis limited.
Type of care: Inpatient; staff consultations to homes.
Fee: None.
Bereavement counseling: Available.

QUEBEC

Montreal

NOTRE-DAME HOSPITAL
L'UNITÉ DE SOINS PALLIATIFS
Maurice Falardeau, M.D., F.R.C.S.(C), Director, Palliative Care Unit
1560, E. Sherbrooke St.
Montreal, Quebec H2L 4K8 Canada
514/876-6607
Scope of care: Cancer patients; prognosis terminal or advanced pre-terminal.
Type of care: Inpatient; home care.
Fee: Sliding scale.
Bereavement counseling: Social worker, volunteers.

PALLIATIVE CARE SERVICE
ROYAL VICTORIA HOSPITAL
Balfour M. Mount, M.D., Director
687 Pine Ave. W
Montreal, Quebec H3A 1A1 Canada
514/842-0863
Scope of care: Adult patients; prognosis limited.
Type of care: Home care; inpatient.
Fee: None.
Bereavement counseling: Available.

PUBLICATIONS

Periodicals

Below is a selected list of U.S. and Canadian professional trade journals that address issues pertinent to death and dying. Only those journals that proved to be particularly useful in researching current issues in this field are included. Except for the publications of some local funeral directors' associations, which focus specifically on death and dying, no state, regional, or provincial periodicals are listed.

Questionnaires were sent to all publishers on this list to verify addresses and telephone numbers. An asterisk (*) preceding an entry indicates no response; the information provided here is the best available from secondary sources.

Because the broad subject of death and dying covers many individual topics and issues, these periodicals are listed alphabetically within subject categories (which are also arranged alphabetically). Publications that fall into more than one category are cross-referenced. In some cases, publications are cross-referenced because of title changes.

AGING/GERONTOLOGY

Readers should also refer to the associations list in this book and to the bibliography for additional publications on aging, gerontology, and geriatrics.

Age
American Aging Association, Inc.
University of Nebraska Medical Center
Forty-second and Dewey Ave.
Omaha, NB 68105
(402) 559-4416

Ageing International
International Federation on Ageing
1909 K St. NW
Washington, DC 20049
(202) 872-4885

Aging
U.S. Administration on Aging
Office of Human Development Services
U.S. Department of Health and Human Services
Washington, DC 20201
(202) 245-1826

*American Geriatrics Society: Journal
American Geriatrics Society
10 Columbus Circle
New York, NY 10019
(212) 582-1333

Canadian Journal on Aging (*see* Death and Dying—General, *Essence* listing)

Essence (*see* Death and Dying—General)

Geriatric Nursing: American journal of care for the aging
American Journal of Nursing Co.
555 W. Fifty-seventh St.
New York, NY 10019
(212) 582-8820

*Gerontopics: A forum of the aging network
Human Sciences Press
72 Fifth Ave.
New York, NY 10011
(212) 243-6000

Gerontologist
The Gerontological Society of America
1835 K St. NW
Washington, DC 20006
(202) 466-6750

International Journal of Aging & Human Development
Baywood Publishing Co., Inc.
120 Marine St.
Box D
Farmingdale, NY 11735
(516) 249-2464

Journal of Gerontological Nursing
C. B. Slack, Inc.
6900 Grove Rd.
Thorofare, NJ 08086
(609) 848-1000

Journal of Gerontology
Gerontological Society of America
1835 K St. NW
Suite 305
Washington, DC 20006
(202) 466-6750

CURRENT ISSUES/CONSUMER ADVOCACY/ PHILOSOPHY

This section includes a wide variety of periodicals that deal with current issues of general and political interest. Readers may find articles on funeral reform, the philosophy of death, death in our society, and other newsworthy topics in these journals.

American Academy of Political and Social Science: Annals (*see* **Sociology/Social Sciences/Social Welfare**)

*Changing Times
The Kiplinger Letter
1729 H St. NW
Washington, DC 20006
(202) 887-6400

Commentary (*see* **Religion**)

Commonweal (*see* **Religion**)

Consumer Reports
Consumers Union
256 Washington St.
Mount Vernon, NY 10550
(914) 664-6400

Consumers Digest
Consumers Digest, Inc.
5705 N. Lincoln Ave.
Chicago, IL 60659
(312) 275-3590

Consumers' Research
Consumers' Research, Inc.
P.O. Box 168
Washington, NJ 07882
(201) 689-3300

Journal of Consumer Affairs
American Council on Consumer Interests
162 Stanley Hall
University of Missouri
Columbia, MO 65211
(314) 882-3817

Journal of Philosophy
Journal of Philosophy, Inc.
720 Philosophy Hall
Columbia University
New York, NY 10027
(212) 280-3188

Moneysworth
Avant Garde Media
251 W. Fifty-seventh St.
New York, NY 10019
(212) 581-2000

New Republic: A journal of opinion
1220 Nineteenth St. NW
Washington, DC 20036
(202) 331-7494

Philosophy & Public Affairs
Princeton University Press
41 William St.
Princeton, NJ 08540
(609) 452-4900

Progressive
Progressive, Inc.
409 E. Main St.
Madison, WI 53703
(608) 257-4626

*Public Opinion Quarterly
Elsevier North-Holland, Inc., New York
52 Vanderbilt Ave.
New York, NY 10017
(212) 867-9040

DEATH AND DYING—GENERAL

Death Education: Pedagogy-counseling-care, an international journal
Hemisphere Publishing Corp.
1025 Vermont Ave. NW
Washington, DC 20005
(202) 783-3958

Essence: Issues in the study of ageing, dying, and death
(Will become **Canadian Journal on Aging**, 1982)
York University
Department of Psychology
Atkinson College
4700 Keele St.
Downsview, Ontario M3J 2R7 Canada

Omega: Journal of death & dying
Baywood Publishing Co., Inc.
Box D, 120 Marine St.
Farmingdale, NY 11735
(516) 249-2464

*Seasons
University of South Florida
Loss and Bereavement Resource Center
Aging Studies Program
Tampa, FL 33620
(813) 974-2011

ETHICS/BIOETHICS

*Bioethics Quarterly
Human Sciences Press
72 Fifth Ave.
New York, NY 10011
(212) 243-6000

Ethics
Publisher:
The University of Chicago Press
5801 S. Ellis Ave.
Chicago, IL 60637
(312) 753-2993
Journal Office:
5828 S. University Ave.
Chicago, IL 60637

Ethics in Science & Medicine
Pergamon Press, Inc.
Journals Division
Maxwell House, Fairview Park
Elmsford, NY 10523
(914) 592-7700

Hastings Center Report
Institute of Society, Ethics, and the Life Sciences
The Hastings Center
360 Broadway
Hastings-on-Hudson, NY 10706
(914) 478-0500

Journal of Medical Ethics
Professional and Scientific Publications
B.M.A. House
Tavistock Square
London WC1H 9JR England

Journal of Medicine and Philosophy
The University of Chicago Press
5801 S. Ellis Ave.
Chicago, IL 60637
(312) 753-3344

Law, Medicine, & Health Care (*see* Law/Taxes)

Man and Medicine: The journal of values and ethics in health care
650 W. 168th St.
New York, NY 10032
(212) 694-3947

Nursing Law & Ethics (*see* Law/Taxes, Law, Medicine & Health Care)

FUNERAL INDUSTRY

This section includes periodicals (mostly trade journals) that contain articles on funeral services, funeral supplies, funeral directors, cemeteries, cremation, etc. State funeral directors' association magazines are included in addition to national publications because the former periodicals focus specifically on death and dying.

American Cemetery
1501 Broadway
New York, NY 10036
(212) 398-9266

American Funeral Director
1501 Broadway
New York, NY 10036
(212) 398-9266

Canadian Funeral Director
1658 Victoria Park Ave.
Suite 5
Scarboro, Ontario M1R 1P7 Canada
(416) 755-7050

*Canadian Funeral News
Sage Brush Ventures Ltd.
Suite 105
Stockmans Centre
2116 Twenty-seventh Ave. NE (Box 6)
Calgary, Alberta T2E 7A6 Canada

*Casket and Sunnyside
274 Madison Ave.
New York, NY 10016
(212) 685-8310

The Catholic Cemetery
National Catholic Cemetery Conference
710 N. River Rd.
Des Plaines, IL 60016
(312) 824-8131

Cemetery Business & Legal Guide
Clark Boardman Co., Ltd.
435 Hudson St.
New York, NY 10014
(800) 221-9428

Champion Bulletins (*see* **Champion Expanding Encyclopedia of Mortuary Practice**)

Champion Expanding Enclopedia of Mortuary Practice
Department of Research & Educational Programs
The Champion Co.
400 Harrison St.
Springfield, OH 45505
(513) 324-5681

The Director
135 W. Wells St.
Suite 600
Milwaukee, WI 53203
(414) 276-2500

*The Dodge Magazine: Dedicated to professional progress in funeral service
Dodge Chemical Co.
165 Rindge Ave. Extension
Cambridge, MA 02140
(617) 661-0500

Florida Funeral Director
P.O. Box 6009
Tallahassee, FL 32301
(904) 878-2163

The Forum
New Jersey State Funeral Directors Association, Inc.
3279 Kennedy Blvd.
Jersey City, NJ 07306
(201) 653-0270

Jewish Funeral Director
122 E. Forty-second St.
Suite 1120
New York, NY 10168
(212) 370-0024

The Knight Letter
The International Order of the Golden Rule
929 S. Second St.
Springfield, IL 62704
(217) 544-7428

Monument Builder News (MB News)
1612 Central St.
Evanston, IL 60201
(312) 869-2031

Morticians of the Southwest
2830 W. Kingsley Rd.
Garland, TX 75041
(214) 840-1060

Mortuary Management
1010 Venice Blvd.
Los Angeles, CA 90015
(213) 746-0691

National Reporter
National Research & Information Center
1614 Central St.
Evanston, IL 60201
(312) 328-6545

The New England Funeral Director
294 Washington St.
Suite 446
Boston, MA 02108
(617) 426-2670

The Oklahoma Director
Oklahoma Funeral Directors Association
1100 Classen Dr.
Suite 209
Oklahoma City, OK 73103
(405) 236-0561

Southern Cemetery
John W. Yopp Publications, Inc.
P.O. Box 7368
Atlanta, GA 30357
(404) 881-9780

The Southern Funeral Director
John W. Yopp Publications, Inc.
P.O. Box 7368
Atlanta, GA 30357
(404) 811-9780

Stone in America
American Monument Association
6902 N. High St.
Worthington, OH 43085
(614) 885-2713

The Tarheel Director
Funeral Information Center
4208 Six Forks Rd.
Suite 357
Raleigh, NC 27609
(919) 781-3549

The Texas Director
The Texas Funeral Directors Association, Inc.
1513 S. Interstate 35
Austin, TX 78741
(512) 442-2304

Thanatos
P.O. Box 6009
Tallahassee, FL 32301

LAW/TAXES

Readers should refer to state bar association journals and university law reviews for additional reading on these subjects.

American Bar Association Journal
American Bar Association
77 S. Wacker Dr.
Chicago, IL 60606
(312) 621-9200

American Journal of Law & Medicine (*see* **Law, Medicine & Health Care** in this section)

*Canadian Bar National
Canadian Bar Foundation
130 Albert St.
Suite 1700
Ottawa, Ontario K1A 0L6 Canada
(613) 237-2925

Canadian Bar Review
Canadian Bar Foundation
130 Albert St.
Suite 1700
Ottawa, Ontario K1A 0L6 Canada
(613) 237-2925

Canadian Family Law Guide
CCH Canadian Ltd.
6 Garamond Ct.
Don Mills, Ontario M3C 1Z5 Canada
(416) 441-2992

*Canadian Journal of Family Law/Revue Canadienne de Droit Familial
Carswell Co., Ltd.
2330 Midland Ave.
Agincourt, Ontario M1S 1F7 Canada

Canadian Society of Forensic Science Journal/Société Canadienne des Sciences Judiciaires Journal
Canadian Society of Forensic Science
171 Nepean St.
Suite 303
Ottawa, Ontario K2P 0B4 Canada
(613) 235-7112

Estate Planning
Warren, Gorham & Lamont, Inc.
1633 Broadway
23rd Floor
New York, NY 10019
(212) 977-7400

Journal of Family Law
University of Louisville School of Law
Louisville, KY 40292
(502) 588-6396

Journal of Psychiatry and Law (*see* **Psychology/Psychiatry**)

Law, Medicine & Health Care (consolidating **Medicolegal News** and **Nursing, Law & Ethics**)
American Society of Law & Medicine, Inc.
765 Commonwealth Ave.
Boston, MA 02215
(617) 262-4990

*****Legal Medical Quarterly**
Jonah Publication Ltd.
620 Sheppard Ave. W
Downsview, Ontario M3H 2S1 Canada

Medico-Legal Bulletin (*see* **Medicine/Life Sciences/Hospitals**)

National Law Journal
New York Law Publishing Co.
111 Eighth Ave.
New York, NY 11201
(212) 741-8300

Nursing, Law & Ethics (*see* **Law, Medicine & Health Care** in this section)

The Review of Taxation of Individuals
Warren, Gorham & Lamont, Inc.
210 South St.
Boston, MA 02111
(617) 423-2020

TRIAL: The national legal newsmagazine
Association of Trial Lawyers of America
1050 Thirty-first St. NW
Washington, DC 20007
(202) 965-3500

*****Trusts and Estates**
Communication Channels, Inc.
6285 Barfield Rd.
Atlanta, GA 30328
(404) 256-9800

MEDICINE/LIFE SCIENCES/HOSPITALS

For additional information, readers may wish to consult the many other medical specialty journals as well as state medical association journals and university publications.

American Family Physician
American Academy of Family Physicians
1740 W. Ninety-second St.
Kansas City, MO 64114
(816) 333-9700

American Journal of Clinical Pathology
J. B. Lippincott Co.
East Washington Sq.
Philadelphia, PA 19105
(215) 574-4270

American Journal of Nursing
American Journal of Nursing Co.
Educational Services Division
555 W. Fifty-seventh St.
New York, NY 10019
(212) 582-8820

American Journal of Public Health
American Public Health Association
1015 Fifteenth St. NW
Washington, DC 20005
(202) 789-5600

*****American Medical News: The newspaper of American medicine**
American Medical Association
535 N. Dearborn St.
Chicago, IL 60610
(312) 751-6000

Annals of Internal Medicine
American College of Physicians
4200 Pine St.
Philadelphia, PA 19104
(215) 243-1200

British Medical Journal
British Medical Association
B.M.A. House
Tavistock Square
London WC1 H9JR England

Canadian Medical Association Journal
The Canadian Medical Association
1867 Alta Vista Dr.
P.O. Box 8650
Ottawa, Ontario K1G 0G8 Canada
(613) 731-9331

Critical Care Medicine
Williams & Wilkins Co.
428 E. Preston St.
Baltimore, MD 21202
(301) 528-4133

Ethics in Science & Medicine (*see* **Ethics/Bioethics**)

Geriatric Nursing (*see* **Aging/Gerontology**)

Hastings Center Report (*see* **Ethics/Bioethics**)

Health and Social Work (*see* **Sociology/Social Sciences/Social Welfare**)

HL: Journal of critical care
C. V. Mosby Co.
11830 Westline Industrial Dr.
St. Louis, MO 63141
(314) 872-8370

Hospitals
American Hospital Publishing, Inc.
211 E. Chicago Ave.
Chicago, IL 60611
(312) 951-1100

JAMA: The journal of the American Medical Association
American Medical Association
535 N. Dearborn St.
Chicago, IL 60610
(312) 751-6000

Journal of Gerontological Nursing (*see* **Aging/Gerontology**)

Journal of Medical Ethics (*see* **Ethics/Bioethics**)

Journal of Medicine and Philosophy (*see* **Ethics/Bioethics**)

Journal of the National Medical Association
Appleton-Century-Crofts
Periodicals Division
292 Madison Ave.
New York, NY 10017
(212) 532-1700

Journal of Pediatrics: Devoted to the problems and diseases of infancy and childhood
C. V. Mosby Co.
11830 Westline Industrial Dr.
St. Louis, MO 63141
(314) 872-8370

Journal of Religion and Health (*see* **Religion**)

Law, Medicine & Health Care (*see* **Law/Taxes**)

Legal Medical Quarterly (*see* **Law/Taxes**)

Man and Medicine (*see* **Ethics/Bioethics**)

Medical Economics
Medical Economics Co.
680 Kinderkamack Rd.
Oradell, NJ 07649
(201) 262-3030

Medical Instrumentation
Association for the Advancement of Medical
Instrumentation
1901 N. Ft. Myer Dr.
Suite 602
Arlington, VA 22209
(703) 525-4890

Medical Sciences Quarterly
Pergamon Press, Inc.
Maxwell House, Fairview Park
Elmsford, NY 10523
(914) 592-7700

Medical Times: A journal for the family physician
Romaine Pierson Publishers, Inc.
80 Shore Rd.
Port Washington, NY 11050
(516) 883-6350

Medical World News: The newsmagazine of medicine
211 E. Forty-third St.
New York, NY 10017
(212) 490-7810

Medico-Legal Bulletin
Department of Health, Medical Examiner Division
9 N. Fourteenth St.
Richmond, VA 23219
(804) 786-3174

*Nation's Health
American Public Health Association
1015 Fifteenth St. NW
Washington, DC 20005
(202) 789-5600

Neurosurgery
Williams & Wilkins Co.
428 E. Preston St.
Baltimore, MD 21202
(301) 528-4116

Nursing, Law & Ethics (*see* **Law/Taxes**)

Nursing Outlook
American Journal of Nursing Co.
555 W. Fifty-seventh St.
New York, NY 10019
(212) 582-8820

Perspectives in Biology and Medicine
Publisher:
The University of Chicago Press
5801 S. Ellis Ave.
Chicago, IL 60637
Editorial Office:
Culver Hall 403
1025 E. Fifty-seventh St.
Chicago, IL 60637
(312) 753-4083

QRB (Quality Review Bulletin): The journal of quality assurance
Joint Commission on Accreditation of Hospitals
875 N. Michigan Ave.
Chicago, IL 60611
(312) 642-6061

RN Magazine
680 Kinderkamack Rd.
Oradell, NJ 07649
(201) 262-3030

*Social Biology
Society for the Study of Social Biology
1180 Observatory Dr.
Room 5440
Madison, WI 53706

*Today's Health
Family Media, Inc.
149 Fifth Ave.
New York, NY 10010
(212) 598-0800

Topics in Clinical Nursing
Aspen Systems Corp.
1600 Research Blvd.
Rockville, MD 20814
(301) 251-5000

Transplantation Proceedings
Grune & Stratton, Inc.
111 Fifth Ave.
New York, NY 10003
(212) 741-4966

PSYCHOLOGY/PSYCHIATRY

American Journal of Community Psychology
Plenum Press
233 Spring St.
New York, NY 10013
(212) 620-8000

Canadian Journal of Psychiatry
Canadian Psychiatric Association
103-225 Lisgar St.
Suite 103
Ottawa, Ontario K2P 0C6 Canada
(613) 234-6644

General Hospital Psychiatry
Elsevier Science Publishing Co., Inc.
52 Vanderbilt Ave.
New York, NY 10017
(212) 867-9040

Journal of Clinical Psychology
Clinical Psychology Publishing Co., Inc.
4 Conant Sq.
Brandon, VT 05733
(802) 247-6871

Journal of Community Psychology
Clinical Psychology Publishing Co., Inc.
4 Conant Sq.
Brandon, VT 05733
(802) 247-6871

Journal of Psychiatry and Law
Federal Legal Publications
157 Chambers St.
New York, NY 10007
(212) 243-5775

Pastoral Psychology (see Religion)

Psychiatry: Journal for the study of interpersonal processes
William Alanson White Psychiatric Foundation
1610 New Hampshire Ave. NW
Washington, DC 20009
(202) 667-3008

Psychological Reports
Box 9229
Missoula, MT 59807

Psychology Today
Ziff Davis Publishing Co.
One Park Ave.
New York, NY 10016
(212) 725-3500

*Suicide and Life Threatening Behavior
Human Sciences Press
72 Fifth Ave.
New York, NY 10011
(212) 243-6000

RELIGION

The periodicals listed below published articles whose subject matter fell within the scope of this book. The list does not necessarily present publications of all religious groups.

America
America Press, Inc.
106 W. Fifty-sixth St.
New York, NY 10019
(212) 581-4640

The Catholic Cemetery (see Funeral Industry)

Christian Century
Christian Century Foundation
407 S. Dearborn St.
Chicago, IL 60605
(312) 427-5380

*Commentary
American Jewish Committee
165 E. Fifty-sixth St.
New York, NY 10022
(212) 751-4000

Commonweal
Commonweal Publishing Co., Inc.
232 Madison Ave.
New York, NY 10016
(212) 683-2042

Jewish Funeral Director (see Funeral Industry)

Journal of Pastoral Care
Association for Clinical Pastoral Education
475 Riverside Dr.
New York, NY 10115
(212) 870-2558

Journal of Religion and Health
Human Sciences Press
72 Fifth Ave.
New York, NY 10011
(212) 243-6000

National Catholic Reporter
National Catholic Reporter Publishing Co.
115 E. Armour Blvd.
Box 281
Kansas City, MO 64141
(816) 531-0538

New Catholic World
Paulist Press
545 Island Rd.
Ramsey, NJ 07446
(201) 825-7300

Pastoral Psychology
Human Sciences Press
72 Fifth Ave.
New York, NY 10011
(212) 243-6000

SCIENCE/TECHNOLOGY

These magazines provide articles on the scientific aspects of death and dying.

Canadian Society of Forensic Science Journal (see **Law/Taxes**)

Forensic Science Society: Journal
Forensic Science Society
Box 41
N. Harrogate, Yorkshire HG1 1BX England

*Science
American Association for the Advancement of Science
1515 Massachusetts Ave. NW
Washington, DC 20005
(202) 467-5220

Science Digest
Hearst Magazines
888 Seventh Ave.
New York, NY 10106
(212) 262-7990

Science News: The weekly summary of current science
Science Service, Inc.
1719 N St. NW
Washington, DC 20036
(202) 785-2255

Scientific American
415 Madison Ave.
New York, NY 10017
(212) 754-0550

SOCIOLOGY/SOCIAL SCIENCES/SOCIAL WELFARE

In these journals, readers will find articles that discuss the relation between society's institutions and death.

American Academy of Political and Social Science: Annals
American Academy of Political and Social Science
3937 Chestnut St.
Philadelphia, PA 19104
(215) 386-4594

American Journal of Community Psychology
Plenum Press
233 Spring St.
New York, NY 10013
(212) 620-8000

American Journal of Sociology
1130 E. Fifty-ninth St.
Chicago, IL 60637
(312) 962-8580

American Sociological Review
American Sociological Association
1722 N St. NW
Washington, DC 20036
(202) 833-3410

Health and Social Work
National Association of Social Workers
Publications Department
257 Park Ave. S
New York, NY 10010
(212) 689-9771
Order Department:
NASW Publications
49 Sheridan Ave.
Albany, NY 12210

Journal of Community Psychology
Clinical Psychology Publishing Co., Inc.
4 Conant Sq.
Brandon, VT 05733
(802) 247-6871

Social Biology (see **Medicine/Life Sciences/Hospitals**)

Social Casework: The journal of contemporary social work
Family Service Association of America
44 E. Twenty-third St.
New York, NY 10010
(212) 674-6100

THANATOLOGY

Journal of Thanatology
Arno Press
Three Park Ave.
New York, NY 10016
(212) 725-2050

Thanatos
P.O. Box 6009
Tallahassee, FL 32301

Bibliography

On the following pages are audiovisual materials and books on the subjects of death and dying. For the most part these publications represent well-known titles that have been published within the last fifteen years, but some older classics are also listed. No periodical articles or pamphlets are included in this bibliography; readers should refer to the list of periodicals and the list of associations in this book for further sources of information.

Audiovisual materials are listed alphabetically but not by subject. Books in this bibliography are classified by subject, but readers should note that these subject headings are not rigid; many books cover a number of subjects, and an attempt has been made to categorize these titles by their major topic only.

AUDIOVISUAL MATERIALS

The following are films, videocassettes, filmstrips, and slide presentations on the subject of death and dying. The listings are arranged alphabetically by author, producer, or director if available; when unavailable, title is listed first.

Advocating Understanding. Available for rent through National Funeral Directors Association. 16mm, color, 32 minutes.

A Life Has Been Lived—A Contemporary Funeral Service. Available for rent through National Funeral Directors Association. 16mm, color, 16 minutes.

And We Were Sad, Remember? Produced by the U.S. Office of Education. Washington, DC: National AudioVisual Center (GSA), 1979. 16mm or videocassette, 29 minutes.

Are You Listening/Widows. Hillsdale, NY: Martha Stuart Communications, Inc. Color, 28 minutes.

Center for Death Education and Research Audiocassette Tape Program. 24 tapes available (e.g., *Dialogue on Death, Stages of Dying, Death and the Family, The Widow-to-Widow Program, Hospice for the Dying: A Living*

Experience, etc.). Bowie, MD: Charles Press Publishers, Inc., Robert J. Brady Co.; purchase only.

Center for Death Education and Research Videocassette Program. 10 tapes available for rent (e.g., *Death in American Society, The Dying Patient, Death and the Care-Giving Professions,* etc.). Minneapolis: Center for Death Education and Research.

Center for Death Education and Research Series of Educational Tapes on Death, Grief, and Bereavement. Bowie, MD: Robert J. Brady Co.

Chait, Michael, and Len Grossman, Ph.D. *A Man.* 1976. 16mm, black and white, 22 minutes.

Chords. Available for rent through the Living Bank. 16mm or videocassette.

Cohen, Maxi, and Joel Gold. *Joe and Maxi.* New York: First Run Features, Inc., 1979. 16mm, 100 minutes.

Couturie, Bill. *Can't It Be Anyone Else?* Santa Monica, CA: Pyramid Films, 1981. 16mm or video, 50 minutes or 30 minutes.

Danska, Herbert, producer. *Nobody Ever Died of Old Age.* 1976. 16mm, color, 58 minutes.

The Day Grandpa Died. Santa Monica, Ca: BFA Educational Media, 1970. Color, 11 minutes.

Death. New York: Filmmakers Library, Inc., 1968. Black and white, 40 minutes.

Death & Dying: Closing the Circle. Guidance Associates, 1976.

Death of a Gandy Dancer. New York: Learning Corporation of America, 1977. 16mm, color, 26 minutes.

Decisions: Life or Death. Crowell-Collier-Macmillan. Available for rent through Association Films, Ridgefield, NJ. Black and white, 30 minutes.

Drayne, Mary, producer (for CBS News). *Hospice*. New York: Carousel Films, 1980. 16mm or videocassette, 13 minutes.

Echoes. Xerox Education Center, 1974. 16mm, color, 11 minutes.

Eisenberg, Ira, producer. *Suicide at 17*. 1977. 16mm, color, 19 minutes.

A Fact of Life. Roanoke, VA: Memorial Society of Roanoke Valley. Film or videocassette, color, 20 minutes.

Feldman, Gene. *Ronnie's Tune*. 1978. 16mm, color, 18 minutes.

The Florida Showcase. Available for rent through National Funeral Directors Association. 16mm, color, 30 minutes.

The Funeral: A Vehicle for the Recognition and Resolution of Grief. Available for rent and purchase through National Funeral Directors Association. 20 35mm slides and manuscript.

The Funeral—From Ancient Egypt to Present Day America. Available for rent and purchase through National Funeral Directors Association. 12 35mm slides and manuscript.

The Funeral Gap. Available for rent through National Funeral Directors Association. 16mm, color, 23 minutes.

Future Shock. Available for rent through National Funeral Directors Association. 16mm, color, 45 minutes.

The Great American Funeral. St. Louis, MO: Mass Media Assn., Inc., 1963. 16mm, 60 minutes.

Gurian/Sholder, producer. *The Garden Party*. 1974. 16mm, color, 24 minutes.

Hoade, Martin, director (for NBC-TV). *On Death and Dying*. Wilmette, IL: Films, Inc., 1977. 16mm and videocassette, 58 minutes.

How Could I Not Be Among You? Briarcliff, NY: Benchmark Films, Inc., 1970. 16mm or videocassette, color, 29 minutes.

Hubley, Faith and John. *Everybody Rides the Carousel*. 1975. 16mm or videocassette, color, 72 minutes.

A Humanist Funeral Service. Available for rent through National Funeral Directors Association. 16mm, color, 15 minutes.

In My Memory (Inside/Out series). Bloomington, IN: Agency for Instructional Television, 1973. Color, 15 minutes.

Inside/Out (A Series). Produced by National Instructional Television Center, 1973. 30 16mm and videocassettes,

color, 15 minutes each.

The Interest in Dying and Death As It Relates to the Funeral. Available for rent through National Funeral Directors Association. 16mm, color, 43 minutes.

An Investment in Sight (An Eye-Bank Film). Iowa City, IA: University of Iowa Media Library, AVC. 16mm, color, 19 minutes.

Jacoby, Alberta, producer. *As Long As There Is Life*. New York: Hospice, 1980. 16mm, 40 minutes.

Jampolsky, Gerald, M.D. *Old Friends . . . New Friends*. Produced by Arthur Barron and Carolyn King. Pittsburgh: Family Communications, 1981. Videocassette, color.

Journey's End. Perrow Productions, 1974. Color, 28 minutes.

Lamb, Derek, and Janet Perlman, producers (for the National Film Board of Canada). *Why Me?* Santa Monica, CA: Pyramid Films and Video, 1979. 16mm and videocassette, 10 minutes.

A Last and Lasting Gift. Redlands, CA: Inland Empire Human Resource Center. Color, 26 minutes.

The Last Days of Living. New York: National Film Board of Canada, 1981. 16mm or videocassette, 57 minutes.

The Last Full Measure of Devotion. Available for rent through National Funeral Directors Association. 16mm, color, 27½ minutes.

The Last Purchase. Washington, DC: NRTA-AARP, 1981. Slides with cassette tape, 20 minutes.

Leaf, Caroline, producer. *The Street*. New York: National Film Board of Canada, 1976. 16mm, 10 minutes.

Live or Die. Wexler Films, 1979. 16mm, 8mm, or videocassette, color, 28½ minutes.

Living. Batesville, IN: Batesville Management Services. Filmstrip (based on Grollman, Earl. *Living—When a Loved One Has Died*). 18 minutes.

Living Together and Dying Alone. Twenty Twenty Media. Available for rent through National Funeral Directors Association. Filmstrip and cassette.

Living With Death. Available for rent through National Funeral Directors Association. 16mm, 45 minutes.

Loss and Grief. Irvine, CA: Concept Media, 1977. 7 filmstrips, 4 cassettes or LPs, discussion manual.

Mason, Edward A. *Films on Death and Dying*. New York: Educational Film Library Association. 40 films available.

Mason, Edward A., M.D. *Widows*. Boston: Documentaries for Learning, 1972. 16 mm and videocassette, 41 minutes.

Meeting Needs . . . Serving People. Educational Perspectives Associates. Available for purchase through National Funeral Directors Association. Slide and cassette presentation.

Mouris, Caroline, and Shelby Leverington. *The Detour*. New York: Phoenix Films, 1977. 16mm and videocassette, 13 minutes.

National Hospice Organization. *Hospice*. New York: Billy Budd Films, 1979. 16mm or videocassette, 26 minutes.

No Longer Alone. Corpus Christi, TX: Del Mar College A-V Dept. Color, 10 minutes.

Not Even Death. Indianapolis: A-V Library, 1976. Color, 30 minutes.

Of Life and Death: the New Catholic Burial Rite. Available for rent through National Funeral Directors Association. 16mm, color, 27½ minutes.

Perspectives on Dying (a series). Irvine, CA: Concept Media. Purchase only. 6 filmstrips with audiocassette or records, instructor's manual, role-playing cards, questionnaires, and text.

Psychosocial Aspects of Death. Indiana University, 1971. Black and white, 39 minutes.

Questions Most Frequently Asked. Available for purchase through National Funeral Directors Association. 16mm, color, 27½ minutes.

Roberts, William L., and Frances M. Darnton. *Conversation With A Widow*. Available through Biomedical Communications, University of Arizona, Tucson, 1976. Videocassette, color, 29 minutes.

St. Pierre, Suzanne, producer (for CBS News). *A Dose of Reality*. New York: Carousel Films, 1978. 16mm and videocassette, 16 minutes.

Sandcastle. New York: Image Publications, Miles-Samuelson, Inc., 1971. Filmstrip, color.

Schiller, Gerald, author and director. *Help Me! The Story of a Teenage Suicide*. 1977. 16mm, color, 25 minutes.

Six American Families—The Stephens Family of Iowa. Westinghouse Broadcasting Co., 1977. 6 59-minute 16mm films, color.

Slote, Alfred H., producer. *To Die with Dignity: To Live with Grief*. Ann Arbor, MI: University of Michigan, 1978. Videocassette, 28 minutes.

Some Day A Future. Available for rent through National Funeral Directors Association. 16mm, color, 30 minutes.

Someone You Love Has Died. Available for rent through National Funeral Directors Association. 16mm, color, 15 minutes.

Soon There Will Be No More Me. Los Angeles: Churchill Films, 1972. Color, 10 minutes.

Sunrise Semester—Featuring Dr. James Carse and Howard C. Raether. Available for rent through National Funeral Directors Association. 16mm, color, 30 minutes.

Talk About. Washington, DC: Widowed Persons Service. Videocassette, 2 parts, each 25 minutes.

Though I Walk Through the Valley. Santa Monica, CA: Pyramid Films, 1972. Color, 30 minutes.

Time of Death. Produced by Korzeniowsky Films. New York: Focus International, 1977. 16mm or videocassette, 16 minutes.

To Be Aware of Death. New York: Billy Budd Films, 1974. 13½ minutes.

To Die Today. Produced by the Canadian Broadcasting Corp. New York: Filmmakers Library, 1973. 16mm and videocassette, black and white, 50 minutes.

Too Personal To Be Private. Available for rent through National Funeral Directors Association. 16mm, color, 28½ minutes.

Towsley, D., R. Larriva, L. Zucker, and M. Lamore, directors. *Uncle Monty's Gone*. Del Mar, CA: CRM/McGraw-Hill Films, 1977. 16mm or videocassette, 14 minutes.

United Methodist Communications. *Portraits of Goodbye*. Baltimore: Mass Media Ministries, 1979. Color, 12 minutes.

University of Southern California Division of Cinema-Television. *Grief*. Los Angeles: USC, 1979. Color, 35 minutes.

Update—Yesterday—Today—Tomorrow. Available for rent through National Funeral Directors Association. 16mm, color, 52 minutes.

Weekend. Produced by Zagreb Films, 1973. 16mm, color, 12 minutes.

Weinstein, Jack. *Hello in There*. Los Angeles: Teleketics, 1979. Color, 21 minutes.

When A Child Dies. Parents Magazine, producer. Milwaukee: National Funeral Directors Association, 1980. 16mm, 27 minutes.

Widows. Boston: Film Program. Black and white, 43 minutes.

WNBC-TV. *What Man Shall Live and Not See Death?* Available through Educational Resources, USF, 1971. Color, 57 minutes.

You Are Not Alone. Available for rent through National Funeral Directors Association. 16mm, color, 30 minutes.

Zalkind, Debra, and Jay Cohen. *Elegy.* New York: Filmmakers Library, 1981. 16mm, 7 minutes.

BOOKS

The books listed below are arranged alphabetically by author, when available. No attempt has been made to be exhaustive in this bibliography. Rather, the list below represents some of the books used most frequently by professionals and scholars in the field of death and dying.

Anatomical Gifts

Fox, Renee C., and Judith P. Swazey. *The Courage to Fail: A Social View of Organ Transplantation and Dialysis.* Chicago: University of Chicago, 1974.

Lyons, Catherine. *Organ Transplants: The Moral Issues.* Philadelphia: Westminster, 1970.

Miller, George W. *Moral and Ethical Implications of Human Organ Transplants.* Springfield, IL: Charles C Thomas, 1971.

Simmons, Roberta. *Gift of Life: The Social and Psychological Impact of Organ Transplantation.* New York: John Wiley and Sons, 1977.

Bibliographies

Bernstein, Joanne E. *Books to Help Children Cope with Separation and Loss.* New York: R. R. Bowker Company, 1971.

Committee on Evolving Trends in Society Affecting Life (Laurens P. White, Chairman). *Death and Dying: Determining and Defining Death—A Compilation of Definitions, Selected Readings and Bibliography.* San Francisco: California Medical Association, 1975.

Franklin Institute, Hyattsville, MD, U.S. Bureau of Health Planning. *Hospices and Related Facilities for the Terminally Ill: Selected Bibliographical References.* Springfield, VA: National Technical Information Service, 1980.

Fulton, Robert, ed. *Death, Grief, and Bereavement: A Bibliography, 1845-1975,* 4th ed. New York: Arno Press, 1977.

Fulton, Robert, ed. *Death, Grief, and Bereavement: Bibliography II, 1975-1980.* New York: Arno Press, 1981.

Goodman, Sara, ed. *On Widowhood.* Longmeadow, MA: Books, Research, and Resources, 1979.

Greene, John T., and John H. Curtis. *Books of Interest to Family Specialists: A Classified and Annotated Bibliography (1980 Supplement).* Blacksburg, VA: Southeastern Council on Family Relations, Virginia Polytechnic Institute and State University, 1980.

Guthman., Robert F., Jr., and Sharon K. Womack. *Death, Dying and Grief: A Bibliography.* Word Serv., 1978.

Harmer, Ruth Mulvey. *A Consumer Bibliography on Funerals.* Washington, DC: Continental Association of Funeral and Memorial Societies, 1977.

Harrah, Barbara K. *Funeral Service: A Bibliography of Literature on Its Past, Present, and Future, The Various Means of Disposition, and Memorialization.* Metuchen, NJ: Scarecrow Press, 1976.

Harrison, Elizabeth A. *Terminal Care (A Bibliography with Abstracts).* Springfield, VA: National Technical Information Service, 1979.

Kastenbaum, Robert, ed. *Death & Dying.* New York: Arno Press, 1977 (40 volumes).

Kutscher, A. H., and A. H. Kutscher, Jr. *A Bibliography of Books on Death, Bereavement, Loss and Grief.* New York: Health Sciences, 1970.

Miller, Albert Jay, and Michael James Acri. *Death: A Bibliographical Guide.* Metuchen, NJ, and London: Scarecrow Press, Inc., 1977.

Poteet, G. Howard. *Death & Dying, A Bibliography.* Troy, NY: Whitston Publishing Co., 1976.

Simpson, Michael A., ed. *Dying, Death and Grief; A Critically Annotated Bibliography and Source Book of Thanatology and Terminal Care.* New York: Plenum Press, 1979.

Strugnell, C., ed. *Adjustment to Widowhood and Related Problems.* New York: Health Sciences Publishing Co., 1974.

Children and Death

The books listed below deal with the subject of children and death, including the death of children, how children can handle the death of family members, etc. Listings marked with an asterisk indicate books meant to be read by children.

Bluebond-Langner, Myra. *The Private Worlds of Dying Children.* Princeton, NJ: Princeton University Press, 1978.

Burton, Lindy, ed. *Care of the Child Facing Death.* London: Routledge & Kegan Paul, 1974.

Cook, Sarah Sheets, ed. *Children and Dying.* New York: Health Sciences, 1974.

Easson, William E. *The Dying Child: The Management of*

the Child or Adolescent Who Is Dying. Springfield, IL: Charles C Thomas, 1970.

Fischhoff, Joseph, and Noreen O'Brien Brohl. *Before and After My Child Died—A Collection of Parents' Experiences.* Detroit: Emmons-Fairfield Publishing Co., 1981.

Furman, Erna. *A Child's Parent Dies: Studies in Childhood Bereavement.* New Haven, CT: Yale University Press, 1974.

Gordon, Audrey K., and Dennis Klass. *They Need to Know: How to Teach Your Children About Death.* Englewood Cliffs, NJ: Prentice-Hall, 1979.

Grollman, Earl A. *Explaining Death to Children.* Boston: Beacon Press, 1967.

Grollman, Earl. *Talking About Death: A Dialogue Between Parent and Child.* Boston: Beacon Press, 1970.

*Harris, Audrey. *Why Did He Die?* Minneapolis: Lerner Publications, 1965.

*Kelin, Stanley. *The Final Mystery.* New York: Doubleday, 1974.

Kooiman, G. *When Death Takes a Father.* Grand Rapids, MI: Baker Book House, 1968.

Kubler-Ross, Elisabeth. *Children & Death.* New York: Macmillan Publishing Co., 1974.

*Langone, John. *Death Is a Noun.* Boston: Little, Brown & Co., 1972.

*LeShan, Eda. *Learning to Say Good-Bye.* New York: Macmillan Publishing Co., 1976.

Schiff, Harriet Sarnoff. *The Bereaved Parent.* New York: Crown Publishers, 1977.

*Stein, Sara B. *About Dying: An Open Family Book for Parents and Children Together.* New York: Walker & Co., 1972.

Death Education

Elin, Caren, and Death Education Directory staff. *Death Educators Directory.* Brooklyn: Highly Specialized Promotions, 1980.

Green, Betty R., and Donald P. Irish. *Death Education.* Cambridge, MA: Schenkman Publishing Co., 1971.

Knott, J. Eugene, Mary C. Ribar, Betty M. Duson, and Marc R. King. *Thanatopics; A Manual of Structured Learning Experiences for Death Education.* Kingston, RI: SLE Publications, 1982.

Morgan, Ernest. *A Manual of Death Education and Simple Burial,* 9th ed. Burnsville, NC: Celo Press, 1980.

Pacholski, Richard, and Charles A. Corr, eds. *New Directions in Death Education and Counseling: Enhancing the Quality of Life in the Nuclear Age.* Arlington, VA: Forum for Death Education and Counseling, 1981.

Wass, Hannelore, et al. *Death Education: An Annotated Resource Guide.* Washington, DC: Hemisphere Publishing Corp., 1980.

Directories and Encyclopedias

Birth, Marriage, Divorce, Death—On the Record. Rye, NY: Reymont Associates, 1977.

Kastenbaum, Robert ed. *Death & Dying.* New York: Arno Press, 1977. (40 volumes.)

Wallis, Charles Langworthy. *The Funeral Encyclopedia: A Source Book.* Grand Rapids, MI: Baker Book House, 1973.

Wass, Hannelore, et al. *Death Education: An Annotated Resource Guide.* Washington, DC: Hemisphere Publishing Corp., 1980.

Ethics and Philosophy

Annas, George J. *The Rights of Hospital Patients (ACLU Guide).* New York: Avon, 1975.

Beauchamp, Tom L., and Seymour Perlin, joint eds. *Ethical Issues in Death and Dying.* Englewood Cliffs, NJ: Prentice-Hall, 1978.

Brim, Orville, G., Jr., ed. *The Dying Patient.* New Brunswick, NJ: Transaction Books, 1980.

Brody, Howard. *Ethical Decisions in Medicine.* Boston: Little, Brown and Co., 1976.

Choron, Jacques. *Death and Modern Man.* New York: Collier Books, 1972.

Congdon, Howard K. *The Pursuit of Death.* Nashville: Abingdon, 1977.

Cutler, Donald R., ed. *Updating Life and Death: Essays on Ethics and Medicine.* Boston: Beacon Press, 1969.

Dumont, Richard. *American View of Death.* General Learning Press, 1972.

Englehardt, H. T., and D. Callahan, eds. *Science, Ethics and Medicine.* New York: The Hastings Center, 1976.

Goldberg, I., S. Malitz, and A. Kutscher, eds. *Psychopharmacologic Agents for the Terminally Ill and Bereaved.* New York: Columbia University, 1973.

Haring, Bernard. *Medical Ethics.* Notre Dame, IN: Fides, 1973.

Holder, Angela Roddey. *Legal Issues in Pediatrics and Adolescent Medicine.* New York: John Wiley and Sons, 1977.

Holder, Angela Roddey. *Medical Malpractice Law.* New York: John Wiley and Sons, 1975.

Hunt, Robert and John Arras, eds. *Ethical Issues in Modern Medicine.* Palo Alto, CA: Mayfield, 1977.

Kastenbaum, Robert J. *Death, Society, and the Human Experience.* St. Louis: C. V. Mosby, 1977.

Katz, Jay, and Alexander Capron. *Catastrophic Diseases: Who Decides What?* New York: Basic Books, 1975.

Kluge, Eike-Henner W. *The Practice of Death.* New Haven, CT: Yale University, 1975.

Ladd, John, ed. *Ethical Issues Relating to Life and Death.* New York: Oxford University Press, 1979.

Leach, Gerald. *The Biocrats: Ethics and the New Medicine.* New York: McGraw-Hill, 1970.

Lunceford, Ronald and Judy. *Attitudes on Death & Dying: A Cross Cultural View.* Los Alamitos, CA: Hwong Publishing, 1976.

Nelson, James B. *Human Medicine: Ethical Perspectives on New Medical Issues.* Minneapolis: Augsburg Publishing House, 1973.

Ramsey, Paul. *Ethics at the Edges of Life; Medical and Legal Intersections.* New Haven, CT: Yale University Press, 1978.

Ramsey, Paul. *The Patient as Person: Explorations in Medical Ethics.* New Haven, CT: Yale University Press, 1970.

Robison, Wade L., and Michael J. Pritchard, eds. *Medical Responsibility: Paternalism, Informed Consent, and Euthanasia.* Clifton, NJ: Humana Press, 1979.

Rostand, Jean. *Humanly Possible.* New York: Saturday Review Press, 1973.

Shannon, Thomas A., ed. *Bioethics.* New York: Paulist Press, 1976.

Stannard, David. *Death in America.* Philadelphia: University of Pennsylvania Press, 1975.

Veatch, Robert M. *Death, Dying and the Biological Revolution: Our Last Quest for Responsibility.* New Haven, CT: Yale University Press, 1976.

Veatch, Robert M., and Roy Branson, eds. *Ethics and Health Policy.* Cambridge, MA: Ballinger Press, 1976.

Weir, Robert F. *Ethical Issues in Death and Dying.* New York: Columbia University Press, 1977.

Euthanasia

Barnard, Christiaan. *Good Life/Good Death: A Doctor's Case for Euthanasia and Suicide.* Englewood Cliffs, NJ: Prentice-Hall, 1980.

Behnke, John, and Sissela Bok, eds. *The Dilemmas of Euthanasia.* New York: Anchor, 1975.

Cohen, B. D. *Karen Ann Quinlan: Dying in the Age of Eternal Life.* Los Angeles: Nash Publishing, 1976.

Cooper, I. S. *It's Hard to Leave While the Music's Playing.* New York: W. W. Norton, 1977.

Downing, A. B., ed. *Euthanasia and the Right to Death: The Case for Voluntary Euthanasia.* Los Angeles: Nash Publishing, 1970. New York: Humanities Press, 1971. London: Peter Owen, Ltd., 1977.

Eisenberg, John. *The Right to Live and Die: Canadian Critical Issues.* Toronto: Canadian Institute for Studies in Education, 1973.

Gould, Jonathan, and Lord Craigmyle, eds. *Your Death Warrant? The Implications of Euthanasia.* New Rochelle, NY: Arlington House, 1971.

Green, William, and Stanley B. Troup. *The Patient, Death, and the Family.* New York: Charles Scribner's Sons, 1974.

Group for the Advancement of Psychiatry. *The Right to Die: Decision and Decision-Makers.* New York: Jason Aronson, 1974.

Heifetz, Milton D., with Charles Mangel. *The Right to Die: A Neurosurgeon Speaks of Death with Candor.* New York: G. P. Putnam's Sons, 1975.

Kohl, Marvin, ed. *Beneficent Euthanasia.* Buffalo, NY: Prometheus, 1975.

Maguire, Daniel C. *Death by Choice.* Garden City, NY: Doubleday, 1974.

Mannes, Marya. *Last Rights: A Case for the Good Death.* New York: Morrow, 1973; New American Library, 1975.

Mitchell, Paige. *Act of Love, The Killing of George Zygmanski.* New York: Alfred A. Knopf, Inc., 1976.

Oden, Thomas C. *Should Treatment Be Terminated? (Moral Guidelines for Christian Families and Pastors).* New York: Harper & Row, 1976.

Russell, O. Ruth. *Freedom to Die: Moral and Legal Aspects of Euthanasia.* New York: Human Sciences Press, 1975.

Society for the Right to Die 1981 Handbook. New York: Society for the Right to Die, 1981.

Superior Court and Supreme Court of New Jersey. *In the Matter of Karen Quinlan, Vols. I and II.* Arlington, VA: University Publications of America, 1976.

Trubo, Richard. *An Act of Mercy: Euthanasia Today.* Los Angeles: Nash, 1973.

Wilson, Jerry B. *Death by Decision.* Philadelphia: The Westminster Press, 1975.

Finance, Law, and Death

Ashley, Paul P. *You and Your Will: The Planning and Management of Your Estate.* New York: McGraw-Hill, 1975; rev. ed., 1978.

A Woman's Guide to Social Security. Washington, DC: U.S. Government Printing Office, 1981.

Brosterman, Robert. *The Complete Estate Planning Guide.* New York: New American Library, 1975.

Clifford, Denis. *Planning Your Estate with Wills, Probate, Trusts & Taxes (California).* Berkeley, CA: Nolo Press, 1980.

Dacey, Norman F. *How to Avoid Probate.* New York: Crown Publishers, 1978.

Flaherty, Patrick F., and Richard S. Ziegler. *Estate Planning for Everyone.* Cambridge, MA: Harper & Row, 1981.

Gollin, James. *Pay Now, Die Later: A Report on Life Insurance, America's Biggest and Strangest Industry.* Baltimore: Penguin Books, 1969.

Howell, John C. *Estate Planning and Will Writing Guide.* Leesburg, VA: Citizens' Law Library, Inc., 1979.

Kahn, Arnold D. *Family Security Through Estate Planning.* New York: McGraw-Hill, 1981.

Klein, Marianne T. *Running Press Glossary of Insurance Language.* Philadelphia: Running Press, 1978.

Lippett, Peter E. *Estate Planning: What Anyone Who Owns Anything Must Know.* Reston, VA: Reston Publishing Co., Inc. (Prentice-Hall), 1979.

McHugh, James T., ed. *Death, Dying, and the Law.* Huntington, IN: Our Sunday Visitor, 1976.

Pedrick, Willard H. *Death, Taxes, and the Living.* Chicago: Commerce Clearing House, 1980.

Simons, Jim, and Denis Clifford. *Planning Your Estate with Wills, Trusts, & Taxes (Texas).* Reading, MA: Addison-

Wesley Publishing Co., 1980.

Social Security in America's Future: Final Report of the National Commission on Social Security, March 1981. Washington, DC: U.S. Government Printing Office, 1981.

Social Security Information for Young Families. Washington, DC: U.S. Government Printing Office, 1980.

Society for the Right to Die. *New York Legislative Manual.* New York: Society for the Right to Die.

Soled, Alex J. *The Essential Guide to Wills, Estates, Trusts, and Death Taxes.* Baltimore: Chancery Publishers, 1981.

State and Local Government Terminations of Social Security Coverage. Washington, DC: U.S. Government Printing Office, 1980.

Taeuber, C., S. Rosoff, R. Veatch, and A. Hellegers. *Death and Dying: An Examination of Legislative and Policy Issues.* Washington, DC: Georgetown University Health Policy Center, 1977.

Your Social Security. Washington, DC: U.S. Government Printing Office, 1979.

You, the Law and Retirement. Washington, DC: U.S. Government Printing Office, 1978.

Funeral Services

Arvio, Raymond. *The Cost of Dying and What You Can Do About It.* New York: Harper & Row, 1974.

Biddle, Perry E. *Abingdon Funeral Manual.* Nashville: Abingdon Press, 1976.

Bowman, Leroy. *The American Funeral.* Westport, CT: Greenwood, 1973.

Brown, Harold W. *How to Sell Cemetery Property before Need.* Topeka, KS: Harold W. Brown, 1975.

Editors of Consumer Reports. *Funerals: Consumers' Last Rights.* Mt. Vernon, NY: Consumers' Union, 1977.

Handbook for Memorial Societies. Washington, DC: Continental Association of Funeral and Memorial Societies.

Harmer, Ruth Mulvey. *The High Cost of Dying.* New York: Collier Books, 1963.

Irion, Paul E. *Cremation.* Philadelphia: Fortress Press, 1968.

Mitford, Jessica. *The American Way of Death.* New York: Simon & Schuster, 1975.

National Funeral Directors Association 21st Century Committee. *Tradition in Transition.* Milwaukee: NFDA, 1981.

"National" Yellow Book of Funeral Directors and Services. Youngstown, OH: Nomis Publications, Inc.

Nelson, Tom. *Your Choice: The Practical Guide to Planning a Funeral.* Glenview, IL: Scott, Foresman & Co., 1982.

NRTA-AARP. *A Consumer's Guide to Funeral Planning.* Washington, DC: NRTA-AARP, 1980.

Pine, Vanderlyn R. *Caretaker of the Dead.* New York: Halstead Press, 1975.

Raether, Howard C., and Robert C. Slater. *The Funeral Director and His Role as a Counselor.* Milwaukee: Bulfin Press, 1975.

Raether, Howard C. *Successful Funeral Service Practice.* Englewood Cliffs, NJ: Prentice-Hall, 1971.

Riley, Miles O'Brien. *Set Your House in Order.* New York: Doubleday, 1980.

Tegg, William. *The Last Act: Being the Funeral Rites of Nations & Individuals.* Detroit: Gale, 1973.

The Price of Death: A Survey Method and Consumer Guide for Funerals, Cemeteries, and Grave Markers. Washington, DC: U.S. Government Printing Office, 1975.

U.S. Department of Housing and Urban Development. *Cemeteries as Open Space Reservations.* Washington, DC: U.S. Government Printing Office, June 1970.

U.S. Department of Housing and Urban Development. *Commemorative Parks from Abandoned Public Cemeteries.* Washington, DC: U.S. Government Printing Office, 1971.

General

Berdes, Celia. *Social Services for the Aged, Dying, and Bereaved in International Perspective.* Washington, DC: International Federation on Ageing, 1978.

Comprehensive Community Services, Inc. *Human Services Directory; Metropolitan Chicago: 1981, 1980.*

Curtin, Sharon R. *Nobody Ever Died of Old Age.* Boston: Atlantic Monthly Press, 1972; Little, Brown and Co., 1973.

Death and Dying A-Z. Queens Village, NY: Croner Publications Incorporated, 1980 (with amendment service).

Dempsey, David. *The Way We Die: An Investigation of Death and Dying in America Today.* New York: Macmillan, 1975.

Elliot, Neil. *The Gods of Life.* New York: Macmillan, 1974.

Facts of Life and Death. Washington, DC: U.S. Government Printing Office, 1978.

Feifel, Herman. *New Meanings of Death.* New York: McGraw-Hill, 1977.

Fleming, Thomas. *Communicating Issues in Thanatology.* Mss Information Corp., 1976.

Fulton, Robert, Eric Markusen, Greg Owen, and Jane Scheiber, eds. *Death and Dying: Challenge and Change.* San Francisco: Boyd and Fraser Publishing Co., 1980.

Green, Betty, and Donald P. Irish, eds. *Death Education: Preparation for Living.* General Learning Press, 1971.

Greenstone, James L., and Sharon Leviton. *Hotline: Crisis Intervention Directory.* New York: Facts on File, 1981.

Greinacher, N., and A. Muller, eds. *The Experience of Dying.* New York: Herder and Herder, 1974.

Grollman, Earl A., ed. *Concerning Death: A Practical Guide for the Living.* Boston: Beacon Press, 1974.

Hendin, David. *Death as a Fact of Life.* New York: Warner Paperbacks, 1973.

Hinton, J. *Dying.* London: Penguin, 1973.

Kalish, Richard A. *Perspectives on Death and Dying* (A Baywood Monograph Series in 3 volumes). Farmingdale, NY: Baywood Publishing Co., Inc., 1979.

Karo, Nancy, and Alvara Michelson. *Adventure in Dying.* Chicago: Moody Press, 1976.

Kastenbaum, Robert, and Ruth Aisenberg. *Psychology of Death.* New York: Springer, 1976.

Kavanaugh, Robert E. *Facing Death.* Baltimore: Penguin Books, 1974.

Kelkeman, Stanley. *Living Your Dying.* New York: Random House, Bookworks, 1974.

Koestenbaum, Peter. *Is There an Answer to Death?* Englewood Cliffs, NJ: Prentice-Hall, 1976.

Kubler-Ross, Elisabeth, M.D. *On Death and Dying.* New York: The Macmillan Company, 1969.

Kubler-Ross, Elisabeth, M.D. *Questions and Answers on Death and Dying.* New York: The Macmillan Company, 1974.

Langone, John. *Death Is a Noun; a View of the End of Life.* Boston and Toronto: Little, Brown and Co., 1972.

Lepp, Ignace. *Death and Its Mysteries.* New York: Macmillan, 1968.

Melby, Lynn L. *Dead Is a Four Letter Word.* Seattle: Dabney Publishing, 1975.

Morse, Theresa A. *Life Is for Living.* Garden City, NY: Doubleday and Co., 1973.

Ostheimer, Nancy and John, eds. *Life or Death: Who Controls?* New York: Springer, 1976.

Pattison, E. Mansell. *The Experience of Dying.* Englewood Cliffs, NJ: Prentice-Hall, 1977.

Pearson, Leonard, ed. *Death & Dying: Current Issues in the Treatment of the Dying Person.* 1977.

Pincus, Lily. *Death and the Family.* New York: Vintage Books, 1976.

Schneidman, Edwin S., ed. *Death: Current Perspectives.* Palo Alto, CA: Mayfield, 1976.

Schneidman, Edwin S. *Deaths of Man.* New York: Quadrangle, 1973.

Sudnow, David. *Passing On.* Englewood Cliffs, NJ: Prentice-Hall, 1967.

Veatch, Robert M. *Death, Dying & the Biological Revolution.* New Haven, CT: Yale University Press, 1976.

Wass, Hannelore, ed. *Dying, Facing the Facts.* Washington, DC: Hemisphere Publishing Co., 1979.

Watt, Jill. *Canadian Guide to Death and Dying.* Vancouver/Toronto: International Self-Counsel Press, 1974.

Weinstein, Stanley E. *Mental Health Issues in Grief Counseling.* Baltimore: National Conference on Mental Health Issues Related to Sudden Infant Death Syndrome, 1979.

Williams, R. H. *To Live and to Die: When, Why, and How.* New York: Springer, 1973.

Wyschogrod, Edith, ed. *The Phenomenon of Death: Faces of Mortality.* New York: Harper & Row, 1973.

Geriatrics and Dying

Butler, Robert N. *Why Survive? Being Old in America.* New York: Harper & Row, 1975.

Innovative Developments in Aging: Area Agencies on Aging. Washington, DC: U.S. Government Printing Office, 1979.

Kart, Cary, and Barbara Manard, eds. *Aging in America: Readings in Social Gerontology.* Port Washington, NY: Alfred, 1976.

Lastenbaum, Robert, with Theodore Barber, Sheryl Wilson, Beverly Ryder, and Lisa Hathaway. *Old, Sick, and Helpless: Where Therapy Begins.* Cambridge, MA: Ballinger Publishing, 1982.

Grief/Bereavement

Adams, Rev. James. *The Sting of Death: A Study Course on Death and Bereavement.* New York: The Seabury Press, 1971.

Anderson, Colena M. *Joy Beyond Grief.* Grand Rapids, MI: Zondervan, 1974.

Antoniak, Helen, et al. *Alone: Emotional, Legal and Financial Help for the Widowed or Divorced Woman.* Millbrae, CA: Les Femmes Celestial Arts, 1979.

Bremer, Maura Scott. *And Send the Sun Tomorrow.* Minneapolis: Winston, 1979.

Brown, Velma. *After Weeping, A Song.* Nashville: Broadman Press, 1980.

Bryant, Betty. *Leaning into the Wind—The Wilderness of Widowhood.* Philadelphia: Fortress Press, 1975.

Burgess, Jane, and Willard Kohn. *The Widower.* Boston: Beacon Press, 1978.

Caine, Lynn. *Lifelines.* New York: Dell Publishing Co., 1977.

Caine, Lynn. *Widow.* New York: William Morrow & Co., Inc., 1974.

Carr, Arthur C., B. Schoenberg, et al. *Grief—Selected Readings on Clinical and Religious Views of Death and Grief.* New York: Health Sciences Publishing Co., 1975.

Champagne, Marion G. *Facing Life Alone: What Widows and Divorcees Should Know.* Indianapolis: Bobbs Merrill, 1964.

Colgrove, Melba, H. Bloomfield, and P. McWilliams. *How to Survive the Loss of a Love.* Allen Park, MI: Leo Press, 1976.

Davidson, Clarissa Stuart. *On Becoming a Widow.* St. Louis: Concordia Publishing House, 1973.

Decker, Bea, and Gladys Kooiman. *After the Flowers Have Gone.* Grand Rapids, MI: Zondervan Publishing, 1973.

Fisher, Ida, and Byron Lane. *The Widow's Guide to Life.* Englewood Cliffs, NJ: Prentice-Hall, 1981.

Glick, I., R. Weiss, and C. M. Parkes. *The First Year of Bereavement.* New York: John Wiley and Sons, 1974.

Grollman, Earl A. *Living When a Loved One Has Died.* Boston: Beacon Press, 1977.

Hellman, Dorothy. *Let Go, My Love.* New York: Bloch Publications Co., 1979.

Hiltz, S. R. *Creative Community Services for Widows.* Port Washington, NY: Kennikat Press, 1977.

Jackson, Edgar Newman. *You and Your Grief.* Great Neck, NY: Channel Per, 1961.

Jackson, Edgar N. *When Someone Dies.* Philadelphia: Fortress Press, 1973.

Kavanaugh, Robert. *Facing Death.* Baltimore: Penguin Books, 1974.

Kirsch, Charlotte. *A Survivors Manual to Wills, Trusts, Maintaining Emotional Stability.* New York: Anchor Press, 1981.

Kohn, Willard K., and Jane Burgess Kohn. *The Widower.* Boston: Beacon Press, 1979.

Kreis, Bernadine. *Up From Grief, Patterns of Recovery.* New York: The Seabury Press, 1969.

Kutner, Luis. *The Intelligent Woman's Guide to Future Security.* New York: Dodd, Mead, 1970.

Kutscher, Austin H. *Death & Bereavement.* Springfield, IL: Charles C Thomas, 1974.

Kutscher, Austin H. *For the Bereaved.* Fell, 1971.

Kutscher, Austin H., and Lillian G. Kutscher. *Religion and Bereavement.* H. S. Publishing Co., 1972.

Lamm, Maurice. *The Jewish Way in Death & Mourning.* Middle Village, NY: Jonathan David, 1969.

Lattanzi, Marcial, and Diane Coffelt. *Bereavement Care Manual.* Boulder County Hospice, Inc., 1979.

Lewis, Alfred A. *Three Out of Four Wives.* New York: Macmillan Publishing Co., Inc., 1975.

Lewis, C. S. *A Grief Observed.* New York: Seabury Press, 1963.

Loewinsohn, Ruth J. *Survival Handbook for Widows (and for Relatives and Friends Who Want to Understand).* Chicago: Follett Publishing Co., 1979.

Lopata, Helena S. *Widowhood in an American City.* Cambridge, MA: Schenkman, 1973.

Lopata, Helena S. *Women as Widows: Support Systems.* New York: Elsevier Publishing Co., 1979.

Margolis, Otto S. *Grief and the Meaning of the Funeral.* Edison, NJ: Mss Information Corp., 1975.

Marshall, Catherine. *To Live Again.* New York: McGraw-Hill, 1957.

Mental Health Issues in Grief Counseling. Washington, DC: U.S. Government Printing Office, 1979.

Meryman, Richard. *Hope—A Loss Survived.* Boston, Toronto: Little, Brown and Co., 1980.

Morris, Sarah. *Grief and How to Live with It.* New York: Grosset & Dunlap, 1972.

Morse, Theresa A. *Life Is for Living.* Garden City, NJ: Doubleday and Co., 1973.

NRTA-AARP. *Widowed Persons Service Organization Manual.* Washington, DC: Widowed Persons Service.

Nye, M. B. *But I Never Thought He'd Die.* Philadelphia: Westminster Press, 1978.

Parkes, M. *Bereavement: Studies of Grief in Adult Life.* New York: International Universities Press, Inc., 1972. London: Tavistock Publications, Ltd., 1972.

Peterson, James A., and Michael Briley. *Widows & Widowhood: A Creative Approach to Being Alone.* New York: Association Press, 1977.

Peterson, James A. *On Being Alone.* Long Beach, CA: Widowed Persons Service.

Phipps, Joyce. *Death's Single Privacy: Grieving and Personal Growth.* New York: Seabury Press, 1974.

Pincus, Lily. *Death and the Family: The Importance of Mourning.* New York: Vintage Books, 1976 (paperback); Pantheon Books, 1974.

Pine, Vanderlyn R., et al., eds. *Acute Grief and the Funeral.* Springfield, IL: Charles C Thomas, 1976.

Schiff, Harriet Sarnoff. *The Bereaved Parent.* New York: Crown Publishers, 1977.

Schoenberg, Bernard. *Anticipatory Grief.* New York: Columbia University Press, 1974.

Schoenberg, Bernard, Arthur C. Carr, David Peretz, and Austin H. Kutscher. *Loss and Grief: Psychological Management in Medical Practice.* New York: Columbia University Press, 1973.

Schoenberg, Bernard, and Irwin Gerber. *Bereavement, Its Psychosocial Aspects.* New York: Columbia University Press, 1975.

Seskin, Jane. *Young Widow.* New York: Ace Books, 1975.

Silverman, Phyllis R. *Helping Each Other in Widowhood.* New York: Health Sciences Publishing Corp., 1974.

Silverman, Phyllis R. *If You Will Lift the Load . . . I Will Lift It Too.* New York: Health Sciences Publishing Corp., 1976.

Simos, Bertha G. *A Time to Grieve: Loss as a Universal Human Experience.* New York: Family Service Association of America, 1979.

Start, Clarissa. *On Becoming a Widow.* St. Louis: Concordia Publishing House, 1973.

Start, Clarissa. *When You're a Widow.* St. Louis: Concordia Publishing House, 1968.

Temes, Roberta. *Living With an Empty Chair.* Amherst, MA: Mandala, 1977.

Wakin, Edward. *Living as a Widow.* Chicago: Claretian Publications, 1976.

Wallant, Louis. *The Human Season.* New York: Harcourt Brace Jovanovich, Inc., 1960.

Weiss, Robert S. *Loneliness: The Experience of Emotional and Social Isolation.* Cambridge, MA: The MIT Press, 1973.

Westberg, Dr. Granger E. *Good Grief: A Constructive Approach to the Problem of Loss.* Philadelphia: Fortress Press, 1979. (Rock Island, IL: Augustana Press, 1962.)

Yates, Martha. *Coping: A Survival Manual for Women Alone.* Englewood Cliffs, NJ: Prentice-Hall, 1976.

Life Span/Population

American Friends Service Committee. *Who Shall Live? Man's Control Over Birth and Death.* New York: Hill and Wang, 1970.

Ettinger, Robert C. W. *The Prospect of Immortality.* New York: McFadden-Bartell, 1966.

Holzer, Hans. *Pattern of Destiny.* Los Angeles: Nash Publishing, 1974.

Kent, Saul. *The Life-Extension Revolution.* New York: William Morrow and Co., Inc., 1980.

Sheskin, Arlene. *Cryonics: A Sociology of Death and Bereavement.* New York: Irvington Publishers, Inc., 1979.

Silverstein, Alvin. *Conquest of Death.* New York: Macmillan Publishing Co., Inc., 1979.

Veatch, Robert M. *Life Span: Values and Life-Extending Technologies.* New York: Harper & Row, 1979.

Psychology/Psychiatry

Alsop, Stewart. *Stay of Execution.* New York: Harper & Row. 1973.

Alvarez, Alfred. *The Savage God: A Study on Suicide.* New York: Bantam Books, 1976.

Anderson, Dorothy B., and Lenora J. McClean, eds. *Identifying Suicide Potential.* New York: Behavioral Publishing, 1971.

Becker, E. *The Denial of Death.* New York: The Free Press, 1973.

Bowles, Elinor. *Self-Help Groups: Perspective and Directions—An Instructional Guide for Developing Self-Help Mutual Aid Groups.* New York: National Self-Help Clearinghouse .

Choron, Jacques. *Suicide.* New York: Charles Scribner's Sons, 1972.

Cutter, Fred. *Coming to Terms with Death.* Chicago: Nelson Hall, 1974.

Douglas, Jack D. *The Social Meanings of Suicide.* Princeton, NJ: Princeton University Press, 1973.

Ellis, Edward Robb, and George N. Allen. *Traitor Within: Our Suicide Problem.* New York: Doubleday, 1971.

Flescher, Joachim, M.D. *Suicide—Man's Fate? Genetic Prevention.* New York: OTRB Editions, 1971.

Fulton, Robert, ed., with Robert Bendiksen. *Death and Identity,* revised 2nd ed. Bowie, MD: Robert J. Brady Co., 1976.

Gartner, Alan, and Frank Riessman. *HELP: A Working Guide to Self-Help Groups.* New York: New Viewpoints, 1979.

Gartner, Alan, and Frank Riessman. *Self-Help in the Human Services.* San Francisco: Jossey-Bass, 1977.

Gordon, David Cole. *Overcoming the Fear of Death.* New York: Macmillan, 1970. Baltimore: Penguin Books, 1970.

Grollman, Earl A. *Suicide: Prevention, Intervention, and Postvention.* Boston: Beacon Press, 1971.

Haim, Andre. *Adolescent Suicide.* New York: International Universities Press, 1974.

Hampe, Johann Christoph. *To Die Is Gain.* Atlanta: John Knox, 1979.

Hendin, Herbert. *Black Suicide.* New York: Basic Books, 1969.

Humm, Andy. *How to Organize a Self-Help Group.* New York: National Self-Help Clearinghouse.

Kastenbaum, Robert, and Ruth B. Aisenberg. *Psychology of Death.* New York: Springer Publishing Co., 1972.

Lester, Gene, and David Lester. *Suicide: The Gamble with Death.* Englewood Cliffs, NJ: Prentice-Hall, 1971.

Lifton, Robert Jay, and Eric Olson. *Living and Dying.* New York: Bantam Books, 1975.

Meyer, J. E. *Death and Neurosis.* New York: International Universities Press, 1975.

Milio, Nancy. *Planning Self-Care Programs: Some Resources for Health Agencies and Community Groups.* New York: National Self-Help Clearinghouse.

Miller, Marv. *Suicide After Sixty—The Final Alternative.* New York: Springer Publishing Co., Vol. 2 in the Springer Series on Death and Suicide, 1979.

Moody, Raymond A., Jr. *Life After Life.* St. Simons Island, GA: Mockingbird Books, 1981.

Neale, Robert E. *The Art of Dying.* New York: Harper & Row, 1973.

Osis, Karlis, and Erlendur Haroldsson. *What They Saw at the Hour of Death.* New York: Avon, 1977.

Portwood, Doris. *Common-Sense Suicide: The Final Right.* New York: Dodd, Mead, & Company, 1978.

Rawlings, Maurice S. *Beyond Death's Door.* Nashville: Nelson, 1978.

Schneidman, Edwin, Norman Farberow, and Robert Littman. *The Psychology of Suicide.* New York: Jason Aronson, 1976.

Schneidman, Edwin. *Voices of Death.* New York: Harper & Row, 1980(?).

Sheehy, G. *Passages.* New York: E. P. Dutton, 1976.

Stone, Howard W. *Suicide and Grief.* Philadelphia: Fortress Press, 1972.

Weisman, Avery D. *The Realization of Death: A Guide for the Psychological Autopsy.* New York: Jason Aronson, 1974.

Weisman, Avery. *On Dying and Denying: A Psychiatric Study of Terminality.* New York: Behavioral Publications, 1972.

Wordon, James, and William Proctor. *PDA—Personal Death Awareness.* Englewood Cliffs, NJ: Prentice-Hall, 1976.

Religion and Death

A Guide to the Church and the Funeral. Knoxville, TN: Christian Witness Committee of the Presbytery of Union, United Presbyterian Church, 1979 (revised).

Bane, J., A. Kutscher, R. Neale, R. Reeves, eds. *Death and Ministry: Pastoral Care of the Dying and the Bereaved.* New York: Seabury Press, 1975.

Bayly, Joseph. *The View from a Hearse: A Christian View of Death.* Elgin, IL: D. C. Cook Publishing Co., 1969; revised 1978.

Console One Another: Guidelines for Christian Burial. Milwaukee: Archdiocese of Milwaukee.

Dedek, John F. *Contemporary Medical Ethics.* New York: Sheed and Ward, 1975.

Doss, Richard. *The Last Enemy: A Christian Understanding of Death.* New York: Harper & Row.

Griffin, William, ed. *Endtime, the Doomsday Catalog.* New York: Macmillan, 1979.

Hardt, Dale V. *Death: The Final Frontier.* Englewood Cliffs, NJ: Prentice-Hall, 1979.

Hunt, Gladys M. *The Christian Way of Death.* Grand Rapids, MI: Zondervan, 1971.

Kavanaugh, Robert E. *Facing Death.* Baltimore: Penguin, 1974.

Lamm, Rabbi Maurice. *The Jewish Way in Death and Mourning.* New York: Jonathan David, 1969.

Mills, Liston O., ed. *Perspectives on Death.* Nashville: Abingdon, 1974.

Reimer, Jack, ed. *Jewish Reflections on Death.* New York: Shocken Books, 1974.

Vaux, Kenneth. *Will to Live, Will to Die.* Minneapolis: Augsburg Publishing House, 1978.

Wallis, Charles Langworthy. *The Funeral Encyclopedia: A Source Book.* Grand Rapids, MI: Baker Book House, 1973.

Society, Culture, and Death

Charmaz, Kathy. *The Social Reality of Death.* Reading, MA: Addison-Wesley, 1980.

Dumont, Richard G., and Dennis C. Foxx. *The American View of Death.*

Kalish, Richard A., and David K. Reynolds. *Death and Ethnicity: A Psychocultural Study.* Los Angeles: Ethel Percy, Andrus Gerontology Center, University of Southern California, 1977.

Kastenbaum, Robert, ed. *Death, Society and Human Behavior.* St. Louis, C. V. Mosby, 1977.

Langone, John. *Vital Signs: The Way We Die in America.* Boston: Little, Brown and Co., 1974.

Mack, Arien, ed. *Death in American Experience.* New York: Shocken Books, 1973.

Marshall, Victor W. *Last Chapters: A Sociology of Aging and Death.* Monterey, CA: Brooks/Cole, 1980.

Stannard, David E., ed. *Death in America.* Philadelphia: University of Pennsylvania Press, 1975.

Terminal Care, Terminal Illness, Hospice

Abrams, Ruth D. *Not Alone with Cancer: A Guide for Those Who Care; What to Expect; What to Do.* Springfield, IL: Charles C Thomas, 1976.

Ajemian, Ina, and Balfour M. Mount, eds. *The R.V.H. Manual on Palliative/Hospice Care: A Resource Book.* New York: Arno Press, 1980.

Back, Sylvia A., and Robert W. Buckingham III. *First American Hospice: Three Years of Home Care.* New Haven, CT: Hospice, Inc., 1978.

Baulch, Evelyn M. *Home Care: A Practical Alternative to Extended Hospitalization.* Millbrae, CA: Celestial Arts, 1980.

Benoliel, Jeanne Quint. *Dealing with Death.* Los Angeles: Ethel Percy, Andrus Gerontology Center, University of Southern California, 1973.

Benton, Richard G. *Death and Dying: Principles and Practices in Patient Care.* New York: Van Nostrand Reinhold Co., 1978.

Browning, Mary H., and Edith P. Lewis. *The Dying Patient: A Nursing Perspective.* New York: American Journal of Nursing Co., 1972.

Cartwright, Ann, et al. *Life Before Death.* London: Routledge & Kegan Paul, 1973.

Cassell, Eric. *The Healer's Art.* Philadelphia: Lippincott, 1976.

Cohen, Kenneth P. *Hospice: Prescription for Terminal Care.* Germantown, MD: Aspen Systems Corp., 1979.

Crane, Diana. *The Sanctity of Social Life: Physicians' Treatment of Critically Ill Patients.* New York: Russell Sage, 1975.

Crichton, Ian. *The Art of Dying.* Atlantic Highlands, NJ: Humanities Press, 1976.

Davidson, Glen W. *The Hospice: Development and Administration.* Washington, DC: Hemisphere Publishing Corp., 1978.

Dempsey, David K. *The Way We Die: An Investigation of Death and Dying and America Today.* New York: Macmillan Publishing Co., 1975.

Dubois, Paul M. *The Hospice Way of Death.* New York: Human Sciences Press, 1980.

Feigenberg, Loma. *Terminal Care: Friendship Contracts with Dying Cancer Patients.* New York: Brunner/Mazel, 1980.

Garfield, Charles, ed. *Psychosocial Care of the Dying Patient: Doctor-Patient Relationships in Terminal Illness.* San Francisco: First National Training Conference for Physicians, University of California Medical School, 1976.

Hamilton, Michael, and Helen Reid, eds. *A Hospice Handbook: A New Way to Care for the Dying.* Grand Rapids, MI: William B. Eerdmans Publishing Co., 1980.

Herhold, Robert. *Learning to Die, Learning to Live.* Philadelphia: Fortress, 1976.

Kelly, Orville. *Until Tomorrow Comes.* New York: Everest House, 1979.

Koff, Theodore H. *Hospice: A Caring Community.* Cambridge, MA: Winthrop Publishers, 1980.

Krant, Melvin J. *Dying & Denying: The Meaning and Control of a Personal Death.* Springfield, IL: Charles C Thomas, 1974.

Krant, Melvin J. *Dying & Dignity.* Springfield, IL: Charles C Thomas, 1974.

Kubler-Ross, Elisabeth. *Death, the Final Stage of Growth.* Englewood Cliffs, NJ: Prentice-Hall, 1975.

Kubler-Ross, Elisabeth. *Images of Growth & Death.* Englewood Cliffs, NJ: Prentice-Hall, 1976.

Kubler-Ross, Elisabeth, and Mel Warshaw. *To Live Until We Say Goodbye.* Englewood Cliffs, NJ: Prentice-Hall, 1978.

Kutscher, Austin H., and Michael Goldberg. *Caring for the Dying Patient and the Family.* New York: Health Science, 1973.

Lack, Sylvia A., and Robert W. Buckingham III. *First American Hospice: Three Years of Home Care.* New Haven, CT: Hospice, Inc., 1978.

National Hospice Organization. *Final Report, September, 1979: Delivery and Payment of Hospice Services: Investigative Study.* Vienna, VA: National Hospice Organization, 1979.

Prichard, Elizabeth R., et al. *Social Work with the Dying Patient and the Family.* New York: Columbia University Press, 1977.

Schoenberg, Bernard, et al. *Psychological Aspects of Termi-nal Care.* New York: Columbia University Press, 1972.

Schut, Henry. *Ten Years to Live.* Grand Rapids, MI: Baker Book House, 1978.

Shepard, Martin, M.D. *Someone You Love Is Dying: A Guide for Helping and Coping.* New York: Harmony Books, 1975.

Simon, Seymour. *Life and Death.* New York: McGraw-Hill, 1976.

Soulen, Richard N. *Care for the Dying: Resources of Theology.* Atlanta: John Knox Press, 1975.

Stoddard, Sandol. *The Hospice Movement: A Better Way of Caring for the Dying.* New York: Vintage Books, 1978.

Wentzel, Kenneth B. *To Those Who Need It Most, Hospice Means Hope.* Charleston, MA: Charles River Books, 1981.

PART 4

GLOSSARY

Glossary

A

Accidental death benefit. A benefit in addition to the face amount of a life insurance policy, payable if the insured dies as the result of an accident. Sometimes referred to as *double indemnity.*

Adjustable life insurance. A type of insurance that allows the insured to switch the type of protection, raise or lower the face amount of the policy, increase or decrease the premium and lengthen or shorten the protection period.

Advisory memorial society. A nonprofit, consumer-oriented organization that advocates and disseminates information about low-cost, simplified alternatives to traditional funeral practices.

Agreement or contract memorial society. A nonprofit organization charging an initial membership fee for contracting with a local mortician to provide a limited range of low-cost funeral services at time of need.

Algor mortis. A postmortem stage following *rigor mortis* that is characterized by the lowering of the body temperature to that of its surroundings.

Anatomical gift. A donated organ or other body part from a deceased person, intended for transplantation or medical study.

Annuitant. The person during whose life an annuity is payable (usually the person to receive the annuity).

Annuity. A contract that provides a periodic income for a specified period of time, such as number of years or for life.

Annuity certain. A contract that provides an income for a specified number of years, regardless of life or death.

Annuity consideration. The payment, or one of the regular periodic payments, an annuitant makes for an annuity.

Assignment. The legal transfer of one person's interest in an insurance policy to another person.

Autopsy. A postmortem examination, usually intended to determine the cause of death or to further medical knowledge of a particular disease or condition present in the human body.

B

Beneficiary. The person named in an insurance policy to receive the proceeds at the death of the insured.

Bereavement. The state of suffering the loss of a loved one through death.

Bereavement counseling. Assistance provided by a trained counselor or experienced professional to help an individual or family respond to grief before and/or after the death of a significant individual.

Bereavement counselor. A trained counselor or experienced professional who assists individuals or families through the grieving process.

Bioethics. The ethics or morality of the life sciences or, more commonly, of medicine. The study of bioethics includes issues concerning the right to live and the right to die, truthtelling in medicine, medical intervention and the lack thereof, and many others.

Brain death. 1) A criterion for defining death based upon total and irreversible cessation of brain function; 2) the irreversible cessation of whole brain function, including that of the brain stem; 3) irreversible total cessation of brain function, heart still beating and respirations totally supported by a respirator.

Burial permit. A legal document authorizing the disposition of individual human remains.

Burial vault. An outer burial container generally constructed of concrete or metal designed to provide additional protection to a casket or to inhibit the sinking of soil above a grave.

Business life insurance. Life insurance purchased by a business enterprise on the life of a member of the firm. It is often bought by partnerships to protect the surviving partners against loss caused by the death of a partner, or by a corporation to reimburse it for loss caused by the death of a key employee.

C

Cash surrender value. The amount available in cash upon voluntary termination of a policy by its owner before it becomes payable by death or maturity.

Casket. A rigid rectangular receptacle designed to hold human remains, usually made of wood or metal and often decorated and lined with fabric.

Cemetery. An area dedicated for the purpose of human burial.

Coffin. An oblong, rigid receptacle designed to hold human remains, usually made of wood or metal and often decorated and lined with fabric.

Cooperative mortuary. A mortuary owned and operated by participating community members for the benefit of cooperating members.

Convertible term insurance. Term insurance which can be exchanged, at the option of the policyholder and without evidence of insurability, for another plan of insurance.

Coroner. A public official who probes, through an inquest, the circumstances surrounding any death whose cause appears not to be natural.

Credit life insurance. Term life insurance issued through a lender or lending agency to cover payment of a loan, installment purchase, or other obligation, in case of death.

Cremation. Reduction of human remains to ashes by incineration. Ashes are normally placed in an urn, which can be subjected to various methods of disposition, above ground or below. *Direct cremation* refers to the practice of cremating the body without prior viewing or visitation.

Crematorium. *See* **Crematory.**

Crematory. 1) An establishment that performs cremation; 2) the furnace for cremating human remains. Synonym: *crematorium.*

Crib death. *See* **Sudden infant death syndrome.**

Cryobiology. The study of the effects of extremely low temperatures on living tissues.

Cryogenics. A science that deals with the effects of low temperatures on various substances and beings.

Cryonics. The practice of freezing dead human bodies so that they can be thawed at some time in the future when the cause(s) of death might be reversible.

Crypt. A burial vault either in a mausoleum or underground. Below-ground crypts are also called *lawn crypts.*

D

Death certificate. A legal document attesting to the date, time and cause of death and signed by a physician, coroner, or medical examiner.

Death education. 1) The name associated with a broad and diverse movement dedicated to increasing personal awareness of the psychological, spiritual, economic and legal ramifications of death; 2) a preventive intervention designed to minimize the variety of problems associated with death and to increase the appreciation of life.

Decedent. A deceased person.

Declination. The rejection by a life insurance company of an application for life insurance, usually for reasons of the health or occupation of the applicant.

Deferred annuity. An annuity providing for income payments to begin at some future date.

Deferred group annuity. A type of group annuity providing for the purchase each year of a paid-up deferred annuity for each member of the group, the total amount received by the member at retirement being the sum of these deferred annuities.

Deposit administration group annuity. A type of group annuity providing for the accumulation of contributions in an undivided fund out of which annuities are purchased as the individual members of the group retire.

Deposit term insurance. A form of term insurance in which the insured pays an additional sum (deposit) with the initial premium. This additional sum, plus interest, is returned to the insured or converted to a cash value of a new whole life policy at the end of the term period; usually 10 years. If the policy does not remain in force for the term period, the additional sum is forfeited.

Dividend. A return of part of the premium on participating insurance to reflect the difference between the premium charged and the combination of actual mortality, expense and investment experience. Such premiums are calculated to provide some margin over the anticipated cost of the insurance protection.

Dividend addition. An amount of paid-up insurance purchased with a policy dividend and added to the face amount of the policy.

DNR. An acronym for "Do not resuscitate," a notation entered on a patient's hospital chart which permits the individual to die naturally, without the intervention of life-preserving measures.

Direct burial/Immediate burial. The immediate removal of the body by a funeral director and delivery of it to the cemetery in a simple container, without viewing, embalming, or cosmetic restoration of the body; generally followed by a memorial service in a home or chapel without the body present.

Donor clearinghouse. A nonprofit registry that coordinates the disposition of anatomical gifts.

E

Embalm. To sanitize and preserve a deceased human body chemically to arrest putrefaction.

Emortality. A coined word meaning freedom from natural death in a futuristic sense (as opposed to *immortality*).

Endowed care. *See* **Perpetual care.**

Endowment. Life insurance payable to the policyholder if living, on the maturity date stated in the policy, or to a beneficiary if the policyholder dies prior to that date.

Euthanasia, active. The act of using certain methods to hasten the death of a terminally-ill patient.

Euthanasia, compulsory. *See* **Euthanasia, involuntary.**

Euthanasia, imposed. *See* **Euthanasia, involuntary.**

Euthanasia, involuntary. An act of mercy-killing not desired or requested by the patient; also called *compulsory* or *imposed euthanasia.*

Euthanasia, passive. The act of withholding life-preserving measures from a dying patient.

Euthanasia, voluntary. An act of mercy-killing sought by the patient.

Extended care facility. *See* **Skilled nursing facility.**

Extended term insurance. A form of insurance available as a nonforfeiture option. It provides the original amount of insurance for a limited period of time.

Eye nucleation. The removal of an eye(s) for the purposes of corneal transplant.

F

Face amount. The amount stated on the face of the policy that will be paid in case of death or at the maturity of the policy. It does not include additional amounts payable under accidental death or other special provisions, or acquired through the application of policy dividends.

Family income policy. A life insurance policy, combining whole life and decreasing term insurance. The beneficiary receives income payments to the end of a specified period if the insured dies prior to the end of the period plus the face amount of the policy—either at the end of the period or at the death of the insured.

Funeral home. A commercial establishment that handles preparations and arrangements for funerals and other ceremonies connected with the disposition of the dead. (*Note:* In the eastern United States, *funeral home* is used almost exclusively; *mortuary* is commonly used in the West.)

Funeral director. An individual who manages funerals and other services associated with the disposition of human remains. Many funeral directors are also embalmers. Synonyms: *mortician, undertaker* (archaic).

Funeral service. Any observance, service, or ceremony held for a deceased human body, usually before burial, cremation, or other final disposition.

G

Geriatrics. A branch of medicine concerned with the special problems of the aged.

Gerontologist. One who studies aging.

Gerontology. The study of aging.

Grace period. A period (usually 30 to 31 days) following the premium due date, during which an overdue premium may be paid without penalty. The policy remains in force throughout this period.

Grave box. A type of outer burial container.

Grave liner. A type of outer burial container.

Grave marker. An upright monument of some sort (in a cemetery) or a bronze plaque laid in the ground (in a memorial park).

Grave opening. The excavation of a designated grave space prior to burial.

Grief. Deep sorrow, usually caused by the loss of a loved one through death.

Grief counselor. *See* **Bereavement counselor.**

Group annuity. A pension plan providing annuities at retirement to a group of people under a master contract. It is usually issued to an employer for the benefit of employees. The individual members of the group hold certificates as evidence of their annuities.

H

Hospice. A program and a philosophy designed to meet the physical, psychological and spiritual needs of the patient and family. The focus is on home care where possible with an emphasis on the relief of pain.

I

Individual policy pension trust. A type of pension plan, frequently used for small groups, administered by trustees who are authorized to purchase individual level premium policies or annuity contracts for each member of the plan. The policies usually provide both life insurance and retirement benefits.

Industrial life insurance. Life insurance issued in small amounts, usually less than $1,000, with premiums payable on a weekly or monthly basis. The premiums are generally collected at the home by an agent of the company. Sometimes referred to as *debit insurance.*

Informed consent. The agreement by a patient to undergo specific medical treatment while understanding what that treatment entails and implies.

Inter-disciplinary care. Usually in a hospice, a physician-supervised program of combined care to meet a patient's physical, psychological and spiritual needs.

L

Level premium life insurance. Life insurance for which the premium remains the same from year to year. The premium is more than the actual cost of protection during the earlier years of the policy and less than the actual cost in the later years. The building of a reserve is a natural result of level premiums. The overpayments in the early years, together with the interest that is to be earned, serve to balance out the underpayments of the later years.

Life annuity. A contract that provides an income for life.

Life span. The average age which a human or other living being can reach.

Limited payment life insurance. Whole life insurance on which premiums are payable for a specified number of years or until death if death occurs before the end of the specified period.

Living will. A document in which an individual specifies that no extraordinary life-sustaining efforts are to be made in the event that he becomes terminally ill and can no longer communicate his desires.

Livor mortis. A postmortem stage following *algor mortis* in which the blood settles, producing a purplish discoloration of the body.

M

Master policy. A policy that is issued to an employer or trustee, establishing a group insurance plan for designated members of an eligible group.

Mausoleum. A building housing crypts, which is owned privately and intended for use by a single family or is owned by a community and large enough to hold many crypts.

Medical examiner. A public official who does postmortem examinations of human bodies to ascertain the cause of death.

Memorial park. A burial ground that contains bronze plaques as grave markers rather than upright monuments and features gardens, trees, and sculpture; also called a *memorial garden.*

Memorial service. An elegiac ceremony that can take place in a home, church, or funeral home, usually in the absence of the body. Frequently a memorial service is held in a private home after direct burial or immediate cremation has taken place.

Memorial society. *See* **Advisory memorial society.**

Mercy-killing. *See* **Euthanasia, voluntary.**

Monument. An inscribed grave marker, usually made of stone.

Mortician. *See* **Funeral director.**

Mortuary. *See* **Funeral home.**

Mourning. The act of feeling or expressing grief, especially during bereavement.

Mutual life insurance company. A life insurance company without stockholders whose management is directed by a board elected by the policyholders. Mutual companies, in general, issue participating insurance.

N

Natural death. A death that ensues without the intervention of life-preserving or death-hastening measures.

Nonforfeiture option. One of the choices available if the policyholder discontinues premium payments on a policy with a cash value. This, if any, may be taken in cash, as extended term insurance or as a reduced paid-up insurance.

Nonmedical limit. The maximum face value of a policy that a given company will issue without the applicant taking a medical examination.

Nonparticipating policy. A life insurance policy in which the company does not distribute to policyholders any part of its surplus. Note should be taken that premiums for nonparticipating policies are usually lower than for comparable participating policies. Note should also be taken that some nonparticipating policies have both a maximum premium and a current lower premium. The current premium reflects anticipated experience that is more favorable than the company is willing to guarantee, and it may be changed from time to time for the entire block of business to which the policy belongs. *See* **Participating policy.**

O

Obituary. A printed notice of an individual's death, commonly including biographical notes.

Organ bank. A private institution to which an individual may donate a particular organ.

Organ donor. An individual who has agreed to have his or her remains donated to a medical school, transplant bank, or other institution after death. *See* **Anatomical gift.**

Outer burial container. Any container designed to be placed in a grave around the casket, such as grave liners and boxes and burial vaults.

P

Paid-up insurance. Insurance on which all required premiums have been paid. The term is frequently used to mean the reduced paid-up insurance available as a nonforfeiture option.

Pallbearer. An individual who helps to carry or escort a coffin during a funeral service.

Palliative care. Care given to ease the pain and suffering of a patient without curing it. The term is often used for the care hospices give patients who are terminally ill.

Participating policy. A life insurance policy under which the company agrees to distribute to policyholders the part of its surplus which its board of directors determines is not needed at the end of the business year. Such a distribution serves to reduce the premium the policyholder had paid. *See* **Policy dividend; Nonparticipating policy.**

Pastoral care. Spiritual and other guidance provided by clergymen to their congregants, especially during times of crisis, such as bereavement or terminal illness.

Permanent life insurance. A phrase used to cover any form of life insurance except term; generally insurance that accrues cash value, such as whole life or endowment.

Perpetual care. An arrangement made with a cemetery or memorial park to maintain a grave over a certain period of time, generally for as long as the cemetery exists.

Policy dividend. A refund of part of the premium on a participating life insurance policy reflecting the difference between the premium charged and actual experience.

Postmortem. After death.

Premium. The payment, or one of the periodic payments, a policyholder agrees to make for an insurance policy.

Premium loan. A policy loan made for the purpose of paying premiums.

Preneed plan. An arrangement made in advance for disposition of one's remains, usually prefinanced. Preneed plans are usually offered by funeral directors; preneed arrangements are made by consumers. Also called a *prearrangement plan.*

R

Rated policy. Sometimes called an "extra-risk" policy, an insurance policy issued at a higher-than-standard premium rate to cover the extra risk where, for example, a policyholder has impaired health or a hazardous occupation.

Reduced paid-up insurance. A form of insurance available as a nonforfeiture option. It provides for continuation of the original insurance plan, but for a reduced amount.

Regional organ procurement agency. A state organization that has teams skilled in the transplant process, such as a kidney retrieval team, a team skilled in removing corneas, etc.

Renewable term insurance. Term insurance which can be renewed at the end of the term, at the option of the policyholder and without evidence of insurability, for a limited number of successive terms. The rates increase at each renewal as the age of the insured increases.

Rider. A special policy provision or group of provisions that may be added to a policy to expand or limit the benefits otherwise payable.

Right to die. The right of human beings to die naturally, without heroic measures to sustain life (usually applied to individuals who are terminally ill). *See* **Living will.**

Rigor mortis. The stiffness in head, neck, and lower extremities that follows death.

Risk classification. The process by which a company decides how its premium rates for life insurance should differ according to the risk characteristics of individuals insured (e.g., age, occupation, sex, state of health) and then applies the resulting rules to individual applications. *See* **Underwriting.**

Rite of passage. A ceremony connected with a major change in a person's status or life, including death.

S

Senescence. 1) The state of being old; 2) the process of aging.

Separate account. An asset account established by a life insurance company separate from other funds, used primarily for pension plans and variable life products. This arrangement permits wider latitude in the choice of investments, particularly in equities.

Settlement options. The several ways, other than immediate payment in cash, which a policyholder or beneficiary may choose to have policy benefits paid. *See* **Supplementary contracts.**

Skilled nursing care facility. An institution that provides nursing services for the sick requiring training, judgment, technical knowledge and skills beyond that of an untrained person.

Stock life insurance company. A life insurance company owned by stockholders who elect a board to direct the company's management. Stock companies, in general, issue nonparticipating insurance, but may also issue participating insurance.

Straight life insurance. Whole life insurance on which premiums are payable for life.

SIDS. *See* **Sudden infant death syndrome.**

Sudden infant death syndrome. The sudden, unexpected death of a sleeping infant (usually less than six months of age) from causes not apparent after a complete autopsy and investigation. Also referred to as *crib death*. Acronym, **SIDS.**

Suicide. The act of intentionally taking one's own life.

Supplementary contract. An agreement between a life insurance company and a policyholder or beneficiary by which the company retains the cash sum payable under an insurance policy and makes payments in accordance with the settlement option chosen.

T

Term insurance. Life insurance payable to a beneficiary only when a policyholder dies within a specific period.

Terminal illness. 1) A disease or other condition for which the prognosis is death; 2) a condition that will eventually directly cause death.

Terminal care. The medical care of a patient who is terminally ill.

Testament. *See* **Will.**

Thanatologist. One who studies death.

Thanatology. The study of death.

Tissue bank. *See* **Organ bank.**

Transplantation. The process of transferring an organ(s) from a donor to a donee (patient) needing the organ(s). The donor's tissue must be compatible with the donee's; there is always a danger of organ or tissue rejection by the donee's immune system of defenses.

Transplant center. Usually affiliated with a major hospital or a medical center, a facility involved in the transplantation of a particular organ.

U

Undertaker. *See* **Funeral director.**

Underwriting. The process by which a life insurance company determines whether or not it can accept an application for life insurance, and if so, on what basis.

Unit of care. A hospice term referring to the treatment of patient and family needs as one.

V

Variable annuity. An annuity contract in which the amount of each periodic income payment may fluctuate. The fluctuation may be related to securities market values, a cost of living index, or some other variable factor.

Variable life insurance. Life insurance under which the benefits relate to the value of assets behind the contract at the time the benefit is paid. The amount of death benefit payable would, under variable life policies that have been proposed, never be less than the initial death benefit payable under the policy.

Variable premium life insurance. A whole life type of protection with premiums geared to the insuring company's rate of return on its investments.

W

Waiver of premium. A provision that under certain conditions an insurance policy will be kept in full force by the company without further payment of premiums. It is used most often in the event of total and permanent disability.

Whole life insurance. Life insurance payable to a beneficiary at the death of the policyholder whenever that occurs. Premiums may be payable for a specific number of years (limited payment life) or for life (straight life).

Widow/widower. One who has lost a spouse through death. In modern usage, *widowed person* is considered preferable to *widow* or *widower.*

Will. A written declaration of an individual's own desires pertaining to disposition of his or her estate/possessions after death.

PART 5

INDEX

Index